T0343158

Performance Evaluation and Attribution of Security Portfolios

Introduction to the Series

The aim of the Handbooks in Economics series is to produce Handbooks for various branches of economics, each of which is a definitive source, reference, and teaching supplement for use by professional researchers and advanced graduate students. Each Handbook provides self-contained surveys of the current state of a branch of economics in the form of chapters prepared by leading specialists on various aspects of this branch of economics. These surveys summarize not only received results but also newer developments, from recent journal articles and discussion papers. Some original material is also included, but the main goal is to provide comprehensive and accessible surveys. The Handbooks are intended to provide not only useful reference volumes for professional collections but also possible supplementary readings for advanced courses for graduate students in economics.

KENNETH J. ARROW and MICHAEL D. INTRILIGATOR

Performance Evaluation and Attribution of Security Portfolios

by

Bernd Fischer and Russell Wermers

Academic Press is an imprint of Elsevier
The Boulevard, Langford Lane,
Kidlington, Oxford OX5 1GB, UK
225 Wyman Street, Waltham, MA 02451, USA

First edition 2013

Copyright © 2013 Elsevier Inc. All rights reserved

SOLNIK, BRUNO, McLEAVEY, DENNIS, *GLOBAL INVESTMENTS, 6th Edition*, © 2009, Reprinted by permission of Pearson Education, Inc., Upper Saddle River, NJ.

No part of this publication may be reproduced, stored in a retrieval system or transmitted in any form or by any means electronic, mechanical, photocopying, recording or otherwise without the prior written permission of the publisher

Permissions may be sought directly from Elsevier's Science & Technology Rights Department in Oxford, UK: phone (+44) (0) 1865 843830; fax (+44) (0) 1865 853333; email: permissions@elsevier.com. Alternatively you can submit your request online by visiting the Elsevier web site at http://elsevier.com/locate/permissions, and selecting *Obtaining permission to use Elsevier material*

Notice

No responsibility is assumed by the publisher for any injury and/or damage to persons or property as a matter of products liability, negligence or otherwise, or from any use or operation of any methods, products, instructions or ideas contained in the material herein. Because of rapid advances in the medical sciences, in particular, independent verification of diagnoses and drug dosages should be made

British Library Cataloguing in Publication Data

A catalogue record for this book is available from the British Library

Library of Congress Cataloging-in-Publication Data

A catalog record for this book is availabe from the Library of Congress

ISBN–13: 978-0-12-744483-3

For information on all Academic Press publications visit our web site at store.elsevier.com

Printed and bound by CPI Group (UK) Ltd, Croydon, CR0 4YY

Working together to grow
libraries in developing countries

www.elsevier.com | www.bookaid.org | www.sabre.org

ELSEVIER BOOK AID International Sabre Foundation

Preface

This book is intended to be the scientific state-of-the-art in performance evaluation—the measurement of manager skills—and performance attribution—the measurement of all of the sources of manager returns, including skill-based. We have attempted to include the best and most promising scientific approaches to these topics, drawn from a voluminous and quickly expanding literature.

Our objective in this book is to distill hundreds of both classic and the best cutting-edge academic and practitioner research papers into a unified framework. Our goal is to present the most important concepts in the literature in order to provide a directed study and/or authoritative reference that saves time for the practitioner or academic researcher. Sufficient detail is provided, in most cases, such that the investment practitioner can implement the approaches with data immediately, without consulting the underlying literature. For the academic, we have provided enough detail to allow an easy further study of the literature, as desired.

We have contributed in two dimensions in this volume—both of which, we believe, are missing in currently available textbooks. Firstly, we provide a timely overview of the most important performance evaluation techniques, which allow an accurate assessment of the skills of a portfolio manager. Secondly, we provide an equally timely overview of the most important and widely used performance attribution techniques, which allow an accurate measure of all of the sources of investment returns, and which are necessary for precise performance reporting by fund managers.

We believe that our text is timely. An estimated $71.3 trillion was invested in managed portfolios worldwide, as of 2009 (source: www.thecityuk.com). Managing this money, thus, is a business that draws perhaps $700 billion per year in management fees and other expenses for asset managers, in addition to a perhaps similar magnitude in annual trading costs accruing to brokers, market makers, and other liquidity providers (i.e., Wall Street and other financial centers). Our book is the first comprehensive text covering the latest science of measuring the main output of portfolio managers: their benchmark-relative performance (alpha). Our hope is that investors use these techniques to improve the allocation of their money, and that portfolio management firms use them to better understand the quality of their funds' output for investors.

We intend this book to be used in at least two ways:

First, as a useful reference source for investment practitioners—who may wish to read only one or a few chapters. We have attempted to make chapters self-contained to meet this demand. We have also included chapter-end questions that both test the reader's understanding and provide examples of applications of each chapter's concepts. The audience for this use includes (at least) those studying for the CFA exams; performance analysts; mutual fund and pension fund trustees; portfolio managers of mutual funds, pension funds, hedge funds, and fund-of-funds; asset management ratings companies (e.g., Lipper and Morningstar); quantitative portfolio strategists, regulators, financial planners, and sophisticated individual investors.

Second, the book serves as an efficient way for mathematically advanced undergraduate, masters, or Ph.D. students to undertake a thorough foundation in the science of performance evaluation and attribution. After reading this book, students will be prepared to handle new developments in these fields.

We have attempted to design each chapter of this book to contain enough detail to bring the reader to a point of being able to apply the concepts therein, including the chapter-end problems. In cases where further detail may be needed, we have cited the most relevant source papers to allow further reading.

We have divided our book into two sections:

Part 1 of the book covers the area of performance evaluation.

Chapter 1 provides a short overview of the basics of empirical asset-pricing as applied to performance assessment, including basic factor models, the CAPM, the Fama-French three-factor model and the research on momentum, and the characteristic-based stock benchmarking model of Daniel, Grinblatt, Titman, and Wermers.

Chapter 2 provides an overview of returns-based factor models, and the issues involved in implementing them. Chapter 3 discusses the issue of luck vs. skill in generating investment returns, and presents the fundamental performance evaluation measures, including those based on the Chapter 2 factor models. In addition, extensions of these factor models are introduced that contain factors that capture the ability of portfolio managers to time the stock market or to time securities over the business cycle.

Chapter 4 presents the latest approaches to using portfolio holdings to more precisely measure the skill of a portfolio manager. Chapter 5 provides a complete system for evaluating the skills of a portfolio manager using her portfolio holdings and net returns.

Many managed portfolios generate non-normal returns. Chapter 6 shows how to apply bootstrap techniques to generate more precise estimates of the statistical significance of manager skills in the presence of non-normal returns and alphas.

Chapter 7 covers a very new topic: how to capture the time-varying abilities of a portfolio manager (as briefly introduced in Chapter 3). Specifically, this chapter shows how to predict which managers are most likely to generate superior alphas in the current economic climate.

Chapter 8 also covers a very recent topic in performance evaluation: the assessment of the proportion of a group of funds that are truly skilled using only their net returns. This approach is very useful in assessing whether the highest alpha managers are truly skilled, or are simply the luckiest in a large group of managers.

Finally, Chapter 9 is a "capstone chapter," in that it provides an overview of the research findings that use the principles outlined in the first 8 chapters. As such, it is a very useful summary of what works (and what does not) when looking for a superior asset manager (a "SAM") and trying to avoid an inferior asset manager (an "IAM").

Part 2 of the book primarily concerns performance attribution and related topics.

Since attribution analysis has become a crucial component within the internal control system of investment managers and institutional clients, ample space is dedicated to a thorough treatment of this field. The focus in this part lies on the practical applications rather than on the discussions of the various approaches from an academic point of view. This (practitioner's) approach is accompanied by a multitude of examples derived from practical experience in the investment industry. Great emphasis was also put on the underlying mathematical detail, which is required for an implementation in practice.

Chapter 10 provides an overview of the basic approaches for the measurement of returns. In particular, the concepts of time-weighted return and internal rate of return, as well as approximation methods for these measures are discussed in detail.

Attribution analysis, in practice, requires a deep understanding of the benchmarks against which the portfolios are measured. Chapter 11 provides an introduction to the benchmarks commonly used in practice, and their underlying concepts.

Chapter 12 covers fundamental models for the attribution analysis of equity portfolios developed by Gary Brinson and others. Furthermore, basic approaches for the treatment of currency effects and the linkage of performance contributions over multiple periods are considered.

Chapter 13 contains an introduction to attribution analysis for fixed income portfolios from a practitioner's point of view. The focus lies on a methodology that is based on a full valuation of the bonds and the option-adjusted spread. In addition, various other approaches are described.

Based on the methodologies for equity and fixed income portfolios, Chapter 14 presents different methodologies for the attribution analysis of balanced portfolios. This chapter also illustrates the basic approaches for a risk-adjusted attribution analysis and covers specific aspects in the analysis of hedge funds.

Chapter 15 describes the various approaches for the consideration of derivatives within the common methodologies for attribution analysis.

The final chapter (Chapter 16) deals with Global Investment Performance Standards, a globally applied set of ethical standards for the presentation of the performance results of investment firms.

The authors are indebted to many dedicated academic researchers and tireless practitioners for many of the insights in this book. Professor Wermers wishes to thank the many investment practitioners that have provided data or insights into the topics of this book, including through their professional investment management activities: Robert Jones of Goldman Sachs Asset Management (now at System Two and Arwen), Rudy Schadt of Invesco, Scott Schoelzel and Sandy Rufenacht of Janus (now retired, and at Three Peaks Capital Management, respectively), Bill Miller and Ken Fuller of Legg-Mason, Andrew Clark, Otto Kober, Matt Lemieux, Tom Roseen, and Robin Thurston of Lipper, Don Phillips, John Rekenthaler, Annette Larson, and Paul Kaplan of Morningstar, Sean Collins and Brian Reid of the Investment Company Institute.

Professor Wermers also wishes to thank all of the classes taught on performance evaluation and attribution since 2001—at Chulalongkorn University (Bangkok); the European Central Bank (Frankfurt); the Swiss Finance Institute/FAME Executive Education Program (Geneva); Queensland University of Technology (Brisbane); Stockholm University; the University of Technology, Sydney; and the University of Vienna. Special thanks are due to students in that first class of the SFI/FAME program during those dark days in September 2001, 10 days after the 9-11 attacks.

Professor Wermers is also indebted to his loving family, Johanna, Natalie, and Samantha, for the endless hours spent away from them while preparing and teaching this subject. He gratefully acknowledges Thomas Copeland and Richard Roll of UCLA and Josef Lakonishok of University of Illinois (and LSV Asset Management) for early inspiration, as well as Wayne Ferson, Robert Stambaugh, Lubos Pastor, and Mark Carhart for their recent contributions to the field. In addition, he owes his career to the brilliant mentoring of Mark Grinblatt and Sheridan Titman at UCLA, pioneers in the subject of performance evaluation. This text would not have been possible from such humble beginnings without their selfless support and guidance.

Dr. Fischer is indebted to his colleagues at IDS GmbH—Analysis and Reporting Services, an international provider of operational investment controlling services. Over the past years he has greatly benefited from numerous discussions surrounding practical applications.

Thanks are also due to Dr. Fischer's former team members at Cominvest Asset Management GmbH. The design and the implementation of a globally applicable attribution software from scratch, and the implementation of the Global Investment Performance Standards were exciting experiences which left their mark on the current treatise.

He also wishes to thank various colleagues (Markus Buchholz, Detlev Kleis, Ulrich Raber, Carsten Wittrock, and others), with whom he co-authored papers in the past. Several sections in this book are greatly indebted to the views expressed there.

Dr. Fischer is also indebted to the CFA institute and the Global Investment Performance Committee for formative discussions surrounding the draft of the GIPS in 1998/1999 and during his official membership term from 2000 to 2004.

Both authors wish to thank J. Scott Bentley of Elsevier, whose vision it was to create such a book, and whose patience it took to see it through.

To those whose contributions we have overlooked, our sincere apologies; such an ambitious undertaking as condensing a huge literature necessitates that the authors choose topics that are either most familiar to us or viewed by us as most widely useful. Surely, we have missed some important papers, and we hope to have a chance to create a second edition that expands on this one.

Finally, to the asset management practitioner: we dedicate this volume to you, and hope that it is useful in furthering your goal of providing high-quality investment management services!

Contents

SECTION 1
Performance Evaluation

Chapter 1

An Introduction to Asset Pricing Models

ABSTRACT

This chapter provides a brief overview of asset pricing models, with an emphasis on those models that are widely used to describe the returns of traded financial securities. Here, we focus on various models of stock returns and fixed-income returns, and discuss the reasoning and assumptions that underlie the structure of each of these models.

Keywords
Asset Pricing Models, CAPM, Factor Models, Fama French three-factor model, Carhart four-factor model, DGTW stock characteristics model, Estimating beta, Expected return and risk.

1.1 HISTORICAL ASSET PRICING MODELS

Individuals are born with a sense of the perils of risk, and they develop mental adjustments to penalize opportunities that involve more risk.[1] For example, farmers do not plant corn, which requires a great deal of rainfall (which may or may not happen), unless the expected price of corn at harvest time is sufficiently high. Currency traders will not take a long position in the Thai baht and short the U.S. dollar unless they expect the baht to appreciate sufficiently. In essence, the farmer and the currency trader are each applying a "personal discount rate" to the expected return of planting corn or investing in baht. The farmer's discount rate depends on his assessment of the risk of rainfall (which greatly affects his total corn crop output) and the risk of a price change in the crop. The currency trader's discount rate depends on the relative economic health of Thailand and the U.S., and any potential government intervention against currency

[1] Gibson and Walk (1960) performed a famous experiment that was designed to test for depth perception possessed by infants as young as six months old. Infants were unwilling to crawl on a transparent glass plate that was placed over a several-foot drop, proving that they possessed depth perception at a very early age. Another inference which can be drawn from this experiment is that infants already perceive physical risks and exhibit risk-averse behavior at a very early age (probably before they are environmentally taught to avoid risk).

Performance Evaluation and Attribution of Security Portfolios. http://dx.doi.org/10.1016/B978-0-12-744483-3.00001-8
© 2013 Elsevier Inc. All rights reserved.
For End-of-chapter Questions: © 2012, CFA Institute, Reproduced and republished with permission from CFA Institute. All rights reserved.

speculation—both of which may carry large risks. Both economic agents" discount rates also depend on their personal aversion to risk, and, thus, may require very different compensations to take similar risks.[2, 3]

Asset managers and investors also understand that some securities are less certain in their payouts than others, and make adjustments to their investment plans accordingly. Short-maturity bank certificates of deposit (CDs), while paying a very low annual interest rate, are attractive because they return the principal fairly quickly and guarantee (with insurance) a particular rate-of-return. Stocks, with not even a promise that they will pay the next quarterly dividend, provide much higher returns than CDs, on average. In general, greater levels of risk in a security or security portfolio—especially those risks that cannot be inexpensively insured—require compensation by risk-averse investors in the form of higher potential future returns.

The most basic approach to an "asset pricing model" that describes the compensation to investors for risk-taking simply ranks securities by the standard deviation of their periodic (say, monthly) returns, then conjectures a particular functional relation between this risk and the expected (average future) returns of securities.[4] But, should the relation be linear or non-linear between standard deviation and expected return? Should there be any credit given to securities that have counter-cyclical risk patterns (i.e., high returns during recessions)? How can we account for offsetting risk patterns between a group of securities, even within a bull market (e.g., technology vs. utility stocks)? Should risk that can be diversified by holding many different investments be rewarded? These questions are the focus of modern asset pricing theory.

The foundations of modern asset pricing models attempt to combine a few very basic and simple axioms that appear to hold in society, including the following. First, that investors prefer more wealth to less wealth. Second, that investors dislike risk in the payouts from securities because they prefer smooth patterns of consumption of their wealth, and not "feast or famine" periods of time. And, third, that investors should not be rewarded with extra return for taking on risk that could be avoided through a smart and costless approach to mixing assets. Our next sections briefly describe the most widely used asset pricing models of today. In discussing these models, we focus on their application to describe the

---

[2] The notion of creating a personal "price of risk", or a required expected reward for taking on a unit of risk, has its mathematical origins at least as long ago as 1738, when Daniel Bernoulli defined the systematic process by which individuals make choices, and, in 1809, when Gauss discovered the normal distribution. For an excellent discussion of the historical origins and development of concepts of risk, see Bernstein (1996).

[3] In cases where bankruptcy is possible, an economic agent may not take a risk that would otherwise be attractive—if credit is not available to forestall the bankruptcy until the expected payoff from the bet. This is the essence of Shleifer and Vishny's (1997) "limits to arbitrage" argument (which might be better referred to as "limits to risky arbitrage").

[4] An *asset pricing model* estimates the future required expected return that must be offered by a security or portfolio with certain observable characteristics, such as perceived future return volatility.

evolution of returns for liquid securities—chiefly, stocks and bonds.[5] However, the usefulness of these models—with some modifications—goes far beyond stocks and bonds to other securities, such as derivatives and less liquid assets such as private equity and real estate.

1.2 THE BEGINNING OF MODERN ASSET PRICING MODELS

A great deal of work has been done, over the past 60 years, to advance the ability of statistical models to explain the returns on securities. Building on Markowitz's (1952) seminal work on efficient portfolio diversification, Sharpe published his famous paper on the capital asset pricing model (CAPM) in 1964 (Sharpe, 1964).[6] These two ideas shared the 1990 Nobel Prize in Economics.

The CAPM says that the expected (average) future excess return, R_t, is a linear function of the systematic (or market-related) risk of a stock or portfolio, β:

$$E\left[R_t\right] = \beta \cdot E\left[RMRF_t\right], \tag{1.1}$$

where R_t = security or portfolio return minus riskfree rate, $RMRF_t$ = market return minus riskfree rate, and $\beta = \frac{cov(R_t, RMRF_t)}{var(RMRF_t)}$ is a measure of correlation of the security or portfolio with the broad market portfolio.[7]

This relation is extremely simple and useful for relating the reward (expected return) that is required of a stock with its level of market-based risk. For instance, if market-based risk (β) is doubled, then expected return, in excess of the risk-free rate, must be doubled for the security or portfolio to be in equilibrium with the market. If T-bills pay 2%/year and a stock with a beta of one promises an average return of 7%, then a stock with a beta of two must promise an average of 12%.

Sharpe's CAPM is simple and is an equilibrium theory, but it depends on several unrealistic assumptions about the economy, including:

1. All investors have the exact same information about possible future expected earnings and their risks at each point in time.
2. Investors are risk-averse and behave perfectly rationally, meaning they do not favor one type of security over another unless the calculated Net Present Value of the first is higher.
3. The cost of trading securities is zero.
4. Investors are mean-variance optimizers (it is sufficient, but not necessary, for this requirement that security returns are normally distributed).

---

[5] For a general review of asset pricing theories and empirical tests of the theories, see, for example, Cochrane (2001) and Campbell et al. (1997).

[6] Apparently, Bill Sharpe, a Ph.D. student in Economics at UCLA, visited Harry Markowitz at the Rand Institute in Santa Monica, California during the early 1960s to discuss Markowitz's paper and Bill's thoughts about an asset-pricing model. This led to Bill's dissertation on the CAPM.

[7] Note that the correlation coefficient between the excess return on a security or portfolio and the excess return on the broad market is defined as $\rho = \frac{cov(R_t, RMRF_t)}{\sqrt{var(R_t) \cdot var(RMRF_t)}}$, which is close to the definition of β.

5. All investors are myopic, and care only about one-period returns.
6. Investors are "price-takers", meaning that their actions cannot influence prices of securities.
7. There are no taxes on holding or trading securities.
8. Investors can trade any amount of an asset, no matter how small or large.

Several of these assumptions may not fit real-world markets, and many papers have attempted, with some—but far from complete—success in extending the CAPM to situations which eliminate one or more of these assumptions. Among these papers are Merton's (1973) intertemporal CAPM (ICAPM), which extends the CAPM to a multiperiod model (to address #5). A good discussion of these extended CAPMs can be found in several investments textbooks, such as Elton et al. (2009).

While there are many extensions of the CAPM that deal with dropping one assumption at a time, it is not at all clear that dropping several assumptions simultaneously still results in the CAPM being a good model that describes the relation of returns to risk in real financial markets. Because of this, recent work has focused on building practical models that "work" with data, even if they are not based on a particular theoretical derivation. Although many attempts have been made, with some success, at creating a new model of asset pricing, no theory has become as universally accepted as the CAPM once was. Hopefully, some future financial economist will create such a new model that reflects real financial markets well. In the meantime, we must rely on either empirical applications of the CAPM, or on other models that have no particular equilibrium theory supporting them.

1.2.1 Estimating the CAPM Model

In reality, we do not know the true values of $E[R_t]$, $E[RMRF_t]$, and β, so we must estimate them somehow from data. This is where a time-series version of the CAPM (also called the Jensen model (Jensen, 1968)) can be used on return data for a security or a portfolio of securities. The time-series version of the CAPM can be written as

$$R_t = \alpha + \beta \cdot RMRF_t + e_t, \tag{1.2}$$

while its application to real-world data can be similarly written as:[8]

$$r_t = \alpha + \beta \cdot rmrf_t + \epsilon_t, \tag{1.3}$$

where we estimate the parameters α (the model intercept) and β (the model slope) using historical values of R_t and $RMRF_t$. (This model is more generally called the "single-factor model", as it does not require that the CAPM is exactly correct to be implemented on real-world data.) A widely used method for doing this is ordinary least squares (OLS), which fits the data with estimated

[8] Note that, in probability and statistics, we use upper case to denote random variables and lower case to denote realizations (outcomes) of these random variables. We will relax this in later chapters, but will use this convention in this chapter to clarify the concepts.

values of α and β, which are denoted as $\widehat{\alpha}$ and $\widehat{\beta}$, such that the sum of the squared residuals from the "fitted OLS regression line" is minimized. Note that Equation (1.1) implies that $\alpha = 0$. We can either impose that restriction before estimating the model, or we can allow the model to estimate $\widehat{\alpha}$, depending on our assumption about how strictly the CAPM model holds in the real world. For instance, if we believe that the CAPM model is mostly correct, but that there are temporary deviations of stocks away from the model, we would allow the intercept, $\widehat{\alpha}$, to be estimated using real data. Even if the CAPM holds exactly at the beginning of each period for, say, Apple, it is easy to understand why there can be several unexpected positive surprises for Apple over a several-month period (such as the unexpected introduction of several innovative products). Such unexpected "shocks" can be captured by the $\widehat{\alpha}$ estimate, which prevents them from affecting the precision of the $\widehat{\beta}$ estimate. In this discussion, we'll stick with the model including an intercept to accommodate such issues.

After we estimate the model, we write the resulting "fitted model" as

$$\widehat{E}[R_t] = \widehat{\alpha} + \widehat{\beta} \cdot E[RMRF_t], \tag{1.4}$$

where we realize that $\widehat{\alpha}$ is just a temporary deviation, and we expect it to be zero in the future. Using this expectation, we can use this model to forecast future returns with:

$$\widehat{E}[R_{t+1}] = \widehat{\beta} \cdot E[RMRF_{t+1}], \tag{1.5}$$

where all we need to do is to estimate one value—the expected excess return of the market portfolio of stocks, $E[RMRF_{t+1}]$. One simple, but not very precise, method of estimating this parameter is to use the average historical values over the past T periods:[9]

$$\widehat{E}[R_{t+1}] = \widehat{\beta} \cdot \frac{1}{T} \sum_{j=t-T}^{t} rmrf_j = \widehat{\beta} \cdot \overline{rmrf}.$$

Other methods of estimating $E[RMRF_{t+1}]$ include using the average return forecast from professionals, such as security analysts, or deriving forecasts from index futures or options markets.

We can also estimate the risk of holding a stock or portfolio—as well as decomposing this risk into market-based and idiosyncratic risk—with this one-factor model by applying the rules of variances to Equation (1.2):

$$V[R_t] = \underbrace{\beta^2 \cdot V[RMRF_t]}_{Systematic\ Risk} + \underbrace{V[e_t]}_{Idiosyncratic(stock\text{-}\ or\ portfolio\text{-}specific)\ risk}. \tag{1.6}$$

[9] This estimator is not precise because of the high variance of monthly values of $rmrf_t$.

Here, we can again use the fitted regression, in conjunction with past values of RMRF and the regression residuals, ϵ_t to estimate the future total risk:

$$\widehat{V}\left[R_{t+1}\right] = \widehat{\beta}^2 \cdot \frac{1}{T-1} \sum_{j=t-T}^{t} \left(rmrf_j - \overline{rmrf}\right)^2 + \frac{1}{T-1} \sum_{j=t-T}^{t} \hat{\epsilon}_j^2. \tag{1.7}$$

Figure 1.1 and Tables 1.1 and 1.2 show an example of a fitted model using Chevron-Texaco (CVX) over the 2007–2008 period. Two approaches to fitting the model of Equation (1.3) using OLS are presented in the graph and in the tables: (1) the unrestricted model, and (2) the restricted model (where α is forced to equal zero):

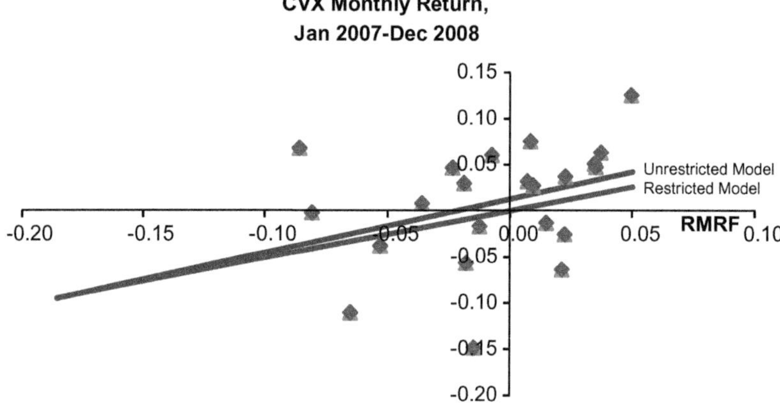

FIGURE 1.1
CAPM Regression Graph for Chevron-Texaco.

Table 1.1 **Unrestricted Ordinary Least Squares CAPM Regression Output for Chevron-Texaco**

Regression Output (Unrestricted Model)				
	Coefficients	**Standard Error**	**t Stat**	**P-value**
Intercept (α)	0.012	0.012	1.0	0.32
RMRF	0.58	0.22	2.58	0.01

Table 1.2 **Restricted Ordinary Least Squares CAPM Regression Output for Chevron-Texaco**

Regression Output (Restricted Model, $\alpha = 0$)				
	Coefficients	**Standard Error**	**t Stat**	**P-value**
Intercept (α)	0	-	-	-
RMRF	0.51	0.21	2.38	0.02

Note that, if we restrict the intercept to equal zero, we get a lower estimate of the slope coefficient on RMRF, $\widehat{\beta}$, since we force the fitted regression line to pass through zero, as shown in the figure above.

In most cases, it is better to allow the intercept to be estimated, since it can be non-zero by the randomness in stock returns, as illustrated by the Apple example discussed previously.

Next, let's model CVX over the following two years, 2009–2010, shown in Table 1.3.

Table 1.3 Unrestricted Ordinary Least Squares CAPM Regression Output for Chevron-Texaco, 2009–2010

Regression Output (Unrestricted Model)

	Coefficients	Standard Error	t Stat	P-value
Intercept (α)	−0.0024	0.01	−0.23	0.32
RMRF	0.81	0.16	5.03	0.00005

Note that both $\widehat{\alpha}$ and $\widehat{\beta}$ have changed from their values during 2007–2008. Does this mean that these parameters actually change quickly for individual stocks? In most cases, no—these changes are the result of "estimation error", which happens when we have a very "noisy" (volatile) y-variable, such as CVX monthly returns,[10] due again to randomness.

Besides using the above regression output in the context of Equation (1.5) to estimate the expected (going-forward) return of CVX, we can also use the regression output to estimate risk for CVX going forward, using Equation (1.6).

The results from the above two regression windows point out an important lesson to remember: individual stock betas are extremely difficult to estimate precisely, which makes the CAPM very difficult to use in modeling individual stocks. There are several ways to attempt to correct these estimated betas while still using the CAPM. One important example is a correction for stocks that respond slowly to broad stock market forces, and might have a lag in their reaction due to their illiquidity. Scholes and Williams (1977) describe an approach to correct for the betas of these stocks by adding a lagged market factor to the CAPM regression,

$$r_t = \alpha + \hat{\beta}_1 \cdot rmrf_{t-1} + \hat{\beta}_2 \cdot rmrf_t + \epsilon_t. \tag{1.8}$$

[10] One example of a case where these parameters could actually change quickly is when a company's capital structure shifts dramatically, which might happen with an extreme stock return, a stock repurchase, or a large issuance of equity or bonds. Theory predicts a change in the CAPM regression slope, β, in all of these cases.

An improved estimate of the beta of a stock, the Scholes-Williams beta ($\widehat{\beta}^{SW}$), is then computed by adding together the estimates of β_1 and β_2 (assuming $rmrf_t$ has trivial serial correlation):

$$\widehat{\beta}^{SW} = \widehat{\beta}_1 + \widehat{\beta}_2 \tag{1.9}$$

There are many other potential problems with estimated betas, and numerous approaches to dealing with them. However, none of these methods, many of which can be complicated to implement, fully correct for the problem of large estimation errors for individual securities, such as stocks.[11] As a result, one should always be very careful about modeling an individual security. When possible, form portfolios of securities, then apply regression models.

1.3 EFFICIENT MARKETS

The notion of market prices efficiently reflecting all available (public) information is likely as old as the notion of capitalism itself. Indeed, if prices swing wildly in a way that is not consistent with the (unknown) expected intrinsic value of assets, then a case can be made for government intervention. Examples of this are the two rounds of "quantitative easing" (QE1 and QE2) that were implemented during 2009 and 2010, during and shortly after the financial crisis of 2008 and 2009.[12]

However, there are many shades of market efficiency, from completely informationally efficient markets to markets that are only "somewhat" informationally efficient.[13] In the world around us, we can easily see that many forms of information are fairly cheap to collect (such as announcements from the Federal Reserve), while many other forms are expensive (such as buying a Bloomberg terminal with all of its models). In their seminal paper, Grossman and Stiglitz (1980) argued that, in a world of costly information, informed traders must earn an excess return, or else they would have no incentive to gather and analyze information to make prices more efficient (i.e., reflective of information). That is, markets need to be "mostly but not completely efficient", or else investors would not make the effort to assess whether prices are "fair". If that were to happen, prices would no longer properly reflect all available and relevant information, and markets would lose their ability to allocate capital efficiently. Thus, Grossman and Stiglitz advocate that markets are likely "Grossman-Stiglitz efficient", which

---

[11] Bayesian models can be very useful for controlling estimation error. A Bayesian prior can be based on the CAPM, or another asset pricing model that is believed to be correct. However, they depend on the researcher having some strong belief in the functional form of one of several possible asset pricing models.

[12] QE1 and QE2 involved the Federal Reserve purchasing long-term government bonds from the marketplace, which is, in essence, placing more money into circulation (i.e., the Fed "printed money").

[13] Informationally efficient markets are those that instantaneously reflect new information that affects market prices, whether this information is freely available to the market or must be purchased or processed using costly means. Such markets may not perfectly know the true value of a security, which would require perfect information on the distribution of cashflows and the proper discount rate, but they use current information properly to estimate these parameters in an unbiased way.

means that costly information is not immediately and freely reflected in prices available to all investors. Indeed, the idea of Grossman-Stiglitz efficient markets is a very useful way for students to view real-world financial markets.

Behavioral finance academics, such as John Campbell and Robert Shiller, have found evidence that markets do not behave "as if" investors are perfectly rational in some Adam Smith "invisible hand" sense—in fact, they believe the evidence makes the potential for efficient markets—Grossman-Stiglitz or other notions of efficiency—very improbable in many areas of financial markets. This evidence is somewhat controversial among academics, although investment practitioners seem to have accepted the idea of behavioral finance more completely than academics. While the field of behavioral finance has become immense, a full discussion of the literature is beyond the scope of this book.[14] However, in the next section, we will discuss some research that documents return anomalies—potentially driven by investor "misbehaviors"—that are directly related to the models used to describe stock and bond returns today—so that the reader will have a better understanding of the origin of these models.[15]

1.4 STUDIES THAT ATTACK THE CAPM

Many financial economists during the 1970s attempted, with some success, to criticize the CAPM as a model that doesn't reflect the real world of stock returns and risk. The reader should note that no one doubted that the mathematics of the CAPM were correct, given its many assumptions. Instead, the model was attacked because it did not work well in the real world of stock, bond, and other security and asset pricing, which means its assumptions were not realistic.

A few of the many famous papers are described here. Most CAPM criticisms have focused on the stock market, mostly because stock price and return data have been studied extensively by academic researchers and such data are of high-quality (i.e., from the Center for Research in Security Prices–CRSP—at the University of Chicago).

First, Banz (1981) studied the returns of small capitalization stocks using the CAPM model. Banz found that a size factor (one that reflects the return difference between stocks with low equity capitalization—price times shares outstanding—and stocks with high equity capitalization) adds explanatory power for the cross-section of future stock returns above the explanatory power of market betas. He finds that average returns on small stocks are too high, even controlling for their higher betas, and that average returns on large stocks are too low, relative to the predictions of the CAPM.

---

[14] Many contributions can be found in the articles and books of Kahneman and Tversky, Shiller, Thaler, Campbell, Barber and Odean, Lo, and several others.

[15] Studies that document anomalies in other markets are much more sparse, such as anomalies in bond or futures markets. To some extent, this is due to the fact that academic researchers have devoted the majority of their time to studying stock prices (due to the high-quality data and transparent markets for stocks, as well as the broad participation of individual investors in stock markets).

Bhandari (1988) found a positive relation between financial leverage (debt to equity ratio) and the cross-section of future stock returns, even after controlling for both size and beta. Basu (1983) finds that the earnings-to-price ratio (E/P) predicts cross-sectional differences in future stock returns in models that include size and beta as explanatory variables. High E/P stocks outperform low E/P stocks.

Keim (1983) finds that about 50% of the size factor return, during 1963–1979, occurs in January. Further, over 50% of the January return occurs during the first week of trading, in particular, the first trading day. And, Reinganum (1983) finds similar results, and also finds that this "January effect" does not appear to be completely explained by investor tax-loss selling in December and repurchasing in January.

1.5 DOES PROVING THE CAPM WRONG = MARKET INEFFICIENCY? OR, DO EFFICIENT MARKETS = THE CAPM IS CORRECT?

Emphatically, no! This is often termed the "joint hypothesis problem", since any empirical test of the CAPM, such as the above-cited studies, is jointly testing the validity of the model and whether violations to the model can be found. Often, students of finance believe in the CAPM so thoroughly (probably through the fault of their professors) that they equate the CAPM's validity to the validity of efficient markets. However, there is no such tie. Markets can be perfectly efficient, and the CAPM model can simply be wrong—it's just that it does not describe the proper risk factors in the economy. For instance, if two risk factors drive the economy, then the CAPM will not work.

If the CAPM is exactly correct, however, markets must be efficient—unless we use an expanded notion of the CAPM that has two versions: one version that is visible to everyone, and another that is visible only to the "informed investors". The CAPM modeled by Sharpe, however, has no such duality—there is one market portfolio and one beta for each security in the economy. In Sharpe's CAPM world, markets are perfectly efficient, and everyone has the same information.[16]

1.6 SMALL CAPITALIZATION AND VALUE STOCKS

In the early 1990s, Fama and French tried to settle the question of the usefulness of the CAPM in the face of all these apparent stock "anomalies". In doing so, Fama and French (FF; 1992) declared that "beta is dead", meaning that the CAPM was a somewhat useless model, at least for the stock market. Instead, FF promoted the use of two new factors to model the difference in returns of different stocks: the market capitalization of the stock (also called "size") and the book-to-market ratio (BTM) of the stock—that is, the accounting book value of equity divided by the market's value of the equity (using the traded market price).

[16] Dybvig and Ross (1985), Mayers and Rice (1979), and Keim and Stambaugh (1986) were among the first to expand the notion of the CAPM to one involving two types of investors, informed and uninformed.

FF used a clever approach to demonstate this argument. Most prior studies of the CAPM first estimate individual stock or stock portfolio betas from the one-factor regression of Equation (1.4), as we did for CVX above, then test whether these betas forecast future stock returns. FF argued that small capitalization stocks tend to have much higher betas than large capitalization stocks, so it might be that small stocks simply have higher returns than large stocks, regardless of their betas.

First, FF estimated each stock's beta with five years (60 months) of past returns, using the one-factor regression model of Equation (1.3). Then, they ranked all stocks by their market capitalization (size), from largest to smallest, then cut these ranked stocks into 10 groups. The top decile group was the group of largest stocks, while the bottom decile was the small stock group.

Next, FF ranked stocks—within each of these decile groups—by the betas of the stocks that they had already computed. Then, FF took the highest 1/10th of stocks, according to their betas, from each of the 10 size deciles (that 1/10th was 1/100 of all stocks)—then, recombined these 10 "high beta" subportfolios into a high beta, mixed size portfolio. This was repeated for the 2nd highest 1/10th of stocks in each portfolio to form the "2nd highest beta" subportfolio with mixed size. And, so on, to the lowest beta 1/10th of stocks to form the "low beta" subportfolio with mixed size. Finally, FF measured the equal-weighted returns of each of these newly constructed 10 portfolios—each of which had stocks with similar betas, but mixed size—during the following 7 years. The objective was to separate the influence of size from beta by "mixing" the size of stocks with similar betas. This procedure is depicted in Figure 1.2.

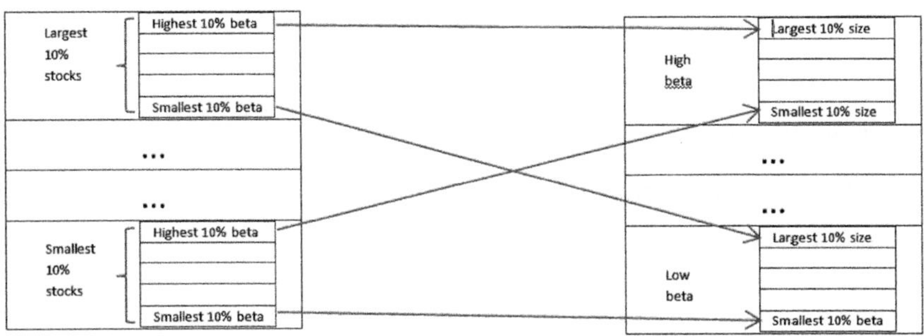

FIGURE 1.2
Fama-French's "Beta is Dead" Slicing Test.

When FF regressed this 7-year future return, cross-sectionally, on the prior equal-weighted betas of these 10 portfolios, they found no significant relation, where the CAPM's central prediction is a strong and positive relation between betas and returns. Thus, according to FF, "beta was dead".[17] Then, FF presented evidence that not only does size work well, but so does BTM ratio; together, they both worked

[17] In fact, to provide a more statistically powerful test, they repeated this similar beta mixed size portfolio construction at the end of each month during 1964 to 1989 to conclude that the evidence of beta being important (or "priced") was, at best, weak.

well, so they appear to be measuring different risks. Finally, FF looked at the return-on-equity (ROE) of small stocks and stocks with a high BTM ratio, and found that the ROE of these stocks was quite low—indicating, perhaps, that they are under financial distress and are at risk of bankruptcy. While not proving anything, FF suggest that size and BTM may be a proxy for financial distress—small stocks with high BTM, for instance, are highly stressed—and this may underlie the usefulness of size and BTM. Simply put, investors demand higher returns for financially distressed stocks, as they are more likely to fail together during a recession.

The reception of the Fama French paper was one of controversy, which still exists today. Most reseachers have admitted that Fama and French are right about what works better in the real world of stocks, but they disagree about why. FF represent one camp with their rational investor, financial distress risk economic story. Another camp believes that investors exhibit behavioral tendencies that color their choice of stocks. Underlying this economic story is the fact that individuals tend to overreact to longer-term trends in the economic fortunes of a corporation, and that they believe that the fortunes of stocks that have become less profitable over the past several years will continue to become worse—thus, they put sell pressure on small stocks and value stocks (high BTM stocks). A third camp believes that small stocks and value stocks have simply gone through a "lucky streak", and that we should not place too much importance on the experience of U.S. stocks in the past few decades.

In an attempt to further test the FF findings, Griffin (2002) studied size and book-to-market as stock return predictors in the U.S., Japan, the U.K., and Canada. He found evidence in all four countries that size and BTM forecast stock returns, consistent with FF's findings in U.S. stocks. However, he also found that returns correlate poorly for size and BTM across these countries, which could be evidence that they are risk-based or that they are due to irrational investor behavior—and country stock markets are segmented, preventing investors from arbitraging across differences in these factor returns across countries.

1.6.1 Momentum Stocks

Notably, Fama and French did not quite find all the important factors that drive stock returns. Jegadeesh and Titman (JT; 1993) found that momentum, measured as the one year past return of a stock is an important predictive variable for the following year's return. In fact, a simple sorting of stocks on their one-year past return, followed by an equal-weighted long position in the top 10% "winners" and a short position in the bottom 10% "losers" of last year provides an "arbitrage" profit of almost 1% per month (i.e., about 10% during the following year).[18]

---

[18] It turns out that momentum, while known for decades by some practitioners and academics (e.g., Levy, 1964), was "discovered" by academics by accident. In conducting research for Grinblatt and Titman's (1993) study of mutual fund performance, a PhD student accidently measured the return of mutual fund positions in stocks held today over the past year (rather than over the next year). The result was that most U.S. domestic equity mutual fund managers were, to some extent, holding larger share positions in last-years winners than in other stocks. Building on this finding, Grinblatt et al. (1995) found that such "momentum-investing funds' also outperformed market indexes in the future—indicating that the stocks that they were buying also outperformed—thus, stock momentum was discovered!

Figure 1.3 illustrates the profitability over numerous portfolios formed over the period 1965–1989. The monthly (not annualized) returns of the long-short portfolio over the 36 event months following the portfolio formation are shown first, followed by the cumulated monthly returns over the same 36 months.[19]

Further evidence supporting momentum in U.S. stocks was found during 1941–1964, although not quite as strong—shown in Figure 1.4.

However, JT found that the depression era did not support their "momentum theory", and, instead, momentum stocks lost considerable money (see Figure 1.5).

JT explained that momentum likely did not work during the depression era because of inconsistent monetary policy that artificially created reversals of stock returns during that time. Specifically, when the stock market dropped, the Fed eased monetary policy, and when it boomed, the Fed strongly tightened. Nevertheless, Daniel (2011) has shown, more recently, that momentum stocks outperformed during 1989–2007, but underperformed (badly) during the financial crisis of 2008–2009.

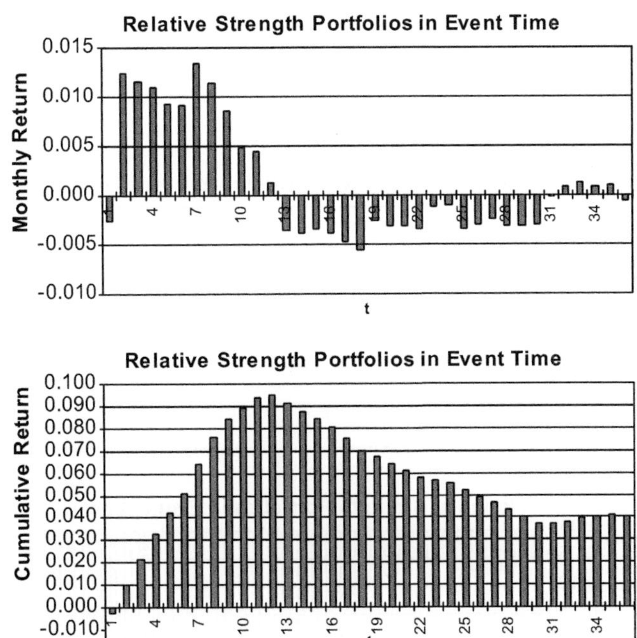

FIGURE 1.3
Monthly and Cumulative Momentum Long/Short Portfolio Returns, 1965–1989.

[19] This ranking and formation strategy is repeated using (overlapping) windows. Specifically, a new portfolio is formed every month, giving (at any point in time) 36 simultaneous (overlapping) portfolio strategies.

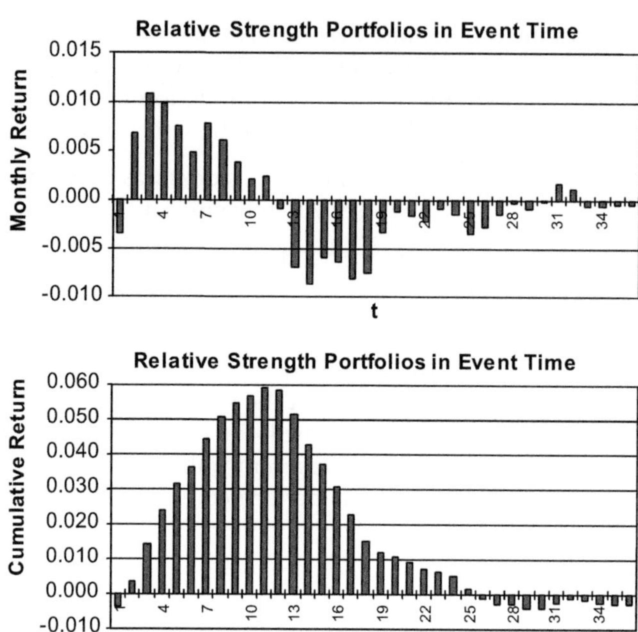

FIGURE 1.4
Monthly and Cumulative Momentum Long/Short Portfolio Returns, 1941–1964.

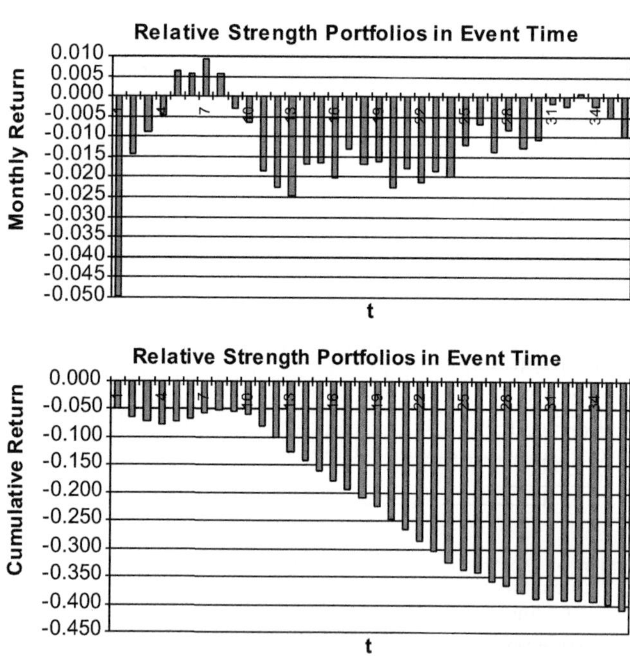

FIGURE 1.5
Monthly and Cumulative Momentum Long/Short Portfolio Returns, 1927–1940.

Further research by Rouwenhorst (1998) found that momentum exists in stocks in Europe, but not in Asia. More recent research seems to find momentum even in Japan (see Asness(2011)).

Today, although the evidence is, at times, inconsistent, momentum is strong enough that most academic researchers appear to accept that it is a reality of markets. One economic explanation of momentum is that investors underreact to short-term news about companies, such as improving earnings or cashflows. Thus, a stock that rises this year has a bright future next year—again, not always, but on average.[20]

Finally, Griffin et al. (GMJ; 2003) examined momentum in the U.S. and 39 other countries, and found evidence that these factors work well in these markets, but that momentum across different countries is only weakly correlated. Therefore, country-level momentum factors work better in capturing momentum, rather than a global momentum factor across all countries. This finding suggests that whatever economics are at play in the risk of stocks, they work a little differently in different countries, but with the same overall result: small stocks outperform large stocks, value stocks outperform growth stocks, and momentum stocks outperform contrarian stocks (all of this is for an average year, but the reverse can occur for any single year or subset of years—such as the superior growth stock returns of the technology boom during the 1990s). Finally, GMJ found that momentum profits tend to reverse in the countries over the following one to four years.

Next, we will describe models that attempt to capture the multiple sources of stock returns noted above. While academics and practitioners do not agree on whether these sources of additional return represent systematic risks or simply return "anomalies", these models have been developed to better describe the drivers of stock returns, regardless of the source of the factors" power.[21]

1.7 THE ASSET PRICING MODELS OF TODAY

The above studies have inspired researchers to add factors to the single-factor model of Equation (1.2) that is, itself, inspired by the CAPM theory. As opposed to this "theory-inspired" single-factor model, almost all recent models are "empirically inspired", which means that they are chosen because they explain the cross-section and/or time-series of security returns while still making economic sense. This means that we don't simply try lots of factors until we find some that work, as this can always be done (and often leads to a breakdown of the model when we try to use it with other data). We carefully examine past

[20] Momentum might also be interpreted as a risk factor. See, for example, Chordia et al. (2002).

[21] The reader should note that there are many more recent papers documenting other anomalies in stock returns. For instance, Sloan (1996) finds that stocks with high accruals—earnings minus cashflows—earn lower future returns than stocks with low accruals. Lee and Swaminathan (2000) find that stocks with lower trading volume (less liquidity) have higher future returns than high trading volume stocks. However, these anomalies are not yet accepted by academics to the point of revising the models that we are about to present in the next section. Or, more accurately, there is not strong agreement that these anomalies are strong enough and are independent of the existing factors to warrant a more complicated model with additional factors.

research for both economic and econometric guidance on the factors that might be used in a model. Fortunately, many researchers have already done this work for us. Almost all models are "multifactor" models, meaning that more than one x-variable ("risk factors") is used to predict the y-variable (security or portfolio excess returns).

1.7.1 Introduction to Multifactor Models

A multifactor model can be visualized as a simple extension of a single factor model, such as the CAPM. However, by using multiple risk factors, we are implicitly rejecting the CAPM and its many assumptions about investors and markets.

The simplest multifactor model is a two-factor model. Let's suppose that we believe that, in addition to the broad stock market, the risk-premium to investing in small stocks drives security returns.

Then, the time-series model would be:

$$R_t = \alpha + \beta \cdot RMRF_t + s \cdot SMB_t + \epsilon_t, \tag{1.10}$$

where s is the exposure of a security, or portfolio, to the "small-capitalization risk-factor". This regression for Chevron-Texaco, implemented using Excel during the 24-month period January 2009 to December 2010, results in the following output Table 1.4.

Table 1.4 Two-Factor Regression for CVX

Regression Output (Unrestricted Model)				
	Coefficients	Standard Error	t Stat	P-value
Intercept	0.00031	0.01	0.03	0.98
RMRF	0.92	0.17	5.32	0.56
SMB	−0.56	0.38	−1.47	−1.35

The adjusted R^2 from this regression is 0.54 (54%), while the adjusted R^2 from the single-factor regression of CVX excess returns on RMRF (from a prior section) is 0.51.[22] Therefore, in this case, the addition of a small-cap factor—to which Chevron-Texaco is negatively correlated—does not matter much. However, since we have estimated the two-factor model, and since its t-statistic is relatively close to −1.645 (the two-tailed critical value for 10% significance), we'll use it.

[22] Note that these R^2 values are very high for an individual stock—likely because CVX is very large cap and had no big surprises during the period, thus, it roughly matched the stock market as a whole. A regression of an individual stock return on the four-factor model usually gives an R^2 of only about 10–20%. As we will see in later chapters, a regression of a managed (long-only) portfolio, such as a mutual fund, using either the one-factor or four-factor models, usually gives an R^2 in excess of 90%. Thus, if you are applying your regression model correctly, you should generally (but not always, as with CVX) see these levels of R^2 values. This is a good diagnostic check of your data work.

Once the model is fitted, the next-period estimated expected return is:

$$\widehat{E}\left[R_{t+1}\right] = \widehat{\beta} \cdot E\left[RMRF_{t+1}\right] + \widehat{s} \cdot E\left[SMB_{t+1}\right], \tag{1.11}$$

or, using the fitted regression from above,

$$\widehat{E}\left[R_{t+1}\right] = 0.92 \cdot E\left[RMRF_{t+1}\right] - 0.56 \cdot E\left[SMB_{t+1}\right]. \tag{1.12}$$

Note that this is an equation of a plane in three-dimensional space, where $\widehat{E}\left[R_{t+1}\right]$ is the vertical axis. The residuals, ϵ_t, are the vertical distance from this plane of the actual month-by-month outcomes, r_t, from the model-predicted values of Equation (1.12).

The next-period estimated total risk, which contains a term for the covariance between RMRF and SMB, is

$$\underbrace{\widehat{V}\left[R_{t+1}\right]}_{\text{Total Risk (Variance)}} = \underbrace{\widehat{\beta}^2 \cdot V\left[RMRF_{t+1}\right] + \widehat{s}^2 \cdot V\left[SMB_{t+1}\right] + 2\widehat{\beta} \cdot \widehat{s} \cdot C\left[RMRF_{t+1}, SMB_{t+1}\right]}_{\text{Systematic Risk}} + \underbrace{V\left[\epsilon_{t+1}\right]}_{\text{Idiosyncratic Risk}}, \tag{1.13}$$

and the next-period estimated systematic (risk-factor related) risk is:

$$\widehat{V}_S\left[R_{t+1}\right] = \widehat{\beta}^2 \cdot V\left[RMRF_{t+1}\right] + \widehat{s}^2 \cdot V\left[SMB_{t+1}\right] + 2\widehat{\beta} \cdot \widehat{s} \cdot C\left[RMRF_{t+1}, SMB_{t+1}\right]. \tag{1.14}$$

Again, following the simple approach of using historical sample data to estimate the above expected returns and variances, the equations for expected return, total, and systematic-only risk become

$$\widehat{E}\left[R_{t+1}\right] = \widehat{\beta} \cdot \overline{rmrf} + \widehat{s} \cdot \overline{smb}, \tag{1.15}$$

$$\widehat{V}\left[R_{t+1}\right] = \widehat{\beta}^2 \cdot \widehat{\sigma}^2_{RMRF} + \widehat{s}^2 \cdot \widehat{\sigma}^2_{SMB} + 2\widehat{\beta} \cdot \widehat{s} \cdot \widehat{\sigma}_{RMRF,\,SMB} + \widehat{\sigma}^2_{\epsilon}, \tag{1.16}$$

and

$$\widehat{V}_S\left[R_{t+1}\right] = \widehat{\beta}^2 \cdot \widehat{\sigma}^2_{RMRF} + \widehat{s}^2 \cdot \widehat{\sigma}^2_{SMB} + 2\widehat{\beta} \cdot \widehat{s} \cdot \widehat{\sigma}_{RMRF,\,SMB}, \tag{1.17}$$

where $\overline{rmrf} = \frac{1}{T}\sum_{t=1}^{T} rmrf_t$,

$$\overline{smb} = \frac{1}{T}\sum_{t=1}^{T} smb_t,$$

$$\widehat{\sigma}^2_{RMRF} = \frac{1}{T-1}\sum_{t=1}^{T}\left(rmrf_t - \overline{rmrf}\right)^2,$$

$$\widehat{\sigma}^2_{SMB} = \frac{1}{T-1}\sum_{t=1}^{T}\left(smb_t - \overline{smb}\right)^2,$$

and $\widehat{\sigma}_{RMRF,SMB} = \frac{1}{T-1}\sum_{t=1}^{T}\left(rmrf_t - \overline{rmrf}\right)\left(smb_t - \overline{smb}\right)$.[23]

---

[23] These sampling statistics are easy to compute in Excel, using the *sample* mean, variance, and covariance functions applied over the time-series of historical data.

1.7.2 Models of Stock Returns

Regression-Based Models Fama and French (1993) designed a widely used multifactor model which adds both the small-capitalization factor (SMB) and a "value stock factor" (HML) to the single-factor model of Equation (1.2).[24]

$$R_t = \alpha + \beta \cdot RMRF_t + s \cdot SMB_t + h \cdot HML_t + e_t. \tag{1.18}$$

However, the most widely used returns-based model for analyzing equities is the four-factor model of Carhart (1997),

$$R_t = \alpha + \beta \cdot RMRF_t + s \cdot SMB_t + h \cdot HML_t + u \cdot UMD_t + \epsilon_t, \tag{1.19}$$

who added a momentum factor (UMD_t) to the three-factor model of Fama and French.[25]

Let's estimate the "Carhart model" for CVX, during 2009–2010 in Table 1.5.

Table 1.5 Four-Factor Regression for CVX

Regression Output (Unrestricted Model)

	Coefficients	Standard Error	t Stat	P-value
Intercept	0.0046	0.0097	0.64	0.98
RMRF	1.1	0.20	5.5	.000026
SMB	−0.61	0.34	−1.8	0.086
HML	0.00028	0.31	0.00090	0.99
UMD	0.31	0.11	2.8	0.012

How did the addition of HML and UMD affect the estimated coefficients on RMRF and SMB ($\widehat{\beta}$ and $\widehat{s}$)? They increased $\widehat{\beta}$ from 0.92 to 1.1, and decreased $\widehat{s}$ from −0.56 to −0.61. Why did these changes occur with the addition of HML and UMD? The answer is that these two new regressors must be correlated, to

[24] One might wonder why Fama and French added back the *RMRF* factor, when their 1992 paper found that beta did not affect stock returns. The reason is that their tests were cross-sectional, meaning that one can assume that the betas of all stocks are unity without much error. In the cross-section, *RMRF* then washes out of differences in stock returns. However, in the time-series, *RMRF* matters for each individual stock or portfolio return. Why don't we force beta to equal one in the time-series regression? For practical reasons, among them, managed funds often carry cashholdings, while others leverage their portfolios, which even Fama and French would admit moves the portfolio beta away from one.

[25] A more detailed description: R_t is the month-t excess return on the stock (net return minus T-bill return), $RMRF_t$ is the month-t excess return on a value-weighted aggregate market proxy portfolio, and SMB_t, HML_t, and UMD_t are the month-t returns on value-weighted, zero-investment factor-mimicking portfolios for size, book-to-market equity, and one-year momentum in stock returns, respectively. This model is based on empirical research by Fama and French (1992, 1993, 1996) and Jegadeesh and Titman (1993) that finds these factors closely capture the cross-sectional and time-series variation in stock returns.

some extent, with RMRF and SMB, thus "stealing" some (pretty small) explanatory power from them, and changing their relation with the predicted variable, R_t.

Also, the four-factor model shows that RMRF and UMD are the most statistically significant explanatory variables, with SMB close behind. HML has no significance, since its p-value is equal to 99% (meaning that the chances of observing a coefficient of $|0.00028|$ or larger by pure randomness, when its actual value is zero, is 99%). So, we conclude that CVX, during 2009–2010, has a beta close to 1 (typical for a stock), is a very large capitalization stock (since its "loading" on SMB is very negative and statistically significant), and it has significant momentum (meaning the prior-year return is high over the period 2009–2010—consistent with increasing oil prices!). Note that, in general, coefficients in this model that are close to (or slightly exceed) one have a large exposure to that risk factor. *However, even coefficients at the level of 0.2 or 0.3 indicate a substantial exposure to a certain risk factor.*

A Stock Characteristic-Based Model Another approach to modeling stocks that is based on the findings noted above (i.e., that market capitalization, value, and momentum drive stock returns) uses the characteristics (observable features) of stocks to assemble them into groups or portfolios of stocks with similar characteristics. Daniel and Titman (1997) found empirical evidence that suggests that characteristics provide better ex-ante forecasts than regression models of the cross-sectional patterns of future stock returns. This evidence indicates that stock factors like equity book-to-market ratio at least partially relate to future stock returns due to investors having behavioral biases against certain types of stocks (e.g., those stocks with recent bad news, which pushes the BTM ratio up "too much").

Following Daniel and Titman, in the characteristic benchmarking approach, the average return of the similar characteristic portfolio is used as a more precise proxy for the expected return of the stock during the same time period. Any deviation of a single stock from this expected return is the stock's "residual", or unexpected return. Daniel et al. (1997) developed such an approach for U.S. equities, and many other researchers have replicated their approach in other stock markets.

First, all stocks (listed on NYSE, AMEX, or Nasdaq) having at least two years of book value of equity information available in the Compustat database, and stock return and market capitalization of equity data in the CRSP database, are ranked, at the end of each June, by their market capitalization. Quintile portfolios are formed (using NYSE size quintile breakpoints), and each quintile portfolio is further subdivided into book-to-market quintiles, based on their most recently available fiscal year-end book-to-market data as of the end of June of the ranking year.[26] Here, we "industry-normalize" the book-to-market ratio, since we would like to classify

---

[26] This usually involves allowing a 30 to 60-day delay in disclosure of fiscal results by corporations.

stocks by how much they deviate from their "industry norms".[27,28] Finally, each of the resulting 25 fractile portfolios are further subdivided into quintiles based on the 12-month past return of stocks through the end of May of the ranking year. This three-way ranking procedure results in 125 fractile portfolios, each having a distinct combination of size, book-to-market, and momentum characteristics.[29] The three-way ranking procedure is repeated at the end of June of each year, and the 125 portfolios are reconstituted at that date.

Figure 1.6 illustrates this process.

A modification of this procedure is to reconstitute these portfolios at the end of each calendar quarter, rather than only once per year on June 30, using updated size, BTM, and momentum data. While the annual sort is closer to an implementable strategy that is an alternative to holding a particular stock, the quarterly sort allows us to more accurately control for the changing characteristics of the stock. For example, the momentum, defined as the prior 12-month return of a stock, can change quickly.

Value-weighted returns are computed for each of the 125 fractile portfolios, and the benchmark for each stock during a given quarter is the buy-and-hold return of the fractile portfolio of which that stock is a member during that quarter. Therefore, the benchmark-adjusted return for a given stock is computed as the buy-and-hold stock return minus the buy-and-hold value-weighted benchmark return during the same quarter.

1.7.3 Models of Bond Returns

Fama and French (1993) found a set of five risk factors that worked well in modeling both stock and bond returns. This includes three stock market factors and two bond market factors:

1. stock market return ($RMRF$),
2. size factor (small cap return minus large cap return) (SMB),
3. value factor (high book-to-market stock return minus low BTM stock return) (HML),

---

[27] Specifically, we compute the book-to-market characteristic as $\frac{\ln(BTM^j_{i,t})-\ln(BTM^j_t)}{\sigma_j\left[\ln(BTM^j_{i,t})-\ln(BTM^j_t)\right]}$, where $BTM^j_{i,t}$ is the book-to-market ratio of stock i, which belongs to industry j on June 30th of year t, and $\ln(BTM^j_t)$ is the log book-to-market ratio of industry j at year t (the aggregate book-value divided by the aggregate market value). Also, $\sigma_j\left[\ln(BTM^j_{i,t}) - \ln(BTM^j_t)\right]$ is the cross-sectional standard deviation of the adjusted book-to-market ratio across industry. This approach was suggested by Cohen and Polk (1998), as well as by discussions with Christopher Polk.

[28] We could industry-normalize the size and momentum of a stock as well, and some researchers have followed this approach. However, the most common approach is to industry-normalize only the book-to-market.

[29] Thus, a stock belonging to size portfolio one, book-to-market portfolio one, and prior return portfolio one is a small, low book-to-market stock having a low prior-year return.

4. bond market maturity premium (10-year Treasury yield minus 30-day T-bill yield) (*TERM*), and
5. default risk premium (Moody's Baa-rated bond yield minus 10-year Treasury yield) (*DEFAULT*).

Panel A

- **Rank all NYSE stocks by Mkt. Cap. -**
  Divide into 5 Quintiles
- **Rank Quintiles = Book Value/Market Value (BTM)**
  Subdivide into 5 more quintiles
- **Rank the 25 fractiles by past year stock return**
  Subdivide into 5 more quintile

A rank of:

Size=5,	BTM=5,	PR1YR=5
Large Cap	High BTM	High Past Return

Panel B

ALL U.S. NYSE/AMEX/NASDAQ STOCKS

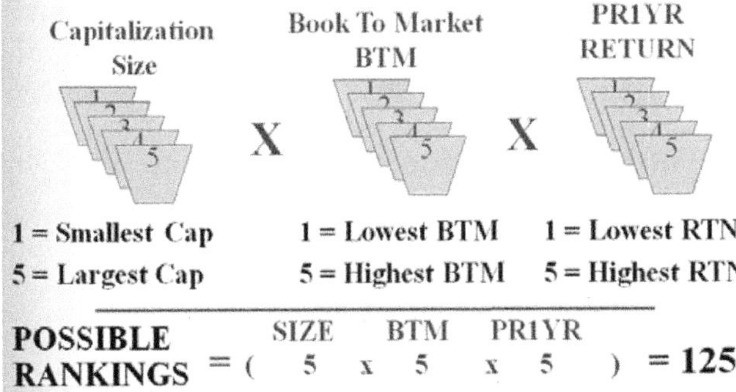

Panel C

Exxon	Size	BTM	PR1YR
1985	5	3	3
1986	5	4	1
1987	5	4	5
1988	5	3	4
1989	5	3	1
1990	5	3	3
1991	5	3	4
1992	5	3	3
1993	5	3	3
1994	5	3	2

Exxon's style?

Consistent Large-Cap

Value Neutral

Changing Momentum

FIGURE 1.6
Daniel, Grinblatt, Titman, and Wermers stock benchmarking procedure.

It is very important to note that Fama and French (1993) modeled the time-series of returns on stocks and bonds, where Fama and French (1992) modeled the cross-sectional (across-stock) differences in returns on stocks—which is why the stock market return is included in the above group, but not in the 1992 paper's factors. In essence, the 1992 paper says that we can assume that beta=1 for all stocks (without a huge amount of error), and, therefore, beta only affects stock returns over time. There is no difference in different stock returns at the same period of time, since they all have assumed betas of one, according to Fama and French (1992).

Fama and French (1993) also find that stock and bond returns are linked together through the correlation of the stock market return with the return on the two bond factors. Interestingly, a large body of other research since then, including Kandel and Stambaugh (1996) has found that broad macroeconomic factors, including the two bond factors noted above, help to forecast the stock market return.

Gruber, Elton, Agrawal, and Mann (2001) find that the three stock risk factors above (1–3) are also useful in modeling corporate bonds—in addition to exposure to potential default and taxation of bond income. Finally, Cornell and Green (1991) find that stock market returns are even more important than government bond market yields in modeling high-yield (junk) bonds.

The above research on bond markets suggest that a five-factor model should be used to model bonds:

$$R_t = \alpha + \beta \cdot RMRF_t + s \cdot SMB_t + h \cdot HML_t + m \cdot TERM_t + d \cdot DEFAULT_t + \epsilon_t. \tag{1.20}$$

Note that there is no momentum factor for bond markets, although some recent papers have also challenged this.

1.8 CHAPTER-END PROBLEMS

1. Download the monthly returns for Exxon-Mobil (XOM) during 2009 and 2010 from CRSP, Yahoo Finance, or another source. Also, download the 30-day Treasury Bill return and the monthly factor returns for RMRF, SMB, HML, and UMD from Ken French's website, http://mba.tuck.dartmouth.edu/pages/faculty/ken.french/.

A. Using Excel or a statistics package, run a single-factor linear regression (ordinary least squares) for XOM (the y-variable is the excess return of XOM, which is the XOM return minus T-Bill return, while the x-variable is the monthly return on RMRF). How does your regression output compare with that of CVX shown in this chapter—what are the differences in the two stocks according to this output?

B. Repeat, using a two-factor model that includes RMRF and SMB. How does your regression output compare with that of CVX shown in this chapter—what are the differences in the two stocks according to this output?

C. Repeat, using the Carhart four-factor model. How does your regression output compare with that of CVX shown in this chapter—what are the differences in the two stocks according to this output?

2. Download monthly returns for Apple (AAPL) during 2009 and 2010, and run a single-factor regression on the S&P 500 as the "market factor". What are the resulting alpha and beta?

3. Using the AAPL data from problem #2, run a four-factor model. What are the coefficients on each factor, and what do they tell you about Apple's stock?

4. Starting with the model of Equation (1.2), derive the risk model shown by Equation (1.6).

5. Starting with the model of Equation (1.10), derive the risk model shown by Equation (1.13).

6. Describe the empirical tests that find violations of the CAPM in stock returns.

7. Describe the empirical approach that Fama and French (1992) used to find that "beta is dead".

8. Discuss each of the assumptions of the CAPM. For each assumption, provide some brief evidence from financial markets that indicates that the assumption may not be correct.

9. Suppose that an institution holds Portfolio K. The institution wants to use Portfolio L to hedge its exposure to inflation. Specifically, it wants to combine K and L to reduce its inflation exposure to zero. Portfolios K and L are well diversified, so the manager can ignore the risk of individual assets and assume that the only source of uncertainty in the portfolio is the surprises in the two factors. The returns to the two portfolios are:

$$R_K = 0.12 + 0.5F_{INFL} + 1.0F_{GDP}$$
$$R_L = 0.11 + 1.5F_{INFL} + 2.5F_{GDP}$$

Calculate the weights that a manager should have on K and L to achieve this goal.

10. Portfolio A has an expected return of 10.25 percent and a factor sensitivity of 0.5. Portfolio B has an expected return of 16.2 percent and a factor sensitivity of 1.2. The risk-free rate is 6 percent, and there is one factor. Determine the factor's price of risk (see Tables 1.4 and 1.5).

Chapter 2

Returns-Based Performance Evaluation Models

ABSTRACT

This chapter provides an introduction to the returns-based models used today to evaluate asset managers: equity and fixed-income mutual fund, hedge fund, and institutional managers. Advanced econometric modifications of such models, designed to accommodate the complexities of asset manager strategies and security characteristics, are also briefly discussed.

2.1 INTRODUCTION

An analysis of the rates-of-return, over time, of an asset manager is the most basic and important starting point for evaluating the performance of that manager. For an index fund, a comparison of returns with those of the index that it tracks informs investors about how efficiently the fund mirrors the index as well as the costs of the fund.

For an actively managed fund, an analysis of returns relative to a benchmark, or set of benchmarks, also addresses the skill level of the manager. Indeed, the return on a fund is the main product provided by that fund, so why not analyze the quality of the product? However, unlike a manufactured good such as an automobile, it is perilously difficult to arrive at a firm conclusion about the quality of a fund manager through an analysis of that manager's returns.[1] This does not mean that such an analysis is without value; on the contrary, *returns-based analysis is an extremely valuable first step in conducting a comprehensive analysis of a manager.*

---

[1] Take, for instance, U.S.-domiciled equity mutual fund managers. Over the 1975–2002 period, Kosowski et al. (2006) show that about 1/3rd of the mutual funds that achieved an alpha greater than 10% per year (net of costs) over (at least) a 5-year period—a seemingly outstanding performance record—were simply lucky! The other 2/3rds were truly skilled managers.

Performance Evaluation and Attribution of Security Portfolios. http://dx.doi.org/10.1016/B978-0-12-744483-3.00002-X
© 2013 Elsevier Inc. All rights reserved.
For End-of-chapter Questions: © 2012. CFA Institute, Reproduced and republished with permission from CFA Institute. All rights reserved.

This chapter introduces some basic models that are used today to arrive at a statistical (quantitative) evaluation of the skills of an asset manager.[2] Here, we present models that only require periodic (e.g., monthly) realized returns of an asset manager to evaluate her performance. In Chapter 4, we present models that require portfolio holdings information. In Chapters 6, 7, and 8, we will return to some of the more sophisticated returns-based models to discuss them in more detail.

Returns-based models are extremely appealing because they are, in general, much simpler to apply than holdings-based models—which require a great deal of data and advanced analysis to apply. In addition, realized returns are almost always available for managed portfolios, either to the public (mutual funds) or to all current investors in the funds (hedge funds). In addition, recent trends are moving asset managers, such as hedge fund managers, toward providing more transparency in their return reporting to the public.[3] Thus, the models below are likely to become even more useful in the future for investors and potential investors to use to evaluate an asset manager's skills.

2.2 GOALS, GUIDELINES, AND PERILS OF PERFORMANCE EVALUATION

Before proceeding with our discussion of benchmarks, performance measures, and models in this paper, let us set out some standards.

2.2.1 Benchmarks

To use a particular benchmark (or set of benchmarks) as a "measuring tape," against which to compare a fund, a manager should be able to "size up" the competition (i.e., the benchmark). Accordingly, Bailey (1995) proposes that a valid benchmark should be:

1. *Unambiguous*: The name and weights of component securities should be known (rules out unknown "derived" benchmarks, such as Arbitrage Pricing Theory factors),
2. *Tradeable:* It should be available as a passive investment alternative for the manager,
3. *Measurable:* One must be able to compute a valid return on the benchmark periodically (might not be possible for benchmarks with illiquid assets),
4. *Appropriate:* Benchmark must reflect the manager's style,
5. *Reflective of current investment opinions:* Manager should be able to form an opinion on the expected rate-of-return on the benchmark, and
6. *Specified in advance:* To give the manager a passive alternative ahead of time, in order to make clear the "measuring tape".

---

[2] Much of the discussion of this chapter follows Wermers (2011), and I acknowledge and thank the Annual Review of Financial Economics (published by Annual Reviews) for permission to use material from that paper.

[3] For instance, several hedge fund databases (e.g., TASS, CISDM, and HFR) provide self-reported monthly returns for a large segment of the hedge fund universe—both on-shore and off-shore domiciled.

Table 2.1 Properties of Several Commonly Used Benchmarks

Benchmark	Unambiguous	Tradeable	Measureable	Appropriate	Reflective	Specified
Peer Group	✓	✓	✓	✓	✓	—
Market Index	✓	Usually	✓	?	?	✓
Statistical Factor[a]	—	—	?	—	—	—
Empirical Factor[b]	—	?	✓	?	?	✓
Macroeconomic Factor	✓	Sometimes	Sometimes	?	?	Sometimes

[a] *For instance, factors derived from factor analysis or principle components analysis.*
[b] *For instance, the Fama and French SMB and HML factors, which attempt to capture the size premium and value premium, or the Barra factors.*

Table 2.1 shows some examples that have been used as returns-based benchmarks for mutual fund managers, as well as whether each fulfills these six principles.

Consider, for example, peer group benchmarks—which are when a fund manager is judged against her peers, who presumably consider a similar set of securities in the market and/or draw from a similar set of strategies. Usually, mutual fund managers self-designate their investment objective to choose the group against which they wish to be compared—as well as to set expectations about their risk and return profile, and how their portfolios might correlate with portfolios of managers in other investment objective categories. An example is aggressive-growth mutual fund managers. To explain further the entries in the above table for peer group benchmarks:

Unambiguous: yes, the names of your peers are known at the beginning of the evaluation period, and usually equal-weighting is used to form the peer benchmark.

Tradeable: yes, usually an equal investment in her peers could (at least in theory) be available to a manager (perhaps, as a set of subadvisors for the fund).

Measurable: yes, mutual fund returns are reported daily.

Appropriate: yes, according to the choice of the manager of that investment-objective category.

Reflective: yes, the manager should be able to forecast returns on his securities and strategies, and, therefore, on his peers.

Specified: no, unless they are passive fund peers

Another example is the use of market indexes as benchmarks. For instance, many mutual fund managers use the Standard and Poor's 500 index as their chosen benchmark to be compared against. However, is this a good benchmark? The evidence is mixed:

Unambiguous: yes, unless the index changes substantially over the performance period.

Tradeable: yes (in the case of the S&P 500, but could be questionable with other less liquid market indexes).

Measureable: yes (with liquid indexes).

Appropriate: questionable. Most mutual fund managers invest outside the S&P 500, especially in smaller-capitalization stocks.

Reflective: questionable. Most mutual fund managers state that they do not attempt to time the market, which implies that they do not forecast the S&P 500's return.

Specified: yes.

So, it is easy to see that some widely used benchmarks do not satisfy all of our requirements for a "good" benchmark. While, at times, we choose to use these benchmarks for other reasons, it is important to understand their limitations.

2.2.2 Performance Measures

Chen and Knez (1996) propose that a performance measure should have, at minimum, four properties:

1. *Fit:* capture the strategies that could reasonably be used by an uninformed investor with "control factors", and assign zero performance to portfolios that result from these simple strategies, whether they be passive or active,
2. *Be scalable:* linear combinations of the manager measures should equal the measure for the same linear combination of their portfolios,
3. *Be continuous:* two managers with arbitrarily close skills should have arbitrarily close performance measures, and
4. *Exhibit monotonicity:* assign higher measures for more-skilled managers.

These properties ensure that performance measures are not easily "gamed" by unskilled asset managers.

For example, suppose that we use the "scoring" system shown in Table 2.2 for fund managers for each year of a two-year period.

Such a scoring system might be appealing for risk-averse investors, who wish to penalize more on the downside than they reward on the upside. However, it is easy to see how such a system could be "gamed" by an unskilled manager—who, let's suppose, has a 50% chance of a "bad" and a 50% chance of a "good" outcome

Table 2.2 Example of Fund Scoring

Outcome	Fund Return (%/yr)	Benchmark Return (%/yr)	Score
Bad	8	10	−4
Mediocre	10	10	0
Good	12	10	2

(i.e., pure luck dictates the outcomes). That manager, facing this concave "scoring curve" would choose to "hug" the benchmark by replicating it, rather than taking a risk which would, on average, score below zero. This is not a bad outcome (a score of zero) for an unskilled manager. However, suppose that a skilled manager has a 60% chance of good and a 40% chance of bad. The above scoring system would assign this manager, on average, a score of

$$Score = 0.6 \cdot 2 + 0.4 \cdot (-4) = -0.4,$$

clearly, a violation of the monotonicity principle #4. Why is this bad? Because it imposes a risk-averse scoring system directly on the total risk of a manager, but much of this risk might be diversified away simply by holding other managers, too. The consequence is that this manager may be wrongly incentivized to not to use his superior skills, which involve taking some risk.

Other examples are commonly used discrete scoring systems, such as Morningstar's star system or Lipper's leader system. With both systems, there is a cutoff for discrete scores, such as the cutoff between Morningstar four- and five-star funds. If this system is applied without exception, then it can provide an incentive for a manager to modify her risks when her fund is close to the border between the star ratings.[4]

2.2.3 Manipulation-Proof Performance Measures

Goetzmann, Ingersoll, Spiegel, and Welch (GISW; 2007) provide further detail of properties of performance measures that resist gaming. An often-quoted way to game a simple returns-based regression model that assumes normally distributed returns, for example, is to sell-short out-of-the-money call or put options on an index, then invest the proceeds in the riskfree asset. This strategy generates left-skewed returns, with greater skewness present for more out-of-the-moneyness of the derivatives; resulting small-sample regression alphas (which assume normality) will be positive (and low volatility) most of the time, even though the strategy requires no real manager skill.

[4] Indeed, a large literature has developed on the tendency of fund managers to attempt to game these measures, called the "mutual fund tournaments" literature. See, for example, Chevalier and Ellison (1997) and Brown, Harlow, and Starks (1996).

Goetzmann, Ingersoll, Spiegel, and Welch (GISW; 2007) ask whether a manipulation-proof performance measure (MPPM) is possible, if we define an MPPM as one that has four properties:

1. The measure should produce a single valued score with which to rank each subject,
2. The score's value should not depend upon the portfolio's beginning dollar value,
3. An uninformed investor cannot expect to enhance his estimated score by deviating from the benchmark portfolio. At the same time informed investors should be able to produce higher scoring portfolios, and can always do so by taking advantage of "arbitrage" opportunities, and
4. The measure should be consistent with standard financial market equilibrium conditions.

GISW find that an MPPM is possible, and that the formula has a simple interpretation: it is the average per period welfare of a power utility investor in the managed fund. Unfortunately, most performance measures used in the literature are not perfectly manipulation proof, which makes it very important to understand the source of the performance of managers. Short of personal knowledge of the portfolio manager (which did not seem to work very well with Madoff's hedge fund), there are two main ways to accomplish this goal. First, extract as much information as possible from the reported returns of the fund. Second, obtain detailed portfolio holdings—or, even better, a complete listing of trades including prices, sizes, and dates. This chapter aims to set out some of the best recent advances in each of these two areas.

2.2.4 Type I or Type II Error (Which Would You Prefer?)

Avoiding manipulation could be clearly accomplished in a very easy way: dogmatically assign all active managers with zero performance, ex-ante. Of course, this comes with a huge price: we miss out on the superior returns of truly skilled managers. So, all performance models and benchmarks must be chosen with an eye toward which is more important: Type I error, falsely identifying a skilled manager, or Type II error, falsely identifying an unskilled manager. Surely, only the most dogmatic investor would completely focus on Type I error, as shown by Baks et al. (2001). But, it would be a bigger mistake to focus completely on Type II error, as shown by Barras et al. (2010). Clearly, models and benchmarks that follow the above guidelines help to reduce both types of errors. Since no model is perfect, however, the researcher should attempt to apply as many models as is practical, reasonably adding and changing assumptions about benchmarks and model specifications.[5] As with the electrical engineering student trying to figure out what is in the "black box" (capacitors, resistors, inductors, etc.), the aggregate evidence should lead to stronger conclusions.

---

[5] For example, Pastor and Stambaugh (2002a) recommend adding non-market benchmarks to improve inferences about manager ability—for example, a technology index when modeling technology funds.

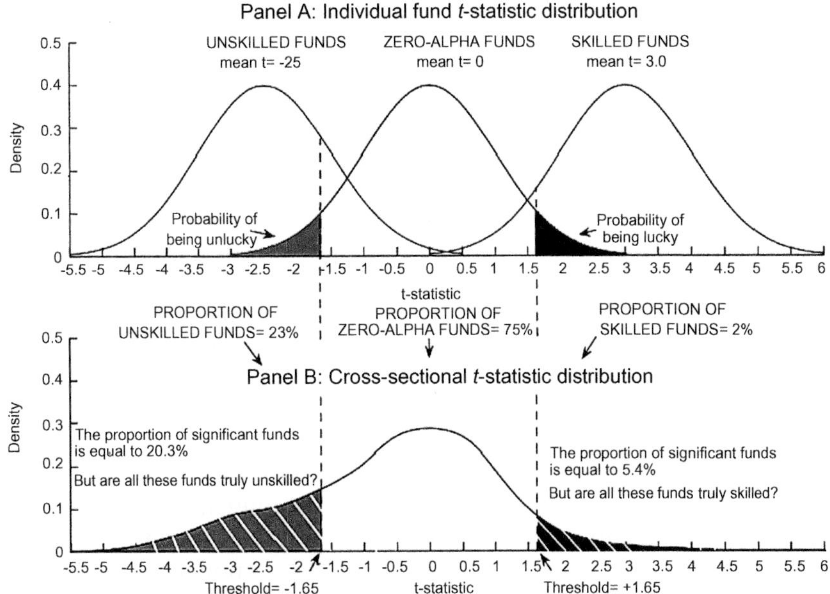

FIGURE 2.1
Three Types of Managers.

Take, for instance, the Figure 2.1 (Panel A) distributions of unskilled, zero-alpha, and skilled fund managers from Barras et al. (2010). These distributions, while hypothetical, attempt to roughly match the distribution and proportion of each fund type as estimated by Barras et al.

Suppose that, as indicated in Panel A, we use a critical value of 1.65 to decide on whether a fund manager is skilled, and a critical value of -1.65 to decide whether the manager is unskilled (has a negative alpha, net of fees). Note, also, that a zero-alpha manager is considered just skilled enough to earn back fees and trading costs.

Note that there is almost no Type I error attributable to unskilled fund managers—it is extremely unlikely for one of these managers to exhibit a t-statistic greater than 1.65. Therefore, in the above graph, Type I error is given by the black area, where a zero-alpha manager is falsely identified as being skilled (positive alpha, net of fees). Type II error is the area to the left of the black shaded region, *but under the skilled fund distributional curve.*

Panel B shows what we observe when we do not know the distribution of alphas for each manager type, nor the proportion of each type. We are faced with a very difficult to comprehend cross-section of t-statistics of alpha, and identifying truly skilled managers (as well as truly unskilled managers) becomes a very complicated statistical problem! In Chapter 8, we address a very powerful and simple approach to this problem.

2.2.5 The Confounding Role of Risk-Aversion

It has long been known that risk-aversion may mitigate a skilled manager's ability to produce alpha. In an extreme example, Verrecchia (1980) shows that a manager with quadratic utility will exhibit a reduction in alpha when the manager receives a signal of a large market return, due to risk-aversion increasing in wealth for quadratic utility.[6] In response, Koijen (2010) applies a structural model, with fund managers having Constant Relative Risk Aversion (CRRA) preferences, that allows the separation of risk-aversion and skill using time-varying alphas, betas, and residual risk. The variation in alphas, betas, and residual risk, together, are informative about the parameters describing preferences, technology (skill and benchmarks), and the incentive contract of the manager. Interestingly, Koijen finds a positive correlation between estimates of ability and risk aversion among U.S. domestic equity mutual fund managers, which indicates that skilled managers may be difficult to locate because they invest rather conservatively. In using Koijen's approach, we must explicitly assume something about the (1) type of preferences (e.g., CRRA), (2) benchmark, and (3) incentive contract of the portfolio manager. In many cases, we do not know these parameters, and Koijen (2010) demonstrates that we must use care in interpreting the results of regression approaches that do not account for the interplay of these three parameters over time, such as the returns-based measures discussed in the next section. Holdings-based performance evaluation, discussed in a later section, allows a more precise (but, still imperfect) inference about ability in the presence of risk-aversion.

2.3 RETURNS-BASED ANALYSIS

All asset managers provide net returns to their clients, and many make these return data public. The widespread availability of returns data makes it imperative to extract the maximum information possible about fund performance, strategy, and risk-taking from returns. This goal involves the application of the best possible models, based on a knowledge of the types of risks taken by fund managers, the statistical distribution of the rewards to those risks, and the breakdown of systematic vs. idiosyncratic risks.

Many biases can result from the improper application of returns-based models, all of which require assumptions about the set of strategies from which a manager generates returns. The most well-documented problem is that of choosing a benchmark, or set of benchmarks, that are mean-variance inefficient when measuring performance with a mean-variance model. Roll (1978) shows how such a choice of inefficient benchmarks can result in any conceivable ranking of investment managers, making performance evaluation an ambiguous undertaking.

[6] Also, Admati and Ross (1985) show, in a one-period model, that alphas are a function of both ability and risk aversion.

Next, we show recent solutions to several of the problems confronting returns-based analysis.[7]

2.3.1 Baseline Models

The most widely used returns-based model among academics in analyzing equity managers is the four-factor model of Carhart (1997),

$$r_t = \alpha + \beta \cdot RMRF_t + s \cdot SMB_t + h \cdot HML_t + u \cdot UMD_t + \epsilon_t, \tag{2.1}$$

where r_t is the month-t excess return on the managed portfolio (net return minus T-bill return), $RMRF_t$ is the month-t excess return on a value-weighted aggregate market proxy portfolio, and $SMB_t, HML_t,$ and UMD_t are the month-t returns on value-weighted, zero-investment factor-mimicking portfolios for size, book-to-market equity, and one-year momentum in stock returns, respectively. This model is based on empirical research by Fama and French (1992, 1993, 1996) and Jegadeesh and Titman (1993) that finds these factors closely capture the cross-sectional and time-series variation in stock returns. A regression of an individual stock return on the four-factor model gives an R-squared of only about 10–20%, but a regression of a managed (long-only) portfolio usually gives an R-squared in excess of 90%.

Does this model fulfill our six requirements for good benchmarks? It turns out that Fama and French formed these benchmarks with this in mind: the factor returns are constructed from long-short positions in actual stocks, although the returns to these positions do not reflect trading costs of rebalancing each month. A further discussion of the construction of these benchmarks can be obtained from Professor Kenneth French's website, as well as in our next chapter and in section 3.5.2.

Hedge funds are notoriously difficult to model. However, in hedge fund studies, a most-popular (current) model has evolved: the seven-factor model of Fung and Hsieh (2004),

$$\begin{aligned} r_t = \alpha + \beta \cdot SPRF_t + s \cdot SMB_t + g \cdot TREAS10YR_t + c \cdot CREDIT_t \\ + b \cdot BONDPTFS_t + d \cdot CURRPTFS_t + o \cdot COMMPTFS_t + \epsilon_t, \end{aligned} \tag{2.2}$$

where the factors are, successively, the S&P 500 return minus risk free rate, Wilshire small cap minus large cap return, change in the constant maturity yield of the 10-year U.S. Treasury, change in the spread of Moody's Baa-rated corporate bonds over the 10-year U.S. Treasury, and three primitive trend-following strategies—derived from bond markets, currency markets, and commodities markets, respectively.

---

[7] However, there are issues that returns-based analysis will not be able to solve. For example, Goetzmann et al. (2000) show that measuring performance on a less-frequent basis than the manager's trading horizon can result in an "interim trading bias' in measured alphas. Such issues require holdings-based analysis, which is discussed in a later section.

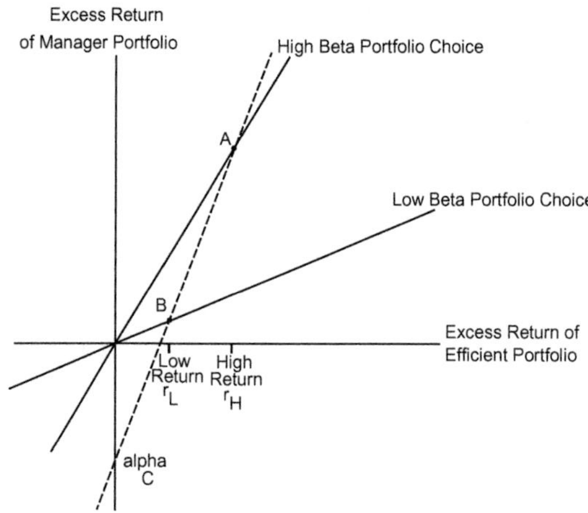

FIGURE 2.2
Timing-Related Biases.

Note that this model, to avoid the data biases in hedge fund databases, constructs benchmarks based on asset returns, rather than hedge fund (Fung and Hsieh, 2004). Fung and Hsieh (2004) find that significant loadings on these seven risk factors are found in 57% of the hedge funds in the TASS database, and 37% of the funds in HFR.

There are many assumptions behind the models represented by Eqs. (2.1) and (2.2). For example, both models assume normally distributed asset and factor returns, as well as constant risk-loadings. Next, we explore the treatments of violations of some assumptions of these models.

2.3.2 Models with Timing Factors

Most prior research on mutual fund performance indicates little evidence that fund managers can time the market. However, if some managers can time the market, this can bias our inferences of selectivity abilities (see, for example, Grinblatt and Titman (1989)). Figure 2.2 shows the usual case—where the market portfolio of stocks outperforms the riskfree asset. In the presence of a skilled timing manager, the alpha of the regression is downward biased.

To control for this possibility, there are two generally used returns-based modifications to models that attempt to capture timing skills separately from selectivity skills.[8] These are the Treynor and Mazuy (TM; 1966) model,

$$r_{i,t} = \alpha_i + b_i \cdot RMRF_t + \gamma_i \cdot [RMRF_t]^2 + \varepsilon_{i,t}, \tag{2.3}$$

[8] Note that, in a model that does not have a timing factor included (e.g., all of the prior models in this chapter), the alpha of the regression will be biased (usually downward) if the manager is a good market timer.

and the Merton and Henriksson (MH; 1981) model,

$$r_{i,t} = \alpha_i + b_i \cdot RMRF_t + \gamma_i \cdot [RMRF_t]^+ + \varepsilon_{i,t}, \tag{2.4}$$

where α_i is the measure of selectivity for the managed portfolio, controlling for any market-timing abilities (under certain assumptions), and $[RMRF_t]^+ = \max(0, RMRF_t)$. What is the difference between these two models? The TM model assumes that a manager is a "proportional timer", meaning that he forecasts RMRF, then adjusts his portfolio beta (b_i) to be proportional to his forecast of RMRF. In other words, for this manager,

$$b_i^{\text{target}} = c \cdot E\left[RMRF_t/I_{mgr}\right],$$

where c=a constant, and $E\left[RMRF_t/I_{mgr}\right]$ = the expected return on the stock market minus the riskfree return, from the point-of-view of the manager (using the manager's information set, I_{mgr}). Substituting this target b_i into the single factor model,

$$r_{i,t} = \alpha_i + b_i \cdot RMRF_t + e_{i,t}, \tag{2.5}$$

gives the TM model.

The MH model assumes that a manager chooses from only two values of b_i^{target}:

$$b_i^{\text{target}} = b_i^{\text{hightarget}}, \textit{if } E\left[RMRF_t/I_{mgr}\right] > 0$$
$$b_i^{\text{target}} = b_i^{\text{lowtarget}}, \textit{if } E\left[RMRF_t/I_{mgr}\right] \leqslant 0,$$

where $b_i^{\text{hightarget}} > b_i^{\text{lowtarget}}$. Neither type of market-timing behavior, TM or MH, is likely to accurately describe actual timing strategies of managers, but they are an attempt to extract some information about timing from returns. Other types of timing measures can be designed by specifying a functional form for the manager's timing strategy.

2.3.3 Return Smoothing

Bollen and Pool (2009) find that return smoothing is common among hedge funds, apparently to fool investors into believing returns are less volatile.[9] Getmansky, Lo, and Makharov (GLM; 2004) suggest that Eq. (2.2), or any chosen model, can be modified to account for return smoothing.

[9] For example, a fund having true returns of +12% and −8% may report (compounded equivalent) returns of +1.51% and +1.51% to lower both the observed fund volatility and the fund's measured exposure to risk-factors.

GLM model the observed hedge fund return as a smoothing of lagged and contemporaneous returns,

$$R_t^O = \theta_0 R_t + \theta_1 R_{t-1} + \theta_2 R_{t-2},$$

where $\theta_0 + \theta_1 + \theta_2 = 1$. GLM show how the seven-factor model (Eq. (2.2)) augmented with the smoothing equation can be estimated with maximum likelihood techniques.

2.3.4 Non-Normal Alphas[10]

Mutual funds, and especially hedge funds, have return distributions that render suspect any analysis using standard assumptions about the shape of these distributions as well as the models and risk-factors that are appropriate to measure performance. There are several irregularities in managed fund returns that deserve attention. First, hedge funds often have a large skewness and/or kurtosis in their alpha distributions. If we do not control for these non-normal distributions, and, instead, measure performance with a standard factor model (that assumes normality), both large Type I and Type II errors can easily result.

Kosowski, Timmermann, Wermers, and White (KTWW; 2006) show how to implement a bootstrap technique with any arbitrary model of returns, in a complicated setting with large numbers of active managers having different (potentially non-normal) distributions. KTWW show that managers with high or low estimated alphas tend to have return distributions that have even greater levels of skewness and kurtosis present—making a bootstrap especially important in the extreme regions of the performance spectrum.

A brief illustration of the bootstrap using the Carhart (1997) four-factor model of Eq. (2.1) follows; the application of the bootstrap procedure to other models is very similar, with the only modification of the following steps being the substitution of the appropriate benchmark model of performance.[11] First, the Carhart model is used to compute ordinary least squares (OLS)-estimated alphas, factor loadings, and residuals using the time series of monthly net returns (minus the T-bill rate) for fund i (r_{it}):

$$r_{it} = \widehat{\alpha}_i + \widehat{\beta}_i RMRF_t + \widehat{s}_i SMB_t + \widehat{h}_i HML_t + \widehat{u}_i UMD_t + \widehat{\epsilon}_{it} \tag{2.6}$$

For fund i, the coefficient estimates, $\{\widehat{\alpha}_i, \widehat{\beta}_i, \widehat{s}_i, \widehat{h}_i, \widehat{u}_i\}$, as well as the time series of estimated residuals, $\{\widehat{\epsilon}_{i,t}, t = T_{i0}, \ldots, T_{i1}\}$, and the t-statistic of estimated alpha, $\widehat{t}_{\widehat{\alpha}_i}$, are saved, where T_{i0} and T_{i1} are the dates of the first and last monthly returns available for fund i, respectively. Next, for each fund i, we draw a sample with

[10] This topic is discussed in detail in Chapter 6.

[11] The simplest bootstrap from KTWW, the residual-only bootstrap, is illustrated. More complicated bootstrapping procedures are also described in KTWW.

replacement from the fund residuals that are saved in the first step above, creating a pseudo time series of resampled residuals, $\{\widehat{\epsilon}_{i,t_\varepsilon}^b, t_\varepsilon = s_{T_{i0}}^b, \ldots, s_{T_{i1}}^b\}$, where b is an index for the bootstrap number (so $b = 1$ for bootstrap resample number one), and where each of the time indices $s_{T_{i0}}^b, \ldots, s_{T_{i1}}^b$ are drawn randomly from $[T_{i0}, \ldots, T_{i1}]$ in such a way that reorders the original sample of $T_{i1} - T_{i0} + 1$ residuals for fund i. Conversely, the original chronological ordering of the factor returns is unaltered.[12]

Next, we construct a time series of pseudo monthly excess returns for this fund, imposing the null hypothesis of zero true performance ($\alpha_i = 0$, or, equivalently, $\widehat{t_{\alpha_i}} = 0$):

$$\{r_{i,t}^b = \widehat{\beta}_i RMRF_t + \widehat{s}_i SMB_t + \widehat{h}_i HML_t + \widehat{u}_i UMD_t + \widehat{\epsilon}_{i,t_\varepsilon}^b\}, \tag{2.7}$$

for $t = T_{i0}, \ldots T_{i1}$ and $t_\varepsilon = s_{T_{i0}}^b, \ldots, s_{T_{i1}}^b$. As Eq. (2.7) indicates, this sequence of artificial returns has a true alpha (and t-statistic of alpha) that is zero by costruction. However, when we next regress the returns for a given bootstrap sample, b, on the Carhart factors, a positive estimated alpha (and t-statistic) may result, since that bootstrap may have drawn an abnormally high number of positive residuals, or, conversely, a negative alpha (and t-statistic) may result if an abnormally high number of negative residuals are drawn.

Repeating the above steps across all funds $i = 1, \ldots, N$, we arrive at a draw from the cross-section of bootstrapped alphas. Repeating this for all bootstrap iterations, $b = 1, \ldots, 1{,}000$, we then build the distribution of these cross-sectional draws of alphas, $\{\widehat{\alpha}_i^b, i = 1, \ldots, N\}$, or their t-statistics, $\{\widehat{t}_{\widehat{\alpha}_i}^b, i = 1, \ldots, N\}$, that result purely from sampling variation, while imposing the null of a true alpha that is equal to zero. For example, the distribution of alphas (or t-statistics) for the top fund is constructed as the distribution of the maximum alpha (or, maximum t-statistic) generated across all bootstraps.[13] (Importantly, this cross-sectional distribution can be non-normal, even if individual fund alphas are normally distributed, as described in KTWW.) If we find that our bootstrap iterations generate far fewer extreme positive values of $\widehat{\alpha}$ (or $\widehat{t_{\alpha}}$) compared to those observed in the actual data, then we conclude that sampling variation (luck) is unlikely to be the sole source of high alphas—genuine stockpicking skills likely exist.

2.3.5 Non-Stable Regression Parameters

The standard assumption of stable model parameters in a linear model is often violated by mutual funds, and, especially, by hedge funds. For instance, hedge

---

[12] The authors also describe a version of the bootstrap that draws the residual from the same time period for all funds (that exist during that period)—a "cross-sectional bootstrap.' Fama and French (2010) further recommend simultaneously drawing factor returns from these randomized time periods for improved inference.

[13] Of course, this maximum alpha can potentially be associated with a different fund during each bootstrap iteration, depending on the outcome of the draw from each fund's residuals.

funds often shift strategies or leverage, which can result in a flawed estimate of alpha by standard fixed-parameter regression techniques.

Bollen and Whaley (2009) demonstrate how a standard linear model can be modified using the changepoint regression technique of Andrews, Lee, and Ploberger (ALP, 1996) to pick up unknown structural shifts in risk-loadings or alphas by funds.[14] For instance, a changepoint regression (in a single factor model) with a single break (changepoint) can be written as:

$$
\begin{aligned}
r_t &= \alpha_1 + \beta_1 F_t + \epsilon_t \qquad \textit{for} \quad t = 1, \ldots, T\pi \\
r_t &= \alpha_1 + \alpha_2 + (\beta_1 + \beta_2) F_t + \epsilon_t \quad \textit{for} \quad t = T\pi + 1, \ldots, T.
\end{aligned}
$$

Then, the econometrician tests the null hypothesis $H_0 : \alpha_2 = \beta_2 = 0$. ALP show how to construct a test for an arbitrary number of changepoints, which is particularly useful for managed funds with long histories and different managers or strategies over time.

2.3.6 Unpriced Benchmarks

Pastor and Stambaugh (2002a) show how the addition of an unpriced benchmark to a regression model can improve inference about manager skills. The key is that the longer history of the unpriced benchmark, relative to an active portfolio that chooses securities in that benchmark, helps to reduce sampling error in the regression. For instance, a technology fund manager in the U.S. may be modeled with the four-factor model of Carhart, augmented with a passive technology index,

$$r_t = \alpha^{PS} + \beta \cdot RMRF_t + s \cdot SMB_t + h \cdot HML_t + u \cdot UMD_t + \eta \cdot TECH_t + \varepsilon_t.$$

The intercept from the above augmented regression, α^{PS}, has tighter standard errors than the intercept from the standard Carhart model,

$$r_t = \alpha + \beta \cdot RMRF_t + s \cdot SMB_t + h \cdot HML_t + u \cdot UMD_t + \varepsilon_t,$$

due to the ability of *TECH* to better capture passive, unpriced risk contained in the active technology portfolio. To apply the augmented model, PS advocate running a first-stage regression of $TECH_t$ on the four factors using the entire time-series for the index (which is usually much longer than that for a managed fund), and saving the regression intercept α^{TECH}. In the second stage, the resulting α^{TECH} is used to adjust the first-stage α of the fund. α^{TECH} helps to control for sampling error that is contained in α.

As another version of this approach, Hunter et al. (2011) suggest augmenting with the unpriced *active* peer-group risk,

$$r_t = \alpha^{HKKW} + \beta \cdot RMRF_t + s \cdot SMB_t + h \cdot HML_t u \cdot UMD_t + \gamma \cdot TECHFUND_t + \varepsilon_t,$$

[14] By structural shifts, we mean intended shifts in model parameters, not those that result from unexpected, temporary shifts in factor loadings of the underlying assets or strategies.

where *TECHFUND* is the residual return of the equal-weighted portfolio of peer funds, after controlling for the four factors in a first-stage regression. There are several advantages of using an active peer-group rather than a passive index. First, adding a peer group factor controls for strategies (both priced and unpriced) used in common by many funds, which can easily be exploited by investing equal amounts in all active funds. Second, estimation errors can be dramatically reduced. For instance, this approach reduces the well-known problem that highly ranked funds tend to have underestimated betas during the ranking period, and, therefore, do not have persistent performance once the higher beta is estimated during the out-of-sample period—the addition of $TECHFUND_t$ helps to capture fund residuals that are, by chance, (negatively) correlated with risk factors.

2.3.7 Bayesian Methods[15]

The large levels of idiosyncratic risk taken by active asset managers means that large estimation errors can result when estimating models. In addition, models and benchmarks never perfectly control for priced risk. While a careful choice of models, as described above, can help to tone down these issues, a Bayesian point-of-view can also be used to mitigate the influence of noise and model misspecification. Pastor and Stambaugh (PS; 2002b) provide a clear demonstration of a Bayesian evaluation of mutual funds, and helped to usher in several further contributions using a Bayesian approach. An appealing feature of their model is that it allows a prior belief to be specified, separately, for the skill of a particular manager and for the ability of a particular model to properly price all passive assets. PS show that optimal portfolios of mutual funds are influenced greatly by prior beliefs about both; this echoes the findings of Baks, Metrick, and Wachter (2001), who find that even a very skeptical investor can substantially improve her expected utility by having access to actively managed funds, rather than being forced to dogmatically accept a prior that no active funds can outperform passive strategies.

To illustrate, we briefly describe a Bayesian approach to alpha estimation, without model uncertainty. Under the Bayesian approach, fund alphas are recognized as random variables, and our objective is to obtain their posterior means. Suppose the investor has prior beliefs about a particular fund's risk-loadings and alphas which are contained in the parameter vector, β. These prior beliefs, suppose, are multivariate normally distributed, $\beta \sim N(\overline{\beta}, \overline{\Sigma}_\beta)$, where $\overline{\Sigma}_\beta =$ the k x k prior belief covariance matrix for a fund's k parameters. Suppose the investor then uses past data to run a linear regression, where the linear regression output for the parameters is $\mathbf{b} \sim N(\overline{\mathbf{b}}, \Sigma_\mathbf{b})$, i.e., $\mathbf{b} =$ the point estimates and $\Sigma_\mathbf{b} =$ the k x k estimated covariance matrix for estimated parameters. Then, the Bayesian

[15] An example application is discussed in detail in Chapter 7.

posterior mean vector, $\overline{\overline{\beta}}$, for the fund's alpha and risk loading parameters, from the point-of-view of that investor, are computed as:

$$\overline{\overline{\beta}} = \left[\overline{\Sigma}_{\beta}^{-1} + \Sigma_{\mathbf{b}}^{-1}\right]^{-1}\left[\overline{\Sigma}_{\beta}^{-1}\overline{\beta} + \Sigma_{\mathbf{b}}^{-1}\mathbf{b}\right] \tag{2.8}$$

Recovering the Bayesian posterior alpha, $\overline{\overline{\alpha}}$ (a scalar value), which is the first element in the column vector, $\overline{\overline{\beta}}$, is computed by premultiplying the above by a (transposed) column vector containing 1 as the first element, and zeros elsewhere, $i_1' = [1\ 0 \ldots 0]$:

$$\overline{\overline{\alpha}} = i_1'(\overline{\Sigma}_{\beta}^{-1} + \Sigma_{\mathbf{b}}^{-1})^{-1}(\overline{\Sigma}_{\beta}^{-1}\overline{\beta} + \Sigma_{\mathbf{b}}^{-1}\mathbf{b}) \tag{2.9}$$

An excellent in-depth discussion of Bayesian methods in asset pricing and investment fund performance evaluation can be found in Avramov and Zhao (2010).

2.3.8 Conditional Returns-Based Performance Measurement

A new class of model examines whether manager skills or risk-taking are different at differing points in the business cycle. Ferson and Schadt (1996) show that asset managers change their risk exposure as the level of various business cycle indicators evolve over time, partly in response to changes in their inflows from investors. Christopherson et al. (1998) show that manager alphas may also change, as managers may have specialized skills that work well only in certain macroeconomic environments.

To the extent that a fund's alpha varies systematically over time, this could be due to either: (1) embedded macro-economic sensitivities (e.g., sector-wide persistent mispricing); (2) time-varying skill; or (3) time-varying opportunities for managers to benefit from their skills. Although all three explanations may play a role, studies lend the most support to the third explanation—namely, that certain environments offer more mispricing opportunities where managers can take advantage of their superior insights. For example, many contrarian managers underperformed during the tech bubble of the late 1990s, when prices diverged significantly from fundamentals, but outperformed by a huge margin when the bubble burst. Did their skills suddenly change so dramatically, or did the market simply provide more opportunities for them in one period versus the other? It is likely the latter.

Studies by Moskowitz (2000) and Kosowski (2006) reveal that the average active manager is more likely to outperform the market during recessions. This is probably not the result of holding cash in down markets, since Kosowski, in particular, adjusts returns for market risk. Instead, it seems likely that recessions are periods of above-average uncertainty, when superior information and analysis can be particularly valuable. Consistent with this explanation, Kosowski (and others) also find that the average active fund performs better in periods of higher return dispersion and volatility, which are also likely to be periods of heightened uncertainty—and opportunity.

Conditional returns-based analysis is simple, and involves a straightforward extension of linear unconditional models. Suppose that we believe that a manager's alpha and beta, in a CAPM setting, dynamically evolve as the level of a particular macroeconomic factor, say, end-of-month t-1 short-term interest rates (z_{t-1}), change through time:

$$\alpha_t = \alpha(z_{t-1})$$
$$\beta_t = \beta(z_{t-1}).$$

We can approximate the functional form through a Taylor-series expansion, assuming it is continuous and differentiable:

$$\alpha_t = \alpha_0 + \alpha_0' \cdot z_{t-1} + \frac{1}{2}\alpha_0'' \cdot {z_{t-1}}^2 + \ldots$$
$$\beta_t = \beta_0 + \beta_0' \cdot z_{t-1} + \frac{1}{2}\beta_0'' \cdot {z_{t-1}}^2 + \ldots$$

Dropping higher-order terms, which means that we assume the manager is not engaging in non-linear strategies with respect to interest rates, then substituting into the Jensen model gives:

$$r_t = \alpha_0 + \alpha_1 \cdot z_{t-1} + \beta_0 \cdot RMRF_t + \beta_1 \cdot z_{t-1} \cdot RMRF_t + \varepsilon_{i,t}, \qquad (2.10)$$

where α_1 and T_i represent the (first-order) sensitivity of fund alpha and beta, respectively, to short interest rates. The above model suggests implementing a three-factor model, in place of the usual one-factor model of Jensen. While this is a simple solution to time-varying skills and risk-taking, it is easy to see that adding more factors and more macroeconomic variables geometrically increases the number of explanatory variables. Thus, factors and macrovariables should be chosen judiciously; some degrees-of-freedom can be saved by limiting the interaction of macrovariables to a subset of the risk factors.[16]

2.3.9 Stochastic Discount Factors

Chen and Knez (1996), Dahlquist and Soderlind (DS; 1999), and Ferson et al. (2006) propose a stochastic discount factor (SDF) approach to measuring performance.[17] The idea is quite elegant: if the law of one price holds, then there

---

[16] For instance, a common approach is to interact the macrovariables only with the market factor in a Carhart four-factor regression.

[17] Grinblatt and Titman (1989b) proposed a time-varying marginal-utility weighted return as a precursor to the SDF approach.

exists a stochastic discount factor, m_t, that prices any passive portfolio (with one-period return ending at t of R_t) either unconditionally,

$$E\left[m_t R_t - 1\right] = 0,$$

or conditional on any vector of public information available at the end of the prior period, $\mathbf{z}_{t-1}$

$$E\left[\mathbf{z}_{t-1} m_t R_t - \mathbf{z}_{t-1}\right] = 0.$$

This set of restrictions implies moment conditions that can be used to estimate the SDF, m_t, with the generalized method of moments, *GMM*. Using *GMM* allows the researcher to avoid choosing a particular assumed distribution for returns of passive or active portfolios, which, as we saw in Section 2.3.4, can be a great advantage with real portfolios of "poorly behaved" securities.[18]

Once the SDF is estimated which prices all passive portfolios and strategies based on public information, it is used to estimate the "alpha" or performance of any active portfolio, p, during time periods $t = 1$ to T as:

$$\alpha^p = \widehat{E}\left[\mathbf{z}_{t-1} m_t R_t^p - \mathbf{z}_{t-1}\right] = \frac{1}{T}\sum_{t=1}^{T}\left(\mathbf{z}_{t-1} m_t R_t^p - \mathbf{z}_{t-1}\right). \qquad (2.11)$$

Further, DS show that, if positivity is not imposed on the SDF, the above test of zero performance can be interpreted in a mean-variance world as whether a managed portfolio expands the mean-variance frontier.[19]

DS study several issues about SDFs with Monte Carlo simulations, including their small-sample properties—which is important in light of managed funds having relatively short histories. They find that a limitation of the SDF approach is that the managed portfolio must have a "considerable" actual alpha over a long period of time for GMM to reject that the fund has zero alpha.

2.3.10 False-Discovery Rate Approach to Measuring Performance of a Group of Funds[20]

Often, a researcher will wish to estimate the number, or proportion, of active fund managers having true skills in beating their benchmarks. Indeed, this is really the central question in the active/passive management debate: does an economically significant number of skilled managers exist, and, if so, can we locate them ahead of time?

[18] In addition to the non-normal distributions mentioned in a prior section, managed (and passive) portfolios can have problems with heteroskedastic and serially correlated returns. These issues pose no large problems when using *GMM*.

[19] In the absence of arbitrage, a positive SDF will exist.

[20] This topic is discussed in detail in Chapter 8.

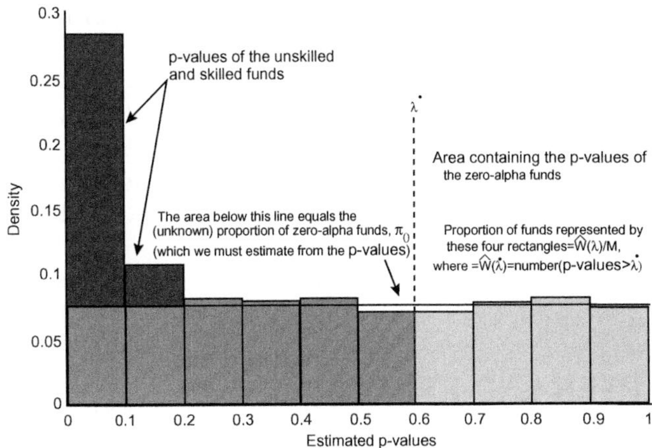

FIGURE 2.3
Alpha p-value Distribution for U.S. Domestic Equity Mutual Funds, 1975–2006.

Barras, Scaillet, and Wermers (2010) address exactly this question with the False-Discovery Rate (FDR) approach. The FDR is a statistical approach that has proven fruitful in studies in other academic areas, where an experiment deals with large numbers of subjects, such as studies of the commonality in DNA subsequences of large groups of people having a common disease.

The idea behind the FDR approach is extremely simple, as is its application, which enhances its appeal. Consider the multiple hypothesis test of skills across M active fund managers,

$$\begin{aligned} &H_{0,1} : \alpha_1 = 0,\ H_{A,1} : \alpha_1 \neq 0, \\ &\ldots : \ldots \\ &H_{0,M} : \alpha_M = 0,\ H_{A,M} : \alpha_M \neq 0. \end{aligned} \tag{2.12}$$

Traditional tests require the inversion of large covariance matrices, which are difficult to construct with hundreds or thousands of funds, many of which do not overlap in time.

The FDR approach, as developed by Storey (2002), instead relies only on the (two-sided) p-values associated with the (alpha) t-statistics of each of the M funds. By definition, zero-alpha funds satisfy the null hypothesis, $H_{0,i} : \alpha_i = 0$, and therefore have p-values that are uniformly distributed over the interval $[0, 1]$, as shown in the (nearly) uniform distribution of an empirical sample from BSW shown in Figure 2.3, over the interval $0.2 < p < 1$.[21] On the other hand, p-values

[21] To see this, we denote by T_i and P_i the t-statistic and p-value of the zero-alpha fund, $\widehat{t_i}$ and $\widehat{p_i}$ their estimated values, and $T_i\ (P_i)$ the t-statistic associated with the p-value, P_i. We have $\widehat{p_i} = 1 - F(\left|\widehat{t_i}\right|)$, where $F(\left|\widehat{t_i}\right|) = prob\left(|T_i| < \left|\widehat{t_i}\right| \middle| \alpha_i = 0\right)$. The p-value P_i is uniformly distributed over $[0, 1]$ since its cdf, $prob(P_i < \widehat{p_i}) = prob(1 - F(|T_i\ (P_i)|) < \widehat{p_i}) = prob(|T_i\ (P_i)| > F^{-1}\left(1 - \widehat{p_i}\right)) = 1 - F\left(F^{-1}\left(1 - \widehat{p_i}\right)\right) = \widehat{p_i}$.

of unskilled and skilled funds tend to be very small because their estimated t-statistics tend to be far from zero, as shown in Figure 2.3. We can exploit this information to estimate π_0 without knowing the exact distribution of the p-values of the unskilled and skilled funds. The FDR approach merely estimates where the horizontal line lies by choosing a λ^*, above which p-values are assumed to all come from unskilled fund managers. Once the hurdle (horizontal density line) is estimated, a simple integration of the density above the hurdle gives the estimated proportion of truly skilled funds.

2.4 CHAPTER-END PROBLEMS

1. Write the 7-factor model of, Fung and Hsieh (2004) for hedge funds. Describe each factor.
2. Suppose that I use a Jensen model to measure the skill of a manager. However, instead of using the true market portfolio, $RMRF_t$, use the S&P 500 index as my benchmark. What biases could I get, and under what conditions would the biases be of a certain sign (i.e., positive bias or negative bias)?
3. Discuss Type I and Type II error in performance evaluation (i.e., what do these two types of error mean?).
4. Write the Treynor-Mazuy model of market timing/security selection. Then, explain how we measure the contribution of (1) market timing and (2) security selection to manager returns.
5. How can a researcher deal with measuring fund alpha when the alpha is non-normally distributed?
6. Suppose you know that a group of fund managers are "convex market timers," each having a beta response function of:

$$\beta_t = b + \gamma r_{f,m,t} + \delta r_{f,m,t}^2$$

   A. Plot their beta response function as a function of $r_{f,m,t}$ (this doesn't have to be accurate, just show the general shape of the function).
   B. Plot their excess return as a function of $r_{f,m,t}$.
   C. Can you derive a modified Jensen regression (as Treynor-Mazuy did for their more simple market timers) that would be appropriate for these convex timers?
   D. Suppose, instead of your proposed model, you decide to simply use the Treynor-Mazuy model to measure stock selection ability (α) as well as market timing ability. Would the measured α from this model be biased? Derive this bias.

7. Describe how to bootstrap the p-value for a hedge fund alpha using a 7-factor Fung and Hsieh model.
8. Briefly discuss the properties that a valid benchmark should have.

9. This is meant to be a question that really makes you think. Suppose that you are given the monthly returns for a portfolio, and you have no idea of the type of portfolio or the strategies employed by the manager. Describe the steps that you might go through to diagnose what is going on in this "black box".

10. Consider funds A and B, as well as the SMB and HML factors of Fama and French below. Which fund (A or B) will show higher performance (alpha) when we use the Fama French model instead of the CAPM (single-factor Jensen) model? Explain why.

Time Period	Return (% Period)			
	A	B	SMB	HML
1	5	12	10	4
2	15	2	2	4
3	12	3	3	2
4	7	7	12	8

11. Kim Lee Ltd., an investment management firm in Singapore managing portfolios of Pacific Rim equities, tells you that its benchmark for performance is to be in the top quartile of its peer group (Singapore managers running portfolios of Pacific Rim equities) over the previous calendar year. Is this a valid benchmark? Why or why not?

Chapter 3

Returns-Based Performance Measures

ABSTRACT

This chapter provides an introduction to measures of performance that are based solely on the realized returns of an asset manager. Here, we start with simple measures that do not require a regression model to be estimated: the Sharpe measure and tracking error. Then, we discuss several of the best performance regression models for equity and fixed-income portfolios. Finally, we present some commonly used measures of performance based on these regressions: alpha, the Treynor ratio, and the Information ratio.

Keywords
Returns-based performance measures, luck vs. skill, Sharpe Ratio, tracking error, Jensen measure, alpha, benchmark choice, Treynor Ratio, information ratio

3.1 INTRODUCTION

Investment returns are the ultimate product provided by asset managers—their main "output" for investors. Measuring the quality of this output can be quite difficult, as the actions of an asset manager—his efforts and skills—are largely unseen by the investor. Even worse, neither the asset manager nor the investor can control random outcomes in the market, which can make the quality of the output difficult to gauge both for the fund manager and for the investor. Simply put, the investor does not know much about the skill of the manager, while the manager's knowledge of his own skills is also far from perfect—and the manager finds it very difficult to signal his quality over all of the noise in market returns!

This chapter is about measures of performance that are based on the observed returns data of a fund manager. These measures are designed to gauge the skills of an active asset manager, or the ability of an index fund to closely track its index. The measures in this chapter, many based on the latest research, are designed, in aggregate, to extract as much information as possible from noisy returns data.

Performance Evaluation and Attribution of Security Portfolios. http://dx.doi.org/10.1016/B978-0-12-744483-3.00003-1
© 2013 Elsevier Inc. All rights reserved.
For End-of-chapter Questions: © 2012. CFA Institute, Reproduced and republished with permission from CFA Institute. All rights reserved.

Table 3.1 Five Famous Mutual Fund Managers

Asset Manager	Fund Name	Asset Class	Time Period	AUM at Begin* ($Billion)	AUM at End* ($Billion)
1. Peter Lynch	Fidelity Magellan	U.S. Domestic Equity, Aggressive Growth	1977–1990	0.022	12.3
2. Bill Miller	Legg Mason Value Trust	U.S. Domestic Equity, Large Cap Value (Concentrated)	1982–2012	0.015	1.9
3. Scott Schoelzel	Janus Twenty	U.S. Domestic Equity, Large Cap Growth (Concentrated)	1997–2007	4.5	12.6
4. Gus Sauter	Vanguard 500 Index	U.S. Domestic Equity, Large Cap (Index Fund)	1987–1991	0.073	4.3
5. Bill Gross	PIMCO Total Return	U.S. Diversified Fixed-Income	1987–2012**	0.013	143.2

Assets under management at start and end of manager tenure.
**Still manager as of August 2012.*

To set up our discussion, let us ask a hypothetical question: in the setting of an active fund manager, why should we care about using a sophisticated model or measure to gauge the performance of an asset manager? As long as an asset manager provides returns that are market-beating, he is skilled, right? The best way to address this question head-on is to show an example of an asset manager with superior returns that were somewhat misleading. But, first, let's introduce five famous asset managers, who we will revisit periodically throughout this chapter to remeasure their skills using increasingly sophisticated methods.

Table 3.1 lists the managers and their funds.[1]

First, note that each of these managers—especially Lynch, Miller, Sauter, and Gross—took a very small fund and built a giant fund. Schoelzel took over a fund that had already experienced several successful years. Obviously, much of this growth occurred from investor inflows into the funds, beyond the high returns that the managers achieved. Investors clearly found these funds attractive.

[1] Results shown in this chapter are computed during the time-period listed for each manager, for the shareclasses represented by tickers: fmagx, lmvtx, javlx, vfinx, and pttrx, respectively. Entire calendar years are used, even if the manager started or departed at some date within the year. For instance, Peter Lynch started in May 1977, but we start the returns in January 1977, since we don't have exact starting dates for all five managers. All computations are based only through September 30, 2011.

Table 3.2 Janus Twenty Fund Returns

Fund/Index	Return (1998)
Janus Twenty	73.4%
Berger Select	72.3
Marsico Focus	51.3
S&P 500 Index	26.7

Let's look further at Schoelzel of the Janus Twenty Fund, ranked the #1 money manager in the world during 1998 by *Mutual Funds* magazine. It is not difficult to understand why when we look at his net returns during that year (in Table 3.2).

In fact, the Janus 20 fund had outstanding returns during each year of the late 1990s. Stories circulated about how Janus could hardly hire enough employees to handle the phone calls of investors wishing to buy shares in their funds, especially the Twenty fund.

Scott's investment style was to buy technology stocks, especially those stocks that had a very high growth outlook due to the increasing popularity of the internet and its implications for e-commerce. He would buy very large positions in individual issues, such as America Online and Hewlett-Packard.[2]

However, when internet and technology stocks collapsed, the 20 fund suffered—and Scott probably could not have exited his positions in an orderly fashion even if he had wanted to. As a result, from July 2000 to July 2001, the Janus 20 fund lost almost 50% of its assets! Thus, the raw return history of the Twenty fund was a poor metric for the ability of Scott, going forward, to outperform. In addition, the poor returns during the first few years of the 21st century may not have been any better an indicator of Scott's skills.[3] The reasoning for this is simple: In any given year, or even calendar quarter, one asset class can outperform another, as shown in Table 3.3.[4]

These return reversals are also common for subgroups within an asset class, such as internet and other technology stocks during the 2000–2003 period.[5] The lesson is that *we must use models that help us to better separate the influence of luck from skill in portfolio returns, else we run the risk of choosing and rewarding lucky managers rather than skilled managers.*

[2] His positions in AOL and Time Warner were so large that Jerry Levin of Time Warner and Steve Case of AOL jointly telephoned Scott shortly after the buyout of Time Warner by AOL was announced, in order to gauge his reaction.

[3] Scott was likely a skilled manager, but his skill was likely highly overstated by his outsized returns during the late 1990s (through being the recipient of an extraordinary level of luck).

[4] Source: Ibbotson Associates.

[5] Still, it is quite amazing that some asset classes exhibit long streaks—such as the four-year streak of large stocks during 1995–1998—which seems to give investors the sense that the streaks will continue even longer.

Table 3.3 Yearly Asset Class Rankings, by Return

	1986	1987	1988	1989	1990	1991	1992	1993
Top	Int'l Stocks	Int'l Stocks	Int'l Stocks	Large Stocks	30-Day T-Bills	Small Stocks	Small Stocks	Int'l Stocks
2nd	LT Gov't Bonds	30-Day T-Bills	Small Stocks	LT Gov't Bonds	LT Gov't Bonds	Large Stocks	LT Gov't Bonds	Small Stocks
3rd	Large Stocks	Large Stocks	Large Stocks	Int'l Stocks	Large Stocks	LT Gov't Bonds	Large Stocks	LT Gov't Bonds
4th	Small Stocks	LT Gov't Bonds	LT Gov't Bonds	Small Stocks	Small Stocks	Int'l Stocks	30-Day T-Bills	Large Stocks
Bottom	30-Day T-Bills	Small Stocks	30-Day T-Bills	30-Day T-Bills	Int'l Stocks	30-Day T-Bills	Int'l Stocks	30-Day T-Bills
	1994	**1995**	**1996**	**1997**	**1998**	**1999**	**2000**	
Top	Int'l Stocks	Large Stocks	Large Stocks	Large Stocks	Large Stocks	Small Stocks	LT Gov't Bonds	
2nd	30-Day T-Bills	Small Stocks	Small Stocks	Small Stocks	Int'l Stocks	Int'l Stocks	30-Day T-Bills	
3rd	Small Stocks	LT Gov't Bonds	Int'l Stocks	LT Gov't Bonds	LT Gov't Bonds	Large Stocks	Small Stocks	
4th	Large Stocks	Int'l Stocks	30-Day T-Bills	30-Day T-Bills	30-Day T-Bills	30-Day T-Bills	Large Stocks	
Bottom	LT Gov't Bonds	30-Day T-Bills	LT Gov't Bonds	Int'l Stocks	Small Stocks	LT Gov't Bonds	Int'l Stocks	

Table 3.4 Statistical Error Types

Error Type	Formal Definition	Casual Definition
Type I	Probability of rejecting the null hypothesis when it is true	Falsely identifying a skilled manager (saying he is skilled when he is really unskilled)
Type II	Probability of accepting (not rejecting) the null hypothesis when it is false	Falsely identifying an unskilled manager (saying he is unskilled when he is really skilled)

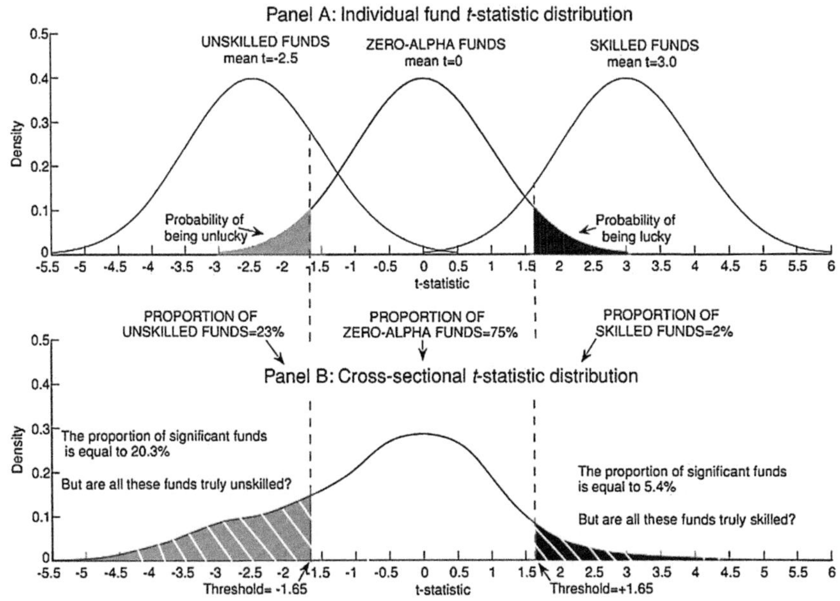

FIGURE 3.1
The Three Types of Fund Managers.

3.2 LUCK VS. SKILL

Let us discuss the issue of luck vs. skill in asset management briefly, before we proceed with presenting measures of skill that help to separate the two. *A very basic issue in performance evaluation is to minimize two types of statistical error.* Table 3.4 defines the types of statistical error, as well as describing it for the null hypothesis of zero performance of an asset manager.

Suppose there are three types of fund managers: skilled (positive true alpha, net of fees); zero true alpha, net of fees; and unskilled (negative true alpha, net of fees). Figure 3.1, Panel A, shows a hypothetical distribution of the t-statistics of estimated alphas (true alpha plus the imprecision that results from using finite samples of noisy returns data) for each type of manager.[6] Recall that a t-statistic in a large sample of data has critical values of -1.65 and 1.65 for a 5% probability (under the null hypothesis of true alpha = 0) of the t-statistic being more extreme in each tail. That is, due to pure luck alone (bad luck), a truly zero-alpha fund would be expected, with 5% probability, to have a t-statistic of its estimated alpha that lies in the grey area to the left of -1.65. Or, it would be expected, with 5% probability to have a purely lucky t-statistic in the black area to the right of 1.65.

Suppose, for a minute, that all fund managers are truly zero-alpha. In this case, if we observe an alpha t-statistic above 1.65, we might erroneously declare (with 95% confidence) that we have found a skilled manager. This is an example of Type I error—concluding that we have a skilled manager when we don't.[7] In Panel A of Figure 3.1, the probability of making this error is shown by the black shaded region labeled "probability of being lucky". Obviously, this conclusion is both wrong and costly in the future—our manager's good luck will surely run out at some point, leaving us to pay his fees for inferior returns. For example, Kosowski, et al. (2006) use a sophisticated bootstrap technique to determine what fraction of managers with a large alpha over a long time period are merely lucky. They found, using actual U.S. domestic equity mutual fund returns, processed using a bootstrap procedure that is described in detail in Chapter 6, that almost all of the roughly 300 funds achieving an estimated alpha of 2% per year over at least a 5-year period during 1975–2002 were simply lucky, using the four-factor Carhart model that we will describe later in this chapter.

An example of Type II error is the opposite. Suppose, now, that some skilled managers exist. In Figure A, Type II error occurs when we observe a fund t-statistic from the skilled fund distribution that, due to bad luck, is below the 1.65 critical value. If we observe an alpha t-statistic below 1.65, we conclude that the manager is a zero-alpha manager, but we have made a mistake. In the above graph, the probability of this erroneous conclusion is the area to the left of the black shaded region, *but under the skilled fund distributional curve*. Here, the manager's skill in picking securities is overwhelmed by unexpected events. We conclude, wrongly, that this manager is unskilled, which could also be costly in the future—we miss investing in a manager that could provide us with benchmark-adjusted returns higher than his fees.

Panel B shows that, if we observe a mixture of the three different types (as in the real world), the probability of Type I and Type II errors will depend on the prevalence of the three types. In the example of Panel B, there are relatively few skilled fund managers (2%), so we observe more left-tail (large negative)

---

[6] This graph is Figure 3.1 from Barras et al. (2010).

[7] In the normal distribution for zero-alpha funds shown in panel A of Figure 3.1, clearly there is a 5% probability of Type I error when using a critical value of 1.65 (which corresponds to the 95th percentile of a standard normal distribution) to reject the null hypothesis.

t-statistics than right-tail t-statistics. And, with few skilled managers, the chances of a high t-statistic fund simply being a lucky zero-alpha fund are increased.

In general, how can we minimize both types of error? Statistical theory tells us that, without good models and statistical measures, we cannot hope to reduce both simultaneously: reducing one type of error increases the other. For instance, an extreme way to eliminate all Type I error is to throw out all managers regardless of their returns—labeling them all unskilled. However, this means that Type II error is increased to 100%, as the probability of throwing out a skilled manager is 100%. Or, an extreme way to eliminate Type II error is to label all managers as being skilled regardless of their returns. In this case, Type I error is 100%, as we have labeled all unskilled managers (as well as all skilled managers) as skilled. Neither of these two extreme rules would be acceptable, unless there were a huge penalty for making one type of mistake, and no penalty for making the other type.

Instead, we strive, in performance evaluation and attribution (henceforth, PEVA), to minimize both Type I and Type II errors simultaneously. The most straightforward way, after obtaining high-quality data over a long time-period for a manager, is to design the best possible models, benchmarks, and measures. Earlier chapters discussed models and benchmarks; here, we discuss some commonly used and effective measures that build on the models and benchmarks.

3.3 THE ULTIMATE GOAL OF PERFORMANCE MEASURES

Usually, the goal of a well-designed performance measure is to rank managers by the accuracy of their private information on future asset returns. The thinking is this: if I find a talented asset manager, then I can allocate a large part of my portfolio toward her, and choose other managers or passive investments to diversify the risk of investing in the talented manager. In fact, Kapur and Timmermann (2005) demonstrate that several active managers that are thought to be skilled, with some statistical precision, may be desired to simultaneously manage portions of an investor's portfolio in order to diversify the alphas (and, thus, deliver a more certain positive portfolio alpha).

However, a confounding problem with ranking managers by their performance measures is the risk-aversion of the fund manager. Simply put, a very talented manager may be very risk-averse, refraining from investing heavily on her ideas; while a less-talented manager may be less risk-averse, aggressively investing on his ideas. The result is that some performance measures may be expected to be higher when applied to the less-talented manager, simply because he "leverages" his ideas by strongly allocating his portfolio to them. Thus, differences in managerial risk-aversion in the cross-section of fund managers can contaminate the information content of some performance measures. We will discuss this point when appropriate in the coverage of each measure that follows.

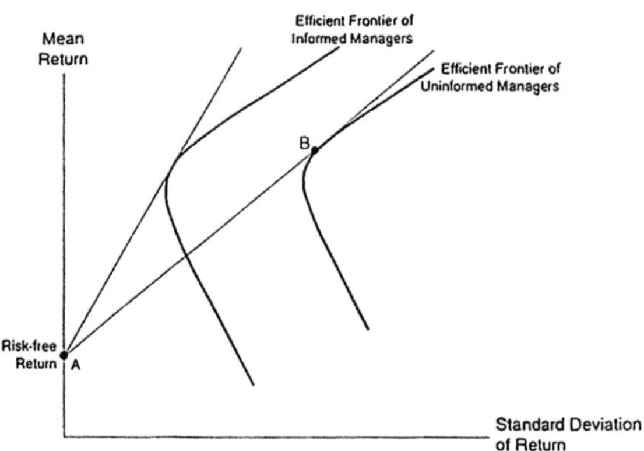

FIGURE 3.2
Efficient Frontiers for Informed and Uninformed Managers.

3.4 TWO NON-REGRESSION APPROACHES

3.4.1 The Sharpe Ratio

The Sharpe Measure or Sharpe Ratio is one of the most widely used measures of investment manager performance.[8] This measure is defined, for a given manager having portfolio returns of R_p, as a population measure and as a sample statistic, respectively, as:

$$SR = \frac{E\left[R_p\right] - R_F}{\sigma_p}, \text{ or}$$

$$Estimated\ SR = \frac{\overline{R}_p - R_F}{\hat{\sigma}_p},$$

where the estimated Sharpe Ratio relies on the sample mean and standard deviation of a manager's returns over a period of time. The Sharpe Ratio, geometrically, is the slope of the ray from the risk-free asset through the expected return of the managed portfolio, as shown in Figure 3.2.[9]

The Sharpe Ratio has some very appealing benefits as a measure of portfolio efficiency. First, it provides a very intuitive reward to risk trade-off, which is also called the "price of risk" of a particular portfolio. For instance, all else held equal, any risk-averse mean-variance investor would rather hold a portfolio with a Sharpe Ratio of 2 than a portfolio with a Sharpe Ratio of 1—each unit of risk is rewarded with double the (excess) return of the lower Sharpe Ratio portfolio.

[8] The Sharpe Ratio was invented by Bill Sharpe (1966) and named by Treynor and Black (1973)—the author confirmed this at a recent Q-Group meeting in a discussion with Jack Treynor.
[9] This graph is reproduced from Grinblatt and Titman (1995).

Table 3.5	Sharpe Ratio Assumptions
1.	The portfolio is the entire portfolio held by an investor, not just a portion
2.	The investor cares only about the mean and standard deviation (or, equivalently, variance) of his entire portfolio (e.g., the CAPM holds in security markets)
3.	The investor is myopic, in that he considers only one-period outcomes without regard to how they may impact periods beyond that

For instance, the graph above shows investment opportunity set lines that mix a riskfree asset with either a skilled (informed) or an unskilled (uninformed) manager. The slope of this line, which is the geometric interpretation of the Sharpe Ratio, is higher for the skilled manager.

Second, the Sharpe Ratio is extremely easy to compute, needing only the time-series of periodic returns of a portfolio. A Sharpe Ratio does not even require an explicit benchmark, although the Sharpe Ratio for a benchmark is usually used to compare a manager against (although the manager may also be compared against his peers in the absence of a benchmark). And, third, the Sharpe Ratio is based on the Capital Asset Pricing Model (CAPM), so there is a well-developed theory behind the measure.

However, there are some key assumptions, shown in Table 3.5, that need to be made before we can accurately apply this measure to individual portfolio managers—whether we wish to measure the efficiency of a portfolio or the skills of an active manager.

These assumptions deserve some explanation. First, if the manager provides a low Sharpe Ratio, but is part of a bigger portfolio, then the Sharpe Ratio can be misleading about the attractiveness of that manager for an investor. Consider, for instance, a portfolio that provides some protection or diversification if the stock market decreases. Risk-averse investors will bid up the price of this portfolio, as with all insurance portfolios, and its future realized returns will then be lower than the stock market's return, on average—but better during bad times. Correspondingly, the Sharpe Ratio of this portfolio will be low, but it will be a very attractive investment portfolio to add to other portfolios that mirror, more closely, the overall stock market return. A partial solution to this issue is to compare the returns of the manager against a prior-defined benchmark—e.g., with the tracking error measure described shortly.

Second, since only the mean and standard deviation enter into the Sharpe Ratio, only these two parameters from a manager's returns are considered by the investor using the Sharpe Ratio. The normal distribution is the only distribution that is fully defined through these two parameters. What type of investor would use this assumption? An investor who either believes that portfolio returns are very nearly normal in their distributions, or an investor that cares only about the standard deviation and expected return properties of a non-normal portfolio return series. As Kosowski, et al. (2006) demonstrate, many skilled and unskilled portfolio managers generate returns and alphas that are very non-normal, bringing the first of these two possibilities into question. (We revisit the approach of Kosowski, et al. in a later chapter).

Third, if the standard deviation and expected return of manager portfolios vary over time, then the one-period Sharpe Ratio can prompt poor fund choices by an investor. For instance, suppose that portfolio returns are expected to be lower than average (but positive) this year, and higher than average next year for the average fund manager. A good strategy would be to keep risk low this year in order to ensure that we have plenty of cash available at the beginning of next year to take advantage of the better returns. The Sharpe Ratio tells us nothing about this multi-period strategy.

Finally, the Sharpe Ratio ignores the agency problem inherent in asset management that was mentioned earlier: a manager may have aversion to taking risk, as he/she may be fired if poor results occur (even simply due to bad luck). For a skilled manager, this may lead to a lower than optimal level of risk-taking as well as expected returns—possibly lowering the Sharpe Ratio.

Nevertheless, the Sharpe Ratio is widely used by practitioners to judge funds. In Table 3.6, we compute the Sharpe Ratios of our five portfolio managers.

Table 3.6 Monthly Sharpe Ratios during Manager Tenure*

Asset Manager	Fund Name	Asset Class	Time Period	SR
1. Peter Lynch	Fidelity Magellan	U.S. Domestic Equity, Aggressive Growth	1977–1990	0.24
2. Bill Miller	Legg Mason Value Trust	U.S. Domestic Equity, Large Cap Value (Concentrated)	1982–2012	0.12
3. Scott Schoelzel	Janus Twenty	U.S. Domestic Equity, Large Cap Growth (Concentrated)	1997–2007	0.14
4. Gus Sauter	Vanguard 500 Index	U.S. Domestic Equity, Large Cap (Index Fund)	1987–1991	0.14
5. Bill Gross	Pimco Total Return (Fixed-Income)	U.S. Diversified Fixed-Income	1987–2012**	0.29

**Beginning of year manager started (if fund existed) or month and year manager started, whichever is earlier, to end of year manager left—or September 30, 2011, whichever is earlier.*

***Still manager as of August 2012.*

Table 3.7 How to Manipulate Sharpe Ratios

1. Change the portfolio risk halfway through the evaluation period
2. Leverage the portfolio
3. Buy a portfolio that has a very small chance of a very big loss, earning, almost always, a small "insurance premium" return ("selling insurance")

What can we make of these levels of Sharpe Ratios? Not much, since no investor would hold these portfolios alone without other diversifying investments.

Manipulating the Sharpe Ratio Beyond these simple problems with the Sharpe Ratio, it is also a measure that a fund manager can manipulate, to some extent. Goetzmann, Ingersoll, Spiegel, and Welch (GISW; 2007) demonstrate how some cleverly chosen trading strategies can lead to improved Sharpe Ratios, even for a manager without skills in selecting securities. Some examples from GISW are shown in Table 3.7.

As an example of the first strategy, suppose that an unskilled equity manager has an expected return of 1% per month—a 25% chance of 0%, a 50% chance of 1%, and a 25% chance of 2%. If the riskfree rate is 0.5% month, then the Sharpe Ratio of this unskilled manager is 0.71. However, now suppose that this manager games the Sharpe Ratio—measured using monthly returns—as follows. Every time his return during the first half of the month is half of 2% (assume the probability of this occurring is 50% with the other 50% on zero), he fully hedges his portfolio to be riskfree and earns 0.25% during the second half of the month. If his return during the first half is 0%, then he continues to "let it ride".

With such a strategy, his expected monthly return will be (ignoring compounding):

$$0.5(1+0.25)+0.25(0+1)+0.25(0+0)=0.875\%,$$

his monthly standard deviation will be:

$$\sqrt{0.5\left[(1+0.25)-0.875\right]^2+0.25\left[(0+1)-0.875\right]^2+0.25\left[(0+0)-0.875\right]^2}=0.515\%,$$

and, his monthly Sharpe Ratio will be:

$$\frac{0.875-0.5}{0.515}=0.73,$$

higher than his original 0.71. The econometrician (investor) would think this manager has skill. Yet, the manager is not any more skilled—he simply reduces his standard deviation more than his expected return through gaming the Sharpe Ratio with a conditional strategy that rebalances more frequently than the frequency of the measurement period.

Table 3.8 Tracking Error Definitions

Tracking-error gain $= \bar{r}_p - \bar{r}_b$

Tracking-error variance $= \text{var}(r_{p,t} - r_{b,t})$, where

$r_{p,t} =$ managed portfolio's return during a given period t

$r_{b,t} =$ benchmark portfolio's return during a given period t

Fortunately, GISW produce a modified Sharpe Ratio, Θ, that is designed to be immune from these problems:

$$\Theta \equiv \frac{1}{(1-\rho)\,\Delta t} \ln\left(\frac{1}{T}\sum_{t=1}^{T}\left[\left(1+r_{ft}\right)^{-1}\left(1+r_{ft}+r_{pt}\right)\right]^{1-\rho}\right), \tag{3.1}$$

where r_{ft} equals the period t riskfree rate (periodic, not annualized), r_{pt} equals the excess return (above the riskfree rate) of the managed portfolio during period t, Δt is the length of time between return observations, and ρ equals the risk aversion coefficient for a power utility function (of the econometrician or investor measuring the performance of the manager). Θ can be interpreted as the annualized continuously compounded certainty equivalent of the portfolio for a power utility investor with risk aversion coefficient ρ.

3.4.2 Tracking Error

Another simple approach to measuring performance is to relate the manager's returns to a benchmark. For retail mutual funds, this would be the self-defined market benchmark that all mutual funds domiciled in the U.S. are required to choose and state in their prospectuses. For institutional funds, this would be the benchmark agreed upon in the contract between the management company and the sponsor.

The most common definitions of tracking error statistics are shown in Table 3.8. Reward is measured through "tracking-error gain", while risk is measured through "tracking error variance" or "tracking-error standard deviation", the latter of which is casually referred to as "tracking error".

A logical way to think of tracking error as an investment objective is to substitute tracking-error gain for average portfolio return, and tracking-error variance for portfolio variance, in the normal Markowitz optimization. Roll (1992) shows that, with the objective of minimizing tracking-error variance while achieving a desired level of tracking-error gain, a fund manager will optimally choose a portfolio that is inefficient, if the benchmark against which he is compared is inefficient see (Figure 3.3).[10]

[10] This figure is from Jorion (2003).

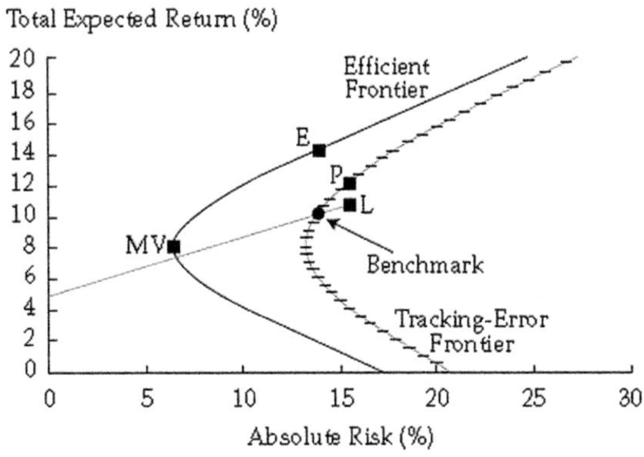

Notes: MV = the global minimum-variance portfolio; E = a portfolio on the efficient frontier with the same level of risk as the benchmark; P = a portfolio with 4 percent tracking error; L = a portfolio leveraged up to have the same risk as Portfolio P.

FIGURE 3.3
Illustration of the Inefficiency Induced by Using Tracking Error.

Note that, in Figure 3.3, the tracking-error variance (TEV) efficient frontier is inefficient everywhere, since it lies to the right of the normal (non-tracking-error optimized) Markowitz efficient frontier.[11] Similarly, a set of managers that optimize against a tracking-error measure will be expected to plot on the Tracking-Error Frontier shown in the diagram; ignoring potential manager skills, the optimal choice of the "right" manager on this curve will always result in a manager with a lower Sharpe Ratio than could be achieved with efficient passive market indexes that are carefully chosen and mixed. Thus, a manager must have enough skill to offset this disadvantage of being tied to the benchmark.

Why are tracking error measures used at all? The answer is that they serve as a simple and often effective way to force a manager to invest reasonably close to a benchmark—that, itself, is acceptable to the investor in terms of the expected return and risk that it offers. The investor may then diversify the overall portfolio through an optimized mixture of the benchmarks. This approach is often used in decentralized asset management in order to benefit from the specialized talents of different fund managers or management companies (see, for example, Sharpe (1981)). However, as shown by van Binsbergen (2008), the cost of using such a decentralized system is that the investor cannot design a perfect contract for each manager that will ensure efficient diversification of his overall portfolio of managers. Thus, although tracking-error methods are simple, widely used (especially among institutions monitoring their managers), and effective in constraining a manager, it is important to ensure that the manager is not gaming the approach, as we will discuss next.

[11] The intuition behind this result is that the portfolio manager will choose to become diversified relative to a benchmark that is not fully diversified, thus, achieving only partial diversification himself.

Table 3.9 Tracking Error Example

Tracking Error Variance	Fund
1 (lowest)	Fidelity Fund
2	Investment Company of America
3	T. Rowe Price Growth Stock Fund
4	Franklin Custodian Fds:Growth Series/II
5	Fidelity Magellan Fund
6 (highest)	Franklin Custodian Fds:Income Series/II

Manipulating Tracking Error Performance Measurement An unskilled, active manager who is judged relative to an inefficient benchmark using tracking error methods, as described above, can easily game the approach. Very simply, the manager chooses a portfolio that has a greater than unity exposure to the inefficient benchmark, when beta is measured in a regression model (i.e., $\beta_P > 1$). One such portfolio is "E" in Figure 3.3. Clearly, the manager will have a superior tracking error gain relative to his tracking error variance, since he is compared against a benchmark assuming his beta $= 1$.

In general, larger and more diversified funds have lower tracking error variances, although a manager could carefully construct a concentrated fund with similar factor exposures as the benchmark. For example, Table 3.9 shows the computed tracking error variance ranking (low to high) of several equity mutual funds over the 1975 to 1994 time period.

Note that specialized growth and income funds have some of the largest levels of tracking error, as would be expected, since they deviate from the market portfolio by definition. Interestingly, the Magellan fund also has high tracking error, which reflects the tendency of Peter Lynch to invest far away from his benchmark while his portfolio was small.

Note that another approach—the information ratio—measures performance relative to a benchmark portfolio that may be arbitrarily chosen. However, the information ratio—in contrast to the tracking error approach—does not assume that the exposure to the benchmark is 1. We discuss the information ratio in detail in a later section.

3.5 REGRESSION-BASED PERFORMANCE MEASURES

The last chapter discussed various regression models used to model securities and portfolios. Here, we briefly discuss these models again, focusing on their application as a measure of performance of a fund. Then, in the following section, we present various measures of performance that use parameters from these models in various ways to measure manager skills.

Table 3.10 Jensen Alphas during Manager Tenure*

Asset Manager	Fund Name	Asset Class	Time Period	α (%/year)
1. Peter Lynch	Fidelity Magellan	U.S. Domestic Equity, Aggressive Growth	1977–1990	11.1**
2. Bill Miller	Legg Mason Value Trust	U.S. Domestic Equity, Large Cap Value (Concentrated)	1982–2012	0.1
3. Scott Schoelzel	Janus Twenty	U.S. Domestic Equity, Large Cap Growth (Concentrated)	1997–2007	3.1
4. Gus Sauter	Vanguard 500 Index	U.S. Domestic Equity, Large Cap (Index Fund)	1987–1991	0.8

**Beginning of year manager started (if fund existed) or date manager started, whichever is earlier, to end of year manager left—or September 30, 2011, whichever is earlier.*
***Significant at the 99% confidence level.*

3.5.1 Single-Factor Alpha ("Jensen Alpha")

The single-factor model assumes that a single systematic risk factor affects all securities, and, thus, all portfolios of these securities:[12]

$$R_{p,t} - R_{F,t} = \alpha_p + \beta_p(R_{B,t} - R_{F,t}) + \varepsilon_{p,t}.$$

We apply this model for a given fund by regressing the excess fund manager return net-of-fees, $R_{p,t} - R_{F,t}$, over periods t=1 to T (usually, months) on the excess return of the benchmark portfolio during the same time period, $R_{B,t} - R_{F,t}$. The estimated intercept from this time-series regression model is the single-factor alpha, usually called the Jensen alpha (since Jensen introduced this measure in his 1968 paper). We have computed the Jensen alpha for the funds once managed by our four famous (equity fund) managers, using the value-weighted index of all NYSE/AMEX/Nasdaq stocks as the benchmark portfolio, and the results are shown in Table 3.10.[13]

[12] Recall from Chapter 1 that a special case of the single-factor model is the CAPM, where $r_{B,t}$ is the market value-weighted portfolio of all assets, traded and non-traded, and α_p is expected to be zero. Here, we discuss a single-factor model where the CAPM may not hold.
[13] We regressed the monthly excess net-of-fee return of each fund on the monthly benchmark returns. The α is the intercept from this model.

What did we find? Only one of the active managers comes out looking very good—beating the benchmark, adjusting for his exposure to the benchmark, β_p, by 11.1% per year over a multi-year period (the other managers have statistically insignificant alphas). This is extraordinary performance for such a long period of time. For instance, if the benchmark returns 12% during an average year, then an 11.1%/year advantage over the S&P would provide an additional 242% of return over a 13-year period.

Note the relatively large (0.8%/year) point estimate for the passive Vanguard fund. This suggests that our single-factor model does not control for some very basic influences on returns in the stock market, influences that are present even in a large-capitalization passive fund. We will further attempt to control for such influences with a four-factor model in a later section.

Benchmark Choice What if we had chosen an equal-weighted index as a benchmark, rather than the value-weighted index we used to evaluate the managers with the single-factor model above? In other words, can we predict what happens when we use the model,[14]

$$R_{p,t} - R_{F,t} = \alpha_p^{valuewt} + \beta_p^{valuewt}(R_{valuewt,t} - R_{F,t}) + \varepsilon_{p,t}, \tag{3.2}$$

vs. the model,

$$R_{p,t} - R_{F,t} = \alpha_p^{equalwt} + \beta_p^{equalwt}(R_{equalwt,t} - R_{F,t}) + e_{p,t}. \tag{3.3}$$

This issue is the central focus of Roll's Ambiguity Paper', Roll (1978), which demonstrates how a single-factor model can be manipulated to dramatically change the estimated alpha of a manager simply by reweighting the benchmark—sometimes very slightly! The key to understanding how $\alpha_p^{valuewt}$ will be greater or less than $\alpha_p^{equalwt}$ is understanding how the benchmark affects the $\beta_p^{valuewt}$ vs. $\beta_p^{equalwt}$. In essence, the regression slope, β_p, is related to the correlation coefficient between the dependent and independent variables, $R_{p,t} - R_{F,t}$ and $R_{valuewt,t} - R_{F,t}$, respectively. So, if the equal-weighted benchmark is more highly correlated with the portfolio manager's returns, then one need only understand whether the value-weighted benchmark or the equal-weighted benchmark performed better over the time period to predict the change in alpha when we switch from the model of Equation (3.2) to the model of Equation (3.3). Table 3.11 helps to understand the direction of change in the alpha when we switch the benchmark from $R_{valuewt,t}$ to $R_{equalwt,t}$.[15]

---

[14] Note that the symbols for the model parameters—intercept, slope, and residuals—are different between the two models, since the choice of benchmark affects all model parameters.

[15] An equation that is simple to derive relates the change in alpha to the betas and benchmark returns:

$$\alpha_p^{equalwt} - \alpha_p^{valuewt} = \beta_p^{valuewt}(\overline{r}_{valuewt} - \overline{r}_F) - \beta_p^{equalwt}(\overline{r}_{equalwt} - \overline{r}_F),$$

where $\overline{r}_{valuewt}$ and $\overline{r}_{equalwt}$ are the average returns of the benchmarks over the time period over which the manager is being evaluated.

Table 3.11 Bias With Incorrect Benchmark

Correlation between	Correlation between	Sign of Average of	Result
$R_{p,t}$ and $R_{valuewt,t}$	$R_{p,t}$ and $R_{equalwt,t}$	$R_{equalwt,t} - R_{valuewt,t}$	$\alpha_p^{equalwt} - \alpha_p^{valuewt}$
Large Positive	Small Positive	Positive	?
Large Positive	Small Positive	Negative	Positive
Small Positive	Large Positive	Positive	Negative
Small Positive	Large Positive	Negative	?

For example (see the second row), if the correlation between $r_{p,t}$ and $r_{valuewt,t}$ is large and positive, then $\beta_p^{valuewt}$ will be close to one—fully adjusting $r_{p,t}$ for the return realized by $r_{valuewt,t}$. Further, if the correlation between $r_{p,t}$ and $r_{equalwt,t}$ is positive, but smaller, then $\beta_p^{equalwt}$ will not fully adjust $r_{p,t}$ for the return realized by $r_{equalwt,t}$. Then, $\alpha_p^{equalwt}$ will reflect (part of) the advantage of $r_{valuewt,t}$ over $r_{equalwt,t}$, since we are basically comparing a portfolio highly similar to the value-weighted benchmark with an equal-weighted benchmark—without fully correcting for this difference in exposure. The result: $\alpha_p^{equalwt}$ will contain both manager skill and the return difference due to this exposure, which is positive in the second row above, while $\alpha_p^{valuewt}$ will contain a return that is (mainly) due to skill. Thus, the benchmark error of using the equal-weighted benchmark when evaluating a manager whose portfolio is more closely aligned with the value-weighted benchmark will incorrectly credit the manager with (part of) the return advantage of the value-weighted benchmark relative to the equal-weighted benchmark. This is exactly the point of Roll's Ambiguity Paper—an improper benchmark will either credit or penalize a manager for benchmark error-based returns.

As another example (see row three), if $r_{p,t}$ is more highly correlated with the equal-weighted benchmark, then the regression of Equation (3.2) will effectively credit, in $\alpha_p^{valuewt}$, part of the difference in returns between $r_{equalwt,t}$ and $r_{valuewt,t}$. This occurs because $r_{p,t}$ is similar to $r_{equalwt,t}$. Figure 3.4 illustrates two security market

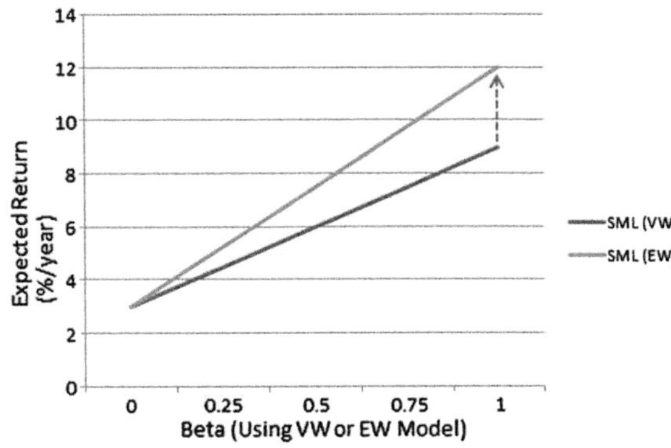

FIGURE 3.4
Security Market Line, VW vs. EW Equity Market Benchmark.

lines that result from the two different benchmarks. Assume that the NYSE/AMEX/Nasdaq value- and equal-weighted portfolios experience a return of 9 and 12%/year, respectively, and that the riskfree return is 3%/year. The lower SML results from using the value-weighted benchmark, while the upper SML results form using the same benchmark, but equal-weighted. Note that the reverse could occur as well—it is simply that this diagram assumes that the equal-weighted benchmark outperformed the value-weighted benchmark during this particular time period (i.e., small stocks outperformed large stocks).

From the perspective of the investor using the value-weighted benchmark, a passive portfolio that is equal-weighted and lands on the top SML will appear to generate alpha, even though the fund has no intention of being active. This means that an unskilled manager can appear to be skilled if he weights his portfolio close to a benchmark that is expected to outperform most of the time. Similarly, an unskilled active manager who tracks the equal-weighted index will also appear to be skilled, if judged using the value-weighted portfolio as a benchmark.

However, from the perspective of the equal-weighted benchmark, there is no alpha. This means that we can artificially generate alpha whenever we wish through a carefully chosen benchmark, which is Roll's point. *The lesson to be learned from this discussion is to carefully choose a benchmark that matches the style or type of securities that the manager chooses from!* For instance, one would never benchmark a small-capitalization stock manager with the S&P 500 index in a single-factor model.

Treynor's Ratio as a Performance Measure Treynor defined a measure of performance that attempts to penalize for systematic risk, rather than the total risk of a manager. Suppose that our model is the single-factor model,

$$R_{p,t} - R_{F,t} = \alpha_p + \beta_p (R_{B,t} - R_{F,t}) + \varepsilon_{p,t}$$

Treynor's ratio is:

$$TR = \frac{E\left[R_p\right] - R_F}{\beta_p}, \text{ or}$$

$$Estimated\ TR = \frac{\bar{r}_p - r_F}{\hat{\beta}_p},$$

which, geometrically, is the slope of the ray from the risk-free asset through the expected return of the managed portfolio on a graph that has expected return as a function of beta (expected return on the y-axis, beta on the x-axis), as in Figure 3.5.[16]

What is the difference between the Treynor Ratio and Jensen's alpha (using a single-factor model)? The Treynor Ratio assumes that we can leverage the manager in our portfolio to achieve whatever level of alpha we wish (along his

[16] This graph is from Grinblatt and Titman (1995).

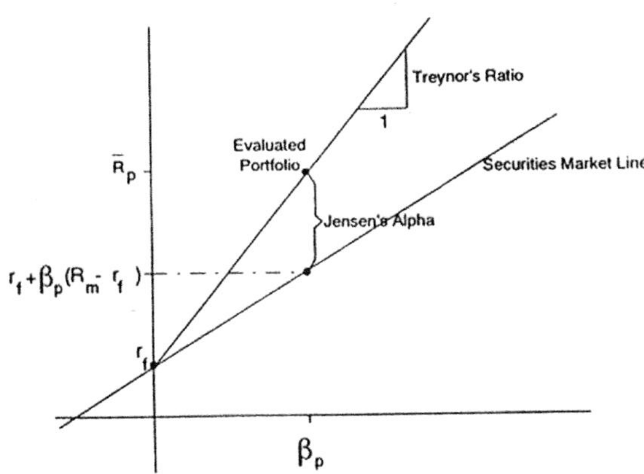

FIGURE 3.5
Geometry of Performance Measures.

allocation line), while the Jensen alpha does not. While Treynor's ratio is limited to a world where we believe that a one-factor model adequately describes asset returns, it recognizes that a manager is likely part of a larger, diversified portfolio of managers. Unfortunately, this measure is rarely used today, as most researchers use multifactor models to describe returns, such as the Carhart model for equities described next.

3.5.2 Multiple-Factor Alpha

Often, we do not know the style or type of securities from which a manager chooses—generally, we may know only the asset class (e.g., U.S. stocks or U.S. fixed income). Or, even if we know the manager's chosen subgroup of securities, a single-factor model may not be sufficient to correct for multiple influences on returns.[17] Both issues are the raison d'être for multiple factor models.

Equity Funds Among equity funds, a workhorse model among academics is the four-factor model (often called the "Carhart model") of Carhart (1997),

$$r_t = \alpha + \beta \cdot RMRF_t + s \cdot SMB_t + h \cdot HML_t + u \cdot UMD_t + \epsilon_t, \tag{3.4}$$

where r_t is the month-t excess return on the managed portfolio (net return minus T-bill return), $RMRF_t$ is the month-t excess return on a value-weighted aggregate market proxy portfolio, and SMB_t, HML_t, and UMD_t are the month-t returns on value-weighted, zero-investment factor-mimicking portfolios for size, book-to-market equity, and one-year momentum in stock returns, respectively. This model is based on empirical research by Fama and French (1992, 1993, 1996) and Jegadeesh and Titman (1993) which finds that these factors closely capture the cross-sectional and time-series variation in stock returns. A regression of a

[17] This issue was discussed in terms of the criticisms of the CAPM model—which has only one benchmark—in Chapter 1.

managed (long-only, equities only) portfolio using Equation 3.4 usually gives an R-squared in excess of 90%, and often in excess of 95%.[18]

A discussion of the formation of these benchmarks reveals what they are trying to capture more clearly. The interested reader can obtain both these benchmark returns and a more complete explanation of their formation from Professor Kenneth French's website (easily found through Google). For RMRF, French uses the value-weighted return on all NYSE, AMEX, and Nasdaq stocks (from CRSP), minus the one-month Treasury bill rate (from Ibbotson Associates).

To construct SMB and HML, French first creates two market capitalization groups (Small and Big, respectively) of all NYSE/AMEX/Nasdaq stocks at the end of June of each year, where stocks are segregated based on the NYSE-only median stock size at that date. Separately, also on June 30th of each year, he creates three book-to-market (BTM) equity groups of NYSE/AMEX/Nasdaq stocks based on NYSE-only BTM breakpoints for the bottom 30% *(Growth)*, middle 40% *(Neutral)*, and top 30% *(Value)*, based on the stock size (market value) at the end of December of the prior year and the book-value of equity at the end of the fiscal year ending during calendar year t-1 (to be sure that these data are known by June of year t). Then, he constructs six portfolios *(SmallValue, SmallNeutral, SmallGrowth, BigValue, BigNeutral, and BigGrowth)* from the intersection of these two size and three BTM groups of stocks. For instance, *SmallValue* contains stocks that are in both the *Small* stock group and the *Value* stock group.

Next, for SMB, he uses the average return on the three small portfolios minus the average return on the three big portfolios,

$$\begin{aligned} SMB &= 1/3(SmallValue + SmallNeutral + SmallGrowth) - \\ &\quad 1/3(BigValue + BigNeutral + BigGrowth), \end{aligned}$$

and, for HML, he uses the average return on the two value portfolios minus the average return on the two growth portfolios,

$$HML = 1/2(SmallValue + BigValue) - 1/2(SmallGrowth + BigGrowth).$$

Although this discussion captures the basics, further details on the formation of these portfolios are available in Fama and French (1993).

The "Carhart alpha" or four-factor alpha of this regression for our four famous funds, shown in Table 3.12, illustrates this measure's usefulness.[19]

With this model, we find that two of the three active managers have statistically significant skills over their entire careers (managers 1 and 3). What should we make of Bill Miller's statistically insignificant performance? It indicates that he picked stocks well enough to cover all transaction costs and fees over a 30-year period, which indicates an impressive level of long-term skills.

---

[18] Thus, if you are applying your regression model correctly, you should see these levels of R^2 values. This is a good diagnostic check of your data work.

[19] We regressed the monthly excess net-of-fee return of each fund on the monthly benchmark returns. The α is the intercept from this model.

Table 3.12 Four-Factor Alphas during Manager Tenure*

Asset Manager	Fund Name	Asset Class	Time Period	α (%/ year)
1. Peter Lynch	Fidelity Magellan	U.S. Domestic Equity, Aggressive Growth	1977–1990	8.2**
2. Bill Miller	Legg Mason Value Trust	U.S. Domestic Equity, Large Cap Value (Concentrated)	1982–2012	0.5
3. Scott Schoelzel	Janus Twenty	U.S. Domestic Equity, Large Cap Growth (Concentrated)	1997–2007	6.4***
4. Gus Sauter	Vanguard 500 Index	U.S. Domestic Equity, Large Cap (Index Fund)	1987–1991	−0.2

**Beginning of year manager started (if fund existed) or date manager started, whichever is earlier, to end of year manager left—or September 30, 2011, whichever is earlier.*
***Significant at the 95% confidence level.*
****Significant at the 99% confidence level.*

Even more impressive is that we have recomputed Miller's alpha over the period 1982–2005, and find that the alpha during this period for Miller's Value Trust fund was 2.9%/year, and statistically significant. The financial crisis was difficult for Value Trust, and maybe we should not make too much of the fact that this short time period of very unique macroeconomic events resulted in very poor results for the fund—especially since the other two active managers had much shorter careers that did not span the financial crisis. In a later chapter, we will explore the idea that fund managers may outperform during certain types of macroeconomic climates, even though they may not outperform during other phases of the business cycle.[20]

Note that the four-factor model reduces the Vanguard 500 index fund alpha to −20 basis points per year, which is closer to the expense ratio charged by the fund—this is good news. Essentially, the Standard and Poor's 500 index has a non-trivial exposure to SMB (negative, due to large stock exposure). The four-factor model corrects for this non-market exposure. We conclude that our three active stock fund managers are skilled—but, we will revisit these managers in a later chapter with other evaluation techniques that use portfolio holdings data.

[20] We also note that Miller's fund became extremely large prior to the financial crisis, making it very difficult for him to adjust the portfolio to changing economic conditions.

Fixed-Income Funds Much less research has been conducted on factor models for fixed income funds, at least among academics. However, as discussed in Chapter 1, Fama and French (1993) found a set of five risk factors that worked well in modeling both stock and bond returns. This includes three stock market factors:

1. stock market return *(RMRF)*,
2. size factor (small cap return minus large cap return) *(SMB)*,
3. value factor (high book-to-market stock return minus low BTM stock return) *(HML)*,
   and two bond market factors:
4. bond market maturity premium (10-year Treasury yield minus 30-day T-bill yield) *(TERM)*, and
5. default risk premium (Baa bond yield minus 10-year Treasury yield) *(DEFAULT)*.

This led to a five-factor model for bonds, as well as for bond funds. The first three stock market factors are of much lesser economic and statistical significance than the last two bond market factors, except for bond portfolios that contain significant allocations to bonds rated Baa or lower. The model is:

$$r_t = \alpha + \beta \cdot RMRF_t + s \cdot SMB_t + h \cdot HML_t + m \cdot TERM_t + d \cdot DEFAULT_t + \epsilon_t.$$

An alternate approach is suggested by Elton, Gruber, and Blake (1995):[21]

$$r_t = \alpha + \beta \cdot RMRF_t + b \cdot FIRF_t + m \cdot TERM_t + d \cdot DEFAULT_t + o \cdot OPTION_t + \epsilon_t. \tag{3.5}$$

FIRF is the excess return of the Lehman (now Barclays) Aggregate Bond Index Total Return. The OPTION factor is included to capture bond optionality features (e.g., among mortgage securities), and is constructed as the difference in return between the Lehman Brothers GNMA index and intermediate government bonds with the same duration. In general, the researcher should add one stock factor (at least), *RMRF*, to the two bond factors when evaluating a bond fund, unless it is known that the fund contains only default-free government bonds or corporate bonds with at least a single-A rating.

Mixed Equity and Fixed-Income Funds A model that can be applied to funds that hold a combination of equities and fixed income securities combines the four-factor equity model of Equation (3.4) and the five-factor fixed-income model of Equation (3.5):

$$\begin{aligned} r_t = \alpha + \beta \cdot RMRF_t + b \cdot FIRF_t + s \cdot SMB_t + h \cdot HML_t \\ + u \cdot UMD_t + m \cdot TERM_t + d \cdot DEFAULT_t + o \cdot OPTION_t + \epsilon_t. \end{aligned} \tag{3.6}$$

[21] EGB find that the term factor is less important, statistically, when the other factors are included, so they drop this factor in their four-factor version of their model. EGB also present other model variants that include unexpected inflation and unexpected real economic growth (unexpected real GNP growth), which marginally improve the model fit for bond fund portfolios, but involve more difficult factor constructions (which are based on consumer expectations measures).

Table 3.13 Fidelity Balanced Fund Model Results, Net of Fees, 1985–2002

	Coefficients	Standard Error	t Stat	P-Value
intercept	-0.784752972	0.984672338	-0.796968638	0.428284477
RMRF	0.551297303	0.026018533	21.18863919	2.07714E-31
FIRF	0.369774675	0.123992105	2.9822437	0.003987322
TERM	-0.274427609	0.309580923	-0.886448707	0.37854657
DEFAULT	0.524221261	0.39460777	1.32846158	0.188532938

Note that the first two slope coefficients (β and b) from this eight-factor model can be used to determine a rough allocation of the fund to various equity and fixed-income sectors, while the remaining coefficients can be used to judge exposures to small, value, and momentum stocks, as well as to the long-term, corporate, and mortgage sectors.

Take, for instance, the example regression,in Table 3.13, for a balanced mutual fund (mixed stocks and bonds). Here, we have used a four-factor version of the above eight-factor model, where all regressors are defined as in the prior subsection.

The adjusted-R^2 from this regression is 87.3%, indicating that the model describes 87% of the variability of the y-variable—a very good fit. Note that the estimated model coefficients, RMRF and FIRF, indicate that the fund is roughly 55% allocated to equities and 37% to fixed-income, respectively. The remaining 8% may be held in cash, although this may also be attributable to the imprecision in the coefficient estimates as well as correlations between these two factors and the remaining two factors, TERM and DEFAULT.[22]

What can we make of the coefficients, TERM and DEFAULT? Both are insignificant, so we can ignore them, and assume that they are zero.

However, what if these coefficients were statistically significant? For the moment, let's assume that the p-values for each are less than 0.05, in order to explore how we would interpret these coefficients in such a case. In this hypothetical case, TERM indicates that the portfolio has a shorter duration than 10 years. In a pure bond portfolio, this would indicate that the weighted-average bond duration is shorter than 10 years. In this portfolio, there are stocks—but, any duration effect of the stocks should be captured by the RMRF term, since individual stocks likely have a duration similar to the overall market (although growth stocks tend to have longer durations, due to their low short-horizon dividends and larger long-horizon dividends). So, we can interpret the −0.27 coefficient on TERM as meaning that the bonds are roughly 73% (100% − 27%) times the

[22] This is, of course, the multicollinearity problem, where correlated regressors compete for explanatory power.

10-year duration of TERM—thus, a duration of 7.3 years. DEFAULT is very likely correlated with RMRF, since bonds tend to default as RMRF performs poorly (a recession indicator). Ignoring this co-linearity effect, it is likely that the fund holds non-Treasurys in large amounts—high-quality corporates plus (perhaps) some high-yield (junk) debt.

Note the remarkable level of information that we are able to extract from such a simple and quick regression analysis! This highlights that there is much information available to the econometrician from even simple OLS regressions, if she takes the time to carefully analyze the output!

Multistrategy Funds Fund managers that engage in multiple strategies, many of which may be hidden from the investor, present a big challenge for the design of performance models, and, thus, for reliable performance measures. For example, the most commonly used hedge fund multi-strategy model is the seven-factor model of Fung and Hsieh (2004),

$$r_t = \alpha + \beta \cdot SPRF_t + s \cdot SMB_t + g \cdot TREAS10YR_t + c \cdot CREDIT_t \qquad (3.7)$$
$$+ b \cdot BONDPTFS_t + d \cdot CURRPTFS_t + o \cdot COMMPTFS_t + \epsilon_t,$$

where the factors are, successively, the S&P 500 return minus riskfree rate, Wilshire small cap minus large cap return, change in the constant maturity yield of the 10-year U.S. Treasury, change in the spread of Moody's Baa-rated corporate bonds over the 10-year U.S. Treasury, and three primitive trend-following strategies—derived from bond markets, currency markets, and commodities markets, respectively. Note that the three trend-following benchmarks are based on a dynamic strategy, and not on a passive index of securities. Thus, Fung and Hsieh (2004) designed this model based on some knowledge of the types of securities and the types of strategies (the three trend-following benchmarks) that are commonly used by multi-strategy hedge funds. The model works fairly well among hedge funds: Fung and Hsieh find that significant loadings on these seven risk factors are found in 57% of the hedge funds in the TASS database, and 37% of the funds in HFR, which is remarkable, given the diverse strategies and securities held by these funds.

In the seven-factor model of Equation (3.7), the α from the model is the fund performance measure. However, as we know from the discussion in Chapter 2 of timing models, it may become necessary to add some timing factors to the model if managers are suspected of attempting to time some of the sectors or strategies represented by the seven factors.

3.5.3 Timing and Selectivity Performance Measures

The above regression models assume that the regression factor-loadings, β_p in the Jensen model do not vary over time. However, this parameter would vary over time—chosen to be higher when the benchmark is expected to experience high returns—by a manager with good benchmark-return forecasting skills. If we use a model with a non-varying benchmark loadings, then both the estimated alpha and beta can be severely biased. For example, Figure 3.6 shows

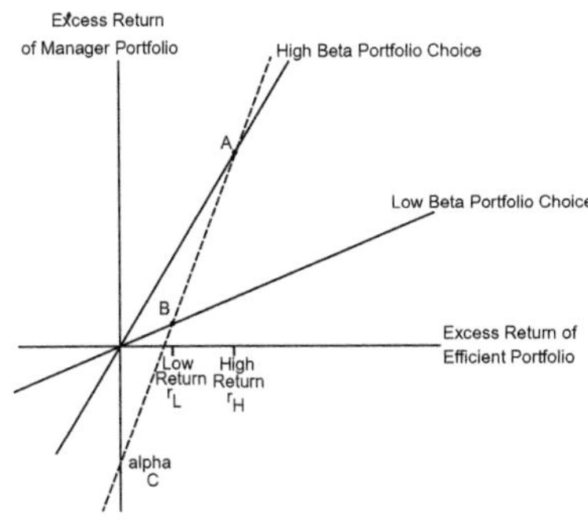

FIGURE 3.6
Potential Bias in Jensen's Alpha when a Manager Times the Market.

the usual outcome in such a case, assuming that the market portfolio of stocks outperforms cash.[23]

While there is little research on the ability of fixed-income or other managers' ability to time fixed-income sectors, some research has been done on U.S.-domiciled domestic equity funds. Almost all of the research that uses returns-based models indicates little evidence that equity fund managers can time the market. However, if some managers can time the market, this can bias our inference of selectivity abilities (see, for example, Grinblatt and Titman (1989)). To control for this possibility, there are two generally used returns-based modifications to models that attempt to capture timing skills separately from selectivity skills.[24]

As described more fully in Chapter 2, these are the Treynor and Mazuy (TM; 1966) model,

$$r_{i,t} = \alpha_i^{TM} + b_i^{TM} \cdot RMRF_t + \gamma_i^{TM} \cdot [RMRF_t]^2 + \varepsilon_{i,t}^{TM}, \tag{3.8}$$

and the Merton and Henriksson (MH; 1981) model,

$$r_{i,t} = \alpha_i^{MH} + b_i^{MH} \cdot RMRF_t + \gamma_i^{MH} \cdot [RMRF_t]^+ + \varepsilon_{i,t}^{MH}, \tag{3.9}$$

where $[RMRF_t]^+ = \max(0, RMRF_t)$. The measure of selectivity performance for the TM model is α_i^{TM}, while the measure of timing performance is $\gamma_i^{TM} \cdot Var[RMRF_t]$. For the MH model, the selectivity measure is α_i^{MH}, while the timing measure is $\gamma_i^{MH} \cdot C[RMRF, T]$, where $C[RMRF, T]$ is the value of an at-the-money call option on the excess market return, RMRF, and T is the performance evaluation period.

3.5.4 Conditional Regression Models

Any of the above regression models can be augmented with macroeconomic factors, if the econometrician (investor) believes that alpha or beta is time-varying

[23] From Grinblatt and Titman (1995).

[24] Note that, in a model that does not have a timing factor included (e.g., all of the prior models), the alpha of the regression will be biased (usually downward) if the manager is a good market timer.

and varies with macroeconomic cycles. While we explore this topic in depth in a Chapter 7, we present some introductory models here.

First, suppose that we believe that asset managers have betas that are a function of one or more macroeconomic variables, such as interest rates, inflation, default spreads, industrial production, consumer confidence, the slope of the term structure of government interest rates, etc. Suppose that we are evaluating U.S. equity managers, and wish to use the four-factor model, augmented with macro factors. Here, we could use a conditional version of the four-factor model that controls for time-varying $RMRF_t$ loadings by a mutual fund, using the technique of Ferson and Schadt (1996) as follows:

$$r_{i,t} = \alpha_i + \beta_i \cdot RMRF_t + s_i \cdot SMB_t + h_i \cdot HML_t + u_i \cdot UMD_t + \sum_{j=1}^{K} B_{i,j}[z_{j,t-1} \cdot RMRF_t] + \varepsilon_{i,t} \tag{3.10}$$

In this model, there are K macro-factors (which must be carefully chosen by the econometrician), and the levels of the macro factors are measured at the end of the prior month, $t-1$. Note that we have assumed that the macro-factors only affect the level of the loading on RMRF, but we could add similar macroeconomic interaction variables for the other three risk factors. For example, we can add $\sum_{j=1}^{K} B_{i,j}[z_{j,t-1} \cdot SMB_t]$ if we think that the small stock premium varies with the macroeconomic cycle.

If we, in addition, believe that manager skills vary with macroeconomic conditions, we can follow the Christopherson, Ferson and Glassman (1998) conditional framework that allows both the alpha and the factor loadings of a fund to vary through time. For example, the above model is modified as follows:

$$r_{i,t} = \alpha_i + \sum_{j=1}^{K} A_{i,j} \cdot z_{j,t-1} + \beta_i \cdot RMRF_t + +s_i \cdot SMB_t + h_i \cdot HML_t + u_i \cdot UMD_t + \sum_{j=1}^{K} B_{i,j}[z_{j,t-1} \cdot RMRF_t] + \varepsilon_{i,t},$$

This model computes the alpha of a managed portfolio, controlling for any investment strategies that use publicly available economic information to change either the portfolio's beta or the portfolio's allocation to individual stocks with abnormally high expected returns, conditional on the information. In this model, the skill of a manager is measured as $\alpha_i + \sum_{j=1}^{K} A_{i,j} \cdot z_{j,t-1}$. The first term, α_i, measures the baseline skill of the manager over all types of business conditions, while the second term, $\sum_{j=1}^{K} A_{i,j} \cdot z_{j,t-1}$, measures the additional skill (which might be negative or positive) due to time-varying skill effects.

3.5.5 The Information Ratio as a Performance Measure

To illustrate the information ratio, suppose the single-factor model is used, where $r_{B,t}$ is the return on some arbitrary benchmark portfolio, which may or may not be mean-variance efficient (for example, the S&P 500 index):

$$R_{p,t} - R_{F,t} = \alpha_p + \beta_p(R_{B,t} - R_{F,t}) + \varepsilon_{p,t}. \quad (3.11)$$

The Treynor and Black (TB: 1973) Appraisal Ratio, better known as the "Information Ratio" (henceforth, IR), is:

$$IR = \frac{\alpha_p}{\sigma_{\varepsilon_p}}, \text{ or} \quad (3.12)$$

$$Estimated\ IR = \frac{\widehat{\alpha_p}}{\widehat{\sigma_{\varepsilon_p}}}.$$

The IR can be viewed as a measure of the "signal-to-noise" ratio of a fund manager, since $\alpha_p + \varepsilon_{p,t}$ is the non-benchmark related return of a manager—where α_p is the mean of this sum (since the mean of $\varepsilon_{p,t}$ is, by assumption of the regression model, equal to zero) and $\varepsilon_{p,t}$ is the period t noise in the underlying performance of the manager, α_p.

In addition, it is important to note that the IR can be computed using any regression model—one factor, four-factor, seven-factor, four-factor with timing, four-factor with timing and conditional alphas and betas, etc. This is a big advantage of this measure. The econometrician can choose the model first, then apply the IR to the chosen model.

There has been some confusion about the definition of the IR over the years. Some practitioners refer to the following as the information ratio:

$$IR\ (Alternative\ Definition) = \frac{R_{p,t} - R_{F,t}}{\sigma_{\varepsilon_p}}.$$

Note that this approach to ranking funds gives the same ordinal ranking as the IR of Equation (3.12) if all funds have a β_p of 1.

Let us return to the first definition of the IR, $IR = \frac{\alpha_p}{\sigma_{\varepsilon_p}}$. One very nice property of this definition is that it is independent of manager aggressiveness in acting on his (perceived) skills. For instance, suppose that a manager leverages his portfolio 2 to 1, such that he doubles α_p in Equation (3.11). If so, he also doubles his residual, $\varepsilon_{p,t}$. What is the effect on the IR? The numerator is doubled, but so is the denominator—since variance of the residual is quadrupled, but standard deviation, σ_{ε_p}, is doubled—thus, the IR stays constant. Thus, the IR controls for differences in risk-aversion among managers, making it a far superior measure to the gross alpha when we are concerned with differential manager risk-aversion.

However, we must be careful to specify the time period over which the IR is computed, since α_p grows proportional to T (the length of the measurement time period), while σ_{ε_p} grows proportional to $\sqrt{T}$. Thus, an annual IR of 1.0 is equivalent to a quarterly IR of 0.5. No matter what time period we choose, we must compare managers using an IR with the same time denomination.

Note, also, that the ex-post estimated IR is closely related to the t-statistic of alpha that is normally provided by any statistics package (and, even Excel!) when running a regression analysis:

$$(Ex - post)\ IR = \frac{\widehat{\alpha}_p}{\widehat{\sigma}_{\varepsilon_p}}, \text{ and}$$

$$t - statistic = \frac{\widehat{\alpha}_p}{\widehat{\sigma}_\alpha}, \text{ thus}$$

$$\frac{IR}{t - stat} = \frac{\widehat{\sigma}_\alpha}{\widehat{\sigma}_{\varepsilon_p}},$$

and

$$\widehat{\sigma}_\alpha \propto \frac{\widehat{\sigma}_{\varepsilon_p}}{\sqrt{T}}, \text{ where T} = \text{\#observations, so}$$

$$\frac{IR}{t - stat} = \frac{\widehat{\sigma}_\alpha}{\widehat{\sigma}_{\varepsilon_p}} \propto \frac{1}{\sqrt{T}}, \text{ or}$$

$$IR \propto \frac{t - stat}{\sqrt{T}}.$$

What does this mean? It means that we can simply compare alpha t-statistics of funds, if they have the same number of time periods under analysis (such as both having 60 months of returns in the regression), and the comparison will be proportionate to a comparison using the IR. If a fund has a t-statistic that is 1.5 times the t-statistic of a second fund, the first fund will also have an IR that is 1.5 times that of the second fund.

Foundations of the Information Ratio As we discussed above, the Sharpe Ratio has its foundations in an equilibrium model, the Capital Asset Pricing Model. While the IR is not derived from such an equilibrium theory, it does have a "partial theory" behind it that is based on benchmark-relative investing—that is, analyzing a manager's skills relative to a (potentially) inefficient benchmark portfolio.

For instance, suppose that we are agnostic about the CAPM, and wish to analyze the value-added and risk of a manager, relative to a potentially inefficient benchmark portfolio. While we might wish that all managers were benchmarked against a mean-variance efficient benchmark, this is not practical in the real world for several good reasons. First, the CAPM may not hold in reality, as discussed earlier. Second, even if the CAPM is a perfect model of the world of investing, it relies on identifying a perfect mean-variance efficient "market portfolio", meaning one that has the lowest variance among all possible portfolios for a given level of desired expected return. Such a M-V efficient portfolio is extremely difficult to locate, in practice, because of the difficulty of estimating security parameters such as expected returns, standard deviations, and correlations, as well as the difficulty in including claims on non- or thinly-traded assets (such as human capital or real estate) in the search for the efficient benchmark. Roll (1977, 1978) discusses the problems involved in using the CAPM in these situations.

Instead, suppose that, which is very common in asset management, we decide to judge a fund manager against a given market index, regardless of whether this index is perfectly efficient.[25] A commonly used inefficient index is the S&P 500 index. Formally, the investor judges managers with the utility function, using estimates from Equation (3.11),

$$U = \widehat{\alpha}_p - \lambda \widehat{\sigma}^2_{\varepsilon_p},$$

where the "hats" emphasize that the investor uses estimated values to rank funds, and where λ equals the risk-aversion or "personal price of risk" for the investor. Note that we can rewrite the above equation as:

$$U = IR_p \widehat{\sigma}_{\varepsilon_p} - \lambda \widehat{\sigma}^2_{\varepsilon_p}.$$

Optimizing (maximizing) the utility for this investor with a fund with this IR, we obtain the optimal residual risk taken:

$$\widehat{\sigma}^*_{\varepsilon_p} = \frac{IR_p}{2\lambda}.$$

Substituting this optimal residual risk value into the above equation for U, we obtain the following maximizing utility level:

$$U^* = \frac{IR_p^2}{4\lambda}.$$

Note that this equation implies that an investor who judges managers relative to a given benchmark, and who can choose only one manager, should choose the manager with the highest IR (relative to that benchmark) and combine with cash to form an optimal investment portfolio.

Figure 3.7 illustrates how a benchmark-relative investor would view the reward-to-risk opportunities offered by a particular fund with an IR of 0.75.[26] Suppose that this fund had a benchmark-relative alpha of $\alpha_p = 8\%/\text{year}$, using the model of Equation (3.11). Note that the investor can mix cash with the active manager to obtain a straight-line investment opportunity set, as shown in Figure 3.7. The investor, who is risk-averse, has a convex indifference curve, as shown in the figure. The investor's optimum choice of the manager plus cash results in a benchmark-adjusted alpha of 3%, and a benchmark-relative standard devation of 4%. This investor has chosen 50% cash and 50% invested in the active manager.

---

[25] One interpretation of benchmark-relative analysis is that the investor can mix together managers having inefficient portfolios (and being judged against an inefficient benchmark) in a way that might result in a M-V efficient portfolio of managers (and non-traded assets).

[26] Note that a manager with a higher IR will provide a higher sloped line in the above opportunity set, since the slope equals the IR of the manager.

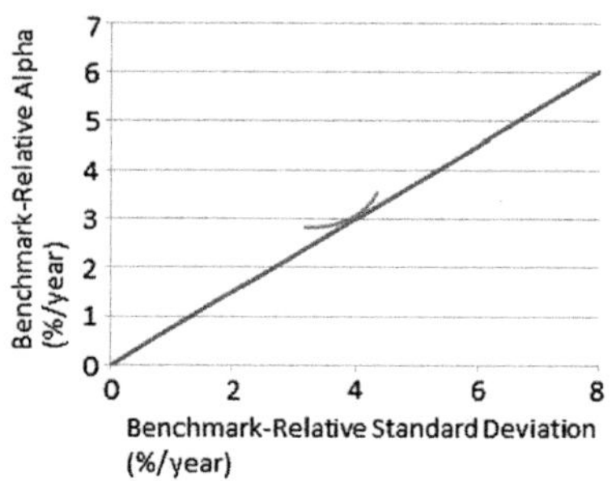

FIGURE 3.7
Information Ratio Investing.

Note that an investor using the IR to evaluate managers does not have to estimate anything about the benchmark—its expected return or its variance—a definite advantage in practice!

Next, let's explore how a set of managers with different information ratios might mix together in a portfolio.[27] Suppose that we are *relative mean-variance optimizers* (M-V optimizers relative to a particular benchmark, as above). In order to choose manager weights, w_i (on N managers, each having (uncorrelated) alphas of α_i and residual variance of σ_i^2) to attain a desired fixed benchmark-relative alpha for our portfolio of managers, α_p, and to minimize the (benchmark-relative) tracking error, our Lagrangian maximization function is as follows:

$$L = \sum_{i=1}^{N+1} w_i^2 \sigma_i^2 - 2\lambda \left(\sum_{i=1}^{N+1} w_i \alpha_i - \alpha_p \right), \tag{3.13}$$

where λ equals the Lagrangian multiplier. Note that the N+1 asset is the benchmark asset itself, which can be used to adjust the total portfolio loading on the benchmark (for example, to create a beta=1.0, if desired).[28] The first term in Equation (3.13) is the residual return variance from the portfolio of managers (since residuals are assumed to be uncorrelated across managers), and the second restricts expected alpha to desired alpha.

Taking the partial differential with respect to w_i, setting equal to zero, and solving, we obtain:

$$w_i = \lambda \frac{\alpha_i}{\sigma_i^2}. \tag{3.14}$$

[27] This discussion outlines the model presented in Treynor and Black (1973).

[28] We define α_{N+1} as the excess expected return on the benchmark, that is, the expected benchmark return minus the riskfree rate. Thus, the N+1 asset (the benchmark) provides the benchmark component of the portfolio, while the other N assets provide the residual return components. The N+1 asset also allows us to adjust the exposure to the benchmark that may be incidental (and perhaps not the desired exposure) to choosing a given set of managers.

With a simple step that recognizes two equations, $\alpha_p = \sum_{i=1}^{N+1} w_i \alpha_i$ and $\sigma_p^2 = \sum_{i=1}^{N+1} w_i^2 \sigma_i^2$, we can solve for the multiplier,

$$\lambda = \frac{\sigma_p^2}{\alpha_p}. \tag{3.15}$$

Now, the optimal allocation to manager i, following Equation (3.14), is

$$w_i = \frac{\alpha_i}{\alpha_p} \frac{\sigma_p^2}{\sigma_i^2}, i = 1, \ldots, n. \tag{3.16}$$

Finally, we can derive a relation between total portfolio Sharpe Ratio and manager information ratios:[29],[30],[31]

$$SR^2 = \left(\frac{\alpha_p}{\sigma_p}\right)^2 = \sum_{i=1}^{N+1} \left(\frac{\alpha_i}{\sigma_i}\right)^2 = \sum_{i=1}^{N+1} IR_i^2. \tag{3.17}$$

This is an important result, as it tells us that a set of managers with higher (uncorrelated) information ratios, weighted optimally, will allow a higher level of Sharpe Ratio (relative to a chosen benchmark) when we combine them. However, the above equation does not tell us what portfolio weight to allocate to each manager—we must use Equation (3.16) for this computation.

What if we choose only a few of the N managers discussed above—perhaps the top IR managers? Treynor and Black (1973) show that this will increase the portfolio variance, σ_p, along with its increase in the portfolio alpha, α_p. The resulting effect on the SR will depend on the tradeoff between these two individual effects. So, we cannot simply choose a subset of managers with the highest IR's without further analysis of these two effects.

Levels of the IR in Practice Grinold and Kahn (2000) find that, among U.S. active equity mutual fund managers (January 1991–December 1993), the top 10% have a pre-fee IR of 1.33 and an after-fee IR of 1.08. Among active equity institutional managers (October 1995–December 1996), the corresponding figures are 1.25 and 1.01, respectively. Among bond mutual fund managers (April 1993–September 1994), the top 10% IRs are 1.14 and 0.5, respectively, and the corresponding institutional bond manager IRs (October 1995–December 1996) are 1.81 and 1.29, respectively. In general, Grinold and Kahn label an IR of 0.5 as "good," 0.75 as "very good," and 1.0 is "exceptional". Roughly, before fees, only 10% of active managers have an IR$>$ 1.0.

---

[29] Note that α_p is total excess return of the portfolio, since the N+1 asset is the benchmark portfolio and that α_{N+1} is defined as the benchmark's excess return, as described in the prior footnote. Also, the sum of the first "N" weights equals one, leaving the weight on the benchmark asset as a free parameter. Similarly, σ_p^2 is total portfolio variance.

[30] See Equation (3.14) and the two expressions in the sentence following that equation to derive this result.

[31] As mentioned by Jack Treynor to the author, Treynor and Black (1973) first coined the term "Sharpe Ratio".

Table 3.14 Information Ratios during Manager Tenure*				
Asset Manager	**Fund Name**	**Asset Class**	**Time Period**	**IR**
1. Peter Lynch	Fidelity Magellan	U.S. Domestic Equity, Aggressive Growth	1977–1990	0.47
2. Bill Miller	Legg Mason Value Trust	U.S. Domestic Equity, Large Cap Value (Concentrated)	1982–2012	0.01
3. Scott Schoelzel	Janus Twenty	U.S. Domestic Equity, Large Cap Growth (Concentrated)	1997–2007	0.22
4. Gus Sauter	Vanguard 500 Index	U.S. Domestic Equity, Large Cap (Index Fund)	1987–1991	0.13
5. Bill Gross	Pimco Total Return (Fixed-Income)	U.S. Diversified Fixed-Income	1987–2012**	0.15

**Beginning of year manager started (if fund existed) or month and year manager started, whichever is earlier, to end of year manager left—or September 30, 2011, whichever is earlier.*
***Still manager as of August 2012.*

The information ratios of the funds once managed by our three famous *active-fund* managers are depicted in Table 3.14.[32]

Again, we show that Lynch exhibited high levels of skill, while Miller's IR suffered from the financial crisis. Since these information ratios used only the value-weighted market portfolio as a benchmark (or the prospectus benchmark, in the case of the Pimco fund), we might suspect that the results may be tainted by style tilts of the managers. When we recompute the IR using the four-factor equity model of Equation (3.4), we find even higher information ratios for Lynch, Miller, and Schoelzel—5.6, 2.4, and 0.4, respectively—but, −0.5 for Sauter. This confirms that we should control for style tilts when measuring performance of managers, including when computing the information ratio.

3.6 CHAPTER-END PROBLEMS

1. Suppose that a large population of fund managers flips a coin each year to determine whether they beat their benchmark or not. "Heads" results in outperformance, "tails" in underperformance.

[32] We regressed the monthly excess net-of-fee return of each fund on the monthly value-weighted CRSP stock returns (for the PIMCO Total Return Fund, the excess return is regressed on the prospectus benchmark, Barclays U.S Aggregate Bond Total Return). The α is the intercept from this model. We form the information ratio as the α divided by the standard error of the regression residual, as specified by the formula for the estimated IR, Equation (3.12).

A. What is the proportion of managers expected to end up with 5 straight years of "outperformance"?
B. What is the proportion of managers expected to end up with 10 straight years of "outperformance"?
C. What is the proportion of managers expected to end up with 15 straight years of "outperformance"?
D. What is the standard deviation of the 15 flips for a given manager?
E. If you randomly chose a manager, how many "heads" would be required out of 15 to reject that he is not skilled at the 95% confidence level?
F. Would your answer in E be different if you first chose the manager who flipped the most "heads"? Why or why not?

2. Suppose that an unskilled manager has an expected return of 9%/year—a 50% chance of 6% and a 50% chance of 12%. If the riskfree rate is 3%/year, then show that the Sharpe Ratio of this unskilled manager is 0.67.

3. Consider the six-factor model for portfolios containing both equities and fixed-income securities.

A. How would you determine what fraction of the portfolio is allocated to equities using the estimated slope coefficients ($\widehat{\beta}, \widehat{s}, \widehat{h}, \widehat{u}, \widehat{m}$, and $\widehat{d}$)?

$$r_t = \alpha + \beta \cdot RMRF_t + s \cdot SMB_t + h \cdot HML_t + u \cdot UMD_t + m \cdot TERM_t + d \cdot DEFAULT_t + \epsilon_t, \tag{3.18}$$

B. How would you determine whether the fund is allocated toward small capitalization stocks?
C. How would you determine whether the fund is allocated toward corporate bonds?

4. Examine the following regression output for a bond fund. From this output, predict what type of fund this is, and provide a detailed answer to support your conclusion.

X-Variable	Coefficients	P-value
Intercept	0.0002	0.55
RMRF	0.25	0.00001
FIRF	0.75	0.004
TERM	0.3	0.05
DEFAULT	0.4	0.05

Regression Statistics	
R Square	0.880
Adjusted R Square	0.873

5. Use Equation (3.1) to show that the dynamic strategy example above the equation will not change Θ, the modified Sharpe Ratio.

Table 3.15 Probability of a Manager Outperforming a Benchmark Given Various Levels of Investment Skills

	Information Ratio					
Year	0.20	0.30	0.40	0.67	0.80	1.00
1.0	57.93	61.79	65.54	74.75	78.81	84.03
5.0	67.26	74.88	81.45	93.20	96.32	98.73
10.0	73.65	82.86	89.70	98.25	99.43	99.92
20.0	81.70	91.01	96.32	99.86	99.98	99.99

6. Given a manager with an IR=0.5, and an investor with a risk-aversion coefficient of 0.1, what is the optimal residual risk taken by this investor using this manager?

7. From Equation (3.13), derive Equation (3.14).

8. From Equation (3.14), derive Equation (3.15).

9. Derive Equation (3.17).

10. A plan sponsor is considering two U.K. investment managers, Manchester Asset Management and Oakleaf Equities, for the same mandate. Manchester will produce on average an annual value-added return of 1.5% over the benchmark, with variability of the excess returns of 2.24%. Oakleaf is expected to produce a higher annual value-added return of 4%, but with variability of excess returns around 10%. Using the information in Table 3.15, determine which manager has a larger chance of underperforming the benchmark over periods of 1, 5, and 10 years. Explain the factor(s) causing the manager you identify to have a larger chance of underperforming for a given time period.

11. A U.S. large-cap value portfolio run by Anderson Investment Management returned 18.9% during the first three quarters of 2003. During the same time period, the Russell 1000 Value Index had returns of 21.7% and the Wilshire 5000 returned 25.2%.

A. What is the return due to style?
B. What is the return due to active management?
C. Discuss the implications of your answers to Parts A and B for assessing Anderson's performance relative to the benchmark and relative to the market.

Chapter 4

Portfolio-Holdings Based Performance Evaluation

ABSTRACT

This chapter reviews recent academic research that uses portfolio holdings to evaluate the performance of an asset manager. These methods overcome the benchmark-choice problem discussed by Roll (1978), as well as exhibiting other advantages over returns-based methods such as providing a much more detailed and precise breakdown of the sources of manager skills. Three main approaches have emerged in the literature. Grinblatt and Titman (1993) develop a method to evaluate performance when the proper benchmarks (or risk factors) for a portfolio are unknown or otherwise unavailable—this approach uses the past portfolio of a manager as the benchmark for her current portfolio. Daniel et al. (1997) build style control portfolios for each stock held by equity managers, based on past research on the style characteristics that are related to the cross-section of stock returns, while Cici and Gibson (2012) build style control portfolios for each bond held by bond fund managers. Although this approach is developed for U.S. domestic equity or bond fund managers, recent papers have applied it to European, Asian, and Australian equity managers. Finally, in contrast to these unconditional performance measures, Ferson and Khang (2002) create a conditional portfolio weight-based performance measure that controls for performance related to macroeconomic variables. This approach credits a manager only for returns in excess of those generated by a strategy of using current macroeconomic information to choose portfolio weights. All three methods of performance evaluation are useful in a wide variety of situations, and can be integrated into the Brinson et al. (1986) method of performance attribution if we allow the benchmark portfolio to evolve through time according to the observed portfolio holdings of the asset manager.

Keywords
Portfolio-holdings performance evaluation, Self-benchmarking, Grinblatt-Titman measure, Copeland-Mayers measure, DGTW benchmarks, characteristic selectivity measure, characteristic timing measure, average style measure

Performance Evaluation and Attribution of Security Portfolios. http://dx.doi.org/10.1016/B978-0-12-744483-3.00004-3

© 2013 Elsevier Inc. All rights reserved.
For End-of-chapter Questions: © 2012. CFA Institute, Reproduced and republished with permission from CFA Institute. All rights reserved.

4.1 INTRODUCTION[1]

Practitioners and academics have long been keenly interested in the value of active portfolio management. Recently, this issue has seemingly become settled, since almost all studies that use returns-based performance analysis methods conclude that actively managed mutual funds (e.g., the Fidelity Magellan fund), on average, underperform their passively managed counterparts (e.g., the Vanguard Index 500 fund). For example, the widely cited Carhart (1997) study finds that the average actively managed U.S. mutual fund underperforms its benchmarks by over one percent per year on a net return basis.[2] However, many individual investors and institutional sponsors are concerned simply with evaluating the set of managers that they currently employ, or might employ in the future to manage their assets. Thus, the past underperformance of the average actively managed fund does not preclude finding subgroups of managers with skills. In addition, returns-based methods used in the past, while perhaps adequately addressing the overall performance of the entire active management industry, or large subgroups of funds, may be too noisy to work well with individual funds or small groups of funds, especially those with a limited history of returns.

Recent advances in methods that examine performance at the security level allow researchers (and investors) to paint a much more detailed picture of the performance of asset managers; these advances make a re-examination of the active/passive issue possible in much the same way that advances in DNA-profiling re-opens many criminal cases for a more thorough analysis of the probable guilt of a defendant beyond more traditional fingerprinting methods. These security-level performance evaluation approaches have become known as "portfolio-holdings based performance evaluation and attribution" or simply "holdings-based performance measurement".

There are several reasons why the use of portfolio holdings data may provide new insights into managed performance, relative to returns-based methods. First, contrary to returns-based methods, recent approaches that use portfolio holdings data address the benchmark-error problem demonstrated by Roll (1978). Specifically, in a mean-variance setting, Roll demonstrates how a benchmark formed from any fixed set of assets can be chosen with similar properties (but different weights on component assets) to a second benchmark, such that the ranking (by the regression alpha) of a group of managers is reversed when moving from the first to the second benchmark, as long as the two benchmarks are both inefficient. Since a truly efficient benchmark is impossible to locate with perfect precision, any ranking of managers with real-world proxy portfolios chosen to represent this unknown efficient portfolio will be flawed; therefore, we cannot blindly trust performance evaluation

---

[1] This chapter is based on Wermers (2006).

[2] Other widely cited studies that examine net returns include Brown and Goetzmann (1995), Grinblatt and Titman (1992), Gruber (1996), and Hendricks et al. (1993).

using market proxies for the true theoretical benchmarks. Returns-based methods cannot overcome this benchmark-choice problem, while portfolio-holdings based methods can.

Second, the style-orientation of a fund may shift non-trivially during short time-periods—such as a value manager who adds technology stocks during the hey-day of growth stocks of the 1990s. Wermers (2011) finds a substantial level of so-called "style drift" among U.S. mutual funds during the 1975 to 2006 period. As shown by Ferson and Schadt (1996), inferences about manager ability may change substantially when we adjust for the shifting style or risk loadings of a professionally managed portfolio.

Third, holdings data allow an examination of fund manager abilities before expenses and trading costs, which can provide important insights about asset allocation or security selection talents. For example, a manager may possess talents in picking securities, but is handicapped by a fund that is too small, making the scale of the fund too expensive to support (through the expense ratio). Identifying such a manager may allow a restructuring of the fund (i.e., through a merger or by creating a new separate account) that overcomes such a friction while retaining the performance-generating aspects of the fund. (We explore the difference between holdings-based and returns-based performance measures, and the information conveyed by this difference, in detail in Chapter 5).

Fourth, an analysis of portfolio holdings adds to our ability to decompose the sources of value added by a manager. For example, a manager may have strengths in choosing technology stocks, but not telecommunication stocks. Or, the manager's performance may be concentrated in her top 10 holdings, rather than being spread more evenly. Such insights may allow us to better predict whether the specific talents in which we are interested are likely to persist.

Finally, benchmarking is more precise when applied on a security-by-security basis, since each security holding constitutes a separate observation about manager ability.[3] Thus, portfolio holdings increase the speed of convergence of the estimated manager ability to her true ability by the law of large numbers.

In the next section, we will review several approaches to measuring and attributing performance using portfolio weights. These methods are derived from recently published academic papers, and should be considered as being state-of-the-art; they are also applicable to a wide variety of practical performance evaluation situations. We will also describe some of the applications of these methods in a section that follows.

---

[3] Although the adding-up constraint implies that the choice of holdings are not truly independent, we can treat them as approximately so since the manager chooses weights from a very large set of securities. Note that this constraint only implies a correlation between weights on the order of 1/N. Thus, even for managers of relatively small portfolios, such as a manager of a biotechnology fund, portfolio weights provide a set of N approximately independent observations of fund manager ability.

4.2 UNCONDITIONAL HOLDINGS-BASED PERFORMANCE MEASUREMENT

A pioneering study that used portfolio holdings data obtained from periodic SEC filings of mutual funds is Grinblatt and Titman (1989a). This paper broke new ground by examining performance at the portfolio holdings level, that is, using holdings applied to changes in the closing price quotations of stocks (plus any cash dividends) to compute the return of an asset manager. Grinblatt and Titman labeled this as the "hypothetical performance" of a fund manager, since the manager (or those who would mimic the manager) could not exactly replicate the performance computed from closing prices due to the reality of trading costs.[4] Grinblatt and Titman (1989a) proceeded to regress these computed hypothetical returns on that of one or more market-based benchmarks to determine the hypothetical, pre-cost alpha of a fund manager. Therefore, while this paper is the first to directly examine portfolio holdings, the authors do not overcome the benchmark-error problem outlined by Roll (1978).

In response to the Roll criticism, academic researchers have built on Grinblatt and Titman (1989a) by developing measures of portfolio performance that allow weights to play a more central role in the formation of the benchmark(s) against which performance is measured. These new portfolio holdings measures (*PHM*) are grounded in the concept of performance being measured as the covariance between lagged weights and current returns,

$$PHM_t = cov(w_{t-1}, R_t).$$

This concept is very simple: a skilled manager will exhibit portfolio weights that move in the same direction as future returns. Of course, since covariances are unscaled (as opposed, for example, to correlation coefficients), such covariance-based measures assign a higher performance to a manager who is more aggressive; a "good" manager who aggressively turns over his portfolio will achieve a higher *PHM* than a "great" manager who is more cautious.[5] This issue aside, the *PHM* may be measured in a few alternative ways, simply by the various approaches to defining covariance, that is,

$$\begin{aligned} PHM_t &= cov(w_{t-1}, R_t) = E\left[w_{t-1}\left(R_t - E\left[R_t\right]\right)\right] = E\left[\left(w_{t-1} - E\left[w_{t-1}\right]\right) R_t\right] \\ &= E\left[\left(w_{t-1} - E\left[w_{t-1}\right]\right)\left(R_t - E\left[R_t\right]\right)\right]. \end{aligned} \tag{4.1}$$

These alternative approaches end up being much more than mathematical technicalities in practice. Specifically, these different expansions of covariance imply very different choices of benchmarks for a managed portfolio, and, therefore, have very different implications when applied to practical performance evaluation problems. For example, it may be easier to estimate expected

[4] Another, less important complication is that closing prices may not reflect the actual value of securities if sufficient liquidity is not present.

[5] We will discuss extensions to pure covariance-based measures that address this issue in a later section of this paper.

portfolio weights, $E[w_{t-1}]$, given available data, than expected security returns, $E[R_t]$—or vice-versa. Also, if precise estimates of both expected weights and expected returns are readily available, then we would expect that the expansion, $PHM_t = E[(w_{t-1} - E[w_{t-1}]), (R_t - E[R_t])]$, might converge more rapidly to the true performance of a manager than the alternative expansions, $PHM_t = E[(w_{t-1} - E[w_{t-1}]) R_t]$ or $PHM_t = E[w_{t-1}(R_t - E[R_t])]$.

Of course, a natural issue that first arises in applying these different approaches is the estimation of $E[w_{t-1}]$ and/or $E[R_t]$. The first, the expected (or "bogey" or "normal") weight of a security in a manager's portfolio may be estimated based on its weight in a commonly used benchmark portfolio, such as a market index. This approach might make sense, and may circumvent the Roll benchmark-choice problem, if the manager's explicit mandate is to track such an index, while adding a higher average return than the index with a controlled tracking error around it.[6] Alternatively, the expected weight may be based on the average or cumulative weights of other managers with the same mandate or self-declared investment objective, as proposed by Kandel et al. (2012). Or, the expected weight might be entirely based on information in the manager's portfolio holdings—using past or future portfolio weights as expected current portfolio weights.

The second estimation, of $E[R_t]$, the expected (or "bogey" or "normal") return of a security in a manager's portfolio may be estimated based on the average of the security's entire history of returns, it's forecasted return based on a factor model, or its single- or multiple-period return during a particular past or future time-period (relative to the period t, the performance evaluation period). We next illustrate two performance evaluation approaches that, while similar in their mathematical formulation, choose to estimate different quantities—one chooses to estimate each security's $E[R_t]$, while the other chooses to estimate each security's $E[w_{t-1}]$ in a given portfolio.

4.2.1 The Self-Benchmarking Method of Performance Evaluation

4.2.1.1 STATISTICAL FOUNDATIONS

Copeland and Mayers (CM; 1982) and Grinblatt and Titman (1993) propose new measures of performance that completely disregard standard market benchmarks (such as the Standard and Poor's 500 index) or peer-group benchmarks (such as the average return of same-objective funds) in favor of a "homemade" or bootstrapped benchmark. The CM approach uses the first expansion of the covariance in Equation (4.1), $PHM_t = cov(w_{t-1}, R_t) = E[w_{t-1}(R_t - E[R_t])]$, while the GT approach builds on the second, $PHM_t = cov(w_{t-1}, R_t) = E[(w_{t-1} - E[w_{t-1}]) R_t]$. Either of these definitions of covariance should be interpreted as a time-series

[6] However, Roll (1992) and Chapter 3 show that managers can game such an explicit benchmark as well, simply by choosing a portfolio with a "beta" greater than unity with respect to the benchmark.

covariance for a single security holding; CM and GT then propose that a manager's performance might reasonably be measured as the "summed covariances" across all security holdings, or:

$$CM = GT = \sum_{j=1}^{N} cov(w_{j,t-1}, R_{j,t}),$$

which measures the aggregate "correctness" of the manager's portfolio bets, across all securities. Of course, the true covariance must be estimated with time-series data, and here is where *CM* and *GT* differ.[7] Specifically, *CM* recommend the estimation,

$$CM = \sum_{j=1}^{N} \frac{1}{T} \sum_{t=1}^{T} w_{j,t-1} \left(R_{j,t} - E\left[R_{j,t}\right]\right),$$

while *GT* favor the estimation,

$$GT = \sum_{j=1}^{N} \frac{1}{T} \sum_{t=1}^{T} \left(w_{j,t-1} - E\left[w_{j,t-1}\right]\right) R_{j,t}. \tag{4.2}$$

Equation (4.2) can be rewritten, for convenience, as:

$$GT = \frac{1}{T} \sum_{t=1}^{T} \sum_{j=1}^{N} \left(w_{j,t-1} - E\left[w_{j,t-1}\right]\right) R_{j,t}.$$

This version of the sample measure allows the easy computation of the GT component for a single time period,

$$GT_t = \sum_{j=1}^{N} \left(w_{j,t-1} - E\left[w_{j,t-1}\right]\right) R_{j,t},$$

such that $GT = \frac{1}{T}\sum_{t=1}^{T} GT_t$. Similarly, the CM component for a single time period is computed as:

$$CM_t = \sum_{j=1}^{N} w_{j,t-1} \left(R_{j,t} - E\left[R_{j,t}\right]\right),$$

with $CM = \frac{1}{T}\sum_{t=1}^{T} CM_t$.

The next step is to decide on a proxy for the expected weight for security *j* at the end of period $t-1$, $E\left[w_{j,t-1}\right]$, or for the expected return of security *j*, $E\left[R_{j,t}\right]$. There are many approaches to this problem, as discussed in the prior section. Grinblatt and Titman (1993) propose that the past weight on security *j* is the best proxy for the security's expected weight. Specifically, using a market- or peer-based benchmark portfolio may allow the manager to game the

---

[7] It is easily shown that, in large samples, the two measures converge.

benchmark by overweighting (relative to the benchmark) securities with higher expected returns, and underweighting securities with lower expected returns.[8] Further, using the manager's future portfolio weights as a proxy for expected current weights biases the GT measure if the manager implements trading strategies based on past security returns. For instance, a manager who overweights securities with high past returns (a relative strength or momentum trader) will exhibit a future weight that is correlated with current returns—thus, spuriously reducing the estimated performance of the manager. For these reasons, GT recommend the past weight of the security in the manager's portfolio as a proxy for current expected, or bogey weight.

For the same reason, *CM* choose the future return of a security as a proxy for its expected return, $E\left[R_{j,t}\right]$. With these proxy choices, note that the *GT* expansion is advantageous, relative to the *CM* expansion, since it does not require a security to survive past the current period, *t*, to be included in the current-period's performance calculation (recall that the *CM* expansion requires the future return of a security for the current period computation). Nevertheless, the *GT* measure has its costs—it requires that the manager must exist for one full period before we can measure performance, while the *CM* requires only a single observation of the manager's weights—at the end of date $t-1$. In most practical situations, we would expect that managers have existed for at least one year before we wish to evaluate them, thus, the *GT* measure is preferred in most situations. As such, we proceed with the *GT* measure, although the application of the *CM* measure follows similar logic.[9]

At this point, we note another nice feature of the *GT* measure: it is exactly equal to the difference between the next period return earned by the current portfolio and a historical portfolio held by a manager, or

$$GT_t = \sum_{j=1}^{N} \left(\tilde{w}_{j,t-1} - \tilde{w}_{j,t-k-1}\right) \widetilde{R}_{j,t}, \tag{4.3}$$

where $\tilde{w}_{j,t-1}$ is the end of month $t-1$ (beginning of month t) portfolio weight of stock j held by the manager, $\tilde{w}_{j,t-k-1}$ is the weight of the same stock lagged k months, and $\widetilde{R}_{j,t}$ is the month t return of stock j. Note that, with this measure, the benchmark used to adjust the return of a portfolio for its risk in a given month is the current month's return earned by the portfolio (held by the same manager) k months prior to the current month's holdings. Taking this interpretation further, the time-series average GT measure, $\overline{GT} = \frac{1}{T-k}\sum_{t=k+1}^{T} GT_t$ represents the mean return of a zero-investment portfolio—long the current portfolio and short the

---

[8] Although a manager could also move toward higher expected return securities over time, thus gaming the past-weight benchmark, such a strategy would be much more difficult to sustain over time unless the manager overweights *temporarily* high-risk securities.

[9] In some cases, if historical portfolio weights and future returns are readily available for all securities held by a manager, the third expansion of Equation (4.1) might be used. If so, the application of this approach would, again, be similar to that shown below for the *GT* measure.

historical portfolio of a given manager. Consider the risk implications of the GT measure: if the systematic risk of the current and benchmark portfolios are the same (plus random noise) for a given manager having no selectivity or timing abilities [as defined by Grinblatt and Titman (1989b)], then the average portfolio represented by $\overline{GT}$ will have diminishing systematic risk, and this average portfolio return will converge to zero as T increases—in small samples, both risk and return will (under certain conditions) be insignificant for that manager, unless (as discussed below) the manager overweights temporarily risky scenarios.

In addition, while prior performance measures are susceptible to benchmark error, à la Roll (1978), and other forms of model misspecification, these errors are much less problematic with the $\overline{GT}$ measure. This results from the form of the $\overline{GT}$ measure—it differences portfolio returns, so any misspecification that remains is due only to differences in loadings (on such an omitted risk factor) between the current and historical portfolios. In effect, past holdings represent the normal or "bogey" risk taken by a particular manager.

Therefore, this measure will be biased only if a manager tilts toward stocks having temporary risk loadings. In such a case, the current portfolio will have a higher systematic risk than the historical portfolio, and the manager will exhibit a $\overline{GT}$ measure that is an upward-biased estimate of manager talent. An approach that can help to correct for such biases in the $\overline{GT}$ measure is to regress the time-series, GT_t, on standard benchmarks. For example, the following four-factor regression from Chapters 2 and 3 can be run:

$$GT_t = \alpha + b \cdot RMRF_t + s \cdot SMB_t + h \cdot HML_t + p \cdot UMD_t + e_t, \tag{4.4}$$

where $RMRF_t$ equals the month t excess return on a value-weighted aggregate market proxy portfolio; and SMB_t, HML_t, and UMD_t equal the month t returns on value-weighted, zero-investment factor-mimicking portfolios for size, book-to-market equity, and one-year momentum in stock returns.[10]

The remaining "benchmark-adjusted $\overline{GT}$ measure", or α, is the manager stock-picking talent, adjusted for any strategy employed by a manager (or, any passive movement in stock risk-loadings over time) that tilts toward stocks with temporarily high loadings on $RMRF$, SMB, HML, or UMD_t. An example of this is a manager who, by chance or by choice, adds stocks with high one-year past returns to her portfolio; the current portfolio will have a higher loading on UMD than the historical portfolio, so GT_t will exhibit a positive p coefficient in Regression (4.4)—but, α in this regression will be "cleaned" of the influence of such a risk-loading.

Note, as mentioned above, that the GT approach has a cost: in this case, the portfolio holdings for the first k months must be set aside as benchmarks for future portfolios. Therefore, the performance of the manager is not available

---

[10] These research returns are available (and updated) via Professor Kenneth French's website at Dartmouth University (http://mba.tuck.dartmouth.edu/pages/faculty/ken.french/).

during these first k months (which also eliminates short-lived funds), making this choice of k important.[11] The choice of k has other implications for this measure as well. If it is chosen to be small, we will eliminate performance that occurs beyond the first k months that a manager holds a stock, since, at that point, the difference in weights from Equation (4.3) will be zero if the manager holds the stock in a constant amount during these k months; if k is large, it is more likely that the measure may include some systematic risk differences in the manager's portfolio over these longer time periods.

When applying this measure to U.S. domestic equity mutual funds, Grinblatt and Titman (1993) find that fund performance appears to increase when varying k from 1 through 12 months, beyond which further increases in fund performance are small. Thus, they recommend a 12-month portfolio lag for these U.S. funds. A similar approach may be used to choose a reasonable value of k in other applications—increasing the chosen k (within reasonable ranges) until further performance changes appear to be negligible or add more noise (increase in standard deviation) than signal (increase in point estimate).

EXAMPLE

Table 4.1 illustrates the application of the GT measure, using $k = 12$ months, for the Janus Twenty fund, a famous fund from the 1990s that benefited greatly from the internet rally. The table shows the stockholdings and prices of each stock at March 31, 1997 (labeled benshares and benprice, respectively) and March 31, 1998 (labeled currshares and currprice), as well as the total dollar position in each stock at each date (labeled dollvalben and dollvalcur).[12]

In the columns, "ben_weight" and "curr_weight", we have calculated the portfolio weights using the price and shareholdings information for the March 31, 1997 and March 31, 1998 dates, respectively, for the Twenty fund. The change in the weight between the two dates, as needed by the term $\tilde{w}_{j,t-1} - \tilde{w}_{j,t-k-1}$ (where $k=12$), is shown in "delta_weight". Note that the Twenty fund initiated a large position in AOL during the year—over \$184 million, priced on March 31, 1998. This is interesting, since Twenty also built a \$174 million position in Time Warner over the same year. In early 2000, AOL would buy Time Warner.[13]

Next, in Table 4.2 let's look at the returns on these positions during the three months of April, May, and June 1998 (return1, return2, and return3, respectively), so that we can complete the calculations for the GT measure of Equation 4.3. In Table 4.2, chngrtn1, chngrtn2, and chngrtn3, for each stock, equal delta_weight multiplied by return1, return2, and return3, respectively, as stipulated by the term $\left(\tilde{w}_{j,t-1} - \tilde{w}_{j,t-k-1}\right) \widetilde{R}_{j,t}$.

---

[11] However, in some cases, various alternative benchmarks might be applied to recover these first k months, such as using peer-group weights.

[12] Currshares and currprice have been adjusted to reverse the effect of stock splits and other stock adjustment events.

[13] After announcing the deal, Jerry Levin of Time Warner and Steve Case of AOL jointly telephoned Scott Schoelzel of Janus Twenty to gauge Scott's sentiment about the impending takeover—so important was the Twenty fund's investment.

Table 4.1 Janus Twenty Fund Stockholdings, March 1997 and 1998

Stock	ben-price	currprice	benshares	currshares	dollvalben	dollvalcur	ben_weight	curr_weight	delta_weight
MICROSOFT CORP	91.6875	179	1,721,400	2,240,000	157,830,863	400,960,000	0.0394	0.0630	0.0236
COCA COLA CO	55.75	77.4375	2,374,200	0	132,361,650	0	0.0331	0.0000	−0.0331
GENERAL ELEC-TRIC CO	99.25	86.1875	1,203,400	3,956,800	119,437,450	341,026,700	0.0299	0.0536	0.0237
INTERNATIONAL BUSINESS MACHS COR	137.25	103.875	475,100	0	65,207,475	0	0.0163	0.0000	−0.0163
PEPSICO INC	32.375	42.6875	7,796,800	0	252,421,400	0	0.0631	0.0000	−0.0631
PHARMACIA CORP	38.25	52	3,991,175	7,982,025	152,662,444	415,065,300	0.0382	0.0652	0.0271
BOEING CO	98.625	52.125	1,862,800	0	183,718,650	0	0.0459	0.0000	−0.0459
U A L CORP	64.5	92.9375	4,773,600	3,679,625	307,897,200	341,975,148	0.0770	0.0538	−0.0232
PFIZER INC	84.125	99.6875	1,985,020	4,346,015	166,989,808	433,243,370	0.0417	0.0681	0.0264
MASSEY EN-ERGY CO	52.5	49.75	100,000	0	5,250,000	0	0.0013	0.0000	−0.0013
CITICORP	108.25	142	2,551,350	2,094,075	276,183,638	297,358,650	0.0690	0.0467	−0.0223
J P MORGAN CHASE & CO	93.875	134.875	2,869,450	0	269,369,619	0	0.0673	0.0000	−0.0673
WELLS FARGO & CO	284.125	331.25	1,512,200	270,875	429,653,825	89,727,344	0.1074	0.0141	−0.0933
LILLY ELI & CO	82.25	59.625	1,644,875	4,061,250	135,290,969	242,152,031	0.0338	0.0381	0.0042
FEDERAL NA-TIONAL MORT-GAGE ASSN	36.125	63.25	2,051,775	4,352,975	74,120,372	275,325,669	0.0185	0.0433	0.0247
MERRILL LYNCH & CO INC	85.875	83	1,558,750	3,660,650	133,857,656	303,833,950	0.0335	0.0478	0.0143

NIKE INC	61.875	44.25	3,066,480	0	189,738,450	0	0.0474	0.0000	−0.0474
INTEL CORP	139.125	78.0625	939,875	0	130,760,109	0	0.0327	0.0000	−0.0327
MIRAGE RE- SORTS INC	21.25	24.3125	4,353,875	0	92,519,844	0	0.0231	0.0000	−0.0231
CISCO SYS- TEMS INC	48.125	68.375	2,472,150	1,605,563	118,972,219	109,780,370	0.0297	0.0173	−0.0125
FIRST DATA CORP	33.875	32.5	3,500,996	395,596	118,596,240	12,856,870	0.0296	0.0020	−0.0276
ELECTRONICS FOR IMAGING INC	39.875	26	1,631,700	0	65,064,038	0	0.0163	0.0000	−0.0163
DANKA BUSI- NESS SYSTEMS PLC	31.4375	18.375	3,078,675	0	96,785,845	0	0.0242	0.0000	−0.0242
FILA HOLDING S P A	54.375	23.4375	407,850	0	22,176,844	0	0.0055	0.0000	−0.0055
ASCEND COM- MUNICATIONS INC	40.75	37.875	4,075,600	0	166,080,700	0	0.0415	−0.0000	−0.0415
GUCCI GROUP N V	72.125	47.5	984,875	0	71,034,109	0	0.0178	0.0000	−0.0178
ASSOCIATES FIRST CAPITAL CORP	43	81.25	1,558,550	0	67,017,650	0	0.0168	−0.0000	−0.0168
WORLDCOM INC GA NEW	22	43.0625	0	700,000	0	30,143,750	0.0000	0.0047	0.0047
DELL INC	67.625	135.5	0	4,219,300	0	571,715,150	0.0000	0.0899	0.0899

(Continued)

Table 4.1 Continued

Stock	ben-price	currprice	benshares	currshares	dollvalben	dollvalcur	ben_weight	curr_weight	delta_weight
DU PONT E I DE NEMOURS & CO	106	68	0	995,375	0	67,685,500	0.0000	0.0106	0.0106
SCHLUMBERG-ER LTD	107.25	75.75	0	4,673,850	0	354,044,138	0.0000	0.0556	0.0556
APPLIED MATE-RIALS INC	46.375	35.3125	0	4,236,050	0	149,585,516	0.0000	0.0235	0.0235
C B S CORP	17.875	33.9375	0	1,800,000	0	61,087,500	0.0000	0.0096	0.0096
COLGATE PAL-MOLIVE CO	99.625	86.75	0	1,000,000	0	86,750,000	0.0000	0.0136	0.0136
HALLIBURTON COMPANY	67.75	50.125	0	844,000	0	42,305,500	0.0000	0.0066	0.0066
WARNER LAM-BERT CO	86.5	170.3125	0	1,880,725	0	320,310,977	0.0000	0.0503	0.0503
TIME WARNER INC	43.25	72	0	2,414,500	0	173,844,000	0.0000	0.0273	0.0273
FEDEX CORP	52.125	71.125	0	1,053,125	0	74,903,516	0.0000	0.0118	0.0118
KONINKLIJKE PHILIPS ELEC N V	44.375	73.4375	0	600,650	0	44,110,234	0.0000	0.0069	0.0069
U S BANCORP DEL	73	124.75	0	642,050	0	80,095,738	0.0000	0.0126	0.0126

HOME DEPOT INC	53.5	67.625	0	700,000	0	47,337,500	0.0000	0.0074	0.0074
S L M CORP	95.25	152.6875	0	1,127,250	0	172,116,984	0.0000	0.0271	0.0271
COCA COLA ENTERPRISES INC	57.375	36.6875	0	2,391,875	0	87,751,914	0.0000	0.0138	0.0138
TELE COMMUNICATIONS INC NEW	12	31.09375	0	762,550	0	23,710,539	0.0000	0.0037	0.0037
AMERICA ONLINE INC DEL	42.5	136.625	0	1,350,000	0	184,443,750	0.0000	0.0290	0.0290
LUCENT TECHNOLOGIES INC	52.5	127.875	0	3,696,075	0	472,635,591	0.0000	0.0743	0.0743
SOLUTIA INC	0	29.75	0	1,829,905	0	54,439,674	0.0000	0.0086	0.0086

Table 4.2 GT Performance Evaluation of Janus Twenty Fund, April–June 1998

Stock	ben_ weight	curr_ weight	delta_ weight	return1	return2	return3	chngrtn1	chngrtn2	chngrtn3
MICROSOFT CORP	0.0394	0.0630	0.0236	0.0070	−0.0589	0.2778	0.0002	−0.0014	0.0065
COCA COLA CO	0.0331	0.0000	−0.0331	−0.0202	0.0329	0.0930	0.0007	−0.0011	−0.0031
GENERAL ELEC-TRIC CO	0.0299	0.0536	0.0237	−0.0116	−0.0213	0.0900	−0.0003	−0.0005	0.0021
INTERNATIONAL BUSINESS MACHS COR	0.0163	0.0000	−0.0163	0.1155	0.0159	−0.0229	−0.0019	−0.0003	0.0004
PEPSICO INC	0.0631	0.0000	−0.0631	−0.0703	0.0283	0.0124	0.0044	−0.0018	−0.0008
PHARMACIA CORP	0.0382	0.0652	0.0271	0.0168	0.0478	0.0090	0.0005	0.0013	0.0002
BOEING CO	0.0459	0.0000	−0.0459	−0.0396	−0.0435	−0.0668	0.0018	0.0020	0.0031
U A L CORP	0.0770	0.0538	−0.0232	−0.0619	−0.0889	−0.0181	0.0014	0.0021	0.0004
PFIZER INC	0.0417	0.0681	0.0264	0.1417	−0.0775	0.0370	0.0037	−0.0020	0.0010
MASSEY ENERGY CO	0.0013	0.0000	−0.0013	−0.0503	0.0093	0.0739	0.0001	0.0000	−0.0001
CITICORP	0.0690	0.0467	−0.0223	0.0640	−0.0083	0.0000	−0.0014	0.0002	0.0000
J P MORGAN CHASE & CO	0.0673	0.0000	−0.0673	0.0326	−0.0189	0.1108	−0.0022	0.0013	−0.0075
WELLS FARGO & CO	0.1074	0.0141	−0.0933	0.1165	−0.0176	0.0193	−0.0109	0.0016	−0.0018
LILLY ELI & CO	0.0338	0.0381	0.0042	0.1667	−0.1151	0.0794	0.0007	−0.0005	0.0003

FEDERAL NATIONAL MORTGAGE ASSN	0.0185	0.0433	0.0247	−0.0493	−0.0010	0.0157	−0.0012	0.0000	0.0004
MERRILL LYNCH & CO INC	0.0335	0.0478	0.0143	0.0594	0.0192	0.0322	0.0008	0.0003	0.0005
NIKE INC	0.0474	0.0000	−0.0474	0.0791	−0.0366	0.0614	−0.0038	0.0017	−0.0029
INTEL CORP	0.0327	0.0000	−0.0327	0.0356	−0.1160	0.0376	−0.0012	0.0038	−0.0012
MIRAGE RESORTS INC	0.0231	0.0000	−0.0231	−0.0925	−0.0567	0.0240	0.0021	0.0013	−0.0006
CISCO SYSTEMS INC	0.0297	0.0173	−0.0125	0.0713	0.0324	0.2174	−0.0009	−0.0004	−0.0027
FIRST DATA CORP	0.0296	0.0020	−0.0276	0.0423	−0.0185	0.0025	−0.0012	0.0005	−0.0001
ELECTRONICS FOR IMAGING INC	0.0163	0.0000	−0.0163	−0.2115	−0.0366	0.0696	0.0034	0.0006	−0.0011
DANKA BUSINESS SYSTEMS PLC	0.0242	0.0000	−0.0242	0.0884	−0.1563	−0.3000	−0.0021	0.0038	0.0073
FILA HOLDING S P A	0.0055	0.0000	−0.0055	0.0080	−0.2540	−0.1328	0.0000	0.0014	0.0007
ASCEND COMMU-NICATIONS INC	0.0415	0.0000	−0.0415	0.1502	−0.0086	0.1476	−0.0062	0.0004	−0.0061
GUCCI GROUP N V	0.0178	0.0000	−0.0178	−0.0197	−0.0255	0.1769	0.0004	0.0005	−0.0031

(Continued)

Table 4.2 Continued

Stock	ben_ weight	curr_ weight	delta_ weight	return1	return2	return3	chngrtn1	chngrtn2	chngrtn3
ASSOCIATES FIRST CAPITAL CORP	0.0168	0.0000	−0.0168	−0.0787	0.0008	0.0284	0.0013	0.0000	−0.0005
WORLDCOM INC GA NEW	0.0000	0.0047	0.0047	−0.0065	0.0636	0.0646	0.0000	0.0003	0.0003
DELL INC	0.0000	0.0899	0.0899	0.1919	0.0205	0.1263	0.0172	0.0018	0.0113
DU PONT E I DE NEMOURS & CO	0.0000	0.0106	0.0106	0.0708	0.0646	−0.0324	0.0008	0.0007	−0.0003
SCHLUMBERGER LTD	0.0000	0.0556	0.0556	0.0957	−0.0572	−0.1249	0.0053	−0.0032	−0.0070
APPLIED MATERI-ALS INC	0.0000	0.0235	0.0235	0.0230	−0.1142	−0.0781	0.0005	−0.0027	−0.0018
C B S CORP	0.0000	0.0096	0.0096	0.0497	−0.1088	0.0000	0.0005	−0.0010	0.0000
COLGATE PALMOL-IVE CO	0.0000	0.0136	0.0136	0.0370	−0.0300	0.0115	0.0005	−0.0004	0.0002
HALLIBURTON COMPANY	0.0000	0.0066	0.0066	0.0923	−0.1324	−0.0619	0.0006	−0.0009	−0.0004
WARNER LAMBERT CO	0.0000	0.0503	0.0503	0.1119	0.0135	0.0872	0.0056	0.0007	0.0044
TIME WARNER INC	0.0000	0.0273	0.0273	0.0903	−0.0076	0.0980	0.0025	−0.0002	0.0027
FEDEX CORP	0.0000	0.0118	0.0118	−0.0439	−0.0570	−0.0214	−0.0005	−0.0007	−0.0003

KONINKLIJKE PHILIPS ELEC N V	0.0000	0.0069	0.0069	0.2272	0.0555	−0.1078	0.0016	0.0004	−0.0007
U S BANCORP DEL	0.0000	0.0126	0.0126	0.0180	−0.0717	0.0990	0.0002	−0.0009	0.0012
HOME DEPOT INC	0.0000	0.0074	0.0074	0.0305	0.1274	0.0581	0.0002	0.0009	0.0004
S L M CORP	0.0000	0.0271	0.0271	−0.0215	−0.0644	0.2314	−0.0006	−0.0017	0.0063
COCA COLA ENTERPRISES INC	0.0000	0.0138	0.0138	0.0290	−0.0050	0.0426	0.0004	−0.0001	0.0006
TELE COMMUNICATIONS INC NEW	0.0000	0.0037	0.0037	0.0372	0.0640	0.1202	0.0001	0.0002	0.0004
AMERICA ONLINE INC DEL	0.0000	0.0290	0.0290	0.1702	0.0422	0.2762	0.0049	0.0012	0.0080
LUCENT TECHNOLOGIES INC	0.0000	0.0743	0.0743	0.1932	−0.0697	0.1727	0.0144	−0.0052	0.0128
SOLUTIA INC	0.0000	0.0086	0.0086	−0.0462	−0.0327	0.0456	−0.0004	−0.0003	0.0004

Table 4.3 Janus Twenty Fund Stockholding-Based Returns, April 1997 and April 1998

Stock	ben_ weight	curr_ weight	return1	return2	return3	curr ret1	ben ret1
MICROSOFT CORP	0.0394	0.0630	0.0070	−0.0589	0.2778	0.0004	0.0003
COCA COLA CO	0.0331	0.0000	−0.0202	0.0329	0.0930	0.0000	−0.0007
GENERAL ELECTRIC CO	0.0299	0.0536	−0.0116	−0.0213	0.0900	−0.0006	−0.0003
INTERNATIONAL BUSINESS MACHS COR	0.0163	0.0000	0.1155	0.0159	−0.0229	0.0000	0.0019
PEPSICO INC	0.0631	0.0000	−0.0703	0.0283	0.0124	0.0000	−0.0044
PHARMACIA CORP	0.0382	0.0652	0.0168	0.0478	0.0090	0.0011	0.0006
BOEING CO	0.0459	0.0000	−0.0396	−0.0435	−0.0668	0.0000	−0.0018
U A L CORP	0.0770	0.0538	−0.0619	−0.0889	−0.0181	−0.0033	−0.0048
PFIZER INC	0.0417	0.0681	0.1417	−0.0775	0.0370	0.0096	0.0059
MASSEY ENERGY CO	0.0013	0.0000	−0.0503	0.0093	0.0739	0.0000	−0.0001
CITICORP	0.0690	0.0467	0.0640	−0.0083	0.0000	0.0030	0.0044
J P MORGAN CHASE & CO	0.0673	0.0000	0.0326	−0.0189	0.1108	0.0000	0.0022
WELLS FARGO & CO	0.1074	0.0141	0.1165	−0.0176	0.0193	0.0016	0.0125
LILLY ELI & CO	0.0338	0.0381	0.1667	−0.1151	0.0794	0.0063	0.0056
FEDERAL NATIONAL MORTGAGE ASSN	0.0185	0.0433	−0.0493	−0.0010	0.0157	−0.0021	−0.0009
MERRILL LYNCH & CO INC	0.0335	0.0478	0.0594	0.0192	0.0322	0.0028	0.0020
NIKE INC	0.0474	0.0000	0.0791	−0.0366	0.0614	0.0000	0.0038
INTEL CORP	0.0327	0.0000	0.0356	−0.1160	0.0376	0.0000	0.0012

MIRAGE RESORTS INC	0.0231	0.0000	−0.0925	−0.0567	0.0240	0.0000	−0.0021
CISCO SYSTEMS INC	0.0297	0.0173	0.0713	0.0324	0.2174	0.0012	0.0021
FIRST DATA CORP	0.0296	0.0020	0.0423	−0.0185	0.0025	0.0001	0.0013
ELECTRONICS FOR IMAGING INC	0.0163	0.0000	−0.2115	−0.0366	0.0696	0.0000	−0.0034
DANKA BUSINESS SYSTEMS PLC	0.0242	0.0000	0.0884	−0.1563	−0.3000	0.0000	0.0021
FILA HOLDING S P A	0.0055	0.0000	0.0080	−0.2540	−0.1328	0.0000	0.0000
ASCEND COMMUNICATIONS INC	0.0415	0.0000	0.1502	−0.0086	0.1476	0.0000	0.0062
GUCCI GROUP N V	0.0178	0.0000	−0.0197	−0.0255	0.1769	0.0000	−0.0004
ASSOCIATES FIRST CAPITAL CORP	0.0168	0.0000	−0.0787	0.0008	0.0284	0.0000	−0.0013
WORLDCOM INC GA NEW	0.0000	0.0047	−0.0065	0.0636	0.0646	0.0000	0.0000
DELL INC	0.0000	0.0899	0.1919	0.0205	0.1263	0.0172	0.0000
DU PONT E I DE NEMOURS & CO	0.0000	0.0106	0.0708	0.0646	−0.0324	0.0008	0.0000
SCHLUMBERGER LTD	0.0000	0.0556	0.0957	−0.0572	−0.1249	0.0053	0.0000
APPLIED MATERIALS INC	0.0000	0.0235	0.0230	−0.1142	−0.0781	0.0005	0.0000
C B S CORP	0.0000	0.0096	0.0497	−0.1088	0.0000	0.0005	0.0000

(Continued)

Table 4.3 Continued

Stock	ben_ weight	curr_ weight	return1	return2	return3	curr ret1	ben ret1
COLGATE PALMOLIVE CO	0.0000	0.0136	0.0370	−0.0300	0.0115	0.0005	0.0000
HALLIBURTON COMPANY	0.0000	0.0066	0.0923	−0.1324	−0.0619	0.0006	0.0000
WARNER LAMBERT CO	0.0000	0.0503	0.1119	0.0135	0.0872	0.0056	0.0000
TIME WARNER INC	0.0000	0.0273	0.0903	−0.0076	0.0980	0.0025	0.0000
FEDEX CORP	0.0000	0.0118	−0.0439	−0.0570	−0.0214	−0.0005	0.0000
KONINKLIJKE PHILIPS ELEC N V	0.0000	0.0069	0.2272	0.0555	−0.1078	0.0016	0.0000
U S BANCORP DEL	0.0000	0.0126	0.0180	−0.0717	0.0990	0.0002	0.0000
HOME DEPOT INC	0.0000	0.0074	0.0305	0.1274	0.0581	0.0002	0.0000
S L M CORP	0.0000	0.0271	−0.0215	−0.0644	0.2314	−0.0006	0.0000
COCA COLA ENTERPRISES INC	0.0000	0.0138	0.0290	−0.0050	0.0426	0.0004	0.0000
TELE COMMUNICATIONS INC NEW	0.0000	0.0037	0.0372	0.0640	0.1202	0.0001	0.0000
AMERICA ONLINE INC DEL	0.0000	0.0290	0.1702	0.0422	0.2762	0.0049	0.0000
LUCENT TECHNOLOGIES INC	0.0000	0.0743	0.1932	−0.0697	0.1727	0.0144	0.0000
SOLUTIA INC	0.0000	0.0086	−0.0462	−0.0327	0.0456	−0.0004	0.0000

The "change returns" can be interpreted as the contribution to portfolio alpha from each stock trade. For instance, a huge contributor to April 1998 alpha for Twenty is that of Dell, since Twenty bought a 9% position in Dell ($572 million) from a small previous-year position ($4 million). And, Dell's April 1998 return was over 19%! Therefore, Twenty made a very good stock purchase decision with Dell, generating a portfolio alpha of 1.72% with only one stock in only one month! Of course, this is a very unusual outcome—in most cases, stock trades generated much more modest contributions to portfolio alpha in the period shown above for the Twenty fund.

The overall April 1998 alpha, according to the GT measure, can be obtained by adding the entries in chngrtn1—it is 0.0422, or 4.22%—again, a very healthy one-month alpha! May and June 1998 alphas are equal to 0.0037 and 0.0299, respectively.

Taking the interpretation of the GT formula further, the time-series average GT measure, $\overline{GT} = \frac{1}{T-k}\sum_{t=k+1}^{T} GT_t$ represents the mean return of a zero-investment portfolio—long the current portfolio and short the historical portfolio of a given manager. Specifically, in the example above, the March 31, 1998 Twenty portfolio generates an April 1998 return of 7.41%, while the March 31, 1997 Twenty portfolio generates an April 1998 return of 3.19%—a difference of 4.22%, consistent with our above result. These returns can be obtained by summing the columns "curr_ret1" and "ben_ret1" in Table 4.3, each of which are obtained by multiplying "curr_weight" and "ben_weight" by "return1", respectively.

4.2.1.2 EMPIRICAL EVIDENCE

Table 4.4 shows the results of the GT measure applied to 155 U.S. domestic equity mutual funds that existed for the entire period from 1975 to 1984.[14] Time-series averages ($\overline{GT}$) of two variants of the GT measure of Equation (4.3) are presented: the first uses a lag of $k = 3$ months, while the second uses a lag of $k = 12$ months. Note that the measure using the 12-month (4 quarter) lag exhibits over four times the level of performance for the average fund (2.04 percent) as the 3-month lag (0.37 percent), indicating that the portfolio choices of the average manager exhibit substantial levels of performance during the remaining 9 months. Thus, using a 3-month lag would result in an underestimation of the skills of the manager. Note, also, that a simple t-statistic is used to determine the statistical precision of the point estimate, since the GT measures for each time period, given by Equation (4.3), are independent under the null hypothesis of no manager ability.

Wermers (1997) updated the *GT* study to include all funds existing between 1975 and 1994, inclusive. He found that the average *GT* measure of U.S. domestic equity funds (equally weighted over all survivors and non-survivors, rebalanced at the beginning of each year) over this period is 1.7 percent per year, using the one-year lagged portfolio weights ($k = 12$), which is similar to the Grinblatt and Titman (1993) result (2.04 percent per year) shown in Table 4.4.

[14] This table is reproduced from Grinblatt and Titman (1993).

Table 4.4 Performance Estimates for 155 Surviving Mutual Funds Grouped by Investment Objective Categories (in % Return per Year)

		Performance Measure					
		Lagged 1 Quarter			Lagged 4 Quarters		
	No. of Funds	Mean Performance	*t*-statistic[a]	Wilcoxon Probability[b]	Mean Performance	t-statistic[a]	Wilcoxon Probability[b]
Total sample	155	.37	1.47	.233	2.04	3.16*	.004
Aggressive growth funds	45	.39	.98	.475	3.40	3.55*	.004
Balanced funds	10	−.48	−1.87	.057	.01	.03	.902
Growth funds	44	.66	2.01*	.017	2.41	2.94*	.009
Growth-income funds	37	.14	.61	.095	.83	1.75	.107
Income funds	13	.54	1.54	.475	1.33	2.64*	.002
Special purpose funds	3	−.10	−.16	.233	.21	.19	.711
Venture capital/ special situation funds	3	1.26	1.07	.812	2.66	1.43	.035

F1-statistic (Abnormal performance in every category = 0)

$F = 3.1438^{*}$

Prob > F = .0028[c]

F2-statistic (Abnormal performance across categories is equal)

$F = 3.6590^{*}$

Prob > F = .0014[c]

---

[a] *The mean over all months divided by the standard error of mean.*

[b] *The probability that the absolute value of the Wilcoxon-Mann-Whitney Rank z-statistic is greater than the absolute value of the observed z-statistic under the null.*

[c] *The probability of the F-statistic being greater than the outcome shown. under the null hypothesis (Type I error).*

* *Type I error < .05.*

4.2.1.3 *RELATION TO THE BRINSON, HOOD, AND BEEBOWER ATTRIBUTION APPROACH*

This GT measure also holds some statistical advantages over standard applications of the Brinson et al. (1986) attribution formulation. That is, commonly used applications of the BHB approach generally involve choosing a market-based index as a benchmark for a manager. Then, taking a pure equity portfolio manager as an example, the stock selection ability of this manager is computed as:

$$BHB_t = \sum_{j=1}^{N} \tilde{w}_{j,t-1}(\widetilde{R}_{j,t} - \widetilde{R}_t^{index}), \tag{4.5}$$

where $\widetilde{R}_t^{index}$ is the return on the benchmark index during month t. Related to our discussion above, if the index is misspecified for this manager (or the proxy for the index is poorly chosen), then the BHB measure will contain a bias that is directly proportional to the loading of the manager on any omitted factors. By contrast, as discussed above, the *GT* measure will contain a bias that is proportional to the difference in loadings between the current and historical portfolios, which will be much smaller in most applications.

In addition, the BHB measure uses a market index chosen to match the manager's stated investment objective at the beginning of the evaluation period—which, clearly, depends on the truthful revelation of such an objective. Thus, the manager might choose to "game" this measure by choosing an index that is expected to underperform his actual chosen portfolio. On the other hand, the GT measure uses an actual past portfolio of a manager as a proxy for the manager's current strategy—making it more difficult for a manager to game the measure for any substantial period of time.[15]

Fortunately, the GT approach can be integrated into a BHB-type attribution system by substituting a historical portfolio return for a market-based index,

$$BHB_t^{GT} = \sum_{j=1}^{N} \tilde{w}_{j,t-1}(\widetilde{R}_{j,t} - \widetilde{R}_t^{historical}),$$

where $\widetilde{R}_t^{historical} = \sum_{j=1}^{N} \tilde{w}_{j,historical}\widetilde{R}_{j,t}$.

The GT measure can also be decomposed into style bets, style timing bets, market timing bets, industry bets, etc., as well as the remaining residual stockpicking bets by simple decompositions of the sum in Equation (4.3). For example, if we wish to decompose into the overall performance from industry bets and the remaining residual stock selectivity bets, we would decompose as,

$$GT_t = \underbrace{\sum_{j=1}^{N} \left(\tilde{w}_{j,t-1} - \tilde{w}_{j,t-k-1}\right) \widetilde{R}_t^{IND(j)}}_{\text{Industry Performance Component}} + \underbrace{\sum_{j=1}^{N} \left(\tilde{w}_{j,t-1} - \tilde{w}_{j,t-k-1}\right) (\widetilde{R}_{j,t} - \widetilde{R}_t^{IND(j)})}_{\text{Stock Selectivity Component}}, \tag{4.6}$$

[15] As mentioned above, however, the manager can game the GT measure if stocks have substantial time-variation in expected returns that are predictable (such as the one-year momentum effect). But, a chosen style index used with the BHB method would likely be even more susceptible to such gaming.

where $\widetilde{R}_t^{IND(j)}$ is the month t return of the industry portfolio to which stock j belongs at the beginning of the month. As with BHB, Equation (4.6) can be decomposed into further partial sums, as desired, to explore the detailed sources of manager returns. Each partial sum is then averaged over all months. Or, if desired, each partial sum can be averaged only over certain months (such as Januaries) or certain time-ranges (such as three-year periods) to analyze the time-series variation in manager performance.

In this section, we have argued that the GT measure holds significant advantages over standard approaches that use market indexes as benchmarks, since the GT approach uses lagged manager weights to form dynamic benchmarks. However, we may wish to use our knowledge of the factors or characteristics that, from past research, are known to drive security returns in order to obtain a more precise measure of performance. For instance, as mentioned above, a manager can potentially game the *GT* measure by overweighting securities with temporarily high levels of risk. To overcome such concerns, we must define the sources of risk in our security universe—in effect, the cost of increased performance evaluation precision is that we must specify the main influences on security returns for all securities in the investable universe of a manager.[16] For some asset managers, this may not be practical—thus, the GT approach may be preferred. However, in the case of U.S. domestic equities, extensive research has documented the most important influences on returns. This research has outlined the drivers of cross-sectional differences in stock returns as well as time-series variation in the returns of a given stock. We next describe an approach for evaluating equity portfolios in the U.S.—with a discussion on extensions in non-U.S. equity markets—that uses the results of this past research.

4.2.2 The DGTW Method of Performance Evaluation for Equity Portfolios

The Daniel et al. (1997) approach applies the results of prior empirical research on the factors that drive stock returns. This research, which includes Fama and French (1993), Fama and French (1996), Ferson and Khang (2002), and Jegadeesh and Titman (1993) shows that the market index as well as indexes that proxy for the size, book-to-market, and momentum effects are sufficient to explain the vast majority of the cross-sectional and time-series variation in U.S. stock returns. International evidence, such as Rouwenhorst (1998), indicates that similar factors also explain non-U.S. stock returns.

[16] This is fairly straightforward for U.S. domestic equities, and (with recent research) for non-U.S. equities in many developed countries. However, the factors that drive bond returns as well as hedge fund returns are not as clearly understood; thus, it is difficult to unambiguously create benchmark portfolios for these markets. In addition, a manager holding a mixed portfolio of both stocks and bonds presents a problem when using defined benchmarks developed for the stock market, although new approaches exist (an approach for bonds is described in Section 4.2.3).

The DGTW portfolio-holdings based measures include three subcomponents:

1. the current portfolio-weighted return on stocks currently held by the fund, in excess of returns (during the same time period) on matched control portfolios having the same style characteristics (selectivity- or stockpicking-based returns),
2. the current portfolio-weighted return on control portfolios having the same characteristics as stocks currently held by the fund, in excess of time-series average returns on those control portfolios (style timing based returns), and
3. the time-series average returns on control portfolios having the same characteristics as stocks currently held (style-based returns),

These three components decompose the return on the portfolio holdings of a fund, thus, they attribute returns before any trading costs or expenses are considered. We describe them next.[17]

4.2.2.1 THE CHARACTERISTIC SELECTIVITY (CS) MEASURE

The first component of performance measures the stock-picking ability of the fund manager, controlling for the particular style used by that manager. This measure of stock-picking ability, which is called the "Characteristic-Selectivity" measure (*CS*), is computed during month *t* as:

$$CS_t = \sum_{j=1}^{N} \tilde{w}_{j,t-1}(\widetilde{R}_{j,t} - \widetilde{R}_t^{b_{j,t-1}}), \tag{4.7}$$

where $\tilde{w}_{j,t-1}$ is the portfolio weight on stock j at the end of month $t-1$, $\widetilde{R}_{j,t}$ is the month t buy-and-hold return of stock j, and $\widetilde{R}^{b_{j,t-1}}$ is the month t buy-and-hold return of a value-weighted portfolio that is matched to stock j based on its characteristics at the beginning of the quarter.

To construct the characteristic-matched benchmark portfolio for a given stock at the beginning of a given quarter, we characterize that stock over three dimensions—the market capitalization of equity (size), the ratio of book-value of equity to market-value of equity, and the prior-year return. Forming these matching portfolios proceeds as follows—this procedure is based on DGTW, and is described in more detail in that paper. First, all stocks (listed on NYSE, AMEX, or Nasdaq) having book value of equity information in Compustat, and stock return and market capitalization of equity data in the Center for Research in Security Prices (CRSP) stock files, are ranked, at the end of each June, by their market capitalization. Quintile portfolios are formed (using NYSE size quintile

[17] These measures are developed in DGTW, and are more fully described there. In that paper, the authors argue that decomposing performance with the use of benchmark portfolios matched to stocks on the basis of the size, book-to-market, and prior-year return characteristics of the stocks is a more precise method of controlling for style-based returns than the method of decomposing performance with factor-based regressions, such as those used by Carhart (1997). See Chapter 5 for an example that compares residuals from both types of models, and confirms that DGTW residuals are smaller for a mutual fund.

breakpoints), and each quintile portfolio is further subdivided into book-to-market quintiles, based on their book-to-market data as of the end of the December immediately prior to the ranking year. Finally, each of the resulting 25 fractile portfolios is further subdivided into quintiles based on the 12-month past return of stocks through the end of May of the ranking year. This three-way ranking procedure results in 125 fractile portfolios, each having a distinct combination of size, book-to-market, and momentum characteristics.[18] The three-way ranking procedure is repeated at the end of June of each year, and the 125 portfolios are reconstituted at that date. Non-June 30 quarter-end rankings are done similarly, except that book-to-market data are not updated.

Value-weighted returns are computed for each of the 125 fractile portfolios, and the benchmark for each stock during a given month is the buy-and-hold return of the fractile portfolio of which that stock is a member during that month (available by Googling "DGTW benchmarks"). Therefore, the characteristic-adjusted return for a given stock is computed as the buy-and-hold stock return minus the buy-and-hold (value-weighted) matched benchmark return during the same month. Finally, the Characteristic Selectivity measure of the stock portfolio of a given mutual fund during month t, CS_t, is computed as the portfolio-weighted characteristic-adjusted return of the component stocks in the portfolio, where the stock portfolio is normalized so that the weights add to one (to focus on the performance of the equity portion of the portfolio).

A caveat is in order regarding the interpretation of the CS measure, as it controls for only three characteristic dimensions of stocks—size, book-to-market, and past returns. Recent research has shown that mutual funds show a distinct preference for other stock characteristics that are related to average returns—for example, stocks with greater liquidity (see Chen et al., 2000 and Wermers, 2000).[19] For example, one might argue that our CS measure underestimates the stock-picking talents of funds since we do not control for the lower average returns that accrue to stocks with greater liquidity. These potential "missing factors" probably do not impact the practical uses of the DGTW approach, but the literature has yet to fully explore such issues.

EXAMPLE

We return to the Janus Twenty fund example used above to illustrate the CS measure. The spreadsheet shown in Table 4.5 illustrates the needed fields to compute the CS measure for April, May, and June 1998. The benchmark return during each of those months is shown in columns "DGTWret1", "DGTWret2", and "DGTWret3", respectively, while the stock return minus DGTW benchmark return $\left(\widetilde{R}_{j,t} - \widetilde{R}_t^{b_{j,t-1}}\right)$ in Equation (4.7) above) is shown in columns "delta_ret1", "delta_ret2", and "delta_ret3", respectively. Then, the current portfolio weight—in this example, the stock weight as of March 31, 1998—is multiplied by the delta return (which itself can be interpreted as the stock-level "alpha"), as shown in Table 4.6 . Note that these portfolio weights are

---

[18] Thus, a stock belonging to size portfolio one, book-to-market portfolio one, and prior return portfolio one is a small, low book-to-market (growth) stock having a low prior-year return.

[19] See Lee and Swaminathan (2000) and Datar et al. (1998) for evidence that more liquid stocks earn lower average returns.

Table 4.5 Janus Twenty Fund Stockholding-Based Returns and Benchmark Returns, April–June 1998

Stock	return1	return2	return3	DGT-Wret1	DGT-Wret2	DGT-Wret3	delta ret1	delta ret2	delta ret3
MICROSOFT CORP	0.0070	−0.0589	0.2778	0.0271	−0.0603	0.1466	−0.0201	0.0014	0.1312
COCA COLA CO	−0.0202	0.0329	0.0930	−0.0254	0.0001	0.0413	0.0052	0.0328	0.0517
GENERAL ELECTRIC CO	−0.0116	−0.0213	0.0900	0.0027	−0.0166	0.0646	−0.0143	−0.0047	0.0254
INTERNATIONAL BUSINESS MACHS COR	0.1155	0.0159	−0.0229	0.0866	−0.0298	0.0276	0.0290	0.0457	−0.0505
PEPSICO INC	−0.0703	0.0283	0.0124	−0.0051	−0.0074	−0.0021	−0.0652	0.0357	0.0145
PHARMACIA CORP	0.0168	0.0478	0.0090	−0.0254	0.0001	0.0413	0.0422	0.0477	−0.0322
BOEING CO	−0.0396	−0.0435	−0.0668	0.0113	−0.0278	−0.0117	−0.0508	−0.0157	−0.0551
U A L CORP	−0.0619	−0.0889	−0.0181	0.0252	−0.0167	0.1030	−0.0871	−0.0722	−0.1211
PFIZER INC	0.1417	−0.0775	0.0370	0.0317	−0.0318	0.0539	0.1099	−0.0457	−0.0169
MASSEY ENERGY CO	−0.0503	0.0093	0.0739	−0.0394	−0.0216	0.0177	−0.0108	0.0309	0.0562
CITICORP	0.0640	−0.0083	0.0000	0.0170	−0.0207	0.0425	0.0470	0.0124	−0.0425

J P MORGAN CHASE & CO	0.0326	−0.0189	0.1108	0.0458	−0.0173	0.0528	−0.0132	−0.0017	0.0580
WELLS FARGO & CO	0.1165	−0.0176	0.0193	−0.0013	0.0090	−0.0027	0.1178	−0.0266	0.0221
LILLY ELI & CO	0.1667	−0.1151	0.0794	0.0866	−0.0298	0.0276	0.0801	−0.0853	0.0518
FEDERAL NATIONAL MORTGAGE ASSN	−0.0493	−0.0010	0.0157	−0.0254	0.0001	0.0413	−0.0240	−0.0012	−0.0256
MERRILL LYNCH & CO INC	0.0594	0.0192	0.0322	0.0027	−0.0166	0.0646	0.0567	0.0358	−0.0324
NIKE INC	0.0791	−0.0366	0.0614	−0.0191	0.0122	0.0374	0.0982	−0.0489	0.0239
INTEL CORP	0.0356	−0.1160	0.0376	0.0271	−0.0603	0.1466	0.0085	−0.0557	−0.1090
MIRAGE RESORTS INC	−0.0925	−0.0567	0.0240	0.0554	−0.0783	0.0199	−0.1479	0.0217	0.0041
CISCO SYSTEMS INC	0.0713	0.0324	0.2174	0.0252	−0.0167	0.1030	0.0461	0.0491	0.1143
FIRST DATA CORP	0.0423	−0.0185	0.0025	−0.0394	−0.0216	0.0177	0.0817	0.0032	−0.0152
ELECTRONICS FOR IMAGING INC	−0.2115	−0.0366	0.0696	−0.0551	−0.0586	−0.0326	−0.1564	0.0220	0.1023

(Continued)

Table 4.5 Continued

Stock	return1	return2	return3	DGTWretl	DGT-Wret2	DGT-Wret3	delta ret1	delta ret2	delta ret3
DANKA BUSINESS SYSTEMS PLC	0.0884	−0.1563	−0.3000	–	–	–	–	–	–
FILA HOLDING S P A	0.0080	−0.2540	−0.1328	–	–	–	–	–	–
ASCEND COMMUNICATIONS INC	0.1502	−0.0086	0.1476	−0.0394	−0.0216	0.0177	0.1896	0.0130	0.1300
GUCCI GROUP N V	−0.0197	−0.0255	0.1769	–	–	–	–	–	–
ASSOCIATES FIRST CAPITAL CORP	−0.0787	0.0008	0.0284	–	–	–	–	–	–
WORLDCOM INC GA NEW	−0.0065	0.0636	0.0646	0.0056	0.0066	0.0091	−0.0121	0.0569	0.0555
DELL INC	0.1919	0.0205	0.1263	0.0271	−0.0603	0.1466	0.1648	0.0808	−0.0203
DU PONT E I DE NEMOURS & CO	0.0708	0.0646	−0.0324	0.0317	−0.0318	0.0539	0.0390	0.0964	−0.0863
SCHLUMBERGER LTD	0.0957	−0.0572	−0.1249	–	–	–	–		
APPLIED MATERIALS INC	0.0230	−0.1142	−0.0781	0.0223	−0.0024	0.0601	0.0007	−0.1118	−0.1382
C B S CORP	0.0497	−0.1088	0.0000	−0.0051	−0.0074	−0.0021	0.0548	−0.1014	0.0021
COLGATE PALMOLIVE CO	0.0370	−0.0300	0.0115	0.0271	−0.0603	0.1466	0.0100	0.0303	−0.1351

HALLIBURTON COMPANY	0.0923	−0.1324	−0.0619	0.0170	−0.0207	0.0425	0.0753	−0.1117	−0.1044
WARNER LAMBERT CO	0.1119	0.0135	0.0872	0.0866	−0.0298	0.0276	0.0254	0.0433	0.0596
TIME WARNER INC	0.0903	−0.0076	0.0980	0.0468	−0.0201	0.0198	0.0435	0.0125	0.0782
FEDEX CORP	−0.0439	−0.0570	−0.0214	−0.0283	−0.0455	0.0346	−0.0156	−0.0115	−0.0560
KONINKLIJKE PHILIPS ELEC N V	0.2272	0.0555	−0.1078	–	–	–	–	–	–
U S BANCORP DEL	0.0180	−0.0717	0.0990	0.0170	−0.0207	0.0425	0.0011	−0.0510	0.0565
HOME DEPOT INC	0.0305	0.1274	0.0581	−0.0105	−0.0289	0.0542	0.0410	0.1562	0.0038
S L M CORP	−0.0215	−0.0644	0.2314	0.0271	−0.0603	0.1466	−0.0486	−0.0041	0.0848
COCA COLA ENTERPRISES INC	0.0290	−0.0050	0.0426	0.0051	−0.0377	−0.0064	0.0239	0.0328	0.0490
TELE COMMUNICATIONS INC NEW	0.0372	0.0640	0.1202	−0.0035	0.0002	0.0327	0.0407	0.0637	0.0875
AMERICA ONLINE INC DEL	0.1702	0.0422	0.2762	−0.0191	0.0122	0.0374	0.1893	0.0300	0.2388
LUCENT TECHNOLOGIES INC	0.1932	−0.0697	0.1727	0.0266	−0.0596	0.1454	0.1666	−0.0100	0.0273
SOLUTIA INC	−0.0462	−0.0327	0.0456	–	–	–	–	–	–

Table 4.6 Janus Twenty Fund Stockholding-Based CS Alpha, April–June 1998

Stock	curr_weight	delta ret1	delta ret2	delta ret3	alphal	alpha2	alpha3
MICROSOFT CORP	0.0678	−0.0201	0.0014	0.1312	−0.0014	0.0001	0.0089
COCA COLA CO	0.0000	0.0052	0.0328	0.0517	0.0000	0.0000	0.0000
GENERAL ELECTRIC CO	0.0577	−0.0143	−0.0047	0.0254	−0.0008	−0.0003	0.0015
INTERNATIONAL BUSINESS MACHS COR	0.0000	0.0290	0.0457	−0.0505	0.0000	0.0000	0.0000
PEPSICO INC	0.0000	−0.0652	0.0357	0.0145	0.0000	0.0000	0.0000
PHARMACIA CORP	0.0702	0.0422	0.0477	−0.0322	0.0030	0.0034	−0.0023
BOEING CO	0.0000	−0.0508	−0.0157	−0.0551	0.0000	0.0000	0.0000
U A L CORP	0.0579	−0.0871	−0.0722	−0.1211	−0.0050	−0.0042	−0.0070
PFIZER INC	0.0733	0.1099	−0.0457	−0.0169	0.0081	−0.0033	−0.0012
MASSEY ENERGY CO	0.0000	−0.0108	0.0309	0.0562	0.0000	0.0000	0.0000
CITICORP	0.0503	0.0470	0.0124	−0.0425	0.0024	0.0006	−0.0021
J P MORGAN CHASE & CO	0.0000	−0.0132	−0.0017	0.0580	0.0000	0.0000	0.0000
WELLS FARGO & CO	0.0152	0.1178	−0.0266	0.0221	0.0018	−0.0004	0.0003

LILLY ELI & CO	0.0410	0.0801	−0.0853	0.0518	0.0033	−0.0035	0.0021
FEDERAL NATIONAL MORTGAGE ASSN	0.0466	−0.0240	−0.0012	−0.0256	−0.0011	−0.0001	−0.0012
MERRILL LYNCH & CO INC	0.0514	0.0567	0.0358	−0.0324	0.0029	0.0018	−0.0017
NIKE INC	0.0000	0.0982	−0.0489	0.0239	0.0000	0.0000	0.0000
INTEL CORP	0.0000	0.0085	−0.0557	−0.1090	0.0000	0.0000	0.0000
MIRAGE RESORTS INC	0.0000	−0.1479	0.0217	0.0041	0.0000	0.0000	0.0000
CISCO SYSTEMS INC	0.0186	0.0461	0.0491	0.1143	0.0009	0.0009	0.0021
FIRST DATA CORP	0.0022	0.0817	0.0032	−0.0152	0.0002	0.0000	0.0000
ELECTRONICS FOR IMAGING INC	0.0000	−0.1564	0.0220	0.1023	0.0000	0.0000	0.0000
DANKA BUSINESS SYSTEMS PLC	0.0000	–	–	–	–	–	–
FILA HOLDING S P A	0.0000	–	–	–	–	–	–
ASCEND COMMUNICATIONS INC	0.0000	0.1896	0.0130	0.1300	0.0000	0.0000	0.0000
GUCCI GROUP N V	0.0000	–	–	–	–	–	–
ASSOCIATES FIRST CAPITAL CORP	0.0000	–	–	–	–	–	–

(*Continued*)

Table 4.6 Continued

Stock	curr_weight	delta ret1	delta ret2	delta ret3	alphal	alpha2	alpha3
WORLDCOM INC GA NEW	0.0051	−0.0121	0.0569	0.0555	−0.0001	0.0003	0.0003
DELL INC	0.0967	0.1648	0.0808	−0.0203	0.0159	0.0078	−0.0020
DU PONT E I DE NEMOURS & CO	0.0115	0.0390	0.0964	−0.0863	0.0004	0.0011	−0.0010
SCHLUMBERGER LTD	0.0000	–	–	–	–	–	–
APPLIED MATERIALS INC	0.0253	0.0007	−0.1118	−0.1382	0.0000	−0.0028	−0.0035
C B S CORP	0.0103	0.0548	−0.1014	0.0021	0.0006	−0.0010	0.0000
COLGATE PALMOLIVE CO	0.0147	0.0100	0.0303	−0.1351	0.0001	0.0004	−0.0020
HALLIBURTON COMPANY	0.0072	0.0753	−0.1117	−0.1044	0.0005	−0.0008	−0.0007
WARNER LAMBERT CO	0.0542	0.0254	0.0433	0.0596	0.0014	0.0023	0.0032
TIME WARNER INC	0.0294	0.0435	0.0125	0.0782	0.0013	0.0004	0.0023
FEDEX CORP	0.0127	−0.0156	−0.0115	−0.0560	−0.0002	−0.0001	−0.0007

KONINKLIJKE PHILIPS ELEC N V	0.0000	–	–	–	–	–	–
U S BANCORP DEL	0.0136	0.0011	−0.0510	0.0565	0.0000	−0.0007	0.0008
HOME DEPOT INC	0.0080	0.0410	0.1562	0.0038	0.0003	0.0013	0.0000
S L M CORP	0.0291	−0.0486	−0.0041	0.0848	−0.0014	−0.0001	0.0025
COCA COLA ENTERPRISES INC	0.0148	0.0239	0.0328	0.0490	0.0004	0.0005	0.0007
TELE COMMUNICATIONS INC NEW	0.0040	0.0407	0.0637	0.0875	0.0002	0.0003	0.0004
AMERICA ONLINE INC DEL	0.0312	0.1893	0.0300	0.2388	0.0059	0.0009	0.0075
LUCENT TECHNOLOGIES INC	0.0800	0.1666	−0.0100	0.0273	0.0133	−0.0008	0.0022
SOLUTIA INC	0.0000	–	–	–	–	–	–

adjusted to compensate for stocks that do not have the required data to be included in a DGTW benchmark cell. Weights of stocks with required data add to 1.

The contribution of each stockholding to the fund alpha for April, May, and June 1998 can be obtained from the columns "alpha1", "alpha2", and "alpha3", respectively. Note that Dell, using the DGTW approach, contributes 1.59% to the fund alpha in April 1998. Summing each of the three columns, "alpha1", "alpha2", and "alpha3", we arrive at the final April, May, and June 1998 alpha for the Twenty fund, according to the CS approach $\left(\sum_{j=1}^{N} \tilde{w}_{j,t-1}\left(\tilde{R}_{j,t} - \tilde{R}_t^{b_{j,t-1}}\right)\right)$, of 5.28%, 0.39%, and 0.93%. These numbers are similar to those using the GT measure, 4.22%, 0.37%, and 2.99%, except for April 1998. Why different in April? First, the CS measure uses DGTW benchmarks, which require that stocks have certain data and characteristics that make them suitable for matching with a "similar" benchmark portfolio. In the case of April, DANKA BUSINESS SYSTEMS PLC, for example, contributed a large amount to fund alpha, computed using the GT measure, since the Twenty fund sold the stock prior to it losing 30%. This stock was an ADR, so it was excluded from the formation of the DGTW benchmarks.[20]

Another reason for the differences in alphas between the GT and CS measures is that the GT measure uses past returns as a proxy for current expected returns. This approach can be somewhat noisy in focused portfolios, such as the Twenty portfolio. In addition, if a fund is using a dynamic strategy based on time-varying expected returns, such as momentum investing, then the GT measure can leave some risk factor loadings in differenced portfolio, as discussed in Section 4.2.1.1.

4.2.2.2 THE CHARACTERISTIC TIMING (CT) MEASURE

The above stock-selectivity measure does not capture the ability of the fund manager to time the various stock characteristics. Indeed, fund managers can generate additional performance if size, book-to-market, or momentum strategies have time-varying expected returns that the manager can exploit by "tilting" portfolio weights toward stocks having these characteristics when the returns on the characteristics are highest. Thus, our second component of performance measures a fund manager's success at timing the different stock characteristics; this component is termed the "Characteristic Timing" (CT) measure. The month t component of this measure is:

$$CT_t = \sum_{j=1}^{N} (\tilde{w}_{j,t-1}\tilde{R}_t^{b_{j,t-1}} - \tilde{w}_{j,t-k-1}\tilde{R}_t^{b_{j,t-k-1}}). \tag{4.8}$$

Note that this expression deducts the month t return of the month $t-k-1$ matching characteristic portfolio for stock j (times the portfolio weight at $t-k-1$) from the month t return of the month $t-1$ matching characteristic portfolio for stock j (times the portfolio weight at $t-1$). Thus, a fund manager who increases the fund's weight on stock j just before the payoff to the characteristics of stock j are highest will exhibit a large CT measure. The choice of k, of course, will depend on the frequency used by the manager to time characteristic-based returns among stocks. For instance, if such timing strategies generally pay

[20] A way to "patch" these instances is to subtract another benchmark return from these non-standard equities, such as the return on a similar ADR.

off within one year, then we might choose $k = 12$, thus, lagging weights four quarters from the current portfolio date, $t - 1$. This choice of k is used by DGTW to evaluate U.S. domestic equity mutual funds.

4.2.2.3 THE AVERAGE STYLE (AS) MEASURE

To measure the returns earned by a fund because of that fund's tendency to hold stocks with certain characteristics, we employ our third performance component, the "Average Style" (AS) return measure. The month t component of this measure is:

$$AS_t = \sum_{j=1}^{N} \tilde{w}_{j,t-k-1} \tilde{R}_t^{b_{j,t-k-1}}. \tag{4.9}$$

Each stock held by a fund at the end of month $t - k$ is matched with its characteristic-based benchmark portfolio of that date. The month t return of this benchmark portfolio is then multiplied by the end of month $t - k - 1$ portfolio weight of the stock, and the resulting product is summed over all stocks held by the fund at the end of month $t - k - 1$ to give the month t AS component. Note that, by lagging weights and benchmark portfolios by k periods, we eliminate returns due to the timing effect described by Equation (4.8). For example, a fund that successfully buys high book-to-market stocks when returns to such a strategy are unusually high will not exhibit an unusually high AS return, since this strategy will most likely involve moving into stocks shortly before the unusually high book-to-market return. However, a fund that systematically holds high book-to-market stocks to boost its portfolio return (without trying to time the effect) will exhibit a high AS Return. Note that k should be chosen to be the same value in both Equations (4.8) and (4.9).

The AS measure of a fund may differ from the return on a broad market index for a couple of reasons. First, the AS measure may contain a compensation for the fund loading on covariance-based risk factors differently than the market portfolio's loadings. And, second, the AS measure may contain return premia for the fund loading on non-covariance-based characteristic factors. We do not attempt to separate these two sources of AS return premia here, but we note it and leave the interpretation to the reader.

4.2.2.4 SUMMING THE COMPONENTS

Note that the sum of the CS, CT, and AS measures equals the total portfolio-weighted (pre-expense and pre-trade cost) return on the stockholdings of a given fund (we also call this the "gross return" of the fund). That is,

$$GR_t = CS_t + CT_t + AS_t.^{21} \tag{4.10}$$

[21] In practice, this equivalence is only approximately true because of the additional requirement that a stock be listed in COMPUSTAT to be included in the calculation of the CS, CT, and AS measures for a fund.

Note, also, that computations of the AS and CT measures begin after a lag of k periods, as we must use k-period lagged portfolio weights to compute these measures.

4.2.2.5 COMPARISON OF DGTW MEASURES WITH FACTOR-BASED REGRESSION APPROACHES

One might reasonably ask why we cannot, more easily, use sophisticated multi-factor returns-based performance evaluation methods to arrive at similar measures—these, of course, do not require gathering and processing portfolio weights! For example, Carhart (1997) develops a four-factor regression method for estimating mutual fund performance. This four-factor model is based on an extension of the Fama and Kenneth (1989) factor model, and is described as,

$$R_{j,t} - R_{F,t} = \alpha_j + b_j \cdot RMRF_t + s_j \cdot SMB_t + h_j \cdot HML_t + p_j \cdot UMD_t + e_{j,t}. \quad (4.11)$$

Here, $R_{j,t} - R_{F,t}$ equals the excess net return of fund j during month t (the fund net return minus T-bills); $RMRF_t$ equals the month t excess return on a value-weighted aggregate market proxy portfolio; and SMB_t, HML_t, and UMD_t equal the month t returns on value-weighted, zero-investment factor-mimicking portfolios for size, book-to-market equity, and one-year momentum in stock returns.

While the Carhart regression approach seemingly controls for known sources of systematic time-series and cross-sectional return variability among U.S. equities, Daniel and Titman (1997) show strong empirical evidence that factor-based risk controls can be beaten with mechanical strategies that, for example, pick certain value stocks. The point of Daniel and Titman is that such strategies will exhibit a positive alpha in a Carhart regression as long as we choose a portfolio of stocks (e.g., value) that has a low covariance with the factors (e.g., HML in the Carhart model) that are designed to capture their common return influences (value). Daniel and Titman find that stocks with "value characteristics", such as those having a high book-value to market-value of equity ratio, generate superior returns to stocks that have "growth characteristics", even if the value stocks have a low covariation with other value stocks. This finding implies that investors do not bid down the prices of value stocks because they have an exposure to an unknown risk factor (such as financial distress), but that they irrationally do so, perhaps due to over-extrapolating recent poor earnings results for such stocks.

Regardless of the interpretation of the Daniel and Titman results, the DGTW approach uses the Daniel and Titman results to benchmark stocks against their "characteristic peers" (e.g., other high book-to-market stocks) rather than against other stocks with which they have a high return covariation. Practically speaking, this means that the DGTW-measured performance controls more accurately for simple, mechanical strategies for which we may not wish to reward a fund manager for undertaking (since many index funds provide bets on these strategies for low cost). Nevertheless, the limited data requirements of the regression approach make it appealing in many practical cases. Therefore, it is important to compare the DGTW and Fama-French/ Carhart approaches to performance evaluation and attribution.

Table 4.7 shows the relation between the DGTW components and the Fama-French/Carhart components. One should note that the dynamic style control approach of DGTW allows for several advantages over the fixed style coefficient regression approach of Fama-French/Carhart. The most important of these advantages are the smaller standard error for the selectivity component, *CS*, relative to α, and the (correspondingly) more precise measure of returns attributable to style loadings, *AS*, relative to the sum of the fixed coefficients times average style return premia of F-F/Carhart (see Table 4.7).

4.2.2.6 *EXTENSIONS*

As with the *GT* performance measure of Equation (4.3), the *CS* performance measure of Equation (4.7) can easily be decomposed into partial sums. This decomposition is a useful technique to determine the attribution of performance in a manager's portfolio. For instance, Sialm, Clemens, Jegadeesh and Titman (1993) find that mutual funds with concentrated holdings in a few industries outperform those with more diverse holdings—suggesting that manager skills are industry-specific. If so, we may wish to measure the performance of stocks held by the manager within a certain industry, ignoring the other holdings of that manager. Alternatively, we may wish to measure the performance of the manager's top 10 holdings, regardless of their sector membership. Further, Wermers (2005) shows that stocks purchased by U.S. mutual fund managers in response to strong cash inflows from investors outperform the other holdings of the managers. In all of these cases, a modification of the performance measures may be used to capture the performance of the subportfolio of interest.

Attributing Subportfolio Performance To illustrate, the characteristic selectivity measure is modified as follows. Suppose that we are interested in measuring the performance of the subportfolio of stocks belonging to set S, where S refers, for example, to a certain sector of the market (e.g., technology stocks). The CS measure is decomposed to measure the partial sum corresponding to stocks within set S.

Table 4.7 Comparison of Attribution by DGTW and Fama-French/Carhart Approaches

	Selectivity	Style Timing	Average Style
DGTW Component	*CS*	*CT*	*AS*
FF/Carhart Component	α	—	$b \cdot \overline{RMRF} + s \cdot \overline{SMB} + h \cdot \overline{HML} + u \cdot \overline{UMD}$
Comments	CS has lower standard errors than α	Assumed constant factor loadings of FF/C doesn't allow timing measures	Dynamic style measurement of AS allows more precise measure than assumed constant b, s, h, and u

That is, the selectivity performance of the manager that is attributable to holding stocks within set S is measured as:

$$CS_{S,t} = \sum_{j \in S} \tilde{w}_{j,t-1}(\tilde{R}_{j,t} - \tilde{R}_t^{b_{j,t-1}}). \tag{4.12}$$

A different question may also be addressed: how skilled (in theory) would this manager be if she were constrained to buy only stocks within set S? A further modification that normalizes set S portfolio weights to add to unity allows an answer:

$$CS'_{S,t} = \frac{\sum_{j \in S} \tilde{w}_{j,t-1}(\tilde{R}_{j,t} - \tilde{R}_t^{b_{j,t-1}})}{\sum_{j \in S} \tilde{w}_{j,t-1}}. \tag{4.13}$$

Normalizing for Turnover An ideal property of a performance measure is to rank managers by the precision of their private information, or simply put, skills that cannot be captured through simple strategies that may be implemented by an uninformed observer. Unfortunately, covariance-based measures assign a higher performance measure to managers implementing higher levels of portfolio turnover, holding constant their actual skills in forecasting security returns. Such differences in turnover can arise from the agency problems inherent in asset management, since most managers own a very small fraction of their managed portfolios. Such agency problems include compensation that is insufficiently sensitive to performance, or the labor-market concerns of a manager (i.e., the manager's reputational concerns or concerns over being fired). These agency problems, in theory, should not affect an investor's performance evaluation, since an investor can scale investments (financed through borrowing or short-selling other funds) to any level to increase or decrease the return desired. However, covariance-based measures, by their very nature, are biased.[22]

In general, it is very difficult to properly adjust for the risk-aversion of a manager, as the manager may not view all investment opportunities with the same level of risk-aversion. For example, a durable-goods manager may be more willing to take a large position in an automobile stock relative to a technology stock with similar prospects. Thus, adjusting the covariance measure would require the knowledge of the manager's risk-aversion with respect to all potential investments.

However, we can easily normalize portfolio-based performance measures for risk-aversion with a simplifying assumption—that a manager views all stocks similarly. This assumption can be relaxed when measuring the performance of subportfolios, as described in the previous section—as such subportfolios likely have much more homogeneous risk characteristics, from the viewpoint of the manager, than securities within the overall portfolio.

[22] It is important to note that returns-based performance measures are also plagued with the risk-aversion problem. One approach to adjusting such measures is to normalize (divide) returns-based regression alphas by the turnover of the manager.

To adjust for turnover, the investor can implement a "turnover-adjusted" version of the portfolio-holdings based measure. To illustrate, the turnover-adjusted *GT* measure during period *t* is computed as:

$$TAGT_t = \frac{GT_t}{\sum_{j=1}^{N} \left(\tilde{w}_{j,t-1} - \tilde{w}_{j,t-k-1}\right)}.$$

Similarly, the *CS* measure, adjusted for turnover, is computed as:

$$TACS_t = \frac{CS_t}{\sum_{j=1}^{N} \left(\tilde{w}_{j,t-1} - \tilde{w}_{j,t-k-1}\right)}.$$

4.2.2.7 EMPIRICAL EVIDENCE

The *CS* measure has been widely applied to evaluate the performance of managed portfolios of securities.[23] As mentioned previously, Kacperczyk et al. (2005) find that mutual funds with concentrated holdings in a few industries outperform those with more diverse holdings—suggesting that manager skills are industry-specific. Kacperczyk et al. (2005) find that the decile of U.S. mutual funds that hold the most industry-concentrated portfolios outperform the decile holding the most industry-diversified portfolios by 1.6 percent per year, according to the difference in *CS* measures.

In recent years, researchers have also applied the *CS* methodology to equity portfolios outside the U.S. by forming the characteristic-based benchmarks in the appropriate country stock market. For example, Wylie (2005) follows DGTW (1997) closely in forming characteristic-based benchmarks for the U.K. market. The procedure is as follows. At the end of June of each year, all London Stock Exchange listed stocks are partitioned into 125 benchmark portfolios by repeated division into quintiles on the basis of market capitalization at the end of June, then book-to-market ratio during the most recent fiscal year-end, then prior 12-month return (ending in May rather than June to avoid the one-month return reversal described in Jegadeesh (1990)).[24] Then, the market capitalization weighted average return of each benchmark portfolio is calculated for each of the 12 months following June to compute benchmark returns for each month of that year. Wylie and Sam (2005) finds that stocks that UK fund managers "herd" into (buy as a group) underperform those they herd out of by 0.8 percent during the following year.

---

[23] The DGTW benchmarks, on which the CS measure is built, have been applied to measure the performance of portfolios of stocks formed as part of an event study, as well as the more conventional application of the benchmarks to measure the performance of an asset manager. For instance, Jeng, Metrick, and Zeckhauser (2003) use the benchmarks to measure the abnormal returns gained by insiders when they trade their company's stock, while Moskowitz and Grinblatt (1999) use the benchmarks to investigate the role of industry in explaining momentum in U.S. equity returns.

[24] Book value is defined as ordinary share capital plus reserves plus deferred and future taxation. Stocks are excluded from the portfolio formation unless they have market capitalization data for June of the current year and December of the preceding year; book value data for the previous 2 years, at least six monthly returns in the year preceding May 31, and are ordinary shares.

Iihara et al. (2004) form characteristic-based portfolios from stocks listed on the Tokyo Stock Exchange to study momentum in Japanese stocks. At the end of each June from 1975 to 1997, all TSE stocks are sorted into five equal groups from small to large based upon their market capitalization. They independently sort TSE stocks into five equal book-to-market (BTM) groups, where BTM is equal to the ratio of book-value to market-value of equity at the end of June for each year. Finally, 25 benchmark portfolios are created from the intersection of the five size and five book-to-market groups. Monthly equal-weighted returns for each of these 25 portfolios are calculated from July of year t to June of year $t + 1$.

Other papers that form characteristic-based benchmarks, in the spirit of the DGTW approach, include Pinnuck (2003), who forms benchmarks in Australia. In addition, Jern (2004) forms benchmarks for Finnish fund managers, while Nitibhon et al. (2005) form benchmarks for Thai equity fund managers. Given the popularity of the DGTW approach, it is likely that further developments in other markets will make these benchmarks more widely available to both academics and practitioners. In addition, once the risk factors in fixed-income markets become widely accepted, it is likely that a similar approach will be feasible for measuring the performance of fixed-income asset managers.

4.2.2.8 THE CORRELATION BETWEEN PERFORMANCE MEASURES

An interesting issue is the correlation, across funds, of performance at the stock-holdings level (DGTW) and performance at the net returns level (F-F/Carhart). Although, at first blush, it would seem that the correlation would be near unity, the issue becomes more interesting if the expenses and transactions costs of funds are also positively correlated with their pre-expense performance. The tendency of funds with superior stock-picking skills to incur higher costs would be consistent with the equilibrium model of Grossman and Stiglitz (1980), where the returns to information-gathering and-processing skills are equal to the costs. Analyzing both the portfolio holdings and the net returns of funds allows deeper insight into an accounting of the sources and uses of returns earned by a portfolio manager.

Table 4.8 investigates this issue by presenting cross-sectional correlations (across funds) between various measures of performance.[25] These performance measures are computed over the entire life of each U.S. domestic equity mutual fund during the 1975 to 1994 period. The only restriction we place on a fund to be included in these correlations is that the fund must have at least 24 valid monthly return observations (both for stockholdings and net returns) in order to provide a reasonable degrees-of-freedom in the regression-based measures.

Panel A of the table presents Pearson correlations between three measures of performance at the stock portfolio level: the Characteristic-Selectivity measure (CS), the Carhart measure using the time-series of excess monthly returns on the stock portfolio as the explained variable ($\alpha_{Carhart}^{Gross}$), and the Jensen measure using

[25] This table is replicated from Wermers (2000).

Table 4.8 Mutual Fund Performance Measure Correlations

In this table, we present cross-sectional correlations (across funds) between different measures of mutual fund performance. The measures included in this table are the Characteristic Selec-tivity measure (CS), the Carhart four-factor regression alpha, and the Jensen regression alpha for the stock portfolio of each mutual fund (labeled "gross" alphas); and the Carhart four-factor regression alpha and the Jensen regression alpha for the realized net returns of the funds (labeled "net" alphas). To compute the characteristic-adjusted return for a given stock during a given month, the buy-and-hold return on a value-weighted portfolio of stocks having the same size, book value to market value of equity, and prior-year return characteristics as the stock is subtracted from that stocks buy-and-hold return during the month. Each mutual funds *CS* measure for a given month, is then computed as the portfolio-weighted characteristic-adjusted return of the individual stocks in the fund's portfolio (normalizing so that the weights of all stocks add to one). Finally, the average monthly *CS* measure is computed for each fund, across all months that fund is in existence. To compute the four-factor Carhart gross alpha, the time series of monthly buy-and-hold excess returns for a given fund (the hypothetical stock returns. using CRSP stock return data applied to fund holdings data, minus the return on T-bills) are regressed on (1) the time series of monthly returns associated with a value-weighted market proxy portfolio minus T-bills, (2) the difference in monthly returns between small- and large-capitalization stocks, (3) the difference in monthly returns between high and low book-to-market stocks, and (4) the difference in monthly returns between stocks having high and low prior-year returns. To compute the Jensen gross alpha, a similar regression is computed on only the first regressor of the Carhart regression. The procedure for computing Carhart and Jensen net alphas is similar, except that the excess net return (net realized return from the CRSP database minus T-bills) is the dependent variable in the regressions. For all regressions, a minimum of 24 months of return observations must be available during the entire life of a given fund to be included—this table includes correlations between performance measures for only those funds having this minimum number of return observations. See Daniel et al. (1997), Fama and French (1993), and Carhart (1997) for further details on these procedures. Panel A provides Pearson correlation coefficients between these measures, across all funds, whereas Panel B provides Spearman rank-correlation coefficients between the measures. All two-tailed p-values in both panels are less than 0.0001.

Panel A. Pearson Correlations

$\rho_{Pearson}$	CS	$\alpha^{Gross}_{Carhart}$	$\alpha^{Net}_{Carhart}$	α^{Gross}_{Jensen}	α^{Net}_{Jensen}
CS	1	—	—	—	—
$\alpha^{Gross}_{Carhart}$	0.57	1	—	—	—
$\alpha^{Net}_{Carhart}$	0.36	0.62	1	—	—
α^{Gross}_{Jensen}	0.58	0.74	0.43	1	—
α^{Net}_{Jensen}	0.33	0.49	0.84	0.63	1

Panel B. Spearman Rank Correlations

$\rho_{Spearman}$	CS	$\alpha^{Gross}_{Carhart}$	$\alpha^{Net}_{Carhart}$	α^{Gross}_{Jensen}	α^{Net}_{Jensen}
CS	1	—	—	—	—
$\alpha^{Gross}_{Carhart}$	0.65	1	—	—	—
$\alpha^{Net}_{Carhart}$	0.46	0.63	1	—	—
α^{Gross}_{Jensen}	0.53	0.67	0.44	1	—
α^{Net}_{Jensen}	0.40	0.49	0.80	0.68	1

the same explained variable ($\alpha^{Gross}_{Carhart}$). In addition, two measures of performance at the net return level are included: the Carhart measure using the time-series of excess monthly net returns as the explained variable ($\alpha^{Net}_{Carhart}$) and the Jensen measure using the same explained variable (α^{Net}_{Jensen}). Panel B presents Spearman rank-correlations between all of these performance measures.

Several observations may be drawn from the two correlation matrices. First, the cross-sectional Pearson correlation (at the gross return level) between the Jensen and Carhart measures is 0.74, which indicates that adding the size, book-to-market, and momentum factors provides a modest increase in the precision of the performance estimate. This result indicates that mutual fund loadings on these omitted variables in the Jensen regression are correlated with the intercept of the Carhart regression. The Spearman rank correlation between these two measures is similar, 0.67.

The correlations between the *CS* measure and the Carhart and Jensen gross performance measures are 0.57 and 0.58, respectively. This lower correlation supports the idea that the *CS* measure provides more precise adjustments for characteristic-based returns than the regression-based methods.[26] Again, Spearman rank-correlations are similar.

At the net return level, the Carhart and Jensen performance measures are again highly correlated, both with the Pearson correlation and with the non-parametric Spearman rank-correlation. A comparison of these measures at the gross stockholdings return level and the net return level provides further insight. For example, the Carhart measure of the stockholdings of funds is highly correlated with the Carhart net return performance measure. The Pearson correlation is 0.62, while the Spearman correlation is 0.63. These high correlations between gross and net performance indicate that the level of mutual fund expenses and transactions costs, while possibly correlated with fund performance at the stockholdings level, do not eliminate the higher benchmark-adjusted net returns provided by funds with stock-picking talents.

4.2.3 The Cici and Gibson Method of Performance Evaluation for Bond Portfolios

Cici and Gibson (2012) create bond benchmark portfolios to measure the characteristic selectivity, characteristic timing, and average style returns of bond fund managers. The bond benchmark portfolios are formed as follows. Every month, each bond is assigned to one of seven credit-quality categories: AAA; AA; A; BBB; BB; B; and below B (i.e., all CCC, CC, C and D rated bonds). Every month each bond is also assigned to one of five duration categories, formed by ranking and sorting bonds into quintiles based on their modified duration, calculated as the Macaulay duration divided by one plus the yield to maturity. As in Gebhardt,

---

[26] See DGTW for evidence that further supports the use of the *CS* measure versus the Carhart and Jensen alphas. The *CS* performance estimates are roughly the same magnitude as the Carhart and Jensen alphas, but the estimated *CS* standard errors are much lower.

Hvidkjaer, and Swaminathan (2005), the credit-quality and duration sorts are conducted independently.

The result is 35 benchmark portfolios categorized by the seven credit-quality categories and five duration categories. The benchmark-adjusted return for each bond is its buy-and-hold return minus the value-weighted buy-and-hold return of the appropriate benchmark portfolio over the same holding period.

Cici and Gibson then apply the same performance attribution measures shown in Equations (4.7)–(4.9) to measure the holdings-based performance of U.S. bond funds from 1995 to 2006. They find only statistically weak evidence that bond fund managers are skilled in their selection of individual bonds.

4.3 CONDITIONAL HOLDINGS-BASED PERFORMANCE MEASUREMENT

The above unconditional performance measures, while straightforward to compute, may be subject to some non-trivial biases. These biases will occur if the manager of the measured portfolio uses macroeconomic information to (dynamically) sharpen her estimates of expected security returns over time. In such a case, the manager can game the unconditional performance measure by overweighting securities that, under current macroeconomic conditions, have higher-than-normal expected returns, and underweighting securities that have lower-than-normal expected returns. Such a strategy will exhibit a positive *unconditional* performance measure, since the manager's weights will be correlated with returns over time even in the absence of any private information (i.e., not based purely on widely available macroeconomic information) about expected stock returns. Prior research by Keim and Stambaugh (1986) and Fama and French (1989) indicates that instruments that are useful in predicting future U.S. marketwide equity returns include the (i) aggregate dividend yield; (ii) default spread; (iii) term spread; and (iv) yield on the three-month T-bill.[27] Further, Ferson and Harvey (1999) find that these variables are relevant in explaining the cross-section of U.S. stock returns.

For instance, suppose that a particular lagged macroeconomic factor (e.g., the T-bill yield) is positively correlated with the next-period return in one sector of the stock market (durable goods stocks), while inversely correlated with the return in another sector (utility stocks). Specifically, assume that the unconditional expected return on each sector is 12 percent per year, while the conditional expected return for durables is 10 percent and 14 percent following low and high T-bill yield realizations (recessions and expansions), respectively, and the reverse is true for nondurables. A manager who uses the T-bill yield level to vary portfolio weights between 30 percent and 70 percent for each sector (averaging

[27] At the end of each month, the dividend yield is measured as the aggregate cash dividends on the value-weighted CRSP index over the previous 12 months divided by the current level of the index, the default spread is the yield differential between bonds rated BAA by Moodys and bonds rated AAA, and the term spread is the yield differential between Treasury bonds with more than ten years to maturity and T-bills that mature in three months.

a 50 percent allocation for each) will appear to be informed, according to the unconditional GT measure described in the last section. Specifically, during a transition from a year (quarters 1 through 4) following a low T-bill yield (a recession) to a year (quarters 5 through 8) following a high bill yield (an expansion), the manager's one-year (industry component) GT measure will be measured as:

$$\begin{aligned} GT_t &= \sum_{j=1}^{2} \left(\tilde{w}_{j,t-1} - \tilde{w}_{j,t-k-1}\right) \widetilde{R}_t^{IND(j)} \\ &= \left(\tilde{w}_{durables,4} - \tilde{w}_{durables,0}\right) \widetilde{R}_{5-8}^{durables} \\ &\quad + \left(\tilde{w}_{nondurables,4} - \tilde{w}_{nondurables,0}\right) \widetilde{R}_{5-8}^{nondurables} \\ &= (0.7 - 0.3)(0.14) + (0.3 - 0.7)(0.10) \\ &= 0.056 - 0.040 = 0.016 = 1.6 \text{ percent} \end{aligned}$$

where $k = 4$ quarters lag between current and historical (benchmark) portfolios. Thus, the manager will exhibit an outperformance of 160 basis points during the year, based simply on using publicly available information on macroeconomic indicators to shift portfolio weights. Over a large number of periods, this performance measure, in the absence of any private-information-based skills possessed by the manager, will converge to the covariance between weights and returns, which is positive by assumption,

$$GT = \sum_{j=1}^{2} cov(\widetilde{w}_{j,t-1}, \widetilde{R}_{j,t}).$$

To further illustrate, suppose that, in the above example, the probabilities of expansion or recession are each 50 percent from the point-of-view of an uninformed observer, but that macroeconomic information gives the manager perfect foresight about whether an expansion or recession will occur during the following year. In this case, the unconditional expected weight, $E\left[\widetilde{w}_{j,t-1}\right]$, equals 0.5 for each industry, and the GT measure will converge to[28]

$$\begin{aligned} GT &= \sum_{j=1}^{2} cov(\widetilde{w}_{j,t-1}, \widetilde{R}_{j,t}) = \sum_{j=1}^{2} E\left[\left(\widetilde{w}_{j,t-1} - E\left[\widetilde{w}_{j,t-1}\right]\right) \widetilde{R}_{j,t}\right] \\ &= (2)\left[0.5\,(0.7 - 0.5)\,(0.14) + 0.5\,(0.3 - 0.5)\,(0.10)\right] \\ &= 0.008 = 0.8 \text{ percent per year.} \end{aligned}$$

Note that this is half the level of the performance measure in the prior example above, since a recession year is equally likely (by assumption) to be followed by another recession year as it is to be followed by an expansion year. If a recession is followed by another recession, the GT measure will assign zero performance

[28] Note that this is half the level of the performance measure in the prior example above, since a recession year is equally likely (by assumption) to be followed by another recession year as it is to be followed by an expansion year. If a recession is followed by a recession, the GT measure will assign zero performance since portfolio weights would not shift from one year to the next for the "perfect foresight" manager.

since portfolio weights would not shift from one year to the next for the "perfect foresight" manager.

If we wish to control for "abnormal returns" derived from manager weight changes that are correlated with shifts in expected returns (predictable using macroeconomic variable information), then we need to adjust our unconditional measures to take account of such predictability-based returns. We can then make the decision of whether or not we should reward the manager for such public-information-based returns; the key is to separate abnormal returns based on public information from those derived from private information. Such private-information-based returns are unambiguously interpreted as "manager skill".

4.3.1 The Ferson-Khang Conditional Portfolio-Holdings Approach

4.3.1.1 DESCRIPTION

In response to the need to separate public- and private-based abnormal returns, Ferson and Khang (2002) developed a conditional portfolio-holdings based performance measurement methodology. FK showed that the relation between unconditional and conditional weight-based covariance measures of performance is:

$$\underbrace{\sum_{j=1}^{N} cov(\tilde{w}_{j,t-1} - E[\tilde{w}_{j,t-1}], \tilde{R}_{j,t})}_{UWM} = \underbrace{\sum_{j=1}^{N} E[cov(\tilde{w}_{j,t-1} - E[\tilde{w}_{j,t-1}], \tilde{R}_{j,t}|Z)]}_{CWM}$$
$$+ \underbrace{\sum_{j=1}^{N} cov(E[\tilde{w}_{j,t-1} - E[\tilde{w}_{j,t-1}]|Z], E[\tilde{R}_{j,t}|Z]).}_{RESID} \tag{4.14}$$

Here, *UWM* is the (summed) covariance-based performance measure of Grinblatt and Titman (1993). The right side of Equation (4.14) decomposes the GT measure of performance into two components. First, *CWM* is the performance of the manager, in excess of that attributable to using public information (Z) to choose holdings. The second, *RESID*, is performance that is due solely to using public information to predict future returns of securities, and varying portfolio weights accordingly. The quality of the manager's private information (skills) is reflected in CWM, while purely mechanical trading strategies are reflected in *RESID*. While the active portfolio manager should clearly be compensated for producing a positive *RESID*, similar rewards for producing *RESID* depend on one's view toward returns that are predictable based on public information variables. An investor should judge the cost of producing such returns, and compare these costs to the fees and other costs charged by the manager who produces returns derived from macroeconomic information that is publicly available.

The *RESID* is the time-series average of its component at time t–1 which, in turn, is written as:

$$CWM_t = E\left[\sum_{j=1}^{N} \left(\widetilde{w}_{j,t-1} - E\left[\widetilde{w}_{j,t-1}\right]\right)\left(\widetilde{R}_{j,t} - E\left[\widetilde{R}_{j,t}|Z_t\right]\right)|Z_{t-1}\right]. \quad (4.15)$$

An analogous expression captures the time t *UWM* component,

$$UWM_t = E\left[\sum_{j=1}^{N} \left(\widetilde{w}_{j,t-1} - E\left[\widetilde{w}_{j,t-1}\right]\right)\left(\widetilde{R}_{j,t} - E\left[\widetilde{R}_{j,t}\right]\right)\right].$$

Note that Equation (4.15) involves working with the conditional expected portfolio weight for each security j, $E\left[\widetilde{w}_{j,t-1}|Z_{t-1}\right]$. In the spirit of Grinblatt and Titman (1993), FK suggest that a good choice of a proxy for these conditional expected weights is the buy-and-hold portfolio weights using the portfolio held k periods ago, and held until the end of period $t-1$, i.e.,

$$\text{proxy for } E\left[\widetilde{w}_{j,t-1}|Z_t\right] \equiv \widetilde{w}_{j,t-1}^{b_k} = \widetilde{w}_{j,t-k-1}\prod_{\tau=t-k}^{t-1}\left(\frac{1+\widetilde{R}_{j,\tau}}{1+\widetilde{R}_{p,\tau}}\right).$$

However, any reasonable proxy for the expected weights in the presence of conditioning variable information may be used—such as the security weights of a conditionally efficient benchmark portfolio according to some asset-pricing model (e.g., the optimal portfolio of stocks and bonds under the conditional CAPM). The key to choosing a good proxy is that is should reflect the advantage of using current macroeconomic information to improve the portfolio allocation, but not any private information contained in the manager's current (or very recent) weights.

4.3.1.2 *ESTIMATION*

FK show that a simple procedure may be used to estimate *CWM* and *UWM*. The procedure is as follows:

1. Estimate the (multivariate) regression, $\widetilde{R}_{j,t} = \alpha_j + \mathbf{b}_j'\mathbf{Z}_{t-1} + e_{j,t}$, for each security, j, saving the fitted coefficient vector, $\widehat{\mathbf{b}}_j$.
2. Estimate the unconditional expected return for each security j using the time-series mean return: $\widehat{E}\left[\widetilde{R}_{j,t}\right] = \frac{1}{T}\sum_{t=1}^{T}\widetilde{R}_{j,t}$.
3. Using the fitted coefficients from step one above, estimate the regression, $\underbrace{\sum_{j=1}^{N}\left(\widetilde{w}_{j,t-1} - \widetilde{w}_{j,t-1}^{b_k}\right)\left(\widetilde{R}_{j,t} - \widehat{\mathbf{b}}_j'\mathbf{Z}_{t-1}\right)}_{y-variable} = \underbrace{CWM}_{intercept} + \boldsymbol{\gamma}'\mathbf{z}_{t-1} + \varepsilon_{j,t}$, to capture the estimated *UWM* (the intercept), where $\mathbf{z}_{t-1}$ is the realization of the vector of macroeconomic variables at the end of time $t-1$, in excess of its long-term (time-series) average.
4. Using the estimated time-series mean return from step two above, estimate t - 1 as the sample mean of $\sum_{j=1}^{N}\left(\widetilde{w}_{j,t-1} - \widetilde{w}_{j,t-1}^{b_k}\right)\left(\widetilde{R}_{j,t} - \widehat{E}\left[\widetilde{R}_{j,t}\right]\right)$.

Estimation of the covariance matrix for the estimated parameters in step 3 above involves simulation methods—the interested reader should refer to FK for details.

4.3.1.3 EMPIRICAL EVIDENCE

Ferson and Khang (2002) show that the use of the conditional portfolio weight measure can make a substantial difference in some situations. For their sample of 60 U.S. pension fund managers from 1985 to 1994, Ferson and Khang find that growth fund managers exhibit a positive unconditional weight measure (UWM), but an insignificant conditional weight measure (CWM). They interpret this difference as evidence that growth fund managers exhibit performance simply by smartly using public information to time their stock purchases. As the Ferson and Khang approach is fairly new, it has not yet been applied by other researchers.

4.4 CHAPTER-END PROBLEMS

1. Suppose that you wish to use the Grinblatt and Titman (1993) "benchmark-free" technique to evaluate the performance of a fund manager. Below are the manager's weights on stocks, as well as the CAPM betas and the returns on those stocks.

A. Compute the performance of the manager during 1977, 1978, and 1979. What do you conclude—is this a manager with talent?
B. What are the potential problems of the GT measure for this manager?
C. How would you correct these problems? Perform the correction.

Portfolio Weights

	$w_{Dec1975}$	$w_{Dec1976}$	$w_{Dec1977}$	$w_{Dec1978}$
Stock 1	0.25	0.50	0.25	0.25
Stock 2	0.25	0.25	0.50	0.25
Stock 3	0.50	0.25	0.25	0.50

Stock CAPM Betas

	$\beta_{Dec1975}$	$\beta_{Dec1976}$	$\beta_{Dec1977}$	$\beta_{Dec1978}$
Stock 1	1.1	1.2	1	1
Stock 2	1.2	1.1	1.2	1.2
Stock 3	1.1	1	1.1	1.1

Rate-of-Return (Full Year)

	R_{1977}	R_{1978}	R_{1979}
Stock 1	25%	20%	15%
Stock 2	12%	25%	15%
Stock 3	20%	10%	17%
"Market" Return	17%	22%	15%
T-bill Yield	5%	5%	5%

2. **A.** Show, mathematically, that the Grinblatt and Titman (1993) and Copeland and Mayers (1982) portfolio-holdings based measures differ only by their endpoints.
   B. Show how the two measures converge as $T \rightarrow \infty$.

3. Assume that Scott Schoelzel's Janus 20 portfolio invests in only six stocks as follows. Assume, for simplicity, that each stock has a market capitalization of $1 billion:

December 31, 1996			December 31, 1995		
DGTW Cell No. 58	Janus Weight	1997 Return	DGTW Cell No. 58	Janus Weight	1996 Return
AOL	$\frac{1}{6}$	−9%	MSFT	$\frac{1}{6}$	15%
CSCO	$\frac{1}{2}$	−6	SUNW	0	12
IBM	$\frac{1}{6}$	−9	IBM	0	18
DGTW Cell No. 59			DGTW Cell No. 59		
MSFT	$\frac{1}{6}$	9%	AOL	$\frac{2}{3}$	18%
SUNW	0	5	CSCO	$\frac{1}{6}$	6
JUNP	0	16	JUNP	0	12

   A. Compute the Characteristic Selectivity (CS) measure of Equation 4.7 for Scott during 1996 and 1997.
   B. Compute the Characteristic Timing (CT) measure of Equation 4.8 for Scott during 1996 to 1997.
   C. What do you conclude about Scott? Is he skilled? Explain fully.

4. Describe how the "Characteristic Selectivity" measure of Equation 4.7 is computed for a portfolio manager.

5. Suppose that you wish to compare the Grinblatt and Titman (1993) "benchmark-free" technique with the Copeland and Mayers (1982) technique to evaluate the performance of a fund manager. Below are the manager's weights on stocks, as well as the returns on those stocks.

   A. Compute the performance of the manager during 1977, 1978, and 1979 with the GT (1993) measure. What do you conclude—is this a manager with talent?
   B. Compute the performance of the manager during 1977, 1978, and 1979 with the CM (1982) measure. What do you conclude—is this a manager with talent?
   C. Why are these two measures different? Which do you think is more appropriate in this example, and why?

Portfolio Weights

	$w_{Dec1975}$	$w_{Dec1976}$	$w_{Dec1977}$	$w_{Dec1978}$
Stock 1	0.25	0.50	0.25	0.25
Stock 2	0.25	0.25	0.50	0.25
Stock 3	0.50	0.25	0.25	0.50

Rate-of-Return (Full Year)

	R_{1977}	R_{1978}	R_{1979}	R_{1980}
Stock 1	25%	20%	15%	−5%
Stock 2	12%	25%	15%	−2%
Stock 3	20%	10%	17%	0%

6. Consider the following 3-stock portfolio held by a manager. The ben_weight and curr_weight are the stock weights, as of March 31, 1997 and March 31, 1998. return1, return2, and return3 are the total returns of each stock (including cash dividends) for April, May, and June 1998. DGTWret1, DGTWret2, and DGTWret3 are the DGTW benchmark (control) portfolio returns during April, May, and June 1998.

Stock	ben_ weight	curr_ weight	return1	return2	re- turn3	DGTWret1	DGTWret2	DGT- Wret3
MICRO- SOFT CORP	0.4000	0.3000	0.0070	−0.0589	0.2778	0.0270709	−0.0603081	0.1465882
COCO COLA CO	0.4000	0.3000	−0.0202	0.0329	0.0930	−0.0253509	0.0001075	0.041256
GENER- AL ELEC- TRIC CO	0.2000	0.4000	−0.0116	−0.0213	0.0900	0.0027231	−0.0165585	0.0645858

A. Compute the Grinblatt-Titman (delta-weight) performance of the fund.
B. Compute the CS (DGTW-adjusted) performance of the fund.

Chapter 5

Combining Portfolio-Holdings-Based and Returns-Based Performance Evaluation (and the "Return Gap")

ABSTRACT

This chapter combines portfolio holdings-based and returns-based performance evaluation measures into a comprehensive system of performance evaluation and attribution analysis. It also allows an analysis of the missing performance due to unobserved actions (the "return gap"). The performance of fund managers is decomposed at the portfolio-holdings level into stockpicking, style-timing, and style-based returns. The performance at the net returns level is decomposed into stockpicking returns and expenses. Finally, an approach to estimate trading costs from the periodic portfolio-holdings data is presented. The component models presented in this chapter apply to U.S. equity funds, but similar approaches can be used for other fund sectors. For instance, Cici and Gibson (2012) develop a similar system for fixed-income funds.

Keywords
Portfolio-holdings performance evaluation, Self-benchmarking, Grinblatt-Titman measure, Copeland-Mayers measure, DGTW benchmarks, Characteristic selectivity measure, Characteristic timing measure, Average style measure

5.1 INTRODUCTION

In Chapter 3, we discussed several approaches to returns-based performance evaluation, while, in Chapter 4, we discussed approaches to holdings-based performance evaluation. How can we integrate these two approaches to learn more about manager skills? For example, a recent paper by Kaczerczyk et al. (2008) finds that the difference in performance between the portfolio-holdings and net returns approaches—called the "return gap"—can help to capture manager skills and predict future performance.

In this chapter, we develop a comprehensive empirical analysis of performance at both the stockholdings level and at the net returns level, then apply it

Performance Evaluation and Attribution of Security Portfolios. http://dx.doi.org/10.1016/B978-0-12-744483-3.00005-5
© 2013 Elsevier Inc. All rights reserved.
For End-of-chapter Questions: © 2012. CFA Institute, Reproduced and republished with permission from CFA Institute. All rights reserved.

(as an example) to the U.S. domestic-equity mutual fund industry.[1] This analysis allows us to empirically decompose performance into several components to analyze the value of active fund management. With this performance decomposition, we provide a more precise analysis of active vs. passive management, as well as addressing the sources of disparity between mutual fund studies that examine security holdings and studies that examine the net returns of funds.

For example, mutual funds tend to systematically follow certain "styles", such as holding small stocks or high past-return stocks (see, for example, Chen et al. (2000)). Indeed, Grinblatt et al. (1995) find that the majority of mutual funds tend to actively invest in high past-return stocks (called "momentum-investing" or "trend-following" strategies), while Carhart (1997) finds that they passively hold on to their high past return stocks when they get lucky. Past research (for example, Fama and French (1992, 1993, 1996), Jegadeesh and Titman (1993), Daniel and Titman (1997), and Moskowitz and Grinblatt (1999)) provides evidence that stocks with certain characteristics (e.g., high book-to-market or momentum stocks) outperform other stocks, at least before trading costs are deducted. Given this evidence, we might expect that mutual funds employing such styles would achieve higher average portfolio returns—however, in practice, they might not deliver superior net returns to investors due to the possibly high costs of analyzing and trading these styles. A full attribution analysis at the portfolio-holdings and net-returns levels allows an exploration into such issues. In addition, an attribution analysis can expose potential "hidden actions" (either good or bad) of a manager and the consequences of these actions on fund performance.

5.2 PERFORMANCE-DECOMPOSITION METHODOLOGY

The fundamental goal of the manager of an actively managed mutual fund is to consistently hold stocks that have higher returns than an appropriate benchmark portfolio for the stocks. However, in pursuing this objective, the fund manager must consider the costs of finding and trading these stocks, since shareholders of the fund care only about the realized net return (the difference between finding and profitably trading attractive stocks is commonly referred to as "the implementation shortfall"). Thus, to understand and to benchmark the performance of an actively managed fund, we must use several different measures that, in combination, quantify the ability of the manager to choose stocks as well as to generate superior performance at the net return level. These measures, in general, separate the return of the stocks held by a mutual fund into several components in order to both benchmark the stock portfolio and to understand how the mutual fund manager generated the level of net returns for the fund.

---

[1] Much of this chapter is distilled from Wermers (2000).

The measures that we employ to decompose the return of a mutual fund include:

1. *Gross return characteristic selectivity*: the portfolio-weighted return on stocks currently held by the fund, in excess of returns (during the same time period) on matched control portfolios having the same style characteristics,
2. *Style timing:* the portfolio-weighted return on control portfolios having the same characteristics as stocks currently held by the fund, in excess of time-series average returns on those control portfolios,
3. *Style:* the time-series average returns on control portfolios having the same characteristics as stocks currently held,
4. *Trading costs:* the transactions costs incurred by the fund,
5. *Fees:* the expense ratio charged by the fund, and
6. *Net selectivity:* the net return to shareholders in the fund, in excess of the return to an appropriate benchmark portfolio.

The first three components above, which decompose the return on the stockholdings before any trading costs or expenses are considered, are briefly described next, and were fully developed in Chapter 4. We estimate the transactions costs of each mutual fund during each quarter by applying research on institutional trading costs to our stockholdings data—also described below. Finally, we use a regression-based performance measure to benchmark-adjust net returns, using models described in Chapter 3.

In the following sections, we describe the system for evaluating stock fund portfolios; however, a similar system can be developed for other types of security portfolios. Indeed, Cici and Gibson (2012) have developed the equations below for bond funds, using appropriate benchmarks for fixed-income.

5.2.1 The Characteristic Selectivity (CS) Measure

The first component of performance measures the gross selectivity ability of the fund manager, controlling for the particular style used by that manager. This measure of stock-picking ability, which is called the "Characteristic-Selectivity" measure (*CS*), is developed in Chapter 4, and is computed during quarter t as:

$$CS_t = \sum_{j=1}^{N} \tilde{w}_{j,t-1}(\widetilde{R}_{j,t} - \widetilde{R}_t^{b_{j,t-1}}), \tag{5.1}$$

where $\tilde{w}_{j,t-1}$ is the portfolio weight on stock j at the end of quarter $t-1$, $\widetilde{R}_{j,t}$ is the quarter t buy-and-hold return of stock j, and $\widetilde{R}_t^{b_{j,t-1}}$ is the quarter t buy-and-hold return of the characteristic-based benchmark portfolio that is matched to stock j at the end of quarter $t-1$.

To construct the characteristic-based benchmark portfolio for a given stock during a given quarter, we characterize that stock over three dimensions—the size, book-value of equity to market-value of equity (BTM) ratio, and prior-year return (momentum) of that stock, at the end of June of each year. Quintile sorts are sequentially implemented on all stocks at that date, first for size, then (within each size quintile) for BTM, then (within each of the 25 size/btm fractiles) for momentum. A stock is then

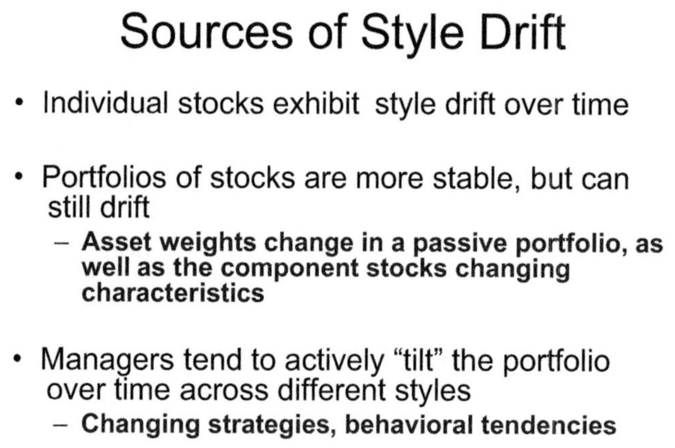

Sources of Style Drift

- Individual stocks exhibit style drift over time
- Portfolios of stocks are more stable, but can still drift
  - **Asset weights change in a passive portfolio, as well as the component stocks changing characteristics**
- Managers tend to actively "tilt" the portfolio over time across different styles
  - **Changing strategies, behavioral tendencies**

FIGURE 5.1
Sources of Style Drift.

assigned a triplet mapping to its benchmark portfolio for that year. The following June 30th, this process is repeating, giving each stock a new mapping each year. For instance, a stock with a triplet mapping of 5,3,1 (the 80th–100th percentile in size, the 40th–60th percentile in BTM, and the 0–20th percentile in momentum) is a member of the largest capitalization of equity quintile, with a middle-quintile (average) value/growth orientation, and a low momentum (prior year return) ranking. This is a large-cap, core, contrarian stock!

There is a big advantage to using portfolio holdings to measure style in this way, relative to using regression-based factor loadings (e.g., Sharpe (1992) rolling regressions)—as long as we can obtain portfolio holdings fairly regularly (at least quarterly for mutual funds, and even monthly for funds with higher levels of turnover)! If the style of a managed portfolio shifts quickly over time, then holdings captures these shifts very accurately, while factor loadings using rolling regressions are slower to adjust. Figure 5.1 shows three reasons why a managed portfolio can experience "style drift".

5.2.1.1 *EXAMPLES OF STYLE DRIFT*

An example of the first effect—the shifting style of an individual stock—is illustrated in Figure 5.2. The quintile mapping of Exxon, on June 30th of each year, is shown. Exxon was a (very!) large capitalization stock during 1985 to 1994, yet it exhibits some small shifts in BTM and large shifts in UMD (prior-year return, or momentum) from year-to-year. These shifts would be difficult to accurately and quickly detect using rolling-window regressions of Exxon monthly returns on these three factors.[2]

---

[2] Daily return regressions can be used to improve the precision of returns-based style evaluation. However, daily returns must be handled with care for many stocks that are thinly traded, as shown by Scholes and Williams (1977).

Exxon	Size	BTM	UMD
1985	5	3	3
1986	5	4	1
1987	5	4	5
1988	5	3	4
1989	5	3	1
1990	5	3	3
1991	5	3	4
1992	5	3	3
1993	5	3	3
1994	5	3	2

Exxon's style?

Consistent Large-Cap

Value Neutral

Changing Momentum

FIGURE 5.2
Style Drift of Exxon.

While these stock-level shifts are somewhat muted in a large portfolio, since style shifts often diversify away, there can still be significant portfolio-level shifts due to a concentration of the portfolio on certain industries. If the industries shift in style, then the portfolio will, too. In addition, a manager"s trades can shift the style of a large portfolio. Grinblatt et al. (1995) documented that U.S. domestic equity mutual funds tend to actively buy momentum stocks—those stocks that have increased in price over the prior year.

Let's take a look at some actual large portfolios to see these effects in action. Figure 5.3 shows an example of an actual (huge) pension fund that exhibited style shifts over 1991–2000. This fund, through (1) shifts in individual stock styles, (2) shifts in stock prices, and (3) active manager trades shows some fairly large drift in the three style dimensions.

While drift in the size dimension is somewhat muted, the fund moved substantially on the BTM dimension from near the median (3.2) to a decidedly growth (2.0, the quintile with the 20th to 40th percentile in BTM) portfolio. It is unlikely that a large portfolio will move this much as a result of the first two driving forces listed in Figure 5.1. More likely, the manager began to chase growth stocks due to the huge rally in growth stock returns during the 1990s (i.e., a momentum strategy!).

Figure 5.4 shows another example—an actual university endowment.

This fund moved substantially in the market cap (size) dimension, which is unusual for a large portfolio. Large cap stocks are stable in value, and trading to a smaller cap portfolio entails substantial trading (mainly market impact) costs. In addition, the manager started implementing momentum trading during the latter years of the 1990s. Unfortunately, this strategy of growth and momentum performed very poorly during 2000 and 2001.

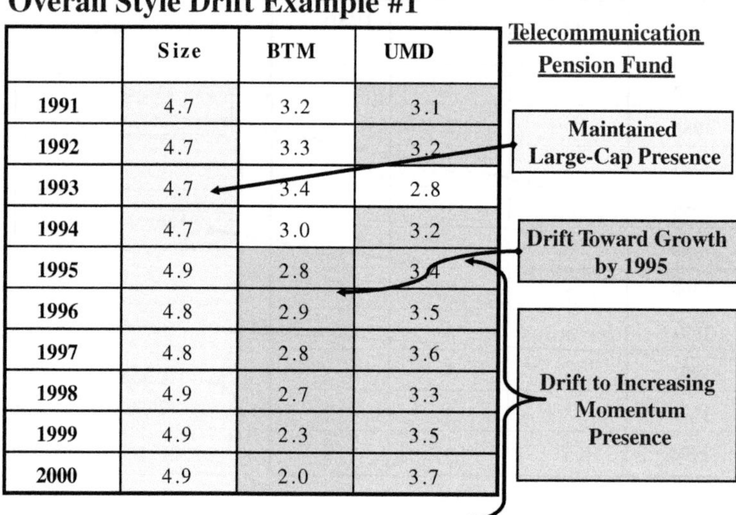

Overall Style Drift Example #1

	Size	BTM	UMD
1991	4.7	3.2	3.1
1992	4.7	3.3	3.2
1993	4.7	3.4	2.8
1994	4.7	3.0	3.2
1995	4.9	2.8	3.4
1996	4.8	2.9	3.5
1997	4.8	2.8	3.6
1998	4.9	2.7	3.3
1999	4.9	2.3	3.5
2000	4.9	2.0	3.7

FIGURE 5.3
Style Drift for a Large Pension Fund.

Overall Style Drift Example #2

	Size	BTM	UMD
1991	4.7	2.3	2.9
1992	4.6	2.5	2.8
1993	4.8	2.4	3.0
1994	4.7	2.4	3.1
1995	4.3	2.6	3.5
1996	4.3	2.4	3.2
1997	4.5	2.5	3.3
1998	3.2	2.4	3.3
1999	3.1	1.8	4.0
2000	3.7	2.0	4.2

University Endowment

Drift to Smaller Cap

Drift to Growth

A Large Drift to Momentum Stocks

FIGURE 5.4
Style Drift for a Large University Endowment.

5.2.1.2 *BENCHMARKING STOCKS (COMPUTING ABNORMAL RETURNS)*

Value-weighted returns are computed for each of the 125 fractile portfolios, and the benchmark for each stock during a given quarter is the buy-and-hold return of the fractile portfolio of which that stock is a member during that quarter. Therefore, the characteristic-adjusted return for a given stock is computed as the buy-and-hold stock return minus the buy-and-hold value-weighted benchmark return during the same quarter. Finally, the Characteristic Selectivity measure of the stock portfolio of a given mutual fund during quarter t, CS_t, is computed as the portfolio-weighted characteristic-adjusted return of the component stocks in the portfolio, where the stock portfolio is normalized so that the weights add to one.

A caveat is in order regarding the interpretation of the *CS* measure, as it controls for only three characteristic dimensions of stocks—size, book-to-market, and past returns. Recent research has shown that mutual funds show a distinct preference for other stock characteristics that are related to average returns—for example, stocks with greater liquidity (see Chen et al. (2000)).[3] For example, one might argue that our *CS* measure underestimates the stock-picking talents of funds since we do not control for the lower average returns that accrue to stocks with greater liquidity.

5.2.1.3 *EXAMPLE OF CS MEASURE FOR U.S. MUTUAL FUNDS (A RETURN TO OUR FAMOUS MANAGERS)*

In Chapter 3, we analyzed the performance of famous fund managers using the intercept (alpha) from two regression models. Here, we re-analyze these funds using their disclosed portfolio holdings.

Table 5.1 shows the *CS* measure for each fund, averaged over the (approximate) period that the manager oversaw the fund. For comparison, we show the single-factor and four-factor alphas computed in Chapter 3. Note that the portfolio approach, *CS*, continues to indicate that Peter Lynch exhibited skilled active management, as did the regression-based approaches of earlier chapters. Lynch's performance is 6%/year, and is statistically significant at the 99% confidence level. The other managers show statistically insignificant performance, using the *CS* measure. Especially puzzling is the drop in evaluated performance of the Janus 20 fund. Upon further inspection of the monthly numbers, this fund exhibited very large spikes in four-factor residuals (and CS measures) during just a relatively few months of the 11-year period. If these performance spikes are due to shifting factor loadings, then the CS measure would exhibit performance closer to zero (as it does) relative to regression-based alphas.

However, before we conclude that Miller and Schoelzel are unskilled, note that the *CS* measure of skill misses any performance implications of round-trip trading ("interim trading") between portfolio disclosure dates, as well as the impact of trading costs, fund expenses, and holdings of securities that are not able to be benchmarked with our CS approach described above. These "missing securities" include derivatives, bonds, and stocks without the required data needed to classify them into one of the 125 style portfolios. Luckily, these securities are generally held in very small proportions by mutual funds, especially very large funds like these). And, large funds likely cannot make large interim trades that would affect their performance substantially. Both the CS measure and the four-factor model may be susceptible to mismeasurement of performance if a

[3] See Lee and Swaminathan (1998) and Datar et al. (1998) for evidence that more liquid stocks earn lower average returns.

Table 5.1 Performance of Four Fund Managers [1]

Asset Manager	Fund Name	Asset Class	Time Period	Single-Factor α (%/year)	Four-Factor α (%/year)	*CS* (%/year)
1. Peter Lynch	Fidelity Magellan	U.S. Domestic Equity, Aggressive Growth	1977–1990	11.1***	8.2***	6.0***
2. Bill Miller	Legg Mason Value Trust	U.S. Domestic Equity, Large Cap Value (Concentrated)	1982–2012	0.1	0.5	2.1
3. Scott Schoelzel	Janus Twenty	U.S. Domestic Equity, Large Cap Growth (Concentrated)	1997–2007	3.1	6.4**	−0.5
4. Gus Sauter	Vanguard 500 Index	U.S. Domestic Equity, Large Cap (Index Fund)	1987–1991	0.8	−0.2	0.1

[1] *Beginning of year manager started (if fund existed) or date manager started, whichever is earlier, to end of year manager left—or September 30, 2011, whichever is earlier. For CS measure, all averages end at the earlier of the end of the year manager left the fund or December 31, 2006. For Lynch, CS measure begins April 1, 1977. For Miller, CS measure begins January 1, 1986.*

***Significant at the 95% confidence level.*

****Significant at the 99% confidence level.*

manager uses a dynamic strategy not captured by these models, such as buying earnings surprise or accrual stocks. A further investigation is warranted into each of these manager's performance numbers to determine whether such a strategy was followed. However, note that we have been able to learn plenty from applying both regression-based and portfolio-holdings-based measures.

It is also notable that the Vanguard 500 index fund has a portfolio-holdings based alpha that is very close to zero (and is statistically insignificant), which is correct, since the fund passively holds an index. While the regression-based alphas are also insignificant, their point estimates are further from zero—suggesting that these approaches result in a noisier estimate of performance than the portfolio-holdings approach. This is confirmed in Figure 5.5, which shows the time-series of monthly CS measures and four-factor residuals (where the four-factor model is estimated over 1980–2011). Note the much larger noise in the four-factor model residuals.

Let's return to all of our funds, and analyze the year-by-year CS measures. These are the quarterly CS measures, computed using Equation (5.1) for quarter *t*, then averaged over the four quarters of each calendar year. This analysis can be incredibly useful, as it informs us of the time-varying skills of each fund manager.

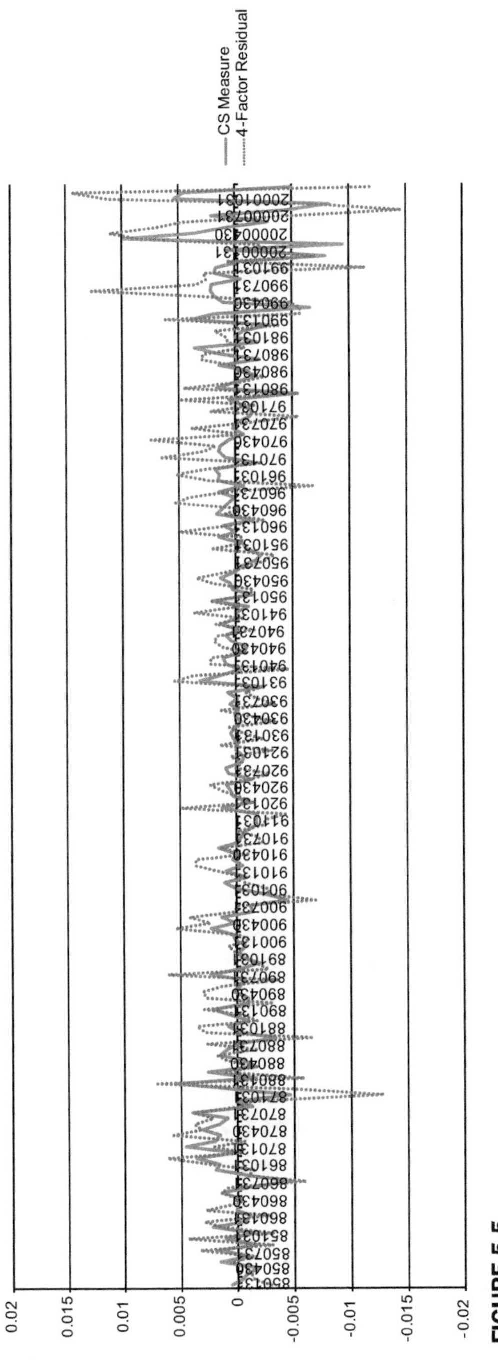

FIGURE 5.5
Comparison of CS Measures and Four-Factor Residuals (Monthly).

The results (Figure 5.6): the Magellan fund showed substantial alphas from 1977 to 1994—during Peter Lynch's, Morris Smith's, and the first couple of years of Jeff Vinik's reign. Afterwards, Magellan generally shows negative alphas—even before trading costs and expenses are deducted! The Janus fund has generally negative alphas after 1992, but has three excellent years—1998, 1999, and 2004. The Value Trust fund shows excellent performance during the post-1990 period. And, as we would expect, the Vanguard index fund shows a CS measure very close to zero every year (with a slight positive alpha during 1987). This fact indicates that the CS measure is doing a very good job of controlling for both systematic and (to a large degree) idiosyncratic risks in fund portfolios.

Can we now conclude that the three active fund managers had skills? Maybe, but we also need to account for the fact that these managers became famous because their returns were high. So, selecting them and labeling them "famous" after the fact may simply reflect the fact that they were the luckiest of the domestic equity funds during this window of time. We return to the issue of controlling for extreme luck among fund managers in Chapter 6.

5.2.1.4 *BENCHMARKING BONDS (COMPUTING ABNORMAL RETURNS)*

Cici and Gibson (2012) construct benchmark portfolios, each month, for corporate bonds. Each corporate bond is assigned, at the beginning of each month, to one of seven credit-quality categories: AAA; AA; A; BBB; BB; B; and below B (i.e., all CCC, CC, C and D rated bonds). Each bond is also assigned, at the beginning of each month, to one of five duration categories. These categories are formed by ranking and sorting bonds into quintiles based on their modified duration, calculated as the Macaulay duration divided by one plus the yield to maturity. Cici and Gibson follow research by Gebhardt, Hvidkjaer, and Swaminathan (2005), in that the credit-quality and duration sorts are conducted independently.

Cici and Gibson's result is 35 benchmark portfolios categorized by the seven credit-quality categories and five duration categories. As with the DGTW benchmark-adjusted returns for stocks discussed in prior sections of this chapter, the benchmark-adjusted return for each bond is its buy-and-hold return minus the value-weighted buy-and-hold return of the appropriate benchmark portfolio over the same holding period.

5.2.2 The Characteristic Timing (CT) Measure

The above stock-selectivity measure does not capture the ability of the fund manager to time the various stock characteristics. Indeed, fund managers can generate additional performance if size, book-to-market, or momentum strategies have time-varying expected returns that the manager can exploit by "tilting" portfolio weights toward stocks having these characteristics when the returns on the characteristics are highest. Thus, our second component of performance measures a fund manager's success at timing the different stock characteristics;

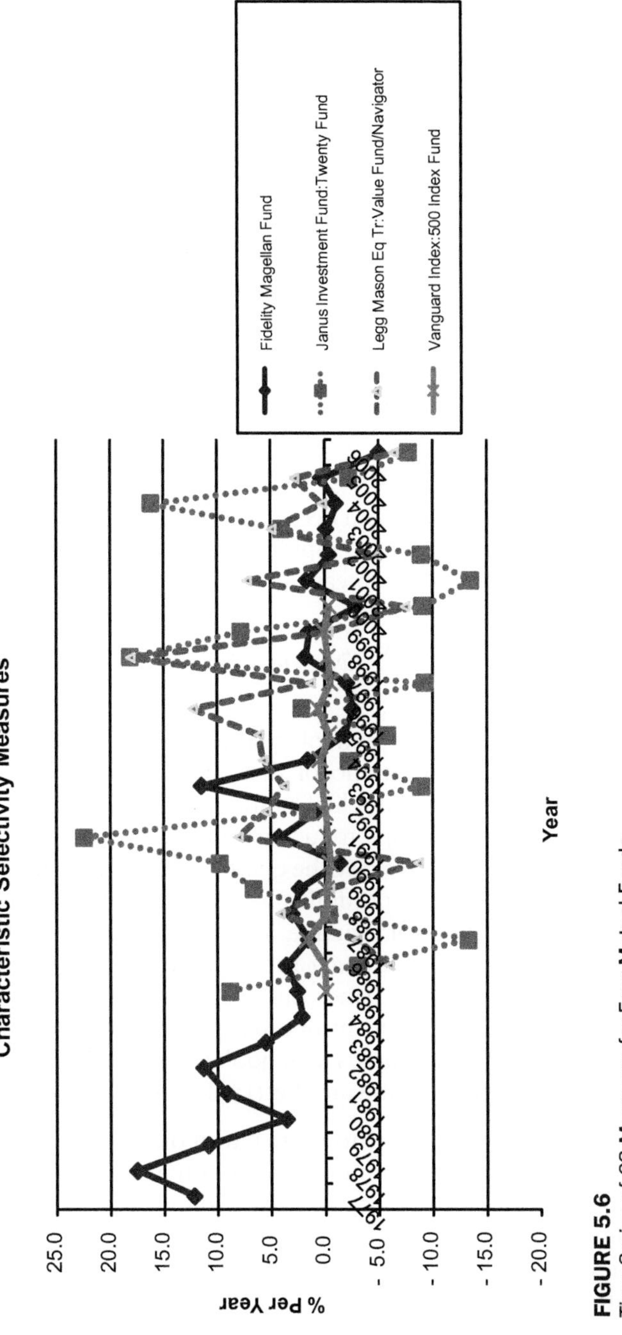

FIGURE 5.6
Time Series of CS Measures for Four Mutual Funds.

this component is termed the "Characteristic Timing" (*CT*) measure. The quarter t component of this measure is:

$$CT_t = \sum_{j=1}^{N} (\tilde{w}_{j,t-1}\tilde{R}_t^{b_{j,t-1}} - \tilde{w}_{j,t-5}\tilde{R}_t^{b_{j,t-5}}). \tag{5.2}$$

Note that this expression deducts the quarter t return of the quarter $t-5$ matching characteristic portfolio for stock j (times the portfolio weight at $t-5$) from the quarter t return of the quarter $t-1$ matching characteristic portfolio for stock j (times the portfolio weight at $t-1$). Thus, a fund manager who increases the fund's weight on stock j just before the payoff to the characteristics of stock j are highest will exhibit a large *CT* measure.

Cici and Gibson (2012) develop a corporate bond-fund *CT* measure that analyzes the ability of funds to time duration and credit quality risk premia.

5.2.3 The Average Style (AS) Measure

To measure the returns earned by a fund because of that fund's tendency to hold stocks with certain characteristics, we employ our third performance component, the "Average Style" (AS) return measure. The quarter t component of this measure is:

$$AS_t = \sum_{j=1}^{N} \tilde{w}_{j,t-5}\tilde{R}_t^{b_{j,t-5}}. \tag{5.3}$$

Each stock held by a fund at the end of quarter $t-5$ is matched with its characteristic-based benchmark portfolio of that date. The quarter t return of this benchmark portfolio is then multiplied by the end of quarter $t-5$ portfolio weight of the stock, and the resulting product is summed over all stocks held by the fund at the end of quarter $t-5$ to give the quarter t *AS* component. Note that, by lagging weights and benchmark portfolios by one year, we eliminate returns due to timing the characteristics. For example, a fund that successfully buys high book-to-market stocks when returns to such a strategy are unusually high will not exhibit an unusually high *AS* return, since this strategy will most likely involve moving into stocks within a year before the unusually high book-to-market return. However, a fund that systematically holds high book-to-market stocks to boost its portfolio return (without trying to time the effect) will exhibit a high *AS* Return.

The *AS* measure of a fund may differ from the return on a broad market index for a couple of reasons. First, the *AS* measure may contain a compensation for the fund loading on covariance-based risk factors differently than the market portfolio's loadings. And, second, the *AS* measure may contain return premia for the fund loading on non-covariance-based characteristic factors. We do not attempt to separate these two sources of *AS* return premia, but we note it and leave the interpretation to the reader (and to further research).

Note that the sum of the *CS*, *CT*, and *AS* measures equals the total portfolio-weighted return on the stockholdings of a given fund (we also call this the "gross return" of the fund).[4] Note, also, that computations of the *AS* and *CT* measures begin in 1976 instead of 1975, as we must use one-year lagged portfolio weights to compute these measures.

Cic and Gibson (2012) develop a corporate bond-fund AS measure that computes the amount of fund performance attributable to duration and credit quality bets away from the time-series average loadings on these risk factors for a given fund.

5.2.4 Trade Execution Costs

Keim and Madhavan (1997; KM) provide a detailed examination of execution costs for a sample of mutual funds during the 1991 to 1993 period. Specifically, KM estimate the cross-sectional dependence of total institutional trading costs (commissions plus market impact) on the market in which a stock is traded (i.e., NYSE or AMEX vs. Nasdaq), the size of the trade, the market capitalization and price of the stock, and whether the trade was a "buy" or a "sell". The total execution cost of a given stock trade is measured by comparing the closing price of the stock on the day prior to the trade-decision date to the actual average execution price of the various separate trades that constituted the entire trade "package".

In addition, Stoll (1995) estimates the time-series trend of total execution costs in the different markets. Specifically, the average cost of executing a trade is documented over time on both the NYSE/AMEX and on the Nasdaq. We combine the results of these two papers to allow an estimate of the cost of a specific stock trade by a mutual fund. For example, suppose our holdings data indicate that the Janus 20 fund bought 10,000 shares of IBM on the NYSE during the first quarter of 1990. We then use those data, along with an estimate of the price and market capitalization of IBM at that time, to apply the execution cost regression of KM (adjusted using the Stoll factor for the year 1990). The resulting estimate is Janus's cost of buying the shares of IBM. Finally, the Janus 20 fund's total trading costs during the first quarter of 1990 are estimated by summing the cost of all trades during that quarter and dividing by the total value of Janus's stock portfolio at the beginning of that quarter.

Specifically, our equation for estimating the total cost of executing a purchase of stock i during quarter t, as a percentage of the total value of the trade, $C^B_{i,t}$, is:

$$C^B_{i,t} = Y^k_t \cdot \Big[1.098 + 0.336 D^{Nasdaq}_{i,t} + 0.092 Trsize_{i,t} \\ -0.084 Logmcap_{i,t} + 13.807\left(\frac{1}{P_{i,t}}\right)\Big]. \tag{5.4}$$

$D^{Nasdaq}_{i,t}$ is a dummy variable that equals one if the trade occurs on Nasdaq, and zero otherwise, $Trsize_{i,t}$ is the ratio of the dollar value of the purchase to the market capitalization of the stock, $Logmcap_{i,t}$ is the natural log of the market

[4] In practice, this equivalence is only approximately true because of the additional requirement that a stock be listed in COMPUSTAT to be included in the calculation of the CS, CT, and AS measures for a fund.

capitalization of the stock (expressed in $thousands), and $P_{i,t}$ is the stock price at the time of the trade. Finally, Y_t^k is the year t trading cost factor for market k (k=NYSE/AMEX or Nasdaq). This factor captures the year-to-year changes in average trading costs over our time period in the different markets—these factors are based on Stoll (1995). Similarly, our equation for estimating the percentage cost of selling stock i during quarter t, $C_{i,t}^S$, is:

$$C_{i,t}^S = Y_t^k \cdot \left[0.979 + 0.058D_{i,t}^{Nasdaq} + 0.214Trsize_{i,t} \right.$$
$$\left. -0.059Logmcap_{i,t} + 6.537\left(\frac{1}{P_{i,t}}\right)\right]. \tag{5.5}$$

Further details on the development of these equations are given in Appendix B.

Cici and Gibson (2012) estimate trade costs of mutual funds for corporate bonds using the TRACE dataset on bond pricing. They estimate quarter-specific spreads for each bond using methods that account for its credit rating, time to maturity, issue size, and age. Then, they estimate the transaction costs of a trade by multiplying the par value of the bond traded multiplied by the estimated half-spread for that bond during that calendar quarter.

5.2.5 Measuring Net Return Selectivity

For stock portfolios, recall from Chapter 1 that the four-factor model is based on an extension of the Fama and French (1993) factor model, and is described as,

$$R_{j,t} - R_{F,t} = \alpha_j + b_j \cdot RMRF_t + s_j \cdot SMB_t + h_j \cdot HML_t + u_j \cdot UMD_t + e_{j,t}. \tag{5.6}$$

$R_{j,t} - R_{F,t}$ equals the excess net return of fund j during month t (the fund net return minus T-bills); $RMRF_t$ equals the month t excess return on a value-weighted aggregate market proxy portfolio; and SMB_t, HML_t, and UMD_t, equal the month t returns on value-weighted, zero-investment factor-mimicking portfolios for size, book-to-market equity, and one-year momentum in stock returns. The Carhart (1997) regression measure of performance, α, is used to estimate the characteristic-adjusted net returns of mutual funds from their net return time-series data. Also, in some instances, we compare the Carhart α, is used estimated for the gross return time-series of mutual fund stock portfolios, to the CS measure described above. In this case, $R_{j,t}$ equals the gross (portfolio-holdings) return of fund j during month t.

For bond portfolios, a model can be adapted from Chapter 3 for bond funds. Cici and Gibson (2012) use a four-factor variant of the Elton, Gruber, and Blake five factor model. They use RMRF, BOND, DEF, and OPTION as their four factors. RMRF is the usual stock market excess return factor. BOND is the excess return on the Lehman (now Barclays) Aggregate bond index. DEF is the return difference between the Lehman High-Yield and Intermediate Government indices. OPTION is the return difference between the Lehman GNMA and Intermediate Government indices.

5.3 APPLICATION TO U.S. DOMESTIC EQUITY MUTUAL FUNDS

To illustrate the integrated performance evaluation system described above, we will use two major mutual fund databases to analyze mutual funds over the 1975–1994 period. These two datasets have been widely used in the academic literature over the past 15 years. The first database contains quarterly portfolio holdings for all U.S. equity mutual funds existing at any time between January 1, 1975 and the present; these data were purchased from Thomson Financial of Rockville, Maryland. The Thomson dataset lists the equity portion of each fund's holdings (i.e., the shareholdings of each stock held by that fund) along with a listing of the total net assets under management and the self-declared investment objective at the beginning of each calendar quarter. Thomson began collecting investment-objective information on June 30, 1980; we supplement these data with investment objective data for January 1, 1975. Further details on the Thomson holdings database are provided in Appendix A, as well as in Wermers (1999).

The second mutual fund database is available from the Center for Research in Securities Prices (CRSP) and is used by Carhart (1997). The CRSP database contains monthly data on net returns, as well as annual data on portfolio turnover and expense ratios for all mutual funds existing at any time between January 1, 1962 and the present. Further details on the CRSP mutual fund database are provided in Appendix A; documentation is also available from CRSP.

These two databases were merged to provide a complete record of the stockholdings of a given fund, along with the fund's turnover ratio, expense ratio, net returns, investment objective, and total net assets under management during each year of the fund's existence during our sample period. In general, funds were matched between the two databases by matching their fund names, although other fund characteristics were also used. Further details on the process used to match funds are provided in Appendix A.[5] Finally, stock prices and returns are obtained from the CRSP NYSE/AMEX/Nasdaq stock files.

We limit our analysis to funds that hold diversified portfolios of U.S. equities. Specifically, during each quarter, we include only mutual funds having a self-declared investment objective of "aggressive growth", "growth", "growth and income", "income", or "balanced" at the beginning of that quarter.[6] We exclude all other funds, which include international funds, bond funds, gold funds, real estate funds, and all other sector funds, as these types of funds generally hold and trade minimal quantities of domestic equities (if any).

Panel A of Table 5.2 provides summary statistics for the merged mutual fund database. In a small number of cases, we could not find a match between funds

[5] The resulting mutual fund links ("MFLINKS") between the two databases are now owned by Wharton Research Data Services (http://www.wrds.wharton.upenn.edu) and can be licensed through WRDS. This linking dataset is updated through 2012 at the time of this writing, and is updated at least annually.

[6] See Grinblatt et al. (1995) for a description of the types of investments made by funds in each category.

Table 5.2 Summary Statistics for Merged Mutual Fund Database

Key statistics are provided below for the merged Thomson holdings and CRSP mutual fund characteristics/net returns databases. For each year, statistics are shown at the beginning of the listed year, except as noted in this legend. The Thomson database, purchased from Thomson Financial includes periodic (usually quarterly) portfolio holdings of equities for all mutual funds. The CRSP database, purchased from the Center for Research in Securities Prices, contains data on mutual fund net returns, turnover ratios, expense ratios, and other fund characteristics. The two databases are merged based on the name and other characteristics of funds. Since CRSP lists net returns and other characteristics for each shareclass of a single mutual fund, these measures are combined based on the relative valuation of the various shareclasses before they are matched to the holdings record for the fund from Thomson. Because Thomson is slower to add some new funds to its database than CRSP, a number of funds have an incomplete data record each year (they are missing shareholdings data)—these fund-years are not included in our analysis. In addition, a small number of funds could not be matched (during their entire existence) between the databases during the last few years of our sample period. Panel A provides, each year, fund counts, total-net-asset (TNA) weighted average yearly net returns, and the median total net assets of the universe of mutual funds contained in the merged database. Every fund existing during a given calendar quarter (and having a complete data record) is included in the computation of that quarter's average net returns, even if the fund does not survive past the end of that quarter (TNA weights are updated at the beginning of each quarter). These quarterly buy-and-hold net returns are compounded to give the quarterly rebalanced annual returns reported below. The panel also provides similar statistics for the CRSP funds that could not be matched (during their entire existence) to a Thomson fund. Panel B provides, at the beginning of each listed year, the number of funds and the number of shareclasses represented by those funds in the merged database. Panel C provides fund counts in each investment objective category, as well as the TNA-average fraction of the mutual fund portfolios that are invested in stocks. In all statistics in all panels of this table, we limit our analysis to funds having a self-declared investment objective of "aggressive growth", "growth", "growth and income", "income", or "balanced" at the beginning of a given calendar quarter. Note, also, that self-declared investment-objective data are available from Thomson starting June 30, 1980, so the 1980 figures are as of that date. Before 1980, funds are classified by their investment objectives as of January 1, 1975 (these data were hand-collected from printed sources).

Panel A. Yearly Mutual Fund Universe Statistics

Year	Merged Database			Unmatched Funds		
	Number	TNA-Averaged Net Return (percent per year)	Median TNA ($millions)	Number	TNA-Averaged Net Return (percent per year)	Median TNA ($millions)
1975	241	30.9	35.5	0	—	—
1976	241	23.0	50.3	0	—	—
1977	226	−2.5	54.5	0	—	—
1978	222	9.0	49.0	0	—	—
1979	219	23.7	44.0	0	—	—
1980	364	31.3	48.9	0	—	—
1981	365	−2.7	44.8	0	—	—
1982	362	24.1	42.1	0	—	—

Table 5.2 Continued

Year	Merged Database			Unmatched Funds		
	Number	TNA-Averaged Net Return (percent per year)	Median TNA ($millions)	Number	TNA-Averaged Net Return (percent per year)	Median TNA ($millions)
1983	347	20.4	52.9	0	—	—
1984	372	−0.1	80.3	0	—	—
1985	391	27.8	77.4	0	—	—
1986	418	15.8	98.2	0	—	—
1987	483	2.4	93.0	0	—	—
1988	543	15.9	83.8	0	—	—
1989	589	25.3	75.7	0	—	—
1990	637	−5.3	84.7	0	—	—
1991	679	32.8	78.5	11	25.2	22.4
1992	815	8.2	88.3	14	7.2	25.9
1993	949	14.2	100.1	31	15.6	9.5
1994	1,279	−1.6	98.5	54	−0.01	12.6
1975–1994	1,788	14.6	—	60	12.0	—

Panel B. Number of CRSP Mutual Fund Shareclasses in Merged Database

Year	Merged Database	
	Number of Funds	Number of Shareclasses
1975	241	241
1980	364	364
1985	391	391
1990	637	638
1991	679	684
1992	815	831
1993	949	996
1994	1,279	1,377

Panel C. Number of Funds and TNA-Average Stockholdings Percentage, by Investment Objective

Year	Universe		AG		G		G & I		I or B	
	Number	Stocks (Pct)	Number	Stocks (Pct)	Number	Stocks (Pct)	Number	Stocks (Pct)	Number	Stocks (Pct)
1975	241	79.9	67	86.9	76	89.1	52	83.8	46	51.0
1980	364	83.8	87	87.1	137	90.7	83	86.9	57	61.6
1985	391	85.4	85	93.4	151	89.5	102	82.0	53	60.8
1990	637	79.8	133	87.3	289	87.8	141	81.2	74	51.4
1994	1,279	82.7	201	92.7	703	90.7	246	82.5	129	54.5

in the Thomson and CRSP files—summary statistics are also provided for these unmatched funds to analyze the potential for biases in our analysis. Specifically, we show statistics on CRSP mutual funds that could not be matched with a Thomson fund, since the reverse situation was rare. We note that the yearly count in the table includes only funds having a complete record containing both Thomson holdings and CRSP net returns and characteristics data for a given year. A number of additional funds have incomplete information during each year—this is especially problematic regarding the Thomson holdings data for new funds, as holdings data are often missing for the first year or two of a fund's existence. These missing data are unlikely to introduce significant biases in our analysis—nevertheless, we focus on the total net asset weighted performance of the mutual fund industry, which minimizes the significance of any small-fund omissions. This issue is discussed in further detail in Appendix A.

Panel A shows the number of funds in the merged database that exist (and have a complete record of Thomson and CRSP data) at the beginning of each year, as well as the average yearly net return, weighted by the total net assets (TNA) of funds. To minimize any survival requirements, we compute quarterly buy-and-hold net returns for each mutual fund that exists during a given quarter, regardless of whether that fund survives the entire year. These quarterly fund returns are then averaged across all funds existing during that quarter, using each fund's total net assets at the beginning of that quarter as that fund's weight. The TNA-averaged quarterly returns are then compounded into yearly returns. Also, at the beginning of each year, the table shows the median TNA of all funds existing (and having a complete record of Thomson and CRSP data) at that time.

The universe of diversified equity mutual funds expanded from 241 funds at the beginning of 1975 to 1,279 funds at the beginning of 1994; the overall total in the merged database is 1,788 distinct funds that existed sometime during the 20-year period. This count includes both funds that survived until the end of 1994, and funds that perished due to a merger or liquidation.[7] As documented in Chen et al. (2000), the proportion of the market value of all U.S. equities (listed in CRSP) held by these funds increased from about 5 percent in 1975 to almost 11 percent in 1994.

Panel A also shows how successful we were in matching the two databases—we matched each mutual fund having an initial listing in the CRSP database before 1991, and having one of the above investment objectives, to a fund in the Thomson database. There are 60 funds with an initial CRSP listing during the 1991 to 1994 period that we could not match to a Thomson fund—this unmatched sample represents only three percent of our sample of 1,788 matched funds. More importantly, the unmatched sample represents 110 "fund-years", which is about one percent of the almost 10,000 fund-years in our matched sample. These unmatched funds are, in general, much smaller than our

[7] This number is slightly smaller than the 1,892 funds reported by Carhart (1997) for the CRSP database. There are a few reasons for this, which we discuss in Appendix A.

matched sample. For example, the median TNA of the unmatched funds existing in 1994 is only $12.6 million, while the median TNA of matched funds is $98.5 million. Thus, the economic relevance of these unmatched funds is quite small, especially since we TNA-weight the majority of results in this chapter.[8]

Panel A also compares the TNA-averaged net return on our matched database to that of the unmatched funds. The unmatched funds have generally lower returns, but not appreciably so, which indicates that the upward bias in estimated returns in our analysis (induced by the exclusion of the unmatched funds) is very small.

Over the past several years, mutual funds have begun to offer different classes of shares in a single mutual fund that appeal to different investor clienteles. These shareclasses confer ownership in the same underlying pool of assets, but have differing expense ratios and load fees. For example, one shareclass may offer a low expense ratio and a high load fee to appeal to long-term investors, while another class offers a high expense ratio and a low load for short-term investors. The CRSP database lists each shareclass separately, while the Thomson database lists only the underlying fund. Panel B illustrates the growth in these shareclasses during the 1990s.[9] For example, in 1994, there are 98 more shareclasses than funds, so many funds have several classes of shares. In such cases, we combine the CRSP net returns, expense ratios, percentage of assets held in stocks, and other characteristics of all shareclasses into the corresponding measures for a given fund. In combining these shareclasses, we weight the return or characteristic of each shareclass by the most recent total net assets of that shareclass. Thus, our analysis uses a mutual fund as the basic unit, and not individual shareclasses.

Finally, Panel C presents both the average asset allocation in stocks (versus bonds, cash, and other investments) and a breakdown of our mutual fund universe into the investment objectives that we include in our analysis.[10] The average fund manager invested almost 80 percent of the fund portfolio in equities in 1975; by 1994, this proportion had increased to almost 83 percent. It is likely that the dismal performance of bonds and cash during this time period provided motivation for the general movement toward becoming more fully invested in stocks.[11] Indeed, we will show, in a later section, that a substantial portion of the

---

[8] In general, Thomson is slower in adding funds to their database than CRSP, although the completeness of the two databases is comparable (as indicated by our successful matching of the two databases for the vast majority of funds). The small unmatched funds during the last few years of our sample period are likely ones that Thomson did not add to their database until after 1994.

[9] We note that some shareclasses are likely to be underrepresented in the CRSP database—especially shareclasses that are offered solely to institutions. These shareclasses are likely to charge lower expenses and loads, which indicates that we overestimate the weighted-average costs of funds.

[10] In this panel, we combine "income" and "balanced" funds, as these two categories generally contain small numbers of funds and hold similar securities.

[11] As of late, equity mutual funds have been relying less on cash holdings to meet uncertain investor redemptions. Most funds now have lines of credit established with banks, and even with other mutual funds. In addition, index funds use options and futures contracts to provide liquidity.

underperformance of mutual funds versus stock indexes can be traced to fund investments in non-stock securities.

The panel also shows that the number of growth-oriented funds (aggressive growth and growth funds) has increased much faster than the number of income-oriented funds (growth and income, balanced, and income funds), probably because of the relatively high returns of growth stocks during our sample period. Also noteworthy is how the asset allocations toward stocks vary across the investment objectives. Growth-oriented funds maintain roughly 90 percent of their portfolios in equities in 1994, while income-oriented funds (true to their investment objectives) maintain lower proportions.

The next section describes the measures we use to decompose the returns generated by the stocks held by a mutual fund. In addition, we describe our method for estimating trading costs for each mutual fund during each quarter.

5.4 EMPIRICAL RESULTS FOR U.S. DOMESTIC EQUITY MUTUAL FUNDS

5.4.1 Overall Mutual Fund Returns

Table 5.3 compares several measures of mutual fund returns to the returns on two market indexes during 1975–1994: the S&P 500 index and the CRSP NYSE/AMEX/Nasdaq portfolio (both value-weighted, with dividends reinvested). The measures of fund returns include the estimated returns on the stock portfolios of the funds (labeled "Gross Returns") as well as the realized net returns of funds.[12] The table presents each return measure, averaged both by the total net assets (TNA) of funds and by using an equal weighting (EW) across all funds. To compute the returns for a given year, we first compute the quarterly buy-and-hold return for the portfolio of all funds existing during the first quarter of that year, regardless of whether those funds survived past that quarter. Weights (TNA or EW) are rebalanced at the end of the first quarter, and the process is repeated for the second quarter (the third and fourth quarters are computed similarly). Finally, the annual return is computed by compounding these quarterly rebalanced, buy-and-hold returns. This procedure minimizes any survival bias, as it includes all funds existing during any given quarter.

The results show that the average mutual fund held stocks that significantly outperformed both market indexes over the 20-year period. First, the TNA-average gross

[12] In estimating the return on the stock portfolio held by a fund during a given quarter, we compute the buy-and-hold return on the stockholdings reported in the most recent portfolio "snapshot" from the merged database for that fund, on or before the beginning of that quarter (using stock returns from the CRSP NYSE/AMEX/Nasdaq stock file to compute buy-and-hold stock returns). In most cases, this snapshot is available at the beginning of the calendar quarter, but, in some cases, the holdings are from an earlier date. A complete description of the limitations of the holdings data is available in Wermers (1999). Also, in computing the return on stockholdings, we normalize portfolio weights so that the weights of stocks held by a given fund add up to one.

Table 5.3 Mutual Fund Returns

Mutual fund returns are provided below for the merged Thomson holdings and CRSP mutual fund characteristics/net returns databases. This table provides, each year, the S&P 500 and CRSP NYSE/AMEX/Nasdaq yearly returns, both value-weighted with dividends reinvested. Also, both gross returns (on stockholdings only) and net reported mutual fund returns are provided for the mutual fund universe for each year, each weighted both by the total net assets (TNA) and by using an equal-weighting (EW) across all mutual funds (weights are updated at the beginning of each quarter). Every fund existing during a given quarter (and having a complete data record) is included in the computation of that quarter's return measures, even if the fund does not survive past the end of that quarter. These quarterly buy-and-hold returns are compounded to give the quarterly rebalanced annual returns reported below. In all statistics in this table, we limit our analysis to funds having a self-declared investment objective of "aggressive growth", "growth", "growth and income", "income", or "balanced" at the beginning of a given calendar quarter. Note, also, that self-declared investment-objective data are available from Thomson starting June 30, 1980, so the 1980 figures are as of that date. Before 1980, funds are classified by their investment objectives as of January 1, 1975 (these data were hand-collected from printed sources).

	Merged Database						
Year	S & P 500 Return	CRSP VW Return	No.	TNA-Avg Gross Returns (pct per year)	EW-Avg Gross Return (pct per year)	TNA-Avg Net Return (pct per year)	EW-Avg Net Return (pct per year)
1975	37.2	37.4	241	38.1	40.1	30.9	31.5
1976	23.8	26.8	241	26.7	28.0	23.0	23.6
1977	−7.2	−3.0	226	−3.0	0.2	−2.5	−0.1
1978	6.6	8.5	222	11.3	12.9	9.0	10.0
1979	18.4	24.4	219	27.9	32.9	23.7	26.2
1980	32.4	33.2	364	37.8	40.1	31.3	31.2
1981	−4.9	−4.0	365	−4.2	−2.3	−2.7	−0.6
1982	21.4	20.4	362	24.0	25.6	24.1	24.9
1983	22.5	22.7	347	23.6	23.9	20.4	20.1
1984	6.3	3.3	372	0.3	−0.6	−0.1	−0.8
1985	32.2	31.5	391	32.0	32.4	27.8	27.7
1986	18.5	15.6	418	17.7	15.8	15.8	14.1
1987	5.2	1.8	483	3.4	2.1	2.4	1.1
1988	16.8	17.6	543	18.7	18.2	15.9	14.5
1989	31.5	28.4	589	29.4	29.2	25.3	24.6
1990	−3.2	−6.0	637	−7.4	−7.4	−5.3	−5.5
1991	30.5	33.6	679	37.5	41.0	32.8	35.2
1992	7.7	9.0	815	9.1	10.0	8.2	9.1
1993	10.0	11.5	949	15.2	13.9	14.2	13.3
1994	1.3	−0.6	1,279	−0.4	−0.8	−1.6	−1.7
1975–1979	15.8	18.8	241	20.2	22.8	16.8	18.2
1980–1984	15.5	15.1	459	16.3	17.3	14.6	15.0
1985–1989	20.8	19.0	676	20.2	19.5	17.4	16.4
1990–1994	9.3	9.5	1,567	10.8	11.3	9.7	10.1
1975–1994	15.4	15.6	1,788	16.9	17.7	14.6	14.9

return on stockholdings averaged 16.9 percent per year over the 20 years, compared to 15.4 and 15.6 percent per year for the S&P 500 and the CRSP indexes, respectively. Indeed, this TNA-average gross return beat the indexes during the majority of the years in our sample period (1975–1994). These return results, although not benchmark-adjusted, are consistent with studies that indicate that mutual funds generally perform well in their choice of stocks.[13] The results for EW-average gross returns are even more promising—here, the average mutual fund holds stocks that outperform the market indexes by over two percent per year.

It is also informative to examine the net returns of the mutual fund industry. For example, a current issue of contention is whether mutual fund expenses and trading costs are excessive, given the level of performance of the funds. Table 5.3 shows that a significant gap indeed exists between the TNA-average net return and the TNA-average gross stock returns of funds over the 20 years. Specifically, gross returns average 16.9 percent per year, while net returns average 14.6 percent per year. However, the yearly differences between these two return measures indicate that the gross return tends to be substantially higher than the net return during years that the stock indexes perform well (which are generally years with a high equity premium over T-bills). For example, in 1975, a very high return year for stocks, the TNA-average gross return is 38.1 percent, versus 30.9 percent for the TNA-average net return. In contrast, the net return of the funds is actually higher than the stock portfolio return during 1977, a very poor return year for stocks. This indicates that the fund holdings of cash and bonds (presumably as a cushion to handle investor inflows and redemptions), which generally performed poorly over this time period (relative to stocks), contributes significantly to the reduced performance of funds on a net return basis.

In unreported tests, we examined seasonal differences between gross and net returns. Consistent with the yearly variation, seasonal differences were substantially larger during calendar months having the largest equity premia over the 1975 to 1994 period (for example, January and December).

Overall, Table 5.3 illustrates the differences between studies that examine the stockholdings of mutual funds and studies that examine the net returns. Specifically, the stockholdings of the mutual fund industry substantially outperform market indexes, yet the net returns significantly underperform the same indexes. The difference between the return on stockholdings and the net return of the funds is 2.3 percent per year, averaged by the total net assets of funds. In a later section of this chapter, we will trace the contribution of expenses and transactions costs to this difference between gross and net returns. First, in the next section, we benchmark-adjust both the gross returns on stockholdings and the net returns to allow a comparison of these measures on a characteristic-adjusted basis.

---

[13] Note, also, that mutual fund returns track the CRSP VW index more closely than the S&P 500 index, due to the small stock holdings of funds.

5.4.2 Benchmark-Adjusted Mutual Fund Returns

Mutual funds tend to hold portfolios of stocks with distinct characteristics. Specifically, Grinblatt et al. (1995) document that the majority of funds buy high past return stocks, while Chen et al. (2000) show that funds prefer growth stocks and large-capitalization stocks as well. Since these characteristics have been shown to be related to average returns during our sample period, the performance of mutual fund stockholdings relative to market indexes may be partly due to the characteristics of the stockholdings. As shown by Fama and French (1992, 1996), Jegadeesh and Titman (1993), Chan et al. (1996), and Daniel and Titman (1997), the size (market capitalization of equity), the ratio of the book-value of equity to the market-value of equity, and the momentum (prior-year return) of stocks are powerful *ex ante* predictors of cross-sectional patterns in common stock returns. In this section, we benchmark-adjust the returns of mutual fund stockholdings to determine the extent to which mutual fund managers choose stocks that outperform stocks having the same characteristics.

Table 5.4 presents yearly average mutual fund Characteristic-Selectivity measures (*CS* measures), weighted by the total net assets (TNA) of each fund. In computing the *CS* measure for a given year, we first compute TNA-average *CS* measures for each quarter of that year, across all funds existing during the quarter. For example, the average *CS* measure for the first quarter of 1975 is computed across all funds existing during that quarter, regardless of whether they survive past the end of the quarter. Similar computations are done for the second, third, and fourth quarters of 1975, and these quarterly TNA-average *CS* measures are then compounded into a quarterly rebalanced annual measure. Also presented are equal-weighted (EW) average *CS* measures—these return averages are computed in a manner similar to that of the TNA-average *CS* measures, but equal weights are applied across mutual funds at the beginning of each quarter. The average *CS* measure shown in Table 5.4 (Panel A) over the entire 1975 to 1994 period, and the averages shown over five-year subperiods (Panel B), are the simple time-series average of the corresponding yearly returns.

The results in Panel A show that the mutual fund industry picks stocks that, on average, outperform their characteristic-matched benchmark portfolios. The TNA-average *CS* measure for the mutual fund universe is 71 basis points per year during the 20-year period—although the funds do not hold stocks that outperform their benchmarks during all years of our sample period, they manage to outperform their benchmarks during the majority of the years. The EW-average *CS* measure is 101 basis points per year, indicating that small funds have better stock-picking talents than large funds during our sample period.[14] Panel B shows that the average *CS* measure is higher during 1975 to 1979 than during the following three five-year subperiods, both for the

[14] However, part of the drag on the performance of larger funds may be due to the lower portfolio turnover rates of these funds. These lower turnover rates are, in turn, likely due to an avoidance of incurring the larger transactions costs they face, relative to small funds, because of the large scale of their investments.

Table 5.4 Mutual Fund Characteristic-Adjusted Performance

Average performance measures for the stockholdings portion of mutual fund portfolios are presented in this table (in percent per year) for the merged Thomson holdings and CRSP mutual fund characteristics/net returns databases. To compute the characteristic-adjusted return for a given stock during a given quarter, the buy-and-hold return on a value-weighted portfolio of stocks having the same size, book-value to market-value of equity, and prior-year return characteristics as the stock is subtracted from that stock's buy-and-hold return during the quarter. Each mutual fund's *CS* measure, for a given quarter, is then computed as the portfolio-weighted characteristic-adjusted return of the individual stocks in the fund's portfolio (normalizing so that the weights of all stocks add to one). Then, the average *CS* measure is computed across the mutual fund universe each quarter, weighted both by the total net assets (TNA) and by using an equal-weighting (EW) across all mutual funds (weights are updated at the beginning of each quarter). Every fund existing during a given quarter (and having a complete data record) is included in the computation of that quarter's average *CS* measure, regardless of whether the fund survived past the end of that quarter. These quarterly buy-and-hold cs measures are compounded to give the quarterly rebalanced annual *CS* measures reported below. Also presented in Panel A are the number of funds existing at the beginning of each listed year (except as noted in this legend). Panel B compares the *CS* measures with the intercept from a Carhart four-factor time-series regression of monthly fund excess returns (TNA-average as well as EW-average across funds) on the monthly excess return associated with a value-weighted aggregate market proxy portfolio; and monthly returns on value-weighted, zero-investment factor-mimicking portfolios for size, book-to-market equity, and one-year momentum in stock returns. Panel B also includes, in the computation of the measures each quarter, all funds existing during that quarter—the count of funds reflects all mutual funds that existed for at least one quarter during each subperiod. In all measures in both panels of this table, we limit our analysis to funds having a self-declared investment objective of "aggressive growth", "growth", "growth and income", "income", or "balanced" at the beginning of a given calendar quarter. Note, also, that self-declared investment-objective data are available from Thomson starting June 30, 1980, so the 1980 figures are as of that date. Before 1980, funds are classified by their investment objectives as of January 1, 1975 (these data were hand-collected from printed sources).

Panel A. Performance of Mutual Fund Stock Portfolios

	Merged Database		
Year	Number	TNA-Avg *CS* Measure (pct/year)	EW-Avg *CS* Measure (pct/year)
1975	241	0.002	0.73
1976	241	0.23	−0.31
1977	226	0.34	1.28
1978	222	3.46	3.64
1979	219	1.79	2.79
1980	364	0.83	1.59
1981	365	0.21	0.87
1982	362	2.53	2.79
1983	347	1.12	1.03
1984	372	−1.15	−1.27
1985	391	−0.07	0.31
1986	418	0.40	0.45

Table 5.4 Continued

Panel A. Performance of Mutual Fund Stock Portfolios

Year	Merged Database		
	Number	TNA-Avg CS Measure (pct/year)	EW-Avg CS Measure (pct/year)
1987	483	1.54	2.10
1988	543	0.20	−0.57
1989	589	−0.26	0.65
1990	637	−0.69	0.97
1991	679	1.95	1.74
1992	815	0.07	0.13
1993	949	1.70	1.02
1994	1,279	0.03	0.23
1975–1994	1,788	0.71**	1.01***

Panel B. Performance of Fund Stock Portfolios vs. Net Fund Performance.

Period	Merged Database				
	Number	TNA-Avg CS Measure (pct/year)	EW-Avg CS Measure (pct/year)	TNA-Avg $\alpha^{Net}_{Carhart}$ (pct/year)	EW-Avg $\alpha^{Net}_{Carhart}$ (pct/year)
1975–1979	241	1.17	1.62*	−0.81	−0.77
1980–1984	459	0.71	1.00	−1.33	−1.14
1985–1989	676	0.36	0.59	−0.73	−1.07**
1990–1994	1,567	0.61	0.82**	−0.71	−0.47
1975–1994	1,788	0.71**	1.01	−1.16	−1.15

*Significant at the 90% confidence level.

**Significant at the 95% confidence level.

*** Significant at the 99% confidence level.

TNA-average and for the EW-average portfolios. However, the average measure is positive during all subperiods for both averaging methods.

In unreported tests, we examined seasonal average *CS* measures. The *CS* measure, averaged across all Decembers from 1975 to 1994, was unusually high (3.56 percent, annualized), but the average May and November were also large (1.60 and 1.68 percent, annualized, respectively). In addition, an F-test could not reject the equality of the monthly *CS* measures (the two-tailed p-value was 29 percent). Thus, December is an anomaly, but it is not the only month with a significant *CS* measure.

In the last section, we found that the TNA-average portfolio of funds outperforms the CRSP value-weighted index by an average of 130 basis points per year. Here, we find an average *CS* measure of 71 basis points per year, which represents the returns on the stockholdings of mutual funds in excess of the returns on their characteristic-matched benchmark portfolios. Based on these results, the remaining 59 basis points per year must be attributable to returns related to the characteristics of stockholdings, either through the ability of funds to time the characteristics (Characteristic Timing, *CT*) or through the long-term holdings of stocks having characteristics with higher average returns (Average Style, *AS*). We will explore these two sources of performance in a later section of this chapter.

Panel B of Table 5.4 compares the average *CS* measure of mutual fund stockholdings to the average Carhart net return performance measure ($\alpha^{Net}_{Carhart}$) of the funds. To compute the Carhart measure for a given period, we regress the monthly time-series of cross-sectional average excess net returns (either TNA- or EW-averaged across funds) on the monthly time-series of returns for the four Carhart factor-mimicking portfolios; the intercept from this regression is the Carhart performance measure for the fund universe. In forming average monthly excess net returns, we include all funds existing during a given month. Panel B reports the resulting Carhart measures (annualized to percent per year).

The Carhart measures vary somewhat across different subperiods; however, the measures are negative in all cases. This finding is consistent with the generally negative net return performance measures reported in Carhart (1997) and elsewhere. Specifically, the TNA-average and the EW-average Carhart measures over the 1975 to 1994 period are −1.16 and −1.15 percent per year, respectively. Both measures are statistically significant at the one percent level. In unreported tests, we found that the Vanguard Index 500 fund has a Carhart net return measure of −29 basis points per year. Thus, the TNA-average mutual fund underperforms the Vanguard fund by 87 basis points per year, adjusted for the characteristics of stockholdings. We will analyze the Vanguard fund in more detail in a later section of this chapter.

Overall, we find that the TNA-average *CS* performance measure, at the stockholdings level, is 71 basis points per year, while the TNA-average Carhart measure, at the net return level, is −116 basis points per year. This difference between the TNA-average characteristic-adjusted returns of fund stockholdings and fund net returns (which also include the return contribution of non-stock holdings of funds)—roughly 1.9 percent per year—can be compared to the difference between the unadjusted returns of fund stockholdings and net returns (presented in the last section)—2.3 percent per year. Thus, about 40 basis points per year of the 2.3 percent per year difference between gross and net returns can be explained by the lower average returns of bonds and cash relative to stocks during this period. In a later section of this chapter, we use a cost-based approach (by deducting, from the 2.3 percent per year, 1.6 percent per year for expenses and transactions costs) to arrive at an estimate of 70 basis points per year being due to the lower average returns of non-stock holdings. Note that these estimates (40 to 70 basis points per year) are roughly consistent with the equity premium over the 1975 to 1994 period (large company stocks minus T-bills), which averaged 7.5 percent per year—mutual funds held 10 to 15 percent T-bills and bonds in their portfolios over the period.

In the remainder of this chapter, we weight each mutual fund measure by the total net assets under management of the fund. Although, in this section, we have found stronger evidence of stock-picking talent when looking at the average mutual fund, we wish to compute measures of return and performance for the average dollar invested in the mutual fund industry.

5.4.3 The Correlation Between Performance Measures

Our results of the last section show strong evidence that, on average, mutual funds pick stocks that outperform their characteristic benchmarks. In addition, net of all expenses and transactions costs, mutual funds underperform their Carhart benchmark portfolios, on average. However, an interesting issue is the correlation, across funds, of performance at the stockholdings level and performance at the net returns level. Although, at first blush, it would seem that the correlation would be near unity, the issue becomes more interesting if the expenses and transactions costs of funds are also positively correlated with their pre-expense performance. The tendency of funds with superior stock-picking skills to incur higher costs would be consistent with the equilibrium model of Grossman and Stiglitz (1980), where the returns to information gathering and processing skills are equal to the costs.

Table 5.5 investigates this issue by presenting cross-sectional correlations (across funds) between various measures of performance. These performance measures are computed over the entire life of each mutual fund during our sample period. The only restriction we place on a fund to be included in these correlations is that the fund must have at least 24 valid monthly return observations (both for stockholdings and net returns) in order to provide a reasonable degrees-of-freedom in the regression-based measures.

Panel A of that table presents Pearson correlations between three measures of performance at the stock portfolio level: the Characteristic-Selectivity measure (CS), the Carhart measure using the time-series of excess monthly returns on the stock portfolio as the explained variable ($\alpha_{Carhart}^{Gross}$), and the Jensen measure using the same explained variable (α_{Jensen}^{Gross}). In addition, two measures of performance at the net return level are included: the Carhart measure using the time-series of excess monthly net returns as the explained variable ($\alpha_{Carhart}^{Net}$) and the Jensen measure using the same explained variable (α_{Jensen}^{Net}). Panel B presents Spearman rank-correlations between all of these performance measures.

Several observations may be drawn from the two correlation matrices. First, the cross-sectional Pearson correlation (at the gross return level) between the Jensen and Carhart measures is 0.74, which indicates that adding the size, book-to-market, and momentum factors provides only a slight increase in the precision of the performance estimate. This result indicates that mutual fund loadings on these omitted variables in the Jensen regression are correlated with the intercept of the Carhart regression. The Spearman rank correlation between these two measures is similar, 0.67.

The correlations between the CS measure and the Carhart and Jensen gross performance measures are 0.57 and 0.58, respectively. This lower correlation supports the idea that the CS measure provides more precise adjustments for

Table 5.5 Mutual Fund Performance Measure Correlations

In this table, we present cross-sectional correlations (across funds) between different measures of mutual fund performance. The measures included in this table are the Characteristic Selectivity measure (*CS*), the Carhart four-factor regression alpha, and the Jensen regression alpha for the stock portfolio of each mutual fund (labeled "gross" alphas); and the Carhart four-factor regression alpha and the Jensen regression alpha for the realized net returns of the funds (labeled "net" alphas). To compute the characteristic-adjusted return for a given stock during a given quarter, the buy-and-hold return on a value-weighted portfolio of stocks having the same size, book-value to market-value of equity, and prior-year return characteristics as the stock is subtracted from that stock's buy-and-hold return during the quarter. Each mutual fund's *CS* measure, for a given quarter, is then computed as the portfolio-weighted characteristic-adjusted return of the individual stocks in the fund's portfolio (normalizing so that the weights of all stocks add to one). Finally, the average quarterly *CS* measure is computed for each fund, across all quarters that fund is in existence. To compute the four-factor Carhart gross alpha, the time-series of monthly buy-and-hold excess returns for a given fund (the hypothetical stock returns, using CRSP stock return data applied to fund holdings data, minus the return on T-bills) are regressed on (1) the time series of monthly returns associated with a value-weighted market proxy portfolio minus T-bills, (2) the difference in monthly returns between small- and large-capitalization stocks, (3) the difference in monthly returns between high and low book-to-market stocks, and (4) the difference in monthly returns between stocks having high and low prior-year returns. To compute the Jensen gross alpha, a similar regression is computed on only the first regressor of the Carhart regression. The procedure for computing Carhart and Jensen net alphas is similar, except that the excess net return (net realized return from the CRSP database minus T-bills) is the explained variable in the regressions. For all regressions, a minimum of 24 months of return observations must be available during the entire life of a given fund to be included—this table includes correlations between performance measures for only those funds having this minimum number of return observations. See Daniel et al. (1997), Fama and French (1993), and Carhart (1997) for further details on these procedures. Panel A provides Pearson correlation coefficients between these measures, across all funds, while Panel B provides Spearman rank-correlation coefficients between the measures. All two-tailed p-values in both panels are less than 0.0001.

Panel A. Pearson Correlations

$\rho_{Spearman}$	***CS***	$\alpha^{Gross}_{Carhart}$	$\alpha^{Net}_{Carhart}$	α^{Gross}_{Jensen}	α^{Net}_{Jensen}
CS	1	—	—	—	—
$\alpha^{Gross}_{Carhart}$	0.57	1	—	—	—
$\alpha^{Net}_{Carhart}$	0.36	0.62	1	—	—
α^{Gross}_{Jensen}	0.58	0.74	0.43	1	—
α^{Net}_{Jensen}	0.33	0.49	0.84	0.63	1

Panel B. Spearman Rank Correlations

$\rho_{Spearman}$	***CS***	$\alpha^{Gross}_{Carhart}$	$\alpha^{Net}_{Carhart}$	α^{Gross}_{Jensen}	α^{Net}_{Jensen}
CS	1	—	—	—	—
$\alpha^{Gross}_{Carhart}$	0.65	1	—	—	—
$\alpha^{Net}_{Carhart}$	0.46	0.63	1	—	—
α^{Gross}_{Jensen}	0.53	0.67	0.44	1	—
α^{Net}_{Jensen}	0.40	0.49	0.80	0.68	1

characteristic-based returns than the regression-based methods.[15] Again, Spearman rank-correlations are similar.

At the net return level, the Carhart and Jensen performance measures are again highly correlated, both with the Pearson correlation and with the non-parametric Spearman rank-correlation. A comparison of these measures at the gross stockholdings return level and the net return level provides further insight. For example, the Carhart measure of the stockholdings of funds is highly correlated with the Carhart net return performance measure. The Pearson correlation is 0.62, while the Spearman correlation is 0.63. These high correlations between gross and net performance indicate that the level of mutual fund expenses and transactions costs, while possibly correlated with fund performance at the stockholdings level, do not eliminate the higher benchmark-adjusted net returns provided by funds with stock-picking talents.[16]

5.4.4 Baseline Mutual Fund Return Decomposition

In this section, we decompose the returns of mutual funds in order to further analyze the value of active stock-picking strategies. Panel A of Table 5.6 provides several different yearly measures for the mutual fund universe, averaged by the total net assets of funds. As discussed in Section 5.4.1, the mutual fund universe held stocks during our sample period with average returns of 16.9 percent per year, using a TNA-weighting across funds. This average return level beats the CRSP value-weighted index by 130 basis points per year. In Section 5.4.2, we showed that the stock-picking talents of fund managers could explain 71 basis points per year of this return difference. However, do these fund managers have the ability to time characteristics—e.g., do they buy momentum stocks just before a high momentum return premium? Panel A addresses this question by presenting yearly average returns associated with characteristic selectivity abilities (*CS*), characteristic timing abilities (*CT*), and the average returns to the characteristics of mutual fund stockholdings (*AS*).

In Table 5.6, we present averages over the 1976 to 1994 period, as the *CT* and *AS* measures require one-year lagged portfolio weights. The corresponding average return of the CRSP index is 14.5 percent per year. Over this period, funds hold stocks with gross returns of 15.8 percent per year—again, 130 basis points per year higher than the CRSP index. Panel A shows that 75 basis points per year can be attributed to the stock-selection talents (the *CS* measure) of fund managers. The table also shows that funds exhibit no abilities in timing the characteristics—these *CT* measures are very close to zero during each five-year

[15] See DGTW for evidence that further supports the use of the *CS* measure versus the Carhart and Jensen alphas. The *CS* performance estimates are roughly the same magnitude as the Carhart and Jensen alphas, but the estimated *CS* standard errors are much lower.

[16] In a later section of this chapter, we will analyze this issue more closely by examining the performance of high-turnover funds, both at the stockholdings and the net returns level. In addition, we will determine the level of expenses and transactions costs for these high-turnover funds, which will allow us to determine whether the higher returns provided by their frequent trades results in higher net returns to investors.

Table 5.6 **Baseline Mutual Fund Return Decomposition**

A decomposition of mutual fund returns and costs is provided below for the merged Thomson holdings and CRSP mutual fund characteristics/net returns databases. Panel A of this table provides, each year, the number of mutual funds (at the beginning of the year, except as described in this legend) in the merged mutual fund database. In addition, the panel shows, weighted by the total net assets (TNA) of mutual funds (updated at the beginning of each quarter), the average annual: return on the stock portfolio of the funds (Gross Return), characteristic selectivity measure (CS), characteristic timing measure (CT), average style measure (AS), expense ratio, estimated transactions costs, net reported return, and portfolio turnover ratio. Every fund existing during a given calendar quarter (and having a complete data record) is included in the computation of that quarter's return measures, even if the fund does not survive past the end of that quarter. These quarterly buy-and-hold returns are compounded to give the quarterly rebalanced annual returns reported below. In all measures in this table, we limit our analysis to funds having a self-declared investment objective of "aggressive growth", "growth", "growth and income", "income", or "balanced" at the beginning of a given quarter (for return and transaction-cost measures) or year (for expense ratio and turnover measures). Note, also, that self-declared investment-objective data are available from Thomson starting June 30, 1980, so the 1980 figures are as of that date. Before 1980, funds are classified by their investment objectives as of January 1, 1975 (these data were hand-collected from printed sources). Panel B presents several comparable measures for the Vanguard Index 500 fund. Time-series inference tests are presented, where appropriate.

Panel A. Mutual Fund Universe (TNA-Averaged)

		Merged Database							
		Transactions							
Year	Number	Gross Return (pct/year)	CS (pct/year)	CT* (pct/year)	AS (pct/year)	Expense Ratio (pct/year)	Costs (pct/year)	Net Return (pct/year)	Turnover (pct/year)
1975	241	38.1	0.002	—	—	0.65	1.40	30.9	32.7
1976	241	26.7	0.23	1.15	25.2	0.64	1.32	23.0	32.6
1977	226	−3.0	0.34	0.52	−4.5	0.65	0.68	−2.5	29.3
1978	222	11.3	3.46	0.61	7.3	0.68	0.88	9.0	39.6
1979	219	27.9	1.79	−1.24	25.7	0.69	0.84	23.7	39.1
1980	364	37.8	0.83	0.13	35.2	0.70	0.96	31.3	53.6
1981	365	−4.2	0.21	−0.52	−4.1	0.70	0.88	−2.7	51.9
1982	362	24.0	2.53	1.83	19.1	0.74	1.20	24.1	60.7
1983	347	23.6	1.12	0.72	22.1	0.73	0.88	20.4	64.8
1984	372	0.3	−1.15	−0.63	2.6	0.80	1.04	−0.1	64.1
1985	391	32.0	−0.07	0.23	32.0	0.77	0.88	27.8	74.7
1986	418	17.7	0.40	−0.96	17.7	0.76	1.28	15.8	75.3
1987	483	3.4	1.54	0.78	1.8	0.81	0.56	2.4	79.2
1988	543	18.7	0.20	−1.07	18.9	0.88	0.56	15.9	68.1

Table 5.6 Continued

		Merged Database							
		Transactions							
		Gross Re- turn	CS	CT*	AS*	Ex- pense Ratio	Costs	Net Re- turn	Turn- over
Year	Num- ber	(pct/ year)	(pct/ year)	(pct/ year)	(pct/ year)	(pct/ year)	(pct/ year)	(pct/ year)	(pct/ year)
1989	589	29.4	−0.26	0.31	29.7	0.88	0.48	25.3	65.1
1990	637	−7.4	−0.69	0.64	−7.0	0.91	0.44	−5.3	69.6
1991	679	37.5	1.95	−0.93	36.4	0.87	0.48	32.8	68.7
1992	815	9.1	0.07	−1.13	10.8	0.94	0.48	8.2	67.8
1993	949	15.2	1.70	0.22	12.1	0.96	0.84	14.2	71.7
1994	1,279	−0.4	0.03	−0.34	0.001	0.99	0.48	−1.6	72.8
1976–1979	241	15.7	1.46	0.26	13.4	0.67	0.93	13.3	35.2
1980–1984	459	16.3	0.71	0.31	15.0	0.73	0.99	14.6	59.0
1985–1989	676	20.2	0.36	−0.14	20.0	0.82	0.75	17.4	72.5
1990–1994	1,567	10.8	0.61	−0.31	10.5	0.93	0.54	9.7	70.2
1976–1994	1,788	15.8	0.75**	0.02	14.8	0.79	0.80	13.8	60.5

Panel B. Vanguard Index 500 Fund

		Vanguard				
	S&P 500	Transactions				
	Return	Gross Return[a]	Expense Ratio	Costs[a]	Net Return	Turn- over
Year	(pct per year)	(pct per year)	(pct per year)	(pct per year)	(pct per year)	(pct per year)
1975	37.2	—	—	—	—	—
1976	23.8	—	—	—	—	—
1977	−7.2	—	0.46	—	−7.8	—
1978	6.6	—	0.36	—	5.9	8
1979	18.4	—	0.30	—	18.1	29
1980	32.4	—	0.35	—	31.7	18
1981	−4.9	−4.5	0.42	0.07	−5.1	12
1982	21.4	22.1	0.39	0.12	21.0	11
1983	22.5	23.2	0.28	0.14	21.4	39
1984	6.3	7.1	0.27	0.09	6.3	14
1985	32.2	32.2	0.28	0.11	31.4	36
1986	18.5	18.5	0.28	0.05	18.1	29
1987	5.2	6.1	0.26	0.06	4.7	15
1988	16.8	16.6	0.22	0.05	16.2	10

(Continued)

Table 5.6 Continued

Panel B. Vanguard Index 500 Fund

	S&P 500	Vanguard				
				Transactions		
	Return	Gross Return[a]	Expense Ratio	Costs[a]	Net Return	Turn-over
Year	(pct per year)	(pct per year)	(pct per year)	(pct per year)	(pct per year)	(pct per year)
1989	31.5	31.4	0.22	0.06	31.4	8
1990	−3.2	−3.6	0.22	0.05	−3.3	23
1991	30.5	30.3	0.20	0.05	30.2	—[b]
1992	7.7	7.3	0.19	0.03	7.4	4
1993	10.0	10.0	0.19	0.02	9.9	6
1994	1.3	1.5	0.19	0.02	1.2	6
1977–1979	5.9	—	0.37	—	5.4	18.5[c]
1980–1984	15.5	12.0[c]	0.34	0.11[c]	15.1	18.8
1985–1989	20.8	21.0	0.25	0.07	20.4	19.6
1990–1994	9.3	9.1	0.20	0.03	9.1	5.3[c]
1977–1994	13.7	14.2[c]	0.28	0.07[c]	13.3	15.3[c]

[a]Vanguard Index 500 fund holdings data are available starting in 1981. [b]Currently unavailable from the CRSP files. [c]Averaged over all available years.

***Significant at the 95% confidence level.*

**The CT and AS measures begin in 1976, since both measures require one-year lagged portfolio weights.*

subperiod and over the entire 20-year period. Thus, the remaining 55 basis point difference (per year) between gross fund returns and the CRSP index can be attributed to the higher average returns earned by the characteristics of the stockholdings of mutual funds, relative to the CRSP index.[17] Specifically, Chen et al. (2000) show that mutual funds exhibit a preference for holding small stocks, growth stocks, and momentum stocks, as compared to the market portfolio. Although growth stocks, with a negative loading on the book-to-market factor, earn lower average returns, small stocks and momentum stocks earn higher average returns. The overall result is that funds hold stocks with characteristics that outperformed the market portfolio during the 20-year period of our sample.

The panel also shows the general trend of expense ratios, transactions costs, and portfolio turnover levels over the period. Expense ratios have increased substantially, rising from 65 basis points per year in 1975 to 99 basis points in 1994. However, the higher proportion of small funds in the sample during later years

[17] Although the *AS* measure exceeds the CRSP VW index by only 30 basis points per year over the 1976 to 1994 period (14.8 vs. 14.5 percent per year), we note that stocks that are omitted from the computation of the *AS* measure are those with missing Compustat or CRSP data. These stocks are generally small stocks, therefore, we infer that they would mainly add to the *AS* measure, if included.

accounts for this increase—as noted by Rea and Reid (1998), expense ratios for the 100 largest U.S. equity mutual funds existing in 1997, and established before 1980, have fallen modestly.

An examination of transactions costs and turnover levels also adds insight. Although the trading activity of the average mutual fund has more than doubled over the 20-year period, estimated transactions costs have decreased substantially. Specifically, the average mutual fund exhibited a yearly turnover level of 35.2 percent during the 1976 to 1979 subperiod, increasing to 70.2 percent during the 1990 to 1994 subperiod. However, while 93 basis points of the total net assets of funds was expended each year on trading costs (including commissions and the market impact of trades) during the first subperiod, only 54 basis points were spent during the last subperiod. Even with substantially higher levels of trading, total transactions costs have roughly been halved from the first to the last five-year subperiod. Certainly, the substantial decrease in transactions costs in the various markets contributed significantly to this trend; however, it is also likely that funds are able to execute trades more carefully with the increased level of technology in use in mutual fund complexes.

Panel A of Table 5.6 also shows the general trend of net mutual fund returns. As noted in a previous section, trends in net returns generally follow those in gross stockholdings returns, although larger differences between the two return measures occur during subperiods with a higher equity premium (large company stocks minus T-bills). Of course, changes in transactions costs and expense ratios also impact the difference between gross and net returns over the sample period. However, the general increase in average expense ratios, and the decrease in average transactions costs have resulted in the sum of these two costs remaining relatively constant over the years.

Finally, a cost-based accounting for the difference between gross and net returns adds further insight. In Table 5.3, we documented a 2.3% per year difference between TNA-averaged gross and net returns over the 1975 to 1994 period. Panel A of Table 5.6 shows that expense ratios and transactions costs each account for roughly 80 basis points per year of this difference. Thus, the remaining 70 basis points per year can be attributed to the lower average returns accruing to non-stock holdings, relative to stocks.

In Figure 5.7, we graphically show the decomposition for the years 1976 to 1994—where the average difference between TNA-averaged gross and net returns was 2% per year. Panel A shows the return sources, while Panel B shows the return uses. First, Panel A shows that 0.6%/year was gained over the S&P 500 index by the (value-weighted) U.S. mutual funds by holding stocks with characteristics that yielded higher returns. Specifically, the funds hold stocks that are, on average, somewhat smaller cap than the S&P 500, as well as investing in stocks with high momentum. Another 0.75%/year is attributable to the stock-picking talents of the managers.

Panel B shows that, in addition to the above-cited 0.8%/year, each, for transactions costs and expense ratios, the funds lost 0.4%/year due to their need to hold

Panel A: Return Sources

Return Sources (*1976* to 1994)
(TNA-average, percent per year)

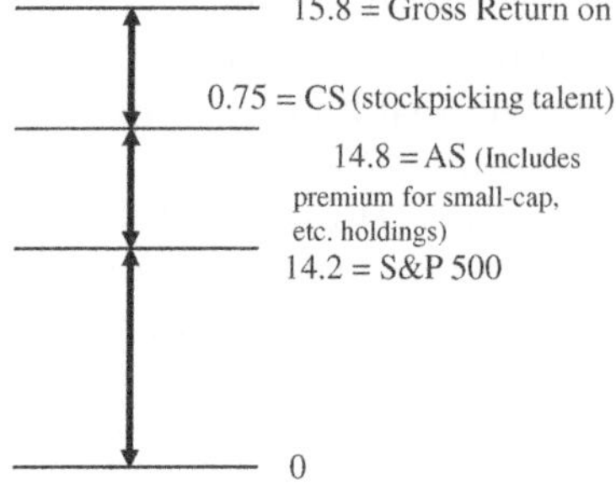

Panel B: Return Uses

Return Uses (*1976* to 1994)
(TNA-average, percent per year)

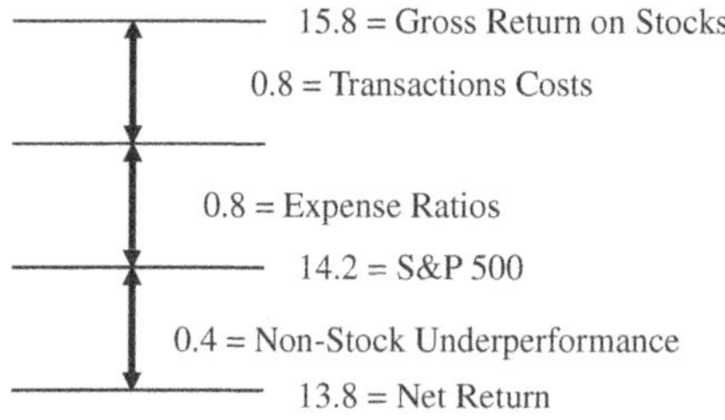

FIGURE 5.7
U.S. Domestic Equity Mutual Fund Performance Attribution.

cash. With open-end mutual funds, some level of cashholdings is usually necessary, in order to be able to meet unforeseen redemptions by fund shareholders. While cashholdings usually amount to less than 5% of fund assets, the effect on fund performance can be substantial (see Edelen (1999) for further details on the drag of cash on performance).

5.4.5 A Comparison of the Average Mutual Fund to the Vanguard Index 500 Fund

An often quoted claim by John Bogle, Senior Chairman of the Vanguard fund family, is that the Vanguard Index 500 fund outperforms the average mutual fund due to the low costs and low trading activity of the fund (see, for example, Bogle (1994)). By making these claims, the implication is that money managers who actively chase stocks do not have the ability to find stocks that outperform the market portfolio by enough to recover their expenses and trading costs. This marketing appeal has been hugely successful—as of November 1999, the Vanguard fund managed $97 billion in assets, placing it within the largest two mutual funds in the U.S.

In Panel B, we examine the returns to the Vanguard Index 500 fund to determine the validity of these claims. Specifically, Panel B decomposes the Vanguard fund returns into several components, as well as providing the turnover level of the fund during various years. Not surprisingly, the gross returns on stockholdings for the Vanguard fund tracks the S&P 500 index very closely. Interesting, however, is the general decrease in expenses charged by the fund, as Vanguard increasingly attempts to compete for investment dollars through a low-cost approach. Specifically, the fund expense ratio decreased from 46 basis points during 1975 to 19 basis points during 1994. Noteworthy is that recent low-cost competitive pressures by ETFs have forced Vanguard and some other index funds to lower fees even further.

The panel also shows that transaction costs incurred by the fund as it responds to fund inflows and outflows (and to changes in the composition of the S&P 500 index) are extremely low. These estimated costs are, in general, below 10 basis points per year. This low-cost item provides a large advantage for the Vanguard fund over actively managed funds.

Our previous analysis showed that, over 1975 to 1994, the TNA-average mutual fund holds stocks that outperform the S&P 500 index by 150 basis points per year. We also showed that 71 basis points of this difference is due to the stock-picking talents of funds, while the remainder is due to the higher average returns associated with the characteristics of the fund stockholdings, relative to the S&P 500 index. However, to determine whether the claim of Vanguard is valid, we must compare net returns between the TNA-average mutual fund and the Vanguard fund.

Since net returns are available in the merged database for the Vanguard fund beginning in 1977, we compare the Vanguard fund to the average mutual fund during the 1977 to 1994 period. Over this time period, the Vanguard fund provided an average net return to investors of 13.3 percent per year. By comparison, the TNA-average mutual fund also returned an average of 13.3 percent per year to investors during the 1977 to 1994 period. As noted in subsection B, however, the TNA-average and EW-average characteristic-adjusted net returns (Carhart measures) over the 1975 to 1994 period are −1.16 and −1.15 percent per year, respectively. In unreported tests, we found that the Vanguard Index 500 fund has a Carhart net return measure of −29 basis points per year.

Thus, we conclude that the claims of the Vanguard fund are not overwhelmingly supported by the unadjusted net returns. Our evidence indicates that the average mutual fund holds stocks with returns that compensate for the higher expenses and trading costs, relative to the Vanguard Index 500 fund. However, if one views the return boost from the characteristics of stockholdings of mutual funds as wholly a compensation for risk, then the funds underperform the Vanguard Index 500 fund by a large 87 basis points per year.

5.4.6 Do Funds that Trade More Frequently Generate Better Performance?

A concept that is central to the idea of actively managed funds outperforming index funds is that higher levels of trading activity are associated with better stock-picking abilities. Do higher levels of mutual fund trading result in higher levels of performance? Our next tests address this issue by examining the performance of high- versus low-turnover funds. If more frequent trading is associated with managers having better stock-picking talents, then we should observe a corresponding increase in performance, at least before trading costs and expenses are factored in. If, instead, managers trade more frequently in an attempt to convince investors that they can successfully pick stocks, we should see no increase in performance before costs and expenses. In this case, we should actually see lower performance, *after* costs and expenses are deducted, for frequent traders. Carhart (1997) finds evidence that supports this view, although his dataset does not allow an examination of performance at the stockholdings level.

We proceed as follows. At the end of each year, beginning on December 31, 1975 and ending December 31, 1993, we rank all mutual funds with at least a one-year history on their turnover level of the prior year (the "ranking year"). Fractile portfolios are formed based on this ranking, then TNA-average fund returns and characteristics are computed over the following year (the "test year"). In computing the test year average returns or performance measures, we first compute TNA-average measures for each quarter of the test year, across all funds that existed during that quarter (whether or not they survived past the end of the quarter) to minimize survival bias. Then, these quarterly TNA-weighted buy-and-hold returns are compounded into a quarterly rebalanced test-year return.

Table 5.7 shows the results of this test, averaged over all test years. Several observations are apparent from these results. First, the highest turnover fund decile has a TNA-average turnover level of 155 percent per year, while the lowest decile has an average turnover level of only 14 percent per year. Thus, high-turnover funds trade roughly ten times as frequently as low-turnover funds. The reader should note that the bottom decile (and perhaps quintile) is populated with several index funds, especially during the later years of our sample period.

Also, high-turnover funds hold stock portfolios that significantly outperform the portfolios of low-turnover funds—specifically, stockholdings of the top turnover decile outperform those of the bottom decile by 4.3 percent per year, on average. An examination of differences in the other measures provides insight into the attribution of this difference—2.2 percent per year is generated by high-turnover funds holding stocks with characteristics that provide higher returns than stocks held by low-turnover funds (the *AS* measure), while another 1.2 percent per year is due to significantly better stock-picking talents (the *CS* measure) of high-turnover funds. The remaining 90 basis points per year can be attributed to the

Table 5.7 Turnover-Sorted Mutual Fund Return Decomposition

A decomposition of mutual fund returns and costs is provided below for the merged Thomson holdings and CRSP mutual fund characteristics/net returns databases. At the end of each year starting December 31, 1975 and ending December 31, 1993, we rank all mutual funds in the merged database that existed during the entire prior year (and had a complete data record during that year) on their portfolio turnover level of that year (the "ranking year"). Then, fractile portfolios are formed, and we compute average return measures (e.g., net returns) for each fractile portfolio during the following year (the "test year"). In computing the average return measure for a given test year, we first compute quarterly buy-and-hold returns for each fund that exists during each quarter of the test year, regardless of whether the fund survives past the end of that quarter. Then, we compute the total net asset-weighted (TNA) average quarterly buy-and-hold return across all funds for each quarter of the test year. Finally, we compound these returns into an annual return that is rebalanced quarterly. Presented in this table are the TNA-average annual: return on the stock portfolio of the funds (Gross Return), characteristic selectivity measure (CS), characteristic timing measure (CT), average style measure (AS), expense ratio, estimated transactions costs, net reported return, Carhart net return alpha, and portfolio turnover ratio. The table presents test year statistics, averaged over all test years. The table also shows the time-series average number of funds within each fractile portfolio. In forming all portfolios in this table, we limit our analysis to funds having a self-declared investment objective of "aggressive growth", "growth", "growth and income", "income", or "balanced" at the beginning of the test year. Note, also, that self-declared investment-objective data are available from Thomson starting June 30, 1980, so the 1980 figures are as of that date. Before 1980, funds are classified by their investment objectives as of January 1, 1975 (these data were hand-collected from printed sources). Time-series inference tests are presented, where appropriate.

Fractile	Avg No	Gross Return (pct/year)	CS (pct/year)	CT (pct/year)	AS (pct/year)	Expense Ratio (pct/year)	Trans. Costs (pct/year)	Net Return (pct/year)	$\alpha^{Net}_{Carhart}$ (pct/year)	Turnover (pct/year)
Top 10 %	42	19.5	1.46*	0.28	16.8	0.97	2.65	15.5	−1.00	155
Top 20 %	84	19.1	1.83***	0.31	16.3	0.94	2.07	15.9	−0.68	132
2nd 20 %	84	17.3	1.33***	0.53*	15.1	0.90	1.12	15.2	−0.98*	82
3rd 20 %	84	16.2	0.89**	0.16	15.1	0.82	0.82	14.3	−1.24**	57
4th 20 %	84	15.8	0.59	−0.07	15.0	0.70	0.92	13.7	−1.40***	33
Bottom 20 %	84	14.8	0.02	−0.06	14.6	0.64	0.33	13.2	−1.01**	18
Bottom 10%	42	15.2	0.24	0.05	14.6	0.69	0.28	13.4	−0.85*	14
Top-Bottom 10%	42	4.3*	1.22	0.23	2.2***	0.28***	2.37***	2.1	−0.15	141***
Top-Bottom 20%	84	4.3**	1.81***	0.37	1.7**	0.30***	1.74***	2.7**	0.33	114***
All Funds	420	16.2	0.79**	0.11	15.0	0.77	0.88	14.2	−1.12	59

*Significant at the 95% confidence level.

**Significant at the 90% confidence level.

***Significant at the 99% confidence level.

slightly higher timing abilities (the *CT* measure) of high-turnover funds as well as to estimation error.[18]

High-turnover funds, however, incur much higher transactions costs than their low-turnover counterparts (a difference of 2.4 percent per year), as well as charging somewhat higher expense ratios (a difference of 28 basis points per year). These factors reduce the net return advantage of high-turnover funds, although they still outperform low-turnover funds by 2.1 percent per year. Although this figure is not statistically significant, the net return difference between the top and bottom turnover quintiles, 2.7 percent per year, is significant at the 95 percent confidence level.

Finally, we benchmark-adjust the TNA-average net returns of each turnover fractile, using the Carhart measure (labeled $\alpha^{Net}_{Carhart}$). Here, there is no significant difference in results between high- and low-turnover funds. Indeed, the Carhart measure is actually lowest for the middle turnover quintiles, which may explain why Carhart (1997) found a negative relation between turnover and benchmark-adjusted net returns (the Carhart measure).

It is interesting to compare the TNA-average net return provided by high-turnover funds to that provided by the Vanguard Index 500 fund. The average unadjusted net returns of the top two turnover quintiles are 15.9 and 15.2 percent per year, respectively. The average net return of the Vanguard fund, assuming that it matches the S&P 500 return in 1976 (our first test year) is 13.8 percent per year; therefore, the top two quintiles of funds, ranked by their turnover level, clearly beat the Vanguard fund on a net return basis. However, only the top quintile of funds has a Carhart performance measure (−68 basis points per year, which is statistically indistinguishable from zero) that is reasonably close to that of the Vanguard fund (−29 basis points per year, also insignificant). Thus, we conclude that actively managed funds beat the Vanguard Index 500 fund on a net return basis, but only before adjusting for the higher average returns accruing to the characteristics of active fund stockholdings.

5.5 RESULTS FOR U.S. DOMESTIC CORPORATE BOND MUTUAL FUNDS

Cici and Gibson (2012) bring many interesting results from their study of corporate bond funds, using the approach described in this chapter. Among these are:

- Bond fund managers, on average, cannot select superior bonds.
- Investment-grade bond fund managers, on average, cannot time duration and credit spreads; however, high-yield managers are able to time these characteristics.

[18] Specifically, the *CS*, *CT*, and *AS* measures include only stocks that are listed in COMPUSTAT and have a one-year return history in CRSP, while the gross return computation includes all stocks having a current-quarter CRSP return. High-turnover funds tend to be smaller funds, which generally have larger holdings of small stocks—this results in a bigger shortfall of the sum of CS+CT+AS as compared to the gross return among high-turnover funds (relative to low-turnover funds). The shortfall is due to the small stock premium that is reflected in the gross return, but not in the *AS* measure.

- Bond fund managers incur a 20 basis point per year transaction cost, on average, of trading bonds (the authors control for the fact that maturing bonds involve no trading when they leave the portfolio).
- Active investment-grade bond fund managers incur fees that average 68 basis points per year, on average—27 basis points per year higher than the combined return contribution from bond selection and duration and/or credit timing.

5.6 APPENDIX A

5.6.1 Description of Matching Process for Thomson and CRSP Mutual Fund Databases[19]

In this section, we describe the process used to match the Thomson mutual fund holdings database and the CRSP mutual fund net returns and characteristics database. The Thomson database consists of the following information for each U.S.-based equity fund at the end of each quarter from December 31, 1974 to the present:

1. Fund name and management company name
2. Date of mutual fund holdings "snapshot" (since June 30, 1979)
3. Total net assets under management
4. Self-declared investment objective (since June 30, 1980, supplemented with data for December 31, 1974)
5. Shares held of each stock by each fund.

The majority of mutual funds use a fiscal quarter that coincides with calendar quarters; therefore, for this study, we use the approximation that all holdings reported within a given calendar quarter are also valid for the end of that calendar quarter. We also note that individual funds are only required to report their holdings to the SEC at the end of each fiscal semiannual period under Section 30 of the Investment Company Act of 1940. However, Thomson obtains more frequent holdings reports from the majority of funds—during most of our sample period, over 80 percent of funds reported holdings on a quarterly basis to Thomson. Further details on the data collection procedure by Thomson are available in Wermers (1999).

The CRSP mutual fund database consists of the following information for each U.S.-based equity fund from January 1, 1962 to the present:

1. Fund name and management company name (management company name only since 1992)
2. Self-declared investment objective (annually)
3. Total net assets under management (monthly)

[19] The latest generation of the below mapping is available from Wharton Research Data Services (WRDS)—named the "MFLINKS" database—developed by WRDS in conjunction with Professor Wermers. See wrds.wharton.upenn.edu.

4. Net return (monthly)
5. Expense ratio (annually)
6. Turnover ratio (annually)
7. Proportion of portfolio allocated to stocks (annually)
8. Total load fee (annually).

Before matching funds between the two databases, we excluded several types of funds from the CRSP database. These funds include international funds, bond funds, money market funds, sector funds, and funds that do not hold the majority of their portfolios in U.S. equities. Such funds were identified through their self-declared investment objective or through a keyword in their name (for example, the "Franklin Gold Fund"); in addition, funds holding less than 50 percent of their total portfolio value in equities during all years that they were in existence (during our sample period) were excluded.

Since the two databases (unfortunately!) have different fund numbering systems, we matched funds between them primarily based on the name of the fund. Occasionally, attempts at matching funds solely with the fund name proved difficult—in such cases, the investment objective, management company name, and total net assets information helped in matching funds between databases.

In matching funds by their names, we implemented a complex matching program that found name similarities between all versions of Thomson fund names and all versions of CRSP fund names. In many cases, the program identified an exact match between names in each database. However, in many other cases, the fund name in one database contained an abbreviation or a contraction, which made matching more difficult. For each fund, we hand-checked potential matches before deciding on the correct match and adding the matched fund to our database.

Panel A of Table 5.2 presents statistics, both for the funds that were successfully matched and for funds in the CRSP database that could not be matched to a Thomson fund during the fund's entire existence. A total of 1,788 funds are included in the matched database, which consists of funds that survive until the end of 1994 and funds that perish due to a merger or liquidation. This number is slightly smaller than the 1,892 funds reported by Carhart (1997) that exist during 1962 to 1993 in the CRSP database, even though we include balanced funds, while Carhart does not. There are a few reasons for this. First, Carhart's time period begins in 1962, while our study begins in 1975. Second, Carhart apparently counts each shareclass in a single fund as a separate "fund". And, third, it is likely that our sample excludes some funds that were erroneously included in Carhart's count, as we use investment objective information from both the Thomson and CRSP databases to decide on funds to include.

The reader should note that the yearly counts (either for matched or for unmatched funds) in Table 5.2, Panel A do not include funds with an incomplete data record during a given year. In general, Thomson is slower in adding funds to their database than CRSP. This results in an incomplete record (missing stockholdings data) for some new funds, which reduces our fund count during most years in the merged database. These fund-year omissions should have a minimal impact on the majority of our results, however, as we average our fund measures by the total net assets of funds (thus, minimizing the importance of small, omitted funds).

The Thomson data omission problem notwithstanding, any funds that could not be matched (during their entire existence) were ones that were listed in the CRSP database, but not in the Thomson database (at least among diversified equity funds). The small, unmatched funds during the last few years of our sample period are likely ones that Thomson did not add to their database until after 1994.

Also noteworthy is that CRSP identifies different shareclasses of the same mutual fund as distinct funds. Table 5.2, Panel B provides counts of the number of shareclasses represented by our mutual fund sample. Such shareclasses, which have become especially prevalent during the 1990s, confer ownership to the same underlying pool of assets while providing different expense ratio and load fee structures in order to appeal to different clienteles. Returns on the various shareclasses corresponding to a single mutual fund are obviously not independent, and Thomson does not separately identify such shareclasses. Therefore, we recombine all CRSP shareclasses of a mutual fund by mapping them to a single Thomson fund. In doing so, we compute net returns, expense ratios, and load fees for the parent Thomson mutual fund by weighting the figures for each shareclass by the most recent total net assets of that shareclass. We note, however, that CRSP likely omits many shareclasses that are offered only to institutions. The impact of this omission is probably an overestimate of fund expenses, however, as institutions generally pay lower expenses and loads.

5.7 APPENDIX B

5.7.1 Description of Execution Cost Estimation Procedure

Keim and Madhavan (1997) provide the following fitted regressions for total institutional execution costs (commissions plus market impact) for a sample of mutual funds during the 1991 to 1993 period:

$$C_{i,t}^{B} = 0.767 + 0.336 D_{i,t}^{Nasdaq} + 0.092 Tr\, size_{i,t} - 0.084 Logmcap_{i,t} + 13.807 \left(\frac{1}{P_{i,t}}\right) + 0.492 D_{i,t}^{Tech} + 0.305 D_{i,t}^{Index}, \tag{B1}$$

and

$$C_{i,t}^{S} = 0.505 + 0.058 D_{i,t}^{Nasdaq} + 0.214 Tr\, size_{i,t} - 0.059 Logmcap_{i,t} + 6.537 \left(\frac{1}{P_{i,t}}\right) + 0.718 D_{i,t}^{Tech} + 0.432 D_{i,t}^{Index}, \tag{B2}$$

where:

$C_{i,t}^{B}$= total costs (in percent of the trade value) of buying stock i during period t,

$C_{i,t}^{S}$= total costs (in percent of the trade value) of selling stock i during period t,

$Trsize_{i,t}$= trade size (dollar value of trade divided by market capitalization of the stock),

$Logmcap_{i,t}$= natural log of the market capitalization of the stock,

$P_{i,t}$=the stock price, and

$D_{i,t}^{Nasdaq}, D_{i,t}^{Tech}, D_{i,t}^{Index}$= dummy variables that equal one if the trade occurred on Nasdaq (as opposed to the NYSE or AMEX), if the trader was a "technical trader", and if the trader was an "index trader", respectively, and zero otherwise.

Since we cannot easily assign trader types (value, technical, or index) to our mutual funds, we use the data on the fraction of each trader type present in the KM study to recompute the fitted regressions without trader dummies. Also, since trading costs declined substantially on all markets over our sample period, we use the results of Stoll (1995), who estimates the time-series trend of total execution costs in the different markets. Specifically, the average cost of executing a trade is documented over time on both the NYSE/AMEX and on the Nasdaq. Using 1992 as our baseline year, we adjust the fitted regressions with a "year factor", Y_t^k, that is equal to the year t average execution cost divided by the 1992 average execution cost for market k (where k=NYSE/AMEX or Nasdaq). These factors are based on Stoll (1995). The resulting fitted regressions are:

$$C_{i,t}^{B} = Y_t^k \cdot \left[1.098+0.336D_{i,t}^{Nasdaq}+0.092Trsize_{i,t}-0.084Logmcap_{i,t}+13.807\left(\frac{1}{P_{i,t}}\right)\right] \tag{B3}$$

and:

$$C_{i,t}^{S} = Y_t^k \cdot \left[0.979+0.058D_{i,t}^{Nasdaq}+0.214Trsize_{i,t}-0.059Logmcap_{i,t}+6.537\left(\frac{1}{P_{i,t}}\right)\right]. \tag{B4}$$

5.8 CHAPTER-END PROBLEMS

1. List the different holdings-based performance components described in this chapter.
2. Suppose that a hedge fund wished to trade a large position in a small stock on Nasdaq. Specifically, suppose the fund wished to purchase 5% of the market cap of a stock trading at $5 per share and having a total market capitalization of $100 million. Compute the percentage trade cost.

3. Repeat problem #2, but this time compute the cost when the hedge fund sells the stock back to the market at $6 per share. What is the net profit achieved?

4. Describe how the "Characteristic Selectivity" measure is computed for a portfolio manager.

5. Consider the following performance evaluation results for the Dimensional Fund Advisors 9–10 fund:

Carhart Regression
US 9-10 Small Company Portfolio

	Coefficients	t Stat	P-value
Intercept	0.31	0.32	0.96
rmrf	0.94	48.47	0.00
smb	0.94	27.37	0.00
hml	0.15	4.23	0.00
pr1yr	-0.09	-3.59	0.00

Portfolio-Holdings Measures

CS	t Stat	AS	CT
0.78	1.11	11.16	0.00

Jensen Regression
US 9-10 Small Company Portfolio

	Coefficients	t Stat
Intercept	-0.81	-0.35
rmrf	1.00	22.6000

Why are alphas of the three different approaches different (list all of the possible reasons)?

6. Assume that Scott Schoelzel's Janus 20 portfolio invests in only six stocks as follows. Assume, for simplicity, that each stock has a market capitalization of $1 Billion, and that each DGTW cell contains only three stocks, a shown:

December 31, 1996			December 31, 1995		
DGTW Cell No. 58	**Janus Weight**	**1997 Return**	**DGTW Cell No. 58**	**Janus Weight**	**1996 Return**
AOL	$\frac{1}{6}$	−9%	MSFT	$\frac{1}{6}$	15%
CSCO	$\frac{1}{2}$	−6	SUNW	0	12
IBM	$\frac{1}{6}$	−9	IBM	0	18

December 31, 1996			December 31, 1995		
DGTW Cell No. 59	**Janus weight**	**1997 Returns**	**DGTW Cell No. 59**	**Janus weight**	**1996 Returns**
MSFT	$\frac{1}{6}$	9%	AOL	$\frac{2}{3}$	18%
SUNW	0	5	CSCO	$\frac{1}{6}$	6
JUNP	0	16	JUNP	0	12

A. Compute the Characteristic Selectivity (CS) measure for Scott during 1996 and 1997.

B. Compute the Characteristic Timing (CT) measure for Scott during 1996 to 1997.

C. What do you conclude about Scott? Is he skilled? Explain fully.

Chapter 6

Performance Evaluation of Non-Normal Portfolios

ABSTRACT

This chapter presents an advanced approach to computing the statistical significance of the estimated performance of a fund manager—the "bootstrap approach". A bootstrap approach is necessary because the cross-section of most managed fund alphas (such as those of a group of ranked mutual funds or hedge funds) has a complex nonnormal distribution due to heterogeneous risk-taking by funds as well as nonnormalities in individual fund alpha distributions. To illustrate the approach, this chapter applies this bootstrap to examine the performance of the U.S. open-end, domestic equity mutual fund industry over the 1975 to 2002 period. The bootstrap approach uncovers findings that differ from many past studies. Specifically, a sizable minority of managers pick stocks well enough to more than cover their costs.

Keywords
Bootstrapping alphas, luck vs. skill, cross-section of alphas, non-normal alphas, residual resampling

6.1 INTRODUCTION

We have previously profiled the performance of the Fidelity Magellan fund in this book. Was Peter Lynch, former manager of Magellan (from 1977–1990), a "star" stockpicker, or was he simply endowed with stellar luck? The popular press seems to assume that Mr. Lynch's fund performed well due to his unusual acumen in identifying underpriced stocks. In addition, Marcus (1990) concludes that the prolonged superior performance of the Magellan fund is difficult to explain as a purely random outcome, that is, a case in which Mr. Lynch and the other Magellan managers have no true stockpicking skills and are merely the luckiest of a large group of fund managers. More recently, the Schroder Ultra Fund topped the field of 6,000 funds (across all investment objective categories) with a return of 107% per year over the three years ending in 2001.

Performance Evaluation and Attribution of Security Portfolios. http://dx.doi.org/10.1016/B978-0-12-744483-3.00006-7
© 2013 Elsevier Inc. All rights reserved.
For End-of-chapter Questions: © 2012. CFA Institute, Reproduced and republished with permission from CFA Institute. All rights reserved.

This fund closed to new investors in 1998 due to overwhelming demand, presumably because investors credited the fund manager as having extraordinary skills.

It is always easy to point to a fund manager with great success in the past. To illustrate, consider a simple thought experiment. We gather 1,024 new MBAs and make them "fund managers". Each year, we have them flip a coin, and all who flip heads survive until the following year, while the remaining "funds" are shut down, and the managers fired. So, we *expect* (i.e., on average) 512 to survive until the second coin toss event at the end of year 2, and 256 to survive until the end of year 3. How many would we *expect* to survive into year 11 (i.e., after 10 coin flip events)? The answer is $1024 \cdot 0.5^{10} = 1$ fund manager (although this number has a large variance). Was Peter Lynch this super-lucky coin-tosser, or was there something more to his performance?

It is tougher to answer this question when funds are taking risks that are not similar to simple coin-tosses. For example, some fund managers—especially hedge fund managers—take option-like risks, where they usually outperform a benchmark by a slight amount, but (rarely) underperform by a large amount.[1] Obviously, the variance in the number of survivors until year 11 in the example above would be much larger in this more complicated setting.

The issues covered by this chapter can be stated very simply: With mutual fund alphas that deviate significantly from normality, how many funds from a large group would we expect to exhibit high alphas simply due to luck, and, how does this figure compare to the number we actually observe?[2] To address these questions, we show how to apply a bootstrap technique to the net returns of fund managers. Then, we illustrate the application of this bootstrap on a panel of U.S. open-end, domestic equity funds during the 1975 to 2002 period—one of the largest panels of fund returns ever analyzed.

To further illustrate the focus of this chapter, suppose that we are told that a particular fund has an alpha of 10% per year over a five-year period. *Prima facie,* this is an extremely impressive performance record. However, if this fund is the best performer among a group of 1,000 funds, then its alpha may not appear to be so impressive. Further, when outlier funds are selected from such an ex post ranking of a large cross-section, the separation of luck from skill becomes extremely sensitive to the assumed joint distribution from which the fund alphas are drawn. Any such analysis must account for non-normality in this distribution, which, as we will show, can result from (1) heterogeneous risk-taking across funds and (2) non-normally distributed individual fund alphas.

[1] One such strategy is writing out options that are deep out-of-the-money on an index, which can create highly non-normal returns. This invalidates the use of performance measures that assume normality, such as the Sharpe Ratio.

[2] This chapter is based on Kosowski et al. (2006).

6.2 BOOTSTRAP EVALUATION OF FUND ALPHAS

6.2.1 Rationale for the Bootstrap Approach

There are many reasons why the bootstrap is necessary for proper evaluation of asset manager skills. These include the propensity of individual funds to exhibit non-normally distributed returns, as well as the cross-section of funds representing a complex mixture of these individual fund distributions. We begin by discussing individual funds. We then progress to the central focus of this chapter, that is, evaluating the cross-sectional distribution of ranked mutual fund alphas, which involves evaluating a complex mixture of individual fund alpha distributions.

In the following discussion, we refer to stocks within equity mutual fund portfolios to simplify and make concrete the discussion. However, all of the below statements can be interpreted as any type of securities within any type of portfolio. For example, Kosowski et al. (2007) apply the bootstrap of this chapter to hedge funds and find that it significantly improves the modeling of the returns of such funds.

6.2.1.1 *Individual Mutual Fund Alphas*

Among U.S. domestic equity mutual funds, Kosowski et al. (2006) find that roughly half have alphas that are drawn from a distinctly non-normal distribution. These non-normalities arise for several reasons. First, individual stocks within the typical mutual fund portfolio realize returns with non-negligible higher moments. Thus, while the central limit theorem implies that an equal-weighted portfolio of such non-normally distributed stocks will approach normality, managers often hold heavy positions in relatively few stocks or industries. Second, market benchmark returns may be non-normal, and co-skewness in benchmark and individual stock returns may result. Further, individual stocks exhibit varying levels of time-series autocorrelation in returns. Finally, funds may implement dynamic strategies that involve changing their levels of risk-taking when the risk of the overall market portfolio changes, or in response to their performance ranking relative to similar funds. Thus, because each of these regularities can contribute to non-normally distributed mutual fund alphas, normality may be a poor approximation in practice, even for a fairly large mutual fund portfolio.

The bootstrap can substantially improve on this approximation, as Bickel and Freedman (1984) and Hall (1986) show. For example, by recognizing the presence of thick tails in individual fund returns, the bootstrap often rejects abnormal performance for fewer mutual funds; we return to this finding in Section 6.4.

6.2.1.2 *The Cross-Section of Mutual Fund Alphas*

While the intuition we gain from the individual fund bootstrap results above is helpful, such intuition does not necessarily carry over to the cross-section of mutual funds. Specifically, the cross-sectional distribution of alphas also carries the effect of variation in risk-taking (as well as sample size) across funds.[3] Furthermore, cross-sectional correlations in residual (fund-specific) risk, although very close to zero on average, may be nonzero in the tails if some funds load on similar non-priced factors. These effects tend to be important because high-risk funds often hold concentrated portfolios that load on similar industries or individual stocks.

That is, while fund-level non-normalities in alphas may imply non-normalities in the cross-sectional distribution of alphas, the reverse need not be true. Even funds that have normally distributed residuals can create non-normalities in the cross-section of ranked alphas. To illustrate, consider 1,000 mutual funds, each existing over 336 months (the time span of our sample period). Suppose each fund has independently and identically distributed (IID) standard normal model residuals, and that the true model intercept (alpha) equals zero for each fund. Thus, measured fund alphas are simply the average realized residual over the 336 months. In this simple case, the cross-sectional distribution of fund alphas would be normally distributed.

However, consider the same 1,000 funds with heterogeneous levels of risk such that, across funds, residual variances range uniformly between 0.5 and 1.5 (i.e., the average variance is unity). In this case, the tails of the cross-sectional distribution of alphas are now fatter than those of a normal distribution. The intuition here is clear: As we move further to the right in the right tail, the probability of these extreme outcomes does not fall very quickly, as high-risk funds more than compensate for the large drop in such extreme outcomes from low-risk funds. Conversely, consider a case in which the distribution of risk levels is less evenly spread out (i.e., more clustered), with 1% of the funds having a residual standard deviation of four, and the remaining 99% having a standard deviation of 0.92 (the average variance across funds remains equal to one). Here, tails of the cross-section of alphas are now thinner than those of a normal. The intuition for these unexpected results is quite simple: The presence of many funds with low risk levels means that these funds' realized residuals have a low probability of lying out in the far tails of the cross-sectional distribution of alpha estimates. At some point in the right tail, this probability decreases faster than can be compensated by the presence of a small group of high-risk funds.

---

[3] It is noteworthy that, even if all funds had normally distributed returns with identical levels of risk, it would still be infeasible to apply standard statistical methods to assess the significance of extreme alphas drawn from a large universe of ranked funds. In this case, the best alpha is modeled as the maximum value drawn from a multivariate normal distribution whose dimension depends on the number of funds in existence. Modeling this joint normal distribution depends on estimating the entire covariance matrix across all individual mutual funds, which is generally impossible to estimate with precision. Specifically, the difficulty in estimating the covariance matrix across several hundreds or thousands of funds is compounded by the entry and exit of funds, which implies that many funds do not have overlapping return records with which to estimate their covariances. Although one might use long-history market indices to improve the covariance matrix estimation as in Pastor and Stambaugh (2002), this method is not likely to improve the covariance estimation between funds that take extreme positions away from the indices.

Finally, consider a larger proportion of high-risk funds than the prior case—suppose 10% of the 1,000 funds have a residual standard deviation of two, while the remaining 90% have a standard deviation of 0.82 (again, the risk continues to be equal to one across all funds). In this case, the cross-section of alphas has five- and three-percentile points that are thinner, but a one-percentile point that is thicker, than that of a normal. Thus, the cross-section of alphas can have thick or thin tails relative to a normal distribution, regardless of the distribution of individual fund returns, as long as risk-taking is heterogeneous across funds.

In unreported tests, we measure the heterogeneity in risk-taking among all U.S. domestic equity mutual funds between 1975 and 2002. We find a heavily skewed distribution of risk-taking; most cluster together with similar levels of risk, while a significant minority of funds exhibit much higher levels of risk. In further unreported tests, we bootstrap the cross-section of fund alphas, where each fund is assumed to have residuals drawn from a normal distribution that has the same moments as those present in the actual (non-normal) fund residuals (using a four-factor model to estimate residuals).[4] The results show that the cross-section of bootstrapped alphas (assuming individual fund alpha normality) has thinner tails relative to a normal distribution, except in the extreme regions of the tails, which are thicker. Therefore, the heterogeneity in risk-taking that we observe in our fund sample generates many unusual non-normalities in the cross-section of alphas, even before considering any non-normalities in individual fund alphas.

It is important to note that similar cross-sectional effects will not result when we assess the distribution of the *t*-statistic of the fund alphas. Since the *t*-statistic normalizes by standard deviation, heterogeneity in risk-taking across funds, by itself, will not bring about non-normalities in the cross-section.[5] However, non-normalities in individual fund residuals—which, as we discuss in a later section, we find for about half of our funds—still imply non-normalities in the cross-section of *t* -statistics.[6]

Thus, many factors, including cross-sectional differences in sample size (fund lives) and risk-taking, as well as fat tails and skews in the individual fund residuals, influence the shape of the distribution of alphas across funds. Given the

---

[4] During each bootstrap iteration, 336 draws (with replacement) are made from a normal distribution with the same mean and variance as each fund's actual four-factor model residuals, and the fund alpha for that iteration is measured as the average of these residuals. This generates one cross-sectional alpha outcome. We repeat this process 1,000 times.

[5] In fact, this points to the superior properties of the *t*-statistic relative to the alpha itself; because of these superior properties, we use this measure extensively in our bootstrap tests in later sections.

[6] For example, suppose that funds have IID thick-tailed residuals that (for each fund) are drawn from a mixture of two normal distributions. The first distribution represents a "high volatility" state, with a standard deviation of three and a probability of 10%, and the second represents a "normal" state, with a standard deviation of 1/3 and a probability of 90% (i.e., the average residual variance remains at unity for each fund). In this case, the cross-sectional distribution of *t*-statistics is thin-tailed relative to a normal, even though the individual fund residuals are fat-tailed. More complex effects, such as small positive correlations in the tails of the residual distributions (across funds) and small negative correlations in the central part of the residual distributions (to yield an overall correlation of zero between funds) can also change the cross-sectional tail probabilities in unexpected ways.

possible interactions among these effects and the added complexity arising from parameter estimation errors, it is very difficult, using an *ex ante* imposed distribution, to credibly evaluate the significance of the observed alphas of funds, since the quantiles of the standard normal distribution and those of the bootstrap need not be the same in the center, shoulders, tails, and extreme tails. Instead, the bootstrap is required for proper inference involving the cross-sectional distribution of fund performance outcomes.

To summarize, it is only in the very special case in which:

1. the residuals of fund returns are drawn from a multivariate normal distribution,
2. correlations in these residuals are zero,
3. funds have identical risk levels, and
4. there is no parameter estimation error, that guarantees that the standard critical values of the normal distribution are appropriate in the cross-section. In all other cases, the cross-section will be a complicated mixture of individual fund return distributions, and must be evaluated with the bootstrap.[7]

6.2.2 Implementation Example: U.S. Domestic Equity Mutual Funds

In this example implementation, we consider two test statistics, namely, the estimated alpha, $\widehat{\alpha}$, and the estimated *t*-statistic of $\widehat{\alpha}, \widehat{t_{\alpha}}$. Note that $\widehat{\alpha}$ measures the economic size of abnormal performance, but suffers from a potential lack of precision in the construction of confidence intervals, whereas $\widehat{t_{\alpha}}$ is a pivotal statistic with better sampling properties.[8] In addition, $\widehat{t_{\alpha}}$ has another very attractive statistical property. Specifically, a fund that has a short life or engages in high risk-taking will have a high variance-estimated alpha distribution, and thus alphas for these funds will tend to be spurious outliers in the cross-section. In addition, these funds tend to be smaller funds that are more likely to be subject to survival bias, raising the concern that the extreme right tail of the cross-section of fund alphas is inflated. The *t*-statistic provides a correction for these spurious outliers by normalizing the estimated alpha by the estimated variance of the alpha estimate. Furthermore, the cross-sectional distribution of *t*-statistics has better properties than the cross-section of alphas, in the presence of heterogeneous fund volatilities due to differing fund risk levels or lifespans. For these reasons, we propose an alternate bootstrap that is conducted using $\widehat{t_{\alpha}}$, rather than $\widehat{\alpha}$. Indeed, the bulk of our tests in this chapter apply to the *t*-statistic.

We apply our bootstrap procedure to monthly mutual fund returns using several models of performance proposed by the past literature. These include the

[7] In addition, refinements of the bootstrap (which we implement in Section 6.5) provide a general approach for dealing with unknown time-series dependencies that are due, for example, to heteroskedasticity or serial correlation in the residuals from performance regressions. These bootstrap refinements also address the estimation of cross-sectional correlations in regression residuals, thus avoiding the estimation of a very large covariance matrix for these residuals.

[8] A pivotal statistic is one that is not a function of nuisance parameters, such as $Var(\varepsilon_{it})$.

simple one-factor model of Jensen (1968), the three-factor model of Fama and French (1993), the timing models of Treynor and Mazuy (1966) and Merton and Henriksson (1981), and several models that include conditional factors based on the papers of Ferson and Schadt (1996) and Christopherson et al. (1998). We present results for two representative models in this chapter; however results for all other models are consistent with those presented.[9] The first model, the main model that we present in this chapter, is the Carhart (1997) four-factor regression

$$r_{i,t} = \alpha_i + \beta_i \cdot RMRF_t + s_i \cdot SMB_t + h_i \cdot HML_t + u_i \cdot UMD_t + \varepsilon_{i,t}, \quad (6.1)$$

where $r_{i,t}$ is the month-t excess return on managed portfolio (net return minus T-bill return), $RMRF_t$ is the month-t excess return on a value-weighted aggregate market proxy portfolio, and SMB_t, HML_t, and UMD_t are the month-t returns on value-weighted, zero-investment factor-mimicking portfolios for size, book-to-market equity, and one-year momentum in stock returns, respectively.

The second representative model is a conditional version of the four-factor model that controls for time-varying $RMRF_t$ loadings by a mutual fund, using the technique of Ferson and Schadt (1996). Hence, the second model extends Equation (6.1) as follows:

$$\begin{aligned} r_{i,t} =& \alpha_i + \beta_i \cdot RMRF_t + s_i \cdot SMB_t + h_i \cdot HML_t + u_i \cdot UMD_t \\ &+ \sum_{j=1}^{K} B_{i,j}[z_{j,t-1} \cdot RMRF_t] + \varepsilon_{i,t} \end{aligned} \quad , \quad (6.2)$$

where $z_{j,t-1} = Z_{j,t-1} - E(Z_j)$, the end of month- $t-1$ deviation of public information variable j from its time-series mean, and $B_{i,j}$ is the fund's "beta response" to the predictive value of $z_{j,t-1}$ in forecasting the following month's excess market return, $RMRF_t$. This model computes the alpha of a managed portfolio, controlling for strategies that dynamically tilt the portfolio's beta in response to the predictable component of market returns.[10]

---

[9] Kosowski et al. (2006) consider 15 different models. In all cases, results are similar to those we present in this chapter. The two representative models that we present are the "best fit" models, according to standard model selection criteria, such as the Schwarz Information Criterion.

[10] We also use model selection criteria to choose the conditioning variables for our representative conditional model. The result, according to this criterion, is that the dividend yield (alone) is the conditioning variable for the preferred model; therefore, the results that we present use $K = 1$. However, we find that results similar to those presented hold for other versions of the conditional model, including a model that uses four conditioning variables as potentially holding predictive value for each of the four factors of the model. Specifically, we consider the following public information variables: (1) the short interest rate, measured as the lagged level of the one-month Treasury bill yield; (2) the dividend yield, measured as the lagged total cash dividends on the value-weighted CRSP index over the previous 12 months divided by the lagged level of the index; (3) the term spread, measured as the lagged yield on a constant-maturity 10-year Treasury bond less the lagged yield on three-month Treasury bills; and (4) the default spread, measured as the lagged yield difference between bonds rated BAA by Moodys and bonds rated AAA. These variables have been shown to be useful for predicting stock returns and risks over time (see, for example, Pesaran and Timmermann (1995)).

We now illustrate the bootstrap implementation with the Carhart (1997) four-factor model of Equation (6.1). The application of the bootstrap procedure to other models is very similar, with the only modification of the following steps being the substitution of the appropriate benchmark model of performance.

To prepare for our bootstrap procedure, we use the Carhart model to compute ordinary least squares (OLS)-estimated alphas, factor loadings, and residuals using the time series of monthly net returns (minus the T-bill rate) for fund i (r_{it}):

$$r_{it} = \widehat{\alpha}_i + \widehat{\beta}_i RMRF_t + \widehat{s}_i SMB_t + \widehat{h}_i HML_t + \widehat{u}_i UMD_t + \widehat{\epsilon}_{i,t}. \tag{6.3}$$

For fund i, the coefficient estimates, $\{\widehat{\alpha}_i, \widehat{\beta}_i, \widehat{s}_i, \widehat{h}_i, \widehat{u}_i\}$, as well as the time series of estimated residuals, $\{\widehat{\epsilon}_{i,t}, t = T_{i0}, \ldots, T_{i1}\}$, and the t-statistic of alpha, $\widehat{t_{\alpha_i}}$, are saved, where T_{i0} and T_{i1} are the dates of the first and last monthly returns available for fund i, respectively.

6.2.2.1 *The Baseline Bootstrap Procedure: Residual Resampling*

Using our baseline bootstrap, for each fund i, we draw a sample with replacement from the fund residuals that are saved in the first step above, creating a pseudo time series of resampled residuals, $\{\widehat{\epsilon}^b_{i,t_\varepsilon}, t_\varepsilon = s^b_{T_{i0}}, \ldots, s^b_{T_{i1}}\}$, where b is an index for the bootstrap number (so $b = 1$ for bootstrap resample number one), and where each of the time indices $s^b_{T_{i0}}, \ldots, s^b_{T_{i1}}$ are drawn randomly from $[T_{i0}, \ldots, T_{i1}]$ in such a way that this reorders the original sample of $T_{i1} - T_{i0} + 1$ residuals for fund i. Conversely, the original chronological ordering of the factor returns is unaltered; we relax this restriction in a different version of our bootstrap in Section 6.5.

Next, we construct a time series of pseudo-monthly excess returns for this fund, imposing the null hypothesis of zero true performance ($\alpha_i = 0$, or, equivalently, $\widehat{t_{\alpha_i}} = 0$):

$$\{r^b_{i,t} = \widehat{\beta}_i RMRF_t + \widehat{s}_i SMB_t + \widehat{h}_i HML_t + \widehat{u}_i UMD_t + \widehat{\epsilon}^b_{i,t_\varepsilon}\}, \tag{6.4}$$

for $t = T_{i0}, \ldots T_{i1}$ and $t_\varepsilon = s^b_{T_{i0}}, \ldots, s^b_{T_{i1}}$. As Equation (6.4) indicates, this sequence of artificial returns has a true alpha (and t-statistic of alpha) that is zero by construction. However, when we next regress the returns for a given bootstrap sample, b, on the Carhart factors, a positive estimated alpha (and t-statistic) may result, since that bootstrap may have drawn an abnormally high number of positive residuals, or, conversely, a negative alpha (and t-statistic) may result if an abnormally high number of negative residuals are drawn.

Repeating the above steps across all funds $i = 1, \ldots, N$, we arrive at a draw from the cross-section of bootstrapped alphas. Repeating this for all bootstrap iterations, $b = 1, \ldots, 1,000$, we then build the distribution of these cross-sectional draws of alphas, $\{\widehat{\alpha}^b_i, i = 1, \ldots, N\}$, or their t-statistics, $\{\widehat{t}^b_{\widehat{\alpha}_i}, i = 1, \ldots, N\}$, that result purely from sampling variation, while imposing the null of a true alpha that is equal to zero. For example, the distribution of alphas (or t-statistics) for the top fund is constructed as the distribution of the maximum alpha (or, maximum t-statistic) generated across all bootstraps.[11] As we note in Section 6.2.1.2, this cross-sectional distribution can be non-normal, even if individual fund alphas are normally distributed. If we find that our bootstrap iterations generate far fewer extreme positive values of $\widehat{\alpha}$ (or $\widehat{t_{\alpha}}$) compared to those observed in the actual data, then we conclude that sampling variation (luck) is not the sole source of high alphas, but rather that genuine stockpicking skills actually exist.

6.2.2.2 *Bootstrap Extensions*

We implement some other straightforward extensions of this bootstrap for our universe of funds as well. These extensions, which we describe in more detail in Section 6.5, include simultaneous residual and factor resampling, as well as a procedure that demonstrates that our results are robust to the presence of a potential omitted factor in our models. We also allow for the possibility of cross-sectional dependence among fund residuals that may be due, for example, to funds holding similar (or the same) stocks at the same time. That is, funds with very high measured alphas might have similar holdings. In addition, we implement a procedure that allows for the possibility that the residuals are correlated over time for a given fund, perhaps due to time-series patterns in stock returns that are not properly specified by our performance models.

6.3 DATA

We examine monthly returns from the Center for Research in Security Prices (CRSP) mutual fund files. The CRSP database contains monthly data on net returns for each shareclass of every open-end mutual fund since January 1, 1962, with no minimum survival requirement for funds to be included. Further details on this mutual fund database are available from CRSP.

Our final database contains fund-level monthly net returns data on 2,118 U.S. open-end domestic equity funds that existed for at least a portion of the period from January 31, 1975 to December 31, 2002. We study the performance of the full sample of funds, as well as funds in each investment objective category. Namely, our sample consists of aggressive-growth funds (285), growth funds (1,227), growth-and-income funds (396), and balanced or income funds (210).[12] Since balanced funds and income funds allocate a significant fraction of assets to non-equity investments, we require that such funds hold at least 50% domestic equities during the majority of their existence to be included in our tests.

[11] Of course, this maximum alpha can potentially be associated with a different fund during each bootstrap iteration, depending on the outcome of the draw from each fund's residuals.

[12] This example combines income funds and balanced funds, as the number in each category is relatively small (and because funds in these two categories make similar investments). Descriptions of the types of investments made by funds in each category are available in Grinblatt et al. (1995).

6.4 RESULTS FOR U.S. EQUITY FUNDS

6.4.1 The Normality of Individual Fund Alphas

Before progressing to our bootstrap tests, we analyze (in unreported tests) the distribution of individual fund alphas generated by the models of Equations (6.1) and (6.2), as well as alphas generated by many other commonly used performance models. We find that normality is rejected for 48% of funds when using either the unconditional or conditional four-factor model; similar results are obtained with all other models that we test. Moreover, we also find that the rejections tend to be very large for many of the funds, especially funds with extreme estimated alphas (either positive or negative). This strong finding of non-normal alpha estimates challenges the validity of earlier research that relies on the normality assumption: In turn, this challenge to standard *t*- and *F*-tests of the significance of fund alphas strongly indicates the need to bootstrap, especially in the tails, to determine whether significant estimated alphas are due, at least in part, to manager skills, or to luck alone. As we apply our bootstrap in the following sections, we will highlight the significant changes in inference that result, relative to the normality assumption.

6.4.2 Bootstrap Analysis of the Significance of Alpha Outliers

We first apply our baseline residual resampling method, described in Section 6.2.2.1, to analyze the significance of mutual fund alphas. In these tests, we rank all mutual funds that have at least 60 months of return observations during the 1975 to 2002 period on their model alphas. It is important to note that, in all of our bootstrap results to come, for each ranked fund we compare *p*-values generated from our cross-sectional bootstrap with standard *p*-values that correspond to the *t*-statistics of these individual ranked funds—these individual fund *t*-tests, of course, do not consider the joint nature of the ex post sorting that we implement. As we discuss in Section 6.2.1, the cross-sectional nature of our bootstrap, along with its ability to model nonnormalities in fund alphas, provides benefits over the casual use of standard *t*-tests applied to individual funds. Since investors and researchers usually examine funds without considering the joint nature of ex post sorts, we use this approach to inference as a benchmark against which to compare the bootstrap. As we will see, in many cases the bootstrap provides substantially different conclusions about the significance of individual ranked-fund performance.

6.4.2.1 *Baseline Bootstrap Tests: Residual Resampling*

Panel A of Table 6.1 shows several points in the resulting cross-section of alphas (using the unconditional and conditional four-factor models of Equations (6.1) and (6.2)), and presents bootstrapped *p*-values ("Cross-sectionally bootstrapped *p*-value"), as well as standard *p*-values that correspond to the *t*-statistic of the individual fund at each percentile point of the distribution ("Parametric (standard) *p*-value"). For example, consistent with the results of Carhart,

1997, the median fund in our sample has an unconditional four-factor alpha of −0.1% per month (−1.2%, annualized), while the bottom and top funds have alpha estimates of −3.6% and 4.2% per month, respectively.[13] Also, as further examples, the fifth-ranked fund and the fund at the one-percentile point in our sample have alphas of 1.3% and 1% per month, respectively.[14] Ranking funds by their *conditional* four-factor alphas of Equation 6.2 results in alphas and p-values (both cross-sectionally bootstrapped and parametric normal) that are remarkably similar to those from the unconditional four-factor alpha sort. This finding indicates that mutual funds do not substantially time the overall market factor according to the level of the lagged dividend yield on the market portfolio. Therefore, for the remainder of this chapter, we present results only for the unconditional four-factor model; however, in all cases, the conditional four-factor model exhibits similar results.

Overall, the results in Panel A show that funds with alphas ranked in the top decile (10th-percentile and above) generally exhibit significant bootstrapped p-values, whether we use the unconditional or conditional four-factor model. However, this is not always the case. For example, the second-ranked fund under the unconditional model displays a large but insignificant alpha; this alpha simply is insufficiently large to reject (based on the empirical distribution of alphas) the hypothesis that the manager achieved it through luck alone. Thus, our bootstrap highlights that extreme alphas are not always significant, and that the bootstrap is important in testing for significance in the tails, which can have quite complex distributional properties.

No funds between (and including) the 20th-percentile and the median exhibit alphas sufficient to beat their benchmarks, net of costs, using either the unconditional or conditional versions of the four-factor model. When we examine funds below the median, using a null hypothesis that these funds do not underperform their benchmarks (net of costs), we find that all bootstrapped p-values strongly reject this null. This finding of significantly negative alphas for below-median funds indicates that these funds may very well be inferior to low-cost index funds. In unreported results (available from the authors upon request), we arrive at the same conclusions with all other performance models, including complex models with both market timing measures and multiple risk factors.

---

[13] This top-ranked fund is the Schroeder Ultra Fund, which the media prominently featured as a fund with extraordinary performance. Although the fund eventually closed to new investments, there were many cases of investors wishing to purchase some shares from current shareholders at exorbitant prices in order to be allowed to add further to those holdings, which was allowed by this fund.

[14] As an example, the cross-sectionally bootstrapped p-value of 0.02 is the probability that the fifth-ranked fund (from repeated *ex post* alpha sorts) generates an estimated alpha of at least 1.3% per month, purely by sampling variation (i.e., with a true alpha of zero). In contrast, the parametric (standard) p-value of 0.01 for this fund is obtained from a simple t-test for this estimated alpha, without regard to the rank of this fund in the cross-section.

Table 6.1 The Cross-Section of Mutual Fund Alphas

In Panel A of this table, all U.S. open-end domestic equity funds that have at least 60 monthly net return observations during the 1975 to 2002 period are ranked on their four-factor alpha. The first to third rows report results when funds are ranked on their unconditional four-factor alphas. The fourth to sixth rows report results when funds are ranked on their conditional four-factor alphas. In Panel A, the first and second rows report the OLS estimate of alphas (in percent per month) and the cross-sectionally bootstrapped p-values of the alphas. For comparison, the third row reports the *p*-values of the *t*-statistic of alphas based on standard critical values of the *t*-statistic. The fourth and fifth rows of Panel A report conditional alphas (in percent per month) and the cross-sectionally bootstrapped *p*-values of conditional alphas. The sixth row reports the *p*-values of the *t*-statistic of alphas, based on standard critical values of the *t-statistic*. In Panel B, all U.S. open-end domestic equity funds that have at least 60 monthly net return observations during the 1975 to 2002 period are ranked on the *t-statistics* of their four-factor alpha (first row). The second row of Panel B shows the cross-sectionally boot*strapped p*-values of the *t*-statistics. For comparison, the third row shows the *p*-values of the *t*-statistic based on standard critical values. Rows four to six show results when funds are ranked based on the *t*-statistic of their conditional four-factor model alpha. Rows four and five report the *t*-statistics of the conditional alpha and the cross-sectionally bootstrapped *p*-value of the *t*-statistic. Row six shows the *p*-values of the *t*-statistic of the conditional alphas, based on standard critical values. In each panel, the first columns on the *left* (right) report results for funds with the five lowest (highest) alphas or *t*-statistics, followed by results for marginal funds at different percentiles in the left (right) tail of the distribution. The cross-sectionally bootstrapped *p*-value is based on the distribution of the best (worst) funds in 1,000 bootstrap resamples. The *t*-statistics of alpha are based on heteroskedasticity- and autocorrelation-consistent standard errors.

	Bottom	2.	3.	4.	5.	1%	3%	5%	10%	20%	30%	40%	Median	40%	30%	20%	10%	5%	3%	1%	5.	4.	3.	2.	Top
Panel A: Funds Ranked on Four-Factor Model Alphas																									
Unconditional Alpha (Pct/Month)	−3.6	−2.7	−2.0	−1.7	−1.5	−0.8	−0.6	−0.5	−0.4	−0.2	−0.2	−0.1	−0.1	0.0	0.1	0.1	0.3	0.4	0.6	1.0	1.3	1.4	1.5	1.6	4.2
Cross-Sectionally Bootstrapped *p*-Value	0.04	<0.01	<0.01	<0.01	<0.01	0.02	<0.01	<0.01	<0.01	<0.01	<0.01	<0.01		1.00	1.00	0.99	0.02	<0.01	<0.01	<0.01	0.02	0.06	0.08	0.19	0.02
Parametric (Standard) *p*-Value	0.04	<0.01	<0.01	<0.01	<0.01	<0.01	0.06	0.01	0.09	<0.01	0.40	0.36		0.50	0.31	0.29	0.12	0.03	0.03	0.01	0.01	<0.01	0.12	0.01	<0.01
Conditional Alpha (Pct/Month)	−4.8	−2.2	−2.0	−1.9	−1.8	−1.0	−0.6	−0.5	−0.4	−0.3	−0.2	−0.1	−0.1	0.0	0.0	0.1	0.3	0 .4	0.6	1.1	1.4	1.5	1.6	1.8	4.2
Cross-Sectionally Bootstrapped *p*-Value	<0.01	0.01	<0.01	<0.01	<0.01	<0.01	<0.01	<0.01	<0.01	<0.01	<0.01	<0.01		1	1	0.88	<0.01	<0.01	<0.01	<0.01	0.01	0.02	0.05	0.09	0.01
Parametric (Standard) *p*-Value	0.01	<0.01	<0.01	<0.01	<0.01	<0.01	0.01	0.05	0.03	0.02	0.12	0.37		0.58	0.40	0.13	0.25	0.09	0.02	0.02	0.15	<0.01	0.01	0.01	<0.01

Panel B: Funds Ranked on the t-Statistics of Four-Factor Model Alphas																									
t-Unconditional Alpha	−7.9	−6.1	−6.0	−4.8	−4.5	−3.6	−3.0	−2.4	−1.9	−1.4	−0.9	−0.6	−0.4	0.0	0.3	0.8	1.4	2.0	2.3	2.8	3.5	3.5	4.1	4.2	6.6
Cross-Sectionally Bootstrapped p-Value	<0.01	<0.01	<0.01	<0.01	<0.01	<0.01	<0.01	<0.01	<0.01	<0.01	<0.01	<0.01		1.00	1.00	1.00	0.25	<0.01	<0.01	<0.01	0.04	0.08	0.01	0.03	<0.01
Parametric (Standard) p-Value	<0.01	<0.01	<0.01	<0.01	<0.01	<0.01	<0.01	0.01	0.03	0.09	0.17	0.26		0.49	0.37	0.23	0.09	0.03	0.01	<0.01	<0.01	<0.01	<0.01	<0.01	<0.01
t-Conditional Alpha	−8.5	−5.8	−5.8	−5.7	−5.2	−3.8	−3.2	−2.7	−2.1	−1.6	−1.1	−0.7	−0.4	−0.1	0.3	0.8	1.4	2.0	2.3	2.9	3.5	3.7	3.9	4.6	5.8
Cross-Sectionally Bootstrapped p-Value	<0.01	<0.01	<0.01	<0.01	<0.01	<0.01	<0.01	<0.01	<0.01	<0.01	<0.01	<0.01		1.00	1.00	1.00	0.04	<0.01	<0.01	<0.01	0.01	0.02	0.02	0.01	0.01
Parametric (Standard) p-Value	<0.01	<0.01	<0.01	<0.01	<0.01	<0.01	<0.01	<0.01	0.02	0.06	0.13	0.23		0.55	0.40	0.22	0.08	0.03	0.01	<0.01	<0.01	<0.01	<0.01	<0.01	<0.01

As we discuss in Section 6.2, we also rank according to a second measure of fund performance, the *t*-statistic for the estimated alpha.[15] Again, the *t*-statistic has some advantageous statistical properties when constructing bootstrapped cross-sectional distributions, since it scales alpha by its standard error (which tends to be larger for shorter-lived funds and for funds that take higher levels of risk). In addition, it is related to the Treynor and Black (1973) information ratio (discussed in Chapter 3), which is prescribed by Brown et al. (1992) for helping to mitigate survival bias problems. Thus, the distribution of bootstrapped *t*-statistics in the tails is likely to exhibit better properties (fewer problems with high variance or survival bias) than the distribution of bootstrapped alpha estimates in that region.

Panel B presents results for funds ranked by their *t*-statistics. In general, right-tail funds continue to exhibit significant performance under a *t*-statistic ranking, as they do in the alpha ranking of Panel A. Most importantly, note that our inference about fund manager talent is somewhat different with the cross-sectional bootstrap than with the standard parametric normal assumption applied to individual fund alpha distributions ("Parametric (standard) *p*-value" in Panel B).[16] Namely, most of the top five funds have bootstrapped *p*-values that are higher than their parametric *p*-values, for both unconditional and conditional model alpha *t*-statistics. In this extreme right tail of the cross-section, the bootstrap uncovers more probability mass (a fatter extreme right tail) than expected under a parametric normal assumption as a result of the complex interaction between non-normal individual fund alphas as well as the complexity of the mixture of these distributions imposed by the cross-sectional draws. The same applies to funds closer to the median. For example, the standard parametric *p*-value for the *t*-statistic (the one-tailed *p*-value for $t = 1.4$ is roughly 9%) indicates that the fund at the 10th-percentile exhibits a significant *t*-statistic, under the unconditional four-factor model. However, the bootstrap does not find this *t*-statistic to be significant, and does not reject the null of no manager talent at the 10th-percentile (this *p*-value equals 25%).

To explore further, Figure 6.1 presents distributions of unconditional four-factor alphas for funds at various points in the cross-section. For example, Panel A1 shows the bootstrapped distribution of the alpha of the bottom-ranked fund across all bootstrap iterations. While the mode of this distribution lies at roughly -1.7% per month, bootstrapped alphas vary from about -1% per month to

---

[15] Reported *t*-statistics use Newey and West (1987) heteroskedasticity- and autocorrelation-consistent standard errors.

[16] Again, in addition to their normality assumption, one should note that these individual fund parametric *p*-values do not account for the ex post, cross-sectional nature of our ranking of funds. For instance, one would not conclude that the three-percentile fund shown in Panel A has a significant alpha simply because its *p*-value is 3%—this would be expected in the absence of any true alpha under an assumption of IID multivariate normal fund returns. However, since ex post individual fund *p*-values are often used to infer talent (rather than a full cross-sectional test statistic across funds), we compare the inference under the cross-sectional bootstrap with this often-used approach.

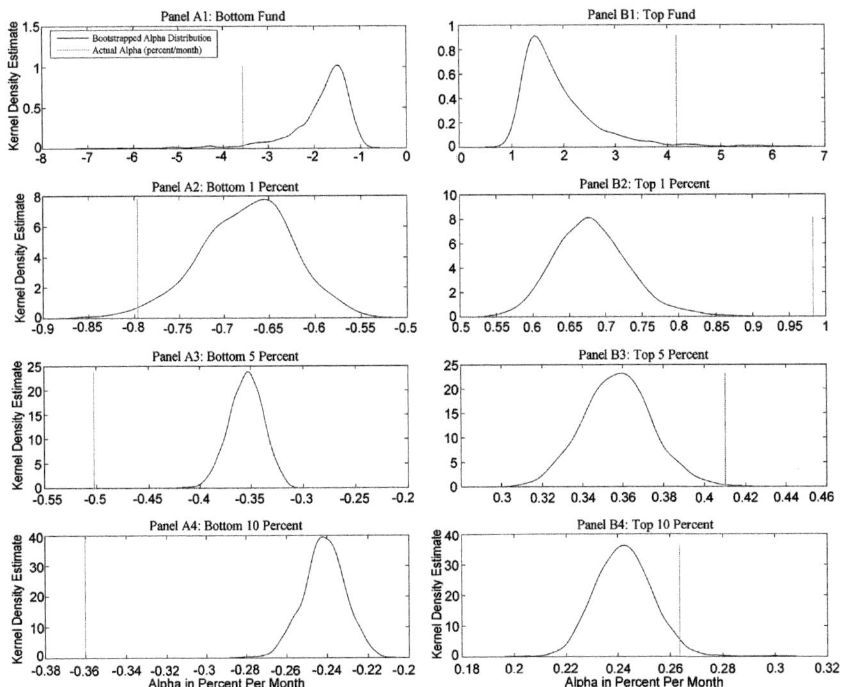

FIGURE 6.1
Estimated alphas vs. bootstrapped alpha distributions for individual funds at various percentile points in the cross-section. This figure plots kernel density estimates of the bootstrapped unconditional four-factor model alpha distribution (solid line) for all U.S. equity funds with at least 60 monthly net return observations during the 1975 to 2002 period. The x-axis shows the alpha performance measure in percent per month, and the y-axis shows the kernel density estimate. The dashed vertical line represents the actual (estimated) fund alpha. Panels A1–A4 show marginal funds in the left tail of the distribution. Panels B1–B4 show marginal funds in the right tail of the distribution. For example, 'Top 1 Percent' in Panel B2 refers to the marginal alpha at the top one percentile of the distribution.

(in rare cases) less than −6% per month. It is easy to see that the actual bottom-fund (estimated) alpha of −3.6% per month (the dashed line in Panel A1) lies well within the left-tail rejection region of the distribution; this rejection is so strong, that a standard t-test also rejects it. However, Panel B4 gives a case in which the bootstrap rejects the null, while the simple t-test does not. In general, as we proceed to the center of the cross-sectional distribution (Panels A1 to A4 and Panels B1 to B4), alpha distributions become more symmetric, but remain markedly non-normal.

As we noted earlier, the extreme deviation from normality that we observe in the extreme top and bottom funds, as ranked by alpha (Panels A1 and B1), is due to those positions generally being occupied by funds that have very risky strategies. This motivates our t-statistic ranking procedure shown in Panel B of Table 6.1. However, we find that bootstrapped t-statistics for funds at various points

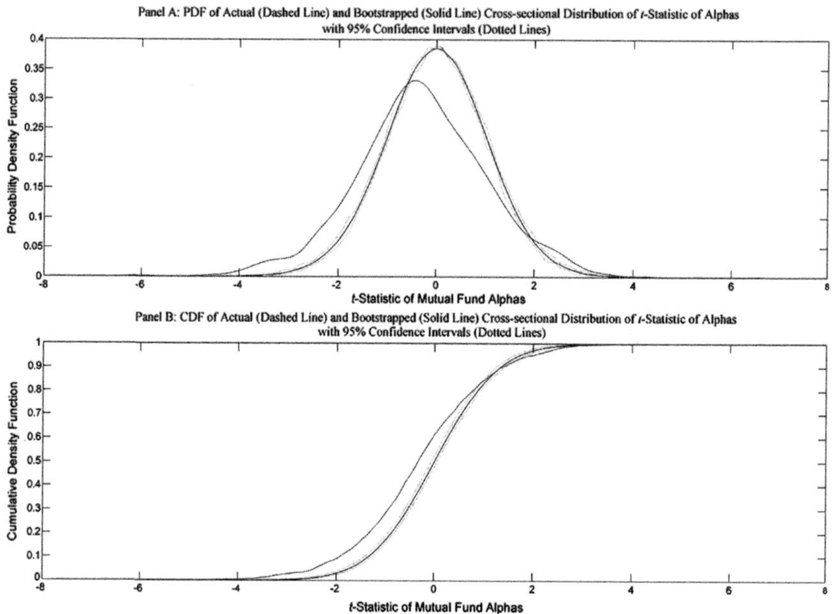

FIGURE 6.2
Estimated vs. bootstrapped cross-section of alpha t-statistics. This figure plots kernel density estimates of the actual (dashed line) and bootstrapped (solid line) cross-sectional distributions of the t-statistic of mutual fund alphas. Panel A shows the kernel density estimate of the probability density function (PDF) of the distributions, and Panel B the kernel density estimate of the cumulative density function (CDF) of the distributions. The alpha estimates are based on the unconditional four-factor model applied to all U.S. equity funds with at least 60 monthly net return observations during the 1975 to 2002 period. The dotted lines give 95% confidence intervals of the bootstrapped distribution.

in the cross-sectional distribution also deviate substantially from normality, as Figure 6.2 illustrates.

Panel A of Figure 6.2 compares the cross-sectional distribution of actual fund t-statistic estimates with the distribution generated by the bootstrap.[17] The two densities in Panel A have quite different shapes. In particular, the distribution of actual t-statistics has more probability mass in the left and right tails, and far less mass in the center, than the bootstrapped distribution. However, this is not the whole story—the distribution of actual t-statistics also exhibits several complex features such as "shoulders" in the tail regions. Thus, our bootstrap inference is different from that based on the normality assumption, not simply because the

[17] The distributions are smoothed with a kernel density estimator. This estimator replaces the "boxes" in a histogram by "bumps" that are smooth, and the kernel function is a weighting function that determines the shape of the bumps. We generate the plot using a Gaussian kernel function. The optimal bandwidth controls the smoothness of the density estimate, and is calculated according to Silverman (1986).

bootstrap more adequately measures fat or thin tails of the actual distribution, but also because the bootstrap more adequately captures the complex shape of the entire cross-sectional distribution of t-statistics (and, especially that of the tails) under the null. The 95% standard error bands around the bootstrapped distribution confirm that the differences between the two distributions are statistically significant.

Overall, this figure illustrates that our sample of funds generates actual t-statistics that have a very non-normal cross-sectional distribution, and that the tails of this actual distribution are not well-explained by random sampling error (which is represented by the bootstrapped distribution). These observations reinforce our prior evidence that many superior and inferior funds exist in our sample. Since our interest is the actual number of funds that exceed a certain level of alpha compared to the bootstrapped distribution, we plot the cumulative density function in Panel B. The results confirm our observations from Panel A that in the far right tail, the actual probability distribution has more weight than the bootstrapped distribution. In addition, as Panel B of Table 6.1 indicates, t-statistics above 1.96 are generally significant, which results in the actual cumulative density function lying below the bootstrapped cumulative density function in that region.

We can also use the bootstrapped distribution of alphas to calculate how many funds (out of the total set of funds with a track record of at least five years) would be expected, by chance alone, to exceed a given level of performance. This number can be compared to the number of funds that actually exceed this level of performance in our sample. Panel A of Figure 6.3 plots the cumulative number of funds from the original and (imputed) from the bootstrapped distribution that perform above each level of alpha, while Panel B plots the cumulative numbers that perform below each level. For example, Panel A indicates that nine funds should have an alpha estimate higher than 10% per year by chance, whereas in reality, 29 funds achieve this alpha, and Panel B indicates that 128 funds exhibit an alpha estimate less than −5% per year, compared to an expected number of 63 funds by chance.

Overall, the results in this section provide strong evidence that many of the extreme funds in our sample exhibit significant positive (or negative) alphas and alpha t-statistics. For example, Panel A of Figure 6.3 indicates that, among the subgroup of fund managers that have an alpha greater than 7% per year over a five-year (or longer) period, about half have stockpicking talent sufficient to exceed their costs, while the other half are simply lucky.

To evaluate the overall potential economic impact of our findings, we approximated the value-added of skilled managers. This is important as, for example, our bootstrap-based evidence of skill might occur primarily among small mutual funds, which might tend to lie further in the tails of the alpha distribution. If so, then our results may not have significant implications for the average investor in actively managed mutual funds. To address this issue, we measure economic impact by examining the difference in value-added between all funds that have a

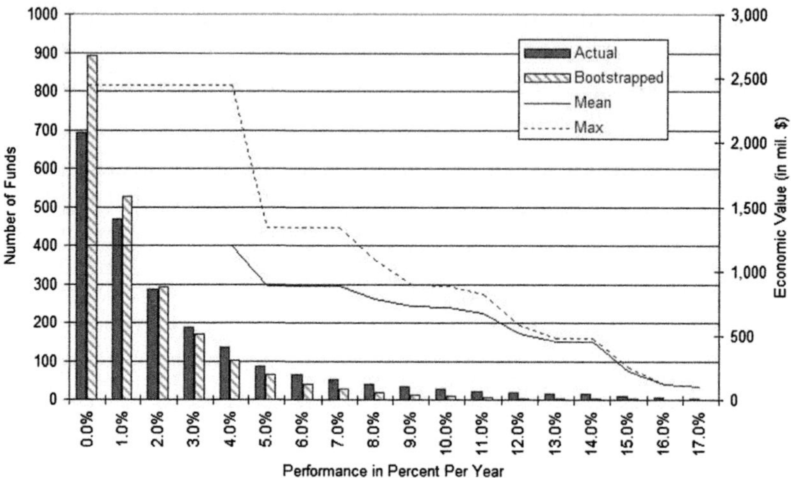

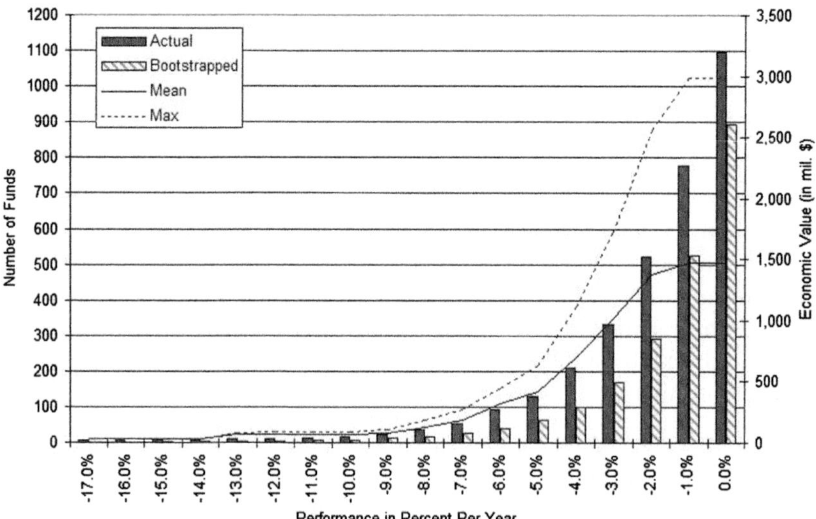

FIGURE 6.3

Cumulative economic value-added by funds above (or below) various alpha levels. This figure presents the number of funds from the original and the bootstrapped cross-sectional distributions (as vertical bars) that surpass (Panel A) or lie below (Panel B) various unconditional four-factor alpha levels. In Panel A, the solid and dashed lines show the cumulative economic value that a hypothetical investor could potentially gain by investing in the difference between the actual and the bootstrapped number of funds in all higher performance brackets. The solid (dashed) line is based on the average (average of a subgroup of the largest funds) total net assets in each performance bracket. In Panel B, the solid and dashed lines show the cumulative value that is potentially lost by the statistically significant underperformance of some funds. The results are based on all U.S. equity funds in our sample between 1975 and 2002 with a minimum of 60 monthly net return observations.

certain level of performance, including lucky and skilled funds, and those funds that achieve the same level of performance due to luck alone (estimated by the bootstrap); this difference estimates skill-based value-added.[18] Panels A and B of Figure 6.3 show the cumulative value-added (value-destroyed) above (below) each point in the alpha distribution. As the figure depicts, we estimate that about \$1.2 billion per year in wealth is generated (see "Mean"), in excess of expenses and trading costs, through true active management skills by funds in the right tail of the cross-section of alphas over the 1975 to 2002 period. By contrast, truly underperforming left-tail funds destroy a total of \$1.5 billion per year by their inability to compensate for fees and trading costs. It should be noted that wealth created in a typical year exceeds wealth destroyed by a greater ratio than these figures, as the average outperforming fund in our sample tends to be longer-lived (and our estimate assumes that all funds in our sample exist in a "typical" year).

One should note, however, that many issues could complicate the interpretation of our baseline bootstrap results above. For example, funds may have cross-sectionally correlated residuals. If so, this could bias our bootstrap results, which (so far) have rested on the assumption of independent residuals. We explore these and other concerns in Section 6.5 of this chapter.

6.5 SENSITIVITY ANALYSIS

Next, we conduct an extensive set of resampling tests to determine the significance of alpha and *t*-statistic outliers. In this section, we test whether our results are sensitive to changes in the nature of the bootstrap procedure, to the assumed return-generating process, or to the set of mutual funds included in the bootstrap tests. In general, we show that our main findings in this chapter are robust to changes in these parameters.

6.5.1 Time-Series Dependence

Our bootstrap results assume that, conditional on the factor realizations, the residuals are independently and identically distributed. While this may seem to be a strong assumption, it allows for conditional dependence in returns through the time-series behavior of the factors. In addition, this simple bootstrap has some robustness properties that apply if the IID assumption is violated (see, for example, Hall (1992)).

---

[18] For example, as we mention, there are 29 funds with alpha estimates greater than or equal to 10% per year, while only nine funds are expected to exhibit such alphas by chance. To approximate the value-added of the additional 20 funds (since we do not know which 20 funds out of the 29 are skilled), we estimate value-added for a given 1% alpha interval as that level of alpha (e.g., 10% per year) multiplied by the average size of all funds lying in the same 1% per year alpha interval, multiplied by the difference between the total number of funds in that interval and the number of "lucky" funds (according to the bootstrap). These interval value-added estimates are cumulated for all alpha intervals above and including a given interval (e.g., the 10% interval), and these cumulative value-added estimates are presented in the graph. For further illustration, we repeat this computation using the average size of the largest funds in each alpha interval in case the 20 skilled funds are generally the largest funds (labeled "Max").

Nevertheless, as a robustness check, we explicitly allow for dependence in return residuals over time by adopting the stationary bootstrap suggested by Politis and Romano (1994), which resamples data blocks (returns) of random length. Specifically, the Politis and Romano approach draws a sequence of IID variables from a geometric distribution to determine the length of the blocks, and draws a sequence from a uniform distribution to arrange the blocks to yield a stationary pseudo-time series.

To explore the sensitivity of our results, we compare the bootstrap results under a block length of one monthly return (which is the same as our previous independent resampling) and for larger block lengths, up to a maximum block length of 10 monthly returns. In unreported results, we find that, with all block lengths greater than one, estimated alphas, *t*-statistics, and bootstrapped *p*-values are almost identical to the results from our baseline block length of one (see Section 6.4).

6.5.2 Residual and Factor Resampling

Next we implement a bootstrap with independent resampling of regression residuals and factor returns. This approach investigates whether randomizing factor returns changes our results, due, perhaps, to breaking a persistence (autocorrelation) in these factor returns.

When resampling factor returns, we use the same draw across all funds (to preserve the correlation effect of factor returns on all funds), giving (for bootstrap iteration b and fund i) independently resampled factors and residuals

$$\{RMRF_t^b, SMB_t^b, HML_t^b, UMD_t^b, t = \tau_{T_{i0}}^b, \ldots, \tau_{T_{i1}}^b\}\text{and}\{\widehat{\epsilon}_{i,t}^b, t = s_{T_{i0}}^b, \ldots, s_{T_{i1}}^b\}. \tag{6.5}$$

Next, for each bootstrap iteration b, we construct a time series of (bootstrapped) monthly net returns for fund i, again imposing the null hypothesis of zero true performance ($\alpha_i = 0$):

$$\{r_{i,t}^b = \widehat{\beta}_i RMRF_{t_F}^b + \widehat{s}_i SMB_{t_F}^b + \widehat{h}_i HML_{t_F}^b + \widehat{u}_i UMD_{t_F}^b + \widehat{\epsilon}_{i,t_\epsilon}^b\}, \tag{6.6}$$

for $t_F = \tau_{T_{i0}}^b, \ldots, \tau_{T_{i1}}^b$ and $t_\varepsilon = s_{T_{i0}}^b, \ldots, s_{T_{i1}}^b$, the independent time reorderings imposed by resampling the factor returns and residuals, respectively, in bootstrap iteration b. Again, in unreported results, we find that this approach exhibits almost identical results (for both left-tail and right-tail funds) to those of our residual-only approach in Section 6.4.

6.5.3 Cross-Sectional Bootstrap

In empirical tests, we find that the cross-sectional correlation between fund residuals is very low; the average residual correlation is 0.09 for the four-factor Carhart model. Nevertheless, we refine our bootstrap procedure to capture any potential cross-sectional correlation in residuals by implementing an extension that draws residuals, across all funds, during identical time periods. For example, funds may herd into, or otherwise hold the same stocks at the same time, inducing correlations in their residuals. This herding may be especially important in the tails of the cross-section of alphas.

In this procedure, rather than drawing sequences of time periods t_i that are unique to each fund i, we draw T time periods from the set $\{t = 1, \ldots, T\}$ and then resample residuals for this reindexed time sequence across *all* funds, thereby preserving any cross-sectional correlation in the residuals. Since, as a result, some funds may be allocated bootstrap index entries from periods when they did not exist or otherwise have a return observation, we drop a fund if it does not have at least 60 observations during the reindexed time sequence. Again, unreported tests show that these results are almost identical to our baseline results of Section 6.4.

6.5.4 Length of Data Records

Short-lived funds tend to generate higher dispersion and, therefore, more extreme alpha estimates, than long-lived funds. This leads to nontrivial heteroskedasticity in the cross-section of alpha estimates. In an attempt to correct for this effect, the baseline bootstrap results impose a minimum of 60 observations in order to exclude funds that are very short-lived; in addition, we base most tests on the t-statistic, which is less sensitive to these variance outliers. However, it is possible that this minimum return requirement may impose a survival bias on our results; bootstrapping may be less (or more) necessary for proper inference when we do not impose such a requirement.

To explore this concern, we vary the return requirement to include funds that have at least 18, 30, 90, and 120 months of observations, respectively. The results (not shown) strongly indicate that our inference about the tails of the performance distribution remains qualitatively similar as we move from a requirement of 18 monthly returns to a requirement of 120 returns. A requirement of 120 months eliminates the extreme left and right tails, but the bootstrap responds by moving deeper into the distribution to identify outperforming funds. Thus, the bootstrap performs consistently across different types of data inclusion rules.

6.5.5 Bootstrap Tests for Stockholdings-Based Alphas

We can also apply the bootstrap to analyze the portfolio-holdings-based alphas of Chapter 4. For instance, the "Characteristic-Selectivity Measure," computed by matching each stock held by a fund with a value-weighted portfolio of stocks that have similar size, book-to-market, and momentum characteristics, is given by:

$$CS_t = \sum_{j=1}^{N} \widetilde{w}_{j,t-1}(\widetilde{R}_{j,t} - \widetilde{R}_t^{b_{j,t-1}}), \tag{6.7}$$

where $\widetilde{w}_{j,t-1}$ is the portfolio weight on stock j at the end of month $t\text{–}1$, $\widetilde{R}_{j,t}$ is the month-t buy-and-hold return of stock j, and $\widetilde{R}_t^{b_{j,t-1}}$ is the month-t buy-and-hold return of the value-weighted matching benchmark portfolio. The construction of the benchmarks follows the procedure in Daniel et al. (1997).

This measure provides not only an analysis of fund returns before all costs, but also an alternative benchmarking approach. Specifically, if portfolios of certain

Table 6.2 The Cross-Section of Stockholdings-Based Performance Measures

In Panel A, all U.S. open-end domestic equity funds that have holdings available for at least five years during the 1975 to 2002 period are ranked on the CS measure introduced by Daniel et al., 1997. The first and second rows of Panel A report the CS measures (in percent per month) and the cross-sectionally bootstrapped *p*-values of the CS measures. For comparison, the third row reports the *p*-values of the *t*-statistic of the CS measures based on standard critical values of the *t*-statistic. In rows four to six funds are ranked on the *t*-statistics of their CS measures. The fourth row shows the *t*-statistics. The fifth row reports the cross-sectionally bootstrapped *p*-values of the *t*-statistic. For comparison, the sixth row shows the *p*-values of the *t*-statistic, based on standard critical values. Panels B, C, D, and E report the same measures as Panel A but for growth, aggressive growth, growth and income, and balanced or income funds, respectively. In each panel, the first columns on the left (right) report results for funds with the five lowest (highest) CS measures or *t*-statistics, followed by results for marginal funds at different percentiles in the left (right) tail of the distribution. The cross-sectionally bootstrapped *p* -value is based on the distribution of the best (worst) funds in 1,000 bootstrap resamples. The *t*-statistics of the CS measure are based on heteroskedasticity- and autocorrelation-consistent standard errors.

	Bottom	2.	3.	4.	5.	1%	3%	5%	10%	20%	20%	10%	5%	3%	1%	5.	4.	3.	2.	Top
PanelA: All Investment Objectives - Funds Ranked on CS Measure																				
CS (Pct/Month)	−2.4	−2.0	−1.6	−1.5	−1.5	−0.7	−0.4	−0.3	−0.2	−0.1	0.2	0.4	0.6	0.7	0.9	1.2	1.3	1.4	1.6	1.7
Cross-Sectionally Bootstrapped *p*-Value	0.29	0.14	0.16	0.09	0.05	0.76	1.00	1.00	1.00	1.00	<0.01	<0.01	<0.01	<0.01	0.19	0.29	0.35	0.40	0.51	0.74
Parametric (Standard) *p*-Value	0.03	<0.01	0.16	<0.01	0.09	0.07	0.06	0.19	0.12	0.14	0.17	0.08	0.01	0.03	<0.01	<0.01	0.21	0.05	0.05	0.07
Funds Ranked on *t*-Statistics of CS Measure																				
t-Unconditional CS	−4.3	−3.2	−3.1	−3.0	−3.0	−2.1	−1.6	−1.4	−1.0	−0.5	1.2	1.7	2.0	2.3	2.9	3.1	3.2	3.3	3.5	3.7
Cross-Sectionally Bootstrapped *p*-Value	0.13	0.76	0.60	0.49	0.49	1.00	1.00	1.00	1.00	1.00	<0.01	<0.01	<0.01	<0.01	<0.01	0.07	0.09	0.18	0.21	0.34
Parametric (Standard) *p*-Value	<0.01	<0.01	<0.01	<0.01	<0.01	0.02	0.06	0.09	0.16	0.32	0.12	0.05	0.02	0.01	<0.01	<0.01	<0.01	<0.01	<0.01	<0.01
Panel B: Growth Funds Ranked on CS Measure																				
CS (Pct/Month)	−2.4	−2.0	−1.5	−1.0	−1.0	−0.8	−0.5	−0.4	−0.2	−0.1	0.3	0.4	0.6	0.7	0.9	1.1	1.2	1.4	1.6	1.7
Cross-Sectionally Bootstrapped *p*-Value	0.14	0.05	0.11	0.78	0.65	0.90	0.94	1.00	1.00	1.00	<0.01	<0.01	<0.01	<0.01	0.25	0.25	0.26	0.21	0.31	0.57
Parametric (Standard) *p*-Value	0.03	<0.01	<0.01	0.18	0.16	0.30	0.03	0.20	0.17	0.22	0.28	0.18	0.03	0.04	0.03	0.01	<0.01	0.05	0.05	0.07

Growth Funds Ranked on *t*-Statistics of CS Measure																				
t-Unconditional CS	−4.3	−3.2	−3.0	−3.0	−2.8	−2.4	−1.7	−1.4	−1.0	−0.5	1.3	1.7	2.0	2.2	2.9	3.1	3.1	3.2	3.3	3.5
Cross-Sectionally Bootstrapped *p*-Value	0.11	0.51	0.40	0.31	0.29	0.78	1.00	1.00	1.00	1.00	<0.01	<0.01	<0.01	0.01	<0.01	0.01	0.05	0.11	0.25	0.42
Parametric (Standard) *p*-Value	<0.01	<0.01	<0.01	<0.01	<0.01	0.01	0.05	0.08	0.17	0.31	0.10	0.05	0.02	0.02	<0.01	<0.01	<0.01	<0.01	<0.01	<0.01
Panel C: Aggressive Growth Funds Ranked on CS Measure																				
CS (Pct/Month)	−1.5	−0.9	−0.7	−0.6	−0.4	−0.7	−0.4	−0.3	−0.2	−0.1	0.2	0.4	0.5	0.7	0.9	0.8	0.9	0.9	0.9	1.0
Cross-Sectionally Bootstrapped *p*-Value	0.2	0.32	0.53	0.82	0.99	0.53	0.97	1.00	1.00	1.00	<0.01	<0.01	<0.01	0.01	0.17	0.06	0.05	0.17	0.39	0.68
Parametric (Standard) *p*-Value	0.09	0.05	0.04	0.20	0.08	0.04	0.06	0.10	0.29	0.40	0.01	0.02	0.09	0.07	0.07	0.01	<0.01	0.07	<0.01	0.07
Aggressive Growth Funds Ranked on *t*-Statistics of CS Measure																				
t-Unconditional CS	−1.8	−1.6	−1.6	−1.6	−1.4	−1.6	−1.3	−1.2	−0.8	−0.4	1.2	1.7	2.1	2.3	2.8	2.5	2.7	2.8	2.9	3.7
Cross-Sectionally Bootstrapped *p*-Value	1.00	1.00	1.00	1.00	1.00	1.00	1.00	1.00	1.00	1.00	<0.01	<0.01	<0.01	0.02	0.04	0.07	0.04	0.04	0.13	0.05
Parametric (Standard) *p*-Value	0.04	0.05	0.05	0.06	0.08	0.05	0.09	0.12	0.21	0.34	0.12	0.04	0.02	0.01	<0.01	0.01	<0.01	<0.01	<0.01	<0.01
Panel D: Growth and Income Funds Ranked on CS Measure																				
CS (Pct/Month)	−1.6	−0.9	−0.4	−0.4	−0.3	−0.4	−0.3	−0.2	−0.2	−0.1	0.1	0.2	0.4	0.5	0.5	0.5	0.5	0.5	0.5	0.7
Cross-Sectionally Bootstrapped *p*-Value	0.15	0.07	0.92	0.92	0.92	0.92	0.98	0.91	0.89	1.00	0.08	0.18	<0.01	0.01	0.40	0.12	0.26	0.40	0.65	0.74

(*Continued*)

Table 6.2 Continued

	Bottom	2.	3.	4.	5.	1%	3%	5%	10%	20%	20%	10%	5%	3%	1%	5.	4.	3.	2.	Top
Parametric (Standard) *p*-Value	0.16	<0.01	<0.01	0.17	0.08	<0.01	0.10	0.03	0.22	0.16	0.15	0.06	0.08	0.01	0.06	0.01	0.06	0.06	0.01	0.04
Growth and Income Funds Ranked on *t*-Statistics of CS Measure																				
t-Unconditional CS	−3.1	−2.6	−2.6	−2.0	−2.0	−2.6	−1.6	−1.5	−1.1	−0.6	1.0	1.6	2.0	2.4	2.7	2.4	2.4	2.7	2.9	3.0
Cross-Sectionally Bootstrapped *p*-Value	0.42	0.55	0.37	0.94	0.86	0.37	0.99	0.97	0.96	1.00	0.02	0.02	0.03	0.02	0.13	0.13	0.26	0.13	0.20	0.49
Parametric (Standard) *p*-Value	<0.01	<0.01	0.01	0.02	0.02	0.01	0.06	0.07	0.13	0.28	0.15	0.06	0.02	0.01	<0.01	0.01	0.01	<0.01	<0.01	<0.01
Panel E: Balanced or Income Funds Ranked on CS Measure																				
CS (Pct/Month)	−0.4	−0.3	−0.3	−0.2	−0.2	−0.4	−0.4	−0.3	−0.3	−0.1	0.2	0.3	0.4	1.3	1.3	0.2	0.2	0.3	0.4	1.3
Cross-Sectionally Bootstrapped *p*-Value	0.69	0.42	0.34	0.49	0.40	0.69	0.69	0.42	0.34	0.79	0.13	0.27	0.39	0.22	0.22	0.13	0.25	0.27	0.39	0.22
Parametric (Standard) *p*-Value	0.23	0.10	0.01	0.17	0.21	0.23	0.23	0.10	0.01	0.24	0.05	0.10	0.03	0.21	0.21	0.17	0.05	0.10	0.03	0.21
Balanced and Income Funds Ranked on *t*-Statistics of CS Measure																				
t-Unconditional CS	−2.4	−1.3	−1.0	−0.8	−0.7	−2.4	−2.4	−1.3	−1.0	−0.7	1.1	1.7	1.9	2.4	2.4	1.3	1.7	1.7	1.9	2.44
Cross-Sectionally Bootstrapped *p*-Value	0.32	0.81	0.88	0.86	0.79	0.32	0.32	0.81	0.88	0.69	0.17	0.18	0.23	0.23	0.23	0.16	0.05	0.18	0.23	0.23
Parametric (Standard) *p*-Value	0.01	0.1	0.17	0.21	0.23	0.01	0.01	0.10	0.17	0.24	0.14	0.05	0.03	0.01	0.01	0.10	0.05	0.05	0.03	0.01

types of stocks, such as small-capitalization value stocks, are able to outperform the Carhart four-factor model, we should observe funds that hold predominantly these stocks in the right tail of our cross-section of alphas. If this outperformance is due to non-linear factor return premia, then the DGTW matching procedure should provide an improved benchmark for such stocks.

Analogous to our prior application of the bootstrap, for each fund we bootstrap the CS performance measure by subtracting the time-series average CS measure from each month's measure to arrive at a demeaned CS residual. Bootstrapping the fund return is then simple—we resample these demeaned residuals to generate a bootstrapped sequence of monthly residuals, and we compute the bootstrapped fund performance as the average residual and the *t*-statistic of the average residual. This procedure is repeated for 1,000 bootstrapped iterations for each fund, and the cross-sectional distribution of CS measures is constructed from these bootstrap outcomes. We repeat this process 1,000 times to construct the cross-sectional empirical distribution of the time-series *t*-statistics of the CS measures.

Table 6.2 reports bootstrap results for the CS performance measures. Again, we focus on a discussion of the distribution of *t*-statistics.

Although the distribution of CS measures is shifted slightly to the right, as we would expect from its pre-cost nature, compared to the unconditional four-factor model of Table 6.1 the right-tail bootstrap results are very consistent with our previous after-cost results. Specifically, according to the bootstrapped *t*-statistic, significant performance now extends to all funds at or above the 20-percentile point (see Panel A), as opposed to the five-percentile cut-off for our after-cost results of Table 6.1. Thus, funds between the 5th and 20th percentiles are skilled, but cannot generate performance sufficient to overcome their expenses and trading costs. It is important to note that the *t*-statistic bootstrap finds no evidence of underperforming mutual funds, gross of expenses and trading costs. It is easy to understand this outcome, as one cannot imagine a fund manager who perversely attempts to underperform her benchmarks. Thus, the significant underperformance documented in Table 6.1 is entirely due to funds that cannot pick stocks well enough to cover their costs, and not to funds that somehow consistently choose underperforming stocks. Again, outperformance is much more prevalent among growth-oriented than income-oriented funds. In addition, inference based on the bootstrap deviates substantially in both the left and right tails of the distributions.

6.6 PERFORMANCE PERSISTENCE

Our analysis in Sections 6.4 and 6.5 demonstrates that the performance of the top aggressive-growth and growth managers is not an artifact of luck. This finding implies that some level of persistence in performance is present as well, although the extent and duration of such persistence is not yet known. Persistence is also an interesting issue in light of Lynch and Musto (2003), who predict persistence among winning funds, but not among losers, and Berk and Green (2004), who predict negligible persistence among winning funds. Following these papers, we measure persistence in fund performance, net of trading costs and fees.

Perhaps the most influential paper on performance persistence is Carhart (1997), which tests whether the alpha from the unconditional four-factor model persists over one- to three-year periods. Carhart's general results are that persistence in superior fund performance is very weak to nonexistent.[19] To test the robustness of Carhart's results, we implement a bootstrap analysis of the Carhart sorting procedure (rather than Carhart's standard t-tests) to evaluate the significance of the future alphas of past winning and losing funds. The application of the bootstrap will sharpen the estimates of p-values, but will not change the alpha point estimates from those of Carhart.[20]

In our baseline persistence tests, we rank funds using the alpha (intercept) of the unconditional four-factor model measured over the three years prior to a given year-end. For example, funds are first ranked on January 1, 1978 by their four-factor alphas over the period 1975 to 1977, and the excess returns of funds are measured over the following year (1978, in this case).[21] We repeat this process through our last ranking date, January 1, 2002. Four-factor alphas are then computed for equal-weighted ranked portfolios in the cross-section, which consists of different funds over time. That is, to remain consistent with Carhart, we form equal-weighted portfolios of funds rather than examine individual funds (as we do in prior sections of this chapter), with the exception of the very top and bottom funds.[22]

---

[19] In general, other studies find similar results: Gruber (1996) finds weak persistence among superior funds; Bollen and Busse (2005) find evidence of very short-term persistence (at the quarterly frequency); Teo and Woo (2001) find that losing funds strongly persist for up to six years; and Wermers (2005) finds strong evidence of multiyear persistence in superior growth funds, but at the stockholdings level (pre-expenses and trading costs).

[20] However, two further differences are also important to note, and they affect the point estimates. First, our data set covers the 1975 to 2002 (inclusive) period, while Carhart's covers the 1962 to 1993 (inclusive) period. Second, and more importantly, we combine shareclasses into portfolios before ranking funds on net returns at the portfolio level, while Carhart ranks shareclasses directly. Our approach therefore reduces the influence of small shareclasses, especially during the latter years of our sample period. In addition, shareclasses of a single portfolio, by construction, have almost perfectly correlated net returns, the only difference being due to uneven changes in expense ratios across the shareclasses during the time period under consideration. This invalidates the assumption of independent residuals in cross-sectional regressions. This consideration is only important during the post-1990 period, when multiple shareclasses became significant in the U.S. fund industry.

[21] Funds are required to have 36 monthly return observations during the four years prior to the ranking date, but need not have complete return information during the test year (to minimize survival bias). Weights of portfolios are readjusted whenever a fund disappears during the test year.

[22] To generate bootstrapped p-values of the t-statistic, we follow a procedure analogous to the bootstrap algorithm described in Section 6.2. Specifically, we bootstrap fund excess returns during the test year using factor loadings estimated during the prior three-year period under the null of a zero true alpha during the test year for each ranked fund or portfolio of funds. This process is repeated for each test year to build a full time series of test-year bootstrapped excess fund (or portfolio of fund) returns over all test years for each ranking point in the alpha distribution. We next estimate the alpha and t-statistic of alpha for each fractile portfolio (or individual fund), then repeat the above for all remaining bootstrap iterations. Thus, funds are ranked on their three-year lagged alphas, but inferences are made based on the bootstrapped distribution of their test-year t-statistics.

Panel A of Table 6.3 shows that the top-ranked fund (the identity of which changes over the years), ranked by its lagged three-year alpha, generates a test-year alpha of 0.48% per month, which is significant using either the cross-sectionally bootstrapped right-tail p-value, or the right-tail p-value that corresponds to a simple t-test (labeled as "one-tailed parametric p-value of alpha). In fact, the standard t-test provides an inference similar to that of the bootstrap for many ranked-fund fractiles, except that the bootstrap provides the very important insight that the top decile consists of skilled funds. Consistent with Carhart, our standard t-test does not reject the null of no performance for these funds, while the bootstrap strongly rejects the null.[23]

Some statistics that describe these fractile portfolio distributions are helpful in understanding why the bootstrap differs from the standard t-test. Panel A provides a normality test (Jarque-Bera) as well as a measure of standard deviation, skew, and kurtosis for each portfolio. Note that the standard deviations indicate heterogeneity in risk-taking in the cross-section, and the skew and kurtosis measures indicate some important non-normalities in portfolio returns. Either of these factors can explain why the cross-sectional bootstrap differs from the standard t-tests implemented by Carhart, as we discuss above in Section 6.2.

Since our alphas (and t-statistics) are computed net of expenses (and security-level trading costs), one might wonder what level of pre-expense alphas our ranked funds generate. This question addresses whether stockpicking skills are present, that is, whether or not expenses effectively capture all of the consumer surplus that is generated. In Panel A, we report the time-series average expense ratio for ranked fractile portfolios. The top decile of funds averages a test-year expense ratio of 97 basis points, which increases our point estimate of alpha to roughly 2% per year (since time-series variability in expense ratios is trivial, this point estimate is also bootstrap-significant).[24] Interestingly, near-median funds (e.g., deciles six and seven) exhibit slightly negative alphas when expenses are added back. Thus, these fund managers appear to have some stockpicking skills, but are too inefficient at picking stocks to justify their costs. With our bottom decile of funds, even adding back expenses does not bring them above water—their trading costs apparently far outweigh any selectivity abilities.

Panel B of Table 6.3 repeats our tests using the one-year past unconditional four-factor alpha as the ranking variable. Shortening the ranking period is important, not from any attempt to try to mine the data for persistence, but rather because it demonstrates that shorter ranking periods result in highly ranked

[23] In general, inferences using standard t-tests agree with those of the bootstrap in the left tail, mainly because their underperformance is so large. These past losing funds exhibit even higher levels of skewness and kurtosis than past winning funds. In addition, we find positive and significant alphas for the spread portfolios (e.g., the top minus bottom 10%, labeled "sprd 10%"), which is not surprising based on the strong results for high- and low-ranked funds.

[24] In unreported tests, we repeat our baseline persistence tests using gross returns, that is, monthly net returns with expense ratios (divided by 12) added back. The bootstrap confirms what we would suspect: All funds, past winners and losers, have higher alphas, but bootstrap p-values do not change very much.

Table 6.3 **Bootstrap Performance Persistence Tests - All Investment Objectives**

In Panel A, mutual funds are sorted on January 1 each year (from 1978 until 2002) into decile portolios based on their unconditional four-factor model alphas estimated over the prior three years. We require a minimum of 36 monthly net return observations for this estimate. For funds that have missing observations during these prior three years, observations from the 12 months preceding the three-year window are added to obtain 36 observations. This assures that funds with missing observations are not excluded. The portfolios are equally weighted monthly, so the weights are readjusted whenever a fund disappears. Funds with the highest past three-year return comprise decile 1, and funds with the lowest comprise decile 10. The '5%ile' portfolio is an equally weighted portfolio of the top 5% funds. The last four rows represent the difference in returns between the top and bottom deciles (10 percentiles, 5 percentiles, 1 percentiles), as well as between the ninth and tenth deciles. In Panel B, the portfolios are formed based on past one-year alphas, and funds are held for one year. Column five reports the one-tailed parametric *p* -value of alpha. Columns six and seven report the cross-sectionally bootstrapped *p*-values for the *t*-statistic of alpha. Column six reports the probability that the bootstrapped *t*-statistic of alpha is lower than (-|*t* (alpha)|), i.e. the left tail of the bootstrapped distribution. Column seven reports the probability that the bootstrapped *t*-statistic of alpha is higher than (+|*t* (alpha)|), i.e., the right tail of the bootstrapped distribution. Columns 12 and 13 report the adjusted R-squared and the annual expense ratio. The expense ratio is calculated as the time-series average of the cross-sectional average of the expense ratios of the funds in the portfolios. The last three columns report the skewness, kurtosis, and the *p*-value of the Jarque-Bera nonnormality statistics. RMRF, SMB, and HML are Fama and French's (1993) market proxy and factor-mimicking portfolios for size and book-to-market equity. PR1 YR is a factor-mimicking portfolio for one-year return momentum. Alpha (in percent per month) is the intercept of the model.

Panel A: Three-Year Ranking Periods, One-Year Holding Period

Fractile	Excess Ret. (Pct/Month)	Std. Dev.	Alpha (Pct/Month)	*t*-Stat of Alpha	One-Tailed Parametric *p*-Value of Alpha	Bootstr. *p*-Value of *t*(Alpha) (Left Tail)	Bootstr. *p*-Value of *t*(Alpha) (Right Tail)	RMRF	SMB	HML	PR1 YR	Adj. R^2	Exp. Ratio	Skew.	Kur.	*p*-Value (JB-Test)
Top	1.04	7.64	0.48	1.5	0.06	0.05	0.04	0.91	0.46	−0.56	0.19	0.65	1.04	0.2	5.2	<0.01
1%ile	0.54	6.79	0.11	0.7	0.24	0.38	0.20	1.03	0.53	−0.45	−0.06	0.89	0.98	−0.2	4.6	<0.01
5%ile	0.58	5.65	0.12	1.3	0.09	0.13	0.03	0.97	0.40	−0.27	−0.04	0.95	1.01	−0.1	5.0	<0.01
1.Dec	0.57	5.17	0.08	1.1	0.13	0.23	0.05	0.95	0.33	−0.15	−0.04	0.96	0.97	−0.2	4.7	<0.01
2.Dec	0.53	4.42	0.02	0.3	0.39	0.60	0.23	0.90	0.15	−0.02	−0.01	0.97	0.87	0.3	4.6	<0.01
3.Dec	0.53	4.21	−0.02	−0.4	0.35	0.45	0.27	0.90	0.10	0.06	0.01	0.98	0.86	0.3	4.7	<0.01
4.Dec	0.50	4.06	−0.02	−0.3	0.38	0.57	0.15	0.88	0.08	0.06	−0.01	0.98	0.84	0.1	4.4	<0.01
5.Dec	0.49	4.13	−0.04	−1.0	0.16	0.32	0.04	0.90	0.05	0.08	−0.01	0.98	0.86	0.3	5.3	<0.01
6.Dec	0.46	4.04	−0.08	−2.3	0.01	0.03	<0.01	0.89	0.03	0.08	0.01	0.98	0.85	0.4	5.8	<0.01
7.Dec	0.48	4.12	−0.09	−1.9	0.03	0.03	<0.01	0.90	0.05	0.10	0.02	0.97	0.88	0.2	4.8	<0.01
8.Dec	0.52	4.08	−0.07	−1.7	0.05	0.07	0.01	0.89	0.10	0.11	0.04	0.97	0.94	0.3	4.7	<0.01
9.Dec	0.50	4.25	−0.09	−1.6	0.06	0.10	0.03	0.90	0.14	0.08	0.03	0.97	1.03	0.5	6.2	<0.01

10.Dec	0.33	4.54	−0.29	−4.2	<0.01	<0.01	<0.01	0.93	0.26	0.08	0.04	0.96	1.30	0.7	5.5	<0.01
95%ile	0.15	4.76	−0.49	−6.0	<0.01	<0.01	<0.01	0.95	0.31	0.06	0.04	0.95	1.50	0.3	4.3	<0.01
99%ile	−0.22	5.66	−0.89	−5.2	<0.01	<0.01	<0.01	1.04	0.40	0.09	0.00	0.81	2.47	1.0	8.2	<0.01
Bottom	−1.02	11.69	−1.38	−2.6	<0.01	<0.01	<0.01	0.87	0.98	−0.42	−0.11	0.32	5.26	2.4	20.5	<0.01
Sprd10%	0.24	1.57	0.37	3.8	<0.01	<0.01	<0.01	0.02	0.08	−0.23	−0.07	0.36	−0.32	−0.3	4.7	<0.01
Sprd5%	0.42	2.10	0.61	4.7	<0.01	<0.01	<0.01	0.01	0.09	−0.33	−0.08	0.36	−0.49	−0.4	4.4	<0.01
Sprd1%	0.76	3.89	1.00	4.0	<0.01	<0.01	<0.01	−0.01	0.14	−0.55	−0.06	0.25	−1.49	−0.8	5.7	<0.01
Dec9_10	0.17	0.85	0.20	4.5	<0.01	<0.01	<0.01	−0.03	−0.12	0.01	0.00	0.27	−0.27	0.0	6.5	<0.01

Panel B: One-Year Ranking Periods, One-Year Holding Period

Fractile	Excess Ret. (Pct/ Month)	Std. Dev.	Alpha (Pct/ Month)	*t*-Stat of Alpha	One-Tailed Parametric *p*-Value of Alpha	Bootstr. *p*-Value of *t*(Alpha) (Left Tail)	Bootstr. *p*-Value of *t*(Alpha) (Right Tail)	RMRF	SMB	HML	PR1 YR	Adj. R^2	Exp. Ratio	Skew.	Kur.	*p*-Value (JB-Test)
Top	0.84	9.14	0.14	0.4	0.36	0.39	0.31	1.10	0.85	−0.27	<0.01	0.55	1.06	0.3	8.7	<0.01
1% ile	0.79	6.50	0.14	0.9	0.19	0.13	0.24	1.04	0.61	−0.26	0.04	0.87	1.26	0.2	3.7	0.01
5% ile	0.82	5.69	0.14	1.5	0.06	0.05	0.06	1.00	0.49	−0.17	0.09	0.93	1.09	0.6	5.1	<0.01
1.Dec	0.78	5.30	0.14	1.9	0.03	0.04	0.01	0.97	0.41	−0.14	0.07	0.95	1.04	0.7	5.9	<0.01
2.Dec	0.66	4.49	0.07	1.5	0.07	0.11	<0.01	0.92	0.20	−0.01	0.03	0.97	0.92	0.4	4.9	<0.01
3.Dec	0.58	4.21	0.03	0.6	0.27	0.53	0.08	0.90	0.12	0.04	0.01	0.97	0.88	0.6	5.4	<0.01
4.Dec	0.54	4.08	<0.01	−0.1	0.46	0.80	0.15	0.89	0.09	0.06	<0.01	0.98	0.86	0.3	5.7	<0.01
5.Dec	0.53	4.01	−0.01	−0.3	0.37	0.62	0.17	0.88	0.07	0.07	<0.01	0.98	0.85	0.5	5.0	<0.01
6.Dec	0.46	3.97	−0.06	−1.8	0.04	0.10	<0.01	0.88	0.06	0.08	<0.01	0.98	0.87	0.2	4.0	<0.01
7.Dec	0.45	4.00	−0.08	−2.0	0.02	0.08	<0.01	0.88	0.06	0.07	<0.01	0.98	0.90	0.3	5.0	<0.01
8.Dec	0.42	4.12	−0.15	−3.1	<0.01	0.01	<0.01	0.90	0.09	0.07	0.02	0.97	0.92	0.0	4.1	<0.01
9.Dec	0.40	4.17	−0.18	−3.2	<0.01	<0.01	<0.01	0.91	0.11	0.09	0.01	0.96	0.95	−0.1	4.2	<0.01
10.Dec	0.28	4.39	−0.30	−3.7	<0.01	<0.01	<0.01	0.92	0.23	0.10	−0.03	0.93	1.22	−0.1	4.5	<0.01
95%ile	0.22	4.57	−0.39	−4.5	<0.01	<0.01	<0.01	0.94	0.28	0.11	−0.03	0.92	1.35	−0.1	4.1	<0.01
99%ile	−0.03	4.96	−0.66	−5.1	<0.01	<0.01	<0.01	0.93	0.41	0.14	−0.04	0.82	1.87	−0.2	4.5	<0.01
Bottom	−0.59	9.96	−1.31	−2.7	<0.01	<0.01	<0.01	1.12	0.25	0.50	−0.17	0.23	2.20	2.8	24.8	<0.01
Sprd10%	0.51	2.22	0.44	3.9	<0.01	<0.01	<0.01	0.05	0.18	−0.24	0.10	0.39	−0.18	0.4	4.5	<0.01
Sprd5%	0.61	2.67	0.53	4.0	<0.01	<0.01	<0.01	0.06	0.21	−0.28	0.12	0.36	−0.26	0.5	4.3	<0.01
Sprd1%	0.82	3.82	0.80	3.9	<0.01	<0.01	<0.01	0.11	0.21	−0.40	0.08	0.28	−0.60	0.2	3.1	0.34
Dec9_10	0.12	0.86	0.12	2.2	0.01	0.01	<0.01	−0.01	−0.12	−0.01	0.04	0.24	−0.26	0.8	7.6	<0.01

funds with alpha distributions that are much more non-normal than those from longer ranking periods, and they have higher risk levels. Specifically, as Panel B shows, the skew and kurtosis deviate much more strongly from normality among almost all highly ranked funds and fund portfolios. Thus, funds with extreme positive lagged alphas, based on short-term rankings, are much more likely to hold stocks, perhaps purposely, with a temporarily high standard deviation, skewness, and kurtosis. This leads us to conclude that the bootstrap is more important when evaluating short-term persistence. Nevertheless, standard *t*-tests agree with most of the bootstrapped results, except that the bootstrap shows that the top three deciles of funds have significant alphas, rather than the top two (as shown by the parametric *t*-test).

6.7 CHAPTER-END PROBLEMS

1. Why is it important to bootstrap the p-values for alphas of performance evaluation regression models?
2. What are the steps involved in the residual-only bootstrap procedure? Assume that we use a single-factor regression model, where the S&P 500 return is the single factor.
3. Why do we have to bootstrap the cross-sectional distribution of past alphas of funds in order to determine the proper *p*-values of funds at each fractile (e.g., the fund at the top 1% point of the distribution)?
4. What is the advantage of bootstrapping *p*-values from the data, relative to running simulations with assumed distributions for the alphas of each fund?
5. Jane Farkas tells Susan DiMarco that she has seen exciting data on the performance of market-neutral, convertible arbitrage, and global macro hedge funds. Farkas states: "The Sharpe ratios of all of these hedge fund strategies are much higher than for traditional equities or bonds, which means they have a great risk/return profile. We should definitely plan a major investment in hedge funds". DiMarco responds: "There are several reasons that the Sharpe ratio may be misleading".

   A. Discuss the situations that could cause an upward bias in the calculation of the Sharpe ratio.
   B. Evaluate the reasons that statistically indicate that the Sharpe ratio is not the most appropriate measure of risk for hedge funds.

Chapter 7

Fund Manager Selection Using Macroeconomic Information

ABSTRACT

It is rare for a fund manager to outperform her benchmarks during all types of market conditions, such as expansions vs. recessions or technology stock vs. financial stock booms. Accordingly, we should look for managers who have outperformed during historical economic conditions that are similar to current conditions for the best chance of finding today's skilled managers. This chapter presents a Bayesian system for predicting managed fund alphas, and for selecting portfolios of fund managers, using information on the macro economy. To illustrate the approach, this chapter applies the system to the choice of U.S. open-end, domestic equity mutual funds over the 1975 to 2002 period. In this example, we choose a portfolio of funds expected to outperform during the next month; the resulting performance of this strategy is 6–8%/year, net of fund-level fees.

Keywords
Macro-alpha, Macroeconomic conditions, Time-varying alpha, Avramov-Wermers model

7.1 INTRODUCTION

This chapter presents a systematic approach to identifying future outperforming managed funds, and optimal portfolios of these funds, using macroeconomic conditions to model their returns.[1] This system builds on methodologies developed by Avramov (2004) and Avramov and Chordia (2005b) for predicting individual stock and stock index returns. Here, we apply the system to managed funds, and bring several methodological contributions, especially in modeling manager skills. The framework shown in this chapter is quite general, and is applicable to investment decisions in real time. Importantly, moments used to form optimal portfolios obey closed-form expressions, which can be used to implement trading strategies across a large universe of managed funds. In addition, our strategies employ long-only positions in managed funds, which implies long-only positions in the underlying stocks (since most managed funds do not short-sell

[1] This chapter is distilled from Avramov and Wermers (2006).

Performance Evaluation and Attribution of Security Portfolios. http://dx.doi.org/10.1016/B978-0-12-744483-3.00007-9

© 2013 Elsevier Inc. All rights reserved.
For End-of-chapter Questions: © 2013. CFA Institute, Reproduced and republished with permission from CFA Institute. All rights reserved.

stocks)—thus, our models derive performance from straightforward and realistic strategies that can be implemented by investing in managed funds or in their underlying stock choices.

7.2 A DYNAMIC MODEL OF MANAGED FUND RETURNS

In this section, we derive a framework within which we assess the economic significance of predictability in managed fund returns as well as the overall value of active management from the perspective of three types of Bayesian optimizing investors who differ with respect to their beliefs about the potential for active fund managers to possess stock picking skills and benchmark timing abilities. Specifically, the investors differ in their views about the parameters in the managed fund return generating model, which is described as:

$$r_{it} = \alpha_{i0} + \alpha_{i1}' z_{t-1} + \beta_{i0}' f_t + \beta_{i1}' \left(f_t \otimes z_{t-1} \right) + v_{it}, \tag{7.1}$$

$$f_t = a_f + A_f z_{t-1} + v_{ft}, \tag{7.2}$$

$$z_t = a_z + A_z z_{t-1} + v_{zt}. \tag{7.3}$$

In this system of equations, r_{it} is the month-t managed fund return in excess of the risk-free rate, z_{t-1} is the information set, which contains M business cycle variables observed at the end of month $t-1, f_t$ is a set of K zero-cost benchmarks, β_{i0} (β_{i1}) is the fixed (time-varying) component of fund risk loadings, and v_{it} is a fund-specific event, assumed to be uncorrelated across funds and over time, as well as normally distributed with mean zero and variance ψ_i. Modeling beta variation with information variables goes back to Shanken (1990). Modeling business cycle variables using a vector autoregression of order one in an investment context has also been applied by Kandel and Stambaugh (1996), Barberis (2000), Avramov (2002, 2004), and Avramov and Chordia (2005b).

The expression $\alpha_{i0}+\alpha_{i1}' z_{t-1}$ in Eq. (7.1) captures manager skills in stock selection and benchmark timing, which may vary in response to changing economic conditions.[2] Superior performance is defined as the fund's expected return (above T-bills), in excess of that attributable to a dynamic strategy with the same time-varying risk exposures that exploit benchmark return predictability. Hence, the measure $\alpha_{i0}+\alpha_{i1}' z_{t-1}$ separates timing- and selectivity-based manager skills from fund returns that are related to predictability in benchmark returns as well as the response of fund risk loadings to changing business conditions.

In particular, note that there are two potential sources of timing-related fund returns that are correlated with public information. The first, predictable fund risk-loadings, may be due to changing stock-level risk loadings, to flows into the

[2] We assume that the benchmarks price all passive investments. Pastor and Stambaugh (2002a,b) note that if benchmarks do not price all passive assets, then a manager could achieve a positive alpha in the absence of any skill by investing in nonbenchmark passive assets with historically positive alphas. Thus, they distinguish between skill and mispricing, which is beyond the scope of this work.

funds, or to manager timing of the benchmarks. The second exploits predictability in the benchmark returns themselves. Such predictability is captured through the time-series regression in Eq. (7.2). Because both of these timing components are assumed to be easily replicated by an investor, we do not consider them to be based on manager "skill". That is, the expression $\alpha_{i0}+\alpha_{i1}'z_{t-1}$ captures benchmark timing and stock picking skills that exploit only the private information possessed by a fund manager. Of course, this private information can be correlated with the business cycle, which is indeed what we show in the empirical section below.

To illustrate the important differences between stock-level predictability, documented by Avramov (2004) and Avramov and Chordia (2005b), and predictability in managed fund returns, we demonstrate that the return dynamics in Eq. (7.1) may obtain even when stock-level alphas are zero and stock-level betas are time invariant. In particular, assume that fund i invests in S individual stocks whose return dynamics conform to the constant-beta model $r_{st} = \beta_s' f_t + v_{st}$, where f_t evolves according to Eq. (7.2) and $E(v_{st}|z_{t-1}) = 0$. That is, this setup assumes that there is no stock-level return predictability based on public information, beyond that implied by the predictability of the benchmarks. Now, let r_t^S, β^S, and v_t^S be the corresponding S-stock versions of r_{st}, β_s, and v_{st}. At time $t-1$, the fund invests in individual stocks using the strategy $\omega_{it-1} = \omega_{i1}(z_{t-1}) + \omega_{i2}(p_{it-1})$, where ω_{it-1} is an S-vector describing the fractions (of total invested wealth) allocated to individual stocks, p_{it-1} denotes private (fund-specific) information available at time $t-1$, and $\omega(x)$ is some function of x. That is, the fund shifts weights across stocks based on public and private information. The time-t return on fund i is $r_{it} = \omega_{it-1}' r_t^S$. It follows that $E(r_{it}|z_{t-1}) = E[\omega_{i2}(p_{it-1})'\beta^S f_t|z_{t-1}] + E[\omega_{i2}(p_{it-1})'v_t^S|z_{t-1}] + \beta_i(z_{t-1})'E(f_t|z_{t-1})$.[3] Note that the expression $\alpha_{i0}+\alpha_{i1}'z_{t-1}$ is related to the first two terms of this equation. That is, even when each stock conforms to a constant-beta model in the absence of private information, private manager skills can induce risk loadings and managerial skills that vary with evolving business conditions. Further, note that abnormal performance is attributed to two sources, $E[\omega_{i2}(p_{it-1})'\beta^S f_t|z_{t-1}]$ and $E[\omega_{i2}(p_{it-1})'v_t^S|z_{t-1}]$, reflecting benchmark timing skills and stock picking skills, respectively (the dichotomy between timing and selectivity abilities is analyzed by, among others, Merton (1981) and Admati et al. (1986)).

Implicit in the above analysis is the assumption that there is significant dependence, either linear or nonlinear, between private (fund-specific) information and the set of publicly available information variables z_t. Empirically, Moskowitz (2000) documents the relation between fund performance and the state of the economy. This relation can be expected if managers in different sectors possess specialized skills that best apply under certain states of the economy. For example, precious metals fund managers may best differentiate among

[3] We treat private manager skills as an unknown stochastic quantity, thus, we form the conditional expected value by conditioning only on public information. Of course, the manager who has a finer information set (private skills) does not perceive stock-level alphas to be zero. That is, the true model that assumes zero stock-level alphas does not condition on private skills.

metals-industry stocks during recessionary periods, whereas technology fund managers may best choose technology stocks during economic expansions. Thus, using macro variables could potentially help investors identify, *ex ante*, the best-performing managers in different economic states.

Overall, the dynamic model for managed fund returns described by Eqs. (7.1)–(7.3) captures potential predictability in managerial skills ($\alpha_{i1} \neq 0$), managed fund risk loadings ($\beta_{i1} \neq 0$), and benchmark returns ($A_f \neq 0$). Indeed, as noted by Dybvig and Ross (1985) and Grinblatt and Titman (1989), among others, using an unconditional approach to modeling managed fund returns may lead to unreliable inference about performance—for example, assigning negative performance to a successful market-timer. In turn, this could lead to a suboptimal selection of managed funds; we demonstrate this below when we apply our proposed framework to our sample of equity mutual funds.

We now turn to our three types of investors, who bring distinct prior beliefs to the managed fund investment decision. Specifically, they have very different views concerning the existence of manager skills in timing the benchmarks and in selecting securities.

7.2.1 The "Dogmatist"

Our first investor, the Dogmatist, has extreme prior beliefs about the potential for manager skill. The Dogmatist rules out any potential for skill, either fixed or time varying, for any fund manager. That is, the Dogmatist's view is that α_{i0} is fixed at $-\frac{1}{12}(\textit{expense} + 0.01 \times \textit{turnover})$ and that α_{i1} is fixed at zero, where *expense* and *turnover* are the fund's reported annual expense ratio and turnover, and where we assume a round-trip total trade cost of 1% (this prior specification is similar to Pastor and Stambaugh (2002a,b)). The Dogmatist believes that a fund manager provides no performance through benchmark timing or stock selection skills, and that expenses and trading costs are a deadweight loss to investors.

We consider two types of Dogmatists. The first is a "No-Predictability Dogmatist (ND)", who rules out predictability, additionally setting the parameters β_{i1} and A_f in Eqs. (7.1) and (7.2) equal to zero. The second is a "Predictability Dogmatist (PD)", who believes that managed fund returns are predictable based on observable business cycle variables. We further partition our PD investor into two types: PD-1, who believes that fund risk loadings are predictable (i.e., β_{i1} is potentially nonzero), and PD-2, who believes that both risk loadings and benchmark returns are predictable (i.e., β_{i1} and A_f are both allowed to be nonzero). Note that our PD investors believe that asset allocation decisions can be improved by exploiting predictability in managed fund returns based on public information, but cannot be improved through seeking managers with private skills.

7.2.2 The "Skeptic"

Our second investor, the Skeptic, brings more moderate views to the managed fund selection mechanism. This investor allows for the possibility of active management skills, time-varying or otherwise. The Skeptic accepts the idea that some fund managers may beat their benchmarks—even so, her beliefs about outperformance (or underperformance) are somewhat bounded, as we formalize below. Analogous to our partitioning of the Dogmatists, we consider two types of Skeptic, a "No-Predictability Skeptic (NS)", who believes that macroeconomic variables should be disregarded, and a "Predictability Skeptic (PS)", who believes that fund risk loadings, benchmark returns, and perhaps even manager skills are predictable based on evolving macroeconomic variables. Specifically, the NS investor looks for managers with potential skills in the absence of macroeconomic variables, while the PS investor believes that asset allocation can be improved by exploiting macroeconomic variables that potentially forecast fund risk loadings, benchmark returns, and private skills of managed fund managers.

Starting with our NS investor, we model prior beliefs similarly to Pastor and Stambaugh (2002a,b). In brief, for this investor, α_{i1} equals zero with probability one, and α_{i0} is normally distributed with a mean equal to $-\frac{1}{12}expense$ and a standard deviation equal to 1%. Note that the NS investor believes that there is no relation between turnover and performance.

Moving to our PS investor, we first note that papers that model informative priors in the presence of i.i.d. managed fund returns essentially assume that manager private skills do not vary over time. In our framework, potential time variation in skills, as specified in Eq. (7.1), calls for a different prior. Specifically, when skill may vary, an investor's prior can be modeled as if that investor has observed a (hypothetical) sample of T_0 months in which there is no manager skill based on either public or private information—the idea of using a hypothetical sample for eliciting prior beliefs is suggested by Kandel and Stambaugh (1996) and implemented by Avramov (2002, 2004). Formally, this implies that the prior mean of α_{i1} is zero and the prior mean of α_{i0} equals $-\frac{1}{12}expense$. The prior standard errors of these parameters depend upon T_0. An investor who is less willing to accept the existence of skill is perceived to have observed a long sequence of observations from this hypothetical prior sample. At one extreme, $T_0 = \infty$ corresponds to dogmatic beliefs that rule out skill, i.e., our Dogmatist of the previous section. At the other, $T_0 = 0$ corresponds to completely agnostic beliefs, which we model in the next section. To address the choice of T_0, we establish an exact link (derived in Part C.2. of the Appendix) between the prior uncertainty about skills, denoted by σ_α, and T_0, which is given by:

$$T_0 = \frac{s^2}{\sigma_\alpha^2}(1 + M + SR_{max}^2), \tag{7.4}$$

where SR_{max} is the largest attainable Sharpe ratio based on investments in the benchmarks only (disregarding predictability), M is the number of predictive variables, and s^2 is the cross-fund average of the sample variance of the residuals in Eq. (7.1). This exact relation gives our prior specification the skill uncertainty interpretation employed by earlier work. To apply our prior specification for the PS investor in the empirical section, we compute s^2 and SR_{max}^2, and set $\sigma_\alpha = 1\%$. Then, T_0 is obtained through Eq. (7.4).

7.2.3 The "Agnostic"

Our last investor is the Agnostic. The Agnostic resembles the Skeptic in that he allows for manager skills to exist, but the Agnostic has completely diffuse prior beliefs about the existence and level of skills (i.e., $T_0 = 0$ in our discussion of the previous section). Specifically, the skill level $\alpha_{i0} + \alpha_{i1}' z_{t-1}$ has mean $-\frac{1}{12}(expense)$ and unbounded standard deviation. Effectively, this means that prior beliefs are noninformative. Hence, the Agnostic allows the data to completely determine the existence of funds that have managers with stock selection and/or benchmark timing skills. As with the Dogmatist and the Skeptic, we further subdivide the Agnostic into two types, the "No-Predictability Agnostic (NA)" and the "Predictability Agnostic (PA)".

Overall we consider 13 investors: three dogmatists, five skeptics, and five agnostics. Table 7.1 summarizes the investor beliefs and the different strategies that they represent.

Table 7.1 List of Investors: Names, Beliefs, and the Different Strategies They Represent

This table describes the various investor types considered in this chapter, each of which represents a unique trading strategy. Investors differ in a few dimensions, namely, their belief in the possibility of active management skills, their belief of whether these skills are predictable, and their belief of whether fund risk loadings and benchmark returns are predictable. Predictability refers to the ability of the four macro variables, the dividend yield, the default spread, the term spread, and the Treasury yield to predict future fund returns. The Dogmatists completely rule out the possibility of active management skills, the Agnostics are completely diffuse about that possibility, and the Skeptics have prior beliefs reflected by $\sigma_\alpha = 1\%$ per month. Here are the investor types:

1. **ND: N**o predictability, **D**ogmatic about no managerial skills.
2. **PD-1: P**redictable betas, **D**ogmatic about no managerial skills.
3. **PD-2: P**redictable betas and factors, **D**ogmatic about no managerial skills.
4. **NS: N**o predictability, **S**keptical about no managerial skills.
5. **PS-1: P**redictable betas, **S**keptical about no managerial skills.
6. **PS-2: P**redictable betas and factors, **S**keptical about no managerial skills.
7. **PS-3: P**redictable alphas, betas, and factors, **S**keptical about no managerial skills.
8. **PS-4: P**redictable alphas, betas, and factors, **S**keptical about no managerial skills.
9. **NA: N**o predictability, **A**gnostic about no managerial skills.
10. **PA-1: P**redictable betas, **A**gnostic about no managerial skills.
11. **PA-2: P**redictable betas and factors, **A**gnostic about no managerial skills.
12. **PA-3: P**redictable alphas, **A**gnostic about no managerial skills.
13. **PA-4: P**redictable alphas, betas, and factors, **A**gnostic about no managerial skills.

7.2.4 Optimal Portfolios of Managed Funds

We form optimal portfolios of managed funds for each of our 13 investor types. The time-t investment universe comprises N_t funds, with N_t varying over time as funds enter and leave the sample through merger or termination. Each of the various investor types maximizes the conditional expected value of the quadratic utility function:

$$U(W_t, R_{p,t+1}, a_t, b_t) = a_t + W_t R_{p,t+1} - \frac{b_t}{2} W_t^2 R_{p,t+1}^2, \tag{7.5}$$

where W_t denotes the time-t invested wealth, b_t reflects the absolute risk aversion parameter, and $R_{p,t+1}$ is (one plus) the realized return on the optimal portfolio of managed funds computed as $R_{p,t+1} = 1 + r_{ft} + w_t' r_{t+1}$, with r_{ft} denoting the riskless rate, r_{t+1} denoting the vector of excess fund returns, and w_t denoting the vector of optimal allocations to managed funds.

Taking conditional expectations of both sides of Eq. (7.5), letting $\gamma_t = \frac{(b_t W_t)}{(1-b_t W_t)}$ be the relative risk-aversion parameter, and letting $\Lambda_t = [\Sigma_t + \mu_t \mu_t']^{-1}$, where μ_t and Σ_t are the mean vector and covariance matrix of future fund returns, yields the following optimization:

$$w_t^* = \arg\max_{w_t} \left\{ w_t' \mu_t - \frac{1}{2(1/\gamma_t - r_{ft})} w_t' \Lambda_t^{-1} w_t \right\}. \tag{7.6}$$

We derive optimal portfolios of managed funds by maximizing Eq. (7.6) constrained to preclude short-selling and leveraging. In forming optimal portfolios, we replace μ_t and Σ_t in Eq. (7.6) by the mean and variance of the Bayesian predictive distribution:

$$p(r_{t+1}|\mathcal{D}_t, \mathcal{I}) = \int_\Theta p(r_{t+1}|\mathcal{D}_t, \Theta, \mathcal{I}) p(\Theta|\mathcal{D}_t, \mathcal{I}) d\Theta, \tag{7.7}$$

where $\mathcal{D}_t$ denotes the data (managed fund returns, benchmark returns, and predictive variables) observed up to (and including) time t, Θ is the set of parameters characterizing the processes in Eqs. (7.1)–(7.3), $p(\Theta|\mathcal{D}_t)$ is the posterior density of Θ, and $\mathcal{I}$ denotes the investor type. Such expected utility maximization is a version of the general Bayesian control problem developed by Zellner and Chetty (1965). Pastor (2000) and Pastor and Stambaugh (2000, 2002b) compute optimal portfolios in a framework in which returns are assumed to be i.i.d., while Kandel and Stambaugh (1996), Barberis (2000), Avramov (2002, 2004), and Avramov and Chordia (2005b) analyze portfolio decisions when returns are potentially predictable.

The optimal portfolio of managed funds does not explicitly account for Merton (1973) hedging demands. Nevertheless, for a wide variety of preferences, hedging demands are small, or even non-existent, as demonstrated by Ait-Sahalia and Brandt (2001), among others. Indeed, in unreported tests, we explicitly derive the hedging demands, following Fama (1996) intuition about Merton's ICAPM.

In particular, we derive an optimal ICAPM portfolio by maximizing Eq. (7.6) subject to the constraint that the optimal portfolio weights times the vector of the factor loadings (corresponding to all benchmarks excluding the market portfolio) is equal to the desired hedge level. For a large range of desired hedge levels, we confirm that the mean-variance portfolio component overwhelmingly dominates any effect from the hedge portfolio component. Let us also note that earlier studies (e.g., Moskowitz, 2003) examine optimal portfolios in the presence of return predictability, focusing on mean-variance optimization excluding hedging demands.

We also note that maximizing a quadratic utility function such as that in Eq. (7.5) ultimately could lead to optimal portfolios that are not only conditionally efficient, but also unconditionally efficient in the sense of Hansen and Richard (1987), who generalize the traditional mean-variance concept of Markowitz (1952, 1959). To see this, note that the conditionally unconstrained optimal portfolio that solves Eq. (7.6) is given by:

$$w_t = (1/\gamma - r_f)\Lambda_t \mu_t.$$

This conditionally efficient portfolio is equivalent to the unconditionally efficient portfolio presented in Eq. (7.12) of Ferson and Siegel (2001), when $\gamma = \frac{1}{\mu_p/\zeta + r_f}$, where μ_p is the excess expected return target and $\zeta = \mathbb{E}(\mu_t{}' \Lambda_t \mu_t) = \mathbb{E}\left[\frac{\mu_t{}' \Sigma_t^{-1} \mu_t}{1+\mu_t{}' \Sigma_t^{-1} \mu_t}\right]$, with $\mathbb{E}$ denoting the expected value taken with respect to the unconditional distribution of the predictors. Since we pre-specify γ, our resulting portfolio is both conditionally and unconditionally efficient to an investor whose expected return target is given by $\mu_p = \zeta(1/\gamma - r_f)$.

What distinguishes our 13 investor types is the predictive moments of future fund returns used in the portfolio optimization. Specifically, different views about the existence and scope of manager skills or about the existence and sources of predictability imply different predictive moments, and, therefore, imply different optimal portfolios of managed funds. Our objective here is to assess the potential economic gain, both *ex ante* and out-of-sample, of incorporating fund return predictability into the investment decision for each investor type.

7.3 EMPIRICAL EXAMPLE: U.S. DOMESTIC EQUITY FUND DATA

To illustrate the application of the methods of this chapter, we will apply the approach to U.S. domestic equity mutual funds, where the benchmarks and models are well-known (and, these are described in earlier chapters). Therefore, for each of the 13 investors, we derive optimal portfolios considering three benchmark specifications, (i) MKT, (ii) MKT, SMB, HML, and (iii) MKT, SMB, HML, UMD, where MKT stands for excess return on the value-weighted CRSP index, SMB and HML are the Fama and French (1993) spread portfolios pertaining to size and value premiums, and UMD is the winner-minus-loser portfolio intended to capture the Jegadeesh and Titman (1993) momentum effect. The importance of model specification in mutual fund research is discussed theoretically by Roll (1978) and documented empirically by Lehmann and Modest (1987). By considering three benchmark specifications under various prior beliefs about manager skills and fund return predictability, we attempt to address concerns about model misspecification.

Our sample contains a total of 1,301 open-end, no-load U.S. domestic equity mutual funds, which include actively managed funds, index funds, sector funds, and ETFs (exchange traded funds). Monthly net returns, as well as annual turnover and expense ratios for the funds, are obtained from the Center for Research in Security Prices (CRSP) Mutual Fund database over the sample period January 1975 through December 2002. Additional data on fund investment objectives are obtained from the Thomson/CDA Spectrum files. In Part A of the appendix, we provide both the process for determining whether a fund is a domestic equity fund as well as a description of the characteristics of our investable equity funds.

Table 7.2 reports summary statistics on the 1,301 funds partitioned by self-declared Thomson investment objectives and by the length of the fund's return history (which roughly corresponds to the fund's age). Our investment objectives are "Aggressive Growth", "Growth", "Growth and Income", and "Metal and Others". The last classification includes precious metals funds, other sector funds (such as health care funds), ETFs, and a small number of funds that have missing investment-objective information in the Thomson files (but that we identify as domestic equity through their names or other information, as explained in the appendix). Note also that the investment objective for a given fund may change during its life, although this is not common. In such cases, we use the last available investment objective for that fund as the fund's objective throughout its life.

In each objective/return-history category, the first row reports the number of funds, the second row displays the cross-sectional median of the time-series average of monthly returns (in %), and the third row shows the cross-sectional median of the time-series average of total net assets (TNA in $ millions). The total number of funds in each age category ranges from 239 to 278. Overall, the sample is roughly balanced between newer and more seasoned funds.

Instruments used to predict future mutual fund returns include the aggregate dividend yield, the default spread, the term spread, and the yield on the three-month T-bill, variables identified by Keim and Stambaugh (1986) and Fama and French (1989) as important in predicting U.S. equity returns. The dividend yield is the total cash dividends on the value-weighted CRSP index over the previous 12 months divided by the current level of the index. The default spread is the yield differential between Moodys BAA-rated and AAA-rated bonds. The term spread is the yield differential between Treasury bonds with more than ten years to maturity and T-bills that mature in three months.

Table 7.2 Summary Statistics for No-Load Equity Mutual Funds

The table reports summary statistics for 1,301 open-end, no-load U.S. domestic equity mutual funds partitioned by the intersection of the fund's return history length and by the following Thompson investment objectives: "Aggressive Growth", "Growth", "Growth & Income", and "Metal and Others". The last classification includes precious metal funds, other sector funds (such as health care funds), Exchange-Traded Funds (ETFs), and a small number of funds that have missing investment objective information in the Thomson files (but that we identify as domestic equity through the fund name and/or through the CRSP investment objective). If the investment objective for a given fund changes during its life, we assign the last investment objective available for that fund as the fund's objective throughout its life. A fund is included in the investment universe if it contains at least 48 consecutive return observations through the investment period, where investments are made on a monthly basis starting at the end of December 1979 and ending at the end of December 2002. In each objective-history category, the first row reports the number of funds, the second displays the cross-sectional median of the time-series average annual return (in %), and the third describes the cross-sectional median of the time-series average total net assets (TNA, in $ million).

	Fund's Return History in Months					
Investment Objective	**48–66**	**67–84**	**85–108**	**109–156**	**157–336**	**All**
Aggressive Growth	8	19	26	24	44	121
	15.2	10.6	11.3	11.5	14.4	12.6
	58.2	35.2	36.1	162.6	264.7	123.1
Growth	146	216	155	144	146	807
	5.7	8.9	10.2	10.3	12.8	10.1
	41.4	69.8	116.6	185.1	267.7	100.0
Growth & Income	19	28	49	72	57	225
	5.4	6.3	10.7	9.8	11.6	10.0
	40.4	151.7	96.8	336.2	249.0	165.4
Metal and Others	99	15	9	10	15	148
	2.1	5.6	8.4	10.5	12.0	5.2
	45.8	54.5	73.9	345.6	139.1	67.4
Total # of Funds	272	278	239	250	262	1301

7.4 EMPIRICAL EXAMPLE: RESULTS FOR U.S. DOMESTIC EQUITY FUNDS

We measure the economic significance of incorporating predictability into the investment decisions of our investor types, i.e., the Dogmatists, the Skeptics, and the Agnostics. Predictability is examined from both *ex ante* and *ex post* out-of-sample perspectives. Our *ex ante* analysis is based upon the formation of optimal portfolios, by each investor type, among 890 equity funds at the end of

December 2002, which is the end of our sample period. Predictive moments are based on prior beliefs for each investor type, revised by sample data that are observed from January 1975 to December 2002. Our out-of-sample analysis relies on a portfolio strategy based on a recursive scheme that invests in 1,301 funds over the December 1979 through November 2002 period, with monthly rebalancing for each investor type, for a total of 276 monthly strategies.

The *ex ante* and out-of-sample analyses rely on portfolio strategies formed by maximizing Eq. (7.6) (subject to no short-selling of funds), while replacing μ_t and Σ_t (for each month, for each investor type) by the updated Bayesian predictive moments that account for estimation risk. Closed-form expressions for the Bayesian moments are derived in the appendix for Dogmatists, Skeptics, and Agnostics when benchmark returns and fund risk loadings are potentially predictable (Appendix B), and for Skeptics and Agnostics when, in addition, manager skills are potentially predictable (Appendix C). Several other scenarios are examined as well (e.g., i.i.d. fund returns), all of which are nested cases. We pick a level of risk aversion that guarantees that, if the market portfolio and a risk-free asset are available for investment in December 2002, an investor's entire wealth will be allocated to the market portfolio.[4]

7.4.1 Optimal Portfolios of Equity Mutual Funds

In this section, we analyze the value of active management and the overall economic significance of predictability in mutual fund returns from an *ex ante* perspective. In particular, Table 7.3 provides optimal portfolio weights across equity mutual funds for each of the 13 investors described in Table 7.1. Optimal weights obtain, assuming these investors use the market benchmark to form moments for asset allocation. That is, f_t in Eq. (7.2) represents the excess return on the value-weighted CRSP index. Weights are shown for the end of December 2002; at this date, the investment universe consists of 890 no-load, open-end equity mutual funds with at least four years of return history. Weights not reported are zero for all investor types. In unreported results (available upon request), we confirm that qualitatively identical findings obtain using the three Fama-French benchmarks as well as the four Carhart benchmarks.

The certainty equivalent loss (shown in Table 7.3 in basis points per month) is computed from the perspective of investors who use the four macro predictive variables noted earlier to choose funds, i.e., PD-, PS-, and PA-type investors, when they are constrained to hold the optimal portfolios of their no-predictability counterparts, ND, NS, and NA, respectively. The Sharpe ratio is computed for the optimal portfolio of each investor based on that investor's Bayesian predictive moments. The certainty equivalent loss and Sharpe ratio measures are based on investment opportunities perceived at the end of December 2002. We also report average values of the certainty equivalent loss and the Sharpe ratio across all 276 months, beginning December 1979 and ending November 2002, as well as for NBER expansion and recession subperiods. These optimal portfolios that invest in 1,301 no-load equity funds also form the basis for our out-of-sample analysis, presented in the next section.

[4] Specifically, $\gamma=2.94$. Experimenting with other values does not change our empirical findings.

Table 7.3 Optimal Portfolios of Mutual Funds Under the CAPM

The table provides optimal portfolio weights across equity mutual funds for each of the 13 investors described in Table 7.1. The optimal weights are presented assuming these investors use the market benchmark to form moments for asset allocation. Weights are provided for the end of December 2002; at this date, the investment universe consists of 890 no-load, open-end equity mutual funds with at least four years of return history. The certainty equivalent loss (in basis points per month) is computed from the perspective of investors who use predictive variables to choose funds, PD-, PS-, and PA-type investors, when they are constrained to hold the optimal portfolios of their no-predictability counterparts, ND, NS, and NA. In addition, the Sharpe ratio is computed for the optimal portfolio of each investor, based on that type's Bayesian predictive moments. These *ex ante* measures of the certainty equivalent loss and of Sharpe ratios are based on investment opportunities perceived at the end of December 2002. We also report average values of the certainty equivalent loss and the Sharpe ratio across all 276 months, beginning December 1979 and ending November 2002, as well as for NBER expansion and recession subperiods.

	The Dogmatist			The Skeptic					The Agnostic				
	ND	PD-1	PD-2	NS	PS-1	PS-2	PS-3	PS-4	NA	PA-1	PA-2	PA-3	PA-4
December 2002 Portfolio Weights (%):													
White Oak Growth	0.0	0.0	19.4	0.0	0.0	0.0	0.0	0.0	0.0	0.0	0.0	0.0	0.0
Scudder Equity 500 Index	4.7	3.8	0.0	0.0	0.0	0.0	0.0	0.0	0.0	0.0	0.0	0.0	0.0
Neuberger Berman Focus	0.0	0.0	35.0	0.0	0.0	0.0	0.0	0.0	0.0	0.0	0.0	0.0	0.0
Flag Investors Communications	0.0	0.0	11.5	0.0	0.0	0.0	0.0	0.0	0.0	0.0	0.0	0.0	0.0
AXP Precious Metals	0.0	0.0	0.0	0.0	0.0	0.0	10.4	7.0	0.0	0.0	0.0	18.0	6.9
Scudder Technology	0.0	0.0	3.8	0.0	0.0	0.0	0.0	0.0	0.0	0.0	0.0	0.0	0.0
Pin Oak Aggressive Stock	0.0	0.0	9.9	0.0	0.0	0.0	0.0	0.0	0.0	0.0	0.0	0.0	0.0
T Rowe Price Science & Technology	0.0	0.0	14.0	0.0	0.0	0.0	0.0	0.0	0.0	0.0	0.0	0.0	0.0
Scudder Gold Precious Metals	0.0	0.0	0.0	0.0	0.0	0.0	28.7	9.0	0.0	0.0	0.0	25.3	0.0
State Farm Growth Fund	13.8	20.9	0.0	0.0	0.0	0.0	0.0	0.0	0.0	0.0	0.0	0.0	0.0
USAA Precious Metals	0.0	0.0	0.0	0.0	0.0	0.0	60.9	65.6	0.0	0.0	0.0	30.8	34.4
Vanguard Institutional Index	20.7	19.7	0.0	0.0	0.0	0.0	0.0	0.0	0.0	0.0	0.0	0.0	0.0

Vanguard Total Stock Market Index	60.8	55.6	0.0	0.0	0.0	0.0	0.0	0.0	0.0	0.0	0.0	0.0	0.0
PIMCO Funds PEA Innovation	0.0	0.0	0.0	0.0	0.0	2.6	0.0	0.0	0.0	0.0	0.0	0.0	0.0
Munder Funds	0.0	0.0	0.0	0.0	0.0	0.0	0.0	4.7	0.0	0.0	0.0	10.8	27.5
Needham Growth Fund	0.0	0.0	0.0	3.7	13.9	3.9	0.0	0.0	0.0	16.6	5.3	0.0	0.0
Bjurman Barry Micro Cap Growth	0.0	0.0	0.0	17.0	4.0	0.0	0.0	0.0	8.6	0.0	0.0	0.0	0.0
Evergreen Small Company Value	0.0	0.0	6.4	0.0	0.0	7.4	0.0	0.0	0.0	0.0	7.2	0.0	0.0
BlackRock US Opportunities	0.0	0.0	0.0	11.6	9.9	0.0	0.0	0.0	13.6	11.4	2.9	0.0	0.0
Morgan Stanley Small Cap Growth	0.0	0.0	0.0	44.7	54.5	38.7	0.0	0.0	52.2	60.2	42.2	0.0	0.0
ProFunds UltraOTC	0.0	0.0	0.0	0.0	0.0	13.0	0.0	13.7	0.0	0.0	11.7	0.0	31.2
Rydex Srs Tr Electronics	0.0	0.0	0.0	0.0	0.0	25.0	0.0	0.0	0.0	0.0	22.7	0.0	0.0
Strong Enterprise	0.0	0.0	0.0	0.0	4.5	0.0	0.0	0.0	0.0	0.0	0.0	0.0	0.0
Kinetics Internet	0.0	0.0	0.0	23.0	13.2	9.4	0.0	0.0	25.6	11.8	8.0	15.1	0.0
December 2002:													
Certainty Equivalent Loss (bp/month)		0.0	15.1		1.3	13.7	89.1	89.6		2.0	11.9	95.0	105.5
Sharpe Ratio (monthly)	0.13	0.13	0.37	0.36	0.44	0.56	0.75	0.81	0.42	0.54	0.64	1.16	1.09
December 1979 to November 2002:													
Average CE Loss (bp/month)													
Overall		0.2	23.5		3.4	23.1	33.9	53.2		3.7	22.6	52.1	74.1
Expansions		0.2	21.1		3.1	22.4	33.6	53.7		3.3	21.8	50.9	74.8
Recessions		0.2	39.0		5.1	27.0	35.9	49.8		5.6	27.2	60.0	69.8
Average Sharpe Ratio (monthly)													
Overall	0.16	0.16	0.05	0.31	0.32	0.26	0.51	0.47	0.33	0.34	0.29	0.69	0.67
Expansions	0.16	0.16	−0.04	0.31	0.30	0.18	0.50	0.42	0.33	0.33	0.21	0.68	0.60
Recessions	0.14	0.14	0.62	0.32	0.39	0.77	0.53	0.79	0.35	0.43	0.81	0.79	1.09

We first examine predictability in fund risk loadings. Note from Table 7.3 that incorporating predictability in fund risk loadings leaves optimal asset allocations nearly unchanged. To illustrate, consider the Dogmatist who incorporates predictable fund risk loadings (PD-1). Forcing this investor to hold the slightly different asset allocation of the no-predictability Dogmatist (ND) does not lead to any utility loss on December 31, 2002. Also, both the ND and PD-1 investors perceive the same *ex ante* Sharpe ratios at this date (0.1) as well as over expansions (0.2 on average) and recessions (0.1 on average).

Next, we examine predictability in both benchmark returns and fund risk loadings. Consider the Dogmatist who believes in such a predictability structure (PD-2). This investor would experience a nontrivial utility loss of 15.1 basis points per month (1.8% per year) in December 2002 if forced to hold the optimal portfolio of the no-predictability Dogmatist (ND). The utility loss is even larger over the course of all 276 monthly investments. This loss averages 21.1 (39) basis points per month over expansions (recessions).

Moreover, the optimal portfolio of the PD-2 investor consists of very different mutual funds, relative to those optimally selected by investors who disallow predictability or who allow predictability only in fund risk loadings. To illustrate, consider the no-predictability Dogmatist (ND). This investor primarily holds index funds, such as the Vanguard Institutional Index fund and the Vanguard Total Stock Market Index fund. When fund risk loading predictability is allowed (see PD-1), the same index funds are still optimally selected, albeit with slightly different weights. However, when predictability in both fund risk loadings and benchmark returns is allowed (see PD-2), the optimal portfolio consists of no index funds. Instead, a large allocation is made to growth, communication, and technology funds, such as the White Oak Growth fund and the T. Rowe Price Science & Technology fund.

Indeed, in the presence of predictability in fund risk loadings and benchmark returns, optimal portfolios consist entirely of actively managed funds even when the possibility of manager skills in stock selection and benchmark timing is ruled out. That is, actively managed funds allow the investor to capitalize on predictability in benchmarks and fund risk loadings in a way that cannot be achieved through long-only index fund positions.

We now turn to analyzing predictability in manager skills. Incorporating such predictability results in asset allocation that is overwhelmingly different from the other cases examined. To illustrate, consider the Agnostic who believes in predictable skills (PA-3). This investor faces an enormous utility loss of 95 basis points per month (or 11.4% per year) if constrained to hold the asset allocation of the no-predictability Agnostic (NA). Focusing on all 276 investment periods, the average utility loss is 50.9 basis points per month over expansions and 60.0 over recessions. Monthly Sharpe ratios are also the largest for investments that allow for predictability in manager skills. The Sharpe ratio is 1.2 on December 31, 2002. The average Sharpe ratio is 0.7 (0.8) over expansions (recessions) as well as 0.7 during all 276 investment periods.

To summarize the findings of this section, we demonstrate that incorporating predictability in mutual fund returns exerts a strong influence on the composition of optimal portfolios of equity mutual funds. The economic significance of predictability is especially strong for investments that allow for predictable managerial skills. In addition, actively managed funds are much more attractive, relative to index funds, in the presence of return predictability. Specifically, the no-predictability Dogmatist (ND) optimally holds index funds only, but when predictability in fund risk loadings as well as in benchmark returns is recognized, the predictability Dogmatists (PD-1 and PD-2) select actively managed funds. Similarly, under predictable manager skills (PS-3, PS-4, PA-3, and PA-4), all the equity funds that are optimally held are actively managed.

7.4.2 Out-of-Sample Performance

Here, we analyze the *ex post*, out-of-sample performance of various portfolios strategies through a sequence of investments with monthly rebalancing. Optimal portfolios are derived first using the initial 60 monthly observations, then using the first 61 monthly observations, and so on, ..., and are finally rebalanced using the first $T - 1$ monthly observations, with $T = 336$ denoting the sample size. Hence, the first investment is made at the end of December 1979, the second at the end of January 1980, and so on, ..., with the last at the end of November 2002. We obtain the month-t realized excess return on each investment strategy by multiplying the portfolio weights of month $t - 1$ by the month-t realized excess returns of the corresponding mutual funds. This recursive scheme produces 276 excess returns on 13 investment strategies that differ with respect to the Bayesian predictive moments used in the portfolio optimization.

Table 7.4 reports various performance measures, described below, for evaluating portfolio strategies that are optimal from the perspective of the 13 investor types as well as for three other strategies for selecting mutual funds that have been proposed in past work. These three strategies include a "hot-hands" strategy of investing in the top decile of funds at the end of each calendar year (Hendricks et al., 1993), based on the compounded net return over that year (H-H), a strategy of investing in the top decile of funds at the end of each year, based on the Carhart alpha (α_{wml}) computed over the prior three-year period, limited to funds that have at least 30 monthly returns available (CAR), and a strategy of investing in funds, each quarter, that have above-median cash inflows (among all positive cash-inflow funds) during the prior three months (SM) (Zheng et al., 1999). The first 13 portfolio strategies are formed assuming that investors use only the market benchmark (MKT) to form moments for asset allocation.

In Table 7.4, μ is the average realized excess return, *SR* is the annual Sharpe ratio, *skew* is the skewness of monthly returns, α_{cpm} ($\tilde{\alpha}_{cpm}$) is the intercept obtained by regressing the realized excess returns on the market factor when beta is constant (when beta is scaled by business cycle variables), α_{ff} and $\tilde{\alpha}_{ff}$ are the same intercepts, but returns are adjusted with the Fama-French benchmarks (MKT, SMB, and HML), and α_{wml} and $\tilde{\alpha}_{wml}$ are the intercepts obtained using the

Table 7.4 Out-of-Sample Performance of Portfolio Strategies

The table reports various performance measures for evaluating portfolio strategies that are optimal from the perspective of the 13 investor types described in Table 7.1, as well as for three strategies for selecting mutual funds advocated in earlier work. These three strategies include a hot-hands strategy of investing in the top decile of funds at the end of each calendar year, based on the compounded net return over that year (H-H); a strategy of investing in the top decile of funds at the end of each year, based on the Carhart alpha (α_{wml}) computed over the prior three-year period, limited to funds having at least 30 monthly returns available (CAR); and a strategy of investing in funds, each quarter, that have above-median cash inflows over the prior three months (SM). Portfolio strategies for the 13 investor types are formed assuming these investors use the market benchmark to form expectations about future moments for asset allocation. Performance is evaluated using 276 *ex post* excess returns generated using a recursive scheme. The evaluation measures are as follows: μ is the annual average realized excess return, *std* is the annual standard deviation, *SR* is the annual Sharpe ratio, *skew* is the skewness of monthly returns, α_{cpm} ($\tilde{\alpha}_{cpm}$) is the annualized intercept obtained by regressing the realized excess returns on the market factor when beta is constant (when beta is scaled by business cycle variables), α_{ff} and $\tilde{\alpha}_{ff}$ are the same intercepts, but returns are adjusted with the Fama-French benchmarks, and α_{wml} and $\tilde{\alpha}_{wml}$ are the intercepts obtained using the Carhart benchmarks. *P*-values are reported below the alphas. Panel A covers the entire investment period, and Panel B (C) focuses on the December 1979 through December 1989 (January 1990 through November 2002) investment period.

	The Dogmatist			The Skeptic					The Agnostic					Previously Studied		
	ND	PD-1	PD-2	NS	PS-1	PS-2	PS-3	PS-4	NA	PA-1	PA-2	PA-3	PA-4	H-H	CAR	SM
	Panel A: The Entire Investment Period															
μ	6.39	6.58	6.74	6.92	5.56	6.06	15.14	11.5	7.07	5.26	5.89	16.52	12.12	8.97	5.42	5.78
std	0.16	0.16	0.16	0.21	0.21	0.18	0.28	0.21	0.21	0.21	0.18	0.28	0.22	0.20	0.19	0.17
SR	0.39	0.41	0.43	0.33	0.27	0.34	0.55	0.54	0.33	0.25	0.33	0.59	0.54	0.44	0.28	0.34
skew	−0.71	−0.68	0.03	−0.20	−0.38	−0.28	1.13	0.32	−0.18	−0.35	−0.31	1.05	0.21	−0.52	−0.57	−0.76
α_{cpm}	−0.23	0.00	1.92	−0.38	−1.89	0.71	8.12	6.48	−0.23	−2.16	0.54	9.46	6.73	1.95	−1.86	−0.99
$P(\alpha_{cpm})$	0.66	1.00	0.38	0.88	0.36	0.79	0.07	0.08	0.93	0.31	0.84	0.04	0.08	0.39	0.26	0.32
α_{ff}	0.60	1.03	0.91	2.33	0.29	−0.51	11.14	6.86	2.49	0.06	−0.46	12.89	7.88	3.48	−0.39	−0.17
$P(\alpha_{ff})$	0.22	0.04	0.68	0.22	0.87	0.85	0.01	0.05	0.20	0.97	0.86	0.00	0.03	0.04	0.74	0.81
α_{wml}	0.37	0.62	3.92	−1.30	−2.49	0.83	5.98	4.95	−1.29	−2.83	0.51	8.46	6.20	−0.99	−0.48	−1.10
$P(\alpha_{wml})$	0.46	0.22	0.07	0.45	0.13	0.76	0.14	0.17	0.47	0.10	0.85	0.04	0.10	0.46	0.69	0.06
$\tilde{\alpha}_{cpm}$	−0.09	0.14	1.85	0.14	−1.75	0.66	9.01	6.36	0.25	−1.99	0.49	10.52	6.76	1.97	−1.50	−0.99
$P(\tilde{\alpha}_{cpm})$	0.87	0.80	0.40	0.96	0.40	0.80	0.05	0.08	0.92	0.35	0.85	0.02	0.08	0.39	0.35	0.32
$\tilde{\alpha}_{ff}$	0.20	0.84	0.91	2.96	1.02	0.29	13.30	9.28	3.10	1.03	0.65	14.84	9.13	4.45	0.30	0.29
$P(\tilde{\alpha}_{ff})$	0.64	0.05	0.62	0.12	0.55	0.90	0.00	0.01	0.11	0.56	0.79	0.00	0.01	0.00	0.79	0.67
$\tilde{\alpha}_{wml}$	0.24	0.69	1.90	−0.84	−1.99	−0.37	9.44	7.88	−0.78	−2.01	−0.19	11.17	7.28	0.08	−0.57	−1.05
$P(\tilde{\alpha}_{wml})$	0.59	0.12	0.30	0.61	0.23	0.88	0.02	0.03	0.65	0.24	0.94	0.00	0.05	0.95	0.61	0.08

Panel B: Dec 1979 through Dec 1989																
μ	7.18	7.68	8.43	7.57	7.88	10.82	12.83	14.85	7.57	7.61	10.78	12.39	15.21	9.40	7.51	7.81
std	0.17	0.17	0.15	0.18	0.21	0.18	0.19	0.19	0.18	0.21	0.18	0.19	0.20	0.20	0.17	0.18
SR	0.43	0.46	0.56	0.43	0.38	0.61	0.69	0.79	0.42	0.37	0.60	0.65	0.76	0.48	0.43	0.44
skew	−0.82	−0.85	−0.05	−1.36	−1.00	−0.36	−1.34	−0.07	−1.41	−1.04	−0.41	−1.36	0.01	−1.43	−0.87	−1.04
α_{cpm}	−0.73	−0.19	2.67	−0.20	−1.20	4.47	5.78	8.51	−0.33	−1.36	4.42	5.41	8.70	0.87	−0.38	−0.45
$P(\alpha_{cpm})$	0.41	0.83	0.36	0.93	0.66	0.24	0.11	0.05	0.90	0.62	0.25	0.18	0.06	0.74	0.85	0.78
α_{ff}	0.26	0.95	2.80	2.08	3.32	4.61	4.49	7.35	1.93	3.18	4.7	3.83	7.60	2.34	1.45	1.49
$P(\alpha_{ff})$	0.76	0.27	0.36	0.30	0.15	0.22	0.22	0.09	0.36	0.17	0.22	0.34	0.12	0.34	0.43	0.23
α_{wml}	0.20	0.79	3.40	−0.58	0.39	4.12	0.52	5.39	−0.85	0.24	4.17	−0.16	5.17	−1.42	−0.10	−0.36
$P(\alpha_{wml})$	0.82	0.36	0.27	0.74	0.85	0.29	0.88	0.22	0.64	0.91	0.29	0.97	0.29	0.48	0.95	0.73
$\tilde{\alpha}_{cpm}$	−0.70	−0.18	1.63	−0.67	−1.48	3.33	5.56	7.08	−0.80	−1.67	3.19	5.16	7.21	0.73	−0.89	−0.74
$P(\tilde{\alpha}_{cpm})$	0.43	0.84	0.56	0.78	0.59	0.36	0.13	0.08	0.75	0.55	0.39	0.20	0.11	0.78	0.66	0.64
$\tilde{\alpha}_{ff}$	−0.27	0.46	−2.30	3.54	5.25	2.39	5.26	5.47	3.35	5.33	2.63	4.98	5.24	6.28	2.14	1.79
$P(\tilde{\alpha}_{ff})$	0.76	0.59	0.38	0.05	0.03	0.50	0.12	0.18	0.08	0.03	0.47	0.20	0.25	0.01	0.28	0.17
$\tilde{\alpha}_{wml}$	0.01	0.76	−1.95	0.95	1.40	1.63	0.88	2.20	0.75	1.46	1.67	0.27	1.04	1.52	−1.23	−1.04
$P(\tilde{\alpha}_{wml})$	0.99	0.39	0.46	0.55	0.54	0.63	0.79	0.61	0.65	0.52	0.63	0.94	0.83	0.48	0.51	0.32
Panel C: Jan 1990 through Nov 2002																
μ	5.78	5.73	5.44	6.55	3.79	2.39	16.45	8.93	6.88	3.44	2.13	19.69	9.83	8.8	4.6	4.69
std	0.16	0.16	0.16	0.23	0.21	0.18	0.32	0.23	0.24	0.22	0.18	0.33	0.25	0.20	0.20	0.16
SR	0.36	0.36	0.34	0.28	0.18	0.13	0.51	0.39	0.29	0.16	0.12	0.59	0.40	0.43	0.23	0.29
skew	−0.61	−0.55	0.08	0.18	0.10	−0.21	1.35	0.51	0.23	0.15	−0.24	1.26	0.31	0.04	−0.44	−0.53
α_{cpm}	0.19	0.17	1.37	−0.31	−2.40	−2.14	10.10	4.90	0.03	−2.74	−2.39	12.83	5.25	2.23	−2.82	−1.62
$P(\alpha_{cpm})$	0.75	0.81	0.66	0.93	0.43	0.55	0.18	0.38	0.99	0.38	0.50	0.09	0.37	0.50	0.20	0.17
α_{ff}	0.91	1.09	0.15	2.04	−1.29	−3.63	13.68	5.47	2.42	−1.61	−3.67	16.99	6.72	3.90	−1.55	−1.04
$P(\alpha_{ff})$	0.09	0.06	0.96	0.48	0.60	0.31	0.03	0.28	0.41	0.53	0.30	0.01	0.20	0.08	0.23	0.14
α_{wml}	0.51	0.45	4.91	−3.26	−4.20	−1.25	6.79	3.65	−3.01	−4.76	−1.90	11.15	5.40	−1.79	−1.25	−2.35
$P(\alpha_{wml})$	0.34	0.44	0.08	0.19	0.08	0.73	0.27	0.49	0.23	0.05	0.60	0.07	0.32	0.28	0.36	0.00
$\tilde{\alpha}_{cpm}$	0.36	0.37	1.82	0.10	−1.64	−1.48	11.90	6.14	0.43	−1.91	−1.68	14.58	6.61	2.28	−2.46	−1.40
$P(\tilde{\alpha}_{cpm})$	0.54	0.59	0.56	0.98	0.58	0.68	0.11	0.27	0.91	0.54	0.63	0.05	0.25	0.49	0.27	0.24
$\tilde{\alpha}_{ff}$	0.67	1.19	1.95	1.42	−1.18	−2.62	17.39	10.28	1.97	−1.32	−2.43	19.77	9.96	3.09	−1.28	−1.04
$P(\tilde{\alpha}_{ff})$	0.07	0.01	0.37	0.59	0.59	0.39	0.00	0.03	0.47	0.56	0.43	0.00	0.05	0.08	0.30	0.09
$\tilde{\alpha}_{wml}$	0.74	0.81	2.14	−3.49	−3.79	−3.66	14.23	8.76	−2.99	−3.66	−3.63	15.83	6.80	−1.21	−1.28	−2.05
$P(\tilde{\alpha}_{wml})$	0.06	0.07	0.34	0.15	0.08	0.24	0.02	0.09	0.23	0.10	0.25	0.01	0.20	0.41	0.32	0.00

Carhart benchmarks (MKT, SMB, HML, and UMD); p-values are reported below the alphas. All alpha measures as well as μ are shown in % per annum. Panel A covers the entire investment period, while Panel B (C) focuses on the December 1979 through December 1989 (January 1990 though November 2002) investment period. The first subperiod corresponds to the time before the discovery of the macro variables by Keim and Stambaugh (1986) and Fama and French (1989). The second subperiod captures the post-discovery period.

Although we form optimal portfolios for believers in the CAPM, out-of-sample *ex post* performance is assessed using the CAPM, the Fama-French three-factor model, and the Carhart four-factor model. That is, we assume that the performance evaluator observes the investment returns, but does not know the model that generates the returns, and therefore, implements various performance measures. Note that a positive and significant α_{cpm} ($\tilde{\alpha}_{cpm}$) implies that the evaluated investment outperforms a static (dynamic) investment in the market benchmark, generating higher payoffs for the same fixed (time-varying) risk exposures. Performance measures under the Fama-French and Carhart models should be similarly interpreted; that is, they imply that the evaluated investment outperforms a static or dynamic investment with the same exposures to the multiple risk sources.

Several insights about the success of the 16 (13+3) portfolio strategies can be inferred from Table 7.4. First, when business cycle variables are excluded, optimal portfolios of mutual funds yield zero and even negative performance. To illustrate, the no-predictability Dogmatist (ND) realizes an insignificant alpha that ranges between −0.23% to 0.60% per year. This suggests that investment opportunities based on i.i.d. mutual fund returns that may be *ex ante* attractive, as advocated by Baks et al. (2001), do not translate into positive out-of-sample alphas. At the same time, we find that incorporating predictability in fund risk loadings and benchmark returns delivers much better out-of-sample performance. Specifically, a Dogmatist who recognizes the possibility of predictable fund risk loadings and benchmark returns (PD-2) realizes an alpha that ranges between 0.91% (α_{ff}) and 3.92% (α_{wml}), where the latter is significant at the 7% level.

It is true that optimal portfolios that reflect predictability in fund risk loadings and benchmark returns do not always beat their benchmarks. However, when we allow for predictability in manager skills, we find that the resulting optimal portfolios consistently outperform strategies that exclude predictability, strategies that account for predictable fund risk loadings and benchmark returns only, static and dynamic investments in the Fama-French and momentum benchmarks, and the three previously studied strategies that we describe above.

To illustrate the strong performance of strategies that account for predictable manager skills, we note that the PA-3 investor selects optimal portfolios that generate $\alpha_{cpm} = 9.46\%$, $\tilde{\alpha}_{cpm} = 10.52\%$, $\alpha_{ff} = 12.89\%$, $\tilde{\alpha}_{ff} = 14.84\%$, $\alpha_{wml} = 8.46\%$, and $\tilde{\alpha}_{wml} = 11.17\%$, all of which are significant at the 5% level. Moreover, the out-of-sample Sharpe ratios of strategies that reflect predictability in manager skills are the largest, consistent with the *ex ante* results described earlier. Take, for instance, the Agnostic investor. When predictability is disregarded altogether

(NA), the annual Sharpe ratio is 0.33. Allowing for predictability in fund risk loadings and benchmark assets (PA-2) does not change this Sharpe ratio. However, allowing for predictability in manager skills (PA-3) delivers a much larger Sharpe ratio of 0.59.

Note, also, that the skewness of investment returns is much larger for strategies that include predictable manager skills. For instance, the level of skewness is 1.05 for investor PA-3, whereas skewness is negative for all investors who disregard predictability, such as investor NA. Although we consider only investor types who are mean-variance optimizers, the higher skewness obtained by PA-3 and other predictable skills strategies indicate that investors who directly include skewness in their preferences (such as those that have a power utility function) would prefer these optimal portfolios relative to those obtained by NA and other no-predictability strategies. That is, the higher levels of skewness indicate that predictable skills strategies may be attractive to an even broader set of investor types than those considered in this chapter.

Interestingly, none of the previously studied strategies, H-H, CAR, and SM, produce performance that matches the optimal portfolios that use predictability in skills. The CAR and SM generate mostly negative alphas. The H-H strategy generates a positive and significant α_{ff} and $\tilde{\alpha}_{ff}$ of 3.48% and 4.45%, respectively. However, this performance becomes insignificant when adding a momentum factor, consistent with Carhart (1997), suggesting that our portfolio strategies are unique, and that they outperform optimal strategies that exclude conditioning information as well as strategies that pick funds based on past returns and flows, as advocated previously in the mutual fund literature.

We conduct two additional experiments. First, we implement the same performance measures for two subperiods, namely, the investment period December 1979 through December 1989 (Panel B, Table 7.4), and the investment period January 1990 through November 2002 (Panel C). Second, we analyze performance (see Table 7.5) when optimal portfolios are formed by the 13 types of investors that believe in the Fama-French model as well as the Carhart four-factor model.

Studying two subperiods is important because the mutual fund industry has grown over time with many more funds available for investment in the second part of the sample. Moreover, through this subperiod analysis, we attempt to address data-mining concerns. Specifically, Schwert (2003) notes that the so-called financial market anomalies related to profit opportunities tend to disappear, reverse, or attenuate following their discovery. For example, he shows that the relation between the aggregate dividend yield and the equity premium is much weaker after the discovery of that predictor by Keim and Stambaugh (1986) and Fama and French (1989).

Observe from Table 7.4, Panel C, that, over the second subperiod, the PA-3 strategy produces robust performance measures. Specifically, the Sharpe ratio attributable to that strategy, 0.59, continues to be the largest across all

Table 7.5 Out-of-Sample Performance of Optimal Portfolio Strategies

The table reports various performance measures for evaluating portfolio strategies that are optimal from the perspective of the 13 investor types described in Table 7.1, using the Fama-French model and the Carhart (1997) models to form moments for asset allocation. Performance is evaluated using 276 *ex post* excess returns generated using a recursive scheme. The evaluation measures are as follows: μ is the average realized excess return, α_{cpm} ($\tilde{\alpha}_{cpm}$) is the intercept obtained by regressing the realized excess returns on the market factor when beta is constant (when beta is scaled by business cycle variables), α_{ff} and $\tilde{\alpha}_{ff}$ are the same intercepts, but returns are adjusted with the Fama-French benchmarks, and α_{wml} and $\tilde{\alpha}_{wml}$ are the intercepts obtained using the Carhart benchmarks. All measures are percent per annum. The symbols * and ** reflect significance at the 5% and 10% level, respectively.

	The Dogmatist			The Skeptic					The Agnostic				
	ND	PD-1	PD-2	NS	PS-1	PS-2	PS-3	PS-4	NA	PA-1	PA-2	PA-3	PA-4
The Fama-French Model													
μ	6.64	6.24	5.86	6.57	4.56	6.25	11.11	10.24	6.65	4.68	6.24	11.17	10.26
α_{cpm}	1.68	1.05	1.00	−0.01	−2.37	0.36	4.57	4.96	−0.10	−2.35	0.30	4.51	4.53
α_{ff}	−2.00	−1.60	−0.71	1.09	−0.99	0.77	8.35*	5.00	1.37	−0.68	0.95	9.09*	5.13
α_{wml}	−1.36	−2.47	−1.56	−1.50	−3.07	−0.11	2.98	3.00	−1.32	−2.65	0.12	4.11	3.10
$\tilde{\alpha}_{cpm}$	1.21	0.61	0.42	0.36	−2.00	0.62	5.67	4.96	0.30	−1.93	0.57	5.70	4.60
$\tilde{\alpha}_{ff}$	−1.33	−0.51	0.82	2.34	1.22	2.92	12.38*	7.67*	2.77	1.65	3.04	12.80*	7.41*
$\tilde{\alpha}_{wml}$	−0.46	−1.30	−1.03	−0.32	−1.71	0.74	8.89*	5.99	0.04	−1.21	0.87	9.35*	5.13
The Carhart Model													
μ	3.43	8.67	5.11	5.82	8.42	5.17	10.80	10.38	5.95	8.35	5.40	11.73	10.62
α_{cpm}	−1.48	3.25	−0.07	−0.75	2.24	−0.92	4.12	4.78	−0.75	2.08	−0.74	5.02	4.45
α_{ff}	−3.41	2.95	−0.50	0.16	4.10**	0.25	7.33**	5.17**	0.47	4.17**	0.56	9.15*	5.80**
α_{wml}	−5.13*	0.27	−3.87	−2.12	2.42	−2.03	2.30	2.49	−1.92	2.68	−1.59	4.16	3.14
$\tilde{\alpha}_{cpm}$	−1.82	3.07	−0.27	−0.39	2.73	−0.61	5.12	4.83	−0.32	2.64	−0.42	6.18	4.67
$\tilde{\alpha}_{ff}$	−2.26	3.98**	1.31	1.69	4.54**	2.17	10.96*	6.97*	2.24	4.63*	2.39	12.96*	6.77*
$\tilde{\alpha}_{wml}$	−3.48	1.60	−2.01	−0.63	2.56	−0.55	7.71*	4.77	−0.19	2.75	−0.21	9.47*	4.56

strategies. In addition, all (annual) alphas are large and significant, given by $\alpha_{cpm} = 12.83\%$, $\tilde{\alpha}_{cpm} = 14.58\%$, $\alpha_{ff} = 16.99\%$, $\tilde{\alpha}_{ff} = 19.77\%$, $\alpha_{wml} = 11.15\%$, and $\tilde{\alpha}_{wml} = 15.83\%$. Indeed, much of the remarkable performance of the PA-3 strategy can be traced to this second subperiod, during which time the predictive variables are already known and available for investment, and when the investment universe contains many more funds.

Finally, observe from Table 7.5 that the superior performance of strategies that allow for predictability in manager skills also obtains when the three Fama-French benchmarks and the four Carhart benchmarks are used to form optimal portfolios. Such strategies consistently deliver positive alphas that are often significant at the 5% or 10% levels. Also note that optimal trading strategies that exclude predictability altogether mostly generate insignificant levels of performance. Overall, the finding that predictability in manager skills is the dominant source of investment profitability still prevails under these alternative models.

We note that the findings in Moskowitz (2000) suggest that fund performance may vary with the business cycle. Moskowitz (2000) uses the NBER characterization for recessionary and expansionary periods, and documents higher performance during recessions, relative to expansions, using the difference in portfolio holdings based performance measures or the difference in net returns. Our work shows that fund performance varies predictably (and substantially) with predetermined macroeconomic variables. Moreover, explicitly incorporating predictability in manager skills using such macro variables leads to dramatically different optimal portfolios of equity mutual funds. In our framework, one can identify *ex ante* the best-performing funds, leading to an optimal fund-of-funds that outperforms dynamic and static investments in passive benchmarks as well as other strategies previously studied in the mutual fund context. Overall, our findings suggest that active mutual fund management adds much more value than previously recognized.

7.4.3 The Determinants of the Superior Predictability-Based Performance

What explains the remarkable performance of strategies that account for predictable skills? In this section, we attempt to address this question. We study the attributes of these strategies at the stock holdings and net returns levels, and we explore inter- and intraindustry effects in their portfolio allocations.

7.4.3.1 *Attributes of Portfolio Strategies*

We first examine the attributes of our optimally selected portfolios of equity mutual funds. Table 7.6 provides time-series average portfolio-level and fund-level attributes across all 276 investment periods (December 1979 to November 2002), as well as averages across NBER expansions only, and across NBER recessions only.

Portfolio holdings attributes of mutual funds include the time-series average characteristic selectivity performance measure of Daniel et al. (1997) in percent

Table 7.6 Attributes of Optimal Portfolios

The table reports several attributes of the portfolio strategies that are optimal from the perspective of the 13 investor types described in Table 7.1, as well as for three strategies for selecting mutual funds that appear in previous studies, as explained in Table 7.4. These attributes include the portfolio-weighted characteristic selectivity measure in percent per year (*CS*), as well as its *p*-value (in parentheses), lagged net return, compounded over the 12 months prior to each portfolio formation date ($Lag_{12}(Ret)$), total net assets in millions of dollars (*TNA*) of funds, portfolio holdings-based DGTW (nonparametric) style attributes in the size (*Size*), book-to-market (*BTM*), and momentum (*MOM*) dimensions, percent monthly fund turnover, computed as annual reported turnover divided by 12 (*Turnover*), monthly percentage net cash inflows (*Flow*), computed as *TNA* minus one-quarter-lagged *TNA* (adjusted for investment returns and distributions), divided by three, fund expense ratio (*ExpenseRatio*), portfolio weight allocation to index funds (*IndexFunds*), and lead manager experience in months (*ManagerExperience*). These attributes are presented for all periods, for expansions only, and for recessions only.

	The Dogmatist			The Skeptic					The Agnostic					Previously Studied		
	ND	PD-1	PD-2	NS	PS-1	PS-2	PS-3	PS-4	NA	PA-1	PA-2	PA-3	PA-4	H-H	CAR	SM
Overall																
CS	0.39	0.26	2.13	0.57	1.47	2.99	7.19	4.38	0.47	1.06	2.78	8.10	6.02	3.30	0.38	1.84
P(CS)	0.28	0.51	0.36	0.72	0.36	0.38	0.09	0.31	0.77	0.51	0.42	0.05	0.19	0.08	0.82	0.05
$Lag_{12}(Ret)$	7.92	8.75	8.54	26.89	22.68	17.53	37.71	28.70	26.69	22.55	17.68	38.73	29.58	29.78	19.33	19.56
TNA	388.73	343.74	201.40	343.47	296.58	224.68	170.39	149.13	318.45	286.68	216.20	146.77	139.68	175.61	195.34	243.97
Size	4.58	4.62	4.05	3.61	4.04	3.69	3.62	3.61	3.52	3.99	3.63	3.55	3.60	3.63	3.68	3.95
BTM	2.70	2.72	2.70	2.51	2.49	2.44	2.45	2.47	2.53	2.49	2.43	2.48	2.44	2.52	2.51	2.62
MOM	3.01	3.03	2.98	3.81	3.88	3.44	3.66	3.35	3.79	3.86	3.45	3.61	3.39	3.70	3.41	3.40
Turnover	1.71	1.91	3.79	9.01	9.29	7.72	8.37	7.85	9.29	9.53	8.05	8.75	7.49	8.43	8.44	7.56
Flow	2.57	2.49	3.51	5.23	4.52	4.67	6.75	6.54	5.47	4.69	4.93	7.28	6.96	5.91	4.54	6.01
ExpenseRatio	0.02	0.02	0.08	0.11	0.11	0.11	0.11	0.11	0.11	0.11	0.11	0.12	0.11	0.11	0.11	0.09
IndexFunds	0.54	0.52	0.15	0.03	0.02	0.02	0.02	0.01	0.03	0.03	0.02	0.02	0.01	0.02	0.01	0.08
ManagerExperience	85.53	88.61	123.46	155.84	179.45	120.79	120.24	111.92	148.33	171.58	117.97	108.92	106.46	99.11	105.77	97.92
Expansions:																
CS	0.23	0.10	1.29	−0.93	−0.11	0.63	5.45	2.68	−0.91	−0.01	0.41	7.19	5.14	2.89	0.37	1.37
P(CS)	0.58	0.82	0.61	0.60	0.95	0.87	0.23	0.56	0.62	0.99	0.92	0.12	0.30	0.16	0.82	0.16
$Lag_{12}(Ret)$	8.94	9.83	10.60	28.86	25.37	20.15	41.76	32.75	28.69	25.23	20.24	42.68	33.73	31.84	21.85	21.88

TNA	403.78	354.54	194.70	375.00	316.34	233.05	180.75	159.07	347.75	304.64	223.50	154.80	144.70	182.07	201.74	250.87
Size	4.59	4.63	4.08	3.70	4.09	3.73	3.68	3.68	3.60	4.03	3.66	3.59	3.66	3.63	3.67	3.97
BTM	2.70	2.73	2.81	2.50	2.55	2.50	2.42	2.51	2.52	2.56	2.49	2.44	2.49	2.52	2.52	2.65
MOM	3.04	3.05	2.95	3.80	3.84	3.41	3.68	3.35	3.78	3.83	3.40	3.62	3.38	3.71	3.44	3.40
Turnover	1.71	1.91	3.79	9.01	9.29	7.72	8.37	7.85	9.29	9.53	8.05	8.75	7.49	8.43	8.44	7.56
Flow	2.63	2.54	3.60	4.89	4.48	4.59	6.75	6.56	5.16	4.63	4.88	7.20	7.09	5.96	4.58	6.09
ExpenseRatio	0.02	0.02	0.08	0.11	0.11	0.11	0.11	0.11	0.11	0.11	0.11	0.12	0.11	0.11	0.11	0.09
IndexFunds	0.56	0.54	0.13	0.04	0.03	0.02	0.02	0.01	0.04	0.03	0.03	0.02	0.01	0.02	0.01	0.09
ManagerExperience	89.67	91.70	120.10	160.45	176.23	117.91	120.57	111.17	152.26	167.70	114.93	105.88	105.11	96.60	102.17	95.34
Recessions:																
CS	1.25	1.07	9.47	9.12	10.25	14.62	11.28	11.99	8.24	7.19	14.38	13.86	8.81	6.63	0.42	4.38
P(*CS*)	0.13	0.18	0.07	0.00	0.07	0.06	0.20	0.31	0.00	0.18	0.05	0.09	0.43	0.00	0.80	0.13
$Lag_{12}(Ret)$	1.53	2.00	−4.36	14.56	5.84	1.10	12.32	3.28	14.19	5.72	1.65	14.00	3.55	16.92	3.54	5.05
TNA	294.91	276.12	242.66	159.24	176.95	176.90	106.01	87.68	155.00	177.99	174.76	91.68	108.41	135.09	155.26	200.77
Size	4.55	4.53	3.82	3.06	3.73	3.49	3.26	3.22	2.98	3.72	3.47	3.31	3.24	3.61	3.75	3.82
BTM	2.74	2.72	2.10	2.62	2.13	2.10	2.65	2.17	2.60	2.09	2.08	2.68	2.16	2.52	2.45	2.48
MOM	2.85	2.89	3.17	3.85	4.08	3.67	3.48	3.39	3.83	4.06	3.69	3.54	3.47	3.64	3.28	3.36
Turnover	2.45	2.39	3.96	7.55	9.37	7.87	9.71	11.00	7.86	9.51	7.95	9.88	9.80	7.97	10.73	7.03
Flow	2.09	2.09	3.00	7.21	4.75	5.08	6.76	6.40	7.21	5.00	5.21	7.89	6.25	5.61	4.35	5.50
ExpenseRatio	0.03	0.03	0.08	0.10	0.10	0.10	0.11	0.11	0.11	0.11	0.11	0.11	0.10	0.11	0.11	0.09
IndexFunds	0.41	0.40	0.24	0.00	0.00	0.00	0.00	0.01	0.00	0.00	0.00	0.00	0.00	0.01	0.02	0.07
ManagerExperience	59.78	68.67	147.42	127.21	199.60	139.71	118.21	116.54	124.74	195.85	137.60	129.70	115.17	114.85	128.32	114.06

per year (*CS*), as well as its *p*-value, and the size (*Size*), book-to-market (*BTM*), and momentum (*MOM*) nonparametric rank characteristics of the stockholdings, as defined by DGTW. To compute the *CS* measure as well as nonparametric characteristics of the stockholdings of each fund, we follow DGTW in creating portfolios, for each stock during each year, that closely match the size, book-to-market, and momentum characteristics of that stock.[5] In turn, these portfolio holdings attributes of funds are weighted by each investor's optimal fund holdings to arrive at investor-level attributes. To illustrate, the ND investor records a *CS* measure of 0.39% per year over the entire investment period, 0.23% over expansions, and 1.25% over recessions.

These portfolio-level and fund-level attributes provide insights into the types of mutual funds that the different optimal strategies choose to hold. Let us start with the *CS* measure. There are two notable findings here. First, the *CS* measure indicates that funds selected by almost all investor types exhibit much higher performance levels during recessions, consistent with the findings of Moskowitz (2000). Second, predictability-based strategies choose funds with higher *CS* measures during both expansions and recessions. Indeed, the highest *CS* measure over the entire investment period is recorded for the PA-3 strategy at 8.1% per year, which is significant at the 5% level. Remarkably, over recessions, the *CS* measure of the PA-2 and PA-3 strategies is 14.38% and 13.86% per year, respectively.

Interestingly, strategies that account for predictable skills, PA-3, PA-4, PS-3, and PS-4, hold funds with the highest past-year returns. This is consistent with Avramov and Chordia (2005a,b) who demonstrate the relation between time-varying alpha and momentum at the stock level. Specifically, the PA-3 investor holds funds with a prior one-year return of 38.73%, on average. The corresponding figure is 26.69% (7.92%) for the NA (ND) investor.[6] Combining the facts that both past returns and current *CS* measures are higher for investors PA-3, PA-4, PS-3, and PS-4 may indicate that these strategies identify fund managers with persistent skills. It should be noted, however, that momentum alone does not explain the entire extraordinary performance of the PA-3 strategy. Observe from Table 7.4 that this strategy generates an excess investment return of 16.52% per year. Adjusting investment returns by the Fama-French

---

[5] To be specific, we sort all CRSP stocks, conditionally, into quintiles based on their size, book-to-market, and momentum characteristics on June 30 of each year, thereby forming 125 portfolios (e.g., the portfolio identified as 5,5,5 is the large-capitalization, high book-to-market, high momentum stock portfolio). Then, the characteristic-adjusted return for each stock, from July 1 to June 30 of the following year, is the return on the stock minus the return on the value-weighted portfolio to which that stock belongs. The *CS* measure for a given fund is computed as the portfolio-weighted characteristic-adjusted return during each month of that fund's existence. The nonparametric size characteristic for a given fund is the quintile size portfolio number to which each stock belongs during a given year, weighted across all stocks held by the fund each month. The *BTM* and *MOM* nonparametric characteristics of each fund are computed similarly.

[6] Indeed, some predictable skill strategies choose funds with prior returns that are higher than those of the H-H strategy. This is explained by the nature of the value weighting of the predictability-based versus the equal weighting of the H-H strategy, as well as the fact that H-H selects the top 10% of funds whereas the predictability-based strategies could select a smaller fraction.

benchmarks yields an alpha of 12.89%; adjusting, in addition, by the momentum factor diminishes the alpha to 8.46%. That suggests that the large average investment return of investor PA-3 is partially explained by momentum. Our focus here is to explain the 8.46% residual performance that already accounts for momentum.

Related to this last point, note that the characteristics of portfolios based on stock holdings, shown by *Size*, *BTM*, and *MOM*, are similar among investor types who allow for active management skills, predictable or not. This reinforces the notion that our results are not driven by taking positions in very specialized style sectors of the market over long time-periods, such as investing in small-cap value strategies. Nor are they driven by switching investment styles over the business cycle.

Next, strategies of Skeptics and Agnostics involve holding smaller funds than strategies of Dogmatists (see *TNA* for NS or NA as compared to ND, as well as for PS-2 or PA-2 as compared to PD-2). Further, investors who allow for predictability hold even smaller funds (e.g., see *TNA* for PA-3 as compared to NA). These findings are consistent with diseconomies of scale in active fund management (see, e.g., Chen et al., 2004).

Moving to turnover, we demonstrate that adding predictability in manager skills (PS-3, PS-4, PA-3, and PA-4) reduces the turnover level of funds optimally held relative to no-predictability strategies (NS and NA), indicating that the former strategies identify managers that have greater skills in picking underpriced stocks over longer holding periods. Note, however, that these investors hold funds with higher levels of turnover during recessions, indicating that fund managers with greater skills during downturns have shorter holding periods. Notice also that almost all investor types hold a smaller allocation of index funds during recessions. This reinforces the notion that active management is much more valuable over recessionary periods (relative to index funds), consistent with Moskowitz (2000).

The pattern of flows indicates that investors who believe in active management skills follow funds with higher levels of lagged net inflows, which is not surprising since they have higher allocations to funds that have high past returns, and flows and past returns have been shown to be highly correlated (see, e.g., Sirri and Tufano, 1998). However, strategies PS-3, PS-4, PA-3, and PA-4 do not merely capture the smart money effect because, as Table 7.4 highlights, a strategy that merely selects funds based on their flows produces negative performance relative to the Fama-French and momentum benchmarks.

The level of manager experience indicates that predictability-based strategies involve choosing fund managers with slightly less experience, but this trend does not seem especially strong.

For comparison purposes, we also present portfolio attributes for the hot-hands, Carhart, and smart money strategies discussed previously. We find that these strategies generally involve holding funds with similar fund-level and portfolio-level attributes as investors PA-3 and PA-4, but that they do not generate similar levels of CS performance. Thus, predictability-based strategies involve selecting from similar groups of funds as the more mechanical hot-hands, Carhart, and smart money strategies, but are much more successful in identifying manager talents.

We summarize the evidence emerging from this section as follows. Strategies that account for predictable manager skills outperform their characteristic-based benchmarks, especially during recessions. Such strategies pick funds with higher past one-year returns and funds with higher new money inflows. Even so, their overall extraordinary performance is unexplained by following mechanical trading strategies based on flows or momentum because the hot-hand and smart money strategies that exploit information in past returns and new money inflows do not produce such robust performance measures. In addition, the outperforming predictability-based strategies hold stocks with similar size, book-to-market, and momentum characteristics as those held by other less-promising strategies. However, although the average *TNA* is different across the strategies, this does not explain the dispersion in performance. Specifically, Chen et al. (2004) find a difference in performance of only 1% per year between the smallest and largest quintiles of mutual funds. Thus, we need to look for other sources, beyond the characteristic styles, past fund returns, and new money inflows, or fund *TNA*, to explain the disparity in performance among the competing strategies. We turn to this issue next.

7.4.3.2 *Industry Allocation Analysis*

Specifically, we examine whether inter- and intraindustry effects can explain the dispersion in performance among trading strategies. In particular, we consider 13 industries based on the Fama-French 12-industry classification, plus a separate industry category for stocks in the metals mining and metals wholesaling businesses.[7] The 13 industries include: computer hardware, software, and other electronic equipment (Buseq); chemicals (Chems); durable goods, including autos, televisions, furniture, and household appliances (Durbl); oil, gas, and coal extraction (Enrgy); healthcare, medical equipment, and drugs (Hlth); machinery, trucks, planes, office furniture, paper, and commercial printing (Manuf); financials (Money); food, tobacco, textiles, apparel, leather, and toys (NoDur); wholesale, retail, and some services such as laundries and repair shops (Shops); telephone and television transmission (Telcm); utilities (Utils); metals mining and wholesaling (Metals); and all other industries (e.g., construction, building materials, transportation, hotels, business services, and entertainment).

Table 7.7 shows the time-series average allocations to industries over all months from December 1979 to November 2002, as well as over expansions and recessions. The allocation to a given industry during a given month is computed by

[7] Metals stocks are extracted from the "Shops" (wholesale, retail, and some service industries) or "Other" categories of the Fama-French 12-industry classification. Stocks with SIC codes of 1000–1049, 1060–1069, and 1080–1099 are extracted from the 'Other' industry category, while SIC codes of 5050–5052 are extracted from "Shops".

Table 7.7 Industry Allocations of Optimal Portfolios

The table reports the industry allocations of portfolio strategies that are optimal from the perspective of the 13 investor types described in Table 7.1, as well as for three strategies for selecting mutual funds that appear in previous studies, as explained in Table 7.4. The industries presented include 13 industries, based on the 12 Fama-French industry classification, plus a separate industry category for stocks in metals mining and metals wholesaling. These metals-industry stocks are extracted from the "energy" or "other" categories of the Fama-French 12 industry classification. The 13 industries include computer hardware, software, and other electronic equipment (Buseq); chemicals (Chems); durable goods, including autos, televisions, furniture, and household appliances (Durbl); oil, gas, and coal extraction (Enrgy); healthcare, medical equipment, and drugs (Hlth); machinery, trucks, planes, office furniture, paper, and commercial printing (Manuf); financials (Money); food, tobacco, textiles, apparel, leather, and toys (NoDur); wholesale, retail, and some services such as laundries and repair shops (Shops); telephone and television transmission (Telcm); utilities (Utils); metals mining and wholesaling (Metals); and, all other industries (e.g., construction, building materials, transportation, hotels, business services, and entertainment). These allocations are computed using the portfolio holdings of the mutual funds, then weighting these fund-level industry characteristics by each investor's optimal portfolio each month. This table shows the time-series average allocations over all months from December 1979 to November 2002, as well as over expansions and recessions.

	The Dogmatist			The Skeptic					The Agnostic					Previously Studied		
	ND	PD-1	PD-2	NS	PS-1	PS-2	PS-3	PS-4	NA	PA-1	PA-2	PA-3	PA-4	H-H	CAR	SM
Overall:																
Buseq	0.24	0.20	0.11	0.19	0.19	0.11	0.17	0.11	0.20	0.19	0.11	0.17	0.12	0.18	0.20	0.16
Chems	0.06	0.07	0.02	0.02	0.03	0.01	0.02	0.01	0.02	0.03	0.01	0.02	0.01	0.03	0.03	0.04
Durbl	0.02	0.03	0.02	0.03	0.03	0.02	0.02	0.01	0.03	0.03	0.02	0.02	0.01	0.03	0.03	0.04
Enrgy	0.07	0.08	0.09	0.04	0.07	0.15	0.08	0.14	0.03	0.08	0.16	0.09	0.14	0.07	0.07	0.07
Hlth	0.13	0.13	0.06	0.10	0.09	0.05	0.07	0.04	0.10	0.09	0.05	0.07	0.04	0.10	0.10	0.08
Manuf	0.12	0.11	0.06	0.11	0.09	0.08	0.09	0.06	0.11	0.09	0.08	0.08	0.06	0.11	0.10	0.12
Money	0.13	0.12	0.24	0.22	0.21	0.25	0.18	0.24	0.22	0.20	0.25	0.18	0.23	0.17	0.16	0.17
NoDur	0.07	0.08	0.04	0.07	0.06	0.06	0.05	0.05	0.06	0.06	0.05	0.04	0.05	0.06	0.07	0.07
Shops	0.05	0.05	0.07	0.09	0.10	0.06	0.05	0.04	0.09	0.10	0.07	0.05	0.04	0.10	0.09	0.10
Telcm	0.04	0.05	0.03	0.06	0.06	0.04	0.06	0.05	0.06	0.06	0.04	0.06	0.05	0.04	0.05	0.04
Utils	0.02	0.04	0.17	0.01	0.01	0.07	0.07	0.07	0.01	0.01	0.07	0.07	0.07	0.04	0.03	0.05
Metals	0.00	0.02	0.11	0.01	0.06	0.17	0.15	0.24	0.01	0.06	0.17	0.16	0.23	0.05	0.07	0.02
Others	0.05	0.05	0.07	0.10	0.10	0.08	0.09	0.09	0.09	0.10	0.08	0.08	0.09	0.10	0.10	0.10

(Continued)

Table 7.7 Continued

	The Dogmatist			The Skeptic					The Agnostic					Previously Studied		
	ND	PD-1	PD-2	NS	PS-1	PS-2	PS-3	PS-4	NA	PA-1	PA-2	PA-3	PA-4	H-H	CAR	SM
Expansions:																
Buseq	0.25	0.21	0.09	0.19	0.18	0.08	0.17	0.09	0.20	0.18	0.09	0.17	0.11	0.19	0.20	0.17
Chems	0.06	0.07	0.03	0.02	0.03	0.01	0.02	0.01	0.02	0.03	0.01	0.02	0.01	0.03	0.03	0.04
Durbl	0.02	0.03	0.02	0.03	0.03	0.02	0.02	0.01	0.03	0.03	0.02	0.02	0.01	0.03	0.03	0.04
Enrgy	0.06	0.07	0.08	0.03	0.06	0.14	0.08	0.14	0.03	0.07	0.15	0.09	0.13	0.06	0.06	0.06
Hlth	0.13	0.13	0.05	0.09	0.08	0.04	0.06	0.03	0.09	0.08	0.04	0.06	0.03	0.10	0.10	0.08
Manuf	0.11	0.11	0.06	0.11	0.09	0.08	0.08	0.06	0.11	0.09	0.08	0.07	0.06	0.11	0.10	0.11
Money	0.14	0.13	0.26	0.23	0.22	0.28	0.19	0.26	0.24	0.22	0.27	0.19	0.26	0.17	0.16	0.17
NoDur	0.07	0.08	0.05	0.07	0.06	0.06	0.05	0.05	0.07	0.06	0.05	0.04	0.05	0.06	0.07	0.07
Shops	0.04	0.05	0.06	0.08	0.10	0.06	0.05	0.03	0.09	0.10	0.06	0.05	0.03	0.10	0.09	0.09
Telcm	0.04	0.05	0.03	0.06	0.06	0.04	0.07	0.05	0.06	0.06	0.04	0.06	0.06	0.04	0.05	0.05
Utils	0.02	0.04	0.20	0.01	0.01	0.08	0.07	0.08	0.01	0.01	0.08	0.07	0.08	0.04	0.03	0.05
Metals	0.00	0.01	0.11	0.01	0.06	0.18	0.16	0.26	0.01	0.06	0.19	0.18	0.25	0.05	0.07	0.02
Others	0.05	0.05	0.06	0.09	0.10	0.08	0.08	0.08	0.09	0.10	0.08	0.07	0.09	0.10	0.10	0.10
Recessions:																
Buseq	0.20	0.16	0.25	0.19	0.23	0.23	0.19	0.23	0.19	0.23	0.23	0.16	0.22	0.13	0.18	0.15
Chems	0.05	0.05	0.02	0.03	0.02	0.01	0.02	0.02	0.03	0.02	0.01	0.02	0.02	0.03	0.03	0.04
Durbl	0.03	0.03	0.01	0.02	0.01	0.01	0.03	0.01	0.02	0.01	0.01	0.02	0.01	0.02	0.02	0.03
Enrgy	0.12	0.18	0.19	0.08	0.14	0.19	0.11	0.20	0.09	0.15	0.20	0.12	0.21	0.12	0.13	0.10
Hlth	0.11	0.11	0.11	0.17	0.13	0.12	0.11	0.10	0.17	0.12	0.11	0.11	0.11	0.09	0.09	0.09
Manuf	0.14	0.13	0.07	0.12	0.09	0.08	0.11	0.07	0.11	0.09	0.08	0.11	0.07	0.11	0.11	0.13
Money	0.11	0.11	0.08	0.10	0.08	0.10	0.13	0.09	0.11	0.08	0.10	0.15	0.10	0.17	0.13	0.13
NoDur	0.08	0.07	0.03	0.06	0.05	0.03	0.07	0.02	0.05	0.04	0.03	0.07	0.02	0.07	0.05	0.07
Shops	0.07	0.07	0.09	0.10	0.09	0.09	0.08	0.07	0.10	0.09	0.09	0.08	0.08	0.10	0.10	0.10
Telcm	0.03	0.04	0.04	0.05	0.07	0.05	0.05	0.04	0.05	0.07	0.05	0.05	0.04	0.03	0.05	0.04
Utils	0.03	0.03	0.01	0.04	0.02	0.02	0.06	0.02	0.04	0.01	0.02	0.06	0.02	0.05	0.03	0.05
Metals	0.01	0.08	0.09	0.02	0.05	0.06	0.09	0.13	0.02	0.06	0.06	0.08	0.11	0.04	0.08	0.02
Others	0.06	0.07	0.11	0.13	0.10	0.10	0.15	0.11	0.13	0.11	0.10	0.15	0.11	0.13	0.12	0.11

multiplying the fund-level industry weight by the investor's optimal weight on that fund, then summing this product over all funds held by the investor. Fund-level industry weights are computed by assigning an industry classification to each stock in the fund's portfolio at the end of each calendar quarter. These fund-level weights are assumed to be constant until the end of the following calendar quarter, while investor-level weights are updated monthly. Quarterly holdings data for mutual funds are obtained from the Thomson/CDA database, and are described in Wermers (1999, 2000), and Chapters 4 and 5.

The evidence shows that no-predictability investors who differ in their outlook toward the value of active management, i.e., ND, NS, and NA, hold similar allocations to industries, both overall, as well as during expansions and recessions. Since the ND investor, who rules out any possibility of active management skills, has industry allocations that are similar to the less dogmatic NS and NA investors, active management skills do not seem to be particularly concentrated in funds with a certain industry tilt when one disregards business cycle variations.

However, predictability-based strategies yield significantly different industry allocations relative to their no predictability counterparts, both during expansions and recessions. For example, investors PA-1, PA-2, PA-3, and PA-4 hold much higher allocations to energy (Enrgy), utilities (Utils), and especially metals (Metals), and a lower allocation to computers and other business equipment (Buseq) than investor NA. Moreover, predictability-based strategies do change their industry tilts over the business cycle. For instance, the PA-3 agent invests about 18% in metals during expansions, and only 8% during recessions. We also formally test whether industry allocations differ more for predictability-based approaches, and find support for this hypothesis.

To summarize, unlike their no-predictability counterparts, investors that use information variables in forming their optimal portfolios exhibit large variation in industry tilts over the business cycle. This suggests that such investors consider a mutual fund's industry orientation as an important characteristic in predicting and ultimately improving performance. Our findings here invite further inquiry into such investor strategies. For example, it is unclear why industry variation enhances performance. It is also unclear whether managers are able to pick funds within the selected industries that ultimately outperform their industry benchmarks. The next section addresses these issues.

7.4.3.3 *Industry Attribution Analysis*

Table 7.8 exhibits performance measures based on an industry-level attribution. The first three rows of the table present time-series average net returns ($\tilde{\mu}$, obtained by adding the annual risk-free rate to μ as reported in Table 7.4), industry-level returns ($\tilde{\mu}^I$), and industry-adjusted net returns ($\tilde{\mu} - \tilde{\mu}^I$). Industry-level returns are computed for each month by multiplying the industry allocations implied by each strategy's holdings of mutual funds by industry-level returns. The reported time-series average of industry-adjusted net returns is obtained as the difference between $\tilde{\mu}$ and $\tilde{\mu}^I$, and represents the net returns accomplished by each strategy above that accomplished through their allocations to industries.

Table 7.8 Industry Attribution Analysis

This table decomposes the net investment returns generated by portfolio strategies that are optimal from the perspective of the 13 investor types described in Table 7.1, as well as for the additional three strategies for selecting mutual funds that appear in previous studies, as explained in Table 7.4. The first three rows of the table present time-series average net returns ($\tilde{\mu}$, the same μ reported in Table 7.4 plus the average annual risk-free rate), industry-level returns, based on a 13-industry classification of the stocks held by funds, weighted by the optimal investor holdings of these funds ($\tilde{\mu}^I$), and industry-adjusted net returns ($\tilde{\mu} - \tilde{\mu}^I$), computed as the difference between these first two return items (its time-series p-value is also shown). The next three rows break down industry-level returns ($\tilde{\mu}^I$) into two components namely, the "industry passive return" ($\tilde{\mu}^{IP}$), which is the industry-level return that accrues to holding the allocation to each industry constant over time (at its time-series average for a given investor), and the 'industry timing return' ($\tilde{\mu}^I - \tilde{\mu}^{IP}$), which is the difference between the industry-level return and the industry passive return (its time-series p-value is also shown). The following three sections report the Carhart alpha (α_{wml}) and associated p-values for investor net returns, as previously reported in Table 7.4, industry-level returns, and industry-adjusted net returns. Slope coefficients for the Carhart model, as well as their p-values, are also shown for industry-level and industry-adjusted returns (β_{mkt}, β_{size}, β_{btm}, and β_{mom} represent loadings on the market, size, book-to-market, and momentum factors).

	The Dogmatist			The Skeptic					The Agnostic					Previously Studied		
	ND	PD-1	PD-2	NS	PS-1	PS-2	PS-3	PS-4	NA	PA-1	PA-2	PA-3	PA-4	H-H	CAR	SM
$\tilde{\mu}$	12.68	12.88	13.02	13.30	11.88	12.33	21.18	17.80	13.48	11.56	12.17	22.82	18.47	15.27	11.72	12.58
$\tilde{\mu}^I$	13.03	12.96	13.93	12.41	12.94	13.40	16.72	15.11	12.13	13.06	13.43	15.72	14.14	13.13	12.81	13.19
$\tilde{\mu} - \tilde{\mu}^I$	−0.34	−0.09	−0.91	0.89	−1.07	−1.07	4.47	2.69	1.35	−1.50	−1.26	7.10	4.33	2.13	−1.09	−0.61
$P(\tilde{\mu} - \tilde{\mu}^I)$	0.50	0.87	0.66	0.70	0.59	0.67	0.23	0.42	0.57	0.46	0.61	0.06	0.18	0.29	0.49	0.51
$\tilde{\mu}^{IP}$	13.72	13.75	13.16	13.98	13.61	13.06	12.73	12.29	13.98	13.58	13.03	12.74	12.31	13.51	13.34	13.69
$\tilde{\mu}^I - \tilde{\mu}^{IP}$	−0.69	−0.79	0.78	−1.57	−0.67	0.34	3.98	2.82	−1.85	−0.52	0.40	2.98	1.82	−0.38	−0.53	−0.49
$P(\tilde{\mu}^I - \tilde{\mu}^{IP})$	0.22	0.19	0.52	0.04	0.36	0.74	0.03	0.07	0.03	0.47	0.74	0.11	0.30	0.68	0.48	0.39
Net return:																
α_{wml}	0.37	0.62	3.92	-1.30	−2.49	0.83	5.98	4.95	−1.29	−2.83	0.51	8.46	6.20	−0.99	−0.48	−1.10
$P(\alpha_{wml})$	0.46	0.22	0.07	0.45	0.13	0.76	0.14	0.17	0.47	0.10	0.85	0.04	0.10	0.46	0.69	0.06

Industry return:																
α_{wml}	0.17	0.00	1.10	−0.79	−0.31	0.34	3.10	1.58	−0.93	−0.20	0.60	2.82	0.46	0.23	0.09	0.25
$P(\alpha_{wml})$	0.41	0.99	0.28	0.24	0.62	0.71	0.06	0.23	0.20	0.74	0.57	0.07	0.77	0.63	0.79	0.10
β_{mkt}	1.01	1.01	1.03	1.06	1.06	1.04	1.03	1.02	1.07	1.05	1.03	1.00	1.03	0.99	0.99	1.00
$P(\beta_{mkt})$	0.00	0.00	0.00	0.00	0.00	0.00	0.00	0.00	0.00	0.00	0.00	0.00	0.00	0.00	0.00	0.00
β_{size}	0.01	0.00	−0.06	−0.02	0.00	−0.05	0.13	0.10	−0.02	0.01	−0.04	0.13	0.09	0.07	0.02	0.00
$P(\beta_{size})$	0.22	0.67	0.03	0.37	0.77	0.04	0.00	0.00	0.28	0.61	0.13	0.00	0.02	0.00	0.01	0.72
β_{btm}	−0.01	−0.01	0.09	−0.04	−0.02	0.07	−0.03	0.09	−0.07	−0.02	0.05	−0.10	0.06	−0.07	−0.07	−0.01
$P(\beta_{btm})$	0.05	0.14	0.00	0.04	0.20	0.02	0.59	0.03	0.00	0.19	0.15	0.03	0.24	0.00	0.00	0.24
β_{mom}	0.00	0.00	−0.06	0.01	0.01	−0.04	0.05	0.00	0.00	0.01	−0.04	0.04	0.02	0.03	0.01	0.00
$P(\beta_{mom})$	0.53	0.34	0.00	0.53	0.48	0.03	0.08	0.91	0.71	0.33	0.03	0.18	0.38	0.00	0.03	0.14
Industry adjusted return:																
α_{wml}	0.20	0.63	2.82	−0.51	−2.18	0.49	2.89	3.37	−0.36	−2.63	−0.09	5.64	5.73	−1.22	−0.58	−1.35
$P(\alpha_{wml})$	0.68	0.22	0.13	0.75	0.16	0.85	0.37	0.29	0.83	0.10	0.97	0.10	0.07	0.34	0.64	0.02
β_{mkt}	−0.04	−0.06	−0.27	−0.12	−0.06	−0.21	−0.21	−0.33	−0.12	−0.07	−0.21	−0.17	−0.31	−0.04	−0.02	−0.03
$P(\beta_{mkt})$	0.00	0.00	0.00	0.00	0.04	0.00	0.00	0.00	0.00	0.03	0.00	0.02	0.00	0.12	0.48	0.00
β_{size}	−0.02	−0.03	0.03	0.48	0.34	0.29	0.62	0.43	0.50	0.35	0.31	0.65	0.42	0.48	0.38	0.24
$P(\beta_{size})$	0.05	0.02	0.57	0.00	0.00	0.00	0.00	0.00	0.00	0.00	0.00	0.00	0.00	0.00	0.00	0.00
β_{btm}	−0.09	−0.12	0.00	−0.24	−0.20	0.09	−0.24	−0.07	−0.20	−0.21	0.09	−0.23	−0.15	−0.03	−0.11	−0.07
$P(\beta_{btm})$	0.00	0.00	0.96	0.00	0.00	0.23	0.01	0.49	0.00	0.00	0.24	0.02	0.12	0.46	0.00	0.00
β_{mom}	0.02	0.03	−0.17	0.26	0.20	−0.07	0.33	0.13	0.28	0.20	−0.03	0.28	0.09	0.30	−0.01	0.10
$P(\beta_{mom})$	0.05	0.01	0.00	0.00	0.00	0.13	0.00	0.02	0.00	0.00	0.43	0.00	0.09	0.00	0.60	0.00

The industry-level returns explain some of the variation in net returns across investor types. For example, investor PA-3 generates an average net return that is 9.3% higher than that of investor NA (22.82%–13.48%). Of this 9.3% difference, 3.6% is due to higher returns generated by industry selection. The remaining 5.7% difference is due to higher returns earned in excess of industry allocations, as shown by the industry-adjusted net returns. That is, investor PA-3 uses business cycle information first to choose industries that significantly outperform those chosen by NA, and then to select individual mutual funds within those well-performing industries that are able to outperform their industry benchmarks. This latter point is especially noteworthy, since the industry benchmarks are gross of any trading costs of implementing such an industry-level mimicking strategy. Specifically, PA-3 chooses individual mutual funds, using business cycle information, that outperform their industry benchmarks by 7.1% per year more than the level of fees and trading costs of the funds.

Next, we break down the monthly industry-level returns ($\tilde{\mu}^I$) into two components. The first component, the "industry passive return" ($\tilde{\mu}^{I_P}$), is computed as the industry-level return that accrues to a passive strategy that merely holds the allocation to each industry constant over time (at its time-series average for a given investor). The second, the "industry timing return" ($\tilde{\mu}^I$-$\tilde{\mu}^{I_P}$), is the difference between the total industry return and the industry passive return. This second component represents the industry-level return earned by timing the industries through holdings of mutual funds, since this return component can only reflect time-series variations in industry allocations relative to passive strategies that merely hold the average allocations.

The evidence shows that the industry passive return component is comparable across all investor types. On the other hand, investors that account for predictability in manager skills actively time industries to enhance performance; for example, PA-3 exhibits an industry timing return of almost 3% per year, while NA exhibits a negative industry timing return. In general, investors using business cycle information generate industry timing returns of 2% to 4% per year.

At this stage, it is an open question as to whether these industry-level returns and/or industry-adjusted returns reflect strategies already documented in previous work, such as the industry-level momentum of Moskowitz and Grinblatt (1999), or, instead, that they indicate genuine skills based on private information. To address this issue, Table 7.8 breaks down the net return alpha (computed using the four-factor Carhart model) into the alpha derived by industry allocations and the alpha derived by allocations to individual mutual funds, controlling for their industry exposures. Alphas are computed by regressing the excess industry-level returns as well as the industry-adjusted returns (both described above) on the four Fama-French and momentum benchmarks. Table 7.8 also presents the factor loadings for each of these two regressions.

We start with the industry-level regressions. We show that almost none of the industry-level timing returns are due to the investors using industry-momentum strategies. In particular, note that the industry return alpha (2.82% per year for PA-3) is very similar to the industry-timing return described previously (2.98% per year). That is, returns attributable to industry timing by strategies that incorporate predictability in manager skills survive the four-benchmark adjustment. This evidence indicates that funds selected by the PA-3 investor load on industries using private information, or at least information unrelated to the standard four benchmarks. Moreover, examining the benchmark loadings reveals no particular tilts toward any style factor.

Next, we consider regression results for the industry-adjusted net returns for each investor type. We demonstrate that the skeptics and agnostics hold mutual funds that have slightly negative market and book-to-market exposures relative to their industries, and positive size and momentum exposures, suggesting that actively managed mutual funds that load on smaller, more growth-oriented stocks that have higher past returns outperform other funds.

However, among actively managed funds, predictability-based strategies have similar exposures to benchmarks as their no-predictability counterparts, indicating that the superior performance of predictability-based strategies is not due to their taking positions in funds with different style characteristics. Further, the majority of industry-adjusted net returns is unexplained by the four benchmarks. In particular, as noted earlier, the industry-adjusted net return for PA-3 is 7.3% per year. When we adjust this return using the four benchmarks, the alpha is 5.6% per year.

To summarize the results of this section, we find that investors who use business-cycle information to choose mutual funds derive their returns from two important sources. First, they vary their allocations to industries over the business cycle. Second, they vary their allocations to individual mutual funds within the chosen industries. Neither source of returns is particularly correlated with the four Fama-French and momentum benchmarks, indicating that the private skills identified by these predictability-based strategies are based on characteristics of funds that are heretofore undocumented by the mutual fund literature.

7.4.4 Survivorship Bias

Survivorship bias has been extensively studied in the context of mutual funds. To be included in our tests, a mutual fund must have at least 48 consecutive months before the investment is made as well as one additional month subsequent to the investment. Hence, a relevant question is: Should performance measures be adjusted to reflect this return requirement? Below, we explain why performance measures need not be adjusted.

In the spirit of Baks et al. (2001), we assume that, conditional on the realized fund returns, the probability of survival is unaffected by conditioning on the true values of the parameters that govern the dynamics of mutual fund returns. Then, by implementing Bayes' rule and by assuming that the residual in Eq. (7.1) is uncorrelated across funds, conditioning on survival has no effect on the posterior distribution of the parameters. Hence, any adjustment to the reported performance measures is not needed.[8]

7.5 CHAPTER-END PROBLEMS

1. Why should fund managers have skills that vary according to macroeconomic conditions? Explain the intuition behind this idea.
2. In Eq. (7.1), z_{t-1} is the vector of lagged macroeconomic variables. In this chapter, we did not de-mean the values of these variables, but one could de-mean them by subtracting their time-series average values. What effect would de-meaning of these variables have on the value and interpretation of α_{i0}?
3. The system of equations, shown by Eqs. (7.1), (7.2), and (7.3), describes the data-generating process that is assumed for the mutual funds, benchmarks, and macroeconomic variables.

   A. What is assumed about the relation between lagged macro factors and the current value of benchmarks by Equation. (7.2)? How could this be extended to a more robust (but, more difficult to estimate) model?
   B. If we assume that a manager does not have a time-varying exposure to risk factors, how is the system of equations modified?
   C. If we assume that factor realizations are independent of macroeconomic variables, how is the system modified?
4. This chapter shows how to find managers with the best current skills, assuming that they have time-varying alphas. Why do we need fund managers at all? That is, why can't we simply use the system of equations, Eq. (7.1), (7.2), and (7.3), to model stocks or stock sector indexes, and directly invest in them? Since there are potentially more degrees-of-freedom with thousands of stocks, would this always improve the alpha of our portfolio, relative to choosing managers using macroeconomic variables?

---

[8] Stambaugh (2003) and Jones and Shanken (2004) explore survival issues in a framework that accounts for prior dependence across funds. Under such dependence, conditioning on survival can affect the posterior distribution of the parameters. Given the vast universe of mutual funds considered here, it is nontrivial to account for such dependence. Indeed, as noted by Stambaugh (2003), further complexities can be studied as computer power allows.

APPENDIX A DESCRIPTION OF MUTUAL FUND DATABASE

This part of the appendix describes the database in detail. Our procedure for building our database begins with the merged CRSP/Thomson open-end mutual fund database described in Chapter 5. This merged database contains monthly fund net returns, self-declared investment objectives (quarterly in Thomson, annually in CRSP), annual turnover and expense ratios, and annual load charges for each shareclass of each fund (from CRSP). Our procedure for classifying and characterizing funds is as follows.

A.1 Investment Objectives

We focus on open-end, no-load U.S.-headquartered domestic equity funds. We exclude balanced or flexible funds because we wish to rule out strategies that involve investments in nonequity securities, such as U.S. government or corporate bonds.

To determine whether a fund qualifies as a domestic equity fund, we proceed through several steps. Then, we determine whether, at the beginning of a given quarter, the fund has a self-declared investment objective that is consistent with investing almost exclusively in domestic equities. In particular, we check the investment objective from the Thomson database, as well as the (somewhat different) investment objective data from the CRSP files to make a first pass at a classification. In doing so, we verify investment objectives for all shareclasses of a given fund (because the data are missing in some cases from some shareclasses in CRSP). Our approach is to use Thomson investment objectives, which are less precise but rarely missing; CRSP investment objectives are more precise, but the large proportion of missing data precludes the wholesale use of these data. Nevertheless, we use CRSP objectives to refine, where possible, our inclusion of funds.

Next, we check the name of the fund for words that indicate that it has an objective other than domestic equity, such as an international growth fund. This step helps us to correct any omissions and/or errors in the Thomson or CRSP investment objectives (i.e., when the investment objective is vague, wrong, or missing). For example, we identify index funds both through CRSP investment objectives and through the names of funds, since Thomson does not identify these funds. Finally, we exclude any shareclasses for such funds that have a nonzero total load (including front-end and deferred) only during the year that the total load is nonzero. We exclude all other funds such as balanced funds, international funds, and bond funds.

A.2 Net Returns

We obtain monthly net returns from the CRSP Mutual Fund database. To compute the net return for a given mutual fund in the linked Thomson/CRSP database, we aggregate the net returns on all no-load shareclasses that exist during that month by value-weighting the shareclass returns using beginning-of-month total net assets (TNA) for each shareclass. Thus, our monthly returns mimic the returns that would have been earned by a pro-rata investment across all no-load shareclasses of a given fund. This approach avoids any biases that might result from using only a single shareclass from a given fund.

When one or more no-load shareclasses has missing returns or total net asset information, we aggregate the net returns for remaining shareclasses that have full data. Finally, when a missing return is indicated for a fund-month for a shareclass in the CRSP files, the first nonmissing return is discarded to alleviate the CRSP approach of filling in a cumulative return at this date, which would introduce large measurement errors.

In forming "hot-hands" and "smart money" portfolios of mutual funds as well as in assessing whether the universe of equity funds provides close substitutes to the Fama-French and momentum benchmarks, we include all shareclasses, including those charging a load. In this case, we reconstruct our shareclass-averaged net returns including all no-load and load shareclasses for each fund.

A.3 Turnover and Expenses

Like net returns, turnover and expenses are shareclass-averaged for each fund, with rebalancing done when a shareclass disappears or has missing data. Shareclass-specific monthly turnover and expenses are derived by dividing the annual numbers (from CRSP) by 12. Weights for shareclass averaging are based on beginning-of-month total net assets (TNA) for the shareclass.

A.4 Flows

Net flows from consumers are estimated with the change in the ratio of total net assets divided by the net asset value per share (i.e., the shares outstanding of the fund) during a month, where the effect of splits during the month are reversed from the end-of-month shares outstanding. In addition, cash distributions are all assumed to be reinvested, meaning that the growth in shares outstanding are net of all distribution-related reinvestments (which are assumed to be 100% reinvested). In other words, reinvested distributions, both capital-gain and dividend, are not counted as flows. Before 1991, total net assets are available only on a quarterly basis, so monthly flows are estimated by dividing the quarterly number by three.

In unreported tests, we compared these estimated flows with the known, actual monthly flows from a large number of funds from a given major mutual fund family. We find that the estimates based on the above procedure are very close to the known actuals for these funds (over 100 funds), which provides reassurance that our computation of flows is more broadly applicable to the universe of funds.

APPENDIX B INVESTMENTS WHEN FUND RISK LOADINGS AND BENCHMARK RETURNS MAY BE PREDICTABLE

This part of the appendix derives moments for asset allocation under the case in which fund risk loadings and benchmark returns could be predictable by business cycle variables, but managerial skill is not.

B.1 Prior Beliefs

First note that $\alpha_{i1} = 0$ in Eq. (7.1) because skill is assumed to be unpredictable. Part C of the appendix relaxes this assumption. The prior on α_{i0} is:

$$p(\alpha_{i0}|\psi_i) \propto (\psi_i)^{-\frac{1}{2}} \exp\left\{-\frac{1}{2\psi_i}(\Gamma_i - \Gamma_{i0})'\Upsilon(\Gamma_i - \Gamma_{i0})\right\}, \tag{7.8}$$

where $\Gamma_{i0} = [\bar{\alpha}_{i0}, 0, \ldots, 0]'$, $\Upsilon = \Delta\Delta'\frac{s^2}{\sigma_\alpha^2}$, Δ is a $(KM + K + 1)$ vector whose first element is one and the rest of the elements are zero, σ_α^2 is the degree of belief about managerial skill, and s^2 is computed as the cross-sectional average of the sample variance of the residuals in Eq. (7.1). Note that the dogmatic (agnostic) case implies that $\sigma_\alpha = 0$ (∞). The skeptic case implies that $0 < \sigma_\alpha < \infty$. (In the empirical application, we set $\sigma_\alpha = 1\%$.) For the Dogmatist, we set $\bar{\alpha}_{i0} = -\frac{1}{12}(expense + 0.01 \times turnover)$, where *expense* and *turnover* are the fund's annual average values of reported expense ratio and turnover. For the Skeptic and Agnostic, we set $\bar{\alpha}_{i0} = -\frac{1}{12}(expense)$. The prior beliefs about all other parameters in Eqs. (7.1), (7.2), and (7.3) are taken to be noninformative. Specifically, the prior is proportional to $(\psi_i)^{-1}|\Sigma_{ff}|^{-\frac{K+1}{2}}|\Sigma_{zz.r.f}|^{-\frac{M+1}{2}}$.

B.2 The Likelihood Function

The sample contains T_i monthly returns of fund i (overall, the investment universe contains $N = 1,301$ no-load, open-end, equity mutual funds) and T monthly observations of K benchmark returns and M business cycle variables. Fund i enters the sample at time t_i and leaves at time $t_i + T_i - 1$, following a merger or termination. The fund may remain until the end of our sample period, December 2002. Let r_i denote the T_i-vector of excess returns on fund i, let $G_i = [G'_{t_i}, \ldots, G'_{t_i+T_i-1}]'$, where $G_t = [1, f'_t, f'_t \otimes z'_{t-1}]'$, let $\Gamma_i = [\alpha_{i0}, \beta'_{i0}, \beta'_{i1}]'$, let $Z = [z'_1, \ldots, z'_T]'$, let $F = [f'_1, \ldots, f'_T]'$, let $X = [x'_0, \ldots, x'_{T-1}]'$, where $x_0 = [1, z'_0]'$ with z_0 being the first observation of the macro predictors, let $V_f = [v'_{f1}, \ldots, v'_{fT}]'$, let $V_Z = [v'_{z1}, \ldots, v'_{zT}]'$, let V_{rz} be a $T \times N$ matrix whose i-th column contains T_i values of v_{it} when returns on fund i are recorded and $T - T_i$ zeros when such returns are missing, let $A_Z = [a_z, A_z]'$, let $A_F = [a_f, A_f]'$, let $Q_{G_i} = I_{T_i} - G_i(G'_iG_i)^{-1}G'_i$, let $Q_X = I_T - X(X'X)^{-1}X$, let $W_Z = [X, V_f, V_{rz}]$, and let $Q_Z = I_T - W_Z\left(W'_ZW_Z\right)^{-1}W'_Z$. The processes for fund returns, benchmark returns, and business cycle predictors characterized in Eqs. (7.1), (7.2), and (7.3) can be rewritten as $r_i = G_i\Gamma_i + v_i$, $F = XA_F + v_f$, and $Z = XA_Z + v_z$, respectively. Then, the likelihood can be factored as:

$$\mathcal{L} \propto \left[\prod_{i=1}^{N}(\psi_i)^{-\frac{T_i}{2}} \exp\left\{-\frac{1}{2\psi_i}\left(r_i'Q_{G_i}r_i + (\Gamma_i - \hat{\Gamma}_i)'G_i'G_i(\Gamma_i - \hat{\Gamma}_i)\right)\right\}\right] \tag{7.9}$$

$$\times \quad |\Sigma_{ff}|^{-\frac{T}{2}} \exp\left\{-\frac{1}{2}\mathrm{tr}\left[\Sigma_{ff}^{-1}\left(F'Q_XF + (A_F - \widehat{A}_F)'X'X(A_F - \widehat{A}_F)\right)\right]\right\}$$

$$\times \quad |\Sigma_{zz.r.f}|^{-\frac{T}{2}} \exp\left\{-\frac{1}{2}\mathrm{tr}\left[\Sigma_{zz.r.f}^{-1}\left(Z'Q_ZZ + (\xi - \hat{\xi})'W_Z'W_Z(\xi - \hat{\xi})\right)\right]\right\},$$

where $\xi = [A_Z', \Sigma_{zf}\Sigma_{ff}^{-1}, \Sigma_{zr}\Psi^{-1}]'$, Ψ is a diagonal matrix whose (i,i)-th element is ψ_i, $\Sigma_{zz.r.f} = \Sigma_{zz} - \Sigma_{zr}\Sigma_{rr}^{-1}\Sigma_{rz} - \Sigma_{zf}\Sigma_{ff}^{-1}\Sigma_{fz}$, Σ_{fz} is the covariance between v_{ft} and v_{zt}, Σ_{zz} is the variance of v_{zt}, and Σ_{rz} is an $N \times M$ matrix whose i-th row contains the covariance between v_{it} and v_{zt}, $\hat{\Gamma}_i = (G_i'G_i)^{-1}G_i'r_i$, $\widehat{A}_F = (X'X)^{-1}X'F$, and $\hat{\xi} = (W_Z'W_Z)^{-1}W_Z'Z$.

B.3 The Predictive Moments

The first two moments of the Bayesian predictive distribution displayed in Eq. (7.7), say at time T, are:

$$\mathbb{E}\{r_{T+1}|\mathcal{D}_T\} = \tilde{\alpha}_0 + \tilde{\beta}_T\widetilde{A}_F'x_T, \tag{7.10}$$

$$\mathbb{V}\{r_{T+1}|\mathcal{D}_T\} = (1+\delta_T)\tilde{\beta}_T\hat{\Sigma}_{ff}\tilde{\beta}_T' + A_T, \tag{7.11}$$

where $\tilde{\alpha}_0$ and $\tilde{\beta}_T$ are the all-fund versions of $\tilde{\alpha}_{i0}$ and $\tilde{\beta}_i(z_T)$ $\left[\tilde{\beta}_i(z_T) = \tilde{\beta}_{i0} + \left(I_K \otimes z_T'\right)\tilde{\beta}_{i1}\right]$, $\tilde{\alpha}_{i0}$, $\tilde{\beta}_{i0}$, and $\tilde{\beta}_{i1}$ are the first element, the next K elements, and the last KM elements in the vector $\tilde{\Gamma}_i = \left(G_i'G_i + \Upsilon\right)^{-1}\left(G_i'r_i + \Upsilon\Gamma_{i0}\right)$, $\delta_T = \frac{1}{T}\left[1 + (\bar{z} - z_T)'\widehat{V}_z^{-1}(\bar{z} - z_T)\right]$, $\widetilde{A}_F = \widehat{A}_F$, $\hat{\Sigma}_{ff} = \frac{F'Q_XF}{T-K-M-2}$, and

A_T is a diagonal matrix whose (i,i) element is:

$$\tilde{\psi}_{i1}\left(1 + \mathrm{tr}\left[\hat{\Sigma}_{ff}\tilde{\Omega}_i\right](1+\delta_T) + \Omega_i^{11} + 2[\Omega_i^{12} + \Omega_i^{13}(I_K \otimes z_T)]\right. \tag{7.12}$$
$$\left. + \widetilde{A}_F'x_T + \mathrm{tr}\left[\widetilde{A}_F'x_Tx_T'\widetilde{A}_F\tilde{\Omega}_i\right]\right).$$

In (7.12), $\tilde{\psi}_{i1} = \frac{\tilde{\psi}_i}{T_i-K-KM-2}$, $\tilde{\psi}_i = r_i'r_i + \Gamma_{i0}'\Upsilon\Gamma_{i0} - \tilde{\Gamma}_i'(G_i'G_i + \Upsilon)\tilde{\Gamma}_i$, $\tilde{\Omega}_i = \Omega_i^{22} + \Omega_i^{23}(I_K \otimes z_T) + \left(I_K \otimes z_T'\right)\Omega_i^{32} + \left(I_K \otimes z_T'\right)\Omega_i^{33}(I_K \otimes z_T)$, and Ω_i^{mn} is a partition of $(G_i'G_i + \Upsilon)^{-1}$ (based on the partitions of $G_{it} = [1;\ f_t';\ f_t' \otimes z_{t-1}']'$) given by:

$$(G_i'G_i + \Upsilon)^{-1} = \begin{pmatrix} \Omega_i^{11} & \Omega_i^{12} & \Omega_i^{13} \\ \Omega_i^{21} & \Omega_i^{22} & \Omega_i^{23} \\ \Omega_i^{31} & \Omega_i^{32} & \Omega_i^{33} \end{pmatrix}. \tag{7.13}$$

APPENDIX C INVESTMENTS WHEN SKILLS MAY BE PREDICTABLE

Here we study the Agnostic and Skeptic investors. Of course, the Dogmatist rules out skill, both fixed and time-varying.

C.1 The Agnostic

The Agnostic investor allows the data to determine the magnitude of skill, both fixed and time-varying. Under that assumption of diffuse priors, the Bayesian predictive mean and variance are given by:

$$\mathbb{E}\{r_{T+1}|\mathcal{D}_T\} = \tilde{\alpha}_0 + \tilde{\alpha}_1 z_T + \tilde{\beta}_T \widetilde{A}'_F x_T, \tag{7.14}$$

$$\mathbb{V}\{r_{T+1}|\mathcal{D}_T\} = (1+\delta_T)\tilde{\beta}_T \hat{\Sigma}_{ff} \tilde{\beta}'_T + A_T, \tag{7.15}$$

where the (i, i) element of the diagonal matrix A_T is given by

$$\tilde{\psi}_{i2}\left(1 + \mathrm{tr}\left[\hat{\Sigma}_{ff}\tilde{\Omega}_i\right](1+\delta_T) + x'_T\Omega_i^{11}x_T + 2x_T[\Omega_i^{12} + \Omega_i^{13}(I_K \otimes z_T)]\right.$$
$$\left.\widetilde{A}'_F x_T + \mathrm{tr}\left[\widetilde{A}'_F x_T x'_T \widetilde{A}_F \tilde{\Omega}_i\right]\right),$$

$\tilde{\psi}_{i2} = \frac{\tilde{\psi}_i}{T_i - K - M - KM - 2}$, and the quantities $\tilde{\psi}_{i2}$ and Ω_i^{mn} are based upon the partitions of $G_{it} = [1, z_{t-1};\ f'_t;\ f'_t \otimes z'_{t-1}]'$. (7.16)

C.2 The Skeptic

Here, prior beliefs about time-varying skill are informative. To simplify the analysis we study the case in which risk premia and fund risk loadings are constant. That is, $\beta_{i1} = 0$ and $A_f = 0$ with probability one. When skill varies over time the investor's prior is modeled as if a hypothetical sample of T_0 months has been observed. In this sample, there is no manager skill in benchmark timing and stock selection based on either public or private information. The mean and variance of fund returns, benchmark returns, and predictive variables in the hypothetical sample are equal to those in the actual sample. Thus, based on that hypothetical sample, the prior on Γ_i is modeled as

$$\Gamma_i|\psi_i \sim N\left[\Gamma_{i0}, \psi_i[G'_{i0}G_{i0}]^{-1}\right], \tag{7.17}$$

where $\Gamma_{i0} = [\bar{\alpha}_{i0}, 0', \bar{\beta}'_{i0}]', \bar{\alpha}_{i0} = -\frac{1}{12}(expense), \bar{\beta}_{i0} = (f'f)^{-1}(f'r_i) - T_i(f'f)^{-1}\bar{f}\bar{\alpha}_{i0}$, and

$$[G'_{i0}G_{i0}]^{-1} = \frac{1}{T_0}\begin{bmatrix} 1 + \bar{z}'\widehat{V}_z^{-1}\bar{z} + \bar{f}'\widehat{V}_f^{-1}\bar{f} & -\bar{z}'\widehat{V}_z^{-1} & -\bar{f}'\widehat{V}_f^{-1} \\ -\widehat{V}_z^{-1}\bar{z} & \widehat{V}_z^{-1} & 0 \\ -\widehat{V}_f^{-1}\bar{f} & 0 & \widehat{V}_f^{-1} \end{bmatrix} \tag{7.18}$$

To address the choice of T_0, we establish an exact link between σ_α (the skill uncertainty entertained by Pastor and Stambaugh (2002a,b)) and T_0. The link is given by

$$T_0 = \frac{s^2}{\sigma_\alpha^2}(1 + M + SR_{max}^2), \tag{7.19}$$

where SR_{max} is the largest attainable Sharpe ratio based on investments in the benchmarks only (disregarding predictability), M is the number of macroeconomic variables that are potentially useful in predicting fund returns, and s^2 is the cross-fund average of the sample variance of the residuals in Eq. (7.1). This exact link gives our prior specification the skill uncertainty interpretation employed by earlier work. To apply our prior specification for the predictability Skeptic investor in the empirical section, we compute s^2 and SR_{max}^2, and set $\sigma_\alpha = 1\%$. Then, we obtain T_0 through Eq. (7.19).

The derivation of the link displayed in Eq. (7.19) is presented below. First note that based on the hypothetical sample, the prior of $\alpha_i = [\alpha_{i0}, \alpha_{i1}']'$ is given by:

$$\alpha_i|\psi_i \sim N\left(\bar{\alpha}_i, \frac{\psi_i}{T_0}\begin{bmatrix} 1 + \bar{z}'\widehat{V}_z^{-1}\bar{z} + \bar{f}'\widehat{V}_f^{-1}\bar{f} & -\bar{z}'\widehat{V}_z^{-1} \\ -\widehat{V}_z^{-1}\bar{z} & \widehat{V}_z^{-1} \end{bmatrix}\right), \tag{7.20}$$

where $\bar{\alpha}_i = [-\frac{1}{12}(expense), 0_{1,M}]'$ and $0_{1,M}$ is an M-row vector of ones. Then, we derive the prior variance of $\alpha_{i0} + \alpha_{i1}'z_{t-1}$ using the steps:

$$\begin{aligned} \mathrm{var}(\alpha_{i0} + \alpha_{i1}'z_{t-1}|\psi_i, \mathcal{D}_0) &= E\left[\alpha_{i0}^2 + \alpha_{i1}z_{t-1}z_{t-1}'\alpha_{i1}' + 2\alpha_{i0}\alpha_{i1}'z_{t-1}\right] - \bar{\alpha}_{i0}^2, \qquad (7.21) \\ &= \frac{\psi_i}{T_0}(1 + \bar{z}'\widehat{V}_z^{-1}\bar{z} + \bar{f}'\widehat{V}_f^{-1}\bar{f}) + \frac{\psi_i}{T_0}\mathrm{tr}\left\{[\widehat{V}_z + \bar{z}\bar{z}'][\widehat{V}_z^{-1}]\right\} - \frac{2\psi_i}{T_0}\bar{z}'\widehat{V}_z^{-1}\bar{z}, \\ &= \frac{\psi_i}{T_0}[1 + M + \bar{f}'\widehat{V}_f^{-1}\bar{f}], \\ &= \frac{\psi_i}{T_0}[1 + M + SR_{max}^2], \end{aligned}$$

where $\mathcal{D}_0$ stands for the information in the hypothetical sample, tr denotes the trace operator, and $\bar{f}'\widehat{V}_f^{-1}\bar{f}$ is the square of the maximal admissible Sharpe ratio obtained by investing in benchmarks only. The link in Eq. (7.19) follows by comparing the unconditional variance derived in Eq. (7.21) with that of Pastor and Stambaugh (2002a,b), which is given by $\psi_i\frac{\sigma_\alpha^2}{s^2}$.

Next, we form posterior densities by combining the hypothetical prior sample with the noninformative prior $\psi_i^{-1}|\Sigma_{ff}|^{-\frac{K+1}{2}}|\Sigma_{zz.r.f}|^{-\frac{M+1}{2}}$ and the actual data. We then find that the Bayesian predictive mean and variance are:

$$\mathbb{E}\{r_{T+1}|\mathcal{D}_T\} = \tilde{\alpha}_0 + \tilde{\alpha}_1 z_T + \tilde{\beta}\bar{f}, \tag{7.22}$$

$$\mathbb{V}\{r_{T+1}|\mathcal{D}_T\} = (1+\frac{1}{T^*})\tilde{\beta}\widetilde{V}_f\tilde{\beta}' + A_T, \quad (7.23)$$

where $\tilde{\alpha}_0$, $\tilde{\alpha}_1$, and $\tilde{\beta}$ are the all-fund versions of $\tilde{\alpha}_{i0}$, $\tilde{\alpha}_{i1}$, and $\tilde{\beta}_i$, obtained as the first column, the next M columns, and the last K columns of $\tilde{\Gamma}_i = \left(G_i'G_i + G_{i0}'G_{i0}\right)^{-1}\left(G_i'r_i + [G_{i0}'G_{i0}]\Gamma_{i0}\right)$,

$$A_T(i,i) = \tilde{\psi}_{i3}\left(1 + \text{tr}\left[\widetilde{V}_f\Omega_i^{22}\right](1+\frac{1}{T^*}) + x_T'\Omega_i^{11}x_T + 2x_T\Omega_i^{12}\bar{f} + \text{tr}\left[\bar{f}\bar{f}'\Omega_i^{22}\right]\right), \quad (7.24)$$

$T_i^* = T_i + T_0$, $T^* = T + T_0$, $\tilde{\psi}_{i3} = \frac{\frac{T_i^*}{T_i}r_i'r_i - \tilde{\Gamma}_i'(G_i'G_i + G_{i0}'G_{i0})\tilde{\Gamma}_i}{T_i^* - K - M - 2}$, $\widetilde{V}_f = \frac{T^*\widehat{V}_f}{T^* - K - 3}$, and the Ω_i^{mn} matrices are obtained by partitioning $(G_i'G_i + G_{i0}'G_{i0})^{-1}$.

Chapter 8

Multiple Fund Performance Evaluation: The False Discovery Rate Approach

ABSTRACT

This chapter develops a simple technique that controls for "false discoveries", or managed funds that exhibit significant alphas by luck alone. The approach presented precisely estimates the proportion of fund managers that are (1) unskilled, (2) zero-alpha, and (3) skilled, even with dependencies in cross-fund estimated alphas. In an application to U.S. domestic equity mutual funds, this approach shows that 75% of funds exhibit zero alphas (net of trading costs and other expenses), consistent with the Berk and Green (2004) equilibrium. Further, we find a significant proportion of skilled (positive alpha) funds prior to 1996, but almost none by 2006. Finally, we show that controlling for false discoveries substantially improves the ability to find funds with superior future performance.

Keywords
False discovery rate, Luck vs. skill, Multiple fund performance evaluation

8.1 INTRODUCTION

Earlier chapters in this book have focused on models and measures of individual fund manager performance. However, suppose that we wish to examine a population of fund managers in its entirety, and not simply one or a few of the managers in the population. In this multiple fund setting, it is natural to wonder how *many* (or what proportion of) fund managers possess true stockpicking skills, and where these funds are located in the cross-section of managers (ranked by their estimated alphas). For instance, do skilled managers exhibit extreme positive estimated alphas, or do they exhibit more moderate positive alphas? This is equivalent to asking the opposite question: do lucky alphas tend to be moderate or extremely large in a particular managed fund sample? From an investment perspective, precisely locating skilled fund managers maximizes our chances of achieving future outperformance and avoiding managers who were simply lucky in the past.

Of course, the main problem is that we cannot observe the *true* alpha of each fund in the population. Therefore, a seemingly reasonable way to estimate the

Performance Evaluation and Attribution of Security Portfolios. http://dx.doi.org/10.1016/B978-0-12-744483-3.00008-0
© 2013 Elsevier Inc. All rights reserved.
For End-of-chapter Questions: © 2012. CFA Institute, Reproduced and republished with permission from CFA Institute. All rights reserved.

prevalence of skilled fund managers is to simply count the number of funds with sufficiently high estimated alphas, $\widehat{\alpha}$. In implementing such a procedure, we are actually conducting a multiple hypothesis test, since we simultaneously examine the performance of all funds in the population (instead of just one fund).[1] However, a simple count of significant-alpha funds does not properly adjust for luck in such a multiple test setting—many of the funds will have significant estimated alphas by luck alone (i.e., their true alphas are zero). To illustrate, consider a population of funds with skills just sufficient to cover trading costs and expenses (truly zero-alpha funds). With the usual significance level of 5%, we should expect that 5% of these zero-alpha funds will have significant estimated alphas—some of them will be unlucky (significant with $\widehat{\alpha} < 0$) while others will be lucky (significant with $\widehat{\alpha} > 0$), but all will be "false discoveries"—funds with significant *estimated* alphas, but zero *true* alphas.

This chapter demonstrates a new approach to controlling for false discoveries in such a multiple fund setting.[2] This approach much more precisely estimates (1) the proportions of unskilled and skilled funds in the population (those with *truly* negative and positive alphas, respectively), and (2) their respective locations in the left and right tails of the cross-sectional *estimated* alpha (or estimated alpha t-statistic) distribution. One main virtue of this approach is its simplicity: to determine the frequency of false discoveries, the only parameter needed is the proportion of zero-alpha funds in the population, π_0. Rather than arbitrarily impose a prior assumption on π_0, our approach estimates it with a straightforward computation that uses the p-values of individual fund estimated alphas—no further econometric tests are necessary. Therefore, the approach outlined in this chapter can be implemented with simple computational tools, such as Excel.

A second advantage of our approach is its accuracy. Using a simple Monte Carlo experiment, we demonstrate that our approach provides a much more accurate partition of the universe of managed funds into zero-alpha, unskilled, and skilled funds than previous approaches that impose an *a priori* assumption about the proportion of zero-alpha funds in the population.

Another important advantage of our approach to multiple testing is its robustness to cross-sectional dependencies among fund estimated alphas. Prior literature indicates that such dependencies, which exist due to herding and other correlated trading behaviors (e.g., Wermers (1999)), greatly complicate performance measurement in a group setting—often, groups of funds get lucky, or unlucky, at the same time! With our approach, the computation of the proportions of

---

[1] This multiple test should not be confused with the joint test of the null hypothesis that all fund alphas are equal to zero in a sample (e.g., Grinblatt and Titman (1989)) or to the (Kosowski et al. (2006; KTWW) test of single-fund performance. The first test addresses whether at least one fund has a nonzero alpha among several funds, but is silent on the prevalence of these nonzero alpha funds. The second test examines the skills of a single fund that is chosen from the universe of alpha-ranked funds. In contrast, our approach simultaneously estimates the prevalence and location of multiple outperforming funds in a group. As such, our approach examines fund performance from a more general perspective, with a richer set of information about active fund manager skills.

[2] This chapter is distilled from Barras et al. (2010).

unskilled and skilled funds only requires the (alpha) p-value for each fund in the population, and not the estimation of the cross-fund covariance matrix. Indeed, the large cross-section of funds in our database makes these estimated proportions very accurate estimators of the true values, even when funds are cross-sectionally correlated. We confirm, with Monte Carlo simulations, that our simple approach is quite robust to cross-fund dependencies.

8.2 THE IMPACT OF LUCK ON MANAGED FUND PERFORMANCE

8.2.1 Overview of the Approach

8.2.1.1 *LUCK IN A MULTIPLE FUND SETTING*

Our objective is to develop a framework to precisely estimate the fraction of managed funds that truly outperform their benchmarks. To begin, suppose that a population of M actively managed funds is composed of three distinct performance categories, where performance is due to stock selection skills. We define such performance as the ability of fund managers to generate superior model alphas, net of trading costs as well as all fees and other expenses (except loads and taxes). Our performance categories are defined as follows:

- Unskilled funds: funds that have managers with stockpicking skills insufficient to recover their trading costs and expenses, creating an "alpha shortfall" ($\alpha < 0$),
- Zero-alpha funds: funds that have managers with stockpicking skills sufficient to just recover trading costs and expenses ($\alpha = 0$), and
- Skilled funds: funds that have managers with stockpicking skills sufficient to provide an "alpha surplus", beyond simply recovering trading costs and expenses ($\alpha > 0$).

Note that our above definition of skill is one that captures performance in excess of expenses, and not in an absolute sense. This definition is driven by the idea that consumers search for actively managed funds that deliver surplus alpha, net of all expenses.[3]

Of course, we cannot observe the true alphas of each fund in the population. So, how do we best infer the prevalence of each of the above skill groups from performance estimates for individual funds? First, we use the t-statistic $\widehat{t}_i = \widehat{\alpha}_i / \widehat{\sigma}_{\widehat{\alpha}_i}$ as our performance measure, where $\widehat{\alpha}_i$ is the estimated alpha for fund i and $\widehat{\sigma}_{\widehat{\alpha}_i}$ is its estimated standard deviation—KTWW show that the t-statistic has superior

[3] However, perhaps a manager exhibits skill sufficient to more than compensate for trading costs, but the fund management company overcharges fees or inefficiently generates other services (such as administrative services, e.g., record-keeping)—costs that the manager usually has little control over. In Section (8.4.4.1), we redefine stockpicking skill in an absolute sense (net of trading costs only) and revisit some of our basic tests to be described.

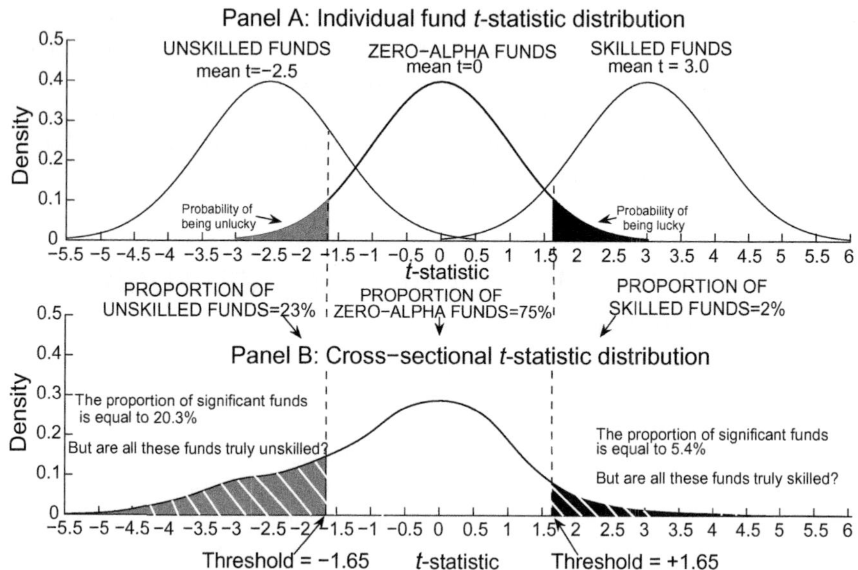

FIGURE 8.1
Panel A: Individual Fund *t*-Statistic Distribution. Panel B: Cross-Sectional *t*-Statistic Distribution.

statistical properties relative to alpha, since alpha estimates have differing precision across funds with varying lives and portfolio volatilities. Second, after choosing a significance level, γ (e.g., 10%), we observe whether $\widehat{t}_i$ lies outside the thresholds implied by γ (denoted by t_γ^- and t_γ^+) and label it "significant" if it is such an outlier. This procedure, simultaneously applied across all funds, is a multiple hypothesis test (for several null hypotheses, $H_{0,i}$, and alternative hypotheses, $H_{A,i}$, $i = 1, \ldots, M$):

$$\begin{aligned} &H_{0,1} : \alpha_1 = 0,\ H_{A,1} : \alpha_1 \neq 0, \\ &\ldots : \ldots \\ &H_{0,M} : \alpha_M = 0,\ H_{A,M} : \alpha_M \neq 0. \end{aligned} \tag{8.1}$$

To illustrate the difficulty of controlling for luck in this multiple test setting, Figure 8.1 presents a simplified hypothetical example that borrows from our empirical findings (to be presented later) over the last five years of our sample period. In Panel A, individual funds within the three skill groups—unskilled, zero alpha, and skilled—are assumed to have true annual four-factor alphas of −3.2%, 0%, and 3.8%, respectively (the choice of these values is explained in Barras et al. (2010)).[4] The individual fund *t*-statistic distributions shown in the panel are assumed to be normal for simplicity, and are centered at −2.5, 0,

[4] Individual funds within a given skill group are assumed to have identical true alphas in this illustration. In our empirical section, our approach makes no such assumption.

and 3.0 (which correspond to the prior-mentioned assumed true alphas; see Barras et al., 2010).[5] The t-distribution shown in Panel B is the cross-section that (hypothetically) would be observed by a researcher. This distribution is a mixture of the three skill group distributions in Panel A, where the weight on each distribution is equal to the proportion of zero-alpha, unskilled, and skilled funds in the population, denoted by π_0, π_A^-, and π_A^+, respectively (specifically, $\pi_0 = 75\%$, $\pi_A^- = 23\%$, and $\pi_A^+ = 2\%$; see Barras et al., 2010).

To illustrate further, suppose that we choose a significance level, γ, of 10% (corresponding to $t_\gamma^- = -1.65$ and $t_\gamma^+ = 1.65$) With the test shown in Equation (8.1), the researcher would expect to find 5.6% of funds with a positive and significant t-statistic.[6] This proportion, denoted by $E(S_\gamma^+)$, is represented by the shaded region in the right tail of the cross-sectional t-distribution (Panel B). Does this area consist merely of skilled funds, as defined above? Clearly not, because some funds are just lucky; as shown in the shaded region of the right tail of Panel A, zero-alpha funds can exhibit positive and significant estimated t-statistics. By the same token, the proportion of funds with a negative and significant t-statistic (the shaded region in the left tail of Panel B) overestimates the proportion of unskilled funds, because it includes some unlucky zero-alpha funds (the shaded region in the left tail of Panel A). Note that we have not considered the possibility that skilled funds could be *very* unlucky, and exhibit a negative and significant t-statistic. In our example of Figure 8.1, the probability that the estimated t-statistic of a skilled fund is lower than $t_\gamma^- = -1.65$ is less than 0.001%. This probability is negligible, so we ignore this pathological case. The same applies to unskilled funds that are very lucky.

The message conveyed by Figure 8.1 is that we measure performance with a limited sample of data, and therefore unskilled and skilled funds cannot easily be distinguished from zero-alpha funds. This problem can be worse if the cross-section of actual skill levels has a complex distribution (and not all fixed at the same levels, as assumed by our simplified example), and is further compounded if a substantial proportion of skilled fund managers have low levels of skill, relative to the error in estimating their t-statistics. To proceed, we must employ a procedure that is able to precisely account for false discoveries, that is, zero-alpha funds that falsely exhibit significant estimated alphas in the face of these complexities.

8.2.1.2 *MEASURING LUCK*

How do we measure the frequency of false discoveries in the tails of the cross-sectional (alpha) t-distribution? At a given significance level γ, it is clear that the probability that a zero-alpha fund (as defined in the last section) exhibits luck

[5] The actual t-statistic distributions for individual funds are non-normal for most U.S. domestic equity funds (KTWW). Accordingly, in our empirical section, we use a bootstrap approach to more accurately estimate the distribution of t-statistics for each fund (and their associated p-values).

[6] From Panel A, the probability that the observed t-statistic is greater than $t_\gamma^+ = 1.65$ equals 5% for a zero-alpha fund and 91% for a skilled fund. Multiplying these two probabilities by the respective proportions represented by their categories (π_0 and π_A^+) gives 5.6%.

equals $\gamma/2$ (shown as the dark shaded region in Panel A of Figure 8.1). If the proportion of zero-alpha funds in the population is π_0, the expected proportion of "lucky funds" (zero-alpha funds with positive and significant t-statistics) equals

$$E(F_\gamma^+) = \pi_0 \cdot \gamma/2. \tag{8.2}$$

To illustrate, if we take our previous example with $\pi_0 = 75\%$ and $\gamma = 0.10$, we find using Equation (8.2) that $E(F_\gamma^+) = 3.75\%$. Now, to determine the expected proportion of skilled funds, $E(T_\gamma^+)$, we simply adjust $E(S_\gamma^+)$ for the presence of these lucky funds:

$$E(T_\gamma^+) = E(S_\gamma^+) - E(F_\gamma^+) = E(S_\gamma^+) - \pi_0 \cdot \gamma/2. \tag{8.3}$$

From Figure 8.1, we see that $E(S_\gamma^+) = 5.6\%$ (the shaded region in the right tail of Panel B). By subtracting $E(F_\gamma^+) = 3.75\%$, the expected proportion of skilled funds, $E(T_\gamma^+)$, amounts to 1.85%.

Since the probability of a zero-alpha fund being unlucky is also equal to $\gamma/2$ (i.e., the gray and black areas in Panel A of Figure 8.1 are identical), $E(F_\gamma^-)$, the expected proportion of "unlucky funds" is equal to $E(F_\gamma^+)$. As a result, the expected proportion of unskilled funds, $E(T_\gamma^-)$, is similarly given by:

$$E(T_\gamma^-) = E(S_\gamma^-) - E(F_\gamma^-) = E(S_\gamma^-) - \pi_0 \cdot \gamma/2. \tag{8.4}$$

The significance level, γ, chosen by the researcher determines the segment of the tail examined for lucky versus skilled (or unlucky versus unskilled) managed funds, as described by Equations (8.3) and (8.4). This flexibility in choosing γ provides us with opportunities to gain important insights into the merits of active fund management. One objective of this chapter—estimating the proportions of unskilled and skilled funds in the entire population, π_A^- and π_A^+—is achieved only by choosing an appropriately large value for γ. Ultimately, as we increase γ, $E(T_\gamma^-)$ and $E(T_\gamma^+)$ converge to π_A^- and π_A^+, thus minimizing Type II error (failing to locate truly unskilled or skilled funds).

Another objective of this chapter—determining the *location* of truly skilled (or unskilled) funds in the tails of the cross-sectional t-distribution—can only be achieved by evaluating Equations (8.3) and (8.4) at several different values of γ. For instance, if the majority of skilled funds lie in the extreme right tail, then increasing the value of γ from 0.10 to 0.20 in Equation (8.3) would result in a very small increase in $E(T_\gamma^+)$, the proportion of truly skilled funds, since most of the additional significant funds, $E(S_\gamma^+)$, would be lucky funds. Alternatively, if skilled funds are dispersed throughout the right tail, then increases in γ would result in larger increases in $E(T_\gamma^+)$.

To illustrate the impact of fund location, consider two different fund populations (A and B) identical to the one shown in Figure 8.1 (with $\pi_0 = 75\%$, $\pi_A^- = 23\%$, and $\pi_A^+ = 2\%$), except that the (true) annual alpha of the skilled funds is equal to 3.8% in A (t-mean of 3.0) and 1.9% in B (t-mean of 1.5). Although these two populations have the same proportion of skilled funds ($\pi_A^+ = 2\%$), their locations differ, since the skilled funds in A are more concentrated in the extreme right tail. This information is useful for investors trying to form portfolios with skilled managers, since, in population A, the skilled funds can be more easily distinguished from the zero-alpha funds. For instance, by forming a portfolio of the significant funds in A at $\gamma = 0.05$ ($t_\gamma^+ = 1.96$) the investor would obtain an expected alpha of 1.8% per year, as opposed to only 45 basis points in population B.[7] Our approach to fund selection presented later (in Section 8.4.3), explicitly accounts for fund location in order to choose the significance level γ used to construct the portfolio.

8.2.1.3 *ESTIMATION PROCEDURE*

The key to our approach to measuring luck in a group setting, as shown in Equation (8.2), is the estimator of the proportion of zero-alpha funds in the population, π_0. Here, we turn to a recent estimation approach developed by Storey (2002), called the "False Discovery Rate" (FDR) approach. The FDR approach is very straightforward, as its sole inputs are the (two-sided) p-values associated with the (alpha) t-statistics of each of the M funds. By definition, zero-alpha funds satisfy the null hypothesis, $H_{0,i} : \alpha_i = 0$, and therefore have p-values that are uniformly distributed over the interval $[0, 1]$.[8] On the other hand, p-values of unskilled and skilled funds tend to be very small because their estimated t-statistics tend to be far from zero (see Panel A of Figure 8.1). We can exploit this information to estimate π_0 without knowing the exact distribution of the p-values of the unskilled and skilled funds.

To explain further, a key intuition of the FDR approach is that it uses information from the center of the cross-sectional t-distribution (which is dominated by zero-alpha funds) to correct for luck in the tails. To illustrate the FDR procedure, suppose we randomly draw 2,076 t-statistics (the number of funds in our sample to be discussed shortly), each from one of the three t-distributions in Panel A of Figure 8.1—with probability according to our estimates of the proportion of unskilled, zero-alpha, and skilled funds in the population, $\pi_0 = 75\%$, $\pi_A^- = 23\%$, and $\pi_A^+ = 2\%$, respectively. Thus, our draw of t-statistics comes from a known frequency of each type (75%, 23%, and 2%, respectively). Next, we apply the FDR technique to estimate these frequencies: from the *sampled* t-statistics, we compute two-sided p-values for each of the 2,076 funds, then plot them in Figure 8.2.

Given the sampled p-values, we estimate π_0 as follows. First, we know that the vast majority of p-values larger than a sufficiently high threshold, λ^* (e.g., $\lambda^* = 0.6$, as

---

[7] From Figure 8.1 (Panel A), the probability of including a zero-alpha fund (skilled fund) in the portfolio equals 2.5% (85%) in population A. This gives $E(T_\gamma^+) = \pi_A^+ \cdot 85\% = 1.7\%$, $E(F_\gamma^+) = \pi_0 \cdot 2.5\% = 1.8\%$, $E(S_\gamma^+) = 3.5\%$, and an expected alpha of $\left(E(T_\gamma^+)/E(S_\gamma^+)\right) \cdot 3.8\% = 1.8\%$ per year.

[8] To see this, we denote by T_i and P_i the t-statistic and p-value of the zero-alpha fund, $\widehat{t}_i$ and $\widehat{p}_i$ their estimated values, and $T_i\,(P_i)$ the t-statistic associated with the p-value, P_i. We have $\widehat{p}_i = 1 - F(|\widehat{t}_i|)$, where $F(|\widehat{t}_i|) = prob(|T_i| < |\widehat{t}_i| \,|\, \alpha_i = 0)$. The p-value P_i is uniformly distributed over $[0, 1]$ since its cdf, $prob(P_i < \widehat{p}_i) = prob(1 - F(|T_i\,(P_i)|) < \widehat{p}_i = prob(|T_i\,(P_i)| > F^{-1}\,(1 - \widehat{p}_i)) = 1 - F\left(F^{-1}\,(1 - \widehat{p}_i)\right) = \widehat{p}_i$.

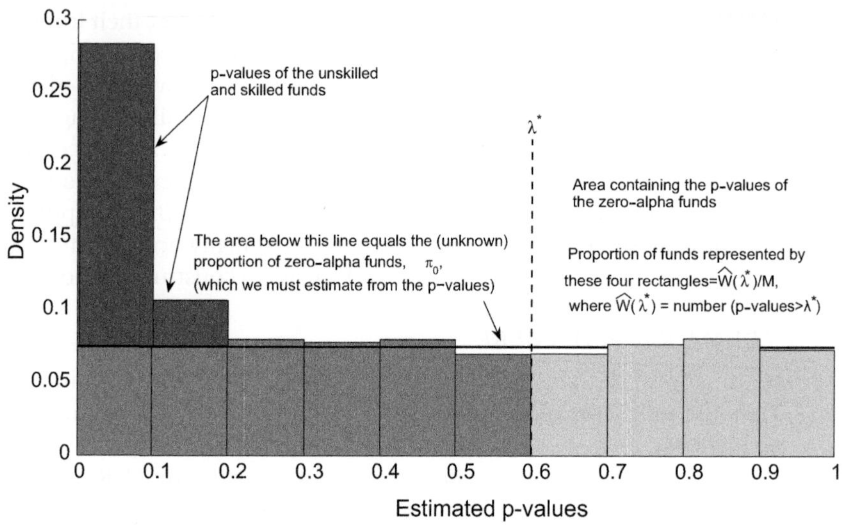

FIGURE 8.2
This figure represents the p-value histogram of M = 2,076 funds (as in our database). For each fund, we draw its t-statistic from one of the distributions in Figure 8.1 (Panel A) according to the proportion of zero-alpha, unskilled, and skilled funds in the population (π_0, π_A^-, and π_A^+). In this example, we set $\pi_0 = 75\%$, $\pi_A^- = 23\%$, and $\pi_A^+ = 2\%$ to match our average estimated values over the final 5 years of our sample. Then, we compute the two-sided p-values of each fund from its respective sampled t-statistic, and plot them in the histogram.

shown in the figure), come from zero-alpha funds. Accordingly, after choosing λ^*, we measure the proportion of the total area that is covered by the four lightest gray bars to the right of λ^*, $\widehat{W}(\lambda^*)/M$ (where $\widehat{W}(\lambda^*)$ equals the number of funds with p-values exceeding λ^*). Note the nearly uniform mass of sampled p-values in intervals between 0.6 and 1—each interval has a mass close to 0.075. Extrapolating this area over the entire region between zero and one, we have

$$\widehat{\pi}_0\left(\lambda^*\right) = \frac{\widehat{W}(\lambda^*)}{M} \cdot \frac{1}{(1-\lambda^*)}, \tag{8.5}$$

which indicates that our estimate of the proportion of zero-alpha funds, $\widehat{\pi}_0(\lambda^*)$, is close to 75%, which is the true (but unknown to the researcher) value of π_0 (since the 75% proportion of zero-alpha funds have uniformly distributed p-values).[9]

To select λ^*, we apply a simple bootstrap procedure introduced by Storey (2002), which minimizes the estimated mean squared error (MSE) of $\widehat{\pi}_0(\lambda)$

[9] This estimation procedure cannot be used in a one-sided multiple test, since the null hypothesis is tested under the least favorable configuration (LFC). For instance, consider the following null hypothesis $H_{0,i}: \alpha_i \leq 0$. Under the LFC, it is replaced with $H_{0,i}: \alpha_i = 0$. Therefore, all funds with $\alpha_i \leq 0$ (i.e., drawn from the null) have inflated p-values that are not uniformly distributed over $[0, 1]$.

(see Barras et al., 2010).[10] While the main advantage of this procedure is that it is entirely data-driven, we find that $\widehat{\pi}_0(\lambda^*)$ is not overly sensitive to the choice of λ^*. For instance, a simple approach that fixes the value of λ^* to intermediate levels (such as 0.5 or 0.6) produces similar estimates (see Barras et al., 2010).

Substituting the resulting estimate, $\widehat{\pi}_0$, in Equations (8.2) and (3), and replacing $E(S_\gamma^+)$ with the observed proportion of significant funds in the right tail, $\widehat{S}_\gamma^+$, we can easily estimate the $E(F_\gamma^+)$ and $E(T_\gamma^+)$ that correspond to any chosen significance level, γ. The same approach can be used in the left tail by replacing $E(S_\gamma^-)$ in Equation (8.4) with the observed proportion of significant funds in the left tail, $\widehat{S}_\gamma^-$. This implies the following estimates of the proportions of unlucky and lucky funds:

$$\widehat{F}_\gamma^- = \widehat{F}_\gamma^+ = \widehat{\pi}_0 \cdot \gamma/2. \tag{8.6}$$

Using Equation (8.6), the estimated proportions of unskilled and skilled funds (at significance level γ) are, respectively, equal to:

$$\begin{aligned} \widehat{T}_\gamma^- &= \widehat{S}_\gamma^- - \widehat{F}_\gamma^- = \widehat{S}_\gamma^- - \widehat{\pi}_0 \cdot \gamma/2, \\ \widehat{T}_\gamma^+ &= \widehat{S}_\gamma^+ - \widehat{F}_\gamma^+ = \widehat{S}_\gamma^+ - \widehat{\pi}_0 \cdot \gamma/2. \end{aligned} \tag{8.7}$$

Finally, we estimate the proportions of unskilled and skilled funds in the entire population as:

$$\widehat{\pi}_A^- = \widehat{T}_{\gamma^*}^-, \qquad \widehat{\pi}_A^+ = \widehat{T}_{\gamma^*}^+, \tag{8.8}$$

where γ^* is a sufficiently high significance level—similar to the choice of λ^*, we select γ^* with a bootstrap procedure that minimizes the estimated *MSE* of $\widehat{\pi}_A^-$ and $\widehat{\pi}_A^+$ (see Barras et al., 2010). While this method is entirely data-driven, there is some flexibility in the choice of γ^*, as long as it is sufficiently high. In Barras et al (2010) it is found that simply setting γ^* to pre-specified values (such as 0.35 or 0.45) produces similar estimates.

8.2.2 Comparison of Our Approach with Existing Methods

The previous literature has followed two alternative approaches when estimating the proportions of unskilled and skilled funds. The "full luck" approach proposed by Jensen (1968) and Ferson and Qian (2004) assumes, *a priori*, that all funds in the population have zero alphas ($\pi_0 = 1$). Thus, for a given significance level, γ, this approach implies an estimate of the proportions of unlucky and lucky funds equal to $\gamma/2$.[11] At the other extreme, the "no luck" approach reports the observed number of significant funds (for instance, Ferson and Schadt (1996)) without making a correction for luck ($\pi_0 = 0$).

[10] The *MSE* is the expected squared difference between $\widehat{\pi}_0(\lambda)$ and the true value, π_0 : $MSE(\widehat{\pi}_0(\lambda)) = E(\widehat{\pi}_0(\lambda) - \pi_0)^2$. Since π_0 is unknown, it is replaced with $\min_\lambda \widehat{\pi}_0(\lambda)$ to compute the estimated *MSE* (see Storey (2002)).

[11] Jensen (1968) summarizes the full luck approach as follows: "...if all the funds had a true α equal to zero, we would expect (merely by random chance) to find 5% of them having *p*-values significant at the 5% level"

What are the errors introduced by assuming, *a priori*, that the proportion of zero-alpha funds, π_0, equals zero or one, when it does not accurately describe the population? To address this question, we compare the bias produced by these two approaches relative to our FDR approach across different possible values for $\pi_0 (\pi_0 \in [0, 1])$ using our simple framework of Figure 8.1. Our procedure consists of three steps. First, for a chosen value of π_0, we create a simulated sample of 2,076 fund t-statistics (corresponding to our mutual fund sample size to be described shortly) by randomly drawing from the three distributions in Panel A of Figure 8.1 in the proportions π_0, π_A^-, and π_A^+. For each π_0, the ratio π_A^- / π_A^+ is held fixed to 11.5 (0.23/0.02), as in Figure 8.1, to ensure that the proportion of skilled funds remains low compared to the unskilled funds. Second, we use these sampled t-statistics to estimate the proportion of unlucky ($\alpha = 0$, significant with $\widehat{\alpha} < 0$), lucky ($\alpha = 0$, significant with $\widehat{\alpha} > 0$), unskilled ($\alpha < 0$, significant with $\widehat{\alpha} < 0$), and skilled ($\alpha > 0$, significant with $\widehat{\alpha} > 0$) funds under each of the three approaches—the no luck, full luck, and FDR techniques.[12] Third, under each approach, we repeat these first two steps 1,000 times, then compare the average value of each estimator with its true population value.

Specifically, Panel A of Figure 8.3 compares the three estimators of the expected proportion of unlucky funds. The true population value, $E(F_\gamma^-)$, is an increasing function of π_0 by construction, as shown by Equation (8.2). While the average value of the FDR estimator closely tracks $E(F_\gamma^-)$, this is not the case for the other two approaches. By assuming that $\pi_0 = 0$, the no luck approach consistently underestimates $E(F_\gamma^-)$ when the true proportion of zero-alpha funds is higher ($\pi_0 > 0$). Conversely, the full luck approach, which assumes that $\pi_0 = 1$, overestimates $E(F_\gamma^-)$ when $\pi_0 < 1$. To illustrate the extent of the bias, consider the case where $\pi_0 = 75\%$. While the no luck approach substantially underestimates $E(F_\gamma^-)$ (0% instead of its true value of 7.5%), the full luck approach overestimates $E(F_\gamma^-)$ (10% instead of its true 7.5%). The biases for estimates of lucky funds, $E(F_\gamma^+)$, in Panel B are exactly the same, since $E(F_\gamma^+) = E(F_\gamma^-)$.

Estimates of the expected proportions of unskilled and skilled funds, $E(T_\gamma^-)$ and $E(T_\gamma^+)$, provided by the three approaches are shown in Panels C and D, respectively. As we move to higher true proportions of zero-alpha funds (a higher value of π_0), the true proportions of unskilled and skilled funds, $E(T_\gamma^-)$ and $E(T_\gamma^+)$, decrease by construction. In both panels, our FDR estimator accurately captures this feature, while the other approaches do not fare well due to their fallacious assumptions about the prevalence of luck. For instance, when $\pi_0 = 75\%$, the no luck approach exhibits a large upward bias in its estimates of the total proportion of unskilled and skilled funds, $E(T_\gamma^-) + E(T_\gamma^+)$ (37.3% rather than the correct value of 22.3%). At the other extreme, the full luck approach underestimates $E(T_\gamma^-) + E(T_\gamma^+)$ (17.3% instead of 22.3%).

Panel D reveals that the no luck and full luck approaches also exhibit a nonsensical positive relation between π_0 and $E(T_\gamma^+)$. This result is a consequence of the low proportion of skilled funds in the population. As π_0 rises, the additional

[12] We choose $\gamma = 0.20$ to examine a large portion of the tails of the cross-sectional t-distribution. As shown in Barras, et al., the results using $\gamma = 0.10$ are similar.

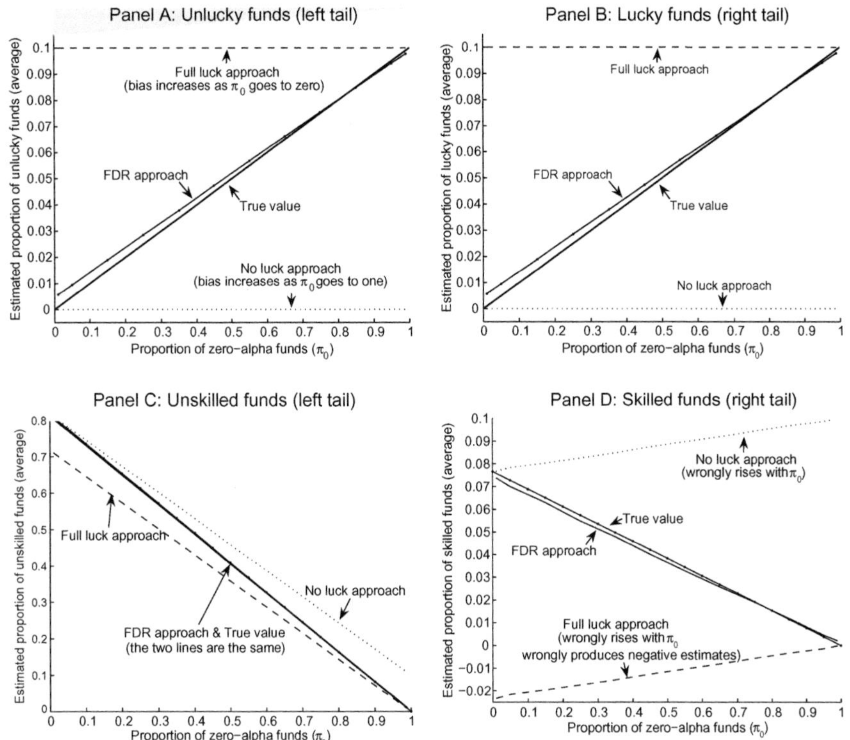

FIGURE 8.3
Panel A: Unlucky funds (left tail), Panel B: Lucky funds (right tail), Panel C: Unskilled funds (left tail), Panel D: Skilled funds (right tail).

lucky funds drive the proportion of significant funds up, making the no luck and full luck approaches wrongly indicate that more skilled funds are present. Further, the excessive luck adjustment of the full luck approach produces estimates of $E(T_\gamma^+)$ below zero.

In addition to the bias properties exhibited by our FDR estimators, their variability is low because of the large cross-section of funds ($M = 2,076$). To understand this, consider our main estimator $\widehat{\pi}_0$ (the same arguments apply to the other estimators). Since $\widehat{\pi}_0$ is a proportion estimator that depends on the proportion of p-values higher than λ^*, the Law of Large Numbers drives it close to its true value with our large sample size. For instance, taking $\lambda^* = 0.6$ and ($\pi_0 = 75\%$), the standard deviation of $\widehat{\pi}_0$, $\sigma_{\pi 0}$, is as low as 2.5% with independent p-values ($1/30^{th}$ the magnitude of π_0).[13] Barras et al. (2010) provide further evidence of the remarkable accuracy of the estimators using Monte Carlo simulations.

[13] Specifically, $\widehat{\pi}_0 = \left(1-\lambda^*\right)^{-1} \cdot 1/M \sum_{i=1}^{M} x_i$, where x_i follows a binomial distribution with probability of success $p_{\lambda^*} = prob(P_i > \lambda^*) = 0.30$, where P_i denotes the fund p-value (p_{λ^*} equals the rectangle area delimited by the horizontal black line and the vertical line at $\lambda^* = 0.6$ in Figure 8.2). Therefore, from the standard deviation of a binomial random variable, $\sigma_x = \left(p_{\lambda^*}\left(1-p_{\lambda^*}\right)\right)^{\frac{1}{2}} = 0.46$ and $\sigma_{\pi 0} = \left(1-\lambda^*\right)^{-1} \cdot \sigma_x/\sqrt{M} = 2.5\%$.

8.2.3 Cross-Sectional Dependence Among Funds

Managed funds can have correlated residuals if they "herd" in their stockholdings (Wermers, 1999) or hold similar industry allocations. In general, cross-sectional dependence in fund estimated alphas greatly complicates performance measurement. Any inference test with dependencies becomes quickly intractable as M rises, since this requires the estimation and inversion of an $M \times M$ residual covariance matrix. In a Bayesian framework, Jones and Shanken (2005) show that performance measurement requires intensive numerical methods when investor prior beliefs about fund alphas include cross-fund dependencies. Further, KTWW show that a complicated bootstrap is necessary to test the significance of fund performance of a fund located at a particular alpha rank, since this test depends on the joint distribution of all fund estimated alphas, that is, cross-correlated fund residuals must be bootstrapped simultaneously.

An important advantage of our approach is that we estimate the p-value of each fund in isolation, avoiding the complications that arise because of the dependence structure of fund residuals. However, high cross-sectional dependencies could potentially bias our estimators. To illustrate this point with an extreme case, suppose that all funds produce zero alphas ($\pi_0 = 100\%$), and that fund residuals are perfectly correlated (perfect herding). In this case, all fund p-values would be the same, and the p-value histogram would not converge to the true p-value distribution, as shown in Figure 8.2. Clearly, we would make serious errors no matter where we set λ^*.

In our sample, we are not overly concerned with dependencies, since we find that the average correlation between four-factor model residuals of pairs of funds is only 0.08. Further, many of our funds do not have highly overlapping return data, thus ruling out highly correlated residuals by construction. Specifically, we find that 15% of the funds pairs do not have a single monthly return observation in common; on average, only 55% of the return observations of fund pairs is overlapping. Therefore, we believe that cross-sectional dependencies are sufficiently low to allow consistent estimators.[14]

However, in order to explicitly verify the properties of our estimators, we run a Monte Carlo simulation. In order to closely reproduce the actual pairwise correlations between funds in our data set, we estimate the residual covariance matrix directly from the data, then use these dependencies in our simulations. In further simulations, we impose other types of dependencies, such as residual block correlations or residual factor dependencies, as in Jones and Shanken (2005). In all simulations, we find both that average estimates (for all of our estimators)

[14] It is well known that the sample average, $\bar{x} = 1/M \sum x_i$, is a consistent estimator under many forms of dependence (i.e., $\bar{x}$ converges to the true mean value when M is large; see Hamilton (1994), p. 47). Since our FDR estimators can be written as sample averages (see footnote 13), it is not surprising that they are also consistent under cross-sectional dependence among funds (for further discussion, see Storey et al. (2004)).

are very close to their true values, and that confidence intervals for estimates are comparable to those that result from simulations where independent residuals are assumed. These results, as well as further details on the simulation experiment, are discussed in Barras et al. (2010).

8.3 AN EMPIRICAL EXAMPLE: U.S. DOMESTIC EQUITY MUTUAL FUNDS

8.3.1 Asset Pricing Models

To illustrate the multiple testing approach outlined in this chapter, as well as to facilitate comparisons with prior chapters, we again turn to the U.S. domestic equity mutual fund universe. To compute fund performance, our baseline asset pricing model is the four-factor model proposed by Carhart (1997):

$$r_{i,t} = \alpha_i + b_i \cdot RMRF_t + s_i \cdot SMB_t + h_i \cdot HML_t + m_i \cdot UMD_t + \varepsilon_{i,t}, \quad (8.9)$$

where $r_{i,t}$ is the month t excess return of fund i over the risk-free rate (proxied by the monthly 30-day T-bill beginning-of-month yield); $r_{m,t}$ is the month t excess return on the CRSP NYSE/Amex/NASDAQ value-weighted market portfolio; and SMB_t, HML_t, and UMD_t are the month t returns on zero-investment factor-mimicking portfolios for size, book-to-market, and momentum obtained from Kenneth French's website.

We also implement a conditional four-factor model to account for time-varying exposure to the market portfolio (Ferson and Schadt (1996)),

$$r_{i,t} = \alpha_i + b_i \cdot RMRF_t + s_i \cdot SMB_t + h_i \cdot HML_t + m_i \cdot UMD_t + B' \left(z_{t-1} \cdot RMRF_t\right) + \varepsilon_{i,t}, \quad (8.10)$$

where z_{t-1} denotes the $J \times 1$ vector of predictive variables measured at the end of month t (minus their mean values over 1975 to 2006), and B is the $J \times 1$ vector of coefficients. The four predictive variables are the one-month T-bill yield; the dividend yield of the CRSP value-weighted NYSE/Amex stock index; the term spread, proxied by the difference between yields on 10-year Treasury's and three-month T-bills; and the default spread, proxied by the yield difference between Moody's Baa-rated and Aaa-rated corporate bonds. We also compute fund alphas using the CAPM and the Fama and French (1993) models. These results are summarized in Section 8.4.4.2.

To compute each fund t-statistic, we use the Newey and West (1987) heteroskedasticity and autocorrelation consistent estimator of the standard deviation, $\widehat{\sigma}_{\widehat{\alpha}_i}$. Further, KTWW find that the finite-sample distribution of the t-statistic is non-normal for approximately half of the funds. Therefore, we use a bootstrap procedure (instead of asymptotic theory) to compute fund p-values for the two-sided tests with equal tail significance level, $\gamma/2$. In order to estimate the distribution of the t-statistic for each fund i under the null hypothesis $\alpha_i = 0$, we use a residual-only bootstrap procedure, which draws with replacement from the regression estimated residuals $\{\widehat{\varepsilon}_{i,t}\}$.[15] For each fund, we implement 1,000 bootstrap replications. The reader is referred to KTWW for details on this bootstrap procedure.

8.3.2 Data

We use monthly mutual fund return data provided by the Center for Research in Security Prices (CRSP) between January 1975 and December 2006 to estimate fund alphas. Each monthly fund return is computed by weighting the net return of its component shareclasses by their beginning-of-month total net asset values. The CRSP database is matched with the Thomson/CDA database using the MFLINKs product of Wharton Research Data Services (WRDS) in order to use Thomson fund investment objective information, which is more consistent over time. Wermers (2000) provides a description of how an earlier version of MFLINKS was created. Our original sample is free of survivorship bias, but we further select only funds having at least 60 monthly return observations in order to obtain precise four-factor alpha estimates. These monthly returns need not be contiguous. However, when we observe a missing return, we delete the following-month return, since CRSP fills this with the cumulated return since the last non-missing return. In results presented in Barras et al. (2010), we find that reducing the minimum fund return requirement to 36 months has no material impact on our main results, and thus we believe that any biases introduced from the 60-month requirement are minimal.

Our final universe has 2,076 open-end, domestic equity mutual funds existing for at least 60 months between 1975 and 2006. Funds are classified into three investment categories: Growth (1,304 funds), Aggressive Growth (388 funds), and Growth & Income (384 funds). If an investment objective is missing, the prior nonmissing objective is carried forward. A fund is included in a given investment category if its objective corresponds to the investment category for at least 60 months.

Table 8.1 shows the estimated annualized alpha as well as factor loadings of equally weighted portfolios within each category of funds. The portfolio is rebalanced each month to include all funds existing at the beginning of that month. Results using the unconditional and conditional four-factor models are shown in Panels A and B, respectively.

Similar to results previously documented in the literature, we find that unconditional estimated alphas for each category are negative, ranging

---

[15] To determine whether assuming homoskedasticity and temporal independence in individual fund residuals is appropriate, we have checked for heteroskedasticity (White test), autocorrelation (Ljung-Box test), and Arch effects (Engle test). We find that only a few funds present such regularities. We have also implemented a block bootstrap methodology with a block length equal to $T^{\frac{1}{5}}$ (proposed by Hall et al. (1995)), where T denotes the length of the fund return time series. All of our results to be presented remain unchanged.

Table 8.1 Performance of the Equally Weighted Portfolio of Funds

Results for the unconditional and conditional four-factor models are shown in Panels A and B for the entire fund population (All funds), as well as for Growth, Aggressive Growth, and Growth & Income funds. The regressions are based on monthly data between January 1975 and December 2006. Each panel contains the estimated annualized alpha ($\widehat{\alpha}$), the estimated exposures to the market ($\widehat{b}_m$), size ($\widehat{b}_{smb}$), book-to-market ($\widehat{b}_{hml}$), and momentum factors ($\widehat{b}_{mom}$), as well as the adjusted R^2 of an equally weighted portfolio that includes all funds that exist at the beginning of each month. Figures in parentheses denote the Newey-West (1987) heteroskedasticity and autocorrelation consistent estimates of p-values under the null hypothesis that the regression parameters are equal to zero.

Panel A. Unconditional Four-Factor Model

	$\widehat{\alpha}$	$\widehat{b}_m$	$\widehat{b}_{smb}$	$\widehat{b}_{hml}$	$\widehat{b}_{mom}$	R^2
All (2,076)	−0.48%	0.95	0.17	−0.01	0.02	98.0%
	(0.12)	(0.00)	(0.00)	(0.38)	(0.09)	
Growth (1,304)	−0.45%	0.95	0.16	−0.03	0.02	98.0%
	(0.16)	(0.00)	(0.00)	(0.15)	(0.07)	
Aggressive Growth (388)	−0.53%	1.04	0.43	−0.17	0.09	95.8%
	(0.22)	(0.00)	(0.00)	(0.00)	(0.00)	
Growth & Income (384)	−0.47%	0.87	−0.04	0.17	−0.03	98.2%
	(0.09)	(0.00)	(0.02)	(0.00)	(0.01)	

Panel B. Conditional Four-Factor Model

	$\widehat{\alpha}$	$\widehat{b}_m$	$\widehat{b}_{smb}$	$\widehat{b}_{hml}$	$\widehat{b}_{mom}$	R^2
All (2,076)	−0.60%	0.96	0.17	−0.02	0.02	98.2%
	(0.00)	(0.00)	(0.23)	(0.08)	(0.09)	
Growth (1,304)	−0.59%	0.96	0.16	−0.03	0.03	98.2%
	(0.00)	(0.00)	(0.08)	(0.05)	(0.10)	
Aggressive Growth (388)	−0.49%	1.05	0.43	−0.19	0.08	96.2%
	(0.24)	(0.00)	(0.00)	(0.00)	(0.00)	
Growth & Income (384)	−0.58%	0.87	−0.04	0.16	−0.03	98.3%
	(0.05)	(0.00)	(0.02)	(0.00)	(0.02)	

from −0.45% to −0.60% per annum. Aggressive Growth funds tilt toward small capitalization, low book-to-market, and momentum stocks, while the opposite holds for Growth & Income funds. Introducing time-varying market betas provides similar results (Panel B). In further tests shown in Barras et al. (2010), we find that using the unconditional or conditional version of the four-factor model has no material impact on our main results. For brevity, in the next section, we present only results from the unconditional four-factor model.

8.4 AN EMPIRICAL EXAMPLE: RESULTS FOR U.S. DOMESTIC EQUITY FUNDS

8.4.1 The Impact of Luck on Long-Term Performance

We begin our empirical analysis by measuring the impact of luck on long-term mutual fund performance, measured as the lifetime performance of each fund (over the period 1975 to 2006) using the monthly four-factor model of Equation (8.9). Panel A of Table 8.2 shows estimated proportions of zero-alpha, unskilled, and skilled funds in the population ($\widehat{\pi}_0, \widehat{\pi}_A^-$, and $\widehat{\pi}_A^+$), as defined in Section 8.2.1.1, with standard deviations of estimates in parentheses. These point estimates are computed using the procedure described in Section 8.2.1.3 while standard deviations are computed using the method of Genovese and Wasserman (2004), which is described in Barras et al (2010).

Among the 2,076 funds, we estimate that the majority—75.4%—are zero-alpha funds. Managers of these funds exhibit stockpicking skills just sufficient to cover their trading costs and other expenses (including fees). These funds, therefore, capture all of the economic rents that they generate, consistent with the long-run prediction of Berk and Green (2004).

Further, it is quite surprising that the estimated proportion of skilled funds is statistically indistinguishable from zero (see "Skilled" column). This result may seem surprising in light of prior studies, such as Ferson and Schadt (1996), which find that a small group of top mutual fund managers appear to outperform their benchmarks, net of costs. However, a closer examination—in Panel B—shows that our adjustment for luck is key in understanding the difference between our approach and prior research.

To be specific, Panel B shows the proportion of significant alpha funds in the left and right tails ($\widehat{S}_\gamma^-$ and $\widehat{S}_\gamma^+$, respectively) at four different significance levels ($\gamma = 0.05, 0.10, 0.15, 0.20$). Similar to past research, there are many significant alpha funds in the right tail—$\widehat{S}_\gamma^+$ peaks at 8.2% of the total population (170 funds) when $\gamma = 0.20$ (i.e., these 170 funds have a positive estimated alpha with a two-sided p-value below 20%).However, of course, "significant alpha" does not always mean "skilled fund manager". Illustrating this point, the right side of Panel B decomposes these significant funds into proportions of lucky zero-alpha funds and skilled funds ($\widehat{F}_\gamma^+$ and $\widehat{T}_\gamma^+$, respectively) using the technique described in Section 8.2.1.3. Clearly, we cannot reject that all of the right tail funds are merely lucky outcomes among the large number (1,565) of zero-alpha funds, and that none have truly skilled managers (i.e., $\widehat{T}_\gamma^+$ is not significantly different from zero for any significance level γ).

It is interesting (Panel A) that 24% of the population (499 funds) are truly unskilled fund managers, unable to pick stocks well enough to recover their trading costs and other expenses.[16] Left tail funds, which are overwhelmingly comprised of

[16] This minority of funds is the driving force explaining the negative average estimated alpha that is widely documented in the literature (e.g., Jensen (1968), Carhart (1997), Elton et al. (1993), and Pastor and Stambaugh (2002a)).

Table 8.2 Impact of Luck on Long-Term Performance

Long-term performance is measured with the unconditional four-factor model over the entire period 1975 to 2006. Panel A displays the estimated proportions of zero-alpha, unskilled, and skilled funds ($\widehat{\pi}_0, \widehat{\pi}_A^-$, and $\widehat{\pi}_A^+$) in the entire fund population (2,076 funds). Panel B counts the proportions of significant funds in the left and right tails of the cross-sectional t-statistic distribution ($\widehat{S}_\gamma^-, \widehat{S}_\gamma^+$) at four significance levels ($\gamma = 0.05, 0.10, 0.15, 0.20$). In the leftmost columns, the significant group in the left tail, $\widehat{S}_\gamma^-$, is decomposed into unlucky and unskilled funds ($\widehat{F}_\gamma^-, \widehat{T}_\gamma^-$). In the rightmost columns, the significant group in the right tail, $\widehat{S}_\gamma^+$, is decomposed into lucky and skilled funds ($\widehat{F}_\gamma^+, \widehat{T}_\gamma^+$). The bottom of Panel B also presents the characteristics of each significant group ($\widehat{S}_\gamma^-, \widehat{S}_\gamma^+$): the average estimated alpha (% per year), expense ratio (% per year), and turnover (% per year). Figures in parentheses denote the standard deviation of the different estimators.

Panel A. Proportion of Unskilled and Skilled Funds

	Zero Alpha ($\widehat{\pi}_0$)	Non-Zero Alpha	Unskilled ($\widehat{\pi}_A^-$)	Skilled ($\widehat{\pi}_A^+$)
Proportion	75.4 (2.5)	24.6	24.0 (2.3)	0.6 (0.8)
Number	1,565	511	499	12

Panel B. Impact of Luck in the Left and Right Tails

	Left Tail				Right Tail				
Signif. Level (γ)	**0.05**	**0.10**	**0.15**	**0.20**	**0.20**	**0.15**	**0.10**	**0.05**	**Signif. Level (γ)**
Signif. $\widehat{S}_\gamma^-$(%)	11.6	17.2	21.5	25.4	8.2	6.0	4.2	2.2	Signif. $\widehat{S}_\gamma^+$(%)
	(0.7)	(0.8)	(0.9)	(0.9)	(0.6)	(0.5)	(0.4)	(0.3)	
Unlucky $\widehat{F}_\gamma^-$(%)	1.9	3.8	5.6	7.6	7.6	5.6	3.8	1.9	Lucky $\widehat{F}_\gamma^+$(%)
	(0.0)	(0.1)	(0.2)	(0.3)	(0.3)	(0.2)	(0.1)	(0.0)	
Unskilled $\widehat{T}_\gamma^-$(%)	9.8	13.6	16.1	18.2	0.6	0.4	0.4	0.3	Skilled $\widehat{T}_\gamma^+$(%)
	(0.7)	(0.9)	(1.0)	(1.1)	(0.7)	(0.6)	(0.5)	(0.3)	
Alpha(% year)	−5.5	−5.0	−4.7	−4.6	4.8	5.2	5.6	6.5	Alpha(% year)
	(0.2)	(0.2)	(0.1)	(0.1)	(0.3)	(0.4)	(0.5)	(0.7)	
Exp.(% year)	1.4	1.4	1.4	1.4	1.3	1.2	1.2	1.2	Exp.(% year)
Turn.(% year)	100	97	95	95	94	95	95	104	Turn.(% year)

unskilled (and not merely unlucky) funds, have a relatively long fund life—12.7 years, on average. Further, these funds generally perform poorly over their entire lives, making their survival puzzling. Perhaps, as discussed by Elton et al. (2004), such funds exist if they are able to attract a sufficient number of unsophisticated investors, who are also charged higher fees (Christoffersen and Musto (2002)).

The bottom of Panel B presents characteristics of the average fund in each segment of the tails. Although the average estimated alpha of right tail funds is somewhat high (between 4.8% and 6.5% per year), this is simply due to very lucky outcomes for a small proportion of the 1,565 zero-alpha funds in the population. It is also interesting that expense ratios are higher for left tail funds, which likely explains some of the underperformance of these funds (we will revisit this issue when we examine pre-expense returns in a later section), while turnover does not vary systematically among the various tail segments.

In further tests reported in Barras et al. (2010), the long-term performance test described above is repeated for investment objective subgroups—Growth, Aggressive Growth, and Growth & Income. The overall results are as follows. Growth funds show similar results to the overall universe of funds: 76.5% have zero alphas, 23.5% are unskilled, while none are skilled. Performance is somewhat better for Aggressive Growth funds, as 3.9% of them show true skills. Finally, Growth & Income funds consist of the largest proportion of unskilled funds (30.7%), but have no skilled funds. The long-term existence of this category of actively managed funds, which includes "value funds" and "core funds" is remarkable in light of these poor results.

As noted by Wermers (2000), the universe of U.S. domestic equity mutual funds has expanded substantially since 1990. Accordingly, the proportions of unskilled and skilled funds estimated over the entire period 1975 to 2006 may not accurately describe the performance generated by the industry prior to this rapid expansion. To address this issue, we next examine the evolution of the long-term proportions of unskilled and skilled funds over time. At the end of each year from 1989 to 2006, we estimate the proportions of unskilled and skilled funds ($\widehat{\pi}_A^-$ and $\widehat{\pi}_A^+$, respectively) using the entire return history for each fund up to that point in time. As we move forward in time, we add new mutual funds once they exhibit a 60-month record. To illustrate, our initial estimates, on December 31, 1989, cover the first 15 years of the sample, 1975 to 1989 (427 funds), while our final estimates, on December 31, 2006, are based on the entire 32 years, 1975 to 2006 (2,076 funds; these are the estimates shown in Panel A of Table 8.2).[17] The results in Panel A of Figure 8.4 show that the proportion of funds with nonzero alphas (equal to the sum of the proportions of skilled and unskilled funds) remains fairly constant over time. However, there are dramatic changes in the relative proportions of unskilled and skilled funds from 1989 to 2006. Specifically, the

[17] The dynamic proportion estimators, $\widehat{\pi}_0$, $\widehat{\pi}_A^-$, and $\widehat{\pi}_A^+$, measured at the end of each year treat the universe of existing funds as a new fund population (to be included, a fund must have at least 60 return observations, ending with that year). For these estimators to be accurate (in terms of bias and variability), it is necessary that the cross-sectional fund dependence at each point in time remains sufficiently low (see Section 8.2.3).

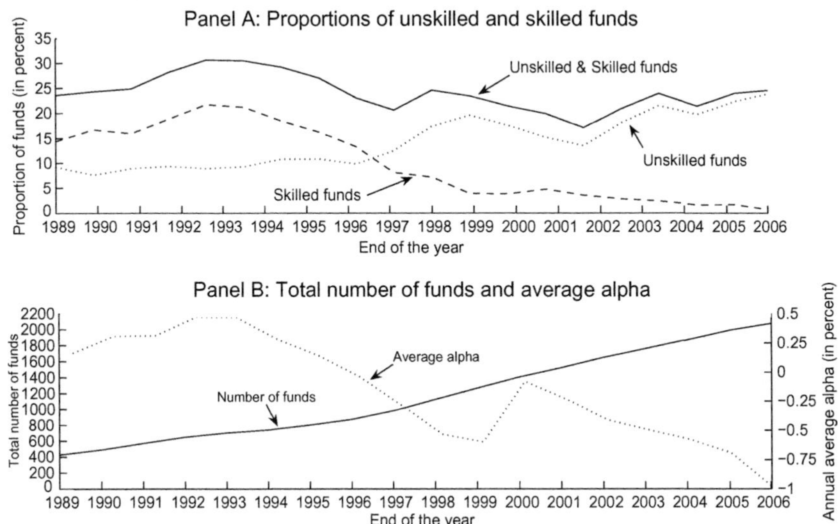

FIGURE 8.4
Panel A: Proportions of Unskilled and Skilled Funds. Panel B: Total Number of Funds and Average Alpha.

proportion of skilled funds declines from 14.4% to 0.6%, while the proportion of unskilled funds rises from 9.2% to 24.0% of the entire universe of funds. These changes are also reflected in the population average estimated alpha, shown in Panel B, which drops from 0.16% to 0.97% per year over the same period.

Further, Panel B shows the yearly count of funds included in the estimated proportions of Panel A. From 1996 to 2005, there are more than 100 additional actively managed domestic equity mutual funds (having a 60-month history) per year. Interestingly, this coincides with the time-variation in the proportions of unskilled and skilled funds shown in Panel A, which can be attributed to two distinct sources. First, new funds created during the 1990s generate very poor performance, as we find that 24% of them are unskilled, while none are skilled (i.e, $\widehat{\pi}_A^- = 24.0\%$ and $\widehat{\pi}_A^+ = 0\%$). Since these 1,328 new funds account for more than 60% of the total population (2,076), they greatly contribute to the performance decline shown in Panel A. Second, our results suggest that the growth in the industry has also affected the alpha of the older funds created before January 1990. While many of these 748 funds exhibit truly positive performance up to December 1996 ($\widehat{\pi}_A^+ = 14.4$, see Panel A), the decline is breathtaking afterwards. Specifically, we estimate that, during 1997 to 2006, 34.8% of these older funds are truly unskilled, while none produces truly positive alphas (i.e., $\widehat{\pi}_A^- = 34.8\%, \widehat{\pi}_A^+ = 0\%$).[18]

[18] Under a structural change, the long-term alpha is a time-weighted average of the two subperiod alphas. A zero or negative performance after 1996 progressively drives the long-term alphas of the skilled funds towards zero. This explains why our estimate of the proportion of skilled funds at the end of 2006 is close to zero ($\widehat{\pi}_A^+ = 0.6\%$). We have verified this pattern using the Monte Carlo setting described in Barras et al. Assuming that all skilled funds become zero-alpha (unskilled) after 1996, we find that the average value of $\widehat{\pi}_A^+$ (1,000 iterations) over the entire period equals 2.9% (0.3%).

Either the growth of the fund industry has coincided with greater levels of stock market efficiency, making stockpicking a more difficult and costly endeavor, or the large number of new managers simply have inadequate skills. It is also interesting that, during our period of analysis, many fund managers with good track records left the sample to manage hedge funds (as shown by Kostovetsky (2007)), and indexed investing increased substantially.

Although increased competition may have decreased the average level of alpha, it is also possible that funds do not achieve superior performance in the long run because flows compete away any alpha surplus. However, we might find evidence of funds with superior short-term alphas before investors become fully aware of such outperformers due to search costs. Since our long-term performance estimates average alphas over time, they are not able to detect such dynamics. To address this issue, in the next section, we investigate whether funds exhibit superior alphas over the short run.[19]

8.4.2 The Impact of Luck on Short-Term Performance

To test for short run mutual fund performance, we partition our data into six non-overlapping subperiods of five years, beginning with 1977 to 1981 and ending with 2002 to 2006. For each subperiod, we include all funds that have 60 monthly return observations and then compute their respective alpha p-values—in other words, we treat each fund during each five-year period as a separate "fund". We pool these five-year records together across all time periods to represent the average experience of an investor in a randomly chosen fund during a randomly chosen five-year period. After pooling, we obtain a total of 3,311 p-values from which we compute our different estimators. The results are shown in Table 8.3.

First, Panel A of Table 8.3 shows that a small fraction of funds (2.4% of the population) exhibit skill over the short run (with a standard deviation of 0.7%). Thus, short-term superior performance is rare, but does exist, as opposed to long-term performance. Second, these skilled funds are located in the extreme right tail of the cross-sectional t-distribution. Panel B of Table 8.3 shows that, with a γ of only 10% (i.e., funds having a positive estimated alpha with a two-sided p-value below 10%), we capture almost all skilled funds, as $\widehat{T}_{\gamma}^{+}$ reaches 2.3% (close to its maximum value of 2.4%). Proceeding toward the center of the distribution (by increasing γ to 0.10 and 0.20) produces almost no additional skilled funds, and almost entirely additional zero-alpha funds that are lucky ($\widehat{F}_{\gamma}^{+}$). Thus, skilled fund managers, while rare, may be somewhat easy to find since they have extremely high t-statistics (extremely low p-values). We will use this finding in our next section, where we attempt to find funds with out-of-sample skills.

---

[19] Time-varying betas may also affect the inference on the estimated alpha. As mentioned earlier, we have measured performance using the conditional version of the four-factor model (Equation (8.10)), and find that the results remained qualitatively unchanged (see Barras et al. for detailed results).

Table 8.3 Impact of Luck on Short-Term Performance

Short-term performance is measured with the unconditional four-factor model over non-overlapping five-year periods between 1977 to 2006. The different estimates shown in the table are computed from the pooled alpha p-values across all five-year periods. Panel A displays the estimated proportions of zero-alpha, unskilled, and skilled funds ($\widehat{\pi}_0$, $\widehat{\pi}_A^-$, and $\widehat{\pi}_A^+$) in the population (3,311 funds). Panel B counts the proportions of significant funds in the left and right tails of the cross-sectional t-statistic distribution ($\widehat{S}_\gamma^-$, $\widehat{S}_\gamma^+$) at four significance levels (γ=0.05, 0.10, 0.15, 0.20). In the leftmost columns, the significant group in the left tail, $\widehat{S}_\gamma^-$, is decomposed into unlucky and unskilled funds ($\widehat{F}_\gamma^-$, $\widehat{T}_\gamma^-$). In the rightmost columns, the significant group in the right tail, $\widehat{S}_\gamma^+$, is decomposed into lucky and skilled funds ($\widehat{F}_\gamma^+$, $\widehat{T}_\gamma^+$). The bottom of Panel B also presents the characteristics of each significant group ($\widehat{S}_\gamma^-$, $\widehat{S}_\gamma^+$): the average estimated alpha (% per year), expense ratio (% per year), and turnover (% per year). Figures in parentheses denote the standard deviation of the different estimators.

Panel A. Proportion of Unskilled and Skilled Funds

	Zero Alpha ($\widehat{\pi}_0$)	Non-Zero Alpha	Unskilled ($\widehat{\pi}_A^-$)	Skilled ($\widehat{\pi}_A^+$)
Proportion	72.2 (2.0)	27.8	25.4 (1.7)	2.4 (0.7)
Number	2,390	921	841	80

Panel B. Impact of Luck in the Left and Right Tails

	Left Tail							Right Tail	
Signif. level (γ)	**0.05**	**0.10**	**0.15**	**0.20**	**0.20**	**0.15**	**0.10**	**0.05**	**Signif. level (γ)**
Signif. $\widehat{S}_\gamma^-$(%)	11.2	16.8	21.4	24.9	9.6	7.8	5.9	3.5	Signif. $\widehat{S}_\gamma^+$(%)
	(0.5)	(0.6)	(0.7)	(0.8)	(0.5)	(0.5)	(0.4)	(0.3)	
Unlucky $\widehat{F}_\gamma^-$(%)	1.8	3.6	5.4	7.2	7.2	5.4	3.6	1.8	Lucky $\widehat{F}_\gamma^+$(%)
	(0.0)	(0.0)	(0.1)	(0.2)	(0.2)	(0.1)	(0.0)	(0.0)	
Unskilled $\widehat{T}_\gamma^-$(%)	9.4	13.2	16.0	17.7	2.4	2.4	2.3	1.7	Skilled $\widehat{T}_\gamma^+$(%)
	(0.6)	(0.7)	(0.8)	(0.8)	(0.6)	(0.5)	(0.4)	(0.3)	
Alpha(% year)	−6.5	−5.9	−5.5	−5.3	6.7	7.0	7.2	7.5	Alpha(% year)
	(0.2)	(0.2)	(0.1)	(0.1)	(0.3)	(0.4)	(0.4)	(0.6)	
Exp.(% year)	1.4	1.3	1.3	1.3	1.2	1.2	1.2	1.2	Exp.(% year)
Turn.(% year)	98	95	94	93	80	80	81	78	Turn.(% year)

In the left tail, we observe that the great majority of funds are unskilled, and not merely unlucky zero-alpha funds. For instance, in the extreme left tail (at $\gamma = 0.05$), the proportion of unskilled funds, $\widehat{T}_{\gamma}^{-}$, is roughly five times the proportion of unlucky funds, $\widehat{F}_{\gamma}^{-}$ (9.4% versus 1.8%). Here, the short-term results are similar to the prior-discussed long-term results: the great majority of left tail funds are truly unskilled. It is also interesting that true short-term skills seem to be inversely related to turnover, as indicated by the substantially higher levels of turnover of left tail funds (which are mainly unskilled funds). Unskilled managers apparently trade frequently, in the short run, to appear skilled, which ultimately hurts their performance. Perhaps the poor governance of some funds (Ding and Wermers (2009)) explains why they end up in the left tail (net of expenses)—they overexpend on both trading costs (through high turnover) and other expenses relative to their skills.

Barras et al. repeat the short-term performance test for investment objective subgroups (Growth, Aggressive Growth, and Growth & Income funds). They find that the proportions of unskilled funds within the three categories are similar to that of the entire universe (from Table 8.3), with some notable differences. While Aggressive Growth funds exhibit somewhat higher skills ($\widehat{\pi}_{A}^{+} = 4.2\%$) than Growth funds ($\widehat{\pi}_{A}^{+} = 2.6\%$), no Growth & Income funds are able to produce positive short-term alphas.

Since we find evidence of short-term fund manager skills that disappear in the long term, it is interesting to further examine the mechanism through which skills disappear. The model of BG provides guidance for how this process may unfold. Specifically, if competing fund investors chase winning funds (which have higher proportions of truly skilled funds), then superior fund management companies (which are in scarce supply) may capture the majority of the rents they produce. We examine this conjecture in Table 8.4. Specifically, at the beginning of each (non-overlapping) five-year period from 1977 to 2006 (similar to Table 8.3), we rank funds into quintiles based on their (1) size (total net assets under management), (2) age (since first offered to the public), and (3) prior-year flows, as a percentage of total net assets. Then, we measure the proportions of zero-alpha, unskilled, and skilled funds ($\widehat{\pi}_0$, $\widehat{\pi}_{A}^{-}$, and $\widehat{\pi}_{A}^{+}$, respectively) within each fund size quintile (Panel A), fund age quintile (Panel B), and fund flow quintile (Panels C and D).

The BG model implies that larger and older funds should exhibit lower alphas, since they have presumably grown (or survived) to the point where they provide no superior alphas, net of fees—partly due to flows that followed past superior performance. Smaller and newer funds, on the other hand, may exhibit some skills before investors learn about their superior abilities. Consistent with this conjecture, Panels A and B show that larger and older funds are populated with far more unskilled funds than smaller and newer funds.

Perhaps more directly, the BG model also implies that flows should disproportionately move to truly skilled funds, and that these funds should exhibit the largest reduction in future skills. Panel C shows, for each past-year flow quintile,

Table 8.4 Fund Characteristics and Performance Dynamics

We examine the relation between short-term performance and fund size (Panel A), age (Panel B), and annual flows (Panels C and D). At the beginning of each non-overlapping five-year period between 1977 to 2006, funds are ranked according to each characteristic and grouped into quintiles (Low, 2, 3, 4, High). Short-term performance is measured with the unconditional four-factor model over the next five years, except for Panel C (Annual Flow-Past Performance), where we use the previous five years. For each quintile, we pool the fund alpha p-values, characteristic levels, and estimated alphas across all five-year periods to compute the estimated proportions of zero-alpha, unskilled, and skilled funds ($\widehat{\pi}_0$, $\widehat{\pi}_A^-$, and $\widehat{\pi}_A^+$), average characteristic levels, and estimated alphas ($\widehat{\alpha}$). Median Size denotes the median quintile total net asset under management (million USD), while Avg. Age and Flow denote the average quintile age (years), and annual flow (%). Figures in parentheses denote the standard deviation of the different estimators.

Panel A. Size (TNA)

Quintile	Low	2	3	4	High	High-Low
Zero-alpha ($\widehat{\pi}_0$)	81.0 (3.5)	72.2 (4.0)	77.7 (3.8)	64.2 (4.2)	62.1 (4.2)	−18.9
Unskilled ($\widehat{\pi}_A^-$)	16.4 (3.1)	23.1 (3.7)	22.3 (3.5)	33.5 (3.9)	34.3 (3.9)	+17.9
Skilled ($\widehat{\pi}_A^+$)	2.6 (1.6)	4.6 (1.7)	0.0 (1.5)	2.3 (1.5)	3.6 (1.6)	+1.0
Median Size (million $)	9.8	52.9	166.0	453.1	1,651.7	+1,641.9
Avg. $\widehat{\alpha}$ (% year)	−0.5 (0.1)	−0.6 (0.1)	−1.1 (0.1)	−1.1 (0.1)	−0.9 (0.1)	−0.4

Panel B. Age

Quintile	Low	2	3	4	High	High-Low
Zero-alpha ($\widehat{\pi}_0$)	79.6 (3.5)	65.0 (4.2)	72.5 (3.7)	70.2 (4.0)	70.1 (4.2)	−9.5
Unskilled ($\widehat{\pi}_A^-$)	16.5 (3.0)	29.8 (3.9)	25.5 (3.4)	26.7 (3.6)	29.9 (4.0)	+13.4
Skilled ($\widehat{\pi}_A^+$)	3.9 (1.7)	5.2 (1.6)	2.0 (1.5)	3.1 (1.5)	0.0 (1.3)	−3.9
Avg. Age (year)	2.1	5.2	8.6	15.5	37.8	+35.7
Avg. $\widehat{\alpha}$ (% year)	−0.3 (0.1)	−0.8 (0.1)	−0.9 (0.1)	−0.7 (0.1)	−1.4 (0.1)	−1.1

Panel C. Annual Flow—Past Performance

Quintile	Low	2	3	4	High	High-Low
Zero-alpha ($\widehat{\pi}_0$)	52.9 (4.0)	73.5 (3.8)	84.0 (2.7)	71.0 (3.8)	78.6 (3.5)	+25.7
Unskilled ($\widehat{\pi}_A^-$)	47.1 (3.8)	26.5 (3.5)	16.0 (2.4)	22.5 (3.5)	3.4 (1.6)	−43.7
Skilled ($\widehat{\pi}_A^+$)	0.0 (1.2)	0.0 (1.2)	0.0 (1.3)	6.5 (1.8)	18.0 (3.0)	+18.0
Avg. Flow (% year)	−26.8	−11.0	−3.2	7.5	67.5	+94.3
Avg. $\widehat{\alpha}$ (% year)	−2.8 (0.1)	−1.7 (0.1)	−0.9 (0.1)	0.1 (0.1)	1.2 (0.1)	+4.0

Panel D. Annual Flow—Future Performance

Quintile	Low	2	3	4	High	High-Low
Zero-alpha ($\widehat{\pi}_0$)	69.9 (4.6)	59.7 (4.4)	70.6 (3.6)	73.8 (4.3)	80.6 (2.9)	+10.7
Unskilled ($\widehat{\pi}_A^-$)	27.0 (4.2)	37.5 (4.0)	26.8 (3.3)	25.7 (3.5)	17.0 (2.5)	−10.0
Skilled ($\widehat{\pi}_A^+$)	3.1 (1.7)	2.7 (1.6)	2.6 (1.6)	0.5 (1.5)	2.4 (1.7)	−0.7
Avg. Flow (% year)	−23.2	−7.1	3.0	24.0	205.3	+228.5
Avg. $\widehat{\alpha}$) (% year)	−0.9 (0.1)	−1.4 (0.1)	−1.0 (0.1)	−1.0 (0.1)	−0.7 (0.1)	+0.2

the proportions of each fund type during the five years ending with the flow measurement year, while Panel D shows similar statistics for these quintiles during the following five years. Here, the results are strongly supportive of the BG model. Specifically, the highest flow quintile exhibits the highest proportion of skilled funds (18%) during the five years prior to the flow year, and the largest reduction in skilled funds during the five years subsequent to the flow year (from 18% to 2.4%). Conversely, funds in the lowest flow quintile exhibit high proportions of unskilled funds prior to the flow year, but appear to improve their skills during the following years (perhaps due to a change in strategy or portfolio manager in response to the outflows). However, consistent with prior research (e.g., Sirri and Tufano (1998)), it appears that investors should have withdrawn even more money from these funds, as they continue to exhibit poor skills (27% are unskilled, compared to 17% for high inflow funds). Although the BG model does not capture the behavior of these apparently irrational investors, our results are generally consistent with the predictions of their model.

8.4.3 Performance Persistence

Our previous analysis reveals that only 2.4% of the funds are skilled over the short term. Can we detect these skilled funds over time, in order to capture their superior alphas? Ideally, we would like to form a portfolio containing only the truly skilled funds in the right tail; however, since we only know in which segment of the tails they lie, and not their identities, such an approach is not feasible.

Nonetheless, the reader should recall from the last section that skilled funds are located in the extreme right tail. By forming portfolios containing all funds in this extreme tail, we stand a greater chance of capturing the superior alphas of the truly skilled funds. For instance, Panel B of Table 8.3 shows that when the significance level γ is low ($\gamma = 0.05$), the proportion of skilled funds among all significant funds, $\widehat{T}_{\gamma}^{+}/\widehat{S}_{\gamma}^{+}$, is about 50%, which is much higher than the proportion of skilled funds in the entire universe, 2.4%.

In order to choose the significance level, γ, that determines the significant funds, S_{γ}^{+}, included in the portfolio, we explicitly account for the location of the skilled funds by using the False Discovery Rate in the right tail, FDR^{+}. The FDR_{γ}^{+} is defined as the expected proportion of lucky funds included in the portfolio at the significance level γ:

$$FDR_{\gamma}^{+} = E\left(\frac{F_{\gamma}^{+}}{S_{\gamma}^{+}}\right). \tag{8.11}$$

The FDR^{+} makes possible a simple portfolio formation rule.[20] When we set a low FDR^{+} target, we allow only a small proportion of lucky funds (false discoveries)

[20] Our new measure, FDR_{γ}^{+}, is an extension of the traditional FDR introduced in the statistical literature (e.g., Benjamini and Hochberg (1995), Storey (2002)), since the latter does not distinguish between bad and good luck. The traditional measure is $FDR_{\gamma} = E\left(F_{\gamma}/S_{\gamma}\right)$, where $F_{\gamma} = F_{\gamma}^{+} + F_{\gamma}^{-}$, $S_{\gamma} = S_{\gamma}^{+} + S_{\gamma}^{-}$.

in the chosen portfolio. Specifically, we set a sufficiently low significance level, γ, so as to include skilled funds along with a small number of zero-alpha funds that are extremely lucky. Conversely, increasing the FDR^+ target has two opposing effects on a portfolio: it decreases the portfolio expected future performance, since the proportion of lucky funds in the portfolio is higher, and it increases the portfolio diversification, since more funds are selected—reducing the volatility of the out-of-sample performance. Accordingly, we examine five FDR^+ target levels, z^+, in our persistence test, namely, $z^+ = 10\%, 30\%, 50\%, 70\%,$ and 90%.[21]

The construction of the portfolios proceeds as follows. At the end of each year, we estimate the alpha p-values of each existing fund using the previous five-year period. Using these p-values, we estimate the FDR_γ^+ over a range of chosen significance levels ($\gamma = 0.01, 0.02, \ldots, 0.60$). Following Storey (2002), we implement the following straightforward estimator of the FDR_γ^+:

$$\widehat{FDR}_\gamma^+ = \frac{\widehat{F}_\gamma^+}{\widehat{S}_\gamma^+} = \frac{\widehat{\pi}_0 \cdot \gamma/2}{\widehat{S}_\gamma^+}, \tag{8.12}$$

where $\widehat{\pi}_0$ is the estimator of the proportion of zero-alpha funds described in Section 8.2.1.3 For each FDR^+ target level z^+, we determine the significance level, $\gamma\left(z^+\right)$, that provides a $\widehat{FDR}_{\gamma(z^+)}^+$ as close as possible to this target. Then, only funds with p-values smaller than $\gamma\left(z^+\right)$ are included in an equally weighted portfolio. This portfolio is held for one year, after which the selection procedure is repeated. If a selected fund does not survive after a given month during the holding period, its weight is reallocated to the remaining funds during the rest of the year to mitigate survival bias. The first portfolio formation date is December 31, 1979 (after five years of returns have been observed), while the last is December 31, 2005.

In Panel A of Table 8.5, we show the FDR level ($\widehat{FDR}_{\gamma(z^+)}^+$) of the five portfolios, as well as the proportion of funds in the population that they include ($\widehat{S}_{\gamma(z^+)}^+$) during the five-year formation period, averaged over the 27 formation periods (ending from 1979 to 2005), and their respective distributions. First, we observe (as expected) that the achieved FDR increases with the FDR target assigned to a portfolio. However, the average $\widehat{FDR}_{\gamma(z^+)}^+$ does not always match its target. For instance, $FDR10\%$ achieves an average of 41.5%, instead of the targeted 10%—during several formation periods, the proportion of skilled funds in the population is too low to achieve a 10% FDR target.[22] Of course, a higher FDR

[21] Besides its financial interpretation, the FDR has also a natural statistical meaning, as it is the extension of the Type I error (i.e., rejecting the null H_0, when it is correct) from single to multiple hypothesis testing. In the single case, the Type I error is controlled by using the significance level γ (i.e., the size of the test). In the multiple case, we replace γ with the FDR, which is a *compound* Type I error measure. In both cases, we face a similar trade-off: in order to increase power, we have to increase γ or the FDR, respectively (see the survey of Romano et al. (2008)).

[22] For instance, the minimum achievable FDR at the end of 2003 and 2004 is equal to 47.0% and 39.1%, respectively. If we look at the $\widehat{FDR}_{\gamma(z^+)}^+$ distribution for the portfolio $FDR10\%$ in Panel A, we observe that in six years out of 27, the $\widehat{FDR}_{\gamma(z^+)}^+$ is higher than 70%.

Table 8.5 Performance Persistence Based on the False Discovery Rate

For each of the five *FDR* **targets ($z^+ = 10\%, 30\%, 50\%, 70\%, and\ 90\%$), Panel A contains descriptive statistics on the** *FDR* **level $\widehat{FDR}^+_{\gamma(z^+)}$ achieved by the chosen portfolio, respectively, as well as the proportion of funds in the population that it includes ($\widehat{S}_{\gamma(z^+)}$). The panel shows the average values of $\widehat{FDR}^+_{\gamma(z^+)}$ and $\widehat{S}^+_{\gamma(z^+)}$ over the 27 annual formation dates (from December 1979 to 2005), as well as their respective distributions. Panel B displays the performance of each portfolio over the period 1980 to 2006. We estimate the annual four-factor alpha ($\widehat{\alpha}$) with its bootstrap** *p***-value, its annual residual standard deviation ($\widehat{\sigma}_\varepsilon$), its annual information ratio (IR $= (\widehat{\alpha}/\widehat{\sigma}_\varepsilon)$), its loadings on the market ($\widehat{b}_m$), size ($\widehat{b}_{smb}$), book-to-market ($\widehat{b}_{hml}$), and momentum factors ($\widehat{b}_{mom}$), and its annual excess mean and standard deviation. In Panel C, we examine the turnover of each portfolio. We compute the proportion of funds that are still included in the portfolio one, two, three, four, and five years after their initial selection.**

Panel A. Portfolio Statistics

	Achieved False Discovery Rate $\left(\widehat{FDR}_\gamma\,(z^+)^+\right)$					Included Proportion of Funds ($\widehat{S}^+_{\gamma(z^+)}$)				
Target (z^+)	Mean	10–30	30–50	50–70	>70%	Mean	0–6	6–12	12–24	>24%
*FDR*10%	41.5%	14	6	1	6	3.0%	25	2	0	0
*FDR*30%	47.5%	8	12	1	6	8.2%	15	7	3	2
*FDR*50%	60.4%	0	14	7	6	20.9%	5	7	4	11
*FDR*70%	71.3%	0	4	12	11	29.7%	1	5	5	16
*FDR*90%	75.0%	0	4	9	14	33.7%	0	3	4	20

Panel B. Performance Analysis

Target (z^+)	$\widehat{\alpha}(p-\text{value})$	$\widehat{\sigma}_\varepsilon$	**IR**	$\widehat{b}_m$	$\widehat{b}_{smb}$	$\widehat{b}_{hml}$	$\widehat{b}_{mom}$	**Mean**	**Std dev**
*FDR*10%	1.45%(0.04)	4.0%	0.36	0.93	0.16	−0.04	−0.02	8.3%	15.4%
*FDR*30%	1.15%(0.05)	3.3%	0.35	0.94	0.17	−0.02	−0.03	8.1%	15.4%
*FDR*50%	0.95%(0.10)	2.9%	0.33	0.96	0.20	−0.06	−0.01	8.1%	16.1%
*FDR*70%	0.68%(0.15)	2.7%	0.25	0.97	0.19	−0.06	−0.01	7.9%	16.1%
*FDR*90%	0.39%(0.30)	2.7%	0.14	0.97	0.19	−0.05	−0.00	7.8%	16.0%

Panel C. Portfolio Turnover

	Proportion of funds remaining in the portfolio...				
Target (z^+)	**After 1 Year**	**After 2 Years**	**After 3 Years**	**After 4 Years**	**After 5 Years**
*FDR*10%	36.7	12.8	3.4	0.8	0.0
*FDR*30%	40.0	14.7	5.1	1.7	1.3
*FDR*50%	48.8	23.5	12.3	4.7	2.6
*FDR*70%	52.2	29.0	17.4	9.5	6.3
*FDR*90%	55.9	33.8	20.4	13.0	8.5

target means an increase in the proportion of funds included in a portfolio, as shown in the rightmost columns of Panel A, since our selection rule becomes less restrictive.

In Panel B, we present the average out-of-sample performance (during the following year) of these five false discovery controlled portfolios, starting January 1, 1980 and ending December 31, 2006. We compute the estimated annualized alpha, $\widehat{\alpha}$, along with its bootstrapped p-value; annualized residual standard deviation, $\widehat{\sigma}_{\varepsilon}$; information ratio, IR= $\widehat{\alpha}/\widehat{\sigma}_{\varepsilon}$; four-factor model loadings; annualized mean return (minus T-bills); and annualized time-series standard deviation of monthly returns. The results reveal that our *FDR* portfolios successfully detect funds with short-term skills. For example, the portfolios *FDR*10% and 30% produce out-of-sample alphas (net of expenses) of 1.45% and 1.15% per year (significant at the 5% level). As the *FDR* target rises to 90%, the proportion of funds in the portfolio increases, which improves diversification ($\widehat{\sigma}_{\varepsilon}$ falls from 4.0% to 2.7%). However, we also observe a sharp decrease in the alpha (from 1.45% to 0.39%), reflecting the large proportion of lucky funds contained in the *FDR*90% portfolio.

Panel C examines portfolio turnover. We determine the proportion of funds that are still selected using a given false discovery rule one, two, three, four, and five years after their initial inclusion. The results sharply illustrate the short-term nature of truly outperforming funds. After one year, 40% or fewer funds remain in portfolios *FDR*10% and 30%, while after three years, these percentages drop below 6%.

Finally, in Figure 8.5, we examine how the estimated alpha of the portfolio *FDR*10% evolves over time using expanding windows. The initial value, on December 31, 1989, is the yearly out-of-sample alpha measured over the period 1980 to 1989, while the final value, on December 31, 2006, is the yearly out-of-sample alpha measured over the entire 1980 to 2006 period (i.e., this is the estimated alpha shown in Panel B of Table 8.5). Again, these are the entire history (back to 1980) of persistence results that would be observed by a researcher at the end of each year. The similarity with Figure 8.4 is striking. While the alpha accruing to the *FDR*10% portfolio is impressive at the beginning of the 1990s, it consistently declines thereafter. As the proportion, π_A^+, of skilled funds falls, the *FDR* approach moves much further to the extreme right tail of the cross-sectional t-distribution (from 5.7% of all funds in 1990 to 0.9% in 2006) in search of skilled managers. However, this change is not sufficient to prevent the performance of *FDR*10% from dropping substantially.

It is important to note the differences between our approach to persistence and that of the previous literature (e.g., Hendricks et al. (1993), Elton et al. (1996), and Carhart (1997)). These prior papers generally classify funds into fractile portfolios based on their past performance (past returns, estimated alpha, or alpha t-statistic) over a previous ranking period (one to three years). The proportionate size of fractile portfolios (e.g., deciles) is held fixed, with no regard to the changing estimated proportion of lucky funds within these fixed fractiles. As a result, the signal used to form portfolios is likely to be noisier than our *FDR* approach. To compare these approaches with ours, Figure 8.5 displays the

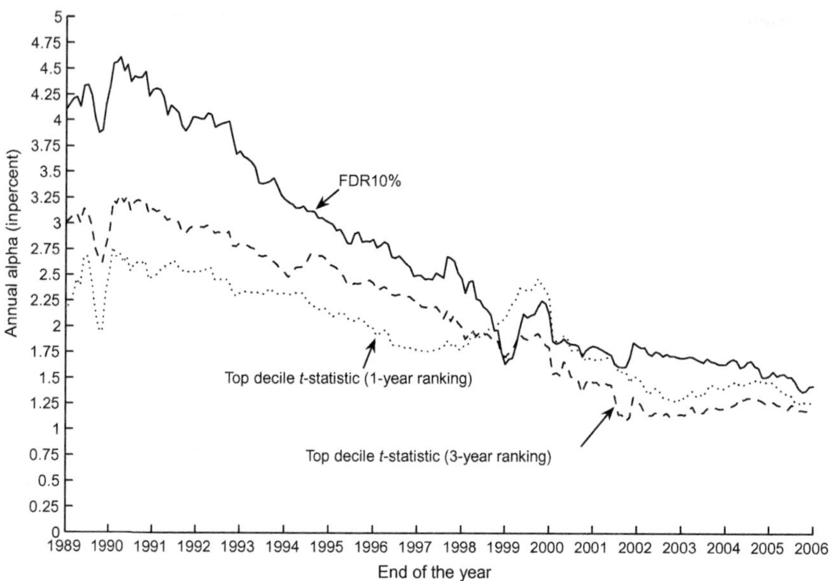

FIGURE 8.5

The graph plots the evolution of the estimated annual four-factor α of the portfolio FDR 10%. To construct this portfolio, we estimate the (α) p-values of each existing fund at the end of each year using the previous five-year period. After determining the significance level, $\gamma_{(z^+)}$, such that the estimated $\widehat{FDR}^+_{\gamma(z^+)}$, is closest to 10%, we include all funds in the right tail of the cross-sectional t-statistic distribution with p-values lower than $\gamma_{(z^+)}$ in an equally-weighted portfolio. At the end of each year from 1989 to 2006, the portfolio alpha is estimated using the portfolio return history up to that point. The initial estimates cover the period 1980-1989 (the first five years are used for the initial portfolio formation on December 31, 1979), while the last ones use the entire portfolio history from 1980 up to 2006. For comparison purposes, we also show the performance of top decile portfolios formed according to a t-statistic ranking, where the t-statistic is estimated over the prior one and three years, respectively.

performance evolution of top decile portfolios that are formed based on ranking funds by their alpha t-statistic, estimated over the previous one and three years, respectively. Over most years, the *FDR* approach performs much better, consistent with the idea that it much more precisely detects skilled funds. However, this performance advantage declines during later years, when the proportion of skilled funds decreases substantially, making them much tougher to locate. Therefore, we find that the superior performance of the *FDR* portfolio is tightly linked to the prevalence of skilled funds in the population.

8.4.4 Additional Results

8.4.4.1 *PERFORMANCE MEASURED WITH PRE-EXPENSE RETURNS*

In our baseline framework described previously, we define a fund as skilled if it generates a positive alpha net of trading costs, fees, and other expenses. Alternatively, skill could be defined in an absolute sense as the manager's ability to produce a positive alpha before expenses are deducted. Measuring performance on a pre-expense basis allows one to disentangle the manager's stockpicking skills from the fund's expense policy, which may be out of the control of the fund manager. To address this issue, we add monthly expenses (1/12 times the most recent reported annual expense ratio) to net returns for each fund, and then revisit the long-term performance of the mutual fund industry.[23]

Panel A of Table 8.6 contains the estimated proportions of zero-alpha, unskilled, and skilled funds in the population ($\widehat{\pi}_0$, $\widehat{\pi}_A^-$, and $\widehat{\pi}_A^+$), on a pre-expense basis. Comparing these estimates with those shown in Table 8.2, we observe a striking reduction in the proportion of unskilled funds, from 24.0% to 4.5%. This result indicates that only a small fraction of fund managers have stockpicking skills that are insufficient to at least compensate for their trading costs. Instead, mutual funds produce negative net-of-expense alphas chiefly because they charge excessive fees in relation to the selection abilities of their managers. In Panel B, we further find that the average expense ratio across funds in the left tail is slightly lower when performance is measured prior to expenses (1.3% versus 1.4% per year), indicating that high fees (potentially charged to unsophisticated investors) are one reason why funds end up in the extreme left tail, net of expenses. In addition, there is no reliable relation between turnover and pre-expense performance, indicating that some unskilled managers trade too much relative to their abilities, although it is also possible that some skilled managers trade too little.

In the right tail, we find that 9.6% of fund managers have stockpicking skills sufficient to more than compensate for trading costs (Panel A). Since 75.4% of funds produce zero net-of-expense alphas, it seems surprising that we do not find more pre-expense skilled funds. However, this is due to the relatively small impact of expense ratios on the performance of funds located in the center of the cross-sectional t-distribution. Adding back these expenses leads only to a marginal increase in the alpha t-statistic, making it difficult to detect the presence of skill.[24]

Finally, Barras et al. find that the proportion of pre-expense skilled funds in the population decreases from 27.5% to 9.6% between 1996 and 2006. This implies that the decline in net-expense skills noted in Figure 8.4 is driven mostly by a reduction in stockpicking skills over time (as opposed to an increase in expenses for pre-expense skilled funds). In contrast, the proportion of pre-expense unskilled funds remains equal to zero until the end of 2003. Thus, poor stockpicking skills (net of trading costs) cannot explain the large increase in the

[23] We discard funds that do not have at least 60 pre-expense return observations over the period 1975 to 2006. This leads to a small reduction in our sample from 2,076 to 1,836 funds.

[24] The average expense ratio across funds with $|\widehat{\alpha}_i| < 1\%$ is approximately 10 bp per month. Adding back these expenses to a fund with zero net-expense alpha only increases its t-statistic mean from 0 to 0.9 (based on $T^{\frac{1}{2}}\alpha_A/\sigma_\varepsilon$, with $T = 384$ and $\sigma_\varepsilon = 0.021$). This implies that the null and alternative t-statistic distributions are extremely difficult to distinguish. To illustrate, for a hypothetical fund with a (pre-expense) t-statistic mean of 0.9, the probability of observing a negative (pre-expense) t-statistic equals 18%.

Table 8.6 Impact of Luck on Long-Term Pre-Expense Performance

We add the monthly expenses to net return of each fund, and measure long-term performance with the unconditional four-factor model over the entire period 1975 to 2006. Panel A displays the estimated proportions of zero-alpha, unskilled, and skilled funds ($\widehat{\pi}_0$, $\widehat{\pi}_A^-$, and $\widehat{\pi}_A^+$) in the entire fund population on a pre-expense basis (1,836 funds). Panel B counts the proportions of significant funds in the left and right tails of the cross-sectional t-statistic distribution ($\widehat{S}_\gamma^-$, $\widehat{S}_\gamma^+$) at four significance levels ($\gamma = 0.05, 0.10, 0.15, 0.20$). In the leftmost columns, the significant group in the left tail, $\widehat{S}_\gamma^-$, is decomposed into unlucky and unskilled funds ($\widehat{F}_\gamma^-$, $\widehat{T}_\gamma^-$). In the rightmost columns, the significant group in the right tail, $\widehat{S}_\gamma^+$, is decomposed into lucky and skilled funds ($\widehat{F}_\gamma^+$, $\widehat{T}_\gamma^+$). The bottom of Panel B also presents the characteristics of each significant group ($\widehat{S}_\gamma^-$, $\widehat{S}_\gamma^+$): the average estimated alpha prior to expenses (in % per year), expense ratio (in % per year), and turnover (in % per year). Figures in parentheses denote the standard deviation of the different estimators.

Panel A. Proportion of Unskilled and Skilled Funds

	Zero Alpha ($\widehat{\pi}_0$)	Non-Zero Alpha	Unskilled $\widehat{\pi}_A^-$	Skilled ($\widehat{\pi}_A^+$)
Proportion	85.9 (2.7)	14.1	4.5 (1.0)	9.6 (1.5)
Number	1,577	259	176	83

Panel B. Impact of Luck in the Left and Right Tails

	Left Tail							Right Tail	
Signif. Level (γ)	**0.05**	**0.10**	**0.15**	**0.20**	**0.20**	**0.15**	**0.10**	**0.05**	**Signif. Level (γ)**
Signif. $\widehat{S}_\gamma^-$ (%)	4.3	7.5	10.2	12.8	17.3	13.1	9.3	5.8	Signif. $\widehat{S}_\gamma^+$ (%)
	(0.5)	(0.6)	(0.7)	(0.8)	(0.9)	(0.8)	(0.7)	(0.5)	
Unlucky $\widehat{F}_\gamma^-$ (%)	2.1	4.3	6.4	8.6	8.6	6.4	4.3	2.1	Lucky $\widehat{F}_\gamma^+$ (%)
	(0.0)	(0.1)	(0.1)	(0.2)	(0.2)	(0.1)	(0.1)	(0.0)	
Unskilled $\widehat{T}_\gamma^-$ (%)	2.2	3.2	3.8	4.2	8.7	6.6	5.0	3.6	Skilled $\widehat{T}_\gamma^+$ (%)
	(0.5)	(0.6)	(0.8)	(0.9)	(1.0)	(0.9)	(0.7)	(0.5)	
Pre Expense Alpha(% year)	−5.9	−5.2	−4.8	−4.5	4.4	4.8	5.0	5.3	Pre Expense Alpha(% year)
	(0.5)	(0.3)	(0.2)	(0.2)	(0.2)	(0.2)	(0.3)	(0.4)	
Exp.(% year)	1.3	1.3	1.3	1.3	1.3	1.3	1.3	1.2	Exp.(% year)
Turn.(% year)	105	107	108	108	90	89	91	84	Turn.(% year)

proportion of unskilled funds (net of both trading costs and expenses) from 1996 onwards. This increase is likely to be due to rising expenses charged by funds with weak stock selection abilities, or the introduction of new funds with high expense ratios and marginal stockpicking skills.

8.4.4.2 PERFORMANCE MEASURED WITH OTHER ASSET PRICING MODELS

Our estimation of the proportions of unskilled and skilled funds, $\widehat{\pi}_A^-$ and $\widehat{\pi}_A^+$, obviously depends on the choice of the asset pricing model. To examine the sensitivity of our results, we repeat the long-term (net of expense) performance analysis using the (unconditional) CAPM and Fama-French models. Based on the CAPM, we find that $\widehat{\pi}_A^-$ and $\widehat{\pi}_A^+$ are equal to 14.3% and 8.6%, respectively, which is much more supportive of active management skills, compared to Section 8.4.1. However, this result may be due to the omission of the size, book-to-market, and momentum factors. This conjecture is confirmed in Panel A of Table 8.7: the funds located in the right tail (according to the CAPM) have substantial loadings on the size and the book-to-market factors, which carry positive risk premia over our sample period (3.7% and 5.4% per year, respectively).

Table 8.7 Loadings on Omitted Factors

We determine the proportions of significant funds in the left and right tails ($\widehat{S}_\gamma^-$, $\widehat{S}_\gamma^+$) at four significance levels ($\gamma = 0.05, 0.10, 0.15, 0.20$) according to each asset pricing model over the period 1975 to 2006. For each of these significant groups, we compute their average loadings on the omitted factors from the four-factor model: size ($\widehat{b}_{smb}$), book-to-market ($\widehat{b}_{hml}$), and momentum ($\widehat{b}_{mom}$). Panel A shows the results obtained with the unconditional CAPM, while Panel B repeats the same procedure with the unconditional Fama-French model.

Panel A. Unconditional CAPM

	Left Tail							Right Tail	
Signif. Level (γ)	**0.05**	**0.10**	**0.15**	**0.20**	**0.20**	**0.15**	**0.10**	**0.05**	**Signif. Level (γ)**
Size ($\widehat{b}_{smb}$)	0.06	0.07	0.09	0.09	0.27	0.28	0.28	0.36	Size $\widehat{b}_{smb}$)
Book ($\widehat{b}_{hml}$)	−0.14	−0.14	−0.13	−0.14	0.34	0.35	0.36	0.37	Book ($\widehat{b}_{hml}$)
Mom. ($\widehat{b}_{mom}$)	0.00	0.00	0.00	0.01	−0.01	−0.01	−0.02	−0.01	Mom. ($\widehat{b}_{mom}$)

Panel B. Unconditional Fama-French model

	Left Tail							Right Tail	
Signif. Level (γ)	**0.05**	**0.10**	**0.15**	**0.20**	**0.20**	**0.15**	**0.10**	**0.05**	**Signif. Level (γ)**
Mom. ($\widehat{b}_{mom}$)	−0.02	−0.03	−0.02	−0.03	0.09	0.10	0.11	0.12	Mom. ($\widehat{b}_{mom}$)

Turning to the Fama and French (1993) model, we find that $\widehat{\pi}_A^-$ and $\widehat{\pi}_A^+$ amount to 25.0% and 1.7%, respectively. These proportions are very close to those obtained with the four-factor model, since only one factor is omitted. As expected, the 1.1% difference in the estimated proportion of skilled funds between the two models (1.7%–0.6%) can be explained by the momentum factor. As shown in Panel B, the funds located in the right tail (according to the Fama-French model) have substantial loadings on the momentum factor, which carries a positive risk premium over the period (9.4% per year).

8.4.4.3 BAYESIAN INTERPRETATION

Although we operate in a classical frequentist framework, our new *FDR* measure, FDR^+, also has a natural Bayesian interpretation.[25] To see this, we denote by G_i a random variable that takes the value of -1 if fund i is unskilled, 0 if it has zero alpha, and $+1$ if it is skilled. The prior probabilities for the three possible values $(-1, 0, +1)$ are given by the proportion of each skill group in the population, π_A^-, π_0, and π_A^+. The Bayesian version of our FDR^+ measure, denoted by fdr_γ^+, is defined as the posterior probability that fund i has a zero alpha given that its t-statistic, denoted by T_i, is positive and significant: $fdr_\gamma^+ = prob\left(G_i = 0 | \, T_i \in \Gamma^+(\gamma)\right)$, where $\Gamma^+(\gamma) = \left(t_\gamma^+, +\infty\right)$. Using Bayes theorem, we have:

$$fdr_\gamma^+ = \frac{prob\left(T_i \in \Gamma^+(\gamma) \middle| \, G_i = 0\right) \cdot prob(G_i = 0)}{prob\left(T_i \in \Gamma^+(\gamma)\right)} = \frac{\gamma/2 \cdot \pi_0}{E(S_\gamma^+)}. \tag{8.13}$$

Stated differently, the fdr_γ^+ indicates how the investor changes his prior probability that fund i has a zero alpha ($G_i = 0$) after observing that its t-statistic is significant. In light of Equation (8.13), our estimator $\widehat{FDR}_\gamma^+ = (\gamma/2 \cdot \widehat{\pi}_0)/\widehat{S}_\gamma^+$ can therefore be interpreted as an empirical Bayes estimator of fdr_γ^+, where π_0 and $E(S_\gamma^+)$ are directly estimated from the data.[26]

In the recent Bayesian literature on mutual fund performance (e.g., Baks et al. (2001) and Pastor and Stambaugh (2002a)), attention is given to the posterior distribution of the fund alpha, α_i, as opposed to the posterior distribution of G_i. Interestingly, our approach also provides some relevant information for modeling the fund alpha prior distribution in an empirical Bayes setting. The parameters of the prior can be specified based on the relative frequency of the three fund skill groups (zero-alpha, unskilled, and skilled). In light of our estimates, an empirically based alpha prior distribution is characterized by a point mass at $\alpha = 0$, reflecting the fact that 75.4% of the funds yield zero alphas, net of expenses. Since $\widehat{\pi}_A^-$ is higher than $\widehat{\pi}_A^+$, the prior probability of observing a

---

[25] Our demonstration follows from the arguments used by Efron et al. (2002) and Storey (2002) for the traditional *FDR*, defined as $FDR_\gamma = E\left(F_\gamma / S_\gamma\right)$, where $F_\gamma = F_\gamma^+ + F_\gamma^-$, $S_\gamma = S_\gamma^+ + S_\gamma^-$.

[26] A full Bayesian estimation of fdr_γ^+ requires that one posits prior distributions for the proportions π_0, π_A^-, and π_A^+, and for the distribution parameters of T_i for each skill group. This method, based on additional assumptions (including independent p-values) as well as intensive numerical methods, is applied by Tang et al. (2007) to estimate the traditional *FDR* in a genomics study.

negative alpha is higher than that of observing a positive alpha. These empirical constraints yield an asymmetric prior distribution. A tractable way to model the left and right parts of this distribution is to exploit two truncated normal distributions in the same spirit as in Baks, Metrick, and Wachter (2001). Further, we estimate that 9.6% of the funds have an alpha greater than zero, before expenses. While Baks, Metrick, and Wachter (2001) set this probability to 1% in order to examine the portfolio decision made by a skeptical investor, our analysis reveals that this level represents an overly skeptical belief.

Finally, we can also interpret the mutual fund selection (Section 8.4.3.) from a Bayesian perspective. In her attempt to determine whether to include fund $i(i = 1, \ldots, M)$ in her portfolio, the Bayesian investor is subject to two sorts of misclassification. First, she may wrongly include a zero-alpha fund in the portfolio (i.e., falsely rejecting H_0). Second, she may fail to include a skilled fund in the portfolio (i.e., falsely accepting H_0). Following Storey (2003), the investor's loss function, *BE*, can be written as a weighted average of each misclassification type:

$$BE(\Gamma^+) = (1 - \psi)\, prob(T_i \in \Gamma^+) \cdot fdr_\gamma^+(\Gamma^+) + \psi \cdot prob(T_i \notin \Gamma^+) \cdot fnr_\gamma^+(\Gamma^+), \tag{8.14}$$

where $fnr^+ \left(\Gamma^+\right) = prob\left(G_i = +1 |\, T_i \notin \Gamma^+\right)$ is the "False Nondiscovery Rate" (i.e., the probability of failing to detect skilled funds), and ψ is a cost parameter that can be interpreted as the investor's regret after failing to detect skilled funds.[27] The decision problem consists of choosing the significance threshold, $t^+(\psi)$, such that $\Gamma^+(\psi) = \left(t^+(\psi), +\infty\right)$ minimizes Equation (8.14) (equivalently, we could work with *p*-values and determine the optimal significance level, $\gamma(\psi)$). Contrary to the frequentist approach used in this chapter, the Bayesian analysis requires an extensive parameterization, which includes, among other things, the exact specification of the null and alternative distributions of T_i, as well as the cost parameter ψ (see Efron et al. (2001) for an application in genomics).

If we decide to make this additional parameterization, we can determine the optimal Bayesian decision implied by the FDR^+ targets used in our persistence tests (($z^+ = 10\%, 30\%, 50\%, 70\%, \text{and } 90\%$). One way to do this is to consider our simple example shown in Figure 8.1, where the null and alternative distributions of T_i are assumed to be normal. We find that a high FDR^+ target z^+ (such as 90%) is consistent with the behavior of a Bayesian investor with a high cost of regret ($\psi(90\%) = 0.997$). Therefore, she chooses a very high significance level (γ (90%) = 0.477), in order to include the vast majority of the skilled funds in the portfolio. In contrast, a low FDR^+ target z^+ (such as 10%) implies a lower regret ($\psi(10\%) = 0.318$), and a lower significance level ($\gamma(10\%) = 0.003$) (further details can be found in Barras, et al.).

[27] See Bell (1982) and Loomes and Sugden (1982) for a presentation of Regret Theory, which includes in the investor's utility function the cost of regret about forgone investment alternatives.

8.5 CHAPTER-END PROBLEMS

1. What are "false discoveries"? What is the "false discovery rate" (FDR)? Why is it important to control for them when assessing the proportion of managers with superior skills?
2. What is the key to the simplicity of the *FDR* approach to multiple hypothesis testing?
3. Prove that the distribution of p-values, under a well-specified null hypothesis, is uniform.
4. What is the "false non-discovery rate" (FNDR)? How can we balance FDR errors with FNDR errors (at least in theory)?
5. Suppose we have 9 fair coins (50% probability of heads and 50% of tails), and a 10th unfair coin (90% probability of heads and 10% of tails). Let us call this unfair coin a "skilled manager". Assuming we know all of the details of these coins, what is the proportion of unskilled managers, π_0?
6. In the above example, if we flip each coin twice, what is the expected proportion of coins that have one heads and one tail flipped? What is the expected proportion that have two heads flipped? That have two tails flipped?
7. In the above example, suppose we know only that there are 10 coins, and we know nothing about the number that are "skilled". We flip each coin twice. Then, suppose that 5 coins flip one heads and one tails, and are labeled "zero alpha" or fair coins (meaning that they truly have an equal probability of heads and tails), while 3 have two heads and 2 have two tails. What is the FDR+ (the expected proportion of two-heads-flipped coins from the 5 zero alpha coins)? What is the FDR– (the expected proportion of two-tails-flipped coins from the 5)? Finally, what is the estimated proportion of truly skilled coins? Of truly unskilled coins?

Chapter 9

Active Management in Mostly Efficient Markets: A Survey of the Academic Literature

ABSTRACT

This chapter surveys the academic literature on the value of active management, using the latest performance evaluation techniques—many of which are described in earlier chapters of this book. The results show that the average active manager does not outperform, but that a significant minority of active managers do add value. Further, academic studies indicate that investors may be able to identify superior active managers (SAMs) in advance using public information. Investors who can identify SAMs should be able to improve their overall Sharpe ratio by including a meaningful exposure to active strategies.

Keywords
Active portfolio management, Efficient markets, Active vs. passive management, The value of active management, Manager selection

9.1 INTRODUCTION

Most debates have a clear winner: Lincoln beat Douglas; Kennedy beat Nixon; and Reagan beat Mondale. But the active-versus-passive debate continues to rage after more than 40 years of contention. Should investors be satisfied with index returns, or should they seek to outperform the indices by gathering and analyzing information that *may* already be reflected in security prices? Adherents on both sides of the issue are dogmatic in their beliefs and provide compelling arguments to support their cases. In this chapter, we survey the academic research on this issue—covering both theory and empirical analysis—in order to offer some practical advice for investors. (This chapter is derived from Jones and Wermers (2011).) Our goal is to answer the following three important questions for investors:

1. Does active management add value?
2. Can we identify superior active managers (SAMs) on an *ex ante* basis?
3. How much active risk should investors include in their portfolios?

Performance Evaluation and Attribution of Security Portfolios. http://dx.doi.org/10.1016/B978-0-12-744483-3.00009-2
© 2013 Elsevier Inc. All rights reserved.
For End-of-chapter Questions: © 2012. CFA Institute, Reproduced and republished with permission from CFA Institute. All rights reserved.

To preview, our main findings are:

1. Consistent with "mostly efficient" financial markets, the average active manager does not add value, net of fees, but a significant minority of active managers do outperform.
2. Academic studies have highlighted a variety of reliable ways to identify outperforming managers on an *ex ante* basis, using a combination of prior performance, macroeconomic forecasting, manager/fund characteristics, and analysis of fund portfolio holdings.
3. If investors can identify SAMs, they can add substantially to portfolio returns with only a moderate increase in total portfolio risk. Investors who pursue active management should consider allocating a meaningful portion of their risk budgets to active strategies.

9.2 SOME CAVEATS

The academic studies on this topic are extensive and, in some cases, the results aren't entirely consistent. The conclusions can often depend on the time period covered, the methodology employed, the universe and type of funds considered, and the author's biases. We have attempted to distill these varied results into practical advice by giving more weight to studies with more extensive data and more robust analysis, but there is always a chance that our own biases may color the results, or that the future will differ significantly from the periods covered in these studies.

Further, due to data availability, most of the existing studies analyze US domestic equity mutual funds. Results for other asset classes (e.g., fixed income, non-US equities, real estate, commodities) and other active vehicles (e.g., separate accounts and hedge funds) are often much more sparse, or even non-existent. Where data do exist, they may contain survivor bias (excludes dead funds or products that are closed for poor performance), self-selection bias (includes only those managers who choose to submit data), and/or have a limited return frequency (annually or quarterly, instead of monthly or daily). Also, we note here that the sample of actively managed ETFs is too small and too recently introduced to conduct a statistically reliable analysis. However, we realize that this concept is receiving a lot of attention in the industry, and should be a focus of future academic research. In general, however, we suspect that many of the results for active mutual funds will also apply to active ETFs, since it is likely that they will be managed using the same managers and strategies.

Where appropriate, we will try to highlight areas where our conclusions likely apply, or do not apply, to these other asset classes and vehicles. In general, however, we should expect institutional funds (e.g., separate accounts or pooled trust funds) to outperform retail funds (e.g., retail mutual funds) because they:

1. usually have lower management fees due to scale economies;
2. can use more performance-sensitive fees to better align the manager's interests with those of the investor; and
3. have lower costs for client accounting, client servicing, and managing daily cash flows.

Finally, even where a study's results are intuitive and statistically significant, they only apply *on average*, not necessarily to a specific manager or fund. For example, one study finds that managers who graduated from colleges with higher average SAT scores outperform other managers.[1] This does not mean, however, that all such managers will outperform, or that managers from other schools won't outperform. Thus, all of our recommendations are generic rather than specific to individual funds or managers.

9.3 DOES ACTIVE MANAGEMENT ADD VALUE?

If we assume that the aggregate of all actively managed funds is equal to the market—that is, active management is a "zero-sum game"—then the aggregate of active fund returns equals the market return, but incurs trading costs and charges fees, so the aggregate will underperform the market by an amount equal to fees and expenses.[2] Empirical studies broadly support this conclusion.

Starting with Jensen's seminal study (Jensen, 1968), numerous papers have reached virtually the same conclusion: *the average actively managed mutual fund does not capture alpha, net of fees and expenses*. Figure 9.1 summarizes results from two recent studies; it shows that neither the average mutual fund nor the average institutional separate account ("ISA") has earned a positive alpha, net of fees and expenses, after adjusting for market and style risks using the four-factor model of Carhart (1997). We do not address the after-tax results in this chapter, but studies (e.g., Dickson and Shoven, 1993) indicate that it is even harder for actively managed funds to outperform passive alternatives on an after-tax basis.

In fact, the average underperformance in these studies is only slightly lower in magnitude than the average fee charged by active managers, implying that the average active manager earns a positive alpha before fees, but this alpha does not quite cover the costs of active management. Further, this conclusion seems to apply equally to domestic equity funds, fixed income funds, international equity funds, balanced funds and possibly even hedge funds and private equity vehicles (although, in these last two cases, the data are not as readily available and the results are less compelling).[3]

Proponents of active management often argue that its benefits are most pronounced in periods of heightened volatility and economic stress. While no

---

[1] Chevalier and Ellison (1999).

[2] French (2008) makes this assumption in computing the "dead-weight loss" from investing in active funds, and concludes that 67 basis points per year is lost from active fund investments. However, a recent paper by Wermers and Yao (2010) indicates large differences in aggregate holdings of active vs. passive funds, making this assumption questionable. For instance, large-cap core stocks are held more heavily by passive funds, while small- and mid-cap stocks are held much more heavily by active funds.

[3] For example, Ferson, Kisgen, and Henry (2006) evaluate a sample of US Government bond funds and find underperformance, net of fees; Phalippou and Gottschalg (2009) find that private-equity funds also underperform, net of fees.

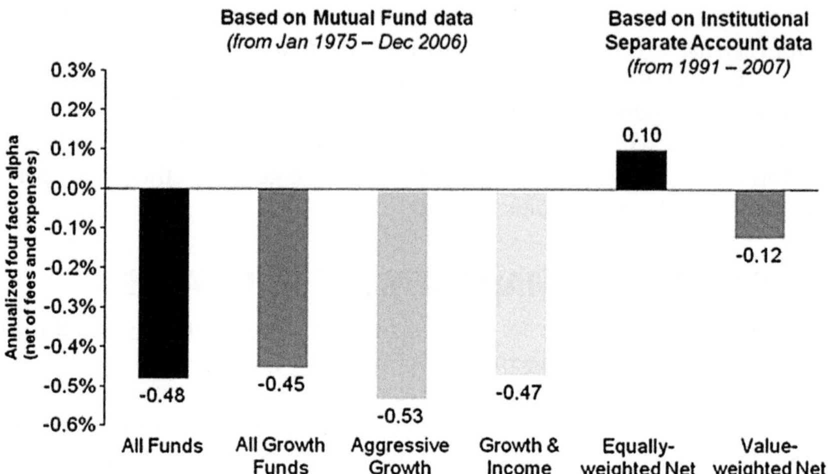

FIGURE 9.1
Four factor alphas, in percent per year, for Active Equity Mutual Funds and Active Equity Institutional Separate Accounts, net of fees and expenses. *Source*: The mutual fund data are from Barras et al., 2010, while the institutional separate account data are from Busse et al., 2010.

academic studies yet exist for the period of the financial crisis (2007–2009), Standard and Poor's has done some comparisons.[4] Their results for the five years ending December 2010 show a fairly balanced "scorecard" for active vs. passive management. Specifically, while the market indices have outperformed a majority of active managers across all major domestic and international equity categories, asset-weighted averages of active managers match or slightly beat the benchmarks in most categories, with the exception of mid-caps, international, and emerging markets.

The five-year results are somewhat worse for actively managed bond funds. With the exception of emerging markets' debt, more than 50% of active managers failed to beat their benchmarks. While five-year asset-weighted average returns are lower for active funds in all but three categories, equal-weighted returns over the same investment horizon lag behind in *every* category.

So, it seems that the most recent five years, which include the financial crisis, have been a bit more favorable to active *equity* management than the much longer period covered by other studies, but not significantly so. Later, we will discuss some research that finds that active funds are more likely to outperform during financial downturns and recessions. Longer-term results, however, that

[4] Standard & Poor's Indices Versus Active Funds Scorecard (SPIVA®), Year-End 2010, available via \ www.standardandpoors.com.

include both "stressed" and "normal" markets, offer little support for the "average" active manager.

9.4 ACTIVE MANAGEMENT AND "MOSTLY EFFICIENT MARKETS"

Of course, the semi-strong form of the efficient market hypothesis—wherein market prices completely and accurately reflect all publicly-available information—predicts that rational investors (without inside information) will always choose passive management over active management. Yet clearly this is not the case. Why not? Are investors that irrational? If so, how can the market be efficient? In their seminal paper, Grossman and Stiglitz (1980) argue that, in a world of costly information, informed traders must earn an excess return or they will have no incentive to gather and analyze information to make prices more efficient (i.e., reflective of information). [5]

That is, markets need to be "mostly, but not completely efficient" or investors would not make the effort to assess whether prices are "fair." If this were to happen, prices would no longer properly reflect all available and relevant information, and markets would lose their ability to efficiently allocate capital. Therefore, although the contest between active managers *might* be a zero-sum game, active management as a whole is definitely not: *By making markets more efficient, active management improves capital allocation, and thereby economic efficiency and growth, resulting in greater aggregate wealth for society as a whole.* Thus, we can view the excess returns earned by informed traders as a kind of economic rent for gathering and processing information, and thereby making markets more efficient.

In the Grossman-Stiglitz (1980) equilibrium, the marginal (least skilled) active manager will earn an excess return that equals the costs of actively managing those assets (i.e., the costs of gathering and analyzing information, including the cost of human capital). Thus, in equilibrium, we should expect to see a (possibly large) group of marginal, yet active, managers who just barely earn back their fees in the form of excess returns. In the real world, however, the average active fund *underperforms* the index net of fees. Why is this?

Funds must provide other benefits—such as liquidity, custody, bookkeeping, scale, optionality, or diversification—that justify their fees. *In fact, virtually 100% of passive funds underperform their relevant indices net of fees,* which can average anywhere from under 15 bps/year for passive mutual funds that invest in large-cap US equities, to over 75 bps/year for passive emerging market funds.[6] Thus, the relevant comparison is to the passive alternative and not to the index itself.

---

[5] Informed traders may have better information and/or a btter ability to assess the implications of information for security prices. We will use the terms "informed trader" and "superior active manager" interchangeably throughout this paper.

[6] Fees are lower for institutional products, under both passive and active management, but the point is the same: active managers should be compared to the passive alternative, not the index itself.

On this basis, the average active fund earns roughly the same return as the average passive fund, net of fees.[7]

Thus, the world we see around us—one filled with active managers who, on average, provide no excess return (versus the passive alternative) net of fees—seems perfectly consistent with the Grossman-Stiglitz model of "mostly efficient" markets, wherein prices may not fully reflect costly information. In the real world, with differential skills among active managers, we expect to (and do) find some informed traders (or "superior active managers") who earn meaningful excess returns commensurate with their superior ability to gather and analyze information. Of course, to the extent that they manage money for others, they are also likely to charge higher fees for their services. Due to randomness in markets, however, it is nearly impossible for investors to perfectly discriminate between superior and inferior active managers; therefore, superior active managers will not be able to capture all of their value added in the form of higher fees.[8] Now the question becomes: can we identify, *ex ante*, superior active managers whose value added is expected to exceed their fees? Academic studies provide some encouraging results, as explained in the next section.

9.5 IDENTIFYING SUPERIOR ACTIVE MANAGERS ('SAM's)

In a zero-sum game, if some investors ("superior active managers," or SAMs) earn positive alphas, other investors ("inferior active managers," or IAMs) must "earn" negative alphas. SAMs can exploit IAMs in one of two ways: (1) by having superior information and/or analytic capabilities, allowing them to better predict future results; or (2) by providing liquidity/immediacy when IAMs need to trade quickly for reasons unrelated to expectations (e.g., to meet redemptions). Of course, the quality of an investor's forecasts can vary across stocks and over time. In addition, today's liquidity suppliers can be tomorrow's liquidity demanders; luck/randomness can also play an important role. Thus, active management amounts to a SAM–IAM contest, where it can be difficult to tell exactly who is who (despite what Horton might hear[9]).

In fact, Chapter 8 of this book argues that some managers do have skills that allow them to outperform the market net of fees, but that it is virtually impossible (with only returns data) to distinguish these skilled managers from other managers who have strong performance simply due to luck. This may be true

---

[7] For instance, Wermers (2000)—contained in Chapter 5 of this book—finds that the asset-weighted average actively managed U.S. domestic equity fund generates a net return, during 1977–1994, that is the same as that of the Vanguard 500 Index Fund.

[8] Berk and Green (2004) present a theoretical model that captures this intuition.

[9] With apologies to Dr. Seuss.

if investors can only work with simple past returns, but academics have identified a number of ways that investors might be able to identify future SAMs using other data and methods. In the following sections, we will discuss four approaches to identifying SAMs, based on:

1. past performance (properly adjusted)
2. macroeconomic forecasting
3. fund/manager characteristics; and
4. analysis of fund holdings.

We recommend that investors consider all of these factors when evaluating active managers.

9.5.1 Past Performance

If SAMs indeed have superior information or analytical capabilities, presumably this advantage should persist through time. If so, then SAMs who outperform in one period will likely outperform in the next period as well. Offsetting this are various agency effects and competitive pressures: Managers at poorly performing funds are more likely to change their strategies or be replaced, resulting in better performance going forward.[10] Managers at top-performing funds may lose their competitive edge—perhaps due to changing technologies for security analysis, diminished motivation, or overconfidence—or they may reduce fund risk in order to protect their reputations and fees. Equally problematic: Top-performing managers may either raise fees or attract too many assets for them to continue to deliver the same *net* excess returns that they had in the past (i.e., at some point there are *diseconomies* of scale in active management). Thus, lack of persistence does not necessarily imply a lack of skill among managers.

The evidence is mixed, but seems to indicate that there is some modest persistence in mutual fund returns, but only if excess returns are adjusted to account for style biases using either the four-factor model of Carhart (1997) or the three-factor model of Fama and French (1993). Although there are many studies, a typical result is that of Harlow and Brown (2006), who find that using style-adjusted returns can improve the odds of finding an outperforming fund from 45% to 60%. Figure 9.2 is from their paper. It shows that the top decile prior-alpha funds produce future alphas of about 150 basis points annually, net of fees. Pastor and Stambaugh (2002) find that adjusting for sector biases can improve these results even further.

Also shown in Figure 9.2 are results from Kosowski et al. (2006) (Chapter 6 of this book), who find that adjusting for non-normality in fund alphas (e.g., skewness and fat tails) improves the odds of identifying funds with greater return persistence. The intuition is that some SAMs may have positively skewed returns,

---

[10] See Lynch and Musto (2003) for a formal model with these predictions.

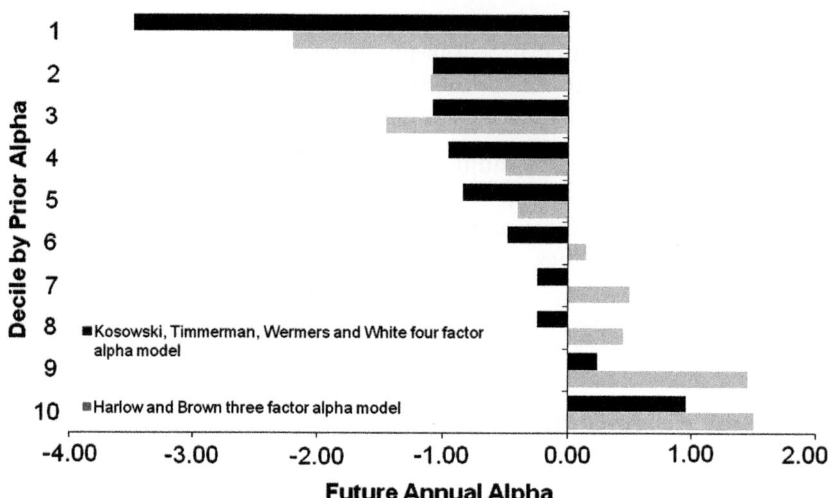

FIGURE 9.2
Persistence in past performance: Harlow and Brown use a three factor alpha methodology rebalanced quarterly using the time period 1979–2003. Kosowski, Timmerman, Wermers and White use a four factor alpha methodology using a three-year ranking period, with a bootstrapping technique to model non-normality, rebalanced annually using the time period 1978–2002.

which are valuable to investors. Therefore, adjusting for "random skewness" (defined as observed fund return skewness that is not statistically significant) should help discriminate between managers who were lucky and those whose active returns actually show a positive bias (or skew).

Although research shows that persistence appears to be strongest at shorter intervals (monthly or quarterly), some studies have been able to document persistence at intervals as long as 3–4 years.[11] None of these studies, however, account for potential fund rebalancing costs, which would reduce the potential value added from picking active managers based solely on (properly adjusted) prior performance.

There is also some evidence of persistent skills among hedge fund managers. Kosowski, Naik, and Teo (KNT; 2007) extend the bootstrap methodology of Kosowski et al. (2006) into the hedge fund universe. It is particularly important to account for non-normal returns with hedge funds, since they often employ dynamic strategies and security choices (e.g., various derivatives) that make their

[11] As an example of short-term persistence, Bollen and Busse (2005) use daily **mutual fund** returns to rank actively managed US domestic equity mutual funds on a quarterly frequency. They find an average abnormal return of the top decile in the post-ranking quarter of 39 basis points (156 bps annually). On longer-term persistence, Wermers (2002) finds that the portfolios of top decile funds, ranked by lagged one-year net return, outperform for three to four years.

portfolio returns distinctly non-normal. KNT find that top decile hedge funds (ranked by adjusted two-year lagged Bayesian posterior alpha) outperform bottom decile funds by 5.8% the following year. There is no significant difference between the top and bottom deciles using a simple ordinary least-squares ranking, illustrating the importance of adjusting for non-normality in hedge fund returns.

Fung et al. (2008) investigate the performance, risk, and capital formation of fund-of-hedge funds from 1995 to 2004 using the seven-factor model of Fung and Hsieh (2004). While the *average* fund-of-funds only delivers alpha during the period between October 1998 and March 2000, a subset of funds-of-funds delivers persistent alpha over longer periods. These alpha-producing funds are also less likely to liquidate and experience steadier capital inflows. Those capital inflows reduce, but do not eliminate, the ability of the alpha producers to deliver alpha in future periods.

Although far fewer in number, studies of other asset classes and vehicles are generally consistent with the results for hedge funds and domestic equity mutual funds. Kaplan and Schoar (2005) find persistence in the performance of funds run by a private-equity management company, although (like hedge funds) general partners can sometimes smooth performance by using smoothed estimates for the "market" values of their investments.[12] It is also unclear whether these GPs choose better investments or exhibit superior skills in overseeing the funded companies (or both).

Bers and Madura (2000) find that actively managed Closed End Funds ('CEF's) exhibit return persistence. This is notable because CEFs (like institutional separate accounts) do not have to deal with regular inflows and outflows, which can make it harder to detect skill (because open-end fund managers need to trade for both liquidity and information purposes). Huij and Derwall (2008) find evidence of persistence in fixed income fund returns, especially high-yield funds, after adjusting for multiple benchmarks.

As presented earlier in Figure 9.1, Busse et al. (2010) is one of the few studies to address institutional separate accounts (ISAs). They find weak persistence out to one year for domestic equity and fixed income funds, but less persistence for international equity funds. They do not adjust for systematic risks (e.g., country, currency, style), however, which may account for the weaker persistence for international fund returns in their study.

Rather than studying persistence itself, Goyal and Wahal (2008) look at the hiring and firing decisions of institutional sponsors. They find that the managers

[12] To attempt to overcome this potential bias, Kaplan and Schoar compute a return based on discounted private equity fund cashflows, rather than potentially biased valuations issued by the fund managers. Nonetheless, the lack of reliable market pricing makes these studies less reliable. Also, the VE data set used in the study is based on *voluntary* reporting of fund returns by the private equity firms (or their general partners), as well as their limited partners.

that institutions hire do not outperform the managers that they fire.[13] Since hiring and firing managers involves search and transactions costs, the implication is that institutions should be less eager to change managers. Because institutions often change managers for reasons other than performance, however, this is not direct evidence against persistence, but it does imply investors should be careful when changing managers. That is, when making manager change decisions, they should properly adjust past returns, and also consider other factors that we discuss below, including transition costs.

When assessing past performance, it can be difficult to distinguish between the contribution of the manager and the contribution of the fund management company—that is, a SAM usually needs a strong support team to perform well. One study that attempts to do this is Baks (2003), who finds that, depending on the investment process, anywhere from 10–50% of return persistence is due to the manager, with the balance attributed to the fund management company or other factors. Thus, investors may want to discount prior performance when there has been a recent change in fund managers, especially for funds that rely on a "star" manager as opposed to a team approach or quant process. Similarly, investors should be cautious about chasing "star" managers when they switch firms.

Table 9.1 summarizes several studies of persistence. Based on these and other studies, we conclude that investors can likely uncover SAMs by analyzing past performance, but they should be careful to account for non-normal return distributions (such as those with skewness or fat tails) and various style/sector biases using a sophisticated performance attribution system. Using less sophisticated techniques greatly diminishes our ability to find true SAMs using past performance. In addition, investors should carefully assess whether any potential improvement from switching managers will cover transition costs.[14]

9.5.2 Macroeconomic Forecasting

Studies in this area try to determine if active managers, in general, perform better in certain environments, and whether it is possible to predict, *ex ante,* which specific managers will perform best in a given environment. That is, can IAMs become SAMs (and *vice versa*) under the right conditions? The results seem quite

---

[13] Stewart et al. (2009) also study the hiring and firing decisions of institutions. As they note, institutional plan sponsors are charged with investing over $10 trillion in assets for pension plans, endowments and foundations. They study a dataset covering 80,000 yearly observations of institutional investment product assets, accounts and returns over the period 1984–2007, and find little evidence of value-added by managers that are picked by the sponsors over time. In fact, the study estimates that over $170 billion were lost over the period examined due to poor manager selection by sponsors.

[14] Transition costs can include the costs of identifying and interviewing new managers, plus the cost of converting the portfolio to a new strategy/manager (trading costs).

Table 9.1 Summary of Persistence Studies Quoted in This Section

Research Paper	Asset Class (Time Period)	Persistence Finding
Bers and Madura (2000)	Active closed-end funds (1976–1996)	Return
Harlow and Brown (2006)	Equity mutual funds (1979–2003)	Style-adjusted RETURN
Huij and Derwall (2005)	Fixed income funds (1990–2003)	Benchmark-adjusted return
Bollen and Busse (2005)	Equity mutual funds (1985–1995)	Raw return during quarter +1
Baks (2003)	Equity mutual funds (1992–1999)	Fund manager-specific return
Kosowski, Timmerman, Wermers, and White (2006)	Equity mutual funds (1975–2002)	Bootstrapping-derived alpha
Busse, Goyal, and Wahal (2007)	Institutional separate accounts (1991–2008)	Weak return for domestic equity
Fung et al. (2008)	Hedge fund of funds (1995–2004)	Alpha
Goyal and Wahal (2008)	Institutional separate accounts (1994–2003)	None for terminations
Jagannathan, Malakhov, and Novikov (2010)	Hedge funds (1996–2005)	Superior funds only
Kosowski et al. (2007)	Hedge funds (1994–2003)	Alpha, computed using Bayesian methods
Kaplan and Schoar (2005)	Private equity funds (1980–2001)	Discounted cash inflows divided by outflows

promising, but the strategies involve considerable manager turnover and may not be as rewarding after deducting manager transition costs.

To the extent that a fund's alpha varies systematically over time, this could be due to either:

1. embedded macro-economic sensitivities (e.g., a persistent overweight in cyclical stocks);
2. time-varying skill; or
3. time-varying opportunities for managers to benefit from their skills.

Although all three explanations may play a role, studies lend the most support to the third explanation—namely, that certain environments offer more mispricing opportunities where managers can take advantage of their superior insights. For example, many contrarian managers underperformed during the tech bubble of the late 1990s, when prices diverged significantly from fundamentals, but outperformed by a huge margin when the bubble burst. Did their skills suddenly change so dramatically, or did the market simply provide more opportunities for them in one period versus the other?

Studies by Moskowitz (2000) and Kosowski (2006) reveal that the average active manager is more likely to outperform the market during recessions. This is probably not the result of holding cash in down markets, since Kosowski, in particular, adjusts returns for market risk. Instead, it seems likely that recessions are periods of above average uncertainty, when superior information and analysis can be particularly valuable. Consistent with this explanation, Kosowski, among others, also finds that the average active fund performs better in periods of higher return dispersion and volatility, which are also likely to be periods of heightened uncertainty—and opportunity.

Figure 9.3 shows Kosowski's results; excess returns are higher in recessions than expansions for all of the major Lipper domestic equity fund categories. Figure 9.4 is from a report by Joseph Gerard Paul at Alliance Bernstein (AB), and shows that the top-quartile manager's alpha tends to be higher in periods of higher return dispersion. In general, Paul (2009) finds that the median active US Domestic Equity fund exhibits an increase in alpha of 11–12 bps per quarter for every 1% increase in the spread between the 25th and 75th percentile stock returns in that quarter.,

The above studies focus on the fund performance during periods of economic stress. Such periods, however, are hard to predict in advance. What if we want to predict fund performance using macro data that are known today?

One of the first studies in the macro forecasting area is Avramov and Wermers (AW; 2006) (Chapter 7 of this book), who identify outperforming funds, *ex ante,* using macro-economic variables that have previously been shown to predict stock returns—namely, the level of short-term rates, the credit default spread, the term structure of interest rates, and the market's dividend yield. AW find that selecting funds based on their prior correlations with these macro variables produces four-factor alphas of more than 600 basis points per year net of fund expenses, but prior to any fund rebalancing costs.

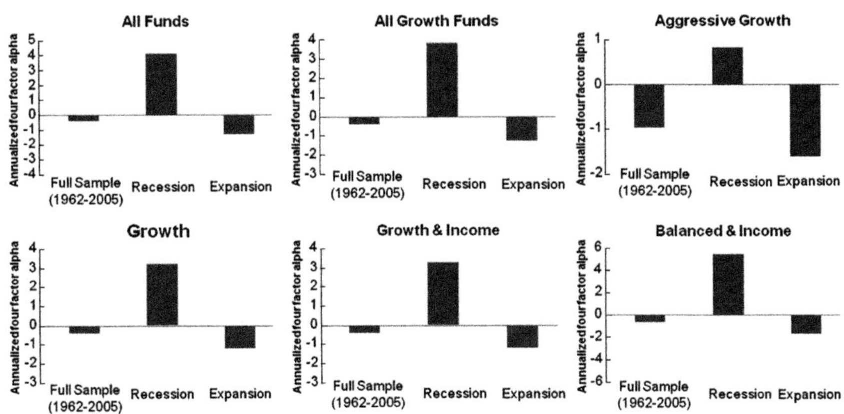

FIGURE 9.3
Alpha Performance in Recession and Expansion Periods, Kosowski (2006).

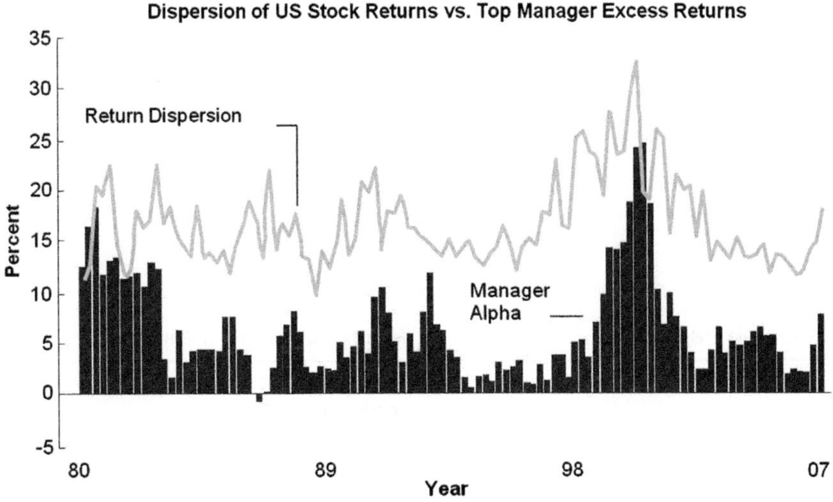

FIGURE 9.4
Manager Alpha Is Greatest in Divergent Markets, 2009; Alliance Bernstein report. *Note:* data are through 31 December 2007. Return dispersion is the difference in quarterly total returns between the 25th and 75th percentiles of stocks in the AllianceBernstein U.S. large-cap universe. Manager alpha is the excess returns of the 25th percentile managers in the eVestment U.S. large-cap equity universe versus the S&P 500 Index. *Source:* Paul (2009).

Banegas et al. (2009) apply the same approach (with additional predictor variables) to European equity funds and find similar levels of outperformance (i.e., roughly 6% per year).

Avramov, Kosowski, and Teo (AKT; 2009) extend the predictability models of Avramov and Wermers (2006) into the hedge fund universe, and find a substantial ability to predict hedge fund outperformance. Specifically, AKT find that several macroeconomic variables, including VIX and credit spreads, allow them to identify hedge funds that outperform their Fung and Hsieh (2004) benchmarks by over 17 percent per year, before considering transition costs, which can be substantial.

It is worth noting that a macro-forecasting strategy can often conflict with a return-persistence strategy for selecting funds. That is, macro forecasts may recommend buying funds that have had poor recent performance, especially when macro economic conditions have recently changed. For example, if we find that some funds have better relative returns when short-term interest rates are low and default spreads are wide, we may decide to invest in such funds when those conditions prevail, even if their recent performance has been weak.

A word of caution is in order, however: Macro-timing strategies can involve considerable fund turnover from one period to the next—i.e., 200–300% annually if implemented without constraints. This could prove difficult if the target funds have flow restrictions in place (e.g., hedge fund lockup periods or early withdrawal penalties).

Thus, for investors who want to pursue this approach, we would recommend investing in a diverse group of funds that do well in different macro environments and re-allocating between them at the margin based on macro forecasts. This more cautious approach may provide less gross alpha, but should also incur significantly lower manager search and transition costs, as well as providing a partial hedge against sudden changes in the macro environment.[15] Table 9.2 summarizes research discussed in this section.

Table 9.2 Summary of Findings Quoted in This Section

Research Paper	Macroeconomic Timing
Moskowitz (2002)	Average active managers outperform in recessions
Kosowski (2006)	Average active managers outperform in recessions, high volatility and dispersion periods
Avramov and Wermers (2006)	Outperformance from identifying funds that do well in certain past environments and choosing them based on the current environment
Avramov, Kosowski, and Teo (2007)	Same as Avramov and Wermers (2006) for hedge funds
Barnegas, Gillen, Timmerman, and Wermers (2012)	Same as Avramov and Wermers (2006) for European equity funds

[15] While the strategies of AW and AKT hedge against potential changes in the macroeconomic environment, a more cautious strategy may provide greater safety in the face of large unexpected shifts.

9.5.3 Fund/Manager Characteristics

Various authors have studied the characteristics of funds, fund management companies and fund managers to see if they can predict future outperformance. Because fund management companies use different techniques and are organized differently, and fund managers come from a variety of backgrounds, it seems likely that certain fund companies and fund managers may be more skilled at collecting and analyzing information. In fact, many studies have found that certain types of funds, fund managers and fund management companies do reliably outperform, on average. This section summarizes those studies. Further, since these approaches involve fairly low levels of manager turnover, we view them as being among the most effective ways to select active managers.

Since unsuccessful **fund managers** (IAMs) are likely to drop out of the pool over time, experienced managers are more likely to be SAMs. Ding and Wermers (2009) find exactly this: experienced managers *of large funds* (i.e., above median AUM) outperform less experienced managers by 92 basis points per year. Interestingly, *for smaller funds*, the opposite is often true. Ding and Wermers attribute this to entrenchment: an experienced manager of a small fund has likely been unsuccessful (which is why the fund is small), but may be difficult to replace for institutional or other reasons. These findings point to a "mostly efficient" market for fund managers, where most (but not all) managers survive based on skill.

Other manager characteristics that can help predict outperformance include social connections, academic background, and co-investment:

- Cohen et al. (CFM; 2008) find that managers take larger positions in companies where they have social connections (i.e., where the officers or board members attended the same college as the manager). Further, these holdings outperform non-connected holdings on average. CFM conjecture that this is because connected managers have better access to private information, or are better able to assess the quality of the company's management team.
- Chevalier and Ellison (1999) find that managers who graduate from colleges where students have higher average SAT scores also tend to outperform, presumably because they are better qualified and thus better able to analyze information.[16]
- Similarly, Gottesman and Morey (2006) find that the quality of a manager's MBA program is positively correlated with future performance. They measure the quality of an MBA program using both the average GMAT score of students in the program and the annual *Business Week* rankings. Interestingly, they find no relation between performance and other graduate degrees (including a PhD degree) or the CFA designation.
- Dincer et al. (DGS; 2010) find that funds managed by CFAs tend to have less tracking risk (better risk management) than other funds. Conversely, funds managed by MBAs (without a CFA) tend to have higher tracking risk,

[16] There are no available data on individual manager SAT scores, so Chevalier and Ellison (1999) use the college average as a proxy.

which may reflect their proverbial overconfidence. DGS find no significant difference in returns (as opposed to risk) attributable to either an MBA or a CFA—or, for that matter, to experience (although, as opposed to Ding and Wermers, they do not adjust for the correlation between experience and fund size).

- A hedge-fund study by De Souza and Gokcan (2003) finds that managers who invest their own capital in their funds are more likely to outperform, possibly because such managers have greater conviction, or because they are more likely to avoid un-compensated risks.

Based on these and other studies, we conclude that investors should look for funds managed by smarter, better-educated managers who have some skin in the game.

Other studies have focused on the characteristics of the **fund management company**. Not surprisingly, funds sponsored by larger fund management companies tend to perform better, probably due to:

1. economies of scale and scope (lower costs/fees);[17]
2. greater resources for gathering and analyzing information;[18] and
3. better technologies for executing trades with less price impact.

In addition, fund companies with a greater number of independent directors also tend to perform better, possibly because they are more demanding of their managers.[19]

Massa and Zhang (2009) find that funds managed by companies with a flatter organizational structure outperform funds managed by companies with a more hierarchical structure. Such funds also tend to be more concentrated and exhibit less herding behavior. *MZ find that each additional layer in the hierarchy reduces average fund performance by 24 basis points per month, or almost 300 basis points per year*. This may be because a hierarchical structure discourages managers from innovating, taking risks and collecting private information—that is, in vertical organizations, managers may not feel as much direct responsibility (ownership) for their funds.

Other studies focus on the characteristics **of the fund itself**. Edelen (1999) finds that cash holdings explain much of the underperformance of the average mutual fund. Thus, funds with large idle cash balances are more likely to lag their benchmarks. If so, then funds that equitize idle cash balances can eliminate this "cash drag" as a source of underperformance. Conversely, if cash is used as a tactical (market timing) tool, then it may be an alpha source.

---

[17] Chen et al. (2004) find economies of scale in management company size.

[18] Busse et al. (2010) find that funds sponsored by companies with broader research capabilities tend to outperform.

[19] Ding and Wermers (2009) find that one additional independent director for a fund is correlated with an additional 20 bps/year in higher pre-expense returns.

Careful attribution analysis should help investors discern if market timing is an alpha source, or whether the manager should be equitizing idle cash balances.

In a well-documented and remarkably objective recent study, Morningstar (Kinnel, 2010) finds that expense ratios (fees) are strong predictors of performance: *The cheapest funds outperformed the most expensive funds in every time period and every fund category*. It was unclear whether Morningstar's star ratings had any additional predictive ability after accounting for the higher net returns of low-fee funds. Given that their star ratings rely solely on past performance, however, we suspect that they would have less predictive ability than a more comprehensive rating methodology.

There are conflicting results when it comes to the issue of specialization versus flexibility. On one hand, we would expect that managers who stick to their areas of expertise (i.e., where they have a competitive advantage) should perform better. On the other hand, any constraint can limit a manager's ability to add alpha. The evidence supports both of these "hands."

Kasperczyk et al. (2005) find that funds that concentrate in certain industries and sectors outperform an appropriate benchmark, indicating that specialization along industry or sector lines improves a manager's ability to gather and analyze information. In addition, some of the macro-based studies (discussed in the prior section) find that different types of managers and funds do better in different environments, when presumably there are more mispricing opportunities in their primary areas of expertise.

Conversely, Wermers (2010) finds that funds that allow the most "style drift" (variation in exposures to style factors, such as value vs. growth) are more likely to outperform their benchmarks. In addition, many studies have shown that eliminating the "no short" constraint can improve a fund's active risk/reward profile.[20] In addition, Liang (1999) finds that hedge funds—which usually have fewer constraints—exhibit more skill and have higher risk-adjusted outperformance than mutual funds. *We conclude that investors should look for funds with few artificial constraints, but where the managers do not stray too far from their primary areas of expertise.*

Finally, there is a large body of research studying the characteristics of top-performing **hedge funds**. The following list summarizes some of these studies:

1. Liang (1999) finds that hedge funds with "high water marks" significantly outperform funds without such structures.[21] He also finds that funds with higher incentive fees and longer lockup periods perform better. *These results indicate that the best-performing funds are those that best align the interests of the manager and the investor.*

---

[20] For example: Hirshleifer et al. (2009) find the accrual anomaly is stronger on the short side; Hong et al. (2000) find the same for momentum; Chordia et al. (2010) find that the value anomaly has been stronger on the short side in recent years.

[21] With a high water mark, the fund does not earn a performance fee until it makes up any prior underperformance.

2. Numerous studies find that larger hedge funds perform better, possibly due to economies of scale.[22] For example, larger funds may be able to attract and retain more and better analysts and managers because of their higher revenue base. Getmansky (2005), however, finds a concave relation between fund size and performance: funds that are either too small or too large underperform, which implies there is an optimal size for most hedge funds. Funds that are too large may run up against liquidity constraints, or possibly lose their competitive edge due to wealth effects (i.e., a wealthy manager with a solid reputation and track record may have little incentive to aggressively seek strong performance).
3. On fund age, there are conflicting results. Howell (2001) finds that younger funds (less than three years since inception) outperform older funds by more than 700 basis points per year, but this could be due to self-selection and backfill bias (after the fact, only successful young funds choose to submit their returns to the database). Conversely, De Souza and Gokcan (2003) find that older funds outperform younger funds on average. Given these conflicting results, we would ignore fund age and focus more on manager experience (and other factors) when selecting hedge funds.

The research quoted in this section is summarized in Table 9.3.

9.5.4 Portfolio Holdings Analysis

Studies in this category look at the holdings of the underlying fund to determine if there is any information that can help predict future performance. Holdings-based analysis generally requires much more detailed (holdings) data and involves additional computational complexity. Results seem quite promising, however, and would seem to justify the additional analysis. In fact, since these approaches involve low manager turnover and get at the heart of a manager's strategy, we view holdings-based analysis as one of the best ways to identify future SAMs. We summarize some of the more interesting findings below.

Kasperczyk et al. (KSZ; 2008) compare the performance of the actual fund to the performance of the publicly disclosed holdings of the fund (the "return gap"). A large negative return gap may indicate sloppy trading, or a manager who is trying to hide bad trades (i.e., "window dressing" at quarter end when holdings are published). Both explanations are cause for concern. KSZ find that funds with a large *negative* return gap underperform by roughly 18 basis points per month (or 216 bps per year), while those with a large *positive* return gap outperform by about 10 bps per month (120 bps annually).

Huang et al. (HSZ; 2010) compare the realized volatility of a fund (based on reported returns) to the volatility calculated using its most recently reported holdings. They find that "risk shifting" funds tend to underperform funds that maintain a stable risk profile. Fund managers who cut risk may be "locking in"

[22] For example: Amenc et al. (2004), Getmansky (2005), and De Souza and Gokcan (2003).

Table 9.3 Summary of Findings Quoted in This Section

Research Paper	Manager/Fund Characteristic Associated with Future Outperformance
Chevalier and Ellison (1999)	Managers from high-average-SAT schools do better
Edelen (1999)	Funds with low cash balances outperform
Liang (1999)	Hedge funds (especially those with higher incentive fees and lock-ups) outperform
Howell (2001)	Younger hedge funds do better
Wermers (2010)	Funds with the most variation in style exposures do better
De Souza and Gokcan (2003)	Managers who invest in their own funds outperform; hedge funds outperform mutual funds; older, larger and higher-incentive-fee hedge funds outperform other hedge funds
Amenc, Curtis and Martellini (2003)	Larger, younger and high-incentive-fee hedge funds outperform
Getmansky (2004)	Hedge funds that are not too large or too small do better
Kasperczyk et al. (2005)	Industry- or sector-concentrated funds do better
Gottesman and Morey (2006)	Managers with better MBA programs outperform
Ding and Wermers (2009)	Experienced managers for large funds outperform; the opposite is true for small funds
Cohen et al. (2008)	Stocks with direct school ties between board members and fund managers outperform
Massa and Zhang (2009)	Funds with flatter organizational structures outperform
Dincer et al. (2010)	Well-trained managers outperform
Morningstar (2010)	Mutual fund managers with lower expense ratios outperform

gains to protect their fees, whereas managers who increase risk may be "doubling down" in a desperate attempt to catch up to other funds. In any case, HSZ conclude that their "results are consistent with the notion that agency problems, rather than the ability to take advantage of changing investment opportunities, are the likely motivation behind risk shifting behavior." *We conclude that investors should select funds that manage risk effectively and maintain a reasonably stable (but not necessarily low) risk profile.*

Managers who have superior information or analytical capabilities are likely to be contrarians. That is, since prices reflect consensus expectations, SAMs will only trade when their views differ from the prevailing consensus. A study by Wei et al. (2009) finds exactly that: contrarian managers outperform herding managers[23] by more than 260 basis points per year. Their research indicates that these excess returns come both from supplying liquidity to the herd, and from superior information collection and analysis—in particular, the companies held by contrarian funds show a much greater improvement in future firm profitability than the holdings of herding funds.

A study by Cremers and Petajisto (2009) finds that managers who take bigger active positions perform better. They define "active share" as the absolute difference between a stock's weight in the portfolio and its weight in the "best fit" market index, cumulated across all stocks in the portfolio and index. They find that funds with the highest aggregate active share outperform those with the lowest active share by roughly 250 basis points per year. They attribute this to greater "conviction" on the part of the manager and conclude that: "the most active stock pickers tend to create value for investors while factor bets and closet indexing tend to destroy value."

There are some important qualifications to their findings, however. First, they did not control for the capitalization of the benchmark. Thus, their results could simply mean that small-cap funds outperform their benchmarks more often than large-cap funds.[24] Such a result, while interesting, is entirely consistent with the "costly information" theory of Grossman and Stiglitz (since small-cap stocks are more costly to research). Second, strong manager "conviction" is not always a good thing. The behavioral literature shows that overconfidence can cause investors to take excessive risk relative to the quality of their information and/or analysis. Therefore, a large active share may indicate a "behaviorally unhumble manager" (BUM) rather than a true SAM. Finally, CP's own analysis does not indicate any return differences between high and low *tracking error* (as opposed to active share) funds, implying that the best funds will have high active shares, but relatively low tracking errors (if the active returns are equivalent, then the lower tracking error funds will have higher information ratios, *ipso facto*).

---

[23] A herding manager is defined as one who trades (i.e., has a change in holdings) in the same direction as the aggregate of other managers. A contrarian manager trades in the opposite direction from the aggregate.

[24] Small-cap funds are likely to have a larger active share because there are more names, with a smaller average weight, in the benchmark.

Table 9.4 Summary of Findings Quoted in This Section

Research Paper	Holdings-Based Result
Cremers and Petajisto (2006)	Funds that take bigger active positions outperform
Kasperczyk, Sialm, and Zheng (2009)	Funds with large "return gaps" between published and holdings-derived performance underperform
Huang, Sialm, and Zheng (2009)	Funds that change risk underperform
Wei et al. (2009)	Contrarian managers (by holdings) outperform

Combining these observations, we conclude that investors should look for funds with a contrarian bent and high active shares but stable tracking errors. Managers of such funds are likely to be adept at risk management—that is, taking large but offsetting bets—but probably not overconfident (because they hedge their largest bets). Investors should also avoid "risk shifters" and funds with a large negative "return gap". A summary of this section's research is provided in Table 9.4.

9.5.5 Active Risk Budgeting[25]

Risk budgeting is the process of allocating risk to different investment alternatives. *Active* risk budgeting means determining how much risk to allocate to and among different *active* strategies—that is, how much and what type of active risk should investors include in their portfolios? The answer will be a function of the expected return to active risk (i.e., the expected information ratio) and the correlation between that active risk and other risks in an investor's portfolio. In essence, then, active risk budgeting is an optimization exercise that requires estimates of the expected returns, volatilities, and correlations of different active strategies.

For investors who are unwilling or unable to devote the level of resources necessary to identify SAMs, the expected return to active management will be zero or negative. Such investors should take little or no active risk, regardless of volatilities and correlations. That is, they should focus on developing an appropriate asset allocation while embracing passive management in each asset class, secure in the knowledge that, by minimizing fees and expenses, they are likely to perform at least as well as the average investor in that asset class (active and passive). Such investors are essentially piggy-backing on "the wisdom of crowds."[26]

[25] For a thorough discussion of active risk budgeting see: "Developing an Optimal Active Risk Budget," by Winkelmann, Chapter 13 in *Modern Investment Management: An Equilibrium Approach*, Litterman et al. (2003).

[26] See "The Wisdom of Crowds" (2004), by James Surowiecki for a cogent explanation of why consensus views are often more accurate than expert opinions.

Table 9.5 Adding Active Risk to a Passive Portfolio

	Passive Portfolio	Active Strategies	Total Portfolio	Incremental Analysis
Return	7.0%	1.5%	8.5%	1.5%
Risk	10.0%	6.0%	11.7%	1.7%
Return/risk	0.70	0.25	0.73	0.88

On the other hand, many of the studies covered in this chapter indicate that there may be reliable ways to identify SAMs on an *ex ante* basis. Investors who can do so successfully should be rewarded with positive expected returns from active management. Further, active risk, almost by definition, should have little correlation to the systematic risks in an investor's portfolio. Similarly, there should be little correlation between the active risks of different active managers that presumably use different strategies.[27] Taken together, these statements imply that active management can provide both positive (active) returns and substantial diversification benefits. For investors who can identify SAMs, then, a thorough risk budgeting exercise would likely recommend a healthy allocation to active strategies.

Table 9.5 shows the potential benefits of adding active risk to a passive portfolio. Assume an investor starts with a passive portfolio that has an expected return of 7% and volatility of 10%. Further, assume that the investor has been able to identify a group of SAMs—which may include hedge funds, active long-only funds, global tactical asset allocation overlay managers, etc.—with an aggregate expected information ratio of 0.25 and no correlation to other risks in the investor's portfolio. If the investor decides to add 6% in active risk to the existing portfolio—without any reduction in other risks—then the portfolio's total expected return improves from 7% to 8.5%, while the expected volatility increases from 10% to 11.7%.[28] Thus, the "incremental return/risk ratio" (or IRRR) is 0.88 (or 1.5%/1.7%). For an investor with a 20-year time horizon, this can lead to a 32% increase in expected terminal wealth—enough to convert an underfunded plan into a fully funded one. Of course, the slightly higher volatility also means a wider range of expected terminal wealth.

Figure 9.5 is from Litterman (2004) and shows the optimal allocation to active risk for a typical equity investor as a function of the expected information ratio.

[27] A more formal risk budgeting exercise would, of course, include explicit estimates of these correlations and related volatilities.

[28] This example assumes the investor can add active risk without reducing systematic risk or return. Under this assumption, total return is 8.5% (7% + 0.25 × 6%). Assuming no correlation between active risk and other portfolio risks, the total risk is the square root of (10% squared plus 6% squared), or the square root of 136 = 11.7%.

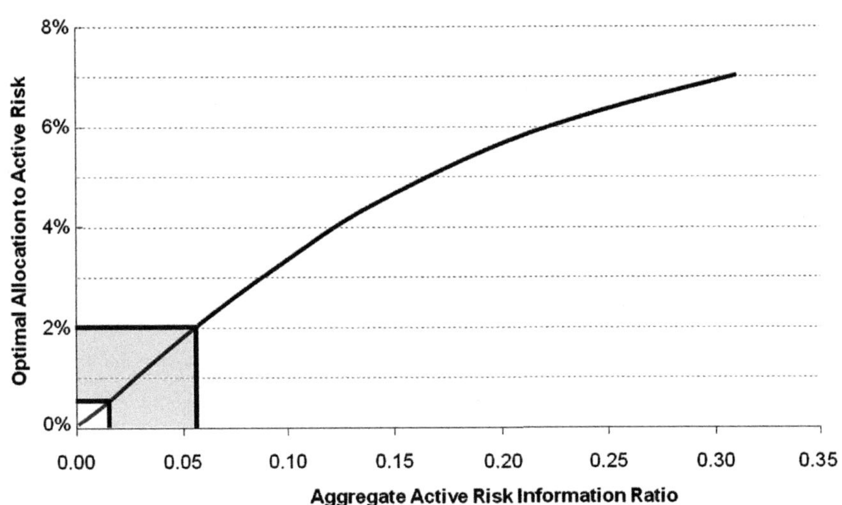

FIGURE 9.5
Optimal Risk Allocations Reveal Modest IR Expectations. *Source:* Goldman Sachs Asset Management.

At an expected IR of 0.25, for example, a typical investor should take more than 6% in active risk, far more than we see in most portfolios.

Litterman calls this "the active risk puzzle." Why do we see the vast majority of investors taking active risk of 2% or less—which implies an expected IR of only about 0.05—instead of a bi-modal distribution where many investors take no active risk and the remaining investors take substantially more active risk? Litterman suspects that agency issues may explain this anomaly—for example, institutional investors may seek to limit career risk by herding with their peers and being overly cautious.[29]

Another possible explanation, however, may be that investors misinterpret the oft-cited Brinson et al. (1986) study, which finds that asset allocation explains more than 90% of a typical plan's return variance over time. Investors may misinterpret this to mean that active management within asset classes has little impact on relative performance; therefore they should focus on setting the right asset allocation and not worry too much about finding SAMs. In fact, however, the BHB results say only that returns to asset classes explain the vast majority of a typical fund's *return variance over time*; they say nothing about cross-sectional differences in *actual long-term returns*.[30]

---

[29] For instance, Brown et al. (2011) find evidence of herding among U.S. domestic equity mutual fund managers with greater career concerns over the 1995–2010 period.

[30] For a more complete discussion, see Xiong et al. (2010), who demonstrate that BHB's results really mean that market movements explain most of a typical plan's returns; a plan's specific asset allocation and active management contribute similar amounts to total active return and risk.

In any case, in recent years (i.e., after the BHB study in 1986) we've seen some investors—primarily individuals, foundations and endowments—take on significantly more active risk, with a substantial impact on their performance. In fact, many of the most successful investors over the past decade (even after the recent crisis) have had substantial exposures to active strategies—including hedge funds, active equity, global tactical asset allocation overlays, currency overlays, private equity, commodities, alternative assets and other sources of active risk. Clearly some of these investors have been able to identify SAMs—as evidenced by their positive active returns—and have done quite well as a result.

Finally, for investors with limited resources, it may make sense to focus the search for SAMs on those asset classes where the rewards to active management are likely to be greatest—that is, asset classes where information gathering and analysis is most difficult and expensive. *It is perfectly rational for an investor to embrace passive management in some asset classes and active management in others.*

9.6 CONCLUSIONS

Our review of academic studies of active management indicates the following.

Active returns across managers and time probably average close to zero, net of fees and other expenses. This is what we should expect in a mostly efficient market, where fierce competition among active managers drives average (net) active returns towards zero in equilibrium. By keeping markets efficient, however, active management provides a critical function in modern capitalist economies; efficient, rational capital allocation improves economic growth and leads to increased wealth for society as a whole.

Thus, to keep the competition fierce, the rewards to superior (as opposed to average) active management must be rich indeed, as in fact they are—for both the manager and the ultimate investor. Superior managers earn high fees and often share in their value added, while inferior managers are soon bereft of both clients and fees. Investors who engage active managers can earn positive alphas with modest additional risk on a total portfolio basis (that is, an attractive incremental return/risk ratio, or "IRRR"). This benefit comes at a cost, however—the risk that active returns may prove negative and lead to lower terminal wealth.

Investors can lessen this risk using some of the research discussed above. In particular, studies indicate that investors may be able to identify SAMs on an *ex ante* basis using:

1. past performance (properly adjusted);
2. macro economic correlations;
3. fund/manager characteristics; and
4. analysis of fund holdings.

We suspect that using a combination of approaches will produce better results than following any one approach exclusively.

Active management will *always* have a place in "mostly efficient" markets. Hence, investors who can identify superior active managers (SAMs) should *always* expect to earn a relative return advantage. Further, this alpha can have a substantial impact on returns with only a modest impact on total portfolio risk. Finding such managers is not easy or simple—it requires going well beyond assessing past returns—but academic studies indicate that it can be done.

9.7 CHAPTER-END PROBLEMS

1. Name the four general areas described in this chapter where we might look for signals of superior fund performance in the future.
2. Within each of the four general areas of problem #1, describe the different approaches outlined in this chapter.
3. What does "mostly efficient markets" mean? Describe the equilibrium from Grossman and Stiglitz (1980) that is consistent with such markets.
4. Describe the predictions of the Berk and Green model for manager skills and after-fee performance.
5. Suppose an investor starts with a passive portfolio that has an expected return of 12% and volatility of 18%. This investor found a group of SAMs with an aggregate expected information ratio of 0.25 and no correlation to other risks in the investor's portfolio. If the investor decides to add 6% in active risk to the existing portfolio—without any reduction in other risks, what is the portfolio's total expected return and volatility? What is the incremental return to risk ratio?

SECTION 2
Performance Analysis and Reporting

Chapter 10

Basic Performance Evaluation Models

ABSTRACT

This chapter introduces the fundamental approaches for the computation of returns. The concepts of the time-weighted returns and the internal rate of return will be described in detail and compared. In practice, due to missing data, it is often not possible to compute these returns in an exact form. Therefore the most common approximation methods will be discussed. Furthermore, continuously compounded returns and different concepts for computing the active return are introduced.

Keywords
Computation returns, time-weighted, internal rate, approximation, continuously compounded returns, active return

10.1 BASIS FORMULA FOR THE CALCULATION OF RETURNS

All measures for the assessment of the return discussed on this chapter are based on a simple formula for the return of a single investment without subsequent withdrawals or contributions ("basis formula"). If I_0 is the initial value of the investment and I_1 the value at a later point in time, then:

$$R = \frac{I_1 - I_0}{I_0} = \frac{I_1}{I_0} - 1 \tag{10.1}$$

is the (simple) return[1] of the investment.

$$R = \frac{I_1 - I_0}{I_0} * 100\% = \left(\frac{I_1}{I_0} - 1\right) * 100\% \tag{10.2}$$

This is basically an identical expression for the return (only in percent). For a formal representation of the return formula (10.1) is often preferable. In this form the income (interests, dividends, etc.) is included in I_1. If one wants to explicitly

[1] This is also called wealth-ratio. In practice this is also sometimes called performance. In the literature (cf. e.g. Wittrock (2000a)) this term refers to a risk-adjusted return.

Performance Evaluation and Attribution of Security Portfolios. http://dx.doi.org/10.1016/B978-0-12-744483-3.00010-9
© 2013 Elsevier Inc. All rights reserved.
For End-of-chapter Questions: © 2012. CFA Institute, Reproduced and republished with permission from CFA Institute. All rights reserved.

Table 10.1 Account Statement Without Cash Flows

Datum	Inventarwert (Mio. €)
t_0	100
t_1	120

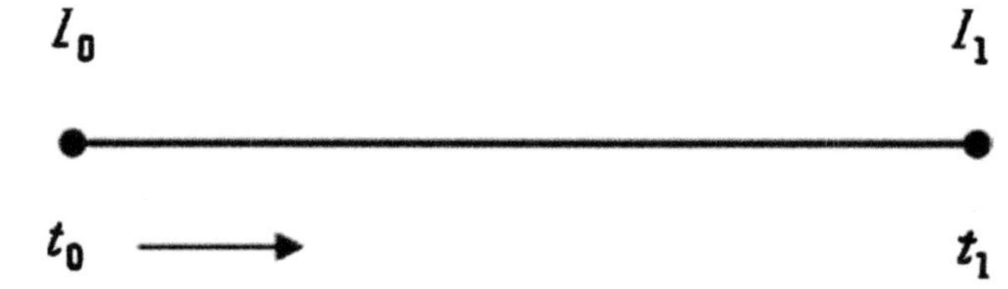

FIGURE 10.1
Basic Adjustment Over Time.

show the income component, then formula (10.2) can be written in the following form (D_1 represents the accumulated income for the period) (see Table 10.1):

$$R = \frac{I_1 + D_1 - I_0}{I_0} * 100\% = \left(\frac{I_1 + D_1}{I_0} - 1\right) * 100\%$$

Example 10.1

Applying the basis formula:

The simple development of the above account statement is illustrated in Figure 10.1. According to formula (10.1) (respectively formula (10.2)) the return R is given by:

$$R = \frac{120 - 100}{100} = 0.2 = 20\%. \tag{10.3}$$

The example illustrates how the expressions $\frac{I_1 - I_0}{I_0}$ and $\frac{I_1 - I_0}{I_0} * 100\%$ are identified with each other. The decimal value $\frac{I_1 - I_0}{I_0} = 0.10$ corresponds to the percentage value of 10%.

If exogenous cash flows[2] (contributions or withdrawals) occur within the time interval from t_0 to t_1, then the above procedure can only be applied to the subintervals between two neighboring cash flows. In the case of portfolios with many cash flows (e.g. investment funds), such a procedure would be quite onerous. The result would be a long list of individual returns, which would not be very

[2] Such exogenous cash flows may be triggered either by the portfolio manager or the client (further endowment of the fund, withdrawal of funds, fund dividends). In the context of an attribution analysis other cash flows must be considered as exogenous (in regard to a fund segment), such as shifting funds between two segments, interest payments, dividends, etc.

An investor is in general interested in the following returns:

1. Average return of his investments over a specific period (or several periods)
2. A return independent of the cash flows and therefore comparable to the return of a benchmark.

useful for either the portfolio manager or the investor. Thus for more complex account statements other return measures are more appropriate.

If the manager of the portfolio has no or little influence on the timing of the exogenous cash flows, then the first number is of little interest to him (cf. Section 10.5). Under these circumstances one should judge the manager's performance solely in comparison to a benchmark by neutralizing the cash flows (cf. Chapter 11).

10.2 GEOMETRIC LINKAGE AND SCALING OF RETURNS

Returns of neighboring periods can be linked in a multiplicative form, if the return is independent of the cash-flows. This assumption is valid for the returns calculated by the basis formula and in general for time-weighted returns (cf. Section 10.4). This assumption is, however, not fulfilled for internal rates of return (cf. Section 10.3).

Example 10.2

Linkage of returns:

In the first quarter of 2006 the DAX achieved a return of $R_1 = 10.39\%$ and in the second quarter a return of $R_2 = -4.80\%$. Based on these values the return for the overall period (first half-year 2006) is computed according to

$$1 + R = (1 + R_1) * (1 + R_2) = 1.1039 * 0.952 = 1.0509.$$

It follows that $R = 5.09\%$.

For the basic formula this is readily proven. Let R_1 and R_2 be the returns for the subintervals and R the overall return. If I_0, I_1 and I_2 denote respectively the net asset value at the beginning of the first interval, the beginning of the second interval (= end of the first interval), and at the end of the second interval, then it holds that:

$$1 + R = \frac{I_2}{I_0} = \frac{I_2}{I_1} * \frac{I_1}{I_0} = (1 + R_1) * (1 + R_2).$$

Often returns are represented in an annualized form. i.e., for returns computed over a longer period, an average yearly return of R_{ann} is calculated. According to the above statements on the linkage of returns it holds that:

$$1 + R = (1 + R_{ann})^n,$$

Table 10.2 Account Statement with One Contribution in the Middle of the Period

Date	Cash Flow	Net Asset Value
01.01.2007		100
30.06.2007	100	?
31.12.2007		250

where n is the number of years comprised in the analysis period. Based on a given return R one obtains the average annualized return according to:

$$1 + R_{ann} = (1 + R)^{\frac{1}{n}} = \sqrt[n]{1 + R}. \tag{10.4}$$

Example 10.3

Annualized returns of the DAX:

On 01.01.1993 and 31.12.2006 the DAX closed at 1545.05 and 6596.92, respectively. Over this period the return of the DAX was thus equal to 326.97%. It holds that

$$1 + R_{ann} = \sqrt[14]{4.2697} \approx 1.10925,$$

so that the average return of the DAX was equal to 10.93% over the analysis period.

An important special case is the relationship between the returns on a daily basis and the annualized returns.

If R is a return in regard to one year (e.g. an annualized return), then the corresponding daily return Q is defined by the following equation:

$$1 + Q = (1 + R)^{\frac{1}{360}} = \sqrt[360]{1 + R}. \tag{10.5}$$

Here it is assumed that the year has 360 days.[3]

10.3 INTERNAL RATE OF RETURN

The internal rate of return is the constant average rate mentioned in Section 10.1. Before the general formula will be introduced, the central idea shall be illustrated by means of a few examples.

Example 10.4

Computation of the internal rate of return with one contribution:

Applying formula (10.1) to the account statement in Table 10.2 is not meaningful. Since for the 30.06.2007 there is no net asset value available (the portfolio was not valuated on

[3] This is a very convenient assumption. In practice there are however many different conventions (cf. e.g. Deutsch (2004, P. 13–17).

Table 10.3 Account Statement with a Withdrawal at the End of the Third Quarter

Date	Cash Flow	Net Asset Value
01.01.2007		100
31.09.2007	−50	?
31.12.2007		40

that day[4]), the formula cannot be applied to the subintervals either. A meaningful question is, however: which average rate Q would have to be applied to both contributions of 100, in order to arrive at final value of 250? This rate follows from solving the following equation:

$$100 * (1 + Q)^{360} + 100 * (1 + Q)^{180} = 250.$$

The substitution:

$$x := (1 + Q)^{180} \tag{10.6}$$

and division by 100 leads to the equation:

$$x^2 + x = 2.5. \tag{10.7}$$

One obtains the solutions of this quadratic equation with the *quadratic formula*:[5] $x = \sqrt{2.75} - 0.5 = 1.1583124$. The internal rate of return in regard to half a year is thus equal to 15.83%. One obtains the rate per day by solving for Q in Equation (10.6):

$$Q \approx 1.1583124^{\frac{1}{180}} - 1 = 0.0008168 = 0.08168\%.$$

This leads to an annualized rate of $R_{ann} = (1 + Q)^{360} - 1 = 0.3417 = 34.17\%$. This value is also called *money-weighted rate of return* for the above account statement.

Example 10.5

Computing the internal rate of return in the case of one withdrawal:

One deals similarly with a withdrawal.

The account statement in Table 10.3 leads to the following equation:

$$100 * (1 + Q)^{360} - 50 * (1 + Q)^{90} = 40. \tag{10.8}$$

The substitution $x = (1 + Q)^{90}$ and a division by 100 lead to the equation $x^4 - 0.5 * x = 0.4$. Although the procedure is completely analogous to the previous example, here one faces a problem, which always occurs (except for some special cases) in the calculation of the internal rate of return: the resulting equations can only be solved by applying an iteration method. The interested reader might refer to Appendix B for a methodology. In this case only the result will be given. The solution of equation (10.8) is Q=-0.033944 %, which translates to an annualized rate of $R_{ann} = -11.50\%$.

[4] Valuation means determination of the unit price based on appropriate price sources. Cf. the explanations in Section 12.5.3.

[5] The quadratic equation $a * x^2 + b * x + c = 0$ has the solutions $x_{1,2} = -\frac{b}{2a} \pm \sqrt{\frac{b^2}{4a} - \frac{c}{a}}$.

Table 10.4 Account Statement with One Contribution and One Withdrawal

Date	Cash Flow (Mio. €)	Net Asset Value (Mio. €)
01.01.1995		100.0
31.12.1995		110.5
01.01.1996	100	210.5
31.12.1996		180.3
01.01.1997	−50	130.3
30.06.1997		145.1

Example 10.6

Internal rate of return with one contribution and one withdrawal:
On 01.01.1995 an investor commissions an investment firm with the management of a fund, which exclusively invests in Japanese equities. The initial volume is 100 Mio. €. At the beginning the fund performs very well, so that on 01.01.1996 the investor puts a further 100 Mio. € into the fund. The timing of this investment was rather unfortunate, however, as the Japanese stock market performed badly in the course of 1996. Out of irritation on 01.01.1997 the impatient investor withdrew 50 Mio. € from the fund. This (pro-cyclic) behavior is reflected in the account statement in Table 10.4.
The average daily interest rate results from the solution of the equation:

$$100 * (1+Q)^{900} + 100 * (1+Q)^{540} - 50 * (1+Q)^{180} = 145.1. \qquad (10.9)$$

The substitution $x = (1+Q)^{180}$ and the division by 100 gives the following equation

$$x^5 + x^3 - \frac{1}{2}x - 1.451 = 0. \qquad (10.10)$$

As already mentioned, in Appendix B to this chapter a methodology for solving such equations is described. Here it shall suffice to simply state the result: $x \approx 0.99339139$. From this results an internal rate of return of –3.26% for the entire period.

The above examples are readily generalized to the general formula for calculating the internal rate of return. As in Section 10.1 let I_0 be the initial value of the account and I_1 the final value. The generalized cash flow is visualized in Figure 10.2.

E_i denotes the contribution i (at t_i^A) and A_i the withdrawal i (at t_i^E). The contributions/withdrawals fall into the interval from 0 to T (cf. Figure 10.2). Q is again the average daily rate. It holds that:

$$I_0 * (1+Q)^T + E_1 * (1+Q)^{T-t_1^E} + E_2 * (1+Q)^{T-t_2^E} + \ldots + A_1 * (1+Q)^{T-t_1^A} + A_2 * (1+Q)^{T-t_2^A} + \cdots = I_1.$$

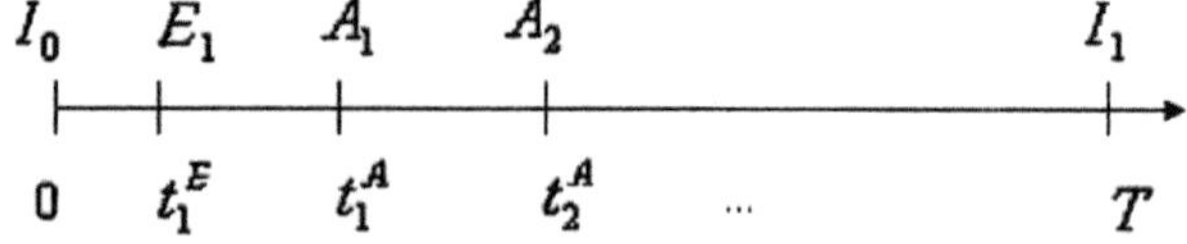

FIGURE 10.2
Cash Flow for an Account Statement with Contributions and Withdrawals.

In a more compact form one obtains

Internal rate of return (Money-Weighted Rate of Return)

$$I_0 * (1+Q)^T + \sum_{i=1}^{N^E} E_i * (1+Q)^{T-t_i^E} + \sum_{i=1}^{N^A} A_i * (1+Q)^{T-t_i^A} = I_1, \quad (10.11)$$

where N^E is the number of contributions and N^A the number of withdrawals. The A_i assume negative values. Q is the internal rate of return scaled to one day. The internal rate of return R^{irr} for the entire interval from 0 to T is defined as follows:

$$1 + R^{irr} := (1+Q)^T.$$

If one writes the above equation in the form:

$$I_0 - \frac{I_1}{(1+Q)^T} + \sum_{i=1}^{N^E} \frac{E_i}{(1+Q)^{t_i^E}} + \sum_{i=1}^{N^A} \frac{A_i}{(1+Q)^{t_i^A}} = 0,$$

it becomes clear that Q is the rate, by which the present value of the cash flows assumes the value zero. To solve the above equation in practice one employs computer programs, which are based on iterative procedures such as Newton's method (cf. Appendix B of this chapter).

10.4 TIME-WEIGHTED RETURN

10.4.1 General Aspects of the Time-Weighted Return

While the internal rate of return represents an average return in regard to the exogenous cash flow, the concept for *time-weighted rate of return* is independent of any cash flows.[6] The underlying basic idea is to track the performance of an initial investment throughout the various subperiods formed by these cash flows. The specific value of the initial investment is irrelevant. The concept will be introduced by means of an example.

Example 10.7

Computation of the time-weighted return:

The account statement of Example 10.6 will also form the basis for this example (see Table 10.5):

[6] Cf. Wittrock (2000a, p. 18 et seq.).

Table 10.5 Account Statement with One Contribution and One Withdrawal

Date	Cash Flow (Mio. €)	Net Asset Value (Mio. €)
01.01.1995		100.0
31.12.1995		110.5
01.01.1996	100	210.5
31.12.1996		180.3
01.01.1997	−50	130.3
30.06.1997		145.1

Instead of measuring the average return for an account statement, the return of a fixed investment of, say 100 €, contributed at the beginning of the period (i.e. on 01.01.1995) and kept until the end of the period (i.e. until 30.06.1997) in the portfolio, will be tracked. According to the cash flows the interval will be split into three subintervals (cf. Figure 10.3).

In the period from 01.01.1995 to 31.12.1995 the original investment of 100.00 € increased to 110.50 €. The corresponding return was thus 10.50%. In the following interval (01.01.1996–31.12.1996) the initial value of 210.50 € declined to 180.30 €. The corresponding return is calculated as follows:

$$R = \frac{180.30 - 210.50}{210.50} = -0.1435 = -14.35\%.$$

According to:

$$110.50 * \left(1 + \frac{-14.35}{100}\right) = 94.64$$

110.50 € would have decreased to 94.64 € in the period. By applying the basis formula one computes the return for the third period in an analogous form:

$$R = \frac{145.10 - 130.30}{130.30} = 0.1136 = 11.36\%.$$

The 94,64 € would have become 105,39 €:

$$94.64 * \left(1 + \frac{11.36}{100}\right) = 105.39$$

Over the entire period 100.00 € would have increased to 105.39 €. The time-weighted return was thus equal to 5.39%.

In order to write this in a systematic form, the value of the initial investment at time t will be denoted by I_t. It holds that:

$$I_{30.06.97} = I_{31.12.96} * \left(1 + \frac{11.36}{100}\right) = I_{31.12.95} * \left(1 + \frac{-14.35}{100}\right) * \left(1 + \frac{11.36}{100}\right).$$

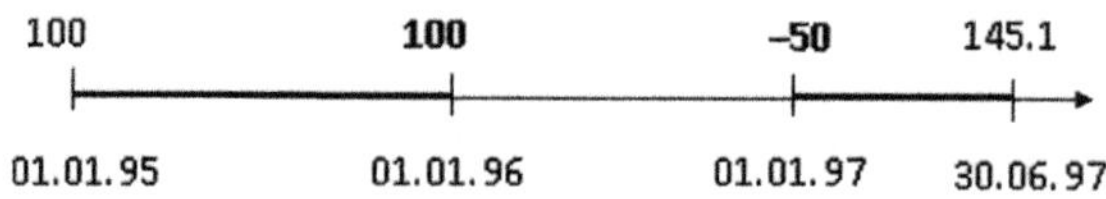

FIGURE 10.3
Partitioning into subintervals.

Table 10.6 Computation of the Time-Weighted Return for the Account Statement in Example 10.6

	Period 1	Period 2	Period 3
Beginning/ end NAV	100.0 110.5	210.5 180.3	130.3 145.1
Period return in %	$100 * \frac{1105-100}{100} = 10.50$	$100 * \frac{180.3-210.5}{210.5} = -14.35$	$100 * \frac{145.1-130.3}{130.3} = 11.36$
Net asset value at the end of the period	$100 * \left(1 + \frac{10.50}{100}\right) = 110.50$	$110.50 * \left(1 + \frac{-14.35}{100}\right) = 94.64$	$94.64 * \left(1 + \frac{11.36}{100}\right) = 105.39$
Cumulated return in %	10.50	–5.36	5.39

One obtains thus:

$$I_{30.06.97} = I_{01.01.95} * \left(1+\frac{10.50}{100}\right) * \left(1+\frac{-14.35}{100}\right) * \left(1+\frac{11.36}{100}\right)$$
$$= 100 * \left(1+\frac{10.50}{100}\right) * \left(1+\frac{-14.35}{100}\right) * \left(1+\frac{11.36}{100}\right)$$

Table 10.6 summarizes the different steps involved in the computation of the time-weighted return.

Finally, the return R will be computed with the formula:

In a symmetric form:

$$R = \frac{I_{30.06.97} - I_{01.01.95}}{I_{01.01.95}}$$
$$= \frac{100 * \left(1+\frac{10.50}{100}\right) * \left(1+\frac{-14.35}{100}\right) * \left(1+\frac{11.36}{100}\right) - 100}{100}$$
$$= \left(1+\frac{10.50}{100}\right) * \left(1+\frac{-14.35}{100}\right) * \left(1+\frac{11.36}{100}\right) - 1.$$

$$1+R = \left(1+\frac{10.50}{100}\right) * \left(1+\frac{-14.35}{100}\right) * \left(1+\frac{11.36}{100}\right)$$

The derived formula can easily be generalized: the period over which the return needs to be calculated will be partitioned into subintervals according to the exogenous cash flows, such that no more cash flows occur within these subintervals. In case of n cash flows $n+1$ such subintervals will result. For these subintervals the $n+1$ returns $R_1, R_2, \ldots$ will be calculated in an elementary way (with the basis formula). These returns will finally be linked multiplicatively according to Equation (10.12). This procedure is called *geometric linkage*:

Time-Weighted Rate of Return

$$1 + R^{tw} := (1 + R_1) * (1 + R_2) * \ldots * (1 + R_{n+1}) = \prod_{i=1}^{n+1} (1 + R_i). \qquad (10.12)$$

With 5.39% the value of the time-weighted rate of return for the account statement in Example 10.6 exceeded by far the internal rate of return (−3.26%) computed in Section 10.3. This difference will be analyzed further in Section 10.5.

10.4.2 Returns for Investment Funds Based On the Unit Price

The central idea on which the time-weighted rate of return is based, is the evaluation of the performance of an individual investment throughout a given (sub) period. This approach corresponds to the unit price method for the return calculation of unit trusts, which will be explained in detail in the following sections. Among the various classes of investment funds mutual funds will serve as a representative.

In general mutual funds have to deal with daily cash flows, which are settled at the given price for a unit determined on that day. The fact that the unit price of mutual fund is in general determined on a daily basis corresponds to the assumption that the period in which no cash flows occurred is at least one day. The time-weighted rates of return are calculated according to formula (10.12). The R_i are daily returns, whose computation is based on the daily net asset values of the funds (expressed by the unit prices I_i). At first, in Sections 10.4.2.1–10.4.2.3 several individual aspects will be treated in isolation. The description of the actual method will follow in Section 10.4.2.4.

10.4.2.1 *CALCULATING RETURNS FOR AN ACCUMULATING INVESTMENT FUND*

An *accumulating investment fund* doesn't pay dividends. The income (interest, stock dividends, rents, etc.) remains within the fund. For such funds the return calculation is straight-forward.[7] If N_i is the number[8] of the distributed fund units between two valuation days, then one calculates:

$$R_i = \frac{N_i * I_{i+1} - N_i * I_i}{N_i * I_i} = \frac{I_{i+1} - I_i}{I_i} = \frac{I_{i+1}}{I_i} - 1$$

[7] Tax aspects will not be considered here.

[8] The number of units is assumed constant within the periods.

Table 10.7 Development of the Unit Price of the Fund FONDAK in the Period from 30.12.2005 to 29.09.2006

Date	Unit Price (€)
30.12.2005	98.02
⋮	⋮
31.07.2006	102.47
01.08.2006	101.49
⋮	⋮
29.09.2006	107.85

for the daily returns. For a period of N days one obtains according to formula (10.12):

$$1+R^{tw}=\prod_{i=1}^{N}(1+R_i)=\prod_{i=1}^{N}\left(1+\frac{I_{i+1}}{I_i}-1\right)=\prod_{i=1}^{N}\frac{I_{i+1}}{I_i}. \tag{10.13}$$

If one expands the last term, then one notices that:

$$1+R^{tw}=\frac{I_{n+1}}{I_n}*\frac{I_n}{I_{n-1}}*\cdots*\frac{I_3}{I_2}*\frac{I_2}{I_1}=\frac{I_{n+1}}{I_1},$$

and thus:

$$R^{tw}=\frac{I_{n+1}}{I_1}-1=\frac{I_{n+1}-I_1}{I_1}.$$

In case of accumulating investment funds the time-weighted return may be calculated directly from the unit prices by means of the basic formula. For dividend-paying investment funds, these dividends need to be considered in addition to the unit prices. The necessary modifications will be outlined in the following section.

10.4.2.2 TREATMENT OF DIVIDENDS

Most investment funds distribute once a year their (ordinary) income (interest, dividends, rent, ...).[9] In this section the methods for considering dividends shall be derived by means of a concrete example. In case of the fund *FONDAK* the unit price developed as follows (see Table 10.7):

$$R=\frac{107.85-98,02}{98.02}=0.1003=10.03\%.$$

[9] Some funds also distribute extraordinary gains such as realized gains resulting from the sale of a property.

Table 10.8 Development of the Additively Adjusted Unit Prices of the Fund FONDAK in the Period from 30.12.2005 to 29.09.2006

Date	Unit Price[a] (€)
30.12.2005	98.02
⋮	⋮
31.07.2006	102.47
01.08.2006	102.55=101.49+1.06
⋮	⋮
29.09.2006	108.91=107.85+1.06

[a] *On the day of the distribution the fund's price is quoted ex dividend (i.e. the price after the distribution is shown).*

On 01.08.2006 a dividend of 1.06€ per unit was distributed.[10] Thus the return over the first three quarters cannot simply be calculated by applying the basis formula

$$R = \frac{107.85 - 98,02}{98.02} = 0.1003 = 10.03\%,$$

since the dividend would then not be considered at all. There are different ways to "correct" the above computation.

10.4.2.3 ADDITIVE ADJUSTMENT

In an additive adjustment the dividend is simply added to those unit prices that follow the day of the distribution. This yields the *additively adjusted time series* (see Table 10.8).

With this adjustment the basis formula can be applied:

$$R = \frac{108.91 - 98.02}{98.02} = 0.1111 = 11.11\%.$$

If the analysis periods comprise several distributions of dividends, then the time series needs to be adjusted for all distributions.

The approach is based on the assumption that the dividends are not reinvested in the fund. They are therefore not submitted to the fund's performance after the distribution.

10.4.2.4 MULTIPLICATIVE ADJUSTMENT (UNIT PRICE METHOD)

The unit price method is based on the assumption that the dividends will be fully reinvested in the fund and thus be submitted to the fund's performance.[11]

---

[10] This dividend is tax-adjusted. Tax aspects will not be discussed in detail.

[11] If one writes the adjusted unit price as at 29.09. in Table 10.9 in the form $107.85 * (1 + 1.06/101.49) = 107.85 + 1.06 * 107.85/101.49$, then it becomes obvious, how the dividend is submitted to the subsequent performance. $107.85/101.49 - 1$ is the fund's return between the distribution date and the end of the analysis period.

Table 10.9 The Additively Backward Adjusted Unit Price of the Fund FONDAK in the Period from 30.12.2005 to 29.09.2006

Date	Unit Price (€)
30.12.2005	98.02
⋮	⋮
31.07.2006	102.47
01.08.2006	102.55=101.49∗1.01044
⋮	⋮
29.09.2006	108.98=107.85∗1.01044

According to the unit price method all unit prices following the day of the distribution would be multiplied by the factor

$$1 + \frac{1.06}{101.49} = 1.01044.$$

The *multiplicatively adjusted time series* would assume the form shown in Table 10.9.

According to the unit price method the return is given by:[12]

$$R = \frac{108.98 - 98.02}{98.02} = 0.11177 = 11.18\%$$

and lies thus 7 basis points (= 11.18%–11.11%) above the value obtained with the additive adjustment. This is plausible, as the reinvested dividend would have "accrued interest" according the general performance of the fund.

Instead of the above "forward adjustment" the original time series could have been submitted to a "backward adjustment". Under this method the preceding unit prices would have been multiplied by the inverse of the "forward factor" (see Table 10.10):

$$\left(1 + \frac{106}{101.49}\right)^{-1} = 0.98966.$$

The calculation of the return by means of the unit price method is independent of the chosen adjustment of the time series. For instance, if one uses the above backward adjusted time series, then the return is given by:

$$R = \frac{107.85 - 97,01}{97.01} = 0.1118 = 11.18\%,$$

which is in agreement with the value computed before.

[12] In order to calculate the return over a certain period, it suffices, of course, to multiply the unit price at the end of the period. It is, however, necessary to multiply the entire time series if one wants to represent the performance graphically.

Table 10.10 The Multiplicatively Backward Adjusted Unit Price of the Fund FONDAK in the Period from 30.12.2005 to 29.09.2006

Date	Unit Price (€)
30.12.2005	97.01=98.02*0.98966
⋮	⋮
31.07.2006	101.412=102.47*0.98966
01.08.2006	101.49
⋮	⋮
29.09.2006	107.85

Analogous to the additive method, also for the unit price method an adjustment factor needs to be defined for each distribution. For a return calculation of, say, n calendar years, the last unit price needs to be multiplied by n adjustment factors before the basis formula can be employed.

Unit price method

The return R of an investment fund over a period with n distributions D_1, D_n is given by[13]

$$R = \frac{I_{n+1} * \prod_{i=1}^{n} \left(1 + \frac{D_i}{I_i}\right) - I_0}{I_0}, \tag{10.14}$$

where:

I_0: unit price of the fund at the beginning of the period

$I_1, \ldots, I_n$: unit price of the fund at the distribution dates

I_{n+1}: unit price of the fund at the end of the period.

It is easy to demonstrate formally, why the return calculation is independent from the chosen adjustment. It suffices to restate the above expression for the return as follows:

$$R = \frac{I_{n+1} * \prod_{i=1}^{n} \left(1 + \frac{D_i}{I_i}\right) - I_0}{I_0} = \frac{I_{n+1} - I_0 * \prod_{i=1}^{n} \left(1 + \frac{D_i}{I_i}\right)^{-1}}{I_0 * \prod_{i=1}^{n} \left(1 + \frac{D_i}{I_i}\right)^{-1}}.$$

The term on the right-hand side of this equation is identical to the expression that one obtains in a "backward adjustment".[14]

[13] This definition implies a forward adjustment.

[14] In case of an additive adjustment the symmetry property between the forward and the backward adjustments is not valid. In this case only the forward adjustment makes sense.

Table 10.11 Unit Prices, Dividends (both in €) and Adjustment Factors for the Fund FONDAK in the Period from 31.01.1996 to 29.09.2006

Date	Dividend	Unit Price	Adjustment Factor	Cumulated Adjustment Factor
31.01.1996		40.11		
01.08.1996	1.12	39.61	1.028	1.028
01.08.1997	1.04	63.92	1.016	1.045
03.08.1998	1.97	74.67	1.026	1.073
02.08.1999	1.26	66.09	1.019	1.093
01.08.2000	1.65	90.19	1.018	1.113
01.08.2001	2.21	81.82	1.027	1.143
01.08.2002	0.77	59.78	1.013	1.158
01.08.2003	0.94	60.24	1.016	1.176
02.08.2004	0.87	68.74	1.013	1.191
01.08.2005	0.95	89.28	1.011	1.203
01.08.2006	1.06	101.49	1.010	1.216
29.09.2006		107.85		

The return calculated with the unit price method is identical to the time-weighted return. This assertion will be proved in Appendix C of this chapter. At this stage formula (10.14) shall be illustrated by means of an example.

Example 10.8

Adjustment of an investment fund over several periods:

Table 10.11 contains the details of the dividend payments of the investment fund *FONDAK* in the period from 31.01.1996 to 29.09.2006. In particular, this entails the days of the dividend payments, the unit prices of these days and the derived adjustment factors. The *cumulated adjustment factor* is the product of the single adjustment factors prior to a given point in time; for the cumulated adjustment factor as at 07.08.1998 one obtains e.g. $1.073 = 1.028 * 1.016 * 1.026$.
According to the unit price method one obtains:

$$\begin{aligned}
R &= \frac{107.85 * \left(1+\frac{1.12}{39{,}61}\right) * \left(1+\frac{1.04}{63.92}\right) * \left(1+\frac{1.97}{74.67}\right) * \cdots * \left(1+\frac{1.06}{101.49}\right) - 40.11}{40.11} \\
&= \frac{107.85 * 1.028 * 1.016 * 1.026 * \cdots * 1.0109 - 40.11}{40.11} \\
&= \frac{107.85 * 1.216 - 40.11}{40.11} = \frac{131.15 - 40.11}{40.11} \\
&= 2.2696.
\end{aligned}$$

Thus the fund achieved a return of 226.96% in the period from 31.01.1996 to 29.09.2006.

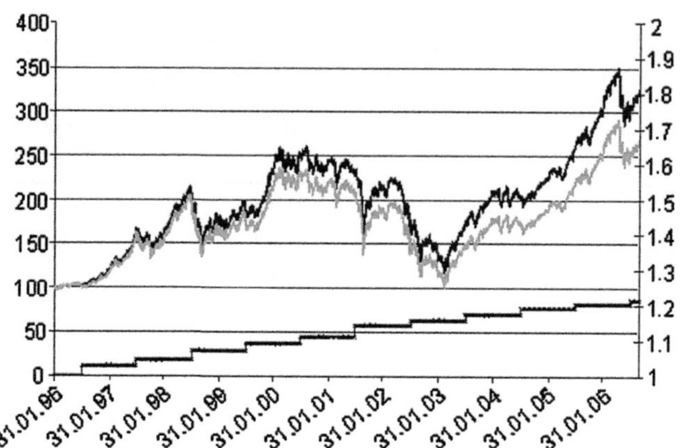

FIGURE 10.4
Time Series of Unit Prices.

In Figure 10.4 the procedure of a multiplicative adjustment will be illustrated by means of the fund *FONDAK*.

Based on the definition the hypotheses of reinvestment of the dividends may be illustrated as follows: at the point in time of the first distribution the net value n units equals $n * (I_1 + A_1)$. Thus the amount $n * A_1$ needs to be reinvested. According to the hypothesis the investor acquires exactly $n * A_1/I_1$ units, such that the number of units that he holds is increased to $n + n * A_1/I_1 = n * (1 + A_1/I_1)$. This procedure is repeated for the next distribution: at this point in time the net investment equals $n * (1 + A_1/I_1) * (I_2 + A_2)$, such that $n * (1 + A_1/I_1) * A_2$ needs to be reinvested. For this amount exactly $n * (1 + A_1/I_1) * A_2/I_2$ units can be acquired, such that after two distributions the investment consists of

$$n * (1 + A_1/I_1) + n * (1 + A_1/I_1) * A_2/I_2 = n * (1 + A_1/I_1) * (1 + A_2/I_2)$$

units. By repeating this procedure one readily derives formula (10.14). The time-series in Figure 10.4 may thus by interpreted as the number of shares that would have resulted simply be reinvesting the dividends according to the reinvestment hypotheses over time. (In the case of the fund *FONDAK* an initial holding of 100 units would have developed into a position of 121.6 units.)

To conclude this section, the key facts of the time-weighted return and the internal rate of return shall be summarized in Table 10.12.

10.5 COMPARISON BETWEEN THE TIME-WEIGHTED RETURN AND THE INTERNAL RATE OF RETURN

In Sections 10.3 and 10.4 it was demonstrated (Examples 10.6 and 10.7), that the time-weighted return and the internal rate of return may diverge considerably for *the same* cash flow. In this section it will be explained how to interpret these divergences.

Table 10.12 Overview of the Properties of the Time-Weighted Return and the Internal Rate of Return

	Time-Weighted Rate of Return (Unit Price Method)	Internal Rate of Return (Money-Weighted Rate of Return)
Basic idea	Performance of *one* initial investment	Average performance of investments with a limited retention time within the account
Assumptions	Knowledge of the net asset values at the points in time at which the exogenous cash flows occur as well as at the beginning and at the end of the analysis period required Knowledge of the values of the exogenous cash flows is required Knowledge of the point in time at which the exogenous cash flows occur not required	Knowledge of the net asset values at the beginning and at the end of the analysis period required Knowledge of the values and the points in time of the exogenous cash flows is required Knowledge of the net asset values at the points in time at which the exogenous cash flows occur not required
Treatment of cash flows	Independent of exogenous cash flows	Exogenous cash flows are determinants of the return
Computation	Multiplicative (geometric) linking of the returns for the periods between cash flows	Determining the zero of a polynomial by means of an iterative procedure (Newton's method)
Formula	$1 + R^{tw} := (1 + R_1) * (1 + R_2) * \ldots * (1 + R_{n+1}) = \prod_{i=1}^{n+1} (1 + R_i)$	$I_0 * (1 + Q)^T + \sum_{i=1}^{N^E} E_i * (1 + Q)^{T - t_i^E} + \sum_{i=1}^{N^A} A_i * (1 + Q)^{T - t_i^A} = I_1 1 + R^{rr} := (1 + Q)^T$

Table 10.13 Account Statement with One Contribution and a Higher Return in the First Subperiod

Date	Cash Flows	Net Asset Value
01.01.2007		100
30.06.2007	100	**170**
31.12.2007		250

The time-weighted return and the internal rate of return are identical in the absence of exogenous cash flows. In the case of exogenous cash flows certain conclusions in regard to timing of the cash flows can be inferred from the relation between the time-weighted return and the internal rate of return. To deduce the principal assertions it suffices to consider an account statement with only one exogenous cash flow. At first a few examples will be given. All examples contain an account statement, for which time-weighted return and the internal rate of return are compared with each other. If for a given date a cash flow is listed, then the value in the right column represents the net asset value immediately *prior* to that cash flow.

Example 10.9

Time-weighted return and internal rate of return in the case of one contribution

(See Table 10.13)

a. The internal rate of return for the above account statement was already computed in Example 10.4: $R^{irr} = 34.17\%$. This return is independent of the net asset value on the day of the cash flow (30.06.2007). The time-weighted return results from linking the return in the single periods:

$$R^{tw} = \frac{170}{100} * \frac{250}{170 + 100} - 1 = 0.5741 = 57.41\%.$$

Thus the time-weighted return exceeds by far the internal rate of return.

Table 10.14 juxtaposes the returns and net asset values for the subperiods resulting from the cash flow. Within the periods the returns are calculated according to the basis formula.

It becomes obvious that the timing of the contribution was unfortunate, as the market started to decline afterwards.

b. In case of the account statement in Table 10.15 the markets[15] were less bullish during the first half-year than during the second.

The time-weighted return, given by

$$R^{tw} = \frac{110}{100} * \frac{250}{110 + 100} - 1 = 0.3095 = 30.95\%,$$

[15] Here it is assumed that the performance is essentially determined by the market performance (benchmark).

Table 10.14 Comparison of Returns and Net Asset Values for the Account Statement in Table 10.13

Period	Return (%)	Initial NAV	Final NAV	Cash Flow at Beginning of the Period
01.01.–30.06.	70.0	100	170	
01.07.–31.12.	−7.4	270	250	+100

Table 10.15 Account Statement with One Contribution and a Higher Return in the Second Subperiod

Date	Cash Flows	Net Asset Value
01.01.2007	⋮	100
30.06.2007	100	**110**
31.12.2007	⋮	250

Table 10.16 Comparison of Returns and Net Asset Values for the Account Statement in Table 10.15

Period	Return (%)	Initial NAV	Final NAV	Cash Flow at Beginning of the Period
01.01.–30.06.	10,0	100	110	
01.07.–31.12.	1,1	210	250	+100

is lower than the internal rate of return of 34.17%.

The returns and net asset values for the subperiods resulting from the cash flow are shown in Table 10.16.

The net asset value was increased at the beginning of the second period, which was characterized by a very strong performance (compared to the first subperiod). Hence this is an example for good market timing.

Example 10.10

Time-weighted return and internal rate of return in the case of one withdrawal

Example 10.9 will be adapted to the case of one withdrawal.

a. For the account statement in Table 10.17 one obtains the following time-weighted return:

$$R^{tw} = \frac{110}{100} * \frac{90}{110 - 50} - 1 = 0.65 = 65\%.$$

This return exceeds the internal rate of return of 51.55% (cf. Exercise 10.1).

The comparison of the period returns with the respective initial net asset values (Table 10.18) clearly shows that the withdrawal was a bad market timing decision.

b. As in Example 10.9 the net asset value on 30.06.2007 will be varied (see Table 10.19):

Table 10.17 Account Statement with One Withdrawal and a Higher Return in the Second Subperiod

Date	Cash Flows	Net Asset Value
01.01.2007		100
30.06.2007	−50	**110**
31.12.2007		90

Table 10.18 Comparison of Returns and Net Asset Values for the Account Statement in Table 10.17

Period	Return (%)	Initial NAV	Final NAV	Cash Flow at Beginning of the Period
01.01.–30.06.	10.0	100	110	
01.07.–31.12.	50.0	60	90	−50

Table 10.19 Account Statement with One Withdrawal and a Higher Return in the First Subperiod

Date	Cash Flows	Net Asset Value
01.01.2007		100
30.06.2007	−50	**150**
31.12.2007		90

Table 10.20 Comparison of Returns and Net Asset Values for the Account Statement in Table 10.19

Period	Return (%)	Initial NAV	Final NAV	Cash Flow at Beginning of the Period
01.01.–30.06.	50.0	100	150	
01.07.–31.12.	−10.0	100	90	−50

In this case one obtains the following time-weighted return:

$$R^{tw} = \frac{150}{100} * \frac{90}{100} - 1 = 0.35 = 35\%.$$

The internal rate of return exceeds the time-weighted return. The withdrawal was thus a bad timing decision. This again becomes clear if one juxtaposes the respective period returns and initial net asset value (Table 10.20).

The investment was reduced before a period of declining prices.

Table 10.21 Account Statement with One Contribution and a Variable Net Asset Value X

Date	Cash Flows	Net Asset Value
01.01.2007		100
30.06.2007	100	X
31.12.2007		250

The examples suggest that the quality of the (relative) market timing decisions is reflected by the relation between the time-weighted return and the internal rate of return.

Time-weighted return > Internal rate of return: Bad timing of the cash flow

Time-weighted return < Internal rate of return: Good timing of the cash flow

In the following this relationship will be examined more closely. For this purpose the above examples will be generalized by keeping the net asset value as at 30.06.2007 variable. The other values are as before. At first the case of a contribution will be considered (see Table 10.21).

From

$$1 + R^{tw} = \frac{X}{100} * \frac{250}{X + 100} = \frac{2.5 * X}{100 + X}$$

one deduces the following functional relationship:

$$R^{tw} = \frac{1.5 * X - 100}{X + 100}.$$

The internal rate of return (34.17%) was already calculated in Example 10.4. Here the reader shall be reminded that the internal rate of return is independent of the valuation result at 30.06.2007. Figure 10.5 illustrates the relationship between the time-weighted return and the valuation X.

The time-weighted return is an increasing function of X, since the increasing return over the first period of x/100 is dominating over the declining return in the second period of $\frac{250}{x+100}$.

For which value of X_{MW} does equality hold between the time-weighted return and the internal rate of return? For this value holds

$$\frac{1.5 * X_{MW} - 100}{X_{MW} + 100} = 0.3417$$

and thus

$$X_{MW} = \frac{134.17}{1.1583} = 100 * \frac{1.3417}{1.1583} = 100 * 1.1583 = 115.83.$$

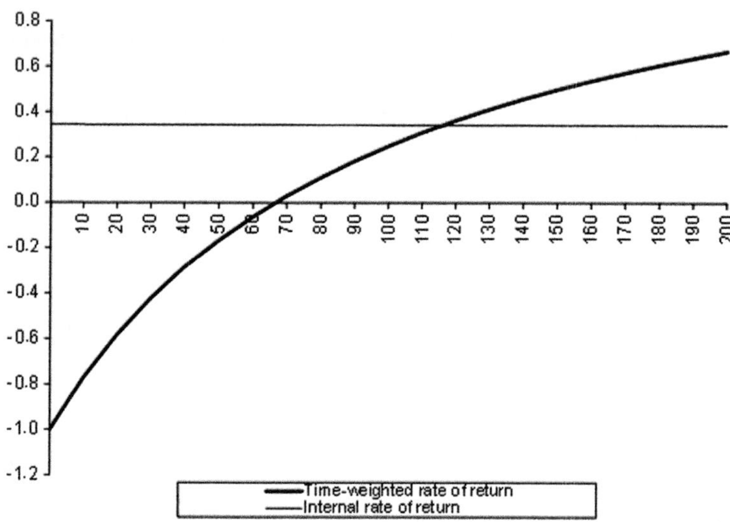

FIGURE 10.5
Time-Weighted Return as a Function of the Variable Net Asset Value X.

The internal rate of return over the full period (1 year) of 34.17% corresponds to a value of 15.83% for the half-yearly period ($1.1583^2 = 1.3417$). Thus the time-weighted return for the account statement equals the internal rate of return, if the valuation of the account at the time of the cash flow is equal to the value that would result from an accrual with the internal rate of return. The interested reader may refer to Appendix A of this chapter for a proof of this assertion. From the above figure one deduces the following relationship:

$X > X_{MW} \Rightarrow$ *Time-weighted return > Internal rate of return*

$X < X_{MW} \Rightarrow$ *Time-weighted return < Internal rate of return.*

Fixing the valuation of X will determine the performance in the respective subperiods. For given net asset values at the end and the beginning of the period it holds: the higher X, the higher the return over the first period and the lower the return in the second period.[16]

If $X > X_{MW}$, then the decision to realize a higher exposure in the first period than in the second period was disadvantageous in regard to the obtained average return compared to an investment without a subsequent cash flow.

In case $X < X_{MW}$ it would have been better to choose a higher volume at the beginning of the second subperiod, since the performance was higher in that period.

[16] The following general (evident) assertion holds: if in all subperiods resulting from the cash flows the performance of the account is identical to the one which one would obtain when applying the internal rate of return, then the time-weighted return is equal to the internal rate of return (if uniquely defined). The converse does not hold.

Table 10.22 Account Statement with One Withdrawal and a Variable Net Asset Value X

Date	Cash Flows	Net Asset Value
01.01.2007		100
30.06.2007	−50	X
31.12.2007		90

One obtains similar conclusions in the case of a withdrawal. In order to illustrate this, the account statement in Example 10.10 will be generalized as follows (see Table 10.22):

It follows that:

$$1 + R^{tw} = \frac{X}{100} * \frac{90}{X - 50} = \frac{0.9 * X}{X - 50},$$

and thus

$$R^{tw} = \frac{50 - 0.1 * X}{X - 50}.$$

In this case the time-weighted return as a function of the net asset value X has the form shown in Figure 10.6.

The assumption of equality between the time-weighted return and the internal rate of return, which according to Example 10.10 equals 51.5%, leads to:

$$\frac{50 - 0.1 * X_{MW}}{X_{MW} - 50} = 0.5155.$$

The solution of this equation equals X_{MW}=123.11. As in the case of a contribution, equality holds thus precisely for the net asset value that would have resulted from an accrual by the internal rate of return, since $1.2311^2 = 1.5155$[17]

From Figure 10.6 one deduces that the time-weighted return exceeds the internal rate of return, if the valuation X renders a value below X_{MW}. In this case the investor would have withdrawn funds right before a strong growth period ("bad timing"). In the converse case ($X > X_{MW}$) the cash flow would have occurred in advance of a period with less growth. This interpretation can be generalized:

If the time-weighted return exceeds the internal rate of return, then this reflects a disadvantageous variation of the invested capital (compared to investments without a subsequent cash flows) ("bad timing"). Conversely, there is a good timing of the cash flows, if the internal rate of return exceeds the time-weighted return.

[17] The withdrawal occurred in the middle of the year, 23.1% is the half-yearly interest rate.

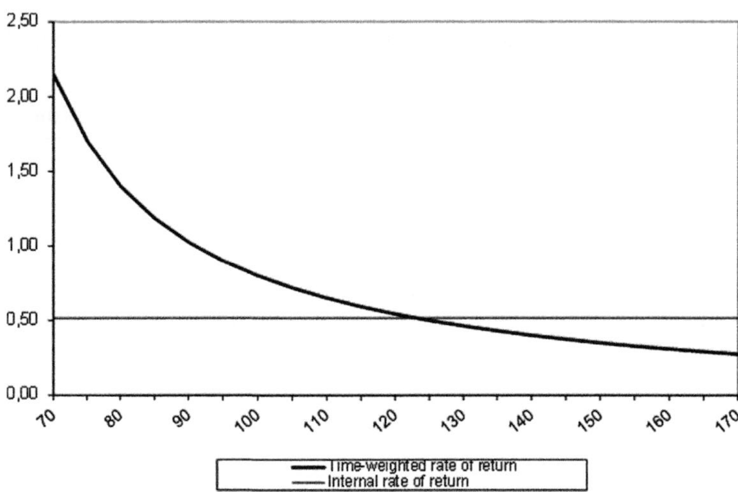

FIGURE 10.6
Time-Weighted Return as a Function of the Net Asset Value X.

Table 10.23 Account Statement with Positive Returns in Both Subperiods

Date	Cash Flow	Net Asset Value
01.01.2007		100
30.06.2007	100	X=130
31.12.2007		250

In praxis one often needs to compare time-weighted returns and internal rates of return, as many institutional investors define a certain target for the average return on the employed capital. Parallel to that they evaluate the fund manager's performance by means of the time-weighted return relative to a benchmark.

In Examples 10.5. and 10.6. a case was described that frequently occurs in practice: while an account has a negative internal rate of return (the investor suffered a loss!), the time-weighted return is positive. In this case the cash flows were badly timed (relatively speaking). An investment without subsequent withdrawals and contributions would have led to a higher internal rate of return. Its value would have been identical to the time-weighted return.

At this stage it must be emphasized that in this section the term timing refers to a variation of the invested capital *relative* to an investment without subsequent cash flows. With a net asset value of e.g. 130 (instead of 170) on 30.06.2007 in Example 10.9 (cf. Table 10.23) the internal rate of return (34.17%) would have been below the time-weighted return of 41.3%.

Obviously, the investment would have yielded a contribution of 20 money units (even if that contribution is below the average return). In case that the additional funds would have been available only as at 30.06.2007, it would be unfair to speak of a bad timing.

Table 10.24 Account Statement with n Exogenous Cash Flows M_i at t_i
I_i are the Net Asset Values at t_i

Date	Cash Flows	Net Asset Value
0		I_0
t_1	M_1	I_1
t_2	M_2	I_2
t_n	M_n	I_n
T		I_{n+1}

10.6 APPROXIMATION METHODS FOR THE COMPUTATION OF THE TIME-WEIGHTED RETURN

As outlined in Section 10.4 (cf. Table 10.12) the time-weighted return of an account (portfolio, portfolio segment, etc.) requires knowledge of the account's net asset value at all points in times at which cash flows occurred. This precondition is, however, often not fulfilled. In practice portfolios are often valuated in a specific frequency, e.g. monthly or weekly.[18]

This problem is especially relevant for performance attribution systems, which often operate on the basis of weekly or monthly valuation data and the transactions that occurred in the analysis period. Under these assumptions one needs to refer to approximation methods when computing the time-weighted return.

In this section various methods for approximating the time-weighted return and the internal rate of return will be described. For this purpose general account statements will be considered, which comprise n exogenous cash flows M_i at t_i in the period from 0 to T (cf. Table 10.24). For a negative value M_i represents a withdrawal, otherwise a contribution. The M_i, thus replace the notation for contributions/withdrawals A_i and E_i used previously in Section 10.3.

The calculation of the time-weighted return is then as follows (cf. Section 10.4): the period for the return calculation will be subdivided according to the cash flows, such that none of the cash flows falls within one of the resulting subintervals. For n cash flows one obtains $n+1$ subintervals (cf. Figure 10.7). Then the $n+1$ returns R_1, R_2, ... are computed according to the basis formula,

$$R_1 = \frac{I_1}{I_0} - 1, \quad R_i = \frac{I_i}{I_{i-1} + M_{i-1}} - 1 \quad \text{for } i = 2, \ldots, n+1,$$

[18] Studies by PricewaterhouseCoopers (PwC) (PwC 2000a, 2000b) showed that in 1999 only 39% of all American asset managers and 24% of all European asset managers valuated the funds daily. The overwhelming majority of the asset managers (54% respectively, 62%) conducted monthly valuations. In 2004 these values were confirmed by a global study: 80% of the asset managers stated that portfolios should be evaluated daily, however, only 35% of the participating organizations actually conducted daily valuations. The majority (ca. 53%) conducted monthly valuations.

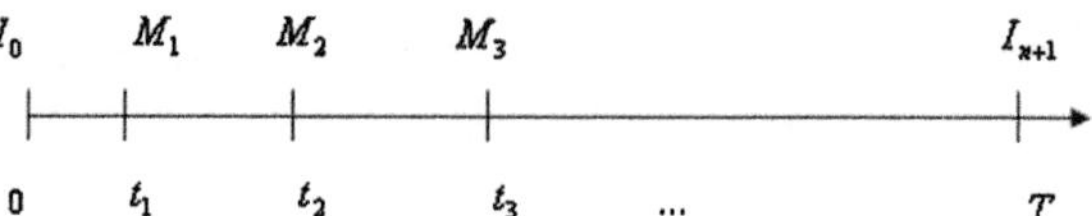

FIGURE 10.7
Account Statement with Cash Flows.

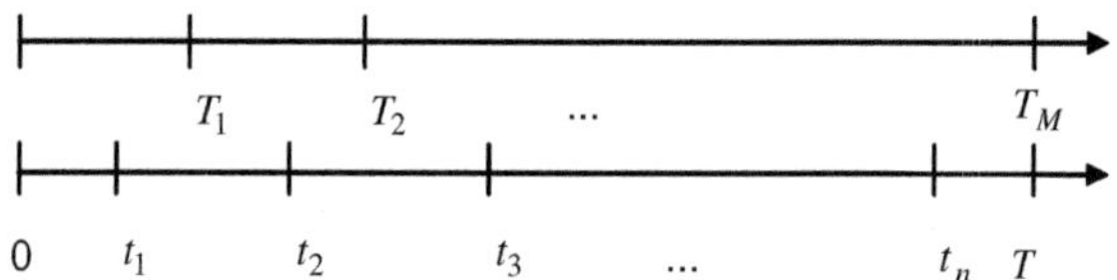

FIGURE 10.8
Valuation Dates.

and linked in a multiplicative form:

$$1 + R^{tw} = (1 + R_1) * (1 + R_2) * \ldots * (1 + R_{n+1}) = \prod_{i=1}^{n+1} (1 + R_i).$$

Computing time-weighted return in an exact form requires thus the knowledge of the net asset values of the account (*market values*) at all points in time in which exogenous cash flow has occurred, as well as the beginning and ending net asset value. Due to the complexity and the costs associated with the valuation, these preconditions are often not fulfilled. The valuation dates T_i usually occur in a certain frequency (e.g. monthly or quarterly), and in general these dates will not cover all days at which exogenous cash flow occurs (Figure 10.8).

The time-weighted return over the entire period from 0 to T is given by:

$$1 + R^{tw} = \prod_{i=1}^{M} (1 + R_i^{tw}), \tag{10.15}$$

where R_i^{tw} denominates the time-weighted return in the interval from T_i–1 to T_i (with $T_0 = 0$). Since the computation of the returns according to formula (10.15) would require that for each cash flow a valuation of the portfolio has been performed, in practice the returns R_i^{tw} in formula (10.15) are often replaced by approximate values R_i^N:

$$1 + R^{tw} \approx \prod_{i=1}^{M} (1 + R_i^N). \tag{10.16}$$

To estimate the R_i^N (respectively, to estimate R^{tw} according to (10.16)) often one of the following methods is used:[19]

1. Internal rate of return
2. Dietz method
3. Modified Dietz method
4. BAI method
5. Second-order Newton approximation to the internal rate of return.

[19] Of course, each commercial performance attribution system has its own approach, which the provider does in general not disclose.

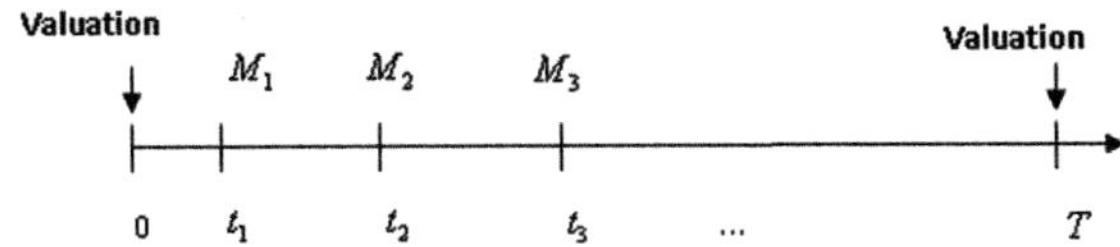

FIGURE 10.9
Exogenous Cash Flows.

The following considerations concern the subperiod between to cash flows. In order to keep the notation as simple as possible, the endpoints of a subperiod shall again be labeled with 0 and T (Figure 10.9).

10.6.1 Approximation of the Time-Weighted Return Based on the Internal Rate of Return

One option for the approximation of the time-weighted returns R_i^{tw} in formula (10.15) is given by the internal rate of return within the single periods. In the following sections it will be described how the other approaches listed above may be interpreted as methods derived from this approach. Hence general aspects of the internal rate of return must be considered in this section.

Based on the explanations in Section 10.3 the internal rate of return scaled to one day[20] Q for the account statement with n contributions in Table 10.24 is given as the solution of the following equation:

$$I_0 * (1+Q)^T + \sum_{i=1}^{n} M_i * (1+Q)^{T-t_i} = I_{n+1} \tag{10.17}$$

The internal rate of return R^{irr} over the entire period is then given by:

$$1 + R^{irr} = (1+Q)^T .$$

After an according substitution equation (10.17) assumes the following form:

$$I_0 * \left(1+R^{irr}\right) + \sum_{i=1}^{n} M_i * \left(1+R^{irr}\right)^{\frac{T-t_i}{T}} = I_{n+1}. \tag{10.18}$$

Dividing by the initial net asset value I_0, assumed different from zero, yields

$$1 * \left(1+R^{irr}\right) + \sum_{i=1}^{n} \frac{M_i}{I_0} * \left(1+R^{irr}\right)^{\frac{T-t_i}{T}} = \frac{I_{n+1}}{I_0}. \tag{10.19}$$

An issue which has not been raised in Section 10.3 concerns the uniqueness of the solution, i.e. the question, whether Equation (10.17) possesses a unique solution for *all* account statements. The following example demonstrates that this is not the case (see Table 10.25).

[20] The method to approximate the time-weighted return by means of the internal rate of return within single periods is also known as the *modified BAI method* (Bank Administration Institute) (cf. e.g. AIMR 1997 or Dietz and Kirschman (1990).

Table 10.25 Account Statement

Date	Cash Flow	Net Asset Value
01.01.2007		10
01.04.2007	8	
01.06.2007	−8	
01.08.2007	−1	
01.10.2007	+1	
31.10.2007		0.2

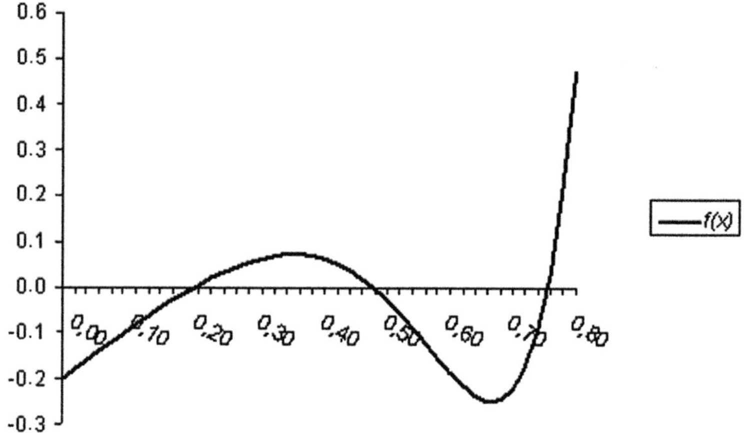

FIGURE 10.10
Graph of the Function *f*.

Example 10.11

Account statement without a unique internal rate of return:

According to Equation (10.17) the account statement in Table 10.25 leads after the substitution $x := (1 + Q)^{30}$ to the equation:

$$10 * x^{10} + 8 * x^7 - 8 * x^5 - x^3 + x = 0.2.$$

The solutions are given by the zeros of the equation $f(x) = 0$ where:

$$f(x) = 10 * x^{10} + 8 * x^7 - 8 * x^5 - x^3 + x - 0.2.$$

Figure 10.10 illustrates that the graph of the function intercepts the x-axis three times on the positive side.

In general the internal rate of return is not uniquely defined. It seems that the question, whether such solutions can be interpreted at all as internal rates of return, has not been fully settled.[21] This is, however, irrelevant for our considerations, since the position taken here is the following: one should be aware of the fact that ambiguous solutions may occur. However, such situations will

[21] cf. e.g. Stucki (1988, Section 1.2) or Rolfes (1992, Section B) for many further references to this topic.

occur only under extreme circumstances with very risky assets. In practice this is almost never the case. The above example shows a typical case: the performance must be quite extreme at least over certain periods. The account suffered a loss of 98% (!) of its entire net contributions.[22]

The question, whether Equation (10.17) possesses a unique solution needs to be answered in each individual case, e.g. by determining all solutions by means of an appropriate numerical procedure such as Sturm's method.

In the following the *normal case* will always be assumed, which is defined as follows: the function resulting from Equation (10.17) possesses a unique zero and is convex around the zero, so that the zero can be found by applying the Newton iteration.

10.6.2 Modified Dietz Method

In the following M^S will denote the sum of all exogenous cash flows,

$$M^S = \sum_{i=1}^{n} M_i,$$

and M^* the sum of all linearly time-weighted exogenous cash flows,

$$M^* = \sum_{i=1}^{n} \frac{T - t_i}{T} * M_i.$$

According to Eadie the return R^{md} representing the subperiod-return R_i^N in formula (10.16) is equal to the return following from the assumption of a linear accrual rate (cf. Section 10.6.2.1):[23]

$$R^{md} = \frac{I_{n+1} - I_0 - M^S}{I_0 + M^*}. \tag{10.20}$$

According to formula (10.16) this term must be calculated for each subperiod, such that every cash flow is considered in the appropriate period.

Example 10.12

Application of the modified Dietz method within one period:

For the account statement in Table 10.26 one obtains:

$$M^* = 20 * \frac{30 - 15}{30} - 10 * \frac{30 - 20}{30} = 10 - 3.33 = 6.67,$$

and thus:

$$R^{md} = \frac{120 - 100 - 20 + 10}{100 + 6.67} = \frac{10}{106.67} = 0.0938 = 9.38\%.$$

Equation (10.20) can be interpreted in a graphic form: The numerator of the expression on the right-hand side $(I_{n+1} - I_0 - M^S)$ represents the *net increase*

---

[22] In such a case the interest in the exact value of the return is probably rather limited.

[23] cf. Eadie (1973).

Table 10.26 Account Statement with One Contribution and One Withdrawal

Date	Cash flow	Net Asset Value
01.09.2007		100
15.09.2007	+20	
20.09.2007	−10	
30.09.2007		120

during the period, while the denominator $I_0 + M^*$ may be interpreted as the *average capital* employed during the period. Due to this vividness the modified Dietz method is very popular in practice.[24] It should be borne in mind, however, that this interpretation is associated rather with the concept of an average interest rate (internal rate of return) than with the concept of the time-weighted return.

As will be shown in the following section, within one subperiod the modified Dietz method may be interpreted as an approximation to the internal rate of return. Such an interpretation is not possible over several linked subperiods. The approximation procedure (as well as the resulting error) shall be illustrated by means of an example:

Example 10.13

Application of the modified Dietz method over two subperiods:

Based on the account statement in Table 10.27 the following approximation values result for the time-weighted return in September and October:

$$R_1^{md} = \frac{130 - 100 - 20}{100 + 20 * \frac{15}{30}} = \frac{10}{110} = 0.0909 = 9.09\%,$$

$$R_2^{md} = \frac{125 - 130 + 10}{130 - 10 * \frac{10}{31}} = 0.394 = 3.94\%.$$

The modified Dietz method yields thus the following approximation to the return over the entire period.

$$R^{md} = \left(1 + R_1^{md}\right) * \left(1 + R_2^{md}\right) - 1 = 1.0909 * 1.0394 - 1 = 0.339 = 13.39\%.$$

How close this value actually lies to the true time-weighted return, depends, however, in an essential form on the realizations of the net asset value at the times of the cash flows X and Y. In order to illustrate the order of magnitude of the error, in the following table the additive error $R^{tw} - R^{md}$ is shown as a function of X and Y (cf. also Figure 10.11). According to formula (10.13) the (true) time-weighted return for the account statement in Table 10.27 is given by:

$$R^{tw} = \frac{X}{100} * \frac{130}{X + 20} * \frac{Y}{130} * \frac{125}{Y - 10} - 1 = 1.25 * \frac{X}{X + 20} * \frac{Y}{Y - 10}.$$

It is obvious that the error is particularly high if the net asset value is submitted to strong fluctuations. In addition to the market volatility, the height of the cash flow in relation to the net asset value plays a crucial role (see Table 10.28).

[24] Cf. e.g. Pieper (2002, p. 1017 et seq.), AIMR (1997) as well as Bacon (2004, p.21 et seq.).

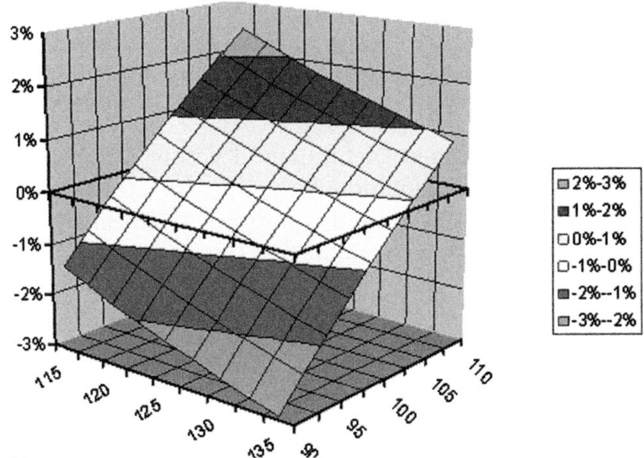

FIGURE 10.11
Error as a Function of the Values of X and Y.

Table 10.27 Account Statement with One Contribution and One Withdrawal Over Two Subperiods

Date	Cash Flow	Net Asset Value
01.09.2007		100
15.09.2007	+20	X
30.09.2007		130
20.10.2007	−10	Y
31.10.2007		125

Table 10.28 Error Resulting from Applying the Modified Dietz Method (in %)

X/Y	115.0	117.5	120.0	122.5	125.0	127.5	130.0	132.5	135.0
90.0	−1.38	−1.60	−1.82	−2.03	−2.22	−2.41	−2.59	−2.77	−2.94
92.5	−0.82	−1.05	−1.27	−1.48	−1.68	−1.87	−2.05	−2.22	−2.39
95.0	−0.29	−0.52	−0.74	−0.95	−1.15	−1.34	−1.52	−1.70	−1.87
97.5	0.21	−0.02	−0.24	−0.45	−0.65	−0.84	−1.02	−1.20	−1.37
100.0	0.70	0.47	0.25	0.04	−0.17	−0.36	−0.54	−0.72	−0.89
102.5	1.16	0.93	0.71	0.50	0.30	0.10	−0.08	−0.26	−0.43
105.0	1.61	1.38	1.16	0.94	0.74	0.55	0.36	0.18	0.01
107.5	2.04	1.81	1.58	1.37	1.17	0.97	0.78	0.61	0.43
110.0	2.45	2.22	1.99	1.78	1.58	1.38	1.19	1.01	0.84

10.6.2.1 *MODIFIED DIETZ METHOD AS A LINEAR APPROXIMATION TO THE INTERNAL RATE OF RETURN*

If one replaces the exponential by a linear accrual of interest, then Equation (10.18) assumes the following form:

$$I_0 * \left(1 + R^L\right) + \sum_{i=1}^{n} M_i * \left(1 + \frac{T - t_i}{T} * R^L\right) = I_{n+1}. \qquad (10.21)$$

For the sake of clarity an index L has been attached to the variable R. The latter equation is readily solved for R^{L}, and the reader can easily verify that R^{L} and R^{md} are identical (cf. Exercise 10.2). This relationship will be considered more closely in the following.

The return used by the modified Dietz method within individual subperiods may be interpreted as an approximation to the internal rate of return. More precisely: The return that follows from the assumption of a linear accrual of interest is identical to the return obtained from the first step in the Newton method. (cf. Appendix B of this chapter). Based on Equation (10.18) and the substitution $x := 1 + R^{iz}$ at first the function $f(x)$ will be defined as:

$$f(x) = I_0 * x + \sum_{i=1}^{n} M_i * x^{\frac{T-t_i}{T}} - I_{n+1}.$$

As the starting point for the Newton iteration the value is chosen, which corresponds to an interest rate level of zero percent: $x = 1$. The derivative of the function $f(x)$ is given by

$$f'(x) = I_0 + \sum_{i=1}^{n} M_i \frac{T - t_i}{T} * x^{\frac{-t_i}{T}},$$

such that the expression resulting from the first step of the iteration (cf. Appendix B of this chapter) is in agreement with formula (10.20)

$$x_1 = 1 - \frac{f(1)}{f'(1)} = 1 + \frac{I_{n+1} - I_0 - \sum_{i=1}^{n} M_i}{I_0 + \sum_{i=1}^{n} \frac{T-t_i}{T} M_i}$$

Figure 10.12 illustrates the relationship between the internal rate of return and the approximation by the modified Dietz method.

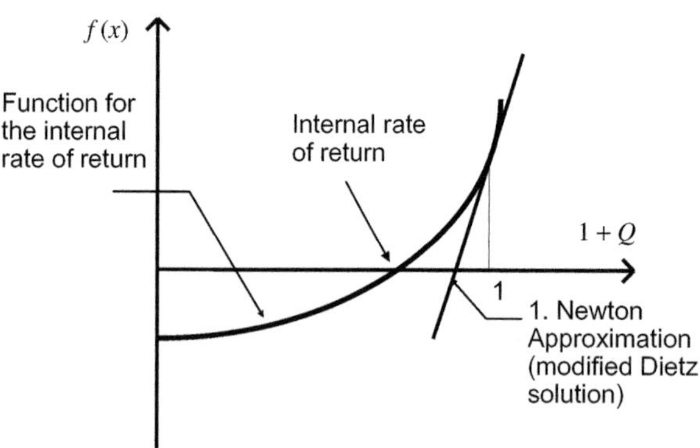

FIGURE 10.12
Illustration of the Modified Dietz Method and the Internal Rate of Return.

Table 10.29 Account Statement with One Contribution

Date	Cash Flow	Net Asset Value
01.09.2007		0
29.09.2007	100	
30.09.2007		110

10.6.2.2 *MODIFICATION OF THE MODIFIED DIETZ METHOD*

When applying the modified Dietz method in practice, often further modifications are made in the case of certain account statements. For instance, if the net asset value equals zero at the beginning of a period, then the modified Dietz formula assumes the following form:

$$R^{md} = \frac{I_{n+1} - M^S}{M^*}.$$

If the contribution occurs near the end of the period, then this will cause a divergence, as the contribution is weighted linearly. In this case it makes sense to replace M^* by M^S.

Example 10.14

Modification of the modified Dietz method in case of one contribution:

For the account statement in Table 10.29 the modified Dietz method yields:

$$R^{md} = \frac{110 - 0 - 100}{0 + 100 * \frac{30-29}{30}} = \frac{10}{3.33} = 300.3\%.$$

In view of the actual performance of the portfolio, this value overestimates the true time-weighted return by far. Modifying the modified Dietz method leads to a more realistic value:

$$R^{md} = \frac{110 - 0 - 100}{0 + 100} = \frac{10}{100} = 10.0\%$$

Analogously one obtains a divergence for the case of a net asset value of zero at the end of the period, if the initial investment was withdrawn at the beginning of the interval ($I_0 \approx -M^*$)):

$$R^{md} = \frac{-I_0 - M^S}{I_0 + M^*}.$$

In this case the formula is often modified by setting $M^* = 0$.

Applying the modified Dietz method is thus especially problematic in those cases where the sequence of cashflows in conjunction with the linear weighting leads to a low "average" capital' in the denominator. A further approximation method consists of dropping the time-weighting altogether by moving all contributions to the beginning of the interval and all withdrawals to the end. This procedure has the advantage that it leads to meaningful results even

Table 10.30 Account Statement, in Which Both the Beginning Net Asset Value and the Ending Net Asset Value are Zero

Date	Cash Flow	Net Asset Value
01.09.2007		0
10.09.2007	100	
15.09.2007	−60	
20.09.2007	−50	
30.09.2007		0

Table 10.31 Simplified Account Statement

Date	Cash Flow	Net Asset Value
01.09.2007		100
30.09.2007		110=60+50

if the beginning or the ending net asset value is zero. Such situations occur quite often in the context of attribution analyses, especially for the segments with a low weight in the portfolio or the benchmark. In such cases the other methods described above provide bad approximations or are not applicable at all.

Example 10.15

Approximation formula in an extreme situation (Table 10.30):

In this scenario the modified Dietz method (10.20) renders an unrealistic estimation:

$$R^{md} = \frac{0-0-100+110}{0+66.667-30-16.67} = \frac{10}{20} = 50\%.$$

Moving the cash flows to the endpoints of the interval yields the account statement in Table 10.31:

In this case the return is estimated at 10% (see Table 10.31).

Further modifications of this kind are possible and indeed used in practice. For instance, some systems apply the above modifications already if the beginning or ending net asset value is small compared with the exogenous cash flows; the condition might for instance be $M^S > KI_0$ for a given threshold K. Analogous modifications are also necessary when applying the BAI method or the method based on the internal rate of return.

10.6.3 Dietz Method Und BAI Method

The Dietz method stipulates that all cash flows between two valuation points occur in the middle of the period. Thus the weighting factor is always 0.5, so that the Dietz formula for the return of a single period assumes the following simple form:[25]

$$R^d = \frac{I_{n+1} - I_0 - M^S}{I_0 + \frac{1}{2}M^S}.$$

Example 10.16

Applying the Dietz method:

In this example the account statement in Table 10.26 will be revisited. Applying the Dietz method one obtains:

$$R^d = \frac{120 - 100 - 20 + 10}{100 + 10 - 5} = \frac{10}{105} = 9.52\%.$$

This value is only slightly different from the one obtained with the modified Dietz method in Example 10.12 (9.38%).

The return obtained with the (*midpoint*) BAI method[26] is the solution of the equation which results from (10.17), if the points in time of the exogenous cash flows are placed in the middle of the period ($t_i = T/2$). If Q^{BAI} denotes the interest rate resulting from the BAI method per time unit, then it holds:

$$I_0 * \left(1 + Q^{BAI}\right)^T + \sum_{i=1}^{n} M_i * \left(1 + Q^{BAI}\right)^{T/2} = I_{n+1}. \tag{10.22}$$

For the return R^{BAI} over the entire period one obtains:

$$1 + R^{BAI} := \left(1 + Q^{BAI}\right)^T.$$

Based on (10.22) one obtains the following equation for R^{BAI}:

$$I_0 * \left(1 + R^{BAI}\right) + \sum_{i=1}^{n} M_i * \left(1 + R^{BAI}\right)^{1/2} = I_{n+1}.$$

After a substitution of variables this equation can be solved by using the quadratic equation for polynomial equations of the second degree. Of the two resulting solutions usually the one closest to zero is the appropriate one.

Between the BAI method and the Dietz method there is a similar relationship as between the internal rate of return and the modified Dietz method: the Dietz method is the linear approximation to the BAI method. The chart is completely analogous to Figure 10.12.

10.6.4 Second-Order Newton Approximation

In Section 10.6.2.1 it was outlined that the modified Dietz formula may be interpreted as the first order Newton approximation to the internal rate of return. It therefore may wonder whether the quality of the approximation (to the

---

[25] cf. Dietz and Kirschman (1990).

[26] cf. Dietz and Kirschman (op. cit).

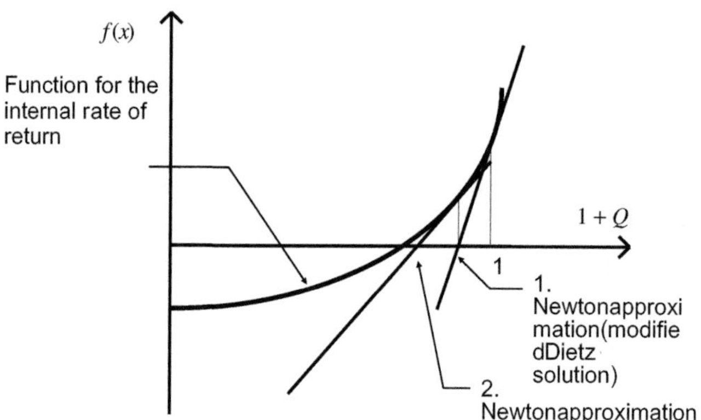

FIGURE 10.13
Illustration of the Modified Dietz Method and the Second-Order Newton Approximation.

Table 10.32 Account Statement with One Contribution

Date	Cash Flow	Net Asset Value
01.09.2007		100
15.09.2007	50	
30.09.2007		110

time-weighted return!) is further increased if one moves on to the second-degree approximation. The formula is given by (cf. Appendix B of this chapter):

$$1 + R^{2n} := x_1 - \frac{I_0 * x_1 + \sum_{i=1}^{n} M_i * x_1^{\frac{T-t_i}{T}} - I_{n+1}}{I_0 + \sum_{i=1}^{n} M_i * \frac{T-t_i}{T} * x_1^{-\frac{t_i}{T}}},$$

$$\text{where } x_1 = 1 + \frac{I_{n+1} - I_0 - \sum_{i=1}^{n} M_i}{I_0 + \sum_{i=1}^{n} \frac{T-t_i}{T} M_i}$$

Thus the approximation is of the form:

Value of the modified Dietz method + additional term.

Example 10.17

Applying the second-order Newton approximation:

For the account statement in Table 10.32 the modified Dietz method yields:

$$R^{md} = \frac{110 - 100 - 50}{100 + \frac{1}{2} * 50} = -\frac{40}{125} = -32.00\%.$$

This yields $x_1 = 0.68$. The second-order Newton approximation provides:

$$1 + R^{2n} = 0.68 - \frac{100 * 0.68 + 50 * 0.68^{0.5} - 110}{100 + 50 * 0.5 * 0.68^{-0.5}} = 0.68 + 0.0059.$$

It follows that $R^{2n} = -31.41\%$.

It's not trivial to make general statements about the accurateness of the approximation methods. The ranking varies from case to case. General assertions can only be made on the basis of statistical considerations.[27]

10.7 ACTIVE RETURN

A central task of the performance analysis for investment funds is the comparison of the portfolio returns and the benchmark returns. The *active return* (or excess return) is the basis for such analyses. In practice one distinguishes between the arithmetic (or additive) and the geometric (or multiplicative) form of the active return. In its arithmetic form the active return D^a is simply the difference between the portfolio and the benchmark return:

$$D^a := RP - RB, \tag{10.23}$$

whereas the geometric form is given by the following expression:

$$1 + D^g := \frac{1 + RP}{1 + RB}. \tag{10.24}$$

Since the return is a ratio, formula (10.24) makes mathematically more sense. (After all, portfolio and benchmark returns over different periods are also linked geometrically.) It would however be wrong to refute formula (10.24) outright. The advantage of the arithmetic form is that the active returns can be compared directly to the portfolio and benchmarks returns. This simplifies the study of performance reports in practice considerably. As regards content the difference of the approaches in practice will be explained in the following.

According to formula (10.24) the geometric active return is given by:

$$D^g := \frac{1 + RP}{1 + RB} - 1 = \frac{RP - RB}{1 + RB} = \frac{D^a}{1 + RB}. \tag{10.25}$$

By means of this expression it becomes obvious that e.g. for a positive benchmark return and a positive value of D^a the relation $D^g < D^a$ holds. Overall there are the cases shown in Table 10.33.

---

[27] See for instance Fischer and Telöken (1999). Under "normal conditions" there are surprisingly only small differences in the degree of approximation of the discussed methods (*modified Dietz method, second-order Newton approximation* and *modified BAI method*). Such conditions are in general not given, if the cash flows are large in comparison to the given net asset value or if the account's net asset value is zero at one of the end points of the interval. Under these circumstances the standard procedure will in general fail.

Table 10.33 Relationship Between the Arithmetic and the Geometric form of the Active Return

	RB>0	RB<0	RB=0
$D^a>0$	$D^g<D^a$	$D^g>D^a$	$D^g=D^a$
$D^a<0$	$D^g>D^a$	$D^g<D^a$	
$D^a=0$		$D^g=D^a=0$	

Example 10.18

Arithmetic vs. geometric form of the active return:

In the following, a portfolio relative to a (benchmark) portfolio will be considered. The benchmark portfolio is assumed to have the same performance as the benchmark and at 100 Mio. € an initial net asset value identical to the portfolio. Let the time-weighted return for the portfolio be 4% and the one for the benchmark portfolio 1%. In the arithmetic form the active return thus equals 3%. In a geometric form one obtains:

$$D^g = \frac{104}{101} - 1 = 0.0297 = 2.97\%.$$

In money units the portfolio and the benchmark portfolio gained 4 Mio. €, respectively 1 Mio. €, which amounts to an excess gain of 3 Mio. €. In contrast to the arithmetic form, which puts the excess gain in relation to the *initial* net asset value, the geometric form uses the initial net asset value adjusted by the benchmark return:

$$D^a = \frac{3}{100} = 3.00\% \quad D^g = \frac{3}{101} = 2.97\%.$$

If one assumes that no cash flows occur, the last statement formally follows from Equation (10.25):

$$D^g = \frac{D^a * I_0}{(1+RB) * I_0}.$$

I_0 denotes the net asset value at the beginning of the period.

An advantage in using the geometric form of the active return is given by the fact that active returns over different periods may be easily linked. This follows directly from Equation (10.24); if $RP_{1,\ldots,n}$ are the portfolio returns over n bordering periods (analogous notation for the benchmark), then it holds that:

$$\begin{aligned} 1 + D^g_{1,\ldots,n} &= \frac{1+RP_{1,\ldots,n}}{1+RB_{1,\ldots,n}} = \frac{1+RP_1}{1+RB_1} * \frac{1+RP_2}{1+RB_2} * \cdots * \frac{1+RP_n}{1+RB_n} \\ &= \left(1+D^g_1\right) * \left(1+D^g_2\right) * \cdots * \left(1+D^g_n\right). \end{aligned} \tag{10.26}$$

There is no such property for the arithmetic returns (see Table 10.34).

Table 10.34 A European Equity Portfolio Compared to Its Benchmark (in %)

Period	RP	RB	D^a	D^g
2005	30.14	25.84	4.30	3.42
2006	18.98	23.02	−4.04	−3.28
2005/2006	54.84	54.81	0.03	0.02

Example 10.19

Linking active returns:

Table 10.34 contains the returns of a European equity portfolio and its benchmark (EURO STOXX TR) (2. and 3. column) for different periods. Columns 4 and 5 contain the values for the arithmetic and geometric active returns respectively. It is obvious that the arithmetic returns for the years 2005 and 2006 cannot simply be combined to obtain the active return for the entire period:

$$4.30\% - 4.04\% \neq 0.03\%.$$

For the active returns in a geometric form one obtains, however:

$$(1 + 3.42\%) * (1 - 3.8\%) - 1 = 0.02\%.$$

A further effect one has to deal with when applying the arithmetic form of the active return is the base effect: the arithmetic active return increases alongside the benchmark return—*independently* of the portfolio manager's performance. This relation is essentially already expressed by Equation (10.25). In order to illustrate this fact, the arithmetic active return over two subperiods will be considered more closely. For the portfolio return over two periods it holds:

$$1 + RP_{1,2} = (1 + RP_1) * (1 + RP_2) = RP_1 + RP_2 + RP_1 * RP_2$$

respectively:

$$1 + RB_{1,2} = (1 + RB_1) * (1 + RB_2) = RB_1 + RB_2 + RB_1 * RB_2,$$

and thus:

$$RP_{1,2} - RB_{1,2} = RP_1 - RB_1 + RP_2 - RB_2 + RP_1 * RP_2 - RB_1 * RB_2.$$

If one assumes that only in the first period an active return different from zero was achieved, such that RP_2 can be identified with RB_2, then the above equation simplifies to:

$$\begin{aligned} RP_{1,2} - RB_{1,2} &= RP_1 - RB_1 + RP_1 * RB_2 - RB_1 * RB_2 \\ &= RP_1 - RB_1 + (RP_1 - RB_1) * RB_2 \\ &= (RP_1 - RB_1) * (1 + RB_2). \end{aligned} \tag{10.27}$$

A positive return during the first period will be amplified by a positive benchmark return in the second period, even if the portfolio manager did not add anything at all toward the active return during the second period. This effect does not show if one applies the geometric form of the active return, as can be readily deduced from Equation (10.26). This aspect will be taken up in Exercises 10.4 and 10.5.

Another relevant aspect in regard to the form of the active return concerns the conversion between currencies. This is for instance required, if portfolios denominated in different currencies, need to be compared with each other. If c is the return of the base currency relative to the currency, in which all portfolios shall be converted, then the portfolio return in the new currency equals $(1 + RP) * (1 + c)$. Since one obtains an analogous expression for the benchmark, $(1 + RB) * (1 + c)$, by means of (10.26) one readily deduces that the geometric active return is unchanged under this conversion. The situation is quite different in case of the arithmetic return, which after the conversion equals $(RP - RB) * (1 + c)$.[28] This circumstance is particularly relevant for internationally operating investment firms. See also Exercise 10.7.

10.8 CONTINUOUSLY COMPOUNDED RETURNS

In the previous sections the valuation of a performance history was in the focus. In this sense both the time-weighted return and the internal rate of return are realizations of a stochastic variable (net asset value), which is, of course, linked itself to other stochastic variables (stock prices, etc.). If one speaks of interest rates or the computation of compounded interest, then one assumes a different point of view: by applying a *given* interest rate one can deduce the value of an investment at a future point in time.

Example 10.20

Discrete compounding:

Let $I_0 = 100Mio.€$ be the value of an investment at $t = 0$. With an interest rate of $i = 5\%$ p.a. after two years the value of the investment will be

$$I_1 = 100Mio.€ * (1 + 5\%)^2 = 100Mio.€ * (1 + 5\%) * (1 + 5\%)$$
$$= 105Mio.€ * (1 + 5\%) = 110.25Mio.€.$$

This representation illustrates that by applying the discrete interest rate one assumes that the interest earned after one year will be reinvested at the same rate. The resulting compound interest equals 0.25 Mio. €.

The example illustrates the underlying assumptions (investment of the interest at the same rate, availability of the interest after one year). In regard to the availability other assumptions can be made that lead to different values of I_1.

[28] The deduction is quite similar to the one, which led to Equation (10.27). One only needs to substantiate RP_2 and RB_2 by c.

In case of a half-yearly payout the value of the investment after two years is as follows:

$$\begin{aligned} I_1 &= 100Mio.€ * (1 + 5\% * 1/2)^{2*2} \\ &= 100Mio.€ * (1 + 5\% * 1/2) * (1 + 5\% * 1/2) \\ &\quad * (1 + 5\% * 1/2) * (1 + 5\% * 1/2) \\ &= 110.38\, Mio.\, € \end{aligned}$$

As the accrued interest can be reinvested earlier, the end value of the investment is higher than in the example. The periodicity for the distribution of interest can be further increased. The computation of the example can be adjusted accordingly:

$$I_1 = 100\ Mio.\ € * (1 + 5\% * 1/m)^{2*m},$$

A value of $m = 4$ means for instance that the interest is distributed quarterly, $m = 12$ implies a monthly frequency and so on. In case of a continuous reinvestment of the accrued interest one speaks of a *continuously compounded interest rate*. This rate follows from a limit consideration:

$$I_1 = \lim_{m \to \infty} 100\ Mio.\ € * (1 + 5\% * 1/m)^{2*m} = 100\ Mio.\ € * e^{2*5\%} = 110,52\ Mio.\ €.$$

In this step the following relation was used:

$$\lim_{n \to \infty} \left(1 + \frac{x}{n}\right)^n = e^x,$$

where e is Euler's number ($e = 2.71828...$). The value of the accrued interest has increased further (to a finite value) compared to the value in the example. For a given (discrete) interest rate p.a. and a period of t years the following relationship holds (see Table 10.35):

$$I_1 = I_0 * e^{i*t}. \tag{10.28}$$

The concept of continuous returns can be transferred to the perspective backward in time. Since in this case the performance is fixed, the resulting interest rate varies with the chosen assumptions on the computation.

Example 10.21

Continuously compounded return:

Let's assume the (discrete) return R_d achieved for an investment in a given period, say from 0 to 1, equals 70%. The growth rate (or continuously compounded return, respectively, logarithmic return) R_{log} necessary to achieve a similar increase in the assets value on a continuous basis follows from equation (10.28) (with $i = R_{log}$):

$$R_{log} = \ln\left(\frac{I_1}{I_0}\right) = \ln(1 + R_d), \tag{10.29}$$

and thus

$$R_{log} = \ln(1 + 70\%) = 53.063\%.$$

Table 10.35 Stepwise Increase of the Periodicity. The Rightmost Column Contains the Discrete Returns

m	Periodicity	Period Rate	I_1	2 Year Return
1	yearly	5%/1 = 5.000%	100 *Mio* € $*(1+5\%*1/1)^{2*1}$	10.250%
2	half-yearly	5%/2 = 2.500%	100 *Mio* € $*(1+5\%*1/2)^{2*2}$	10.381%
4	quarterly	5%/4 = 1.125%	100 *Mio* € $*(1+5\%*1/4)^{2*4}$	10.449%
12	monthly	5%/12 = 0.417%	100 *Mio* € $*(1+5\%*1/12)^{2*12}$	10.494%
52	weekly	5%/52 = 0.096%	100 *Mio* € $*(1+5\%*1/52)^{2*52}$	10.512%
365	daily	5%/365 = 0.014%	100 *Mio* € $*\ (1+5\%*1/365)^{2*365}$	10.516%
∞	continuously	-	100 *Mio* € $*\ e^{2*5\%}$	10.517%

In Figure 10.14 the different compounding forms are illustrated graphically. The straight line represents the uniform accrual in case of a simple (linear) compounding ($t * 70\%$), the sloped curve represents the continuously growing graph resulting from the continuous compounding ($\exp(t * 53.063\%)$).

It shall be noted that each rate of return may be expressed in a discrete or continuous form. Equation (10.29) describes how a discrete rate can be transformed into a continuous one. Conversely one readily obtains the corresponding discrete rate from the continuous one:

$$R_d = e^{R_{\log}} - 1.$$

In the following further properties of the logarithmic returns will be described.

a. (Additivity of logarithmic returns)

Discrete returns are linked multiplicatively. If for $n > 0$

$$(1 + R_d) = (1 + R_{d1}) * (1 + R_{d2}) * \cdots * (1 + R_{dn})\,.$$

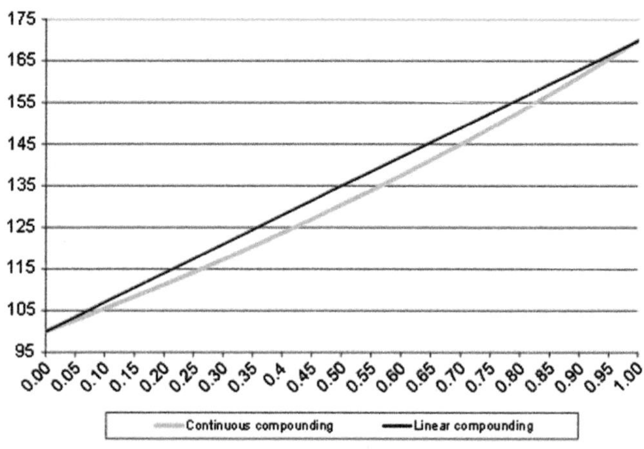

FIGURE 10.14
Different Accruals Over Time.

By means of a well-known property of the logarithm function one obtains[29]

$$\begin{aligned} R_s &= \ln(1+R_d) = \ln((1+R_{d1})*(1+R_{d2})*\cdots*(1+R_{dn})) \\ &= \ln(1+R_{d1}) \ + \ln(1+R_{d2}) + \cdots + \ln(1+R_{dn}) \\ &= R_{s1} + R_{s2} + \cdots + R_{sn}. \end{aligned}$$

Logarithmic returns over different periods are thus linked in an additive form:

$$R_s = R_{s1} + R_{s2} + \cdots + R_{sn}. \tag{10.30}$$

b. (Symmetry of the return calculation)

An increase of the price of a given security from 1000 Euro to 1200 Euro corresponds to a discrete return of 20.0%. Vice versa, for a decrease in price from 1200 Euro to 1000 Euro a discrete return of −16.67% is shown. For the logarithmic return one obtains, however:

$$R_{s1} = \ln\left(\frac{1200}{1000}\right) = -\ln\left(\frac{1000}{1200}\right) = -R_{s2}.$$

In numerical terms:

$$R_{s1} = 18.23\% \text{ and } R_{s2} = -18.23\% \tag{10.31}$$

c. (Graphic representation of the performance)

Also in the graphic representation of the performance of an investment fund using logarithmic returns has some advantages. This will be illustrated by means of an example.

Example 10.22

Comparison portfolio vs. benchmark:

Table 10.36 contains the discrete and logarithmic returns of a portfolio, which invests in US stocks, and its benchmark (S&P 500) in the period from 01.01.1995 to 31.12.2006. The graphic representation in Figure 10.15 clearly illustrates that the positive active return results primarily from the outperformance in the years from 1995 until 1998. During the following years the fund performance followed the benchmark very closely. (After 1998 the graphs are almost parallel.) Obviously the fund management strategy was switched to a passive approach. This is clearly confirmed by the listing of the performance values for the individual calendar years (Figure 10.16).

If one looks at the same graph showing the discrete return over time the effect doesn't become at all apparent. This is the consequence of the so-called base-effect already described in Section 10.7. Due to the positive return in the following year the achieved return (computed on an arithmetic basis) is increased again further. From then on there is at first a contraction (until 2003) and afterwards again an expansion of the active return, only a small fraction of which is attributable to the manager's performance. It is therefore not possible to assess the manager on the basis of Figure 10.17 without further information.

---

[29] $\ln(a*b) = \ln(a) + ln(b)$ for $a, b > 0$.

Table 10.36 Returns of the S&P 500 and a Portfolio Consisting of US Stocks (in %)

Year	S&P 500		Portfolio	
	Discrete Return	Logarithmic Return	Discrete Return	Logarithmic Return
1995	37.58	31.90	45.03	37.18
1996	22.96	20.67	30.56	26.67
1997	33.36	28.79	37.89	32.13
1998	28.58	25.14	34.19	29.41
1999	21.04	19.10	20.87	18.95
2000	−9.10	−9.55	−10.10	−10.65
2001	−11.89	−12.65	−13.12	−14.06
2002	−22.10	−24.97	−22.56	−25.57
2003	28.68	25.22	29.05	25.50
2004	10.88	10.33	11.34	10.74
2005	4.91	4.79	4.80	4.69
2006	15.80	14.67	16.01	14.85

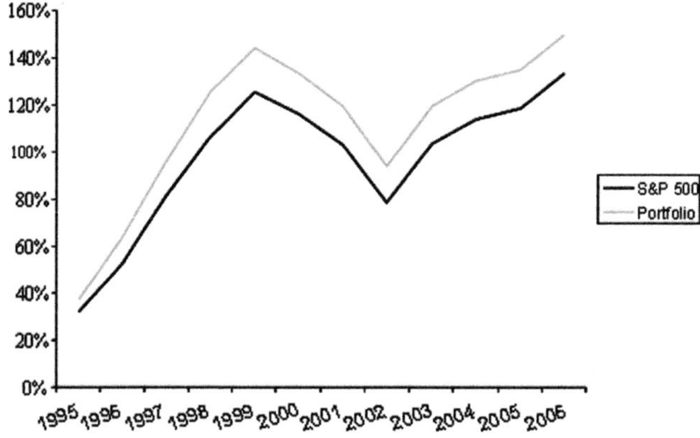

FIGURE 10.15
Cumulated Logarithmic Returns Over Time.

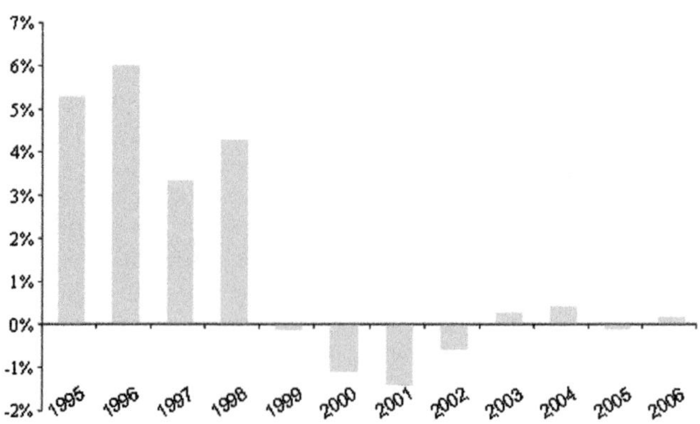

FIGURE 10.16
Active (discrete) Return in a Single Calendar Year.

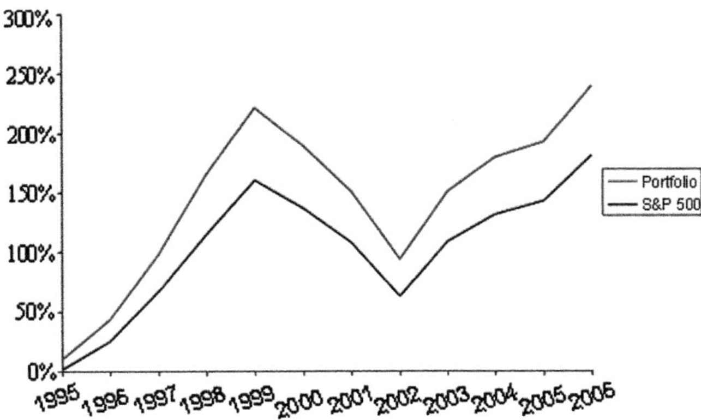

FIGURE 10.17
Cumulated Discrete Returns Over Time.

In the academic literature one often assumes that the distribution of logarithmic returns is closer to the normal distribution than the distribution of the discrete returns.[30] Research articles are thus in general based on logarithmic returns.

APPENDIX A EQUALITY BETWEEN THE TIME-WEIGHTED RETURN AND THE INTERNAL RATE OF RETURN

In this appendix the proof of the assertion in regard to the equality of the time-weighted rate of return and the internal rate of return made in Section 10.5 will be sketched:

Table 10.37 General Account Statement with One Cash-Flow

Time	Cash Flow	Net Asset Value
0		I_0
t	M	X
T		I_1

For the account statement in Table 10.37 with only one exogenous cashflow M (M may represent a contribution or a withdrawal) the internal rate of return and the time-weighted rate of return are identical, if and only if the net asset value X at t is identical to the value obtained through the internal rate of return (based on the initial net asset value I_0)[31]:

$$X = I_0 * (1 + Q)^t .$$

Q is the internal rate of return scaled to one day (cf. Section 10.3).

[30] Cf. e.g. Poddig et al. (2003, p. 105).

[31] It will be assumed that the internal rate of return is uniquely defined (cf. Section 10.6).

According to Section 10.3 the internal rate of return is defined as follows:

$$I_0 * (1+Q)^T + M * (1+Q)^{T-t} = I_1 \quad R^{irr} = (1+Q)^T .$$

A transformation of the first equation yields

$$(1+Q)^T * \left(I_0 * (1+Q)^t + M\right) = I_1 * (1+Q)^t . \tag{10.32}$$

If one sets $X = I_0 * (1+Q)^t$, then Equation (10.31) assumes the following form:

$$(1+Q)^T * (X+M) = I_1 * \frac{X}{I_0},$$

and thus

$$(1+Q)^T = \frac{X}{I_0} * \frac{I_1}{X+M}.$$

The right-hand side of this equation is identical to the time-weighted return, so that $R^{irr} = R^{tw}$ follows.

If one now assumes that the time-weighted return and the internal rate of return are identical, i.e.

$$(1+Q)^T = \frac{X}{I_0} * \frac{I_1}{X+M},$$

then it follows that:

$$\frac{I_1}{I_0} * X = (1+Q)^T * (X+M)$$

and thus:

$$X = \frac{(1+Q)^T * M}{\frac{I_1}{I_0} - (1+Q)^T} = I_0 * (1+Q)^t * \frac{M * (1+Q)^{T-t}}{I_1 - I_0 * (1+Q)^T} = I_0 * (1+Q)^t .$$

In the last step the defining equation of Q (10.31) was used, which can be stated in the following form:

$$\frac{M * (1+Q)^{T-t}}{I_1 - I_0 * (1+Q)^T} = 1.$$

This proves the assertion.

APPENDIX B SOLVING POLYNOMIAL EQUATIONS FOR THE DETERMINATION OF INTERNAL RATE OF RETURN

In Section 10.3 it was already mentioned that the equations which arise when calculating the internal rate of return (10.11) can be solved by iterative procedures. In the following this shall be explained in some detail. The account statement in Example 10.4 led to the equation $x^2 + x - 2.5 = 0$, which was solved by means of the *quadratic formula* (cf. Example 10.4).

The "simplicity" of the equation in Example 10.4 is due to the fact that only one cash flow occurred and that this cash flow fell right into the middle of the interval. In contrast to this, the account statement in Example 10.5, which includes a cash flow at the end of the third quarter, led to the equation:

$$x^4 - \frac{1}{2}x - 0.4 = 0.$$

There are also formulas for the solution of third-and fourth-degree polynomial equations.[32] Since these are quite involved and in praxis polynomial equations for account statements often have a very high degree, they will not be discussed in detail.[33] One therefore needs to refer to alternative methods, such as computer-based iterative procedures. One of them is Newton's method.

B.1 Newton's Method

Newton's method[34] is an iterative procedure, by which the zeros for a large class of mathematical functions can be determined. It is always applicable to the equations (polynomial equation) for the internal rate of return. In general, equations of the type *f(x)=0* are considered. (*f* is assumed twice differentiable.) The following steps must be carried out.

At first two values x_0 und x_1 must be found for which respectively $f(x_0) > 0$ and $f(x_1) < 0$ hold. If the function f is concave or convex[35] in the interval from x_0 to x_1 (this is precisely the case, if for all points in this interval for the second derivative of the function f holds: $f'' \geqslant 0$ or $f'' \leqslant 0$), then the (unique) zero in this interval can be found by the following iteration: at first one selects a value x_2 between x_0 and x_1. Then the sequence

$$x_3 = x_2 - \frac{f(x_2)}{f'(x_2)}, x_4 = x_3 - \frac{f(x_3)}{f'(x_3)}, \ldots, x_{n+1} = x_n - \frac{f(x_n)}{f'(x_n)} \quad (10.33)$$

converges toward the desired zero.

In the following example this method will be applied to find the solution of Equation (10.10) in Example 10.6.

Example 10.23

Determining the internal rate of return:

The starting point is the following equation, which resulted from the account statement in Table 10.4:

$$x^5 + x^3 - \frac{1}{2}x - 1.451 = 0. \quad (10.10)$$

---

[32] cf. Rottmann (1960, p. 14 et seq).

[33] At the beginning of the 19. Century the mathematicians Galois and Abel were able to show that no such formulas exist for polynomial equations of degree five or higher (cf. Bastida 1984).

[34] cf. Forster (1983, p. et seq).

[35] This can always be achieved for polynomials. One just needs to select points x_0 and x_1 sufficiently close to each other.

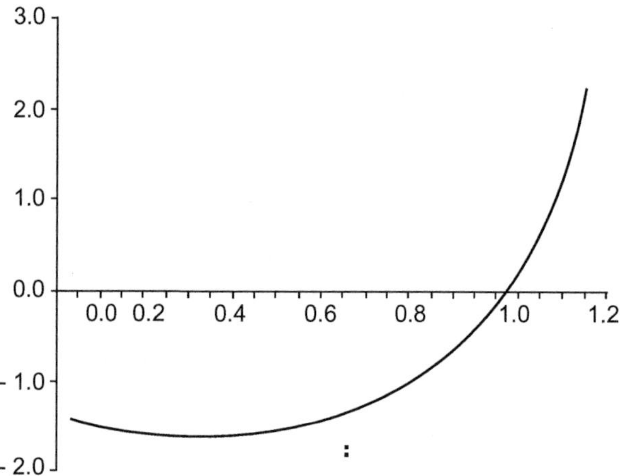

FIGURE 10.18
Graph of the Function *f*.

The function on the left-hand side of the equation, in the following denoted by *f(x)*, is mapped in Figure 10.18. The graph of the function is "convex", i.e., it "bends away" from the x-axis. To solve equation (10.10) a simple Excel spreadsheet suffices! It is readily shown that:

$$f'(x) = 5x^4 + 3x^2 - \frac{1}{2}.$$

By trial and error one obtains $f(1)=0.049$ and $f(0.9)=-0.581$, and thus appropriate starting points $x_0 = 0.9$ and $x_1 = 1.0$. Let $x_2 = 0.95$. This value will be entered into the first column of the spreadsheet in Table 10.38. After that the functions f and f' are valuated at x_2 (entries in the second and third column). Finally x_3 is determined according to equation (10.32) (entry in the fourth column). This value (or rather the formula) must then be copied into the second line of the first column. By dragging down the function values from the first column x_4 will be determined. By dragging down all four entries one can proceed to any given step in the iteration. Newton's method is characterized by a rapid convergence. Already the fourth iteration step results in a value, which is correct to the eighth digit! It follows that

$$x \approx 0.99339139.$$

Table 10.38 **Excel Spreadsheet for the Solution of the Polynomial Equation $x^5 + x^3 - \frac{1}{2}x - 1.451 = 0$**

	x	f(x)	f'(x)	x-f(x)/f'(x)
x_2	0.95000000	−0.29484406	6.14465625	0.99798382
x_3	0.99798382	0.03393138	7.44168905	0.99342418
x_4	0.99342418	0.00024039	7.31098117	0.99339130
x_5	0.99339130	−6.2632E−07	7.31004445	0.99339139
x_6	0.99339139	1.6764E−09	7.31004689	0.99339139
x_7	0.99339139	−4.4869E−12	7.31004689	0.99339139

This yields a daily interest rate of $Q = x^{\frac{1}{180}} - 1 = -0.0000368357 = -0.00368357\%$, from which the rate for the entire period, $(1+Q)^{900} - 1 = -0.0326 = -3.26\%$, and the annualized rate, $(1+Q)^{360} - 1 = -0.0137 = -1.317\%$, are readily derived.

APPENDIX C TIME-WEIGHTED RETURN AND THE UNIT PRICE METHOD

In Section 10.4 the unit price method for the return computation was described and it was asserted that this return corresponds to the time-weighted return. The case without dividends was already treated in Section 10.4. In the following it will be shown that this assertion holds in general. For this purpose the return obtained from the unit price method will be denoted by R^{up} and the time-weighted return by R^{tw}. According to the definition of R^{tw}(10.13) it holds that:

$$1 + R^{tw} = \left(1 + \frac{I_{n+1} - I_n}{I_n}\right) * \prod_{i=1}^{n}\left(1 + \frac{I_i + D_i - I_{i-1}}{I_{i-1}}\right) = \frac{I_{n+1}}{I_n} * \prod_{i=1}^{n} \frac{I_i + D_i}{I_{i-1}}. \tag{10.33}$$

One thus obtains

$$\begin{aligned}
1 + R^{tw} &= \frac{I_{n+1}}{I_n} * \frac{I_n + D_n}{I_{n-1}} * \cdots * \frac{I_1 + D_1}{I_0} \\
&= \frac{I_{n+1}}{I_{n-1}} * \frac{I_n + D_n}{I_n} * \frac{I_{n-1} + D_{n-1}}{I_{n-2}} * \cdots * \frac{I_1 + D_1}{I_0} \\
&= \frac{I_{n+1} * \left(1 + \frac{D_n}{I_n}\right)}{I_{n-1}} * \frac{I_{n-1} + D_{n-1}}{I_{n-2}} * \cdots * \frac{I_1 + D_1}{I_0} \\
&= \frac{I_{n+1} * \left(1 + \frac{D_n}{I_n}\right)}{I_{n-2}} * \frac{I_{n-1} + D_{n-1}}{I_{n-1}} * \frac{I_{n-2} + D_{n-2}}{I_{n-2}} * \cdots * \frac{I_1 + D_1}{I_0} \\
&= \frac{I_{n+1} * \left(1 + \frac{D_n}{I_n}\right) * \left(1 + \frac{D_{n-1}}{I_{n-1}}\right)}{I_{n-2}} * \frac{I_{n-2} + D_{n-2}}{I_{n-3}} * \cdots * \frac{I_1 + D_1}{I_0} \\
&= \frac{I_{n+1} * \left(1 + \frac{D_n}{I_n}\right) * \left(1 + \frac{D_{n-1}}{I_{n-1}}\right) * \cdots * \left(1 + \frac{D_1}{I_1}\right)}{I_0} \\
&= 1 + \frac{I_{n+1} * \prod_{i=1}^{n}\left(1 + \frac{D_i}{I_i}\right) - I_0}{I_0} \\
&= 1 + R^{up}.
\end{aligned}$$

It shall be emphasized again that the above derivation essentially depends on the assumption that each dividend is treated like a withdrawal and that the unit prices are adjusted accordingly ("reinvestment of the dividends").

10.9 CHAPTER-END PROBLEMS

1. (Internal rate of return, Example 10.10): Compute the internal rate of return for the account statement in Table 10.17 and confirm the value given in Example 10.10. Use the convention that a year consists of 360 days and a month of 30 days.
2. (Linear accrual): Using equation (10.21) in Section 10.6.2.1 show that the return based on the assumption of a linear accrual is identical to the one obtained when applying the modified Dietz method (10.20) over a single period.
3. (Unit price method):

   A. On 16.02.2006 the unit price of a fund was equal to 165.58 € and on 31.07.2007 169.68 €. On 15.02.2007 the fund distributed a dividend of 4.61€ per unit. A unit price of 158.60€ was published on that day. Which return did the fund achieve in the period from 16.02.2006 to 31.07.2007?

   B. On 17.02.2005 the unit price of a fund was equal to 134.64 €. On 16.02.2006 the fund distributed a dividend of 3.84 € per unit. A unit price of 165.58 € was published on that day. Which return did the fund achieve in the period from 17.02.2005 to 31.07.2007?

4. (Active return in a multiplicative form): A portfolio manager's annual bonus payment is usually based (among others) on the active return of the portfolios which he oversees. Table 10.39 shows the returns of two portfolios in the period from 01.01.1997 to 31.12.1997, which are respectively invested in German (A) and Japanese (B) equities.
   Compute the values X and Y of the active return in multiplicative form and show that the portfolio manager of fund B has achieved a higher (multiplicative) active return than the portfolio manager of portfolio A: $Y>X$.
   To what extend did the general market development (different returns in the markets) contribute toward the active return ("base effect")? Which measure is more suitable to neutralize the market effects?
   Finally: To whom would you allocate the higher bonus payment?
5. (Base effect): This exercise will illustrate the influence of the absolute return of a portfolio (respectively a benchmark) on the active return. The analysis period will be split in two subperiods. While during the first period the portfolio manager was able to realize an active return of +1% (+1% vs. 0%),

Table 10.39 Returns (in %) of a German (A) and a Japanese Equity Portfolio (B) Compared to its Respective Benchmark (DAX, TOPIX). Column 4 contains the Additive Active Return, D^m Denotes the Active Return in Multiplicative form

Portfolio	Portfolio Return	Benchmark Return	D^a (%)	D^m (%)
A (German stocks)	49.61	48.11	1.50	X
B (Japanese stocks)	−19.12	−20.12	1.00	Y

Table 10.40 Returns (in %) of a Portfolio and its Benchmark Over Two Periods

	Return 1. Period	Return 2. Period A	B	C	D
Benchmark	0	−50	0	50	100
Portfolio	1	−50	0	50	100

Table 10.41 Portfolio Returns (%) Over the Entire Period

Scenario	Benchmark	Portfolio	D^a	D^m
A	−50.0	−49.5		
B	0.0	1.0		
C	50.0	51.5		
D	100.0	102.0		

Table 10.42 Account Statement with One Contribution

Date	Cash Flow	Net Asset Value
01.04.2007		100
10.04.2007	E	120
30.04.2007		230

Table 10.43 Returns in US$ (in %)

	Fund A	Fund B	Benchmark
Return	12.0	8.0	7.0
Active return (additive form)	5.0	1.0	

during the second period the portfolio return was identical to the benchmark return. Four scenarios (A–D) will be considered for the development of the portfolio in the second period (see Table 10.40).
Compute the active returns in an arithmetic and in a geometric form, and complete Table 10.41.
Which conclusions can be drawn from this?

6. (Timing of an investment): Consider the account statement in Table 10.42 and decide, whether the cash flow *E* at 10.04.2007 was a good market timing decision. Approximate the internal rate of return with the modified Dietz method. The time-weighted return was 32%.
7. (Active return under a currency conversion): For two investment funds of a globally operating US American investment firm the following US dollar-based returns are exhibited (see Table 10.43).

Table 10.44 Returns in € (in %)

	Fund A	Fund B	Benchmark
Return	14.24	10.16	9.14
Active return (additive form)	5.10	1.02	

Over the analysis period the US$ appreciated by 2.0% against the Euro. Verify that on a €-Basis the returns are as shown in Table 10.44. The size of the active return depends thus on the currency, in which it is expressed. Recalculate these values by using the geometrical form of the active return. At which conclusions do you arrive?

CFA Institute

8. Mary Nesbitt has an investment account with a local firm, and she makes contributions to her account as funds become available. Self-employed, Mary receives money from her clients on an irregular basis. She began the month of September with a balance in her account of $100,000. She received funds in the amount of $3,000 and made a deposit into her account on September 14th. Next, she received a payment of $2,500 on the September 21st and made another contribution. The value of her account after the first contribution was $105,000, and the account value was $108,000 after the second contribution. The account was valued at $110,000 at the end of the month. Mary believes that it will be difficult, if not impossible,to determine an accurate rate of return of her account, since her cash flows do not occur on a regular basis.

A. State and justify whether an accurate rate of return can be calculated.
B. If an accurate rate of return can be calculated, determine that rate of return.

9. An investment manager has time-weighted returns for the first six months of the year as follows:

January	1.25%
February	3.47%
March	−2.36%
April	1.89%
May	−2.67%
June	2.57%

A. Calculate a time-weighted rate of return for the investment manager by chain-linking the monthly time-weighted returns.
B. Compare and contrast the time-weighted rate of return with a calculation involving adding the monthly rates of return.

10. Swennson, who manages a domestic equities portfolio of Swedish shares, has had fairly volatile returns for the last five years. Nevertheless, Swennson claims that his returns over the long run are good. Another Swedish equity manager, Mattsson, has had less volatile returns.Their records are as follows:

Year	Swennson	Mattsson
1	27.5%	5.7%
2	−18.9%	4.9%
3	14.6%	7.8%
4	−32.4%	−6.7%
5	12.3%	5.3%

Assume no interim cash flows.

A. Calculate the annualized rates of return for Swennson and Mattsson.

B. State which manager achieved a higher return over the five-year period.

Chapter 11
Indices and the Construction of Benchmarks

ABSTRACT

Managing and analyzing a portfolio against a given benchmark require detailed knowledge of the latter's composition, and an attribution analysis for a portfolio typically requires selecting an appropriate benchmark. This chapter provides an overview of benchmarks commonly used in portfolio management and analysis. Some particularly important indices are described, and a number of further indices are given in tabular form. The criteria for selecting an index are also described.

Keywords
Portfolio,
Benchmark,
Attribution analysis,
Market index,
Index selection

11.1 BASIC CONCEPTS

Both managing and analyzing a portfolio against a given benchmark require the detailed knowledge of the latter's composition. If, for example, the benchmark is an equity or bond index, one needs to know the constituent securities and their weights. The benchmark concept is also central to GIPS, as these standards require, among others, to compare the returns of a composite with those of an appropriate benchmark.[1] In addition, an attribution analysis for a portfolio typically requires the selection of an appropriate benchmark (with relevant constituent data being known).[2] Therefore, before discussing the important areas of attribution analysis and Investment Performance Standards in greater detail, we will provide the necessary overview of benchmarks commonly used in portfolio management and analysis.

In the following paragraphs, we will describe several such benchmarks and benchmark families for the equity, bond, and money markets.[3] We will discuss to what extent they meet the requirements necessary for the purposes of portfolio

[1] See CFA Insitute (2010, 5.A.1) and the discussion in Chapter 16.
[2] See Chapter 12.
[3] Benchmarks for alternative asset classes will not be discussed. For an overview of hedge fund benchmarks, see Lhabitant (2002, Chapter 11), for example.

Performance Evaluation and Attribution of Security Portfolios. http://dx.doi.org/10.1016/B978-0-12-744483-3.00011-0
© 2013 Elsevier Inc. All rights reserved.
For End-of-chapter Questions: © 2012. CFA Institute, Reproduced and republished with permission from CFA Institute. All rights reserved.

management and analysis. A complete and detailed discussion of all indices for these markets would, however, go far beyond the scope of this book. We will therefore only be able to describe some particularly important indices in detail, and a number of further indices in tabular form. The reader may be warned at this point that the descriptions of the indices refer to the time when this chapter was written (Spring 2012). Index rules and names, however, change quite often. For instance, following the dramatic events surrounding the shares of VW in October 2008, Deutsche Börse changed the rules regarding the exclusion of stocks from the DAX index. In the fixed income space, the traditional Lehman Indices were rebranded as *Barclays Capital Indices* early in 2009.[4] Often, indices disappear from the scene, as did DAX 100 or the *Neuer Markt* indices (NEMAX 50, NEMAX All Share), which existed just a few years. On the other hand, new indices are constantly being developed for increasingly specific market segments. Moreover, other changes like, for example, a new sector classification of companies are always possible. Index users should therefore make themselves acquainted in advance with the current rules. After these notes of caution, let us now address the requirements which indices should meet in practice.

Basic criteria which need to be considered when selecting a benchmark for a portfolio of securities include:[5]

1. The benchmark should be defined before investment decisions are taken.
2. It should be subject to the same restrictions as the portfolio.
3. It should exist in the long run.
4. It should be broadly diversified (and difficult to beat).
5. It should be possible to actually purchase its constituents and thus to replicate the benchmark.
6. The purchase of the benchmark constituents should be possible at low transaction costs.
7. Index levels should be published at a sufficient frequency.
8. Index compositions should be published at a sufficient frequency.
9. Sub-indices for sectors, maturity classes or country segments should be published sufficiently.
10. The history of the index should be sufficient.
11. Replication of the index over the course of time should be feasible with limited turnover.

Indices are used to describe the performance of certain groups of securities ("market segments"). DAX, for example, represents the group of German equities with very high market capitalization. Most indices are calculated essentially as (market-weighted) averages of the prices of a sample of securities which is considered to represent a market segment (see Figure 11.1).

---

[4] We cite just a few examples, which arose when this chapter was rewritten. Further examples could be added at will.

[5] See Sharpe (1992): "A benchmark portfolio should be 1) a viable alternative, 2) not easily beaten, 3) low in cost and 4) identifiable before the fact." This is reflected in items 1–6 of the following list. Properties 7–11 are additional demands often made by portfolio managers or performance analysts in practice. Item 11 is relevant to index funds, in particular.

The selection of a benchmark for a portfolio predetermines the market segment and thus, to a large extent, the absolute performance of the portfolio. Therefore, comparisons of portfolio and benchmark returns serve the sole purpose of measuring "management performance", i.e. assessing the portfolio manager's capability of varying the composition of the portfolio relative to that of the benchmark within given limits ("investment guidelines"). Investment guidelines often allow investments in off-benchmark assets. In this regard, it has to be borne in mind that, in general, comparisons of portfolio and benchmark returns only make sense if portfolio and benchmark risks are of a similar magnitude.

The problem of measuring the performance of market segments is complicated (as is similarly the case with the measurement of investment fund returns) by the fact that they typically do not constitute closed systems, the prices of most securities (e.g. stocks, bonds) being affected by coupon or dividend payments (Figure 11.1).

The construction of indices thus involves the principal question of whether (and how) these distributions are included in the calculation of the index. An index calculated without including any distributions is called a *price index*, while an index which includes distributions is called a *performance index* or *total return index* (see Figure 11.2).

$$\text{Total Return} = \text{Price Return} + \text{Income Return}$$

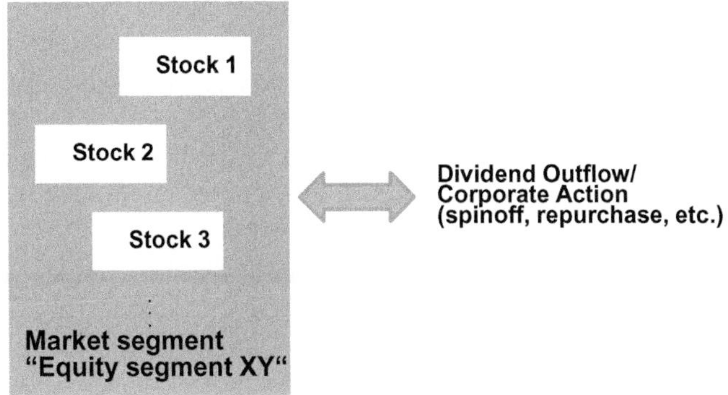

FIGURE 11.1
A Group of Securities Does Not form a Closed System (Example: Equity Market).

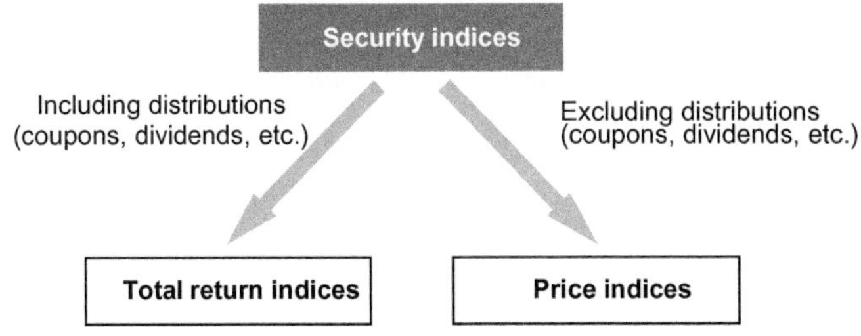

FIGURE 11.2
Basic Types of Security Indices.

Example 11.1

Including distributions in index calculations

1. The **DAX** is a performance index. Hence, dividends and bonuses (cash distributions without deduction of capital gains tax) are included in the index calculation. In addition, a DAX price index is also published. The performance index is calculated continuously once a second, whereas computation of the price index is carried out once a day, at the close of trading.
2. The **MSCI Indices** (all but a few exceptions) are published in three variants. In addition to the price indices, there are two types of performance indices, which are distinguished by the name extensions "Gross" and "Net". Essentially, the "Net Indices" include dividends *after* deduction of withholding tax, while the "Gross Indices" include dividends *before* deduction of withholding tax. The Gross Indices approximate the maximum possible dividend reinvestment. The amount reinvested is the entire dividend distributed to individuals resident in the country of the company, but does not include tax credits. For the net Indices the dividend is reinvested after deduction of withholding tax, applying the rate to non-resident individuals who do not benefit from double taxation treaties.[6]

11.2 EQUITY INDICES

11.2.1 Indices of the Dow Jones Industrial Average Type (Price-Weighted Indices)

In most equity market indices, the weight of each security is determined by its market capitalization or its free float. Important exceptions are the *Dow Jones Industrial Average* ("Dow Jones") and the *Nikkei 225*, which are calculated essentially by averaging the prices of a certain number of representative stocks.

Example 11.2

Dow Jones Industrial Average

The *Dow Jones Industrial Average* is probably the most well-known security index in the world. It dates from a time[7] when complex calculations, such as adjusting time series for dividends etc., could only be performed with great effort, as electronic computing devices did not then exist. This explains the simple calculation methodology of that index. The Dow Jones Industrial Average is calculated by averaging the share prices of 30 industrial companies (see Table 11.1). Stock splits are adjusted for by introducing a multiplier, to avoid discontinuities in the index.[8] There are no adjustments for dividends, etc.

---

[6] See MSCI (2012).

[7] The Dow Jones Industrial Average was devised by Charles H. Dow in 1896 (Dow Jones 2009).

[8] This adjustment was, however, introduced not until 1928 Dow Jones (2009). Changes in the index composition also involve the introduction of an adjustment factor.

Table 11.1 Constituents of the Dow Jones Industrial Average and their Share Prices as at 29/02/2007

3M Co.	74.08	E.I. DuPont de Nemours & Co.	50.75	JPMorgan Chase & Co.	49.40
Alcoa Inc.	33.41	Exxon Mobil Corp.	71.68	McDonald's Corp.	43.72
Altria Group Inc.	84.28	General Electric Co.	34.92	Merck & Co. Inc.	44.16
American Express Co.	56.87	General Motors Corp.	31.92	Microsoft Corp.	28.17
American International Group Inc.	67.10	Hewlett-Packard Co.	39.38	Pfizer Inc.	24.96
AT&T Inc.	36.80	Home Depot Inc.	39.60	Procter & Gamble Co.	63.49
Boeing Co.	87.27	Honeywell International Inc.	46.44	United Technologies Corp.	65.63
Caterpillar Inc.	64.42	Intel Corp.	19.85	Verizon Communications Inc.	37.43
Citigroup Inc.	50.40	International Business Machines Corp.	93.01	Wal-Mart Stores Inc.	48.30
Coca-Cola Co.	46.68	Johnson & Johnson	63.05	Walt Disney Co.	34.26

Dow Jones calculation formula

The Dow Jones Industrial Average DJ is the average of 30 share prices

K_i, adjusted for stock splits:

$$DJ = \frac{F}{30} * \sum_{i=1}^{30} K_i = \frac{1}{(30/F)} * \sum_{i=1}^{30} K_i, \qquad (11.1)$$

where F is the product of all adjustment factors since 1928.

If, for example, stock $j(1 \leqslant j \leqslant 30)$ has a two-for-one split, the shares are suddenly priced at half of their previous level. This results in the adjustment factor:

$$f = \frac{\frac{1}{30} * \sum_{30}^{i=1} K_i}{\frac{1}{30} * \left(\sum_{\substack{i=1 \\ i \neq j}}^{30} K_i + \frac{K_j}{2} \right)},$$

where the share prices immediately before the split are used. Beginning with the split, the adjustment factor F in Equation (11.1) is equal to its value before the split, multiplied by f. With f always being greater than one, the value of F is constantly growing. In other words: the sum of the 30 share prices included in the Dow Jones Industrial Average is divided by a factor which is getting smaller and smaller. On 29 February 2007, for example, the adjustment factor F was equal to 240.34. Thus, the sum of the 30 share prices included in the Dow Jones Industrial Average is divided by 0.12482483 until the next stock split or constituent change.

Using the share prices in Table 11.1, it is easy to calculate the value of the Dow Jones Industrial Average as at 29 February 2007:

$$\frac{1}{0,12482483} * (74,08 + 33,41 + \cdots + 34,26) = 12268,63.$$

As can be seen from Table 11.1, the stocks of General Electric and General Motors are included in the index with roughly equal weights, which by no means reflects the real importance of these companies. As of the reference date, General Electric had a market capitalization of more than EUR 269 billion, against only EUR 13.4 billion for General Motors.

In spite of all its popularity, the Dow Jones Industrial Average is not suitable for portfolio management purposes. In the above-mentioned case of a split of stock j, any discontinuity in the index is avoided by lowering the divisor. However, at the split date, the weight of stock j in the index falls to roughly half its previous level, i.e., going forward, any change in the share price of this stock will affect the index level only about half as strongly as it did before the split. Thus, for example, a slight underweight in this stock within a portfolio would turn into a significant overweight at the date of split. This would no longer represent the portfolio manager's view. Realigning the portfolio to the new benchmark weighting would involve additional transaction costs and would thus weigh on performance.

11.2.2 Market Capitalization Weighted Indices

The great majority of indices used in the practice of portfolio management are capitalization-weighted indices, i.e. the share prices of the index constituents are included in the calculation formula according to market capitalization or free float (cf. Example 11.3).[9]

Capitalization-weighted indices are based on the idea to represent a market or market segment by a portfolio consisting of a representative cross-section of stocks. The performance of the index is calculated as the weighted average performance of the stocks included in the portfolio, with each stock being weighted according to its market capitalization. Thus, the performance of the index reflects the "investment reality" faced by the average investor. If, for example, a highly capitalized stock appreciates in value, the index performance will reflect it accordingly.

In the following, we will explain the principle of calculating market capitalization indices. The index level at time t is given by

$$Index(t) = \sum_{i=1}^{N} K_i(t) * n_i, \qquad (11.2)$$

[9] A different approach (*fundamental indexing*) is propagated by Arnott, Hsu and West. They advocate benchmark weighting schemes based on business data for the constituent companies, such as revenues, dividends, and book values (see Arnott/Hsu/West 2008).

where $K_i(t)$ denotes the share price of stock i at time t, and n_i denotes the number of shares of that stock. We will for now ignore details like capital changes, dividends, stock splits, etc., as this would obstruct the view of the vital points. Regarding the performance of the index over a time interval from 0 to t, Equation (11.2) allows to explain the above-mentioned key aspect of the calculation methodology. Using Equation (11.2), the index return over the period from 0 to t can be expressed as follows:

$$\text{Return} = \frac{Index(t)}{Index(0)} - 1 = \underbrace{\sum_{i=1}^{N} \left(\frac{K_i(t)}{K_i(0)} - 1 \right)}_{\text{Return of stock } i} * \underbrace{\left(K_i(0) * n_i \Big/ \sum_{j=1}^{N} K_j(0) * n_j \right)}_{\text{Relative market capitalization of stock } i}. \tag{11.3}$$

Thus, the returns of the constituent stocks contribute to the return of the index according to their (relative) market capitalization. By means of the DAX indices, we will explain how this approach is implemented in practice.

Derivation of Equation (11.3):

$$\begin{aligned}
\frac{Index(t)}{Index(0)} - 1 &= \frac{\sum_{i=1}^{N} K_i(t) * n_i}{\sum_{i=1}^{N} K_i(0) * n_i} - 1 \\
&= \frac{\sum_{i=1}^{N} \frac{K_i(t)}{K_i(0)} * K_i(0) * n_i}{\sum_{i=1}^{N} K_i(0) * n_i} - 1 \\
&= \sum_{i=1}^{N} \frac{K_i(t)}{K_i(0)} * \frac{K_i(0) * n_i}{\sum_{j=1}^{N} K_j(0) * n_j} - 1 \\
&= \sum_{i=1}^{N} \frac{K_i(t)}{K_i(0)} * \frac{K_i(0) * n_i}{\sum_{j=1}^{N} K_j(0) * n_j} - \frac{\sum_{i=1}^{N} K_i(0) * n_i}{\sum_{j=1}^{N} K_j(0) * n_j} \\
&= \sum_{i=1}^{N} \left(\frac{K_i(t)}{K_i(0)} - 1 \right) * \left(K_i(0) * n_i / \sum_{j=1}^{N} K_j(0) * n_j \right).
\end{aligned}$$

Example 11.3

The equity indices of Deutsche Börse (DAX Indices)

The equity indices of Deutsche Börse are principally performance indices.[10] Unlike the Dow Jones Industrial Average, the indices are calculated including dividends and bonuses. The indices comprise stocks which are listed in the *Prime Standard* segment of the Frankfurt Stock Exchange and issued by German companies or by EU- or EFTA-based companies with a major share of their stock exchange turnover at the Frankfurt Stock Exchange.

[10] Most of them are also calculated as price indices. This calculation is, however, carried out only once a day, at the close of trading.

Within the Regulated Market, Deutsche Börse defines segments with different admission requirements. *Prime Standard* is the segment with the highest transparency standards. The requirements for admission to *General Standard* are lower. *Entry Standard* is a segment of the Open Market and thus requires significantly lower admission standards.

The DAX is a benchmark for the performance of stocks with very high market capitalization ("blue chips"). It represents the largest and most actively traded companies that are listed at the Frankfurt Stock Exchange.[11] The MDAX comprises 50 mid-cap stocks which, in terms of size and turnover, rank below the DAX. The segment below the MDAX is represented by the SDAX, which also comprises 50 stocks. The TecDAX tracks the 30 largest and most liquid technology stocks beneath the DAX.[12] All the constituents of the indices mentioned above are listed in the Prime Standard segment.

In addition to the *Selection indices*, there is a range of "broader" indices (in particular the *All Share Indices*, which comprise all the stocks of a specific market segment). The CDAX, for example, covers all the stocks listed in the Prime Standard and General Standard segments, while the HDAX is the aggregate of DAX, MDAX and TecDAX. Furthermore, there are All Share Indices for the technology, Prime Standard,[13] General Standard, and Entry Standard segments.[14]

The weight of each constituent in the DAX indices is determined by its *Free Float*,[15] i.e. the freely available and tradable portion of the capital stock.[16] However, the weight of any single company in DAX, MDAX, SDAX, HDAX and TecDAX is capped to 10 percent of the index capitalization. There are no cap limits for the broader indices.

The basis of the DAX index formula, which we will explain in the following, is given by Equation (11.2). However, the derivation of the final formula requires a number of adjustments, which will be introduced step by step.

1. Adjustments for changes in the number of shares
2. Free float adjustments
3. Adjustments for price-relevant exogenous influences resulting in capital changes ("corporate actions")
4. Standardization of the time series as of a base date

The number of shares is updated quarterly at fixed dates (third Friday of the last month of a quarter, i.e. the expiration date of the Eurex equity index futures). In addition, extraordinary adjustments may occur. The time of the adjustment immediately before the calculation at time t is denoted by τ. Thus, τ assumes at least four different values over the course of the year. With this modification, Equation (11.2) becomes

$$Index(t) = \sum_{i=1}^{N} K_i(t) * n_i(\tau), \tag{11.4}$$

---

[11] See Deutsche Börse (2011, p. 21 et seq.) for the selection criteria and the exit/entry rules for the constituents of the DAX and the other selection indices described here.

[12] The TecDAX was introduced in March 2003 to succeed the ill-famed NEMAX50.

[13] Stocks included in the DAX are not included in the Technology All Share and in the Classic-All-Share indices

[14] For a complete list of all indices published, see Deutsche Börse (2011, p. 8 et seq.).

[15] Exceptions are the *Entry Standard Index* and the *Entry All Share Index*, whose constituents are equally weighted. Until 2002, the index calculation was based on total capital stock.

[16] For the exact definition, see Deutsche Börse (2011, p. 15 et seq.).

where $n_i(\tau)$ denotes the number of shares of company i at the adjustment time τ.[17] The sum in (11.4) includes all the companies constituting the index at time t. When the index calculation was converted to a free float weighting basis, so-called free float factors $ff_i(\tau)$ were introduced, which measure the free float of the stocks as a fraction of their market capitalization. The free float factors are updated together with the number of shares. With these factors, (11.4) becomes:

$$Index(t) = \sum_{i=1}^{N} K_i(t) * n_i(\tau) * ff_i(\tau). \tag{11.5}$$

Between two regular adjustment dates, price-relevant exogenous influences (corporate actions) may occur, for which the index has to be adjusted. Deutsche Börse distinguishes the following events:[18]

1. Cash dividends and other distributions
2. Stock dividends
3. Capital increases
4. Capital reductions
5. Nominal value changes and stock splits
6. Subscription rights on other share classes
7. Spin-offs
8. Subscription rights on fixed-income instruments
9. Subscription rights on instruments with embedded options

In addition, there are special rules for distributions which exceed 10 percent of the market capitalization of the distributing company, as well as for extraordinary free float adjustments.

Each of these events concerning stock i is adjusted for by means of an appropriate correction factor $c_i(t)$, with which the i-th summand in (11.5) is multiplied until the next adjustment of $n_i(\tau)$. For example, the correction factor for a distribution (dividend, bonus, or special distribution) of company i is given by:

$$c_i(t) := \frac{K_i(t-1)}{K_i(t-1) - D_i(t)},$$

where $K_i(t-1)$ is the closing price of stock i on the day before the ex date and $D_i(t)$ is the distribution on day t. This adjustment is based on the assumption that the distribution is reinvested in the same stock (*operation blanche*[19]). If multiple events within a quarter require adjustments, the product of the respective correction factors is also denoted by $c_i(t)$. Including the correction factors, the index Equation (11.5) becomes:

$$Index(t) = \sum_{i=1}^{N} K_i(t) * n_i(\tau) * ff_i(\tau) * c_i(t). \tag{11.6}$$

As soon as the numbers of shares are updated in the last month of a quarter, all correction factors are set to 1. This means that the accumulated income from distributions

---

[17] In addition to the quarterly adjustment dates, the number of shares may also be adjusted in the event of extraordinary circumstances, such as mergers or extraordinary free float adjustments (see Deutsche Börse (2010, S. 41 et seq.)).

[18] See Deutsche Börse (2011).

[19] See Loistl (1990, p. 26 et seq., p 473 et seq.). If the distribution accounts for more than 10 percent of the market capitalization of the distributing company, the part of the distribution exceeding the 10 percent will not be reinvested in a single stock, but in the overall index portfolio per unscheduled chaining date (see Deutsche Börse (2011, p. 41)).

and capital changes is allocated to the index constituents according to the respective new weights. A *chaining factor* needs to be introduced to avoid a gap between the index values before and after the adjustment of the numbers of shares. Equation (11.6) is thus expanded to:

$$Index(t) = V(t) * \sum_{i=1}^{N} K_i(t) * n_i(\tau) * ff_i(\tau) * c_i(t). \tag{11.7}$$

$V(t)$ denotes the chaining factor valid at time t. The chaining factor is modified only at a few adjustment dates. Besides the days on which the numbers of shares are updated, these are the dates on which the index composition changes. To avoid gaps in the index, the following must hold on the chaining dates on which the numbers of shares are updated:

Index value at the end of the chaining date with the old chaining factor =
Index value at the end of the chaining date with the new chaining factor.

Thus,

$$V(\tau) * \sum_{i=1}^{N} K_i(t) * n_i(\tau) * ff_i(\tau) * c_i(t) = V(\tau+1) * \sum_{i=1}^{N} K_i(t) * n_i(\tau+1) * ff_i(\tau+1), \tag{11.8}$$

where the prices $K_i(t)$ are the closing prices on the chaining date. The new chaining factor $V(\tau + 1)$ is derived from Equation (11.8) and is valid from the beginning of the day after the chaining date. An analogous procedure is applied on the dates on which the index composition changes.

The only thing left to do is the standardization of the indices. For example, the DAX, MDAX, TecDAX, and SDAX are standardized so that they assume a base value of 1000 on 30 December 1987. This leads to the final index formula:

DAX index formula (*Laspeyres* index formula[20])

The DAX indices are calculated according to the following formula:

$$Index(t) = V(t) * \frac{Base}{\sum_{i=1}^{N} K_{i,0} * n_{i,0}} * \sum_{i=1}^{N} K_i(t) * n_i(\tau) * ff_i(\tau) * c_i(t), \tag{11.9}$$

where:
$K_i(t)$: share price of stock i at time t
$K_{i,0}$: closing price of stock i before the first inclusion in an index of Deutsche Börse
$n_i(\tau)$: number of shares of company i at time τ
$n_{i,0}$: number of shares of company i before the first inclusion in an index of Deutsche Börse
$ff_i(\tau)$: free float factor of stock i at time τ
$c_i(t)$: correction factor of stock i at time t
$V(t)$: chaining factor at time t
τ: date of last adjustment of the numbers of shares before time t
Base: index value as of 30 December 1987.

[20] See Bamberg/Baur (1998, p. 55 et seq.) and (Hartung (1999, p. 63 et seq.).

For the Prime Standard segment as well as for a portfolio comprising all companies listed in Prime Standard, General Standard and Entry Standard, Deutsche Börse calculates 18 sector indices and 63 subsector indices, which are designed as All Share indices. In addition, nine so-called supersector indices consisting of companies with an average daily trading volume of at least EUR 1 million are calculated for the Prime segment.

In the practice of asset management, these broad indices are not commonly used as benchmarks. This is the domain of the traditional Prime Standard selection indices, for which Deutsche Börse does not calculate any (official) sector indices. Such indices are, however, required to perform a sector-based attribution analysis according to Brinson et al. (cf. Chapter 12). Therefore, many users in practice calculate these indices themselves, applying the DAX index formula.

Besides the Laspeyres formula, there are still other formulas for the calculation of equity indices. The most well-known ones are the Paasche and value index formulas. The value index formula differs from the Laspeyres formula only in that the number of shares is updated continuously. This reduces (compared with the Laspeyres formula) the number of correction factors required. For example, the value index formula is applied to calculate to S&P 500. We will not go into the details of the Paasche method, as it is very rarely used for the calculation of equity market indices.[21]

Example 11.4

STOXX indices

The STOXX index family was launched in 1998. The indices are designed and compiled by STOXX Ltd., a joint venture between Deutsche Börse and SIX Group AG. In advance of the creation of the Eurozone, STOXX initially focused on European indices, but now offers a comprehensive global family of equity indices.

Of central importance to the index family is the *Industry Classification Benchmark (ICB)*, which classifies companies on four hierarchy levels: industries, supersectors, sectors, and subsectors. A number of regional and sector indices, in particular sub-indices for supersectors and sectors, are derived from this classification scheme.[22] This is illustrated in Figure 11.3, which, by way of example, illustrates the classification of the Finnish paper company *Ahlstrom*. As such, it is included in the *Paper* subsector, which comprises "producers, converters, merchants and distributors of all grades of paper"[23] and is

[21] For these indices, see Loistl and Kobinger (1993), Bamberg/Baur/Krapp (2009, p. 50 et seq.), and Hartung (1999, p. 63 et seq.). The calculation formula for the Paasche index can be derived from Equation (11.3) by substituting the end period weights for the weights at the beginning of the observation period. This is relevant, for example, when the price development of a basket of goods is measured based on the basket's composition in the current reporting period (rather than the base year). A Paasche index used in finance is, by way of example, the FAZ index, which has been compiled by the *Frankfurter Allgemeine Zeitung* on a daily basis since 1961. Another example is the SSE Composite Index of the Shanghai stock exchange (cf. Table 11.6).

[22] The indices of FTSE Group, a subsidiary of the London Stock Exchange, are also based on the ICB scheme. We will not regard this index family in more detail, although it is of similar importance to the financial industry as the STOXX and MSCI families.

[23] It "excludes makers of printed forms [...] and manufacturers of paper items such as cups and napkins ..." These are classified under different subsectors (*Nondurable Household Products, Business Support Services*, see STOXX (2012, p. 82).

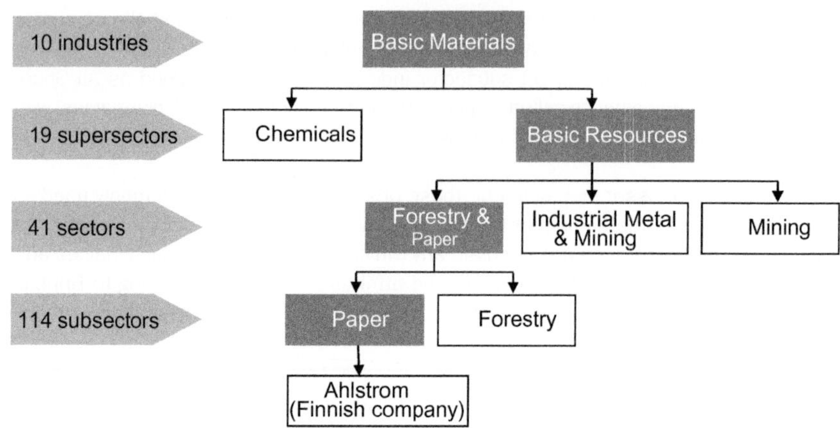

FIGURE 11.3
ICB Sector Classification.

contained in the *Forestry & Paper* sector. This is a part of the *Basic Resources* supersector, which, together with the *Chemicals* supersector, forms the *Basic Materials* industry.[24]

The *STOXX Global 1800 Index* contains the 600 largest companies (in terms of free float) from the developed markets of each of the regions *Europe* (Austria, Belgium, Denmark, Finland, France, Germany, Greece, Iceland, Ireland, Italy, Luxembourg, the Netherlands, Norway, Portugal, Spain, Sweden, Switzerland, United Kingdom), *North America* (USA, Canada) and *Asia/Pacific* (Australia, Hong Kong, Japan, New Zealand, Singapore). For select European regions (Europe, Eurozone, Europe ex UK, etc.) so-called Total Market Indices (TMI) are compiled, which cover 95 percent of the free float market capitalization of the respective investible stock universe by region (STOXX Europe TMI, EURO STOXX TMI, etc.). The STOXX indices are calculated with the Laspeyres index formula.

In addition to the indices mentioned above, STOXX publishes a variety of further indices. The most well-known of these are arguably the blue-chip indices STOXX Europe 50 and EURO STOXX 50, which consist of 50 stocks covering the largest supersector leaders in Europe and the Eurozone, respectively. The weight of each constituent company is again determined by its free float market capitalization, with a weighting cap factor of 10% of the total free float of the index. No sector indices are published for the blue-chip indices.

The Total Market indices are also the basis of so-called style indices. These are derived by classifying all stocks by means of a multivariate data analysis (based on six factors such as dividend yield, price/book ratio, earnings growth, etc.) into one of five clusters: strong growth and weak growth, strong value and weak value, and neutral. In addition, there are a number of indices with a fixed number of stocks, such as the STOXX 600, the STOXX Eastern Europe 300, etc. For all TMI indices the indices for the corresponding industries, supersectors, sectors and subsectors are calculated and (provided the indices have enough components) disseminated. Furthermore for all TMI indices size indices covering different ranges of total or free float market capitalization (large, mid and small) are available. For a complete overview of the STOXX indices, see STOXX (2012).

---

[24] For the sake of simplicity, we will not subdivide the *Chemicals, Industrial Metals & Mining* and *Mining* sectors.

Example 11.5

MSCI Indices

Another very comprehensive family of equity indices is provided by MSCI. The company uses a different company classification scheme than STOXX, namely the so-called *Global Industry Classification Standard (GICS)*. GICS also comprises four hierarchy levels (sectors, industry groups, industries, sub-industries), which, however, differ from the ICB classification (also in terminology). This is illustrated in Figure 11.4, again using the Finnish company *Ahlstrom* as an example. It is listed in the *Paper Products* sub-industry, which comprises all paper manufacturers excluding those specializing in paper packaging. The latter are classified in a separate sub-industry. The *Paper Products* sub-industry is included (together with *Forest Products*) in the *Paper & Forest Products* industry, which in turn is a component of the *Materials* industry group. In this case, the industry group is identical with the sector, which is also termed *Materials*.[25]

The MSCI indices cover 24 developed markets and 21 emerging markets. The country and regional indices are calculated in USD, EUR, and other terms. These country indices are aggregated into a number of major regional indices, a selection of which are presented in Table 11.2. In addition to these indices MSCI computes and publishes also indices for 31 so-called *Frontier markets*, which includes countries like Tunisia, Lebanon, Nigeria, and Vietnam.

In addition, the developed market country indices and most of the regional indices are segmented into sector indices according to the GICS classification (sectors, industry groups, and industries). These indices are therefore particularly suitable for the purpose of attribution analyses.

Like the DAX and STOXX indices, all MSCI indices are calculated using the Laspeyres index formula with a free float-adjusted market capitalization weighting scheme.

The MSCI indices capture various degrees of the overall free-float adjusted market capitalization. The *MSCI Global Standard indices* cover around 85% and the *MSCI Global Investment Market indices* around 99%. The *MSCI Small Cap indices* include those stocks in the Investment Market index which are not included in the standard indices.

The indices are calculated both as price and as performance indices (see Example 11.1).

For each segment, MSCI Barra calculates size indices covering different ranges of market capitalization (Micro, Small, Mid and Large Cap). In addition, a comprehensive set of style indices (Value, Growth) is published. For each developed market as well as several emerging markets, MSCI also calculates so-called hedged indices, which are

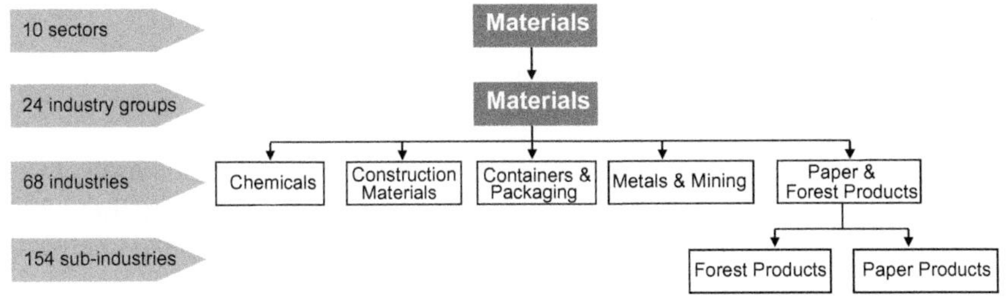

FIGURE 11.4
GICS Sector Classification.

[25] See http://www.msci.com/products/indices/sector/gics/gics_structure.html.

Table 11.2 MSCI Regional Indices

Index Name	Countries	Number of Constituents	Number of Countries
MSCI World	Global developed markets	1613	24
MSCI Europe	European developed markets	449	16
MSCI EMU	Eurozone countries	250	11
MSCI EAFE[a]	Developed markets in Europe, Australia and the Far East	924	22
MSCI EM	All emerging markets	825	21
MSCI North America	USA, Canada	689	2
MSCI ACWI[a]	Global developed and emerging markets	2433	45

[a]*EAFE = Europe, Australia, Far East; ACWI = All Countries World Index (www.msci.com as of March 2012).*

hedged against exchange rate fluctuations (relative to the base currency). For example, fully or partially hedged indices are available for the EAFE Index and its components. The hedge is accomplished by selling the full currency exposures of the index in the one-month forward market at each end of month.

Besides the above-mentioned families of cross-country equity indices, there are a number of country-specific indices usually published by local stock exchanges. Several indices for the German equity market have already been described in Example 11.3. Further indices for major capital markets are shown in Table 11.3. While being widely known, many of these indices are not suitable for the purpose of portfolio analysis, as no sector indices are available. This holds in particular for indices which, like DAX 30, CAC 40, or S&P/MIB, comprise only a few stocks but are perceived by the general public as barometers of their respective local market. Moreover, they are often available only as price indices.

Almost a plethora of indices is available for the US equity market, the by far most important equity market in the world. Table 11.4 contains a (limited) selection of major indices. For select emerging market indices see Table 11.5.

11.3 BOND INDICES

Bond indices which are based on real bonds[26] (so-called basket indices) are calculated in a similar way as market capitalization-weighted equity indices. By way of example, we illustrate the calculation of the *FTSE Global Bond Index Series*.

[26] Deutsche Börse also calculates synthetic bond indices like the REX. In view of their decreasing practical importance, we will not discuss these indices.

Table 11.3 Equity Indices of Major Capital Markets

Country	Index	Description
Japan	TOPIX(Tokyo Stock Price Index)	Broad Japanese equity index comprising all companies listed on the first section of the Tokyo Stock Exchange (around 1700 stocks as of February 2012)
	Nikkei 225	Blue chip index (price-weighted average of highly liquid stocks)
United Kingdom	FTSE 100(Financial Times Stock Exchange Index)	Blue chip index of the 100 most highly capitalized stocks (price index; total return version available)
	FTSE All-Share	Broad equity index; aggregation of the FTSE 100, FTSE 250 and the FTSE Small Cap Indices (price index; total return version available)
France	CAC 40	Blue chip index (price index, also available as a total return index)
	SBF 120	Large/mid cap index comprising the 40 stocks in the CAC 40 and a selection of 80 additional, particularly liquid stocks listed on the Premier Marché (price index, also available as a total return index (gross and net))
Italy	FTSE MIB	Blue chip index comprising the 40 most liquid stocks listed on the Milan stock exchange (price index; successor to S&P MIB)
	FTSE Italia All Share	Broad Italian equity index (price index successor to MIBTEL)
Switzerland	SPI	Total market index for the Swiss equity market (total return index)
	SMI	Blue chip index comprising the 20 largest and most liquid stocks from the large/mid cap segment of the SPI; price index, also available as a total return index
Netherlands	AEX(Amsterdam Exchange Index)	Blue chip index comprising up to 25 of the most liquid stocks traded on the Euronext Amsterdam (price index)
Spain	IBEX 35	Blue chip index of the 35 most important Spanish companies (free float-weighted price index)

Table 11.4 A Selection of Major US Equity Indices

Index	Description
Dow Jones Industrial Average	Price-weighted average of 30 blue chip stocks
Dow Jones Transportation Average	Price-weighted average of major transportation stocks
Dow Jones Utility Average	Price-weighted average of major utility stocks
Dow Jones Composite Average	Price-weighted average of all stocks included in the other Dow Jones Averages
Standard & Poor's 500 (S&P 500)	Comprises 500 stocks selected on the basis of market capitalization, liquidity and sector representation; free float market capitalization-weighted index calculated as a price index and in two performance index versions (total return and net total return).
Standard & Poor's 100 (S&P 100)	Index of 100 blue chips included in the S&P 500
Russell 3000	Performance index comprising the 3000 most highly capitalized US stocks (in terms of free float)

(Continued)

Table 11.4 Continued

Index	Description
Russell 2000	Small cap performance index comprising all constituents of the Russell 3000 Index except for those included in the Russell 1000
Russell 1000	Performance index comprising the 1000 most highly capitalized US stocks (in terms of free float)
Dow Jones Wilshire 5000 Composite Index	Comprises the primary equity issues (common stock, REIT or limited partnership) of all US companies; various versions: price index, performance index, market capitalization/free float weighting
Dow Jones Wilshire 4500 Composite Index	Comprises all constituents of the Dow Jones Wilshire 5000 Composite Index except for those included in the S&P 500
Nasdaq Composite	Comprises all stocks and similar securities (ADRs, limited partnerships, REITs, tracking stocks) listed exclusively on the Nasdaq; market capitalization-weighted price index
NYSE Composite	Comprises all common stocks listed on the New York Stock Exchange; free float market capitalization-weighted; calculated both as a price index and as a performance index
MSCI USA	Country index from the MSCI index family

Table 11.5 Equity Indices of Select Emerging Markets

Country	Index	Description
Brasil	Bovespa	Broad Brazilian equity index representing about 70% of the market capitalization of the stocks listed on the São Paulo stock exchange (total return index)
China	SSE Composite Index	Comprises all A and B shares listed on the Shanghai stock exchange. The calculation is based on the Paasche index formula (price index)
Hong Kong	Hang Seng Index	Comprises 45 companies which represent around 60% of the overall market capitalization of the Hong Kong stock exchange (free float market capitalization-weighted price index)
India	BSE Indey	Free float market capitalization-weighted selection index of 30 companies listed on the Bombay stock exchange (price index)
South Korea	KOSPI	The Korea Composite Index (KOSPI) comprises all stocks listed on the Korea stock exchange (price index)
Singapore	FTSE Straits Times Index	Capitalization-weighted index comprising the top 30 companies on the Singapore exchange ranked by market capitalization
Mexico	IPC	The índice de Precios y Cotizaciones (IPC) comprises the 35 largest and most liquid stocks of the Mexican stock exchange (price index)

(Continued)

Table 11.5 Continued

Country	Index	Description
Taiwan	TAIEX	The Taiwan Capitalization Weighted Stock Index (TAIEX) comprises all stocks listed on the Taiwan stock exchange (with a few exceptions) (price index)
South Africa	FTSE/JSE All-Share Index	Capitalization-weighted composite index of the Johannesburg Securities Exchange (price index)
Thailand	Stock Exchange of Thailand (SET)	Composite index of the Stock Exchange of Thailand (SET (price index)

Example 11.6

FTSE Global Bond Index Series

The *FTSE Global Bond Index Series* is divided into four index families.[27] One of them is the family of government bond indices (*FTSE Global Government Bond Indices*), which consists of 22 country indices and five regional indices (Global, Eurozone, Europe ex Eurozone, North America, and Asia Pacific). In addition, there are the family of Pfandbrief indices (*FTSE Covered Bond Indices*: 14 country indices), the family of corporate bond indices (*FTSE Corporate Bond Indices*: *Euro Corporate* and *Sterling Corporate*), and the index family of EUR-denominated emerging market bonds (*FTSE Euro Emerging Market Bond Indices*).

The FTSE Global Bond Indices are calculated using the methodology proposed by the *European Federation of Financial Analysts Societies* ("EFFAS standardized rules").[28] All indices have sub-indices for the following maturity bands: 1–3, 3–5, 5–7, 7–10, and 10+ years. For the *Corporate Bond Indices*, additional sub-indices are calculated for the maturity bands 1–5, 5–10, 5–15, 10–15, and 15+ years. Moreover, these indices have sub-indices for the ten ICB industries. The *Corporate Bond Indices* and the *Euro Emerging Market Bond Indices* also cover rating sub-indices.

In general, bullet bonds maturing in one year or more are considered for inclusion in the FTSE Global Bond Index Series.[29] Zero coupon bonds and strippable bonds are eligible, more complex types such as convertible bonds, variable interest bonds, etc. are, however, excluded from the indices.

Each index is calculated as a clean price index (capital index) and as a total return index. The clean price index reflects only the price changes of the bonds in the index. Based on its value at time $t-1$, the clean price index $CI(t)$ at time t is calculated as follows:

$$CI(t) = CI(t-1) * \frac{\sum_i P_i(t) * N_i(t-1)}{\sum_i P_i(t-1) * N_i(t-1)}, \tag{11.10}$$

where

$P_i(t)$: "clean price"[30] of bond i at time t

$N_i(t)$: nominal amount outstanding of bond i at time t.

[27] See, generally, FTSE (2006) for a background to this presentation.

[28] See Brown (2002).

[29] An exception is the Turkish Lira Government Bond Index, with minimum maturity eligibility being six months.

[30] Value of the bond without accrued interest.

The total return index RI includes both accrued interest and coupon payments. Based on its value at time $t-1$, the total return index at time t is calculated as follows:

$$RI(t) = RI(t-1) * \frac{\sum_i (P_i(t) + A_i(t) + CP_i(t) + C_i(t)) * N_i(t-1)}{\sum_i (P_i(t-1) + A_i(t-1) + CP_i(t-1)) * N_i(t-1)} \quad (11.11)$$

where
$A_i(t)$: accrued interest of bond i at t
$C_i(t)$: coupon payment of bond i from $t-1$ to t
$CP_i(t)$: correction term for coupon payments in the ex-dividend period.[31]

Further important bond indices are described in the following example.

Example 11.7

Further bond indices

1. J.P. Morgan Government Bond Index Series
The *J.P. Morgan Government Bond Index Series* is probably the most important family of international bond indices.[32] The broad index (*Broad*) includes government bonds from 27 countries. The classical global index is focused on 13 developed countries (Australia, Belgium, Canada, Denmark, France, Germany, Italy, Japan, Netherlands, Spain, Sweden, the United Kingdom, and the USA). Additional indices include the *J.P. Morgan EMU Government Bond Index*, which covers government bonds from the 17 (as of April 2012) member states of the European Monetary Union, which fulfill certain liquidity standards. Only bullet bonds maturing in one year or more are considered for inclusion in the indices.[33] The index calculation is based on the closing prices (mid prices) in the respective locations of J.P. Morgan.[34] The WM/Reuters exchange rates as at 16.00 (London time) are used for currency translation. Only bonds which are officially quoted and tradable in the short term qualify for the indices.

To calculate the indices, the bonds dirty prices are weighted by the respective market values (nominal amounts outstanding). A comprehensive set of maturity sub-indices (1–3, 3–5, 5–7, 7–10, 1–5, 1–7, 1–10, 10–15, 3+, 5+, 7+, 10+, 15+ years) is calculated for each index.

2. Barclays Capital Indices (formerly: Lehman Brothers Indices)
A very popular index, especially in North America, is the *US Aggregate Index*,[35] which covers a wide range of USD-denominated investment grade bonds. It comprises primarily government and corporate bonds, but also certain *mortgage-* and *asset-backed securities* (MBS, ABS) as well as *commercial mortgage-backed securities* (CMBS). Specific indices are calculated for the individual segments.

[31] The coupon payment is already included in the bond price, but has not yet been effected. See the discussion in Section 16.4.1.
[32] All information given here is based on JPMorgan (2002) and JPMorgan (2007) or has been researched from the (restricted) website https://mm.jpmorgan.com (access in February 2009).
[33] In particular, variable interest bonds, convertible or callable bonds, perpetuals, or bonds issued in local markets for tax purposes are not eligible for the indices.
[34] There are exceptions from this rule in certain markets (see JPMorgan (2002)).
[35] See Barcleys (2012).

The index is also weighted by market capitalization (including accrued interest) and usually based on bid prices. Interest and principal payments are held in the index without a reinvestment return until month-end when it is removed from the index.

The *US Aggregate Index* is a component of the *Global Aggregate Index*. Additional indices include the *Pan-European* and the *Asian-Pacific Aggregate Index*. They require rather high nominal amounts outstanding, namely at least EUR 300/£ 200 million for the Pan-European Aggregate Index and at least JPY 35 billion for the Asian-Pacific Aggregate Index.

3. Markit iBoxx EUR Benchmark Indices

The *Markit iBoxx EUR Benchmark Indices* cover four important bond segments: sovereigns, sub-sovereigns (supranationals, regions, public banks, agencies, etc.), collateralized, and corporates. Besides the overall index, there are sub-indices such as maturity band indices (1–3, 3–5, 5–7, 7–10, 10+ years) as well as various sector and rating indices. Well-known examples include the *iBoxx € Corporates* and the *iBoxx € Sovereigns*.[36]

The indices are calculated using bid prices, with the (bid *and* ask) quotes provided by the banks being filtered in a consolidation process. The bonds in these indices, too, are market capitalization-weighted (based on nominal amounts outstanding).

Bonds eligible for the indices include fixed coupon bonds, zero coupon bonds, step-ups, as well as dated and undated subordinate corporate bonds. Undated bonds must be callable. In the index calculation, these bonds are always assumed to redeem at the first call date. The indices may also include event-driven bonds, such as rating- or tax-driven bonds with a maximum of one coupon change per period. At each rebalancing date, bonds maturing in less than one year are removed from the index.

All bonds must be rated investment grade by at least one rating agency (Standard & Poor's, Moody's or Fitch). If a bond is rated by several agencies, then the average rating is attached to the bond.[37]

The *Markit iBoxx EUR Liquid Indices* are derived from some of the benchmark indices, including only particularly liquid issues and applying stricter inclusion criteria (higher minimum amount outstanding for corporates, longer minimum time to maturity, maximum age conditions).

4. eb.rexx index family

Since 2002, Deutsche Börse has been calculating an index family which in many respects resembles the iboxx family. The *eb.rexx index family* comprises overall indices as well as special indices for the government bond *(Government)* segment, the asset-covered issues *(Collateralized)* segment, and the government-guaranteed bonds *(Sub-Sovereigns)* segment.[38] The indices include bonds traded on the Eurex Bonds platform. Eligible for inclusion are fixed-income bonds with a maturity of at least 1.5 years, an investment grade rating, and a minimum amount outstanding of EUR 4 billion for governments and EUR 1.5 billion for non-governments. Selection indices are calculated for the *Government* and *Pfandbriefe* segments: *eb.rexx Government Germany (Select)* and *eb.rexx Jumbo Pfandbriefe (Select)* comprise the 25 most liquid government bonds and Jumbo Pfandbriefe issues, respectively, with a time to maturity between 1.5 and 10.5 years. The indices are calculated as basket indices in price and performance index versions. The calculation methodology is in line with the EFFAS standardized rules described above.

[36] The information given here is based on Markit (2012).

[37] Prior to 1 January 2008, the lowest rating was used in these cases. No rating is required for Eurozone sovereigns.

[38] The information given here is based on Deutsche Börse (2009).

If applicable, sub-indices for the maturity bands 1 month–1 year, 1.5–2.5, 2.5–5.5, 5.5–7.5, 7.5–10.5, 5.5–10.5, and 10.5+ years are calculated for each bond index.

5. Citigroup Indices (formerly: Salomon Smith Barney Indices)
Citigroup publishes another comprehensive family of bond indices. While many of them are focused on the US bond market, a number of international indices are calculated, too. In the following, we will take a closer look at two indices.[39]

Similar to Barclays" *US Aggregate Index*, Citigroup's *US Broad Investment-Grade (USBIG) Bond Index* covers the segment of investment grade bonds denominated in USD. In particular, the index includes among others US Treasury and agency (e.g. Fannie Mae) issues, ABS and MBS, Yankee bonds, corporates, and supranationals. Coupon payments are "reinvested at the daily average of the one-month Eurodeposit rate for the calculation period". Eligible for inclusion in the index are bullet bonds, bonds with embedded options, and sinking bonds.

The *World Government Bond Index* covers the most important and liquid investment grade government bond markets (23 countries as of April 2012). Like the USBIG index, it applies a market capitalization weighting scheme with monthly updates. Coupon payments are reinvested at the daily average of local currency one-month Eurodeposit rate (except Australia). Also like the USBIG index, the World Government Bond Index includes bullet bonds, bonds with embedded options, and sinking bonds.

Colin warns—and the authors of this work agree with him—that the inclusion of coupon payments and treatment of cash positions constitute a general problem in the calculation of a bond index.[40] Given the differences in the individual coupon payments (odd first coupon, differences in the treatment of the ex-dividend period, etc.), calculating a bond index is a very complex thing to do. Some index providers do not publish all the information needed to recalculate or replicate the indices.[41] Also, the quality of a bond index depends on the quality of the prices used. Many bonds are very seldom traded. The index provider thus needs to have suitable, up-to-date price sources covering a sufficiently large universe.[42] For this reason, many major bond indices are calculated by big brokers like Citigroup, J. P. Morgan or Merrill Lynch, which, thanks to their extensive bond dealing, dispose of adequate price information.

11.4 MONEY MARKET INDICES

Money market funds are investment funds which invest primarily in term deposits and very short-dated bonds. The benchmarks used for these funds are therefore based on the reference interest rates for the money market.

[39] The presentation in this paragraph is based on Citigroup (2011). Merrill Lynch publishes a similarly important and comparable index family, which, however, will not be discussed here (see http://www.mlindex.ml (restricted webpage)

[40] See Colin (2005, p. 118 et seq.).

[41] This results in a further requirement for indices, which may be added to the ones listed in section 11.1. See also Citigroup (2003, p. 9).

[42] This is less important for equity indices, as stocks are listed on a stock exchange and thus have publicly available prices.

Example 11.8

EONIA, EURIBOR, and LIBOR indices, eb.rexx Money Market

a. Every day, a group of so-called panel banks report data (total volume, weighted average lending rate) on their overnight unsecured lending transactions in the interbank market to the European Central Bank. EONIA (Euro Overnight Index Average) is then computed by the ECB as the average of these overnight lending rates[43] weighted by the respective transaction volumes.

b. The same panel banks which quote for EONIA also report daily quotes of the rate that each panel bank believes one prime bank is quoting to another prime bank for interbank term deposits within the euro zone. The maturity spectrum covers one, two and three weeks as well as the twelve maturities from one to twelve months. The EURIBOR (*Euro Interbank Offered Rate*) for each maturity is calculated as the equal weighted average of the bank quotes, after eliminating the highest and lowest 15% of these quotes.[44] The so-called EURIBID (*Euro Interbank Bid Rate*) is a reference rate which is not officially published but often used in practice. It is calculated by subtracting a specifically chosen cost charge from EURIBOR (e.g. EURIBOR – 20 bps[45]) and may be interpreted as the interest rate at which a bank is willing to borrow from other banks.

c. LIBOR[46] may be regarded as the counterpart to EURIBOR. LIBOR (London Interbank *Offered Rate)* is the average interest rate offered by several commercial banks in the London interbank market. It is calculated for ten currencies (e.g. EUR, USD, JPY). The panel banks are chosen individually for each currency. Maturities include

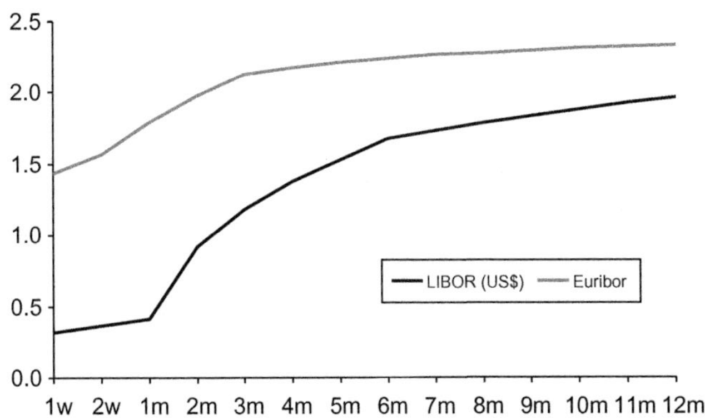

FIGURE 11.5
EURIBOR and LIBOR (USD) Interest Rates by Maturity as at 27/01/2009.

---

[43] See http://www.euribor.org. As of March 2012, the website lists 44 panel banks.
[44] See also http://www.euribor.org.
[45] The abbreviation bps stands for "basis points" (e.g. 10 bps are equal to 0.10%).
[46] See www.bbalibor.com.

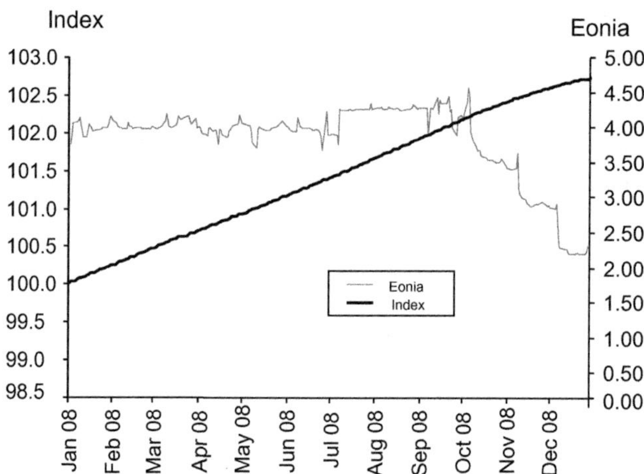

FIGURE 11.6
EONIA from 31 December 2005 to 31 December 2008 and the Corresponding Performance Index (left hand scale).

one day (overnight), one and two weeks, as well as one to twelve months. Like EURIBID, LIBID *(London Interbank Bid Rate)* is calculated in practice by subtracting an appropriate cost charge from LIBOR.

d. Besides the above-mentioned bond indices, Deutsche Börse calculates the money market index *eb.rexx Money Market*, which includes highly liquid German government bonds. Eligible bonds must have a maturity between one month and one year and an amount outstanding of at least EUR 4 billion. The bonds are market capitalization-weighted, with a maximum weight of 30 percent.

Unlike their equity and bond market counterparts, money market benchmarks are initially given only in terms of interests (Figure 11.5). Therefore, the interest rate series needs to be transformed into a performance series to obtain an index which can be compared with the share price series of a portfolio. For that purpose, a given base value (e.g. 100) is compounded with the one-day interest rates resulting from the interest rate series. In doing so, the applicable interest rate conventions have to be taken into account (Figure 11.6).[47]

11.5 PEER GROUP COMPARISONS AND FUND UNIVERSES

To better allow for an absolute return view, management performance is often measured against the results of comparable competitor portfolios (so-called *peer group comparisons*). This requires the maintenance of so-called *fund universes*.

[47] EURIBOR, for example, is quoted on an ACT/360 (ACT = Actual) day-count convention, i.e. the year is assumed to have 360 days and each month is calculated on an actual day count basis.

In practice, however, peer groups are often defined on the basis of very loose entry criteria. As a result, a peer group may consist of a very broad range of portfolios with widely divergent risk levels. Peer group comparisons also suffer from *survivorship bias:* poor-performing portfolios are closed more often than well-performing portfolios, which results in an increasingly good peer group performance in the course of time. For these reasons, peer groups earn some criticism.[48]

Example 11.9

Peer group comparison at IDS

IDS constructs peer group comparisons for its customers by means of a so-called box-and-whisker diagram, a common form of representation for such purposes. The funds—in this case an European bond fund and a global bond fund, respectively—are compared to a suitable universe of funds. The bottom and top of the box represent the 25th and 75th percentile, so that the boxes represent the funds in the second and third quartile. The whiskers are defined by the funds in the universe with the maximal, respectively minimal performance. They represent thus the first, respectively last quartile of the fund universe. The line in the box is the median of the return distribution (see Figure 11.7).

The box-and-whisker diagram provides a good overview of the positioning of the fund and the benchmark relative to the peer group. The quality of this representation depends on the quality of the underlying fund universe. In case of the Global bond portfolio, e.g., the vast dispersion of the returns—especially in the fourth quartile—is particularly striking. This skewness needs to be investigated further in the performance evaluation.

Also widely used in practice, a bar chart illustrates performance over different time periods. An example is given in Figure 11.8. It presents a fund which outperformed both its benchmark and the median of its peer group consistently over longer periods. Only year-to-date, it lags the benchmark and the peer group median.

Peer group comparisons violate many of the benchmark criteria listed at the beginning of this chapter. In particular, portfolio managers cannot assume a neutral position. Also, they typically do not know the investment decisions of their competitors. Thus, an investment objective defined in terms of a peer group comparison (e.g. a first-quartile ranking) does not constitute a benchmark in the strict sense. If, however, there is no adequate benchmark (i.e. a combination of suitable capital market indices) which fulfills the criteria mentioned, then a peer group comparison can be a useful alternative. Absolute return portfolios are a case in point.

Generally, it should be noted that the strategic decision to invest in the market segments represented by the benchmark has to be evaluated largely independently from management performance. The portfolio's position within the peer group is then the combined result of this allocation decision and the active manager return.

[48] See e.g. Spaulding (1997, p. 141 et seq.) or (Bacon 2008, p. 48 et seq.).

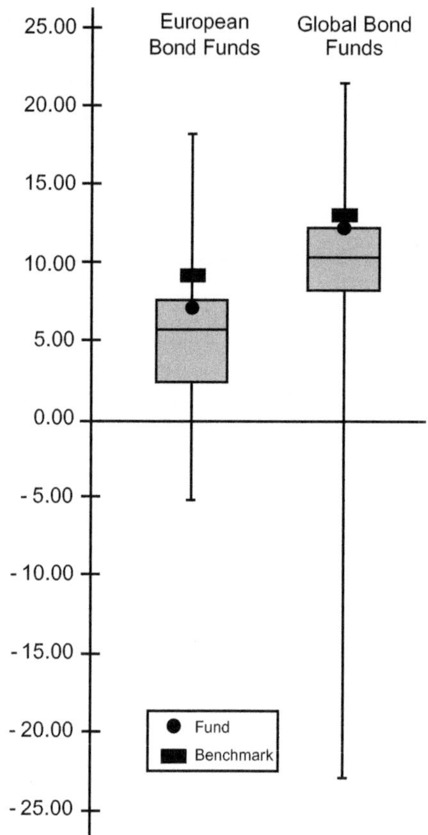

FIGURE 11.7
Peer Group Comparison for Bond Portfolios.

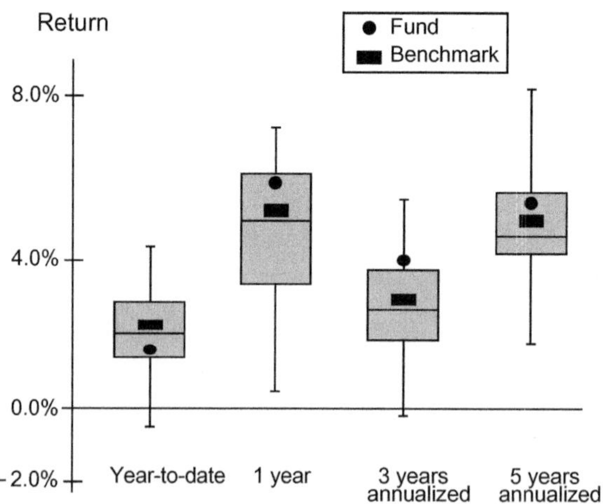

FIGURE 11.8
Peer Group Comparison by Means of a Bar Chart.

11.6 BENCHMARKS FOR PORTFOLIOS INVESTING IN MULTIPLE ASSET CLASSES

Indices for different asset classes are often combined to obtain benchmarks for so-called multi-asset or *balanced portfolios.*

> **Balanced portfolios**
>
> Balanced portfolios are portfolios which invest in securities from multiple asset classes. The asset mix is usually designed to provide a risk level which meets the investor's personal preferences. This is done in practice by combining high-risk assets (e.g. equities) with low-risk assets (e.g. bonds).

If investment risk is measured by return volatility, then the total risk σ of a portfolio with two components is given by

$$\sigma = \sqrt{x^2 * \sigma_1^2 + (1-x)^2\sigma_2^2 + 2 * x * (1-x) * Cov_{12}}, \qquad (11.12)$$

where σ_1 and σ_2 denote the return volatility of the two components; Cov_{12} is their covariance; and x is the portfolio weight of the first component. $1-x$ is then the portfolio weight of the second component.

Any risk level between σ_1 and σ_2 or, possibly, even below their minimum can be realized by appropriately selecting the weighting factor x. However, the portfolio weights need to be rebalanced on a regular basis to avoid undue fluctuations in the risk level.[49]

Example 11.10

Balanced portfolio of German bonds and equities

The following table shows the return and risk of German equities and bonds. The calculation was based on monthly returns of DAX and REXP over the period from 1 January 2001 to 31 December 2008 (see Table 11.6).

The covariance between the two return series over the observation period was −0.40.

By combining the two asset classes, an investor can realize his preferred risk level according to Equation (11.12). Leaving short positions out of account, Figure 11.9 shows all the volatility levels that can be realized by combining equities and bonds. Volatility is shown as a function of the equity weight x.

The end points represent pure equity and bond investments.

The performance of a balanced portfolio should be evaluated against a benchmark combining indices for different asset classes, i.e. a so-called composite

[49] In practice, however, it will hardly be possible to keep risk levels constant, as the empirical variance and covariance parameters of security market indices fluctuate over time.

Table 11.6 Return and risk of German Equities and Bonds (Observation Period: 1 January 2001 to 31 December 2008)

	Return p.a.	Volatility
German equities (DAX)	−3.57%	23.8%
German bonds (REXP)	5.26%	3.2%

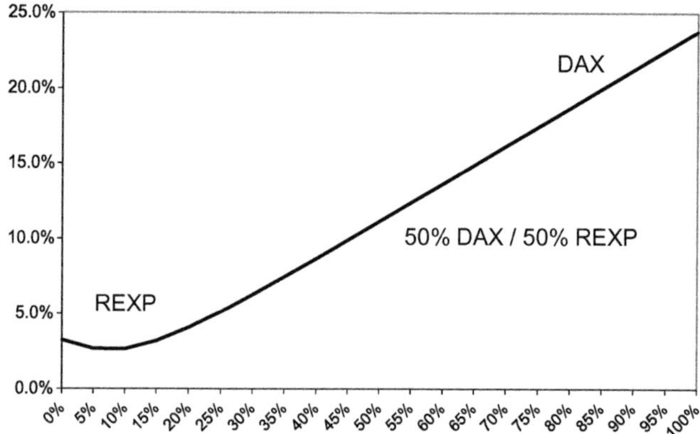

FIGURE 11.9
Risk Level of a Combined Equity and Bond Investment Depending on the Equity Weight x.

or *customized benchmark*. As already mentioned, the customized benchmark and the balanced portfolio need to be rebalanced on a regular basis in order to (approximately) maintain the target risk level. In the process, the benchmark and portfolio weights are periodically reset to their original values. There are different possibilities to choose the rebalancing frequency. An important aspect to consider is transaction costs. Higher frequencies (e.g. daily rebalancing) can result in significantly higher transaction costs, which detract from performance. Thus, in practice, benchmarks are often rebalanced on a monthly basis.

Generally, the "right" rebalancing frequency depends on the underlying management style. If a portfolio is managed very actively (e.g. with daily transactions as is the case with many balanced mutual funds), it can make sense to choose a high—perhaps daily—rebalancing frequency.

The return R of a customized benchmark with N segments between two rebalancing dates is given by:

$$R = \sum_{i=1}^{N} w_i * r_i,$$

where r_i is the return and w_i is the weight of segment i.

Benchmarks can also be customized to consider investment restrictions.

Example 11.11

Customized benchmark considering investment restrictions

An investor intends to launch a portfolio which invests in CDAX stocks. However, investments in construction stocks are excluded. The portfolio is to be benchmarked against the CDAX excluding construction stocks. As this index is not published by Deutsche Börse, the asset manager calculates it himself according to the calculation methodology for the DAX indices.

This type of a customized benchmark also needs to define the rebalancing frequency. The return over multiple periods is calculated on the basis of the formula for the time-weighted return.

11.7 CHAPTER-END PROBLEMS

(Rebalancing of a Customized Benchmark)

The managing director of an asset management company receives a phone call from a client with a balanced portfolio. The portfolio is measured against the customized benchmark 50% DAX/50% REXP.

The client points out that the return calculated by himself differs from the figure reported in the company's statement of net assets. Both the client and the asset management company use the data shown in Table 11.7.

The return figure calculated by the client, −10.29%, is almost half a percentage point higher than the figure reported in the statement of net assets (−10.77%). How do you explain this discrepancy?

Table 11.7 Returns of REXP and DAX. (Figures in%)

	Month 1	Month 2
REXP	2,46	1,14
DAX	−17,05	−8,64

(Treatment of Cash positions in Benchmark Calculations)

The calculation of the J.P. Morgan bond indices is based on the assumption that coupon payments and other cash flows are held as (non-interest-bearing) cash positions until month end when they are removed from the index. Is this method principally to the advantage of the fund manager? How does the calculation methodology used for the FTSE indices compare in this regard (Example 11.6)? Are there further alternatives?

Chapter 12

Attribution Analysis for Equity Portfolios According to the Brinson Approach

ABSTRACT

In this chapter the fundamental approach to attribution analysis as developed by Brinson and others will be introduced. At first, simple ways for decomposing a return on a segment basis will be described. Based on these preliminary considerations, the basic features of the Brinson approach will be derived by means of an allocation and a selection portfolio, representing the characteristic aspects of the underlying investment process. The resulting interaction effects will be discussed in detail. Furthermore, basic approaches to consider currency effects will be outlined. The formalism will then be extended to the multi-period-case. Finally, approaches for a geometric attributions analysis will be considered.

Keywords
approach
attribution analysis,
decomposing,
return, segment,
Brinson approach,
allocation,
selection portfolio,
interaction effects,
geometric
attributions analysis

12.1 INTRODUCTION TO ATTRIBUTION ANALYSIS

12.1.1 Goals of an Attribution Analysis

Attribution analysis is defined as the ascertainment, the description and the quantification of key factors on the returns of investment portfolios.[1] In general it is not the absolute but the active return[2], which will be analyzed. The central question of an attribution analysis is thus:

> To which investment decisions can the active return of a portfolio relative to its benchmark be traced over a given period?

Chapter 12, Exercises 12.5 and 12.6: SOLNIK, BRUNO, McLEAVEY, DENNIS, *GLOBAL INVESTMENTS, 6th Edition*, © 2009, Reprinted by permission of Pearson Education, Inc., Upper Saddle River, NJ.

[1] Instead of attribution analysis, also the term performance analysis is used.
[2] Cf. Section 10.7.

Performance Evaluation and Attribution of Security Portfolios. http://dx.doi.org/10.1016/B978-0-12-744483-3.00011-0

© 2013 Elsevier Inc. All rights reserved.
For End-of-chapter Questions: © 2012. CFA Institute, Reproduced and republished with permission from CFA Institute. All rights reserved.

In this generality it is a very demanding task. The performance analyst has to trace every decision of the portfolio managers very carefully. This will be especially difficult and cumbersome if the analyst has to cover different portfolios, which do not follow a systematic investment process.

If the investment decisions are made according to a systematic investment process, then the goal of an attribution analysis can be described as follows: to what extend have the components of the investment process contributed to the active return achieved?

Typical components of investment processes are for example:

- Weighting of portfolio segments relative to a benchmark
- Selection of individual securities
- Active currency management
- Active variation of the overall invested capital (leveraging of the portfolio).

In this and in the following chapters a number of different investment processes and their corresponding forms of attribution analysis will be described. The focus of these considerations will be on the methodology of Brinson et al. and its pertinent investment processes.[3]

The quality of an analysis depends decisively on the degree of the adaptation to the investment process. In every specific case one needs to determine the appropriate framework for an analysis. The desire to obtain information about all factors, which can influence the investment return, in a comprehensive form, needs to be balanced against the requirement to present the information in an efficient and graphic form. In practice it is often difficult to determine the right level, as the respective requirements may vary among the different recipients. Senior management will in general require, for instance, a more top-level report than the portfolio manager.

12.1.2 Overall Return as the Weighted Sum of Individual Returns

The linking of individual segment returns to obtain an overall portfolio return is fundamental for attribution analysis. In the following a formula will be derived, by which the overall return of a portfolio can be derived by means of the initial weights of the securities.

At first, for the sake of simplicity we will look at the special case, where the portfolio consists of two segments. The return of the two segments (e.g. equity and bond segment) in the interval from 0 to T will be denominated by srp_1 and srp_2, respectively (see Table 12.1).

The notation for the net asset values (or Inventory) of the segments is given in the following table.

If the weights of the segments at the beginning of the period are denoted by swp_1 and swp_2 then the following holds:

$$swp_1 = \frac{I_1^0}{I_1^0 + I_2^0}, \text{ respectively } swp_2 = \frac{I_2^0}{I_1^0 + I_2^0}.$$

[3] Cf. e.g. Brinson and Fachler (1985) and Brinson et al. (1986).

SRP Segment Return Portfolio	SRB Segment Return Benchmark
SGP Segment Weight Portfolio	SGB Segment Weight Benchmark

FIGURE 12.1
Notation for Key Parameters.

At this stage it is assumed that no exogenous cash-flows occur in each of the segments. Under this assumption the returns srp_1 and srp_2 are given by:

$$srp_1 = \frac{I_1^T - I_1^0}{I_1^0}, \text{ respectively } srp_2 = \frac{I_2^T - I_2^0}{I_2^0}.$$

The return RP of the overall portfolio is given by:

$$RP = \frac{I_1^T + I_2^T - I_1^0 - I_2^0}{I_1^0 + I_2^0}.$$

In order to derive the desired formula for the overall return of a portfolio with two segments, the expression on the right-hand side of this equation will be modified as follows:

$$RP = \frac{I_1^T - I_1^0}{I_1^0 + I_2^0} + \frac{I_2^T - I_2^0}{I_1^0 + I_2^0} = \frac{I_1^0}{I_1^0 + I_2^0} * \frac{I_1^T - I_1^0}{I_1^0} + \frac{I_2^0}{I_1^0 + I_2^0} * \frac{I_2^T - I_2^0}{I_2^0}$$
$$= swp_1 * srp_1 + swp_2 * srp_2.$$

Under the assumption that no exogenous cash flows have occurred, the overall return of a portfolio broken down in several segments is thus identical to the weighted sum of the individual segment returns. In particular:

Segment contribution = initial weight of the segment * segment return.

In the following we make the assumption that the weights of the segments at the beginning of the period are based on the closing prices of the assets of the previous trade day. The calculation of the return contributions over the period from 01.07.2007 to 31.07.2007 is for instance based on the weightings derived from closing prices as at 30.06.2007 (cf. the following example).

Table 12.1 Notation for the Net Asset Value of the Portfolio Segments

	Net Asset Value at t=0	Net Asset Value at t=T
Segment 1	I_1^0	I_1^T
Segment 2	I_2^0	I_2^T

Table 12.2 Weightings and Returns of a Balanced Portfolio (%)

Segment	Weighting as at 30.06.2007	Return 01.07.2007–31.07.2007
Equity	40	10.8
Bonds	50	−2.3
Cash	10	0.3

Example 12.1

Return contributions for a balanced portfolio:

On 30.06.2007, 50% of a balanced portfolio[4] was invested in German bonds, 40% in German equity, and 10% in cash. The segment returns for the period until 31/07/07 are listed in Table 12.2.[5]

The overall return RP is thus given by[6]

$$RP = 40\% * 10.8\% + 50\% * (-2.3\%) + 10\% * 0.3\% = 3.2\%.$$

These considerations can easily be generalized to a return decomposition for a portfolio with an arbitrary number of segments.

Representation of the overall return as the sum of return contributions

The return RP of a portfolio consisting of n segments over a period, in which no exogenous cash-flows have occurred, is given by the weighted sum of the segment returns.

$$RP = swp_1 * srp_1 + swp_2 * srp_2 + \cdots + swp_n * srp_n = \sum_{i=1}^{n} swp_i * srp_i, \qquad (12.1)$$

where:

srp_i : return of the portfolio segment i over the period

swp_i : weighting of the portfolio segment i at the beginning of the period $\left(\sum_{i=1}^{n} swp_i = 1\right)$.

The terms $swp_i * srp_i$ are called *return contributions* of the portfolio segments.

The return contributions of the individual benchmark components are computed analogous to those of the portfolio, such that the return RB of the benchmark over a period, in which no adjustment of the weights has occurred (cf. Equation (12.1)), is given by:

$$RB = swb_1 * srb_1 + swb_2 * srb_2 + \cdots + swb_n * srb_n = \sum_{i=1}^{n} swb_i * srb_i, \qquad (12.2)$$

[4] The balanced portfolio will be analyzed according to the standard Brinson approach. A methodology specifically tailored to balanced portfolios will be described in Chapter 14.

[5] This calculation is based on the assumption that no exogenous cash-flows have occurred in July.

[6] The Equation for three segments is given by: $RP = swp_1 * srp_1 + swp_2 * srp_2 + swp_3 * srp_3$.

	Positive return $srb_i > 0$	Negative return $srb_i < 0$
overweighting $swp_i > swb_i$	+	–
underweighting $swp_i < swb_i$	–	+

FIGURE 12.2
Sign of the Relative Contribution According to Equation (12.4).

where:

srb_i : return of the benchmark segment i over the period
swb_i : weighting of the benchmark segment i at the beginning of the period $\left(\sum_{i=1}^{n} swb_i = 1\right)$
n: number of segments within the benchmark and the portfolio.[7]

The terms $swb_i * srb_i$ are called return contributions of the benchmark segments.

The goal of an attribution analysis relative to a benchmark is to find out, how the different weightings of the segments have contributed toward the active return

$$RP - RB = \sum_{i=1}^{n} swp_i * srp_i - swb_i * srb_i. \tag{12.3}$$

The terms on the right-hand side

$$swp_i * srp_i - swb_i * srb_i \tag{12.4}$$

represent the differences of the return contributions of the individual segments.

In the following we will consider the special case, in which all segments consist of a single stock. In this case the returns srb_i and srp_i are identical, so that Equation (12.3) can be written in a simplified form:

$$RP - RB = \sum_{i=1}^{n} (swp_i - swb_i) * srb_i. \tag{12.5}$$

In regard to the sign of $(swp_i - swb_i) * srb_i$ four different cases need to be distinguished.

The return contribution of $(swp_i - swb_i) * srb_i$ is positive, if the portfolio was overweight in the stock i and the stock had a positive return, or if the portfolio was underweight and the stock had a negative return. It is negative, if the portfolio was overweight in case of a negative stock return, or if the portfolio was underweight in case of a positive stock return.

[7] At this stage we will assume for the sake of simplicity that the number of portfolio segments is identical to the number of benchmark segments. In practice this is, however, often not the case. A generalized view is described in Section 12.2.2.

There is, however, a problem with this equation. An overweight sector with a positive benchmark return will give a positive contribution even if the stock underperforms the benchmark. This will be avoided if one uses in Equation (12.5) the active returns relative to the benchmark, $srb_i - RB$, instead of the absolute returns srb_i. Then the return contributions will have the following form:

$$(swp_i - swb_i) * (srb_i - RB). \tag{12.6}$$

Also the modified return contributions in (12.6) sum up to the active return $RP - RB$. According to Equation (12.5) it holds that:

$$RP - RB = \sum_{i=1}^{n} (swp_i - swb_i) * srb_i.$$

Using this identity we obtain:

$$\begin{aligned}\sum_{i=1}^{n} \left(swp_i - swb_i\right) * (srb_i - RB) &= \sum_{i=1}^{n} \left(swp_i - swb_i\right) * srb_i - \sum_{i=1}^{n} \left(swp_i - swb_i\right) * RB \\ &= RP - RB - (1-1) * RB \\ &= RP - RB,\end{aligned}$$

according to the claim.

Example 12.2

Decomposition of the active return for a DAX portfolio:

We consider a portfolio investing in German stocks that are included in the DAX, which represents the 30 most important German stocks. DAX will also be the benchmark of the portfolio. Table 12.3 shows the modified relative return contributions in the period from 01.03.2007 to 31.03.2007 computed according to Equation (12.6).

For the position in stocks of the company Metro for instance, a negative contribution is exhibited. This reflects the fact that the return of the (overweight) stock was below the average return of the stocks in the benchmark. Likewise, the positive contribution of SAP is due to the underweighting of a stock performing much worse than the benchmark.

To conclude both approaches for a relative attribution methodologies are summarized.

Return contributions of individual stocks to the active return

The relative return contributions of the single stocks toward the active return of a portfolio relative to its benchmark (in a period without exogenous cash-flows) can be calculated in two different ways:

The (absolute) return of a stock is multiplied by the initial active weight as at the beginning of the period:

$$(swp_i - swb_i) * srb_i. \tag{12.7}$$

The return of a stock relative to a benchmark is multiplied by the initial active weight as at the beginning of the period:

$$(swp_i - swb_i) * (srb_i - RB), \tag{12.8}$$

where:
RB : benchmark return over the period
srb_i : return of the stock i over the period
swb_i : weighting of the stock i in the benchmark at the beginning of the period

$$\left(\sum_{i=1}^{n} swb_i = 1\right)$$

swp_i : weighting of the stock i in the portfolio at the beginning of the period

$$\left(\sum_{i=1}^{n} swp_i = 1\right)$$

n : number of stocks in the benchmark and the portfolio.
In both cases the relative contributions add up to the active return.

Table 12.3 Return Contributions of a Portfolio Relative to the DAX (in %)

Stock	Portfolio Weight	DAX Weight	Return	Relative Return Contribution
Adidas	2.00	1.08	10.26	0.07
Allianz	12.50	10.06	−5.57	−0.21
Altana	2.00	0.46	6.27	0.05
BASF	2.00	5.51	9.67	−0.23
BMW	0.00	2.02	0.59	0.05
Bayer	3.00	4.75	10.05	−0.12
Commerzbank	2.50	2.68	6.15	−0.01
Continental	3.00	1.98	2.60	0.00
Daimler	2.00	6.98	19.43	−0.82
Deutsche Bank	4.00	7.40	1.60	0.05
Deutsche Börse	4.00	2.21	13.31	0.18
Deutsche Post	1.00	2.68	−6.05	0.15
Deutsche Postbank	3.00	0.75	2.71	−0.01
Deutsche Telekom	8.00	5.40	−8.70	−0.30
E.ON	2.50	9.32	2.66	0.02
Fresenius Medical Care	4.00	0.94	1.79	−0.04
Henkel Vz.	3.00	0.91	3.64	0.01
Hypo Real Estate	4.00	0.92	−0.29	−0.10
Infineon	0.00	1.24	0.43	0.03
Linde	3.00	1.23	4.73	0.03
Lufthansa	4.00	1.34	−0.64	−0.10
MAN	1.00	1.39	7.23	−0.02
Metro	3.00	1.21	1.40	−0.03
Münchener Rück	1.50	3.58	5.13	−0.04
RWE	4.00	5.13	2.71	0.00
SAP	3.00	4.41	−4.14	0.10
Siemens	8.00	9.71	0.34	0.05

Table 12.3 Continued

Stock	Portfolio Weight	DAX Weight	Return	Relative Return Contribution
ThyssenKrupp	4.00	2.14	−0.03	−0.06
TUI	2.00	0.57	4.99	0.03
VW	4.00	2.02	18.00	0.30
Total	100.00	100.00		−0.96

12.2 SINGLE-PERIOD ATTRIBUTION ANALYSIS ACCORDING TO THE BRINSON APPROACH

12.2.1 Allocation and Selection

The approaches discussed so far focused on the (relative) contributions of individual stocks. This can be helpful for a portfolio manager, who is interested in a detailed breakdown of the portfolio performance. In case of portfolios with many positions this information level might, however, be too detailed. The standard attribution analysis according to Brinson et al. is thus based on a modified approach,[8] according to which the securities contained in the portfolio (respectively in the benchmark) are first grouped in different sectors classified, e.g. according to currencies, maturity buckets,[9] etc. The analyses contain information on:

- the success of the allocation of the invested capital among the individual segments relative to the benchmark,
- stock selection based on the allocation decisions,
- currency contributions, etc.

At first the focus will be on the determination of the allocation and selection contributions. Currency effects will be covered not until Section 12.2.5. The methodology will again be developed by means of examples.

Example 12.3

Breakdown of the DAX into sectors:

Although Deutschen Börse AG does not explicitly publish sector indices for the DAX, with the data in Table 12.3 it is, however, possible to calculate such indices by oneself. Since the number of defined sectors is lower than the number of the individual stocks (fourteen instead of thirty) the extent of the resulting analysis will be reduced considerably (see Table 12.4).

The classification of the different titles to the sectors could be even more differentiated (or coarser). A further refinement (e.g. by mapping *Allianz* and *Munich Re* to separate sectors *Insurance* and *Reinsurance*) would increase that data amount. This would have an impact on the clarity of the analysis. For a benchmark with a limited number of titles like the DAX – which we rely on heavily in this chapter just because of this

[8] Cf. e.g. Brinson and Fachler (1985) and Brinson et al. (1986).

[9] This chapter will primarily deal with equities. Asset classes will be discussed only occasionally, but are treated in detail in the following chapters.

Table 12.4 Weighting of the DAX Sectors as at 28.02.2007

DAX Sector	Weight (%)	Stock
Automobile	13.00	BMW, Continental, Daimler, VW
Banks	10.82	Commerzbank, Deutsche Bank, Deutsche Postbank
Chemicals	10.26	BASF, Bayer
Consumer	1.99	Adidas, Henkel Vz.
Financial Service	3.13	Deutsche Börse, Hypo Real Estate
Industrial	14.48	Linde, MAN, Siemens, ThyssenKrupp
Insurance	13.64	Allianz, Munich Re
Pharma & Healthcare	1.40	Altana, Fresenius Medical Care
Retail	1.21	Metro
Software	4.41	SAP
Technology	1.24	Infinion
Telecommunication	5.40	Deutsche Telekom
Transportation & Logistics	4.59	Deutsche Post, Lufthansa, TUI
Utilities	14.45	E.ON, RWE

simplicity—the danger of a negative impact is limited. If the benchmark encompasses a much higher number of different stocks (e.g. the *MSCI Europe* with 592 titles (as of 24.04.2007)), then there is a real danger that the additional detailed information obscures the essential messages of the analysis.

Based on the sector weightings the manager of a portfolio benchmarked against the DAX may over- or -underweight a specific sector (*allocation decisions*). In a second step he may decide how to change the weighting of individual stocks within the individual sectors (*selection decisions*), thereby respecting the set weights for the sectors. In the following it will be described how to measure the success of these investment decisions. To illustrate the underlying idea we will consider first a quite simple case, in which both the portfolio and the benchmark consist of only two sectors containing two stocks each. The initial weighting of the stocks within the benchmark is set at 25% for each title.

Example 12.4

Allocation and selection decisions for a two sector portfolio:

Based on the information in Table 12.5, the performance of the portfolio manager responsible for the portfolio structure below (Table 12.6) shall be evaluated.

Table 12.5 Weightings Within the Benchmark. The Returns are Calculated for the Period from 01.03.2007 Until 31.03.2007 with Weights as at 28.02.2007 (Values in %)

Sector	Sector Weighting	Sector Return	Stock	Stock Weighting	Stock Return
Chemicals	50	9.86	BASF	25	9.67
			Bayer	25	10.05
Insurance	50	−0.22	Allianz	25	−5.57
			Munich Re	25	5.13

Table 12.6 Weightings Within the Portfolio. Returns and Weights Are Calculated as Above (Values in %)

Sector	Sector Weighting	Sector Return	Stock	Stock Weighting	Stock Return
Chemicals	40	9.77	BASF	30	9.67
			Bayer	10	10.05
Insurance	60	−2.00	Allianz	40	−5.57
			Munich Re	20	5.13

The overall returns of the benchmark and the portfolio are calculated to 4.82% and 2.70%, respectively, so that the active return is given by −2,12%. In each sector the stock with the highest return (*BASF*, *Allianz*) was overweight relative to the benchmark. In addition the sector with lower performance (*insurance*) was overweight.

In order to illustrate the different decision levels (allocation and selection), based on the portfolio structure two theoretical portfolios will be formed: the "allocation"—and the "selection portfolio". Based on these two portfolios the respective contributions are easily derived.

Allocation portfolio: In this portfolio only the weights of the benchmark segments are altered. The weighting of the stocks within each segment is preserved, so that the returns of the respective portfolio and the benchmark segments are identical.

Selection portfolio: In this portfolio the weights of the benchmark segments are preserved. Only the weighting of the stocks within the sectors is changed.

Figure 12.3 illustrates those investment decisions graphically. The quadrants of the upper square represent the four sectors within the benchmark comprising two stocks each. It is assumed that both the sectors and the stocks are equally weighted. In the allocation portfolio the (equal) weighting of the stocks within the sectors is preserved, the weighting of the sectors has, however, changed. (The area representing the sectors has changed.) In the selection portfolio the weighting of the sectors is preserved (partitioning into quadrants), the weighting of the stocks within the sectors has changed, however. It needs to be emphasized that, according to the classical Brinson approach, selection and allocation portfolio are viewed as on the same decision level. This reflects the independence of the decision-making processes.

The manager responsible for the selection decisions (i.e. the manager of the selection portfolio) will be called *selection manager*. Similarly, we will call the manager responsible for the allocation decisions (i.e. the manager of the allocation portfolio) the *allocation manager*. If these decisions are indeed made by different portfolio managers for the real portfolio, then the selection and

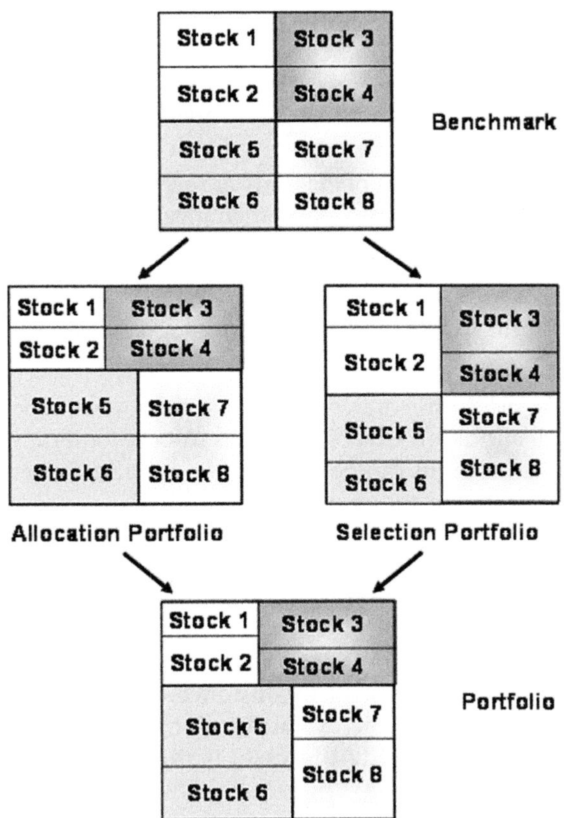

FIGURE 12.3
Illustration of the Allocation and Selection Portfolios.

allocation managers are real managers, whose performance can be evaluated by the performance contributions assigned to them. Should the portfolio be managed by a single portfolio manager, then the terms selection and allocation manager have only theoretical meaning. In this case the contributions derived from them measure the performance of a single manager in different areas.

According to Equation (12.2) the overall return of the benchmark *RB* over a single period is given by:

$$RB = \sum_{i=1}^{n} swb_i * srb_i,$$

where:

srb_i: return of the benchmark segment i over the period
swb_i: weight of the benchmark segment i at the beginning of the period
n: number of benchmark segments.

Under the assumptions outlined above, the overall return of the allocation portfolio *RAP* is given by:

$$RAP = \sum_{i=1}^{n} swp_i * srb_i, \tag{12.9}$$

where swp_i represents the weight of the portfolio segment *i*. The overall contribution from the allocation decisions *AC* is then given by the active return of the allocation portfolio relative to the benchmark:

$$AC = RAP - RB = \sum_{i=1}^{n} \left(swp_i - swb_i\right) * srb_i. \tag{12.10}$$

The terms $\left(swp_i - swb_i\right) * srb_i$ are contributions from the individual segments toward the overall allocation effect. Analogous to the modification expressed in Equation (12.8) these terms can be modified by subtracting the overall benchmark return *RB* from the sector returns:[10]

$$RAP - RB = \sum_{i=1}^{n} \left(swp_i - swb_i\right) * (srb_i - RB). \tag{12.11}$$

The reasoning behind this modification has already been illustrated. Overweighting a specific segment will, for instance, result in a positive contribution if the return is above the overall benchmark return. If one employs Equation (12.10) this is already the case, if the return of the segment is positive.

In a similar way one deals with the selection portfolio. According to the hypotheses the return of the selection portfolio *RSP* is defined as:

$$RSP = \sum_{i=1}^{n} swb_i * srp_i, \tag{12.12}$$

so that the selection contribution *SC* is given by

$$SC = RSP - RB = \sum_{i=1}^{n} swb_i * \left(srp_i - srb_i\right). \tag{12.13}$$

The terms $swb_i * \left(srp_i - srb_i\right)_i$ represent the selection contributions of individual segments. The allocation and selection terms do, however, *not* sum up to the overall active return $RP - RB$. In fact, the following holds:

$$RP - RB = AC + SC + IT(1),$$

---

[10] Cf. Brinson and Fachler (1985).

where the so-called *interaction term* $IT(1)$ is defined as follows:[11]

$$IT(1) := \sum_{i=1}^{n} \left(swp_i - swb_i\right) * \left(srp_i - srb_i\right). \tag{12.14}$$

This results from the following transformation:

$$\begin{aligned}
RP - RB - AC - SC &= \sum_{i=1}^{n} swp_i * srp_i - swb_i * srb_i \\
&\quad - \sum_{i=1}^{n} \left(swp_i - swb_i\right) * srb_i - \sum_{i=1}^{n} swb_i * \left(srp_i - srb_i\right) \\
&= \sum_{i=1}^{n} swp_i * srp_i - swp_i * srb_i - swb_i * srp_i + swb_i * srb_i \\
&= \sum_{i=1}^{n} swp_i * \left(srp_i - srb_i\right) - swb_i * \left(srp_i - srb_i\right) \\
&= \sum_{i=}^{n} \left(swp_i - swb_i\right) * \left(srp_i - srb_i\right).
\end{aligned}$$

In particular, it holds:

$$IT(1) = RP - RB - AC - SC = (RP - RAP) + (RB - RSP). \tag{12.15}$$

Using Equations (12.10), (12.13) and (12.14) one readily deduces the following representation of the effects on the top level:

$$RP - RB = \underbrace{(RAP - RB)}_{AC} + \underbrace{(RSP - RB)}_{SC} + \underbrace{(RP - RAP) + (RB - RSP)}_{IT(1)}. \tag{12.16}$$

From an absolute return standpoint one obtains the following ordering:

$$RP = RB + (RP - RB) = RB + AC + SC + IT(1). \tag{12.17}$$

Formally, the interaction terms can be regarded as second-order effects, as they contain—other than the selection and allocation terms—only differential expressions of the weights and returns. This does not imply, however, that they are *necessarily* small compared to the allocation and selection contributions. This will, in particular, be unlikely if the portfolio manager has implemented a portfolio structure with considerable deviations relative to the benchmarks. In practice, the interaction terms are often combined with the selection terms (occasionally also with the allocation terms). The implications of these procedures will be

---

[11] The *interaction terms* are also known as *cross products* (cf. Bacon (2004, p. 90 et seq.) and (Burnie et al. (1998)).

discussed in detail in Section 12.2.3. The following summery contains the major results (cf. also Table 12.7):

Allocation and selection contributions over a single period (without separating currency effects)

The allocation contribution ac_i of the segment i of a portfolio is given by

$$ac_i := (swp_i - swb_i) * srb_i. \tag{12.18}$$

Alternatively one can base the allocation contribution on the segment return relative to the overall benchmark return. Then the (relative) allocation contribution assumes the form:

$$acr_i := (swp_i - swb_i) * (srb_i - RB). \tag{12.19}$$

The selection contribution sc_i of the segment i is given by

$$sc_i := swb_i * (srp_i - srb_i). \tag{12.20}$$

The interaction terms are defined as

$$it(1)_i := (swp_i - swb_i) * (srp_i - srb_i) \quad \text{(Variant 1) respectively} \tag{12.21}$$

$$it(1)_i := (swp_i - swb_i) * (srp_i - srb_i + RB) \quad \text{(Variant 2).} \tag{12.22}$$

RB: benchmark return over the period
swb_i: weight of the benchmark segment i at the beginning of the period
swp_i: weight of the portfolio segment i at the beginning of the period
srb_i: return of the benchmark segment i over the period
srp_i: return of the portfolio segment i over the period
n: number of portfolio/benchmark segments

Using the allocation term ac_i, the sum of the contributions (allocation, selection, interaction) within the segments equals exactly the difference of the contributions of the portfolio and benchmark, respectively:

$$ac_i + sc_i + it(1)_i = swp_i * srp_i - swb_i * srb_i. \tag{12.23}$$

If instead the allocation terms acr_i are employed, then this is no longer the case. Using this term one obtains:

$$\begin{aligned} acr_i + sc_i + it(1)_i &= swp_i * srp_i - swb_i * srb_i - \left(swp_i - swb_i\right) * RB \\ &= swp_i * \left(srp_i - RB\right) - swb_i * (srb_i - RB). \end{aligned}$$

In this case the return contributions of the segments are compared to those contributions that would have been obtained, if all portfolio and benchmark segments had achieved the average benchmark return RB. The return contribution $acr_i + sc_i + it(1)_i$ will, for instance, only then be positive, if the contribution $swp_i * srp_i - swb_i * srb_i$ exceeds the average contribution $\left(swp_i - swb_i\right) * RB$.

If one prefers that the effects on the segment level add up to the return contribution of the segment, then this can be realized simply by adding the term

Table 12.7 Components of an Attribution Analysis (Without Separating Currency Effects)

Term	Bezeichnung	Interpretation
$ac_i = (swp_i - swb_i) * srb_i$	allocation contribution = active weight * benchmark return	The allocation contribution is defined as the return contribution, which results from the different weighting of the segments relative to the benchmark
$acr_i = (swp_i - swb_i) * (srb_i - RB)$	(relative) allocation contribution = active weight * relative benchmark return	As above; the segment return is, however, considered relative to the benchmark
$sc_i = swb_i * (srp_i - srb_i)$	selection contribution = benchmark weight * active return	The selection contribution is defined as the return contribution, which results from the different weightings within the segments (stock picking)
$it(1)_i = (swp_i - swb_i) * (srp_i - srb_i)$ (Variant 1) respectively $(swp_i - swb_i) * (srp_i - srb_i + RB)$ (Variant 2)	interaction term = active weight * active return variant 2 only in conjunction with the relative allocation contribution	The interaction term results from the "interaction" between the allocation (1. factor) and the selection (2. factor)

$(swp_i - swb_i) * RB$ (the term that was in effect subtracted from the original allocation contribution) to the respective interaction contribution:

$$\begin{aligned} it(1)_i &= (swp_i - swb_i) * (srp_i - srb_i) + (swp_i - swb_i) * RB \\ &= (swp_i - sgb_i) * (srp_i - srb_i + RB) . \end{aligned}$$

The sum of the return contributions over all segments equals in any case (independently of the chosen form of the allocation term) the overall active return:

$$\sum_{i=1}^{n} (acr_i + sc_i + it(1)_i) = \sum_{i=1}^{n} (ac_i + sc_i + it(1)_i) = RP - RB.$$

Example 12.5

Allocation and selection analysis of the portfolio in Example 12.4:

Tables 12.5 and 12.6 contained the initial weights and the returns of a portfolio, consisting of two sectors, and its benchmark. The various return contributions of the segments are computed according to the formula in Table 12.7. At first Equation (12.18) will be employed for the calculation of the allocation effect. For the segment *Insurance* the allocation contribution is then calculated as:[12]

$$ac_2 = (60\% - 50\%) * (-0.22\%) = -0.02\%.$$

[12] In the numbering of the segments *Chemicals* is the first and *Insurance* the second sector.

Table 12.8 Attribution Analysis for the Portfolio in Example 12.4. The Allocation Effect is Computed According to Equation (12.18) (in %)

Sector	Selection	Allocation	Interaction	Total
Chemicals	−0.05	−0.99	0.01	−1.02
Insurance	−0.89	−0.02	−0.18	−1.09
Total	−0.94	−1.01	−0.17	−2.12

Table 12.9 Attribution Analysis for the Portfolio in Example 12.4. The Allocation Effect is Computed According to Equation (12.19), Interaction Terms According to (12.21) (in %)

Sector	Selection	Allocation	Interaction	Total
Chemicals	−0.05	−0.50	0.01	−0.54
Insurance	−0.89	−0.50	−0.18	−1.57
Total[a]	−0.94	−1.01	−0.17	−2.12

[a] *It is a common effect in practice that, due to rounding errors, the sum of the exhibited individual contributions may equal only approximately the overall effect.*

According to Equation (12.20) the selection contribution of the segment *Chemicals* is given by:

$$sc_1 = 50\% * (9.77\% - 9.86\%) = -0.05\%.$$

If one employs Equation (12.19) for the allocation effect, then the (relative) allocation contribution of, e.g., the segment *Insurance* is given by:

$$acr_2 = (60\% - 50\%) * (-0.22\% - 4.82\%) = -0.50\%.$$

The results illustrate the differences of the two equations for the allocation effect: due to the low absolute return of the segment *Insurance* within the benchmark there is only a small allocation contribution shown in Table 12.8.[13] In Table 12.9 the return relative to the overall return of the benchmark is considered. Since the active return of the segment *Insurance* relative to the benchmark was given by −5.04%, the allocation decision in regard to this segment (overweighting) must be regarded critically. In Table 12.9 this is appropriately reflected by the distinct negative contribution of −50 bp.

Horizontally the contributions add up to the overall (relative) contribution of the segment and vertically to the overall contribution of the attribution effect. Both the sum of the segment contribution and the sum of the overall attribution effects (allocation, selection, interaction) equal the active return of −2.12%. Compared to the overall active return the interaction terms (−0.17% in total) are small.

[13] Had, e.g., the segment return within the benchmark been equal to 0 %, then the allocation decision, to weight this segment differently from the benchmark, would always have led to an indifferent judgment, since the allocation contribution would have always been equal to 0 %—regardless of the overall benchmark return!

Example 12.6

Allocation and selection analysis for the DAX-Portfolio in Example 12.2:

Table 12.10 lists the return contributions from the sector allocation and the stock selection within the sectors. The allocation contributions in Table 12.10 are calculated according to Equation (12.18). The weights of the DAX sectors were taken from Example 12.2 (Tables 12.3 and 12.4).

If the allocation contribution is based on the return relative to the benchmark average (Equation (12.19)), then one obtains (in conjunction with the second variant of the formula for the interaction term (12.22)) the analysis in Table 12.11.

The sum of the allocation, selection and interaction terms equals the active return:[14]

$$-0.18\% - 0.71\% - 0.07\% = -0.96\%.$$

The negative active return is primarily due to bad allocation decisions:

- Underweighting *Automobile* (allocation contribution of −0.55%, respectively −0.43%)
- Underweighting *Chemicals* (−0.52%, respectively −0.36%)
- Overweighting *Telecommunication* (−0.23%, respectively −0.30%)

Table 12.10 Attribution Analysis for the DAX-Portfolio in Example 12.2. The Allocation Contributions are Based on Equation (12.18) (in %)

Sector	Weight		Return		Contributions			Total
	DAX	Portfolio	DAX	Portfolio	Selection	Allocation	Interact	
Automobile	13.00	9.00	13.72	13.18	−0.07	−0.55	0.02	−0.60
Banks	10.82	9.50	2.80	3.15	0.04	−0.04	0.00	0.00
Chemicals	10.26	5.00	9.85	9.90	0.01	−0.52	0.00	−0.52
Financial Service	3.13	8.00	9.31	6.51	−0.09	0.45	−0.14	0.23
Retail	1.21	3.00	1.40	1.40	0.00	0.03	0.00	0.03
Industrial	14.48	16.00	1.32	1.50	0.03	0.02	0.00	0.05
Consumer	1.99	5.00	7.24	6.29	−0.02	0.22	−0.03	0.17
Pharma & Healthcare	1.40	6.00	3.27	3.29	0.00	0.15	0.00	0.15
Software	4.41	3.00	−4.14	−4.14	0.00	0.06	0.00	0.06
Technology	1.24	0.00	0.43	0.43	0.00	−0.01	0.00	−0.01
Telecommunication	5.40	8.00	−8.70	−8.70	0.00	−0.23	0.00	−0.23
Transportation & Logistics	4.59	7.00	−3.10	0.20	0.15	−0.07	0.08	0.16
Insurance	13.64	14.00	−2.76	−4.43	−0.23	−0.01	−0.01	−0.24
Utilities	14.45	6.50	2.68	2.69	0.00	−0.21	0.00	−0.21
Total	100.00	100.00			−0.18	−0.71	−0.07	−0.96

[14] As a reminder: the returns of the portfolio and the benchmark were equal to 2.04% and 3.00%, respectively.

Table 12.11 Attribution Analysis of the Portfolio in Example 12.2 Relative to the DAX. The (relative) Allocation Contributions are Based on Equation (12.19) and the Interaction Terms on Equation (12.22) (in %)

Sector	Weight		Return		Contributions			Total
	DAX	Portfolio	DAX	Portfolio	Selection	Allocation	Interact	
Automobile	13.00	9.00	13.72	13.18	−0.07	−0.43	−0.10	−0.60
Banks	10.82	9.50	2.80	3.15	0.04	0.00	−0.04	0.00
Chemicals	10.26	5.00	9.85	9.90	0.01	−0.36	−0.16	−0.52
Financial Service	3.13	8.00	9.31	6.51	−0.09	0.31	0.01	0.23
Retail	1.21	3.00	1.40	1.40	0.00	−0.03	0.05	0.03
Industrial	14.48	16.00	1.32	1.50	0.03	−0.03	0.05	0.05
Consumer	1.99	5.00	7.24	6.29	−0.02	0.13	0.06	0.17
Pharma & Health-care	1.40	6.00	3.27	3.29	0.00	0.01	0.14	0.15
Software	4.41	3.00	−4.14	−4.14	0.00	0.10	−0.04	0.06
Technology	1.24	0.00	0.43	0.43	0.00	0.03	−0.04	−0.01
Telecommunica-tion	5.40	8.00	−8.70	−8.70	0.00	−0.30	0.08	−0.23
Transportation & Logistics	4.59	7.00	−3.10	0.20	0.15	−0.15	0.15	0.16
Insurance	13.64	14.00	−2.76	−4.43	−0.23	−0.02	0.00	−0.24
Utilities	14.45	6.50	2.68	2.69	0.00	0.03	−0.24	−0.21
Total	100.00	100.00			−0.18	−0.71	−0.07	−0.96

The stock picking also yields a negative contribution. Two sectors stand out:

- Selection contribution of −0.23% of the segment *Insurance*; this reflects the overweighting of *Allianz* vs. *Munich Re*.
- Selection contribution of 0.15% of the segment *Transportation & Logistics* (overweighting *TUI* and *Lufthansa* vs. *Deutsche Post*)

For the segments *Financial Service* and *Transportation & Logistics* the interaction terms turn out quite large with −0.14%, respectively −0.08%, as in those sectors significant sector bets (overweighting by ca. 4.9% respectively 2.4%) and stock bets (with the corresponding differences in the returns) were realized.

In Table 12.10 a positive allocation contribution (0.03%) is shown for the segment *Retail*, since the portfolio manager overweighted this positively performing sector. However, the return was lower than the overall benchmark return, which led to the negative (relative) allocation contribution of −0.03% in Table 12.11.

Compared with more detailed analyses as in Example 12.2 it is evident that within a Brinson type analysis the information is presented in a more systematic and compact form. It is thus much easier to draw conclusions in regard to the success of the determinants of the investment process (weighting of the sectors, stock selection). In particular, only in this approach do the allocation decisions become fully transparent. In practice it is important to present the information

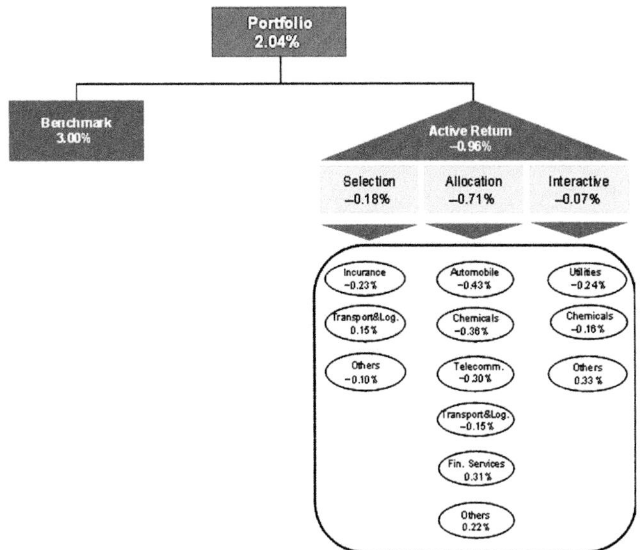

FIGURE 12.4
Key Factors of the Attribution Analysis in Table 12.11.

in a form as compact as possible. By restraining the presentation to the really significant factors it is possible to compress it further (Figure 12.4).

One point of critique often made in regard to the analysis framework of Brinson et al. concerns the treatment of transaction costs.[15] From the formulas for the contribution types it becomes obvious that these costs have an impact only on the selection contributions, not on the allocation contributions: only the returns of the portfolio segments, srp_i, but not the benchmark returns, srb_i, are affected by these costs.[16] While the allocation contributions are based on the benchmark returns, the selection contributions are dependent on the portfolio returns. This asymmetry puts the "selection manager" at a disadvantage compared to the "allocation manager".

Unfortunately there is no fully satisfactory solution for this problem. One could partially meet this criticism by switching to adjusted returns (i.e. returns adjusted by transaction costs). The effect of transaction costs could be listed as a separate effect of the analysis or combined with the cash position. One should bear in mind, however, that transaction costs are closely linked to the investment process. If the process involves a high trading frequency, then the resulting

[15] This question is addressed in different so-called "presentation standards" for attribution analysis. Cf., e.g., Spaulding (2002/03, recommendation 3.B.6) or a draft of the EIPC (European Investment Performance Committee) (Illmer and Senik 2004, p. 55). These (non-binding) standards contain in essence recommendations for the disclosure of the methodology for treating transactions costs and the assumptions made.

[16] At least, this is the case for the transaction-based approaches. Purely position-based systems are in general not affected by this problem, since all (portfolio and benchmark) positions are valuated with a unique price source.

transaction costs should be brought in relation to the generated return. Thus a complete separation of the transaction costs must be regarded critically.[17] Theoretically one could record for each transaction whether it's for the implementation of a selection decision or an allocation decision and record the transaction costs accordingly. Especially for a large number of portfolios this might prove a challenge.

12.2.2 Dealing With Titles Outside the Benchmark and Portfolio Segments with a Zero Weight

The considerations of the previous sections were implicitly based on the assumption that all titles of the portfolios are also constituents of the benchmark (cf. Figure 12.3). In practice, this assumption is, however, often not fulfilled. There are several ways to extend the framework. One needs to distinguish between two basic cases.

For stocks not included in the benchmark, which can be mapped in a unique form to benchmark segments (example: In case of the DAX the MDAX-stock *Hannover Rück* could be mapped in a unique way to the segment *Insurance*), there is no need for a modification: all parameters necessary for an attribution analysis as described in Section 12.2 are given in a unique way.

If it's not possible to associate the stock outside the benchmark with a benchmark segment (example: a portfolio, containing stocks from the segment *Construction*, is compared to the DAX (which does not include stocks from this segment)), then additional assumptions must be made. In this case often the number of benchmark segments is formally increased by the segments of the stocks that can't be mapped to the genuine benchmark segments. As these additional segments carry a zero weighting, it is called a "formal" extension. In order to conduct the attribution analysis further assumptions regarding the returns of these additional segments must be made. Setting these returns equal to zero (in analogy the "zero-weight postulate") would, however, entail that all (absolute) allocation contributions and all selection contributions would also be equal to zero, such that the entire contribution would be reflected by the interaction term.[18] As there are obviously both allocation and selection decisions involved with the selection of titles outside the benchmark, this is not common practice. Instead one often sets the returns of the formal benchmark segments identical to the returns of the corresponding portfolio segments. This implies that all

[17] In this context it should be mentioned that the GIPS standards consider the calculation of gross-of-fee returns on a portfolio level, but that the deduction of trading expenses is not permissible (CFA Institute 2010, 2.A.5).

[18] In this case the relative allocation terms would assume the form $acr_i = -swp_{n+i} * RB$. Thus, using the relative approach does not lead to a meaningful breakdown either.

selection and interaction terms are equal to zero, and that the entire contribution is reflected by the allocation term:[19]

$$ac_{n+i} = swp_{n+i} * srp_{n+i} \quad (i > 0). \tag{12.24}$$

In a relative form one obtains:

$$acr_{n+i} = swp_{n+i} * \left(srp_{n+i} - RB\right). \tag{12.25}$$

In this approach the contributions from stock picking are included in the allocation contribution. In order to split off these contributions one may chose a broader benchmark that contains the missing segment(s). In the above example of the segment *Construction*, which has formally been attached to the DAX, one may chose the sector *Construction* from the broader market segment *Prime Standard* in order to compute the selection contributions. The index of this segment is called *Prime Construction Performance Index.*[20] Within the allocation portfolio described in Section 12.2.1 the segment *Construction* would have a weight identical to the weight of the stocks of this industry in the portfolio.

Under these assumptions the Equation for the allocation contribution assumes the following form:[21]

$$ac_{n+i} = swp_{n+i} * \widetilde{srb}_{n+i}, \tag{12.26}$$

where $\widetilde{srb}_{n+i}$ are the returns of the respective segments in the broader benchmark. The selection contribution is then defined as the difference of the terms on the right-hand side of the Equations (12.24) and (12.26):

$$sc_{n+i} = swp_{n+i} * \left(srp_{n+i} - \widetilde{srb}_{n+i}\right). \tag{12.27}$$

If one uses the relative allocation terms, then Equation (12.25) assumes the following form:

$$acr_{n+i} = swp_{n+i} * \left(\widetilde{srb}_{n+i} - RB\right). \tag{12.28}$$

Example 12.7

Attribution analysis with stocks outside the benchmark:

In this example we come back to the portfolio already described in Example 12.4. Here we assume, however, that the portfolio is invested also in stocks that belong to a sector (*Construction*[22]) which is not included in the benchmark (see Table 12.12).

Analogous to the procedure in Example 12.5 one obtains the attribution analysis (based on the relative allocation contributions) in Table 12.14. The portfolio return is 2.19% compared to a benchmark return of 4.82%. Thus the active return is −2.63%).

[19] In addition to the original n benchmark segments, the indexation also includes the additional segments.

[20] Cf. DB (2006).

[21] In order to keep the notation simple, the notation ac_{n+i} is kept.

[22] This sector will be represented by the *Prime Construction Performance Index.*

Table 12.12 Portfolio Consisting of Stocks of the Sectors *Chemicals*, *Insurance* and *Construction*. The Analysis Period is 01.03. to 31.03.2007 (in %)

Sector	Sector Weight	Sector Return	Stock	Stock Weight	Stock Return
Chemicals	30	9.77	BASF	22.5	9.67
			Bayer	7.5	10.05
Insurance	60	−2.00	Allianz	40.0	−5.57
			Munich Re	20.0	5.13
Construction	10	4.64	Bilfinger & Berger	5.0	8.21
			HeidelbergCement	5.0	1.07

Table 12.13 Benchmark Components. Apart from the Official Benchmark of the Portfolio, the Index Prime Construction is used to Cover the Stocks Outside the Benchmark (in %)

Sector	Sector	Sector Weight	Sector Return	Stock Weight	Stock Return	Sector
Chemicals	Benchmark sector	50	9.86	BASF	25	9.67
				Bayer	25	10.05
Insurance	Benchmark sector	50	−0.22	Allianz	25	−5.57
				Munich Re	25	5.13
Construction	Prime Construction		9.47			

Table 12.14 The (Relative) Allocation Contributions (in %) are Calculated According to Equation (12.19); for the Segment Construction Equation (12.28) was Used

Sector	Selection	Allocation	Interaction	Total
Chemicals	−0.05	−1.01	0.02	−1.04
Insurance	−0.89	−0.50	−0.18	−1.57
Construction	0.00	−0.02	0.00	−0.02
Total[a]	−0.94	−1.53	−0.16	−2.63

[a] *It is a common effect that due to rounding differences in an attribution analysis, that often the sum of the listed individual contributions equals the overall effect only approximately.*

Table 12.15 Relative Attribution Analysis with an Additional Index for the Sector Construction (in %)

Sector	Selection	Allocation	Interaction	Total
Chemicals	−0.05	−1.01	0.02	−1.04
Insurance	−0.89	−0.50	−0.18	−1.57
Construction	0.48	−0.47	0.00	−0.02
Total	−0.94	−1.53	−0.16	−2.63

	positive active return $srp_i > srb_i$	negative active return $srp_i < srb_i$
Overweighting $swp_i > swb_i$	+	–
Underweighting $swp_i < swb_i$	–	+

FIGURE 12.5
Sign of the Interaction Terms.

The addition of titles of the segment construction thus had a negligible impact on the active return.

One obtains, however, a more differentiated picture if one chooses an appropriate index for the sector *Construction*. The return of the *Construction Performance Index* was 9.47% over the analysis period. Based on Equations (12.27) and (12.28) the attribution analysis assumes the form exhibited in Table 12.1.

This information gives a much more detailed view on the quality of the management decisions. The idea to add stocks from the segment *Construction* was basically a good one: an investment in the (average) construction sector would have yielded an allocation contribution of 47 basis points. This positive return contribution was, however, entirely eliminated by the poor title selection. Especially the selection of the stock *HeidelbergCement* was disadvantageous, since this stock performed much worse than other stocks in his sector.

Another problem occurs if the portfolio manager has not selected any title from a benchmark segment ($swp_i = 0$); in this case the return of the portfolio segment, (and thus the selection and interaction terms) are not defined. It is, however, easy to address this issue, since it wouldn't make sense at all to assign to the selection contribution (or to the interaction term) a contribution different from zero. Thus the return of the portfolio can (at least formally[23]) be set equal to the return of the corresponding benchmark segment. As a consequence, the contribution of such a segment will be fully reflected by the allocation contribution.

12.2.3 Interpretation of the Interaction Terms

The signs of the interaction terms (cf. Table 12.7)

$$it(1)_i := \left(swp_i - swb_i\right) * \left(srp_i - srb_i\right)$$

can be illustrated analogous to Figure 12.2 (cf. Figure 12.5).

[23] This return is needed only for conducting the attribution analysis. It should not be listed in other client reports. Cf. also Laker (2006).

Table 12.16 Initial Weights and Returns of a 2-Sector-Portfolio and Its Benchmark for a Period, in Which Both Sectors Consisted of Two Titles Each

Sector	Stocks		Benchmark			Portfolio		
			Weight (%)		Return (%)	Weight (%)		Return (%)
	Title	Return (%)	Title	Sector	Sector	Title	Sector	Sector
1	1	20	25	50	10	40	60	13.33
	2	0	25			20		
2	3	10	25	50	5	20	40	5
	4	0	25			20		

Table 12.17 Attribution Analysis; the Allocation Contributions are Based on Equation (12.19) (in %)

Sector	Selection	Allocation	Interaction	Total
1	1.67	0.25	0.33	0.25
2	0.00	2.25	0.00	0.25
Total	1.67	0.50	0.33	2.50

Example 12.8

Interaction terms:

In order to illustrate the role of the interaction terms, we will consider again the simple case of a portfolio consisting of two sectors with two stocks each (see Table 12.16).

At the beginning of the period the portfolio manager has made the following decisions:

- Overweighting sector 1;
- Overweighting stock 1 within sector 1;
- No active stock selection in sector 2.[24]

The return of the benchmark was 7.5% and the portfolio return 10.0%. This yields an active return of 2.5%.

Using Equations (12.19), (12.20) and (12.21) one obtains the return contributions shown in Table 12.17.

The investment decisions to overweight sector 1 relative to sector 2 and stock 1 relative to stock 2 have contributed the lion's share of the active return. According to the additive decomposition outlined in Section 12.2.1 the allocation and selection decisions cannot be separated entirely. It remains an interaction term of 0.33%.

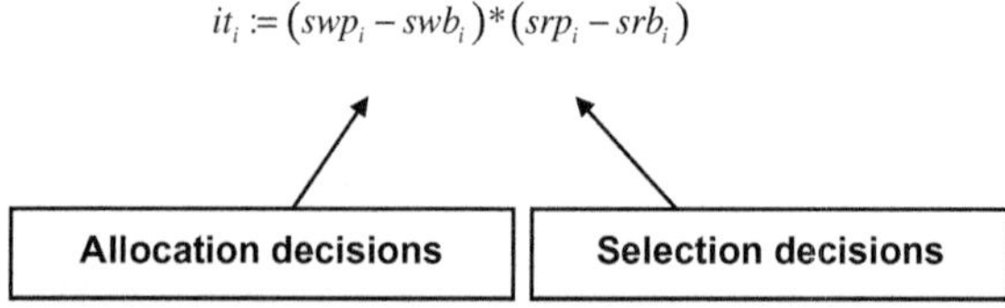

FIGURE. 12.6
Components of the "Allocation/Selection Interaction Terms".

[24] Both stocks of this sector have equal weights within the portfolio and the benchmark. The different absolute levels of the weighting (25% vs. 20%) are a result of the allocation decisions.

Under the assumptions made so far the interaction terms (Figure 12.6) cannot be linked in a unique way to the parameters of the investment process; although they contain "allocation factors" $(swp_i - swb_i)$, these are weighted by factors $(srp_i - srb_i)$ clearly attributed to the selection process. What they precisely mean and the requirements for a mapping of the effects to the standard contributions of an attribution analysis shall be deduced by means of a (drastic) example.

Example 12.9

Significance of the interaction terms:

The return of the portfolio described in Table 12.18 was −0.05% and the return of its benchmark 0.50%. Table 12.19 contains the results of the attribution analysis.

Even though both the overall allocation contribution and the selection contributions are positive (0.50%, respectively 1.40%), the portfolio manager is credited with a negative active return of −0.55%! This is due to the extraordinarily high interaction terms, which accounted in sum for −2.45% of the active return. In order to explain how these interaction terms came about, first the allocation and selection contributions will be analyzed:

Allocation contributions: The portfolio manager has taken a drastic overweight position in the sector with the higher return (Sector 2) and a corresponding underweight position in the weaker sector. The successful allocation decisions are reflected in the positive allocation contribution of 0.50%.

Table 12.18 Initial Weights and Returns of a 2-Sector-Portfolio for a Period Over Which Both Sectors Consisted of Two Stocks Each

Sector	Stocks		Benchmark			Portfolio		
			Weight (%)		Return (%)	Weight (%)		Return (%)
	Title	Return (%)	Title	Title	Sector	Title	Sector	Sector
1	1	−11	25	50	−0.5	5	**25**	5.8
	2	10	25			20		
2	3	12	25	50	1.5	25	**75**	−2.0
	4	−9	25			50		

Table 12.19 Attribution Analysis for the Portfolio in Example 12.18. The Allocation Contributions is Based on Equation (12.19) (in %)

Sector	Selection	Allocation	Interaction	Total
1	3.15	0.25	−1.58	1.83
2	−1.75	0.25	−0.88	−2.38
Total	1.40	0.50	−2.45	−0.55

Selection contributions: Within Sector 1 the stock picking was very successful. The portfolio manager took an overweight position in the outperforming stock 2, whereas the weaker stock 1 was underweighted.
In Sector 2 there a mixed picture; the portfolio manager took an overweight position in the low performing stock 4. The exceptional selection in Sector 1, however, more than makes up for the bad selection in Sector 2, so that the overall contribution from stock picking is positive.

The decisive point is that the positive stock selection occurred in Sector 1, for which the portfolio manager took a drastic underweight position. Although the latter doesn't impact the selection contribution, in regard to the overall result it makes a big difference. Through the corresponding overweight position in Sector 2 the bad stock selection is de facto *leveraged*. The resulting contribution is not attributable to either allocation or selection decisions, but rather to the (in this case unfortunate) concurrence of these decisions. This is why the corresponding term is called the interaction term. It refers to the quasi interaction between allocation and selection decisions. In a nutshell: The analysis shows that both the allocation and selection decisions were successfull; the latter, however, predominantly within the underweighted sectors. This is the reason for the negative active return.

The effect from Example 12.9 is also present in Example 12.8 – although to a lesser extent: the interaction term of 33 basis points results from the overweight position of the segment with the superior stock selection (Sector 1). The positive selection effect is leveraged by the allocation.

Figure 12.7 contains the allocation portfolio and the selection portfolio of the 2-sector-portfolio in Table 12.18. The selection portfolio has to preserve the sector weightings. The allocation portfolio represents solely the weighting of the portfolio sectors.

At this stage it is necessary to consider the investment process pertinent to the analysis of Brinson et al. more closely. It assumes that all titles in the benchmark

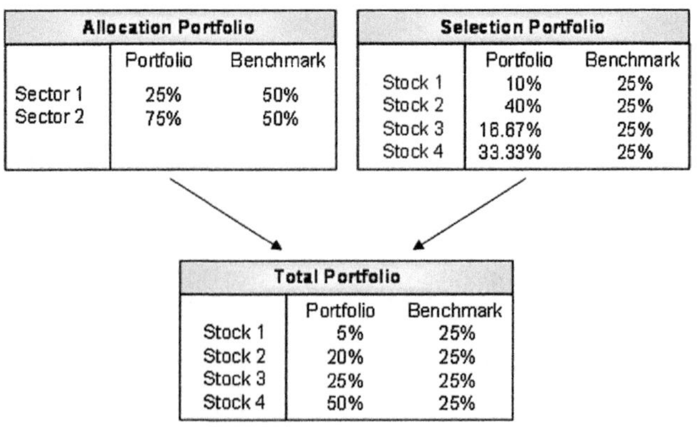

FIGURE 12.7
Break-Down in the Associated Allocation and Selection Portfolios.

and the portfolio can be broken down according to a specified scheme (e.g. according to the sector or country specification).[25] Under this assumption the choices of the portfolio manager can be reduced to two different types: he may change the weights of the segments relative to the benchmark (*allocation*), or he may change the weights of the titles *within* these segments (*stock selection*).[26] The selection contribution is based on the sector weights of the benchmark (cf. Equation (12.20)), which leads directly to the appearance of interaction terms. If the return of the selection portfolio is compared to the original benchmark (the same benchmark as the one for the allocation portfolio), then it makes sense to list the interaction terms separately. In this case these contributions represent the "interaction" between the allocation and selection decisions taken independently.

The methodology of Brinson et al. can be characterized by the following properties.

Properties of the attribution analysis according to Brinson et al. over a single period

I. The active return is represented as the sum of the return contributions.
II. The success of the decisions made within the investment process is quantified by the individual contributions. The investment process is based on allocation decisions in regard to the segments and on selection decisions within the segments.
III. The contribution for a determinant of the attribution analysis over a single period is independent of the decisions in regard to the other determinants.
IV. The contributions for an attribution determinant (e.g. selection within a segment) over multiple periods may be linked, such that they are independent of the decisions in regard to another determinant (e.g. allocation).
V. The total contribution for a determinant of an attribution analysis (e.g. selection) over a single period is identical to the sum of the contributions over the individual segments of this determinant.
VI. The absolute value of the contributions depends on the absolute value of benchmark return, respectively on the return of the benchmark segments.[27]

The use of the benchmark weights in the definition of the selection contributions reflects the independence between the selection and allocation decisions. Waiving the condition of independence has an impact on the treatment of the interaction terms. If, for instance, the allocation decisions are regarded as part of the background on which the selection manager derives his decisions, then it is meaningful to combine the selection and interaction contributions. In this

[25] This view is essentially determined by the partitioning of the investment universe. A further level is added in case of a balanced portfolio, where one needs to distinguish between the equity and the fixed income portion (cf. Chapter 14). A differentiation between different asset managers (*multi manager approach*) would lead yet to a further level.

[26] It is important to stress this point as it is not a selection *per se*. Cf. e.g. Brinson et al. (1986).

[27] Cf. Section 10.7.

approach the benchmark assigned to the selection manager is identical to the allocation portfolio:[28]

$$RAP = \sum_{i=1}^{n} swp_i * srb_i. \tag{12.29}$$

The benchmark portfolio is based on the decisions of the allocation manager (made *prior* to the stock picking), and does not include any selection decisions. Under these assumptions the selection contribution is given by:[29]

$$SC^{alt} = RP - RAP = \sum_{i=1}^{n} swp_i * \left(srp_i - srb_i\right) = \sum sc_i^{alt}. \tag{12.30}$$

The term (12.30) is equal to the sum of the original selection contribution (12.13) and the interaction term (12.14):

$$\begin{aligned} SC + IT(1) &= \sum_{i=1}^{n} swb_i * \left(srp_i - srb_i\right) + \sum_{i=1}^{n} \left(swp_i - swb_i\right) * \left(srp_i - srb_i\right) \\ &= \sum_{i=1}^{n} swp_i * \left(srp_i - srb_i\right) \\ &= SC^{alt}. \end{aligned}$$

Formally only the benchmark weight is replaced by the respective portfolio weight in the formula for the selection contribution. This procedure is applied often in practice perhaps due to this suggestive substitution.

On the level of the overall effects, this approach yields the following breakdown (cf. Equation (12.16)):

$$RP - RB = \underbrace{(RAP - RB)}_{AC} + \underbrace{(RP - RAP)}_{SC^{alt}}. \tag{12.31}$$

Table 12.20 Attribution Analysis for the Portfolio in Example 12.8. The Selection Contributions are Calculated According to Equation (12.29) (in %)

Sector	Selection	Allocation	Total
1	2.00	0.25	2.25
2	0.00	0.25	0.25
Total	2.00	0.50	2.50

[28] Under this premise the original portfolio benchmark is no longer relevant for the selection manager, which leads to an asymmetrical consideration of the selection and allocation management.
[29] cf. Fischer (2002).

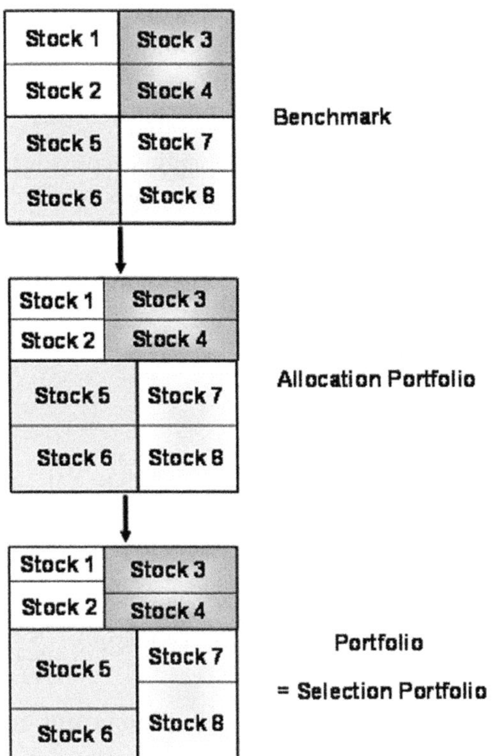

FIGURE 12.8
Investment Process According to Brinson et al. in A Hierarchical Ordering (The Results of the Allocation Process Form the Basis of the Selection Process).

Example 12.10

Combining selection and interaction:

Under the premise of integrating the interaction terms into the selection contributions, the attribution analysis in Example 12.8 assumes the form shown in Table 12.20).

As the (positive) interaction effect arising from the overweighting of sector 1 is added to the selection contribution, this term is higher than the one listed in Example 12.8.

In face of the purported plausibility of this analysis form the reader might ask why it is not generally used in order to do away with the interaction terms. Figure 12.8 illustrates the mentioned interaction effects: the quadrant on the upper-left side (segment 1) is, for instance, considerably underweight and the sector on the lower-right side (segment 2) considerably overweight. Therefore the selection decisions taken in segment 2 have a much larger impact on the overall performance than the ones in segment 1. In the extreme case that a segment would be assigned a zero weight or a weight near zero (allocation weight equal to or near zero), the selection decisions taken in this segment would have no impact on the overall performance whatsoever (or very little)! In this approach the evaluation of the selection manager is strongly influenced by the allocation decisions. The selection manager(s) might find this arbitrary or unjust.

An alternative approach to weaken the independence principle for the selection and allocation decisions is given by reversing the process described above. Thus the allocation decisions would be based on the selection decisions (made prior to the allocation decisions). In this approach the benchmark assigned to the allocation manager is identical to the selection portfolio:

$$RSP = \sum_{i=1}^{n} swb_i * srp_i.$$

This benchmark portfolio is based on the (already taken) decisions of the selection manager and does not express any allocation decisions.[30] To compute the allocation contribution (based on Equation (12.10)), *RAP* must be replaced by *RP* and *RB* by *RSP*.[31] Under these assumptions it is given by:

$$AC^{alt} = RP - RSP = \sum_{i=1}^{n} (swp_i - swb_i) * srp_i = \sum_{i=1}^{n} ac_i^{alt}. \quad (12.32)$$

The term (12.32) is the sum of the original allocation contribution (12.10) and the interaction term (12.14):

$$\begin{aligned} AC + IT(1) &= \sum_{i=1}^{n} (swp_i - swb_i) * srb_i + \sum_{i=1}^{n} (swp_i - swb_i) * (srp_i - srb_i) \\ &= \sum_{i=1}^{n} (swp_i - swb_i) * srp_i = AC^{alt}. \end{aligned} \quad (12.33)$$

In this approach the investment process stipulates that the allocation manager has the obligation to assess the strengths and weaknesses of the selection manager(s), and to consider these while implementing his allocation decisions.

In this case there are options in regard to the treatment of the interaction terms. These terms measure the ability of the allocation manager to assess the competency of the selection manager(s) in selecting titles within the various segments. If he succeeds in overweighting those segments, where the stock picking is particularly successful, then this will be reflected by positive interaction terms. Vice versa, misjudging the stock picking skills will lead to negative interaction terms. If the portfolio is managed by a single portfolio manager, this interpretation of

[30] This benchmark portfolio is sometimes called selection notional fund (cf. e.g. Bacon 2008, p. 119). The assertion of footnote 30 applies mutatis mutandis.

[31] See also Fischer (2002).

the interaction terms holds generally[32], as a breakdown of the investment process is of limited use in this case.

On the level of the overall effects this approach results in the following breakdown (cf. Equation (12.16)):

$$RP - RB = \underbrace{(RP - RSP)}_{AC^{alt}} + \underbrace{(RSP - RB)}_{SC}. \qquad (12.34)$$

The investment process is illustrated in Figure 12.9.

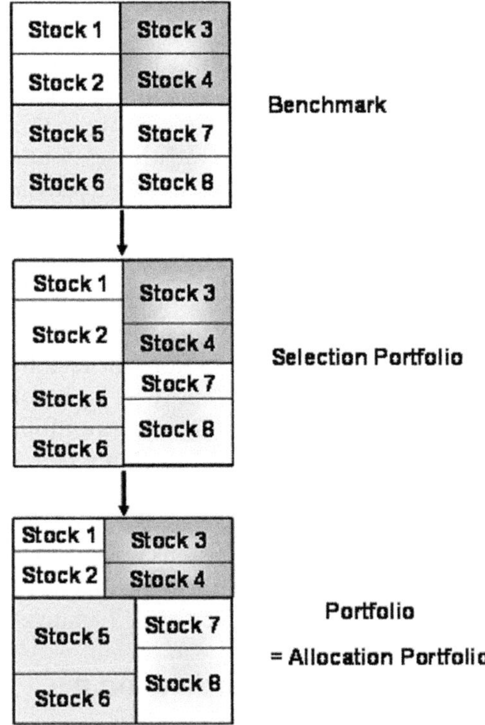

FIGURE 12.9
Investment Process According to Brinson et al. in A Hierarchical Ordering (the Results of the Selection Process Form the Basis of the Allocation Process).

Table 12.21 Attribution Analysis for the Portfolio in Example 12.8. The Allocation Contributions are Calculated According to Equation (12.32) (in %)

Sector	Selection	Allocation	Total
1	3.15	−1.33	1.83
2	−1.75	−0.63	−2.38
Total	1.40	−1.95	−0.55

[32] Cf. Ankrim 1992. In the general case the interaction terms can always be listed separately.

Example 12.11

Combining allocation and interaction:

Under the premise of integrating the interaction terms into the allocation contributions, the attribution analysis in Example 12.8 assumes the form shown in Table 12.21.

Since in this case the contributions resulting from the overweighting of sector 1 and the underweighting of sector 2 need to be assigned to the allocation contributions, the results are much worse than in Example 12.8. This reflects the poor judgement of the portfolio manager (or allocation manager) in regard to his stock picking abilities (respectively the one of his colleagues) (see Table 12.21).

These considerations make it clear that the simplicity in combining the selection (or allocation) terms with the interaction terms comes at a certain price: the performance assessment of the selection manager (respectively the allocation manager) is no longer independent. Especially in those cases, where the interaction makes the figures look worse (as in Example 12.11), discussions between the portfolio managers and management or the controlling department in regard to the soundness of the measurement are very likely.

We conclude this section with a general remark: a difficulty in communicating the Brinson concept of distinguishing between an allocation and a selection portfolio in practice (say, vis-à-vis an investor) originates from the fact that sometimes the selection decisions can be observed only indirectly in a portfolio. This shall be briefly illustrated with the help of Example 12.9. The portfolio manager took, for example, an underweight position in stock 3 within sector 2 of the selection portfolio (16.67% vs. 25%). In the real portfolio this underweight position is, however, somewhat hidden due to the decision to take an overweight position in sector 2. In fact, the net effect of these two decisions was that in the real portfolio stock 3 ended up with the same weight as in the benchmark. The selection decision can only be deduced from the weighting of stock 3 relative to stock 4.

12.2.4 Breakdown of the Contributions on a Single-Stock-Level

Part of the motivation for an attribution analysis is the desire to represent the information about the success of the investment manager in a compact form. However, sometimes it is desirable to take a deeper look into segments with a significant performance contribution. Then it is required to go back on a single-position level. The Brinson-type analysis can be modified for this purpose. In the following this will be illustrated in case of the allocation contribution (Equation (12.18)):

$$ac_i := \left(swp_i - swb_i\right) * srb_i.$$

If one substitutes the return of the benchmark segment by the expression

$$srb_i = \sum_{j=1}^{N_i} \frac{wb_{ij}}{swb_i} * rb_{ij}, \tag{12.35}$$

(if $swb_i \neq 0$), where:

wb_{ij}: weight of the title j in the benchmark segment i at the beginning of the period

rb_{ij}: return of the title j in the benchmark segment i over the period
N_i: number of titles in the segment i (contains by definition all titles of the benchmark and the portfolio in this segment),then Equation. (12.18) assumes the following form:

$$ac_i := \sum_{j=1}^{N_i} (swp_i - swb_i) * \frac{wb_{ij}}{swb_i} * rb_{ij}. \tag{12.36}$$

From this one readily deduces the terms that may be identified as the allocation contribution ac_{ij} of the stock j toward the allocation contribution of the segment i:

$$ac_{ij} := (swp_i - swb_i) * \frac{wb_{ij}}{swb_i} * rb_{ij}. \tag{12.37}$$

It holds $\sum_{j=1}^{N_i} wb_{ij} = swb_i$.

One deals similarly with the selection contributions:

$$sc_i := swb_i * (srp_i - srb_i). \tag{12.38}$$

Here one substitutes the terms srb_i and srp_i by the expression in (12.35), respectively by:

$$srp_i = \sum_{j=1}^{N_i} \frac{wp_{ij}}{swp_i} * rb_{ij},$$

(assuming that $swp_i \neq 0$), where:
wp_{ij}: weight of the title j in the portfolio segment i at the beginning of the period
rb_{ij}: return of the title j in the portfolio segment i over the period.[33]
One obtains:

$$sc_i := swb_i * \sum_{j=1}^{N_i} \left(\frac{wp_{ij}}{swp_i} * rb_{ij} - \frac{wb_{ij}}{swb_i} * rb_{ij} \right) = swb_i * \sum_{j=1}^{N_i} rb_{ij} * \left(\frac{wp_{ij}}{swp_i} - \frac{wb_{ij}}{swb_i} \right). \tag{12.39}$$

From this the selection contributions sc_{ij} of the stocks j toward the selection contribution of the segment i are readily deduced:

$$sc_{ij} := swb_i * rb_{ij} * \left(\frac{wp_{ij}}{swp_i} - \frac{wb_{ij}}{swb_i} \right) = swb_i * \left(\frac{wp_{ij}}{swp_i} * rb_{ij} - \frac{wb_{ij}}{swb_i} * rb_{ij} \right). \tag{12.40}$$

The interaction terms are deduced in a similar way:

$$\begin{aligned} it(1)_{ij} &:= (swp_i - swb_i) * \left(\frac{wp_{ij}}{swp_i} * rb_{ij} - \frac{wb_{ij}}{swb_i} * rb_{ij} \right) \\ &= (swp_i - swb_i) * \left(\frac{wp_{ij}}{swp_i} - \frac{wb_{ij}}{swb_i} \right) * rb_{ij}, \end{aligned} \tag{12.41}$$

[33] The return of a title is independent of whether it is part of the benchmark or the portfolio. This return will uniformly be denoted by rb_{ij}.

and it is readily verified that:

$$ac_{ij} + sc_{ij} + it(1)_{ij} = wp_{ij} * rb_{ij} - wb_{ij} * rb_{ij}, \tag{12.42}$$

which is to say, that the individual contributions sum up to the overall contribution of a stock.

The allocation contribution can again be written in a relative form. One obtains an expression similar to the one in Equation (12.19):

$$acr_i := \sum_{j=1}^{N_i} \left(swp_i - swb_i\right) * \frac{wb_{ij}}{swb_i} * \left(rb_{ij} - RB\right), \tag{12.43}$$

respectively on a single-title basis:

$$acr_{ij} := \left(swp_i - swb_i\right) * \frac{wb_{ij}}{swb_i} * \left(rb_{ij} - RB\right). \tag{12.44}$$

In this case the sum of the contributions yields:[34]

$$acr_{ij} + sc_{ij} + it(1)_{ij} = wp_{ij} * rb_{ij} - wb_{ij} * rb_{ij} - \left(swp_i - swb_i\right) * \frac{wb_{ij}}{swb_i} * RB. \tag{12.45}$$

In agreement with the approach in Section 12.2.1 the interaction terms may also be defined as follows:

$$\begin{aligned} it(1)_{ij} &:= \left(swp_i - swb_i\right) * rb_{ij} * \left(\frac{wp_{ij}}{swp_i} - \frac{wb_{ij}}{swb_i}\right) + \left(swp_i - swb_i\right) * \frac{wb_{ij}}{swb_i} * RB \\ &= \left(swp_i - swb_i\right) * \left(rb_{ij} * \left(\frac{wp_{ij}}{swp_i} - \frac{wb_{ij}}{swb_i}\right) + \frac{wb_{ij}}{swb_i} * RB\right). \end{aligned} \tag{12.46}$$

If one uses this expression instead, then the sum of the contributions will add up again to the overall contribution of the segment (Equation (12.5)). In agreement with the notation in Section 12.2.1, the variant of Equation (12.41) will be labeled variant 1 and the one of (12.46) variant 2.

Example 12.12

Breakdown of the contributions on a single-stock basis:

This approach shall be illustrated by means of the German equity portfolio analyzed in Example 12.6.

Table 12.22 contains a breakdown to a single-stock-level for a number of segments. The breakdown was applied only to those segments where the individual titles contributed significantly (> 10 basis points). In a computer-aided report (e.g. Excel) the user may choose the detail level in a flexible way.

Although the interpretation of the single-stock contributions might be problematic (especially of the allocation and interaction terms), the user can in general infer useful

[34] The interpretation of this expression is analogous to the one outlined in Section 12.2.1.

Table 12.22 Attribution Analysis of the DAX-Portfolio in Example 12.2 Relative to the DAX. The (Relative) Allocation Contributions are Based on Equations (12.19) and (12.44) (in %)

Sector	Weight		Return		Contributions			Total
	DAX	Portfolio	DAX	Portfolio	Selection	Allocation	Interact.	
Automobile	13.00	9.00	13.72	13.18	−0.07	−0.43	−0.10	−0.60
BMW	2.02	0.00	0.59		−0.01	0.01	−0.01	−0.01
Continental	1.98	3.00	2.60		0.06	0.00	−0.04	0.03
Daimler	6.98	2.00	19.43		−0.80	−0.35	0.18	−0.97
VW	2.02	4.00	18.00		0.68	−0.09	−0.23	0.36
Banks	10.82	9.50	2.80	3.15	0.04	0.00	−0.04	0.00
Chemicals	10.26	5.00	9.85	9.90	0.01	−0.36	−0.16	−0.52
BASF	5.51	2.00	9.67		−0.14	−0.19	−0.02	−0.34
Bayer	4.75	3.00	10.05		0.14	−0.17	−0.15	−0.18
Financial Service	3.13	8.00	9.31	6.51	−0.09	0.31	0.01	0.23
Deutsche Börse	2.21	4.00	13.31		−0.09	0.35	−0.03	0.24
Hypo Real Estate	0.92	4.00	−0.29		0.00	−0.05	0.04	−0.01
Retail	1.21	3.00	1.40	1.40	0.00	−0.03	0.05	0.03
Industrial	14.48	16.00	1.32	1.50	0.03	−0.03	0.05	0.05
Consumer	1.99	5.00	7.24	6.29	−0.02	0.13	0.06	0.17
Pharma & Health-care	1.40	6.00	3.27	3.29	0.00	0.01	0.14	0.15
Software	4.41	3.00	−4.14	−4.14	0.00	0.10	−0.04	0.06
Technology	1.24	0.00	0.43	0.43	0.00	0.03	−0.04	−0.01
Telecommunica-tion	5.40	8.00	−8.70	−8.70	0.00	−0.30	0.08	−0.23
Transportation & Logistics	4.59	7.00	−3.10	0.20	0.15	−0.15	0.15	0.16
Deutsche Post	2.68	1.00	−6.05		0.12	−0.13	0.11	0.10
Lufthansa	1.34	4.00	−0.64		−0.01	−0.03	0.02	−0.02
TUI	0.57	2.00	4.99		0.04	0.01	0.03	0.07
Insurance	13.64	14.00	−2.76	−4.43	−0.23	−0.02	0.00	−0.24
Allianz	10.06	12.50	−5.57		−0.12	−0.02	0.00	−0.14
Munich Re	3.58	1.50	5.13		−0.11	0.00	0.00	−0.11
Utilities	14.45	6.50	2.68	2.69	0.00	0.03	−0.24	−0.21
Total	100.00	100.00			−0.18	−0.71	−0.07	−0.96

information. He recognizes for instance that within the segment *Insurance* the stock picking was uniformly bad (overweight position in *Allianz*, underweight position in *Munich Re*), while the stock picking results in the sector *Automobile* were quite heterogeneous. The listing of the allocation and interaction contributions on a single-stock-level serves primarily the purpose of achieving mathematical consistency, since all contributions indeed add up to the overall contribution toward the active return.

In the concrete structuring of a reporting of the findings of an attribution analysis the type of benchmark plays a crucial role. In the example above, the portfolio was benchmarked against the DAX, which is an index with an unusually low number of constituents (which is the reason why we chose this benchmark so often). A broadly diversified index like the MSCI Europe or the Stoxx 600 carries a considerably higher number of constituents than the DAX (cf. Chapter 11) (and in general also more titles than the portfolio). Thus one always faces the danger that an analysis on a single-stock-level contains a plethora of completely useless information that only obscures the essential facts.

12.2.5 Separation of the Currency Contributions in Attribution Analysis with a Passive Management Approach

In Section 12.2.1 a form of attribution analysis was described which contained implicit currency effects but didn't make them transparent. This approach will be briefly reviewed for an international equity portfolio in order to illustrate the necessity for a separation of the currency contributions.

Table 12.23 Portfolio Data for the Period from 01.03.2007 to 31.03.2007. Returns are Calcu-Lated in Base Currency (€). The Bottom Line Shows the Overall Return of the Portfolio und the Benchmark (in %)

Portfolio Segment	Weight		Return	
	Portfolio	Benchmark	Portfolio	Benchmark
USA	70	50	2.50	−0.96
Germany	30	50	2.00	3.00
Total	100	100	2.35	1.02

Table 12.24 Return Contributions According to Section 12.2.1. The Contributions of the Segment *USA* Contain Currency Components. The Allocation Contribution is Based on Equation (12.18) (in %)

Portfolio Segment	Selection	Allocation	Interaction	Total
USA	1.73	−0.19	0.69	2.23
Germany	−0.50	−0.60	0.20	−0.90
Total	1.23	−0.79	0.89	1.33

Table 12.25 Return Contributions According to Section 12.2.1. The Contributions of the Segment *USA* Contain Currency Components. The Allocation Contribution is Based on Equation (12.19) (in %)

Portfolio Segment	Selection	Allocation	Interaction	Total
USA	1.73	−0.40	0.69	2.23
Germany	−0.50	−0.40	0.20	−0.90
Total	1.23	−0.79	0.89	1.33

Example 12.13

Attribution analysis for a 2-country portfolio:

In this example we will consider an international equity portfolio, which consists of two country segments only: *USA* and *Germany*. The benchmark consists of 50% S&P 500 and 50% DAX (see Table 12.23).

The active return of 1.33% will be decomposed according to the methodology outlined in Section 12.2.1 (allocation terms (12.18) and (12.19)) (Table 12.24 and Table 12.25).

Over the analysis period the US$ depreciated against the Euro by −1.94%. This had an impact on the performance of the segment *USA* both in the benchmark and the portfolio, since all returns are calculated on an €-basis. Currency effects are thus included in all contributions in this segment.

Consequently, this approach doesn't yield clarity in regard to the impact of the developments on the currency markets on the portfolio performance. This makes it hard to properly evaluate the management skills. The approach depends (as always) on the investment strategy and the desired level of detail of the analysis. If, for instance, the allocation decisions are made independently of currency aspects, then it makes sense to list currency contributions separately. On the other hand, if currency management is part of the allocation process (and not of the selection process), then currency and allocation contributions may be combined. A separate listing of the currency contributions is in any case at least informative. Most commercial analysis systems have this functionality available. In the following it will be explained how to split off the currency effects from the contributions of a Brinson-type analysis, in order to report them separately. A crucial assumption in this context is that the performance is analyzed from the standpoint of a fixed base currency (in general the currency of the investor's home country). The requirements on an analysis system can be quite demanding, if a detailed analysis is required for a portfolio with an active currency management. This case will be treated in a simplified form in Section 12.2.6 and (in more detail) in Chapter 15. In this section, the simple case of "passive" currency management will be treated, i.e., a management, in which the currency contributions solely arise from the direct investment in the assets with a denomination in local currencies. It has already been pointed out that the returns pertinent to the analysis in Section 12.2.1 are all assumed to be calculated relative to the base currency of the portfolio. Thus a distinction between *local currencies* (currencies, in which the individual investments are denominated) and the base currency was not required in this section, and therefore the returns were not specifically labeled. In this section it will, however, be necessary to distinguish between the local currencies and the base currency, in order to define the currency contributions. The following general relationship holds:

Relationship between the return in local currency and in base currency

srp_i^B : return of the portfolio segment i in base currency

$$1 + srp_i^B = \left(1 + srp_i^L\right) * (1 + c_i). \tag{12.47}$$

srp_i^L : return of the portfolio segment i in local currency

c_i : return of the local currency of the portfolio segment i relative to the base currency[35]

The notation for the corresponding benchmark terms will be analogous.

Example 12.14

Local currency and base currency:

On a Euro basis the return of the benchmark segment *USA* in Example 12.13 was equal to −0.96%. In the period from 01.03.2007 until 31.03.2007 the value of the US$ decreased by 1.94% relative to the base currency €. It follows that

$$1 - 0.96\% = \left(1 + srp_i^L\right) * (1 - 1.94\%).$$

For the return in US$ one obtains:

$$srp_i^L = \frac{1 - 0.96\%}{1 - 1.94\%} - 1 = 1.00\%.$$

From the perspective of an investor with base currency US$ the return of S&P 500 was thus equal to 1.00%.

The starting point for deriving an attribution analysis with separate currency contributions is the difference in contributions from the individual segments:

$$swp_i * srp_i^B - swb_i * srb_i^B.$$

In this expression the return in base currency srp_i^B will be substituted according to Equation (12.47) as follows:

$$srp_i^B = \left(1 + srp_i^L\right) * (1 + c_i) - 1.$$

The benchmark return will be dealt with similarly.[36] It follows that:

$$\begin{aligned} & swp_i * srp_i^B - swb_i * srb_i^B \\ &= swp_i * \left(\left(1 + srp_i^L\right) * (1 + c_i) - 1\right) - swb_i * \left(\left(1 + srb_i^L\right) * (1 + c_i) - 1\right) \\ &= \left(swp_i * srp_i^L - swb_i * srb_i^L\right) + \left(swp_i - swb_i\right) * c_i + \left(swp_i * srp_i^L - swb_i * srb_i^L\right) * c_i. \end{aligned} \tag{12.48}$$

[35] This parameter will also be called currency return.

[36] It should be stressed that only unhedged benchmarks are considered at this stage.

Table 12.26 Contributions of an Attribution Analysis with a Split-off of Currency Contributions

Term	Term	Interpretation
$swp_i * srp_i^L - swb_i * srb_i^L$	Active Return in local currency	According to the approach in Section 12.3 this term may be broken down in an allocation, a selection and an interaction term.
$(swp_i - swb_i) * c_i$	Currency contribution	This term reflects the contribution caused by the appreciation/depreciation of an investment currency relative to the base currency.
$(swp_i * srp_i^L - swb_i * srb_i^L) * c_i$	Interaction(2)	Interaction(2) is caused by the interaction of the allocation, selection and currency decisions.

The currency contribution cc_i and a further interaction term $it(2)_i$ can be readily deduced from this decomposition:

$$cc_i := (swp_i - swb_i) * c_i, \tag{12.49}$$

$$it(2)_i^L := (swp_i * srp_i^L - swb_i * srb_i^L) * c_i. \tag{12.50}$$

Table 12.26 contains the interpretation of the individual terms of the decomposition (12.48).
The decomposition of the active return in local currency, expressed by the term $swp_i * srp_i^L - swb_i * srb_i^L$, is exactly the same as the one outlined in Section 12.2.1. The following terms are involved:

$$ac_i^L := (swp_i - swb_i) * srb_i^L, \tag{12.51}$$

$$sc_i^L := swb_i * (srp_i^L - srb_i^L) \tag{12.52}$$

and

$$it(1)_i^L := (swp_i - swb_i) * (srp_i^L - srb_i^L). \tag{12.53}$$

The returns in these terms are calculated in local currency, which is highlighted by the additional index L. It then follows that:

$$ac_i^L + sc_i^L + it(1)_i^L = swp_i * srp_i^L - swb_i * srb_i^L.$$

Analogous to the approach in Section 12.2.1 one can also use the (relative) allocation contributions acr_i. In this case one must keep in mind to subtract the benchmark return based on the *local* returns:

$$acr_i^L := (swp_i - swb_i) * (srb_i^L - RB^L), \tag{12.54}$$

where (n equals the number of benchmark segments):

$$RB^L := swb_1 * srb_1^L + \cdots + swb_n * srb_n^L. \tag{12.55}$$

This leads to a decomposition of the active return in base currency into five terms:

$$swp_i^* srp_i^B - swb_i * srb_i^B = ac_i^L + sc_i^L + it(1)_i^L + cc_i^L + it(2)_i. \tag{12.56}$$

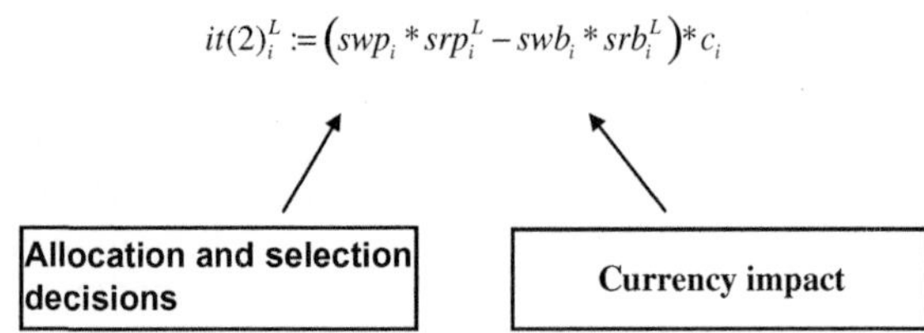

FIGURE 12.10
Components of the "Currency/Allocation/Selection Interaction".

If one uses the relative allocation contribution (Equation (12.54)), then one obtains:

$$\begin{aligned} acr_i^L + sc_i^L + it(1)_i^L + cc_i^L + it(2)_i^L &= swp_i * srp_i^B - swb_i * srb_i^B - (swp_i - swb_i) * RB^L \\ &= swp_i * (srp_i^B - RB^L) - swb_i * (srb_i^B - RB^L) . \end{aligned}$$

The attribution methodology in Table 12.26 corresponds to the methodology developed by Brinson et al.[37]

The ambiguous nature of the interaction terms is highlighted in Figure 12.10.

Table 12.27 Data of a 2-Country-Portfolio in the Period from 01.03.2007 to 31.03.2007 (in %)

Portfolio Segment	Weight		Return (Local Currency)	
	Portfolio	Benchmark	Portfolio	Benchmark
USA	70	50	4.53	1.00
Germany	30	50	2.00	3.00

Table 12.28 Attribution Analysis for the Portfolio in Table 12.27 (in %)

Portfolio Segment	Selection	Allocation	Currency	Interaction (1)	Interaction (2)	Total
USA	1.76	0.20	−0.39	0.71	−0.05	1.83
Germany	−0.50	−0.60	0.00	0.20	0.00	−0.50
Total	1.26	−0.40	−0.39	0.91	−0.05	1.33

Table 12.29 Attribution Analysis for the Portfolio in Table 12.27 with the Relative Allocation (in %)

Portfolio Segment	Selection	Allocation	Currency	Interaction (1)	Interaction (2)	Total
USA	1.76	−0.20	−0.39	0.71	−0.05	2.23
Germany	−0.50	−0.20	0.00	0.20	0.00	−0.90
Total	1.26	−0.40	−0.39	0.91	−0.05	1.33

[37] Cf. Brinson et al. (1991). Although currency contributions are not explicitly treated in the articles by Brinson et al., this is a natural extension. For an approach quite similar to the one described here, cf. Pieper (1998).

Example 12.15

Attribution analysis for a 2-country-portfolio with currency effects:

In this example we will revisit the 2-country-portfolio from Example 12.13. Contrary to the analysis there the currency contributions will be split off in this example. The data in Table 12.27 form the starting point.

Table 12.28 contains the results of the attribution analysis with a split-off of the currency contributions. The (absolute) allocation contributions are calculated according to Equation (12.51).

The contributions of the segment *Germany* are unchanged compared to the attribution analysis in Table 12.24, since for this segment local currency and base currency (€) coincide.

In Table 12.24 the allocation contribution of the segment *USA* was listed at −0.19%. The above analysis shows that the allocation (overweight position) in this local market has even led to a positive contribution of 0.20%. This contribution was, however, more than wiped out by the loss due to the depreciation of the US$ relative to the base currency of the investor (currency contribution = −0.39%).

The attribution analysis that results if one uses the allocation contribution in its relative form (Equation (12.54)), is given in Table 12.29. The allocation contribution was calculated using the benchmark return in local currency:

$$RB^L = 50\% * 1.0\% + 50\% * 3.0\% = 2.0\%.$$

The negative allocation contributions clearly show that the allocation of the segment weights was unfortunate: the portfolio manager took an overweight position in the stock market with a performance below average (*USA*: 1.00% vs. 2.00%) and an overweight position in the market with an above average performance (*Germany*: 3.00% vs. 2.00%).

Compared to the analysis in Example 12.13 the selection contributions remain nearly unchanged. This is due to the fact that the returns enter these terms only in a differential form ($srp_i^L - srb_i^L$, respectively $srp_i - srb_i$). Thus the currency effects cancel each other out for the most part.

12.2.6 Separation of the Currency Contributions in Attribution Analysis with an Active Management Approach

In case of an active currency management the deduction of the return contributions is much more involved than in the passive case. Such an attribution methodology poses also much higher demands in regard to the required position data. In this section a simplified method will be described that can be regarded as a straight-forward generalization of the Brinson methodology (Section 12.2.5). The much more involved approaches by Karnosky and Singer and Ankrim and Hensel, in which the contributions of the hedging instruments are explicitly quantified, will be discussed in Chapter 15.

The deduction of the currency contributions in Section 12.2.5 (Equation (12.49)) was based on the assumption that the currency returns (c_i) generated by the impact of the appreciation or depreciation of the local currency against the base currency are identical for the corresponding benchmark and portfolio segments. In case of an active currency management this assumption can no longer be sustained. Thus, in this section a distinction between the currency return of the benchmark segment (cb_i) and the currency return of the portfolio segment (cp_i) has to be made. These terms are defined by:

$$1 + srb_i^B = \left(1 + srb_i^L\right) * (1 + cb_i), \tag{12.57}$$

and:

$$1 + srp_i^B = \left(1 + srp_i^L\right) * \left(1 + cp_i\right). \tag{12.58}$$

The differences between the cp_i and the cb_i result in practice from the employment of currency forwards or similar derivatives. This is, however, irrelevant in the context of this simplified consideration.

In generalization of Equation (12.49) the contribution of the active currency management is then defined as follows:

$$cc_i := swp_i * cp_i - swb_i * cb_i. \tag{12.59}$$

Apart from Interaction (2) the other attribution terms (allocation, selection and Interaction (1)) remain unchanged. Interaction (2) assumes the following form (cf. Exercise 12.1):

$$it_i(2) = swp_i * srp_i^L * cp_i - swb_i * srb_i^L * cb_i.$$

In [Pieper 98] the currency contribution cc_i^{Bri} and the (overall) interaction term over one period it_i^{Bri} are defined as follows:

$$cc_i^{Bri} := swp_i * \left(srp_i^B - srp_i^L\right) - swb_i * \left(srb_i^B - srb_i^L\right), \tag{12.60}$$

$$it_i^{Bri} := \left(swp_i - swb_i\right) * \left(srp_i^L - srb_i^L\right). \tag{12.61}$$

Equation (12.60) follows from (12.59) if one substitutes cp_i and cb_i through the approximation terms $srp_i^B - srp_i^L$ respectively $srb_i^B - srb_i^L$ (cf. Exercise 12.2).

Table 12.30 Portfolio and Benchmark Data (in %)

Portfolio Segment	Weight		Return (Local Currency)		Return (Base Currency)	
	Portfolio	Benchmark	Portfolio	Benchmark	Portfolio	Benchmark
USA	70	50	4.53	1.00	4.12	−0.96
Germany	30	50	2.00	3.00	2.00	3.00

Table 12.31 Attribution Analysis of the Portfolio in Table 12.30. The Allocation Term is Based on Equation (12.51) (in %)

Portfolio Segment	Selection	Allocation	Currency	Interaction (1)	Interaction (2)	Total
USA	1.76	0.20	0.70	0.71	0.00	3.36
Germany	−0.50	−0.60	0.00	0.20	0.00	−0.90
Total	1.26	−0.40	0.70	0.91	0.00	2.46

Table 12.32 Breakdown of the Currency Contribution into a Market Component and an Active Management Component (in %)

Currency/Passive	Currency/Active	Currency/Total
−0.39	1.09	0.70
0.00	0.00	0.00
−0.39	1.09	0.70

Example 12.16

Currency contributions in case of an active currency management:

Here Example 12.13 will be considered once again. In this case the portfolio manager has, however, hedged a substantial portion of the currency risks through currency forwards. This limits the loss in the segment *USA* caused by the currency movements. This is reflected by the attribution analysis, although it doesn't contain specific information on the currency hedges (see Table 12.31).

The currency contribution described in Table 12.31 reflects the aggregated effect of the currency exchange rates movements and the active currency management. A further refinement can be achieved by splitting off the "passive" contribution from this term. The resulting contribution is given by the difference of the terms (12.59) and (12.49) (see Table 12.32).

$$\overline{cu}_i := swp_i * cp_i - swb_i * cb_i - (swp_i - swb_i) * cb_i = swp_i * (cp_i - cb_i)\,. \qquad (12.62)$$

12.2.7 Approach to Global Performance Attribution in the CFA Course

Arguing that many benchmarks are price indices (cf. Chapter 11), the approach in the course material for the CFA exam distinguishes between a capital gain (price appreciation) and yield component ((accrued) interests, dividends, etc.).[38] In general, the return of a portfolio segment in a period from 0 to T in local currency can be represented as follows.

$$\begin{aligned} srp_j^L &= \frac{I_j^T - I_j^0 + D_j}{I_j^0} \\ &= \frac{I_j^T - I_j^0}{I_j^0} + \frac{D_j}{I_j^0} \\ &= p_j + d_j \end{aligned} \qquad (12.63)$$

[38] The outline here follows the one in CFA Institute (2009, p. 207 et seq.).

Here I denotes the net asset value of the segment j at time O/T. D is the amount of interest, accrued income, etc. earned in the period from 0 to T. p_j denotes the capital gain (due to price appreciation) and d_j the "yield" component.

If S denotes the exchange rate of the segment j relative to the base currency of the portfolio at time 0/T, then the segment's return in base currency can be represented as:

$$srp_j^B = \frac{I_j^T * S_j^T + D_j * S_j^T - I_j^0 * S_j^0}{I_j^0 * S_j^0}. \tag{12.64}$$

This return can be written in the following form:

$$srp_j^B = p_j + d_j + cp_j, \tag{12.65}$$

where:

$$cp_j = \frac{I_j^T + D_j}{I_j^0} * \left(\frac{S_j^T}{S_j^0} - 1\right). \tag{12.66}$$

With these preliminary remarks the attribution analysis can be outlined. At first the overall portfolio return can be written as:

$$\begin{aligned} RP &= \sum_j sgp_j * srp_j^B = \sum_j sgp_j * (p_j + d_j + cp_j) \\ &= \sum_j sgp_j * p_j + \sum_j sgp_j * d_j + \sum_j sgp_j * cp_j \end{aligned} \tag{12.67}$$

highlighting the capital gain component, yield component, and currency component of the portfolio return, respectively. Next, the benchmark will be introduced. First, Equation (12.65) will be rewritten by using the local benchmark return of the segment j:

$$srp_j^B = srb_j^L + \left(p_j - srb_j^L\right) + d_j + cp_j, \tag{12.68}$$

so that the overall return in (12.67) may be rewritten as:

$$RP = \sum_{swp_j * srb_j^L} + \sum_j swp_j * \left(p_j - srb_j^L\right) + \sum_j swp_j * d_j + \sum_j swp_j * cp_j. \tag{12.69}$$

If one now adds the following expression to the right-hand side of (12.69)[39]

$$\begin{aligned} 0 = RB - RB &= \sum_j swb_j * srb_j^B - \sum_j swb_j * srb_j^B \\ &= \sum_j swb_j * srb_j^B - \sum_j swb_j * \left(srb_j^L + cb_j\right) \end{aligned} \tag{12.70}$$

[39] The decomposition of the benchmark return is analogous to Equation (12.66).

then one obtains the desired break-down:[40]

$$RP = \sum_j swb_j * srb_j^B + \sum_j (swp_j - swb_j) * srb_j^L + \sum_j swp_j * (p_j - srb_j) + \sum_j swp_j * d_j + \sum_j swp_j * cp_j - swb_j * cb_j. \tag{12.71}$$

The method will be applied in the exercise section (see problem 5).

12.3 MULTI-PERIOD ATTRIBUTION ANALYSIS ACCORDING TO BRINSON ET AL.

12.3.1 Basic Formulas for Linking Contributions in the Multi-Period Case

The attribution methodology described in the papers by Brinson et al. for the single-period case[41] is by far not sufficient for practical applications, since over a longer period (without an appropriate break-up into sub-periods) the involved computations lead to inexact results due to exogenous cash-flows and management actions (e.g. adaptation of the allocation and selection decisions, dividend or interest payments).[42] In the past decade, a multitude of different approaches have been published. It must be added, however, that some of the methodologies have been applied in practice for many years. Some authors even (probably ignorantly) picked up well-known and published methodologies and rebranded them, so that some methods are referred to under differing names. This, of course, is not exactly helpful when trying to obtain an overview of the various approaches. With some distance from the details, one notices, however, that all methodologies can be grouped according to a few general principles. This will be illustrated in the following sections. In doing so, some of the articles that were primarily published in the *Journal of Performance Measurement* will be treated in some detail.

The starting point for all approaches is the assumption of a valid attribution model for a single period (e.g. the Brinson model). Analogous to the computation of the time-weighted return (Section 10.4) the overall period can be partitioned into sub-periods according to the exogenous cash-flows. The aim of a multi-period model is to derive aggregated terms by means of linking the contributions calculated with the single-period model with each other,[43] such that the final result will provide an attribution analysis for the entire period. In the

---

[40] Note that it is implicitly assumed that the benchmark is a price index. The formalism is, however, readily extended to the more general case of a total return benchmark.

[41] Cf. e.g. Brinson and Fachler (1985) and Brinson et al. (1986).

[42] Cf. the explanation in Section 10.6.

[43] A simple summation of the contributions is not meaningful, as the period returns must be linked multiplicatively (cf. Section 10.4).

following the basic mathematical foundation will be outlined. In order to illustrate the general problems that one faces, at first the cases of linking results over two, respectively three periods will be considered.

If the portfolio weights at the beginning of the first and the second period are denoted by swp_i^1 and swp_i^2 (i runs over the n different portfolio segments) and the segment returns[44] within the periods by srp_i^1, respectively srp_i^2, then the return RP_1 of the overall portfolio over the first period is given by (cf. Equation (12.1)):

$$RP_1 = \sum_{i=1}^{n} swp_i^1 * srp_i^1, \tag{12.72}$$

and the return RP_2 over the second period by:[45]

$$RP_2 = \sum_{i=1}^{n} swp_i^2 * srp_i^2. \tag{12.73}$$

The portfolio return RP over both periods is obtained by geometrically linking these returns:

$$1 + RP = (1 + RP_1) * (1 + RP_2). \tag{12.74}$$

Using the expressions in (12.72) and (12.73) one obtains:

$$\begin{aligned} 1 + RP &= \left(1 + \sum_{i=1}^{n} swp_i^1 * srp_i^1\right) * \left(1 + \sum_{i=1}^{n} swp_i^2 * srp_i^2\right) \\ &= 1 + \sum_{i=1}^{n} swp_i^1 * srp_i^1 + \sum_{i=1}^{n} swp_i^2 * srp_i^2 * (1 + RP_1), \end{aligned}$$

and thus:

$$RP = \sum_{i=1}^{n} swp_i^1 * srp_i^1 + \sum_{i=1}^{n} swp_i^2 * (1 + RP_1) * srp_i^2. \tag{12.75}$$

This illustrates once again that the return over both periods is *not* identical to the sum of the contributions generated in the periods viewed independently of each other:

$$RP \neq \sum_{i=1}^{m} swp_i^1 * srp_i^1 + \sum_{i=1}^{m} swp_i^2 * srp_i^2.$$

Before combining all contributions, the ones of the second period (viewed in isolation) have to be multiplied by the factor $1 +$ *Total return in the first period*. This reflects the "base effect" resulting from the geometric linkage of the returns.[46] The derived assertion is readily generalized to the case of an arbitrary number of sub-periods.

---

[44] All returns in this section are assumed to be calculated in the base currency.

[45] The possibility that the number of segments changes over time will not be considered here.

[46] Cf. the remarks in Section 10.7. There are, however, different approaches for breaking down the linked returns, which leads to the different methodologies in the multi-period case.

Representation of the return as the weighted sum of contributions in single periods

If the measurement period is partitioned in m sub-periods (according to exogenous cash-flows), then the following representation of the portfolio return RP holds:

$$RP = \sum_{j=1}^{m} \left(1 + RP^{j-1}\right) * RP_j = \sum_{j=1}^{m} \left(1 + RP^{j-1}\right) \sum_{i=1}^{n} swp_i^j * srp_i^j, \tag{12.76}$$

where:

RP^j : Portfolio return over the first j periods (RP^0 is set equal to 0)
RP_j : Portfolio return over period j
swp_i^j : Weight of the portfolio segment i at the beginning of period j
srp_i^j : Return of the portfolio segment i over period j
m: Number of sub-periods ($m \geqslant 1$)
n: Number of segments within the benchmark and the portfolio ($n \geqslant 1$).

Equation (12.76) follows from a transformation of the expression, which results from a geometric linkage of the individual returns. For the return RP^j it holds that:[47]

$$1 + RP^j = (1 + RP_1) * (1 + RP_2) * \cdots * \left(1 + RP_j\right).$$

In addition the following identities hold:

$$1 + RP^j = \left(1 + RP^{j-1}\right) * \left(1 + RP_j\right) and 1 + RP = 1 + RP^m.$$

$$\begin{aligned}
&1 + RP = 1 + RP^m \\
&= \left(1 + RP^{m-1}\right) * (1 + RP_m) \\
&= \left(1 + RP^{m-1}\right) + \left(1 + RP^{m-1}\right) * RP_m \\
&= \left(1 + RP^{m-2}\right) * (1 + RP_{m-1}) + \left(1 + RP^{m-1}\right) * RP_m \\
&= \left(1 + RP^{m-2}\right) + \left(1 + RP^{m-2}\right) * RP_{m-1} + \left(1 + RP^{m-1}\right) * RP_m \\
&\vdots \\
&= \left(1 + RP^1\right) + \left(1 + RP^1\right) * RP_2 + \cdots + \left(1 + RP^{m-1}\right) * RP_m \\
&= 1 + \sum_{i=1}^{n} swp_i^1 * srp_i^1 + \left(1 + RP^1\right) * \left(\sum_{i=1}^{n} swp_i^2 * srp_i^2\right) + \cdots + \left(1 + RP^{m-1}\right) \\
&* \left(\sum_{i=1}^{n} swp_i^m * srp_i^m\right).
\end{aligned}$$

Solving for RP yields Equation (12.76).

Based on this formula, the terms of the attribution analysis relative to a benchmark derived in Sections 12.2.1 and 12.2.5 may be generalized to the multi-period

[47] In order to help understanding, it shall be repeated that RP_j denotes the return within the period j and RP^j denotes the return that the portfolio achieved in the period including the period j.

case. At first the multi-period benchmark return RB will be expressed in analogous form to Equation (12.76):

$$RB = \sum_{j=1}^{m} \left(1 + RB^{j-1}\right) * RB_j = \sum_{j=1}^{m} \left(1 + RB^{j-1}\right) \sum_{i=1}^{n} swb_i^j * srb_i^j, \quad (12.77)$$

where:
RB^j : Benchmark return over the first j periods (RB^0 is set equal to 0)
RB_j : Benchmark return over period j
swb_i^j : Weight of the benchmark segment i at the beginning of period j
srb_i^j : Return of the benchmark segment i over period j
m: Number of sub-periods ($m \geqslant 1$)
n: Number of segments within the benchmark and the portfolio ($n \geqslant 1$).

One obtains thus the following expression for the active return of a portfolio relative to its benchmark:

Basic formula I

$$\begin{aligned} RP - RB &= \sum_{j=1}^{m} \left(\left(1 + RP^{j-1}\right) * RP_j - \left(1 + RB^{j-1}\right) * RB_j\right) \\ &= \sum_{j=1}^{m} \sum_{i=1}^{n} \left(swp_i^j * \left(1 + RP^{j-1}\right) * srp_i^j - swb_i^j * \left(1 + RB^{j-1}\right) * srb_i^j\right). \end{aligned} \quad (12.78)$$

This formula forms the basis for two different linkage methodologies that will be described in Section 12.3.2. It does, however, by no means represent the only approaches for linking contributions. An alternative, elaborated on in Section 12.3.3, is given by:

Basic formula II

$$\begin{aligned} RP - RB &= RP^m - RB^m \\ &= (1 + RB_m) * \left(RP^{m-1} - RB^{m-1}\right) + (RP_m - RB_m) * \left(1 + RP^{m-1}\right). \end{aligned} \quad (12.79)$$

It results from a simple transformation:

$$\begin{aligned} RP^m - RB^m &= \left(1 + RP^m\right) - \left(1 + RB^m\right) \\ &= \left(1 + RP^{m-1}\right) * (1 + RP_m) - \left(1 + RB^{m-1}\right) * (1 + RB_m) \\ &= -(1 + RB_m) * \left(1 + RB^{m-1}\right) + (1 + RB_m) * \left(1 + RP^{m-1}\right) \\ &\quad + \left(1 + RP^{m-1}\right) * (1 + RP_m) - (1 + RB_m) * \left(1 + RP^{m-1}\right) \\ &= (1 + RB_m) * \left(RP^{m-1} - RB^{m-1}\right) + \left(1 + RP^{m-1}\right) * (RP_m - RB_m). \end{aligned} \quad (12.80)$$

In the third step the term $(1+RB_m)*\left(1+RP^{m-1}\right)-(1+RB_m)*\left(1+RP^{m-1}\right)$ was formally added.

A further alternative to Equation (12.78) was described by Kahan.[48] Although in his article only the case of absolute contributions was treated, his considerations can easily be generalized to the linking of attribution contributions in the multi-period case (cf. Section 12.3.4). First the special cases of two and three sub-periods will be considered by means of introduction. In the case of two sub-periods one obtains:

$$\begin{aligned}
RP &= (1+RP_1)*(1+RP_2)-1 = RP_1+RP_2+RP_1*RP_2\\
&= RP_1*\left(1+\frac{1}{2}*RP_2\right)+RP_2*\left(1+\frac{1}{2}*RP_1\right)\\
&= \sum_{i=1}^{n} swp_i^1 * srp_i^1 * \left(1+\frac{1}{2}*RP_2\right)\\
&\quad + \sum_{i=1}^{n} swp_i^2 srp_i^2 * \left(1+\frac{1}{2}*RP_1\right).
\end{aligned} \tag{12.81}$$

According to Kahan the mixed terms will be distributed uniformly to the individual periods. The generalized contributions for the segment i are thus given by $swp_i^1 * srp_i^1 * (1+1/2*RP_2)$ and $swp_i^2 * srp_i^2 * (1+1/2*RP_1)$.

Over three periods one obtains in a similar way:

$$\begin{aligned}
RP &= (1+RP_1)*(1+RP_2)*(1+RP_3)-1\\
&= RP_1+RP_2+RP_3+RP_1*RP_2+RP_2*RP_3+RP_1\\
&\quad *RP_3+RP_1*RP_2*RP_3\\
&= RP_1*\left(1+\frac{RP_2+RP_3}{2}+\frac{RP_2*RP_3}{3}\right)\\
&\quad +RP_2*\left(1+\frac{RP_1+RP_3}{2}+\frac{RP_1*RP_3}{3}\right)\\
&\quad +RP_3*\left(1+\frac{RP_1+RP_2}{2}+\frac{RP_1*RP_2}{3}\right).
\end{aligned} \tag{12.82}$$

The individual contributions can be deduced similarly to the two-period case.[49]

If one denotes by bp^j the generalized overall contribution in the period j and by bp^j the generalized overall contribution of the segment i in the period j, then

[48] See Kahan (2006).

[49] Differing from the form described here, in Kahan (2006) the contributions are derived based on the infinitesimal contributions toward the return in a linear progression.

the generalized formula for contributions over m periods according to Kahan is given by:[50]

$$bp^j = RP_j * \left(1 + \sum_{l=1}^{m-1}\left(\frac{1}{l+1} * \prod_{\substack{1 \leqslant k_1 < k_2 < \cdots < k_l \leqslant m \\ k_i \neq j}} RP_{k_1} * \cdots * RP_{k_l}\right)\right)$$

$$= \sum_{i=1}^{n} swp_i^j * srp_i^j * \left(1 + \sum_{l=1}^{m-1}\left(\frac{1}{l+1} * \prod_{\substack{1 \leqslant k_1 < k_2 < \cdots < k_l \leqslant m \\ k_i \neq j}} RP_{k_1} * \cdots * RP_{k_l}\right)\right), \tag{12.83}$$

and:

$$bp_i^j = swp_i^j * srp_i^j * \left(1 + \sum_{l=1}^{m-1}\left(\frac{1}{l+1} * \prod_{\substack{1 \leqslant k_1 < k_2 < \cdots < k_l \leqslant m \\ k_i \neq j}} RP_{k_1} * \cdots * RP_{k_l}\right)\right). \tag{12.84}$$

It is straight-forward to show that the sum of the bp^j equals indeed the overall return over m periods:

$$\sum\nolimits_{j=1}^{m} bp^j = \sum_{j=1}^{m} RP_j * \left(\sum_{l=0}^{m-1}\left(\frac{1}{l+1} * \prod_{\substack{1 \leqslant k_1 < k_2 < \cdots < k_l \leqslant m \\ k_i \neq j}} RP_{k_1} * \cdots * RP_{k_l}\right)\right)$$

$$= \sum_{j=1}^{m}\left(\sum_{l=0}^{m-1}\left(\frac{1}{l+1} * \prod_{\substack{1 \leqslant k_1 < k_2 < \cdots < k_l \leqslant m \\ k_i \neq j}} RP_{k_1} * \cdots * RP_{k_l} * RP_j\right)\right)$$

$$= \sum_{l=1}^{m}\left(\frac{1}{l+1} * (l+1) \prod_{1 \leqslant k_1 < k_2 < \cdots < k_l \leqslant m} RP_{k_1} * \cdots * RP_{k_l}\right)$$

$$= \sum_{l=1}^{m}\left(\prod_{1 \leqslant k_1 < k_2 < \cdots < k_l \leqslant m} RP_{k_1} * \cdots * RP_{k_l}\right)$$

$$= \prod_{j=1}^{m}(1 + RP_j) - 1$$

$$= RP. \tag{12.85}$$

[50] This formula was not given in [Kahan 06].

An analogous consideration yields for the benchmark:

$$bb^j = \sum_{i=1}^{n} swb_i^j * srb_i^j * \left(1 + \sum_{l=1}^{m-1}\left(\frac{1}{l+1} * \prod_{\substack{1\leqslant k_1<k_2<\cdots<k_l\leqslant m \\ k_i\neq j}} RB_{k_1} * \cdots * RB_{k_l}\right)\right). \tag{12.86}$$

One thus obtains yet a further representation of the active return:

$$\begin{aligned} RP - RB &= \sum_{j=1}^{m} bp^j - bb^j \\ &= \sum_{j=1}^{m} RP_j * \left(1 + \sum_{l=1}^{m-1}\left(\frac{1}{l+1} * \prod_{\substack{1\leqslant k_1<k_2<\cdots<k_l\leqslant m \\ k_i\neq j}} RP_{k_1} * \cdots * RP_{k_l}\right)\right) \\ &\quad - \sum_{j=1}^{m} RB_j * \left(1 + \sum_{l=1}^{m-1}\left(\frac{1}{l+1}^{*} \prod_{\substack{1\leqslant k_1<k_2<\cdots<k_l\leqslant m \\ k_i\neq j}} RB_{k_1} * \cdots * RB_{k_l}\right)\right) \end{aligned} \tag{12.87}$$

Basic formula III

$$\begin{aligned} RP - RB = &\sum_{j=1}^{m} RP_j * \left(1 + \sum_{l=1}^{m-1}\left(\frac{1}{l+1} * \prod_{\substack{1\leqslant k_1<k_2<\cdots<k_l\leqslant m \\ k_i\neq j}} RP^*_{k_1} \cdots * RP_{k_l}\right)\right) \\ &- \sum_{j=1}^{m} RB^*_j \left(1 + \sum_{l=1}^{m-1}\left(\frac{1}{l+1}^{*} \prod_{\substack{1\leqslant k_1<k_2<\cdots<k_l\leqslant m \\ k_i\neq j}} RB^*_{k_1} \cdots * RB_{k_l}\right)\right). \end{aligned} \tag{12.88}$$

Based on these introductory explanations the various methodologies will be explained in detail in the following sections. It is possible to group the different procedures into four categories. The first three are linked to the respective basic formula. The methodologies of the fourth category aim for a scaling of the contributions by means of mathematical smoothing algorithms based on the contributions in the single sub-periods. Figure 12.11 provides an overview of the individual methodologies as well as of the denominations by which they are quoted in the literature or in practice.

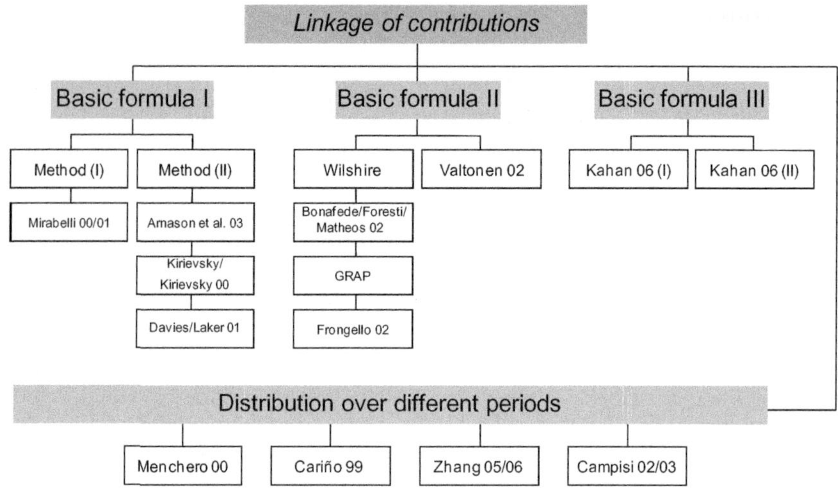

FIGURE 12.11
Approaches for the Linkage of Return Contributions in the Multi-Period Case.

12.3.2 Approach According to Basic Formula I

12.3.2.1 VARIANT 1

A single term of the expression on the right-hand side of Equation (12.78)

$$swp_i^j * \left(1 + RP^{j-1}\right) * srp_i^j - swb_i^j * \left(1 + RB^{j-1}\right) * srb_i^j$$

may be interpreted as a (generalized) contribution of the segment i toward the active return in the period j. According to the "compound interest effects", which result from the multiplicative linkage of the returns, the weights are, however, adjusted by the returns of the portfolio, respectively the benchmark achieved in the period prior to the respective sub-period..

Based on the expression for the active return in (12.78) it suggests itself to generalize the single-period allocation, selection and interaction terms of Section 12.2.1 as follows for a period consisting of m sub-periods ($1 \leqslant j \leqslant m$):[51]

$$ac_i^j := \left(swp_i^j * \left(1 + RP^{j-1}\right) - swb_i^j * \left(1 + RB^{j-1}\right)\right) * srb_i^j, \tag{12.89}$$

$$sc_i^j := swb_i^j * \left(1 + RB^{j-1}\right) * \left(srp_i^j - srb_i^j\right), \tag{12.90}$$

$$it(1)_i^j := \left(swp_i^j * \left(1 + RP^{j-1}\right) - swb_i^j * \left(1 + RB^{j-1}\right)\right) * \left(srp_i^j - srb_i^j\right). \tag{12.91}$$

[51] This methodology is identical to the "new mirroring approach" described by Mirabelli (cf. Mirabelli (2000/01).

Table 12.33 Portfolio and Benchmark Data Over Two Periods (in %)

Sector	Period 1				Period 2			
	Portfolio		Benchmark		Portfolio		Benchmark	
	Weight	Return	Weight	Return	Weight	Return	Weight	Return
1	30.0	4.0	60.0	−4.0	20.0	20.0	60.0	5.0
2	70.0	10.0	40.0	−10.0	80.0	5.0	40.0	−5.0
Total	100.0	8.2	100.0	−6.4	100.0	8.0	100.0	1.0

The terms ac_i^j, sc_i^j, $it(1)_i^j$ may be interpreted as (generalized) allocation, selection and interaction terms of the portfolio segment i toward the active return in the period j. A simple calculation confirms that:

$$ac_i^j + sc_i^j + it(1)_i^j = swp_i^j * \left(1 + RP^{j-1}\right) * srp_i^j - swb_i^j * \left(1 + RB^{j-1}\right) * srb_i^j. \tag{12.92}$$

The sum of the $ac_i^j + sc_i^j + it(1)_i^j$ (i=1,...,n and j=1,...,m) equals thus the active return (12.78). Equation (12.92) may be interpreted as a generalization of Equation (12.23).

Analogous to the approach in Section 12.2.1 an attribution analysis over multiple periods may be calculated in a relative form. In this case the allocation contribution is based on the return of the benchmark segment relative to the overall benchmark return:

$$acr_i^j := \left(swp_i^j * \left(1 + RP^{j-1}\right) - swb_i^j * \left(1 + RB^{j-1}\right)\right) * \left(srb_i^j - RB_j\right). \tag{12.93}$$

This necessitates, however, a modification of the interaction terms, since otherwise the sum of the allocation, selection and interaction terms would not equal the active return.

$$it(1)_i^j \rightarrow it(1)_i^j + \left(swp_i^j * \left(1 + RP^{j-1}\right) - swb_i^j * \left(1 + RB^{j-1}\right)\right) * RB_j. \tag{12.94}$$

Example 12.17

Linkage over two periods I:

Starting point is a comparison of a portfolio relative to its benchmark over two periods given in Table 12.33.

The portfolio clearly outperformed its benchmark in each period (see Table 12.34).

The positive active return can be exclusively ascribed to the stock picking. On the sector level one obtains the representation shown in Table 12.36.

The other linkage methodologies will also be illustrated by means of this example.

Table 12.34 Portfolio and Benchmark Data Over Two Periods (in %)

Period	Portfolio return	Benchmark return	Active return
1	8.20	−6.40	14.60
2	8.00	1.00	7.00
Total	16.86	−5.46	22.32

Table 12.35 Results of the Attribution Analysis. The Computation of the Adjusted Contributions is Based on Equations (12.89)–(12.91) (in %)

Period	Allocation	Selection	Interaction	Total
1	−1.80	12.80	3.60	14.60
2	−4.00	13.00	−2.00	7.00
2 adjusted	−4.18	12.17	−0.27	7.72
Total	−5.98	24.97	3.33	22.32

Table 12.36 Results of the Attribution Analysis on a Sector Level for the Entire Period (in %)

Sector	Allocation	Selection	Interaction	Total
1	−0.53	13.22	−7.58	5.12
2	−5.46	11.74	10.91	17.20
Total	−5.98	24.97	3.33	22.32

12.3.2.2 *VARIANT 2*

12.3.2.2.1 General Considerations

In the preceding section the allocation contribution of the segment i in the period j toward the active return was defined as:

$$ac_i^j := swp_i^j * \left(1 + RP^{j-1}\right) * srb_i^j - swb_i^j * \left(1 + RB^{j-1}\right) * srb_i^j. \qquad (12.95)$$

The main argument for this definition was the analogy to the formula for the computation of the return contributions in the multi-period case (Equation (12.76)). This definition is, however, in contradiction to the original idea to base the computation of the allocation contribution on an "allocation portfolio", in which only the segment weights may be altered relative to the benchmark. Through the scaling of the terms $swp_i^j * srb_i^j$ by the "total portfolio return" $\left(1 + RP^{j-1}\right)$ achieved prior to the period j the selection decisions of that period do have an impact on the allocation contribution. The scaling may alternatively be based solely on the return of the allocation portfolio. According to Section 12.2.1 the return RAP_j of the allocation portfolio in the period j is given by

$$RAP_j = \sum_{i=1}^{n} swp_i^j * srb_i^j,$$

and the return RAP^j *including* the period j by:

$$1 + RAP^j = (1 + RAP_1) * (1 + RAP_2) * \cdots * \left(1 + RAP_j\right).$$

Thus, when using the return of the allocation portfolio, the (generalized) allocation contribution of the segment i in the period j is given by:

$$\widetilde{ac}_i^j := swp_i^j * \left(1 + RAP^{j-1}\right) * srb_i^j - swb_i^j * \left(1 + RB^{j-1}\right) * srb_i^j. \qquad (12.96)$$

In order to distinguish these terms from the attribution contributions in (12.89) a tilde has been added to the expression ac_i^j. From Equation (12.78) it readily follows that:

$$\sum_{j=1}^{m}\sum_{i=1}^{n} \widetilde{ac}_i^j = RAP - RB. \qquad (12.97)$$

This equation clearly demonstrates that the terms $\widetilde{ac}_i^j$ may be viewed as the generalization of the allocation terms, since $RAP - RB$ is a natural definition of the overall allocation contribution according to Brinson et al. in the multi-period case.[52]

The selection contributions are dealt with in a similar way: the contributions are weighted with the returns of the selection portfolio instead of with the returns of the overall portfolio. By this the selection contributions are computed independently of the allocation contributions achieved prior to the respective period. The return RSP_j of the selection portfolio in the period j is given by:

$$RSP_j = \sum_{i=1}^{n} swb_i^j * srp_i^j,$$

and the return RSP^j *including* the period j follows from the geometric linkage:

$$1 + RSP^j = (1 + RSP_1) * (1 + RSP_2) * \cdots * \left(1 + RSP_j\right).$$

Using these factors, the (generalized) selection contribution $\widetilde{sb}_i^j$ is defined as

$$\widetilde{sc}_i^j := swb_i^j * \left(1 + RSP^{j-1}\right) * srp_i^j - swb_i^j * \left(1 + RB^{j-1}\right) * srb_i^j. \qquad (12.98)$$

Analogous to the property for the allocation contributions (12.97) it holds that:

$$\sum_{j=1}^{m}\sum_{i=1}^{n} \widetilde{sc}_i^j = RSP - RB. \qquad (12.99)$$

The terms $\widetilde{sc}_i^j$ may thus be viewed as the generalization of the Brinson selection terms in the multi-period case, since $RSP - RB$ is a natural definition of the overall selection contribution, which is in agreement with the Brinson approach.

---

[52] This view is also expressed in Davies and Laker (2001).

The modifications of the allocation and selection contributions relative to the definition in Section 12.3.2.1 also require a modification of the definition of the interaction terms. A simple calculation shows that these have to be of the form:

$$\begin{aligned}\widetilde{it(1)}_i^j &:= it(1)_i^j + swp_i^j * srb_i^j * \left(RP^{j-1} - RAP^{j-1}\right) - swb_i^j * srp_i^j * \left(RSP^{j-1} - RB^{j-1}\right)\\ &= swp_i^j * \left(srp_i^j * \left(1 + RP^{j-1}\right) - srb_i^j * \left(1 + RAP^{j-1}\right)\right)\\ &\quad - swb_i^j * \left(srp_i^j * \left(1 + RSP^{j-1}\right) - srb_i^j * \left(1 + RB^{j-1}\right)\right),\end{aligned}$$

if one demands that the terms $\widetilde{ac}_i^j$, $\widetilde{sc}_i^j$, $\widetilde{it(1)}_i^j$ add up to the (generalized) return difference:

$$\widetilde{ac}_i^j + \widetilde{sc}_i^j + \widetilde{it(1)}_i^j = swp_i^j * \left(1 + RP^{j-1}\right) * srp_i^j - swb_i^j * \left(1 + RB^{j-1}\right) * srb_i^j.$$

In particular it holds that:

$$\sum_{j=1}^{m} \sum_{i=1}^{n} \widetilde{it(1)}_i^j = (RP - RAP) + (RB - RSP)\,. \tag{12.100}$$

Also in this approach the allocation contribution may be defined "relative to the benchmark" in a way completely analogous to the procedure in the last section:

$$\widetilde{acr}_i^j := \left(swp_i^j * \left(1 + RAP^{j-1}\right) - swb_i^j * \left(1 + RB^{j-1}\right)\right) * \left(srb_i^j - RB_j\right). \tag{12.101}$$

The interaction terms have to be modified as follows (for $j > 1$):

$$\widetilde{it(1)}_i^j \rightarrow \widetilde{it(1)}_i^j + \left(swp_i^j * \left(1 + RAP^{j-1}\right) - swb_i^j * \left(1 + RB^{j-1}\right)\right) * RB_j. \tag{12.102}$$

This is required to ensure that the individual contributions add up to the overall active return.

In summary, one can say that the described method transforms the Brinson approach in a natural way to the multi-period case.[53] On the level of the sub-sectors this holds only partially, since the allocation contributions in a given sector (although independent of the selection decisions) still depend on the allocation decisions made in regard to the other sectors. An analogous assertion holds for the selection contributions.

[53] The approach pertinent to this methodology was already described by Davies and Laker in 2001. In their article a detailed break-down was, however, not provided (Davies and Laker 2001; cf. also Laker 2005). Thus, occasionally this methodology is also referred to as the Davies Laker method (cf. e.g. Bacon 2004). In Valtonen (2002) this approach is taken up and at least a break-down of the terms for the overall period was given. Finally in Arnarson et al. (2003) the breakdown on a segment level given here is described. The latter break-down is also the subject of the analyses in the articles by David and Broberg (David 2006, Broberg 2006).

Example 12.18

Linkage over two periods II:

In this example the linking methodology will be applied to the portfolio in Example 12.17. As expected, the selection term is larger than the term that was shown in analysis in Example 12.17 and also the allocation term has increased. Due to the strong stock picking in the first sub-period the factor based on the selection is much bigger than the factor based on the overall performance. This explains why the selection contribution is bigger than in Example 12.17. A similar reasoning applies to the allocation contribution. The sum of the adjusted contributions equals the one in Example 12.17, but the individual contributions appear somewhat more realistic due to the use of the specific weighting factors (instead of employing the portfolio return across-the-board).

The breakdown on sector level is given in Table 12.37.

Compared to the analysis in Table 12.36 this analysis does not lead to a drastically changed assessment of the strength of the investment results. But there are some differences. For the allocation and selection terms, for instance, higher values are shown than in Table 12.36 (at the expense of the interaction term).

Table 12.37 Results of the Attribution Analysis (in %)

Period	Allocation	Selection	Interaction	Total
1	−1.80	12.80	3.60	14.60
2	−4.00	13.00	−2.00	7.00
2 adjusted	−3.69	13.96	−2.55	7.72
Total	−5.49	26.76	1.05	22.32

12.3.2.2.2 Approach of Kirievsky and Kirievsky

The methodology of Kirievsky and Kirievsky[54] is also based on the approach outlined in the previous section. Their breakdown at the segment level is, however, closer to the original Brinson approach. They attempt to base the linking exclusively on segment effects. The disadvantage of this procedure is, however, that the resulting contributions do not add up to the overall effects.

According to Equation (12.13) the selection contribution SC over m periods is defined as follows:

$$SC = RSP - RB,$$

where:

$$RSP = \prod_{j=1}^{m}\left(1 + \sum_{i=1}^{n} swb_i^j * srp_i^j\right) - 1 \quad \text{and} \quad RB = \prod_{j=1}^{m}\left(1 + \sum_{i=1}^{n} swb_i^j * srb_i^j\right) - 1.$$

Based on this expression the authors aim to separate the contribution that results from the stock picking in a single segment k:

[54] cf. Kirievsky and Kirievsky (2000).

Table 12.38 Results of the Attribution Analysis (in %)

Sector	Allocation	Selection	Interaction	Total
1	−0.69	14.76	−8.95	5.12
2	−4.80	12.00	10.00	17.20
Total	−5.49	26.76	1.05	22.32

$$RSP_{(k)} = \prod_{j=1}^{m}\left(1+\left(\sum_{i=1}^{n} swb_i^j * srb_i^j\right) - swb_k^j * \left(srb_k^j - srp_k^j\right)\right) - 1. \quad (12.103)$$

In the expression above all terms are identical to the respective terms in the formula for the benchmark return with the exception of the term k, where the allocation decision is represented by the portfolio weight. This leads to the following definition of the selection contribution of the segment k:

$$SC_k = RSP_{(k)} - RB. \quad (12.104)$$

As mentioned above, in general the sum of the SB_k does not equal the overall selection contribution:

$$\sum_{k=1}^{n} SC_k \neq SC. \quad (12.105)$$

The difference may be quite significant! In order to reduce this difference the authors extend the expression in (12.104) by part of the effects that result from the interaction of parallel changes in weight. They define:

$$RSP_{(k)\perp} = \prod_{j=1}^{m}\left(1+\left(\sum_{i=1}^{n} swb_i^j * srp_i^j\right) - swb_k^j * \left(srp_k^j - srb_k^j\right)\right) - 1 \quad (12.106)$$

and (put in a way that appears somewhat arbitrary):

$$SC_k = \frac{1}{2} * \left[\left(RSP_{(k)} - RB\right) + \left(RSP - RSP_{(k)\perp}\right)\right]. \quad (12.107)$$

The procedure is similar for the allocation contribution. The starting point is in this case:

$$AC = RAP - RB,$$

where:

$$RAP = \prod_{j=1}^{m}\left(1+\sum_{i=1}^{n} swp_i^j * srb_i^j\right) - 1 \quad \text{and} \quad RB = \prod_{j=1}^{m}\left(1+\sum_{i=1}^{n} swb_i^j * srb_i^j\right) - 1.$$

Again, the authors aim to separate the effect that results from the allocation decision in a single segment k:[55]

$$RAP_{(k)} = \prod_{j=1}^{m}\left(1 + \left(\sum_{i=1}^{n} swb_i^j * srb_i^j\right) + \left(swp_k^j - swb_k^j\right) * \left(srb_k^j - RB^j\right)\right) - 1. \tag{12.108}$$

This leads to the following definition of the allocation contribution of the segment k:

$$AC_k = RAP_{(k)} - RB. \tag{12.109}$$

In order to reduce the difference between AC and the sum of the AC_k, the authors alter the definition in line with the procedure in the case of the selection contribution:

$$AC_k = \frac{1}{2} * \left[\left(RAP_{(k)} - RB\right) + \left(RAP - RAP_{(k)^{\perp}}\right)\right], \tag{12.110}$$

where:

$$RAP_{(k)^{\perp}} = \prod_{j=1}^{m}\left(1 + \left(\sum_{i=1}^{n} swp_i^j * srb_i^j\right) - \left(swp_k^j - swb_k^j\right) * \left(srb_k^j - RB^j\right)\right) - 1. \tag{12.111}$$

As already mentioned, the approach of Kirievsky and Kirievsky possesses the weakness that the aggregation of segment contributions does not match the overall contribution in a category. Mapping certain components of the residuum to the contributions could point the way toward a meaningful amendment of the methodology. It would for instance be worthwhile considering whether a scaling of the segment contributions according to the Menchero approach (Section 12.3.5) (to achieve the additivity property) would be such a meaningful amendment. This would, of course, add further to the complexity of the methodology.[56]

Example 12.19

Linkage over two periods III:

Applying the unadjusted formula yields the results shown in Table 12.39.[57]

Employing Equations (12.107) and (12.110) lead to the analysis in Table 12.40.

One notices that the smoothing results in minor changes only. Also compared to the other linkage methodologies the differences are rather small.

---

[55] Kirievsky and Kirievsky consider only the relative allocation contribution.

[56] Menchero doubts that this could be meaningful (Menchero 2002), a comprehensive investigation of this question is, however, still outstanding.

[57] In the article (Kirievsky and Kirievsky 2000) the interaction term is not explicitly defined. A natural definition would be to define this term as the differential between the contribution of the segment and the sum of the allocation and selection contribution within a period.

Table 12.39 Results of the Attribution Analysis (in %)

Sector	Allocation	Selection
1	−0.68	13.70
2	−4.84	12.14
Total	−5.53	25.85

Table 12.40 Results of the Attribution Analysis (in %)

Sector	Allocation	Selection
1	−0.67	14.16
2	−4.82	12.60
Total	−5.49	26.76

12.3.3 Approach According to Basic Formula II

12.3.3.1 *WILSHIRE LINKING ALGORITHM*

A further linking algorithm has been applied in their analysis tools by the company Wilshire since the early 1980s. The goal of this approach is to derive a multi-period methodology based on Equation (12.79). For a single period j the standard breakdown serves as the base:[58]

$$RP_j - RB_j = ac_j + sc_j + it_j. \tag{12.112}$$

If one chooses the notation as expressed in the following equation for the multi-period case of m sub-periods,

$$RP^m - RB^m = AC^m + SC^m + IT^m, \tag{12.113}$$

then one obtains a recursive formula for the individual contributions over m periods by means of (12.79):

$$\begin{aligned} AC^m + SC^m + IT^m = & (1 + RB_m) * \left(AC^{m-1} + SC^{m-1} + IT^{m-1}\right) \\ & + (ac_m + sc_m + it_m) * \left(1 + RP^{m-1}\right). \end{aligned} \tag{12.114}$$

In the next step the different contribution effects are separated, which (exemplified by the allocation contribution) leads to the following expression:[59]

$$AC^m = (1 + RB_m) * AC^{m-1} + ac_m * \left(1 + RP^{m-1}\right). \tag{12.115}$$

[58] Obviously this approach corresponds to the Brinson model without separation of the currency terms. Any other model with an additive breakdown into an arbitrary number of effects would do, however.

[59] This is the central Equation (1) in (Bonafede et al. 2002).

The other contributions can be derived in a similar way. In a differential form one obtains:[60]

$$AC^m - AC^{m-1} = RB_m * AC^{m-1} + ac_m * \left(1 + RP^{m-1}\right). \tag{12.116}$$

From this equation follows the explicit form of the (generalized) allocation contribution by means of mathematical induction (other contributions follow again analogously):

$$AC^m = \sum_{j=1}^{m} ac_j * \left(1 + RP^{j-1}\right) * \frac{1 + RB}{1 + RB^j}. \tag{12.117}$$

The case ($m = 1$) is trivial. Let's assume the assertion holds for $m - 1$:

$$AC^{m-1} = \sum_{j=1}^{m-1} ac_j * \left(1 + RP^{j-1}\right) * \frac{1 + RB^{m-1}}{1 + RB^j}. \tag{12.118}$$

The induction step follows from:

$$\begin{aligned} AC^m &= (1 + RB_m) * AC^{m-1} + ac_m * \left(1 + RP^{m-1}\right) \\ &= (1 + RB_m) * \sum_{j=1}^{m-1} ac_j * \left(1 + RP^{j-1}\right) * \frac{1 + RB^{m-1}}{1 + RB^j} + ac_m * \left(1 + RP^{m-1}\right) \\ &= \sum_{j=1}^{m-1} ac_j * \left(1 + RP^{j-1}\right) * \frac{1 + RB^m}{1 + RB^j} + ac_m * \left(1 + RP^{m-1}\right) \\ &= \sum_{j=1}^{m} ac_j * \left(1 + RP^{j-1}\right) * \frac{1 + RB}{1 + RB^j}. \end{aligned} \tag{12.119}$$

From (12.119) and the analogous formula for the selection term and the interaction term it follows that:[61]

$$RP - RB = \sum_{j=1}^{m} \left(RP_j - RB_j\right) * \left(1 + RP^{j-1}\right) * \frac{1 + RB}{1 + RB^j}. \tag{12.120}$$

---

[60] This is the central equation on page 13 in Frongello (2002a). (See also Frongello 2002b). The "Frongello linking algorithm" (denotation according to Frongello (2002a) is thus identical to the Wilshire methodology, as has already been pointed out in Bonafede et al. (2002).

[61] This equation as well as Equation. 12.117 is also known as the GRAP-methodology (GRAP = *Groupe de Réflexion en Attribution de Performance*, a French working group) (cf. e.g. Bacon 2004, p. 112). The GRAP-methodology and the Wilshire method are thus identical.

The Wilshire scaling suggests a very tempting "interpretation": the allocation contribution from the period j is scaled by the portfolio return in previous $j-1$ sub-periods and by the benchmark return in the subsequent $m-j$ periods. The allocation effect in the period j is thus taken in relation to overall accumulated portfolio volume at this stage $(ac_j * (1 + RP^{j-1}))$, and one subsequently "accrues" the "interest" by using the benchmark return as the accrual factor.

This scaling procedure is totally different from the one described in Section 12.3.2.2.1. Let's recall: in this formalism, which (on the overall level) conforms to the Brinson approach, the allocation contribution in one sub-period assumes the following form:

$$\widetilde{ac}^j = RAP_j * \left(1 + RAP^{j-1}\right) - RB_j * \left(1 + RB^{j-1}\right), \qquad (12.121)$$

where $\widetilde{ac}^j := \sum_{i=1}^n \widetilde{ac}_i^j$. The scaling is thus based on the returns achieved in the previous sub-periods. The sum of the allocation terms yields is in agreement with the overall Brinson approach.

$$\sum_{j=1}^{m} \widetilde{ac}^j = RAP - RB, \qquad (12.122)$$

which is not the case for the Wilshire methodology: $AC^m \neq RAP - RB$. It is characteristic for the Wilshire approach that the returns of the allocation and benchmark portfolio are scaled by the *same* factor:

$$ac_j * \left(1 + RP^{j-1}\right) * \frac{1 + RB}{1 + RB^j} = \left(RAP_j - RB_j\right) * \left(1 + RP^{j-1}\right) * \frac{1 + RB}{1 + RB^j}.$$

One can assume that the motivation for this algorithm was the desire to subject the individual period contributions to a scaling that is as little as possible influenced by the overall contributions. While the terms in (12.121) grow proportional to the active return between the allocation and the benchmark portfolio, the scaling effect in (12.119) will be limited, as both terms are scaled by the same factor. The fact that the past periods are scaled by the portfolio return and the periods following the period j are scaled by the benchmark returns is probably owed to the existence of a consistent mathematical linking algorithm (12.114).

Example 12.20

Linkage over two periods IV:

Applying the Wilshire linking algorithm to the portfolio in Example 12.17 yields the analysis in Table 12.41.

With this methodology the exhibited values differ somewhat more from the results obtained in Tables 12.36 and 12.38 than was the case with the other methodologies (especially on the segment level). The allocation is, e.g., viewed more negatively and

Table 12.41 Results of the Attribution Analysis (in %)

Sector	Allocation	Selection	Interaction	Total
1	−0.95	14.59	−8.92	4.72
2	−5.19	12.41	10.39	17.60
Total	−6.15	26.99	1.47	22.32

selection more positively. The assessment of the management success is, however, not fundamentally changed.

12.3.3.2 VALTONEN LINKING ALGORITHM

Valtonen chooses an approach, which can be viewed as the analog of the methodology described in Section 12.3.2.2.1.[62] The starting point is the well-known Equation (12.31):

$$RP^m - RB^m = AC^m + SC^m = \left(RAP^m - RB^m\right) + \left(RP^m - RAP^m\right).$$

(As a reminder: in this form the selection contribution is linked to the interaction terms.) Valtonen considers the terms on the right-hand side of the equation separately by applying Equation (12.79) to them. This yields the following recursive equation:

$$\begin{aligned} AC^m &= RAP^m - RB^m \\ &= (1 + RB_m) * \left(RAP^{m-1} - RB^{m-1}\right) + (RAP_m - RB_m) * \left(1 + RAP^{m-1}\right), \end{aligned} \qquad (12.123)$$

and

$$\begin{aligned} SC^m &= RP^m - RAP^m \\ &= (1 + RAP_m) * \left(RP^{m-1} - RAP^{m-1}\right) + (RP_m - RAP_m) * \left(1 + RP^{m-1}\right). \end{aligned} \qquad (12.124)$$

Using Equation (12.117) one obtains *mutatis mutandis* the following formulas:

$$AC^m = \sum_{j=1}^{m} ac_j * \left(1 + RAP^{j-1}\right) * \frac{1 + RB}{1 + RB^j} \qquad (12.125)$$

and:

$$SC^m = \sum_{j=1}^{m} sc_j * \left(1 + RP^{j-1}\right) * \frac{1 + RAP}{1 + RAP^j}. \qquad (12.126)$$

The generalization to the case of a complete Brinson breakdown (i.e. with a split-off of the interaction terms) based on equation (12.16) is similar:

$$RP - RB = \underbrace{(RAP - RB)}_{AC} + \underbrace{(RSP - RB)}_{SC} + \underbrace{(RP - RAP) + (RB - RSP)}_{IT(1)}. \qquad (12.127)$$

---

[62] See Valtonen (2002).

In this case the selection contribution assumes the following form:

$$SC^m = \sum_{j=1}^{m} sc_j * \left(1 + RSP^{j-1}\right) * \frac{1 + RB}{1 + RB^j}. \tag{12.128}$$

Each term of the interaction term has to be dealt with separately. By setting $IT(1)_1 = RP - RAP$ and $IT(1)_2 = RB - RSP$ one obtains the following breakdown:[63]

$$RP - RB = \sum_{j=1}^{m} ac_j * \left(1 + RAP^{j-1}\right) * \frac{1 + RB}{1 + RB^j} + \sum_{j=1}^{m} sc_j * \left(1 + RSP^{j-1}\right) * \frac{1 + RB}{1 + RB^j}$$
$$+ \sum_{j=1}^{m} it1_j * \left(1 + RP^{j-1}\right) * \frac{1 + RAP}{1 + RAP^j} + \sum_{j=1}^{m} it2_j * \left(1 + RB^{j-1}\right) * \frac{1 + RSP}{1 + RSP^j}. \tag{12.129}$$

In his article Valtonen notices also that (12.79) (basis Equation II) and thus (12.120) surprisingly still holds if the variables for the portfolio and benchmark returns are swapped:

$$\begin{aligned} RP - RB &= RP^m - RB^m \\ &= (1 + RP_m) * \left(RP^{m-1} - RB^{m-1}\right) + (RP_m - RB_m) * \left(1 + RB^{m-1}\right). \end{aligned} \tag{12.130}$$

The deduction is analogous to (12.80):

$$\begin{aligned} RP^m - RB^m &= \left(1 + RP^m\right) - \left(1 + RB^m\right) \\ &= \left(1 + RP^{m-1}\right) * (1 + RP_m) - \left(1 + RB^{m-1}\right) * (1 + RB_m) \\ &= \left(1 + RP^{m-1}\right) * (1 + RP_m) - (1 + RP_m) * \left(1 + RB^{m-1}\right) \\ &\quad - (1 + RB_m) * \left(1 + RB^{m-1}\right) + (1 + RP_m) * \left(1 + RB^{m-1}\right) \\ &= (1 + RP_m) * \left(RP^{m-1} - RB^{m-1}\right) + \left(1 + RB^{m-1}\right) * (RP_m - RB_m) \end{aligned} \tag{12.131}$$

If one follows the steps in (12.118) and (12.119) that led to Equation (12.120), then one obtains the desired expression:

$$RP - RB = \sum_{j=1}^{m} (RP_j - RB_j) * \left(1 + RB^{j-1}\right) * \frac{1 + RP}{1 + RP^j}. \tag{12.132}$$

The fact that portfolio and benchmark returns are interchangeable in Equation (12.120) reflects the fact that these linking procedures are not rooted in economical insights but rather in mathematical finesse.

---

[63] The overall selection and allocation terms are identical to the ones obtained by the methodology described in Section 12.3.2.2.1. It is the breakdown on a segment level where the differences occur.

Table 12.42 Results of the Attribution Analysis (in %)

Sector	Allocation	Selection	Interaction	Total
1	−0.62	14.42	−8.32	5.48
2	−4.87	12.34	9.37	16.84
Total	−5.49	26.76	1.05	22.32

Valtonen goes one step further by forming convex sums of the expressions (12.79) and (12.130). He thus obtains a family of linking Equations. For $x \in [0, 1]$ it holds that:

$$\begin{aligned} RP - RB &= RP^m - RB^m \\ &= x * \left[(1 + RP_m) * \left(RP^{m-1} - RB^{m-1}\right) + (RP_m - RB_m) * \left(1 + RB^{m-1}\right)\right] \\ &\quad + (1 - x) * \left[(1 + RB_m) * \left(RP^{m-1} - RB^{m-1}\right) + (RP_m - RB_m) * \left(1 + RP^{m-1}\right)\right] \\ &= (1 + x * RP_m + (1 - x) * RB_m) * \left(RP^{m-1} - RB^{m-1}\right) \\ &\quad + \left(1 + x * RB^{m-1} + (1 - x) * RP^{m-1}\right) * (RP_m - RB_m) \\ &= (1 + RB_m + x * (RP_m - RB_m)) * \left(RP^{m-1} - RB^{m-1}\right) \\ &\quad + (RP_m - RB_m) * \left(1 + RB^{m-1} + (1 - x) * \left(RP^{m-1} - RB^{m-1}\right)\right). \end{aligned} \tag{12.133}$$

Based on this identity Valtonen speaks of a *x-cumulative* linkage method, if for the effects (illustrated by the allocation contribution *AC*, other effects analogously) the following relationship holds:

$$\begin{aligned} AC^m &= (1 + RB_m + x * (RP_m - RB_m)) * AC^{m-1} \\ &\quad + ac_m * \left(1 + RB^{m-1} + (1 - x) * \left(RP^{m-1} - RB^{m-1}\right)\right) \end{aligned} \tag{12.134}$$

If $x = 1$ (i.e. the case treated above) he speaks of a cumulative linkage method. Valtonen shows that the linkage method by Cariño (described in the following section) can be approximately viewed as a 1/2-cumulative linkage method; further applications are not given in his article.

Example 12.21

Linkage over two periods V:

Applying this methodology to the standard example (Example 12.17) yields the analysis in Table 12.42.

Compared to the other linking algorithms the application of this methodology doesn't result in substantially different numerical values, either. The overall contributions for the selection and the allocation are identical to those in Table 12.38, as expected.

12.3.4 Approach According to Basic Formula III

12.3.4.1 APPROACH ACCORDING TO KAHAN (I)

Analogously to the procedure in Section 12.3.2, the approach by Kahan for the breakdown of the contributions (Equation (12.88)) defined in Section 12.3.1[64] can be extended to the Brinson analysis in the multi-period case. If one sets:

$$FP^j = \sum_{l=1}^{m-1} \left(\frac{1}{l+1} * \prod_{\substack{1 \leqslant k_1 < k_2 < \cdots < k_l \leqslant m \\ k_i \neq j}} RP_{k_1} * \cdots * RP_{k_l} \right) \tag{12.135}$$

and:

$$FB^j = \sum_{l=1}^{m-1} \left(\frac{1}{l+1} * \prod_{\substack{1 \leqslant k_1 < k_2 < \cdots < k_l \leqslant m \\ k_i \neq j}} RB_{k_1} * \cdots * RB_{k_l} \right), \tag{12.136}$$

then the attribution effects can be defined as follows:

$$ac_i^j := \left(swp_i^j * \left(1 + FP^j\right) - swb_i^j * \left(1 + FB^j\right)\right) * srb_i^j, \tag{12.137}$$

$$sc_i^j := swb_i^j * \left(1 + FB^j\right) * \left(srp_i^j - srb_i^j\right), \tag{12.138}$$

$$it(1)_i^j := \left(swp_i^j * \left(1 + FP^j\right) - swb_i^j * \left(1 + FB^j\right)\right) * \left(srp_i^j - srb_i^j\right). \tag{12.139}$$

In regard to the scaling outlined in Section 12.3.2.1 it is often criticised that in case of a positive return development the interaction terms resulting from the linking of the periods are distributed mainly to the sub-periods at the end of the analysis period. In the approach of Kahan all periods are treated equally, by distributing the interaction terms uniformly to them. This implies, however, that with the addition of sub-periods all generalized contributions of the previous periods have to be computed anew.

Example 12.22

Linkage over two periods V:

Once again the portfolio in Example 12.17 will be used to illustrate this methodology (see Table 12.43).

Compared to the results in Table 12.38 the differences are minor.

[64] Cf. Kahan (2006). The attribution analysis is, however, not explicitly treated there.

Table 12.43 Results of the Attribution Analysis (in %)

Sector	Allocation	Selection	Interaction	Total
1	−0.70	13.54	−7.92	4.92
2	−5.49	11.91	10.98	17.40
Total	−6.19	25.45	3.06	22.32

12.3.4.2 APPROACH ACCORDING TO KAHAN (II)

Based on the methodology outlined in the previous section, the transition to a linking algorithm, in which the selection and allocation contributions are scaled solely by the respective returns achieved for these attribution effects, is completely analogous to the procedure described in Section 12.3.2.2.

The attribution terms are as follows:

$$\overline{ac}_i^j := swp_i^j * \left(1 + FAP^{j-1}\right) * srb_i^j - swb_i^j * \left(1 + FB^{j-1}\right) * srb_i^j, \tag{12.140}$$

$$\overline{sc}_i^j := swb_i^j * \left(1 + FSP^{j-1}\right) * srp_i^j - swb_i^j * \left(1 + FB^{j-1}\right) * srb_i^j, \tag{12.141}$$

$$\begin{aligned} \overline{it(1)}_i^j = {} & swp_i^j * \left(srp_i^j * \left(1 + FP^{j-1}\right) - srb_i^j * \left(1 + FAP^{j-1}\right)\right) \\ & - swb_i^j * \left(srp_i^j * \left(1 + FSP^{j-1}\right) - srb_i^j * \left(1 + FB^{j-1}\right)\right), \end{aligned} \tag{12.142}$$

where the factors FAP and FSP are defined as follows:

$$FAP^j = \sum_{l=1}^{m-1} \left(\frac{1}{l+1} * \prod_{\substack{1 \leqslant k_1 < k_2 < \cdots < k_l \leqslant m \\ k_i \neq j}} RAP_{k_1} * \cdots * RAP_{k_l} \right), \tag{12.143}$$

respectively

$$FSP^j = \sum_{l=1}^{m-1} \left(\frac{1}{l+1} * \prod_{\substack{1 \leqslant k_1 < k_2 < \cdots < k_l \leqslant m \\ k_i \neq j}} RSP_{k_1} * \cdots * RSP_{k_l} \right). \tag{12.144}$$

For the advantages of this approach compared to the one described in the last section see Section 12.3.2.2.1.

Table 12.44 Results of the Attribution Analysis (in %)

Sector	Allocation	Selection	Interaction	Total
1	−0.72	14.46	−8.83	4.92
2	−4.78	12.30	9.88	17.40
Total	−5.49	26.76	1.05	22.32

Example 12.23

Linkage over two periods VII:

Based on the portfolio Example 12.17 this linking algorithm yields the analysis in Table 12.44.

12.3.5 Linking algorithms by Menchero and Cariño

In contrast to the consideration in Sections 12.3.2 and 12.3.4, the approaches by Menchero and Cariño are not based on the decomposition of the linked returns over several sub-periods (Equations (12.78), (12.79) and (12.88)). Instead they attempt to apply certain mathematical smoothing algorithms, in order to obtain a consistent linkage of the *active* returns for the individual sub-periods – and thus an attribution analysis without residuum. The starting point of their considerations is again an arbitrary attribution model for one period, which decomposes the active return in a finite number of effects. In case of the Brinson model the break-down is given by:

$$RP_j - RB_j = ac^j + sc^j + it^j. \tag{12.145}$$

ac^j, sc^j and it^j denominate the allocation, selection and interaction contributions in the period j. As is well-known, the sum of the active returns achieved in the individual sub-periods does in general not equal the active return in the overall period:

$$RP - RB \neq \sum_{j=1}^{m} RP_j - RB_j. \tag{12.146}$$

The simplest approach for obtaining a consistent analysis by means of an appropriate scaling is based on the following factor:

$$A := \frac{RP - RB}{\sum_{j=1}^{m} RP_j - RB_j} \tag{12.147}$$

(the term in the denominator is assumed different from zero). One then obviously obtains:

$$RP - RB = A * \sum_{j=1}^{m} RP_j - RB_j = A * \sum_{j=1}^{m} ac^j + sc^j + it^j, \tag{12.148}$$

and the definition of the generalized contribution effects can easily be derived. For instance would $A * ac^j$ be the generalized allocation contribution for the period j and $A * \sum_{j=1}^{m} ac^j$ the generalized overall allocation contribution etc.

Unfortunately, this simple approach (promulgated by Campisi) is not suitable for the requirements in practice.[65] It is, for instance, not very hard to construct cases, in which A assumes a negative value, so that the return effects would not only be scaled but submitted to a change in sign (which would turn the original valuation of an effect into the opposite).

A further similar approach was proposed by Zhang. For each attribution effect he defines a specific factor:[66]

$$(f_{ac} := \prod_{j=1}^{m} (1 + ac^j) \quad f_{sc} := \prod_{j=1}^{m} (1 + sc^j) \quad f_{it} := \prod_{j=1}^{m} (1 + it^j). \qquad (12.149)$$

He furthermore sets $F := f_{ac} + f_{sc} + f_{it}$ and defines the attribution affects over the entire period as follows:

$$ac := f_{ac} * \frac{RP^m - RB^m}{F}, \quad sc := f_{sc} * \frac{RP^m - RB^m}{F}, \quad it := f_{it} * \frac{RP^m - RB^m}{F}. \qquad (12.150)$$

These terms clearly add up to the total overall active return:

$$ac + sc + it = \frac{(f_{ac} + f_{sc} + f_{it})}{F} * (RP^m - RB^m) = RP^m - RB^m. \qquad (12.151)$$

However, in many cases the scaling in (12.150) has far-reaching consequences. On inspection already the multiplicative linkage of the contributions in (12.149) is questionable (returns are linked geometrically, *not* the contributions). Furthermore the factors can lead to considerable distortions of the results. For instance, in case $RP^m - RB^m = 0$ (and $F \neq 0$) all effects are shown as zero (even in the case that the active return is due, say, to a good selection and a bad allocation). Further problematic cases are readily constructed, so that all in all, this algorithm is also unsuitable for practical applications.

Menchero chooses a more nimble approach.[67] He starts from the assumption that the sum of the single-period active returns is close to the geometric return scaled down to a single period and multiplied by the number of sub-periods:[68]

$$\sum_{j=1}^{m} RP_j - RB_j \approx m * \left((1 + RP)^{1/m} - (1 + RB)^{1/m}\right), \qquad (12.152)$$

[65] Cf. Campisi (2002/03). The reasons for the impracticality of this approach are outlined in Menchero (2003). There also an example is given.
[66] See Zhang, (2005/06) (especially Eq. 23). Zhang considers a general group of factors. Without loss of generality here the approach is discussed in the concrete Brinson case.
[67] See Menchero (2000).
[68] In regard to the question, whether the right-hand side of this equation is a suitable statistical estimator, only general consideration is given in Menchero (2000). The question of whether it is an optimal estimator is not considered at all.

and thus

$$RP - RB \approx \frac{(RP - RB)}{m * \left((1+RP)^{1/m} - (1+RB)^{1/m}\right)} * \sum_{j=1}^{m} \left(RP_j - RB_j\right). \quad (12.153)$$

The left-hand side and the right-hand side of this formula will in general not be identical, and it is not possible to choose a single scaling factor. In order to obtain identity, Menchero makes the assumption that all periods should be weighted as evenly as possible, an assumption which he calls intuitive. Mathematically he chooses the following approach:

$$RP - RB = \sum_{j=1}^{m} \left(A + \alpha_j\right) * \left(RP_j - RB_j\right), \quad (12.154)$$

where:

$$A := \begin{cases} \frac{(RP-RB)/m}{(1+RP)^{1/m}-(1+RB)^{1/m}} & RP \neq RB \\ (1+RP)^{\frac{m-1}{m}} & RP = RB. \end{cases} \quad (12.155)$$

A is thus the quotient of the mean arithmetic and the mean geometric active return for a sub-period and assumes only positive values. According to the second premise, the α_j will be determined by means of a quadratic optimization, such that the sum of the squares of the α_j is minimized under the constraint (12.154). The solution to this problem is readily found by the well-known method of Lagrange multipliers.[69] It is given by:

$$\alpha_i = \frac{RP - RB - A * \sum_{j=1}^{m} \left(RP_j - RB_j\right)}{\sum_{j=1}^{m} \left(RP_j - RB_j\right)^2} * RP_i - RB_i. \quad (12.156)$$

Based on the terms in the one-period case, according to (12.145) and (12.154) the generalized attribution terms are given by $\left(A + \alpha_j\right) * ac^j$, $\left(A + \alpha_j\right) * sc^j$ and $\left(A + \alpha_j\right) * it^j$. $\left(A + \alpha_j\right) * ac^j$ is for instance the generalized allocation contribution for the period j and $\sum_{j=1}^{m} \left(A + \alpha_j\right) * ac^j$ the generalized allocation contribution for the overall period, etc.[70]

---

[69] For the method of Lagrange multipliers see e.g. the source given in Menchero (2000).

[70] The approach by Menchero (and the one by Cariño, too) is somewhat similar to the linking algorithms proposed by Kahan as described in Sections 12.3.4.1 and 12.3.4.2. It is also Kahan's objective to distribute the interaction terms as evenly as possible to the different sub-periods. Menchero's scaling is, however, based on the effects, whereas in the Kahan approach the portfolio and benchmark terms are scaled separately.

Menchero refers in his article to statistical computations conducted by himself according to which the coefficients $A + \alpha_j$ assume negative values only in extreme performance scenarios, such that the criticism that led to a refutation of the naive approach (12.147) is not applicable here (respectively only to a very limited extent).

As in the case of Menchero's algorithm, the base for Cariño's[71] approach is not precise mathematical or economical reasoning, but rather a clever intuitive approach. His reasoning is as follows: for the geometric active return over a single period approximately the following relationship holds (especially for small values):

$$\frac{1+RP_j}{1+RB_j} \approx e^{RP_j - RB_j}. \tag{12.157}$$

To obtain an exact identity in (12.157), Cariño introduces a correction factor k_j:

$$\frac{1+RP_j}{1+RB_j} = e^{k_j*(RP_j - RB_j)}. \tag{12.158}$$

It is readily shown that these factors assume the following form:

$$k_j = \begin{cases} \frac{\ln(1+RP_j)-\ln(1+RB_j)}{RP_j - RB_j} & RP_j \neq RB_j \\ \left(1+RP_j\right)^{-1} & RP_j = RB_j. \end{cases} \tag{12.159}$$

Multiplying the expressions in (12.158) over m periods provides the following identity:

$$\frac{1+RP}{1+RB} = \prod_{j=1}^{m} \frac{1+RP_j}{1+RB_j} = \prod_{j=1}^{m} e^{k_j*(RP_j - RB_j)} = e^{\sum_{j=1}^{m} k_j*(RP_j - RB_j)}. \tag{12.160}$$

If one applies the natural logarithm function, one obtains:

$$\ln\left(\frac{1+RP}{1+RB}\right) = \ln(1+RP) - \ln(1+RB) = \sum_{j=1}^{m} k_j * \left(RP_j - RB_j\right). \tag{12.161}$$

By means of a further factor:

$$k = \begin{cases} \frac{\ln(1+RP) - \ln(1+RB)}{RP - RB} & RP \neq RB \\ (1+RP)^{-1} & RP = RB \end{cases} \tag{12.162}$$

one finally obtains the desired identity:

$$RP - RB = \sum_{j=1}^{m} \frac{k_j}{k} * \left(RP_j - RB_j\right). \tag{12.163}$$

[71] Cf. Cariño (1999, 2002).

Table 12.45 Results of the Attribution Analysis (in %) (Menchero)

Sector	Allocation	Selection	Interaction	Total
1	−0.82	14.24	−8.67	4.76
2	−5.17	12.40	10.33	17.56
Total	−5.98	26.64	1.66	22.32

Table 12.46 Results of the Attribution Analysis (in %) (Cariño)

Sector	Allocation	Selection	Interaction	Total
1	−0.76	14.09	−8.56	4.77
2	−5.15	12.40	10.30	17.55
Total	−5.91	26.49	1.75	22.32

In this approach the problem of a sign reversal is completely excluded: the factors k_j and k are always positive. The generalized attribution terms are given by $k_j/k * ac^j$, $k_j/k * sc^j$ and $k_j/k * it^j$. ($k_j/k * ac^j$ is the generalized attribution term for the period j, $\sum_{j=1}^{m} k_j/k * ac^j$ the generalized attribution term for the overall period, etc.)

As already indicated, the methodology in Cariño (1999) is ultimately not based on an economical foundation. In summary, the main argument for this approach is that the scaling has a limited impact on the effects.

In Menchero (2000) various statistical considerations based on normally distributed portfolio and benchmark returns are discussed. It is assumed that the standard deviations of these returns correspond to the average (monthly) returns. These quantities assume values from −10% to 2%. In summary the author concludes that the resulting mean values of the Menchero and Cariño coefficients are very close to each other. Menchero points out that in those cases, where the average portfolio and the average benchmark return are close to each other – a standard situation for portfolio managed close to their benchmarks – the variance of the Menchero factors is less than the variance of the Cariño factors. The value of an attribution analysis in practice cannot, however, solely be measured by statistical averages. It must contain more or less reasonable values in all effect categories. This is certainly a point in favor of the Menchero methodology (compared to the Cariño linking algorithm).

Example 12.24

Linkage over two periods VIII:

Applying the Menchero approach to the standard example (Example 12.17) yields the analysis in Table 12.45.

With the Cariño linking algorithm one obtains the results in Table 12.46.

Both methods lead to results that lie well within the range of the results obtained with the other methods.

Table 12.47 Portfolio and Benchmark Data Over Two Periods (in %)

Sector	Period 1				Period 2			
	Portfolio		Benchmark		Portfolio		Benchmark	
	Weight	Return	Weight	Return	Weight	Return	Weight	Return
1	58.0	−6.00	60.0	4.20	58.0	5.20	60.0	5.00
2	42.0	−10.00	40.0	10.40	42.0	−4.50	40.0	−11.00
Total	100.0	−7.68	100.0	6.68	100.0	1.13	100.0	−1.40

Table 12.48 Portfolio and Benchmark Data Over Two Periods (in %)

Period	Portfolio Return	Benchmark Return	Active Return
1	−7.68	6.68	−14.36
2	1.13	−1.40	2.53
Total	−6.64	5.19	−11.83

12.3.6 Concluding Remarks on the Linking Algorithms

In view of the small differences that were obtained by applying the various linking algorithms to the portfolio in Example 12.17 (after all, a portfolio with significant bets relative to the benchmark), one could indeed agree with Campisi's view that it's hardly worth the effort to implement an involved linking algorithm, since the quality of the results will only be marginally enhanced.[72] In general, this assertion is, however, misleading, as will be illustrated by the following example.

Example 12.25

Multiplicative Linkage:

The starting point is again the analysis of a portfolio relative to its benchmark over two periods (see Table 12.47).

During the first period the portfolio underperformed its benchmark considerably, whereas for the second period an outperformance was achieved. The management approach, primarily driven by the title selection with moderate allocation bets, is clearly reflected by the results of the analysis (see Table 12.48).

If one analyses this portfolio based on the different linking algorithms (Table 12.49), then it becomes apparent that the results scatter significantly. The selection contributions are, however, always the dominating factors. For the allocation decision in regard to the segment 2 according to "Method 1" and "Kahan I" a positive contribution

[72] Cf. Campisi (2002/03).

Table 12.49 Results According to the Various Linking Algorithms (in %)

		Allocation	Selection	Interaction
Method 1	Segment 1	−0.61	−5.99	0.18
	Segment 2	0.64	−5.39	−0.66
	Total	0.03	−11.38	−0.48
Method 2	Segment 1	−0.19	−6.44	0.21
	Segment 2	−0.03	−5.13	−0.25
	Total	−0.22	−11.57	−0.04
Kirievsky/ Kirievsky	Segment 1	−0.26	−4.63	
	Segment 2	−0.30	−4.23	
	Total	−0.56	−8.86	
Wilshire	Segment 1	−0.18	−5.92	0.20
	Segment 2	0.00	−5.65	−0.28
	Total	−0.17	−11.57	−0.08
Valtonen	Segment 1	−0.19	−5.92	0.37
	Segment 2	−0.03	−5.64	−0.41
	Total	−0.22	−11.57	−0.04
Kahan I	Segment 1	−0.36	−5.95	0.12
	Segment 2	0.37	−5.42	−0.58
	Total	0.00	−11.37	−0.46
Kahan II	Segment 1	−0.19	−6.22	0.21
	Segment 2	−0.03	−5.34	−0.25
	Total	−0.22	−11.57	−0.04
Menchero	Segment 1	−0.18	−5.99	0.20
	Segment 2	−0.01	−5.56	−0.28
	Total	−0.19	−11.55	−0.08
Cariño	Segment 1	−0.18	−5.99	0.20
	Segment 2	−0.01	−5.56	−0.28
	Total	−0.19	−11.55	−0.08

is shown. However, a negative result is obtained by the methodology of Kirievsky/ Kirievsky. All other methodologies have a neutral (or, respectively, a slightly negative) view on that decision. Also, in regard to the first segment of the allocation decision the judgement is not uniform, although it is negative in all cases. (The range is in this case −0.18% to −0.61%.)

Similar variations can be observed in case of the selection contributions (viewed absolutely). As these effects assume much higher absolute values, the impact on the quality of the analysis is, however, not that significant.

In itself the considered portfolio is not at all unrealistic: significant stock selection bets are accompanied by moderate allocation decisions. The stock picks were chosen that strong merely to illustrate the effects more clearly. In real portfolios one usually finds a larger number of (more moderate) bets. The effect will in practice also show up in portfolios without such extreme stock picks. This is due to accumulation effects over longer periods as well as to the tendency that contributions often assume small values over longer periods.

Another point of criticism, which is brought up against the methodology described in Section 12.3.2.2.1, is the appearance of interaction terms even in situations where no interaction terms are shown for the individual sub-periods.[73]

Table 12.50 Portfolio and Benchmark Data Over Two Periods (in %)

Sector	Period 1				Period 2			
	Portfolio		Benchmark		Portfolio		Benchmark	
	Weight	Return	Weight	Return	Weight	Return	Weight	Return
1	75.0	−4.0	60.0	−4.0	60.0	12.0	60.0	5.0
2	25.0	−10.0	40.0	−10.0	40.0	9.0	40.0	−5.0
Total	100.0	−5.5	100.0	−6.4	100.0	10.80	100.0	1.0

Example 12.26

Interaction terms and multiplicative linkage:

The data in Example 12.25 are modified in a way, so that for the first period the selection contribution and for the second period the allocation contribution equals zero (as is readily shown). As a consequence, in the individual periods no interaction terms appear. Depending on the chosen linking algorithm such interaction terms might be generated (see Tables 12.50 and 12.51).

The example illustrates that only with the linking algorithms according to Wilshire, Menchero and Cariño the appearance of interaction terms, which are solely due to the linking, is excluded.[74] As mentioned above, in the minds of the authors promulgating these approaches, this is an advantage of their algorithm. In lack of a guiding economical principle a final evaluation of this property is, however, difficult. In any case, it is by no means *a priori* clear that a linking algorithm should possess this property. One should be aware of the fact that interaction terms appear inevitably if one links two periods in which allocation and selection contributions ($AC_{1/2}, SC_{1/2}$) were generated, but no interaction terms.

$$\frac{1+RP}{1+RB} - 1 = \frac{1+RP_1}{1+RB_1} * \frac{1+RP_2}{1+RB_2} - 1$$
$$= (1 + AC_1 + SC_1) * (1 + AC_2 + SC_2) - 1.$$

Although the interaction terms ($AC_1 * SC_2 + AC_2 * SC_1$) are not the same interaction terms as in Table 12.51, their appearance makes it comprehensible that such interaction terms appear in the multi-period case.

[73] Cf. e.g. Bonafedeet al. (02, p. 18).

[74] The method of Kirievsky/Kirievsky is not considered in this context, as the interaction terms are not explicitly listed in their article.

Table 12.51 Results on the Portfolio Level (in %)

	Allocation	Selection	Interaction
Method 1	0.91	9.17	0.09
Method 2	0.91	9.17	0.09
Wilshire	0.91	9.26	0.00
Valtonen	0.91	9.17	0.09
Kahan I	0.64	9.49	0.04
Kahan II	0.91	9.17	0.09
Menchero	0.89	9.28	0.00
Cariño	0.95	9.22	0.00

A significant disadvantage of the linking algorithms by Menchero and Cariño is that the correction factors must be recalculated for each sub-period added to the analysis period, which causes a higher computational effort. It furthermore entails that the partial results of the previous sub-periods are subject to a recalculation, so that these figures will change over time. This has some grave consequences. It, for instance, often occurs in practice that the portfolio managers invest in certain segments only for a limited period. If one applies the methods of Menchero and Cariño to a portfolio with segments that were invested only in the past, the historical contributions of these segments will still be changed with every new sub-period added to the overall analysis period. As these changes are unrelated to the investment decisions, they are hard to explain to the portfolio manager or the client.[75]

A concluding systematic analysis of the effects is still outstanding. Such an analysis is significantly handicapped (if not made impossible) by the fact that there is no agreement in the literature in regard to the economic principles on which an evaluation should be based.[76] This makes it in particular impossible to judge which value of the allocation effect shown in Example 12.26 comes closest to the "real" value, since the latter cannot be measured independently of a model! It was furthermore outlined that the approach by Kirievsky/Kirievsky leads to a non-additive methodology. Hence it is clear that the natural approach by Brinson et al. cannot be extended in a direct form to the multi-period case. The last word has certainly not been spoken about linking algorithms. It is, however, questionable, whether a final consensus can be achieved in this area.

[75] In this context Broberg gives the example of an attribution analysis for a portfolio, whose sub-segments are managed by different portfolio managers. The management contract of one of these managers was terminated in the middle of the period (cf. Broberg 2006).

[76] This was pointed out by several authors. See for instance Valtonen (2002, p. 79): "There exists no absolute yardstick against which to benchmark the methods."

12.4 ATTRIBUTION ANALYSIS IN A GEOMETRIC FORM

12.4.1 Method of Burnie et al.

For an attribution analysis in geometric (or multiplicative) form instead of the arithmetic (or additive) form of the active return, $RP - RB$, the geometric (or multiplicative) form is used:[77]

$$\frac{1+RP}{1+RB} - 1 = \frac{RP - RB}{1+RB}. \tag{12.164}$$

As was the case for the Brinson analysis, the aim of the approach by Burnie et al. is the breakdown of the active return, such that the single components can be linked to determinants of the underlying management process.[78] The main difference is that the authors use a geometric approach.

The formulas for this analysis form follow to a large extent from the Brinson formulas by implementing the transition from the arithmetic to the geometric form of the active return,

$$R_1 - R_2 \rightarrow (1+R_1)/(1+R_2) - 1, \tag{12.165}$$

and by linking of the overall contributions in a geometric form. The following representation is based on the article by Burnie, Knowles and Teder. At first the transformation of Equations (12.16), (12.19) and (12.20) to the multiplicative case will be considered.

Multiplicative attribution analysis with separation of the interaction terms

$$\frac{1+RP}{1+RB} = \underbrace{\frac{1+RAP}{1+RB}}_{1+ACM} * \underbrace{\frac{1+RSP}{1+RB}}_{1+SCM} * \underbrace{\frac{1+RP}{1+RAP} * \frac{1+RB}{1+RSP}}_{1+ITM}, \tag{12.166}$$

$$acmr_i := (swp_i - swb_i) * \left(\frac{1+srb_i}{1+RB} - 1\right), \tag{12.167}$$

$$scm_i := swb_i * \frac{srp_i - srb_i}{1+RB}. \tag{12.168}$$

[77] Cf. also the explanations in Section 10.7.

[78] Cf. e.g. Burnie et al. (1998). There the notation "geometric attribution" is used, whereas in the article by Buhl et al. (2000) the term *multiplicative* attribution is used. Both expressions are used in Bacon (2002). For a similar approach, which also considers currency effects, see McLaren (2001).

Equations (12.166) and (12.167) follow directly from Equations (12.16) and (12.19) by applying the premise on the (multiplicative) linkage of returns and the representation of the active return in (12.165). This is, however, not the case for the selection terms in (12.168), whose form is essentially determined by the requirement that they add up to the overall selection contribution. The following calculation confirms that this is indeed the case.[79]

$$\sum_{i=1}^{n} scm_i = \frac{1}{1+RB} * \sum_{i=1}^{n} \left(swb_i * srp_i - swb_i * srb_i\right) = \frac{RSP - RB}{1+RB}$$
$$= \frac{1+RSP}{1+RB} - 1 = SBM.$$

Had the definition of the selection contributions for the portfolio segments been based on the transformation (12.165), then one would have obtained the following expressions:

$$scm_i := swb_i * \left(\frac{1+srp_i}{1+srb_i} - 1\right) = swb_i * \frac{srp_i - srb_i}{1+srb_i}. \tag{12.169}$$

With the definition of the allocation and selection contributions in (12.167) and (12.168) it follows that these contributions – as well as the active return (12.164) – can be deduced from the arithmetic contributions via a scaling by the factor 1+*RB*:

$$ACM = \frac{AC}{1+RB}, \text{ respectively } SCM = \frac{SC}{1+RB}. \tag{12.170}$$

This also holds for the selection and attribution contributions on a segment level:

$$acmr_i = \frac{acr_i}{1+RB}, \text{ respectively } scm_i = \frac{scr_i}{1+RB}. \tag{12.171}$$

Due to multiplicative form, a meaningful break-down of the interaction terms in Equation (12.166) seems to be unfeasible.

Example 12.27

Attribution analysis in a geometric form according to Burnie et al.:

In this example an equity portfolio will be considered which consists of the two segments *Germany* and *Euroland ex Germany*. The management process includes selection and allocation decisions in regard to those segments. Two different portfolio managers are responsible for the stock picking within the respective segments. Both regions are assumed to be equally weighted within the benchmark. Furthermore, it will be assumed that the segment *Germany* within the benchmark achieved a return of 20% in the analysis period and the segment *Euroland ex Germany* a return of –20%.

[79] In a similar way one shows that $\sum_{i=1}^{n} acmr_i = ACM$.

Table 12.52 Comparison of the Selection Contributions (in %)

Sector	Return		Selection contribution	
	BM	PF	Multiplicative (12.169)	Burnie (4.168)/ Additive (12.20)
Germany	20	40	8.33	10.00
Euroland ex Germany	−20	0	12.50	10.00

Table 12.53 Portfolio and Benchmark Data (in %)

Sector	Return		Weight	
	BM	PF	BM	PF
Germany	50	40	50	70
Euroland ex Germany	−40	0	50	30

Table 12.54 Comparison of the Selection and Allocation Contributions (in %)

Sector	Selection			Allocation	
	Multiplicative (12.169)	Multiplicative Burnie (12.168)	Additive (12.20)	Multiplicative Burnie (12.167)	Additive (12.19)
Germany	−3.33	−4.76	−5.00	8.57	10.00
Euroland ex Ger.	33.33	19.05	20.00	8.57	8.00

The overall return of the benchmark is thus equal to 0%, which implies that the selection contributions computed according to the additive method are identical to the ones computed on the basis of Equation (12.168). The manager of the segment *Germany* achieved a return of 40% and the manager of the segment *Euroland ex Germany* a return of 0%. Table 12.52 contains the selection contributions calculated according to Equation (12.168), respectively Equation (12.169). Currency contributions do not incur, and other contributions (allocation, interaction) are not considered for the sake of simplicity.

It becomes clear that simplification made in the selection term (12.169) can have a significant impact on the result.

Also the effects listed in Table 12.54 for the portfolio in Table 12.53 illustrate that the contributions computed according to the methodology by Burnie et al. differ only slightly from the additive contributions, but that the selection contributions are much different to those computed by Equation (12.169).

Some of the properties I–VI in Section 12.2.3 are not (respectively, only partially) valid for this approach. The active return over a single period is not represented as the sum of the contributions, but as the product of the contributions

Multiplicative attribution analysis, in which the interaction and selection terms are combined

$$\frac{1+RP}{1+RB} = \underbrace{\frac{1+RP}{1+RAP}}_{1+SCM^{alt}} * \underbrace{\frac{1+RAP}{1+RB}}_{1+ACM}, \tag{12.172}$$

$$acmr_i := (swp_i - swb_i) * \left(\frac{1+srb_i}{1+RB} - 1\right), \tag{12.173}$$

$$scm_i^{alt} := swp_i * \frac{srp_i - srb_i}{1+RAP}. \tag{12.174}$$

(allocation, selection, interaction) on the overall level. The latter terms (with the exception of the interaction term) can in turn be represented in the form of a sum (property I). In regard to property V it has already been pointed out that the computation of the selection contributions on the segment level is not in agreement with the premise of computing all contributions based on the multiplicative active return. This property only holds for the contributions on the portfolio level (total allocation, selection and interaction contribution) and for the individual allocation contributions. One goal of the multiplicative attribution analysis is to define the contributions in such a way that they only depend on the active return and not on the absolute return of the benchmark (property VI). This, again, is only the case for the overall contributions and for the allocation contributions, and not for the selection terms.

The transformation of the additive attribution analysis, where the selection and interaction terms are combined (Equations (12.19), (12.30), (12.31)), is analogous to the previous case.[80]

The definition of the individual selection contributions safeguards the additivity property:

$$\begin{aligned}\sum_{i=1}^{n} scm_i^{alt} &= \frac{1}{1+RAP} * \sum_{i=1}^{n} \left(swp_i * srp_i - swp_i * srb_i\right) = \frac{RP - RAP}{1+RAP} \\ &= \frac{1+RP}{1+RAP} - 1 = SCM^{alt}.\end{aligned}$$

Due to the similarities between Equations (12.166)–(12.168) and Equations (12.172)–(12.174) the considerations made for those are readily applied to the present situation. In contrast to Equation (12.168) the definition of the selection contribution is based on the return of the allocation portfolio rather than on the segment return. The sole motivation for this modification is again the preservation of the additivity. This procedure is thus also not in agreement with

[80] Cf. Burnie et al. (98, p. 61). This analysis form coincides with the one outlined in Bacon (2008).

the premise of basing the individual contributions on the multiplicative form of the active return.

12.4.2 Approaches According to Menchero and Cariño

With the methodology of Burnie et al. the approach to substitute the additive by the multiplicative active return (Equation (12.165)), was realized only partially. The overall contributions were still broken down in an additive form. Menchero goes one step further by also applying the substitution in Equation (12.165) to the formulas for the contributions of individual segments. He does, however, not apply the formula to the (active) returns, but to the contributions. Based on Equations (12.18)–(12.22) he obtains for the selection contribution (Equation (12.20))[81]

$$sc_i = swb_i * srp_i - swb_i * srb_i \rightarrow \widetilde{scm}_i := \frac{1 + swb_i * srp_i}{1 + swb_i * srb_i} - 1 \qquad (12.175)$$

and analogously for the allocation contribution (Equation (12.19))

$$acr_i \rightarrow \widetilde{acmr}_i : \frac{1 + swp_i * srb_i}{1 + swb_i * srb_i} * \frac{1 + swb_i * RB}{1 + swp_i * RB} - 1. \qquad (12.176)$$

The goal of this procedure is to represent the contributions on a higher level also as the product of the individual contributions. This can only be achieved by introducing appropriate correction factors K_i^{SCM}, respectively K_i^{ACM}.[82]

$$1 + ACM = \prod_{i=1}^{n} \left(1 + \widetilde{acmr}_i\right) * \left(1 + K_i^{ABM}\right), \qquad (12.177)$$

$$1 + SCM = \prod_{i=1}^{n} \left(1 + \widetilde{scm}_i\right) * \left(1 + K_i^{SCM}\right). \qquad (12.178)$$

This leads to:

$$\prod_{i=1}^{n} \left(1 + K_i^{SCM}\right) = \frac{1 + SCM}{\prod_{i=1}^{n} \left(1 + \widetilde{scm}_i\right)}, \quad \text{respectively}$$

$$\prod_{i=1}^{n} \left(1 + K_i^{ACM}\right) = \frac{1 + ACM}{\prod_{i=1}^{n} \left(1 + \widetilde{acmr}_i\right)}. \qquad (12.179)$$

The individual correction factors are basically freely definable, merely Equations (12.177) and (12.178) must be fulfilled. Menchero chooses an approach,

---

[81] Cf. Menchero (2000/01). In order to differentiate the notation from the one in the previous section a tilde is added to the terms.

[82] n represents again the number of segments.

in which the overall factor is distributed uniformly to the individual terms. He sets

$$1 + K_i^{SCM} : \sqrt[n]{\frac{1+SCM}{\prod_{i=1}^{n}(1+\widetilde{scm}_i)}}, \text{ respectively } 1 + K_i^{ACM} : \sqrt[n]{\frac{1+ACM}{\prod_{i=1}^{n}(1+\widetilde{acmr}_i)}}. \tag{12.180}$$

The allocation and selection terms will thus be modified as follows:

$$\begin{aligned} 1 \quad + \quad & \widetilde{acmr}_i \rightarrow (1+\widetilde{acmr}_i) * (1+K_i^{ACM}) \\ = \quad & \frac{1+swp_i * srb_i}{1+swb_i * srb_i} * \frac{1+swb_i * RB}{1+swp_i * RB} * \sqrt[n]{\frac{1+ACM}{\prod_{i=1}^{n}(1+\widetilde{acmr}_i)}} \end{aligned} \tag{12.181}$$

respectively

$$1+\widetilde{scm}_i^{alt} \rightarrow (1+\widetilde{scm}_i) * (1+K_i^{SCM}) = \frac{1+swb_i * srp_i}{1+swb_i * srb_i} * \sqrt[n]{\frac{1+SCM}{\prod_{i=1}^{n}(1+\widetilde{scm}_i)}}. \tag{12.182}$$

The procedure for the interaction term is analogous. Formally it is defined by:

$$it_i \rightarrow \widetilde{itm}_i := \frac{1+swp_i * srp_i}{1+swp_i * srb_i} * \frac{1+swb_i * srb_i}{1+swb_i * srp_i} - 1. \tag{12.183}$$

The definition of the correction terms is analogous and will therefore be left to the reader. Similarly, the analysis where selection and interaction terms are combined, will not be considered here in detail.[83]

Menchero points out in his article that by means of simulations one can show that under realistic conditions the correction terms assume an expected value near zero with a limited variance.[84] This does, however, not exclude that under certain conditions (especially over longer periods) the correction factors may cause significant distortions. Unfortunately, such (singular) cases can undermine the credibility of the performance analysis. This needs to be considered when applying this methodology in practice.

Of the properties I–VI listed in Section 12.2.3 properties I–V also hold (approximately) *mutatis mutandis* (substitution of the term "sum" by "product" etc.) for the methodology by Menchero. That assumes, however, that the impact of the correction factors is small. Property VI does not hold for this methodology.

---

[83] Only this case is treated in the article by Menchero explicitly.

[84] Cf. Menchero (2000/01, p. 25 et seq).

Table 12.55 Portfolio and Benchmark Data (in %)

Sector	Portfolio		Benchmark	
	Weight	Return	Weight	Return
1	50.0	44.0	5.0	40.0
2	50.0	15.0	85.0	–10.0
Total	100.0	30.0	100.0	–2.5

Table 12.56 Results of the Attribution Analysis (in %)

Sector	Selection			Allocation		
	Additive	Menchero (unscaled)	Menchero	Additive	Menchero (unscaled)	Menchero
1	0.60	0.57	–0.05	14.88	14.21	14.24
2	21.25	23.22	22.47	2.63	2.91	2.91
Total	21.85	23.92	22.41	17.50	17.53	17.56

Example 12.28

Geometric attribution analysis according to Menchero:

Table 12.56 contains the Menchero attribution analysis for the portfolio in Table 12.55. The separate listing of the unscaled "Menchero contributions" illustrates the influence of the scaling. An effect appears that already showed up in the discussion of the linking algorithms in the multi-period case: the scaling has only a small impact on the large contributions (selection sector 2, allocation sector 1). The impact is, however, noticeable in the case of the smaller contributions. For instance, the (negative!) selection contribution exhibited for sector 1 is an obvious contradiction to the positioning of the portfolio (segment return clearly exceeds the benchmark). This can bring the portfolio analyst into trouble when explaining his findings in front of the portfolio manager or the client!

In the article already discussed in the context of linking attribution effects in the multi-period case (Section 12.3.5), Cariño describes a simple model for a geometric attribution analysis that will be sketched briefly.[85] Based on the Brinson model he defines the following overall effects:

$$ACM := e^{k*AC} - 1, \tag{12.184}$$

$$SCM := e^{k*SC} - 1, \tag{12.185}$$

$$ITM := e^{k*IT} - 1, \tag{12.186}$$

[85] See Cariño (1999).

where k is again the correction factor defined in Section 12.3.5:

$$k = \begin{cases} \frac{\ln(1+RP)-\ln(1+RB)}{RP-RB} & RP \neq RB \\ (1+RP)^{-1} & RP = RB. \end{cases} \tag{12.187}$$

Here the period index j used in Section 12.3.5 is eliminated, since only the one-period case is considered. It readily follows that the multiplicative linking of the contributions yields the active return:

$$\begin{aligned}(1+ACM)*(1+SCM)*(1+ITM) &= e^{k*AC} * e^{k*SC} * e^{k*IT} \\ &= e^{k*(AC+SC+IT)} \\ &= e^{k*(RP-RB)} \\ &= e^{\frac{\ln(1+RP)-\ln(1+RB)}{RP-RB}*(RP-RB)} \\ &= e^{\ln(1+RP)-\ln(1+RB)} \\ &= \frac{1+RP}{1+RB}.\end{aligned} \tag{12.188}$$

The approach can readily be extended to the segment level, as will be demonstrated for the allocation contribution (other contributions analogously). If one assumes $AC = \sum_{i=1}^{n} ac_i$, then it follows that:

$$1+ACM := e^{k*AC} = e^{k*\sum_{i=1}^{n} ac_i} = \prod_{i=1}^{n} e^{k*ac_i} = \prod_{i=1}^{n} (1+acm_i), \tag{12.189}$$

where:

$$acm_i := e^{k*ac_i} - 1. \tag{12.190}$$

12.5 FURTHER ASPECTS OF ATTRIBUTION ANALYSIS

12.5.1 Position-Based vs. Transaction-Based Attribution Analysis

An important aspect in the implementation of the methodologies discussed in the preceding sections is the data basis which it requires. Simply speaking, in order to compute the returns and weights required for an attribution analysis detailed and valid information on the position and transaction data (both, transactions within the fund and exogenous cash-flows) as well as the appropriate conversion by an interface is required. The actual "data procurement task" in practice is, of course, much bigger, since the computation of the desired attribution effects hinges also on the appropriate input in regard to corporate actions, dividend and interest rate payments and an extensive set of static data for the individual securities (time to maturity, sector, etc.). However, a detailed consideration of the data requirements in general goes far beyond the scope of this treatise. Instead the consideration will focus on one important general aspect, which determines the data requirements to a large degree.

Position-Based Approach

In this approach a certain standard period length is defined (in general one day[86]). The computation of the returns is then based on the premise that within the standard periods the weights of the positions are not influenced by exogenous cash-flows (transactions, dividend or interest payments etc.), respectively that the cash-flows occur at the end of the standard periods. Transactions are thus considered by updating the weights at the beginning of the standard periods. Position-based approaches are thus also known as buy-and-hold approaches. Among the advantages of the position-based approaches are the robustness against strong cash-flows on a segment level (especially in case of segments with a small weight within the portfolio) and the fact that they are (relatively) easy to implement.[87] A disadvantage of this approach is the fact that the sum of the attribution effects does not necessarily replicate the official portfolio return based on the unit prices. In case of an active portfolio management style and volatile markets the discrepancy can be quite significant. For a portfolio manager, who requires some information on the success of his management process, this might not be a problem. Investors, however, often do not accept it.

Transaction-Based Approach

Also in this approach a certain period length is defined. In addition, the transactions occurring within the standard periods are taken into account by applying the approximation methods described in Section 10.6 on the segment level. The implementation of such an approach in practice is much harder than the implementation of a position-based approach, as it requires to accurately transfer all transitions via the interface (in a timely manner).

For both approaches the accuracy increases proportionally to the valuation frequency.[88] Whether position-based approaches (with a daily valuation frequency)

[86] In most papers on the position-based approach it is tacitly assumed that position data are available on a daily basis (e.g. Menchero and Hu 2003 and Bonafede and McCarty 2003), since a lower frequency may lead to inacceptable results due to the transactions. This is also a central assertion in Zangari and Bayraktar (2005/06).

[87] Attribution systems based on a factor system are usually position-based (Examples: Wilshire Axiom, Vestek Portfolio Analyzer), while systems based on a Brinson-type segmentation usually also consider transactions, (Examples: PEARL of the firm ORTEC Finance, Socrates of the firm Microgen). Some firms offer systems for both approaches (Example: Factset).

[88] This view seems to be generally accepted in the literature (cf. e.g. the quoted papers in the preceeding footnotes as well as Bacon (2008, p. 210). It seems that only diBartolomeo has uttered a deviating opinion (diBartolomeo (2003)). He refers to the data procurement problems (general impreciseness of the data; stocks traded on different exchanges, etc.) and draws the conclusion that the daily valuation frequency is suboptimal. We don't agree with this conclusion, as we regard the issues raised by diBartolomeo as solvable data issues. For a refutation of the arguments by diBartolomeo see also Zangari and Bayraktar (2005/06). Also in the GRAP standards a high valuation frequency is recommended (cf. e.g. GRAP 2004 or Giguère 2005), provided that "accurate prices" for the investments are available.

or transaction-based approaches (with a daily or weekly valuation) provide a more exact analysis is discussed controversially in the literature.[89]

A further advantage of the position-based approach is the limited computational effort, which matters even in times of ever-increasing computer capacity. Another positive aspect is high flexibility in regard to the segmentation of the portfolio and the benchmark. Many transaction-based systems are limited to the segmentations of the benchmarks.[90] This is, of course, a limitation for the potential break-downs.

The simplicity of the position-based approach, respectively of the resulting systems in general allows for a high flexibility in regard to the segmentation. Some systems provide, e.g., the option to base the segmentation on fundamental data such as market capitalization, price/earnings ratio or dividend yield. This enables one to verify that, say, the supposedly good stock picking within several segments is in the end the result of a (risky) overweighting of equities with a low market capitalization, which (accidentally) achieved a higher return then the market average during the analysis period.

It seems impossible to answer the question of which approach (position-based vs. transaction-based) provides a better quality of results in practical applications, since for each there exist numerous distinct practical performance systems. Due to practical restrictions it is very hard to assess the quality of a methodology in a systematic way. The results depend, for instance, on the type of the portfolios and the management style. Transaction-based systems may run into problems for portfolios with a high transaction frequency. Problematic also are portfolios, where certain segments are invested in only temporarily. As is well-known, the employed approximation methods may produce erroneous results in these cases. It is furthermore a very complex task to collect the data for an appropriate comparison: for the computation of actual time-weighted segment returns it would be required to evaluate the portfolio, respectively its segments, for every cash-flow. It is probably due to this reason that the literature doesn't really go far beyond the narration of personal impressions or opinions.[91]

A final remark on the advantages of the transaction-based method: an important measure for the assessment of the data quality is the difference between the sum of the attribution effects and the official return. For quality-assured systems

---

[89] Menchero and Hu (Vestek) as well as Bonafede and McCarthy (Wilshire) prefer position-based approaches, while Bacon (Statpro), Giguère (Financial Models Company) and Zangari und Bayraktar (Goldman Sachs Asset Management) are in favor of transaction-based approaches (cf. Giguère 2003) and the papers quoted before). See also Spaulding (2003) for a general overview.

[90] A higher degree of flexibility in transaction-based systems can be obtained by computing the benchmark segments oneself. This can, of course, be quite onerous.

[91] This holds for all articles quoted in this section. In Menchero and Hu (2003) it is only shown that the modified Dietz Equation leads with a high probability in certain situations to unsatisfactory results. There is, however, no generality in this assertion, as a transaction-based approach is by no means synonymous to modified Dietz approach. Another problem is that there is no generally accepted method for linking performance contributions. Due to these reasons we also can add only a further opinion.

this difference should be close to zero. If significant differences occur, then this points to corrupted input data sets or to an inappropriate quality control. For a position-based analysis system this control step is not available, as one couldn't assume the equality between the sum of the effects and the official return in the first place.[92]

12.5.2 Factor-Based Attribution Analysis

The attempt to apply the *Arbitrage Pricing Theory* (APT)[93] in practice led in the 1980s to the development of the so-called multifactor risk models, which provide implicitly an attribution analysis. In the APT theory it is postulated that the excess return (return above the risk-free rate) of a single security can be represented as a linear combination of weighted factor returns. The weights of the factor returns are derived from the so-called sensitivities or *exposures* of a security to the various factors. Within the model the underlying factors are identical for all securities:

$$r_i - r^f = \sum_{l=1}^{M} \beta_i^l F^l + \varepsilon_i$$

(r_i = return of the security i, r^f = risk-free rate, β_i^l = sensitivity of the security i to the factor l, F^l = factor return of the factor l, ε_i = residual return of the security i). According to this approach the factors capture the commonalities of the securities, while the residuum reflects that part of the return, which is unique to the security, such that the residual returns of the different securities have nothing in common. If one applies this break-down to the active return of a portfolio relative to its benchmark, then (in analogy to Brinson approach) the factor returns may be interpreted as the allocation contributions and the residual return (also known as specific or unsystematic return) as the selection contribution.[94]

The difficulty in applying the APT model in practice results from the task of identifying those factors that cover the commonalities of the securities (and fulfill the model requirements, which will not be discussed in detail). In practice at least three different approaches are applied.

In the so-called *fundamental* or *microeconomic models* the factors are chosen, such that the sensitivities are observable and the factor returns can be estimated by means of suitable statistical procedures. Providers that use this approach in their risk models and their associated multi-factor attribution analyses are, for instance, Barra and Wilshire. Factors used in equity models are, e.g., sectors, countries, currencies or fundamental values like market capitalization or price-earnings-ratio.

---

[92] This was also pointed out by Bacon (cf. Bacon 2008, p. 210). Of course, it is not sufficient to regard this quantity in isolation. It needs to be complemented by further quality checks in practice.

[93] cf. Ross (1976, 1977). Section 12.5.2 and 12.5.3 are based on the which by Fischer and Bacon(2011).

[94] It should be clear that we consider the differential terms (weighted portfolio returns minus the weighted benchmark returns).

Macroeconomic models pursue the opposite approach, i.e., they use statistical methods to estimate the sensitivities of individual securities based on factors with observable returns. An example of a provider whose models are essentially based on such an approach is Northfield Inc. This model employs sector and country indices, too. As opposed to the microeconomic models, the factor returns are not estimated by means of statistical methods. Rather *observable* returns, derived, e.g., from MSCI sector or country indices are employed. They are complemented by other factors such as oil price, natural resources indices, government bond yields, different currencies and/or time to maturities as well as other rather macroeconomic quantities.

The *third model type* is based on a completely different approach. Instead of estimating them in advance, under this approach the factors as well as their returns and the associated sensitivities are extracted from the available time series of returns. A provider of risk measurement systems, who employs such a model, is APT Ltd., a subsidiary of SunGard Inc.

An obvious disadvantage of the first two approaches results from the need to select factors, respectively from the risk of choosing an incomplete set of factors or the wrong factors. The big advantage is, however, that the chosen factors are more accessible to the persons involved in steering the investment processes. The latter is obviously not the case for purely statistical models.

A more detailed analysis is beyond the scope of this section. Suffice it to say that the fit of the individual approaches depends on the specific investment approach. Analyzing portfolios from different angles by applying several different methodologies simultaneously can sometimes be meaningful in practice. There are providers like Axioma Inc. that offer different types of risk models.

Example 12.29

Factor Analysis via Wilshire Axiom:

In order to illustrate the factor-based attribution analysis by means of an example we will analyze a portfolio and its benchmark with the Wilshire "Global 6-Regions Equity"-model. The model will be applied to a fairly simple portfolio and a corresponding benchmark (see Table 12.57).

Both the portfolio and the benchmark consist of two segments with two stocks each. At the beginning of the period in consideration the portfolio manager took an overweight-position in the sector capital goods. He furthermore showed a clear preference for the

Table 12.57 Portfolio and Benchmark Structure as at 31.12.2009 (%)

Sector	Stock	Stock Weight		Sector Weight	
		P	BM	P	BM
Banks	Commerzbank	10	25	40	50
	Deutsche Bank	30	25		
Capital goods	MAN	40	25	60	50
	Siemens	20	25		

Table 12.58 Returns in the Period from 31.12.2009 to 29.01.2010 (%)

Sector	Stock	Stock	Sectors		Total	
			P	BM	P	BM
Banks	Commerzbank	−4.21	−8.71	−7.22	−7.06	−5.38
	Deutsche Bank	−10.21				
Capital goods	MAN	−10.80	−5.97	−3.55		
	Siemens	3.70				

Table 12.59 Contributions According to the Global 6-Regions Equity-Model (Wilshire Atlas)

Factors	Portfolio Exposure[99]	Benchmark Exposure	Factor Return (%)	Contribution (%)
Currency				
EUR	100.0%	100.0%	0.00	0.00
Region:				
Europe	100.0%	100.0%	−2.01	0.00
Countries				
Germany	1.459	1.479	−0.68	0.01
Sectors:				
Banks	10.0%	25.0%	−3.36	0.50
Diversified financials	30.0%	25.0%	−6.10	−0.30
Capital goods	60.0%	50.0%	−0.09	−0.01
Fundamental:				
Size	−0.166	−0.155	−2.06	0.02
Price-earnings	−0.389	−0.765	0.07	0.03
Price-to-book	1.245	1.810	0.66	−0.38
Volatility	1.889	2.200	−1.05	0.33
Momentum	0.7266	0.401	0.30	0.10
Sum factors				0.30
Residual return(%)	−1.25	0.74		−1.98
Sum overall				−1.68

[99] *The derivation of the exposures and sensitivities for the individual factors cannot be discussed in detail. Suffice it to say that currency, regional and sector exposures are derived straight from the securities weights. For the country factors country-betas are employed, i.e. the sensitivities of the stock returns to the respective countries. Exposures in regard to the fundamental factors are derived as so-called Z-scores.*

stocks of *Deutsche Bank* and *MAN* within the sectors. No transactions occurred in the analysis period from 31.12.2009 to 29.01.2010. The returns are shown in Table 12.58.

This Wilshire “Global 6-Regions Equity”-model is based on ca. 400 factors grouped in 5 different segments. Wilshire subdivides the investment universe in to 6 regions, which form the first factor group. Country and currency are two further factor groups,

Table 12.60 Attribution Analysis according to Brinson, Hood and Beebower (%)

Sector	Selection	Allocation	Interaction	Total
Banks	−0.75	0.72	0.15	0.12
Capital goods	−1.21	−0.35	−0.24	−1.80
Total	−1.96	0.37	−0.09	−1.68

sectors within the regions are the fourth and fundamental values the fifth factor group. For each region five fundamental indicators are used: market capitalization as a size indicator, price-earnings ratio and price-to-book value as indicators for the investment style (growth vs. value) as well as momentum and volatility.[95] A more detailed description of the individual factor group is outside the scope of this example. In the following the results of the analysis of the portfolio for the month of January 2010 are shown and discussed in detail.

In this example the factor-based attribution analysis (Table 12.59) provides a similar picture as the Brinson-type analysis, which for the sake of comparison is given in Table 12.60.

Over the analysis period the total overall active return resultes from the selection (residual return); the allocation (sum of the factor contributions) provides a slightly positive contribution of 0.30%. Also, this analysis approach underlines that the allocation is primarily generated by the sector allocation. The detail level reveals, however, some additional details compared to the Brinson analysis. The overweight-position of *capital goods*, for instance, did not yield a significant allocation contribution. This is attributable to the fact that the return of the sector *capital goods* estimated by the model is very small (−0.09%), so that the overweight-position of 10% doesn't translate into a significant contribution. According to the model the positive effect resulted rather from the fact that true *banks* (Commerzbank) outperformed diversified financials (Deutsche Bank). The return of the sector banks for the month January 2010 was estimated at −3.36% and exceeded thus the return of the factor "diversified financials" (which came out at −6.1%) by almost 3%. Underweighting banks by 15% thus yielded a positive contribution, which clearly exceeded the negative effect resulting from the 5% overweight-position of diversified financials.

Even though the contributions toward the active return for the five fundamental factors neutralize each other, at least two have a significant contribution. The overweight position in growth stocks[96] resulted in a contribution of −0.38%, which was, however, cancelled out by the contribution resulting from underweighting stocks with

[95] Momentum is the stock return during the previous 12 months and volatility the dispersion of the monthly returns of a stock over the previous 24 months. The idea behind this choice of factors is the observation that stocks respectively with a high or low momentum or with a high or low volatility behave similarly in certain market situations, so that they classify as potential market factors according to the APT.

[96] For the portfolio a smaller exposure (1,245) to the factor price-to-book is shown than for the benchmark. This reflects the fact that the stocks in the portfolio have on average a lower price-to-book-ratio than the benchmark constituents. A lower price-to-book-ratio results in general from underweighting value stocks and overweighting growth stocks.

a high volatility (0.33%). Similarly to the sectors, the results for the fundamental factors have a dependency on the relative exposure to the respective factor and on the estimated return of the factor. Even though their relative exposures[97] are similar, the contributions of the factors volatility and momentum are quite different, reflecting the fact that the model estimation came up with different returns. The return of the factor momentum was estimated at 0.30%, while for the factor volatility a return of −1.05% was exhibited.

For the analysis period January 2010 the Wilshire model estimates residual returns in the range from −7.87% (MAN SE) to 8.23% (Siemens) for the four titles contained in the portfolio and the benchmark. The return of Deutsche Bank is nearly in its entirety explained by the model factors, so that only a very small residual return of −0.02% is left over. In contrast, the residual return of Commerzbank was equal to 2.61% for the analysis period. The portfolio had thus an overweight position in titles with a negative residual return and an underweight position in titles with a positive residual return, which led to a significant negative selection contribution of −1.98%.

A characteristic of the attribution analysis according to Brinson et al. is the dependence of the results on the chosen partitioning of the investment universe. It is, for instance, possible that for a global equity fund significant interaction terms occur in a sector-based approach, while when switching to a country-segmentation, interaction terms are close to zero. Factor-based attribution analyses do not depend so much on the chosen factors. Since they are all derived from the APT model, they deliver similar results for the distribution of allocation and selection effects. Depending on the chosen factors the allocation results may change, however, on a detail level.

A further big advantage of the factor-based attribution analysis is the possibility of basing the analysis on a variety of factors, or factor groups. The allocation is not seen only in relation to a segment, but in relation to several factor groups. In this respect the break-down of the allocation results is given not only in reference to the sectors or countries, as is the case for the Brinson-type analysis. The allocation effect will rather be allocated simultaneously to the sectors, countries and other factors, such that it becomes transparent whether the country allocation had a stronger or weaker impact than the sector allocation, or whether completely different factors were dominant. Its disadvantages are the difficulty in interpreting the results as well as the dependence of the results on the chosen model. As already mentioned there is the general danger of choosing the wrong factors in the model construction.

Due to these restrictions, in practice the attribution analyses of equity portfolios are mostly based on the Brinson approach. For bond portfolios, this is, however, increasingly not the case. On the one hand this is due to the limited explanatory power of a pure Brinson analysis for such portfolios, and on the other hand to the increasing acceptance of factor models in the analysis of bond portfolios. The returns of bonds can much better be approximated by mathematical models

---

[97] Relative exposure volatility: 1.889 − 2.200 = −0.311; relative exposure momentum: 0.7266 − 0.401 = 0.3265.

than equity returns, which implies that the risk of a model misspecification in a multi-factor model is much less for bonds than for equities.

Occasionally factor models are specifically tailored for the investment process of an investment firm. There are companies like Alpha Strategies LLC, which have specialized in implementing client-specific models. The advantage of such an approach is that the success of the investment process can be validated by means of the bespoke model. There is, however, the risk of ignoring important factors that might influence the performance considerably. In order to mitigate that risk one should also use a standard model by way of comparison.

12.5.3 Attribution Analysis and Valuation Questions

An often underestimated issue concerns the valuation of the securities in a portfolio or benchmark. In this context valuation of a fund means the determination of the unit price based on appropriate price sources. It is generally problematic if one uses different price sources for the portfolio and the benchmark, respectively for the underlying indices.

Indices are usually priced on the basis of closing prices at the respective bourses. The coverage depends, however, on the market conditions. In the case of equity indices, the prevailing liquidity has the consequence that for different indices nearly identical prices are used (even if the providers are different). For bond indices this is, however, generally not the case, as such indices often contain illiquid titles, which need to be valued by the index provider. Investment funds are valued by a custodian, who may use intraday prices or even prices of the previous day, depending on the market conditions. What makes it even worse is that providers use different sources for the exchange rates and employ different methodologies for the treatment of dividend or coupon accruals. Given all these aspects in portfolio/benchmark valuation, it becomes clear that the actually exhibited active return for a given period is only partially dependent on the investment decisions. These so-called valuation differences may have a significant share in the active return.

In this respect, the investor has to answer the fundamental question of whether the requirement of replicating the return delivered by the custodian or the investment firm is really indispensible.[98] Under this premise it will in general not become obvious which component of the active return is caused by valuation difference and which one is generated by the investment process. For that reason portfolio managers in most cases require a uniform valuation basis. There are two general approaches to achieving this: one either revalues the benchmark (with the portfolio prices) or the portfolio (with the benchmark prices). In practice one usually chooses the second approach, i.e., one submits the portfolio to a

---

[98] This would be ensured if the portfolio holdings would be valued exclusively with the prices provided by the custodian.

re-valuation. This means that the analysis will not reproduce the official portfolio return delivered by the custodian. The (official) benchmark return will, however, be preserved.

In this context re-valuation is understood as a valuation as much in accordance with the specific methodologies applied by the respective index providers as possible.[99] The difference between the revalued return and official return computed by the custodian then reflects the valuation discrepancies. The attribution analysis based on the difference between the revalued return of the portfolio and the benchmark return enables the portfolio manager or the performance analyst to analyze and monitor the success of the portfolio manager's strategy.

Although a portfolio revaluation is a very demanding task, such a service is offered by several providers of attribution analyses or in the context of middle-office-services.

A special case form the position-based analysis systems discussed in the previous section. Such systems (e.g., Wilshire or FactSet) often use a uniform methodology for the valuation of portfolio and benchmark positions. In this respect these systems are implicitly based on a re-evaluation. This can lead to the fact that the performance shown for a specific index alters from the official performance published by the provider.

Against the background of an increasing usage of financial derivatives the revaluation is gaining in importance. Many of these instruments are either quite illiquid or not traded on a bourse, so that daily prices are not available. However, in order to come up with meaningful analyses also for such instruments sufficient (daily) prices are needed. Thus within the revaluation process market-like prices for these instruments must be generated (even if true market prices are not available). This is a further complexity, which needs to be considered when choosing a suitable revaluation methodology, respectively a provider for such services.

12.6 CHAPTER-END PROBLEMS

1. (Interaction (2) in case of an active currency management):
   Review the derivation of the different terms of the attribution analysis in case of a passive currency management (Section 12.2.5). Then use distinct currency returns cp_i and cb_i for the portfolio and benchmark segments as in Section 12.2.6 and modify the equations accordingly. You should in particular derive Equation (12.59). Show that Interaction (2) then assumes the following form:

$$it_i(2) = swp_i * srp_i^L * cp_i - swb_i * srb_i^L * cb_i.$$

[99] At least the sources for the prices and the currency exchange rates should be identical (including the valuation times).

2. (Attribution analysis according to Brinson, Hood and Beebower I):
In Section 12.2.6 the following expression for the contribution of an active currency management (over one period) was derived (Equation (12.59)):

$$cc_i := swp_i * cp_i - swb_i * cb_i.$$

The corresponding expression in the approach of Pieper in Section 12.2.6 (Equation (12.60)) is:[100]

$$cc_i^{Bri} := swp_i * \left(srp_i^B - srp_i^L\right) - swb_i * \left(srb_i^B - srb_i^L\right).$$

Show (e.g. by means of a Taylor approximation), that for small values of x and y $(0 < x, y < 1)$ the following relationship holds approximately:

$$\frac{1+x}{1+y} \approx 1 + x - y.$$

Based on the definition of the terms cp_i and cb_i (equations (12.57) and (12.58)) show that the expression on the right-hand side of equation (12.59) passes over to the expression on the right-hand equation (12.60) when using the above approximation.

3. (Attribution according to Brinson, Hood und Beebower II):
Show that the currency contributions cu_i^{Bri} defined in Section 12.2.6 include the terms Interaction(2):

$$cc_i^{Bri} = cc_i + it(2)_i.$$

Use equation (12.59) to show that cc_i^{Bri} is influenced by both selection and allocation decisions.

4. (Currency attribution):
Compare the approaches in Sections 12.2.6 and 12.2.7. What are the differences?

5. An American investor has invested $100,000 in a global equity portfolio made up of U.S., Asian, and European stocks. On December 31, the portfolio is invested in 500 IBM shares listed in New York, 200 Sony shares listed in Tokyo, and 50 BMW shares listed in Frankfurt. He wants to beat the World index used as benchmark. This index has a 50 percent weight in the U.S. stock index, a 25 percent weight in the Japanese stock index, and a 25 percent weight in the European stock index. The country

[100] cf. Pieper (1998).

components of the portfolio have average risk relative to their respective country indexes. He uses the U.S. dollar as base currency. On March 31, his portfolio has gained 4.065 percent, while the World index gained only 0.735 percent in dollars.
He wishes to understand why his portfolio had such a good performance over the quarter. All necessary data are given in the following tables. There were no cash flows in the portfolio, nor any dividends paid.

A. Decompose the total return on the portfolio into capital gains (in local currency) and currency contribution.
B. What is the contribution of security selection?
C. Attribute the performance relative to the benchmark (World index) to the various investment decisions.

Global Equity Portfolio: Composition and Market Data

		Price (in Local Currency)		Portfolio Value on Dec. 31		Portfolio Value on Mar. 31	
Portfolio	**Number of Shares**	**Dec. 31**	**Mar. 31**	**Local Currency**	**Dollar**	**Local Currency**	**Dollar**
U.S. stocks							
IBM	500	100	105	50,000	50,000	52,500	52,500
Japanese stocks							
Sony	200	10,000	11,000	2,000,000	20,000	2,200,000	20,952
European stocks							
BMW	50	600	600	30,000	30,000	30,000	30,612
Total					*100,000*		*104,065*

Market Data	**Dec. 31**	**Mar. 31**
World index ($)	100	100.735
U.S.index ($)	100	103
Japanese index (¥)	100	105
European index (€)	100	95
Yen per dollar	100	105
Euro per dollar	1	0.98

6. Your discussion with a client has turned to the measurement of investment performance, particularly with respect to international portfolios.

Performance and Attribution Data: Annualized Returns for Five Years Ended 12/31/2008

International Manager/Index	Total Return	Country/Security Selection	Currency Return
Manager A	–6.0%	2.0%	–8.0%
Manager B	–2.0	–1.0	–1.0
EAFE index	–5.0	0.2	–5.2

A. Assume that the data in this table for Manager A and Manager B accurately reflect their investment skills and that both managers actively manage currency exposure. Briefly describe one strength and one weakness for each manager.

B. Recommend and justify a strategy that would enable the fund to take advantage of the strength of each of the two managers while minimizing their weaknesses.

Chapter 13

Attribution Analysis for Fixed Income Portfolios

ABSTRACT

In this chapter an introduction to the attribution analysis of fixed income portfolios is given. After an introduction to yield curves and related topics, the methodology of a yield-curve based analysis, which relies on the full valuation of the bonds in the portfolio and the benchmark and the option-adjusted spreads, is given. The standard methods for the modeling of a yield curve and their application in the attribution analysis are described. The chapter closes with a brief description of alternative approaches.

Keywords
attribution analysis, fixed income portfolio, yield curve, methodology, bond, benchmark, option-adjusted spread, modeling.

13.1 INVESTMENT PROCESSES FOR FIXED INCOME PORTFOLIOS

13.1.1 Determinants of Investment Processes for Fixed Income Portfolios

13.1.1.1 *YIELD CURVES*

The positioning of the term structure is at the core of an analysis of the investment processes for fixed income portfolios. An adequate understanding of yield curves is a prerequisite for describing the resulting effects, thus here follows a brief digression on this subject. The *interest rate structure* is the functional dependence of the internal rate of return of a zero-coupon bond on the duration of its term. In the graphical representation of the interest rate structure, it is called a *yield curve*. Generally, there are three types of model yield curve. In a *flat yield curve*, the interest rate is independent of its term, while in the *inverted yield curve* the interest rate declines with the term. In practice, this hardly ever happens, because the interest rate usually increases over time. In the latter situation a yield curve is therefore referred to as a *normal* (or *rising*) *yield curve* (cf. Figure 13.1).

Performance Evaluation and Attribution of Security Portfolios. http://dx.doi.org/10.1016/B978-0-12-744483-3.00013-4
© 2013 Elsevier Inc. All rights reserved.
For End-of-chapter Questions: © 2012. CFA Institute, Reproduced and republished with permission from CFA Institute. All rights reserved.

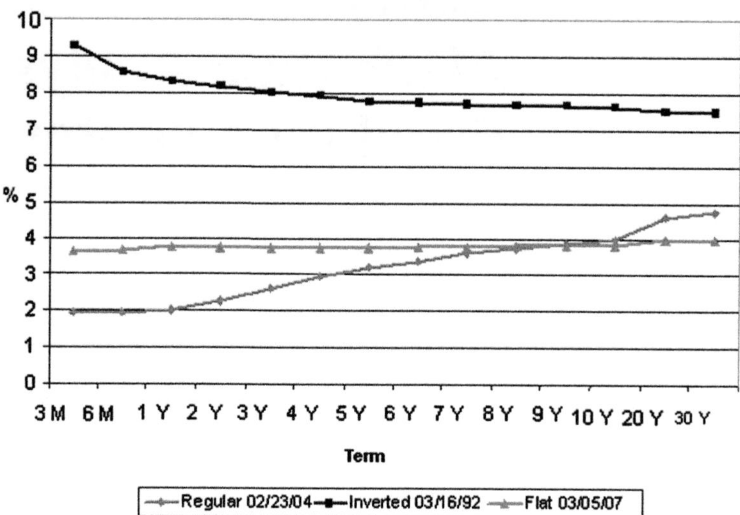

FIGURE 13.1
Yield Curves (EUR German Sovereign) at Different Times.

The analysis of the economic causes of different types of yield curve is not the subject of this essay. It is only mentioned here that an inverted yield curve is generally considered as an indication of a recession.[1]

One should, however, bear in mind that in practice yield curves do not always appear in one of these "smooth" textbook shapes. For one, a discrete interest term is provided, and, for the other, yield curves often have special features, which, in the case of a simple linear interpolation, do not conform to the model patterns (see Figure 13.2).

If, as is usual in practice and in the specialist literature, one uses a present value model as a basis, then the (theoretical) value of a bond is calculated as the discounted sum of the future payments from the bond (coupons, nominals), using market-based interest rates.[2] Here a significant difference to equity portfolios becomes apparent. Due to the (in general) limited term and the fixed coupon payments, the speculative element in determining the value of bonds is much less important than with stocks. In the case of bonds with low risk of default or nonpayment by the borrower, the value, and therefore the price alteration, is largely determined through the dynamics of the yield curve. Thus, one can identify the most important determinants of the performance of a bond portfolio, and hence the basic factors of an investment process, i.e. over- or underweighting the maturities segments of the yield curve relative to the benchmark, where the portfolio manager expects a relatively strong rise or fall in interest rates.[3]

[1] For a brief but concise presentation of the theoretical approaches, see Fabozzi (1998, p. 537 et seq.).

[2] See the discussion in Section 13.2.1.

[3] A falling interest rate means a rise in the price of a zero-coupon bond in the respective maturity segment. When interest rates rise, it is the other way around.

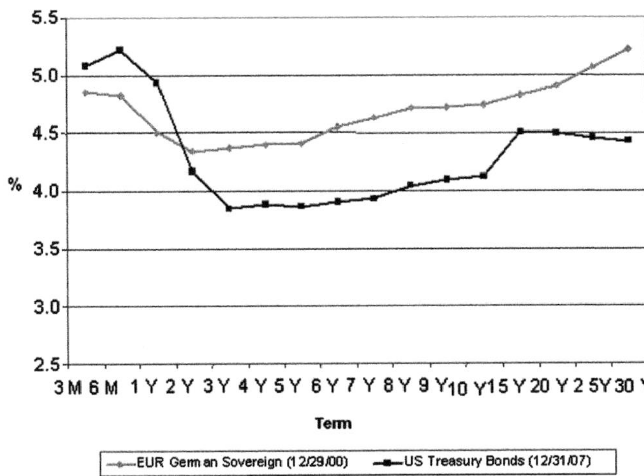

FIGURE 13.2
Yield Curves Not Appearing in Standard Forms.

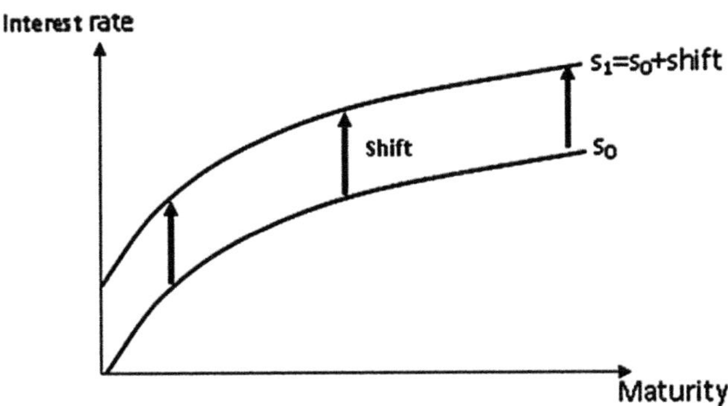

FIGURE 13.3
Parallel Movement of a Yield Curve.

In addition to these yield curve effects, bond-specific factors such as the creditworthiness of the issuer or the liquidity of a bond play a role.[4] And, of course, as with stocks, the adjustment of the currency exposures is an important determinant of the investment process.

It is a common procedure to highlight characteristic movements[5] of a yield curve. A distinction is made here between a parallel movement (*shift*), a rotation (*twist*) and a change in the curvature of the yield curve (*curvature*) (see Figures 13.3–13.5).

---

[4] Other specific aspects, such as termination rights with bonds or the possibility of partial payments in securitization (ABS), etc. cannot be included as part of this discussion.

[5] See, for instance Fabozzi (1998 p. 572 et seq.) and Hagenstein and Bangemann (2000, p. 11 et seq.)

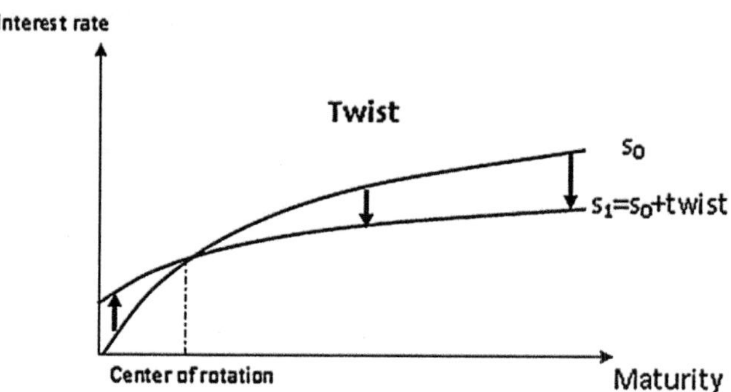

FIGURE 13.4
Rotation of a Yield Curve.

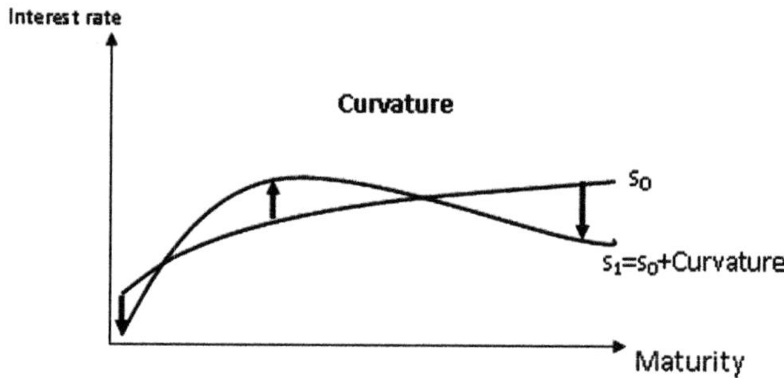

FIGURE 13.5
Change in Curvature.

Figure 13.3 depicts a parallel shift, in which the interest rate has increased uniformly. This is coupled with falling bond prices (negative *shift return*). Conversely, uniformly falling interest rates would result in a general price increase.

Pending such a curve movement, the obvious strategy is to construct the portfolio primarily with securities in the lower maturity or term range, since such bonds suffer less from rising interest rates than securities with long maturities. This therefore amounts to taking a bet in regard to the average maturity or duration. Should the opposite effect (lowering of the curve) be expected, then the portfolio manager would accordingly take an overweight position in securities with a long maturity in order to benefit here from an above-average increase in prices.

Figure 13.4 illustrates another characteristic movement of a yield curve. Here, the curve is rotated through a certain point. Pending such a curve movement, the portfolio manager would take an overweight position in bonds with shorter maturities. Accordingly he would take an underweight position in that segment in the case of an expected counter-rotation of the curve.

The so-called *Barbell strategy* is a strategy for utilization of the curve movement shown in Figure 13.5. Here, the short and long maturities would be

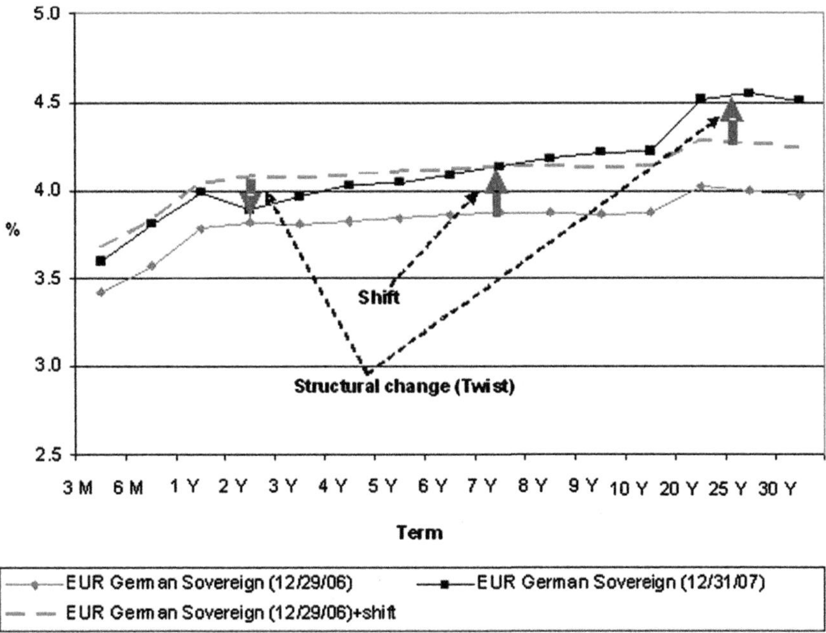

FIGURE 13.6
Movement of the EUR-German Sovereign Curve 2007.

overweighted and the medium term range underweighted (or not considered at all). For the curve movement diametrically opposed to the one shown in Figure 13.5 (rising interest rates in the segments of long and short maturities, interest rates falling in the middle segment) the so-called *Bullet Strategy* is appropriate, whereby the portfolio concentrates on the medium-term maturities segment.

In practice, these movements occur seldom in their pure form. Usually the curve movements overlap and there are other effects that are not covered by these standard movements. Particularly, there is a strong correlation between the parallel displacement and the rotation, which entails that strategies must be coordinated with each other.[6]

Figure 13.6 illustrates the change in the yield curve for German government bonds in 2007, which was characterized by a general rise in interest rates of an average 29 basis points (shift). With regard to the curve displaced by the shift (dashed line), it is clear that a change in the structure has also occurred (especially with the long maturities), partly due to a rotation of the curve with a rotation center at a maturity of about seven years.

---

[6] See Jones (1991) and Litterman and Scheinkman (1991). According to Jones, an increase in the interest rate (positive shift) is correlated with a flattening of the curve and a reduction in the curvature (positive butterfly). Conversely, a decrease in the interest rate (negative shift) is correlated with a steepening of the curve and an increase in the curvature (negative butterfly).

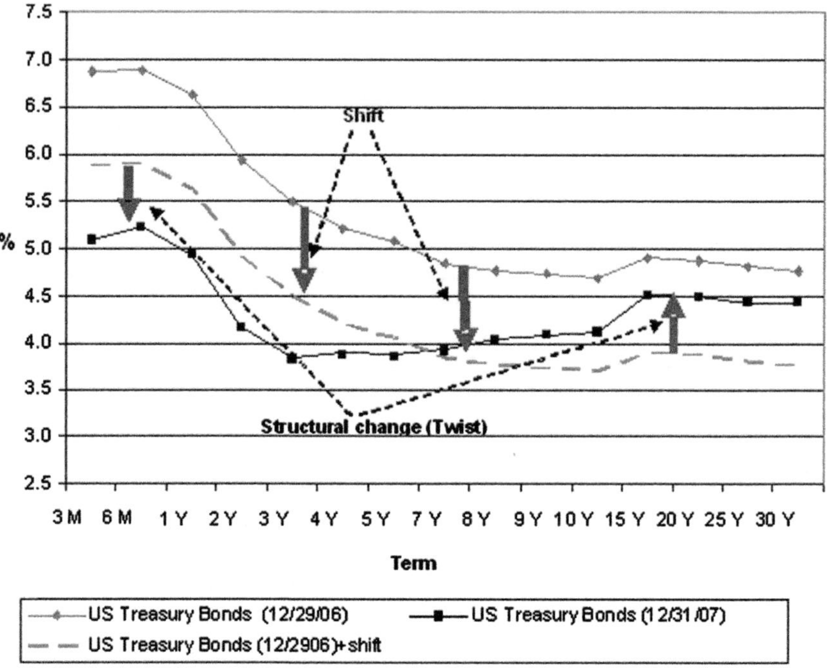

FIGURE 13.7
Movement of the U.S. Treasury Curve 2007.

In Figure 13.7, the corresponding movement of the yield curve is shown for US government bonds. Here, a significant drop in interest rates by an average of 103 basis points was observed. However, interest rates fell much more at the short end of the curve than at the long end. The parallel movement is accompanied by a strong rotation and a minor curvature movement. From a pure mathematical point of view one can easily imagine other forms of decomposition into a parallel and a rotary movement, such as that the original curve is shifted until the level of the December curve is at the short end of the curve, followed by a rotation. This illustrates a fundamental problem of the decomposition of yield curves, which is addressed again later.

In addition to these yield curves, there are a number of other interest rate curves, which are important. For example, a yield curve can express the functional dependence of the yield to the remaining term for a particular class of bonds (e.g. government bonds). The so-called *par yield curve* is a special yield curve, in which the coupons of certain loans are modified so that they write (with a present value calculation) at par.[7] In this case, the bond's yield (internal rate) is identical to the coupon. In general, the *par rate* is different from the yield of the original bond.[8]

[7] In the case of the U.S. Treasury curve these are the most liquid government bonds (On-the-Run Treasury Issues). See Fabbozzi (2000, p. 201 et seq).

[8] Equality holds only if the bond trades at par. For a proof see Deutsch (2004, p. 75 et seq).

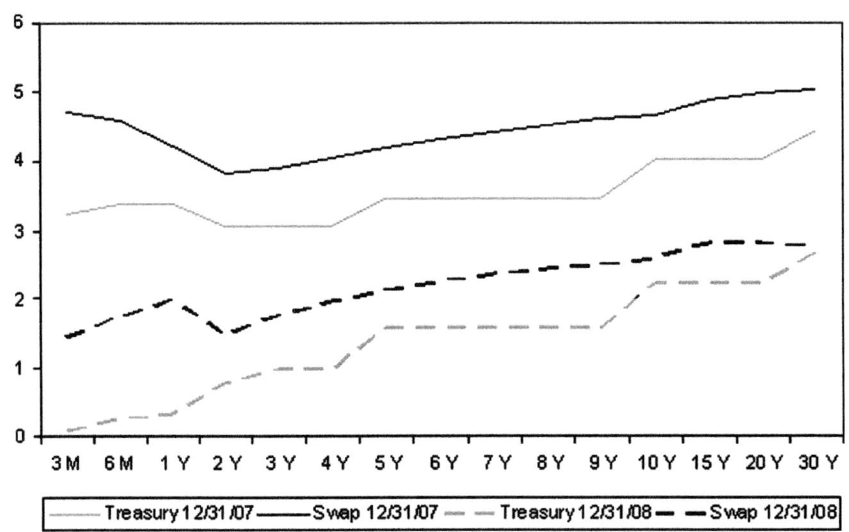

FIGURE 13.8
Swap Curve vs. U.S. Treasury Curve.

Swap curves are of great importance to fixed income management. A swap curve represents the fixed swap rate (the fixed rate) which the seller of a swap is willing to pay in exchange for the payment of a variable LIBOR rate, as a function of maturity. As illustrated in Figure 13.8, the swap curve is usually above the yield curve, which (compared with government bonds) reflects the higher credit risk of banks with good creditworthiness. In addition to the credit rating, LIBOR forward rates are important factors for the swap rates.

Yield curves can also be constructed for individual enterprises, provided that there are sufficiently many bonds outstanding.

13.1.1.2 FORWARD RATES AND IMPLICIT FORECASTS

An equivalent representation to the yield curves based on forward rates is provided in this section. The consideration of forward rates is the starting point of many yield curve models, such as that of Nelson and Siegel (Section 13.3.1). Forward rates are interest rates over a period in the future. They are determined by the current yield curve. $f_t(t_n)$ denotes the forward rate for the period from t_{n-1} to t, and $s_t(t_n)$ the spot rates ($n = 1, 2, \cdots$) at time t, therefore:

$$(1 + s_t(t_n))^{t_n} = (1 + s_t(t_{n-1}))^{t_{n-1}} * \left(1 + f_t(t_n)\right), \tag{13.1}$$

or:

$$1 + f_t(t_n) = \frac{(1 + s_t(t_n))^{t_n}}{(1 + s_t(t_{n-1}))^{t_{n-1}}} \tag{13.2}$$

$f_t(t_n)$ is thus the interest rate resulting from the current yield curve for the period from t_{n-1} to t_n. From Equation (13.1) it follows directly:

$$(1+s_t(t_n))^{t_n} = (1+f_t(t_1)) * (1+f_t(t_2)) * \cdots * (1+f_t(t_n)) \qquad (13.3)$$

Another (again equivalent) form of representation of the yield structure is obtained by using the *discount factors*, where:[9]

$$d_t(t_n) = \frac{1}{(1+s_t(t_n))^{t_n}}.$$

The discount factors have the advantage that the valuation formula for a bond (the present value formula, see Section 13.2.1), has a linear relationship with them; their dependence on the interest rates is non-linear.

Finally, there is the possibility of determining the yield curve by using *market implicit forecasts* $\hat{s}_t(t_m)$, which are defined by the following equations:

$$(1+s_t(t_n))^{t_n} * \left(1+\hat{s}_{t_n}(t_m)\right)^{t_m} = (1+s_t(t_n+t_m))^{t_n+t_m}. \qquad (13.4)$$

The market implicit forecast is therefore the spot rate which results from the reinvestment assumption according to Equation (13.4) based on the current spot rates.

It can easily be demonstrated that the market implicit forecasts can be expressed by the forward rates (Exercise 13.2):

$$\left(1+\hat{s}_{t_n}(t_m)\right)^{t_m} = (1+f_t(t_{n+1})) * \cdots * (1+f_t(t_n+t_m)) \qquad (13.5)$$

13.1.2 Comparison with the Methodology for Equity Portfolios

Although the models of the attribution analyses by Brinson, Beebowes, Hood, Fachler, et al., described in detail in Chapter 12, were primarily developed for equity portfolios, they can also be applied in the case of fixed income portfolios.[10] As described, the approach of Brinson et al. is based on the division of a given investment universe into separate groups (called "buckets") corresponding to the investment process. Usually this is based on the country or sector classification of a specified benchmark.

An obvious approach for the transfer of this methodology to the case of bond portfolios is given by classifying the loans according to their maturity.[11] The actual shape is usually determined by the benchmark's maturities breakdown (cf. the

[9] Here, in the form that results from a discrete compounding of interest.

[10] See for example Lehman (1998). Campisi still stating in 2000: "Many performance attribution systems use the same process for stocks as they do for bonds" (Campisi 2000, p. 14). However, this approach is also addressed in recent publications, such as in Murira and Sierra (2006/2007) and—in conjunction with the CMS BondEdge Performance Analysis System—in Geske (2006). The Barra Enterprise Performance System uses a modified Brinson approach (see Section 13.4.2).

[11] Alternatively, the classification can be based on the duration. Since the methodology is completely analogous, without loss of generality only the case of a classification according to the time to maturity will be considered. Bonds with a variable interest rate can thereby be classified according to the distance in time between two interest rate adjustment dates.

Table 13.1 Portfolio and Benchmark Data

Bond		Detailed Information				Nominal (Mn€)	
ISIN	Name	Coupon (%)	Maturity	Price 04/01	Price 10/31	Portfolio	Benchmark
IT0001448619	BUONI POLIENNALI DEL TES	5.500	11/01/10	100.88	107.47	1.0	1.0
IT0001338612	BUONI POLIENNALI DEL TES	4.250	11/01/09	93.44	99.69	0.5	1.0
DE0002317807	DEUTSCHE TELEKOM INT FIN	5.250	05/20/08	94.65	95.70	1.4	0.1
DE0001135036	BUNDESREPUB. DEUTSCHLAND	6.000	07/04/07	104.98	109.19	2.0	0.1
DE0001134963	BUNDESREPUB. DEUTSCHLAND	7.375	01/03/05	107.16	108.53	0.1	0.1
XS0086832473	OLIVETTI INTERNATIONAL	6.025	05/22/03	100.92	101.11	0.1	0.1
DE0001134880	BUNDESREPUB. DEUTSCHLAND	7.125	12./20/02	102.35	100.47	0.1	1.0
DE0001135069	BUNDESREPUB. DEUTSCHLAND	5.625	01/04/28	100.40	106.49	1.0	1.0
DE0001135135	BUNDESREPUB. DEUTSCHLAND	5.375	01/04/10	101.40	106.66	3.0	2.0
DE0001135093	BUNDESREPUB. DEUTSCHLAND	4.125	07/04/08	95.30	100.63	1.0	0.1
DE0001135010	BUNDESREPUB. DEUTSCHLAND	6.250	04/26/06	105.24	108.59	2.0	0.1
DE0001141356	BUNDESOBLIGATION	5.000	05/20/05	101.26	104.11	0.1	0.1
DE0001090082	TREUHANDANSTALT	6.750	05/13/04	104.75	105.32	1.0	2.0
DE0001090025	TREUHANDANSTALT	7.125	01/29/03	102.63	100.89	0.0	0.1
IT0001273363	BUONI POLIENNALI DEL TES	4.500	05/01/09	95.65	101.63	0.0	1.0
IT0001448619	BUONI POLIENNALI DEL TES	5.500	11/01/10	100.88	107.47	0.0	1.0
XS0063078330	KONINKLIJKE PHILIPS ELEC	7.125	02/06/08	107.01	111.34	3.0	0.1
XS0102706776	VOLVO TREASURY AB	5.125	10/12/04	99.31	102.33	0.1	0.1
XS0120883961	UNILEVER PLC	5.375	12/01/03	101.18	101.93	0.1	0.1
DE0004104708	VOLKSWAGEN INTL FIN NV	7.000	05/26/03	102.80	101.85	0.1	0.1

example in Section 11.3). In addition to the distinction between the different currencies in which the bonds are priced (analogous to equities) and the maturity categories, further characteristics such as the creditworthiness may be used for the definition of a sector.

Example 13.1

Transfer of the Brinson Approach to a Fixed Income Portfolio[12]

To illustrate this methodology (and its limitations), a portfolio is considered that consists of 17 different bonds. A portion of these bonds are sovereign bonds, the remainder corporate bonds. It is assumed that the portfolio in Table 13.1 was created on 04/01/2002. The benchmark of the portfolio consists essentially of the same bonds (with only three additional positions), but with a different weighting of the individual securities.[13] The performance is analyzed over the period 04/01/2002 to 10/31/2002.

The bonds are classified according to the remaining term by forming the intervals [0, 1.5] and [1.5, 2.5] etc.[14] For the sake of simplicity it was assumed that the remaining term of a bond remains constant throughout the analysis period. Thus each bond will remain in the segment to which it was initially assigned. Since this premise was applied not only to the bonds in the portfolio but also for the benchmark, this simplifying assumption is reasonable for the short analysis period. When dealing with real portfolios in practice, it is, however, generally necessary to consider these changes adequately, especially with such changes arising at periodic intervals in common benchmarks. Therefore, it is necessary to divide the time interval according to the breaks generated by these changes, before calculating the individual contributions of each of the resulting sub-periods.[15] The weight distribution of the portfolio under analysis and its benchmark at the beginning of the period under analysis are illustrated in Table 13.2. The accrued interest is considered in the weight calculation. It is evident that the portfolio manager has applied a so-called Bullet Strategy: clearly overweighting bonds with a medium term (from 3.5 to 6.5 years), and underweighting those with a long or short term (Figure 13.9).

Figure 13.10 shows that the strategy of the portfolio manager was successful. There was a general decline of interest rates in the Eurozone during the observed period with the medium term bonds benefiting above the average.

The results of Brinson et al.'s attribution analysis (Equations (12.18) (12.20) and (12.21)) can partly be seen in Table 13.3: The portfolio achieved an active

[12] The example is taken from the article (Buchholz et al. 2004).

[13] In contrast to the examples for equity portfolios, the use of common indices in practice must unfortunately be omitted here. Although a breakdown of the DAX with 30 stocks is still possible in a concise form, this approach is impracticable for a typical bond index such as the JP Morgan Europe, which features more than 200 loans (as of 10.20.2008).

[14] The first group thus consists of bonds with a remaining term up to 1.5 years (exclusive), the second with a remaining term between 1.5 years (inclusive) and 2.5 years (exclusive), etc.

[15] In Section 12.3 various methods for linking the contributions are discussed in detail.

Table 13.2 Weights of the Portfolio and Benchmark Maturity Segments on 04/01/2002 (%)

Remaining Term	[0.0–1.5)	[1.5–2.5)	[2.5–3.5)	[3.5–4.5)	[4.5–5.5)	[5.5–6.5)	[6.5–7.5)	[7.5–8.5)	[8.5–9.5)	>=9.5
Portfolio	1.8	6.9	1.8	12.7	12.5	32.1	0.0	20.4	5.9	5.8
Benchmark	11.8	20.0	2.7	1.0	0.9	2.6	8.4	26.0	17.8	8.8
Difference	−9.9	−13.1	−0.9	11.8	11.6	29.5	−8.4	−5.6	−11.9	−3.0

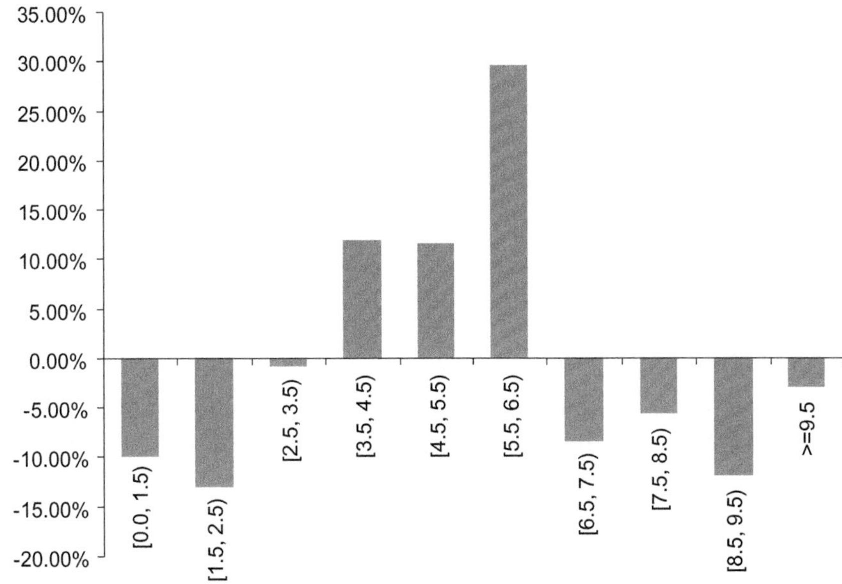

FIGURE 13.9
Active Weights on 04/01/2002.

return of 0.16% against the benchmark, of which 0.12% is attributable to the allocation decisions taken.

The significant negative contribution of the selection of bonds with a maturity of 6.5 to 7.5 years, and that of the interaction term with identical value but with the opposite sign, are particularly prominent. The explanation for this somewhat strange result is the apportionment chosen in conjunction with the (arbitrary) assumption that the return of the segment in the portfolio amounted to 0%.[16] This is one of the reasons why the selection terms are often combined with the interaction terms (cf. Section 12.2.3).

[16] See the discussion in Section 12.2.2.

Table 13.3 Results of the Attribution Analysis (Values in %)

	Returns		Contributions			
Remaining Term	Benchmark	Portfolio	Total	Allocation	Selection	Interaction
[0.0 – 1.5)	2.4	2.9	−0.22	−0.23	0.07	−0.06
[1.5 – 2.5)	4.3	4.2	−0.56	−0.56	0.00	0.00
[2.5 – 3.5)	5.6	5.6	−0.05	−0.05	0.00	0.00
[3.5 – 4.5)	6.6	6.6	0.77	0.77	0.00	0.00
[4.5 – 5.5)	7.3	7.3	0.84	0.84	0.00	0.00
[5.5 – 6.5)	6.8	7.0	2.08	2.01	0.01	0.07
[6.5 – 7.5)	9.0	0.0	−0.76	−0.76	−0.76	0.76
[7.5 – 8.5)	8.5	8.3	−0.52	−0.48	−0.06	0.01
[8.5 – 9.5)	9.7	9.7	−1.16	−1.16	0.00	0.00
>=9.5	9.2	9.2	−0.27	−0.27	0.00	0.00
Total	7.1	7.26	0.16	0.12	−0.74	0.78

Generally, the information content of such a term analysis is rather limited. For instance, it is not clear which components of the active return are attributable to the active decisions in respect to the duration and the term structure. Further, the selection effect combines different performance effects, which should be listed individually or not be included at all. The latter are contribution components resulting from structural decisions. Also, it is not clear what contributions would result from the spread effects.

Another issue stems from the rigid demarcation of subintervals. Consider, for instance, the case where the maturity of a benchmark bond is just above one of these limits. If the portfolio manager, influenced by this bond, acquires a paper

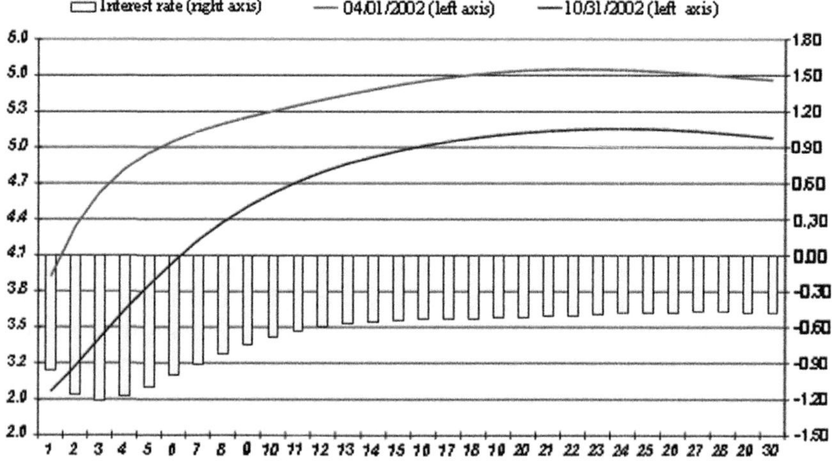

FIGURE 13.10
Change of Yield Curves in the Period Between 04/01/2002 and 12/31/2002.

with similar features from a risk-return point of view, but with a slightly shorter remaining term, then this would result in a distorted representation of the return contributions, since the return contribution of the portfolio bond would be shown in another subinterval than the contribution of the benchmark bond.

By further refining the subdivision of the bond universe,[17] the listed criticisms are not invalidated. Although the decomposition would, indeed, be much more detailed, the contributions actually corresponding to the investment process would still not become transparent or could at the best be deduced by (significant) additional effort from the listed results.

Despite these criticisms, this term methodology is still used in practice (see footnote 10). The major reason for this is—apart from the analogy to the analysis methodology for stocks—its simple implementation. Nowadays, however, yield curve based methods dominate the development and practical applications in this market segment.[18]

13.2 YIELD CURVES BASED ATTRIBUTION ANALYSIS USING AN OAS VALUATION APPROACH

In this section the consideration of attribution analysis for bond portfolios is based on a standard procedure for the (theoretical) valuation for a given bond based on a (temporally variable) yield curve.[19] This process is explained and illustrated with examples, especially since it serves as a reference point in the presentation of alternative approaches (Section 13.4).

---

[17] For example, in the presentation in Lehman (1998) the methodology of Brinson et al. is applied to a bond portfolio where the bond universe is classified by several parameters. This approach can be visualized as a subdivision into individual cells. The discussion in the cited article focuses on the case where the duration and the general segment (government bonds, corporate bonds, MBS, ABS, etc.) form this parameter set. A similar approach is described in Murira and Sierra (2006/07), recommending that the term or duration bands should not be longer than six months.

[18] For a more detailed description of the differences between stock and bond portfolios and the resulting need for different analytical approaches, see Campisi (2000) or Colin (2005, p. 36 et seq).

[19] The discussions in this chapter are based on the presentation in Buchholz et al. (2004). A similar approach is described in Merrill Lynch (2000). The method described in Burns and Chu (2005) is largely identical to the one presented here, but it contains a slightly different approach to the analysis of spread effects, based on peer groups, and discusses a volatility parameter. A similar method is depicted in Hansen and Søgaard-Andersen (2006), where an additional effect, "view", is introduced, the result of a differing development of the yield curve movement compared to a projected form (view). Another approach, similar to the one presented here, can be found in Cubilier (2005/06). The article by Khoury, Veilleux, and Viau provides an overview of important factors that must be considered in the analysis of bond portfolios (Khoury et al. 03). For a general study on attribution analysis for bond portfolios (derived from the so-called GRAP recommendations (GRAP 2004), with many parallels to the method presented here, see Giguère (2005). For a further analysis approach which defines the management effect as a contribution exceeding common market yields see Fong et al. (1983). In this approach contributions are broken down into an expected ("market implicit") and an "unexpected" contribution, the latter reflecting unexpected changes in futures rates. The management contribution is broken down into contributions that correspond to the maturity and spread management plus the selection of specific titles. Another "classical" approach is described in Dietz et al. (1980), where the returns are decomposed into a yield effect ("yield to maturity"), an interest rate effect, a sector effect and a residual term.

13.2.1 Model Evaluation

As part of the discussion below, the price (so-called *clean price*) of a bond at a given time t is called $P(t)$. The accrued interest at time t is denoted by $AI(t)$, so that $P(t)$ and $AI(t)$ combined correspond to the (market) resale value of the bond at time t (so-called *dirty price* value). The yield curve, based on time t, will be referred to as s_t. The theoretical (clean) price of a bond at time t, evaluated with respect to the yield curve s_t, is denoted by $T(t, s_t)$. It is defined as the sum of the future cash flows of the bond discounted by means of the yield curve s_t minus the interest claims $AI(t)$ accrued up to time t, and corresponds to the current value of the bond at time t:[20]

$$T(t, s_t) := \sum_{i=1}^{N} (1 + s_t(t_i)/m)^{-t_i * m} * Z_{t_i} - AI(t), \tag{13.6}$$

where the Z_{t_i} denote the N payments (coupon, nominal) of the bond at times t_i and $s_t(t_i)$ the interest rates congruent to the term t_i. The number of coupon payments per year is denoted by m. If T refers to the maturity of a bond, then the t_i can be expressed as follows:[21]

$$t_i = \mathrm{T} - i + 1, \quad i = 1, \cdots, N, \text{ which } N = [\mathrm{T}] + 1.$$

Without consideration of the specific trade practices, the accrued interest (based on the coupon C) shall be defined by:

$$AI(t) = C * ([\mathrm{T}] + 1 - \mathrm{T}).$$

Usually the actual observable bond prices do not agree with the theoretical prices, since, in the theoretical calculation, the specific characteristics of the bond, such as the specific risk or liquidity specifications, are ignored. A common measure for quantifying this difference is the option-adjusted spread (OAS),[22] which is defined as follows:

Option-Adjusted Spread

The option-adjusted spread OAS_t of a bond at time t is implicitly defined by the following equation:

$$P(t) = T(t, s_t + OAS_t). \tag{13.8}$$

OAS_t is thus the spread, which needs to be added uniformly to the spot rates of the underlying interest rate curve, in order to obtain the true market value.

---

[20] See Fabozzi (1999, p. 533 et seq). Options and tax issues are ignored in this form. See also Vasicek and Fong (1982). In the case of maturities of less than one year, the discount factor is linearized : $1 + t_i * s_t(t_i)$, which leads to significant deviations only for high nominal interest rates (see EUREX 2008, p. 12).

[21] For a real number x $[x]$ is the largest integer less than or equal to x. This function is known as the Floor Function.

[22] See Fabozzi (1999, p. 554 et seq).

Table 13.4 Interest Rates

	6 Months	1 Year	2 Years	3 Years
04.01.2002	3.59	3.92	4.34	4.62
10.31. 2002	3.12	2.96	3.17	3.41

A positive spread may, for example, reflect a lower credit rating, liquidity or profile of a bond.

The notation comes from the field of mortgage bonds (mortgage-backed securities). The mortgage holders have the right to redeem their mortgage when it is beneficial for them (for example due to a fall in interest rates) and thus unfavorable for the bond holders. In other words, the holders of the bonds have given them an option. However, the calculation of the option-adjusted spreads for such a bond is much more complicated than for ordinary ones: it involves the simulation of interest rate paths, and a model of the early repayments.[23]

Example 13.2

Determination of the Theoretical Price of a Bond/Option-Adjusted Spread

For the bond *Volvo Treasury AB* in Example 13.1 the *option-adjusted spread* at 01/04/2002 and at 10/31/2002 is calculated. The relevant data for the yield curve are given in Table 13.4 (see also Figure 13.10):

The discount interest rates are calculated by linear interpolation. The bond pays a coupon of 5.125% once a year. The time to maturity is equal to 2.53 years (at 04.01), respectively 1.95 years (at 10.31). The accrued interest equals 2.40% (on 04.01), respectively and 0.27% (at 10.31). At the beginning of the period the OAS equals 0.93%:

$$
\begin{aligned}
99.31\% &= \frac{105.125\%}{(1+4.49\%+0.93\%)^{2.53}} + \frac{5.125\%}{(1+4.14\%+0.93\%)^{1.53}} \\
&\quad + \frac{5.125\%}{(1+3.77\%+0.93\%)^{0.53}} - 2.40\%.
\end{aligned}
$$

At the end of the period the OAS equals 0.70%.

$$
102.33\% = \frac{105.125\%}{(1+3.16\%+0.70.\%)^{1.95}} + \frac{5.125\%}{(1+2.97\%+0.70\%)^{0.95}} - 0.27\%.
$$

13.2.2 Description of the Effects

This section describes a basic method for decomposing the return of a bond into individual contributions, which are attributable to certain characteristic changes in the yield curve (parallel shifts, structural changes, etc.) or bond-specific effects

[23] See Lakhbir (2001, p. 34 et seq).

Table 13.5 Summary of Notation

Variable	Explanation
$P(t)$	Price of the bond at time t
$C(t_1, t_2)$	Coupon payments in the period from t_1 to t_2
$AI(t)$	Accrued interest at time t
s_t	Yield curve at time t
$T(t, s_t)$	Theoretical price of the bond at time t evaluated with respect to the yield curve s_t
OAS_t	Option-adjusted spread at time t

(interest claims, roll-down effect, spread changes). The aim, similar to stock portfolios, is to calculate individual effects independently. For this purpose, a (AAA-rated) government bond based yield curve is used. Thus, the spread of a bond (see below) is generally determined relative to the segment with the highest credit rating. However, depending on the investment spectrum, other definitions are possible. Alternatively, for example, a swap curve can be applied.[24] The choice of a yield curve with a maximum credit rating has the advantage that all bonds facing such a curve usually have a positive spread, and thus, to a certain extent, a calibration is achieved.

The total contribution of a bond in a period from t_0 to t_1 is calculated as follows:

$$total = P_1 - P_0 + AI(t_1) - AI(t_0) + C(t_0, t_1)^{25}$$

The return is obtained by dividing by the initial price:

$$R = \frac{P_1 - P_0 + AI(t_1) - AI(t_0) + C(t_0, t_1)}{P_0 + AI(t_0)}. \tag{13.9}$$

In the following the total contribution will be broken down into the individual effects.

Roll-Down Effect/Pull-to-Par Effect

The term "roll-down effect" describes the price changes due to a shortening of the maturity of a bond over a particular period. In a normal yield curve, this effect would yield a positive contribution, and in an inverse yield curve a negative one (Figure 13.11).[26] When monitoring this effect, it must also be considered that the yield curve will change over the observation period. Thus, in the strict sense the calculation of the resulting price follows from an integration of infinitesimal roll-down effects. For reasons of practicality, however, such a complex method will not be considered. Instead, the yield curve over the observation

[24] See the discussion in Section 13.1.1.1.

[25] Ideally, the term $C(t_0, t_1)$ also includes the interest income on the coupon payment earned over the period.

[26] See Leibowitz (1992, p. 98).

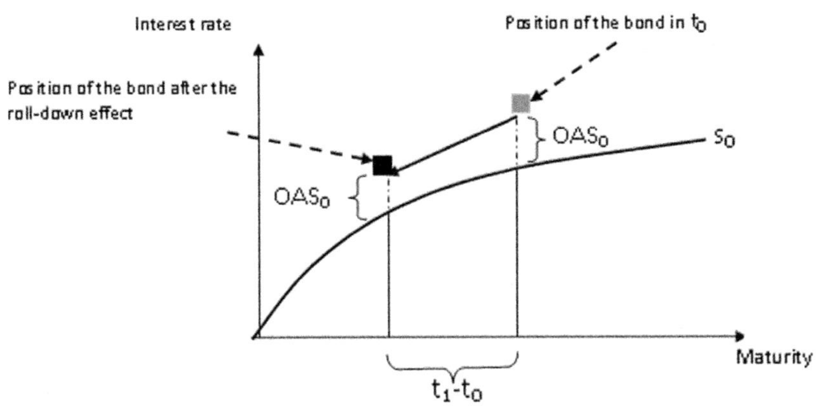

FIGURE 13.11
Illustration of the roll-down effect, using a zero-coupon bond (square). (In a strict sense, the positioning of a bond in a remaining term / spot rate chart is reserved only for zero-coupon bonds; this can, however, be extended to coupon bonds by selecting a representative spot rate (e.g. present value weighted spot rate)).

period is taken as constant. Formally, the (absolute) roll-down effect for a bond is determined as:

$$rolldown = T(t_1, s_0 + OAS_0) - T(t_0, s_0 + OAS_0). \qquad (13.10)$$

Thus, the spread OAS_0 is initially determined by using the price of the bond. Next the theoretical price of the bond at the end of the analysis period (at t_1) is determined, based on the yield curve at t_0 and the assumption of a constant spread (see Figure 13.11). The difference between these values is the roll-down effect, which (in this definition) includes the so-called pull-to-par effect. The pull-to-par effect quantifies the convergence of the bond price towards the nominal value (100) with decreasing maturity (regardless of the actual shape of the yield curve).[27] The above definition is also based on the yield curve at the beginning of the period analyzed.[28] However, it could also be based on the yield curve at any other fixed point in time within the analysis period (e.g. the end or the middle of the interval). Choosing the yield curve at the beginning of the period[29] has the advantage that the roll-down effect can be estimated in advance.

[27] See Rathjens (1998, p. 632). The roll-down effect (in the strict sense) and the pull-to-par effect may be offsetting. In the case of a normal yield curve, this will be the case if the bond is traded at a premium (*premium bond*). At prices below par (*discount bond*), the effects are in alignment. In an inverted yield curve, the statements are reversed.

[28] This is one of the most frequently used definitions in the literature. For roll-down effect see for example Leibowitz (1992, p. 98). In this context, see the article by Carpenter (2003), in which one finds a more detailed explanation regarding the importance of roll-down effects in the practice of portfolio management.

[29] Here, it is assumed that the portfolio was structured at the initial point of the analysis period.

The pull-to-par effect can also be calculated and reported separately. To do this, the original interest rate is taken as constant over time

$$pulltopar = T(t_1, \tilde{s_0} + OAS_0) - T(t_0, s_0 + OAS_0), \tag{13.11}$$

with

$$\tilde{s_0}(t_i) = s_0\,(t_i + (t_1 - t_0))$$

The (actual) roll-down effect is then the size difference between (13.10) and (13.11).

Parallel Effect

The parallel effect describes the outcomes which are the sole result of the parallel shift of a given yield curve, while maintaining the original spread of the bond (see Figure 13.12).

$$parallel = T(t_1, s_0 + OAS_0 + shift) - T(t_1, s_0 + OAS_0) \tag{13.12}$$

This break-down has the character of a model. From a mathematical perspective the breakdown into a roll-down and a parallel effect is not unique, as the change of the yield curve over the period is a continuous process. To calculate it in a realistic form, one has to rely on practical approximation methods. The procedure described here is based on the stipulation that first the roll-down effect is calculated (which is based on the yield curve at t_0) and then the parallel effect (at time t_1). In practice, the calculation may be based on other conventions (see Figure 13.13). As long as the time interval between t_0 and t_1 is not too long, the process should lead to meaningful approximations.

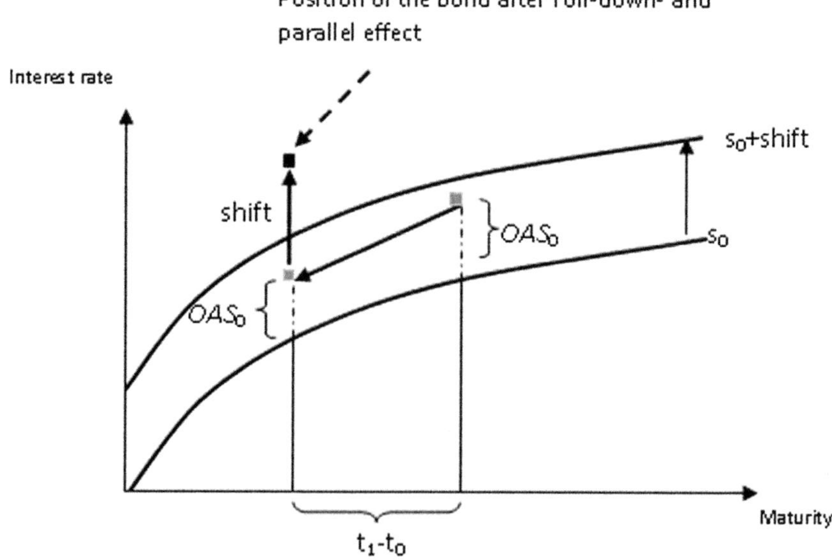

FIGURE 13.12
Illustration of the Definition of the Parallel Effect.

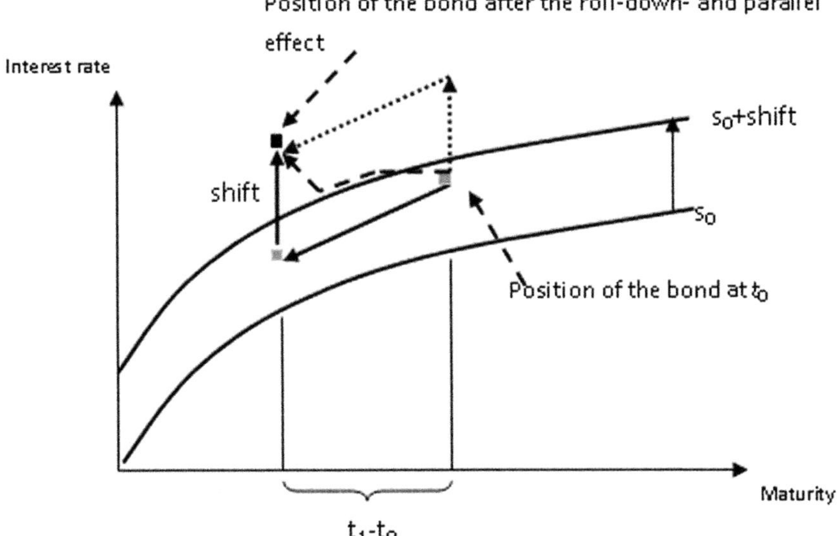

FIGURE 13.13
Different Paths from the Starting Position to the Position of the Bond After the Roll-Down and the Parallel Effect.

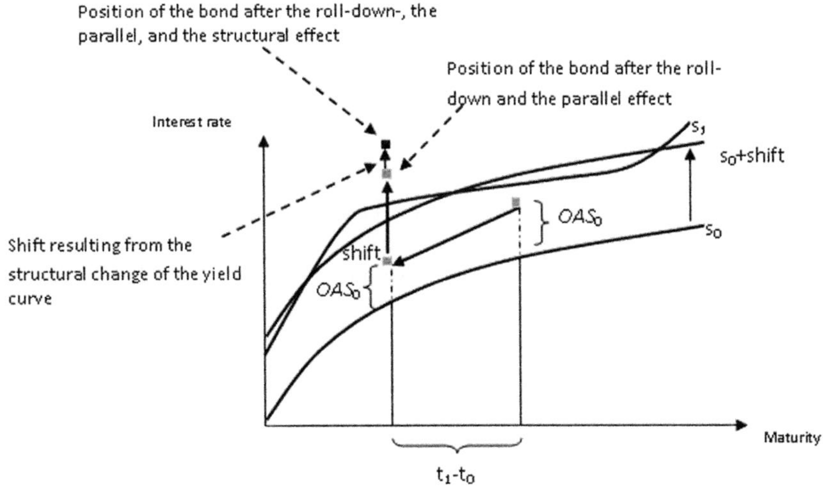

FIGURE 13.14
Illustration of the Structural Effect.

Structural Effect

The structural effect is the return component, which results from the curve movement complementary to the parallel movement of the yield curve.

$$structure = T(t_1, s_1 + OAS_0) - T(t_1, s_0 + OAS_0 + shift) \qquad (13.13)$$

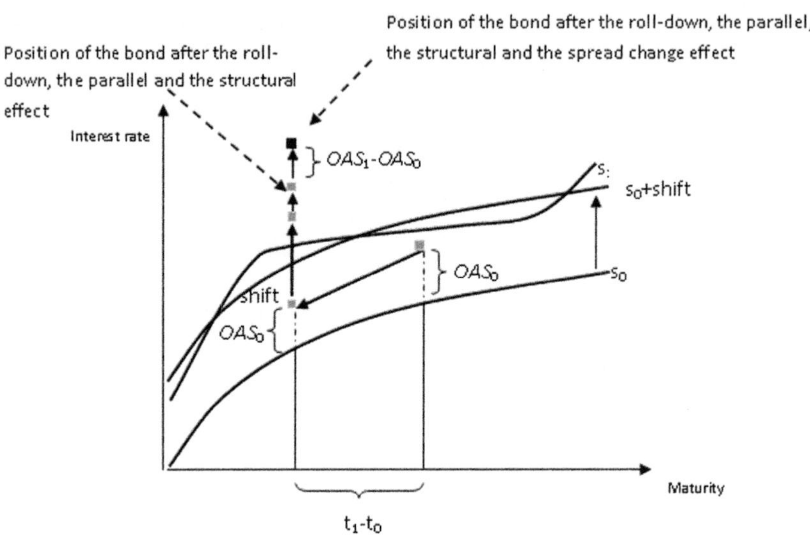

FIGURE 13.15
Illustration of the Spread Change Effect.

The effect is illustrated in Figure 13.14. Basically, this contribution can be disaggregated in any number of other more sophisticated return contributions, which reflect characteristic movements of a yield curve.[30]

Spread Change Effect

The effects described above, *roll-down, parallel* and *structure,* explain the return effects, which can be directly attributed to the shape and movement of the yield curve. The remaining spread change effect quantifies the component of the change in bond price, which cannot be explained by the movement of the yield curve. The spread change effect is, therefore, a residual, i.e., the difference between the actual price (clean price) of the bond at time t_1 and the theoretical price of the bond at time t_1 using an unchanged spread from the initial starting point:

$$spread = T(t_1, s_1 + OAS_1) - T(t_1, s_1 + OAS_0) = P_1 - T(t_1, s_1 + OAS_0). \quad (13.14)$$

The term reflects the change in spread relative to the given yield curve in t_1. For a widening of the spread this is illustrated in Figure 13.15.

Consideration of Accrued Income and Interest Coupon Payments

After the presentation of the various yield curve induced effects, respectively spread effects, the treatment of accrued interest and interest coupon payments needs to be addressed:

$$coupon = AI(t_1) - AI(t_0) + K(t_0, t_1) \quad (13.15)$$

---

[30] See the discussion in Section 13.1.1.1. This point is explained in Example 13.3 in a simplified form and in a detailed form in Section 13.3 by using methods for the determination of interest rate curves.

Table 13.6 Interest Rate Curve

Term (Years)	Interest Rate Curve (%) $t=0$	$t=1$
0.5	1.7	2.0
1.0	2.0	2.5
2.0	4.0	4.5
3.0	4.5	6.0
4.0	5.5	7.5

Example 13.3

Effects for a Single Bond I

The methodology will be explained by means of an elementary example. It is based on the yield curve change over a period of one year as shown in Table 13.6.

Consider a bond with a remaining term of two years at the beginning of the period. The nominal equals 100 and the coupon 3%. At $t = 0$, the price of the bond is 97.61%, so that the valuation model (13.6) delivers an OAS of 0.30%:

$$97.61\% = \frac{3\%}{1 + 2.0\% + 0.3\%} + \frac{103\%}{(1 + 4.0\% + 0.3\%)^2}.$$

At $t=1$ the price of the bond equals 99.90% and the OAS 0.60%:

$$99.90\% = \frac{103\%}{1 + 2.5\% + 0.6\%}.$$

Coupon Effect

Since there is no accrued interest at either the starting or ending time of the accounting period, only the actual coupon payments must be taken into account:

$$coupon = 3\%.$$

Roll-Down Effect

According to (13.10) the roll-down effect is calculated as follows:

$$\begin{aligned} rolldown &= \frac{103\%}{1 + 2.0\% + 0.3\%} - 97.61\% \\ &= 100.68\% - 97.61\% \\ &= 3.07\%. \end{aligned}$$

If one calculates the pull-to-par effect separately, then according to Equation (13.11):

$$pull\text{-}to\text{-}par = \frac{103\%}{1 + 4.0\% + 0.3\%} - 97.61\% = 1.14\%.$$

The roll-down effect is obtained by forming the difference of these quantities (1.93% = 3.07%–1.14%). In any case, this effect contributes significantly to the total return, reflecting the considerable slope of the curve. The amount is roughly equivalent to the interest rate differential between the terms of one and two years.

The pull-to-par effect is also significant, as is frequently the case with bonds of short maturity. Generally speaking, this effect is positive if the coupon rate is below the market interest rate (as in the present case, where the coupon is about 1% lower than the market rate) and negative in the opposite case.

Parallel Effect

The average rise in interest rates (shift) is calculated as follows:

$$shift = \frac{1}{5} * ((2.0\% - 1.7\%) + (2.5\% - 2.0\%) + \cdots + (7.5\% - 5.5\%)) = 1.06\%.$$

A negative parallel effect at a comparable magnitude corresponds to this shift:

$$\begin{aligned} parallel &= \frac{103\%}{1 + 2.0\% + 1.06\% + 0.3\%} - \frac{103\%}{1 + 2.0\% + 0.3\%} \\ &= 99.65\% - 100.68\% \\ &= -1.03\%. \end{aligned}$$

Structural Effect

According to (13.13) the structural effect is calculated as:

$$\begin{aligned} \text{structure} &= \frac{103\%}{1 + 2.5\% + 0.3\%} - \frac{103\%}{1 + 2.0\% + 1.06\% + 0.3\%} \\ &= 100.19\% - 99.65\% \\ &= 0.54\%. \end{aligned}$$

Spread Change Effect

Finally, according to (13.14) the spread change effect is given by:

$$\begin{aligned} spread &= 99.90\% - \frac{103\%}{1 + 2.5\% + 0.3\%} \\ &= 99.90\% - 100.19\% \\ &= -0.29\%. \end{aligned}$$

This result reflects quite accurately the expansion of the OAS by 30 basis points.

Breakdown of the Structural Effect

The structural effect can be broken down further. Without anticipating the discussion in Section 13.3, a simple, intuitive approach is described here. Figure 13.16 shows that the original yield curve, after being moved by a parallel shift, can be transferred into the yield curve at time $t = 1$ through an additional rotation (with a rotation center around two years). Taking the average of the endpoints' differences (terms 0.5 and 4.0 years), then this rotation causes an additional change of–0.85% and 0.85%, respectively in

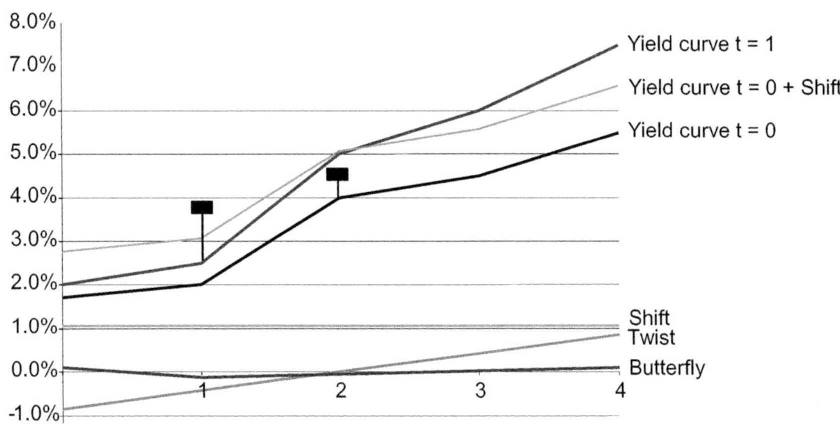

FIGURE 13.16
Characteristic Movements in the Yield Curve.

the terms 0.5 and 4.0 years.[31] Accordingly, the displacement in the terms 1.0 and 3.0 years amounts to −0.425% and 0.425%, respectively (cf. Figure 13.16). The residual movement (here called Butterfly) is minimal.

The resulting effect of the rotation of the yield curve is then calculated as:

$$\begin{aligned} twist &= \frac{103\%}{1 + 2.00\% + 1.06\% - 0.43\% + 0.30\%} - \frac{103\%}{1 + 2.00\% + 1.06\% + 0.30\%} \\ &= 100.06\% - 99.65\% \\ &= 0.41\%. \end{aligned}$$

The remaining curve effect is obtained by forming the difference of the two effects:

$$butterfly = structure - twist = 0.13\%.$$

Figure 13.16 illustrates the position of the bond (rectangle) at the beginning and end of the period. The coordinate point on the term axis is determined by the time to maturity of the bond. The specific spread (OAS) is indicated above the corresponding point of the relevant yield curve Table 13.7 provides a summary of the effects.

Calculation of Returns

The return contributions are given by the quotient of the absolute contributions and the price of the bond (*dirty price*) at the beginning of the period. A distinction between a yield curve and a spread-induced component is made.

[31] Here the simplifying assumption of equal distances between the nodes 0.5, 1, 2, etc. is made.

Table 13.7 Summary of the Effects

Effect	Return (%)
Coupon	3.00
Roll-down	3.07
Pull-to-par	1.14
Roll-down (mod)	1.93
Parallel	−1.03
Structure	0.54
Twist	0.41
Butterfly	0.13
Spread change	−0.29
Sum	5.29

The total yield effect, r_{coupon}, which results from the coupon payments and the change in accrued interest, is calculated by:

$$r_{coupon} = \frac{AI(t_1) - AI(t_0) + C(t_0, t_1)}{P_0 + AI(t_0)} \tag{13.16}$$

It is clear that this effect is strongly dependent on the bond's market value at the beginning of the period. For example, if the bond is traded well below par, then it will be much bigger than in the case of a notation near par. For a bond priced above par, the effect would be opposite. According to the desired distinction the yield curve induced coupon effect is defined as:

$$r_{coupon,yci} = \frac{AI(t_1) - AI(t_0) + C(t_0, t_1)}{T(t_0, s_0) + AI(t_0)} \tag{13.17}$$

In other words the absolute contribution is divided by theoretical value of the bond, which has the consequence that the return is independent on the specific spread of the bond. The component of the spread induced effect $r_{coupon,spread}$ is then obtained as a residual:

$$r_{coupon,spread} := r_{coupon} - r_{coupon,yci} \tag{13.18}$$

If necessary, a further breakdown of the effect of coupon / accrued interest is possible by considering the income in relation to the nominal value of the bond. The yield curve induced component is then perceived as a resulting difference term:

$$\begin{aligned} r_{coupon,nominal} &:= \frac{AI(t_1) - AI(t_0) + C(t_0, t_1)}{Nominal} \\ \widetilde{r}_{coupon,yci} &:= \frac{AI(t_1) - AI(t_0) + C(t_0, t_1)}{T(t_0, s_0) + AI(t_0)} - r_{coupon,nominal} \end{aligned}$$

The spread-induced component follows again as a residual term and remains unchanged with regard to the expression (13.18):

$$\begin{aligned} r_{coupon,spread} &:= r_{coupon} - r_{coupon,nominal} - \widetilde{r}_{coupon,yci} \\ &= r_{coupon} - r_{coupon,yci}. \end{aligned}$$

Table 13.8 Yield Effects. A Breakdown of the Roll-Down Effect is Omitted Here

		Total	Yield Curve Induced	Spread Induced
Return effects due to passage of time	Coupon/ Accrued interest	$\frac{AI(t_1)-AI(t_0)+C(t_1,t_0)}{P_0+AI(t_0)}$	$\frac{AI(t_1)-AI(t_0)+C(t_1,t_0)}{T(t_0,s_0)+AI(t_0)}$	Total – Yield Curve Induced
	Roll-down	$\frac{T(t_1,s_0+OAS_0)-T(t_0,s_0+OAS_0)}{P_0+AI(t_0)}$	$\frac{T(t_1,s_0)-T(t_0,s_0)}{T(t_0,s_0)+AI(t_0)}$	Total – Yield Curve Induced
Return effects due to changes in the interest rates	Parallel	$\frac{T(t_1,s_0+OAS_0+shift)-T(t_1,s_0+OAS_0)}{P_0+AI(t_0)}$	Total	––
	Structural	$\frac{T(t_1,s_1+OAS_0)-T(t_1,s_0+OAS_0+shift)}{P_0+AI(t_0)}$	Total	––
	Spread Change	$\frac{P_1-T(t_1,s_1+OAS_0)}{P_0+AI(t_0)}$	––	Total

In a similar way, the roll-down effect can be decomposed into a yield curve and a spread-induced component. In Table 13.8 an overview of the different return effects is provided.

While the *coupon/accrued income* and *roll-down* returns are a direct consequence of the passage of time, the other effects (parallel, structural, and spread change) only arise if the interest rate environment or the spread levels change; an explicit time dependency does not exist.[32] Thus, these five return effects can be divided into two groups: time-dependent effects and those that are induced by changes in interest rates and spreads (Table 13.8). The sum of the effects equals the total return (13.9) of the bond.

Example 13.4

The case of a Single Bond I

The calculation of the effects for the bond in Example 13.3 leads to the return breakdown in Table 13.9.

13.2.3 Attribution Relative to A Benchmark

In a yield-curve based attribution the returns shown in Table 13.8 must be calculated for each bond in the portfolio and in the benchmark, and subsequently aggregated using the weights. Table 13.10 contains the notation for the returns of individual titles according to Table 13.8.

[32] The return of a portfolio via the so-called "carry" is always the sum of two components, coupon/ accrued interest and roll-down.

Table 13.9 Summary of the Return Effects

	Effect	Yield (%)
Coupon		3.07
	Yield Curve Induced	3.06
	Spread Induced	0.02
Roll-down		3.14
Pull-to-par		1.17
	Yield Curve Induced	1.16
	Spread Induced	0.01
Roll-down (mod)		1.98
	Yield Curve Induced	1.97
	Spread Induced	0.01
Parallel		−1.06
Structure		0.56
	Twist	0.42
	Butterfly	0.13
Spread Change		−0.30
Sum		5.42

Table 13.10 Details of the Effects on Portfolio and Benchmark Level

	Total	Yield Curve Induced	Spread Induced
Coupon/Accrued interest	r^{co}	$r^{co,yc}$	$r^{co,sp}$
Roll-down	r^{rd}	$r^{rd,yc}$	$r^{rd,sp}$
Parallel	r^{pa}	---	---
Structure	r^{st}	---	---
Spread Change	r^{sp}	---	---

If wp_i and wb_i denote the weights of the individual securities in the portfolio, respectively in the benchmark, then their contributions at the portfolio level are computed as shown in Table 13.11. This consideration is based on the assumption that all bonds occuring in the portfolio and in the benchmark are counted with an index i, using values from 1 to N. For a bond, which is not included in the portfolio, the weight will be set to zero (similarly for the benchmark).

The level of detail can be augmented by a further breakdown according to specified portfolio / benchmark sectors (such as class of issuer, term structure, industries, etc.). In regard to the contributions resulting from spread changes, a further breakdown of the effects based on the Brinson approach can be of interest. To this end, the totality of the N bonds, which form the benchmark/portfolio universe will be decomposed into M segments G_i ($i = 1, \cdots, M$). Each of the N bonds will be assigned to exactly one of these segments.[33] Then, the segment

[33] It therefore holds $\bigcup_{i=1}^{M} G_i = \{1, \cdots, N\}$.

Table 13.11 Return Contributions on the Portfolio – and Benchmark Level

	Portfolio	Benchmark	Relative Contribution
Coupon/ Accrued Interest (Interest Rate Curve Induced)	$RP^{co.yc} = \sum_{i=1}^{N} wp_i * r_i^{co.yc}$	$RB^{co.yc} = \sum_{i=1}^{N} wb_i * r_i^{co.yc}$	$B^{co.yc} = RP^{co.yc} - RB^{co.yc} = \sum_{i=1}^{N} (wp_i - wb_i) * r_i^{co.yc}$
Coupon/ Accrued Interest(Spread Induced)	$RP^{co.sp} = \sum_{i=1}^{N} wp_i * r_i^{co.sp}$	$RB^{co.sp} = \sum_{i=1}^{N} wb_i * r_i^{co.sp}$	$B^{co.sp} = RP^{co.sp} - RB^{co.sp} = \sum_{i=1}^{N} (wp_i - wb_i) * r_i^{co.sp}$
Roll-down (Yield Curve Iinduced)	$RP^{rd.yc} = \sum_{i=1}^{N} wp_i * r_i^{rd.yc}$	$RB^{rd.yc} = \sum_{i=1}^{N} wb_i * r_i^{rd.yc}$	$B^{rd.yc} = RP^{rd.yc} - RB^{rd.yc} = \sum_{i=1}^{N} (wp_i - wb_i) * r_i^{rd.yc}$
Roll-down (Spread induced)	$RP^{rd.sp} = \sum_{i=1}^{N} wp_i * r_i^{rd.sp}$	$RB^{rd.sp} = \sum_{i=1}^{N} wb_i * r_i^{rd.sp}$	$B^{rd.sp} = RP^{rd.sp} - RB^{rd.sp} = \sum_{i=1}^{N} (wp_i - wb_i) * r_i^{rd.sp}$
Parallel	$RP^{pa} = \sum_{i=1}^{N} wp_i * r_i^{pa}$	$RB^{pa} = \sum_{i=1}^{N} wb_i * r_i^{pa}$	$B^{pa} = RP^{pa} - RB^{pa} = \sum_{i=1}^{N} (wp_i - wb_i) * r_i^{pa}$
Structure	$RP^{st} = \sum_{i=1}^{N} wp_i * r_i^{st}$	$RB^{st} = \sum_{i=1}^{N} wb_i * r_i^{st}$	$B^{st} = RP^{st} - RB^{st} = \sum_{i=1}^{N} (wp_i - wb_i) * r_i^{st}$
Spread Change	$RP^{sp} = \sum_{i=1}^{N} wp_i * r_i^{sp}$	$RB^{sp} = \sum_{i=1}^{N} wb_i * r_i^{sp}$	$B^{sp} = RP^{sp} - RB^{sp} = \sum_{i=1}^{N} (wp_i - wb_i) * r_i^{sp}$

weights and returns are calculated (assuming the corresponding weights are not equal to zero):

$$swp_i := \sum_{j \in G_i} wp_j \quad swb_i := \sum_{j \in G_i} wb_j$$

$$srp_i^{sp} := \frac{\sum_{j \in G_i} wp_j * r_j^{sp}}{swp_i} \quad srb_i^{sp} := \frac{\sum_{j \in G_i} wb_j * r_j^{sp}}{swb_i}$$

The allocation, selection, and interaction terms are calculated in accordance with the formulas (12.19) – (12.21). In this approach it seems reasonable to calculate the allocation contributions based on the returns relative to the benchmark average,[34] $srb_i^{sp} - RB^{sp}$, instead of on the absolute segment returns, srb_i^{sp}, so that the spread change induced contributions are as shown in Table 13.12:

Example 13.5

Yield curve based analysis

Once again the portfolio in Example 13.1 will be considered. This time the breakdown is carried out, however, according to the procedure described in the previous section's yield curve based methodology. For simplicity, it is assumed that the weights will not be

[34] See the discussion in Section 12.2.1.

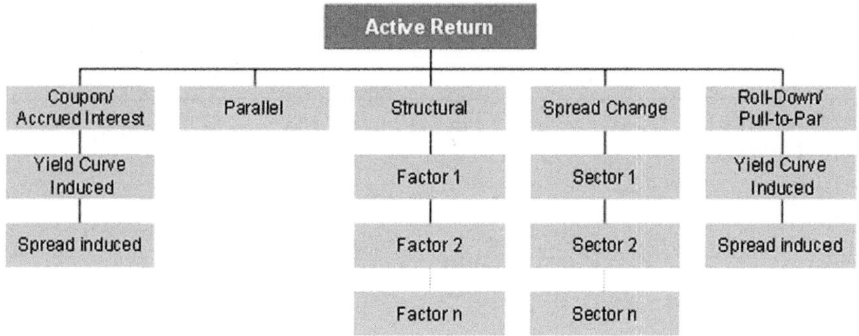

FIGURE 13.17
Overview of the Effects.

Table 13.12 Return Contribution at Portfolio and Benchmark Level

	Contribution via Spread Change
Allocation Contribution	$B_i^{sp,all} = (swp_i - swb_i) * \left(srb_i^{sp} - RB^{sp}\right)$
Selection Contribution	$B_i^{sp,sel} = swb_i * \left(srp_i^{sp} - srb_i^{sp}\right)$
Interaction term	$B_i^{sp,it} = (swp_i - swb_i) * \left(srp_i^{sp} - srb_i^{sp}\right)$

Table 13.13 Results of the Yield Curve Based Attribution Analysis (Values in %)

	Portfolio			Benchmark			Portfolio vs. Benchmark		
Contributions	**Yield Curve**	**Spread**	**Total**	**Yield Curve**	**Spread**	**Total**	**Yield Curve**	**Spread**	**Total**
Roll-down	−0.37	0.15	−0.22	−0.45	0.05	−0.40	0.08	0.09	0.17
Coupon/ Accrued Interest	3.26	0.06	3.32	3.24	0.03	3.27	0.02	0.03	0.05
Parallel	3.52		3.52	3.53		3.53	−0.01		−0.01
Structure	1.38		1.38	0.91		0.91	0.47		0.47
Spread Change		−0.73	−0.73		−0.22	−0.22		−0.51	−0.51
Time	2.89	0.22	3.11	2.79	0.09	2.86	0.10	0.13	0.23
Yield curve / spread	4.89	−0.74	4.15	4.44	−0.22	4.22	0.45	−0.52	−0.07
Total	7.78	−0.52	7.26	7.23	−0.13	7.10	0.55	−0.39	0.16

adjusted for coupon payments and that these payments bear no interest in the period analyzed.

The results in Table 13.13 are based on the formulas in Table 13.8 and Table 13.11.

Table 13.14 Spread Change Contributions by Segment (Values in %)

	Total	Allocation	Selection	Rest
Government Bonds Germany (Bunds)	−0.02	−0.01	−0.01	0.00
Government Bonds Eurozone ex Germany	−0.07	−0.08	0.04	−0.03
Automobile	0.00	0.00	0.00	0.00
Telecommunications	−0.32	−0.32	0.00	0.00
Technology	−0.09	−0.02	−0.01	−0.06
Retail	0.00	0.00	0.00	0.00
Total	−0.51	−0.43	0.02	−0.09

The result shows that the entire active return of 0.16% is mainly due to the carry components roll-down and coupon/accrued interest (passage of time effects of 0.23%).

Among the other effects, the yield curve and the spread change effects neutralized each other. A major positive contribution to the return was generated through the realization of a Bullet Strategy (structural effect of 0.47%). The overweight position in corporate bonds, however, generated a negative contribution of −0.51% in the spread change, because the spreads increased over the period. A breakdown of this contribution in accordance with the methodology in Table 13.12 is shown in Table 13.14. It is evident that the change in spread contribution is primarily due to the positioning in the telecommunications sector.

The parallel component of the yield curve change resulted in a negligible contribution. This was expected since the modified duration of the portfolio coincided with the modified duration of the benchmark at the beginning of the analysis period.[35]

Despite a normal yield curve the contributions to the absolute return through the roll-down-/pull-to-par effect, are negative, since the positive return effect (roll-down) resulting from the rolling-down to a lower interest rate is overcompensated by a negative effect, caused by the convergence of the above par bonds toward their nominal value (pull-to-par). The latter effect corresponds to a positive coupon effect.

In individual cases, it may be instructive to analyze the development of the (relative) return effects over time (Figure 13.18). This may, for example, indicate whether the return effects have been achieved over a longer period in a consistent form, or whether they are simply due to special circumstances (such as specific market conditions, increased cash position due to inflows, etc).

[35] The value of the modified duration was 5.09 years for both the portfolio and the benchmark.

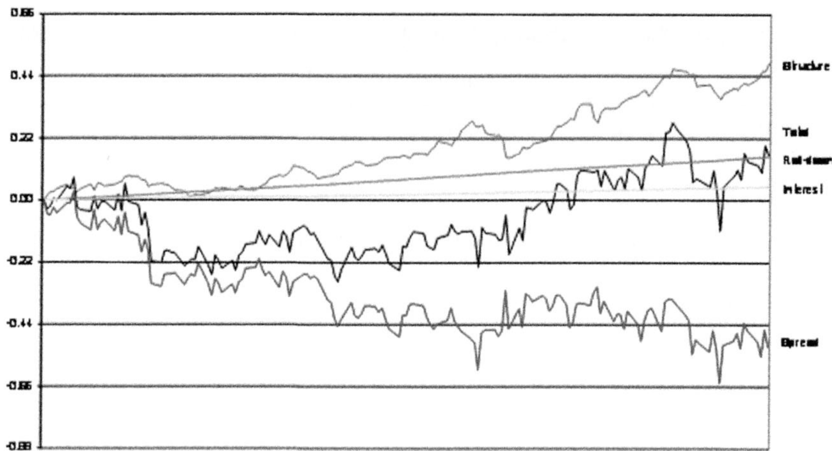

FIGURE 13.18
Development of the Effects Over Time.

13.2.4 Analysis with A Separation of the Interaction Terms

The analysis described in the preceding sections is quite simple and can be easily extended to any number of iterations. If Δs_i ($i = 1, \ldots, n$) are the individual steps in the transformation of the yield curve between 0 to 1, then one obtains:

$$s_1 = s_0 + \Delta s_1 + \Delta s_2 + \cdots + \Delta s_n = s_0 + \sum_{i=1}^{n} \Delta s_i. \tag{13.19}$$

The coupon and the roll-down effect remain unchanged and are not included in (13.19). The other (curve-based) effects in Section 13.2.2 can be generalized as follows:

$$\begin{aligned}
Eff_1 &= T(t_1, s_0 + \Delta s_1 + OAS_0) - T(t_1, s_0 + OAS_0),\\
Eff_2 &= T(t_1, s_0 + \Delta s_1 + \Delta s_2 + OAS_0) - T(t_1, s_0 + \Delta s_1 + OAS_0), \cdots,\\
Eff_k &= T(t_1, s_0 + \Delta s_1 + \Delta s_2 + \cdots + \Delta s_k + OAS_0)\\
&\quad - T\left(t_1, s_0 + \Delta s_1 + \Delta s_2 + \cdots + \Delta s_{k-1} + OAS_0\right)\\
&= T\left(t_1, s_0 + \sum_{j=1}^{k} \Delta s_j + OAS_0\right) - T\left(t_1, s_0 + \sum_{j=1}^{k-1} \Delta s_j + OAS_0\right), \cdots,\\
Eff_n &= T(t_1, s_1 + OAS_0) - T\left(t_1, s_0 + \sum_{j=1}^{n-1} \Delta s_j + OAS_0\right).
\end{aligned}$$

In this way, the yield curve effects are represented in the form of a telescopic sum.[36] The spread change effect remains unchanged:

$$Eff_{n+1} = T\left(t_1, s_1 + OAS_1\right) - T\left(t_1, s_1 + OAS_0\right).$$

In this approach, due to the progressive accumulation of the effects , the residual terms are integrated in the individual contributions. If one follows the procedure for the derivation of the Brinson terms for equity portfolios (Section 12.2), then an alternative approach (for $k=2, \ldots, n$) is given by:

$$\widetilde{Eff_k} = T\left(t_1, s_0 + \Delta s_k + OAS_0\right) - T\left(t_1, s_0 + OAS_0\right). \tag{13.20}$$

Based on the yield curve and the spread at time zero, only the substep k is added, which entails that the effect k is determined independently of the other effects. (The effects 1 and $n+1$ are identical in both cases.) A drawback to this analysis is, however, the appearance of interaction terms, which are defined as the differences between Eff_k and $\widetilde{Eff_k}$.

Example 13.6

Yield-curve based Analysis with a Separation of the Interaction Terms

Only minimal changes will result for the portfolio in Example 13.3, when applying this systematics: instead of 0.41% the twist effect here is 0.42%, and the entire structural effect is 0.55% instead of 0.54%.

This representation illustrates the options for an expansion of the analysis in regard to the spread change effects. Instead of using the simple Brinson approach, the breakdown can also be based on additional interest rate curves. For example, the spread change in a bond issued by a bank (against government bonds) can be further broken down relative to a swap curve and/or a curve representing the industry of the issuer.[37]

13.2.5 Generalization of Portfolios with Different Currency Segments

It is preferable not to base the calculation of the contributions defined in Section 13.2.4 on a single, globally applicable yield curve, but on several yield curves adjusted to the respective segments. For Eurozone bonds, for example, the Eurozone yield curve can be applied, for US $-denominated bonds, the Treasury curve, etc. The contributions of the individual segments can first be calculated separately based on local returns (without taking account of currency hedges) for each segment, and then be aggregated by using appropriate weighting factors. The analysis methods for currency effects are discussed in detail in Chapters 12 and 15. To illustrate the approach, therefore, here only local returns will be considered. In the following a portfolio will be considered with investments in N different currency zones. The weights are denoted by swp_i and the returns by srp_i^L (benchmark analog).[38]

[36] A related approach, based on the key rate durations, however, is described in Keller and Schlatter (1999).

[37] For a similar procedure see the approach by Lord in Section 13.4.2.

[38] It is only considered a period of decline.

The active return is thus as follows:

$$
\begin{aligned}
RP^L - RB^L
&= \sum_{i=1}^{N} swp_i{*}srp_i^L - swb_i{*}srb_i^L \\
&= \sum_{i=1}^{N} swb_i{*}\left(srp_i^L - srb_i^L\right) + \sum_{i=1}^{N}\left(swp_i - swb_i\right){*}srp_i^L \\
&= \underbrace{\sum_{i=1}^{N} swb_i{*}\left(srp_i^L - srb_i^L\right)}_{\text{Basis for the yield-curve analysis}} + \underbrace{\sum_{i=1}^{N}\left(swp_i - swb_i\right){*}srb_i^L}_{\text{market allocation}} + \underbrace{\sum_{i=1}^{N}\left(swp_i - swb_i\right){*}\left(srp_i^L - srb_i^L\right)}_{\text{interaction terms}}.
\end{aligned}
\tag{13.21}
$$

The differential of the returns in the first term can decomposed further by using suitable yield curves, according to the method described above. The second term measures the contribution from the market allocation. Here one can also return to the method based on the returns relative to the overall benchmark:

$$\sum_{i=1}^{N}\left(swp_i - swb_i\right){*}\left(srb_i^L - RB^L\right) \tag{13.22}$$

The third term contains the interaction terms, which reflects the interaction between the allocation decisions and the positioning in regard to the yield curve.

Example 13.7

Multi-Currency Portfolio Segments

In this example a portfolio is considered with investments in three currency segments (Euro, US $, Yen). The Euro components of the portfolio and the benchmark are identical to those in Example 13.5. Also, the analysis period is identical, so that the results can be copied from this example. The weighting of the individual blocks is shown in Table 13.15, in which also the local returns of the segments are listed. Currency effects will not be considered here. Table 13.16 contains the (unweighted) effects calculated according to the methodology described in Section 13.2.4.

Based on the terms in (13.21) (in conjunction with (13.22)), one obtains the results shown in Table 13.17.

The largest contribution to the active return of 1.21% resulted from the allocation of market weights (underweight position in the weakly performing Yen segment and the overweight position in the Euro segment). Except for the *spread change* effect, other effects have contributed relatively evenly to the positive result. Only for the Yen segment a significant interaction term is shown, which is due to the significant difference between the portfolio and the benchmark return in that segment.

In this approach, it is assumed that the effects caused by the change in interest rate and spread levels are calculated separately for each currency segment. In particular, it is assumed that there is no duration decision on the overall portfolio level and thus no leveraging of the exposure in regard to individual segments. The latter justifies the

Table 13.15 Weights and Local Returns (Values in %)

	Weight		Returns	
	Portfolio	Benchmark	Portfolio	Benchmark
Euro	60	40	7.26	7.10
US$	30	30	6.63	6.10
Yen	10	30	3.41	2.70
Total	100	100	6.69	5.48

Table 13.16 Effects for the Different Segments (Values in %)

	Roll-down	Coupon	Parallel	Structure	Spread	Total
Euro	0.17	0.05	−0.01	0.47	−0.51	0.17
US$	0.21	0.02	0.20	0.30	−0.20	0.53
Yen	0.10	0.01	0.10	0.20	0.30	0.71

Table 13.17 Weighted Effects for the Different Segments (Values in %)

	Roll-down	Coupon	Parallel	Structure	Spread	Allocation	Interaction	Total
Euro	0.07	0.02	0.00	0.19	−0.20	0.32	0.03	0.42
US$	0.06	0.01	0.06	0.09	−0.06	0.00	0.00	0.16
Yen	0.03	0.00	0.03	0.06	0.09	0.56	−0.14	0.63
Total	0.16	0.03	0.09	0.34	−0.17	0.88	−0.11	1.21

procedure for calculating the attribution contributions according to (13.21) and (13.22). A distinct methodology was introduced by van Breukelen.[39] An introduction to this (quite different) approach is given in Section 13.4.1.

13.3 INCLUSION OF MODELS FOR THE ESTIMATION OF YIELD CURVES

13.3.1 The Methods of Nelson and Siegel, And Svensson

The representation of the yield curves in Figure 13.1 was based on a simple method of linear interpolation between the nodes. In practice, however, other, more complex procedures are used, leading to smoother curves. The main application areas illustrate the central importance of these methods:

- Visualization and forecasting procedures at central banks
- Valuation of derivatives based on an arbitrage-free interest rate
- Valuation of coupon bonds

[39] See Van Breukelen (2000).

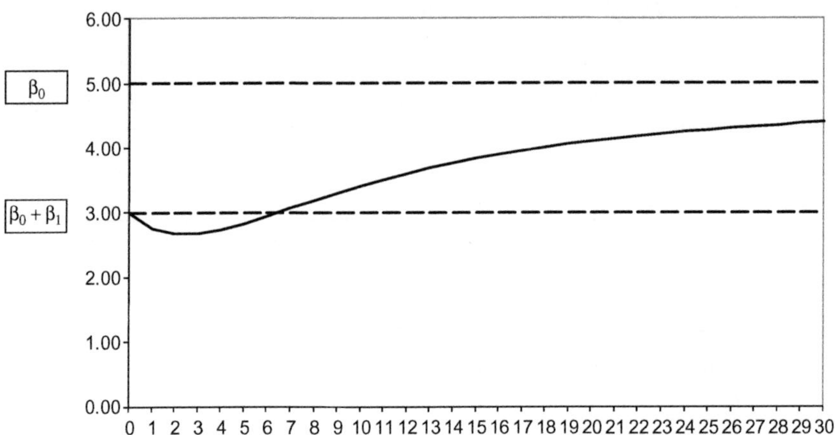

FIGURE 13.19
Yield Curve by Nelson and Siegel (with $\beta_0 = 5$, $\beta_1 = -2$, $\beta_2 = -4$ and $\tau = 3$).

- Fixed-income portfolio management
- Performance analysis

The best known methods, used by various central banks, are the polynomial method, and the methods introduced by Vasicek and Fong, Nelson and Siegel, and Svensson.[40] The method developed by Nelson and Siegel will be illustrated in detail, as it is quite relevant for practical applications in the field of attribution analysis.

Nelson and Siegel postulate the following model for the description of forward rates as a function of the different terms.[41]

$$f(t) = \beta_0 + \beta_1 * e^{-\frac{t}{\tau}} + \beta_2 * \frac{t}{\tau} * e^{-\frac{t}{\tau}} \tag{13.23}$$

The model provides the description of the yield curve by means of a simple integration:

$$\begin{aligned} s(t) &= \frac{1}{t} \int_0^t f(x)dx \\ &= \beta_0 + (\beta_1 + \beta_2) * \left(1 - e^{-\frac{t}{\tau}}\right) / (t/\tau) - \beta_2 * e^{-\frac{t}{\tau}} \\ &= \beta_0 + \beta_1 * \left(1 - e^{-\frac{t}{\tau}}\right) / (t/\tau) - \beta_2 * \left(\left(1 - e^{-\frac{t}{\tau}}\right) / (t/\tau) - e^{-\frac{t}{\tau}}\right). \end{aligned} \tag{13.24}$$

There are the constraints $\beta_0 > 0$, $\beta_0 + \beta_1 > 0$ and $\tau > 0$.

---

40 See Vasicek and Fong (1982), Svensson (1994) and Nelson and Siegel (1987). For a detailed presentation of methods for an estimation of yield curves, see the monograph by James and Webber (James and Webber (2000)).

41 See Nelson and Siegel (1987), where primarily the short end of the yield curve is considered.

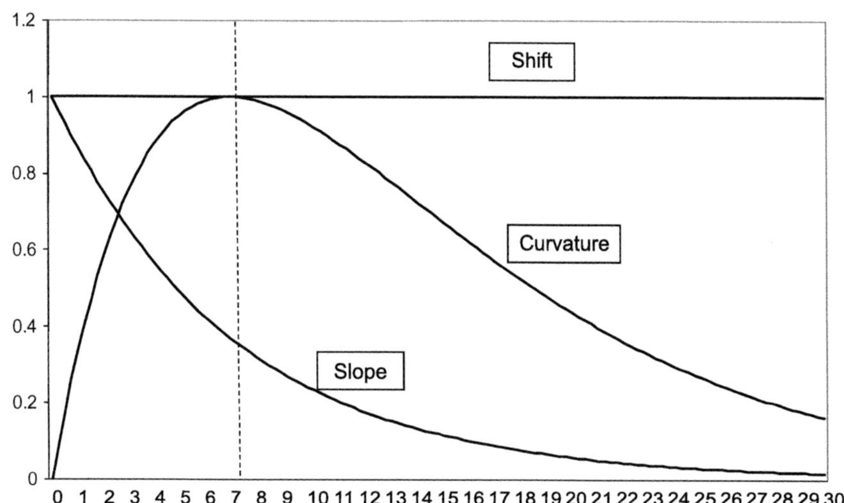

FIGURE 13.20
Nelson and Siegel Factors ($\tau = 7$).

β_0 corresponds to the long-term interest rate and $\beta_0 + \beta_1$ to the interest rate at $t=0$. Thus, β_1 represents the difference between long-and short-term interest rates. The position of the bulge is essentially determined by parameter τ and the height and the direction (up or down) by the parameter β_2 (cf. Figure 13.19).

Kuberek uses this approach for the definition of a factor model, which explains the *change* of the yield curve (see Section 13.2.5) based on a model for forward interest rates (13.23):

$$\Delta s(t) = \beta_0 + \beta_1 {*} e^{-\frac{t}{\tau}} + \beta_2 {*} \frac{t}{\tau} {*} e^{-\frac{t}{\tau}} \tag{13.25}$$

The first factor (*shift*) describes a uniform change in interest rates, the second (*slope*) a change in the slope or rotation, and the third (*curvature*) a change in the curvature of the yield curve. Figure 13.20 presents a graphical representation of these factors. An alternative approach to (13.25)—on which the following discussion is based – is given by

$$\Delta s(t) = (\beta_0 + \beta_1) + \beta_1 {*} \left(e^{-\frac{t}{\tau}} - 1\right) + \beta_2 {*} \frac{t}{\tau} {*} e^{-\frac{t}{\tau}} \tag{13.26}$$

In this representation $\beta_0 + \beta_1$ is to be regarded as a shift. It has the advantage that here the slope factor starts at zero.[42]

On the one hand the value of τ represents the maximum of the third factor, and on the other hand the decay rate for the second factor. Basically, this factor, as

[42] An equation of this form is also used in the Wilshire Axiom System (see for example Kuberek a and McCarthy (2003, p. 5).

well as the factors β_0, β_1 and β_2, is determined by applying suitable regression techniques. Due to its nonlinear form, these are quite involved. Thus, in practice, τ is often fixed *a priori*. Making a general statement about the choice of τ is difficult. Kuberek selected this factor so that a wide variety of different change scenarios can be illustrated by the three-factor model. According to Colin, the factor should be around 30% of the maximum term.[43]

Svensson extended Nelson and Siegel's model by introducing an additional exponential term with two additional parameters τ_2 and β_3. Thus, the shape of the forward rates can be described as follows:[44]

$$f(t) = \beta_0 + \beta_1 * e^{-\frac{t}{\tau_1}} + \beta_2 * \frac{t}{\tau_1} * e^{-\frac{t}{\tau_1}} + \beta_3 * \frac{t}{\tau_2} * e^{-\frac{t}{\tau_2}}. \qquad (13.27)$$

Through an integration similar to (13.24) one again obtains the shape of the yield curve:

$$s(t) = \beta_0 + \beta_1 * \left(1 - e^{-\frac{t}{\tau_1}}\right) / (t/\tau_1) - \beta_2 * \left(\left(1 - e^{-\frac{t}{\tau_1}}\right) / (t/\tau_1) - e^{-\frac{t}{\tau_1}}\right)$$
$$+ \beta_3 * \left(\left(1 - e^{-\frac{t}{\tau_2}}\right) / (t/\tau_2) - e^{-\frac{t}{\tau_2}}\right). \qquad (13.28)$$

The additional parameters open up the possibility to model an additional hump in the yield curve. In particular, this has advantages for the modeling of the volatile short end of the curve. However, the computational effort is considerably higher than for the Nelson and Siegel method.

Svensson's method is used, for example, by the Deutsche Bundesbank in modeling yield curves.[45]

With these approaches, it is possible to describe the characteristic movements of yield curves introduced at the beginning of this chapter in a quantitative form.

Example 13.8

Application of the Methods of Nelson and Siegel, and Svensson

Figure 13.21 shows the shape of the yield curve at 10/14 and 10/21/2008 for the different models. If one simply uses the method of linear interpolation (splines), then it becomes obvious that the curves have discontinuities, particularly at the short end. The striking elements are the comparatively high interest rates with maturities close to zero. The curves[46] produced by the Nelson and Siegel method have no such discontinuities. The approximation at the short end of the yield curve is, however, rather weak.

[43] See Colin (2005, p. 61).
[44] See Svensson (1994).
[45] For an overview of the methods used by various central banks, see Zimmeres and Hertlein (2007).
[46] The required parameters are determined by the method of least squares. For the sake of simplicity it was assumed that $\tau = 3.33$. The calculated parameters are $\beta_0 = 5.02$, $\beta_1 = -2.21$ and $\beta_2 = -0.26$ on 10/14, respectively $\beta_0 = 5.16$, $\beta_1 = -2.15$ and $\beta_2 = -1.72$ on 10/21.

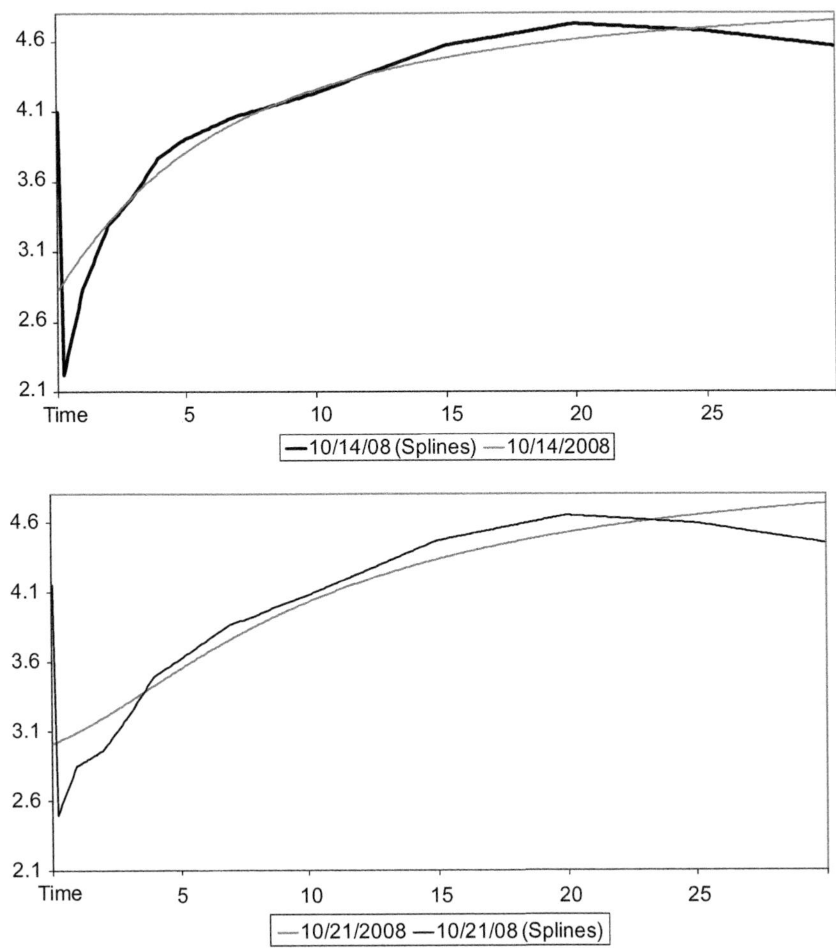

FIGURE 13.21
Yield Curves of the Eurozone at 10/14 and 10/21/2008 Determined with Linear Interpolation (Splines) and the Nelson and Siegel Method ($\tau = 3.33$).

Figure 13.22 illustrates the factor transitions separately. If one equips the parameter β_i with an additional index indicating the date of the computation (t_0 at the beginning of the period, t_1 at the end), then the transitions related to the expression in formula (13.24) are as follows:

$$\beta_0^{t_0} \to \beta_0^{t_1} + \beta_1^{t_1} - \beta_1^{t_0} \text{ ('shift')} \tag{13.29}$$

$$\beta_1^{t_0} * \left(1 - e^{-\frac{t}{\tau}}\right) / (t/\tau) \to \beta_1^{t_1} * \left(1 - e^{-\frac{t}{\tau}}\right) / (t/\tau) - \beta_1^{t_1} + \beta_1^{t_0} \text{ ("slope")} \tag{13.30}$$

$$\beta_2^{t_0} * \left(\left(1 - e^{-\frac{t}{\tau}}\right) / (t/\tau) - e^{-\frac{t}{\tau}}\right) \to \beta_2^{t_1} * \left(\left(1 - e^{-\frac{t}{\tau}}\right) / (t/\tau) - e^{-\frac{t}{\tau}}\right) \text{ ("curvature")} \tag{13.31}$$

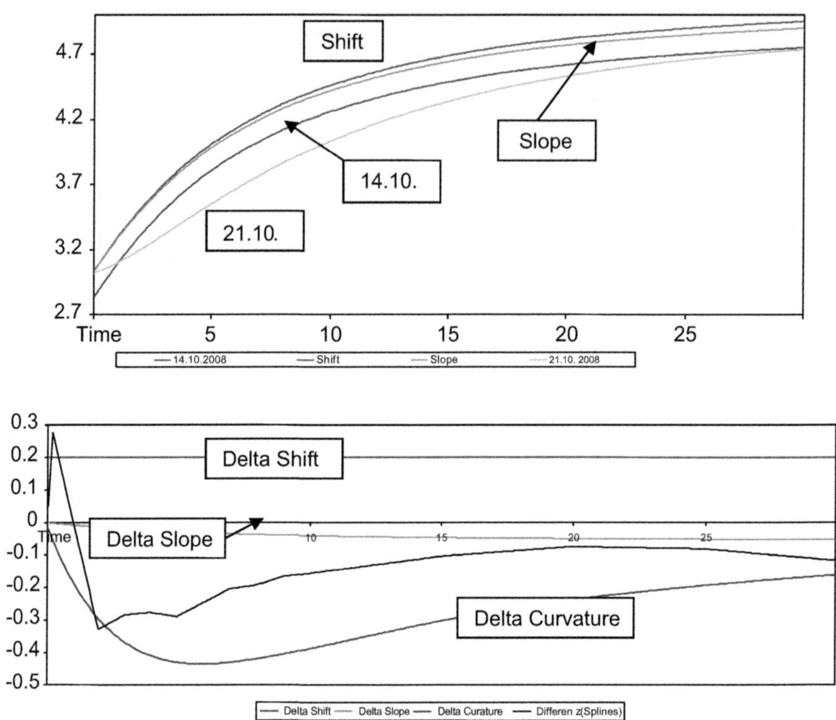

FIGURE 13.22
Illustration of the Shift and Slope. Factors the Lower Graph Demonstrates the Pure Effects.

Figure 13.23 shows of the yield curve estimated according to Svensson.[47] It is evident that due to the additional degree of freedom particularly the short end is far better approximated. This is underlined by Figure 13.24. It is striking that in this approximation the shift effect is negative. This is perhaps more intuitive than the positive effect in the case of Nelson and Siegel. It is also due to the better approximation at the short end of the yield curve. The last two terms in (13.28) are summarized under *curvature*.

The decomposition by Nelson and Siegel, respectively by Svensson can be transferred into an attribution analysis by means of the methodology described in Section 13.2.5. This entails, as shown graphically in Figure 13.24, that the telescopic breakdown is based on the respective (delta) curve terms. The definition of the transitions is analogous to (13.29)–(13.31). Again the lower half of the graph represents the pure effects.

---

[47] The calculation was performed again by using the method of least squares, where $\tau_1 = 3.33$ and $\tau_2 = 0.33$ were computed. The parameters are $\beta_0 = 5.03$, $\beta_1 = -0.15$, $\beta_2 = -1.82$ and $\beta_3 = -8.50$ as at 10/14, respectively $\beta_0 = 5.17$, $\beta_1 = -0.40$, $\beta_2 = -3.03$ and $\beta_3 = -7.20$ as at 10/21.

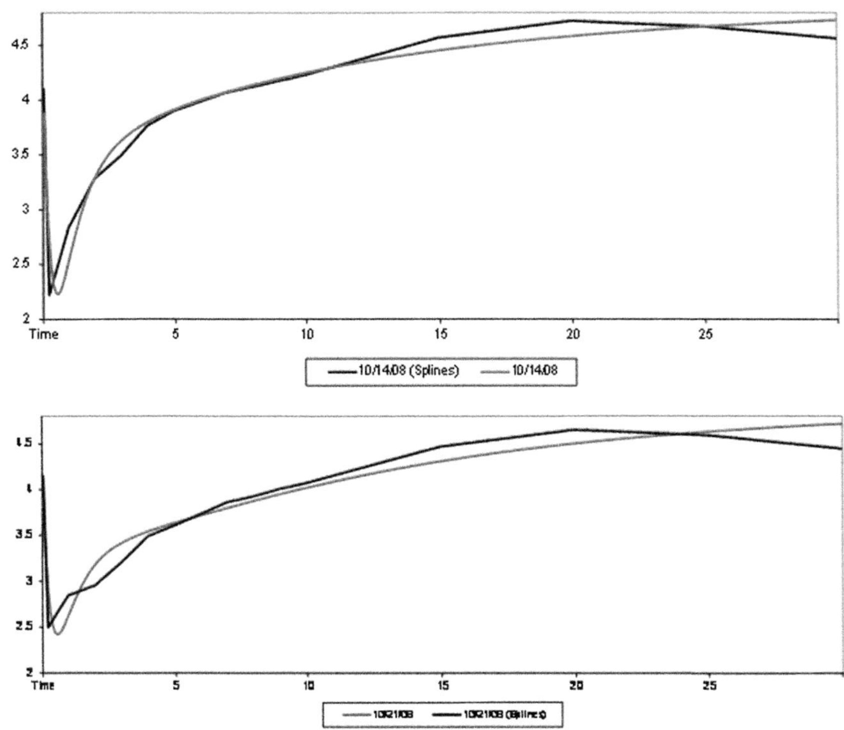

FIGURE 13.23
Yield curves of the Eurozone at 10/14 and 10/21/2008, Determined by Linear Interpolation (Spline) and Svensson's Method ($\tau_1 = 3.33$, $\tau_2 = 0.33$).

13.3.2 Principal Component Analysis

An important alternative method for determining characteristic analysis factors, used by MSCI Barra in particular, is Principal Component Analysis.[48] The idea behind this method is to attribute the change in interest rates in defined maturities to a limited number of fundamental factors. The change of the yield curve with m maturities is represented as follows:

$$\Delta s = (\Delta s(t_1), \Delta s(t_2), \cdots, \Delta s(t_m)) = \sum_{i=1}^{m} \Delta s(t_m) * e_i \qquad (13.32)$$

In which e_i represent the m basis vectors:

$$e_1 = (1, 0, \cdots, 0), \quad e_2 = (0, 1, 0, \cdots, 0) \text{ etc.}$$

[48] See Deutsch (2004, p. 615 et seq). For similar approaches see Litterman and Scheinkman (1991), Lehman (1996, p. 5 et seq), and Kahn (1991).

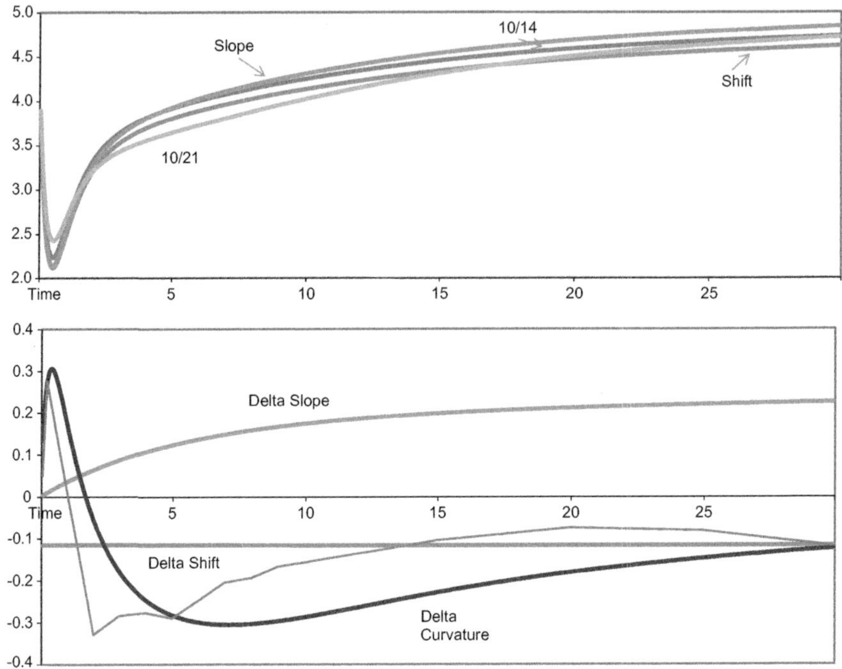

FIGURE 13.24
Yield Curves of the Eurozone at 14/10. and 10/21/2008, Determined by the Svensson Method ($\tau_1 = 3.33$, $\tau_2 = 0.33$). The graphs show the Shift and Slope factors (Top), As Well as the Shift, Slope, and Curvature Factors for the Transition Between the Yield Curves.

The new vectors $\widetilde{e}_i$ are determined by using Principal Component Analysis. This set of basis vectors, is orthonormal (i.e., the vectors are normalized such that two different vectors are orthogonal to each other). These vectors represent typical movements of the yield curve. Vector $\widetilde{e}_1$ explains the highest share of the observed variance, vector $\widetilde{e}_2$ the second highest, and so on. Due to the high correlation between interest rate movements in different terms (interest rates for bonds with a three-year maturity behave in most cases much like the interest rates with a two- or four-year maturity, etc.), in practice, it is sufficient to consider just a few factors. In general, one takes the first three factors into account: *shift, twist* and *butterfly* (see Figure 13.25):

$$\Delta s = \sum_{i=1}^{m} w_i{*}\widetilde{e}_i \approx w_1{*}\widetilde{e}_1 + w_2{*}\widetilde{e}_2 + w_3{*}\widetilde{e}_3 \qquad (13.33)$$

This clearly means that a given movement of the yield curve can be replicated to a high degree by the movement $\widetilde{e}_1$ (scaled by w_1). A consideration of $\widetilde{e}_2$ leads to a further approximation, and with $\widetilde{e}_3$ often a reasonable degree of accuracy already will have been achieved.[49]

[49] See e.g. Buhler and Zimmermann (1996) for an examination of changes in interest rates in Germany and Switzerland.

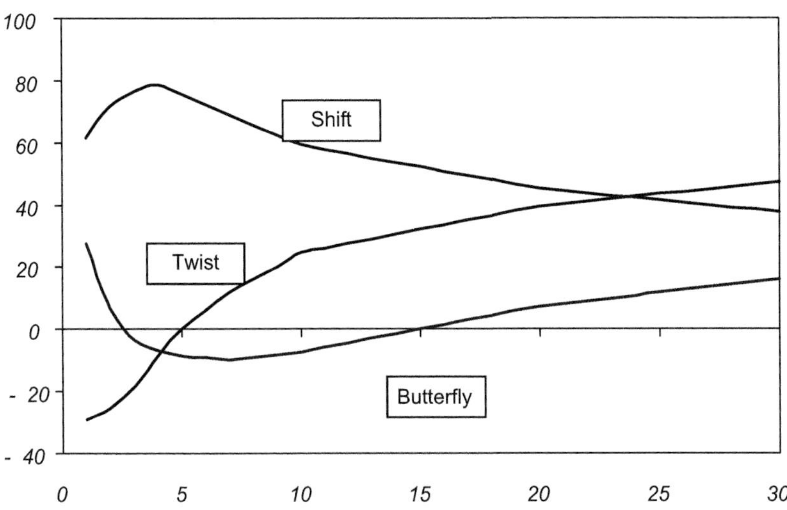

FIGURE 13.25
Main Components of the Yield Curve Movement of German Government Bonds.

There is a certain parallel to the method of Nelson and Siegel described above. However, here the *shift* factor represents no uniform change in interest rates, since interest rates of shorter terms are clearly more significantly changed than those for the longer maturities. The *butterfly* factor describes a reverse movement of the long and short term interest rates on the one hand and the medium term interest rates on the other hand. The effect of the second factor (*twist*), similiar to the *slope* factor, can be interpreted as an approximate rotation, but with a different center of rotation. It should also be emphasized that the results of a Principal Component Analysis are strongly dependent on the underlying observation period and the specific yield curve. For the Japanese yield curve, for instance, one obtains quite different factors than for the US-American treasury curve. These points—the fuzzy meaning of the factors and the dependency on the underlying data—are often listed as negative aspects of this method.

The above decomposition can be incorporated into the analysis method illustrated in Section 13.2 analogous to the considerations in Section 13.2.5. It is only necessary to determine and measure the parameters w_1, w_2 and w_3 for each sub-period. The additional Δs_i can then be determined according to (13.33), and the additional effects are then calculated as the terms of the telescoping sum.[50]

[50] The calculation of the *Wilshire Axiom* System is nevertheless different. Here the returns of the factors are determined by a factor analysis. The contributions follow from the sensitivities of the individual factors plus an income term (see Kuberek b).

13.4 ALTERNATIVE APPROACHES

13.4.1 Consideration of Reference Portfolios

13.4.1.1 *VAN BREUKELEN APPROACH*

In addition to the methods presented in Section 13.2, which were based on the gradual valuation of individual instruments, there is another, slightly less involved methodology that is based on the auxiliary portfolios corresponding to the investment process (as in the Brinson approach). A well-known example is the method presented in van Breukelen's article, which is used in the Dutch investment company Robeco.[51] It is based on a top–down investment approach: first, at the level of the total portfolio, a total duration (across the currency areas) is set. Based on this, weighting and duration decisions are made in regard to the local markets[52], and finally the selection decisions are implemented. The methodology aims to quantify the effects caused by the changing interest rates by means of the sensitivities (modified durations). For a single bond van Breukelen stipulates the following relationship:

$$rp = r + D*(-\Delta y); \tag{13.34}$$

Here r represents the return corresponding to the risk-free investment, D the modified duration, and Δy the (initially undetermined) change in market interest rates. Since the expression on the left-hand side can be observed independently, van Breukelen uses this equation to determine Δy:

$$\Delta y = -\frac{rp - r}{D}. \tag{13.35}$$

The total return of a portfolio consisting of n segments is given by:[53]

$$RP = \sum_{i=1}^{n} swp_i * \left(srp_i^L + c_i\right),$$

where c_i is the currency return of the currency i. There is an analogous expression for the benchmark. If one assumes that the currency returns are identical for the portfolio and benchmark segments, then (analogous to (13.34)) the active return , can be written in the following form:

---

[51] See van Breukelen (2000).

[52] According to van Breukelen, these markets are determined by the currency. They could also be formed by term segments.

[53] As in the article by van Breukelen the interaction terms will be neglected.

$$
\begin{aligned}
RP - RB &= \sum_{i=1}^{n} swp_i * \left(srp_i^L + c_i\right) - \sum_{i=1}^{n} swb_i * \left(srb_i^L + c_i\right) \\
&= \sum_{i=1}^{n} swp_i * \left(srp_i^L - r_i\right) \\
&\quad + \sum_{i=1}^{n} swp_i * (r_i + c_i) - \sum_{i=1}^{n} swb_i * \left(srb_i^L - r_i\right) - \sum_{i=1}^{n} swb_i * (r_i + c_i) \\
&= \sum_{i=1}^{n} swp_i * D_{P_i} * (-\Delta y)_{P_i} - \sum_{i=1}^{n} swb_i * D_{BM_i} * (-\Delta y)_{BM_i} \\
&\quad + \sum_{i=1}^{n} \left(swp_i - swb_i\right) * (r_i + c_i).
\end{aligned}
\tag{13.36}
$$

From the last term of the expression on the right-hand side van Breukelen derives the currency contribution (similarly to Karnosky and Singer[54]):

$$
\sum_{i=1}^{n} \left(swp_i - swb_i\right) * \left(r_i + c_i - \overline{r_i + c_i}\right),
$$

in which:

$$
\overline{r_i + c_i} := \sum_{i=1}^{n} swb_i * (r_i + c_i).
$$

The other contributions are derived from the first two terms of the expression on the right-hand side of (13.36). For this the overall duration of both the portfolio and the benchmark (D_P or D_{BM}), as well as the average change in interest rates on the benchmark side, ($(-\Delta y)_{BM}$) are needed:

$$
\begin{aligned}
&\sum\nolimits_{i=1}^{n} swp_i * D_{P_i} * (-\Delta y)_{P_i} - \sum_{i=1}^{n} swb_i * D_{BM_i} * (-\Delta y)_{BM_i} \\
&= \sum_{i=1}^{n} \left(swb_i * D_{BM_i} * \frac{D_P}{D_{BM}} - swb_i * D_{BM_i} \right) * (-\Delta y)_{BM_i} \\
&\quad + \sum_{i=1}^{n} \left(swp_i * D_{P_i} - swb_i * D_{BM_i} * \frac{D_P}{D_{BM}} \right) * \left((-\Delta y)_{BM_i} - (-\Delta y)_{BM}\right) \\
&\quad + \sum_{i=1}^{n} swp_i * D_{P_i} * \left((-\Delta y)_{P_i} - (-\Delta y)_{BM_i}\right).
\end{aligned}
$$

[54] See Section 15.1.1.2.

A slight transformation provides the following breakdown:

$$\underbrace{\sum_{i=1}^{n}\left(swb_i{*}\frac{D_P}{D_{BM}}-swb_i\right){*}D_{BM_i}{*}(-\Delta y)_{BM_i}}_{\text{Overall duration effect}}$$
$$+\underbrace{\sum_{i=1}^{n}\left(swp_i{*}\frac{D_{P_i}}{D_{BM_i}}-swb_i{*}\frac{D_P}{D_{BM}}\right){*}D_{BM_i}{*}\left((-\Delta y)_{BM_i}-(-\Delta y)_{BM}\right)}_{\text{Market allocation}}$$
$$+\underbrace{\sum_{i=1}^{n}swp_i{*}D_{P_i}{*}\left((-\Delta y)_{P_i}-(-\Delta y)_{BM_i}\right).}_{\text{Selection}} \tag{13.37}$$

Van Breukelen's approach is thus based on scaling the weights with appropriate factors to achieve comparability from the point of view of duration leverage. Thus, the method is based on factor weights. The *overall duration effect* quantifies the effect that one would achieve, if the duration factor changed gradually, while the benchmark segments remained unchanged.[55] In the term *market attribution effect* (the analogue to the allocation contribution in Brinson's analysis) the weights are also scaled by the relative duration factor, so that the benchmark weights are evenly adjusted to the portfolio level.

In van Breukelen's article the form of selection contribution is illustrated as follows: he considers a portfolio and a benchmark with only one bond each. The bonds are assumed to have the same duration but different returns. It is assumed further that the return of the portfolio is higher than the benchmark return. If one assumes in addition that the returns are identical to the internal rates of return, then this would also correspond to a larger factor $-\Delta y$ on the part of the portfolio. Via the transition to these factors (13.35), the return is then replaced by the duration-adjusted return in the traditional Brinson terms.

Example 13.9

van Breukelen Analysis

Table 13.18 contains the basic data for a fixed income portfolio, which consists of three currency segments.

The values in the column interest rate change follow from the other data by means of (13.35).

Dominant among the results shown in Table 13.19 is the *overall duration effect* contribution at 1.04%. Also, the selection contributions are remarkable. The positive contribution of the US $ segment highlights spread narrowing, the negative contributions in other segments reflecting spread widening.

---

[55] Theoretically, one thus acquires $swb_i{*}D_P/D_{BM}$ units of weight in one segment. However, in practice, such duration decisions are usually implemented through derivatives (bond futures).

Table 13.18 Portfolio and Benchmark Data (Values in %)

	Weighting		Duration		Local Return		Interest Rate Change Δy			
	Portfolio	BM	Portfolio	BM	Portfolio	BM	Portfolio	BM	Currency	Risk-Free Interest Rate
Euro	50	30	7.0	4.0	8.0	6.0	−0.9	−1.0	0.0	2.0
US$	20	30	5.0	6.0	7.0	5.0	−1.2	−0.7	2.0	1.0
Yen	30	40	6.0	5.0	5.0	6.0	−0.5	−0.8	3.0	2.0
Total	100	100	6.3	5.0				−0.8	1.8	1.7

Table 13.19 Attribution Analysis According to Van Breukelen (Values in %)

	Total Duration	Market Attribution	Selection	Currency	Sum
Euro	0.31	0.36	−0.30	−0.30	0.07
US$	0.31	−0.15	0.80	0.05	1.01
Yen	0.42	−0.04	−0.72	−0.15	−0.49
Sum	1.04	0.17	−0.22	−0.40	0.59

Van Breukelen's method represents an interesting alternative to the more accurate valuation-based procedures, because it is relatively easy to implement. However, it does not offer the possibility of a further breakdown of the structural effects. This is a significant limitation, since duration decisions implemented through a bond future will always have an impact on the structural effects.[56] Further, the postulated relationship between the local return and the duration is only an approximation.

13.4.1.2 MCLAREN APPROACH

McLaren has described a method in which the Brinson et al. model is generalized by incorporating an appropriate yield curve.[57] In the following the procedure will be outlined for a portfolio, whose titles are denominated in a single currency.

The central idea is to set the returns of individual maturity classes of the portfolio and its benchmark in relation to the return determined by the yield curve. To describe this in detail, the returns for the term classes (or duration classes), as calculated on the basis of the yield curve, are denominated by sry_i $(i = 1, \cdots, n)$.[58] $\overline{sry}$ indicates

[56] Cf. the discussion in Section 15.2.4.

[57] See McLaren (2002). Here also the general case of a portfolio with different currency segments is discussed.

[58] For practical purposes the (synthetic) bonds may be placed in the middle of the maturity bands and their returns may be estimated by the change of the yield curve.

Table 13.20 Attribution Analysis According to McLaren

Contributions	Formula
Duration	$Du_i^{ML} := (swp_i - swb_i) * (sry_i - \overline{sry})$
Spread	$Spread_i^{ML} := (swp_i - swb_i) * (srb_i - sry_i)$
Selection	$Selection_i^{ML} := swb_i * (srp_i - srb_i)$
Interaction	$IT_i^{ML} := (swp_i - swb_i) * (srp_i - srb_i)$

Table 13.21 Results of the Analysis (Values in %)

Remaining Term	Yield Curve	Contributions				
		Total	Duration	Spread	Selection	Interaction
[0.0.1.5)	2.66	−0.22	0.58	0.03	0.07	−0.06
[1.5.2.5)	4.11	−0.56	0.57	−0.02	0.00	0.00
[2.5.3.5)	5.45	−0.05	0.03	0.00	0.00	0.00
[3.5.4.5)	6.52	0.77	−0.23	0.01	0.00	0.00
[4.5.5.5)	7.26	0.84	−0.14	0.00	0.00	0.00
[5.5.6.5)	7.72	2.08	−0.22	−0.27	0.01	0.07
[6.5.7.5)	7.98	−0.76	0.04	−0.09	−0.76	0.76
[7.5.8.5)	8.10	−0.52	0.02	−0.02	−0.06	0.01
[8.5.9.5)	8.15	−1.16	0.04	−0.18	0.00	0.00
>=9.5	9.33	−0.27	−0.03	0.00	0.0 0	0.00
Total		0.16	0.66	−0.54	−0.74	0.78

the average of these returns. Otherwise the notation of the Brinson approach, introduced in Section 12.2, is carried over to the maturity segments (Table 13.20).

The selection and intesaction terms are apparently formally identical to the Brinson terms defined in Section 12.2. The duration term approximately summarizes the contributions (*structural, parallel*) resulting from the change in interest the rate structure.

Example 13.10

Attribution Analysis According to McLaren Approach

The portfolio previously investigated in Example 13.1 and Example 13.5 is considered again. Table 13.21 lists the return contributions, calculated according to the formulas in Table 13.20.

A comparison with the results reported in Table 13.13 demonstrates that the total *structure* and *spread* contributions are nearly identical.[59] The discrepancies are partly due to the fact that under the method described in Section 13.2, the interest rate effects and the roll-down/pull-to-par effect are spun off. The problem of selection and residual contributions has already been discussed in Example 13.1. If one combines the interaction terms and the selection contributions (see the remarks in Example 13.1), then one obtains an (insignificant) selection contribution of 0.04%.

It should also be noted that the parallel contribution in this example is approximately zero (Table 13.13), so that the duration contribution coincides roughly with the structural contribution in Table 13.13. This will, however, not be the case in general.[60]

As the example highlights, McLaren's approach has more similarities with the one described in Section 13.2 than with the one by van Breukelen. With the latter it has in common that the required set of data is limited. However, in neither approach are the effects of the passage of time clearly separated.

13.4.2 Duration-Based Approaches

In practice, other models are employed, which quantify the essential contributions through sensitivities (durations) (in a simpler form as described in the previous models). Their advantage is that they are usually easy to implement. A well-known model—that of Lord—is discussed below.[61]

The principal idea of Lord's approach is similar to that of the model described in Section 13.2. Lord, however, avoids the (involved) evaluation of all the bonds, by assigning to each bond in the portfolio and its benchmark (via the duration) an appropriate government bond (*duration-matched Treasury* (DMT)), by which he estimates the curve and spread effects[62].

The DMT is defined as a synthetic government bond (with no rights of termination) with a duration identical to the duration of the bond to which it is assigned at the beginning of the observation period. It is derived from the *par yield curve* of government bonds.[63]

Figure 13.26 illustrated the effects of Lord's attribution analysis. The excess return is defined as the difference between the total return of the bond and its associated DMT. The total return is broken down into an income component (coupon / accrued interest) and a price component (similar to Section 13.2). The breakdown of the latter is also comparable to that in Section 13.2. The yield curve induced component of the return, referred to by Lord as the *duration return*, is split into a

---

[59] The structural effect must be compared with the duration effect in the McLaren analysis (see above).

[60] Although McLaren's example explicitly shows a duration term, he does not indicate how this is precisely defined. Presumably, it is based on the average of the individual duration contributions.

[61] See Lord (1997). For simpler approaches, in which the calculation of the effects is also based on the duration, see Geske (2001) and Campisi (2000).

[62] Lord's approach is based on the *effective duration*.

[63] See Section 13.1.1.1.

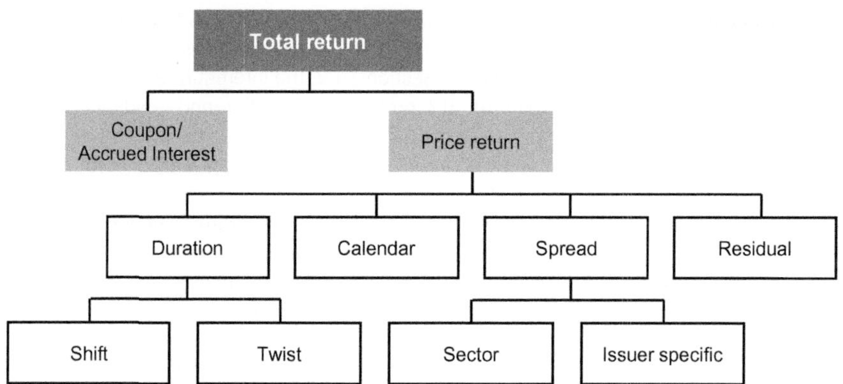

FIGURE 13.26
Attributions Model According to Lord (*Source:* (Lord 1997, p. 47)).

parallel and a structural component (*shift and twist return*). In addition, a spread-induced return is reported, which in turn is broken down into a sector-induced and a specific component. There is furthermore a residual contribution.

The formulas for the return effects in Table 13.22 are again emphasizing the similarity with the model[64] described in Section 13.2. According to Lord the required cells for the return effect *sector* are formed based on the bonds of an index: corporate bonds are allocated to the corporate bonds sector, *collateralized mortgage obligations* to the mortgage sector, etc. Within the sector, there is a subdivision according to the duration and quality (rating).

Therefore, in general terms, the Lord model (as the approach in Section 13.2 and in contrast to van Breukelen's or McLaren's methodology) is a "bottom-up" model, as all the effects are determined for each bond individually. The results can then be aggregated in various ways by computing market-value weighted averages at the portfolio level. Lord regards this flexibility a decisive advantage of his method. Since the calculation methodology is relatively simple, it shall suffice here to refer to the examples in Lord's paper.

Another approach is based on the use of *key rate durations* instead of the *effective duration*.[65] Such an approach is used by the firm *MSCI Barra* in their system *Barra Enterprise Performance*.[66] Based on the key rate durations KRD_i (i represents the term) the following return on an exposure basis is calculated for a bond:

$$R_j = \sum_{i=1}^{N} -KRD_i * \Delta r_i, \tag{13.38}$$

[64] In a way, Lord's method is a simplified version of the method in Section 13.2, with the important difference that it does not allow for a more detailed analysis of the curve effects.

[65] See Appendix D to this chapter.

[66] See the discussion in Davis (2005).

Table 13.22 Contributions of Attribution Analysis, According to Lord

Return effect $= -D * \Delta y$

Duration	$\Delta y = y_{DMT,t} - y_{DMT,t-1}$	Change of the internal rate of return of the DMT
Shift	$\Delta y = y^{PC}_{5y,t} - y^{PC}_{5y,t-1}$	Change of interest rate on the par yield curve at $t = 5$ years
Spread	$\Delta y = S_{DMT,t} - S_{DMT,t-1}$	Change in spread between the bond and its DMT
Sector	$\Delta y = OAS_{i,t} - OAS_{i,t-1}$	Average change in the OAS of the indexed bonds in the cell to which the bond is assigned

in which Δr_i represents the change in the prime rate (key rate) in the term i. The bonds are marked with the index j. Based on this estimate (the equation holds only approximately for small Δr_i) a parallel effect can be defined as:

$$R_{j,par} = \sum_{i=1}^{N} -KRD_i * \Delta r_{par}, \tag{13.39}$$

that is by replacing the variable interest rate changes with a constant rate change, Δr_{par}, which can be defined in agreement with the investment process.[67] The contributions from the non-parallel shift in the yield curve are calculated as the difference between Equations (13.38) and (13.39).

The calculation of the contributions not induced by the yield curve is carried out by a modified Brinson model, where the weights are replaced by contributions to the spread (spread duration × weight) and returns by returns per unit of spread duration.

APPENDIX: DURATION MEASURES

A Macauley Duration

An important measure for the determination of the risk of a bond portfolio is the Macauley Duration. In order to introduce this measure and to derive an interpretation, first the present value of a bond with corresponding payments Z_{t_j} will be considered. It is assumed that the bond holder receives annual payments (coupon, nominal) Z_{t_1}, Z_{t_2}, etc. In case of N (annual) payments the present value K is as follows:

$$K = \frac{Z_{t_1}}{1+s} + \frac{Z_{t_2}}{(1+s)^2} + \cdots + \frac{Z_{t_N}}{(1+s)^N} = \sum_{j=1}^{N} \frac{Z_{t_j}}{(1+s)^j}. \tag{13.40}$$

[67] In practice, views on how the spread change shall be defined, which enters the definition of the parallel shift, vary considerably. In addition to the approaches, which are based on an average of the displacements of key rates, there is also the variant where the spread change is linked to on a fixed term (like Lord's approach).

Macauley Duration[68]

The Macauley Duration D is a measure for the price change δR, which results from an unexpected shift in the yield curve[69]. It holds:

$$\delta R = \frac{dK}{K} = -D * \Delta s, \text{ where } \Delta s := \frac{d(1+s)}{1+s}. \tag{13.41}$$

The mathematical unit of the Macauley duration is years.

To simplify the formalism, it was assumed that there is no accrued interest at the given point in time. Z_{t_N} includes the redemption payment of the bond. By means of the discount factor s the (standard) assumption for the derivation of the formula for the Macauley Duration becomes evident: the consideration is based on a parallel (flat) interest rate curve, i.e., all spot rates are assumed equal.

Example 13.11

Sensitivity of zero-coupon bond

In this example a zero-coupon bond will be considered with a time to maturity of 5 years and a nominal payment of 150€. The discount rate s shall be equal to 5%. The price K of the zero-coupon bond (= present value) is then given by:

$$K = \frac{150}{1.05^5} = 117.53.$$

How does the price of this bond react to changes in the market rates? Two scenarios will be considered by means of example.

Scenario 1 (Rising interest rates): Assuming that the flat interest rate curve is shifted parallel upward by +1% (s = 6%), one obtains:

$$K = \frac{150}{1.06^5} = 112.09.$$

The price of the bond thus falls by 5.44€, or by 4.63%. Approximately it holds $\Delta s \approx 0.01/1.05$ and thus $D \approx 4.63 * 1.05 = 4.86$.

Scenario 2 (Falling interest rates): Assuming that the flat interest rate curve is shifted parallel downward by −1% (s = 4%), one obtains:

$$K = \frac{150}{1.04^5} = 123.29.$$

The price of the bond rises thus by 5.76€ or by 4.90%. It holds $\Delta s \approx -0.01/1.05$ and thus $D \approx 4.90 * 1.05 = 5.15$.

---

[68] Cf. Elton and Gruber (1995, Chapter 21). The transition to the second order in Equation (13.41) leads to a more exact relationship of the price changes as a function of changes in the interest rate level. The corresponding sensitivity is called convexity.

[69] The definition implies that the relationship only holds for infinitesimal shifts and under the assumption of a flat yield curve. Even though this assumption is hardly ever fulfilled in praxis, the measure is quite popular in practice.

An unexpected change in the interest rate by ±1% thus leads to a change in the price of the bond by ∓5∗Δs%.

The precise value of the Macauley duration is indeed $D = 5$, as will be shown in following computation. Based on:

$$K = 150*(1+s)^{-5}$$

the chain rule for derivatives yields:

$$\frac{dK}{d(1+s)} = \frac{dK}{ds} = -5*150*(1+s)^{-6},$$

and thus:

$$dK = -5*150*(1+s)^{-5}*\frac{ds}{1+s} = -5*K*\Delta s.$$

A comparison with the defining Equation (13.41) yields $D=5$ years.

The above calculation can easily be generalized to the case of an arbitrary zero-coupon bond.

For a zero-coupon bond the Macauley duration is identical to the time to maturity.

In the following the general case of a bond with a time to maturity of N years and annual coupon payments will be considered. In order to keep the considerations as simple as possible, the observation date will be chosen such that there is no accrued interest. According to Equation (13.40) one obtains:

$$K = \sum_{j=1}^{N} Z_{t_j} * (1+s)^{-j}.$$

Using again the chain rule one obtains:

$$\frac{dK}{ds} = \sum_{j=1}^{N} -j*Z_{t_j} * (1+s)^{-j-1},$$

and thus:

$$dK = \sum_{j=1}^{N} -j*Z_{t_j} * (1+s)^{-j}*\frac{d(1+s)}{1+s}.$$

A division by K leads to:

$$\delta R = \frac{dK}{K} = -\frac{\sum_{j=1}^{N} j*Z_{t_j}*(1+s)^{-j}}{\sum_{j=1}^{N} Z_{t_j}*(1+s)^{-j}}*\Delta s.$$

From this equation the well-known formula for the Macauley duration can be derived:

$$D = \frac{\sum_{j=1}^{N} j*Z_{t_j}*(1+s)^{-j}}{\sum_{j=1}^{N} Z_{t_j}*(1+s)^{-j}}. \tag{13.42}$$

If one writes Equation (13.42) in the form:

$$D = \sum_{j=1}^{N} j * w_{t_j}, \tag{13.43}$$

where

$$w_{t_j} = \frac{Z_{t_j} * (1+s)^{-j}}{\sum_{i=1}^{N} Z_{t_i} * (1+s)^{-i}}, \tag{13.44}$$

then it becomes obvious, that the Macauley Duration may be interpreted as the weighted average maturity of cash flows. The Macauley duration is always smaller than the time to maturity of the bond. Since, as has already been mentioned, the assumption of a parallel interest rate curve is usually not fulfilled in practice, one often identifies s with the internal rate of return.

Factors with an impact on the duration:[71]

1. An increase of the coupon on the account of nominal (with constant discount rate and constant time to maturity) leads to a decrease of the duration.
2. An increase of the nominal on the account of the coupon (with constant discount rate and constant time to maturity) leads to an increase of the duration.
3. An increase of the discount rate s (with constant coupon, constant nominal and constant time to maturity) leads to a decrease of the duration.
4. An increase of the time to maturity N (with constant coupon, constant nominal, and constant discount rate) leads to an increase of the duration.

Example 13.12

Duration of a German treasury bond

On 02.06.2009 a German treasury bond with a maturity date of 20.06.2016 and an (annual) coupon of 6% was priced at 116.85% with a corresponding yield of 3.25%. The time to maturity was 7.05 years. On this date the present value of the bond was approximately given by:[70]

$$6\% * (1.0325)^{-1} + 6\% * (1.0325)^{-2} + \cdots + 106\% * (1.0325)^{-7} = 116.97\%,$$

in agreement with the actual price of the bond. Furthermore:

$$6\% * (1.0325)^{-1} + 2 * 6\% * (1.0325)^{-2} + \cdots + 7 * 106\% * (1.0325)^{-7} = 702.98\%,$$

so that according to Equation (13.42) the Macauley Duration is approximately given by $D = 702.98/\ 116.97$ years $= 6.01$ years.

[70] The accrued interest is neglected.

[71] Cf. Uhlir and Steiner (1994, Section 2.6.6).

Next, the duration concept will be applied to a bond portfolio.

Macauley Duration for a Bond Portfolio[72]

The Macauley Duration D_P of a bond portfolio is the weighted average of the Macauley duration over the M bonds contained in the portfolio:

$$D_P = \sum_{i=1}^{M} w_i * D_i, \tag{13.45}$$

with

w_i : weight of the bond i in the portfolio

D_i : duration of the bond i in the portfolio.

This is still based on the usage of a uniform interest rate level.[73]

The duration of a portfolio is a measure of the *absolute* risk, since it measures the sensitivity of the portfolio's net asset value to an (unexpected) *small* shift in the interest rates. In practice one usually assumes a relative perspective, as a portfolio manager's performance is usually compared to a benchmark. In order to limit the tracking error, the portfolio manager often has to obey certain duration limits.

B Modified Duration

There are many more duration measures. Of particular importance is the *Modified Duration* D_{mod}. It is defined by:

$$D_{\text{mod}} = -\frac{1}{K} * \frac{dK}{ds}, \tag{13.46}$$

so that the price change of a bond resulting from an unexpected shift in the yield curve is given by:[74]

$$\delta R = \frac{dK}{K} = -D_{\text{mod}} * ds. \tag{13.47}$$

The modified duration follows from the Macauley Duration after a division by $1+s$:

$$D_{\text{mod}} = \frac{D}{1+s}.$$

---

[72] Cf. Elton and Gruber (1995, Chapter 21). The duration of a composite may be defined similarly.

[73] Cf. in some detail Deutsch (2004, p. 81et seq.)

[74] For the sake of completeness, it shall be pointed out that $K * D_{\text{mod}}$ is sometimes called the absolute duration or Dollar duration (cf. Albrecht and Maurer (2008, p. 442).

Thus one can multiply the (modified) duration directly by the (infinitesimal) interest rate change ds instead of by the factor $\Delta s := \frac{d(1+s)}{1+s}$. For the bond in Example 13.12 the modified Duration equals 5.82 years.

C Effective Duration

A special case is given by bonds that are equipped with one or several termination rights of the issuer or the bond holder (call or put). The calculation of the duration requires specific valuation models for these options. The *effective duration* represents a discrete approximation:

$$D_{effective} = \frac{K_- - K_+}{2*K_0*\Delta s}. \tag{13.48}$$

K_- and K_+ represent the prices after an increase/decrease of the interest rate level by $-\Delta s$ respectively Δs. (In the following Δs will be considered as a finite shift of the interest rate level.) K_0 is the original price of the bond. For the computation of K_- und K_+ a valuation model for the options (e.g. a binominal model) is required.[75] The usage of the term duration is not uniform. If one uses in Equation (13.42) instead of a constant interest rate the effectively given interest rate curve, then the resulting duration measure is also known as the *effective duration*:[76]

$$D_{effective} = \frac{\sum_{j=1}^{N} j*Z_{t_j}*(1+s_j)^{-j}}{\sum_{j=1}^{N} Z_{t_j}*(1+s_j)^{-j}}. \tag{13.49}$$

The further assumptions made for the Macauley Duration – i.e.: sensitivity to a parallel shift, small shifts only – must be also made here. For a parallel shift the following relationship must hold:[77]

$$\frac{ds_1}{1+s_1} = \frac{ds_2}{1+s_2} = \cdots = \frac{ds_N}{1+s_N}. \tag{13.50}$$

D Key Rate Duration

With the so-called *key rate durations* the assumption in regard to a horizontal interest rate curve with a parallel shift is waived. The key rate duration in regard to the key rate i represents the sensitivity of the bond price in regard to a change of this rate:[78]

$$KRD_i = -\frac{1}{K}*\frac{\partial K}{\partial s_i}. \tag{13.51}$$

From this definition it follows immediately that key rate durations of a portfolio are given by the present-value weighted sum of the key rate durations of the

[75] Cf. in detail Fabozzi (2000, p. 353 et seq.).
[76] Cf. Bühler and Hies (1995). This measure is also called *Fisher-Weil* or *Macauley-Weil Duration* (cf. Bacon (2008, p. 105) and Albrecht and Maurer (2008, p. 492).
[77] Cf. Bühler and Hies op. cit., footnote 4.
[78] Cf. Bühler and Hies, op. cit.

Table 13.23 Computation of the Key Rate Durations by Means of Equation (13.54)

Key Rates	Spot Rates	Payments	Discounted payments	Key Rate Durations
1	0.91	6	5.95	0,05
2	1.41	6	5.83	0,10
3	1.92	6	5.67	0,14
4	2.36	6	5.47	0,18
5	2.73	6	5.24	0,22
6	3.05	6	5.01	0,25
7	3.41	106	83.80	4,85
			116.97	5.79

individual bonds. Furthermore, the change in the present value of the bond is approximately given by:

$$\frac{dK}{K} \approx \frac{1}{K} * \sum_{i=1}^{N} \frac{\partial K}{\partial s_i} * ds_i = -\sum_{i=1}^{N} KRD_i * ds_i. \tag{13.52}$$

This definition resembles the one of the modified duration. In a special case – if the payments occur precisely on the dates corresponding to the key rates – based on

$$K = \sum_{j=1}^{N} \frac{Z_{t_j}}{(1+s_j)^j} \tag{13.53}$$

a closed formula for the key rate durations can be derived:

$$KRD_i = -\frac{1}{K} * \frac{\partial K}{\partial s_i} = -\frac{1}{K} * (-i) * Z_{t_i} * (1+s_i)^{-i-1} = \frac{i * Z_{t_i} * (1+s_i)^{-i-1}}{\sum_{j=1}^{N} Z_{t_j} * (1+s_j)^{-j}}. \tag{13.54}$$

Thus one obtains:

$$\sum_{i=1}^{N} (1+s_i) * KRD_i = \frac{\sum_{i=1}^{N} i * Z_{t_i} * (1+s_i)^{-i}}{\sum_{j=1}^{N} Z_{t_j} * (1+s_j)^{-j}} = D_{effective}.$$

In the special case of a parallel displacements as in Equation (13.50) it holds:

$$\sum_{i=1}^{N} KRD_i * ds_i = D_{effective} * \frac{ds_1}{1+s_1} = \cdots = D_{effective} * \frac{ds_N}{1+s_N}.$$

Example 13.13

Key Rate Durations I

Here the bond in Example 13.12 will again be considered, for which the assumptions for the application (13.54) are approximately fulfilled. The computation steps and the key rate durations are given in Table 13.23.

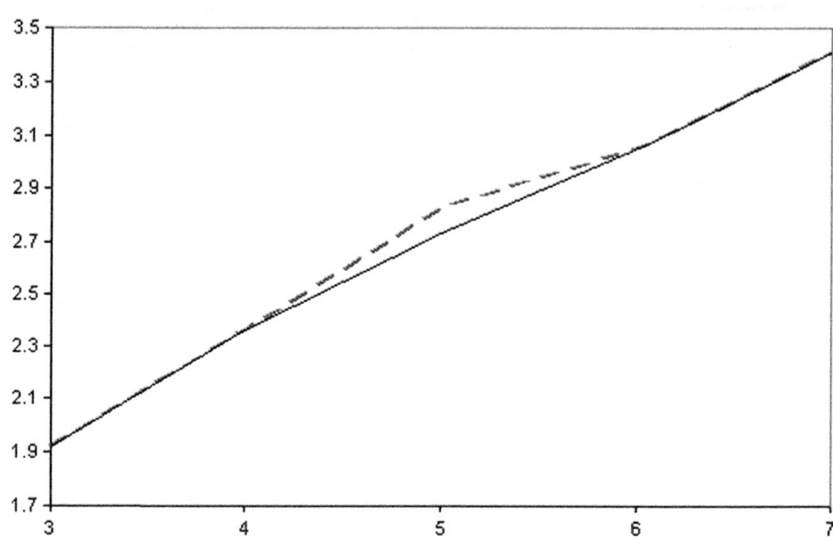

FIGURE 13.27
Definition of a Key Rate Shifts.

Table 13.24 Computation of the Key Rate Durations According to Equation (13.54)

Key Rates	Spot Rates	Payments	Discounted payments	Key Rate Durations
1	0.91	6	5.95	0.05
2	1.41	6	5.83	0.10
3	1.92	6	5.67	0.14
4	2.36	6	5.47	0.18
5	2.73	6	5.24	0.22
6	3.05	6	5.01	0.25
7	3.41	106	83.80	4.85
			116.97	5.79

Table 13.25 Computation of the Key Rate Durations According to Equation (13.55)

Key Rates	Spot Rates	Payments	Discounted Payments
1	0.91	6	5.95
2	1.41	6	5.83
3	1.92	6	5.67
4	2.36	6	5.46
5	2.73+0.10	6	5.22
6	3.05	6	5.00
7	3.41	106	83.80
			116.94

The effective duration is thus equal to 5.79 years.

In the general case the computation of the key rate durations can be based on the following formula:

$$KRD_i = -\frac{1}{\Delta s_i} * \frac{K_i - K_0}{K_0}, \tag{13.55}$$

where K_0 is the price of the bond at the given interest rates level, and K_i the price, which one obtains after the displacement of the key rate i by Δs_i (Figure 13.27).

Example 13.14

Key Rate Durations II

In order to apply Equation (13.55) the key rate duration, which corresponds to a term of 5 years will be considered. The corresponding spot rate will be increased by 10 basis points. The steps of the computation and the key rate durations are given in Table 13.25.

It follows that

$$KRD_5 = -\frac{1}{0.10} * \frac{116.94 - 116.97}{116.97} = 0.22, \tag{13.56}$$

in agreement with the results in Table 13.24.

E Spread Duration

Finally, the spread duration measures the sensitivity of a bond price to the option-adjusted spread introduced in Section 13.2.[79] For a bond without rights of termination the effective duration and the spread duration are identical, as it makes no difference whether one shifts the interest rate curve or increases the OAS. For corporate bonds with rights of termination, mortgage-backed securities, etc., a change of the OAS may have an impact on the cash flows. In these cases the computation of the spread duration must be based on specific valuation models.

13.5 EXERCISES FOR CHAPTER-END PROBLEMS

Exercise 13.1 (Roll-Down Effect):

A. Show that the roll-down effect over a period is identical to the forward rate.

B. Show that the roll-down effect can be interpreted as the slope of the yield curve.[80]

---

[79] Cf. Leibowitz et al. (1990).

[80] See the discussion in Zimmerer (2003).

Exercise 13.2 (Market Implicit Interest Rates):

Show that the following relationship holds between the market implicit interest rates and the forward rates:

$$\left(1+\hat{s}_{t_n}(t_m)\right)^{t_m} = \left(1+f_t(t_{n+1})\right) * \cdots * \left(1+f_t(t_n+t_m)\right)$$

Exercise 13.3 (Nelson-Siegel Method):

A. Determine the local extreme value for the function in Equation (13.24).

B. Prove the statements made in Section 13.3.1:

$$\lim_{t\to 0} f(t) = \beta_0 + \beta_1$$

$$\lim_{t\to \infty} f(t) = \beta_0$$

Exercise 13.4 (Svensson's Method):

A. Integrate the Equation (13.27) analogous to Equation (13.24) and determine the local extreme points of this function.

Chapter 14

Analysis of Multi-Asset Class Portfolios and Hedge Funds

ABSTRACT

In this chapter the traditional Brinson approach to attribution analysis will be extended to funds invested in several asset classes. Furthermore, approaches will be sketched for the incorporation of the risk dimension into the attribution analysis. Finally certain aspects surrounding the analysis of hedge funds will be introduced. Several new risk and performance measures will be critically discussed in this context.

Keywords
attribution analysis, Brinson approach, fund, asset class, risk, hedge fund risk, performance measure

14.1 BASIC CONSIDERATIONS

So far only portfolios with one category of securities (stocks or bonds) have been considered (if one disregards here the cash segment, which was occasionally included in the considerations). In reality, many portfolios invest in several asset classes (balanced portfolios), the weights of which are set by the portfolio manager. For such portfolios the investment process has an additional decision level, which has not been considered in the methodologies described so far.

The approach described in the following is a generalization of the Brinson approach, by introducing an additional effect, which measures the allocation decision in regard to the asset class. For the purpose of this treatment this allocation effect will be called global allocation, and the resulting contributions, global allocation contributions.[1] Figure 14.1 illustrates the investment process with this additional decision level.

In the following, a portfolio with two decision levels (in the concrete case of a *balanced portfolio* with stocks and bonds) will be considered. In the subsequent

[1] The term "*global allocation*" is not widely used in practice. This neutral notation will be used in order to avoid discussions about its appropriateness. In (Levecq 2004) the terms "strategic" and "tactical allocation" are used. Menchero considers subsegments of sectors, which formally amounts to the same and speaks of a "nested attribution analysis" (Menchero 2004). For a similar approach see also (Geenen et al., 2001).

Performance Evaluation and Attribution of Security Portfolios. http://dx.doi.org/10.1016/B978-0-12-744483-3.00014-6
© 2013 Elsevier Inc. All rights reserved.
For End-of-chapter Questions: © 2012. CFA Institute, Reproduced and republished with permission from CFA Institute. All rights reserved.

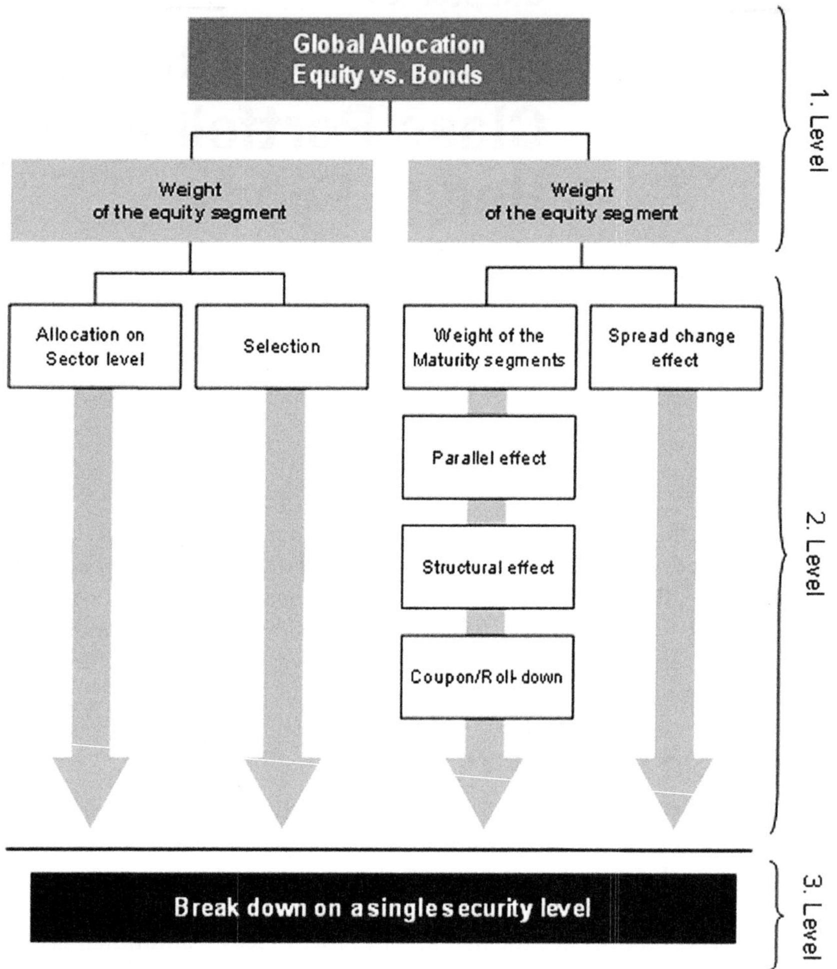

FIGURE 14.1
Decision Levels for a Balanced Portfolio (Equity/Bonds).

sections the approach will be generalized to three levels (break down on a single security level) and to the multi-currency case.

14.2 ATTRIBUTION ANALYSIS ON TWO LEVELS

14.2.1 Contributions without Separating the Currency Components

The global allocation decision consists in fixing the weights of the bond and the equity segment of the portfolio:[2]

[2] For the sake of simplicity, an (additional) cash segment will not be considered. It is, however, a straight-forward matter to generalize the methodology to this case.

$$WP_e := \sum_{i=1}^{N_A} swp_{ei}, \quad WP_b := \sum_{i=1}^{N_b} swp_{ri}$$

relative to the respective benchmark weights:

$$WB_e := \sum_{i=1}^{N_e} swb_{ei}, \quad WB_b := \sum_{i=1}^{N_b} swb_{ri},$$

Where:

swp_{ei}/swb_{ei}: weight of the equity segment i in the portfolio/benchmark
swp_{bi}/swb_{bi}: weight of the bond segment i in the portfolio/benchmark
N_e: number of equity segments in the portfolio/benchmark
N_b: number of bond segments in the portfolio/benchmark.[3]

In the definition of the contributions, it will be assumed that for each level shown in Figure 14.1 the decisions are taken independently. (For example by different portfolio managers of one company or by different companies.) The formulas will be derived step by step.

14.2.1.1 GLOBAL ALLOCATION CONTRIBUTIONS

On this level the weights of the equity and the bond segments are determined relative to the benchmark. The quantification of these contributions is based on a portfolio (*global allocation portfolio*), which reflects exclusively the *global allocation*, i.e., both the weights of the individual segments (for example the weights of the industry sectors or the weights of the maturity segments) and the weights of individual titles within the segments remain unchanged relative to the benchmark (cf. Figure 14.2).

If RB_e and RB_b denote the return of respectively the equity and bond segment, then the return $RGAP$ of the global allocation portfolio is given by:

$$RGAP = WP_e * RB_e + WP_b * RB_b.$$

The overall global allocation contribution GAC follows after subtracting the benchmark return $RB = WB_e * RB_e + WB_b * RB_b$ from $RGAP$:

$$GAC = (WP_e - WB_e) * RB_e + (WP_b - WB_b) * RB_b. \tag{14.1}$$

$$gac_e := (WP_e - WB_e) * RB_e$$

and:

$$gac_b := (WP_b - WB_b) * RB_b$$

[3] For the sake of simplicity it will be assumed that both the equity and the bond segment consist of the same number of subsectors as the respective segment in the benchmark.

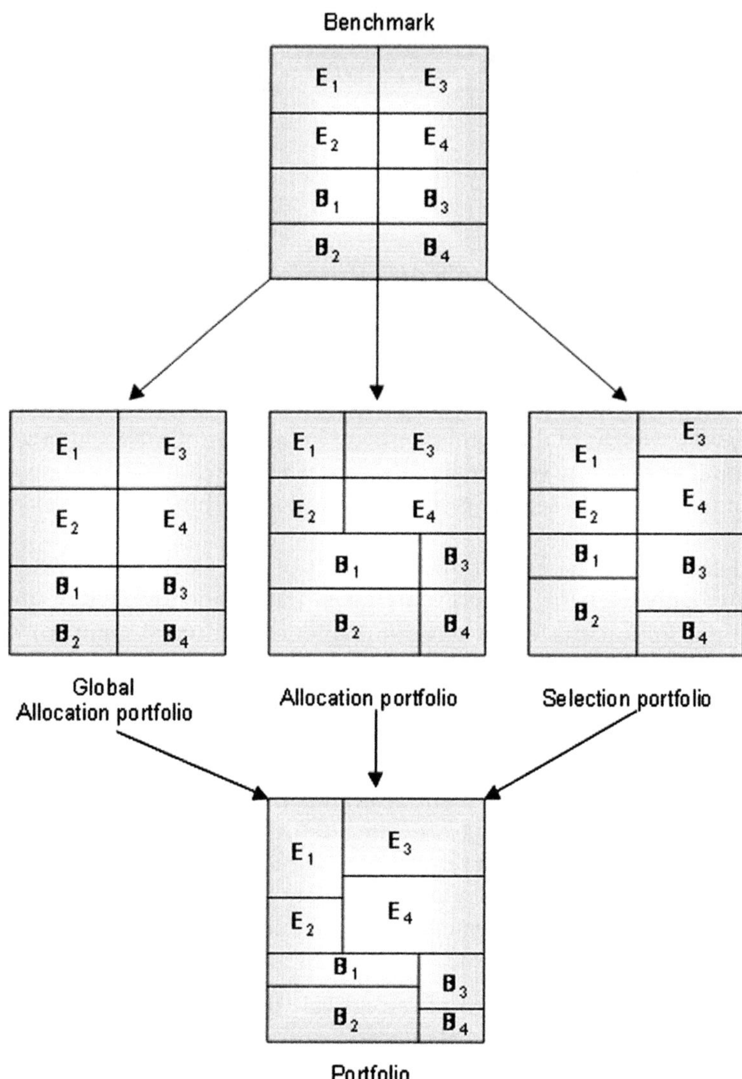

FIGURE 14.2
Illustration of the Allocation Decisions for a Balanced Portfolio Without Currency Effects.

are the components of the global allocation contribution, which are attributable to the equity, respectively the bond segment. Analogous to the procedure in Section 12.2 these terms can be modified by subtracting the overall benchmark return from the return of the segments:

$$gac_e^r := (WP_e - WB_e)*(RB_e - RB),$$

and:

$$gac_b^r := (WP_b - WB_b)*(RB_b - RB).$$

The sum of these relative global allocation contributions again yields the overall global allocation contribution. For the signs of these terms one obtains a diagram analogous to the one in Figure 12.2.

In order to determine the components of the global allocation contribution, which can be attributed to the individual segments of the equity, respectively the bond segment, the term in Equation (14.1) will be expressed by means of the segment returns and weights. The return of the bond segment may be represented as the sum of the products between the weights and the returns of the individual segments. Here the weights of the bond segment viewed on a stand-alone basis need to be used. These weights are obtained by normalizing the weights swb_{bi}:

$$swb_{bi} \to \frac{swb_{bi}}{WB_b}.$$

One deals similarly with the equity segment, such that:

$$RB_b = \sum_{i=1}^{N_b} \frac{swb_{bi}}{WB_b} * srb_{bi} \tag{14.2}$$

$$RB_e = \sum_{i=1}^{N_e} \frac{swb_{ei}}{WB_e} * srb_{ei}, \tag{14.3}$$

The term in Equation (14.1) can be written in the following form:

$$GAC = (WP_e - WB_e) * \sum_{i=1}^{N_e} \frac{swb_{ei}}{WB_e} * srb_{ei} + (WP_b - WB_b) * \sum_{i=1}^{N_b} \frac{swb_{bi}}{WB_b} * srb_{bi}. \tag{14.4}$$

For the portfolio return one obtains analogous breakdowns to Equations (14.2) and (14.3): $RP = WP_e * RP_e + WP_b * RP_b$, where:

$$RP_b = \sum_{i=1}^{N_b} \frac{swp_{bi}}{WP_b} * srp_{bi} \tag{14.5}$$

and

$$RP_e = \sum_{i=1}^{N_e} \frac{swp_{ei}}{WP_e} * srp_{ei}. \tag{14.6}$$

From Equation (14.4) it becomes apparent that the components of the global allocation contributions attributable to the equity and bond segment are respectively given by:

$$gac_{ei} := (WP_e - WB_e) * \frac{swb_{ei}}{WB_e} * srb_{ei}, \tag{14.7}$$

and:

$$gac_{bi} := (WP_b - WB_b)*\frac{swb_{bi}}{WB_b}*srb_{bi}. \tag{14.8}$$

In a relative form one obtains:

$$gac^r_{ei} := (WP_e - WB_e)*\frac{swb_{ei}}{WB_e}*(srb_{ei} - RB), \tag{14.9}$$

and:

$$gac^r_{bi} := (WP_b - WB_b)*\frac{swb_{bi}}{WB_b}*(srb_{bi} - RB). \tag{14.10}$$

14.2.1.2 *ALLOCATION CONTRIBUTIONS*

Analogous to the procedure in Section 12.2 the computation of the allocation contributions within the equity and bond segments[4] will be based on an allocation portfolio. This portfolio reflects the altered weights of the individual segments within the global segments (bonds, equities). Both the global segments as well as the weights of individual titles within the segments remain unchanged (cf. Figure 14.2). Under this premise the return *RAP* of the allocation portfolio is given by:

$$RAP = WB_e*RAP_e + WB_b*RAP_b = WB_e*\sum_{i=1}^{N_e}\frac{swp_{ei}}{WP_e}*srb_{ei} + WB_b*\sum_{i=1}^{N_b}\frac{swp_{bi}}{WP_b}*srb_{bi}.$$

The overall allocation contribution follows from subtracting the benchmark return:

$$\begin{aligned}AC &= RAP - RB\\ &= (WB_e*RAP_a + WB_b*RAP_b) - (WB_e*RB_e + WB_b*RB_b)\\ &= WB_e*\sum_{i=1}^{N_e}\left(\frac{swp_{ei}}{WP_e} - \frac{swb_{ei}}{WB_e}\right)*srb_{ei} + WB_b*\sum_{i=1}^{N_b}\left(\frac{swp_{bi}}{WP_b} - \frac{swb_{bi}}{WB_b}\right)*srb_{bi},\end{aligned}$$

such that the allocation contributions of the individual segments may be defined as follows:

$$ac_{ei} := WB_e*\left(\frac{swp_{ei}}{WP_e} - \frac{swb_{ei}}{WB_e}\right)*srb_{ei} \tag{14.11}$$

and:

$$ac_{bi} := WB_b*\left(\frac{swp_{bi}}{WP_b} - \frac{swb_{bi}}{WB_b}\right)*srb_{bi} \tag{14.12}$$

---

[4] In order to keep the presentation as simple as possible, the basic Brinson approach will be also applied to the bond segment. The approach can, however, be altered by using one of the approaches outlined in Chapter 13.

Analogous to the procedure in Section 14.2 one can switch to the relative form by subtracting the return of the equity benchmark RB_e, respectively the return of the bond benchmark RB_b from the returns in Equations (14.11) and (14.12).

$$ac^r_{ei} := WB_e * \left(\frac{swp_{ei}}{WP_e} - \frac{swb_{ei}}{WB_e}\right) *(srb_{ei} - RB_e) \tag{14.13}$$

and:

$$ac^r_{bi} = WB_b * \left(\frac{swp_{bi}}{WP_b} - \frac{swb_{bi}}{WB_b}\right) *(srb_{bi} - RB_b). \tag{14.14}$$

It can readily be verified that the sum of these contributions equals the overall allocation contribution.

14.2.1.3 SELECTION CONTRIBUTIONS

In comparison to the benchmark portfolio, the selection portfolio features different weights within the equity and bond segments, however, the weights of the global segments as well as the segment weights within the global segments (bonds, equities) remain unchanged (cf. Figure 14.2). Under these conditions the return RSP of the selection portfolio is given by:

$$\begin{aligned} RSP &= WB_e * RSP_e + WB_b * RSP_b \\ &= WB_e * \sum_{i=1}^{N_e} \frac{swb_{ei}}{WB_e} * srp_{ei} + WB_b * \sum_{i=1}^{N_b} \frac{swb_{bi}}{WB_b} * srp_{bi} \\ &= \sum_{i=1}^{N_e} swb_{ei} * srp_{ei} + \sum_{i=1}^{N_b} swb_{bi} * srp_{bi}. \end{aligned}$$

One obtains the overall selection contribution SC by subtracting the Benchmark return from RSP:

$$SC = RSP - RB = \sum_{i=1}^{N_e} swb_{ei} *(srp_{ei} - srb_{ei}) + \sum_{i=1}^{N_b} swb_{bi} *(srp_{bi} - srb_{bi}).$$

The terms:

$$sc_{ei} := swb_{ei} *(srp_{ei} - srb_{ei}) \tag{14.15}$$

and:

$$sc_{bi} := swb_{bi} *(srp_{bi} - srb_{bi})$$

are the selection contributions of the individual equity and bond segments. Thus, unlike the allocation contributions, the selection contributions are formally unchanged compared to the definition in Section 14.2.

14.2.1.4 INTERACTION TERMS

Apart from the interaction terms already introduced in Section 14.2, which were attributable to the "interaction" between selection and allocation decisions, an attribution analysis of balanced portfolios requires additional interaction terms. These are caused by the "interaction" between the global allocation decisions and the sectorial allocation and selection decisions.

First the well-known interaction terms from Section 14.2 will be adjusted to the case of a balanced portfolio. If one considers the equity segment as a stand-alone portfolio, then the following interaction term results from the allocation and selection decisions:

$$(RP_e - RSP_e) + (RB_e - RAP_e).$$

One obtains an analogous expression for the bond segment, when regarded as a stand-alone portfolio:

$$(RP_b - RSP_b) + (RB_b - RAP_b).$$

Weighting these contributions with the global benchmark weight yields the interaction term $IT(1)$, which reflects the "interaction" of selection and sectorial allocation decisions:

$$\begin{aligned} IT(1) &= WB_e*((RP_e - RSP_e) + (RB_e - RAP_e)) \\ &+ WB_b*((RP_b - RSP_b) + (RB_b - RAP_b)) \\ &= WB_e*\sum_{i=1}^{N_e}\left(\frac{swp_{ei}}{WP_e} - \frac{swb_{ei}}{WB_e}\right)*(srp_{ei} - srb_{ei}) \\ &+ WB_b*\sum_{i=1}^{N_b}\left(\frac{swp_{bi}}{WP_b} - \frac{swb_{bi}}{WB_b}\right)*(srp_{bi} - srb_{bi}). \end{aligned}$$

Thus the interaction terms for the segments may be defined as:

$$it(1)_{ei} := WB_e*\left(\frac{swp_{ei}}{WP_e} - \frac{swb_{ei}}{WB_e}\right)*(srp_{ei} - srb_{ei}), \tag{14.16}$$

$$it(1)_{bi} := WB_b*\left(\frac{swp_{bi}}{WP_b} - \frac{swb_{bi}}{WB_b}\right)*(srp_{bi} - srb_{bi}) \tag{14.17}$$

A simple calculation shows:

$$\begin{aligned} RP - RB - GAC - AC - SC - IT(1) = &(WP_e - WB_e)*(RP_e - RB_e) \\ &+(WP_b - WB_b)*(RP_b - RB_b), \end{aligned}$$

from which one readily deduces the form of the additional interaction term, which will be denoted by $IT(2)$:

$$IT(2) := (WP_e - WB_e)*(RP_e - RB_e) + (WP_b - WB_b)*(RP_b - RB_b).$$

By means of Equations (14.1), (14.2), (14.5), and (14.4) one obtains:

$$cIT(2) = (WP_e - WB_e)*\left[\sum_{i=1}^{N_e}\frac{swp_{ei}}{WP_e}*srp_{ei} - \sum_{i=1}^{N_e}\frac{swb_{ei}}{WB_e}*srb_{ei}\right] + (WP_b - WB_b)*\left[\sum_{i=1}^{N_b}\frac{swp_{bi}}{WP_b}*srp_{bi} - \sum_{i=1}^{N_b}\frac{swb_{bi}}{WB_b}*srb_{bi}\right].$$

Based on this one can define these interaction terms for the individual segments i as follows:

$$it(2)_{ei} := (WP_e - WB_e)*\left(\frac{swp_{ei}}{WP_e}*srp_{ei} - \frac{swb_{ei}}{WB_e}*srb_{ei}\right), \tag{14.18}$$

and:

$$it(2)_{bi} := (WP_b - WB_b)*\left(\frac{swp_{bi}}{WP_b}*srp_{bi} - \frac{swb_{bi}}{WB_b}*srb_{bi}\right). \tag{14.19}$$

Table 14.1 summarizes the different terms for the equity portion of the portfolio (bonds analogously).

A simple calculation shows that the sum of the terms assigned to one segment is equal to the total contribution of that segment, $swp_{ei}*srp_{ei} - swb_{ei}*srb_{ei}$ (bond segment analogously).

Example 14.1

Attribution analysis for a balanced portfolio

In this example a portfolio will be considered, which consists of an equity and a bond segment with two subsegments each. Within the bond segment we will distinguish between investment grade corporate bonds (B1, B2) and non-investment grade corporate bonds (B3, B4).[5] The equity segment consists of two sectors with two titles each (E1 and E2, respectively E3 and E4). Table 14.2 contains the required data for the benchmark associated with the portfolio and Table 14.3 the required portfolio data.

A simple calculation shows that the portfolio achieved a return of 2.15% and the benchmark a return of 0.75%, so that the active return equals 1.40%. The results obtained from an attribution analysis based on the relative form of the allocation contribution are summarized in Table 14.4.

[5]According to the classification by the rating agency Moody's a bond has an *investment grade*, if its rating is above Ba1. In the S&P classification this corresponds to a rating above BB+ (cf. Fabozzi 1996, p. 142 et seq).

Table 14.1 Terms of an Attribution Analysis (Equities) for a Balanced Portfolio

	Total	Segment
Global Allocation	$(WP_e - WB_e) * RB_e$	$(WP_e - WB_e) * \frac{swb_{ei}}{WB_e} * srb_{ei}$
Allocation	$\sum_{i=1}^{N_e} WB_e * \left(\frac{swp_{ei}}{WP_e} - \frac{swb_{ei}}{WB_e}\right) * srb_{ei}$	$WB_e * \left(\frac{swp_{ei}}{WP_e} - \frac{swb_{ei}}{WB_e}\right) * srb_{ei}$
Selection	$\sum_{i=1}^{N_e} swb_{ei} * (srp_{ei} - srb_{ei})$	$swb_{ei} * (srp_{ei} - srb_{ei})$
Interaction (I)	$WB_e * \sum_{i=1}^{N_e} \left(\frac{swp_{ei}}{WP_e} - \frac{swb_{ei}}{WB_e}\right) * (srp_{ei} - srb_{ei})$	$WB_e * \left(\frac{swp_{ei}}{WP_e} - \frac{swb_{ei}}{WB_e}\right) * (srp_{ei} - srb_{ei})$
Interaction (II)	$(WP_e - WB_e) * (RP_e - RB_e)$	$(WP_e - WB_e) * \left(\frac{swp_{ei}}{WP_e} * srp_{ei} - \frac{swb_{ei}}{WB_e} * srb_{ei}\right)$

Table 14.2 Weights and Returns for a Mixed Benchmark

			Weight (%)			Returns (Base Currency %)		
Global Segment	Segment (Industries/ Rating)	Title	Global Segment	Segment (Industries/ Rating)	Title	Global Segment	Segment (Industries/ Rating)	Title
Bonds	Investment	B1	50	25	12.5	5.75	5.00	7.0
	Grade	B2			12.5			3.0
	< Investment	B3		25	12.5		6.50	5.0
	Grade	B4			12.5			8.0
Equities	Sector 1	E1	50	25	12.5	−4.25	−7.00	−6.0
		E2			12.5			−8.0
	Sector 2	E3		25	12.5		−1.50	−2.0
		E4			12.5			−1.0

Table 14.3 Weights and Returns for a Mixed Portfolio

			Weight (%)			Returns (Base Currency %)		
Global Segment	**Segment (Industries/ Rating)**	**Title**	**Global Segment**	**Segment (Industries/ Rating)**	**Title**	**Global Segment**	**Segment (Industries/ Rating)**	**Title**
Bonds	Investment Grade	B1	60	25	10	5.83	4.60	7.0
		B2			15			3.0
	< Investment Grade	B3		35	15		6.71	5.0
		B4			20			8.0
Equities	Sector 1	E1	40	15	10	−3.38	−6.67	−6.0
		E2			5			−8.0
	Sector 2	E3		25	10		−1.40	−2.0
		E4			15			−1.0

Table 14.4 Results of the Attribution Analysis (in %)

Portfolio Level			GAC	AC	SC	IT(1)	IT(2)	Total
	Bonds		**0.58**	**0.06**	**−0.05**	**0.03**	**0.01**	**0.63**
		Investment Grade	0.25	−0.21	−0.10	0.02	−0.06	**−0.10**
		< Investment Grade	0.33	0.27	0.05	0.01	0.07	**0.73**
	Equities		**0.43**	**0.34**	**0.11**	**−0.01**	**−0.09**	**0.78**
		Sector 1	0.35	0.44	0.08	−0.02	−0.10	**0.75**
		Sector 2	0.08	−0.09	0.03	0.01	0.01	**0.03**
Total			**1.00**	**0.41**	**0.06**	**0.01**	**−0.08**	**1.40**

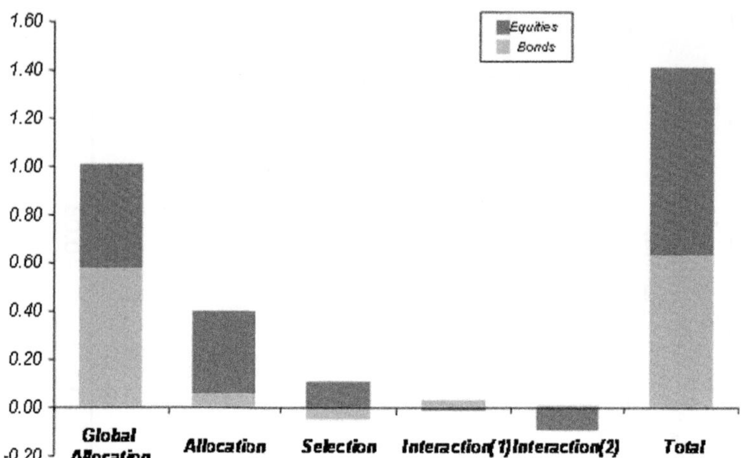

FIGURE 14.3
Results of the Attribution Analysis.

The figure clearly illustrates that the overwhelming portion of the active return stems from the global allocation decision. A significant portion also results from the equity sector allocation. The other contributions are negligible.

14.2.2 Contributions after Separating Currency Effects

The separation of currency contributions is similar to the methodology described in Section 12.2.6. Therefore it shall suffice to sketch the details only for the equity portion. The treatment of the bond terms is analogous. The derivation is based on a simple transformation, which enable one to use the formulas already derived in Section 14.2.1. The starting point is the relationship between the return in local currency and the return in base currency introduced in Section 12.2.6:

$$srb^B_{ei} = srb^L_{ei} + cb_{ei} + srb^L_{ei} * cb_{ei},$$

and:

$$srp^B_{ei} = srp^L_{ei} + cp_{ei} + srp^L_{ei} * cp_{ei}.$$

In order to simplify the notation a little bit, in the following the index B will be dropped for the terms in base currency. For the return of the equity segment of the benchmark one first obtains:

$$RB_e = \sum_{i=1}^{N_e} \frac{swb_{ei}}{WB_e} * srb_{ei} = \sum_{i=1}^{N_e} \frac{swb_{ei}}{WB_e} * (srb^L_{ei} + cb_{ei} + srb^L_{ei} * cb_{ei})$$

$$= RB^L_e + CB_e + \sum_{i=1}^{N_e} \frac{swb_{ei}}{WB_e} * srb^L_{ei} * cb_{ei},$$

with:

$$CB_e := \sum_{i=1}^{N_e} \frac{swb_{ei}}{WB_e} * cb_{ei} \text{ and } RB^L_e := \sum_{i=1}^{N_e} \frac{swb_{ei}}{WB_e} * srb^L_{ei}.$$

The portfolio terms are analogous:

$$RP_e = \sum_{i=1}^{N_e} \frac{swp_{ei}}{WP_e} * srp_{ei} = \sum_{i=1}^{N_e} \frac{swp_{ei}}{WP_e} * (srp_{ei}^L + cp_{ei} + srp_{ei}^L * cp_{ei})$$

$$= RP_e^L + CP_e + \sum_{i=1}^{N_e} \frac{swp_{ei}}{WP_e} * srp_{ei}^L * cp_{ei},$$

with:

$$CP_e := \sum_{i=1}^{N_e} \frac{swp_{ei}}{WP_e} * cp_{ei} \text{ and } RP_e^L := \sum_{i=1}^{N_e} \frac{swp_{ei}}{WP_e} * srp_{ei}^L.$$

A simple transformation yields:

$$\begin{aligned} & WP_e * RP_e - WB_e * RB_e \\ &= \sum_{i=1}^{N_e} swp_{ei} * srp_{ei} - \sum_{i=1}^{N_e} swb_{ei}^* srb_{ei} \\ &= \sum_{i=1}^{N_e} swp_{ei} * (srp_{ei}^L + cp_{ei} + srp_{ei}^L * cp_{ei}) - \sum_{i=1}^{N_e} swb_{ei} * (srb_{ei}^L + cb_{ei} + srb_{ei}^L * cb_{ei}) \\ &= (WP_e * RP_e^L - WB_e * RB_e^L) + (WP_e * CP_e - WB_e * CB_e) \\ &\quad + (\sum_{i=1}^{N_e} swp_{ei} * srp_{ei}^L * cp_{ei} - swb_{ei} * srb_{ei}^L * cb_{ei}). \end{aligned}$$

The term in the first bracket will be decomposed according to the Brinson systematics. This procedure could also be applied to the second term. We will refrain from doing so, however, as in Section 15.1 more suitable procedures for analyzing the currency contributions will be described. Table 14.5 summarizes the different contributions.

Example 14.2

Attribution analysis for balanced portfolio in Example 14.1

Here Example 14.1 will be revisited. This time we will distinguish between the returns in base currency and the ones in local currency (see Table 14.6).

After separating the currency terms according to the described methodology, the attribution analysis in Example 14.1 assumes the form shown in Table 14.7.

Compared to the analysis in Example 14.1, it becomes obvious that the currency effects had a significant impact on the different contributions. This is especially true for the global allocation effect, which has become much smaller. But also the allocation and the selection contribution were overestimated in Example 14.1.

14.3 ATTRIBUTION ANALYSIS ON THREE LEVELS

In this section the methodology described in the previous sections will be extended by an additional analysis level. There are many reasons for such an extension. A given country breakdown in the equity portion of a balanced portfolio could e.g. be refined by a sector or single-security breakdown. Alternatively, a sector-breakdown

Table 14.5 Terms of an Attribution Analysis (Equity) of a Balanced Portfolio After Separating the Currency Contributions (Bonds Analogously)

	Total	Segment
Global Allocation	$(WP_e - WB_e) * RB_e^L$	$(WP_e - WB_e) * \frac{swb_{ei}}{WB_e} * srb_{ei}^L$
Allocation	$\sum_{i=1}^{N_e} WB_e * \left(\frac{swp_{ei}}{WP_e} - \frac{swb_{ei}}{WB_e}\right) * srb_{ei}^L$	$WB_e * \left(\frac{swp_{ei}}{WP_e} - \frac{swb_{ei}}{WB_e}\right) * srb_{ei}^L$
Selection	$\sum_{i=1}^{N_e} swb_{ei} * \left(srp_{ei}^L - srb_{ei}^L\right)$	$swb_{ei} * (srp_{ei}^L - srb_{ei}^L)$
Currency	$WP_{ei} * CP_e - WB_e * CB_e$	$swb_{ei} * cp_{ei} - swb_{ei} * cb_{ei}$
Interaction (I)	$WB_e * \sum_{i=1}^{N_e} \left(\frac{swp_{ei}}{WP_e} - \frac{swb_{ei}}{WB_e}\right) * \left(srp_{ei}^L - srb_{ei}^L\right)$	$WB_e * \left(\frac{swp_{ei}}{WP_e} - \frac{swb_{ei}}{WB_e}\right) * (srp_{ei}^L - srb_{ei}^L)$
Interaction (II)	$(WP_e - WB_e) * (RP_e^L - RB_e^L)$	$(WP_e - WB_e) * \left(\frac{swp_{ei}}{WP_e} * srp_{ei}^L - \frac{swb_{ei}}{WB_e} * srb_{ei}^L\right)$
Interaction (III)	$\sum_{i=1}^{N_e} swp_{ei} * srp_{ei}^L * cp_{ei} - swb_{ei} * srb_{ei}^L * cb_{ei}$	$swp_{ei} * srp_{ei}^L * cp_{ei} - swb_{ei} * srb_{ei}^L * cb_{ei}$

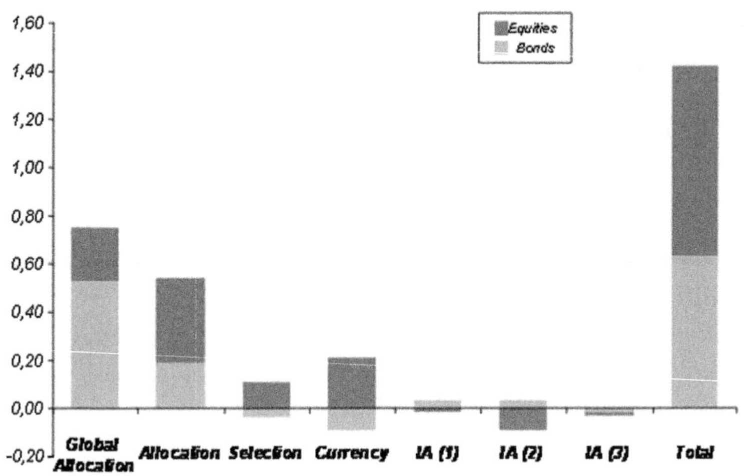

FIGURE 14.4
Results of the Attribution Analysis with the Separation of Currency Effects.

could be broken down further by means of a country or a refined sector breakdown.[6] A further application is given for the so-called multimanager funds, in which different investment styles are implemented in different segments of the funds. For such funds one needs to distinguish between the different portfolio managers

[6] In this context see also Example 14.5 as well as the explanations in Examples 11.4 and 11.5 in Chapter 11.

Table 14.6 Local Returns of the Portfolio and the Benchmark (in %)

Portfolio Level		Benchmark		Portfolio	
Bonds		Local Return	Currency Return	Local Return	Currency Return
	Investment Grade	3.05	1.89	2.66	0.00
	< Investment Grade	7.50	−0.93	7.71	−0.09
Equities					
	Sector 1	−5.00	−2.11	−4.67	−2.10
	Sector 2	0.60	−2.09	0.70	−2.09

Table 14.7 Results of the Attribution Analysis After Separating Currency Effects (in %)

Portfolio Level		GAC	AC	SC	CC	IT(1)	IT(2)	IT(3)	Total
Bonds		**0.53**	**0.19**	**−0.04**	**−0.09**	**0.03**	**0.03**	**−0.01**	**0.63**
	Investment Grade	0.15	−0.13	−0.10	0.00	0.02	−0.04	0.00	−0.10
	< Investment Grade	0.38	0.31	0.05	−0.09	0.01	0.08	−0.01	0.73
Equities		**0.22**	**0.35**	**0.11**	**0.21**	**−0.01**	**−0.09**	**−0.01**	**0.79**
	Sector 1	0.25	0.31	0.08	0.21	−0.02	−0.08	−0.01	0.76
	Sector 2	−0.03	0.04	0.03	0.00	0.01	−0.01	0.00	0.03
Total		**0.75**	**0.54**	**0.06**	**0.12**	**0.01**	**−0.06**	**−0.02**	**1.40**

responsible for the segments (with corresponding (global) allocation terms, which result from the specific weighting segments allocated to the portfolio manager).

This approach can also be applied to the so-called *overlay mandates*. An *overlay mandate* is given, if the responsibility for a certain area of the portfolio is delegated to another manager (so-called *overlay manager*). Typical examples are *currency overlay mandates* or *asset allocation overlay mandates*. If the overlay manager has full discretion over his decisions in regard to this area, then the described methodology is directly applicable. In case of hybrid form (e.g., if allocation decisions are partially made by the portfolio manager and by the overlay manager), the methodology needs to be adopted in such a way that the allocation decisions implemented by the portfolio manager serve as a benchmark for the overlay manager.

For the derivation of the details it will be assumed that the additional analysis level reflects individual stocks. This assumption is, however, not essential. It merely has the purpose of avoiding an abstract referencing. The explanations in Section 14.2.2 will form the basis for the methodology.

14.3.1 Contributions without Separating the Currency Effects

Although the original idea of an attribution analysis is to provide information in an aggregated form, sometimes in praxis there is a desire to obtain a breakdown of (significant) attribution effects to individual securities. Although there is no clear economic principle for such a breakdown, it is possible to derive a (natural) mathematical procedure, which provides a rough overview over the distributions of the effects. This will be explained for the case of the equity segment (the bond segment follows analogously).

In the following the return of the stock j in segment i will be denoted by rp_{eij} and its portfolio weight by wp_{eij}. The analogous benchmark terms will be denoted similarly by rb_{eij} and wb_{eij}, respectively. It holds that:

$$srb_{ei} = \sum_{j=1}^{N_{e_i}} \frac{wb_{eij}}{swb_{ei}} * rb_{eij}, \tag{14.20}$$

where N_{e_i} denotes the number of titles in segment i. If one substitutes the expression on the right-hand side of Equation (14.11), then one obtains:

$$\begin{aligned} ac_{ei} &= WB_e * \left[\frac{swp_{ei}}{WP_e} - \frac{swb_{ei}}{WB_e} \right] * \sum_{j=1}^{N_{e_i}} \frac{wb_{eij}}{swb_{ei}} * rb_{eij} \\ &= \sum_{j=1}^{N_{e_i}} WB_e * \left[\frac{swp_{ei}}{WP_e} - \frac{swb_{ei}}{WB_e} \right] * \frac{wb_{eij}}{swb_{ei}} * rb_{eij}. \end{aligned}$$

Thus it appears natural to assign to the stock j in segment i the allocation contribution:

$$ac_{eij} = WB_e * \left[\frac{swp_{ei}}{WP_e} - \frac{swb_{ei}}{WB_e} \right] * \frac{wb_{eij}}{swb_{ei}} * rb_{eij}. \tag{14.21}$$

One deals similarly with the selection and interaction terms. Employing Equation (14.20) and the relationship:

$$srp_{ei} = \sum_{j=1}^{N_{e_i}} \frac{wp_{eij}}{swp_{ei}} * rp_{eij}, \tag{14.22}$$

then it follows from Equation (14.15) that:

$$\begin{aligned} sc_{ei} &= swb_{ei} * \left(\sum_{j=1}^{N_{e_i}} \frac{wp_{eij}}{swp_{ei}} * rp_{eij} - \sum_{j=1}^{N_{e_i}} \frac{wb_{eij}}{swb_{ei}} * rb_{eij} \right) \\ &= \sum_{j=1}^{N_{e_i}} swb_{ei} * \left(\frac{wp_{eij}}{swp_{ei}} * rp_{eij} - \frac{wb_{eij}}{swb_{ei}} * rb_{eij} \right), \end{aligned}$$

such that the following selection contribution can be attributed to stock j in segment i:

$$sc_{eij} = swb_{ei} * \left(\frac{wp_{eij}}{swp_{ei}} * rp_{eij} - \frac{wb_{eij}}{swb_{ei}} * rb_{eij} \right).$$

The shape of the term Interaction (1) follows from Equations (14.16), (14.20), and (14.22):

$$it(1)_{ei} = \sum_{j=1}^{N_{e_i}} WB_e * \left(\frac{swp_{ei}}{WP_e} - \frac{swb_{ei}}{WB_e}\right) * \left(\frac{wp_{eij}}{swp_{ei}} * rp_{eij} - \frac{wb_{eij}}{swb_{ei}} * rb_{eij}\right),$$

so that the share of Interaction (1), attributable to stock j in segment i equals:

$$it(1)_{eij} = WB_e * \left(\frac{swp_{ei}}{WP_e} - \frac{swb_{ei}}{WB_e}\right) * \left(\frac{wp_{eij}}{swp_{ei}} * rp_{eij} - \frac{wb_{eij}}{swb_{ei}} * rb_{eij}\right).$$

A simple calculation shows:

$$ac_{eij} + sc_{eij} + it(1)_{eij} = \frac{WB_e}{WP_e} * wp_{eij} * rp_{eij} - wb_{eij} * rb_{eij}.$$

In order to obtain a complete break-down of the overall active contribution one needs to attribute the components from the global allocation and Interaction (2) to the stock j. For the global allocation term one obtains by means of Equation (14.7):

$$\begin{aligned} gac_{ei} &= (WP_e - WB_e) * \tfrac{swb_{ei}}{WB_e} * srb_{ei} \\ &= (WP_e - WB_e) * \tfrac{swb_{ei}}{WB_e} * \textstyle\sum_{j=1}^{N_{e_i}} \tfrac{wb_{eij}}{swb_{ei}} * rb_{eij} \\ &= \tfrac{(WP_e - WB_e)}{WB_e} * \textstyle\sum_{j=1}^{N_{e_i}} wb_{eij} * rb_{eij}, \end{aligned}$$

such that the following contribution may be assigned to stock j in this segment:

$$gac_{ei} := (WP_e - WB_e) * \frac{wb_{eij}}{WB_e} * rb_{eij}.$$

One finally needs to settle the break-down of Interaction (2). By means of Equations (14.18), (14.20), and (14.22) one obtains:

$$\begin{aligned} it(2)_{ei} &= (WP_e - WB_e) * \left(\frac{swp_{ei}}{WP_e} * srp_{ei} - \frac{swb_{ei}}{WB_e} * srb_{ei}\right) \\ &= (WP_e - WB_e) * \left(\frac{swp_{ei}}{WP_e} * \sum_{j=1}^{N_{e_i}} \frac{wp_{eij}}{swp_{ei}} * rp_{eij} - \frac{swb_{ei}}{WB_e} * \sum_{j=1}^{N_{e_i}} \frac{wb_{eij}}{swb_{ei}} * rb_{eij}\right) \\ &= (WP_e - WB_e) * \left(\sum_{j=1}^{N_{e_i}} \frac{wp_{eij}}{WP_e} * rp_{eij} - \sum_{j=1}^{N_{e_i}} \frac{wb_{eij}}{WB_e} * rb_{eij}\right). \end{aligned}$$

Thus the following share of Interaction (2) may be assigned to stock j:

$$it(2)_{eij} = (WP_e - WB_e) * \left(\frac{wp_{eij}}{WP_e} * rp_{eij} - \frac{wb_{eij}}{WB_e} * rb_{eij}\right).$$

An again simple calculation shows that with the additional global allocation term and the interaction term the breakdown of the relative contribution stock j in segment i is now complete:

$$ac_{eij} + sc_{eij} + it(1)_{eij} + gac_{eij} + it(2)_{eij} = wp_{eij}*rp_{eij} - wb_{eij}*rb_{eij}.$$

This relationship enables the user of the attribution analysis to bring the more complex contributions of the allocation, selection and interaction terms in relation to the more graspable relative contributions of individual securities.

Example 14.3

Attribution analysis for the balanced portfolio in Example 14.1 on a single security level

By applying the above formulas, the attribution analysis of the balanced portfolio in Example 14.1 assumes the form shown in Table 14.8.

On a segment level the contribution by sector 1 in the equity sector stands out. The 75 basis points are almost entirely attributable to stock E2 with almost equal contributions from each category (allocation, selection, global allocation).

14.3.2 Contributions after Separating Currency Effects

Strictly speaking it would be necessary to use for each stock its specific currency return in order to separate the title-specific currency contribution. Due to transactions or approximation methods these will in general be different from the currency returns of the segment. This would also result in additional interaction terms. Since these interaction terms would in general be small, a simplifying assumption will be made. Instead of the title-specific currency return the

Table 14.8 Results of the Attribution Analysis on a Single Security Level (in%)

Portfolio Level		GAC	AC	SC	IT(1)	IT(2)	Total
Bonds		**0.58**	**0.06**	**−0.05**	**0.03**	**0.01**	**0.63**
	Investment Grade	**0.25**	**−0.21**	**−0.10**	**0.02**	**−0.06**	**−0.10**
	B1	0.18	−0.15	−0.18	0.03	−0.06	−0.18
	B2	0.08	−0.06	0.08	−0.01	0.00	0.08
	< Investment Grade	**0.33**	**0.27**	**0.05**	**0.01**	**0.07**	**0.73**
	B3	0.13	0.10	−0.09	−0.01	0.00	0.13
	B4	0.20	0.17	0.14	0.02	0.07	0.60
Equities		**0.43**	**0.34**	**0.11**	**−0.01**	**−0.09**	**0.78**
	Sector 1	**0.35**	**0.44**	**0.08**	**−0.02**	**−0.10**	**0.75**
	E1	0.15	0.19	−0.25	0.06	0.00	0.15
	E2	0.20	0.25	0.33	−0.08	−0.10	0.60
	Sector 2	**0.08**	**−0.09**	**0.03**	**0.01**	**0.01**	**0.03**
	E3	0.05	−0.06	0.05	0.01	0.00	0.05
	E4	0.03	−0.03	−0.03	−0.01	0.01	−0.03
Total		**1.00**	**0.41**	**0.06**	**0.01**	**−0.08**	**1.40**

segment return will be used for all stocks. According to this assumption the currency contributions of the stocks are given by:

$$cc_{eij} := wp_{eij}*cp_{ei} - wb_{eij}*cb_{ei}$$

and the respective terms interaction (3) by:

$$it(3)_{ij} = wp_{eij}*rp^{L}_{eij}*cp_{ei} - wb_{eij}*rb^{L}_{eij}*cb_{ei}.$$

Example 14.4

Attribution analysis for the balanced Portfolio in Example 14.1, broken down to a single security level with a separation of currency contributions

After separating out the currency contributions, the attribution analysis of the balanced portfolio in Example 14.3 assumes the form shown in Table 14.9.

If one picks again stock E2, then it becomes apparent that a significant portion of the contributions listed in Table 14.8 is in fact attributable to currency effects.

Example 14.5

Breakdown to a subsector level

Table 14.10 contains the analysis of an equity portfolio, which is entirely invested in stocks from the Eurozone. Since the base currency is also the Euro, there are no currency contributions. At first the analysis will be based on the MSCI sectors (GICS classification) on the highest level (level I, sectors). The results in Table 14.10 show that the most significant contribution stems from the segment "Consumer discretionary".

Table 14.9 Results of the Attribution Analysis on a Single Security Level with a Separation of Currency Effects (in %)

Portfolio Level		GAC	AC	SC	CC	IT(1)	IT(2)	IT(3)	Total
Bonds		**0.53**	**0.19**	**−0.04**	**−0.09**	**0.03**	**0.03**	**−0.01**	**0.63**
	Investment Grade	**0.15**	**−0.13**	**−0.10**	**0.00**	**0.02**	**−0.04**	**0.00**	**−0.10**
	B1	0.13	−0.10	−0.13	−0.05	0.02	−0.04	0.00	−0.17
	B2	0.03	−0.02	0.03	0.05	0.00	0.00	0.00	0.07
	< Investment Grade	**0.38**	**0.31**	**0.05**	**−0.09**	**0.01**	**0.08**	**−0.01**	**0.73**
	B3	0.15	0.13	−0.11	−0.02	−0.02	0.00	0.00	0.13
	B4	0.23	0.19	0.16	−0.07	0.03	0.08	−0.01	0.60
Equities		**0.22**	**0.35**	**0.11**	**0.21**	**−0.01**	**−0.09**	**−0.01**	**0.79**
	Sector 1	**0.25**	**0.31**	**0.08**	**0.21**	**−0.02**	**−0.08**	**−0.01**	**0.76**
	E1	0.10	0.13	−0.17	0.05	0.04	0.00	0.00	0.15
	E2	0.15	0.19	0.25	0.16	−0.06	−0.08	−0.01	0.60
	Sector 2	**−0.03**	**0.04**	**0.03**	**0.00**	**0.01**	**−0.01**	**0.00**	**0.03**
	E3	0.00	0.00	0.00	0.05	0.00	0.00	0.00	0.05
	E4	**−0.03**	**0.03**	**0.03**	**−0.05**	**0.01**	**−0.01**	**0.00**	**−0.02**
Total		**0.75**	**0.54**	**0.06**	**0.12**	**0.01**	**−0.06**	**−0.02**	**1.40**

Table 14.10 Attribution Analysis Based on MSCI-Sectors (Level I) (in%)

Portfolio Level			AC	SC	IT	Total
	Sector	Consumer discretionary	−0.25	−3.31	0.24	−3.32
		Consumer staples	−0.04	0.05	0.00	0.01
		Energy	0.61	−0.26	−0.03	0.32
		Financials	0.11	0.15	−0.42	−0.16
		Health care	0.23	0.05	−0.03	0.25
		Industrials	−0.38	0.32	−0.22	−0.28
		Information technology	0.09	−0.07	−0.11	−0.09
		Materials	0.04	−0.30	−0.19	−0.45
		Telecommunication services	−0.15	−0.10	−0.05	−0.30
		Utilities	−0.85	−0.45	0.24	−1.06
		Others	−0.06	0.00	0.00	−0.06
Total			**−0.65**	**−3.92**	**−0.57**	**−5.14**
	Cash					0.21
	Fees					−0.93
Total						**−5.86**

This negative contribution of −3.32% is almost entirely due to bad selection decisions. The portfolio manager (or the investor) has therefore the desire to see a more refined breakdown for this segment. The result will thus be broken down further by employing additional subsectors (level II, industry groups). With this extra information it becomes clear that the lion's share of the contribution results from the segment "automobiles & components"(cf. Table 14.11). A more refined breakdown to single stocks (or an even more refined sector classification; level III or IV, industries, respectively sub-industries) is also possible, although it will not be carried out here.

For an application of this systematics to an extremely nested investment process see the article by Geenen et al.[6a]

14.4 IMPLEMENTATION IN PRACTICE

The level of complexity for the actual implementation strongly depends on the number and complexity of the portfolios to be analyzed. In general one can state that the implementation becomes much more involved with each additional layer. One just needs to remind oneself of the onerous task of adapting the employed approximation procedures (including the distribution of the residua) to the new scheme!

If a portfolio manager has a considerable leeway for positioning portfolios relative to the benchmark, then it might occur that the results of the attribution analysis are hard "to sell" to a client or a portfolio manager (which can also be the case for the classical Brinson methodology). If, for instance, a portfolio manager implements very distinct allocation bets, then this can lead to dominating interaction terms. This problem can be resolved by combining the interaction

[6a] Cf. Greenen et al. (2001).

Table 14.11 Attribution Analysis Based on MSCI–Sectors (Level II) (in %)

Portfolio Level		AC	SC	IT	Total
Consumer discretionary					
	Automobiles & components	−0.51	−2.98	0.63	−2.86
	Consumer durables & apparel	0.01	−0.11	−0.04	−0.14
	Consumer services	−0.01	0.03	−0.01	0.01
	Media	−0.06	0.00	0.00	−0.06
	Retailing	−0.28	0.00	0.00	−0.28
Total		**−0.25**	**−3.31**	**0.24**	**−3.32**

terms with the global allocation terms (at least partially). The modification should, however, be in agreement with the investment process.[7]

14.5 RISK-ADJUSTED ATTRIBUTION ANALYSIS BASED ON THE SYSTEMATIC RISK

14.5.1 Introduction

As already pointed out, in practice and in the corresponding literature, the term attribution analysis in general refers to a breakdown of the return. Risk is considered only in an indirect way. The global allocation contribution for a balanced portfolio is, for instance, the reflection of a weighting decision in regard to the more risky asset class relative to the less risky one. In case of a bond portfolio the contributions from the term structure (duration), for instance, are associated with a chosen risk level. Of course, focusing on the return is in stark contrast to the generally accepted necessity to judge a portfolio manager on the basis of risk-adjusted performance measures.[8] In a certain way this fact was already pointed out in the seminal article by Brinson et al.[9]—even if only in a general form (specifically in the case of cash positions). The inclusion of a risk measure is (for reasons to be explained later), however, not without complications, so that there are relatively few articles on this subject matter. Prominent is certainly the article by Ankrim,[10] in which a breakdown of the contributions on a segment level on the basis of a measure for the systematic (equity) risk is described.

In the following section an intuitive approach for the generalization of the Brinson process will be described, which will already provide the essential results of the Ankrim methodology. Then, in Section 14.5.3 the aforementioned approach by Ankrim will be described in detail. Finally, in Section 14.6 a methodology is

[7] Cf. the explanations in Section 12.2.3 as well as Exercise 12.2.
[8] For instance the standard measures defined in Chapter 3.
[9] See Brinson et al. (1991).
[10] Cf. Ankrim (1992). For a modified form of this methodology see Obeid (2005).

outlined, which—unlike the approach by Ankrim—is based on a measure that has the form of a quotient (Sharpe ratio).

14.5.2 Intuitive Derivation via the Investment Process

According to the methodology by Brinson et al., the contributions from the risk positioning are distributed to the individual effects (selection, allocation, interaction). The goal of this section is to define the contribution resulting from setting the risk level relative to the benchmark properly, and to adjust the effects from the Brinson type analysis accordingly.

As in the analysis of a balanced portfolio, the approach will be illustrated by separating the different decision levels of the investment process, as shown in Figure 14.5 for an equity portfolio, which consists of four segments with two stocks each. The benchmark is similar, but, contrary to the portfolio, in the benchmark all stocks are assumed to be equally weighted. Compared to the decision process in Section 14.2 a further level has been added reflecting the variable systematic risk. The decisions can, for instance, be implemented by keeping a cash position, by leveraging (credit), by purchasing/selling of futures contracts, or through the over- or under-weighting of stocks with a particularly high/low contribution toward the systematic risk (relative to the benchmark). The figure illustrates the case of lowering the systematic risk. Based on the benchmark, these decisions can be illustrated by means of a suitable cash position: the area representing the stocks will be reduced relative to the benchmark area; the resulting cash position is marked.

According to the single-index model, the decision to realize a specific beta corresponds to the following expected return:

$$\beta C := r_f + \beta_P * (RB - r_f) - RB. \tag{14.23}$$

Here r_f is the risk-free interest rate, RB the expected benchmark return, and β_P the portfolio beta.

If one, for the sake of simplicity, neglects the risk-free interest rate, then this relation simplifies to:

$$\beta C = (\beta_P - 1) * RB. \tag{14.24}$$

Both allocation decisions (e.g. overweighting of sectors with a high beta) and selection decisions (e.g. addition of stocks with a low beta) contribute toward the positioning in regard to the systematic risk. The decisive step in adjusting the classical attribution terms consists in finding a relationship between the resulting betas and the overall beta. The starting point is the well-known relationship from Section 12.2.1:

$$RP = RB + \underbrace{(RAP - RB)}_{AC} + \underbrace{(RSP - RB)}_{SC} + \underbrace{(RP - RAP) + (RB - RSP)}_{IT}. \tag{14.25}$$

It holds that:

$$\beta_P = \frac{Kov(RP, RB)}{Var(RB)}. \tag{14.26}$$

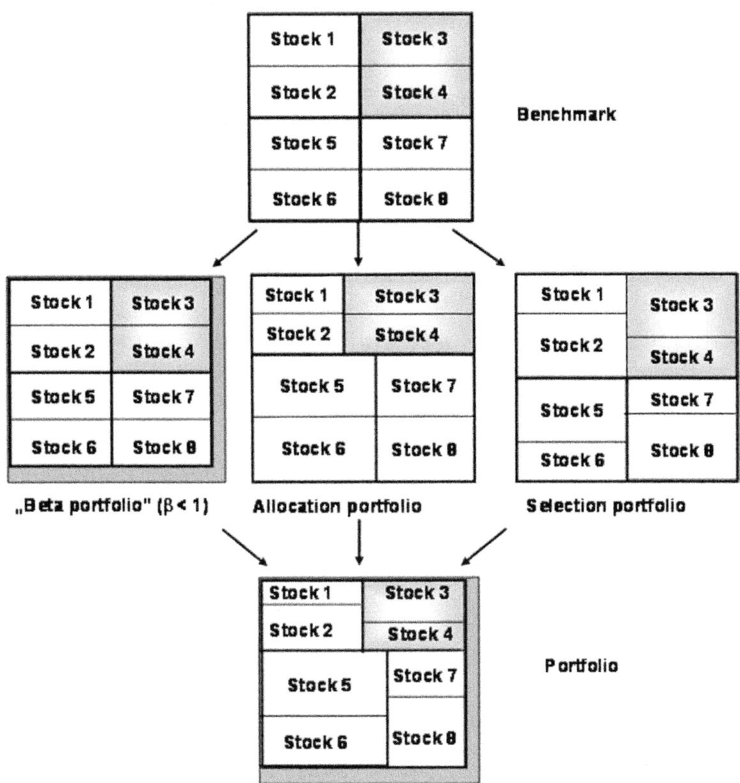

FIGURE 14.5
Illustration of the Decision Process for an Equity Portfolio Without Currency Effects.

If one substitutes for *RP* the expression on the right-hand side of Equation (14.25), then one obtains:

$$\begin{aligned}\beta_P * Var(RB) &= Kov(RP, RB)\\ &= Kov(RB, RB) + Kov(RAP - RB, RB) + Kov(RSP - RB, RB)\\ &\quad + Kov(RP - RAP + RB - RSP, RB).\end{aligned}$$

A simple transformation yields:

$$\beta_P - 1 = \underbrace{\frac{Kov(RAP, RB)}{Var(RB)}}_{=\beta_{AI}} - 1 + \underbrace{\frac{Kov(RSP, RB)}{Var(RB)}}_{=\beta_{Sel}} - 1 + \underbrace{\frac{Kov(RP - RAP + RB - RSP, RB)}{Var(RB)}}_{:=\Delta\beta_{IA}}, \tag{14.27}$$

So that one finally obtains the following relationship:

$$\beta_P - 1 = (\beta_{AI} - 1) + (\beta_{Sel} - 1) + \Delta\beta_{IA}. \tag{14.28}$$

As was to be expected, an interaction term also appears in the analysis of the systematic risk, which reflects the impact of the interaction between allocation and selection decisions on the systematic risk. The expression in Equations (14.28) and (14.25) will be modified as follows:

$$\begin{aligned} RP - RB &= RB*(\beta_P - 1) + ((RAP - RB) - RB*(\beta_{AI} - 1)) + ((RSP - RB) \\ &\quad - RB*(\beta_{Sel} - 1)) + ((RP - RAP) + (RB - RSP) - RB*\Delta\beta_{IA}) \\ &= \underbrace{RB*(\beta_P - 1)}_{\beta B} + \underbrace{RAP - RB*\beta_{AI}}_{AB'} + \underbrace{RSP - RB*\beta_{Sel}}_{SB'} \\ &\quad + \underbrace{(RP - RAP) + (RB*(1 - \Delta\beta_{IA}) - RSP)}_{IT'}. \end{aligned} \tag{14.29}$$

One can readily deduce the modified attribution terms; in order to distinguish them from the traditional terms, the new effects will be denoted by AB' etc. The allocation contribution depends on the relative scaled (via β_{AI}) benchmark return. This entails that the allocation decisions have an impact on the relevant "benchmark return" ($\beta_{AI}*RB$). An analogous assertion holds for the selection term.

For the "allocation beta" and the "selection beta" the following relationships hold:

$$\begin{aligned} \beta_{AI} &= \frac{Kov(RAP, RB)}{Var(RB)} = \frac{Kov(\sum_{i=1}^{N} swp_i*srb_i, RB)}{Var(RB)} \\ &= \frac{\sum_{i=1}^{N} swp_i*Kov(srb_i, RB)}{Var(RB)} = \sum_{i=1}^{N} swp_i*\beta_{BM,i}, \end{aligned} \tag{14.30}$$

and:

$$\begin{aligned} \beta_{Sel} &= \frac{Kov(RSP, RB)}{Var(RB)} = \frac{Kov(\sum_{i=1}^{N} swb_i*srp_i, RB)}{Var(RB)} \\ &= \frac{\sum_{i=1}^{N} swb_i*Kov(srp_i, RB)}{Var(RB)} = \sum_{i=1}^{N} swb_i*\beta_{P,i}, \end{aligned} \tag{14.31}$$

where $\beta_{BM,i}$ is the beta of the benchmark segment i and $\beta_{P,i}$ the beta of the portfolio segment i. β_{AI} represents the component of the portfolio beta (relative to the benchmark), which results from altering the weights of the individual segments and β_{Sel} the one, which results from changing the title weights within the segments (with constant segment weights). These relationships will be revisited later on in this presentation.

The "interaction beta" follows from a similar transformation:

$$\Delta\beta_{IA} = \frac{Kov(RP - RAP + RB - RSP, RB)}{Var(RB)} = \sum_{i=1}^{N} (swp_i - swb_i)*(\beta_{P,i} - \beta_{BM,i}). \tag{14.32}$$

In the transformation (14.30) (analog in Equation (14.31) and (14.32)) it was assumed that

$$Kov(swp_i*srb_i, RB) = swp_i*Kov(srb_i, RB) \tag{14.33}$$

holds. This in turn is based on the assumption that the computation is made for individual periods, in which the weights are approximately constant (in agreement with the Brinson approach). If the weights are treated as stochastic variables (as is the case in the approach by Ankrim), then Equation (14.33) does not hold in this generality. This aspect will also be taken up again after the description of the Ankrim approach.

The analysis methodology described will correspond to the investment process, if—apart from the portfolio beta—the components of the systematic risk, which result from the allocation and selection decisions, figure among the process parameters. In praxis, this will in general not be the case. One needs to emphasize, however, that the modification of the allocation and selection terms are a direct consequence of the separation of the overall beta contribution. Consequently, *if* the portfolio beta is an explicit factor in the investment process, then the impact of the allocation and selection decisions on the portfolio beta is of decisive importance (cf. Figure 14.6) and should be considered in one way or the other.

It is already obvious that Jensen's alpha will play a decisive role in this breakdown. In order to illustrate this further, Equation (14.3.3) will be considered in slightly revised form:

$$\begin{aligned} RP - RB - RB*(\beta_P - 1) = RP - \beta_P RB = RAP - RB*\beta_{Al} + RSP - RB*\beta_{Sel} \\ + (RP - RAP) + (RB*(1 - \Delta\beta_{IA}) - RSP). \end{aligned} \tag{14.34}$$

According to Equation (14.28) the terms corresponding to the risk-free interest rate (neglected so far) will now be added:

$$\begin{aligned} RP - \beta_P*RB - (1 - \beta_P)*r_f = RAP - RB*\beta_{Al} - (1 - \beta_{Al})*r_f + RSP - RB*\beta_{Sel} \\ - (1 - \beta_{Sel})*r_f + (RP - RAP) + (RB*(1 - \Delta\beta_{IA}) - RSP) + \Delta\beta_{IA}*r_f. \end{aligned}$$

Due to Equation (14.28), the terms that were added on the right-hand side equal $-(1 - \beta_P)*r_f$. A regrouping leads to:

$$\begin{aligned} RP - r_f - \beta_P*(RB - r_f) &= RAP - r_f - \beta_{Al}*(RB - r_f) + RSP - r_f - \beta_{Sel}*(RB - r_f) \\ &\quad + (RP - RAP) + (RB*(1 - \Delta\beta_{IA}) - RSP) + \Delta\beta_{IA}*r_f \\ &= RAP - r_f - \beta_{Al}*(RB - r_f) + RSP - r_f - \beta_{Sel}*(RB - r_f) \\ &\quad + (RP - RAP) - (RSP - \Delta\beta_{IA}*r_f - (1 - \Delta\beta_{IA})*RB). \end{aligned} \tag{14.35}$$

With this representation the relationship between the breakdown of the portfolio beta and Jensen's alpha becomes obvious:

$$j\alpha^{Port} = j\alpha^{Sel} + j\alpha^{Al} + \Delta j\alpha^{IA}, \tag{14.36}$$

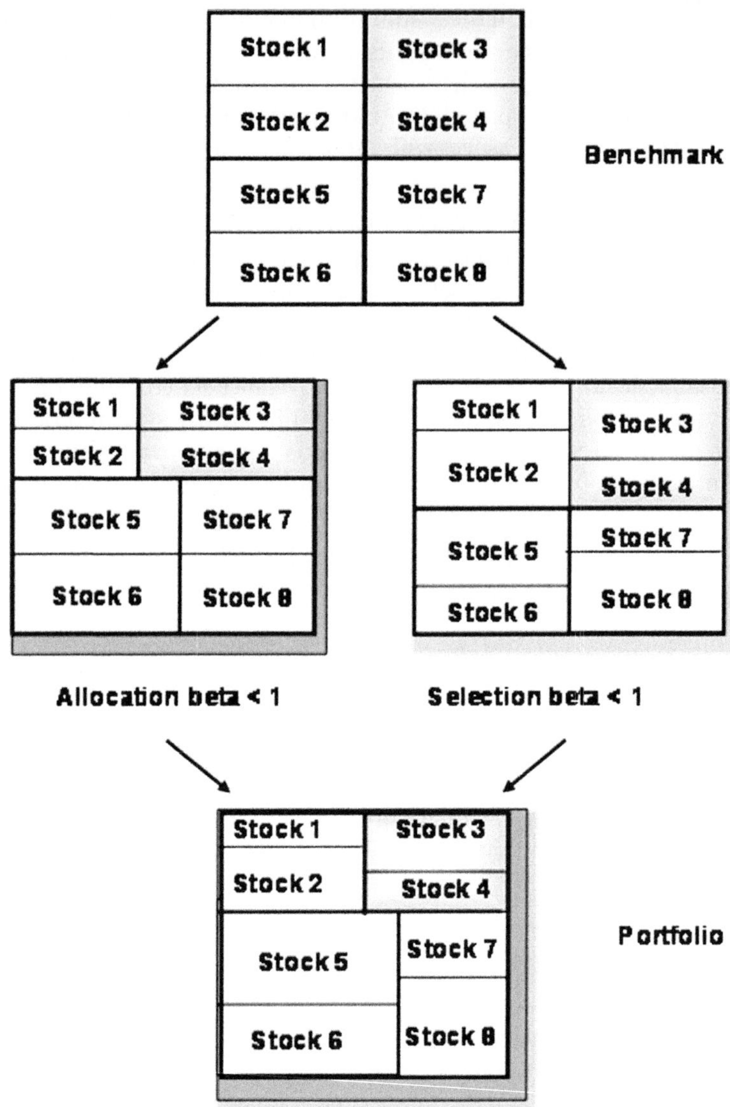

FIGURE 14.6
Decision Process in Regard to the Portfolio Beta in Case of an Equity Portfolio Without Currency Effects (Assumption: $\Delta\beta_{IA}=0$).

where:

$$\Delta j\alpha^{IA} := (RP - RAP) - (RSP - \Delta\beta_{IA} * r_f - (1 - \Delta\beta_{IA}) * RB). \quad (14.37)$$

In practice there are two variants of the beta-adjusted analysis, depending on whether or not one disregards the risk-free interest rate. The latter variant (inclusion of the risk-free rate) is, of course, more in agreement with the theoretical concept of the CAPM. It is, however, often difficult to obtain acceptance among the portfolio managers for this variant, so that we will only consider the variant where the risk-free rate equals zero. At first the allocation contribution will be derived:

$$AC' = RAP - RB*\beta_{AI} = \sum_{i=1}^{N} swp_i*srb_i - \sum_{i=1}^{N} swb_i*srb_i*\beta_{AI} = \sum_{i=1}^{N} (swp_i - \beta_{AI}*swb_i)*srb_i. \tag{14.38}$$

As a consequence one obtains the allocation contribution on a segment level (segment i):

$$ac_i' := (swp_i - \beta_{AI}*swb_i)*srb_i. \tag{14.39}$$

The implementation of the allocation beta (without implementing further allocation or selection decisions) may be interpreted as a scaling of all benchmark weights by β_{AI}. (For a given portfolio, the level β_{AI} is realized by the specific segment weights (allocation portfolio).) It is thus only logical to measure the allocation contribution relative to the scaled benchmark.

The transition to the relative allocation contribution is analogous to the procedure described in Section 14.2. Accordingly, the allocation contribution will be measured in comparison to the contribution, which would result from an investment in the (average) benchmark with the given weight differentials (without beta adjustment):

$$acr_i' := (swp_i - \beta_{AI}*swb_i)*srb_i - (swp_i - swb_i)*RB. \tag{14.40}$$

These contributions add up to the overall allocation contribution, since the sum of the terms $(swp_i - swb_i)*RB$ equals zero. The other contributions are derived analogously. Table 14.12 provides an overview.

Example 14.6

Beta-adjusted attribution analysis

In this example a portfolio will be analyzed, which is exclusively invested in titles of its benchmark (DAX). Over the analysis period (31.03.2009–30.04.2009) nearly all stocks gained considerably in value. Apart from the weights and returns, Table 14.13 contains also estimates for the stock-specific betas, which were computed with the risk software Barra Total Risk; they are assumed constant over the analysis period. In Table 14.14 these betas are shown in aggregated form on a sector level. One can readily verify that:

$$\beta_{AI} = 1.11$$

and:

$$\beta_{Sel} = 1.05;$$

$\Delta\beta_{IA}$ is close to zero, while the portfolio beta equals 1.16, so that the beta contribution equals:[11]

$$\beta C = 0.16*16.75\% = 2.81\%.$$

Table 14.14 contains the results of the risk-adjusted attribution analysis.

[11]The riskless rate of return is neglected here.

Table 14.12 Contributions of the Risk-Adjusted Analysis without Separating Currency Effects

Term	Description	Interpretation
$\beta c_i = (\beta_P - 1) * swb_i * srb_i$	Beta contribution = Beta differential $*$ contribution of the benchmark segment	The beta contribution is the return contribution, which results from the realized level of systematic risk
$ac_{i'} = (swp_i - \beta_{Al} * swb_i) * srb_i$	Allocation contribution = Modified weight differential $*$ Benchmark return	The allocation contribution is the return contribution, which results from altering the benchmarks weights
$acr_{i'} := (swp_i - \beta_{Al} * swb_i) * srb_i - (swp_i - swb_i) * RB$	(Relative) Allocation term = Allocation term – weighted Benchmark return	As above; additionally the return will be modified by a term reflecting the overall benchmark return
$sc_{i'} = swb_i * (srp_i - \beta_{Sel} * srb_i)$	Selection contribution = Benchmark weight $*$ Modified return differential	The selection contribution is the return contribution, which results from the selection of specific title weights within the segments (stock picking)
$it(1)_{i'} = (swp_i - swb_i) * (srp_i - srb_i) - \Delta\beta_{IT} * swb_i * srb_i$	Interaction term = weight differential $*$ return differential –adjustment term	The interaction term results from the "interaction" between the allocation (1. factor) and title selection (2. factor) as well as from a beta-adjusted term

The sum of the contributions equals the active return of 5.76%. A comparison between the above results and the ordinary Brinson-type analysis in Table 14.15 clearly shows that to a large extent the Brinson terms are attributable to the risk leveraging of the portfolio. Since the lion's share of the levering was implemented via the allocation decisions, the allocation contribution has been affected most (1.92% of 3.10%!). But also the selection contribution was to a large degree coupled to a leveraging effect, due to the selection of stocks with a high beta.

The question whether one prefers to split off the beta contributions or to keep them as components of the other contributions must be decided for each case, in accordance with the investment process. If the systematic risk represents a determinant of the investment process, then one should consider separating these effects. One objection that can be made in regard to the separation concerns the often rather weak correlation between the expected $(\beta * (RB - r_f) + r_f)$ and the actual returns (especially, if the portfolio disposes of a significant unsystematic risk). But even for benchmarked portfolios with such a characteristic one could argue (analogous to Ankrim and Hensel in the case of their analysis

Table 14.13 Data on a Security Level

Titles	Sector	Weight (%) Portfolio	BM	Return (%)	Beta
BMW	Automobile	1.88	4.00	20.47	1.10
Daimler	Automobile	4.37	8.00	45.76	1.36
VW	Automobile	5.35	3.00	4.27	0.74
Commerzbank	Banks	0.72	5.00	28.36	1.94
Deutsche Bank	Banks	4.57	9.00	34.16	1.61
BASF	Chemicals	5.62	6.00	25.36	0.98
Bayer	Chemicals	7.39	4.00	4.47	0.78
K+S	Chemicals	1.15	1.00	30.40	1.22
Linde	Chemicals	2.31	1.00	17.88	0.86
Deutsche Börse	Financial Services	2.38	4.00	23.40	1.18
Salzgitter	Basic Resources	0.43	0.50	28.18	1.36
Metro	Retail	0.74	0.50	29.58	0.80
MAN	Industrial	0.87	3.00	50.98	1.31
Siemens	Industrial	9.41	4.00	18.65	1.27
ThyssenKrupp	Industrial	1.18	5.00	23.31	1.33
Adidas	Consumer	1.30	0.50	14.21	0.99
Beiersdorf	Consumer	0.74	0.00	−7.78	0.44
Henkel	Consumer	0.98	0.00	2.99	0.64
Fresenius Medical Care	Pharma & Healthcare	1.47	2.00	1.67	0.42
Fresenius	Pharma & Healthcare	0.75	3.00	12.96	0.59
Merck	Pharma & Healthcare	1.15	0.00	4.43	0.53
SAP AG O.N.	Software	6.01	4.00	8.79	0.91
Deutsche Telekom	Telecommunications	7.48	2.00	−2.25	0.60
Deutsche Post	Transport & Logistics	1.83	6.00	15.19	1.25
Lufthansa	Transport & logistics	1.00	2.00	27.78	1.00
Allianz	Insurance	7.69	10.00	15.78	1.33
Hannover Rück	Insurance	0.39	0.00	2.37	0.93
Münchener Rück	Insurance	4.83	5.00	20.59	0.85
E.ON	Utilities	10.23	7.50	22.62	0.94
RWE	Utilities	5.78	0.00	12.25	0.71

of the currency management) that the expected return can be achieved *de facto*, as long as the investment guidelines allow for suitable leverage instruments.

One furthermore needs to take into account that the betas of individual stocks are likely to fluctuate considerably over time. It is therefore necessary to require a certain minimum size of the portfolio and benchmark segments, in order to ensure a sufficient stochastic stability. In particular, a further breakdown of the betas to a single-stock level does not appear meaningful.

The analysis approach described above for a single period can be generalized to the multi-period case with the procedures described in Section 14.3.

Table 14.14 Beta-Adjusted Analysis

	Weight (%)		Return (%)		Beta		Contribution (%)		
Sector	**Portf.**	**BM**	**Portf.**	**BM**	**Portf.**	**BM**	**Alloc.**	**Selection**	**IA**
Automobile	15.00	11.61	30.72	22.53	1.0	1.2	0.46	0.81	0.28
Banks	14.00	5.29	32.09	33.37	1.7	1.7	2.71	−0.16	−0.11
Chemicals	12.00	16.47	18.20	15.30	0.9	0.9	−0.97	0.34	−0.13
Financial Services	4.00	2.38	23.40	23.40	1.2	1.2	0.32	−0.03	0.00
Basic Resources	0.50	0.43	28.18	28.18	1.4	1.4	0.01	−0.01	0.00
Retail	0.50	0.74	29.58	29.58	0.8	0.8	−0.10	−0.01	0.00
Industrial	12.00	11.46	28.67	21.58	1.3	1.3	−0.17	0.68	0.04
Consumer	0.50	3.02	14.21	5.19	0.7	1.0	−0.15	0.26	−0.23
Pharma & Healthcare	5.00	3.37	8.45	5.12	0.5	0.5	0.06	0.10	0.05
Software	4.00	6.01	8.79	8.79	0.9	0.9	−0.24	−0.03	0.00
Telecommunications	2.00	7.48	−2.25	−2.25	0.6	0.6	0.14	0.01	0.00
Transport & logistics	8.00	2.83	18.34	19.65	1.2	1.2	0.95	−0.07	−0.07
Insurance	15.00	12.91	17.38	17.18	1.1	1.2	0.10	−0.09	0.01
Utilities	7.50	16.01	22.62	18.88	0.9	0.1	−1.95	0.44	−0.32
	100.00	100.00	22.52	16.75	1.2	1.0	1.18	2.24	−0.46

14.5.3 Approach According to Ankrim

Ankrim's starting point for his adaptation of the Brinson approach is Fama's approach for the performance measurement as outlined in detail in Fama (1972). In turn, Fama bases his considerations on the CAPM, according to which the measurement of the portfolio manager's performance ("selectivity") must be carried out relative to a benchmark with the same systematic risk expressed by the portfolio beta.

The starting point is again given by the well-known formulas of the Brinson type analysis in Section 12.2.1., which shall be recapitulated here.

$$AC = \sum ac_i = \sum (swp_i - swb_i) * srb_i, \tag{14.41}$$

$$SC = \sum sc_i = \sum swb_i * (srp_i - srb_i), \tag{14.42}$$

$$IT = \sum it(1)_i = \sum (swp_i - swb_i) * (srp_i - srb_i). \tag{14.43}$$

Both the returns and the weights will be considered as stochastic variables. In the following they will therefore be characterized by a tilde. By linking the

Table 14.15 Attribution Analysis According to Brinson et al.

Sector	Contributions (%)		
	Allocation	Selection	Interaction
Automobile	0.76	0.95	0.28
Banks	2.91	−0.07	−0.11
Chemicals	−0.68	0.48	−0.13
Financial Services	0.38	0.00	0.00
Basic Resources	0.02	0.00	0.00
Retail	−0.07	0.00	0.00
Industrial	0.12	0.81	0.04
Consumer	−0.13	0.27	−0.23
Pharma & Healthcare	0.08	0.11	0.05
Software	−0.18	0.00	0.00
Telecommunications	0.12	0.00	0.00
Transport & logistics	1.02	−0.04	−0.07
Insurance	0.36	0.03	0.00
Utilities	−1.61	0.60	−0.32
	3.10	3.15	−0.48

representation of the segment returns as a function of the individual stock returns,[12]

$$\widetilde{srb_i} = \sum \widetilde{wb}'_{ij} * \widetilde{rb}_{ij}, \tag{14.44}$$

with the expression of the equilibrium return of a risky asset according to the CAPM,

$$\widetilde{rb}_{ij} = r_f + \beta_{ij} * (\widetilde{RB} - r_f) + \widetilde{\varepsilon}_{ij}, \tag{14.45}$$

one obtains:

$$\widetilde{srb_i} = \sum \widetilde{wb}'_{ij} * (r_f + \beta_{ij} * (\widetilde{RB} - r_f) + \widetilde{\varepsilon}_{ij}). \tag{14.46}$$

The weights $\widetilde{wb}'_{ij}$ are already normalized in regard to the weight of the segment i, which is already reflected in the notation (wb prime). β_{ij} represents the beta of the stock j in segment i, and $\widetilde{\varepsilon}_{ij}$ the specific fluctuations of the stock (residuum). r_f is the (constant) risk-free rate of return. For the residuum the usual assumptions are made.[13]

[12] The notation is the same as in Section 12.2.4.

[13] Cf. e.g. Zimmermann (1997).

By means of the above formula, the expression for the allocation contribution in Equation (14.41) assumes the following form:

$$\widetilde{AC} = \sum_i (\widetilde{swp}_i - \widetilde{swb}_i) * \sum_j \widetilde{wb}'_{ij} * (r_f + \beta_{ij} * (\widetilde{RB} - r_f) + \tilde{\varepsilon}_{ij}). \tag{14.47}$$

Based on the assumption that no stock selection occurred, one can show that the non-measurable expected value of this expression assumes the following form (cf. Exercise 14.3):

$$\begin{aligned} E(\widetilde{AC}) &= \sum_i E(\widetilde{swp}_i - \widetilde{swb}_i) * E(\beta_{BM,i} * (\widetilde{RB} - r_f)) \\ &\quad + \sum_i Cov(\widetilde{swp}_i - \widetilde{swb}_i,\ \beta_{BM,i} * (\widetilde{RB} - r_f)). \end{aligned} \tag{14.48}$$

$\beta_{BM,i}$ represents the weighted sum of the betas for all stocks in this segment ($\beta_{P,i}$ analogous):

$$\beta_{BM,i} = \sum_j \widetilde{wb}'_{ij} * \beta_{BM,ij}. \tag{14.49}$$

According to Obeid the second term in the breakdown (14.48) may be interpreted as the portfolio manager's ability to implement allocation decisions in practice,[14] so that the first factor represents the desired adjustment factor for the allocation contribution. By forming the arithmetic average (indicated by the overbar) one finally arrives at the following expression of the risk adjusted allocation contribution:

$$\begin{aligned} AC_\beta &= \sum (swp_i - swb_i) * srb_i - \sum E(\widetilde{swp}_i - \widetilde{swb}_i) * E(\beta_{BM,i} * (\widetilde{RB} - r_f)) \\ &= \sum (swp_i - swb_i) * srb_i - \sum \overline{(swp_i - swb_i)} * \overline{(\beta_{BM,i} * (RB - r_f))}. \end{aligned} \tag{14.50}$$

One obtains similar expressions for the selection and the interaction terms:

$$\begin{aligned} SC_\beta &= \sum swb_i * (srp_i - srb_i) - E\left(\sum \widetilde{swb}_i * (\tilde{\beta}_{P,i} - \tilde{\beta}_{BM,i}) * (\widetilde{RB} - r_f)\right) \\ &= \sum swb_i * (srp_i - srb_i) - \overline{swb_i * (\beta_{P,i} - \beta_{BM,i}) * (RB - r_f)}, \end{aligned} \tag{14.51}$$

$$\begin{aligned} IT_\beta &= \sum (swp_i - swb_i) * (srp_i - srb_i) - E\left(\sum (\widetilde{swp}_i - \widetilde{swb}_i) * (\tilde{\beta}_{P,i} - \tilde{\beta}_{BM,i}) * (\widetilde{RB} - r_f)\right) \\ &= \sum (swp_i - swb_i) * (srp_i - srb_i) - \overline{(swp_i - swb_i) * (\beta_{P,i} - \beta_{BM,i}) * (RB - r_f)}. \end{aligned} \tag{14.52}$$

[14] In the article by Ankrim this term is shown in a slightly different way. For a comparison see the article by Obeid in the place cited.

Based on the Equations (14.50), (14.51), and (14.52) one can readily deduce the transition to the terms sketched in Table 14.12. If one chooses a sufficiently small period under consideration, the averaged quantities in Equation (14.50) may be approximated by the values at the beginning of the period or another constant value, and if one neglects in addition the risk-free interest rate, then one obtains for the allocation contribution:

$$\begin{aligned} AC_\beta &= \sum (swp_i - swb_i)*srb_i - \sum (swp_i - swb_i)*\beta_{BM,i}*RB \\ &= \sum (swp_i - swb_i)*srb_i - (\beta_{AI} - 1)*RB \\ &= \sum (swp_i - swb_i)*srb_i - (\beta_{AI} - 1)*\sum swb_i*srb_i \\ &= \sum (swp_i - \beta_{AI}*swb_i)*srb_i. \end{aligned} \tag{14.53}$$

This expression is identical to the one in Table 14.12. The transformation of the other attribution effects is analogous.

In practice the application of the adjustment terms is problematic. Firstly, taking an average is always at the cost of losing information. An average beta of 1 does *not* imply the realization of the same systematic risk as for the benchmark. While this aspect of the beta gets lost to a large extent in the Ankrim approach, the approach sketched in Section 14.5 reflects it more appropriately. Since the general Brinson approach is not based on average values (for instance, one does not consider the effect of an average overweight position), it appears that the approach delineated in Section 14.5 complements the Brinson methodology better than the approach of Ankrim. This latter approach also has the possibility of showing results for individual sub-periods, which can be linked with any of the standard methodologies described in Section 12.3.

14.6 RISK-ADJUSTED ATTRIBUTION ANALYSIS BASED ON THE INFORMATION RATIO

Based on a suitable breakdown of the tracking error, Menchero outlines an approach for a risk-adjusted attribution analysis on the basis of the information ratio.[15] The starting point is an abstract form of an attribution analysis, in which the attribution effects obtained for the period t are denominated by Q_{it} (i represents the attribution effect). The only requirement is that the active return of the period t, RA_t, can entirely be broken down by means of the Q_{it}:

$$RA_t = RP_t - RB_t = \sum_i Q_{it}. \tag{14.54}$$

The standard example for such a breakdown is, of course, the attribution analysis according to Brinson et al. Further examples are the breakdowns for balanced and bond portfolios described in Chapter 12 and section 14.1 and 14.2, respectively.

[15] Cf. Mechero (2006/07).

In Section 12.3 different methodologies for the linking of contributions in the multi-period case were described. In simplified terms, most procedures amounted to a suitable scaling of the individual terms for the periods. Thus:

$$Q_i = \sum_t \gamma_t * Q_{it} \tag{14.55}$$

represents the aggregated overall effect over time, so that for the overall active return, *RA*, one obtains:

$$RA = RP - RB = \sum_i Q_i. \tag{14.56}$$

In another article, Menchero and Hu demonstrated that the breakdown of the return both in its ex ante form and in its ex post form can be transformed into a breakdown of risk measures. Based on the breakdown

$$RA = R - R^{bm} = \sum_i Q_i, \tag{14.57}$$

one obtains the following representation of the tracking error:[16]

$$TE = \sigma(RA) = \sum_i \sigma(Q_i) * \rho(Q_i, RA). \tag{14.58}$$

From (14.56) and (14.57) then readily follows the desired representation of the information ratio:

$$IR = \frac{RA}{TE} = \frac{\sum_i Q_i}{\sigma(RA)} = \sum_i \underbrace{\frac{\sigma(Q_i) * \rho(Q_i, RA)}{\sigma(RA)}}_{u_i} * \underbrace{\frac{Q_i}{\sigma(Q_i) * \rho(Q_i, RA)}}_{IR_i}. \tag{14.58}$$

One obtains the following suggestive relationship:

$$IR = \sum_i u_i * IR_i. \tag{14.59}$$

Menchero refers to the terms u_i as *risk weights* and to the terms IR_i as *component information ratio*. Some caution is in order, however. Although the terms u_i add up to one, they have a strong dependence on the factors, which also influence the terms IR_i. Furthermore, the latter terms are not quite the "stand alone" information ratios, since due to the scaling in Equation (14.55) they are also dependent on the other effects. In regard to the breakdown in Equation (14.58) there is another critical aspect, which was pointed out in the article by Menchero.[17] Correlations near zero can lead to singularities in the risk weights. Furthermore, under certain circumstances, estimation errors for the correlations can be quite significant, such that the reliability of the results in practice is limited.

---

[16] Cf. Menchero and Hu (2006), Xiang (2005/06) as well as Grégoire and van Oppens.

[17] Cf. Menchero (2006/07, p. 27). Cf. also this article for a detailed example.

14.7 SPECIAL ASPECTS IN THE ANALYSIS OF HEDGE FUNDS

14.7.1 Attribution Analysis for Portfolios with Short Positions

In Chapter 15 examples for building up short positions with derivatives will be given. The methodology described so far can be adopted (with a few modifications) to cover these situations as well. In the case of portfolios consisting of a short and a long position, it can be meaningful to analyze both components separately, especially if there is a similar structure on the benchmark side. In order to arrive at a meaningful analysis without "singularities", it is, however, mandatory to consider an appropriate cash position.[18]

If the long and the short components of a portfolio are measured against different benchmarks (one attached with a positive, the other with a negative weight), then the methodology for balanced funds described in previous sections of this chapter may be applied.[19]

14.7.2 Risk Measures Based on the Drawdown

14.7.2.1 *MOTIVATION*

It is often claimed that for hedge funds, the traditional performance measures described in Chapter 3 lead to inadequate results.[20] Thus for the performance and risk measurement for hedge funds new measures were suggested. These measures are principally applicable to all funds, but in practice they are primarily used for hedge funds and absolute return funds. They provide a ranking of different funds, such that the fund with the highest value also assumes the top position in the ranking.

14.7.2.2 *DRAWDOWN, MAXIMUM DRAWDOWN, CALMAR, STERLING AND BURKE RATIO*

If a_i denotes time series of unit prices (adjusted by dividends) of a fund, then the *drawdown* (D_j) for the unit price j (for $1 \leqslant j \leqslant N$) is defined as follows:[21]

$$D_j := \max_{j \leqslant i \leqslant N} \{r_{ij} := -\frac{a_i}{a_j} + 1, 0\} \tag{14.60}$$

---

[18] Cf. Menchero (2002/03).

[19] In this case, the portfolio can be regarded as a balanced fund with the components "long equity", "short equity" and a cash position. The adaption of this methodology is straight-forward and will not be described in detail cf. (Exercise 14.4).

[20] Cf. e.g. Lo, (2002). The author demonstrates that due to the autocorrelations the Sharpe ratios of many hedge funds are significantly overestimated.

[21] Cf. e.g. Magdon-Ismail et al. (2004) and Magdon-Ismail and Atiya 2004).

The *maximum drawdown* (*MD*) is defined as the loss, which an investor would have suffered in the worst combination for the start, respectively termination of an investment in the history of the fund. It holds that:

$$MD = \max_{1 \leqslant j \leqslant N} (D_j). \tag{14.61}$$

A local maximum of the time series is also called *high watermark*.

When using the maximum drawdown it should always be made transparent on which period the computation was based (since inception of the fund, last three, five, or ten years, etc.). Figure 14.7 illustrates that this loss occurs between a local maximum and local minimum.

The *time to recovery* is defined as the length of the period necessary to recover from the maximum drawdown, starting from the point in time where the high watermark was reached.

The drawdown forms the basis for a number of risk measures. The *Calmar ratio*[22] is for instance defined as the quotient formed by the annualized return and the maximum drawdown over the last 36 months:[23]

$$CR = \frac{R_{ann}}{MD}. \tag{14.62}$$

A modified approach is pursued by the so-called *Sterling Ratio* (*SterR*). It is similar to the Calmar ratio. The maximum drawdown is, however, replaced by the average of the largest drawdowns ($\overline{D}$) over a defined period plus a fixed absolute charge of 10%:

$$SterR = \frac{R_{ann}}{\overline{D} + 10\,\%}. \tag{14.63}$$

$\overline{D}$ can for instance be based on the maximum drawdown following a high watermark (cf. Figure 14.7). In practice, there are many different variants of this definition.[24]

---

[22] Calmar stands for CALifornia Managed Accounts Reports. California Managed Accounts and is an American investment firma (cf. Young (1991)).

[23] Cf. e.g. Kestner (1996). In practice, however, also other conventions are used. The period under consideration can for instance comprise the entire available data history. Often the numerator is defined analogous to the Sharpe ratio by subtracting the risk-free return (see e.g. Eling and Schuhmacher (2007)). For a derivation of expected values and a discussion of the scaling properties for variable periods cf. the article by Magdon-Ismail et al.

[24] In Magdon-Ismail and Aiya (2004) and Heidorn et al. (2006), instead of the average drawdown, the maximal drawdown over the analysis period minus (absolute) 10% is used. In Kestner (1996) the ratio is (somewhat artificially) based on the average maximal drawdown of the three preceding calendar years. In Eling and Schuhmacher (2007) the denominator just contains the average drawdown without the subtraction of a constant term. Furthermore, occasionally the active return relative to a risk-free interest rate is used instead of the absolute return (cf. e.g. Eling and Schuhmacher (2007). According to the entry in the German version of Wikipedia, the denominator is defined as $\overline{D}$ - 10% (German page as of 17.01.2012), (which opens up the possibility of an infinite Sterling Ratio). The English version (same point in time) contains two versions (–10% and no subtraction at all). An older version of English Wikipedia site (21.04.2009) introduces yet another version of the denominator (+$\overline{D}$, volatility of the benchmark).

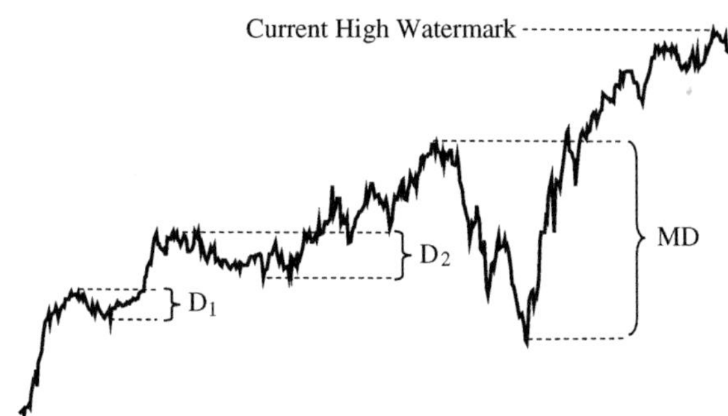

FIGURE 14.7
Illustration of the Maximum Drawdown by Means of the Time-Series of a Hedge Fund.

The Burke ratio uses the square root of the sum of the squares of the n largest (maximum) drawdowns, where n is user-defined[25]. It would make sense to compute the maximum drawdown with a high watermark as the starting point and to pick only one value for each trend channel; in Figure 14.7, for instance, the three largest drawdowns would be MD, D_1, and D_2.

$$BR = \frac{R_{ann} - r_f}{\sqrt{\sum_{i=1}^{n} MD_i^2}}. \tag{14.64}$$

In this definition, due to the squaring, the maximum drawdown still has a significant impact on the classification of the portfolios, it is, however, not as dominating as in the Calmar ratio.

14.7.2.3 ULCER INDEX AND MARTIN RATIO

These measures are based on the time-series of drawdowns in (14.60). The ulcer index[26] is defined as the square root of the average of the squares of the drawdowns:

$$UI = \sqrt{\frac{1}{n} * \sum_{i=1}^{n} \tilde{D}_i^2}, \tag{14.65}$$

where $\tilde{D}_i$ denotes the drawdown of the unit price starting from the last high watermark. (In this context drawdown means: decrease of the unit price relative to the last high watermark. Also this drawdown assumes positive values.)

Due to the division by the number of data points, this measure is principally suitable for all data frequencies. Martin recommends a high frequency, however (daily or weekly). If the valuation of the fund leads to a unit price above the high

---

[25] Cf. Burke (1994) and Eling and Schumacher (2007).

[26] For the ulcer index and the Martin ratio see Martin and McCann (1989) and Martin (2004).

watermark relevant at this point in time, then $\widetilde{D}_i = 0$ and there is no contribution to the sum in Equation (14.65). If the unit price is significantly lower than the high watermark, then, due to the quadratic form of the terms, this will result in a significant increase of *UI*. During long periods of weak performance the ulcer index increases considerably. This is illustrated in Figure 14.8, the lower part of which shows the ulcer index over time.

The definition of the Martin ratio is similar to the one of the Sharpe ratio. Volatility is replaced by the ulcer index:

$$MR = \frac{R_{ann} - r_f}{UI} = \frac{R_{ann} - r_f}{\sqrt{\frac{1}{n} * \sum_{i=1}^{n} \widetilde{D}_i^2}}. \tag{14.66}$$

A risk measure similar to the ulcer index, which will not be discussed in detail, was defined by Becker.[27] In its discrete form the so-called *pain index* is defined by:

$$PI = \frac{1}{n} * \sum_{i=1}^{n} \widetilde{D}_i. \tag{14.67}$$

The corresponding risk measure $MR = \left(R_{ann} - r_f\right) / PI$ is called the *pain ratio*.

14.7.2.4 LAKE RATIO

A further risk measure was defined by Seykota. He interprets the profile of a time-series graphically as a mountain region, which he fills up with water in

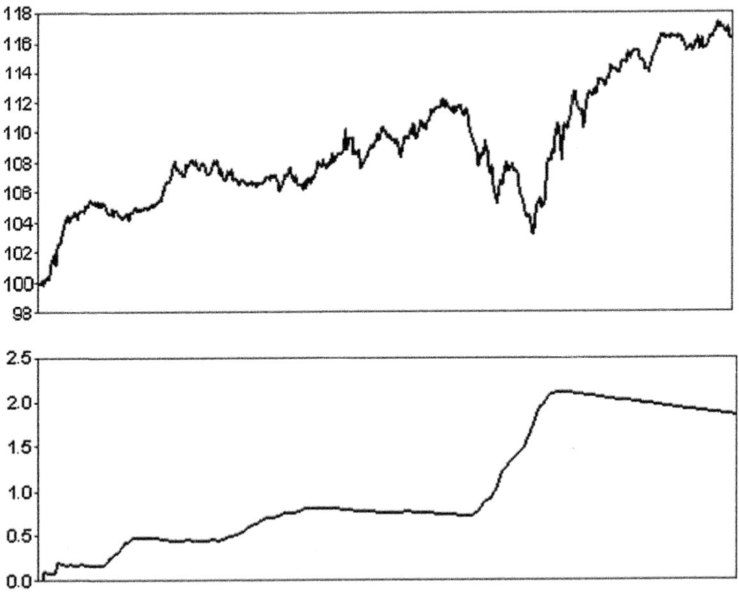

FIGURE 14.8
Illustration of the Ulcer Index by Means of the Time-Series of a Hedge Fund.

[27] Cf. Becker (2006).

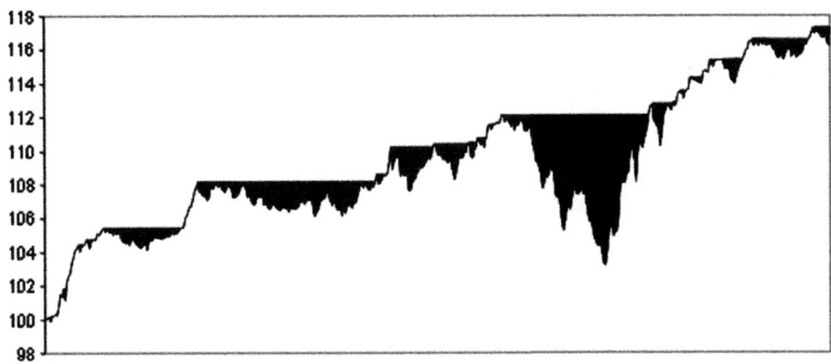

FIGURE 14.9
Illustration of the Lake Index by Means of the Time-Series of a Hedge Fund.

those regions, where the time-series shows a negative return and moves away from the high watermark. In this way "lakes" are created, which explains the name of the risk measure.[28] Seykota calls the quotient formed by the cross-sections of the lakes and the mountain regions, respectively, *lake ratio* (Figure 14.9).

The lake ratio is problematic. If a risky fund shows a strong performance (with few lakes, so to speak) at the beginning of the period under consideration, then this would suggest that the fund entails few risks.

The question, whether these new measures will lead to a really new appraisal of the performance and risk compared to the traditional measures described in Chapter 3, seems to be still open. However, several studies did not support this assertion.[29]

14.8 CHAPTER-END PROBLEMS

1. (Brinson Fachler approach):

Show that the sum of the contributions in Equations (14.13) and (14.14),

$$ac^r_{ei} := WB_e * \left(\frac{swp_{ei}}{WP_e} - \frac{swb_{ei}}{WB_e}) * (srb_{ei} - RB_e\right),$$

and

$$ac^r_{bi} = WB_b * \left(\frac{swp_{bi}}{WP_b} - \frac{swb_{bi}}{WB_b}\right) * (srb_{bi} - RB_b),$$

equals the overall allocation contribution.

[28] Cf. http://www.seykota.com/tribe/risk/index.htm.

[29] Cf. e.g. Eling and Schuhmacher (2007). In this study several of the alternative measures described in this section were investigated by means of the rank correlation. The authors conclude that the new approaches essentially lead to the same ranking as the Sharpe ratio. A similar conclusion is drawn in Heidorn/Hoppe/Kaiser (2006).

Table 14.16 Weights and Returns of the Balanced Benchmark

			Weight (%)			Returns (Base Currency %)		
Global Segment	Segment (Industries/ Rating)	Title	Global Segment	Segment (Industries/ Rating)	Title	Global Segment	Segment (Industries/ Rating)	Title
Bonds	Investment	B1	50	25	12.5	5.75	5.00	7.0
	Grade	B2			12.5			3.0
	< Investment	B3		25	12.5		6.50	5.0
	Grade	B4			12.5			8.0
Equities	Sector 1	A1	50	25	12.5	−4.25	−7.00	−6.0
		A2			12.5			−8.0
	Sector 2	A3		25	12.5		−1.50	−2.0
		A4			12.5			−1.0

Table 14.17 Weights and Returns of the Balanced Portfolio

			Weight (%)			Returns (Base Currency %)		
Global Segment	Segment (Industries/ Rating)	Title	Global Segment	Segment (Industries/ Rating)	Title	Global Segment	Segment (Industries/ Rating)	Title
Bonds	Investment	B1	15	10	5			7.0
	Grade	B2			5			3.0
	< Investment	B3		5	2			5.0
	Grade	B4			3			8.0
Equities	Sector 1	A1	85	65	25			−6.0
		A2			40			−8.0
	Sector 2	A3		20	10			−2.0
		A4			10			−1.0

The breakdown to a single stock level in Equation (14.21) resulted in the following contribution for an individual title:

$$ac_{eij} = WB_e * \left[\frac{swp_{ei}}{WP_e} - \frac{swb_{ei}}{WB_e}\right] * \frac{wb_{eij}}{swb_{ei}} * rb_{eij}.$$

It would be meaningful to consider the return of the stock relative to its segment:

$$ac^r_{eij} = WB_e * \left[\frac{swp_{ei}}{WP_e} - \frac{swb_{ei}}{WB_e}\right] * \frac{wb_{eij}}{swb_{ei}} * (rb_{eij} - srb_{ei}).$$

What would be the mathematical consequences of this alteration?

2. (Limitation of the analysis):

Tables 14.16 and 14.17 contain the data required for an analysis of a balanced portfolio relative to its benchmark.

A. Determine the missing segment returns in Table 14.17 and produce an attribution analysis, which contains the global allocation contributions.
B. In view of these results, discuss the limitations of the methodology.
C. Consider how the approach could be modified, in order to provide meaningful results in such situations?

3. (Allocation contribution according to Ankrim):

A. Derive Equation, (14.48) based on Equation (14.47) and the assumption that no stock picking took place:30

$$(E(\widetilde{AC}) = \sum E(\widetilde{swp}_i - \widetilde{srb}_i) * E(\beta_{BM,i} * (\widetilde{RB} - r_f)) + \sum Cov(\widetilde{swp}_i - \widetilde{swb}_i,\ \beta_{BM,i} * (\widetilde{RB} - r_f))$$

B. Sketch the transition of the selection and interaction contributions according to Ankrim into the contributions defined in Section 14.5 (analogous to the transformation in Equation (14.53)).

4. Analysis of a long/short equity portfolios:

Generalize the attribution analysis described in Section 14.2.1 to the case of a long/short equity portfolio with a cash position, where the benchmark components are different on the long and the short side.

[30] Cf. [Obeid 05].

Chapter 15

Attribution Analysis with Derivatives

ABSTRACT

A delineation of common methodologies in the field of attribution analysis would be incomplete without a discussion of the role of derivatives in the steering of investment portfolios. Due to the immense number of different types of derivative, we focus on the most basic instruments. These include interest rate futures, certain swaps, futures, and options on single stocks and stock indices. Furthermore currency forward contracts will be considered, which are essential in the steering of currency risk. The methodologies described for these instrument types may be adopted for the analysis of other derivatives.

The starting point is the Brinson-type attribution analysis described in Chapters 14 and 16 and the approach for an analysis of bond portfolio in Chapter 15. In the case of options it will become particularly obvious how the spectrum of the analysis parameters is expanded by adding a limited number of essential valuation parameters explicitly to the analysis framework.

Keywords
Currency premium, currency surprise, forward premium, currency forwards, Ankrim and Hensel approach, Singer and Karnosky approach, currency hedging, cost of carry, single-stock futures.

15.1 ATTRIBUTION ANALYSIS WITH DERIVATIVE-BASED CURRENCY MANAGEMENT

15.1.1 Currency Premium and Currency Surprise

An important instrument for managing currency positions in international investment portfolios is given by currency forwards (FX forwards). A currency forward is a binding agreement to exchange one currency for another at a specified date in the future at a price (exchange rate) that is fixed on the purchase date. These instruments have a crucial role in the hedging of currency risks. In the following, the basic notation and relationships important to the analysis approaches, will be introduced.

Performance Evaluation and Attribution of Security Portfolios. http://dx.doi.org/10.1016/B978-0-12-744483-3.00015-8

© 2013 Elsevier Inc. All rights reserved.
For End-of-chapter Questions: © 2012. CFA Institute, Reproduced and republished with permission from CFA Institute. All rights reserved.

If S^0 denotes the exchange rate of the (local) currency relative to the base currency at the beginning of the period,[1] and F^t the exchange rate, which (at the beginning of the period) can be realized at the end of the period via a currency forward, then the so-called *currency premium* (or *forward premium*) f is given by:

$$f := \frac{F^t - S^0}{S^0}. \tag{15.1}$$

It represents (apart from counterparty risks) the "safe" currency return, which can be locked in by means of currency forwards. In case $F^t > S^0$ f is positive, for $F^t < S^0$ negative. If one assumes that there are no arbitrage opportunities, then, according to the interest rate parity theorem, it holds that:[2]

$$(1 + r_b) = (1 + r_i) * (1 + f), \tag{15.2}$$

where r_i denotes the riskless rate of return in the local currency and r_b the riskless rate of return in the base currency (both with the same term). The expected currency return is thus a reflection of the difference between the (risk-free) rates of the same maturity in different currencies (currency regions). In a region with a higher interest rate, the currency will devalue, for a currency with a lower interest rate level the opposite effect will be expected. If one uses continuously compounded instead of discrete returns, then (keeping the notation) the above equation assumes the form:

$$r_b = r_i + f. \tag{15.3}$$

If, as in Section 12.2.5, c is the *actual* return obtained in a period relative to the base currency, then it holds that:

$$c := \frac{S^t - S^0}{S^0}. \tag{15.4}$$

If one accepts the concept of a currency premium f, then it is natural to define the component of the currency return, which exceeds the currency premium as the *currency surprise*:

$$cs := \frac{S^t - F^t}{S^0}. \tag{15.5}$$

Consequently it holds that:

$$c = cs + f. \tag{15.6}$$

The return of a currency forward contract is given by:

$$r^{for} := \frac{S^t - F^t}{F^t}. \tag{15.7}$$

According to Equation (15.1) one obtains:

$$r^{for} := \frac{S^t - F^t}{S^0} * \frac{S^0}{F^t} = \frac{cs}{1 + f}, \tag{15.8}$$

[1] More generally S^t denotes the exchange rate at t.

[2] Cf. Eun and Resnick (1994).

and thus:

$$1 + r^{for} = 1 + \frac{cs}{1+f} = 1 + \frac{c-f}{1+f} = \frac{1+c}{1+f}, \tag{15.9}$$

so that one obtains the following relationship, if one uses continuously compounded returns instead of discrete returns (and relationship (15.3)):

$$r^{for} = c - f = c + r_i - r_b \tag{15.10}$$

and:

$$c = r^{for} - r_i + r_b. \tag{15.11}$$

15.1.1.1 APPROACH OF ANKRIM AND HENSEL

An approach to analyzing currency effects of international portfolios was introduced by Ankrim and Hensel.[3] When calculating the currency contributions they distinguish, as described in the previous section, between the currency premium and the currency surprise. According to Ankrim and Hensel the assessment of the currency managers should focus on their ability to predict currency surprises. The contributions due to the currency premiums should be split off and listed separately. Overall, their analysis contains the following effects, which will be explained in detail:

- Forward premium
- Currency management
- Allocation
- Selection
- Interaction.

The section will close with a critical appraisal of this approach.

15.1.1.1.1 Forward Premium Effect

According to Ankrim and Hensel the Forward Premium Effect plays the role of a quasi-benchmark for the currency manager, or the currency management (if different persons are involved). It is determined solely by the allocation manager and the given currency premiums.[4]

$$fp_i^{ah} := (swp_i - swb_i) * (f_i - F),$$

---

[3] Cf. Ankrim and Hensel (1994).

[4] The notation is basically the same as for the Brinson-type analysis in Chapter 12. Thus swp_i again denotes the weight of the portfolio segment i and swb_i the corresponding benchmark weight. In order to distinguish the contributions to the Ankrim-Hensel analysis from the Brinson terms, an index ah is added to the notation. For the returns the traditional notation is kept. For instance, the return of the portfolio segment i in base currency i is denoted by srp_i. An index L is added to the variables that represent the returns in local currency.

where:

$$F := \sum_{i=1}^{n} swb_i * f_i \tag{15.12}$$

is the weighted average of the currency premiums of the segments (f_i). An overweight position results in a positive contribution, only if the respective market segment features a currency premium above average. These terms represent currency contributions which a portfolio manager could lock in with certainty.

15.1.1.1.2 Currency Management Effect

The currency management effect measures the ability of the manager to select currencies, which experience an above average appreciation relative to the base currency (currency surprise). In other words, it quantifies the ability to generate a surplus performance to the currency premium by means of currency forwards (or similar instruments). As for the currency premium, the term is based on the return (currency surprise) in relation to the average:

$$cm_i^{ah} := (swp_i - swb_i) * (cs_i - CS) + (hwp_i - hwb_i) * (r_i^{for} - CS), \tag{15.13}$$

where:

$$CS := \sum_{i=1}^{n} swb_i * cs_i.$$

Relative to the currency i the variables hwp_i and hwb_i denote the additional exposures of the portfolios and the benchmark generated via currency forwards (positive sign), respectively hedged into the base currency (negative sign).

15.1.1.1.3 Allocation Effect

The allocation contribution is formally identical to the Brinson-term:

$$ac_i^{ah} := (swp_i - swb_i) * (\widetilde{srb_i^L} - \widetilde{RB^L}). \tag{15.14}$$

In the approach by Ankrim and Hensel the local returns are, however, defined differently from the Brinson approach:

$$\widetilde{srb_i^L} = srb_i - c_i = srb_i - cs_i - f_i \tag{15.15}$$

and:

$$\widetilde{RB} = \sum_{i=1}^{n} swb_i * \widetilde{srb_i^L}. \tag{15.16}$$

Thus the effect resulting from the interaction between the segment returns in local currency and the currency returns are incorporated into the segment returns, which leads to a significant simplification of the formal representation.

When implementing this approach in practice, it makes sense to use the set of formulae based on the separation of the interaction terms.

15.1.1.1.4 Selection Effect

The selection contribution is formally identical to the corresponding Brinson term:

$$sc_i^{ah} := swb_i * (\widetilde{srp_i^L} - \widetilde{srb_i^L}), \tag{15.17}$$

but also this term is based on the modified returns:

$$\widetilde{srp_i^L} = srp_i - c_i = srp_i - cs_i - f_i. \tag{15.18}$$

15.1.1.1.5 Interaction Effect

The interaction terms are defined in an analogous form:

$$it_i^{ah} := (swp_i - swb_i) * (\widetilde{srp_i^L} - \widetilde{srb_i^L}). \tag{15.19}$$

It can be readily verified that the different effects add up to the active return:

$$\sum_{i=1}^{n} fp_i^{ah} + cm_i^{ah} + ac_i^{ah} + sc_i^{ah} + it_i^{ah} = \sum_{i=1}^{n} (swp_i * srp_i - swb_i * srb_i) + (hwp_i - hwb_i) * r_i^{for}.$$

Example 15.1

Attribution analysis according to Ankrim and Hensel

An international equity portfolio investing in five countries will be considered as an example. The following tables contain all the data necessary for an analysis according to Ankrim and Hensel. The risk-free investment rates correspond to the rates available in June 1999 for an investment period of one year. The weights refer to the beginning of the period. The calculation of the contributions is based on the discrete returns shown in Tables 15.1 and 15.2. The additional interaction terms will not be considered, as they are very small.

Effects resulting from the currency hedges have an impact on the portfolio segment in base currency (in this case: Euro), since a trade in a (local) currency forward always has an effect on the base currency exposure (respectively on the currency, associated to the forward contract).

The portfolio/benchmark return was equal to 13.29%/14.68%, which resulted in an active return of −1.39%.

By hedging the currency risk in the Japan segment, a currency management contribution of 1.49% was achieved. Currency positioning in the segment *USA* has likewise led to a positive contribution of 0.80%, but the full hedging of the Sterling risk resulted in a negative contribution (−1.51%) (Table 15.3).

The central idea of the approach is the separation of the *currency premium*. However, its role within common investment processes is not fully clear.

Table 15.1 Holding Data and Returns for an International Equity Portfolio (Values in %)

	Weight		Currency Hedge		Return Riskless Asset		Return (in Local Currency)		Local Currency vs. Base Currency
	Portf.	BM	Portf.	BM	Portf.	BM	Portf.	BM	
UK	10	20	−10	−10	5.35	5.25	25	20	15
USA	38	20	−20	−10	5.75	5.50	10	20	10
Switzerland	10	20	0	−10	1.50	1.40	18	25	−5
Japan	8	20	−8	−10	0.12	0.17	−10	−5	−10
Germany	30	20	38	40	2.85	2.88	15	5	0
Cash	4	0	0	0	2.85	2.88	2	0	0
Total	100	100	0	0					

Table 15.2 Components of the Currency Return (Values in %)

	Currency Premium	Currency Surprise	r^{for}
UK	−2.25	17.25	17.65
USA	−2.48	12.48	12.80
Switzerland	1.46	−6.46	−6.37
Japan	2.71	−12.71	−12.37
Germany	0.00	0.00	0.00
Cash	0.00	0.00	0.00

Table 15.3 Attribution Analysis According to Ankrim and Hensel (Values in %)

	Allocation	Selection	Active Currency Management	Currency Premium	Interaction
UK	−0.70	1.00	−1.51	0.21	−0.50
USA	1.26	−2.00	0.80	−0.43	−1.80
Switzerland	−1.20	−1.40	0.01	−0.16	0.70
Japan	2.16	−1.00	1.49	−0.34	0.60
Germany	−0.80	2.00	−0.17	0.01	1.00
Cash	−0.52	0.00	−0.08	0.00	0.08
Total	0.20	−1.40	0.53	−0.69	0.08

Ankrim and Hensel's approach is based on the premise that the allocation decisions are independent of the expectations regarding the development of the exchange rates. It is doubtful whether this is the case for the investment processes in practice. It is also hard to see why the currency premium must be viewed in relation to the average premium. It is furthermore assumed that the

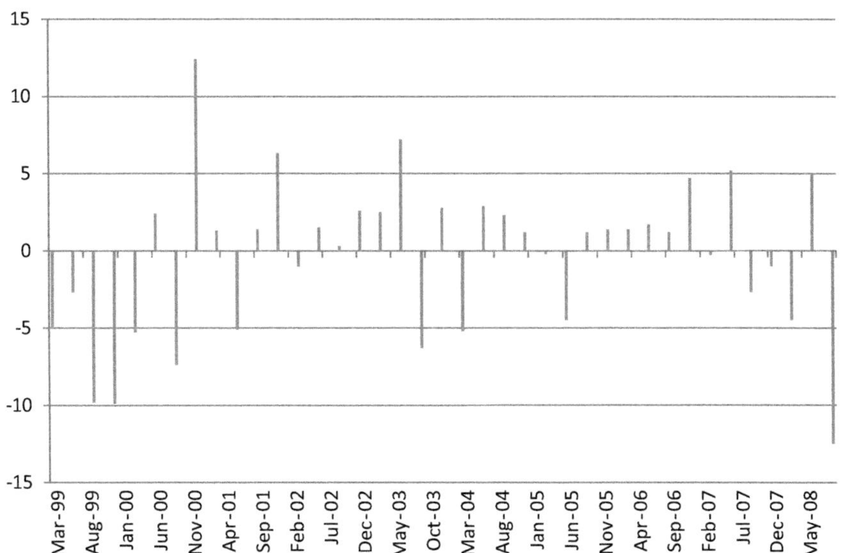

FIGURE 15.1
Quarterly Currency Returns of the Yen Relative to the Euro (Minus the Currency Premium).

entire currency exposure can always be hedged. This is, however, unrealistic in practice (and theoretically not possible for a risky asset).[5]

Over and above this a general question arises: is the currency premium actually a significant factor in the development of exchange rates? If not, this would be another reason (next to the lack of relevance to the investment processes in practice) for not separating these terms.

Example 15.2

Significance of the currency premium

Figure 15.1 depicts the currency returns of the Yen relative to the Euro (minus the currency premium) for each quarter since the introduction of the Euro. In this period the quarterly forward premium is between 0.60% and 1.00%. Obviously the currency surprise is far bigger than the currency premium.

15.1.1.2 *APPROACH OF SINGER AND KARNOSKY*

A further important approach to the analysis of currency effects was introduced by Singer and Karnosky.[6] Their approach also takes the framework developed by

[5] This assumption is not made in the approach of Singer and Karnosky described in the following section.

[6] See Singer and Karnosky (1995). In this context, the article by Allen (1991) should be mentioned. In the article the different effects related to management decisions are quantified by means of "theoretical portfolios', which partially mirror these decisions.

Brinson et al. as a starting point. The SK approach considers local returns relative to the riskless rate of return (excess return). Furthermore, not only the *currency selection* is made transparent, but also the *hedge selection*. The former is motivated by the Capital Asset Pricing Model (CAPM). Singer and Karnosky consider Euro deposits in local currency as their riskless investments.

To understand this approach better, it is helpful to take a look at the example in the article by Singer and Karnosky. They consider a US investor (base currency=US dollar), who holds assets denominated in US dollars, sterling and yen. Without hedging, the return of this portfolio would be as follows:

$$R_{\$} = swp_{\$} * srp^L_{\$} + swp_{£} * (srp^L_{£} + c_{\$,£}) + swp_{¥} * (srp^L_{¥} + c_{\$,¥}), \quad (15.20)$$

where:

$R_{\$}$: portfolio return in US dollars

swp_i: weight of the country segment i in the portfolio

srp^L_i: return of the country segment i in local currency

$c_{\$,i}$: currency return of the local currency against the US dollar.

A complete hedging of the currency risk against the US dollar would result in the following return:

$$R_{\$} = swp_{\$} * srp^L_{\$} + swp_{£} * (srp^L_{£} + f_{\$,£}) + swp_{¥} * (srp^L_{¥} + f_{\$,¥}), \quad (15.21)$$

where $f_{\$,i}$ represents the forward premium of currency i against the US\$.

In order to illustrate the different strategic options for the currency management, the yen segment will be considered in detail. According to Singer and Karnosky the investor has three options:

1. Yen strategy: maintaining the unhedged yen position (assumption: the yen will appreciate in value against the US dollar)
2. US dollar strategy: hedging the yen position into the US dollar
3. Sterling strategy: hedging the yen position into the sterling (so-called *cross-hedge* into a third currency).

The resulting returns are as follows:

1. $R^1_{\$,¥} = srp^L_{¥} + c_{\$,¥}$
2. $R^2_{\$,¥} = srp^L_{¥} + f_{\$,¥}$
3. $R^3_{\$,¥} = srp^L_{¥} + (f_{£,¥} + c_{\$,£})$.

If one expresses the forward premium by the returns resulting from the differences in the term interest rates according to Equation (15.3), then one obtains:

1. $R^1_{\$,¥} = (srp^L_{¥} - rp_{¥}) + (rp_{¥} + c_{\$,¥})$
2. $R^2_{\$,¥} = (srp^L_{¥} - rp_{¥}) + rp_{\$}$
3. $R^3_{\$,¥} = (srp^L_{¥} - rp_{¥}) + (rp_{£} + c_{\$,£})$

From this, Singer and Karnosky conclude that the riskless rates of return on a US dollar basis $(rp_i + c_{\$,i})$ and the risk premiums $(srp_i^L - rp_i)$ must be viewed as the basic measures for an evaluation of the different currency strategies, respectively for the determination of the pure market performance on the basis of the local returns.

The different terms of the attribution analysis will be labeled with an additional index "ks", in order to set them apart from the Brinson terms. The individual terms will be described in some detail. As in the article by Singer and Karnosky this will be carried out on the basis of continuously compounded returns, which, due to their additivity, leads to a much simpler formal representation than if discrete returns were used.[7] Using Equation (15.10) and the assumption that $\sum_{i=1}^{n} hwp_i * r_b = 0$ holds, one obtains:

$$\begin{aligned}
RP &= \sum_{i=1}^{n} swp_i * srp_i + \sum_{i=1}^{n} hwp_i * r_i^{for} \\
&= \sum_{i=1}^{n} swp_i * (srp_i^L + c_i) + \sum_{i=1}^{n} hwp_i * (c_i + rp_i - r_b) \\
&= \sum_{i=1}^{n} swp_i * (srp_i^L - rp_i) + \sum_{i=1}^{n} swp_i * (c_i + rp_i) + \sum_{i=1}^{n} hwp_i * (c_i + rp_i) \\
&= \sum_{i=1}^{n} swp_i * (srp_i^L - rp_i) + \sum_{i=1}^{n} (swp_i + hwp_i) * (c_i + rp_i),
\end{aligned} \tag{15.22}$$

where:

rp_i: riskless rate of return for the portfolio segment i.

An analogous expression is obtained for the benchmark return:

$$\begin{aligned}
RB &= \sum_{i=1}^{n} swb_i * (srb_i^L - rb_i) + \sum_{i=1}^{n} swb_i * (c_i + rb_i) + \sum_{i=1}^{n} hwp_i * (c_i + rb_i) \\
&= \sum_{i=1}^{n} swb_i * (srb_i^L - rb_i) + \sum_{i=1}^{n} (swb_i + hwb_i) * (c_i + rb_i),
\end{aligned} \tag{15.23}$$

where:

rb_i: riskless rate of return for the benchmark segment i.

---

[7] The assumption of continuously compounded returns is already included in Equation (15.21). However, in a strict sense this form of calculating contributions only holds for discrete returns. Therefore the deduced relationships hold only approximately. For application it is thus necessary to reformulate (in fact: correct) the method on the basis of discrete returns with a precise description of the interaction terms. This is not a straight-forward task and will not be discussed here. For two (strongly differing) attempts see e.g. Paape (2003) and Menchero and Davis (2009).

Based on this representation, the active return will be broken down into a component comprising the market effects in local currency, and a component comprising the currency effects.

$$RP - RB = \underbrace{\sum_{i=1}^{n} swp_i * (srp_i^L - rb_i) - \sum_{i=1}^{n} swb_i * (srb_i^L - rb_i)}_{M} - \sum_{i=1}^{n} swp_i * (rp_i - rb_i)$$

$$+ \underbrace{\sum_{i=1}^{n} (swp_i + hwp_i) * (rp_i + c_i) - \sum_{i=1}^{n} (swb_i + hwb_i) * (rb_i + c_i)}_{W}.$$

In the article by Singer and Karnosky, M is interpreted as the overall market contribution on the basis of the local currencies, and W as the overall currency contribution. It is obvious that in this approach a small residual remains. A breakdown of the currency contribution yields:

$$W = \sum_{i=1}^{n} (swp_i + hwp_i) * (rp_i + c_i) - \sum_{i=1}^{n} (swb_i + hwb_i) * (rb_i + c_i)$$

$$= \underbrace{\sum_{i=1}^{n} (swp_i + hwp_i - swb_i - hwb_i) * (rb_i + c_i)}_{W_1} + \sum_{i=1}^{n} (swp_i + hwp_i) * (rp_i - rb_i)$$

$$= W_1 + \underbrace{\sum_{i=1}^{n} (swb_i + hwb_i) * (rp_i - rb_i)}_{W_2}$$

$$+ \underbrace{\sum_{i=1}^{n} (swp_i + hwp_i - swb_i - hwb_i) * (rp_i - rb_i)}_{W_3}.$$

One deals similarly with the market allocation terms:

$$M = \sum_{i=1}^{n} swp_i * (srp_i^L - rb_i) - \sum_{i=1}^{n} swb_i * (srb_i^L - rb_i)$$

$$= \underbrace{\sum_{i=1}^{n} swb_i * (srp_i^L - srb_i^L)}_{M_1} + \sum_{i=1}^{n} swp_i * (srp_i^L - rb_i) - \sum_{i=1}^{n} swb_i * (srp_i^L - rb_i)$$

$$= M_1 + \underbrace{\sum_{i=1}^{n} (swp_i - swb_i) * (srb_i^L - rb_i)}_{M_2} + \underbrace{\sum_{i=1}^{n} (swp_i - swb_i) * (srp_i^L - srb_i^L)}_{M_3}.$$

Based on this breakdown the different contributions will be defined.

15.1.2.1 Active Currency Selection

Based on W_1 the "active currency selection" in Segment i is defined as follows:

$$ca_i^{ks} = (swp_i + hwp_i - swb_i - hwb_i) * (rb_i + c_i - C),$$

with:

$$C := \sum_{i=1}^{n} swb_i * (rb_i + c_i)$$

representing the "aggregate passive benchmark Euro deposit return, in base currency".

The employment of currency forwards alters the weighting of the different currency segments, so that it is justified to speak of an allocation decision in regard to the currencies. ca_i^{ks} is the contribution, which one obtains, if the resulting exposure is invested in the local currencies.

15.1.2.2 Hedge Selection

The terms for the contribution from the hedge selection (encompassing the contribution resulting from the selection of different currency forwards relative to the benchmark) follow from W2:

$$\begin{aligned} hs_i^{ks} &= (swb_i + hwb_i) * (rp_i - rb_i) \\ &= (swb_i + hwb_i) * (rp_i + c_i) - (swb_i + hwb_i) * (rb_i + c_i). \end{aligned}$$

The calculation is based on the benchmark weights.

15.1.2.3 Interaction (Currency)

The interaction terms follow from W_3:

$$\begin{aligned} it(2)_i^{ks} &= (swp_i + hwp_i - swb_i - hwb_i) * (rp_i - rb_i) \\ &= (swp_i + hwp_i - swb_i - hwb_i) * ((rp_i + c_i) - (rb_i + c_i)). \end{aligned}$$

In an analogous form to the interaction terms in the Brinson-type analysis described in Chapter 12, they reflect the interaction between the currency selection and the hedge selection.

The other terms are similar to the ones in the Brinson-type analysis.

15.1.2.4 Allocation (Market)

The allocation terms follow from M_2:

$$ac_i^{ks} = (swp_i - swb_i) * (srb_i^L - rb_i - KRP),$$

with:

$$KRP = \sum_{i=1}^{n} swb_i * (srb_i^L - rb_i)$$

representing the "aggregate passive benchmark local-currency return premium".

Table 15.4 Attribution Analysis According to Singer and Karnosky (Values in %)

	Allocation	Selection	Currency Selection	Hedge Selection	Interaction (1)	Interaction (2)
UK	−0.48	1.00	−1.52	0.01	−0.50	−0.01
USA	0.82	−2.00	0.84	0.03	−1.80	0.02
Switzerland	−1.36	−1.40	0.00	0.01	0.70	0.00
Japan	1.82	−1.00	1.49	−0.01	0.60	0.01
Germany	−0.78	2.00	−0.17	−0.02	1.00	0.00
Cash	−0.51	0.00	−0.09	0.00	0.08	0.01
Total	−0.51	−1.40	0.54	0.02	0.08	0.01

15.1.2.5 Selection (Market)

These terms follow from M_1:

$$sb_i^{ks} = swb_i * (srp_i^L - srb_i^L) = swb_i * ((srp_i^L - rb_i) - (srb_i^L - rb_i)).$$

15.1.2.6 Interaction (Market)

Finally, the interaction terms (or cross-product terms) follow from M_3:

$$\begin{aligned} it(1)_i^{ks} &= (swp_i - swb_i) * (srp_i^L - srb_i^L) \\ &= (swp_i - swb_i) * ((srp_i^L - rb_i) - (srb_i^L - rb_i)). \end{aligned}$$

Formally the market contributions coincide with the Brinson terms. They are, however, based on excess returns. Furthermore there is the additional residual term mentioned above.

Example 15.3

Singer-Karnosky attribution analysis

This method will be illustrated by means of the portfolio introduced in Example 15.2. Table 15.4 contains the results of the Singer-Karnosky attribution analysis. Again the discrete returns are used in the calculation of the contributions. The resulting additional interaction terms (overall around 10 basis points) will be disregarded.

The selection terms coincide with the ones in the analysis by Ankrim and Hensel; the terms *currency selection* and *active currency management* are also nearly identical. The differences in the allocation terms are due to the use of the excess returns in the analysis according to Singer and Karnosky.

The contributions due to the hedge selection are negligible.

Exercise 15.1 contains a further example of the Singer-Karnosky attribution analysis.

15.2 TREATMENT OF FUTURES AND FORWARDS

15.2.1 Cost of Carry

A futures contract is a standardized binding contract traded on a stock exchange between two parties to exchange a specified asset of standardized quantity and quality for a price agreed today with delivery occurring at a specified future date. Valuation approaches for futures contracts are based on a consideration of the *cost of carry*. This terminology stems from trading commodities such as basic resources (e.g. oil or gold) or agricultural products (e.g. orange juice, pork belly). In these cases, carrying the goods generates non-negligible costs such as rents, cooling costs, insurance, etc. In the following sections, only futures in which the underlying is given by financial instruments such as stocks, equity indices, bonds, etc. will be considered, for which such costs are of a very limited relevance. Nevertheless for these contracts the terminology *cost of carry* is also used. In such cases the term represents the net income, if the underlying is not purchased via a futures contract, but by a spot transaction and held to the maturity of the futures contract. Thus the income derived from the underlying (interest payments, dividends, etc.) and the cost of financing of the spot purchase is set in relation.[8] Under the assumption that there are no arbitrage opportunities, it holds that the investment in the underlying delivers the same return as the investment in a futures contract, and a cash position corresponding to the nominal of the underlying. It thus holds:

$$\textit{Futures Price} = \textit{Spot Price} + \underbrace{\textit{Cost of Financing} - \textit{Income Underlying}}_{\textit{Cost of Carry}}. \tag{15.24}$$

The risk of a deviation of the observed futures price from the theoretical price is called *basis risk*. If the cost of financing exceeds the income of the underlying, then one speaks of a *negative cost of carry*, or in the converse case, a *positive cost of carry*.[9] According to the described approach, the price of the futures contract with delivery date t at t_0 ($t_0 < t$) is given by:[10]

$$F_{t_0} = \left(B_{t_0} - \frac{E}{(1 + r_{fin})^{t_1 - t_0}} \right) * (1 + r_{fin})^{t - t_0},$$

in which:

F_{t0}: Price of the futures contract according to the cost of carry approach at t_0
B_{t_0}: Price of the underlying at t_0
r_{fin}: Cost of financing p.a.
E: Income of the underlying (e.g. dividends)
t_1: Date of the cash flow.

---

[8] Here the case of a futures long position is implicitly considered. In case of a futures short position the relation of the various positions must be adapted accordingly.

[9] Cf. EUREX (2008a, p. 26 et seq.)

[10] See e.g. Deutsch (2004. S. 84 et seq.) In the literature regarding performance attribution, this relationship is occasionally presented in a highly simplified form: $F_{t_0} = B_{t_0} * (1 + r_{fin} - r_e)$, where r_{fin} and r_e represent respectively the cost of financing and the income of the underlying (see e.g. Stannard (1996)).

At the transaction date a so-called margin account needs to be set up (initial margin). The position is valued daily, gains and losses are settled on each exchange trading day. In case of strong losses, the investor needs to transfer further cash (or bonds of a high credit quality) to this account, in order to prevent his position being automatically closed. Since the invested capital in the form of a margin account is much smaller than the investment in the form of the underlying, the employment of futures contracts is associated with leverage.

A forward contract (or *forward*) is a non-standardized (and non-exchange traded) contract between two parties to buy or sell an asset at a specified future time at a price agreed today. At the transaction date, the valuation of similar forwards and futures leads to identical results. Forwards are not traded on margin. The settlement occurs at the delivery date; the economic risk may, however, be eliminated by means of a suitable countertrade.[11]

Example 15.4

DAX-Future

DAX futures have a contract value of 25 "DAX stocks". The maximal risk in a purchase of a contract at a DAX level of, e.g., 5000€ is thus 125,000€. The expiration dates of the DAX contracts fall on the third Friday of the delivery months. Delivery months are March, June, September, and December. The overall term of the futures contract is nine months. Gains or losses at the delivery month are settled in cash (*cash settlement*).

In Figure 15.2 the course of the DAX-Futures (December contract 2008) is compared to the DAX itself. At the beginning of the period, the price of the futures contract is noticeably above the price of the DAX, which reflects the negative cost of carry resulting from the financing cost. (Dividend payments do not play a role, since the DAX is a performance index.) The relative representation in the figure below illustrates the basis risk as a deviation of the theoretical price. Due to the shortage of VW stocks, which resulted from a spectacular takeover attempt by the much smaller firm Porsche, at the beginning of November, extreme discrepancies between the futures price and the DAX were observed.

15.2.2 Single-Stock Futures

Single-stock futures are (exchange-traded) futures contracts of various sizes, in which the underlying consists of a single stock. Like all exchange-traded futures they are traded on margin, so that their employment is associated with a leverage effect. Single-stock futures are traded on a number of exchanges such as the EUREX or OneChicago.[12] These instruments are commonly used in practice to build up short positions in a portfolio. Alternative instruments for this purpose are single-stock forwards; in the framework of an attribution analysis they can be considered in a similar way as single-stock futures. The procedure for single-stock futures will be described in this section. Contrary to stock market index

[11] For the differences in the valuation of futures and forwards see Deutsch (2004, p. 86).

[12] See e.g. EUREX (2008b, p. 7 et seq.).

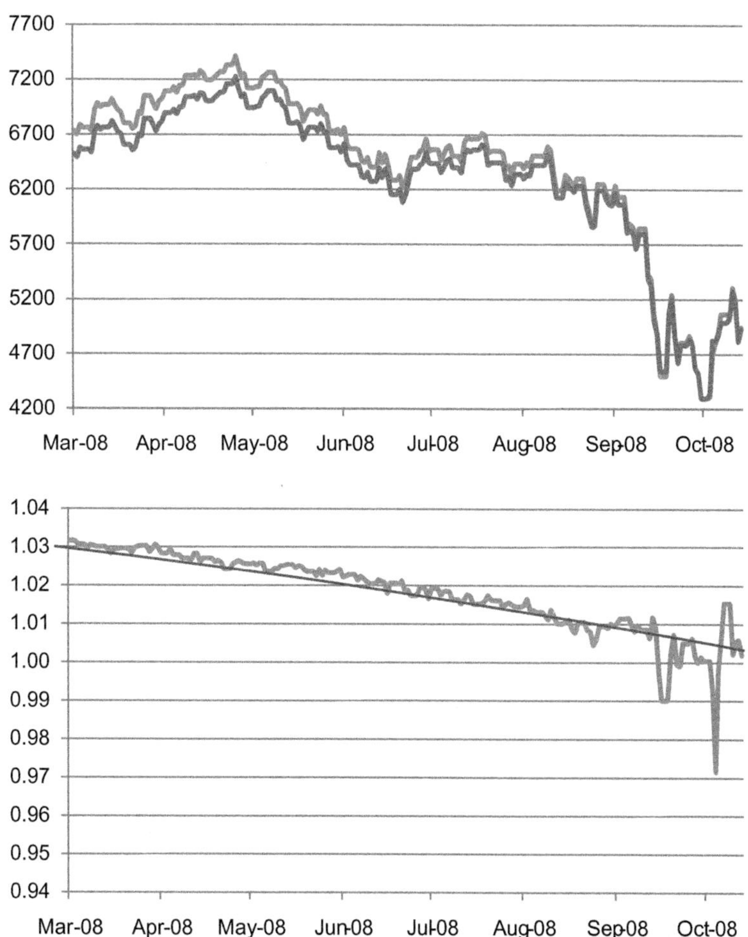

FIGURE 15.2
Prices of the DAX-08 Futures contract and the DAX in the period from 03/25/08 to 11/07/08 (above in absolute terms, below in a representation relative to the theoretical price of the DAX-Futures contract on the basis of a cost of carry approach).

futures, single-stock futures are associated with positioning in regard to stock selection and segment allocation. This means that *all* terms of the Brinson-type attribution will be affected (cf. Figure 15.3); from a perspective of a Brinson-type analysis, the consideration of single-stock futures is thus the most general case (among futures with an equity underlying). The analysis of the balanced portfolio described in Section 14.2 (Table 14.1) will serve as a basis for this analysis.

In regard to a single futures position (with the underlying in stock i_j in segment i), the following return can be calculated on an exposure basis:

$$rf_{ei_j} = \frac{F_{t,i_j} - F_{t_0,i_j}}{F_{t_0,i_j}}, \tag{15.25}$$

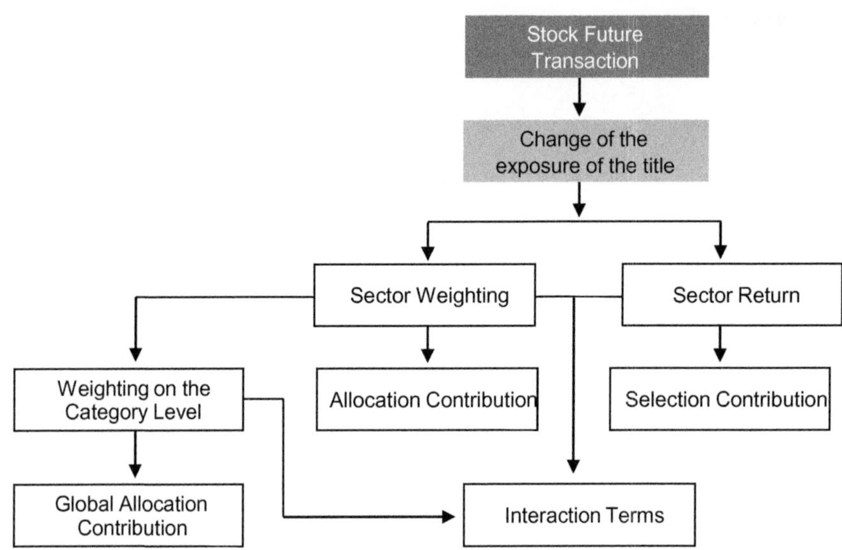

FIGURE 15.3
Impact of a Transaction in Stock Futures.

where F_{t_0,i_j} denotes the price of the future (forward price) in regard to stock i_j in segment i at t_0, and F_{t,i_j} the price at t. One obtains a similar expression for the weight (on an exposure basis):

$$hwp_{ei_j} = \frac{K_{i_j} * F_{t_0,i_j}}{I_{t_0}}. \tag{15.26}$$

(K_{i_j} denotes the product of the number of futures contracts and the contract size, and I_{t_0} the net asset value at the beginning of the period). Equation (15.26) reflects the case of a long position. For a short position the expression on the right-hand side should be negative. A mirroring position with the opposite sign needs to be generated in the (synthetic) cash position. In total one obtains the following contribution from the futures position:[13]

$$hwp_{ei_j} * rf_{ei_j} = \frac{K_{i_j} * F_{t_0,i_j}}{I_0} * \frac{F_{t,i_j} - F_{t_0,i_j}}{F_{t_0,i_j}} = \frac{K_{i_j} * (F_{t,i_j} - F_{t_0,i_j})}{I_0}.$$

On a segment level one obtains the additional weight (exposure) generated by the single-stock futures (hwp_{ei}) by summing up the terms in Equation (15.26). Similarly, the weight on the category level (HP_e) is obtained by a summation over the different segments. For an application of the Brinson methodology the

[13] Exogenous cash flows will not be considered.

segment returns are also required. By incorporating the futures exposures one obtains:[14]

$$\widetilde{srp}_{ei} = \frac{\sum_{j=1}^{N_i} (swp_{ei_j} + hwp_{ei_j}) * rp_{ei_j}}{swp_{ei} + hwp_{ei}}. \tag{15.27}$$

The weights $\widetilde{swp}_{ei}$ are defined analogously:

$$\widetilde{swp}_{ei} = swp_{ei} + hwp_{ei}. \tag{15.28}$$

The contribution generated by Equation (15.27) is identical to the numerator:

$$\sum_{j=1}^{N_i} (swp_{ei_j} + hwp_{ei_j}) * rp_{ei_j} = swp_i * srp_i + \sum_{j=1}^{N_k} hwp_{ei_j} * rp_{ei_j}, \tag{15.29}$$

so that, after introducing a correction term ϑ, one obtains the following representation on an overall level:

$$\begin{aligned}\widetilde{WP}_e * \widetilde{RP}_e + \vartheta &= \sum_{i=1}^{N_e} \widetilde{swp}_{ei} * \widetilde{srp}_{ei} + \vartheta \\ &= \sum_{i=1}^{N_e} (swp_{ei} * srp_{ei} + \sum_{j=1}^{N_i} hwp_{ei_j} * rp_{ei_j}) + \vartheta \\ &= \sum_{i=1}^{N_e} swp_{ei} * srp_{ei} + \sum_{i=1}^{N_e} \sum_{j=1}^{N_i} hwp_{ei_j} * rp_{ei_j} + \vartheta. \end{aligned} \tag{15.30}$$

(N_e denotes the number of stock segments and N_i the number of stocks in segment i.) This approach is based on the assumption that the exposure generated via the futures is considered at the level of the underlying. The deviating performance of the futures contracts relative to the underlying will be captured by an adjustment term. If one expresses the portfolio return through the factual contributions of the futures positions, then one obtains:

$$WP_e * RP_e + \mathit{Future\ contributions} = \sum_{i=1}^{N_e} swp_{ei} * srp_{ei} + \sum_{i=1}^{N_e} \sum_{j=1}^{N_i} hwp_{ei_j} * rf_{ei_j}. \tag{15.31}$$

[14] Here it is assumed that the expression in the denominator is not zero. If this is not the case, then the analysis must be conducted exclusively on the contribution level. A similar assumption will be made for all comparable cases considered here.

Table 15.5 Terms of an Attribution Analysis (Stocks) for a Balanced Portfolio with Single-Stock Futures (Bonds Analogously)

	Overall	Segment
Global Allocation	$(\widetilde{WP}_e - WB_e) * RB_e$	$(\widetilde{WP}_e - WB_e) * \frac{swb_{ei}}{WB_e} * srb_{ei}$
Allocation	$\sum_{i=1}^{N_e} WB_e * \left(\frac{\widetilde{swp}_{ei}}{\widetilde{WP}_e} - \frac{swb_{ei}}{WB_e}\right) * srb_{ei}$	$WB_e * \left(\frac{swp_{ei}}{WP_e} - \frac{swb_{ei}}{WB_e}\right) * srb_{ei}$
Selection	$\sum_{i=1}^{N_E} swb_{ei} * (\widetilde{srp}_{ei} - srb_{ei})$	$swb_{ei} * (srp_{ei} - srb_{ei})$
Interaction (I)	$\sum_{i=1}^{N_e} WB_e * \left(\frac{\widetilde{swp}_{ei}}{\widetilde{WP}_e} - \frac{swb_{ei}}{WB_e}\right) * (\widetilde{srp}_{ei} - srb_{ei})$	$WB_e * \left(\frac{swp_{ei}}{WP_e} - \frac{swb_{ei}}{WB_e}\right) * (srp_{ei} - srb_{ei})$
Interaction (II)	$(\widetilde{WP}_e - WB_e) * (\widetilde{RP}_e - RB_e)$	$(\widetilde{WP}_e - WB_e) * \left(\frac{\widetilde{swp}_{ei}}{\widetilde{WP}_e} * \widetilde{srp}_{ei} - \frac{swb_{ei}}{WB_e} * srb_{ei}\right)$
Synthetic Cash	$-HP_e * r_{cash}$	$-hwp_{ei} * r_{cash}$
Futures Basis risk	$\sum_{i=1}^{N_e} \sum_{j=1}^{N_i} hwp_{ei_j} * \left(rf_{ei_j} + r_{cash} - srp_{ei_j}\right)$	$\sum_{j=1}^{N_i} hwp_{ei_j} * \left(rf_{ei_j} + r_{cash} - srp_{ei_j}\right)$

A comparison of the Equations (15.30) and (15.31) yields:

$$\begin{aligned} \vartheta &= \sum_{i=1}^{N_e} \sum_{j=1}^{N_i} hwp_{ei_j} * (rf_{ei_j} - rp_{ei_j}) \\ &= \underbrace{\sum_{i=1}^{N_e} \sum_{j=1}^{N_i} hwp_{ei_j} * (rf_{ei_j} + r_{cash} - rp_{ei_j})}_{\textit{Futures basis risk}} - \underbrace{\sum_{i=1}^{N_e} \sum_{j=1}^{N_i} hwp_{ei_j} * r_{cash}}_{\textit{Synthetic cash position}} . \end{aligned} \tag{15.32}$$

This expression reflects the return components of the futures, which are not in line with the cost of carry valuation, and the synthetic cash position.

It is now clear how the approach in Section 14.2 may be generalized to cover also futures transactions. The following transformations were carried out:

$$WP_e \rightarrow \widetilde{WP}_e = WP_e + HP_e \tag{15.33}$$

$$swp_{ei} \rightarrow \widetilde{swp}_{ei} = swp_{ei} + hwp_{ei} \tag{15.34}$$

$$srp_{ei} \rightarrow \widetilde{srp}_{ei} \tag{15.35}$$

$$RP_e \rightarrow \widetilde{RP}_e \tag{15.36}$$

$$\widetilde{WP}_e * \widetilde{RP}_e - WB_e * RB_e + \vartheta = \sum_{i=1}^{N_e} \widetilde{swp}_{ei} * \widetilde{srp}_{ei} - \sum_{i=1}^{N_e} swb_{ei} * srb_{ei} + \vartheta. \tag{15.37}$$

The terms of the analysis are shown in Table 15.5.

Table 15.6 Structure of the Portfolio/Benchmark (in %)

	Weighting w/o Stock Futures		Weighting incl. Stock Futures	
	Portfolio	Benchmark	Portfolio	Benchmark
Siemens	15	10	20	10
SAP	20	10	20	10
Technology Sector	35	20	40	20

Table 15.7 Initial Weights and Returns for the Period 11/01–11/30/08 (Including the Futures Contracts on Siemens (in %)

	Portfolio		Benchmark	
	Weight	Return	Weight	Return
Siemens	20	11.04	10	11.04
SAP	20	−1.22	10	−1.22
Technology Sector	40	4.12	20	4.12

Example 15.5

Employment of Stocks Futures

On 10/31/08 the technology sector of the equity component in a balanced portfolio had the structure shown in Table 15.6.

The fund manager decides to reduce the exposure to Siemens to the benchmark level as at 11/01/08. Since he held an underweight position in that stock (relative to the overall weighting in the segment),[15] he builds up a corresponding long position via EUREX-listed futures on the Siemens stock (December contracts) (Table 15.7).

It is obvious that all of the allocation, selection and interaction terms are equal to zero. The "synthetic" position (futures + cash) has, however, performed differently to the underlying. The futures contract has achieved a return of 9.45%. Given a return of the (synthetic) cash position (1 month Euribor) of 0.37%, according to (15.32) one obtains for the "futures basis risk":

$$5\% * (9.45\% + 0.37\% - 11.04\%) = -0.06\%.$$

For the synthetic cash position a contribution of −0.02% is listed. The other contributions (global allocation, contributions of the bond segments) will not be considered here.

The described breakdown is, however, only one potential approach (for a specific investment process). One alternative variant would, e.g., be given by basing the calculation of the allocation contributions on the original weights (without

[15]The apparent overweight position (15% vs. 10%) is a result of the allocation decision to take an overweight position in that sector (35% vs. 20%). Since the weighting of the SAP stock remained constant, the transaction in the futures contracts on Siemens also led to a reduction of the weight of the SAP stock in the sector.

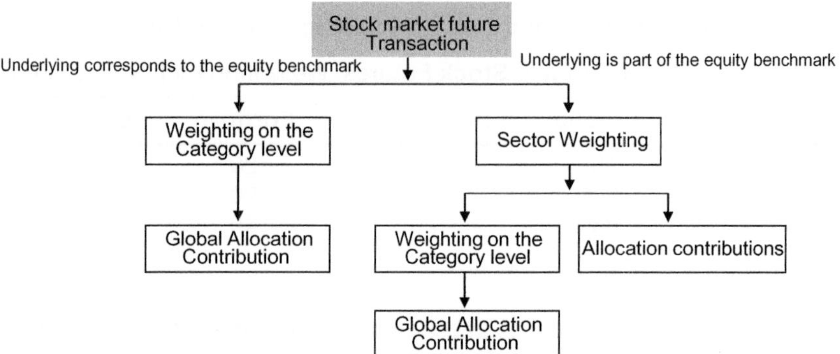

FIGURE 15.4
Impact of a Transaction in Stock Market Index Futures.

the futures exposure). In this case the contributions of the futures positions would be attributed entirely to the selection term, and there would be no need to calculate the exposures. This would make sense, if for instance the allocation decisions were regarded as a general framework defined by the actually held securities; derivative transactions would then automatically be regarded as selection decisions. Furthermore, a breakdown of the effects on the securities level similar to the one described in Section 12.2.4 would be feasible. The details will be left to the reader.

15.2.3 Stock Market Index Futures

15.2.3.1 *UNDERLYING ASSET OF THE FUTURES CONTRACT IS IDENTICAL TO THE EQUITY BENCHMARK*

As the name suggests, the underlying of a stock market index futures is formed by a stock market index; i.e. a basket of (weighted) stocks. When dealing with stock market index futures in the context of an attribution analysis, two general cases need to be distinguished. If the equity benchmark corresponds to the underlying of the stock market index futures, then the effects caused by the futures transaction should only be considered on the category level, as the fund manager does not associate an impact on the sector or stock selection with it.[16] Consequently, the allocation and selection terms are not affected by such a transaction. This case is illustrated in Example 15.6. In the second case the underlying of the stock market index future covers only part of the range of the equity benchmark. This case will be treated in Section 15.2.3.2. A summary of stock market index future approaches is shown in Figure 15.4.

[16] Should this be necessary, then the futures position can be broken down on the single stocks of the underlying according to the approach mentioned in Section 15.3.2.

Table 15.8 Breakdown of the Absolute Return (in %)

Selection	Allocation	Interaction	Futures Basis Risk	Synthetic Cash	Total
−0.18	−0.71	−0.07	0.40	0.31	−0.25

Table 15.9 Breakdown of the Relative Return (in %)

Selection	Allocation	Interaction	Futures	Synthetic Cash	Total
−0.18	−0.71	−0.07	−2.60	0.31	−3.25

Example 15.6

Employment of stock market index futures in an equity portfolio

Here the portfolio introduced in Example 12.2 and thoroughly analyzed in Example 12.6 will be considered once again. This time it will be assumed that the portfolio manager attempted to hedge his portfolio completely (without considering the portfolio beta) by selling futures contracts on the DAX (September contracts),[17] such that the portfolio was effectively invested at 100% in synthetic cash. The futures position was opened on 03/01/07 at a DAX level of 6886.5 and closed on 03/31/07 at a level of 7044. The (absolute) portfolio return can be broken down as follows:

$$\begin{aligned}\widetilde{RP} &= RP - rf\\ &= (RP - RB) + ((-rf - r_{fin}) + RB) + r_{fin}\\ &= SC + AC + IT + ((-rf - r_{fin}) + RB) + r_{fin}.\end{aligned}$$

where $\widetilde{RP}$ denotes the return of the portfolio including the futures contract. The futures contract achieved a return of −2.29%. After carrying charges this value is reduced to −2.60%,[18] so that one obtains the breakdown shown in Table 15.8.

Overall the portfolio lost −0.25% in value. Since the return of the futures contract was slightly below the DAX return, the portfolio has to a certain extent profited from the hedging measure (not in the originally intended form, however, since the overall market went up). This has led to a reduction of the original (structural) active return of −0.96%. In a representation relative to the benchmark one obtains:

$$\begin{aligned}\widetilde{RP} - RB &= RP - rf - RB\\ &= (RP - RB) + (-rf - r_{fin}) + r_{fin} \qquad (15.38)\\ &= SC + AC + IT + (-rf - r_{fin}) + r_{fin}.\end{aligned}$$

This yields the breakdown shown in Table 15.9.

This analysis can also be presented in a form similar to the one in Section 15.2.2, the main difference being that the term "global allocation contribution" is adjusted for the return of the benchmark (DAX); in Table 15.9 the contribution "futures" reflects

[17] Cf. Example 15.4.

[18] On 03/01/07 the rate of the Euribor (1 month) was 3.7%; over the analysis period the DAX achieved a return of 3.00%.

Table 15.10 Breakdown of the Relative Return (in %)

Selection	Allocation	Interaction	GAP (Stocks)	GAP (Cash)	Futures basis risk	Total
−0.18	−0.71	−0.07	−3.00	0.31	0.40	−3.25

Table 15.11 Terms of an Attribution Analysis (Stocks) for a Balanced Portfolio with Stock Market Index Futures (Underlying Asset = Stock Benchmark)

	Overall	Segment
Global Allocation	$(\widetilde{WP}_e - WB_e) * RB_e$	$(\widetilde{WP}_e - WB_e) * \frac{swb_{ei}}{WB_e} * srb_{ei}$
Allocation	$\sum_{i=1}^{N_e} WB_e * \left(\frac{swp_{ei}}{\widetilde{WP}_e} - \frac{swb_{ei}}{WB_e}\right) * srb_{ei}$	$WB_e * \left(\frac{swp_{ei}}{WP_e} - \frac{swb_{ei}}{WB_e}\right) * srb_{ei}$
Selection	$\sum_{i=1}^{N_e} swb_{ei} * (srb_{ei} - srb_{ei})$	$swb_{ei} * (srb_{ei} - srb_{ei})$
Interaction (I)	$\sum_{i=1}^{N_e} WB_e * \left(\frac{swp_{ei}}{WP_e} - \frac{swb_{ei}}{WB_e}\right) * (srp_{ei} - srb_{ei})$	$WB_e * \left(\frac{swp_{ei}}{WP_e} - \frac{swb_{ei}}{WB_e}\right) * (srp_{ei} - srb_{ei})$
Interaction (II)	$(\widetilde{WP}_e - WB_e) * (RP_e - RB_e)$	$(\widetilde{WP}_e - WB_e) * \left(\frac{swp_{ei}}{WP_e} * srp_{ei} - \frac{swb_{ei}}{WB_e} * srb_{ei}\right)$
Synthetic Cash	$-HP_e * r_{cash}$	$-hwp_{ei} * r_{cash}$
Futures Basis risk	$Hp_e * (rf_e + r_{cash} - RP_e)$	$hwp_{ei} * (rf_e + r_{cash} - RP_e)$

the differential return (+ interest) generated by the futures contracts. In this case the breakdown corresponding to the one in Equation (15.38) is as follows:

$$\begin{aligned}\widetilde{RP} - RB &= RP - rf - RB \\ &= (RP - RB) + (-rf - r_{fin}) + r_{fin} \\ &= SC + AC + IT + (-rf - r_{fin}) + r_{fin} \\ &= SC + AC + IT + \underbrace{(-rf - r_{fin} + RB)}_{\text{Futures basis risk}} - \underbrace{(RB - r_{fin})}_{\text{Global allocation contribution}}.\end{aligned} \tag{15.39}$$

The effect generated by the difference in performance of the futures contract and its underlying is listed separately in Table 15.10 (futures basis risk[19]).

In the general case of a balanced portfolio the contributions are defined in Table 15.11. Compared to the representation in Table 14.1 in Chapter 14 only the global allocation terms and *Interaction* (II) are modified. The breakdown of the terms *synthetic cash* and *futures basis risk* on a segment level is a purely mathematical one. Equation (15.39) is

[19] This contribution will in general also entail a timing component resulting from the specific timing of the transaction.

Table 15.12 Portfolio Weighting at 09/30/08 (in %)

	Portfolio	Benchmark
Cash	5	0
Bonds	65	50
Stocks	30	50
Total	100	100

Table 15.13 Portfolio Weighting at 10/01/10 and Returns in the Period 10/01–10/31/08 (in %)

	Weight		Return	
	Portfolio	Benchmark	Portfolio	Benchmark
Cash	5	0	0.43	0.43
Synthetic Cash	−20	0	0.43	0.43
Bonds	65	50	−7.56	−9.34
Stocks	50	50	−10.66	−14.46
Total	100	100	−11.15	−11.90

a special case of the above decomposition.[20] The component *synthetic cash* can (and will in the following) be regarded as a component of the global allocation.

Example 15.7

Employment of stock market index futures in a balanced portfolio

In order to give a further example of the described methodology, a balanced portfolio will be considered, which on 09/30/08 was invested as shown in Table 15.12.

The portfolio's benchmark is an (equally weighted) combination of the *DAX* and the *JP Morgan Euro Emerging Markets Bond Index Europe*.

On 10/01 the portfolio manager decides to "neutralize" the equity component (i.e., lower the exposure to the benchmark level), without touching the bond segment. By acquiring a corresponding number of DAX future contracts (December contracts) he realizes the weight distribution shown in Table 15.13.

Over the analysis period the DAX realized a return of −14.46%, while the bond index achieved a return of −9.34%. The return of the DAX future amounted to −13.98%. For the Euribor (1 month) a rate of 5.09% was listed on 10/01/08. To simplify, it was assumed that the Euribor interest rate also applies to the actual cash position. The negative net cash position of −15% can be regarded as the leverage degree of the portfolio (115% of the net asset value of the portfolio was invested in risky assets).

As the structure of the underlying securities remains unchanged, there is also no change in regard to the contributions generated by the respective asset classes (allocation, selection, interaction). In the following summary (Table 15.14) these will be shown in an aggregated form (segment contribution stocks, bonds, and cash).

In practice a potential (simplifying) variant could be to omit the cash component in the calculation of the term "futures basis risk". Then the disclosure of the component

[20]This approach is similar to the one described in Stannard (1996, 1997).

Table 15.14 Contribution Analysis (in %)

	Segment	Contribution
Segment contribution	Bonds	0.89
	Stocks	1.90
Global Allocation	Bonds	−1.40
	Stocks	0.00
	Cash	−0.06
Interaction(II)	Bonds	0.27
	Stocks	0.00
	Cash	0.00
Futures basis risk		−0.65
Total		0.95

"synthetic cash" (whose potential negative values might be hard to communicate to a client!) could be dispensed with.

The divergence between the performance of the synthetic position (futures + cash) and the performance of the associated portfolio segment in this case has led to a non-negligible contribution of −65 basis points.

15.2.3.2 UNDERLYING ASSET OF THE FUTURES CONTRACT IS DIFFERENT FROM THE EQUITY BENCHMARK

In this case the employment of the futures contracts will have an impact on the allocation decisions on a category *and* a segment level, not on the selection decisions, however. The derivation of the formulas for the breakdown of the effects is similar to the one in Section 15.2.2 Note, however, that the returns of the portfolio segments are not impacted by the employment of the futures (Table 15.15).[21]

The term *futures basis risk* can be broken down further:

$$\sum_{i=1}^{N_e} hwp_{ei} * (rf_{ei} + r_{cash} - srp_{ei}) = \sum_{i=1}^{N_e} hwp_{ei} * (rf_{ei} + r_{cash} - srb_{ei}) + \sum_{i=1}^{N_A} hwp_{ei} * (srb_{ei} - srp_{ei}). \quad (15.40)$$

The first term on the right-hand side of this equation measures the deviation of the synthetic position to the benchmark index.[22] In case this index differs from the basis value of the future, a further term analogous to Equation (15.40) may

[21] Provided the data for the composition of the future are available, a mapping of the component weights to the single stocks of the segments is feasible. In this case also the segment returns would be altered and the general methodology would be identical to the one described in Section 15.2.2. In general, this procedure would, however, not be in agreement with the most common investment processes.

[22] If the basis value is not covered by the equity benchmark, then the analysis might be extended according to the procedures described in Section 12.2.2.

Table 15.15 Attribution Analysis for a Balanced Portfolio with Stock Market Index Futures, Whose Underlying is Different from the Equity Benchmark

	Overall	Segment
Global Allocation	$(\widetilde{WP}_e - WB_e) * RB_e$	$(\widetilde{WP}_e - WB_e) * \frac{swb_{ei}}{WB_e} * srb_{ei}$
Allocation	$\sum_{i=1}^{N_e} WB_e * \left(\frac{\widetilde{swp}_{ei}}{\widetilde{WP}_e} - \frac{swb_{ei}}{WB_e}\right) * srb_{ei}$	$WB_e * \left(\frac{\widetilde{swp}_{ei}}{\widetilde{WP}_e} - \frac{swb_{ei}}{WB_e}\right) * srb_{ei}$
Selection	$\sum_{i=1}^{N_e} swb_{ei} * (srp_{ei} - srb_{ei})$	$swb_{ei} * (srp_{ei} - srb_{ei})$
Interaction (I)	$\sum_{i=1}^{N_e} GB_e * \left(\frac{\widetilde{swp}_{ei}}{\widetilde{WP}_e} - \frac{swb_{ei}}{WB_e}\right) * (srp_{ei} - srb_{ei})$	$GB_e * \left(\frac{\widetilde{swp}_{ei}}{\widetilde{WP}_e} - \frac{swb_{ei}}{WB_e}\right) * (srp_{ei} - srb_{ei})$
Interaction (II)	$(\widetilde{WP}_e - WB_e) * (\widetilde{RP}_e - RB_e)$	$(\widetilde{WP}_e - WB_e * \left(\frac{\widetilde{swp}_{ei}}{\widetilde{WP}_e} * \widetilde{srp}_{ei} - \frac{swb_{ei}}{WB_e} * srb_{ei}\right)$
Synthetic Cash	$-HP_e * r_{cash}$	$-hwp_{ei} * r_{cash}$
Futures Basis risk	$\sum_{i=1}^{N_e} hwp_{ei} * (rf_{ei} + r_{cash} - srp_{ei})$	$hwp_{ei} * (rf_{ei} + r_{cash} - srp_{ei})$

be introduced, quantifying this discrepancy. The second term on the right-hand side reflects the achieved active return.

Example 15.8

Employment of stock market index futures

The following example will consider a balanced portfolio with a net asset value of 100 Mio. € managed relative to its benchmark (75% *EURO STOXX* 50/25% *REXP*[23]). The analysis period is 01/21 to 01/28/09. At the beginning of the period the portfolio already held an overweight position in stocks. With the purchase of 40 DAX futures contracts (March 09) on 01/21 the portfolio manager increased this position even further. In particular the overweight position in the segment Germany was accentuated.

On 01/21 the price of the futures contract was 4262.5 and the exposure generated by this position was given by

$$Exposure = 40 * 25 * 4262.5 = 4.26\,Mio.\,€ \cong 4.26\%.$$

On 01/28 the price of the futures contract reached 4523.0, such that on an exposure basis the futures contract achieved a return of 6.11%. Table 15.16 contains the information on the weighting and the returns of the portfolio and benchmark segments.

The active return was equal to 2.03%. One can readily verify that $\widetilde{RP}_e = 7.84\%$. With these data the formulae in Table 15.15 can be computed (See Table 15.17).

The futures position generated a contribution of 0.26% (= 4.26% * 6.11%). In the analysis in Table 15.17 this contribution is mainly reflected by the global allocation contribution

[23]In this example, the equity component of the benchmark is computed in a simplified form by only considering the segments that the portfolio was actually invested in. Thus the listed return differs from the official return of the *EURO STOXX* 50.

Table 15.16 Portfolio and Benchmark Data

Segment	Weight (w/o Futures)		Weight (incl. Futures)		Return (w/o Futures)	
	Portfolio	Benchmark	Portfolio	Benchmark	Portfolio	Benchmark
Stocks	80.00	75.00	84.26	75.0	7.89	6.25
Belgium	1.60	0.20	1.60	0.20	5.60	13.64
Finland	2.66	2.41	2.66	2.41	−3.68	−3.23
France	26.02	27.00	26.02	27.00	9.07	5.74
Germany	31.33	21.66	35.59	21.66	6.79	6.05
Italy	6.87	8.35	6.87	8.35	6.63	5.39
Luxemburg	1.74	0.86	1.74	0.86	12.59	15.96
Netherlands	1.81	3.87	1.81	3.87	31.13	10.41
Spain	7.97	10.66	7.97	10.66	7.50	8.37
Bonds	20.00	25.00	20.00	25.00	−0.50	−1.02
Synth. Cash	0.00	0.00	−4.26	0.00	0.04	
Total	100.00	100.00	100.00	100.00	6.47	4.44

and the allocation term for the segment *Germany*. Apart from the selection term of the segment *France* and the allocation term *Spain* these are the only noticeable contributions. The contributions from the synthetic cash and the futures basis risk are negligible.

15.2.4 Interest Rate Futures

Interest rate futures are futures contracts with an interest-bearing instrument as the underlying asset. Within an attribution analysis, interest rate futures can be considered on the basis of an exposure consideration by a mapping to the notional bond. Alternatively, the mapping might be based on a real bond from the basket of deliverable bonds specified by the exchange. Since the price of an interest rate future is closely linked to the price of the cheapest to deliver bond (CTD bond), choosing this specific bond provides another option for the mapping. From a basket of deliverable bonds, the CTD bond is the one, which causes the least cost in physical delivery upon expiry. This bond might, however, vary frequently over time.

For a balanced portfolio, the methodology described in Section 15.2.2 (Table 15.5) may be applied, which assumes that the bond segment is equipped with a segmentation according to maturity or a similar parameter. This approach can also be applied to the methodology outlined in Section 13.2, which is based on the characteristic movements of yield curves. This will be illustrated by means of an example.

Example 15.9

Euro Bund Future I

The *Euro Bund Future* is a futures contract on a hypothetical obligation of the Federal Republic of Germany with a coupon of 6%. The term range of the deliverable bonds is 8.5–10.5 years; the contract value is 100.000 €. Only bonds issued by the Federal Republic

Table 15.17 Attribution Analysis

Segment	Country	Allocation	Selection	Interaction (I)	Total
Stocks		0.01	1.82	−0.64	1.19
	Belgium	0.17	−0.02	−0.10	0.05
	Finland	0.00	−0.01	0.00	−0.01
	France	−0.22	0.90	−0.13	0.55
	Germany	0.61	0.16	0.07	0.84
	Italy	−0.12	0.10	−0.03	−0.04
	Luxemburg	0.11	−0.03	−0.02	0.06
	Netherlands	−0.24	0.80	−0.47	0.10
	Spain	−0.30	−0.09	0.03	−0.36
Bonds					0.13
Global allocation					0.63
Bonds	Stocks				0.58
	Bonds				0.05
Futures basis risk					−0.03
Interaction (II) (Stocks)					0.15
Interaction (II) (Bonds)					−0.03
Total					2.04

of Germany with a nominal value of at least five billion euros are eligible.[24] Since for this futures contract the notional bond is not uniquely defined – contrary, e.g., to the US Treasury Future[25] – there are choices for the mapping. For the purpose of an attribution analysis the notional bond may, for instance, be defined as a (hypothetical) federal bond with a time to maturity of 9.5 years and a coupon of 6%, i.e., in terms of the remaining term the bond will be placed in the middle of the spectrum. The advantage of this fixation is that one realizes a constant mapping (in regard to the target) over the course of time. If one realizes the mapping via the CTD-bond, then the mapping must be adjusted for each change in the CTD-bond. If this is considered too tedious for use in practice, then there is the further option of mapping the futures contract to a fixed bond in the basket of deliverable bonds.

In the following, the portfolio in Example 13.1 will be revisited.[26] It will be assumed, however, that the portfolio manager bought ten contracts of the Euro Bund Future (December contract). On 04/01/02 the price of the future was equal to 104.47,[27] which leads to the following initial exposure E_0 (in Euro) generated by the futures contracts:

$$E_0 = 10 * 100,000 * \frac{104.47}{100} = 1,044,700.$$

On 10/31/02 the price of the future was 111.43, from which a return (gains/loss in relation to the exposure E_0) of 6.66% is derived. By mapping the futures exposures to the maturity segment (≥9.5) years (see above) only the weight of this segment will be affected.[28] The other weights listed in Table 13.2 are unchanged. The contribution resulting from the futures position is assigned directly to this segment. In order to

[24]Cf. EUREX (20/08a,b).
[25]In case of the US treasury bond future the notional bond is a (hypothetical) treasury bond with a time to maturity of exactly 20 years and a coupon of 8% (cf. Fabozzi (1999, p. 631)).
[26]This and the following example are taken from Buchholz et al. (2004).
[27]The future was not traded on 04/01/02, which causes a slight inconsistency.
[28]The futures transaction led to an increase of the duration from 5.09 years to ca. 5.51 years.

Table 15.18 Portfolio and Benchmark Weights of the Term Segments at 04/01/02 (in %)

Rem. term	Cash	[0.0, 1.5)	[1.5, 2.5)	[2.5, 3.5)	[3.5, 4.5)	[4.5, 5.5)	[5.5, 6.5)	[6.5, 7.5)	[7.5, 8.5)	[8.5, 9.5)	≥=9.5
Portfolio	−6.0	1.8	6.9	1.8	12.7	12.5	32.1	0.0	20.4	5.9	11.8
Benchmark	0.0	11.8	20.0	2.7	1.0	0.9	2.6	8.4	26.0	17.8	8.8
Difference	−6.0	−9.9	−13.1	−0.9	11.8	11.6	29.5	−8.4	−5.6	−11.9	3.0

Table 15.19 Modified Return Contributions Due to the Futures Transaction (in %)

	Allocation	Selection	Interaction	Total
Cash	−0.08	0.00	0.00	−0.08
≥9.5 Years	0.28	−0.04	−0.03	0.13

preserve the consistency of the analysis, it is, however, necessary to introduce a synthetic cash position mirroring the negative futures exposure. In the general case, this synthetic position might be combined with the generic cash position. A negative cash position may be interpreted as a *leveraging* of the portfolio (Table 15.18).

Of the returns listed in Table 13.2 only the one for the portfolio segment ≥9.5 years is changed. The computation of this return can be based on the *cost of carry approach,* which means that in addition to the futures return, a return component of the cash position corresponding to the futures exposure must be considered.[29] This additional cash contribution is neutralized, however, by the synthetic cash position, such that there is no impact on the overall return. The return $srp_{\geqslant 9.5}$ of the portfolio segment ≥ 9.5 years is thus calculated as follows:

$$srp_{\geqslant 9.5} = \frac{\Delta Bond + \Delta Future + \Delta Cash\ position}{11.8\% * I_0}, \tag{15.41}$$

where the numerator contains the gains/losses and earned interest of the bonds in the segment ($\Delta Bond$), gains/losses of the futures contracts ($\Delta Future$) and the interest payments on the synthetic cash position ($\Delta Cash\ position$). In the denominator the additional exposure generated by the futures contracts is considered. (I_0 denotes the initial net asset value of the portfolio.[30]) If one assumes that the interest earned on the (synthetic) cash position corresponding to the futures contracts can be calculated by means of the EONIA, then the return is given by $srp_{\geqslant 9.5} = 8.70\%$.

Relative to the results in the attribution analysis in Table 13.3, only the term for the segment ≥9.5 years has changed. However, a term reflecting the synthetic cash position is added as shown in Table 15.19.[31]

[29] As explained in the preceding section, the underlying can be replicated—at least theoretically—by the combination of the futures and a cash position. Margin payments are neglected in this consideration, which is, e.g., justified if the margin is formed by the securities contained in the portfolio.

[30] Exogenous cash flows will not be considered here.

[31] The computation of the return of the cash position is based on the formula $srp_C = \Delta Cash\ position/E_0$. The return contribution follows from a multiplication by the weight $-E_0/I_0$. In the computation of the various contributions according to the methodology in Section 12.2 the assumption was made that the corresponding (synthetic) cash segment has a zero weight in the benchmark and a return identical to the return of the cash segment in the portfolio. With these assumptions the return contributions of the segments, which are not contained in the benchmark, will always be subsumed among the allocation contributions (cf. Section 12.2.2).

By assigning the entire contribution to the maturity segment a different approach was taken to that of the analysis of the portfolio with the single-stock-futures. Thus in this case there is no need to introduce an adjustment term (futures basis risk). Alternatively one could use the contribution generated by the notional bond in (Equation (15.41) and introduce an adjustment term, which subsumes the difference in contribution.

Example 15.10

Euro Bund Future II:

In this example, the impact of the additional futures position will be quantified by an attribution analysis; this time the interest rate curve based approach (Example 13.5) will serve as the general framework. Once again it is necessary to map the futures position to a concrete bond. For this purpose the hypothetical bond of the Federal Republic of Germany with a remaining term of 9.5 years and a coupon of 6% will again be used. In order to compute the return effects in Section 13.2.3 it is necessary to make certain assumptions:

- The valuation of this hypothetical bond is entirely based on the interest rate curve.
- As an interest rate derivative to a sector with a very high credit quality the Bund future is assumed to have no spread induced return component.

One also needs to pay attention to the shortening of the remaining term of the notional bond over time. In practice, at the beginning of each sub-period the notional bond could be adjusted, if one wants to avoid this effect. The remaining term is then reduced by no more than the length of the sub-period.

In the present example it was assumed that the exposure of the futures contracts is mapped via the notional bond with a shortening of the remaining term over time. Due to the deviating performance of the futures contract and the notional bond, a small residual remains, which will not be broken down further.

The extra exposure generated by the futures contracts has thus led to an additional contribution of 40 basis points relative to the benchmark (Table 15.20). As was to be expected, due to the modified duration this is primarily reflected by the parallel contribution.

For a balanced portfolio, which contains, e.g., stocks and bonds, there are options in regard to the assignment of the effects. The concrete realization must

Table 15.20 Return Effects with Futures Positions (in %)

Effect	Return	Return Contribution (Portfolio Level)
Coupon/Accrued interest	2.10	0.13
Roll down	−0.14	−0.01
Parallel	4.59	0.28
Structural	0.97	0.06
Spread change	0.00	0.00
Residual	−0.86	−0.05
Total	6.66	0.40

be in agreement with the investment process. Based on the methodology outlined in Section 14.2 a transaction in a bond future (similar to a single stock future) has an impact on *all* contribution effects:

- Selection contribution (bond future is considered on a position level)
- Allocation contribution (impact on the weightings of the segments)
- Global allocation (impact on the weight of the bond category)
- Interaction terms (as a consequence of the other contributions).

The methodology described in Section 15.2.2 can be carried over to the present case. Whether all contributions actually need to be modified depends on the investment process, respectively on the intention behind the transaction. If the futures position is solely intended to increase the exposure to the bond segment, then this position should only have an impact on the global allocation contribution. If it is, however, intended to control the duration positioning within the bond segment, then the global allocation contribution should not be affected at all. In the extreme case, there are various derivative positions, each one having a specific purpose. Ideally, these trades are classified by the portfolio manager or trader, when placing the orders in the order management system. Of course, this is only useful if the attribution system is able to assign the various effects according to these data.

15.3 TREATMENT OF OPTIONS

15.3.1 Options and Their Valuation

The buyer of an (American) option acquires the right (but not the obligation), to purchase an asset (basis value) during a fixed period at a specified price (call option), or to sell the asset at a specified price (put option). A European option may be exercised only at the expiry date of the option, a Bermudan option at a set number of (discrete) times. Similar to futures, in the settlement one needs to distinguish between cash settlement and delivery of the underlying. Options on indices are usually subject to cash settlement.

Options are traded in standardized contracts on derivatives exchanges like the EUREX or OneChicago. These options should be distinguished from so-called OTC-options (over the counter), for which an individual contract is signed between the option buyer and the option seller.[32] Furthermore, options and OTC-options are derivatives, whereas warrants are securitized options.

[32] Consequently a counterparty risk arises from this transaction.

According to the well-known model of Black and Scholes the valuation formula for a European call option, which entitles the holder to purchase a stock (without dividend payments) after $T-t$ years at the price B:[33]

$$C_t = K_t * N(d_1) - B * e^{-r*(T-t)} * N(d_2) \tag{15.42}$$

where:

C_t : Price of the call option at t (Option premium)
K_t : Spot price of the underlying asset (stock) at t
B: Strike price of the option
r: Risk free rate p.a.
σ: Expected volatility of returns of the underlying stock p.a.
T-t: Time to maturity of the option.

Furthermore:

$$d_1 = \frac{\ln(B/K_t) + (r + 0,5 * \sigma^2) * (T-t)}{\sigma * \sqrt{T-t}}$$

and:

$$d_2 = \frac{\ln(B/K_t) + (r - 0,5 * \sigma^2) * (T-t)}{\sigma * \sqrt{T-t}}$$

in which N is the cumulative distribution function of the standard normal distribution.

The Black and Scholes model is based on the assumption that the stock prices follow a geometric Brownian motion (Wiener process) with constant drift and volatility. This is a continuous stochastic process, in which the returns at different times are normally distributed and independent of each other. The model assumes furthermore that the returns are log-normally distributed.

The price of a corresponding put option is given by:

$$P_t = B * e^{-r*(T-t)} * N(-d_2) - K_t * N(-d_1) \tag{15.43}$$

As in the case of futures, the question arises of how to consider options in the context of an attribution analysis (e.g., based on the Brinson approach). Of course, there are different approaches in practice. The concrete choice depends on the extent and frequency of the use of these derivatives, and, as is usually

---

[33] Cf. Black and Scholes (1973). Further valuation models will not be considered in the context of this chapter. For an extension of the Black-Scholes model to dividend paying stocks see e.g. Albrecht and Maurer (2008, p. 639 et seq.) or Wilmott (1999, p 115 et seq.) In practice different models for the valuation of American options are applied. The binomial model by Cox, Ross and Rubinstein is very commonly applied (cf. e.g. Deutsch (2004, p. 323 et seq.) or Wilmott (1999, p 163)). For Bermuda options there is (also) no closed-form solution. These options must be valued by means of involved numerical procedures. Further variants (Barrier options, lookback options, Cliquet options etc.) will not be considered in the context of this chapter. For details, see e.g. Deutsch (2004, p. 341 et seq.) or the textbook by Wilmott.

the case in the context of attribution analysis, on the investment process. If, for instance, the use of the derivatives is intended for selection and allocation decisions (with underlying assets that typically also belong to the portfolio), then the allocation of the contributions generated by these derivatives to the basic effects of a Brinson analysis (or a similar analysis) might be meaningful. If (complex) derivatives are frequently employed in order to implement specific trading strategies, which are not captured by the standard Brinson framework, then it is necessary to consider a (potentially tedious) breakdown of the derivative's return according to its specific valuation parameters. It generally needs to be stressed that—unlike in the case of futures—transactions in options are accompanied by an actual cash flow, which needs to be considered separately.

The sensitivities of the derivatives are of crucial importance for an attribution analysis. A sensitivity quantifies the impact of a small (infinitesimal) change in a given underlying parameter to the derivative's price. For options most sensitivities are denoted by Greek letters; in this context the term "Greeks" is used synonymously with sensitivities.[34] Of particular importance is the sensitivity of the option price (call delta or hedge ratio) to changes in the price of the underlying asset (i.e. the price of the stock):

$$\delta_C = \frac{\partial C}{\partial K} \tag{15.44}$$

According to the model of Black and Scholes (15.42) it holds that:

$$\delta_C = N(d_1) \tag{15.45}$$

δ_C thus has a dependency on the stock price, the strike price, the time to maturity, the riskless rate of return and the volatility. A call option with a strike price significantly below the market price of the stock is called *deeply in the money*, δ_C is close to one. In the opposite case (*deeply out of the money*) δ_C is close to zero. If the strike price equals the market price of the stock (*at the money*), then δ_C is equal to 0.5.

With this quantity a locally riskless portfolio can be constructed. It holds that:[35]

$$\delta_C * Stock - Call = Locally\ riskless\ return\ on\ net\ position. \tag{15.46}$$

From the perspective of an option seller, an options position can be hedged by acquiring δ_C stocks. To put it another way, similar to the case of futures, an exposure to the underlying asset may be generated by a call option and a cash position. This, however, works only locally, i.e., the above relationship is true only for minor changes in the underlying parameters.

[34] See Deutsch (2004, p. 195 et seq.) or Wilmott (1999, p. 91).

[35] See Albrecht and Maurer (2008, p. 638).

The sensitivity of a put option to a change in price of the underlying is given by:

$$\delta_P = \frac{\partial P}{\partial K} = -N(-d_1) = \delta_C - 1 \tag{15.47}$$

Also in this case a locally riskless portfolio can be constructed:[36]

$$Put + \delta_P * Stock = Locally\ riskless\ return\ on\ net\ position.$$

15.3.2 Options on a Single Stock

Stock options are common instruments for the implementation of selection decisions in practice. Unlike single-stock futures the market value of these derivatives is not zero. In the following, an approach for the inclusion of such instruments into a Brinson-type analysis will be described, in which the option position is transferred into an unleveraged stock position (exposure basis) by means of a sensitivity (delta). Here, it is assumed that the option position can be approximated in a meaningful way through its delta-equivalent.[37] Similarly to the case of single-stock futures, the employment of stock options has an impact on the sectorial and global allocation decisions. The analysis is similar to the one described in Section 15.2.2. Only long positions will be considered.

The exposure generated by a long-position is given by:[38]

$$hwp_{ei_j} = \frac{\delta_{i_j} * N_{i_j} * K_{t_0,i_j}}{I_{t_0}}, \tag{15.48}$$

in which:

δ_{i_j}: Delta of the option with underlying stock j in the segment i
N_{i_j}: Number of options multiplied by the contract size
K_{t_0,i_j}: Spot price of the stock at t_0
I_{t_0}: Net asset value of the overall portfolio at the beginning of the period.

The exposures on a segment and category level follow from summing up the terms in Equation (15.48). With these substitutions, the attribution analysis in Table 15.5 can be directly transferred to the case of stock options. Only the term ϑ assumes a slightly different form. Cash positions (especially the synthetic position – exposure of the option minus its price) shall again be subject to a uniform return r_{Cash}. K_{t,i_j}, and P_{t,i_j} shall denote the prices of the underlying, respectively the option at t ($t = t_0$ or $t = t_1$). If wo_{ei_j} denotes the weight of the option at the beginning of the analysis period and ro_{ei_j} its return, then the portfolio return

[36] For detailed explanations to options and their sensitivities see e.g. EUREX (2007)

[37] See also the considerations in Section 15.3.4.

[38] For a short position the right-hand side of Equation (15.45) must have a minus sign. The essential difference between a long and a short position results from the treatment of the option premium. In case of a short position the portfolio obtains this premium first. Within an attribution analysis this contribution must be assigned to the appropriate contribution effect(s).

based on the effective return contribution generated by the option position (analogous to Equation (15.31)) is as follows:[39]

$$
\begin{aligned}
&WP_e * RP_e + \textit{Option contributions}\\
&= \sum_{i=1}^{N_e} swp_{ei} * srp_{ei} + \sum_{i=1}^{N_e}\sum_{j=1}^{N_i} wo_{ei_j} * ro_{ei_j}\\
&= \sum_{i=1}^{N_e} swp_{ei} * srp_{ei} + \sum_{i=1}^{N_e}\sum_{j=1}^{N_i} \frac{N_{i_j} * P_{t_0,i_j}}{I_0} * \frac{P_{t_1,i_j} - P_{t_0,i_j}}{P_{t_0,i_j}}\\
&= \sum_{i=1}^{N_e} swp_{ei} * srp_{ei} + \sum_{i=1}^{N_e}\sum_{j=1}^{N_i} \frac{N_{i_j}}{I_0} * (P_{t_1,i_j} - P_{t_0,i_j}) = \sum_{i=1}^{N_e} swp_{ei} * srp_{ei}\\
&+ \sum_{i=1}^{N_e}\sum_{j=1}^{N_i} \frac{\delta_{i_j} * N_{i_j}}{I_0} * \left(\frac{1}{\delta_{i_j}}(P_{t_1,i_j} - P_{t_0,i_j} + r_{cash} * (K_{t_0,i_j} - P_{t_0,i_j})) - \frac{1}{\delta_{i_j}} * r_{cash} * (K_{t_0,i_j} - P_{t_0,i_j})\right)\\
&= \sum_{i=1}^{N_e} swp_{ei} * srp_{ei} + \sum_{i=1}^{N_e}\sum_{j=1}^{N_i} \frac{\delta_{i_j} * N_{i_j}}{I_0} * \left((K_{t_1,i_j} - K_{t_0,i_j}) - \frac{1}{\delta_{i_j}} * r_{cash} * (K_{t_0,i_j} - P_{t_0,i_j})\right) + \vartheta_1\\
&= \sum_{i=1}^{N_e} swp_{ei} * srp_{ei} + \sum_{i=1}^{N_e}\sum_{j=1}^{N_i} \left(\frac{\delta_{i_j} * N_{i_j} * K_{t_0,i_j}}{I_0} * \frac{K_{t_1,i_j} - K_{t_0,i_j}}{K_{t_0,i_j}} - \frac{N_{i_j} * r_{cash} * (K_{t_0,i_j} - P_{t_0,i_j})}{I_0}\right) + \vartheta_1\\
&= \sum_{i=1}^{N_e} swp_{ei} * srp_{ei} + \sum_{i=1}^{N_e}\sum_{j=1}^{N_i} \left(hwp_{ei_j} * rp_{ei_j} - \frac{N_{i_j} * r_{cash} * (K_{t_0,i_j} - P_{t_0,i_j})}{I_0}\right) + \vartheta_1.
\end{aligned}
\tag{15.49}
$$

ϑ_1 represents the correction term, which measures the difference between the change in price of the option and the linearized price change (δ-risk):

$$
\vartheta_1 = \sum_{i=1}^{N_e}\sum_{j=1}^{N_i} \left(wo_{ei_j} * ro_{ei_j} + \frac{N_{i_j} * r_{cash} * (K_{t_0,i_j} - P_{t_0,i_j})}{I_0} - hwp_{ei_j} * rp_{ei_j}\right).
\tag{15.50}
$$

The last expression in Equation (15.49) can be transformed as follows.

$$
\begin{aligned}
&\sum_{i=1}^{N_e} swp_{ei} * srp_{ei} + \sum_{i=1}^{N_e}\sum_{j=1}^{N_i} \left(hwp_{ei_j} * rp_{ei_j} - \frac{N_{i_j} * r_{cash} * (K_{t_0,i_j} - P_{t_0,i_j})}{I_0}\right) + \vartheta_1\\
&= \sum_{i=1}^{N_e}\sum_{j=1}^{N_i} (swp_{ei} + hwp_{ei_j}) * rp_{ei_j} - \sum_{i=1}^{N_e}\sum_{j=1}^{N_i} \frac{N_{i_j} * r_{cash} * (K_{t_0,i_j} - P_{t_0,i_j})}{I_0} + \vartheta_1\\
&= \sum_{i=1}^{N_e} \widetilde{swp}_{ei} * \widetilde{srp}_{ei} \underbrace{- \sum_{i=1}^{N_e}\sum_{j=1}^{N_i} \frac{N_{i_j} * r_{cash} * (K_{t_0,i_j} - P_{t_0,i_j})}{I_0} + \vartheta_1}_{\vartheta}.
\end{aligned}
\tag{15.51}
$$

[39] I_0 denotes the net asset value at the beginning of the analysis period. Exogenous cash flows will not be considered here.

Thus one obtains an expression analogous to Equation (15.32):

$$\vartheta = \sum_{i=1}^{N_e}\sum_{j=1}^{N_i}\left(wo_{ei_j} * ro_{ei_j} + \frac{N_{i_j} * r_{cash} * (K_{t_0,i_j} - P_{t_0,i_j})}{I_0} - hwp_{ei_j} * rp_{ei_j}\right)$$
$$-\sum_{i=1}^{N_e}\sum_{j=1}^{N_i}\frac{N_{i_j} * r_{cash} * (K_{t_0,i_j} - P_{t_0,i_j})}{I_0}. \quad (15.52)$$

Thus the transformations (15.33)–(15.36) can be applied here in a completely analogous form, which means that the analysis of futures in Table 15.5 an be carried forward to the case of options (with a definition of the adjustment term as in Equation (15.52); the synthetic cash term is given by the expression in the second row).[40]

Example 15.11

Employing a stock option in a balanced portfolio

On 01/21/09 the manager of a balanced portfolio, consisting of stocks and bonds, purchases 10,000 contracts of call options on the Allianz stock via the stock exchange. The contract size is 10 stocks per option. On 01/21 the prices of the option and the stock are 0.93€ respectively 60.32€ and on 01/28 2.23€ respectively 70.00€. On 01/21 the option delta is given by 0.1093. With a strike price at 82€, the option is *deeply out of the money*.

If the net asset value of the portfolio is equal to 10 Mio. €, then the option position will have a weight of 0.93% (=10,000 ∗ 10 ∗ 0.93/10,000,000) and generate an exposure of 6.59% (=0.1093 ∗ 10,000 ∗ 10 ∗ 60.32/10,000,000). This means that the weighting of the Allianz stock as well as the sector and category weighting are increased by 6.59%. Accordingly, the synthetic cash will assume a weight of 5.66%.

The contribution "δ-risk" was equal to 0.24% and thus is not entirely negligible.

15.3.3 Options on Stock Indices

Apart from stock market index futures, options on a stock market index are an instrument for implementing allocation decisions. The treatment of these instruments is quite similar to the methodology of Section 15.2.3. Based on the sensitivity of the option the exposure of the option is calculated, which enters as a weight-equivalent into the analysis. Again, the cases outlined in Section 15.2.3 need to be distinguished. If the underlying of the option is identical to the equity benchmark, the analysis in Table 15.11 can readily be adapted to the present situation by means of the following substitution:

$$HP_e = \frac{\delta_e * N * K_{t_0}}{I_{t_0}}$$

where δ_e symbolizes the sensitivity of the option to the equity index and N is the number of options (multiplied by the contract size). Of the generic analysis

[40] This approach resembles the one described in Stannard (1996, 1997). See also the recommendations in LIFFE (1994) in this context.

terms only those for the global allocation and Interaction (II) change. The global allocation term is as follows:

$$(\widetilde{WP}_e - WB_e) * RB_e = (WP_e + HP_e - WB_e) * RB_e.$$

If wo_e denotes the weight of the option position and ro_e its return, then, analogous to Equation (15.52), the adjustment term ϑ may be defined by:

$$\vartheta = \underbrace{\left(wo_e * ro_e + \frac{N * r_{cash} * (K_{t_0} - P_{t_0})}{I_0} - HP_e * RP_e \right)}_{\delta - Risk} - \underbrace{\frac{N * r_{cash} * (K_{t_0} - P_{t_0})}{I_0}}_{Synthetic\ Cash} \quad (15.53)$$

which includes the terms *δ-risk* and *synthetic cash*. The other terms in Table 15.11 remain formally unchanged.

If the underlying of the option represents only one component of the benchmark, adaptation of the results in Section 15.2.3.2 is also straight-forward. The expression for the adjustment term analogous to Equation (15.53) is as follows:

$$\vartheta = \sum_{i=1}^{N_e} \left(wo_{ei} * rp_{ei} + \frac{N_i * r_{cash} * (K_{t_0,i} - P_{t_0,i})}{I_0} - hwp_{ei} * rp_{ei} \right) - \sum_{i=1}^{N_e} \frac{N_i * r_{cash} * (K_{t_0,i} - P_{t_0,i})}{I_0} \quad (15.54)$$

Hence the contributions to the *δ-risk* and the *synthetic cash* can be readily derived. The other terms in Table 15.15 are formally identical.

Example 15.12

Employment of an option on the DAX in a balanced portfolio

Again the portfolio of Example 15.8 will be considered; instead of futures contracts this time 100 exchange traded put options on the DAX (March 09) with a strike price of 4500 are acquired. The analysis period is again 01/21 to 01/28/2009.

On 01/21 the prices of the option and the DAX were 351.0 and 4261.0 respectively, and on 01/28 160.8 and 4518.7 respectively. On 01/21 the put delta was equal to 0.59. At an assumed net asset value of 100 Mio. € and a contract size of 5 the option position had a weight of 0.18% ($=351 * 5 * 100/100{,}000{,}000$) and a corresponding exposure of $-0.59 * 5 * 100 * 4261 = -1.26\%$.

The portfolio achieved an active return of 1.67%, which is broken down in Table 15.21. As expected, the most significant differences compared to Example 15.8 arise in the terms global allocation *Stocks* and, most significantly, in the segment *Germany* (allocation).[41] In this case the δ-risk is negligible.

[41]In this segment the put reduces the overweight-position relative to the benchmark, which results (among others) in a lower allocation contribution.

Table 15.21 Attribution Analysis

Segment	Country	Allocation	Selection	Interaction (I)	Total
Stocks		0.02	1.82	−0.60	1.24
	Belgium	0.18	−0.02	−0.11	0.06
	Finland	0.00	−0.01	0.00	−0.02
	France	−0.13	0.90	−0.07	0.70
	Germany	0.42	0.16	0.05	0.64
	Italy	−0.10	0.10	−0.02	−0.02
	Luxemburg	0.13	−0.03	−0.03	0.07
	Netherlands	−0.22	0.80	−0.45	0.13
	Spain	−0.26	−0.09	0.03	−0.32
Bonds					0.13
Global allocation					0.28
	Stocks				0.23
	Bonds				0.05
σ-risk					0.01
Interaction (II) (stocks)					0.06
Interaction (II) (Bonds)					−0.03
Total					1.67

15.3.4 Limitations of the Approach and Possible Extensions

The described approach could in principle also be applied to other derivatives. The methodology described in Section 15.3 can, for instance, be applied to forwards, which, like options, have a market value different from zero, by setting $\delta = 1$. The approach reaches its limitation, if the strategies pursued by the employment of derivatives aim at factors different from the price of the underlying.

Example 15.13

Employment of an option on the DAX in a balanced portfolio:

A fund manager sells options which he considers "overpriced". This trade is based on the perception that the realized volatility of stocks is often lower than the implied volatility derived from the option price theory. He hedges his position against the risk of a price change in the stock by means of a delta hedge. Such a strategy would not become adequately transparent within the framework described so far, since the factor "volatility" would be "buried" in the residual term in Equation (15.54).

Analogously to the procedure for the delta, the methodology can be extended by means of a sensitivity consideration. The sensitivity to the volatility is called vega. Although vega is not a Greek letter, it is expressed by one (nu, ν):

$$\nu_C = \nu_P = \frac{\partial C}{\partial \sigma}.$$

For European options without dividend payments, the Black-Scholes model provides the following formula:

$$\nu_C = \nu_P = K_t * \sqrt{T-t} * n(d_1), \tag{15.55}$$

where n denotes the density function of the standard normal distribution. Vega effects are especially pronounced if the stock price is close to the strike price. As Equation (15.55) illustrates, the effect levels off as the option reaches its maturity.

In this approach an increase in the volatility by $\Delta\sigma$ results in a contribution of $\nu_C * \Delta\sigma$. The adjustment term in Equation (15.54) would need to be reduced by this contribution.

In this way, further sensitivities, e.g., to the passage of time (theta) or to the risk free interest rate (rho), as well as second order effects (e.g. gamma) can be included in a Brinson-type analysis.

A further approach for the inclusion of derivatives is given by a reevaluation of the option (with only a change in a specific parameter) based on the valuation Equations (15.42) and (15.43) by keeping the remaining parameters constant. This procedure leads to more exact results, but requires greater computational capacity. This approach can also be applied to other (non-linear) derivatives.[42]

15.4 SWAPS

A swap is an agreement between counterparties to exchange defined cash flows in the future. Swaps are closely linked to futures contracts, since in the latter, the counterparties agree to exchange cash flows at *one* point in time. To value a swap it is necessary to value both payment streams separately, which provides an indication for the inclusion of swaps in a Brinson-type analysis, i.e., the assignment of the different components to appropriate sectors.

Example 15.14

Interest rate swaps

In a "*plain vanilla*" (or standard) interest rate swap, one counterparty pays the other a fixed rate loan at a certain frequency (often semiannually) in exchange for a floating rate loan on a defined[43] nominal. For instance, the floating rate loan may be defined as LIBOR + x basis points (London Interbank Offered Rate).[44] In this case the value of the swap is given by the difference between the present value of the "separated" fixed rate loan and the floating rate note. In a Brinson-type attribution analysis both loans can be assigned to the appropriate term segment. Since the procedure is similar to the one for interest rate futures, the details will not be presented here. It should be mentioned, however, that due to deviating valuation prices, the overall contribution of the swap might be different from the contribution based on the broker valuation. Therefore yet another adjustment term needs to be introduced.

[42] If there is no closed valuation formula for a derivative, then the sensitivities must be estimated by appropriate numerical procedures (e.g. a Monte Carlo simulation).

[43] A variant is the amortization swap, in which the notional principal for the interest payments declines during the life of the swap.

[44] Cf. e.g. Hull (2001, p. 224 et seq.) For the LIBOR see the explanations in Section 11.4.

Table 15.22 Holdings of an International Equity Portfolio and other Data Required for a Singer-Karnosky Analysis (Values in %)

	Weight		Currency Hedge		Return Euro Deposit		Return (in Local Currency)		Local Currency vs. Base Currency
	Portf.	BM	Portf.	BM	Portf.	BM	Portf.	BM	
UK	10	20	−10	−20	5.35	5.25	25	20	15
USA	50	20	−20	−20	5.75	5.5	10	20	10
Switzerl.	10	20	0	−20	1.50	1.40	18	25	−5
Japan	8	20	−10	−20	0.12	0.17	−10	−5	−10
Germany	20	20	40	80	2.85	2.88	15	5	0
Cash	2	0	0	0	2.85	2.88	2	0	0
Total	100	100	0	0					

15.5 CHAPTER-END PROBLEMS

1. (Attribution analysis according to Karnosky and Singer):
   Compute all components of the Singer-Karnosky attribution analysis for a portfolio on the basis of the data listed in Table 15.22. Compared to the benchmark the portfolio manager has taken considerable currency risks. Is this reflected by the results?
2. (Attribution analysis according to Ankrim and Hensel):
   Verify that the terms in the attribution analysis according to Ankrim and Hensel give in sum the active return.

Chapter 16

Global Investment Performance Standards (GIPS)

ABSTRACT

This chapter deals with the Global Investment Performance Standards (GIPS). GIPS are ethical standards for the presentation of the results of investment firms. Firstly, the historical development which led to the GIPS in its current form is briefly described. Then the key characteristics of the standards are addressed: definition of the firm, definition of composites and the computation of composite returns. The chapter closes with a description of the most common dispersion measures and an overview of the provisions for the presentation of risk in the firm's investments.

Keywords
Global Investment Performance Standards, ethical, results, investment, firm, composites, composite return, dispersion measure, risk, investment

16.1 BACKGROUND

16.1.1 History

This chapter deals with performance presentation by asset managers. The term "Performance Presentation" includes all forms of presentation, such as publication of company performance via the media and individual presentation of performance data to customers. The discourse centers around the *Global Investment Performance Standards* (GIPS), which set forth "ethical" principles for calculation and presentation of performance results.[1] Asset managers are encouraged to voluntarily apply these standards. Review by an independent expert is also recommended, but not a required part of implementation. The standards are meant to promote comparability of asset manager performance on an equal level playing field worldwide. They were created with the motivation to establish an example of self-regulation for the industry (rather than relying on the dictates of regulatory agencies).

[1] Cf. CFA Institute (2010, p. IV).

Performance Evaluation and Attribution of Security Portfolios. http://dx.doi.org/10.1016/B978-0-12-744483-3.00016-X
© 2013 Elsevier Inc. All rights reserved.
For End-of-chapter Questions: © 2012. CFA Institute, Reproduced and republished with permission from CFA Institute. All rights reserved.

The standards make a formal distinction between "requirements" and "recommendations". For an asset manager to be in compliance with the standards, all of the requirements must be satisfied and the recommendations acknowledged. This includes implementation of the updates, reports, guidance statements, questions and answers (Q&As), and the clarifications published by the CFA Institute and GIPS Executive Committee.[2]

The main beneficiaries of the standards are (potential) clients and investment advisors, who are given an objective insight into an asset manager's performance capabilities. The asset manager also benefits from this transparency (especially in very large organizations, where complexity obscures the view); likewise, the manager can make advantageous use of the analysis and structuring of investment processes and data flows that are part of implementing the GIPS.

Efforts to establish such voluntary *Performance Presentation Standards* (PPS) have been ongoing in the United States since the end of the 1980s.[3] They were initiated and driven by the *Association for Investment Management and Research* (AIMR) (now *CFA Institute*[4]). This was a response to the deliberately manipulative performance presentation by some asset managers at the time.[5] A typical example of this practice is selecting a non-representative portfolio displaying good performance over a given period. Selection of specific periods is another example.

The work of the AIMR culminated in 1993 with publication of a set of standards (the AIMR-PPS), which were very well-received in the US and abroad. In 1997, the AIMR published a second, greatly expanded version of the PPS.[6]

In the United Kingdom, the *National Association for Pension Funds* (NAPF) in 1992 drafted comparable rules for calculation and reporting of performance results for *Pension Funds*, which were well-received and expanded in 1996.[7] These standards were soon replaced as of 1 January 2000 by new standards (*UKIPS*) that were nearly identical with the GIPS.[8] Other countries, such as Germany and Switzerland, also published their own PPS. These standards were motivated in no small part by the success of the AIMR-PPS and exhibit very close similarities to those standards.[9]

In order to transfer the AIMR-PPS—at least the basic terms—to other countries, the AIMR at the end of 1995 formed a commission to draft the GIPS, the members of which were representatives of nearly every important capital market worldwide.

---

[2] Implementation of the recommendations is deemed to be "best practice", but the previously intent to see them incorporated as requirements has been abandoned in the 2010 version (cf. CFA Institute (2010, p. 2)).
[3] The standards (FAF 1987) released in 1987 by the Financial Analysts Federation constitute a first version of the AIMR-PPS.
[4] The organization was renamed in 2004.
[5] See e.g. Caccese (1997).
[6] Cf. AIMR (1997).
[7] See NAPF (1996).
[8] The only difference between the GIPS and the British UKIPS was that verification was mandatory for compliance with the UKIPS (cf. UKIPS 2000, p. 5).
[9] Cf.Swiss PPS (1996) and DVFA (2000).

FIGURE 16.1
Nations with Country Sponsors for the GIPS (status: January 2010, CFA Institute 10, p. 4 et seq.), resp. http://gipsstandards.org/about/governance/sponsors/sponsors.html).

These standards became effective on 1 January 2000.[10] In order to allow as many asset managers as possible to comply with the standards in the various countries, the commission intentionally tried to define a "lowest common denominator", trusting that the requirements can become more stringent as accounting and PMI systems improve over time. The GIPS thus comprised a series of recommendations with a specific deadline for adoption as mandatory guidelines. Note as well that the standards are continually updated, with new versions appearing every five years. The version on which this chapter is based was published in 2010.[11]

When it became apparent that the proliferation of local standards ran contrary to the original motivation of establishing a uniform set of standards worldwide, the AIMR set up a second global committee (the Investment Performance Council—IPC), which was charged with modifying the GIPS in such a way that the local standards became obsolete. This aim has been achieved, as the majority of national investment or analysts associations acting as so-called "Country Sponsors" abolished their local standards or "Country Versions" (slightly modified versions authorized by the IPC), and replaced them with an authorized translation of the GIPS (cf. Figure 16.1). This version is the first to contain specialized standards for the market segments Private Equity und Real Estate.[12] It must, however, be stated that the harmonization process resulted in a significant weakening of the standards.

---

[10] Cf. AIMR (1999).

[11] Cf. CFA Institute (2010). The 2005 standards were expanded, amended and interpreted, without changing their fundamental character. The numbering of the standards, however, was jumbled, making a comparison between these two versions difficult.

[12] These standards (CFA Institute 2010, pp. 16–23) will only be treated peripherally here.

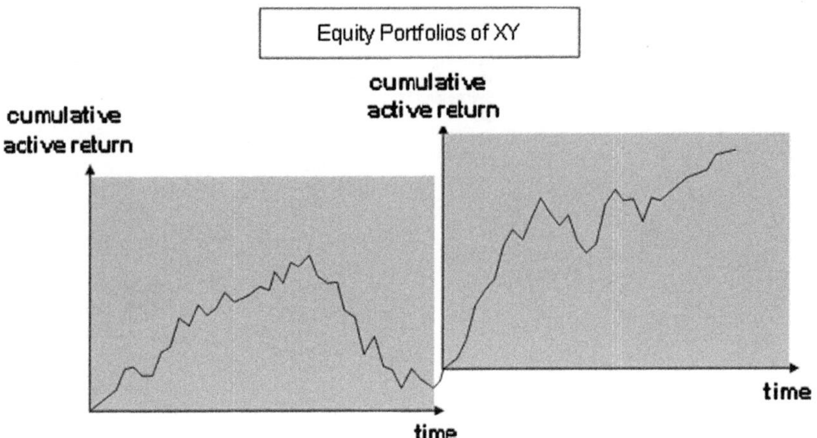

FIGURE 16.2
Presentation of Selective Periods (Only the Right Section is Shown).

In 2006, the IPC became the *GIPS Executive Committee*. Together with the four permanent *Subcommittees*, this body acts as the formal decision maker on issues relating to the GIPS. These standards, which were released in 2005 entered into force on 1 January 2006, form the basis for the present descriptions.

16.1.2 Fundamental Features of the Standards

The idea of performance presentation standards grew out of the desire to create rules that call on asset managers to objectively present their management performance. Without such rules of conduct, there is always a danger that managers will present themselves only "in a good light", and cherry-pick portfolio data as "proof" of their management performance. By setting up strict rules, the GIPS endeavors to counter the primary forms of cherry-picking.

- Presentation of selected portfolios

The GIPS require disclosure of composite returns as a measure of average management performance. A composite should encompass all discretionary portfolios managed by a comparable investment process or sharing a comparable investment objective. Only portfolios displaying severe exogenous cash flows or similar effects can be temporarily omitted from this scheme (3.A.1).

- Survivorship Bias

New portfolios should be promptly integrated into a composite after launch. Discontinued portfolios must remain in their composite until the end of the last full management period. Information on performance in periods prior to portfolio liquidation must *not* be deleted from the performance data for the discontinued portfolio. Since portfolios exhibiting unsatisfactory performance are more likely to be discontinued than those with good performance, deletion of such

Table 16.1 Minimum Period for Presentation

Period Since Initial Compliance Statement	Minimum Period for Presentation
1 year	6 years
2 years	7 years
3 years	8 years
4 years	9 years
5 years	10 years
> 5 years	10 years

data would result in a so-called "survivorship bias", i.e. the reported performance values would overstate the quality of management performance (3.A.5, 3.A.6).

- *Presentation of selective periods*

If a presentation is based on selected time intervals in which above-average results are achieved, then its management is not objective (Figure 16.2). This approach also represents "cherry-picking." Therefore, the GIPS require the presentation of standardized periods with a long history.

- Returns must be calculated for all calendar years included in the presentation. Returns for periods of less than one year may not be annualized (5.A.1, 5.A.4).
- Beginning with the compliance statement by an asset manager, the GIPS require disclosure of returns for at least five calendar years. The track record must then be successively expanded until it encompasses a period of at least the last ten calendar years (see Table 16.1).

Shorter periods may only be presented if, at the time of the compliance statement, the period since creation of the firm is shorter than the number of required full calendar years or if all portfolios assigned to a composite were launched after the start of the first required calendar year. In such cases, the standards require disclosure of the entire history since foundation of the company or the maximum composite history (5.A.1).

- *Change of composite definition*

A further manifestation of cherry-picking can be changing of the composite definition. This would be the case if modification of the composite definition had the potential to assign particularly weak-performing portfolios, for instance, to a less important composite. Consequently, the GIPS require disclosure of the date of the composite creation (4.A.10). For every change, both the date and the grounds for the change must be given (4.A.17). Furthermore, all changes of the composite name must be disclosed (4.A.18). Thus, frequent changes to the composite definition can be tracked by observers.[13]

[13] Possible reasons for a change of composite definition include, e.g. expansion of the investment universe, change of benchmark, or merging with another composite.

16.2 DEFINITION OF FIRM

The first important task when implementing the GIPS is the definition of the firm. If the relevant asset manager is an independent company with a homogenous business model, this is a very simple matter. If, however, the manager is part of a larger group or network that conducts a variety of business activities, then the issue of a reasonable definition is not as easy to resolve. In the version of the AIMR-PPS from 1997, companies were permitted only very limited discretion when it came to answering this question, as the consensus at the time was that formation of sub-firms represented another form of cherry-picking, by way of which companies could create (at least temporary) comparative advantages.

According to the GIPS, a firm must be defined "as an investment firm, subsidiary or division held out to clients or prospective clients as a distinct business entity'.[14] A further interpretation was provided in a *Guidance Statement* by the IPC.[15] Other criteria for determining the firm include, in accordance with this opinion, status as a separate legal entity, a special group of customers, focus on a particular market or a separate investment approach.

In Standard 0.B.3, however, the firm is strongly encouraged;

> "to adopt the broadest, most meaningful definition of the firm. The scope of this definition should include all geographical (country, regional, etc.) offices operating under the same brand name regardless of the actual name of the individual investment management company".

Example 16.1

Definition of a firm:

a. Branch office as independent firm
The New York branch of "Bonus Bank" declares compliance with the GIPS, although the parent itself has never claimed compliance. In presentations to (potential) clients, "Bonus Banks New York Branch" represents itself as an independent firm and provides information on assets under management of that branch only. All portfolios under discretionary management at the New York branch, including the advisory mandate for other branches, must be taken into account for the creation of the composites.

b. Institutional asset management as firm
The units of Bonus Bank in charge of institutional asset management are merged to create a firm (rather a network) "Bonus Bank Institutional Asset Management (BBIAM)". The thus defined firm has its own autonomous investment process. In presentations, assets under management are stated as the sum of all assets managed by the companies belonging to BBIAM.

c. Global group of companies
The Asian subsidiaries of the globally operating Bonus Bank will in the foreseeable future no longer be capable of implementing the GIPS. The bank thus defines the firm

---

[14] Cf. CFA Institute (2010, 0.A.12).
[15] Cf. the "Guidance statement on the definition of the Firm" (2010 version).

"Bonus Bank ex-Asian units" for presentation purposes, and aggregates composites for this firm. The assets under Management at the Asian subsidiary, however, may not be included in presentations for this firm.

d. Limitation to a single asset form
An asset management company manages both equity and fixed income portfolios, but plans to formally define a firm under which all equity management activities are subsumed. This, however, is prohibited under the GIPS, as the company does not normally present itself to investors in this form.[16]

The GIPS place great emphasis on disclosing the definition of the presented firm, and set forth additional transparency requirements in this regard.

- The definition of the firm must be included in the presentation materials (4.A.2).
- "Firms must disclose that the firms list of composite descriptions is available upon request" (4.A.11).
- The volume of the composite and the related total assets under management must be presented (5.A.1.g,h).[17]
- Changes to the definition of the firm are possible; however, in such a case, the date and reasons should be indicated (4.A.16). Generally it must be checked whether the changes are extensive enough to require a new definition.

In this context, it should also be noted that the firms, since 1 January 2006, must "disclose the use of a sub-advisor and the periods a sub-advisor was used" (4.A.25). This information can be particularly useful if the investor wants to evaluate the role of the firm within the group, which may also offer advisory services. The procedure with respect to sub-advisory mandates was long unclear and was not clearly defined until release of the above Guidance Statement. If the firm has full discretion over an appointment of the sub-advisor (i.e. authority to "hire and fire"), then this portfolio must be assigned to one of the firm's composites. If, however, the sub-advisor is defined by the client, assignment to a composite is prohibited. In practice, it is nonetheless customary that such mandates are included in reported assets under management. Conversely, advisory mandates must be assigned to a composite of the advisor and included in his reported assets under management.

Finally, the issue must be addressed as to what happens when two firms merge. To clarify this question and define criteria relating to the conditions under which the performance history of an acquired firm may be transferred to the buyer, the IPC developed criteria and published a related Guidance Statement.[18]

---

[16] Cf. "Guidance statement on the definition of the Firm" (2010 version), p. 1.

[17] As an alternative to a statement of the total assets under management, the percentage of composites in total assets can also be given. Together with the composite volume provided, one can then easily compute the total assets.

[18] Cf. "Guidance statement on the performance record portability" (2010 version).

Standard 5.A.8:

a. *Performance of a past firm or affiliation must be linked to or used to represent the historical performance of a new or acquiring firm if, on a composite-specific basis:*
   i. *Substantially all of the investment decision makers are employed by the new or acquiring firm (e.g., research department staff, portfolio managers, and other relevant staff);*
   ii. *The decision-making process remains substantially intact and independent within the new or acquiring firm; and*
   iii. *new or acquiring firm has records that document and support the performance.*

b. *If a firm acquires another firm or affiliation, the firm has one year to bring any non-compliant assets into compliance.*

Thus, a firm may only assume the performance history of a predecessor firm if the above criteria are satisfied. This can also apply to individual composites carried on by the new firm ("surviving composites"). If the criteria have not been met, then the performance history of the predecessor firm may only be presented in the form of supplementary information. This standard has been more specifically defined as compared to the 2005 version (previous number 5.A.4) to require portability tests directly on a composite-specific basis. This is to account for the argument that the acquiring firm generally only takes over a (small) portion of personnel from the target company.

16.3 CREATION OF COMPOSITES

16.3.1 Identification of Discretionary Portfolios

Now that we have a definition of firm, and thus the general scope of the work at hand, the next important step is to select the discretionary portfolios. The following GIPS standard provides the basis for this:

> *All actual, fee-paying, discretionary portfolios must be included in at least one composite. Although non-fee-paying discretionary portfolios may be included in a composite (with appropriate disclosure), non-discretionary portfolios must not be included in a firm's composites. (3.A.1).*

Thus, an asset manager must independently decide for each of the portfolios it manages whether it can be assigned to a composite. In this context, there is an option to define a minimum volume for each composite, below which a portfolio is not included.[19] This assignment must be carried out in accordance with criteria defined by the asset manager, which must be documented in the firm's policies and procedures.[20]

[19] Retrograde changes to the minimum volume are not permissible. It must also be applied consistently, i.e. no portfolio that falls below the threshold may be allocated to a composite (cf. CFA Institute 2010, 3.A.9). Both the thresholds and any changes to them must be disclosed (CFA Institute 2010, 4.A.19).

[20] Cf. CFA Institute (2010), 0.A.5.

Example 16.2

(Composite Formation with Restrictions):

A client engages asset manager XY to manage a portfolio investing exclusively in DAX shares. The only restriction to which the manager is subject states that no insurance shares (Allianz, Munich Re) are to be purchased. The DAX is defined as the benchmark. XY already manages two portfolios with this restriction.

Under the GIPS,21 asset manager XY has several possibilities with respect to the assignment of the portfolio.

a. As a result of the considerable restriction of the investment universe (together, Allianz and Munich Re make up roughly 8.7% of the DAX (status: February 2012)), XY does not consider the performance of these portfolios to be representative of its management performance in the segment "German equities". It thus decides not to assign this portfolio to a composite. Consequently, the same rule must be applied to all funds managed in accordance with the same restriction. Thus, the two other portfolios with the same restrictions also must not be assigned to any composite.

b. Since XY now manages three portfolios in this particular segment, it creates the composite "DAX ex-insurance companies" and uses it to represent its management expertise in this area. As a benchmark, XY uses the index "DAX ex insurance companies", which it calculates by himself in a transparent form.

c. XY considers the restriction as irrelevant for the purposes of the GIPS and reallocates all three portfolios to his DAX composite.

For reasons of transparency, the solutions in a) and b) are the best forms for taking the portfolio into account when creating composites. Solution c)—although generally permissible under the standard—could result in significant consequences for the DAX composite. For instance, it must be expected that both the range of returns within the composite and the volatility of returns for the entire composite would increase over time. Moreover, the issue would arise as to whether the DAX is a suitable benchmark to compare the risk of the investment process.

An asset manager must deal in a similar way with other forms of restrictions. Some examples of restrictions are:

- Client defines required characteristics of the securities that lead to inadequate coverage of the benchmark (e.g. no investment in so-called "sin stocks" (alcohol, tobacco, etc.) or companies that violate certain environmental standards, etc.);
- Derivatives are prohibited;
- Client-specific investment degree that fails to correspond with the benchmark;
- Client prescribes a minimum rate of return;
- Substantial, permanent client restrictions are defined in a side letter;
- Restrictions on foreign currency investments;
- Client imposes a ceiling on investment in certain asset classes (precluding total coverage of the benchmark);

[21]See also the "Guidance statement on composite definition" (2010 version).

- Restrictions with respect to the maturity spectrum or defining minimum rating for bond portfolios (not in line with the benchmark);
- Consideration of individual aspects of investor taxation, which limit the discretionary scope of the firm.

Example 16.3

(Composite Creation in Connection with Tax Restrictions):

In many countries, price gains are subject to taxation at the point of realization. This leads to a situation in which many investors prevent portfolio managers from disposing of equities that have seen long periods of substantial rises in price. In the US, this is also known as a "low cost stock". If cash is to be withdrawn from the portfolio, equities are sold off that have not yet seen any significant rise in value. In many cases, this leads to an enormous weighting of low cost stocks in some portfolios.

Portfolios may also be generally treated as non-discretionary if managed according to tax criteria and there is no explicit consideration of tax-related criteria in the firm's investment processes.

If portfolios experience substantial exogenous inflows and outflows, the performance achieved in the restructuring period may not fully reflect the capabilities of the manager. If, for instance, an equity portfolio is launched during a period of rising prices, there is a danger that the manager is unable to invest the additional sums quickly enough, so that performance lags the benchmark as a result of the high cash ratio. In "tight" segments, such as certain emerging market segments or European small caps, it may only be reasonable to invest larger sums (i.e. without artificially inflating the price of the target stocks) by distributing the transactions over an extended period of time.

Similar effects occur in phases of falling prices, only in this case, managers can benefit from the increased cash ratio. As a result, however, it must be stated that the track record, here as well, does not reflect solely the capability of the manager. Sometimes such risks can be reduced via futures and other derivatives. This requires, however, adequate liquidity and the permissibility of such instruments under the investment guidelines.

The GIPS therefore provide for the possibility to designate the relevant funds as non-discretionary over a certain period, and thus eliminate them from calculation of composite returns. In this context, it must be noted that the guidance statement "On the Treatment of Significant Cash Flows" (2010 version) requires firms to document:

- *"The date of the significant cash flow, the date the firm removes the portfolio from the composite, and the date the firm returns the portfolio to the composite,*
- *Depending upon the firm's definition of significant cash flow, the amount of the significant cash flow or the amount of the significant cash flow as a percentage of the most recent portfolio value, and*
- *If the significant cash flow is moving into or out of the portfolio."*

At the request of the client, the firm must also disclose not only the number of portfolios, but also how often such eliminations were undertaken due to significant fund flows, as well as the volume of portfolio assets affected.

Elimination of portfolios from the composites, however, is only one of the options available under the GIPS, and in no way the preferred alternative. What is recommended is creation of so-called temporary accounts. This method remains controversial to this day. It harkens back to the AIMR-PPS, but was not included in the 1998 GIPS.[22] It reappeared in the GIPS version from 2002 and was kept in the 2005 and 2010 versions.[23] According to the process described in these standards, temporary accounts should be created for severe exogenous flows. Here one needs to differentiate between contributions and withdrawals:

Contributions: A contribution is initially transferred to a separate account. Within the account, securities are then acquired. Only when this investment process has been completed is the separate account transferred to the "core portfolio".

Withdrawals: If a significant portion of the portfolio must be disposed of to cover planned outflows, then the positions designated for liquidation may initially be transferred to a separate account from which they may be sold in stages. The amounts realized from the sales then flow back into the core portfolio.

Practical implementation of this process is very resource intensive given that two sub-portfolios must be created in the event of severe fund flows. Moreover, it must be specified how the returns for the artificial portfolio are to be calculated from these sub-portfolios; in particular, there must be decided how the trading costs incurred in the temporary accounts are dealt with.

In this context, it must be noted that, according to a study by Pricewaterhouse Coopers,[24] only a minority of asset managers are prepared to abide by this GIPS recommendation. According to the study, roughly 19% of all asset managers who participated in the survey have eliminated portfolios from composites in the event of critical exogenous fund flows. Only 11% create temporary accounts in such cases. The vast majority of the other asset managers kept portfolios with extreme cash flows in their composites, without setting up a temporary account. In another PwC survey, it was demonstrated that the majority of asset managers welcome the possibility to temporarily remove portfolios from their

[22] Cf. AIMR (1999) and AIMR (1997, p. ix).

[23] Cf., AIMR (2002, section 5-5), CFA Institute (2006, p. 240 et seq.) and the current guidance statement mentioned above. In the 2002 version it was "anticipated that the Investment Performance Council (IPC) will adopt a requirement to use Temporary New Account to handle significant cash flows beginning 1 January 2010" (section 5-5). In the 2006 version this was changed to "The removal of portfolios due to significant cash flows may no longer be permitted at some point in the future". This is identical to the corresponding assertion in the current guidance statement.

[24] Cf. PwC (2000a); all asset managers reported by *Pensions&Investments* to have more than on billion US$ in tax exempt assets under management were contacted. Of these managers, 30% responded. See also PwC (2000b).

composites.[25] The results of this survey were recently corroborated in a study by Spaulding Group,[26] according to which 28.8% of the 102 participating asset managers use the option of removing portfolios from composites, with only 7.7% setting up temporary accounts.

Severe fund inflows and outflows are the primary reason for temporary elimination of portfolios from composites. There are, however, other criteria that may lead to such elimination, which are not subject to disclosure under the GIPS. An example here would be material changes to a benchmark as a result of restructuring of indexes by the index provider.[27] In such cases, the portfolio manager must reallocate the portfolio for reasons outside his control, and is thus unable to pursue the intended management approach. Accordingly, the situation is the same as in the case of benchmark changes by customers. As with the issue of exogenous fund flows, the firm should define a quantitative threshold for this in the corporate policies and procedures.

In the Q&As, several statements were made with respect to temporary elimination of portfolios in the context of the 2007–2009 financial market crisis. For instance, a portfolio may be declared non-discretionary if the custodian bank or broker becomes insolvent or is taken over by another company, because in such cases it can be expected that the investment strategy can no longer be fully implemented as a result of restrictions on disposition. As soon as the restrictions are no longer in place, the portfolio must be included once again in the composites (Q&A database, June 2009). Conversely, portfolios may not be designated non-discretionary if individual securities are illiquid or counterparties enter insolvency.[28]

In closing, a word about the special treatment of non-*fee*-paying *portfolios*. Unlike portfolios for which fees are charged, non-fee-paying portfolios *may* be included in composites, but are not required to be. What is meant here are portfolios for which no fees are charged or will be charged in general, and not those for which fee collection has been suspended temporarily, e.g. as a gesture of goodwill to a client[29]. If a firm resolves to include its non-fee-paying portfolios in the composites, it must disclose the proportion of such portfolios in the annual composite reporting. The firm may, however, exercise selectivity with respect to the non-fee-paying portfolios that it intends to include in its composites. If it has allocated a certain non-fee paying portfolio to a specific composite, then all other such portfolios that meet the specific criteria must also be included.

---

[25] Cf. PwC (2001); the study was based on 69 responses to the PwC survey of asset managers with between 3 and 200 billion US$ under management.

[26] Cf. Spaulding Group (2005); 64% of participants in the study were North American asset managers and 30% European, with the remainder based in Australia, East Asia, and South Africa.

[27] Such significant changes are rare. Such a situation occurred, e.g. in September 1999, when the provider implemented material changes to its STOXX 50 and EURO STOXX 50 indices.

[28] Cf. PwC (2010).

[29] Cf. CFA Institute (2006, p. 97). Examples here are the pension fund of the firm or portfolios managed for friends or employees.

The discussion with respect to treatment of non-fee-paying portfolios is as old as the idea of the GIPS. The specific justification for this special treatment of such portfolios is not included in any of the standards. In hindsight, it can only be assumed that the original PPS advocates had the (vague) concern that fraud could be perpetrated with such portfolios (e.g. through preferred attribution of particularly strong performing securities or IPOs), and this position was included with no further reflection in all versions of the GIPS.

16.3.2 Criteria for Allocation of Portfolios to Composites

The criteria to be observed when allocating portfolios managed by a portfolio manager to a composite were already mentioned in Section 16.1. In this context, the portfolios aggregated to a composite must share a comparable investment style or common investment objective,[30] so that the resulting "superportfolio"[31] can be associated with a specific investment style or objective. The 2010 version was the first to expressly include the possibility of creating composites according to the type of vehicle. Some examples for criteria for composite creation are:[32]

- *same or similar geographical asset classes (e.g. European equities, USD bonds);*
- *same or similar strategies (e.g. growth stocks, value stocks);*
- *weighting range of asset classes (e.g. 10–20% bonds, 80–90% equities), in the case of balanced portfolios;*
- *same benchmark;*
- *similar use of derivatives;*
- *similar use of currency hedging instruments;*
- *comparable risk classes (e.g. expressed as standard deviation, probability of default);*
- *comparable investment approach (e.g. active, low tracking error, passive);*
- *similar investment objectives (e.g. excess returns over a local bond market through additions of up to x% equities and/or forex positions, achievement of a minimum return target).*

The GIPS emphasize a hierarchical order of composites, but otherwise give an asset manager considerable freedom in the formation of composites. In principle, the transfer of a portfolio between two composites is possible. The requirement, however, is that the changes in the investment policy of portfolios (based on client instructions) are well documented. In the event of such a change, the performance history remains with the old composite.[33]

The rules for creation of composites must be defined in the corporate policies and procedures,[34] which must also specify the timeframe within which new portfolios are added to the composite (3.A.5).

---

[30] Cf. CFA Institute (2010, 3.A.4).

[31] Cf. Wittrock et al. (1998a,b).

[32] According to CFA Institute (2006, p. 100 et seq.) and DVFA (2000, 7.2). For further criteria see the "Guidance statement on composite definition" (2010 version).

[33] See CFA Institute (2010, 3.A.6).

[34] See "Guidance statement on composite definition" (2010 version).

Table 16.2 German Equity Portfolios Managed by XY

Portfolio	Return (%)*	Asset Value (Mio. €)	Fee p. a. (%)**	Type***	Investment Style
Portfolio 1	4.0	70	0.3	I	German blue chips supplemented with European blue chips; investment degree often well over 100%
Portfolio 2	2.0	210	0.2	I	DAX stocks supplemented with MDAX stocks
Portfolio 3	−10.4	320	1.0	R	DAX stocks
Portfolio 4	10.2	80	0.3	I	HDAX equities supplemented with German fixed income
Portfolio 5	8.0	600	0.2	I	German broad market equities
DAX	−3.8				
HDAX	−4.0				
CDAX	−1.6				

*Unit price return in the period from 99/01/01–08/12/31; **In percent of portfolio value; includes management fees and other volume-based charges; ***R: Retail fund, I: Institutional funds and other institutional portfolios.

Example 16.4

(Presentation of management performance):

Asset manager XY wants to present its performance in the "German equities" segment using characteristic performance indicators. XY manages five equity portfolios targeting the German equities segment. Table 16.2 contains further information about these portfolios.

Asset manager XY has a number of options available for the allocation of the portfolios to composites.

a. Benchmark-based allocation
XY seeks to ensure that the portfolios in the composite structurally deviate as little as possible from the benchmark on which the composite is based.
He forms four composites (Figure 16.3). Since these are narrowly defined, the number of portfolios in each composite (and thus the volume contained) is relatively small. He achieves, however (in three composites in trivial ways), that all portfolios of a composite are very similar in their investment style.

b. Allocation by investment objective
XY comes to an agreement with each investor that the benchmark will serve as investment objective and as the basis for the investment policies of the portfolios. The possibility of adding non-benchmark stocks is also an integral component of each such investment strategy. Consequently, XY creates only two composites (see Figure 16.4).
As the investment objective is crucial to this method, a composite contains portfolios with different management approaches. Therefore, a wide dispersion of performance results can be expected.

c. Composites with different levels of allocation
To provide the most detailed illustration possible of management performance, XY creates both the composites under b) and the sub-composites under a). Such a differentiation

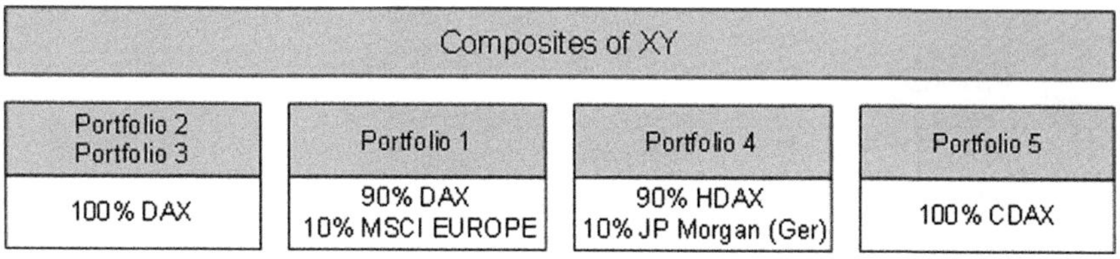

Composites of XY

Portfolio 2
Portfolio 3
100% DAX

Portfolio 1
90% DAX
10% MSCI EUROPE

Portfolio 4
90% HDAX
10% JP Morgan (Ger)

Portfolio 5
100% CDAX

FIGURE 16.3
Allocation of the Portfolios According to the Investment Style.

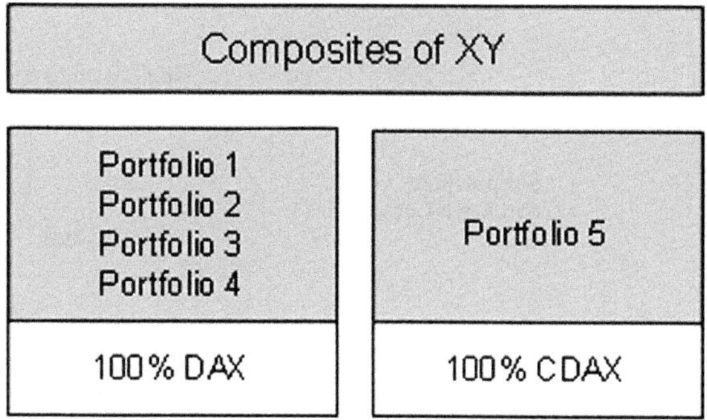

FIGURE 16.4
Allocation of Portfolios to Composites by Investment Objective.

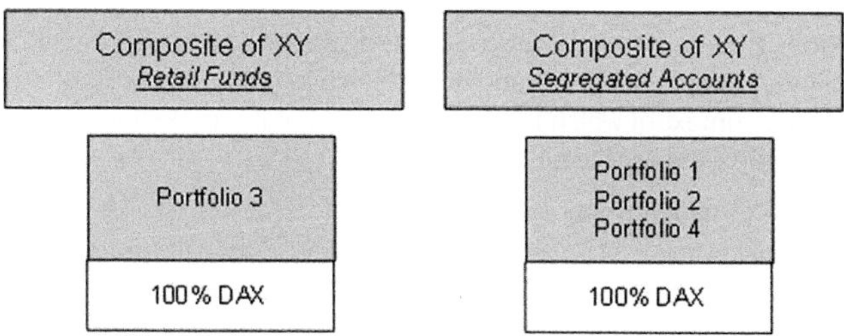

FIGURE 16.5
Alternative Breakdown of the DAX-Portfolios.

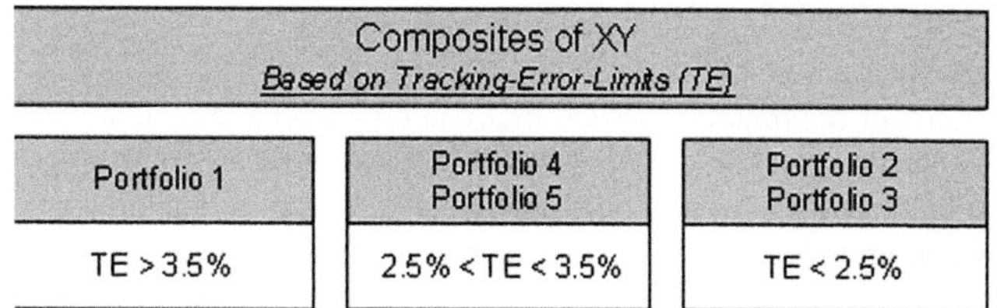

FIGURE 16.6
Classification of Portfolios According to Tracking Error Limit.

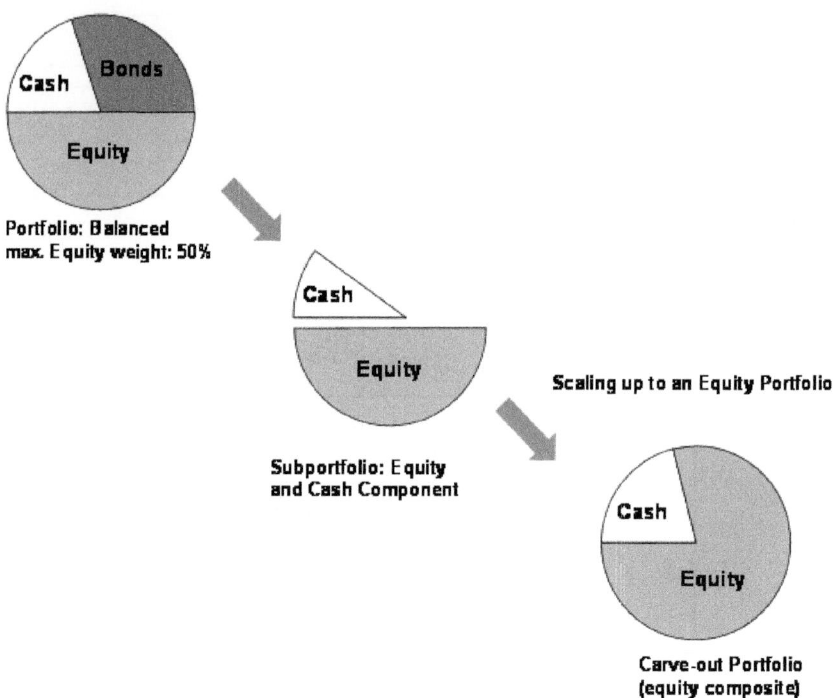

FIGURE 16.7
Formation of Carve-Outs from a Balanced Portfolio.

of investment segments, however, is associated with an increased administrative burden. The (voluntary) presentation of additional levels is thus an important strategic decision for XY, in the context of which the future benefits of its marketing activities must be weighed against the increased cost.

d. Separation by portfolio type
XY presents the performance of its retail fund separately,[35] through creation of an additional composite on the basis of the DAX composite in b). This is only allowed, however, if different types of portfolios are managed according to different styles. If portfolio 3 is no longer taken into account in the original DAX composite, it must be renamed (see Figure 16.5):

e. Consideration of the investment degree
Since the management approach for Portfolio 1 involves a wide variation in investment degree, XY decides to form a separate composite for this portfolio and make this feature part of the composite definition.

f. Allocation using a risk measure
The management approach employed by XY is characterized by risk considerations. Through the specific selection of DAX stocks and supplementation with non-index positions, XY seeks to ouperform the index, in conjunction with a defined limit on tracking error, which can vary from portfolio to portfolio. XY defines the following limits (see Table 16.3).

[35]This is permissible, whereas a separation by type of client alone would be prohibited (cf. "Guidance statement on composite definition" (2010 version), p. 6).

Table 16.3 Tracking-Error-Limits of the Portfolios

	Tracking Error p. a. Against the DAX (%)
Portfolio 1	4.0
Portfolio 2	2.5
Portfolio 3	2.0
Portfolio 4	3.0
Portfolio 5	3.0

XY therefore creates the composites shown in Figure 16.6, all of which are compared against the DAX.

A division of portfolios into composites based on different risk levels is particularly useful for portfolios whose investment objective is to earn the highest possible return at a defined risk level, but in which neither the investment objective nor the investment strategy will be defined by means of a benchmark, such as absolute return funds or hedge fund.

In breaking down the portfolios to composites one should try not to make an assignment only for the moment without considering their overall structure and stability in the future.

16.3.3 Carve-Outs

In order to enable asset managers to present their management performance in as comprehensive a manner as possible, the GIPS permit the assignment of individual portfolio segments to composites.[36] The precondition for this, however, is that these segments are managed independently of other segments. For periods prior to January 1, 2010, the cash segments must be consistently attributable to the segments of the portfolios. A separate segment, together with the corresponding cash position and other accompanying positions such as derivatives, is referred to as a *carve-out*. Since January 1, 2010, the GIPS only permit the use of carve-outs under the condition that the segment maintains its own cash position, via which the transactions for the segment are settled.[37]

If the ideal situation, fully autonomous segments with their own, directly attributable dedicated cash bucket, is not in place ("bookkeeping assignment"), as is the case with sub-funds, the liquidity position can be attributed using a clearly defined, uniform method ("mathematical attribution"). Definition of the rules for attribution of cash positions should correspond with the relevant management process and be anchored in the corporate policies and procedures.[38] If available, the cash weighting of the pure segment (i.e., "non-carve-out") portfolio should be used as a basis. In general, the GIPS require that the management

[36] Cf. CFA Institute (2010, 3.A.8).

[37] Cf. CFA Institute (2010, 3.A.8). According to the original GIPS, this more stringent rule was supposed to enter into force much earlier, namely January 1, 2005. The transitional period was extended given that many investment companies were deemed to be unable to fulfill the requirement.

[38] Cf. CFA Institute (2010, 4.A.23). See also the "Guidance Statement on Treatment of Carve-outs" (2010 version).

style of the carve-out portfolio be representative of the segment to which it is attributed. In other words, a carve-out from a global equity portfolio of a "Japanese equities" segment containing only ten stocks with the Nikkei 225 (225 stock index) as a benchmark would be extremely dubious in this context (see Figure 16.7).

The following options apply to the assignment of individual cash segments:[39]

a. Assignment according to the benchmark weights at the beginning of each period.
b. Assignment according to the portfolio segment weights at the beginning of each period, or according to the average weights.
c. Fixed attribution that does not change over time and corresponds to the investment process represented by the composite.
d. Use of the cash segment to cover the difference between portfolio and benchmark weighting. Portfolio segments that exceed the benchmark weighting even without attribution of a cash segment are deemed fully invested. Calculation of portfolio segment weightings may take cash flows into account.[40]

Example 16.5

(Allocation of cash in formation of carve-out portfolios):

Given the growth of investment in European equities, asset manager XY considers it important to highlight its expertise in this market segment. However, XY manages only a handful of portfolios dedicated exclusively to European stocks; these are benchmarked against the *EURO STOXX*. Therefore, the manager decides to create a carve-out portfolio from the equity side of a balanced portfolio and assign it to the composite *EURO STOXX*. The allocation of the cash segment is described using data from the months of September and October 2008, which are included in Table 8.4. The benchmark of the balanced portfolio consists of 50% *JP Morgan Europe* and 50% *EURO STOXX*; it is subject to monthly rebalancing (see Table 16.4).

The following presents the options for dividing the cash segment.

a. The cash segment is allocated according to the benchmark weighting
In this case, always 50% of the cash position and the resulting return contributions are added to the "European equity" segment. Thus, at the beginning of September the constructed carve-out portfolio consists of 100 * 30/35% = 85.71 European equities and 100 * 5/35% = 14.29% liquid assets. The return on the carve-out portfolio for the month of September is then:

$$85.71\% * 6.9\% + 14.29\% * 0.3\% = 5.96\%.$$

With this rate of return and the net asset value at the beginning of September (= asset value of the equity segment + 50% * of the cash asset value), the portfolio can be integrated into the *EURO STOXX* composite. The procedure for October is similar.

---

[39] These procedures are taken from the notes to the DVFA PPS (DVFA 2000, p. 67). Methods a) and d) feature explicitly in the "Guidance Statement on Carve-outs" (2010 version).
[40] This alternative is sensible if there is no potential for "negative cash positions" (debts).

Table 16.4 Data for Balanced Portfolio with Benchmark 50% JP Morgan Europe/50% EURO STOXX, for the Months of September and October 2008. Information on the Returns of the Bond Segment is Omitted as not Needed (Values in %)

	Weight 08/31/08	Return September 08	Weight 09/30/08	Return October 08
Bonds Europe	60		50	
Equities Europe	30	6.9	45	12.0
Cash	10	0.3	5	0.4

b. The cash segment is allocated according to the portfolio weighting
XY regards the actual weighting of the segments in the portfolio as relevant to the distribution of the cash segment. At the beginning of September a third of the cash will be added to the carve-out portfolio, and at the beginning of October 45 * 100/95% = 47.37%. The calculation for the September return of the carve-out portfolio shall serve as an example:

$$\frac{30}{33.33} * 6.9\% + \frac{3.33}{33.33} * 0.3\% = 6.24\%.$$

c. Fixed assignment
The variation of the investment degree is not part of the management approach of the composite *EURO STOXX*. Therefore, XY decides to allocate a cash component to the equity segment with a constant weight of 1%. Thus at the beginning of September the carve-out portfolio consists of 100 * 30/31% European stocks and 100 * 1/31% liquidity. In this case the return for September is given by:

$$\frac{30}{31} * 6.9\% + \frac{1}{31} * 0.3\% = 6.69\%.$$

d. Covering differences to the benchmark
Since in September and October the bond segment exceeded the benchmark weighting, or was identical, with this allocation method in both periods the entire cash segment will be assigned to the equity segment:

$$\frac{30}{40} * 6.9\% + \frac{10}{40} * 0.3\% = 5.25\%.$$

It is clearly demonstrated that the carve-out return depends considerably on the method of calculation.

The investment manager may also assign the bond segment to a corresponding fixed-income composite, provided that the investment process applied to the bond component corresponds to the relevant target composite. Although this seems a logical consequence, the GIPS do not require this.

Because of the potential inaccuracies in the assignment of the contributions of the cash and derivatives segments, the carve-out formation in the form admissible for the periods until 01/01/2010 cannot be considered an optimal form of representation of management performance. For this reason, in the presentation of composites, which include carve-out portfolios, for the period between 01/01/2006 and 01/01/2010, it must be specified what percentage of volume these carve-outs are taking up within the composite.[41]

16.4 DETERMINATION OF COMPOSITE RETURN

16.4.1 Standards for the Valuation of Portfolios

The GIPS demand the calculation of time-weighted returns for the portfolios of a composite.[42] As explained in Section 10.4, the condition for the exact calculation of this return is that the portfolio is valued whenever an exogenous cash flow occurs. In practice, however, this condition is often not met because many asset managers value their portfolios on a regular basis, e.g. weekly or monthly.[43]

The GIPS recommend that "firms should value portfolios on the date of all exogenous cash flows". For periods beginning on or after 01/01/2001 portfolios must at least be valued on a monthly basis. For the prior periods a quarterly valuation would be sufficient. Finally, for periods beginning on or after 01/01/2010 it is furthermore required to value portfolios on the date of all "large" external cash flows.[44]

Approximation methods are acceptable to calculate the time-weighted rate of return (e.g. the methods described in Section 10.6). Within a period between two valuation dates exogenous (the GIPS prefer the term external) cash flows must be taken into account as follows:

- For periods prior to 1/1/2005 external fund flows must only be considered in the adjustment of time-weighted returns (without further specification).
- For periods beginning 1/1/2005 firms must calculate portfolio returns "that adjust for daily-weighted external cash flows."
- For the period from 01/01/2010 firms must value portfolios at the time of significant external cash flows.[45]

---

[41] See CFA Institute (2010, 5.A.5).

[42] See CFA Institute (2010, 2.A.2); the exceptions are private equity portfolios. Since the manager of a private equity fund has discretion over the fund inflows, here the internal rate of return from the inception of the composite shall be reported. Since in the case of private equity a composite usually consists of a single fund or a partnership, this is equivalent to the statement of the internal interest rate for a fund or a partnership (see CFA Institute (2006, p. 146)).

[43] See the discussion in Section 10.6.

[44] See CFA Institute (2010, 1.A.3). It is therefore necessary to distinguish between the terms "large cash flow" and "significant cash flow". A significant cash flow leads to the classification of a portfolio as non-discretionary, a large cash flow to a revaluation. The determination of when a fund movement should be considered as "large" depends on the firm. The criteria for each composite must be documented in the company's guidelines. The "real estate" and "private equity" market segments are subject to different requirements. Since 01/01/2008 real estate must be valued quarterly; for prior periods an annual evaluation is sufficient (CFA Institute 2010, 6.A.1., 6.A.2). Private equity must be valued at least annually (CFA Institute 2010, 7.A.2). Both asset classes must be valued according to the GIPS Valuation Principles (see below).

[45] See CFA Institute (2010, 1.A.3, 2.A.2) and (AIMR 1999, 2.A.2).

For periods before 2005, for example, even the simple Dietz Method (see Section 10.6.3) can be applied. For periods after this date at least the modified Dietz Method or a similar method must be used. This is a good example for the evolution of requirements over time in the GIPS.

Over time more stringent requirements in regard to the update frequency of the weighting factors for portfolio returns in a calculation of the composite returns came into effect. For periods beginning on or after 01/01/2010, the weighting factors must be updated at least monthly. For periods before this a quarterly (since 01/01/2006) respectively an annual update are required.[46] The GIPS also call for the calculation of the total return of the portfolio.[47] This implies that at the valuation of the securities, all cash, realized and unrealized capital gains, and all the income (interest, dividends, rents, etc.) must be considered.

The term valuation needs to be explained. Ideally, the securities of a portfolio and the exchange rates required for the conversion of their prices into the base currency are taken from the same price source.[48] Given the fact that in practice this often can be done only with great difficulty, the GIPS limit the requirement for the firm "to disclose and describe any known inconsistency in the exchange rates used between the portfolios within a composite and between the composite and the benchmark."[49] Against the backdrop of the financial market crisis 2007–2009, which is primarily considered a liquidity crisis by many observers, the GIPS Executive Committee has developed extensive additional guidelines for the valuation of portfolios, which have been compiled in a separate section (GIPS Valuation Principles). These guidelines are based on the valuation principles of the International Accounting Standard Board (IASB) and the Financial Accounting Standards Board (FASB) (see Figure 16.8).[50]

The methodology described in a)—if market data are available—is mandatory for the firms. The further steps in the hierarchy are to be regarded as recommendations. The firms may thus also apply their own classification scheme, but must from 01/01/2011 disclose "material differences" to the procedure outlined in Figure 16.8 (4.A.28). Thereafter, the firms must also disclose the use of subjective estimates for the valuation of investments (4.A.27), if these are of material importance. In addition, they must also disclose the relevant company policies upon request (4.A.12). The experiences of the financial crisis in 2007–2009 have shown that the valuation can be very sensitive to the assumptions made so that the materiality threshold may be exceeded very quickly.

---

[46] See CFA Institute (2010, 2.A.7) or AIMR (1999, 2.A.4).

[47] See CFA Institute (2010, 2.A.1).

[48] The commentary to the 2006 version of the GIPS mentions the spot rates from WM/Reuters (4 p.m. London), which are used by many index providers (FTSE, MSCI, Standard & Poor's, etc.), but without expressing a clear recommendation (CFA Institute 2006, p. 115).

[49] See CFA Institute (2010, 4.A.21). From this the recommendation for the equality of sources used for the prices and exchange rate can be deduced indirectly. For periods from 01/01/2011, the disclosure is required only if the differences are material.

[50] Cf. CFA Institute (2010, p. 25).

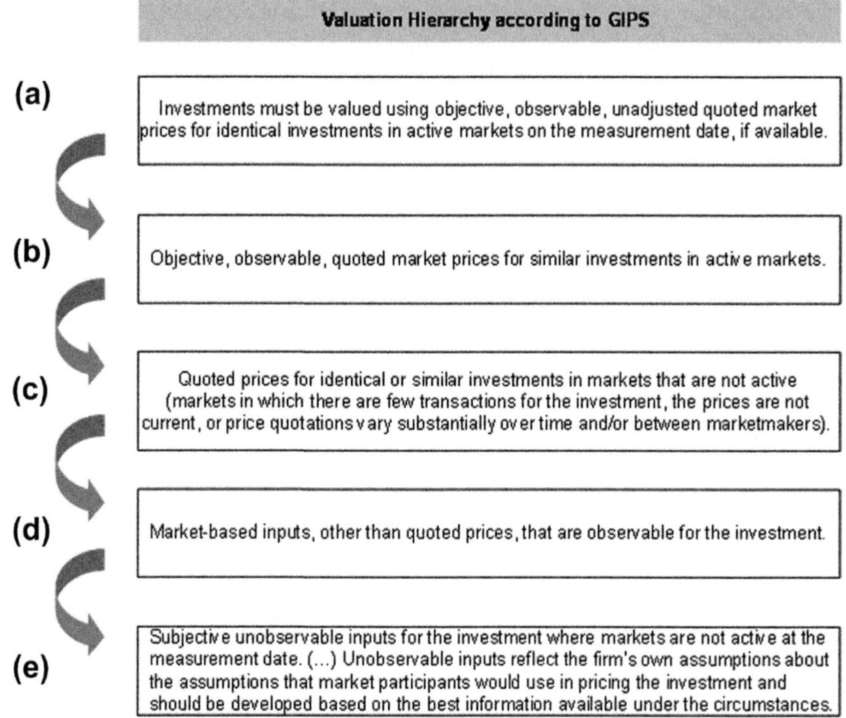

FIGURE 16.8
GIPS Valuation Recommendations.

According to standard 1.A.5, from 01/01/2005 firms must use trade date accounting (i.e., record securities transactions on the day of trading). Due to practical considerations the requirement is considered fulfilled when the trades are entered within three days of the date the transaction is made.[51] Further, from 01/01/2010 portfolios must be valued at the end or on the last trading day of each month (1.A.4). Discrepancies for periods prior to 01/01/2010 must be disclosed (4.A.26).

Period-compatible Accrual of Financial Transactions (Accrual Accounting)

The GIPS contain various requirements and recommendations for dealing with financial transactions (dividends and interest payments, refund of withholding taxes), to which there is a legal claim, but which will be recorded at a later date:

- For fixed-interest securities and other assets that accrue interest claims, period-compatible[52] accrual accounting of the claims must be made in the valuation. The market values of fixed-income securities must include interest claims (1.A.6).

[51] See CFA Institute (2006, p. 79).

[52] In the GIPS the term accrual accounting is defined as follows: "The recording of financial transactions as they come into existence rather than when they are paid or settled." (CFA Institute 2010, p. 36).

- For dividends, period-compatible accrual accounting should be used on the ex-dividends date in the valuation (1.B.3]).[53] Dividends should therefore be taken into consideration in the valuation from the ex-dividend date. (If not, the asset value of the fund would be too low until the dividends are entered in the bookkeeping system.)
- Returns should be calculated after deducting non-reclaimable withholding taxes on dividends, interest and capital gains. Reclaimable withholding taxes should undergo period-compatible accrual accounting (2.B.1).[54]

16.4.2 Calculation Methodology

A composite can be regarded as a result of merging similarly managed portfolios. In this way, all constituents and transactions are combined to a "superportfolio". In this context, removing a portfolio from or adding a portfolio to a composite means nothing more than an exogenous fund flow. In principle, the return of a composite is calculated by the same mathematical methods as those used for a single portfolio.[55] According to the GIPS time-weighted returns should be calculated for portfolios and composites.[56]

An alternative method of calculation, which represents an approximation of the described aggregation method, is to weight the returns of all portfolios of a composite with the asset values within individual periods and combine the resulting composite returns geometrically over the periods under consideration.[57] The weighting should be calculated on the basis of either asset values at the beginning of a period or asset values at the beginning of a period *plus* the time-weighted cash flows.[58] To illustrate the general approach, first the simple case of the composite in Example 16.4 will be considered.

Example 16.6

(Calculation of Composite Return):

For the composite in Example 16.4, case b), which consists of Portfolios 1–4, on the basis of the given data the asset-weighted rate of return is calculated as:

$$R = \frac{70}{680} * 4.0\% + \frac{210}{680} * 2.0\% + \frac{320}{680} * (-10.4\%) + \frac{80}{680} * 10.2\% = -2.66\%.$$

---

[53] In the original edition of GIPS it was planned to convert this on 01/01/2005 into a requirement (AIMR 1999, 1.A.6). The IPC was apparently of the view that the technical capabilities of many investment firms would not permit this.

[54] According to Standard 4.A.20, the firms must "outline all the relevant details of the treatment of withholding taxes on dividends, interest and capital gains."

[55] See the "Guidance Statement on Calculation Methodology" (2010 version).

[56] See CFA Institute (2010, 2.A.2 and 2.A.6). The only exceptions are private equity portfolios and composites, which are not examined any further in the context of this discussion. Here the internal interest rate method is used (CFA Institute 2010, 7.A.3).

[57] This is the actual method intended by GIPS. See CFA Institute (2010, 2.A.6) and CFA Institute (2006, pp. 91 et seq.).

[58] See CFA Institute (2010, 2.A.6).

Table 16.5 Composite of Two Portfolios

Portfolio	Return September 2008	Asset Value 08/31 2008 in Million €	Cash Flow in Million € / Date
A	20%	2	
B	10%	10	06 / 09/15/2008

When determining the return of a real composite, the weighting by means of asset value must, however, be more differentiated. The following is an example that has been taken from Wittrock et al. (1998b).

Example 16.7

(Calculation of Composite Return):

In this example, a composite was formed from two portfolios (A and B) for a single period (in the notation for the general case described below: $j = 1$ and $N_1 = 2$). On 09/15/2008 an exogenous cash flow entered Portfolio B ($T_1 = 30$ days, $t_1^{21} = 15$ days, $M_1^{21} = 6$ million €).

For the composite described in Table 16.5 the return will be calculated by using the asset value at the beginning of the period (method a)):

$$R_1^C = 0.20 * \frac{2}{10+2} + 0.10 * \frac{10}{10+2} = 11.67\%.$$

If the cash flows within the period (inflow of € 6 million to 09/15) are considered (method b)), then the return is calculated as:

$$R_1^C = 0.20 * \frac{2}{10 + \frac{1}{2} * 6 + 2} + 0.10 * \frac{10 + \frac{1}{2} * 6}{10 + \frac{1}{2} * 6 + 2} = 11.33\%.$$

The general case is as follows.

Calculation of Composite Return

a. If the weightings are based on the initial asset values and on returns of individual portfolios, then the return R_j^C of a composite within the period j is calculated according to

$$R_j^C = \sum_{i=1}^{N_j} I_i^j * R_i^j / \sum_{i=1}^{N_j} I_i^j, \tag{16.1}$$

where:

I_i^j: Net asset value of portfolio i in the composite at the beginning of period j

R_i^j: return of portfolio i over period j

N_j: Number of portfolios in the composite over period j.

If the exogenous (or: external) cash flows are to be considered in the portfolio calculation, this is achieved by the following substitutions in Equation (16.1):

$$I_i^j \to I_i^j + \sum_{k=1}^{N_{ij}} \frac{T_j - t_k^{ij}}{T_j} * M_k^{ij}, \tag{16.2}$$

where:

M_k^{ij} : cash flow k for the portfolio i at time t_k^{ij}
N_{ij} : number of exogenous cash flows in portfolio i in period j
T_j : length of period j.
The return R^C of the composite over N periods follows from geometrically linking the period returns:

$$1 + R^C = (1 + R_1^C) * (1 + R_2^C) * \cdots * (1 + R_N^C).$$

The GIPS require that the composite returns are compared with the returns of a representative benchmark. Only if the asset manager believes that no "representative benchmark" exists, can the comparison be dispensed with. The reasons for such an approach, however, must then be given in a presentation. If the benchmark is calculated by the asset managers themselves ("customized benchmark"), then the calculation method and the rebasing procedure must be disclosed.[59]

The GIPS also recommend, for each composite, disclosure of the equal-weighted returns and the median of the individual returns.[60] By comparing the median with the asset-weighted return, it might become evident whether individual funds with a very high asset value have led to a distorted picture.

16.4.3 Gross vs Net Return

The GIPS distinguish between three main types of fees or costs:

- Investment management fees
- Administrative fees
- Trading expenses.

The GIPS emphasize that in the manager's performance measurement only the fees, which he can influence directly, should be considered.[61] This is not the case for most of the administrative fees as the custodian fees, for example, if the investment managers are not involved in the selection process. The GIPS put it in a very general way:

> "In some situations, the only fees that the firm controls are the investment management fees and the trading expenses."

The actual separation between fees, which he can influence and other fees must be made in each specific case individually.

---

[59] See CFA Institute (2010, 5.A.1.e, 4.A.29, 4.A.31). It is also required that in the event of a change in a benchmark, the firm must disclose the date and the reason for the change. (CFA Institute 2010, 4.A.30).
[60] See CFA Institute (2010, 5.B.2).
[61] See "Guidance statement on Fees" (2010 version).

According to the GIPS other forms of administrative fees are (guidance statement, p. 1):

- Accounting fees
- Auditing fees
- Consulting fees
- Legal fees
- Performance measurement fees.

Further examples for retail funds are, e.g.:

- Costs of price announcements
- Costs of printing prospectuses, and annual or biannual reports.

The GIPS recommend reporting the *gross-of-fees return* on the composite.[62] The *gross-of-fees return* is defined as the "return on investments reduced by any trading expenses". In other words, the *gross-of-fees return* is the return before deduction of the investment management fees, administrative costs and reclaimable taxes. In general, "returns should be calculated net of non-reclaimable withholding taxes on dividends, interests, and capital gains" (recommendation 2.B.1). Since the calculation of the benchmark return does usually not consider costs, *the gross-of-fees return* is the appropriate measure for performance evaluation. Transaction costs must be considered in any case because these are regarded as an integral part of the management approach.[63] Estimation methods for determining transaction fees are not permitted.[64]

Instead of the *gross-of-fees return* also the net return may be presented, which is defined as the *gross-of-fees return* reduced by the investment management fees incurred. The fees include the performance-based fees and carried interest. Investment management fee is defined as the fee that the firm receives for the management of a portfolio. It is typically given as a percentage of the managed volume and possibly a performance-based fee.[65] The net return is usually *not* identical to the return calculated on the basis of the unit prices. The latter (unit price return) is obtained if, in addition to management fees, administrative fees are also deducted (cf. Figure 16.9). One needs to acknowledge, however, that the above-mentioned principle of the GIPS, to consider fees if and only if the firm can influence them, leaves room for different interpretations. For example, there are different opinions as to whether custodian bank charges must be taken into account when calculating the net return. The asset managers or the investment company may influence these to a certain extent. This is evident when, for example, the size of the custodian fee is transaction-dependent, as in this case

[62] See CFA Institute (2010, 5.B.1).

[63] Simply speaking: if a management approach is based on a high transaction turnover, then the corresponding costs must be reflected in performance assessment. Transaction-based custodian fees are, however, considered as custodian fees (CFA Institute 2010, p. 38).

[64] See CFA Institute (2010, 2.A.4).

[65] See CFA Institute (2010, p. 40).

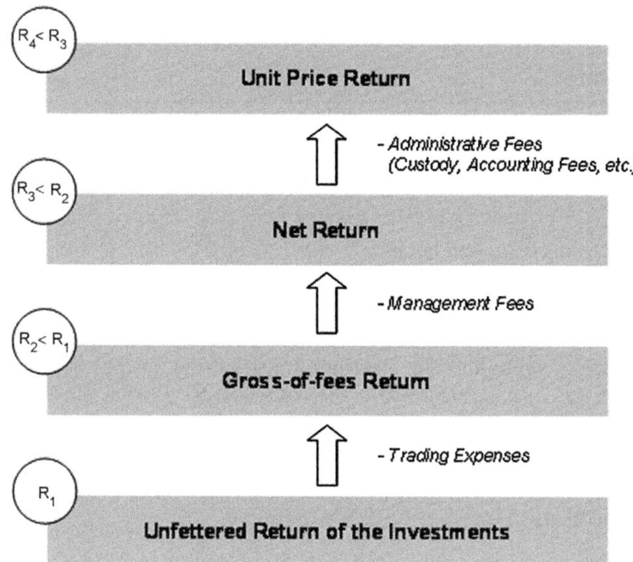

FIGURE 16.9
Relationship Between Different Forms of Return from the Perspective of the GIPS.

the manager determines the size of the turnover. In addition, custodian fees can be adjusted by means of an all-in-fee agreement (see Figure 16.9).

The management fee is often negotiated on an individual basis with the client, where factors such as asset volume, reporting expenses, etc. play a role. The average cost ratio for a composite usually does not correspond to the amount that could be agreed with a (potential) client. Based on the reported gross return, he can easily determine the return that would have resulted based on his specific fee ratio.

The logic of the GIPS does not necessarily correspond to the usual procedure in practice. Often the return on the basis of the unit price is given; the gross return is then deduced from this return via a fee adjustment.

Example 16.8

(Gross-of-fees vs. net return):

In Example 16.6, the volume-weighted return was calculated for the composite in Example 16.4, case b), which consists of Portfolios 1–4. All portfolios have different fee agreements (see Example 16.4). The composite is considered *de facto* a total portfolio, whose fees or charges K correspond to the average rate of the individual portfolios contained in the composite:

$$K = \frac{1}{680} * (70 * 0.3\% + 210 * 0.2\% + 320 * 1.0\% + 80 * 0.3\%) = 0.6\%.$$

Table 16.6 Comparison of Annualized Returns

DAX Composite	DAX
0.33% p.a.	–0.39% p.a.

Over a period of ten years, one obtains:[66]

$$R^{gross} = (1 - 2.66\%) * (1 + 0.60\%)^{10} - 1 = 3.32\%,$$

which corresponds to an annualized gross-of-fees return of 0.33% (see Table 16.6). Based on these values and the relevant fees for the client, the (hypothetical) net return can be easily calculated.[67] If, for example, one assumes a fee ratio of 0.40% p.a., then the theoretical annualized net return would be approximately -0.07% $(= (1 + 0.33\%)/(1 + 0.4\%) - 1)$).

a. Adjustment of the Time Series of Unit Prices

Analogous to the procedure for dividends (see Section 10.4.2.4) on days when management or administrative fees are deducted from a portfolio, an adjustment factor in the form

$$1 + \frac{K(t)}{I(t)}$$

may be formed. For the purpose of return calculation, unit prices following the fee deduction may be multiplied[68] by this adjustment factor, analogous to the approach of the unit price method. This method provides accurate values for gross and net returns, provided accurate information on the fees is available. The approach will be illustrated by an example.

Example 16.9

(Adjustment for dividends and management fees):

The investment fund in Table 16.7 had to record a dividend in February and an outflow of fees at the end of the first quarter.

The gross-of-fees return R^{gross} of the fund (return adjusted by the dividend and the fees) in the period from 01/01/2008 to 04/30/2008 is calculated according to:

$$R^{gross} = \frac{130 * 1.01613 * 1.00236 - 120}{120} = 10.34\%,$$

[66]This calculation approach illustrates the basic procedure, which is known in the GIPS as "grossing-up" (cf. CFA Institute 2006, p. 166).

[67]It should be noted, however, that with this approach only the volume-based fees are included. The unrecognized costs must be allocated in accordance with CFA Institute (2010, 4.A.5).

[68] At this point, only the "forward adjustment" is outlined. The "backward adjustment" is analogous to the procedure in Section 10.4.2.4.

Table 16.7 Unit Prices, Dividends, and Fees of an Investment Fund

Date	Unit Price	Dividend per Unit	Investment Management /Administrative Fees per Unit	Adjustment Factor
12/31/2007	120			
02/15/2008	124	2		$1+\frac{2}{124}=1.01613$
03/31/2008	127		0.3	$1+\frac{0.3}{127}=1.000236$
04/30/2008	130			

and the unit price return R^{up} (return adjusted for the dividend) according to:

$$R^{up} = \frac{130^{*}1.01613 - 120}{120} = 10.08\%.$$

a. Approximation Methods

The GIPS do not elaborate on methods for calculating the gross return for a given net or unit price return. In the corresponding Guidance Statement the recommendation is made that for a single portfolio the method used over time should remain unchanged. However, a composite may comprise portfolios, for which the gross return is determined by different methods.[69]

For adjusting fees, which are calculated on the basis of a fixed percentage, approximation methods were described in the original version of the DVFA-PPS. For example, to an annual fixed fee G^C corresponds the fee factor $\sqrt[12]{1+G^C}$, by which the monthly net returns can be adjusted as follows:[70]

$$1 + R^{gross} = (1 + R^{up}) * \sqrt[12]{1 + G^C}.$$

Under the assumption that the fee ratio of the annual administrative and custodian fee for the portfolio in Example 16.9 is equal to 0.95% the fee factor is calculated as:

$$\sqrt[12]{1 + \frac{0.95}{100}} = \sqrt[12]{1.0095} = 1.00078824.$$

As a result, based on a unit price return of 10.08%, the following approximate value for the gross return over the four-month period considered in Example 16.9 is:

$$(1 + \frac{10.08}{100})^{*}1.00078824^{4} - 1 = 10.43\%.$$

[69] Cf. "Guidance Statement on calculation methodology" (2010 version), page 9.

[70] The DVFA-PPS also describe an alternative form of adjustment DVFA (2000, 7.3.2), whereby the monthly net returns are adjusted as follows: $1 + R^{gross} = (1 + R^{up}) / \sqrt[12]{1 - K^C}$. This approach is especially preferred when the costs are taken principally at the beginning of a period. The numerical differences between these adjustment methods are generally small.

In an adjustment by only the fixed percentage fee factors, the variable costs (such as those for the audit of the portfolio accounts) remain unconsidered. (These costs are in practice usually much lower than the management fee.) When it follows this procedure, the firm presents its results as potentially worse than they really are. For this reason, the GIPS require to disclose the neglected types of fees. This applies to both net and gross returns.[71]

Example 16.10

(Determination of the Gross return, based on the unit price return):

Table 16.8 contains the monthly returns of a portfolio calculated according to the unit price method over a period of one year. Until the end of June the agreed constant annual charge set for administration and custodian fees was 1.0% of the portfolio value. Due to an additional fund inflow at this time a reduced annual management fee of 0.7% was agreed. Column 4 shows the applicable monthly cost factor, with which the gross returns were determined.

The GIPS require that at each presentation the firm discloses an appropriate fee schedule.[72]

A special case is portfolios with a so-called *Bundled Fee*. In a bundled fee various types of charges are linked together in a total fee. Examples of bundled fees are the *all-in fee* and the *wrap fee* (a specific investment product in the US). The all-in fee usually combines (or bundles) the administration fee, trading expenses, and

Table 16.8 Conversion of Net Returns to Gross Returns Using the Current Cost Rates (Values in %)

	Net Return	Annual Cost	Monthly Cost	Gross Return
January	4.00	1.0	0.083	4.09
February	5.30	1.0	0.083	5.39
March	−2.80	1.0	0.083	−2.72
April	−0.80	1.0	0.083	−0.72
May	3.70	1.0	0.083	3.79
June	2.50	1.0	0.083	2.59
July	10.30	0.7	0.058	10.36
August	−7.50	0.7	0.058	−7.45
September	1.90	0.7	0.058	1.96
October	4.30	0.7	0.058	4.36
November	8.90	0.7	0.058	8.96
December	−10.60	0.7	0.058	−10.55
Total	18.49			19.50

[71] See CFA Institute (2010, 4.A5, 4.A.6).
[72] See CFA Institute (2010, 4.A.9).

other administrative costs.[73] In cases where the actual trading expenses cannot be determined separately, the entire bundled fee (or the identifiable component, of which the trading expenses are part of) must be used to calculate gross and net return.[74]

Total Expense Ratio (TER)

The Total Expense Ratio is a ratio designed to mirror the entire costs incurred in an investment fund. It is often associated with the fund research firm Lipper Fitzrovia. The German Federal Association for Investment and Asset Management (BVI) has adopted the disclosure of the TER in its good conduct rules.[75] The calculation formula is as follows:

$$TER = \frac{GK_n}{FV} * 100,$$

where:

TER: Total Expense Ratio as a percentage, following the BVI method (unit price method)

GK_n: actual loaded cost in fund currency

FV: average fund volume during the reporting period in fund currency.

The costs comprise all management and administrative charges, with the exception of performance-related fees. The latter should be reported separately as a percentage of average fund volume.

Since transaction costs are disregarded in the BVI TER, there is a clear parallel to the GIPS. Through an adjustment of the unit price return by means of the TER, one approximately obtains the gross return.

16.4.4 Presentation of Performance Results after Currency Conversion

A particular problem in the presentation of performance results is caused by the introduction of a new currency. Portfolios or composites which, in the context of currency reform, are submitted to a switch in their base or reporting currency, lose their performance history in the strict sense, because the base currency is an essential characteristic of the portfolio and thus the performance achieved. However, in practice calculation methods are often used, which pretend the continuity of the history.

A particular example is the introduction of the Euro on January 1, 1999, when the currency of eleven European nations was transformed. Due to ongoing

---

[73] This is mainly relevant for countries with a universal banking system, where the depositary bank, the asset manager, and the broker are part of the same company (cf. "Guidance statement on fees" (2010 version), p. 3.

[74] See "Guidance statement on fees" (2010 version), p. 3.

[75] See BVI (2002). The TER definitions of the BVI and of Lipper Fitzrovia differ, however. In contrast to the BVI TER, the latter includes also transaction costs.

Table 16.9 Official Euro Exchange Rates for DM and Lira

Lira	DM
1936.27	1.95583

Table 16.10 Performance of the Unit Prices of Portfolio 1 and Portfolio 2

	Unit Price (Base Currency)		Return (Base Currency) 01/01/1995–12/31/1998
	12/31/1994	12/31/1998	
Portfolio 1	100.00	230.44	130.44%
Portfolio 2	100.000.00	220.500.00	120.50%

inclusion of additional countries in the monetary union this example is still very relevant. The Permanent Commission on Performance Measurement of the European Federation of Financial Analysts" Societies (EFFAS) set up recommendations for the presentation of performance results for portfolios or composites whose base currency had changed due to the introduction of the Euro.[76] Their purpose is to make the underlying assumptions to presentations as transparent as possible. The main focus of the commission is to convert the original input data prior to 01/01/1999 "into one single pre-ECD[77] currency, using the historical exchange rate, before converting to Euro at the fixed conversion rate". This statement refers explicitly to the Euro. It also applies to similar cases.

To explain the basic problem and the EFFAS recommendations, two portfolios will be considered in the following examples, both of which invest in Italian stocks.[78] Portfolio 1 traded until 12/31/1998 in DM and portfolio 2 in Italian lira. To make the presentation as simple as possible, both portfolios are assumed to be accumulative. This avoids having to adjust the returns for fund dividends. Table 16.9 contains the official exchange rates required for the conversion.

The unit price development for the two portfolios in the period 12/31/1994 to 12/31/1998 is shown in Table 16.10.

The backward adjustment with the conversion rates as of 12/31/1998 leads to the unit prices and returns exhibited Table 16.11.

Since in this approach all unit prices before 01/01/1999 are multiplied by constant factors, the returns after the conversion are, of course, unchanged from the returns in the original base currencies. It is evident, that the resulting time series

[76] See EFFAS (1998). See also MacKendrick (1998); the EFFAS recommendations are included here as an attachment. A slightly modified version of these recommendations has been adopted as a GIPS Guidance Statement ("Guidelines in respect of the impact of Euro Conversion").

[77] ECG = Euro conversion date (01/01/99).

[78] The presentation is based on statements in Fischer and Lilla (1999).

Table 16.11 Unit Prices and Returns of Portfolio 1 and Portfolio 2 After Division by Constant Conversion Factors (Exchange Rates at 12/31/1998)

	Unit Price ("Euro")		Return ("Euro")
	12/31/1994	12/31/1998	01/01/1995–12/31/1998
Portfolio 1	51.13	117.82	130.44%
Portfolio 2	51.65	113.88	120.50%

are not really Euro time series. This fact is expressed by the inverted commas around "Euro".

Generally, in this approach the return R of a portfolio over a period including 01/01/1999 is determined by the following linkage relationship:

$$1 + R = (1 + R^{ac})*(1 + R^{e}), \qquad (16.3)$$

with:

R^{ac}: Return on the basis of the old base currency until 12/31/1998

R^{e}: Return on Euro basis from 12/31/1998.

In a presentation as in Table 16.11, which suggests a history on a "Euro" basis, the development of the lira/DM exchange rate is disregarded. The returns in Table 16.11 reflect the performance from the perspective of the investor, who, prior to 01/01/1999, had been using lira or DM to assess the success of an investment. A sensible comparison of the returns in Table 16.11 will not be achieved with this method.

Example 16.11

(Comparability of Performance Values (I)):

A French institutional investor is awarding a European equity mandate. A number of European asset managers pitch for this mandate. They present their performance results on a "Euro" basis. If the values are calculated according to Equation (16.3) and the respective "ante-currencies" are not explicitly stated, there is no possibility for the investor to make a sensible comparison of "Euro" returns.

To take the changes in exchange rates into account in a performance comparison, according to the EFFAS recommendations the following procedure should be used: the time series of the unit prices of the considered portfolios must first be converted into a common currency, before converting them into "Euro" time series based on the exchange rates from 12/31/1998. The resulting returns are heavily dependent on the currency used in the intermediate step. In the following, the conversion for the portfolios of the above example will be based on the "intermediate currencies" DM and lira, respectively. On the key dates 12/31/1994 and 12/31/1998 the lira/DM exchange rates were respectively 0.95 DM and 1.01 DM per 1000 lira. In case of the DM as "intermediate currency" one obtains the results in Table 16.12.

Table 16.12 Conversion of the Original Lira/DM Time Series into "Euro" Time Series with the Intermediate Step of Conversion to DM Time Series. The Inter-Mediate Step is Shown in the Middle Row of Each of the Two Blocks

	Currency	Unit Price 12/31/94	Unit Price 12/31/98	Return
Portfolio 1	DM	100.00	230.44	130.44 %
	DM	100.00	230.44	
	Euro	51.13	117.82	
Portfolio 2	Lira	100.000.00	220.500.00	134.43 %
	DM	95.00	222.71	
	Euro	48.57	113.87	

Table 16.13 Conversion of the Original Lira/DM Time Series to "Euro" Time Series with the Intermediate Step of Conversion into Lira Time Series. The Intermediate Step is Given in the Middle Row of Each of the Two Blocks

	Currency	Unit Price 12/31/94	Unit Price 12/31/98	Return
Portfolio 1	DM	100.00	230.44	116.76%
	Lira	105,263.16	228,158.42	
	Euro	54.36	117.82	
Portfolio 2	Lira	100,000.00	220,500.00	120.50%
	Lira	100,000.00	220,500.00	
	Euro	51.65	113.88	

The information obtained by using the lira as intermediate currency is shown in Table 16.13.

The example illustrates how the absolute returns depend considerably on the chosen "intermediate currency." The difference between the returns in Table 16.13 and the ones reported in Table 16.12 is due to the appreciation of the lira against the DM, which in that period amounted to 6.32%. In principle, any currency can serve as the intermediate currency. In particular, it can also be a "synthetic currency", such as a (simulated) "synthetic Euro." For the conversion only a sufficiently long history of exchange rates against the base currencies of related portfolios is needed. While the absolute returns depend on the particular selection of intermediate currency, the ranking among the portfolios is independent of this choice. This is illustrated by the preceding example: in both cases (Table 16.12 and Table 16.13) the return of portfolio 2 exceeds that of portfolio 1.

Using an intermediate currency, the return R of a portfolio over a period including 01/01/1999 is calculated as follows:

$$1 + R = (1 + R^{ac}) * (1 + c^{ic}) * (1 + R^{e}), \tag{16.4}$$

where c^{ic} refers to the performance of the old base currency against the "intermediate currency" up to 12/31/1998.

The choice of the "intermediate currency" for conversion depends on the context of a presentation. In a presentation to a client from a country belonging to the EU, it seems sensible to choose the currency, which up to 12/31/1998 was the base currency for this client. According to the EFFAS recommendations both the original currencies and the intermediate currency should be disclosed.

Example 16.12

(Comparability of Performance Values (II)):

If all asset managers competing for the mandate described in Example 16.11 converted their historical time series using a single currency (e.g. French francs) first, then the returns would be directly comparable. This intermediate step could be executed by the investor himself (using Equation (16.4)), if for each return the "ante base currency" is specified.

For time series, portfolios, composites, etc., whose base currency remained unchanged in the course of the introduction of the Euro (e.g., if the base currency was US dollars, yen or sterling), the introduction of the Euro caused no breaks.

The procedures shown in the above example for individual portfolios can also be applied to composites. It must be noted, however, that according to the EFFAS recommendations, portfolios combined into a composite or comparable composites must have similar investment objectives or styles.[79]

16.5 FURTHER DISCLOSURE REQUIREMENTS FOR COMPOSITE STRUCTURE AND SAMPLE PRESENTATIONS

16.5.1 GIPS Requirements and Recommendations

In addition to the information requirements of the GIPS described so far, there are a number of additional transparency obligations, of which only the most important ones shall be discussed here:

- For each composite it must be specified in which currency the returns are calculated (4.A.7). Further, there should be a clear distinction between gross and net returns (5.A.1.b). The description of the composite must be disclosed (4.A.3).
- It is permissible to provide information for periods prior to the year 2000 that are not compliant with the GIPS. This, however, must be disclosed (4.A.15). Likewise, the non-compliant (to GIPS) presentation contents, which are

---

[79] See Fischer and Lilla (1999) and "Guidelines in Respect of the Impact of Euro Conversion" (2001 version).

required by a local law, must be labeled as such. In particular, the discrepancies with the GIPS must be indicated (4.A.22).

- The firms must hold a full list of composites with descriptions. Its availability must be disclosed (0.A.10, 4.A.11). Further, the availability of information on the policies for the valuation and for calculating returns must be disclosed. (4.A.12).
- For a composite, the number of portfolios (if greater than five) and its volume as of each annual period end must be disclosed. In addition, either the total firm assets or the composite assets as a percentage of the total firm assets must be disclosed as of each annual period end (5.A.1).
- If a composite contains portfolios with bundled fees, the firm must disclose the percentage of composite assets represented by such portfolios. Further, the firm must identify the types of fees included in bundled fee (5.A.7, 4.A.24).

In addition, the GIPS contain several requirements and recommendations for the presentation of the risks of composites or the portfolios they contain and the dispersion of returns within a composite. These will be discussed separately in Sections 16.8 and 16.9.

In the GIPS version of 2006 (Standard 5.B.1) it was also recommended that firms identify country and sector weights on the composite level. This was already a significant weakening of the original requirement in the GIPS (1999 version), according to which "for composites managed against a specific benchmark, the percentage of the composites not invested in countries or regions not included in the benchmark" had to be disclosed (AIMR 1999, 4. A.10). The intention was to make transparent to what extent the benchmark universe has also served as the investment universe. In the 2010 version of the GIPS even the recommendation 5.B.1 was cancelled.

16.5.2 Supplemental Information

In addition to the information required or recommended by the GIPS, the firm may choose to provide supplemental information. In a Guidance Statement, the IPC has formulated criteria, with which the firms need to comply.[80] However, this statement explicitly deals only with "performance-related" information. With regard to general information about the firm, the investment process, etc., the firm has considerable freedom.

No misleading or false information may be given. This includes, for example, that the performance of model portfolios or a nontransferable performance history of acquired[81] firms may not be connected with the current performance history (unless this is explicitly requested by a prospective client[82]). Further examples of supplemental information are listed in the guidance statement (p. 2):

---

[80] "Guidance statement on the use of supplemental information" (2010 version).

[81] See the discussion in Section 16.2.

[82] The general principle is that the provision of all information requested by potential clients is permitted, provided it is accompanied by a GIPS compliant presentation (cf. "Guidance statement on the use of supplemental information" (2010 version), p. 2).

- Carve-out returns that exclude cash
- Representative portfolio information (portfolio-level country/sector weightings or risk measures)
- Attribution
- Composite or portfolio specific holdings
- Peer group comparisons
- Ex ante risk and ex ante risk-adjusted return measures.

Supplemental information—in contrast to the applied recommendations—is not subject to verification.[83]

According to the guidance statement, non-performance-related information needs not be labeled or identified as supplemental or separate from the compliant information. General information about the firm, staff biographies, details about the investment process and ownership structure are listed as examples for that type of information. In general, in view of the above examples (bullet points) the term "performance-related information" seems to be a bit too opaque.

Example 16.13

Turnover coefficient for a Portfolio/Composite:

An example of supplemental information (that is not required by the GIPS) is the specification of the turnover coefficient. It provides information on the extent to which the portfolio managers make reallocations (purchases, sales) within a portfolio:

$$TC := \frac{\textit{Total purchases} + \textit{Total sales}}{2 * \textit{Average asset value}}. \tag{16.5}$$

In practice, this coefficient is usually determined with respect to a calendar year. There may be an averaging over various calendar years. However, the significance of this value can be limited in case of high inflows or withdrawals. The calculation is often refined in practice by first constructing values for smaller intervals (months, weeks), which are subsequently transformed into annualized quantities. A turnover coefficient of 1 means, for instance, that the portfolio is reallocated on average once within a year (if the transactions were not primarily caused by exogenous fund flows).

Transactions resulting from contributions or withdrawals are incorporated in the definition (16.5). As they are not characteristic of the investment process, the formula may be adjusted for such transactions:

$$TC^{adj} := \frac{\textit{Total purchases} + \textit{Total sales} - \textit{Withdrawals} - \textit{Contributions}}{I_0 + I_1 + \textit{Withdrawals} - \textit{Contributions}}. \tag{16.6}$$

---

[83] See "Guidance Statement on the Use of Supplemental Information" (2010 version), p. 3.

I_0 and I_1 represent the asset value respectively at the beginning and at the end of the overall period. In the denominator the cash flows—similar to the procedure for the modified Dietz Method—could be considered on a time-weighted basis.

For instance, if for an international equity portfolio with an average asset value of €150 million, which is being compared with the MSCI World Index, €65 million of shares are acquired and shares equal to €40 million are sold, then the turnover coefficient specified in Equation (16.5) is calculated as

$$TC = \frac{65 + 40}{2 * 150} = 0.35 .$$

Thus approximately 35% of the portfolio was reallocated in this period, a comparatively moderate value,[84] which suggests that the portfolio manager pursues a long-term oriented investment style for the portfolio. This impression is reinforced by consideration of the adjusted turnover coefficient because the portfolio has recorded an inflow of €50 million (at an initial asset value of €100 million and a closing valuation of €200 million):

$$TC^{adj} - \frac{65 + 40 - 50}{100 + 200 - 50} = 0.22 .$$

Therefore, a considerable proportion of the transactions resulted from the inflow; the transactions driven by implementing the investment strategy led to a reallocation of approximately only 22% of the portfolio.

Finally, it should be noted that in extreme cases the application of Equation (16.6) can result in negative values. This artifact can be addressed by shortening the interval period (e.g. to weeks rather than months).

At the composite level, specifying the average turnover coefficients may be useful (possibly with maximum and minimum values at the portfolio level).

16.5.3 GIPS Advertising Guidelines

To counter the misuse of the term GIPS in advertising, the IPC has formulated guidelines on this topic.[85] Firms wishing to use the term GIPS in their promotional materials must comply with these guidelines. The primary requirement is the disclosure of standardized performance values for composites and benchmarks used in the composite presentations. Either one-, three-, and five-year cumulative annualized returns, or five individual annual returns may be reported. Further, the (non-annualized) returns for the current year should be presented. The period-end date for the returns must be clearly identified. The advertisement must contain a definition of the firm and both composite

---

[84] Turnover coefficients for an actively managed international equity portfolio are in practice often around 1 and, with very actively managed portfolios or with hedge funds, can be significantly higher.
[85] See CFA Institute (2010, pp. 29 et seq. and pp. 64 et seq.) (GIPS Advertising Guidelines).

and benchmark must be described. If the firm determines that no appropriate benchmark exists, then the reasons for this judgment must be disclosed in the advertisement. In addition, the currency in which the returns were calculated must be given, and the use of derivatives and/or leverage instruments must be declared and quantified, insofar as these have a significant impact on the performance. It must also be disclosed whether gross or net returns are reported.

Furthermore, it must be specified how a potential investor can obtain a GIPS-compliant composite presentation and a complete list and description of all composites. It must be disclosed, if periods are presented (prior to 1 January 2000), which are not in compliance with the GIPS, or whether regulatory requirements have caused the firm to deviate from GIPS requirements.

Sample Presentations

Based on the fictitious investment company Bonus an example of the statement of composites required by the GIPS is provided in Figure 16.10. One can clearly see the hierarchical structure. This is followed by a sample presentation for the composite *Germany Blue Chips Stocks.*

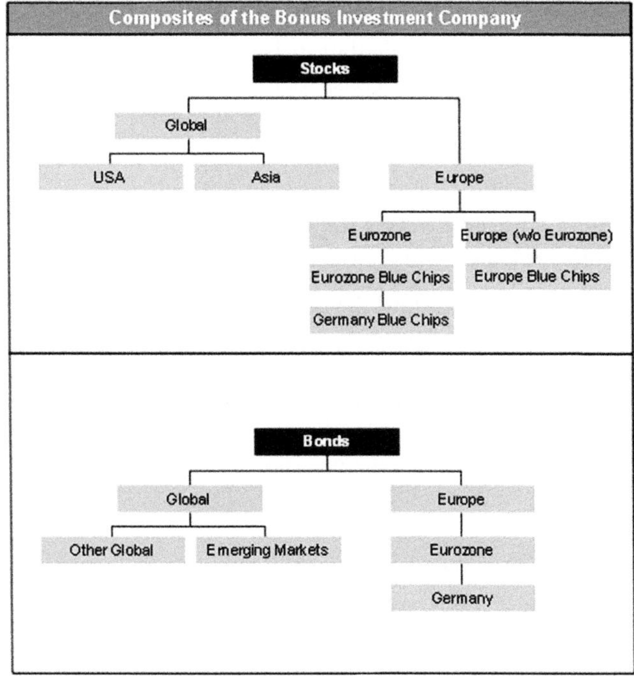

FIGURE 16.10
Overview of Composites of the Bonus Investment Company.

Bonus Investment Company Composite Germany Blue Chips Stocks						
Year	**Number of Portfolios**	**Asset Value at Year End (Billion €)**	**Share of Assets Under Management at Year End (%)**	**Dispersion (%)**	**Composite Return (%)**	**Benchmark Return (DAX) (%)**
1998	6	0.56	4.3	14.11/26.20	16.73	17.71
1999	7	1.21	3.9	32.79/45.67	40.10	39.10
2000	10	1.65	4.9	3.21	–6.54	–7.54
2001	11	1.58	4.8	5.67	–17.44	–19.79
2002	13	0.96	4.3	8.39	–44.45	–43.94
2003	15	1.56	5.0	5.69	35.88	37.08
2004	14	1.72	5.1	4.30	13.02	7.34
2005	18	2.35	5.6	5.78	30.30	27.07
2006	19	3.34	6.1	4.32	19.56	21.98
2007	19	4.20	6.2	3.45	21.33	22.29

Description of the composite: Portfolios in this composite invest exclusively in shares included in the DAX 100. There are no restrictions on the selection of securities, which is based on a fundamental "bottom-up approach". The portfolios are always almost entirely invested. The composite was created on 01/01/1999.

Calculation method: The return calculation is based on the unit price method. Shown are gross returns on a Euro basis before deduction of management fees (investment management fees, custodian fees and others). The fee schedule is as follows: 1.20% for volumes of less than €50 million, 0.80% for other volumes.

Reclaimable taxes: Domestic withholding tax is always treated as reclaimable. Regarding foreign withholding taxes for all countries with which there is a double taxation agreement, a claim is booked.

Dispersion: Asset-weighted standard deviation of portfolio returns on a monthly basis, if more than ten portfolios were included in the composite for the entire period; otherwise the minimum and the maximum returns are reported (high-low-range). Portfolios are only included in the calculation if they were in the composite throughout the entire calendar year.

Cumulative Figures 1998–2007				
	Cumulative Return	**Annualized Return**	**Volatility***	**Tracking Error* Against DAX**
Composite	103.47	7.36	26.45	3.8
DAX	89.86	6.62	25.67	–

*Tracking Error and Volatility were calculated from monthly data. (Values in %).

16.6 MAINTENANCE OF COMPOSITES

The time and effort for the maintenance of composites within a firm should not be underestimated, especially if the composite data also provide the basis for flexible control processes within portfolio management and is used to answer inquiries from potential clients or consultants on current performance results. In this case, all alterations in the management of portfolios, such as a change in investment strategy (or benchmark), the introduction or waiving of restrictions, a change in the fee scheme (such as switching to an all-in fee) or changing investment management advisors must be immediately recorded in the relevant systems. This naturally also applies to the launch or closure of investment portfolios. In addition, it requires a continuous review of the correspondence between the composite structure and established investment processes.

According to requirement 1.A.1 "all data and information necessary to support all items included in a compliant presentation must be captured and maintained." The details are outlined in the "Guidance Statement on recordkeeping requirements" (2010 version).

Also, no matter how carefully approached, the GIPS-compliant documents are in practice rarely entirely accurate. For dealing with errors, the Executive Committee has drafted a Guidance Statement, which sets internal guidelines for significance criteria for errors.[86] There are four essential steps. The lowest level (minor error) does not indicate measures that must be taken, while with a material error (fourth step) correction of the presentation must be made with an additional disclosure of the changes. Such adjustments may occur, for example, due to incorrect allocation of portfolios to composites, incorrect calculation of benchmarks, wrong currency exchange rates, and so on. Clients who have received an erroneous presentation, must be given a corrected version.

16.7 INDEPENDENT VERIFICATION OF COMPLIANCE WITH THE STANDARDS

Just as with the use of the GIPS, the so-called verification of correct application of the standards is on a voluntary basis.[87] The firm may select a verifier, who has the necessary skills and needs to be independent of the firm.[88]

The scope and content of the audit are defined in a separate Guidance Statement,[89] according to which verification is defined as

[86] See "Guidance Statement on Error correction" (2010 version).

[87] See CFA Institute (2010, 0.B.2).

[88] The requirements for the auditor are further specified in a Guidance Statement ("Guidance Statement on verifier Independence" (2005 version)).

[89] "Guidance Statement on Verification" (2010 version).

> " a process by which the verifier assesses whether the firm has complied with all the composite construction requirements of the GIPS standards on a firm-wide basis, and the firm's policies and procedures are designed to calculate and present performance in compliance with the GIPS standards."

Although the verifier may use samples, the examination must extend across the entire firm, and not be limited to certain composites.

In the Guidance Statement it is explicitly explained, what verification does not mean, namely the examination of specific performance values. This is seen in the GIPS as a "performance examination." The details of such a review are outlined in a further Guidance Statement ("Guidance for Performance Examinations" (2006 version)). Such a performance examination can be applied to individual composites.[90] However, it is at the discretion of the firms whether they extend the verification by such an examination. [91]

16.8 MEASUREMENT OF THE HOMOGENEITY OF THE INVESTMENT PROCESS

The GIPS require the presentation of a measure for the spread (dispersion) of portfolio returns within a composite for each of the presented calendar years. [92] No specific measure is prescribed for this. Accordingly, no limits are set for the dispersion of a composite, nor is the firm required to define such limits. A change in the measure is possible at any time by providing the reasons. For the sake of comparability, the firm should try to retain the chosen measures over time. If both the gross and net returns are reported, the asset manager may use either of these in the calculation of dispersion. The selection must be disclosed.

The calculating of the dispersion must be based on the values (returns, asset values) of those portfolios that were assigned to the underlying composite during the entire period (one year). If there are only five or fewer portfolios in the composite over an entire calendar year, then the firm is not required to present a dispersion measure, indicating this in a corresponding note.

The dispersion of a composite can provide some indication of how the asset manager pursues a clearly defined investment style in managing the portfolio. The smaller the dispersion, the more uniformly the portfolios aggregated in the composite are managed. Investment consultants involved in the manager selection process typically pay attention to that kind of information.

Different measures will be discussed in relation to the composite shown in Table 16.14.

The benchmark achieved a return of 11.80% in the reporting period.

---

[90] It is thus similar to the Level II Verification of AIMR-PPS (see AIMR (1997, p. 119)).

[91] This section is partly based on Wittrock et al. (1998b).

[92] See CFA Institute (2010, 5.A.1.i) and CFA Institute (2006, pp. 127 et seq.). As a supplement the explanations in AIMR (1997, pp. 97 et seq.) are also helpful.

Table 16.14 The Composite Consists of Six Portfolios. Asset Value Refers to the Beginning of a Period (Calendar Year)

Portfolio	Return (%)	Asset Value in Million €	Share of Composite Volume (%)
A	20	150	15
B	18	50	5
C	15	200	20
D	12	300	30
E	11	100	10
F	9	200	20
Total		1000	100

16.8.1 High-Low Range

With this measure simply the highest and the lowest returns are presented. It is especially suitable for composites with a small number of portfolios.[93]

For the composite in Table 16.14 one obtains $R_{high} = 20\%$ and $R_{low} = 9\%$.

16.8.2 Standard Deviation

The (empirical) standard deviation S_C is suitable as a dispersion measure for composites with a large number of portfolios. It is calculated according to

$$S_C = \sqrt{\sum_{i=1}^{N} \frac{1}{N} * (R_i - \mu)^2}, \tag{16.7}$$

where R_i are the returns of the N portfolios, which were assigned to the composite over the entire period. μ is the arithmetic mean of these returns. The active return of the composite achieved against the benchmark can (formally analogous to the procedure for the Information Ratio) be set in relation to the dispersion by defining:

$$\Delta^{S_C} := \frac{\mu - R^{bm}}{S_C}.$$

The higher the value Δ^{S_C}, the greater the proportion of portfolios that have outperformed the benchmark. For instance, a value of $\Delta^{S_C} = 1$ implies that approximately 84% of all portfolios in the composite outperformed the benchmark..

In the case of the composite in Table 16.14 one obtains $\mu = 14.17\%$ and $S_C = 3.89\%$, and thus $\Delta^{S_C} := \frac{14.17-11,80}{3.89} = 0.61$. It follows that about 73% of the portfolios outperformed the benchmark.[94]

[93] This measure is required for real estate funds (CFA Institute 2010, 6.A.16,a).

[94] One can see this in Table 16.14. However, a (potential) client generally has no insight into the spectrum of the composite returns.

16.8.3 Asset-Weighted Standard Deviation

With this measure, the squares of the differences in return in Equation (16.7) are not weighted by the constant factor $1/N$, but with the asset values:

$$S_C^{aw} = \sqrt{\sum_{i=1}^{N} q_i * (R_i - \mu^{aw})^2}, \tag{16.8}$$

with:

$$q_i = \frac{\textit{Asset value portfolio i}}{\textit{Asset value composite}}$$

and $\mu^{aw} = \sum_{i=1}^{N} q_i^* R_i$.

The calculation of the weighting factors q_i is analogous to the calculation of the weighting factors in determining the composite return. One can for instance use the asset values at the beginning of a calendar year (Equation (16.1)) are the initial asset values plus the time-weighted cash flow (Equation (16.2).

To set the active return of the composite against the benchmark in relation to the resulting dispersion, as in the previous section, the quotient of these quantities can be considered:

$$\Delta^{S_C^{aw}} := \frac{\mu^{aw} - R^{bm}}{S_C^{aw}}.$$

The higher the value of $\Delta^{S_C^{aw}}$, the greater the fraction (in terms of asset size) of the composite, which has achieved a higher return than the benchmark. For instance, a value of $\Delta^{S_C^{aw}} = 1$, indicates that approximately 84% of the composite volume has exceeded the benchmark return.

For the composite in Table 16.14 one calculates $\mu^{aw} = 13.40\%$ and $S_C^{aw} = 3.62\%$ and consequently $\Delta^{S_C^{aw}} := \frac{13.40-11.80}{3.62} = 0.442$. Thus, approximately 67% of the composite assets outperformed the benchmark.

16.8.4 Quartile Representation

With this method, the composites will be divided according to their asset size and returns into quartiles, i.e. the portfolios are first listed according to their returns in descending order. Then the first portfolio is allocated to the first quartile. If its net asset value exceeds a quarter of the total portfolio asset value, then the maximum permitted share is assigned to this quartile. The remainder of the portfolio is then allocated to the second quartile. If the asset value of the first portfolio falls below a quarter of total asset value, then the second portfolio, or an appropriate portion of it, is allocated to the first quartile. This process is continued analogously until all portfolios are divided into quartiles. For each quartile the asset-weighted return is shown.[95]

[95] Alternatively, the returns of the first and fourth quartile can be presented.

Table 16.15 Classification into Quartiles of the Composite in Table 16.14

Quartile	Composition of Quartiles
1	Portfolios A, B and 25% of Portfolio C
2	75% of Portfolio C and 33.33% of Portfolio D
3	66.66% of Portfolio D and 50% of Portfolio E
4	50% of Portfolio E and Portfolio F

Table 16.16 Returns of the Quartiles in Table 16.15

Quartile	Asset-Weighted Return (%)
Quartile 1	18.6
Quartile 2	13.8
Composite	13.4
Quartile 3	11.8
Quartile 4	9.4

The procedure is explained on the basis of the composite in Table 16.14. In this case the four quartiles are constructed as shown in Table 16.15.

Each quartile thus has a net asset value of €250 million.

According to this classification, the asset-weighted returns are calculated as follows:

$$Quartile1 : R = \frac{150}{250} * 20\% + \frac{50}{250} * 18\% + \frac{50}{250} * 15\% = 18.6\% \text{ etc.}$$

The results are summarized Table 16.16.

The questions, which measure is most suitable to reflect the performance dispersion within a composite, must be answered by the firm for each composite individually. Measures, like the standard deviation or the asset-weighted standard deviation, are, for example, suitable only for composites with a sufficiently large number of portfolios. The high-low range is in turn very sensitive to extreme values. Therefore, in practice, the quartile presentation enjoys a certain popularity, since this method results in meaningful statements with both a large and an average number of portfolios.

Example 16.14

(Selection of the dispersion measure):

Table 16.17 contains the data needed to calculate the measures of dispersion.
The standard deviations for this composite are listed in Table 16.18.
The break down into quartiles is shown in Table 16.19.

Table 16.17 Composite Consisting of Seven Portfolios. The Asset Values Refer to the Beginning of a Period (Calendar Year)

Portfolio	Return (%)	Asset Value in Million €	Share of Composite Volume (%)
A	–3	10	6.25
B	8	30	18.75
C	10	30	18.75
D	4	20	12.50
E	5	40	25.00
F	9	20	12.50
G	12	10	6.25
Total		160	100.00

Table 16.18 Values for Standard Deviation and Asset-Weighted Standard Deviation

Arithmetic Calculation		Asset-Weighted Calculation	
Return	Standard deviation	Return	Standard deviation
6.81%	4.62%	6.43%	3.50%

Table 16.19 Classification of the Portfolios from Table 16.17 in Quartiles

	Portfolios	Asset Value		Return (%)
		Quartile	Total	
Quartile 1	G, C	10/30	40	10.50
Quartile 2	F, 66.67% of B	20/20	40	8.50
Quartile 3	33.33 % of B, 75% of E	10/30	40	5.75
Quartile 4	25% of E, D, A	10/20/10	40	2.50

Further $R_{high} = -3\,\%$ and $R_{low} = 12\,\%$. However, the reported range of 15% exaggerates the dispersion somewhat, since the portfolios, for which these results were reported, represent only a small proportion of the total composite. This is also reflected in the value of the asset-weighted standard deviation, which is significantly lower than that of the standard deviation. In this case, the asset-weighted standard deviation and the quartile presentation are the most appropriate to express the dispersion of the portfolio returns.

16.8.5 Combination of Different Measures of Dispersion

To obtain an adequate presentation of the dispersion of composite returns, combining different dispersion measures is often recommended. This can be particularly useful if the number of portfolios taken into account in the calculation of the dispersion (portfolios assigned to the composite for the entire calendar year) varies considerably over time.

Composite "Global Equity Portfolios"

Year	Number of Portfolios	Dispersion (%)*	Composite return (%)
2008	26	2.8	12.5
2007	22	4.0	42.6
2006	17	18.5/24.4	20.5
2005	20	2.8	8.3
2004	5	–4.9/0.4	–2.6

*Dispersion: Asset-weighted standard deviation of portfolio returns on a monthly basis, if more than twenty portfolios were included in the composite for the entire period, otherwise the minimum and the high-low range is reported.

FIGURE 16.11
Presentation of Dispersion of a Global Equity Portfolios Composite.

Example 16.15

Use of Different Measures of Dispersion in a Composite:

Due to the limited explanatory power of the standard deviation for a small number of portfolios, an investment manager represents the dispersion by means of the high-low range, if there are fewer than twenty returns (i.e. fewer than twenty portfolios assigned to the composite for the entire calendar year) (see Figure 16.11).

In some cases it may also be useful to provide several measures of dispersion displayed side by side.

Example 16.16

(Use of Different Measures of Dispersion Side by Side):

To document that the investment strategy for the composite "German stocks" is implemented in an almost identical manner for all equity portfolios with corresponding

Composite "German Equity Portfolios"

Year	Share of Assets under Management	Min/Max Return	Standard Deviation of Portfolio Returns	Composite Return	Benchmark Return
1998	14.3	15.36/18.40	1.2	16.73	16.81
1997	15.9	41.60/46.80	1.8	44.12	43.78
1996	12.3	22.20/26.26	1.4	24.35	24.23
1995	10.8	6.32/8.50	0.9	7.45	7.25
1994	10.3	–4.65/–3.76	0.4	–4.32	–4.89

FIGURE 16.12
Presentation of Dispersion of the German Equity Composite Using Two Different Measures (Values in %).

investment objectives, an asset manager decides to present the standard deviation of returns alongside the high-low range for each of the calendar years. The small ranges between the respective minimum and maximum returns emphasize that there were no extreme performance outliers (see Figure 16.12).

16.9 PRESENTATION OF RISKS ACCORDING TO THE GIPS

An appropriate presentation of the performance of an investment manager would be incomplete without the consideration of the inherent risks. The Investment Performance Council (IPC) was well aware of this fact when working on the various GIPS versions. The aspects of risks were covered in different subcommittees, the recommendations of which formed the basis of the discussions in the IPC. Despite the considerable efforts that went into these discussions, the resulting standards, listed below, are quite general.

- *4.A.5 (Requirement): "Firms must disclose the presence, use, and extent of leverage, derivatives, and short positions, if material, including a description of the frequency of use and characteristics of the instruments sufficient to identify risks."*
- *4.A.14 (Requirement): "Firms must disclose all significant events that would help a prospective client interpret the compliant presentation."*
- *5.A.1 (Requirement): "Firms must present a measure of internal dispersion".*
- *5.B.3 (Recommendation): "For periods prior to 1 January 2011, firms should present the three-year annualized ex-post standard deviation (using monthly returns) of the composite and the benchmark as of each annual period end."*
- *5.B.6 (Recommendation): "Firms should present additional relevant composite-level ex-post risk measures."*

This generality is due to the fact that it is much harder to find generally accepted risk measures than it is to agree on standards for the presentation of returns. Furthermore, different fund types require different risk measures. After a long controversy, in the 2010 version finally a concrete ex-post risk measure for market risk (standard deviation) was introduced.

Further, the GIPS expect the firms to disclose the leverage exerted in the funds (4.A.13). The notes on this (CFA Institute 2006 p. 114) are, however, rather vague. Various attempts by the CFA Institute to develop concrete recommendations have already failed.

A prominent role has been for the "general" risks which might jeopardize future performance, of which a potential investor should be informed (4.A.14). In general, events affecting the entire firm should be mentioned in the context of the description of the firm. In the case of events that only affect specific composites, it is more appropriate to refer to them in a presentation of the respective composites. Here are some examples:

Example 16.17

(Personnel Changes):

Investment company XY has an excellent track record in the "European stocks" segment. The portfolio manager, who for years has been mainly responsible for the portfolios of this segment, has recently left the company. Because of this management change there is the risk that the future management team will not be able to maintain the current level of performance. In this case, the composites concerned should at least be provided with appropriate information.

Similar risks arise if there is a significant change in the trading desk or investment company analyst teams. In this case, it should be examined whether a notice needs to be given in regard to the description of the firm.

If the personnel changes are recent and not yet included in the certified documents, then the firm should follow the recommendation of the GIPS and disclose the change of staff in actual presentations on the *European Stocks* composite and indicate how the continuity of management and the investment process are maintained.

Example 16.18

Change of Ownership Structure:

Investors are confronted with additional risks when the ownership structure of an investment company changes. If a successful investment company is, e.g., acquired by a larger firm, then there is the risk that due to the restructuring substantial changes will occur in the investment management area. For example, the restructuring can cause the departure of successful portfolio managers, traders, and analysts (cf. Example 16.17). Since this is a comprehensive event, the changes resulting from such a corporate action should be featured in the presentation of the firm. In particular, the consequences for the management of portfolios should be indicated.

Apart from risks that are directly related to the company, there might be other general risks for investors, which the firm should be aware of and which it should disclose.

Example 16.19

(Significant Change in the Legal Framework):

If the exploitation of special aspects of the legal framework regarding the taxation of capital gains or income from certain securities constitutes an essential component of the investment style of a composite, then it should be noted in the description of the composite required by the GIPS.[96] If a firm has reason to believe that a change to their framework can jeopardize the future performance (such as when legislation in this respect is discussed in public), then it should point this out in the presentation of the composite, showing the impact that this change could have on the composite's management.

---

[96]See CFA Institute (2010, 4.A.3).

In this context, also the disclosure of credit or counterparty risks can occur (absolute or relative to the benchmark). This might entail a description of the rating structure or the expression of the results of further risk analysis (specifying the model used).

16.10 CHAPTER-END PROBLEMS

1. (Composite return) (see Table 16.20):

Table 16.20 shows the returns of three equity portfolios over the period of one year and the asset values of the portfolios at selected points in time (at the beginning of each period, prior to the cash flows).

Determine the return of the composite over the entire period from January to December. Conduct the computation in two ways by applying two of the three methods described in Section 16.4.2.

If you assume that, except for the exogenous cash flows presented, no other inflow or outflow has occurred, verify that under these conditions the information provided is sufficient to determine the return of the composite.

The benchmark of the composite has achieved a return of 34.00% in this period. How do you assess the performance of the manager?

2. (Return of a Carve-out Portfolio):

Table 16.21 provides the basic data for the carve-out portfolio "Global equity". Use the mathematical procedure described in Section 16.3.3 for the allocation

Table 16.20 Data for a Composite Consisting of Three Portfolios

Period	Portfolio A			Portfolio B			Portfolio C		
	Return	Asset Value	Cash Flow	Return	Asset Value	Cash Flow	Return	Asset Value	Cash Flow
Jan.–June	20%	100	0	10%	200	0	12%	200	0
July	10%	120	100/ 07/10	10%	220	0	25%	224	0
Aug.–Dec.	8%	230	0	5%	242	0	–4%	280	0

Table 16.21 Data for Balanced Global Portfolios (Values in %)

	Weight 06/01/2008	Return June 2008	Weight 07/01/2008	Return July 2008	Weight 08/01/2008	Return August 2008
Bonds	40	–1.5	50	–2.0	50	0.3
Stocks	40	–1.8	30	–18.8	40	–5.3
Funds	20	0.3	20	0.3	20	0.3

Malus-Invest

Equity Composite "German Blue Chips"

Year	Number of Portfolios	Asset Values in Million €)	Dispersion	Composite Return	Benchmark Return
2008	16	2.56	3.7%	16.73%	11.24%
2004–2007	6	0.52		75.80%	30.37%

Description of composite: Portfolios of this composite are invested exclusively in German stocks. There are no restrictions on the selection of securities, which is based on a fundamental "bottom-up approach." The portfolios are almost always invested entirely. The composite was created on 01/01/1999.

Calculation method: The return calculation is based on the unit price method. The returns shown are net, i.e. after deduction of management fees (investment management fees and custodian fees).

FIGURE 16.13
Equity Composite "German Blue Chips' of Malus-Invest.

of contributions from the cash position. Calculate the return over the period June–August 2008 and compare the results according to the different types of distribution of the cash inflows.

Is it really possible to derive a valid evaluation of the performance of the manager? Can you recognize why, according to the GIPS, since 2010 the formation of carve-outs should be permitted only if each segment has a separate cash position?

3. (Presentation of Composite Performance according to the GIPS):

The fund company Malus-Invest presents its performance results as shown in Figure 16.13 and claims to be "in compliance" with the GIPS. Do you agree?

4. The GIPS standards prohibit including nondiscretionary portfolios in composites. IPS restrictions do not necessarily render a portfolio nondiscretionary. It is up to the investment management firm to define discretion and to determine whether it has the discretion to implement the investment strategy, given the restrictions of the IPS. In this case, however, it appears likely that SMERF's policy requiring transactions to be approved in advance by the Investment Committee and the pension plan's liquidity needs prevent Midwest National Bank from fully implementing the investment objective of achieving long-term capital appreciation through active management. If so, Midwest National Bank should classify the SMERF portfolio as nondiscretionary and exclude and execute it from all composites.

5. The head of performance measurement is correct in stating that the GIPS standards require the presenting firm to disclose significant events that may assist a prospective client in interpreting the performance record (Provision II.4.A.19). Such events include, but are not limited to, the loss of key personnel such as portfolio managers. In this case, the small firm lost not one but seven investment decision-makers. Shelbourne Capital Company must

include a disclosure that equity investment professionals left the firm, and it must indicate when they left.

6. The report has a significant number of omissions and errors.
Omissions that prevent the Bristol Capital Management performance report from being GIPS-compliant are as follows:

- The availability of a complete list and description of all of Bristol's composites is not disclosed as is required (Provision II.4.A.2).
- The availability of additional information regarding policies for calculating and reporting returns in compliance with the GIPS standards is not disclosed (Provision II.4.A.17).
- Although Bristol does disclose the use of derivatives, the firm has omitted the required description of the extent of use, frequency, and characteristics of the instruments that must also be disclosed in sufficient detail to identify the risks (Provision II.4.A.5).
- If the firm has included non-fee-paying accounts in its composite, the percentage of the composite represented by these accounts must be disclosed as of the end of each annual period (Provision II.5.A.7).
- The composite creation date must be disclosed (Provision II.4.A.24).
- Because the composite represents a global investment strategy, the presentation must include information about the treatment of withholding tax on dividends, interest income, and capital gains (Provision II.4.A.7).
- A description of the composite's strategy must be disclosed (Provision II.4.A.20).

Items included in the Bristol Capital Management performance report that are *not compliant* with GIPS are as follows:

- The GIPS standards state that performance periods of less than one year must not be annualized, as Bristol does for the first quarter of 2007 (Provision II.5.A.3).
- GIPS verification cannot be performed for a single composite as is stated in the notes to the Bristol report. Third-party verification is performed with respect to the entire firm (Provisions IILA.l and III.C).
- For periods beginning 1 January 2001, portfolios must be valued at least monthly. Bristol is valuing portfolios quarterly (Provision II.1.A.3).
- A firm must use the compliance statement as specified in the GIPS. There are no provisions for partial compliance. If a firm does not meet all the GIPS requirements, then it is not in compliance with the GIPS standards. Bristol's use of the "except for" compliance statement violates the Standards (Provisions II.0.A.7-8).
- The firm must disclose which measure of composite dispersion is presented (Provision II.4.A.26).
- The GIPS standards state that accrual accounting must be used for fixed-income securities and all other assets that accrue interest income (Provision II.1.A.6). Bristol states that it uses cash-basis accounting for the recognition of interest income.

Bibliography

Admati, A., Bhattacharya, S., Pfleiderer, P., Ross, S., 1986. On timing and selectivity. Journal of Finance 41, 715–730.

Admati, Anat R., Ross, Stephen A., 1985. Measuring investment performance in a rational expectations equilibrium model. Journal of Business 58, 1–26.

Ait-Sahalia, Y., Brandt, M., 2001. Variable selection for portfolio choice. Journal of Finance 56, 1297–1351.

Amenc, Noel, Curtis, Susan, Martellini, Lionel, 2004. The Alpha and the Omega of Hedge Funds Performance. Unpublished paper, EDHEC, February.

Andrews, Donald W.K., Lee, Inpyo, Ploberger, Werner, 1996. Optimal change-point tests for normal linear regression. Journal of Econometrics 70, 9–38.

Avramov, D., 2002. Stock return predictability and model uncertainty. Journal of Financial Economics 64, 423–458.

Avramov, D., 2004. Stock return predictability and asset pricing models. The Review of Financial Studies 17, 699–738.

Avramov, D., Chordia, T., 2005a. Asset pricing models and financial market anomalies. Forthcoming in the Review of Financial Studies.

Avramov, D., Chordia, T., 2005b. Predicting stock returns. Forthcoming in Journal of Financial Economics.

Avramov, D., Russ Wermers, 2006. Investing in mutual funds when returns are predictable. Journal of Financial Economics 81, 339–377.

Avramov, D., Zhao, G., 2010. Bayesian portfolio analysis. Annual Review of Financial Economics, forthcoming.

Avramov, Doron, Kosowski, Robert, Naik, Narayan Y., Teo, Melvyn, 2007. Investing in Hedge Funds When Returns Are Predictable. Unpublished paper. University of Maryland, Imperial College, London Business School and Singapore Management University, February.

Avramov, Doron, Kosowski, Robert, Naik, Narayan, Teo, Melvyn, 2011. Hedge funds, managerial skills, and macroeconomic variables. Journal of Financial Economics 99, 672–692.

Avramov, Doron, Wermers, Russ, 2006. Investing in mutual funds when returns are predictable. Journal of Financial Economics, 339–377. August.

Avramov, Doron, Wermers, Russ, 2006. Investing in mutual funds when returns are predictable. Journal of Financial Economics 81 (2), 339–377.

Bailey, J., 1995. Manager Universes: The solution or the problem? In: Performance Evaluation, Benchmarks, and Attribution Analysis, Association for Investment Management and Research (AIMR).

Bajgrowicz, Pierre, Scaillet, Olivier, 2009. Technical Trading Revisited: False Discoveries, Persistence Tests, and Transaction Costs. University of Geneva. Working paper.

Baks, K.P., Metrick, A., Wachter, J., 2001. Should investors avoid all actively managed mutual funds? A study in Bayesian performance evaluation. Journal of Finance 56, 45–85.

Baks, Klaas P., Metrick, Andrew, Wachter, Jessica, 2001. Should investors avoid all actively managed mutual funds? A study in Bayesian performance evaluation. Journal of Finance 56, 45–85.

Baks, Klaas, 2003. On the Performance of Mutual Fund Managers. Unpublished paper, Emory University, March.

Baks, Klaas, Metrick, Andrew, Wachter, Jessica, 2001. Should investors avoid all actively managed mutual funds? a study in Bayesian performance evaluation. Journal of Finance 56, 45–86.

Banegas, Ayelen, Gillen, Ben, Timmermann, Allan, and Wermers, Russ, et al., 2010. Mutual Fund Return Predictability In Partially-Integrated Markets. Working paper.

Banegas, Ayelen, Gillen, Benjamin, Timmerman, Allen G., Wermers, Russ, 2009. The Performance of European Equity Mutual Funds. Unpublished paper, University of California, San Diego and University of Maryland, March.

Barberis, N., 2000. Investing for the long run when returns are predictable. Journal of Finance 55, 225–264.

Barras, Laurent, Scaillet, Olivier, Wermers, Russ, 2010. False discoveries in mutual fund performance: Measuring luck in estimated alphas. Journal of Finance, 179–216. February.

Barras, Laurent, Scaillet, Olivier, Wermers, Russ, 2010. False discoveries in mutual fund performance: measuring luck in estimated alphas. Journal of Finance 65, 179–216.

Barras, Laurent, Scaillet, Olivier, Wermers, Russ, 2010. False discoveries in mutual fund performance. Measuring luck in estimated alphas. Journal of Finance 65 (1), 179–216.

Bell, David E., 1982. Regret theory in decisionmaking under uncertainty. Operations Research 30, 961–981.

Benjamini, Yoav, Hochberg, Yosef, 1995. Controlling the false discovery rate: A practical and powerful approach to multiple testing. Journal of the Royal Statistical Society 57, 289–300.

Berk, Jonathan B., Green, Richard C., 2004. Mutual fund flows and performance in rational markets. Journal of Political Economy 112, 1269–1295.

Berk, Jonathan, Green, Richard, 2004. Mutual fund flows and performance in rational markets. Journal of Political Economy 112 (6), 1269–1295.

Bernstein, Peter, 1996. Against the Gods: The Remarkable Story of Risk. John Wiley & Sons, Inc.

Bers, Martina, Madura, Jeff, 2000. Why does performance persistence vary among closed-end funds? Journal of Financial Services Research 17 (2), 127–147.

Bickel, Peter J., Freedman, David A., 1984. Some asymptotics on the bootstrap. Annals of Statistics 9, 1196–1271.

Blake, Christopher, Elton, Edwin, Gruber, Martin, 1995. Fundamental economic variables, expected returns, and bond fund performance. Journal of Finance 50, 1229–1256.

Blake, David, Timmermann, Allan, 2005. International asset allocation with time-varying investment opportunities. Journal of Business 78, 71–98.

Blake, David, Tonks, Ian, Timmermann, Allan, Wermers, Russ, 2011. Decentralized Investment Management: Evidence from the Pension Fund Industry. Working Paper.

Bollen, Nicholas P., Pool, Veronika K., 2009. Do hedge fund managers misreport returns? evidence from the pooled distribution. Journal of Finance 64, 2257–2288.

Bollen, Nicholas P., Whaley, Robert, 2009. Hedge fund risk dynamics: Implications for performance appraisal. Journal of Finance 64, 987–1037.

Bollen, Nicholas, Busse, Jeffrey A., 2005. Short-term persistence in mutual fund performance. Review of Financial Studies 18, 569–597.

Bollen, Nicolas P.B., Busse, Jeffrey A., 2005. Short-term persistence in mutual fund performance. Review of Financial Studies 18 (2), 569–597.

Brinson, Gary P., Hood, Randolph, Beebower, Gilbert L., 1986. Determinants of portfolio performance. Financial Analysts Journal 42 (4), 39–48. Reprinted in Financial Analysts Journal, vol. 51, no. 1 (January/February 1995, 50th anniversary issue):133–138.

Brinson, Gary P., Randolph Hood, L., Beebower, Gilbert L., 1986. Determinants of portfolio performance. Financial Analyst Journal 42, 39–44.

Brown, Nerissa, Wei, Kelsey, Wermers, Russ, 2011. Analyst Recommendations, Mutual Fund Herding, and Overreaction in Stock Prices. Unpublished paper, University of Maryland, March.

Brown, Stephen J., Goetzmann, William N., 1995. Performance persistence. Journal of Finance 50, 679–698.

Brown, Stephen J., Goetzmann, William N., Ibbotson, Roger G., Ross, Stephen A., 1992. Survivorship bias in performance studies. Review of Financial Studies 5, 553–580.

Busse, Jeffrey A., Goyal, Amit, Wahal, Sunil, 2010. Performance and persistence in institutional investment management. Journal of Finance 65 (2), 765–790.

Busse, Jeffrey, 1999. Volatility timing in mutual funds: Evidence from daily returns. Review of Financial Studies 12, 1009–1041.

Busse, Jeffrey, Goyal, Amit, Wahal, Sunil, 2010. Performance and persistence in institutional investment management. Journal of Finance 65, 765–790.

Campbell, John, Lo, Andrew, MacKinlay, Craig, 1997. The Econometrics of Financial Markets and Craig MacKinlay. Princeton University Press.

Carhart, M., 1997. On persistence in mutual fund performance. Journal of Finance 52, 57–82.

Carhart, Mark M., 1997. On persistence in mutual fund performance. Journal of Finance 62 (1), 57–82.

Carhart, Mark M., Carpenter, Jennifer N., Lynch, Anthony W., Musto, David K., 2002. Mutual fund survivorship. Review of Financial Studies 15, 1439–1463.

Chan, Louis K.C., Jegadeesh, Narasimhan, Lakonishok, Josef, 1996. Momentum strategies. Journal of Finance 51, 1681–1713.

Chen, Hsiu-Lang, Jegadeesh, Narasimhan, Wermers, Russ, 2000. An examination of the stockholdings and trades of fund managers. Journal of Financial and Quantitative Analysis 35, 343–368.

Chen, Hsiu-Lang, Jegadeesh, Narasimhan, Wermers, Russ, 2000. The value of active mutual fund management: An examination of the stockholdings and trades of fund managers. Journal of Financial and Quantitative Analysis 35, 343–368.

Chen, J., Hong, H., Huang, M., Kubik, J., 2004. Does fund size erode mutual fund performance? The role of liquidity and organization. American Economic Review 94, 1276–1302.

Chen, Joseph, Hong, Harrison, Huang, Ming, Kubik, Jeffrey, 2004. Does fund size erode mutual fund performance? The role of liquidity and organization. American Economic Review 94 (5), 1276–1302.

Chen, Zhiwu, Knez, Peter, 1996. Portfolio performance measurement: Theory and applications. Review of Financial Studies 9, 511–556.

Chevalier, Judith A., Ellison, Glenn, 1997. Risk taking by mutual funds as a response to incentives. Journal of Political Economy 105, 1167–1200.

Chevalier, Judith, Ellison, Glenn, 1999. Are some mutual fund managers better than others? cross-sectional patterns in behavior and performance. Journal of Finance 54, 875–899.

Chevalier, Judith, Ellison, Glenn, 1999. Are some mutual fund managers better than others? Cross-sectional patterns in behavior and performance. Journal of Finance 54 (3), 875–899.

Chordia, Tarun, Roll, Richard, Subrahmanyam, Avanidhar, 2000. Commonality in liquidity. Journal of Financial Economics 56, 3–28.

Chordia, Tarun, Subrahmanyam, Avanidhar, Tong, Qing, 2010. Trends in the Cross-Section of Expected Stock Returns. Unpublished paper, Emory University, UCLA and Singapore Management University, November.

Christoffersen, Susan E.K., Musto, David K., 2002. Demand curves and the pricing of money management. Review of Financial Studies 15, 1495–1524.

Christopherson, Jon A., Ferson, Wayne, Glassman, Debra, 1998. Conditioning manager alphas on economic information: Another look at the persistence of performance. Review of Financial Studies 11, 111–142.

Cici, Gjergji, Gibson, Scott, 2012. The performance of corporate-bond mutual funds: Evidence based on security-level holdings. Journal of Financial and Quantitative Analysis, pp. 159-178.

Clements, J., 1999. Stock funds just don't measure up. Wall Street Journal october 5.

Clifford, De Souza., Gokcan, S., 2003. How some hedge fund characteristics impact performance. AIMA Journal.

Cochrane, John, 2001. Asset Pricing. Princeton University Press.

Cohen, Lauren, Frazzini, Andrea, Malloy, Christopher, 2008. The small world of investing: Board connections and mutual fund returns. Journal of Political Economy 116, 951–979.

Cohen, Lauren, Frazzini, Andrea, Malloy, Christopher, 2008. The small world of investing: board connections and mutual fund returns. Journal of Political Economy 116 (5), 951–979.

Cohen, Randolph, Coval, Joshua, Pastor, Lubos, 2005. Judging fund managers by the company they keep. Journal of Finance 60, 1057–1096.

Copeland, Thomas E., Mayers, David, 1982. The ValueLine enigma (1965–1978): A case study of performance evaluation issues. Journal of Financial Economics 10, 289–322.

Cornell, Bradford, Green, Kevin, 1991. The investment performance of low-grade bond funds. Journal of Finance 46, 29–48.

Cremers, Martijn, Petajisto, Antti, 2009. How active is your fund manager? a new measure that predicts performance. Review of Financial Studies 22, 3329–3365.

Cremers, Martijn, Petajisto, Antti, 2009. How active is your fund manager? A new measure that predicts performance. Review of Financial Studies 22 (9), 3329–3365.

Dahlquist, Magnus, Soderlind, Paul, 1999. Evaluating portfolio performance with stochastic discount factors. Journal of Business 72, 347–383.

Daniel, K., Grinblatt, M., Titman, S., Wermers, R., 1997. Measuring mutual fund performance with characteristic-based benchmarks. Journal of Finance 52, 1035–1058.

Daniel, Kent, 2011. Momentum Crashes, Columbia University, Working Paper.

Daniel, Kent, Grinblatt, Mark, Titman, Sheridan, Wermers, Russ, 1997. Measuring mutual fund performance with characteristic-based benchmarks. Journal of Finance 52, 1035–1058.

Daniel, Kent, Titman, Sheridan, 1997. Evidence on the characteristics of cross sectional variation in stock returns. Journal of Finance 52, 1–33.

Datar, Vinay, Naik, Narayan Y., Radcliffe, Robert, 1998. Liquidity and stock returns: An alternative test. Journal of Financial Markets 1, 203–219.

De Souza, Clifford, Gokcan, Suleyman, 2003. How some hedge fund characteristics impact performance. AIMA Journal (September).

Dickson, Joel, Shoven, John, 1993. Ranking Mutual Funds on an After-Tax Basis. NBER Working Paper, July.

Dincer, Oguzhan, Gregory-Allen, Russell B., Shawky, Hany A., 2010. Are You Smarter Than a CFA'er. Unpublished paper, Illinois State University, Massey University and SUNY at Albany, January.

Dincer, Oguzhan, Russell B. Gregory-Allen, Hany A. Shawky, 2010. Are You Smarter Than a CFA'er? Working Paper.

Ding, Bill, Wermers, Russ, 2009. Mutual Fund Performance and Governance Structure: The Role of Portfolio Managers and Boards of Directors. Working Paper.

Ding, Bill, Wermers, Russ, 2009. Mutual Fund Performance and Governance Structure: The Role of Portfolio Managers and Boards of Directors. University of Maryland. Working paper.

Ding, Bill, Wermers, Russ, 2009. Mutual Fund Performance and Governance Structure: The Role of Portfolio Managers and Boards of Directors. Unpublished paper, SUNY at Albany and University of Maryland, November.

Dybvig, P., Ross, S., 1985. Performance measurement using differential information and a security market line. Journal of Finance 40, 383–399.

Edelen, Roger M., 1999. Investor flows and the assessed performance of open-end mutual funds. Journal of Financial Economics 53 (3), 439–466.

Edelen, Roger, 1999. Investor flows and the assessed performance of open-end mutual funds. Journal of Financial Economics 53, 439–466.

Efron, Bradley, Tibshirani, Robert, 2002. Empirical Bayes methods and false discovery rates for microarrays. Genetic Epidemiology 23, 70–86.

Efron, Bradley, Tibshirani, Robert, Storey, John D., Tusher, Virginia, 2001. Empirical Bayes analysis of a microarray experiment. Journal of the American Statistical Association 96, 1151–1160.

Elton, Edwin J., Gruber, Martin J., Blake, Christopher R., 1996. The persistence of risk-adjusted mutual fund performance. Journal of Business 69, 133–157.

Elton, Edwin J., Gruber, Martin J., Blake, Christopher R., 2007. Participant reaction and the performance of funds offered by 401(k) plans. Journal of Financial Intermediation 16, 249–271.

Elton, Edwin J., Gruber, Martin J., Busse, Jeffrey, 2004. Are investors rational? Choices among index funds. Journal of Finance 59, 261–288.

Elton, Edwin J., Gruber, Martin J., Das, Sanjiv, Hlavka, Matthew, 1993. Efficiency with costly information: A reinterpretation of evidence from managed portfolios. Review of Financial Studies 6, 1–22.

Elton, Ned, Gruber, Martin, Brown, Steven, Goetzmann, William, 2011. Investments and Portfolio Management.

Fama, E., 1996. Multifactor portfolio efficiency and multifactor asset pricing. Journal of Financial and Quantitative Analysis 31, 441–465.

Fama, E., French, K., 1989. Business conditions and expected returns on stocks and bonds. Journal of Financial Economics 19, 3–29.

Fama, E., French, K., 1993. Common risk factors in the returns on stocks and bonds. Journal of Financial Economics 33, 3–56.

Fama, Eugene F., French, Kenneth R., 1989. Business conditions and expected returns on stocks and bonds. Journal of Financial Economics 19, 3–29.

Fama, Eugene F., French, Kenneth R., 1992. The cross-section of expected stock returns. Journal of Finance 47, 427–465.

Fama, Eugene F., French, Kenneth R., 1993. Common risk factors in the returns on stocks and bonds. Journal of Financial Economics 33, 3–56.

Fama, Eugene F., French, Kenneth R., 1993. Common risk factors in the returns on stocks and bonds. Journal of Financial Economics 33 (1), 3–56.

Fama, Eugene F., French, Kenneth R., 1996. Multifactor explanations of asset pricing anomalies. Journal of Finance 51, 55–84.

Fama, Eugene F., French, Kenneth R., 2009. Luck versus skill in the cross-section of mutual fund returns. Journal of Finance 65, 1915–1945.

Ferson, W., Siegel, A., 2001. The efficient use of conditioning information in portfolios. Journal of Finance 56, 967–982.

Ferson, Wayne E., and Qian, Meijun, 2004. Conditional performance evalution revisited. In: Research Foundation Monograph of the CFA institute.

Ferson, Wayne E., Schadt, Rudi W., 1996. Measuring fund strategy and performance in changing economic conditions. Journal of Finance 51, 425–461.

Ferson, Wayne E., Schadt, Rudy W., 1996. Measuring fund strategy and performance in changing economic conditions. Journal of Finance 51, 425–461.

Ferson, Wayne, Harvey, Campbell, 1999. Conditioning variables and the cross-section of stock returns. Journal of Finance 54, 1325–1360.

Ferson, Wayne, Henry, Terry R., Kisgen, Darren J., 2006. Evaluating government bond fund performance with stochastic discount factors. Review of Financial Studies 19 (2), 423–455.

Ferson, Wayne, Henry, Tyler, Kisgen, Darren, 2006. Evaluating government bond fund performance with stochastic discount factors. Review of Financial Studies 19, 423–455.

Ferson, Wayne, Khang, Kenneth, 2002. Conditional performance measurement using portfolio weights: evidence for pension funds. Journal of Financial Economics 65, 249–282.

French, Kenneth R., 2008. Presidential address: The cost of active investing. Journal of Finance 63, 1537–1573.

French, Kenneth, 2008. Presidential address: the costs of active investing. Journal of Finance 63 (4), 1537–1573.

Fung, William, Hsieh, David A., 2004. Hedge fund benchmarks: a risk based approach. Financial Analysts Journal 60, 65–80.

Fung, William, Hsieh, David A., Naik, Narayan Y., Ramadorai, Tarun, 2008. Hedge funds: Performance, risk, and capital Formation. Journal of Finance 63, 1777–1803.

Fung, William, Hsieh, David A., Naik, Narayan Y., Ramadorai, Tarun, 2008. Hedge funds: performance, risk, and capital formation. Journal of Finance 63 (4), 1777–1803.

Fung, William, Hsieh, David, 2000. Performance characteristics of hedge funds and CTA funds: Natural versus spurious biases. Journal of Financial and Quantitative Analysis 35, 291–307.

Fung, William, Hsieh, David, 2004. Hedge fund benchmarks: A risk-based approach. Financial Analysts Journal 60, 65–80.

Genovese, Christopher, Wasserman, Larry, 2004. A stochastic process approach to false discovery control. Annals of Statistics 32, 1035–1061.

Getmansky, Mila, 2005. The Life Cycle of Hedge Funds: Fund Flows, Size and Performance. Unpublished paper, University of Massachusetts at Amherst, January.

Getmansky, Mila, Liang, Bing, Schwarz, Chris, Wermers, Russ 2011. Investor Flows and Share Restrictions in the Hedge Fund Industry. Working Paper.

Getmansky, Mila, Lo, Andrew W., Makarov, Igor, 2004. An econometric model of serial correlation and illiquidity in hedge fund returns. Journal of Financial Economics 74, 529–610.

Gibson, E.J., Walk, R.D., 1960. The Visual Cliff. Scientific American.

Goetzmann, W., Ingersoll, J., Ivkovic, Z., 2000. Monthly measurement of daily timers. Journal of Financial and Quantitative Analysis 35, 257–290.

Goetzmann, W., Ingersoll, J., Spiegel, M., Welch, I., 2007. Portfolio performance manipulation and manipulation-proof performance measures. Review of Financial Studies 20, 1503–1546.

Gottesman, Aron, Morey, Matthew R., 2006. Manager education and mutual fund performance. Journal of Empirical Finance 13, 145–182.

Gottesman, Aron, Morey, Matthew R., 2006. Manager education and mutual fund performance. Journal of Empirical Finance 13 (2), 145–182.

Goyal, Amit, Wahal, Sunil, 2008. The selection and termination of investment management firms by plan sponsors. Journal of Finance 63 (4), 1805–1847.

Graham, John, Harvey, Campbell, 1996. Market timing ability and volatility implied in investment newsletters' asset allocation recommendations. Journal of Financial Economics 42, 397–421.

Griffin, John, 2002. Are the Fama and French factors global or country specific? Review of Financial Studies 15, 783–803.

Griffin, John, Spencer Martin, J., Ji, Susan, 2003. Momentum investing and business cycle risk: evidence from pole to pole. Journal of Finance 43, 2515–2547.

Griffin, John, Xu, Jin, 2009. How smart are the smart guys? a unique view from hedge fund stock holdings. Review of Financial Studies 22, 2531–2570.

Grinblatt, M., and Titman, S., 1995. Performance Evaluation. In: Jarrow, R. et al., (Ed.), Handbooks in OR and MS, Vol. 9.

Grinblatt, M., Keloharju, M., Linnainmaa, J., 2011. IQ, trading behavior, and performance. Journal of Financial Economics. forthcoming.

Grinblatt, M., Titman, S., 1989. Mutual fund performance: an analysis of quarterly portfolio holdings. Journal of Business 62, 394–415.

Grinblatt, Mark, Titman, Sheridan, 1989. Mutual fund performance: an analysis of quarterly portfolio holdings. Journal of Business 62, 394–415.

Grinblatt, Mark, Titman, Sheridan, 1989. Mutual fund performance: An analysis of quarterly portfolio holdings. Journal of Business 62, 393–416.

Grinblatt, Mark, Titman, Sheridan, 1989a. Mutual fund performance: An analysis of quarterly portfolio holdings. Journal of Business 62, 394–415.

Grinblatt, Mark, Titman, Sheridan, 1989b. Portfolio performance evaluation: Old issues and new insights. Review of Financial Studies 2, 393–422.

Grinblatt, Mark, Titman, Sheridan, 1992. The persistence of mutual fund performance. Journal of Finance 47, 1977–1984.

Grinblatt, Mark, Titman, Sheridan, 1993. Performance measurement without benchmarks: An examination of mutual fund returns. Journal of Business 66, 47–68.

Grinblatt, Mark, Titman, Sheridan, Wermers, Russ, 1995. Momentum investment strategies, portfolio performance, and herding: A study of mutual fund behavior. American Economic Review 85, 1088–1105.

Grinold, Richard C., Kahn, Ronald N., 2000. Active Portfolio Management. McGraw-Hill.

Grossman, Sanford J., Stiglitz, Joseph E., 1980. On the impossibility of informationally efficient markets. American Economic Review 70, 393–408.

Grossman, Sanford J., Stiglitz, Joseph E., 1980. On the impossibility of informationally efficient markets. American Economic Review 70 (3), 393–408.

Gruber, Martin J., 1996. Another puzzle: the growth of actively managed mutual funds. Journal of Finance 51, 783–810.

Hall, Peter, 1986. On the bootstrap and confidence intervals. Annals of Statistics 14, 1431–1452.

Hall, Peter, 1992. The Bootstrap and Edgeworth Expansion. Springer Verlag, New York.

Hall, Peter, Horowitz, Joel L., Jing, Bing-Yi, 1995. On blocking rules for the bootstrap with dependent data. Biometrika 82, 561–574.

Hamilton, James D., 1994. Times-Series Analysis. Princeton University Press, Princeton.

Hansen, L., Richard, S., 1987. The role of conditioning information in deducing testable restrictions implied by dynamic asset pricing models. Econometrica 55, 587–613.

Harlow, W.Van, Brown, Keith C., 2006. The right answer to the wrong question: identifying superior active portfolio management. Journal of Investment Management 4 (4 (Fourth Quarter)), 15–40.

Hendricks, D., Patel, J., Zeckhauser, R., 1993. Hot hands in mutual funds: the persistence of performance, 1974-88. Journal of Finance 48, 93–130.

Hendricks, Darryll, Patel, Jayendu, Zeckhauser, Richard, 1993. Hot hands in mutual funds: The persistence of performance, 1974–88. Journal of Finance 48, 93–130.

Hirshleifer, David, Teoh, Siew Hong, Yu, Jeff Jiewei, 2009. Short arbitrage, return asymmetry and the accrual anomaly. Review of Financial Studies 24 (7), 2429–2461.

Hong, Harrison, Lim, Terence, Stein, Jeremy, 2000. Bad news travels slowly: size, analyst coverage, and the profitability of momentum strategies. Journal of Finance 55 (1), 265–295.

Horowitz, Joel L., 2003. Bootstrap methods for Markov processes. Econometrica 71, 1049–1082.

Howell, Michael J., 2001. Fund age and performance. Journal of Alternative Investments 4 (2), 57–60.

Huang, J., Sialm, C., Zhang, H., 2010. Risk shifting and mutual fund performance. Review of Financial Studies. forthcoming.

Huang, Jennifer, Sialm, Clemens, Zhang, Hanjiang, 2010. Risk Shifting and Mutual Fund Performance. Unpublished paper, University of Texas at Austin, May.

Huij, Joop, Derwall, Jeroen, 2008. Hot hands in bond funds. Journal of Banking and Finance 32 (4), 559–572.

Hunter, David, Kandel, Eugene, Kandel, Shmuel, Wermers, Russ, 2012. Endogenous Benchmarks. Working paper

Ibbotson, Roger, 2010. The importance of asset allocation. Financial Analysts Journal 66 (2), 1–3.

Iihara, Yoshio, Kato, Hideaki K., Tokunaga, Toshifumi, 2004. The winner-loser effect in Japanese stock returns. Japan and the World Economy 8, 471–485.

Iihara, Yoshio, Kato, Hideaki K., Tokunaga, Toshifumi, 2004. The winner-loser effect in Japanese stock returns. Japan and the World Economy, 471–485.

Investment strategies, portfolio performance, and herding: A study of mutual fund behavior, American Economic Review 85, 1088–1105.

Investment Company Institute, 2004. Mutual Fund Fact Book. Washington, D.C.

Jagannathan, Ravi, Malakhov, Alexey, Novikov, Dimitry, 2010. Do hot hands exist among hedge fund managers? An empirical evaluation. Journal of Finance 65 (1), 217–255.

Jagannathan, Ravi, Malakhov, Alexey, Novikov, Dmitry, 2010. Do hot hands exist among hedge fund managers? an empirical examination. Journal of Finance 65, 217–255.

Jegadeesh, N., Titman, S., 1993. Returns to buying winners and selling losers: implications for stock market efficiency. Journal of Finance 48, 65–91.

Jegadeesh, Narasimhan, 1990. Evidence of predictable behavior of security returns. Journal of Finance 45, 881–898.

Jegadeesh, Narasimhan, Titman, Sheridan, 1993. Returns to buying winners and selling losers: implications for stock market efficiency. Journal of Finance 48, 65–91.

Jensen, Michael C., 1968. The performance of mutual funds in the period 1945–1964. Journal of Finance 23, 389–416.

Jensen, Michael C., 1968. The performance of mutual funds in the period 1945–1964. Journal of Finance 23 (2), 389–416.

Jenson M.C., 1969. Risk, the pricing of capital assests, and the evalution of investment portfolios. Journal of Business 42, 167–247.

Jern, B., 2002. Can past performance be used to find the winners among international stock funds? Ekonomiska Samfundets Tidskrift 55, 77–97.

Jones, C.S., Shanken, J., 2004. Mutual fund performance with learning across assets. Forthcoming in Journal of Financial Economics.

Jones, Christopher S., Shanken, Jay, 2005. Mutual fund performance with learning across funds. Journal of Financial Economics 78, 507–552.

Jorion, Philippe, 2003. Portfolio optimization with tracking-error constraints. Financial Analysts Journal, 70–82. September/October.

Kacperczyk, Marcin, Sialm, Clemens, Zheng, Lu, 2005. On the industry concentration of actively managed equity mutual funds. Journal of Finance 60, 1983–2012.

Kaczerczyk, Marcin, Sialm, Clemens, Zheng, Lu, 2008. Unobserved actions of mutual funds. Review of Financial Studies 21, 2379–2416.

Kandel, S., Stambaugh, R., 1996. On the predictability of stock returns: an asset allocation perspective. Journal of Finance 51, 385–424.

Kaplan, Steven N., Schoar, Antoinette, 2005. Private equity performance. returns, persistence and capital flows. Journal of Finance 60 (4), 1791–1823.

Kapur, S., Timmermann, A., 2005. Relative performance evaluation contracts and asset market equilibrium. Economic Journal 115, 1077–1102.

Kasperczyk, Marcin, Sialm, Clemens, Zheng, Lu, 2005. On the industry concentration of actively managed equity mutual funds. Journal of Finance 60 (4), 1983–2011.

Kasperczyk, Marcin, Sialm, Clemens, Zheng, Lu, 2008. Unobserved actions of mutual funds. Review of Financial Studies 21 (6), 2379–2416.

Keim, D., Stambaugh, R.F., 1986. Predicting returns in the stock and the bond markets. Journal of Financial Economics 17, 357–390.

Keim, Don, 1983. Size-related anomalies and stock return seasonality: further empirical evidence. Journal of Financial Economics 12.

Keim, Donald B., Madhavan, Ananth, 1997. Transactions costs and investment style: an inter-exchange analysis of institutional equity trades. Journal of Financial Economics 46, 265–292.

Kent, Daniel, Grinblatt, Mark, Titman, Sheridan, Wermers, Russ, 1997. Measuring mutual fund performance with characteristic-based benchmarks. Journal of Finance 52, 1035–1058.

Kinnel, Russel, 2010. How Expense Ratios and Star Ratings Predict Success. Unpublished paper, Morningstar, Inc.

Koijen, Ralph, 2010. The Cross-Section of Managerial Ability, Incentives, and Risk Preferences. Working Paper.

Kosowski, Robert, 2006. Do Mutual Funds Perform When it Matters Most to Investors? US Mutual Fund Performance and Risk in Recessions and Expansions. Working Paper.

Kosowski, Robert, 2006. Do Mutual Funds Perform When it Matters Most to Investors? US Mutual Fund Performance and Risk in Recessions and Expansions. Unpublished paper, Imperial College Business School, August.

Kosowski, Robert, Allan Timmermann, Hal White, Russ Wermers, Can Mutual Fund "Stars" Really Pick Stocks? New Evidence from a Bootstrap Analysis. Journal of Finance 61, 2551–2596.

Kosowski, Robert, Naik, Narayan, Teo, Melvyn, 2007. Do hedge funds deliver alpha? a Bayesian and bootstrap analysis. Journal of Financial Economics 84, 229–264.

Kosowski, Robert, Naik, Narayan, Teo, Melvyn, 2007. Do hedge funds deliver alpha? A Bayesian and bootstrap analysis. Journal of Financial Economics 84 (1), 229–264.

Kosowski, Robert, Timmerman, Allan G., Wermers, Russ, White, Hal, 2006. Can mutual fund "Stars" really pick stocks? New evidence from a bootstrap analysis. Journal of Finance 66 (6), 2551–2595.

Kosowski, Robert, Timmermann, Allan, Wermers, Russ, White, Hal, 2006. Can mutual fund "stars" really pick stocks? new evidence from a bootstrap analysis. Journal of Finance 61, 2551–2596.

Kosowski, Robert, Timmermann, Allan, Wermers, Russ, White, Halbert, 2006. Can mutual fund stars really pick stocks? New evidence from a bootstrap analysis. Journal of Finance 61, 2551–2595.

Kostovetsky, Leonard, 2007. Brain Drain: Are Mutual Funds Losing their Best Minds? Princeton University. Working paper.

Kothari, S.P., Warner, Jerold, 2001. Evaluating mutual fund performance. Journal of Finance 56, 1985–2010.

Lee, Charles M.C., Swaminathan Bhaskaran, 2000. Price momentum and trading volume. Journal of Finance 55, 2017–2069.

Lee, Charles, Swaminathan Bhaskaran, 1998. Price Momentum and Trading Volume. Working paper, Cornell University.

Lehmann, B., Modest, D., 1987. Mutual fund performance evaluation: a comparison of benchmarks and benchmark comparisons. Journal of Finance 42, 233–265.

Liang, Bing, 1999. On the performance of hedge funds. Financial Analysts Journal 55 (4), 72–85.

Liang, Bing, 2000. Hedge funds: The living and the dead. Journal of Financial and Quantitative Analysis 35, 309–326.

Litterman, B., et al., 2003. Modern Investment Management: An Equilibrium Approach. John Wiley and Sons.

Litterman, Robert B., 2004. The active risk puzzle. Journal of Portfolio Management 30 (5), 88–93 (September, 30th Anniversary Issue).

Loomes, Graham, Sugden, Robert, 1982. Regret theory: An alternative theory of rational choice under uncertainty. Economic Journal 92, 805–824.

Lynch, Anthony W., Musto, David K., 2003. How investors interpret past fund returns. Journal of Finance 58, 2033–2058.

Lynch, Anthony W., Musto, David K., 2003. How investors interpret past fund returns. Journal of Finance 58 (5), 2033–2058.

Marcus, Alan J., 1990. The Magellan fund and market efficiency. Journal of Portfolio Management 17, 85–88.

Markowitz, H.M., 1952. Portfolio selection. Journal of Finance 7, 77–91.

Markowitz, H.M., 1959. Portfolio Selection: Efficient Diversification of Investments. Yale University Press, New Haven, CT.

Massa, Massimo, Zhang, Lei, 2009. The Effects of Organizational Structure on Asset Management. Working Paper.

Massa, Massimo, Zhang, Lei, 2009. The Effects of Organizational Structure on Asset Management. Unpublished paper, INSEAD and Nanyang Technological University, October.

Mayers, David, Rice, Edward, 1979. Measuring portfolio performance and the empirical content of asset pricing models. Journal of Financial Economics, 3–28.

Merton, R.C., 1973. An intertemporal capital asset pricing model. Econometrica 41, 867–887.

Merton, R.C., 1981. On market timing and investment performance part I: an equilibrium theory of value for market forecasts. Journal of Business 54, 263–289.

Merton, Robert C., Henriksson, Roy D., 1981. On market timing and investment performance II: Statistical procedures for evaluating forecasting skills. Journal of Business 54, 513–533.

Moskowitz, T., 2000. Discussion: Mutual fund performance: an empirical decomposition into stock-picking talent, style, transactions costs, and expenses. Journal of Finance 55, 1695–1703.

Moskowitz, T., 2003. An analysis of covariance risk and pricing anomalies. Review of Financial Studies 16, 417–457.

Moskowitz, T., Grinblatt, M., 1999. Do industries explain momentum?. Journal of Finance 54, 1249–1290.

Moskowitz, Tobias J., 2000. Mutual fund performance: An empirical decomposition into stock-picking talent, style, transactions costs, and expenses: discussion. Journal of Finance 55, 1695–1703.

Moskowitz, Tobias J., Grinblatt, Mark, 1999. Do industries explain momentum? Journal of Finance 54, 1249–1290.

Moskowitz, Tobias, 2000. Discussion of mutual fund performance. An empirical decomposition into stock- picking talent, style, transactions costs, and expenses. Journal of Finance 55 (4), 1695–1704.

Newey, Whitney K., West, Kenneth D., 1987. A simple, positive semi-definite, heteroskedasticity and autocorrelation consistent covariance matrix. Econometrica 55, 703–708.

Nitibhon, Chakramon, Tirapat, Sunti, Wermers, Russ, 2005. Secrets of Thai equity funds revealed: An analysis of performance, persistence, and flows. Working Paper.

Pastor, L., 2000. Portfolio selection and asset pricing models. Journal of Finance 55, 179–223.

Pastor, L., Stambaugh, R., 2000. Comparing asset pricing models: an investment perspective. Journal of Financial Economics 56, 335–381.

Pastor, L., Stambaugh, R., 2002a. Mutual fund performance and seemingly unrelated assets. Journal of Financial Economics 63, 315–349.

Pastor, L., Stambaugh, R., 2002b. Investing in equity mutual funds. Journal of Financial Economics 63, 351–380.

Pastor, Lubos, Stambaugh, Robert F., 2002. Mutual fund performance and seemingly unrelated assets. Journal of Financial Economics 63, 315–349.

Pastor, Lubos, Stambaugh, Robert, 2002. Mutual fund performance and seemingly unrelated assets. Journal of Financial Economics 63 (3), 315–349.

Pastor, Lubos, Stambaugh, Robert, 2002a. Mutual fund performance and seemingly unrelated assets. Journal of Financial Economics 63, 315–349.

Pastor, Lubos, Stambaugh, Robert, 2002b. Investing in equity mutual funds. Journal of Financial Economics 63, 351–380.

Paul, Joseph Gerard, 2009. No Time to Be Passive—Get Active Now. AllianceBernstein, January).

Pesaran, M. Hashem, Timmermann, Allan, 1995. Predictability of stock returns: Robustness and economic significance. Journal of Finance 50, 1201–1228.

Phalippou, Ludovic, Gottschalg, Oliver, 2009. The performance of private equity funds. Review of Financial Studies 22 (4), 1747–1776.

Pinnuck, M., 2003. An examination of the performance of the trades and stockholdings of fund managers: Further evidence. Journal of Financial and Quantitative Analysis 38, 811–828.

Politis, Dimitris N., Romano, Joseph P., 1994. The stationary bootstrap. Journal of the American Statistical Association 89, 1303–1313.

Rea, John D., Reid, Brian K., 1998. Trends in the ownership cost of equity mutual funds, Investment Company Institute Perspective. (November).

Robert, Kosowski, Naik, Narayan, Teo, Melvin, 2007. Do hedge funds deliver alpha? A Bayesian and bootstrap analysis. Journal of Financial Economics 84, 229–264.

Roll, Richard, 1978. Ambiguity when performance is measured by the securities line. Journal of Finance 33, 1051–1069.

Roll, Richard, 1992. A mean/variance analysis of tracking error. Journal of Portfolio Management 18, 13–23.

Romano, Joseph P., Shaikh, Azeem M., Wolf, Michael, 2008. Formalized data snooping on generalized error rates. Econometric Theory 24, 404–447.

Rouwenhorst, Geert, 1998. International momentum strategies. Journal of Finance 53, 267–284.

Ryan, Sullivan, Timmermann, Allan, White, Halbert, 1999. Data-snooping, technical trading rule performance and the bootstrap. Journal of Finance 54, 1647–1691.

Schwert, G.W., 2003. Anomalies and market efficiency. In: Constantinides, G.M., Harris, M., Stulz, R. (Eds.), Handbook of economics and finance. Elsevier., pp. 937–972.

Shanken, J., 1990. Intertemporal asset pricing: an empirical investigation. Journal of Econometrics 45, 99–120.

Silverman, Bernard W., 1986. Density Estimation for Statistics and Data Analysis. Chapman and Hall, London.

Sirri, E., Tufano, P., 1998. Costly search and mutual fund flows. Journal of Finance 53, 1589–1622.

Stambaugh, R.F., 2003. Inference About Survivors. Unpublished working paper. The Wharton School.

Stewart, Scott D., Neumann, John J., Knittel, Christopher R., Heisler, Jeffrey, 2009. Absence of value: an analysis of investment allocation decisions by institutional plan sponsors. Financial Analysts Journal 65 (6), 34–51.

Stoll, Hans R., 1995. The importance of equity trading costs: evidence from securities firms' revenues. In: Schwartz, Robert A. (Ed.), Global Equity Markets Technological Competitive and Regulatory Challenges. Irwin Professional Publishing, New York.

Storey, John D., 2002. A direct approach to false discovery rates. Journal of the Royal Statistical Society 64, 479–498.

Storey, John D., 2003. The positive false discovery rate: A Bayesian interpretation and the q-value. Annals of Statistics 31, 2013–2035.

Storey, John D., Taylor, Jonathan E., Siegmund, David, 2004. Strong control, conservative point estimation and simultaneous conservative consistency of false discovery rates: A unified approach. Journal of the Royal Statistical Society 66, 187–205.

Surowiecki, James, 2004. The Wisdom of Crowds. Random House, Inc., New York.

Sullivan Ryan, Allan Timmermann, and Halbert white, 1999, Data-snooping, technical trading rule performance and the bootstrap, Journal of Finance 54, 1647–1691.

Tang, Yongqiang, Ghosal, Subhashis, Roy, Anindya, 2007. Nonparametric Bayesian estimation of positive false discovery rates. Biometrics 63, 1126–1134.

Teo, Melvyn, and Sung-Jun Woo, 2001. Persistence in style-adjusted mutual fund returns, unpublished manuscript, Harvard University.

Titman, Sheridan, Tiu, Cristian, 2011. Do the best hedge funds hedge?. Review of Financial Studies 24, 123–168.

Treynor, J., Kay Mazuy, 1966. Can mutual funds outguess the market? Harvard Business Review 44, 131–36.

Treynor, Jack L., Black, Fischer, 1973. How to use security analysis to improve portfolio selection. Journal of Business, 66–68. January.

Treynor, Jack L., Black, Fischer, 1973. How to use security analysis to improve portfolio selection. Journal of Business 46, 66–86.

Verrecchia, Robert, 1980. The mayers-rice conjecture: A counterexample. Journal of Financial Economics 8, 87–100.

Wei, Kelsey, Wermers, Russ, Yao, Tong, 2009. Uncommon Value: The Investment Performance of Contrarian Funds. Unpublished paper, University of Texas at Dallas, University of Iowa, and University of Maryland, November.

Wermers, R., 1999. Mutual fund herding and the impact on stock prices. Journal of Finance 55, 581–622.

Wermers, R., 2000. Mutual fund performance: an empirical decomposition into stock-picking talent, style, transactions costs, and expenses. Journal of Finance 55, 1655–1695.

Wermers, Russ, 1997. Momentum Investment Strategies of Mutual Funds, Performance Persistence, and Survivorship Bias. Working Paper.

Wermers, Russ, 1997. Momentum Investment Strategies of Mutual Funds, Performance Persistence, and Survivorship Bias. Working paper, University of Colorado.

Wermers, Russ, 1999. Mutual fund herding and the impact on stock prices. Journal of Finance 54, 581–622.

Wermers, Russ, 2000. Mutual fund performance. an empirical decomposition into stock-picking talent, style, transaction costs, and expenses. Journal of Finance 55 (4), 1655–1695.

Wermers, Russ, 2000. Mutual fund performance: An empirical decomposition into stock-picking talent, style, transactions costs, and expenses. Journal of Finance 55, 1655–1695.

Wermers, Russ, 2002. Is Money Really "Smart"? New Evidence on the Relation Between Mutual Fund Flows, Manager Behavior, and Performance Persistence. Unpublished paper, University of Maryland, May.

Wermers, Russ, 2005. Is Money Really "Smart"? New Evidence On The Relation Between Mutual Fund Flows, Manager Behavior, and Performance Persistence. Working Paper.

Wermers, Russ, 2004. Is money really smart? New evidence on the relation between mutual fund flows, manager behavior, and performance persistence, unpublished manuscript, University of Maryland.

Wermers, Russ, 2006. Performance evaluation with portfolio holdings information. North American Journal of Economics and Finance, 207–230. August.

Wermers, Russ, 2006. Performance evaluation with portfolio holdings information. North American Journal of Economics and Finance, 207–230.

Wermers, Russ, 2010a. A Matter of Style: The Causes and Consequences of Style Drift in Institutional Portfolios. Working Paper.

Wermers, Russ, 2010. A Matter of Style: The Causes and Consequences of Style Drift in Institutional Portfolios. Unpublished paper, University of Maryland, May.

Wermers, Russ, 2011. A Matter of Style: The Causes and Consequences of Style Drift in Institutional Portfolios. Working Paper.

Wermers, Russ, Yao, Tong, 2010b. Active vs. Passive Investing and the Efficiency of Individual Stock Prices. Unpublished paper, University of Iowa and University of Maryland, May.

Wylie, Sam, 2005. Fund manager herding: a test of the accuracy of empirical results using U.K. data. Journal of Business 78, 381–403.

Xiong, James, Ibbotson, Roger G., Idzorek, Thomas, Chen, Peng, 2010. The equal importance of asset allocation and active management. Financial Analysts Journal 66 (2), 22–30.

Zellner, A., Chetty, V.K., 1965. Prediction and decision problems in regression models from the Bayesian point of view. Journal of the American Statistical Association 60, 608–615.

Zheng, L., 1999. Is money smart? A study of mutual fund investors' fund selection ability. Journal of Finance 54, 901–933.

Index

A

B

G

H

I

N

S

T

U

Printed and bound by CPI Group (UK) Ltd, Croydon, CR0 4YY
08/05/2025
01864772-0001